Harlequins

Cover photographs

Top – Richard Moon scores the match winning try against Wasps in the John Player Special Cup semi-final at Sudbury in March 1988. © F.X. Cross

Bottom – Chris Robshaw kisses the Aviva Premiership trophy after victory over Leicester in May 2012. © Colorsport

Dedication

To Rob, Jean, Elaine and Kate – you are my world, I love you all.

Foreword

Image courtesy of Will Carling

I still remember being told by the then Chairman of England selectors that I needed to get club rugby experience, hence he would recommend that I go and play for Harlequins. A good idea, if you were not a student at Durham University!

So, I started making my three weekly train trips up and down to training and playing, I got to know that route pretty well.

One of my first games, against Waterloo, was an education in how to control nerves, the like of which I had never had. All was under control until I tried to be clever with a quick drop out which ended in a try for them!

Not long after, we made it to the John Player Cup Final and it was a classic case of smash and grab Quins up against the forward might of Bristol. I ended up scoring two tries, one made by the brilliant counter-attacking of the likes of Harriman, Thresher, Davis and Salmon and the other from the attacking play of Adrian Thompson. It was a brilliant day, a great win, the Quins' first and a triumph for our "run everything" policy that day, bravely instigated by Dick Best.

My time at Harlequins coincided with some truly great players, from Loveridge and Salmon, through the likes of Winterbottom, Skinner, Ackford, Moore, Leonard, Olver, Pears and Harriman, to the great club men such as Langhorn, Wright, Luxton and Sheasby.

The list of great names and players goes on; at the end Zinzan Brooke and Dan Luger were involved, two World Cup winners.

I only ever played club rugby for Harlequins, not that I was never tempted by the lure of France and even some other English clubs. For me however, it was more to do with the understanding treatment that I was always afforded at the club as a young England captain, alongside the desire to play attacking, adventurous rugby.

Hugely proud to have worn that iconic shirt, very lucky to have played alongside great characters and special players and very excited to read this book about the most famous club side in England !!

Will Carling OBE
January 2016

Preface

In life, some decisions are made early and they affect the rest of your life. When I was five, my Dad took me to see Harlequins play Wilmslow at Twickenham in the RFU Knockout Cup competition. From that point on, the Quins were my team even though most people had never heard of them. Little did I know then that it would be my destiny to write a book covering the first 150 years of the Club. His other choice for me was The Arsenal so, despite all the frustrating defeats over the years, success followed for both so he didn't do too badly!

As my Dad had done back in the 1950s, he introduced me to the art of newspaper cuttings and scrapbooks – hours and hours of fun! I was regaled with stories of the time he saw the Busby Babes beat Arsenal at Old Trafford; of travelling all the way to Blackheath in the late 1950s only to find the game had been called off due to a frozen pitch; of Micky Grant producing a piece of string from his pocket when his shorts fell down; of Ricky Bartlett and his cross-field kick; of the Harlequin style of play – real running rugby and the true Harlequin way of snatching defeat from the jaws of victory. As you will see, not much has changed there! I was convinced we could beat anyone and by and large, we could.

In the days before the internet, the only way to track the progress of your side was by newspaper and actually going to the game; there was virtually no coverage of club rugby anywhere else. It all seems so strange now but that's the way it was and I loved it. I started getting excited about the next game almost as soon as the previous one had finished. The cup ties were the only fixtures where anything but pride and the satisfaction of beating your opponents counted and if you were lucky, there would be an article on Quins in one or more papers in the build up to the game. It is amazing to see how the coverage of rugby has changed over the last 44 years.

My favourite Quins moment? It has to be the 1988 John Player Special Cup Final as it was the first big trophy we had won (closely followed by the Aviva Premiership victory in 2012).

I decided to write an up to date history and first put pen to paper back in 1987 when I had enough material on the early days to begin piecing together the start of our wonderful history. As I worked my way through it, I discovered so much unknown and long forgotten information that I found I was fascinated by the whole subject. I used to spend weeks going through the old newspapers in the British Museum Newspaper Library at Colindale and spent nearly as long on the Northern Line tubes as a result. Sadly, this fantastic resource is no longer available.

In 1988, I became the Club historian and took on the unenviable task of trying to uncover what sort of archive the club had. The answer was not very much apart form a lot of programmes, photographs, old minute books and other memorabilia. Gradually, with no money (it was still the amateur era remember), I sorted out the archive and secured a different room in the old West stand so the damp affecting it was no longer a threat.

Many pictures were reframed and hung in the bar at the top of the old stand along with club shields and other items being placed in the various cabinets. It was a regular family event when we had to polish the silverware for the start of each season.

In 1995, I was joined by Basil Lambert and together, as a team, we began the task of securing funding to bring the various boards up to date and invent new ones such as the internationals board. We also answered historical questions and started to prepare for the 150th anniversary which was fast approaching after the game went professional.

The period January 2013 to February 2015 was an extremely difficult one as the Trustees (including Roger Looker and Colin Herridge) and the Chief Executive Officer (David Ellis) had decided that they wanted to replace myself and Basil as the Club's Historians with a man by the name of Graeme Roberts (who was involved with the Harlequin Players' Association and pretended to know about the history of the Club). David Ellis even went to the lengths of locking us out of the archive store and lying about it. I will never forgive them for the way they treated Basil and me – they should all hang their heads in shame!

As I continued my quest to finish the book and get more information, Roberts, Herridge and Malcolm Wall even told people not to talk to me as we were in dispute (there was no dispute, they had effectively kicked me out). If you were one of those who never responded because of this, I hope you now regret your decision. Fortunately, there were many who did make the effort to speak and went against the bullying tactics of the so-called Harlequins who treated one of their own so badly – I thank them from the bottom of my heart, you restored my faith!

Unfortunately, it was not possible to include all the statistics in this volume due to space limitations. I have relied upon my vast records dating back to the very beginning for most of the detail (obviously, details for games played before I was able to write were gleaned from various programmes and newspaper reports!). I have counted all appearances and scores in a 1st XV match towards a player's total figure. From the beginning of the 2011/12 season, it was decided by the Director of Rugby that friendlies would no longer count as a professional appearance and so from then on, the only appearances in non-league and cup games that I have counted are those against international sides. Of course, as is always the case, there will be errors and I hold my hand up to these so if you do spot one or would like to share additional information, I can be contacted at harlequinstats@outlook.com.

To help the reader understand the scoring and results abbreviations and values (further explanations follow in the text), I list them here:-

Results

A	Abandoned
C	Cancelled
D	Drawn
DA	Drawn Against
DIF	Drawn In Favour
L	Lost
P	Postponed
W	Won

Scoring

DG Dropped Goal
DSG Disputed Goal
DST Disputed Try
DSTD Disputed Touchdown
FAFC From A Fair Catch
FAFK From A Free Kick
MG Goal from a Mark
MT Try from a Mark
G Goal
PG Penalty Goal
PS Poster
R Rouge
T Try
TD Touchdown
TIG Touch In Goal

Values (points scoring did not begin until 1886/87 season)

Seasons	Try	Conversion	Penalty	Dropped goal	Goal from a mark
1886/87-1888/89	1	2	-	3	3
1889/90-1890/91	1	2	2	3	3
1891/92-1892/93	2	3	3	4	4
1893/94-1904/05	3	2	3	4	4
1905/06-1947/48	3	2	3	4	3
1948/49-1970/71	3	2	3	3	3
1971/72-1976/77	4	2	3	3	3
1977/78-1991/92	4	2	3	3	-
1992/93 to date	5	2	3	3	-

This book has been 29 years in the making, I have tried to recreate the story from start to finish with no stone left unturned and I hope you enjoy reading it as much as I enjoyed writing it.

Here's to the next 150 years – COME ON YOU QUINS!!

Nick Cross
Worcester Park
July 2016

Acknowledgements

When writing a book like this, there are so many people to thank, they are often far too numerous to mention and this volume is no exception.

I am going to start with my wonderful wife Elaine who has supported me through this process. Without her unwavering loyalty, I doubt it would have been finished on time! A big thank you to my step daughter Kate for sorting out the publishing side of things and Robin Burrows for the cover design.

Of course, Jean and Rob (my Mum and Dad) have been there since the beginning and have always been there for me and for that I thank them. An extra special thanks to Mum for reading the book and being my strongest critic – it was just what I needed! My brother Frank has accompanied me on more than a few long journeys to away games and I thank him for providing the inspiration for the title to Chapter 47!

The following Harlequin players all replied to my requests for help over the years (some sadly no longer with us and two through their scrapbooks from the early 1900s) – John Adcock, Albert Agar, Adrian Alexander, John Bazalgette, C.G. Bellamy, Graham Birkett, David Brooks, Billy Bushell, Geoff Butler, D. Bulmer, Harold Caccia, Mickey Claxton, Terry Claxton, David A. Cooke, David H. Cooke, Simon Cooke, John Cox, Pat Cleaver, Maurice Daly, Phil Davies, Andre Dent, Ray Dudman, Harry Eden, Neil Edwards, M.R.M. Evans, Malcolm Foulkes-Arnold, Rob Glenister, Mark Green, Ken Granger, Alan Grimsdell, Paul Grant, Bob Hiller, Chris Horner, Martin Jackson, Paul Jackson, Reg Kindred, Gerry Loader, Hugh McHardy, Mike Mason, Richard Moon, Grahame Murray, Joe Mycock, Basil Napper, Nigel O'Brien, John Olver, Colin Payne, George Plumtree, Bob Read, Ray Relf, Richard Riddell, Herbert Sibree, Mickey Skinner, Adrian Stoop, P.D. Strang, John Simons, Iestyn Thomas, Alex Woodhouse, Peter Woodruff, Roger Whyte, Derek Whiting, Peter Whiting, Steve Wilcock and Rhys Williams.

Of those, an extra big thanks to Adrian, Mickey, Terry and Mark (who spent a day with me reliving the good old days) and David H. Cooke for all ignoring the demands not to speak to me.

To Mark Evans, thank you for supporting me during your time as CEO at Quins and for giving me some of your valuable time when your role had finished.

My great friend and colleague Basil Lambert who went through the trauma with me as part of the archives team and was an invaluable sounding board. Andrew Davie, an exceptional film maker but sadly another unappreciated resource – thank you for your help and support.

Thanks to John Christy and Roy Croucher for your assistance along the way – it has been a great journey.

Of the host of others who have supplied information, special mention must go to Stuart Farmer of Leicester (Mr Sports Statistician) with whom I have been swapping information for over twenty years – I really appreciate your help and assistance. To Julian Easterbrook of the original Harlequin Supporters' Club and long-time reporter for various newspapers, thank you for sharing your notes with me. Also to Alun Rees who tried to help with the Canadian tours, Bill Good for his help with the tour to the USA in 1980 and Walter Gebhardt of Deutsches Rugby Museum Heidelberg for help with the early German tours. Alasdair Norrie of Colorsport and Phil McGowan from the Museum of Rugby at Twickenham, thank you for your help with photographs.

Thanks to the rest of you who all contributed in one way or another and I am sorry if I have forgotten anyone.

During my research, I consulted the Rugby Museum at Twickenham and the British Museum Newspaper Library at Colindale; I would like to thank all the staff there for the help and assistance provided.

All mainstream British newspapers were sourced at some point with most help coming from The Sportsman, The Field, the Daily and Sunday Telegraph, The Times and the Saturday pink and green papers from Bristol, Gloucester and Leicester, the Middlesex Chronicle, Surrey Comet and Richmond and Twickenham Times.

Finally to those who wish to remain anonymous – Thank you for everything!!

1

The Beginning and a Change of Name 1866-1871

It all started a long time ago - some time in 1865, 1866 or 1867. In an article from a newspaper called "Flood and Field" dated November 1890, the following information is given at the start of an article about the Quins - "In 1865 arose what was known as the Hampstead Football Club with ground adjoining Finchley Road Station, the site of which is now occupied by St. John's Wood C.C. and T.C.". In H.B.T. Wakelam's original "Harlequin Story", he says that "A close search of our own records, however, reveals the fact that the Hampstead Club actually played first in 1866, on the ground now used by the Hampstead Cricket Club, and as the Rugby Union itself did not come into being until 1871, it seems fair to assume that the date in our records is the correct one".

In "Baily's Magazine of Sports and Pastimes" from April 1921, an article written by An Old Campaigner sheds some interesting light on the whole subject. He states that we were founded under the title of Hampstead Club in August 1867 and played on Hampstead Heath with a membership of thirty. Further research tells us that there was a Hampstead Cricket Club renting a field north of England's Lane in what is now London NW3. As there was very little housing in this area compared to now, it is likely that this could have been the spot although without a very detailed description, we cannot be absolutely certain. One thing that there can be no doubt about is that it cannot have been the ground where Hampstead Cricket Club now play as they did not move to Lymington Road until 1877 (the current clubhouse was built in 1927). The colours adopted were gold and black barred cap (these were said to be long worsted caps similar in shape to those of stage smugglers or brewers' draymen) and jersey.

The "Flood and Field" also mentions that when the Hampstead Club split, one half became Harlequin F.C. and the other members went off to become Wasps. This is quite simply not true as Wasps were formed around the same time as Hampstead and were never any other club apart from Wasps according to one of their founders.

In one reference book from 1913 (The Rugby Football Annual), the date of our formation is given as 1867 (under title of Hampstead) changed to Harlequins 1870. So, no one is quite sure but one thing is certain, the first recorded game of the Hampstead Football Club took place on 16th November 1867 on Hackney Downs and the opponents were Clapton. The result was a win for Clapton by two goals to nil. Going by this date, it would seem that the most likely year of formation would be 1867 and the first season 1867/68. A man by the name of E. Ellice Clark was said to be the probable founder of the Club; he was the first Honorary Secretary and captained the side for the first two seasons.

During that first season, a total of four games were played, two being lost and two 0-0 draws. One of those came after two hours play against Clapton when it was reported that both clubs had strong teams who contested so evenly, that at the end of two hours the game was drawn. In those days these scoreless draws were commonplace. As you could only win a game by scoring more goals than your opponents, most games were either straight draws, drawn in favour or drawn against. In total we had only three fixtures at Hampstead and as, on two occasions, the games were cancelled, we only actually played there once and this was in the 1868/69 season.

At the start of Hampstead's last season (1869/70), a meeting was held at which it was decided to change the name of the Club, as the membership was no longer a purely local one. At the same time, it was agreed that it would be a shame to dispose of the "H.F.C." monogram and the "Nunquam Dormio" (I Never Sleep) motto already in use. A dictionary was produced and the "Hs" were read out. When the reader got to "Harlequin" he was stopped and, at once, all those present gave their approval. At the same meeting, in place of the old Hampstead black and gold, new colours were chosen, the ones which we wear today (the pantone numbers are given for reference - light blue (291), chocolate (469), French grey (422) and magenta (201) reversed on back, sleeves light green (363) and black reversed). It is said that the change of name attracted a lot of new members and the Club took on a new lease of life. This is probably the true story although, as with most organisations or societies, there was a fabled version. It was said that we came into being under a lamp-post in Hampstead at two o'clock one morning and that this probably accounted for our colours, name and also our motto. "The Sportsman" from Tuesday, November 30th 1869 reported under the heading "Hampstead Football Club" that "A special meeting of the above club will be held on Thursday evening next the 2nd of December, at the Eyre Arms, St. John's Wood, at which all members are particularly requested to be present". Whether this refers to the above meeting is unclear but I believe there is a good chance it does. Unfortunately, there was no follow up report to confirm what happened at the meeting. The Eyre Arms lasted until the 1920s before being demolished. An upmarket development called Eyre Court now stands on the site which is opposite St. John's Wood Station although the exact spot where the pub was is actually a branch of HSBC Bank. The home games during this season were played on the borrowed Parkfield Club ground at Finchley Road. One game that season was played by Harlequins against Christ's College at Finchley. This is believed to be the first game played by Harlequins under that name. The report which follows comes from "The Field" of Saturday, February 12th:

"This match was played at Finchley on Wednesday last, and resulted in a draw in favour of the college by one touchdown and two rouges. The ball was started shortly after three by the Harlequins, who were, however, soon driven back to their lines, and a touchdown obtained; but the place kick was missed. Half time being called and ends changed, the Harlequins got better together, and for some time kept the ball in close proximity to the college goal; but Hornsby, by a good run, carried it to neutral ground, where it mostly remained until the end of the game. The field was covered with snow, causing play on both sides to be anything but good; the college more especially were in very bad form. G.F. Henderson and A. Hornsby for their respective sides rendered themselves most conspicuous throughout the game".

Both sides played only seven men so were somewhat short. The Harlequin team was E.E. Clark (who captained the side), G.F. Henderson (back), A. Trinder, R. Snagg, E.H. Oldham, J.L. Zwinger and E.H. Bubb. Shortages in those days were by no means a rare occurrence. In fact, it seemed to be more common for there to be one or more short on both sides. An example of this came on March 28th 1868 when we played three short in a game against City of London School in Victoria Park. This turned out to be another 0-0 draw.

1867/68 (Hampstead)

161167	CLAPTON	HACKNEY DOWNS	L	0-2G
080268	UNIVERSITY COLLEGE	PRIMROSE HILL	L	1G-2G1DG
210368	CLAPTON	HACKNEY DOWNS	D	0-0
280368	CITY OF LONDON SCHOOL	VICTORIA PARK	D	0-0

In the 1868/69 season, membership had increased to sixty. The Old Campaigner from "Baily's" goes on to say that in 1869 the colours were altered to a yellow and black hooped jersey and stockings. This is the only mention of a change of colours by Hampstead but there is no reason to dispute the fact. We played against such teams as Heath Brow School, Mars, Parkfield, Gipsies and Red Rovers. As well as a captain in the games against Heath Brow School and City of London School, we played two sub captains. This also happened when we played Clapton on 7th November 1868. The result was a draw, each side having scored one rouge. A rouge (which later became a touchdown when a touchdown became known as a try) was where the attacking team forced their opponents to touchdown behind their own goal line. In the return match against Clapton on 16th January 1869, the Hampstead captain (E.E. Clark) met with an accident, breaking one of his fingers by coming into contact with the iron railing. The particular newspaper report goes on to say "It would be as well if the Clapton men were to play more in the centre of the downs, where there is plenty of room". Nowadays, I suppose the equivalent of this would be crashing into the advertising hoardings! In this game, ends were changed not just once but twice. It appears that in these early days it was common practice to change ends after a goal had been scored. It's a good job this rule does not still apply! When we played City of London School on 30th January there was a curious incident. Before Madden (one of four emergencies to make up our numbers) scored his touchdown, there was a maul in goal which lasted for a full 15 minutes.

1868/69

171068	HEATH BROW SCHOOL		D	1TD-1TD
241068	ST.BARTHOLOMEW'S HOSPITAL	MIDDLESEX COUNTY CRICKET GROUND	C	
311068	CITY OF LONDON SCHOOL	VICTORIA PARK	D	0-0
071168	CLAPTON	HACKNEY DOWNS	D	1R-1R
141168	HEATH BROW SCHOOL	HAMPSTEAD	C	
211168	MARS	HACKNEY DOWNS	U	
281168	PARKFIELD	FINCHLEY ROAD	W	4G-0
051268	GIPSIES	HAMPSTEAD	DA	0-4TD
121268	MARS	HAMPSTEAD	C	
191268	ST.BARTHOLOMEW'S HOSPITAL	MIDDLESEX COUNTY CRICKET GROUND	DA	7R-1TD2R
160169	CLAPTON	CLAPTON DOWNS	W	2G4R-3R
230169	RED ROVERS	VICTORIA PARK	C	
300169	CITY OF LONDON SCHOOL	VICTORIA PARK	DIF	1G5TD-1DG2TD

060269	RED ROVERS	VICTORIA PARK	DA	2R-6R
130269	UNIVERSITY COLLEGE SCHOOL	PRIMROSE HILL	DIF	1TD13R-2R
060369	GIPSIES	FINCHLEY ROAD	DIF	3R-1R1DSG
130369	RAVENSCOURT PARK	STAMFORD BROOK	C	
270369	UNIVERSITY COLLEGE SCHOOL	PRIMROSE HILL	C	

Our ground was now a field adjoining Finchley Road Station (as mentioned in "Flood and Field") but we would only stop here for one season. W. E. Titchener was captain for this season only. We were moving from strength to strength as regards the playing of matches and went from four known games in 1867/68 to twelve in 68/69 and actually played twenty three in 69/70. The first of these was on 2nd October and was against Clapham Rovers. This was their first game played according to Rugby rules and they duly defeated us by three touchdowns (tries) to nil, although this only counted as a draw in their favour as a goal had to be scored before you could win in these early games. The match had started at half past three and continued until ten to five when an accident to one of Clapham's men caused it to finish. On the 16th October we played against Red Rovers in a game which had been postponed from the previous Saturday owing to our opponents having a paper chase! One of our backs, C.E. Atkinson, ran 100 yards for his touchdown in this game in which we ran out comfortable winners by three goals and four touchdowns to nil. On 27th November, we met Richmond for the first time. The game was played at the Old Deer Park, we numbered ten against their eleven and the result was a scoreless draw. In at least eleven games during this season we could not manage to put out a full fifteen but as we only lost three games it doesn't seem to have had much effect on us. In the game against Burlington House on 20th November, Percy Wilkinson made his debut. He was our first international and appears to have made the switch from us to Law Club during the season in which he won his only cap for England against Scotland.

1869/70

021069	CLAPHAM ROVERS	CLAPHAM COMMON	DA	0-3TD
161069	RED ROVERS	FINCHLEY ROAD	W	3G4TD-0
231069	ROYAL NAVAL SCHOOL	FINCHLEY ROAD	DIF	1TD3R-1R
301069	BLACKHEATH PROPRIETARY SCHOOL	BLACKHEATH	DA	0-2TD1DSG
061169	WHITTON PARK	FINCHLEY ROAD	W	1G1TD-0
131169	GIPSIES	PECKHAM RYE	L	0-1G2TD
201169	BURLINGTON HOUSE	FINCHLEY ROAD	W	2G6TD-0
271169	RICHMOND	OLD DEER PARK	D	0-0
041269	ROYAL NAVAL SCHOOL	NEW CROSS	D	0-0
111269	EALING WANDERERS	FINCHLEY ROAD	D	1R-1R
181269	MARS	CLAPTON DOWNS	W	1G1T-0
010170	OAKFIELD	FINCHLEY ROAD		
080170	CLAPTON	HACKNEY DOWNS	DA	0-1TD2R
150170	EDMONTON AND TOTTENHAM	FINCHLEY ROAD	L	0-1G2TD
220170	GIPSIES	FINCHLEY ROAD	D	0-0

290170	RED ROVERS		DIF	1TD-0
050270	WHITTON PARK	WHITTON	L	1TD-1G4TD
120270	UNIVERSITY COLLEGE SCHOOL	PRIMROSE HILL	C	
190270	CITY OF LONDON SCHOOL	VICTORIA PARK	C	
230270	GODOLPHIN SCHOOL	FINCHLEY ROAD	DIF	5TD-0
260270	BURLINGTON HOUSE	SPRING GROVE	W	1G3TD-1TD
050370	ST.MARY'S HOSPITAL	ETON AND MIDDLESEX CRICKET GROUND	W	4G-0
120370	OAKFIELD	CROYDON	W	1G-0
160370	GODOLPHIN SCHOOL	HAMMERSMITH	DIF	1TD2R-3R
190370	G M WHITE'S TEAM	BATTERSEA PARK	W	1G1TD-0
260370	EDMONTON AND TOTTENHAM	EDMONTON	W	1G2TD-0

1869/70 (Harlequin)

090270	CHRIST'S COLLEGE	FINCHLEY	DA	0-1TD2R

At the start of season 1870/71, we had a new name and a new ground at The Old Sluice House, Highbury Vale. From looking at maps around this time, it would appear that our ground was located in the area surrounded by Queen's Drive, Brownswood Road, Wilberforce Road and Somerfield Road in London N4. We were destined to stay at this location for just one season. Our first game in this season was played against E.E. Clark's team. Clark was one of our early stalwarts and made appearances in the first four seasons. The game resulted in a win for the Harlequins by one goal and a touchdown to a touchdown. In fact, we remained unbeaten at Highbury Vale and, in the eleven games we played there, we were victorious in six and drew the other five in our favour. On 10th December 1870 we played Epsom away and whilst playing twelve to their fifteen and coming away with a draw in our favour, the game only lasted 45 minutes as two inches of snow had fallen. Percy Wilkinson captained the side and scored 18 touchdowns (this was a new Club record for an individual) beating his previous season's score of 10. The side managed 60 touchdowns and this record was to stand until 1905/06 when 97 tries were scored, although it was equalled in 1897/98.

In these early games, it was not at all unusual for us to lend or borrow substitutes or "emergencies" as they were sometimes called. On 17th December, for example, we lent E.E. Clark and Rose to St. Thomas's Hospital to make their numbers up to fourteen. We still ran out easy winners by four goals (one from a mark) and two touchdowns to nil. Again, on 21st January 1871, Wimbledon Hornets made use of G.F.Henderson and W.Richard to bring their numbers up to eleven, just one short of ours. The result this time was a more resounding victory for us by five goals and four touchdowns to nil. In the return match against Epsom at Highbury Vale in February, we only played ten men for the first half until two more turned up. Epsom, incidentally, played a full side but still we managed somehow a draw in our favour by three rouges to one.

With all this talk of shortages, there was in fact an occasion on 23rd October 1869 in a 2nd XV game against Oakfield when, by some oversight of our captain, we played seventeen men. This appears to have been returned on 4th March 1871 when we were playing away to Hornsey as it was discovered near the end of the game that the Hornsey Club had been playing 16 men. Perhaps these were merely oversights or were they early examples of gamesmanship?! We still won against Hornsey, though only just, by one goal to two rouges. Interestingly, the rules of the Hornsey Club stated that there be a change of ends whenever a goal was scored. It appears that, contrary to what has been written earlier, not all clubs instigated this rule. We were due to finish the season with a game against the Blackheath Proprietary School at Blackheath but, unfortunately, it was cancelled. In this season, five prize caps were given to Percy Wilkinson, E. Walker, W.E. Titchener, C.E. Atkinson and W.A. (William) Smith. Sometime in 1871, Atkinson, who was Club secretary, left the country and Smith was elected to the post. Upon his retirement from this post in 1876, he was presented with a handsome testimonial and made a life member of the Club (he had also been a racing cyclist in the early penny-farthing days).

As a footnote to the 1870/71 season, on the 26th January a meeting was held at the old Pall Mall restaurant, Charing Cross. The following clubs were represented: Blackheath, Richmond, Wellington College, Guy's Hospital, Harlequins, King's College, St. Paul's, Civil Service, Marlborough Nomads, Queen's House, West Kent, Wimbledon Hornets, Gipsies, Clapham Rovers, Flamingoes, Law, Lausanne, Addison, Mohicans and Belsize Park. This meeting founded the Rugby Union, the first of all such bodies, so never to be called the "English Rugby Union". So, as can be seen, we really were in at the beginning and are the only club to have survived who are not named after a district or particular organisation. One name which does not appear in the list above is that of the Wasps. The official Centenary History of the Rugby Football Union states the following:

"There would have been twenty-two clubs represented at the meeting if the staff work of the Wasps had been a trifle less vague. In the event their party turned up at the wrong rendezvous on the wrong day at the wrong time".

As regards playing strength in the first four seasons, we managed fifteen, thirty eight, sixty two and fifty different players respectively.

1870/71

240970	E E CLARK'S TEAM	HIGHBURY VALE	W	1G1TD-1TD
011070	BURLINGTON HOUSE	HIGHBURY VALE	DIF	1TD-0
081070	CLAPHAM ROVERS	CLAPHAM COMMON	L	0-1G3TD
121070	ROYAL NAVAL SCHOOL	NEW CROSS	L	1R-2G
151070	RAVENSCOURT PARK	STAMFORD BROOK	L	0-1G4TD
221070	CHRIST'S COLLEGE	FINCHLEY	D	1G-1G
261070	GODOLPHIN SCHOOL	HAMMERSMITH	C	
291070	RICHMOND	OLD DEER PARK	C	
051170	EALING	HIGHBURY VALE	D	1TD-1TD
091170	ROYAL NAVAL SCHOOL	NEW CROSS	W	1G2TD-0
121170	FLAMINGOES	HIGHBURY VALE	DIF	5R-1R
161170	ST.BARTHOLOMEW'S HOSPITAL	HIGHBURY VALE	W	2G2DG7TD-0
191170	CHRIST'S COLLEGE	HIGHBURY VALE	DIF	2TD2R-0
261170	HORNSEY	HIGHBURY VALE	W	1G5TD-1DSG
031270	CRESCENT	HIGHBURY VALE	W	2G8TD-0
071270	ST.BARTHOLOMEW'S HOSPITAL	BATTERSEA PARK	W	1G-0
101270	EPSOM COLLEGE	EPSOM	DIF	2TD1R-5R
141270	GODOLPHIN SCHOOL	HAMMERSMITH	W	1G2TD-1TD

171270	ST.THOMAS'S HOSPITAL	HIGHBURY VALE	W	3G1MG2TD-0
241270	BELSIZE PARK	BELSIZE ROAD	C	
311270	EALING WANDERERS	EALING	C	
070171	LAUSANNE	HIGHBURY VALE	C	
140171	CRESCENT	BATTERSEA PARK	W	2G2TD-0
210171	WIMBLEDON HORNETS	HIGHBURY VALE	W	5G4TD-0
250171	LAW	HIGHBURY VALE	C	
280171	LAUSANNE	ROSEMARY BRANCH	C	
040271	BURLINGTON HOUSE	SPRING GROVE	W	2G1TD-0
110271	EPSOM COLLEGE	HIGHBURY VALE	DIF	3R-1R
180271	ST.GEORGE'S HOSPITAL	BATTERSEA PARK	C	
250271	FLAMINGOES	BATTERSEA PARK	DA	0-1TD2R
040371	HORNSEY	HORNSEY	W	1G-2R
110371	CLAPHAM ROVERS	HIGHBURY VALE	DIF	1TD-0
180371	WIMBLEDON HORNETS	WIMBLEDON	L	0-2G1DG
250371	BLACKHEATH PROPRIETARY SCHOOL	BLACKHEATH	C	

2

Changes of Ground but Still No Games Outside the South 1871-1875

In season 1871/72 we started off with a game against a team called Football Company. They were captained by E.E. Clark who himself had captained Hampstead in their first two seasons. We went on to lose this game by two goals (one dropped) and a touchdown to nil. This was the first ever game played under the rules of the newly formed Rugby Football Union.

In these early years, scoring was possible by such things as posters (where the ball went over the top of one of the posts in an attempt at goal), touch in goal (where the ball went into touch in goal), rouges (see earlier) as well as the recognised forms of touchdowns (later to become tries) and goals (kicked from a fair catch, dropped or converted from a touchdown). It is interesting to note that touchdowns and goals were sometimes registered as disputed. This was where one side disputed the score and so it could not be agreed that one had been made. This was obviously before independent referees were used.

E. Walker captained the side in this and the next season and played in at least 30 of the 47 games played. Page's Cricket Ground at Tufnell Park was our home for 1871/72 (this was situated in the area around Anson Road, N7). In the game against Flamingoes on 14th October at Battersea Park, one of our players (W.E. Titchener) found his shirt ripped from his back and the writer of the report in "The Sportsman" (an excellent coverage of all sports was given in this newspaper right up until its merger with the "Sporting Life" in the 1920s) quoted verse as follows "Like the poor Injun, whose untootered mind, Clothes him in front, but leaves him bare behind". This game was lost by two goals (one dropped) and four rouges to two rouges. It seems to have gone unnoticed that we played fifteen against their sixteen. We also played two backs and two half backs. After playing and defeating Belsize Park at home on 13th January (although it was only a draw in our favour) by five touchdowns to nil, it seems they disbanded shortly afterwards and several of their players came and joined us. These included J.E. Gorton, G.W. Perham, R.L. Pugh and H.L. Wynne. New teams appearing on our fixture list this season were Carlton Hill, Civil Service, Football Company, Guy's Hospital, Oakfield, Pirates, Rangers, Wasps and Wimbledon School.

1871/72

300971	FOOTBALL COMPANY	PECKHAM RYE	L	0-1G1DG1TD
071071	BELSIZE PARK	BELSIZE ROAD	W	1G1TD-0

141071	FLAMINGOES	BATTERSEA PARK	L	2R-1G1DG4R
281071	CHRIST'S COLLEGE	FINCHLEY	DIF	1R-0
041171	PIRATES	TUFNELL PARK	DA	0-4R1DSTD
111171	ST.BARTHOLOMEW'S HOSPITAL	TUFNELL PARK	W	1DG-0
181171	ST.THOMAS'S HOSPITAL	CLAPHAM COMMON		
251171	EALING	EALING	DIF	2TD-0
021271	WIMBLEDON SCHOOL	WIMBLEDON	DA	
091271	HORNSEY	HORNSEY		
161271	FLAMINGOES	TUFNELL PARK	D	1G-1G
231271	ST.BARTHOLOMEW'S HOSPITAL	BATTERSEA PARK		
301271	OAKFIELD	CROYDON	L	0-1G
060172	PIRATES	ENFIELD	DA	0-1TD3R
130172	BELSIZE PARK	TUFNELL PARK	DIF	5TD-0
200172	EALING	TUFNELL PARK	W	4G8TD-0
270172	LAUSANNE	PECKHAM RYE	W	2G-0
030272	WASPS	HAMPSTEAD	DIF	1TD2R-0
100272	CIVIL SERVICE	TUFNELL PARK	D	1G-1DG
170272	CARLTON HILL	TUFNELL PARK	L	1TD5R-1G
240272	CHRIST'S COLLEGE	TUFNELL PARK	W	1G1R-1TD
020372	HORNSEY	TUFNELL PARK	DIF	2TD-0
090372	WASPS	TUFNELL PARK		
160372	LAUSANNE	TUFNELL PARK		
230372	GUY'S HOSPITAL	TUFNELL PARK		
300372	RANGERS		DA	

Season 1872/73 saw us on the move again, this time to Belsize Road, Swiss Cottage. We made use of changing and other facilities supplied by "The Britannia" public house, Belsize Park. Again, this ground failed to hold us for more than a season as we moved on to Putney Heath to use "The Green Man" public house at the top of Putney Hill. 1872/73 saw Addison, Old Paulines, West Kent and, most importantly, Cambridge University added to our opponents. We played the University on 2nd November at Cambridge and lost by one goal and two touchdowns to nil. In our first game of this season, we played against Hornsey and one of our two touchdowns was described as being "from a fair catch" - what exactly this means is not clear.

A fixture card from this season belonging to one G.H. (George) Rope who was with us for a number of years and made at least eight appearances for the first team gives us an insight into the early days. It would seem that the majority of the time he was a second team regular and played mostly as a half-back but was noted playing as a quarter-back and a forward on other occasions. The fixture card is just a piece of card folded in half and on the front page is the name "Harlequin" with our monogram and motto and "Rules: Rugby Union" at the bottom. The inside double spread gives the matches for the season 1872-3 and at the bottom is printed "N.B. - Members when asked to play in any match are requested to send a written answer as early as possible". The back page gives the captain and his address as well as that of the Honorary Treasurer, whilst at the bottom the Committee is listed.

Our 2nd XV played a match against Somerset at Highbury on 16th November and won by a goal and two touchdowns to nil. It is not clear if this was the County of Somerset. This appears to mark the existence of a second team being run by the Club and during this season they appeared to have at least eight games in their list. In our return match at home to Old Paulines on 18th January, it was reported that after a few minutes play, during which time the Harlequins had obtained a goal, kicked by Walker from a try by Pugh, they beat a retreat against their captain's wishes. Even after this occurrence, the result was listed as a win for us by that goal to nil.

1872/73

051072	HORNSEY	BELSIZE ROAD	DIF	2TD(1FAFC)-0
121072	ADDISON	WORMWOOD SCRUBS	D	0-0
191072	FLAMINGOES	BATTERSEA PARK	DIF	1TD-0
261072	CIVIL SERVICE	LILLIE BRIDGE	W	1G2TD-0
021172	CAMBRIDGE UNIVERSITY	CAMBRIDGE	L	0-1G2TD
091172	OAKFIELD	CROYDON	W	1G-1TD
161172	WIMBLEDON SCHOOL	WIMBLEDON	D	0-0
231172	OLD PAULINES	BATTERSEA PARK	DIF	3R-0
301172	CHRIST'S COLLEGE	BELSIZE ROAD	DIF	1TD4R-0
071272	WASPS	HAMPSTEAD	DA	1TD1R-1TD3R1PS
111272	BLACKHEATH PROPRIETARY SCHOOL	BLACKHEATH	DIF	1G6TD-1DG
141272	CHRIST'S COLLEGE	FINCHLEY	W	1G3TD1DSTD-0
211272	BLACKHEATH PROPRIETARY SCHOOL	BLACKHEATH	C	
211272	RICHMOND	BELSIZE ROAD	C	
281272	PIRATES	BELSIZE ROAD	C	
281272	RICHMOND	OLD DEER PARK	D	0-0
040173	OAKFIELD	BELSIZE ROAD	C	
110173	BELSIZE PARK	PRIMROSE HILL	DIF	3TD-0
180173	OLD PAULINES	BELSIZE ROAD	W	1G-0
250173	HORNSEY	BELSIZE ROAD	DIF	1TD-0
010273	WASPS	BELSIZE ROAD	C	
080273	EALING	EALING	DIF	1TD-0
150273	WEST KENT	CHISLEHURST	L	0-1G
220273	ADDISON	BELSIZE ROAD	W	2G2TD1TIG-0
010373	FLAMINGOES	BATTERSEA PARK	W	1G1MG2TD1TIG-0
080373	KING'S COLLEGE	VICTORIA PARK	C	
150373	BELSIZE PARK	LILLIE BRIDGE	W	1G-1TD
220373	PIRATES	ENFIELD	C	
290373	ST.ANDREW'S ROVERS	PECKHAM RYE	C	

The following season saw us play Wimbledon School twice, both times at Wimbledon. In these games we had several Old Wimbledonians playing for us and they were listed as E.C. Bidwell, J.W. Courtenay, A.F. Dalgetty, D.Hervey, H.A.F.Hervey, F.H. Wheeler, C.S. (Charles) Wheler, A.H. Wilson, W.Y. Winthrop and H.L. Wynne who captained the side on both occasions. Incidentally, although W.Watson was Club captain, he only appears to have played in the first game of the season after which Wynne took over and captained the side in at least 18 games. Our first game at Putney Heath was against Christ's College and, with both teams fielding 16, we drew the game in our favour with four tries (touchdowns had now become tries and rouges had become touchdowns) to nil. Our only outright defeat at this ground came in our tenth and last game there. The opponents were Addison on 7th March and, after going ahead in the second half with a try by H.P. Northcott, F. Hervey dropped a goal for the visitors and that was the result. During this season Richmond were met on three occasions. Once we played eighteen to their fourteen and the others were seventeen and eighteen-a-side games. All three games were drawn, the first in Richmond's favour and the others in ours. Oxford University were to have been met on 29th November away but the game was cancelled and we didn't actually play them for the first time until February 1876.

1874 was the season of gigantic forwards, E.J. Kennedy, W. Lawson and W.Y. Winthrop averaging about fifteen stones; while the lightweights numbered C.E. Grasemann, Frank Lloyd, P.C. Oswald, F. Pennell, A.F. Somerville and A. Woodward all over twelve stones each. These were seen as a rather formidable contingent in these days of heavy scrummaging. It was also thought by some that Frank Lloyd's play at the time should have gained him his International Cap but our single international this season was W.C. (Con) Hutchinson. He was to gain his two England caps in 1876 and 1877 when he played for the Royal Indian Engineering College.

1873/74

041073	ST.THOMAS'S HOSPITAL	CLAPHAM COMMON	W	1G1TIG-0
111073	KING'S COLLEGE SCHOOL	BATTERSEA PARK	D	0-0(10 MINS)
181073	WIMBLEDON SCHOOL	WIMBLEDON	DIF	1T1PS1DST-0
251073	RICHMOND	OLD DEER PARK	DA	1TD-4T1MT
011173	HORNSEY	HORNSEY		
081173	FLAMINGOES	BATTERSEA PARK	W	1G1T-0
151173	CHRIST'S COLLEGE	FINCHLEY	DIF	1T-0
191173	CIVIL SERVICE	LILLIE BRIDGE	L	0-2G1T1PS
221173	OLD CHELTONIANS	PUTNEY HEATH	D	0-0
291173	OXFORD UNIVERSITY	OXFORD	C	
061273	CHRIST'S COLLEGE	PUTNEY HEATH	DIF	4T1PS-0
131273	QUEEN'S HOUSE	PUTNEY HEATH	D	0-0
201273	RICHMOND	OLD DEER PARK	DIF	2TD1PS1DSG-0
261273	RICHMOND	OLD DEER PARK	DIF	1TD-0
271273	FLAMINGOES	PUTNEY HEATH	D	1G1T1PS-1G1T
030174	STREATHAM	STREATHAM	W	4G-0
100174	OLD CHELTONIANS	PUTNEY HEATH	D	2T-2T
170174	ST.GEORGE'S HOSPITAL	PUTNEY HEATH	W	1G1DG1T1G1DST-0
240174	CIVIL SERVICE	PUTNEY HEATH	DA	3TD-4T1TD1DST

310174	HORNSEY	PUTNEY HEATH	DIF	1T1PS-0
070274	STREATHAM	PUTNEY HEATH	W	1G1T-1T
140274	ADDISON	PUTNEY HEATH	DIF	3T-0
210274	QUEEN'S HOUSE	BLACKHEATH	L	0-1G
280274	WIMBLEDON SCHOOL	WIMBLEDON	DIF	1T1G1DST-0
070374	ADDISON	PUTNEY HEATH	L	1T-1DG
140374	ST.GEORGE'S HOSPITAL	BATTERSEA PARK		
210374	WIMBLEDON HORNETS	WIMBLEDON	DA	0-2T4TD1DSG

The hooligan element raised its head again in the following season (1874/75) when we met Flamingoes at Battersea Park on 7th November. The game was terminated 15 minutes before the appointed time because of the unruly behaviour of the mob. Another newspaper says that the Quins refused to carry on playing because of encroachments of the spectators. I doubt very much that there were the same scenes that have been witnessed in and around many football grounds up and down the country. In those days, it appears that in the excitement of trying to get a better view of the game the crowd were described as a mob and unruly.

The Indian Civil Engineering College appear on our fixture list for the first time, the game being played at Cooper's Hill near Staines and this resulted in a 0-0 draw, one of four in this season. We also played against the Stock Exchange in Battersea Park, winning by a goal and three tries to nil. Another first in this season was the game against the Royal Military College at Sandhurst - no reports have been traced on this game but we know that we lost by a dropped goal to nil. Other teams we had fixtures against were Beckenham, University College Hospital, London International College, Streatham, Sydenham Hill and Hermits. We had now moved to Kensal Green where we stayed for two seasons (our most permanent home so far!). The changing facilities were located at the "William the Fourth" tavern.

At a Committee meeting held on 6th March 1875, it is noted that W. Watson was resigning from the captaincy and leaving for California and that the Club expressed a wish to make him a gift in recognition of his past services. The report goes on to say that Mr. Watson intimated that he would be glad if the testimonial took the form of a revolver! Watson played at least 51 games for the Club and, although he was captain for these last two seasons, he only captained the side on seven occasions. His playing career lasted from October 1870 until his last game against Gipsies on 27th February 1875.

The Club had now established itself among the leaders of the day, with a membership of 109 and 19 new elections.

1874/75

031074	BECKENHAM	BECKENHAM	DIF	3T1TD1PS-1T
101074	STOCK EXCHANGE	BATTERSEA PARK	W	1G3T-0
171074	UNIVERSITY COLLEGE HOSPITAL		DIF	1T1DST-0
241074	RICHMOND	OLD DEER PARK	L	1T-1DG1TD
311074	INDIAN CIVIL ENGINEERING COLLEGE	COOPER'S HILL	D	0-0
041174	ROYAL MILITARY COLLEGE	SANDHURST	L	0-1DG

071174	FLAMINGOES	BATTERSEA PARK	DA	1TD-1T1G1TD
141174	BECKENHAM	KENSAL GREEN		
141174	ROYAL NAVAL SCHOOL	NEW CROSS	W	1G4T-0
211174	GUY'S HOSPITAL	KENSAL GREEN	L	4TD-2G
281174	LONDON INTERNATIONAL COLLEGE	KENSAL GREEN	W	3G1DG2T-0
051274	WIMBLEDON SCHOOL	WIMBLEDON	DIF	1T-0
121274	ST.ANDREW'S ROVERS	KENSAL GREEN		
191274	RICHMOND	OLD DEER PARK		
020175	STREATHAM	STREATHAM		
090175	STOCK EXCHANGE	KENSAL GREEN		
160175	GUY'S HOSPITAL	BLACKHEATH	DIF	1G1T-1G
230175	SYDENHAM HILL	KENSAL GREEN	D	0-0
300175	FLAMINGOES	KENSAL GREEN	DA	0-4TD
060275	HERMITS	LADYWELL	DIF	4TD-0
060275	STREATHAM	KENSAL GREEN		
130275	UNIVERSITY COLLEGE HOSPITAL	KENSAL GREEN	W	1G1T-0
200275	WIMBLEDON SCHOOL	KENSAL GREEN	D	0-0
270275	GIPSIES	KENSAL GREEN	D	0-0
060375	ADDISON	KENSAL GREEN		
130375	CHRIST'S COLLEGE	FINCHLEY	DIF	1T1TD-0
200375	LONDON INTERNATIONAL COLLEGE	ISLEWORTH		

3

Still on the Move but Slowing Down 1875-1879

G.W. Perham was our new captain but was not a new face as he had made his debut in 1871/72. Another old fixture card is from the 1875/76 season and again belonged to George Rope. As well as showing the captain, it gives P.C. Oswald as vice-captain and lists the honorary secretary, his assistant and the honorary treasurer. The Committee had grown from six to eleven. The bottom of the front of the card states "The ground is at Kensal Green, and the Dressing room at the William the Fourth Tavern, a few minutes' walk from the Station on the London and North Western, from Broad Street. Trains, 2.10, 2.25". The games are then listed in date order with two games being played on most Saturdays as we were running two teams at this point.

We were due to start against the Old Harleyburians but the match was cancelled. Richmond, Guy's Hospital, Wasps and Oxford University were teams due to be played in this season who became very regular opponents in the years ahead. Unfortunately, only Wasps are on our fixture list nowadays. The game against St. Andrew's Rovers on 6th November was due to be played on their ground at Nunhead but the pitch was under water so was played at Kensal Green. Bad drainage must have been a severe problem in these early days. We eventually drew this game in the Rovers' favour nil to one try and two touchdowns. Lack of floodlights caused the game against Walthamstow to be stopped about five minutes before the appointed time - the game didn't kick-off until a quarter to four and darkness had crept in. We were left as winners by a goal and a touch in goal to one touchdown. When we met Oxford University on 16th February, we had three substitutes to make us up to a full complement. At this time, both Oxford and Cambridge had outstanding sides and we were given a sound thrashing by two goals and six tries to nil (in modern day scoring that's 44-0). We seem to have been a bit upset about this result as we didn't play them again until February 1885.

An extract from "The Field" of Saturday, March 25 1876 says by way of describing our game against Christ's College at Finchley: "This match was played at Finchley, on Saturday last. As the visitors were very slow in turning up, play did not commence till a few minutes to five. After a good game, the Harlequins obtained one touchdown to nothing. For the Harlequins, Richmond, West, and Smith (behind), Forbes and Tillyer played well while Henry and Coates played well for the college".

Some of our leading players in this season were A.F. Bassano (11 appearances), A.F. Browne (13), P.C. Oswald (13), G.W. Perham (eleven), C. Tillyer (13) and E. Wheler (12). Perham and Wheler were backs and the others were forwards.

1875/76

021075	OLD HARLEYBURIANS	KENSAL GREEN	C	
091075	BECKENHAM	BECKENHAM	W	2G2T-0
161075	RICHMOND	OLD DEER PARK	D	1T1G-1TD
231075	UNIVERSITY COLLEGE HOSPITAL	KENSAL GREEN	C	
301075	FLAMINGOES	KENSAL GREEN	DIF	1T-0
061175	ST.ANDREW'S ROVERS	KENSAL GREEN	DA	0-1T2TD
131175	WIMBLEDON SCHOOL	WIMBLEDON	DIF	5TD-0
201175	ROYAL NAVAL COLLEGE	GREENWICH	DIF	1TD-0
271175	ST.THOMAS'S HOSPITAL	KENSAL GREEN	W	1G1T2TD-1T1TD
041275	GUY'S HOSPITAL	ILFORD	C	
111275	ST.ANDREW'S ROVERS	KENSAL GREEN	C	
181275	WASPS	STAMFORD BROOK	DA	0-3T
231275	VAMPYRES	KENSAL GREEN	DIF	1T-0
010176	WALTHAMSTOW	WALTHAMSTOW	W	1G1T1G-1TD
080176	BECKENHAM	KENSAL GREEN	C	
150176	WASPS	LILLIE BRIDGE	C	
170176	VAMPYRES	BEAUFORT HOUSE	C	
220176	RICHMOND	OLD DEER PARK	D	0-0
290176	GUY'S HOSPITAL	BLACKHEATH	W	1G1TD-0
020276	ST.BARTHOLOMEW'S HOSPITAL		L	
050276	WIMBLEDON SCHOOL	WIMBLEDON	W	1G1DG2T2/3TD-1G
120276	FLAMINGOES	NUNHEAD	C	
160276	OXFORD UNIVERSITY	OXFORD	L	0-2G6T
190276	LONDON INTERNATIONAL COLLEGE	BEAUFORT HOUSE	W	5G4T1T1G8TD-0
260276	UNIVERSITY COLLEGE HOSPITAL	VICTORIA PARK	C	
040376	ROYAL NAVAL COLLEGE	BEAUFORT HOUSE	DIF	1MT1T1G2TD-0
110376	GIPSIES	PUTNEY	W	
180376	CHRIST'S COLLEGE	FINCHLEY	DIF	1TD-0
250376	BELSIZE	KENSAL GREEN	C	

The 1876/77 season saw the re-appearance of R.T. Manley who, according to newspapers of the time had last played for us in 1869. Perham captained the side again and made it three seasons in a row the next year. We used at least seventy eight players during the course of this season although this was still two short of our record of at least eighty in 1873/74. 1876 was the first year that teams in all games (including club games) were fifteen-a-side. The previous number was said to be twenty, but we have no record of ever having played against or fielded a team of this size. It was not until 1892 that a law appeared stating that "The game should be played by 15 players on each side".

On the whole this was a disappointing season as only one game out of seventeen known as having been played was won. This was against Guy's Hospital on 14th October in only the second game. P.P. Sharpe dropped a goal and kicked a goal from a try by Perham, while Guy's could only manage a touchdown. As well as Manley making his comeback, another old Hampstead player, William Smith, was in our team. The two had played together as far back as 5th March 1870 against St. Mary's Hospital at the Eton and Middlesex Cricket Ground. Of the remaining matches, three were drawn in our favour, eight were drawn against and five were lost. In one of the matches drawn against, our opponents were a team called "Vampyres". This match, by the courtesy of the Wasps F.C., was played on their ground at Beaufort House. They scored a touchdown to nil. On 23rd December we were due to play what must rank as one of the strangest named opponents we have had - the German Gymnastic Society at Haverstock Hill. Unfortunately this match was cancelled and this is believed to have been the fate of the return on the 10th March. On 6th February what is described as a "scratch team" played against East Sheen at Mortlake. We played eleven against their twelve and lost by two goals, two tries and four touchdowns to nil. In this season we still occasionally played two backs, two quarter backs and two three quarter backs but this did tend to vary from game to game.

It was noted that the subscription was put up this season from 7s 6d to 10s. At the end of the previous season we had moved again, this time to Stamford Brook. It is believed the ground was in the area between the Chiswick High Road and the Goldhawk Road. We changed and refreshed at "The Queen of England". This ground held us for the following season (1877/78) as well.

1876/77

071076	QUEEN'S HOUSE	STAMFORD BROOK	DA	0-1T2TD
141076	GUY'S HOSPITAL	STAMFORD BROOK	W	1G1DG-1TD
211076	ST.ANDREW'S ROVERS	STAMFORD BROOK	L	0-1G3T2TD
281076	BECKENHAM	BECKENHAM		
281076	CLEVEDON	RAVENSCOURT PARK	DA	0-2T3TD
041176	WIMBLEDON SCHOOL	WIMBLEDON	L	1T-1G
111176	UNIVERSITY COLLEGE HOSPITAL	STAMFORD BROOK		
181176	WALTHAMSTOW	STAMFORD BROOK	DA	
251176	GUY'S HOSPITAL	BLACKHEATH		
021276	ST.THOMAS'S HOSPITAL	LAMBETH	DIF	1T1TD-0
091276	FLAMINGOES	STAMFORD BROOK	DIF	1T1TD-0
161276	ST.BARTHOLOMEW'S HOSPITAL	BATTERSEA PARK		
181276	VAMPYRES	BEAUFORT HOUSE	DA	0-1TD
231276	GERMAN GYMNASTIC SOCIETY	HAVERSTOCK HILL	C	
301276	QUEEN'S HOUSE	BLACKHEATH	DA	0-1T3TD
060177	CLEVEDON	BLACKHEATH		
130177	WASPS	BEAUFORT HOUSE		
200177	ST.BARTHOLOMEW'S HOSPITAL	STAMFORD BROOK		
270177	RICHMOND	OLD DEER PARK	DA	1TD-3TD
270177	W W NORTHCOTT'S TEAM	STAMFORD BROOK		
030277	ST.THOMAS'S HOSPITAL	CLAPHAM	DIF	1T-2TD
060277	EAST SHEEN	MORTLAKE	L	0-2G2T4TD

100277	UNIVERSITY COLLEGE HOSPITAL	STAMFORD BROOK		
170277	ST.THOMAS'S HOSPITAL	STAMFORD BROOK		
170277	WALTHAMSTOW	WALTHAMSTOW	DA	0-1T6TD
240277	BECKENHAM	STAMFORD BROOK		
240277	WASPS			
030377	MARLBOROUGH NOMADS	BLACKHEATH	L	0-1G1DG
030377	QUEEN'S HOUSE	BLACKHEATH	L	0-1G1TD
100377	GERMAN GYMNASTIC SOCIETY	STAMFORD BROOK		
100377	WIMBLEDON SCHOOL	WIMBLEDON		
170377	FLAMINGOES	BATTERSEA PARK	DA	2TD-3TD

For our second game we played Wasps at Putney and it was interesting to note that one of their team was unavoidably detained in town until half time. Their captain on the day, B.J. Angle, was to make one appearance for us later in the season on 23rd March when he lent us their ground for a game. A lot of the newspaper reports in these relatively early days would just give a very brief description of the game and then list the teams. One example of this came on 13th November in "The Sportsman", covering our game against King's College, when it was stated that "A drawn game was the result of the meeting of the clubs on Saturday, at Battersea Park, the heavy ground preventing a point to either side".

Another example of a sixteenth man can be found on 22nd December against Lausanne. This was a game lasting only forty minutes and the discrepancy was not discovered until after the match. For our last game of the season, on 23rd March against Colville Grasshoppers, we had to borrow the Wasps Club ground at Putney (as mentioned earlier and described in a report as their "territory" and lent for the purpose by Mr. B.J. Angle) owing to the fact that our ground was under repair for the ensuing Cricket season. This one lasted seventy minutes. We managed to win this, our only game against the Grasshoppers, by one goal and five touchdowns to one touchdown. This was our fourth victory of the season against five losses, while two games each were drawn and drawn against.

1877/78

061077	WIMBLEDON SCHOOL	WIMBLEDON	W	1G1TD-0
201077	WASPS	PUTNEY	DA	1TD-1T6TD
101177	KING'S COLLEGE	BATTERSEA PARK	D	0-0
171177	ST.ANDREW'S ROVERS	PECKHAM RYE	L	0-1G1T
241177	FLAMINGOES	BATTERSEA PARK	L	0-1DG1TD1T1G
081277	ST.BARTHOLOMEW'S HOSPITAL	BATTERSEA PARK		
151277	KENSINGTON	ADDISON ROAD	D	0-0
221277	LAUSANNE	DULWICH	L	0-1G2TD1DST
291277	QUEEN'S HOUSE	STAMFORD BROOK		
020178	RAVENSCOURT PARK	STAMFORD BROOK		
190178	FLAMINGOES	PUTNEY HEATH	DA	0-2TD
230178	RAVENSCOURT PARK	STAMFORD BROOK		
260178	ST.ANDREW'S ROVERS	STAMFORD BROOK		

020278	WASPS	PUTNEY HEATH	W	1G-0
090278	CLEVEDON	STAMFORD BROOK		
160278	KING'S COLLEGE	BATTERSEA PARK	L	1T2TD1T1G- 1DG2TD1T1G
230278	GUY'S HOSPITAL	BLACKHEATH		
020378	KENSINGTON	ADDISON ROAD	L	0-3G3T
090378	ROCHESTER HOUSE	PUTNEY HEATH	W	1G4TD1T1G-1TD
230378	COLVILLE GRASSHOPPERS	PUTNEY	W	1G5TD-1TD

Season 1878/79 found us on the move yet again, this time to Turnham Green but, unlike our previous ones, this was to be for five seasons. We started with a draw in our favour away to Flamingoes at Battersea Park and then for our first game at our new home we played against Kensington. This game was played on 2nd November resulting in a reverse to the tune of three goals (one dropped) to nil. The scorer of the two tries and consequent goals was G.F. Griffin who made five appearances for us in the 1875/76 season. He did, in fact, come back and "guest" for us in a game against University College Hospital on 11th March 1882 and scored two tries in an easy win. On 9th November, another significant event occurred as we met London Scottish for the first time. The game was played on our home ground and was drawn in favour of the visitors by two touchdowns to nil. We had to wait until the following season for a return as this was the only fixture in this one. Who would have thought then that, almost 120 years later to the day, we would be meeting each other on a ground that we both played on? C.E. Grasemann was captain for this and the following season which proved to be his last. He made at least 41 appearances for us between 1873 and 1879, 19 of these as captain. He played among the forwards who, in these early days, were not the specialists of today. It appears that when a scrummage was formed players just gathered round and attempted to push their opponents back. Even as far back as 1874 it was not lawful in a scrummage to touch the ball with the hand under any circumstance whatever.

In the game against London International College on 16th November, one of the college players was G.B. James. He eventually made his debut for us on 24th September 1881 against the college and was the first Harlequin player to play in 100 games, his final total being 102. He captained the Club in the 1886/87 season in which he made thirteen appearances. We had a return against East Sheen from the 1876/77 season on 15th January and, although having borrowed four men from them, we still played one short of their thirteen. The result was a not surprising heavy defeat for us by three goals and seven tries to nil. The game against Wasps and the returns with Flamingoes and Kensington were cancelled so, out of the ten known games, we only had three victories to show. At least 47 players were used in the first team during this season, the more prominent of which were F.W. Burnand, P.G.C. Burnand, C.E. Grasemann, C.E. Macrae, A. Tillyer, F.S. Watts and Harry Watts. C. Job, who made two appearances was to go on and become our President for the last few years of the 1880's.

The next season saw the end of the 1870's and the start of the decade that would see the introduction of points scoring.

1878/79

191078	FLAMINGOES	BATTERSEA PARK	DIF	1T4TD-0
021178	KENSINGTON	PUTNEY HEATH	L	0-2G1DG
091178	LONDON SCOTTISH	PUTNEY HEATH	DA	0-2TD
161178	LONDON INTERNATIONAL COLLEGE	PUTNEY HEATH	DIF	2TD-0
231178	RAVENSCOURT PARK	PUTNEY HEATH	C	
231178	F WATTS'S XV	TURNHAM GREEN	W	2G1T3TD-1G2TD
071278	ST.ANDREW'S ROVERS	TURNHAM GREEN	DA	1T-1T2TD
141278	ST.THOMAS'S HOSPITAL	TURNHAM GREEN		
261278	RICHMOND	OLD DEER PARK		
040179	KING'S COLLEGE	STAMFORD BRIDGE		
110179	LAUSANNE	TURNHAM GREEN		
150179	EAST SHEEN	TURNHAM GREEN	L	0-3G7T
180179	FLAMINGOES	TURNHAM GREEN	C	
250179	KENSINGTON	ADDISON ROAD	C	
010279	WASPS	TURNHAM GREEN	C	
080279	ST.BARTHOLOMEW'S HOSPITAL	TURNHAM GREEN	L	0-1G7TD
150279	LAUSANNE	TURNHAM GREEN	W	1DG2TD-4TD
220279	ST.BARTHOLOMEW'S HOSPITAL	BATTERSEA PARK		
010379	QUEEN'S HOUSE	TURNHAM GREEN		
080379	GUY'S HOSPITAL	TURNHAM GREEN		
150379	ROCHESTER HOUSE	TURNHAM GREEN	W	1G2T2TD-2TD
220379	ST.ANDREW'S ROVERS	PECKHAM RYE		

4

On the Verge of Points and Getting More Adventurous 1879-1886

We were still at Turnham Green for the start of the 1879/80 season and, as mentioned earlier, C.E. Grasemann was captain. We started against Queen's House at Blackheath on 4th October and went down two tries to nil. In all we played them nine times and the best we managed was a 0-0 draw in the first encounter, the remainder being either lost or drawn against. It must also be recorded that we never scored anything against them at all! The game against Flamingoes on 18th October is noteworthy in that it was the first game recorded where an umpire is mentioned. His name was H.B. Bromhead. Up until umpires were brought in it was up to the two captains to decide any problems or disputed points. This is why there are so many examples of disputed tries and goals: they just could not agree. The problem of short teams was still happening and when we met and were defeated by Walthamstow on 3rd January, we played eleven to their fifteen. Our captain only appears to have played up to 1st November. It is not known if he retired or an injury forced him out but C.E. Macrae captained the side for the rest of the games. A total of 42 players were used in fourteen known games, top appearances were by C.E. Macrae and F.S. Watts, both with twelve.

1879/80

041079	QUEEN'S HOUSE	BLACKHEATH	L	0-2T
111079	UNIVERSITY COLLEGE HOSPITAL	TOTTENHAM	D	0-0
181079	FLAMINGOES	WILLESDEN	L	0-1T
251079	LAUSANNE	DULWICH	L	2TD-1G2TD1T1G
011179	ST.BARTHOLOMEW'S HOSPITAL	TURNHAM GREEN	D	0-0
081179	LONDON INTERNATIONAL COLLEGE	TURNHAM GREEN	DA	0-1TD
151179	WASPS	TURNHAM GREEN	D	0-0
221179	KENSINGTON	ADDISON ROAD		
061279	LONDON SCOTTISH	CLAPHAM JUNCTION		
131279	GUY'S HOSPITAL	BLACKHEATH	C	

201279	ST.ANDREW'S ROVERS	TURNHAM GREEN	C	
261279	RICHMOND	OLD DEER PARK		
271279	WASPS	PUTNEY		
030180	WALTHAMSTOW	WALTHAMSTOW	L	0-3G2DG4T
100180	ST.THOMAS'S HOSPITAL	LAMBETH	L	0-1G2T
170180	ST.BARTHOLOMEW'S HOSPITAL	TURNHAM GREEN	W	1G2TD1DST-1TD
240180	ST.ANDREW'S ROVERS	PECKHAM RYE		
070280	FLAMINGOES	TURNHAM GREEN	L	0-3T5TD
140280	UNIVERSITY COLLEGE HOSPITAL	TURNHAM GREEN	W	1T-0
210280	LONDON INTERNATIONAL COLLEGE	ISLEWORTH	W	1T-0
280280	LAUSANNE	TURNHAM GREEN		
060380	GUY'S HOSPITAL	TURNHAM GREEN		
130380	BELSIZE	PRIMROSE HILL		
200380	KENSINGTON	TURNHAM GREEN	D	0-0

The next season although not showing a change of venue showed a change of captain with the appointment of A. Tillyer. The minutes for this year showed that the annual general meeting took place on 9th September 1880 at the Bedford Head Hotel, Maiden Lane, Covent Garden at 8.30 p.m. Thirteen gentleman were present and C.E. Grasemann was in the chair. After electing the Officers and Committee for the 1880/81 season, the question of the ground was discussed and a sub-committee was elected to look at the new ground to see if it was worth taking. After this, Caps for the previous season were voted for and awarded to F.W. Burnand, Harry Watts and Percy Boville. Finally, a vote of thanks was passed to Mr. Grasemann for the able way in which he had taken the chair.

This season's new opponents were to have been Arabs at Turnham Green but there is no record of the fixture being played. After losing to Queen's House and drawing our games with Kensington and University College Hospital, we went on to win the remaining eight games known to have been played. This included two victories over Richmond, the first of which on 23rd October at the Old Deer Park proved to be a complete walkover by one goal and ten tries to nil. For the record our tries were scored by H. Bell-Irving, H.R. Hedderwick, J.T. Hughes, R.V.K. Stewart, H.L. Stoddart (2), A. Tillyer (who also kicked the goal) (2) and Harry Watts (2). Both sides played full fifteens which were split six backs to nine forwards.

R.T. Manley made his last appearance against UCH. His career had spanned some thirteen seasons although he had a gap of six seasons when he failed to play in the first team. Another player who made his last appearance for us was W.A. Smith and, unlike Manley, he had played in ten out of his career spanning twelve seasons. A.E. (Andrew) Stoddart, the famous English international, made his debut for us against Richmond on 27th December, having been elected as a member on 2nd October. Although he is listed as a Blackheath player, he actually played for us in both the 1884/85 and 1885/86 seasons when he gained his first caps. He was also the first captain of England to have played for us. H.L. Stoddart and Harry Watts shared the most tries with three apiece while Andrew Stoddart and Harry Watts each dropped a goal and A. Tillyer kicked one conversion. The team scored seventeen tries, which was the first time since 1875/76 they had managed more than six!

1880/81

021080	QUEEN'S HOUSE	BLACKHEATH	L	0-1G2T
091080	KENSINGTON	TURNHAM GREEN	D	0-0
161080	UNIVERSITY COLLEGE HOSPITAL	TOTTENHAM	DIF	1TD-0
231080	RICHMOND	OLD DEER PARK	W	1G10T-0
301080	LONDON INTERNATIONAL COLLEGE	ISLEWORTH	W	1T-0
061180	WASPS	TURNHAM GREEN	W	
131180	LONDON SCOTTISH	LEE		
201180	ST.BARTHOLOMEW'S HOSPITAL	TURNHAM GREEN		
271180	FLAMINGOES	WILLESDEN		
041280	LONDON SCOTTISH	TURNHAM GREEN	W	1G-1T
111280	GUY'S HOSPITAL	BLACKHEATH		
181280	ARABS	TURNHAM GREEN		
271280	RICHMOND	OLD DEER PARK	W	1DG2T3TD-1TD
010181	BELSIZE	TURNHAM GREEN		
080181	WASPS	PUTNEY		
150181	LAUSANNE	TURNHAM GREEN	C	
290181	UNIVERSITY COLLEGE HOSPITAL	TURNHAM GREEN	C	
050281	FLAMINGOES	TURNHAM GREEN	W	1T2TD-0
120281	LAUSANNE	DULWICH		
190281	KING'S COLLEGE	TURNHAM GREEN	W	1T-0
260281	KENSINGTON	TURNHAM GREEN		
050381	GUY'S HOSPITAL	TURNHAM GREEN		
120381	KING'S COLLEGE	TURNHAM GREEN		
260381	LONDON INTERNATIONAL COLLEGE	TURNHAM GREEN	W	1DG1T4TD-0

The 1881/82 season brought us fixtures for the first time against two of our most famous opponents. On 8th October we met Blackheath away and were duly dispatched by five goals and two tries to nil. This result was not too surprising as Blackheath were certainly amongst the top two or three clubs in the country at this time and had a number of current or future international players playing for them. On 1st April came our first match against those Welsh giants - Cardiff. The game was played (as a report in "The Sportsman" states) "At Cardiff on Saturday in the presence of about 1500 spectators. As this was the first occasion on which a metropolitan rugby team had visited Wales, considerable interest was manifested in the event. The result was a draw, Cardiff scoring two touches in self-defence to their opponents' one touch-down in self-defence and one touch in goal". On 29th October we met the Royal Military Academy at Woolwich for the first time. Harry Watts led the side and was a three quarter back alongside Andrew Stoddart. The Academy proved too strong for us and ran out winners by two goals and one try to one goal. The week before this we had played our first game against Maidstone at Turnham Green and run out winners by a goal and seven tries to nil. Another first appearance was made on our fixture list by London Athletic Club. We were due to meet them on a home and away basis but no record of these games taking place has been discovered.

At a meeting on 1st September 1881, among the elected officers were H. Watts as Honorary Secretary and vice-captain and F. Watts as captain of the 2nd XV. Caps were awarded to H.L. Stoddart and E. Kell for the 1880/81 season. The question of the ground was again entered into but was left over to the Committee to decide. A Committee meeting was held on 7th December at 9 Gracechurch Street, London where subscriptions towards Club funds were made. C. Job contributed £2 and F.W. Burnand, A. Copland, H.K. Gow, G.B. James, C.E. Macrae, William Smith, Andrew Stoddart, H.L. Stoddart, Frank Watts, F.S. Watts and Harry Watts gave £1.

Andrew Stoddart topped the try scoring with seven and was joint leading appearance maker with his brother, H.L. on fourteen. A. Tillyer was in his second season as captain and we were in our fourth season at Turnham Green.

1881/82

240981	LONDON INTERNATIONAL COLLEGE	TURNHAM GREEN	W	2T-0
011081	QUEEN'S HOUSE	BLACKHEATH	L	0-1G1DG
081081	BLACKHEATH	BLACKHEATH	L	0-5G2T
151081	LONDON SCOTTISH	TURNHAM GREEN		
221081	MAIDSTONE	TURNHAM GREEN	W	1G7T-0
291081	ROYAL MILITARY ACADEMY	WOOLWICH	L	1G-2G1T
051181	KENSINGTON	TURNHAM GREEN	W	1G1T-0
121181	LONDON ATHLETIC CLUB	STAMFORD BRIDGE		
191181	WASPS	TURNHAM GREEN	W	2G4T-0
261181	FLAMINGOES	PUTNEY	W	1DG-0
031281	LONDON INTERNATIONAL COLLEGE	ISLEWORTH	W	1DG3T-1T
101281	UNIVERSITY COLLEGE HOSPITAL	TOTTENHAM		
171281	LONDON SCOTTISH	LEE		
261281	RICHMOND	OLD DEER PARK	W	1G2T-0
311281	MARLBOROUGH NOMADS	TURNHAM GREEN	L	1T-1G
140182	WASPS	PUTNEY		
210182	MAIDSTONE	MAIDSTONE	D	1T-1T
040282	FLAMINGOES	TURNHAM GREEN		
110282	LONDON ATHLETIC CLUB	TURNHAM GREEN		
180282	LAUSANNE	DULWICH		
250282	KENSINGTON	TURNHAM GREEN	L	0-1G2T
040382	LAUSANNE	TURNHAM GREEN		
110382	UNIVERSITY COLLEGE HOSPITAL	TURNHAM GREEN	W	2G2DG3T-0
180382	RICHMOND	OLD DEER PARK	L	0-2G3T
250382	WEST KENT	CHISLEHURST	W	2DG-0
010482	CARDIFF	CARDIFF	D	1TD1T1G-2TD

When we began our next season, it was to be our last at Turnham Green but the first of two for Harry Watts as captain. F. W. Burnand was vice-captain and the captain of the 2nd XV was C. Gossage. A fixture card from the 1882/83 season is stuck into the minute book covering this period. It is a simple card affair stretching to four sides. On the front page it lists the Officers and Committee, in the middle it lists the 1st and 2nd XV fixtures for the season and on the back page it is noted that the ground is two minutes' walk from the station and the dressing room is at the "Pack Horse and Talbot". There is also a note requesting members to play in the Club colours and stating that these can be obtained from Goy's, 21, Leadenhall Street. At the bottom of the page it says that trains leave Mansion House for Turnham Green at 3, 15 and 33 minutes past the hour.

We began with our obligatory loss to Queen's House and Blackheath only scored three tries to nil against us so it augured well for a good season. Eleven victories followed as opposed to three losses, two draws in our favour and one draw. Out of those victories came two in our only ever fixtures against Turnham Green and Twickenham, both being easily beaten. We met Cardiff at home, losing by a goal and a try to a try whilst the return was a scoreless draw. In a newspaper report of the home game, umpires are mentioned as well as a referee. They were G.W. Perham for Harlequins and A. Duncan for Cardiff and the referee was W. Wallace who is noted as the Honorary Treasurer of the Rugby Football Union.

J.T. Trotman was top appearance maker with 18 and A.E. Stoddart scored 17 tries. The team managed 45 tries which was their highest total since the first Harlequin season of 1870/71. A future English international made his debut for us against Turnham Green on 23rd December, he was G.L. (George) Jeffery. Although he played for us after winning his first cap in 1885/86 he is listed as a Blackheath player. Another player making his debut in this season was that famous Harlequin half back, A.B. Cipriani. After his first appearance on 4th November, he went on to play no fewer than 195 games for the Club over the next 15 seasons. Caps were presented, as usual, to C. Job, Andrew Stoddart and L. Weber for the last season.

1882/83

300982	QUEEN'S HOUSE	BLACKHEATH	L	0-1G1T
071082	BLACKHEATH	BLACKHEATH	L	0-3T
141082	WEST KENT	TURNHAM GREEN	W	1G5T-0
211082	LONDON INTERNATIONAL COLLEGE	TURNHAM GREEN	W	3T-0
281082	UNIVERSITY COLLEGE HOSPITAL	TURNHAM GREEN	W	1G5T-1DSG
041182	WIMBLEDON SCHOOL	WIMBLEDON	W	1T-0
111182	CARDIFF	CARDIFF	C	
181182	WASPS	TURNHAM GREEN	W	3G4T-0
251182	FLAMINGOES	PUTNEY	DIF	1DST-0
021282	LONDON INTERNATIONAL COLLEGE	ISLEWORTH	C	
091282	KENSINGTON	WOOD LANE	L	0-1T
161282	MAIDSTONE	MAIDSTONE		
231282	TURNHAM GREEN	TURNHAM GREEN(A)	W	2G3T-0

301282	TWICKENHAM	TURNHAM GREEN	W	4G5T-0
060183	CLAPHAM ROVERS	WANDSWORTH COMMON	C	
130183	EALING	TURNHAM GREEN	W	2G3T-0
200183	MAIDSTONE	TURNHAM GREEN	C	
270183	ST.THOMAS'S HOSPITAL	LAMBETH	C	
030283	FLAMINGOES	TURNHAM GREEN	W	2G2T-1T
100283	UNIVERSITY COLLEGE HOSPITAL	TOTTENHAM	W	2G-0
170283	CARDIFF	CARDIFF	D	0-0
240283	KENSINGTON	TURNHAM GREEN	L	0-1G2T
030383	WEST KENT	CHISLEHURST	DIF	1T-1DST
100383	WASPS	PUTNEY	C	
170383	RICHMOND	OLD DEER PARK	W	2G-0
240383	CARDIFF	TURNHAM GREEN	L	1T-1G1T

The next season (1883/84) saw us playing at Devonshire Park, Chiswick. At the A.G.M. on 30th August, as well as electing the Officers and Committee and awarding Caps to H.K. Gow and Frank Watts, it was proposed by William Smith (the motion being seconded and carried) that he draft out a set of rules to lay before the Committee and that a General meeting be called to pass same. These appear to be the original rules of the Club and as such are listed below.

1. - That the Club be called the HARLEQUIN FOOTBALL CLUB.
2. - That all matches be played under the Rules of the Rugby Football Union.
3. - That the Club consist of Active, Honorary and Life Members.
4. - That the Officers of the Club consist of the President, Captain, Vice-Captain, Secretary, Treasurer, Captain of 2nd XV, and Committee of eight Members.
5. - That the annual subscription for Active Members be half-a-guinea, and for Honorary Members five shillings.
6. - That all subscriptions become due and payable on the 1st of October in each year, and that any Member failing to pay his subscription within three calendar months from that date, be liable to have his name posted in the Club-room.
7. - That each candidate for election be proposed and seconded by a Member of the Club, and balloted for at the Committee Meeting next following his nomination. One black ball in three to exclude. On election his subscription becomes due.
8. - That Members whose subscriptions are unpaid at the date of the Annual General Meeting after due application has been made by the Treasurer, shall be posted as defaulters, and their names read out at such meeting.
9. - That the proposer of a new Member shall in case of that Member's default be liable for his first annual subscription.
10. - That the Annual General Meeting for the election of Officers, confirmation of matches arranged, and other business be held as near the first week in September in each year as possible.

11. - That the Club colours be light blue, chocolate, French grey and magenta reversed on back, sleeves light green and black reversed; dark blue knickerbockers and dark stockings, and that all Members be requested to wear the same.
12. - That the Committee shall elect two Members from the body of the Club, who shall audit the Accounts, and sign balance sheet, which shall be produced at the Annual General Meeting.
13. - That any Member having promised to play in a match, and failing to do so without a satisfactory explanation, be liable to a fine of 2s. 6d.
14. - That five form a quorum at a Committee Meeting.
15. - That no rule be altered or rescinded without the consent of two-thirds of a General Meeting.
16. - That after each Match a Committee Meeting be held for the election of new Members only.
17. - That a Special General Meeting shall be called either at the discretion of the Hon. Sec., or within fourteen days of the receipt by him of a written requisition, signed by ten Members, stating the reasons for which such Meeting is to be called. Not less than seven clear days' shall be given to the Members of any Special General Meeting, and of the purpose of that Meeting.
18. - That the Committee shall have power to make regulations and bye-laws in accordance with these Rules, and so settle any disputed points not otherwise provided for by these Rules.
19. - That present Public-School men can become Members of the Club without Subscription after being proposed and balloted for in the usual manner.
20. - That notice shall be sent to each Member on his election, with a copy of these Rules, and a request for payment of his Subscription and Entrance Fee. Such payment to be held as a submission to the Rules of the Club.

The meeting took place on Tuesday 30th October at the Bedford Head Hotel, the above Rules were confirmed and it was resolved that they should form the code of Rules for the Club. At the same meeting it was also resolved that the Captain and Secretary pick the teams.

On the 26th and 27th October we appear to have undertaken our first "mini" tour to Wales when we played Newport and Cardiff. Newport were met for the first time on the Friday and dispatched us to the tune of four tries to nil. We had to make up our numbers with the addition of E. James at back and F. Williams in the forwards, both of whom were from the Cardiff Club but neither played the next day against us. Eleven of the side did play the next day and managed a respectable draw, each side scoring one try. We met Old Cheltonians for the first time in nine years on 24th November and this game is recalled as it was the last game we drew in our favour by virtue of a disputed goal to nil. The following week against University College Hospital at Tottenham we trailed at half-time by a goal to nil but in the second half managed to tie things up when F.H. Johnstone kicked a goal from a free kick. It appears that this method was succeeded by the penalty kick. On 13th October a certain W. Williams made his first appearance for us against West Kent. This was the "Billy" Williams of Cabbage Patch (Twickenham) fame. Of this, more later. He went on to play over 50 games for the first team in the next seven years. Another famous Quin, A.A. Surtees made his debut on 29th December against Middlesex Wanderers and scored two tries in a comfortable win. Frank Watts made 13 appearances and six players scored two tries each to share the top spot. Overall, nine games were won, seven drawn and three lost. Those losses were against Blackheath, Cardiff and Newport, while some of the most impressive results were against Wasps, West Kent and Wimbledon School.

Amongst the archives there is a "request to play" letter. It was sent out by Frank Watts, the Honorary Secretary, to someone asking them to play in the fixture on 3rd November against the Wimbledon School. It says that you had to dress at "The Rose and Crown" and that the train from Waterloo to Wimbledon was at 2.32. The match was to commence at three o'clock, wet or fine so even if the ground was right next to the station, it didn't leave an awful lot of time to get changed and be ready for the start!

1883/84

061083	BLACKHEATH	BLACKHEATH	L	0-2G2T
131083	WEST KENT	DEVONSHIRE PARK	W	1T-0
201083	QUEEN'S	WESTCOMBE PARK	W	1G-0
261083	NEWPORT	NEWPORT	L	0-4T
271083	CARDIFF	CARDIFF	D	1T-1T
031183	WIMBLEDON SCHOOL	WIMBLEDON	W	2T-0
101183	WASPS	DEVONSHIRE PARK	W	4T-0
171183	FLAMINGOES	DEVONSHIRE PARK	W	1G-0
241183	OLD CHELTONIANS	MITCHAM	DIF	1DSG-0
011283	UNIVERSITY COLLEGE HOSPITAL	TOTTENHAM	D	1G(FAFK)-1G
081283	KENSINGTON	WOOD LANE	D	0-0
151283	MAIDSTONE	MAIDSTONE	C	
291283	MIDDLESEX WANDERERS	DEVONSHIRE PARK	W	3G1T-0
120184	WASPS	PUTNEY	W	1T-0
260184	ST.THOMAS'S HOSPITAL	LAMBETH	D	0-0
020284	FLAMINGOES	PUTNEY	D	0-0
090284	MAIDSTONE	DEVONSHIRE PARK	C	
160284	UNIVERSITY COLLEGE HOSPITAL	DEVONSHIRE PARK	C	
230284	KENSINGTON	DEVONSHIRE PARK	W	1T-0
010384	WEST KENT	CHISLEHURST	C	
080384	QUEEN'S	DEVONSHIRE PARK	W	3T-0
150384	RICHMOND	DEVONSHIRE PARK	D	0-0
220384	CARDIFF	DEVONSHIRE PARK	L	0-2G1T

For our second and last season at Devonshire Park, we showed F.W. Burnand as captain of the side, G.B. James as vice-captain, H.C. Tress as captain of the 2nd XV and for the first time, as noted in Rule 4, a President whose name was W.J. Compton. In the fifteen games out of twenty one we have a full side for, Burnand played in each one.

For these early years press reports were sketchy. For example, when we played against Old Cheltonians on 13th December, the game was described as being "pleasantly contested"; you don't often see a game like that today! When we defeated the Honourable Artillery Company at Finsbury Square on 24th January good play was said to have been out of the question due to the state of the ground. Two weeks before this we had played Wasps and our old friend "shortages" was back with a vengeance. While the Wasps played a full fifteen, we were poorly represented and played three short up to half time and four short afterwards. Despite this we somehow managed to win by a goal and a try to a try. Three weeks later we were four short again, this time against West Kent at Chislehurst. The home side were themselves two short and we won again by two goals to a try. When we met Blackheath away on 14th March, Andrew Stoddart appeared at three quarter back for the home team. He scored two tries and two conversions in their score of three goals, one dropped goal and a try to nil to leave us with our fifth defeat against them in as many games. It is interesting that a week later we met Cardiff at home and Stoddart turned out for us and helped us to record our first win over them by four tries to one. Our next victory over Cardiff was in 1924!

Out of seventeen games played at Devonshire Park, we managed to win eleven, draw two and lose three. The clubs to lower our colours were Cardiff, Kensington and London Hospital. J.S. (Sydney) Smith of Wales was our first foreign international, making three appearances in this season and returning to make six more the following season. E. Liddiatt scored nine tries and F. Watts made most appearances with 17.

1884/85

041084	BLACKHEATH	BLACKHEATH	L	1T-1G
111084	DULWICH COLLEGE	DULWICH	W	1G1T-0
181084	QUEEN'S	WESTCOMBE PARK	L	0-1DG
251084	MARLBOROUGH NOMADS	DEVONSHIRE PARK	W	1T-0
011184	RICHMOND	OLD DEER PARK	L	0-1DG
081184	ST.THOMAS'S HOSPITAL	DEVONSHIRE PARK	W	3T-0
151184	LONDON SCOTTISH	LEE	L	0-1DG
221184	KENSINGTON	WOOD LANE	D	0-0
291184	WEST KENT	DEVONSHIRE PARK	D	0-0
061284	CARDIFF	CARDIFF	L	0-1DG6T
131284	OLD CHELTONIANS	DEVONSHIRE PARK	W	2G6T-0
201284	ARABS	DEVONSHIRE PARK		
271284	MIDDLESEX WANDERERS	DEVONSHIRE PARK	C	
100185	WASPS	DEVONSHIRE PARK	W	1G1T-1T
170185	LONDON HOSPITAL	DEVONSHIRE PARK	L	0-3G2T
240185	HONOURABLE ARTILLERY COMPANY	FINSBURY SQUARE	W	1G1T-0
310185	WEST KENT	CHISLEHURST	W	2G-1T
070285	OXFORD UNIVERSITY	OXFORD	L	0-2G1DG1T
210285	KENSINGTON	DEVONSHIRE PARK	L	0-1T
280285	ROYAL MILITARY COLLEGE	SANDHURST	W	1G-0
070385	QUEEN'S	DEVONSHIRE PARK	L	0-1DG
140385	BLACKHEATH	BLACKHEATH	L	0-3G1DG1T
210385	CARDIFF	DEVONSHIRE PARK	W	4T-1T

Season 1885/86 saw another move to a new ground, this time the venue was Chiswick Park. This was to be a period of stability for the Club and we were to remain here until the end of the 1896/97 season when the ground was sold over our heads to St. Thomas's Hospital. We started against Blackheath and, in our usual fashion, lost to them, this time by one goal and four tries to nil. We, in fact, lost twenty two out of our first twenty three games against Blackheath, the other being a scoreless draw. We had to wait until 1904 to gain our first victory and we only managed to score in eight of those first twenty three fixtures. This really is a testament to the strength of the Blackheath Club in those days when they were probably the best side in the country. Cambridge and Oxford Universities were met in the same season for the first time. Alas, both games were duly lost. The games against London Scottish at Lee on 10th October and Kensington at Chiswick Park on 24th October were refereed by Mr. George Jones from Cardiff. It appears that the referees travelled great distances even if some of the players did not! Mr. G. Rowland Hill who was the Honorary Secretary of the Rugby Football Union refereed a few of our games in this season.

On 14th November we played West Kent at Chislehurst and although the game was won reasonably easily by us, it was of only 40 minutes duration "on account of the very unfavourable conditions as regards weather". Darkness caused the stoppage of a game against Marlborough Nomads a few minutes before the end the next weekend and this appears to have been a continuing problem because fifteen minutes before the scheduled finish of the fixture with the Royal Naval College two weeks later play was stopped owing to the light being so bad.

F.W. Burnand had captained the side again whilst H. Gurney, G.B. James and R.T. Walker were our most regular players with 14 appearances each. Overall, this had turned out to be a most disappointing season with four games being won, five drawn and eleven lost. It proved to be our worst for tries since 1879/80 with only six being scored and luckily, we have not stooped so low since in a full season. More internationals played for us in this season, W.R.M. (William) Leake and W.G. (William) Mitchell from England and F.T. Purdon (who was a sub from Newport in the game against Cardiff) from Wales. Leake was our first international who was actually named as playing for the Harlequins at the time he was first capped in 1891. Mitchell only made one appearance for us and that was in the match with his club, which happened to be Richmond. He went on to be capped first in 1890. Purdon had already been capped in 1881, 82 and 83 and his international career had finished.

1885/86

031085	BLACKHEATH	BLACKHEATH	L	0-1G4T
101085	LONDON SCOTTISH	LEE	D	0-0
171085	RICHMOND	OLD DEER PARK	L	0-1G2T
241085	KENSINGTON	CHISWICK PARK	W	1T-0
311085	QUEEN'S	WESTCOMBE PARK	L	0-1G
041185	CAMBRIDGE UNIVERSITY	CAMBRIDGE	L	0-3G2DG3T
071185	DULWICH COLLEGE	DULWICH	D	0-0
141185	WEST KENT	CHISLEHURST	W	1G3T-0
211185	MARLBOROUGH NOMADS	SURBITON	W	1DG-0
281185	ROYAL MILITARY COLLEGE	SANDHURST	D	
051285	ROYAL NAVAL COLLEGE	GREENWICH	D	0-0
121285	OLD CHELTONIANS	CHISWICK PARK	C	
191285	KENSINGTON	WOOD LANE	D	0-0
090186	LONDON HOSPITAL	CHISWICK PARK	C	
160186	RICHMOND	OLD DEER PARK	L	0-2G1DG

Nick Cross

230186	CARDIFF	CARDIFF	L	0-3G3T
300186	LONDON SCOTTISH	CHISWICK PARK	L	0-3G1T
060286	OXFORD UNIVERSITY	OXFORD	L	0-1T
130286	CARDIFF	CHISWICK PARK	L	0-1T
200286	QUEEN'S	CHISWICK PARK	W	1G1T-0
270286	WEST KENT	CHISWICK PARK	C	
060386	MIDDLESEX WANDERERS	CHISWICK PARK	L	0-1T
130386	BLACKHEATH	CHISWICK PARK	L	0-1T

5

Points Scoring Introduced 1886-1897

For the first time points scoring had been introduced. It meant that, whereas in the past you had to score a goal or a try to win a game, this was not now so. If you outscored your opponents on points you won the game. The points were awarded as follows: try - 1 point, conversion - 2 points, dropped goal - 3 points, goal from a mark - 3 points. It had been proposed as far back as 1874 that scoring should be by points, but this was rejected. It was also proposed that three touchdowns should count as one goal, this was also rejected. It was noted that one team (Cheltenham College) had been scoring by points ever since the 1860's.

Our fixture list now included teams like Birkenhead Park, Dulwich College, Old Cheltonians, Old Rugbeians and the Royal Indian Engineering College. Moseley and Suffolk County were to have been met away but the weather intervened and the games were cancelled. We started off with three straight defeats against Blackheath, London Scottish and Richmond and all we had to show for these was a dropped goal by William Leake against the Scots. He therefore became the first Harlequin player to score points in a Rugby match. In the defeat against London Scottish, we started with fifteen men but, due to injuries, finished with only thirteen. This was a case of shortages in reverse! Our first win came against Dulwich College on 3rd November by a goal to a try, or 3-1. For the record, F.H. Merk scored the try and C.J. Carver kicked the goal. For the remainder of the season we managed to defeat only Marlborough Nomads, Old Cheltonians and Old Rugbeians, all of which were at home. Both Oxford and Cambridge beat us as did Queen's. The game against Old Rugbeians was worthy of note because both the umpires and the referee were Harlequins, namely D.A.J. Bacon, William Smith and H.S. Johnstone.

During this season, G.B. James was captain and played in at least thirteen games, although most appearances were by H.P. Surtees with sixteen. A.B. Cipriani, M. Walker and F.W. Weekes shared the most tries with two each while James (two conversions) and S.G. Manfield (one try and one dropped goal) shared the most points with four. The team managed seven conversions from fourteen tries which was a vast improvement on the previous season's one from six! We had used 57 different players during the course of the nineteen games of this season. We consistently used less than this until the 1898/99 season when 69 were used. Making his debut was Rowland Hill, who was said to have been one of the greatest administrators in the game and someone whose worth to it and work for it on that side of things were above possible valuation. Unfortunately, he played just nine games for us, all in this season.

1886/87

021086	BLACKHEATH	BLACKHEATH	L	0-2G2T(8)
091086	LONDON SCOTTISH	LEE	L	1DG(3)-1G1DG2T(8)
161086	RICHMOND	CHISWICK PARK	L	0-2G(6)
231086	KENSINGTON	CHISWICK PARK	D	0-0
301086	ROYAL INDIAN ENGINEERING COLLEGE	COOPER'S HILL	L	0-1G1DG1T(7)
031186	DULWICH COLLEGE	DULWICH	W	1G(3)-1T(1)
061186	CAMBRIDGE UNIVERSITY	CAMBRIDGE	L	1T(1)-3G1T(10)
131186	ROYAL MILITARY ACADEMY	WOOLWICH	D	0-0
201186	MARLBOROUGH NOMADS	CHISWICK PARK	W	1DG(3)-1T(1)
271186	ROYAL MILITARY COLLEGE	SANDHURST	L	0-1T(1)
041286	BIRKENHEAD PARK	CHISWICK PARK	L	0-3T(3)
111286	OLD CHELTONIANS	CHISWICK PARK	W	2G2T(8)-0
271286	SUFFOLK COUNTY	IPSWICH	C	
010187	MOSELEY	MOSELEY	C	
080187	MIDDLESEX WANDERERS	CHISWICK PARK	C	
150187	RICHMOND	OLD DEER PARK	C	
190187	ST.THOMAS'S HOSPITAL	CHISWICK PARK	D	1G(3)-1G(3)
290187	LONDON SCOTTISH	CHISWICK PARK	L	0-2G1DG(9)
050287	OXFORD UNIVERSITY	OXFORD	L	0-3T(3)
120287	LONDON WELSH	CHISWICK PARK	D	1T(1)-1T(1)
190287	QUEEN'S	CHISWICK PARK	L	0-1T(1)
260287	OLD RUGBEIANS	CHISWICK PARK	W	2G3T(9)-1T(1)
050387	KENSINGTON	CHISWICK PARK	L	1G(3)-1DG2T(5)
120387	BLACKHEATH	CHISWICK PARK	C	

A.B. Cipriani was captain for season 1887/88 and made at least fourteen appearances in the twenty one games played. We also had a new President, C. Job replacing W.J. Compton. His Presidency was to last for four seasons, the same as Compton's had. Unlike his predecessor, Job actually played for the first team. He made his debut against London Scottish on 9th November 1878 and made the last of his 66 appearances on 13th March 1886 against Blackheath. On the first five Saturdays of the season we lost, conceding 64 points and scoring none. The heaviest defeat was against London Scottish by seven goals and a try to nil. In this game, according to newspaper reports of the time, one of the Scottish forwards was a man by the name of J.H. "Haggis". This is assumed to be a non de plume and did happen quite regularly, our favourite being A.R. le Quin! Our one victory in the opening month was a Wednesday game against the Royal Military Academy at Woolwich by 6-3. We did manage to defeat Cambridge University at Cambridge by a single point as well as Marlborough Nomads and the Old Cheltonians before going on a short pre-Christmas tour to Liverpool. We were due to meet Birkenhead Park on the Saturday and Liverpool Old Boys on the Monday but, in the event, only the former were met as the weather got the better of the second game, the result being a narrow win for our hosts. In this game we had to borrow two players from them as we were men short. On Boxing Day 1887, we travelled down to Weston-Super-Mare and in winning 3-2 we inflicted on them their first defeat of the season and their first home defeat for four years. Our thirst for travelling was undiminished and we visited Ipswich to play against Suffolk County, winning easily. At the Annual General Meeting the Honorary Treasurer was able to report that for the first time for many years the Club had a balance in hand. H.S. Johnstone was top appearance maker with eighteen, he also captained the side on five occasions. Most tries were scored by F.W. Weekes with six, while S.G. Manfield got five conversions which, along with a dropped goal, made him top points scorer with thirteen.

This was the year the first British Isles team ventured on tour. The destination was Australia and New Zealand and joining the tour party (who were really an English side not a British side) was our first "Lion", Andrew Stoddart. He was playing for and captaining the English Cricket team touring Australia and actually took over the captaincy of the Rugby side when the captain, R.L. Seddon was tragically drowned in a boating accident during the Australian part of the tour. He was also to prove to be the star of the tour. When a member of the Stock Exchange he very sadly committed suicide in April 1915.

1887/88

011087	BLACKHEATH	BLACKHEATH	L	0-3G2DG(15)
081087	LONDON SCOTTISH	LEE	L	0-7G1T(22)
121087	ROYAL MILITARY ACADEMY	WOOLWICH	W	2DG(6)-1G(3)
151087	RICHMOND	CHISWICK PARK	L	0-1G2DG4T(13)
221087	KENSINGTON	CHISWICK PARK	L	0-1G1T(4)
291087	ROYAL INDIAN ENGINEERING COLLEGE	COOPER'S HILL	L	0-3G1T(10)
051187	CAMBRIDGE UNIVERSITY	CAMBRIDGE	W	1G(3)-2T(2)
121187	MIDDLESEX WANDERERS	CHISWICK PARK	D	0-0
191187	MARLBOROUGH NOMADS	CHISWICK PARK	W	2G2T(8)-0
261187	ROYAL MILITARY COLLEGE	SANDHURST	L	1T(1)-1G1T(4)
101287	OLD CHELTONIANS	CHISWICK PARK	W	2G(6)-1T(1)
171287	BIRKENHEAD PARK	BIRKENHEAD	L	1T(1)-1DG(3)
191287	LIVERPOOL OLD BOYS	LIVERPOOL	C	
261287	WESTON-SUPER-MARE	WESTON-SUPER-MARE	W	1G(3)-2T(2)
311287	CLAPHAM ROVERS	CHISWICK PARK	C	
070188	SUFFOLK COUNTY	IPSWICH	W	3G7T(16)-0
110188	ST.THOMAS'S HOSPITAL	CHISWICK PARK	C	
140188	RICHMOND	OLD DEER PARK	L	0-1G(3)
210188	MIDDLESEX WANDERERS	RICHMOND	D	0-0
280188	LONDON SCOTTISH	CHISWICK PARK	D	0-0
040288	OXFORD UNIVERSITY	OXFORD	L	0-2T(2)
110288	DULWICH COLLEGE	DULWICH	W	4T(4)-0
180288	QUEEN'S	CHISWICK PARK	W	1G1T(4)-0
250288	LONDON WELSH	CHISWICK PARK	C	
030388	KENSINGTON	WOOD LANE	W	3T(3)-0
100388	BLACKHEATH	CHISWICK PARK	C	

For season 1888/89, A.A. Surtees started his four season reign as captain. Indeed, his last playing season was 1891/92 and this was his last as captain. He made nineteen appearances in this season, being beaten by H.P. (Henry) Surtees and F.B. Hannen (who appeared in every game) to the most appearances by one. On the pitch we did not have a bad season as we won eight, drew two and lost nine with one game (against Middlesex Wanderers) being abandoned seven minutes from the end with us leading 3-0. Our biggest win proved to be against the Royal Indian Engineering College when we won 6-0. As was now becoming usual we played both the Universities away and Blackheath and London Scottish at home and away. As was also becoming usual, all six matches were lost. We did journey to Weston-Super-Mare again on Boxing Day and after borrowing W. Aldridge from them to make up our numbers, we dispatched them again, this time 3-1. As well as the two Surtees' and Hannen, our other top appearance makers were H.B. Lawrell (18), G.B. James (17), A.B. Cipriani and H. Stocken (16) and A.C. Broadbent, C.J. Carver and J.K. Gregory (15). A.A. Surtees got four tries and S. Kent kicked four conversions making him top points man with eight. The team had managed 22 tries in all, which was seven down on the previous season, and our conversion total of six was not particularly good either! Making his farewell appearance for us against Richmond on 2nd February was Billy Williams although he features again in our story when we talk about his "Cabbage Patch".

1888/89

290988	BLACKHEATH	BLACKHEATH	L	0-3G3DG3T(21)
061088	LONDON SCOTTISH	BRONDESBURY	L	0-1G1DG4T(10)
131088	RICHMOND	CHISWICK PARK	L	1G(3)-1G2T(5)
201088	KENSINGTON	CHISWICK PARK	L	0-2G2T(8)
271088	ROYAL INDIAN ENGINEERING COLLEGE	COOPER'S HILL	W	1DG3T(6)-0
031188	MIDDLESEX WANDERERS	CHISWICK PARK	A	1G(3)-0
101188	CAMBRIDGE UNIVERSITY	CAMBRIDGE	L	1T(1)-2T(2)
171188	MARLBOROUGH NOMADS	CHISWICK PARK	W	3T(3)-0
241188	BIRKENHEAD PARK	CHISWICK PARK	W	1G1T(4)-0
011288	OXFORD UNIVERSITY	OXFORD	L	0-1DG1T(4)
081288	OLD CHELTONIANS	CHISWICK PARK	W	1T(1)-0
221288	ROYAL MILITARY ACADEMY	WOOLWICH	C	
261288	WESTON-SUPER-MARE	WESTON-SUPER-MARE	W	1G(3)-1T(1)
291288	BLACKHEATH	CHISWICK PARK	L	0-1G2T(5)
050189	SHERBORNE SCHOOL	CHISWICK PARK	C	
120189	QUEEN'S	CHISWICK PARK	D	0-0
190189	MIDDLESEX WANDERERS	RICHMOND	W	1G3T(6)-1T(1)
260189	LONDON SCOTTISH	CHISWICK PARK	L	0-1G(3)
020289	RICHMOND	OLD DEER PARK	D	0-0
090289	DULWICH COLLEGE	DULWICH	C	
160289	MARLBOROUGH NOMADS	CHISWICK PARK	C	
230289	LONDON WELSH	CHISWICK PARK	W	2T(2)-1T(1)
020389	KENSINGTON	WOOD LANE	W	2T(2)-1T(1)
090389	ST.THOMAS'S HOSPITAL	CHISWICK PARK	L	1G(3)-2G(6)

As the decade came to an end, so our fortunes dipped very slightly as we managed to win only seven games out of nineteen, draw two and lose ten in the following season. Our fixture list was now starting to take on almost the same look every season. London Welsh were regular opponents as were St. Thomas's Hospital. Newport were met for the first time in six years and Lansdowne from Dublin were to have been played for the first time on 3rd December at Chiswick Park but, unfortunately, the game was called off. The Old Leysians were played for the first time on 23rd November and ran out winners by six points to nil. A week after this we played at Oxford against the University in our seventh meeting. We had failed to score in the six previous meetings so things did not look good. In those days the two university sides from Oxford and Cambridge were rarely weak and this time was no exception. The Oxford team contained five current or future internationals, three from England and two from Scotland while we fielded a side which had William Leake at half-back and was led by A.A. Surtees. In the first half Leake got a try and R. "Fale" (who was later identified as H.B. Lawrell) kicked the goal for a lead of 3-0. Henry Surtees scored our second try to extend the lead by one point before A.M. Paterson got one for Oxford to leave the final score at 4-1 in our favour. Interestingly, this was to prove our only success against them until after the turn of the Century. The game against Queen's which was due to take place on 11th January was cancelled due to the winding up of that Club.

No one managed to appear in all nineteen games this season although three players (T.A.M. Forde, F.B. Hannen and Henry Surtees) played in eighteen. The captain managed fifteen while Cipriani and J.K. Gregory (16) and Lawrell (17) were other leading players. Henry Surtees got six tries and Gregory with five conversions and two tries was top points scorer with twelve. The total tries for the season reached 26 and our points total of 55 equalled our best of 1887/88 in the four seasons since points scoring was introduced.

This season had seen the introduction of a penalty goal whose value was 2 points. This was despite the fact that three years earlier the Rugby Football Union had said that they would oppose any proposition whereby a goal from a try should count more than another goal and "...which we trust will never be sanctioned". The International Board which England had not yet joined still declined to allow a goal from a penalty to score. England were to join the Board in 1890 who then had to accept the scoring for a goal from a penalty.

This season was also to see the founding of the famous Barbarians Club. Their first tour, which was to the North of England, was to take place during Christmas 1890. The Club was the brainchild of Percy Carpmael of Blackheath who organised a scratch side to play against Burton, Moseley, Wakefield Trinity and Huddersfield over Easter 1890. The scratch team were called various things on this first tour, "Carpmael's London team" (at Burton), "a Blackheath team" (at Moseley), "W.P. Carpmael's County and International Team" (at Wakefield) and "The Southern Nomads" (at Huddersfield). Among those taking part were William Mitchell and William Leake. These two became our first "Barbarians" because, although the Barbarian Football Club was not formed until after the Nomads tour had finished, they were there at the very beginning in the Alexandra Hotel, Bradford at two o'clock in the morning on the 9th April.

1889/90

280989	OLD CHELTONIANS	CHISWICK PARK	C	
051089	LONDON SCOTTISH	OLD DEER PARK	L	1T(1)-1G3T(6)
121089	RICHMOND	CHISWICK PARK	W	1G2T(5)-1T(1)
191089	KENSINGTON	CHISWICK PARK	L	0-1T(1)
231089	ROYAL MILITARY ACADEMY	WOOLWICH	W	3T(3)-0

261089	ROYAL INDIAN ENGINEERING COLLEGE	COOPER'S HILL	W	1G1T(4)-1G(3)
021189	NEWPORT	NEWPORT	L	0-4T(4)
091189	CAMBRIDGE UNIVERSITY	CAMBRIDGE	L	0-2G1T(7)
161189	MARLBOROUGH NOMADS	CHISWICK PARK	W	4G1T(13)-1T(1)
231189	OLD LEYSIANS	CHISWICK PARK	L	0-1G3T(6)
301189	OXFORD UNIVERSITY	OXFORD	W	1G1T(4)-1T(1)
031289	LANSDOWNE	CHISWICK PARK	C	
071289	BIRKENHEAD PARK	BIRKENHEAD	L	1G(3)-1G2T(5)
141289	LONDON WELSH	CHISWICK PARK	L	1G(3)-1G1T(4)
211289	OLD CHELTONIANS	CHISWICK PARK	D	1G1T(4)-1G1T(4)
281289	BLACKHEATH	CHISWICK PARK	C	
040190	BLACKHEATH	BLACKHEATH	L	1T(1)-1G1T(4)
110190	QUEEN'S	CHISWICK PARK	C	
180190	MIDDLESEX WANDERERS	CHISWICK PARK	W	2G1T(7)-0
250190	LONDON SCOTTISH	CHISWICK PARK	L	0-2G(6)
080290	ROYAL MILITARY COLLEGE	SANDHURST	C	
150290	MARLBOROUGH NOMADS	CHISWICK PARK	W	1G1T(4)-0
220290	MIDDLESEX WANDERERS	CHISWICK PARK	D	1DG(3)-3T(3)
010390	KENSINGTON	WOOD LANE	C	
080390	ST.THOMAS'S HOSPITAL	CHISWICK PARK	L	0-3G1T(10)

The next season covering 1890/91 proved to be somewhat shortened as six games were lost to the weather between 13th December and 24th January. Obviously, the means of pitch protection in these days were virtually non-existent. We still managed to defeat Kensington, Richmond (twice) and Birkenhead Park. Newport, Cambridge University, London Scottish and Oxford University were all played away and all matches were lost, the first two by just a single point. Forty eight players were used in the first team during the course of the season the most prominent of whom were F.B. Hannen (full back), A.B. Cipriani and William Leake (half back) and P.E. Bodington, A.C. Broadbent, N.L. Garrett, A.A. Surtees and D.W. Williams (forwards). Twenty one of these players were making their debuts for the First XV, one of whom was S.B. Peech who went on to make 103 appearances over the next seven seasons. Our top try scorer was W.F. Surtees with just two, while G.B. James got a goal from a mark and a penalty goal (our first since the introduction of such in 1889/90 and scored against Clapham Rovers on 6th December) for a total of six points.

As mentioned before, the Barbarians went on their first tour to the North of England. They played against Hartlepool Rovers and Bradford and Andrew Stoddart captained the side. By this time other original members of the Barbarians had been elected and these included the following Harlequins - F.B. Hannen and A.A. Surtees.

This season saw Leake make his only three appearances for England, playing against Wales, Ireland and Scotland (France did not join to make the four nations five until the 1905/06 season). After an excellent debut and creating the first try against Wales (England winning 7-3) he was then part of the team which went to Lansdowne Road and did very well to win against Ireland 9-0 (five tries being scored). His last game at Richmond Athletic Ground was one where the home side was completely outclassed by the visiting Scots. This team was said to be the most disappointing English side since 1871. This is probably the reason he got only those three caps and why ten players in total from this team were dropped and never gained another international cap. The match against Wales was played at Rodney Parade, Newport and this is a ground where we have only ever been victorious once as a club. Therefore, Leake and Mitchell (who played at full back in that game) must be two of very few Quins to have been in a side to win there.

1890/91

041090	OLD LEYSIANS	CHISWICK PARK	L	0-1T(1)
111090	KENSINGTON	CHISWICK PARK	W	1G(3)-2T(2)
181090	RICHMOND	CHISWICK PARK	W	2T(2)-0
221090	ROYAL MILITARY ACADEMY	WOOLWICH	W	1DG1T(4)-2T(2)
251090	ROYAL INDIAN ENGINEERING COLLEGE	COOPER'S HILL	D	0-0
011190	NEWPORT	NEWPORT	L	0-1T(1)
081190	CAMBRIDGE UNIVERSITY	CAMBRIDGE	L	1MG2T(5)-1G1DG(6)
151190	LONDON SCOTTISH	OLD DEER PARK	L	1T(1)-2G(6)
221190	BIRKENHEAD PARK	CHISWICK PARK	W	1G1T(4)-0
061290	CLAPHAM ROVERS	WANDSWORTH COMMON	W	1PG1T(3)-0
131290	LONDON WELSH	CHISWICK PARK	C	
271290	MARLBOROUGH NOMADS	CHISWICK PARK	C	
030191	BLACKHEATH	BLACKHEATH	C	
100191	NEWPORT	CHISWICK PARK	C	
170191	MIDDLESEX WANDERERS	RICHMOND	C	
240191	LONDON SCOTTISH	CHISWICK PARK	C	
310191	RICHMOND	OLD DEER PARK	W	1G1T(4)-0
070291	OXFORD UNIVERSITY	OXFORD	L	0-5T(5)
140291	ST.THOMAS'S HOSPITAL	CHISWICK PARK	L	0-4G1T(13)
210291	MIDDLESEX WANDERERS	CHISWICK PARK	L	0-1G1T(4)
280291	KENSINGTON	CHISWICK PARK	L	0-1G(3)

During the Summer of 1891 the first British team toured South Africa, playing twenty games (one unofficial) including three test matches, winning all twenty and scoring 226 points for with just one point against. On this tour William Mitchell was one of the full backs and A.A. Surtees one of the forwards. Both men played in all three tests against South Africa, Mitchell getting a goal from a mark in the second. The captain, W.E. Maclagen, was handed a cup donated by Sir Donald Currie of the Union Castle Shipping Line, this was to be awarded to the colonial club who performed best against the team. Griqualand West were defeated 3-0 and so were deemed to have won the cup. This cup was to be held by the club until the next season when it was to be competed for by the clubs of South Africa. This cup (known, of course, as the Currie Cup) is now the trophy for the South African Provincial Championship. After this, our next tourist was J.S.R. Reeve who went on the 1930 tour to Australia and New Zealand.

For Season 1891/92, four sides were listed in the fixture card, 1st, "A", 2nd XV and 3rd XV as the membership grew. The last season of A.A. Surtees's leadership of the Club (he had managed 82 appearances, 63 as captain) saw the debut of C.M. (Cyril) Wells. Wells was recruited by Leake through his connection to Dulwich College and, similarly to Leake, also played for Cambridge, although made only two appearances in the Varsity match as opposed to Leake's three. When Wells made his debut for us against Richmond on 17th October 1891, he played as a three quarter but he was to make his name at half back. He was still at Cambridge and one of his two other appearances for us in this season was against his University when he played in the position now known as a wing three quarter. Unfortunately we were well beaten by three goals (15) to nil. His third appearance came against London Scottish where he teamed up at half back with Cipriani. We were going through a rather difficult patch at this time and were again easily beaten by 0-19, our heaviest defeat of the season. He still managed to play in the Varsity match for a victorious light blues team.

In a letter written by Wells, he describes the ground at Chiswick Park as always being in good condition and the grass being short and thick with the ground level almost like a cricket ground. As for the accommodation, he describes this as being rather primitive with only four or five small basins with cold water for the whole fifteen! Later, a hip bath with hot water was introduced but the changing arrangements were never good. He didn't seem to think the players were so particular in those days. As for half back play of the time, it was normal practice for both half backs to stand close to the scrummage. Towards the end of his career he used to stand back from the scrum when in the opponents twenty five to receive the ball from the other half back as soon as he could get it. Perhaps this was the origin of the present stand-off half. He goes on to mention that although not a strong side in those days, we were not easy to defeat and might at any time pull a match out of the fire. The two best seasons we had during his career were 1895/96 and when he captained the side in 1896/97. Coincidentally, these were the two he played most in.

Newport handed us a heavy defeat at their hands in what was our last game against them for nineteen years. This was hardly surprising as they included three current and eight future Welsh internationals. They were still able to lend us J.E. (James) Webb (an old Welsh international) to make up our numbers as we had arrived one short. Rosslyn Park were played and beaten for the first time and the famous Old Merchant Taylors were to have been met at Chiswick Park on 5th March but the fixture was cancelled. Another first was the visit of Dublin Wanderers who came on tour in December. We met them at Chiswick on 9th December and although we fielded quite a strong team including Hannen, Cipriani, Leake, A.A and Henry Surtees and Peech, we could not match a strong Irish side containing at least two current and two future international players and ended up losing by the narrowest of margins - a try to nil. Cipriani managed to get three tries and E.H.D. Sewell with ten points (a goal from a mark and two conversions) were the top in those respective areas. Top appearances were by Cipriani and A.A. Surtees (16) and Hannen, R.W. Hunt and G.W.T. Pimbury (14). Interestingly, Surtees played in our first game of the season (against Old Leysians) just five days after returning from the arduous tour of South Africa. Two players who made their debuts were R.W. Hunt (on 3rd October against Old Leysians) and J.R. Pank (on 27th February against London Scottish), who went on to make 112 and 126 appearances respectively.

The minutes for this season recorded that at the end of this season we had 263 members and a balance of £1 12s 3d in the bank. A further item in the balance sheet indicating the share of gate up to December 1891 - £2 18s 10d - is interesting as it appears we shared the money with the Chiswick Park Cricket Club which used the ground in the summer months.

The fixture card from the 1891/92 season was of a more solid nature than those before. On the front it simply states: Harlequin Football Club - Season 1891-92. It opens out to give fixtures for the 1st, A, 2nd and 3rd XVs. On the reverse of one of the outer flaps is given the President - F.S. Watts (this was his first season, he made 51 appearances between 1878 and 1887), Vice Presidents - F.W. Burnand, H.K. Gow, H.S. Johnstone and W.R.M. Leake, Captain - A.A. Surtees and Vice-Captain - A.B. Cipriani as well as the names of the Honorary Secretary, Honorary Treasurer, Captain A Team, the Committee and the Honorary Auditors. On the other flap are details of the ground and the notation that it is close to Chiswick Station, London & South Western Railway, and ten minutes' walk from Gunnersbury Station, where Club Colours are available from (C. Lewin & Co., 29, King William Street, E.C.) and the departure time from Waterloo of the train for Chiswick on the loop line.

At about this time the points system was updated by the International Board and adopted by other Unions. The changes were 2 points for a try (up from 1), 3 points for a conversion (up from 2), 3 points for a penalty goal (up from 2) and 4 points for both a dropped goal and a goal from a mark (both up from 3).

1891/92

031091	OLD LEYSIANS	CHISWICK PARK	L	1G3T(11)-2G1T(12)
101091	KENSINGTON	CHISWICK PARK	L	0-1T(2)
171091	RICHMOND	CHISWICK PARK	W	1T(2)-0
211091	ROYAL MILITARY ACADEMY	WOOLWICH	W	1DG1T(6)-2T(4)
241091	ROYAL INDIAN ENGINEERING COLLEGE	COOPER'S HILL	D	0-0
311091	NEWPORT	NEWPORT	L	1T(2)-1G6T(17)
071191	CAMBRIDGE UNIVERSITY	CAMBRIDGE	L	0-3G(15)
141191	LONDON SCOTTISH	OLD DEER PARK	L	0-3G2T(19)
211191	BIRKENHEAD PARK	BIRKENHEAD	L	0-2T(4)
281191	OXFORD UNIVERSITY	OXFORD	L	0-2T(4)
051291	ROSSLYN PARK	CHISWICK PARK	W	1G1T(7)-0
091291	DUBLIN WANDERERS	CHISWICK PARK	L	0-1T(2)
121291	CLAPHAM ROVERS	CHISWICK PARK	L	2T(4)-1G(5)
191291	LONDON WELSH	CHISWICK PARK	C	
261291	MARLBOROUGH NOMADS	CHISWICK PARK	C	
160192	MIDDLESEX WANDERERS	RICHMOND	C	
230192	KENSINGTON	CHISWICK PARK	D	1T(2)-1T(2)
300192	RICHMOND	OLD DEER PARK	W	2G(10)-0
060292	BLACKHEATH	BLACKHEATH	L	1T(2)-1G1T(7)
130292	ST.THOMAS'S HOSPITAL	CHISWICK PARK	L	1MG(4)-2G1T(12)
200292	MIDDLESEX WANDERERS	CHISWICK PARK	C	
270292	LONDON SCOTTISH	CHISWICK PARK	L	1T(2)-1G(5)
050392	OLD MERCHANT TAYLORS	CHISWICK PARK	C	

For the next two seasons, Cipriani was back as captain following his first outing as such in 1887/88. We began season 1892/93 with our best start since the Club was formed with six wins out of six, defeating Old Leysians, Kensington, Richmond, Royal Military Academy, Royal Indian Engineering College and Old Cheltonians, the latter by forty points to nil! Between November and February we played some of the stronger sides in the country and came off second best, losing to both Cambridge and Oxford Universities, London Scottish, Birkenhead Park and Blackheath. The Old Merchant Taylors were played for the first time and although we were to lose, revenge would be ours the following season. In the last five fixtures we managed to win four (including London Welsh and the return with Richmond) and draw with London Scottish. Three scoreless draws with them were the best we had managed in the last sixteen meetings. The twelve wins equalled a Club record set in the 1870/71 season, although it took twenty five games that year as opposed to just twenty this time. Top appearance makers were T. Hemmant, who appeared in all twenty games as a forward, S.B. Peech (19), Cipriani and Henry Surtees (18) and N.L. Garrett (16). Cipriani and C.D.E. Grose scored six tries apiece (Grose got four of those and four conversions in the thrashing of the Old Cheltonians to set a new Club record for individual points (20) in one match) and the captain went on to set a new points record in a season with 33 (made up of those six tries and seven conversions). Things were definitely on the up as the team scored 42 tries which was the best for ten years and the points for the season was a record number of 136 whilst 90 were conceded.

The England game against Scotland on 4th March saw the debut of Cyril Wells. Over the next five seasons he was to gain six caps, four against Scotland and two against Wales but none against Ireland. It would appear that he was dropped twice for games against the Irish (1894 and 1897) and the players who replaced him gained their solitary caps in those matches.

1892/93

011092	OLD LEYSIANS	STAMFORD BRIDGE	W	1G2T(9)-0
081092	KENSINGTON	CHISWICK PARK	W	1G2T(9)-0
151092	RICHMOND	OLD DEER PARK	W	3T(6)-0
191092	ROYAL MILITARY ACADEMY	WOOLWICH	W	1G3T(11)-1G(5)
221092	ROYAL INDIAN ENGINEERING COLLEGE	COOPER'S HILL	W	1G2T(9)-1G(5)
291092	OLD CHELTONIANS	CHISWICK PARK	W	6G5T(40)-0
051192	CAMBRIDGE UNIVERSITY	CAMBRIDGE	L	0-1G1T(7)
121192	LONDON SCOTTISH	OLD DEER PARK	L	0-4G1T(22)
191192	BIRKENHEAD PARK	CHISWICK PARK	L	1T(2)-1DG2T(8)
261192	OXFORD UNIVERSITY	OXFORD	L	0-1G2T(9)
031292	ROSSLYN PARK	ACTON	W	1T(2)-0
101292	CLAPHAM ROVERS	WANDSWORTH COMMON	W	2T(4)-0
241292	MARLBOROUGH NOMADS	CHISWICK PARK	C	
311292	CLAPHAM ROVERS	CHISWICK PARK	C	
070193	BLACKHEATH	CHISWICK PARK	C	
140193	MIDDLESEX WANDERERS	RICHMOND	L	0-1G1T(7)
210193	KENSINGTON	WOOD LANE	C	
280193	OLD MERCHANT TAYLORS	CHISWICK PARK	L	0-2T(4)
040293	BLACKHEATH	BLACKHEATH	L	0-2G2T(14)
110293	ST.THOMAS'S HOSPITAL	CHISWICK PARK	W	2G1T(12)-0

180293	MIDDLESEX WANDERERS	CHISWICK PARK	W	1G1T(7)-2T(4)
250293	LONDON SCOTTISH	CHISWICK PARK	D	0-0
040393	RICHMOND	CHISWICK PARK	W	1G1DG(9)-1G(5)
110393	LONDON WELSH	CHISWICK PARK	W	2G3T(16)-0

Following on from the successful start of the previous season was always going to be difficult and so it proved. Well, to begin with anyway. By the turn of the year we had managed seven victories, two draws and five defeats. One of these losses was against Dublin Wanderers who had returned after their narrow success in 1891. Their side contained three current and one future Irish internationals, ours contained none. By half time the visitors had scored a goal and two tries (11) to our solitary try (3). We could make no further impression after the break while the Wanderers added a goal and a dropped goal to win by 20 points to 3. After the cancellation of the games against Clapham Rovers and Blackheath (a blessing in disguise!) we managed to win six out of seven, losing only to St. Thomas's Hospital. Out of the wins, the most remarkable was the victory over London Welsh by the score of 41-0. The Welsh did play two men short and this probably accounted for the large score, but, for the record our try scorers were A.E. Earnshaw, E.G. Kent (3), William Leake, S.B. Peech and C.E. Wilson (3) while H.W. Burness dropped a goal and A.B. Cipriani kicked five conversions. This win eclipsed the previous number of victories in a season by one. The record of twelve, equalled the previous season, now stood at thirteen.

In total this season, 46 players were used in the 21 games played by the first XV. Of those making their debuts, J.J. (James) Gowans the Scottish international three quarter was noteworthy in that he played for us in the first three games of the season and by 4th November he was playing against us for Cambridge University and managed to score a try in their victory. Cipriani set a record number of conversions with fourteen, while E.G. Kent got most tries with six. The team set a new points record with 180 and twenty conversions beat the previous best of nineteen set in 1870/71. On the appearance front, J.R. Pank was the only ever present and T. Hemmant (20), H.S.P. (Henry) Hindley (19), T.H.C. Dunn (18) and S.B. Peech (17) were the best of the rest. The points system was given a very minor overhaul at the start of this season when the try became worth 3 points and the conversion dropped down to 2. All the other values remained the same and it was to be twelve years before any more changes were made.

1893/94

300993	OLD LEYSIANS	CHISWICK PARK	W	1G4T(17)-1DG(4)
071093	KENSINGTON	CHISWICK PARK	W	2G2T(16)-0
141093	RICHMOND	CHISWICK PARK	D	1T(3)-1PG(3)
181093	ROYAL MILITARY ACADEMY	WOOLWICH	L	0-1G(5)
211093	ROYAL INDIAN ENGINEERING COLLEGE	COOPER'S HILL	W	1G(5)-0
281093	MARLBOROUGH NOMADS	CHISWICK PARK	W	3G1T(18)-0
041193	CAMBRIDGE UNIVERSITY	CAMBRIDGE	L	0-2G(10)
111193	LONDON SCOTTISH	OLD DEER PARK	L	1T(3)-2G1T(13)
181193	BIRKENHEAD PARK	BIRKENHEAD	D	0-0
251193	OXFORD UNIVERSITY	OXFORD	L	1T(3)-1G3T(14)
021293	ROSSLYN PARK	CHISWICK PARK	C	

091293	CLAPHAM ROVERS	WANDSWORTH COMMON	W	1G1T(8)-0
141293	DUBLIN WANDERERS	CHISWICK PARK	L	1T(3)-2G1DG2T(20)
161293	OLD LEYSIANS	STAMFORD BRIDGE	W	1G2T(11)-1G(5)
231293	OLD CHELTONIANS	CHISWICK PARK	W	2G2T(16)-2G(10)
301293	CLAPHAM ROVERS	CHISWICK PARK	C	
060194	BLACKHEATH	CHISWICK PARK	C	
130194	MIDDLESEX WANDERERS	RICHMOND	W	2G(10)-1DG(4)
200194	KENSINGTON	WOOD LANE	W	1G1T(8)-2T(6)
270194	OLD MERCHANT TAYLORS	STAMFORD BRIDGE	W	1T(3)-0
100294	ST.THOMAS'S HOSPITAL	CHISWICK PARK	L	0-2G1PG1T(16)
170294	MIDDLESEX WANDERERS	CHISWICK PARK	W	1G1T(8)-1T(3)
240294	LONDON SCOTTISH	CHISWICK PARK	C	
030394	RICHMOND	RICHMOND	W	1DG1T(7)-1G(5)
100394	LONDON WELSH	CHISWICK PARK	W	5G1DG4T(41)-0

The number of teams we ran dropped to three with the disappearance of the 3rd XV. After two reasonably successful seasons, it was time for our fortunes to take a dip. We started well enough with our first home victory over the Old Merchant Taylors by a goal to nil but then lost eight out of our next ten games. The last of these was against Coventry on our first Christmas tour of the Midlands. This match took place on 26th December and we went down 3-11. The next day the tour moved to Rugby, we proved more successful here and ran out winners 11-0. The playing members of this first tour were the forwards, P.E. Bodington, R.N. Douglas, A.E. (Alfred) Eiloart, J.N. (Norman) Hill, A.C. Hunter, C.N. Jeffcoat, S.B. Peech (who was in his first of two seasons as Club captain), J.L. Phillips and H.R. Wood and the backs, A.B. Cipriani, H.N. Clarke, William Leake, J.R. Pank, W.F. Surtees, Clifford Wells and his brother Cyril Wells. After this just four out of eleven games were played, three were won and one was a scoreless draw against Richmond. These cancellations brought the number for the season to eleven, so this can probably be stated as the reason for our low number of wins, although it must also be mentioned that both Blackheath games and one of the London Scottish fixtures were amongst them. Going on form these games would probably have been lost anyway so our losses would have been much higher than the previous two seasons. Another of the matches lost was to be against Dulwich College. It would have been nice to have seen this match go ahead as we hadn't played them since 1888. All these scratched matches didn't help appearances or scores for this season. Only H.N. Clarke out of forty players managed to appear in each game while Cipriani, Pank and Peech missed just one. The team got seventeen tries, and with just six being converted, this translated into only 63 points from sixteen matches. Points conceded were 119 (this was mainly due to both Oxford and Cambridge defeating us heavily). H.N. Clarke and Cyril Wells got four tries apiece and as Wells got four conversions as well he finished top points scorer with twenty.

1894/95

290994	OLD MERCHANT TAYLORS	CHISWICK PARK	W	1G(5)-0
061094	KENSINGTON	CHISWICK PARK	L	1T(3)-2T(6)
131094	RICHMOND	RICHMOND	L	0-1G3T(14)

201094	ROYAL INDIAN ENGINEERING COLLEGE	COOPER'S HILL	L	0-1T(3)
271094	MIDDLESEX WANDERERS	RICHMOND	W	1G2T(11)-1G(5)
031194	CAMBRIDGE UNIVERSITY	CAMBRIDGE	L	1T(3)-4G4T(32)
101194	LONDON SCOTTISH	RICHMOND	L	0-1T(3)
141194	ROYAL MILITARY ACADEMY	WOOLWICH	C	
171194	BIRKENHEAD PARK	CHISWICK PARK	L	1T(3)-2G2T(16)
241194	OXFORD UNIVERSITY	OXFORD	L	0-4G1PG1T(26)
011294	ROSSLYN PARK	CHISWICK PARK	D	0-0
081294	CLAPHAM ROVERS	WANDSWORTH COMMON	C	
151294	OLD LEYSIANS	STAMFORD BRIDGE	C	
221294	OLD CHELTONIANS	CHISWICK PARK	C	
261294	COVENTRY	COVENTRY	L	1T(3)-1G2T(11)
271294	RUGBY	RUGBY	W	1G2T(11)-0
291294	CROYDON	CHISWICK PARK	W	1G2T(11)-1T(3)
050195	BLACKHEATH	CHISWICK PARK	C	
120195	LONDON SCOTTISH	CHISWICK PARK	C	
190195	KENSINGTON	WOOD LANE	W	1G(5)-0
260195	OLD MERCHANT TAYLORS	OLD DEER PARK	W	1G1T(8)-0
020295	BLACKHEATH	BLACKHEATH	C	
090295	ST.THOMAS'S HOSPITAL	CHISWICK PARK	C	
160295	DULWICH COLLEGE	DULWICH	C	
230295	MARLBOROUGH NOMADS	CHISWICK PARK	C	
020395	RICHMOND	CHISWICK PARK	D	0-0
090395	LONDON WELSH	CHISWICK PARK	C	

Compared with the previous season, the 1895/96 one was to be near perfect. We played twenty five games and only three were cancelled. We won ten out of twelve games at home and nine out of thirteen away to set a new record of nineteen wins in a season, a record that was to stand for thirteen years. Other notable events were our first "double" over London Scottish, our first win against Dublin Wanderers and two of the Hospitals, St. Bartholomew's and Guy's were met for the first time since 1880 and 1881 respectively. In the match at Chiswick against the touring Wanderers from Dublin on Thursday 5th December, we ran out winners by 13 points to nil. We mainly had Cyril Wells to thank for this as he (according to a newspaper report of the game) was much too clever for his opponents at every point. He scored two tries and kicked two conversions, the other try coming from wing three quarter P.S. Saward. The Wanderers had played and been beaten by Cambridge University the day before and were due to play Richmond to finish off their tour on the Saturday, this was some schedule and, not surprisingly, were showing the effects of the Cambridge game when they played us. The report also mentions that their forwards played with that spirit in the open which has long been a characteristic of the Irish rugby footballer, a tradition which still lives on today.

We went on our second Christmas tour to the Midlands and this time fitted in an extra game against a team who have long since been our opponents, Leicester. We started off against Coventry on 26th December and with

Wells in fine form again we came away with a 13-0 win. The next day we met Rugby and although making two changes we managed to win by two goals and three tries (19) to nil, with Wells again doing well and adding another seven points to the ten he got in the first game. With the game at Leicester on the following day, it was a truly gruelling schedule. It must have been a testament to the fitness of the players that twelve of the seventeen who were in the party played in all three matches. Our first meeting with Leicester was to prove a fruitful one for us and with tries coming from Leake and Wells in the first half, we ran out winners 6-0. This tour has to go down as one of, if not, the most successful ever undertaken by a Quins team. Again, a fixture was due to be fulfilled against Dulwich College but again it was to be scratched and we have not played them since. Even though this season was so successful, it was not without its low points. We still lost to Birkenhead Park (our fourth in five games), Oxford and Cambridge Universities defeated us by twenty five and eighteen points to nil and of course we lost to Blackheath (but only by a goal to nil). Apart from season 1867/68, this proved to be the season with the lowest number of players used up to the Second World War, just 36. Pank, Peech and J.D. (John) Whittaker (a captain of the Club in the not too distant future) appeared in all twenty five games and Henry Surtees (24), H.N. Clarke (22), R.W. Hunt (21) and P.S. Saward (20) all made significant contributions. In his seventeen appearances, Cyril Wells managed to score eleven tries and thirteen conversions to set a new Club record of 59 points in a season. This was the most tries an individual had scored since Andrew Stoddart's seventeen in 1882/83. The team set a record number of points in a season with 181, this beat the previous best set in 1893/94 by a single point.

1895/96

280995	OLD MERCHANT TAYLORS	CHISWICK PARK	L	0-1T(3)
051095	KENSINGTON	CHISWICK PARK	W	1G1T(8)-0
121095	RICHMOND	RICHMOND	W	1G(5)-0
191095	ROYAL INDIAN ENGINEERING COLLEGE	COOPER'S HILL	W	1G(5)-0
021195	ROSSLYN PARK	CHISWICK PARK	W	1MG(4)-0
091195	LONDON SCOTTISH	RICHMOND	W	2T(6)-1T(3)
161195	BIRKENHEAD PARK	BIRKENHEAD	L	0-1G1T(8)
231195	OXFORD UNIVERSITY	OXFORD	L	0-5G(25)
301195	CAMBRIDGE UNIVERSITY	CAMBRIDGE	L	0-6T(18)
051295	DUBLIN WANDERERS	CHISWICK PARK	W	2G1T(13)-0
071295	CROYDON	CHISWICK PARK	W	1T(3)-0
141295	OLD LEYSIANS	STAMFORD BRIDGE	W	2G(10)-1G(5)
211295	ST.BARTHOLOMEW'S HOSPITAL	CHISWICK PARK	W	2G2T(16)-0
261295	COVENTRY	COVENTRY	W	2G1T(13)-0
271295	RUGBY	RUGBY	W	2G3T(19)-0
281295	LEICESTER	LEICESTER	W	2T(6)-0
040196	BLACKHEATH	CHISWICK PARK	C	
110196	LONDON SCOTTISH	CHISWICK PARK	W	3G1T(18)-0
150196	ROYAL MILITARY ACADEMY	WOOLWICH	C	
180196	GUY'S HOSPITAL	CHISWICK PARK	W	1G3T(14)-0

250196	OLD MERCHANT TAYLORS	OLD DEER PARK	W	1T(3)-0
010296	BLACKHEATH	BLACKHEATH	L	0-1G(5)
080296	ST.THOMAS'S HOSPITAL	CHISWICK PARK	W	3T(9)-0
150296	DULWICH COLLEGE	DULWICH	C	
220296	MARLBOROUGH NOMADS	CHISWICK PARK	W	1G2T(11)-1G(5)
290296	RICHMOND	CHISWICK PARK	L	0-2G1DG(14)
070396	KENSINGTON	WOOD LANE	W	3T(9)-0
140396	OLD LEYSIANS	CHISWICK PARK	W	3T(9)-1G(5)

The 1896/97 season was to be our last at Chiswick Park, the ground was sold over our heads to St. Thomas's Hospital. Not only were we going to lose our ground but also the services of Cipriani, Leake and Peech who all played their final games for the first team during this season. Between them they had made over 350 appearances so a wealth of experience was also being lost. Cyril Wells was to be captain but, unlike the three previous post holders, he only lasted for one season. The only notable victory was that against Birkenhead Park by eight points to five in the final game of the season on 20th March. We received a visit from another Irish side in the form of Monkstown on 28th November and after a close game we lost 3-8. It was our third tour of the Midlands at Christmas and this time we played at Coventry, Leicester and, for the first time, Northampton. Again, it was a reasonably successful tour and, after defeating Coventry (6-3), we went on to draw at both Leicester (0-0) and Northampton (6-6). Making one appearance for us this season was J.C. Marquis, who gained two caps for England against Ireland and Scotland in 1900. He is listed as playing for Birkenhead Park as he, in fact, did when they met us in March. He played on the wing that day whereas when he played for us against Cambridge University he was at centre. On the appearance side of things, only Pank appeared in all twenty two games while Norman Hill and John Whittaker (21), C.B. Gervis (19) and Cipriani, R.W. Hunt and Wells (17) were all prominent. Wells topped the try chart with six and the points with 28 (five conversions to add to his tries) while Pank set a new number of penalty goals kicked in a season with two. In our twelve seasons at Chiswick Park we played 110 games, winning 53, drawing 14 and losing 42 with one match being abandoned. Additionally, 39 matches were cancelled which is an amazingly high percentage.

From the fixture card of this season we know that the annual subscription had stayed the same as it was in 1883 with an additional charge for life members of five guineas. We ran four sides, the 1st XV, "A" XV, 2nd XV and one described as "B" XV. This last one is a manuscript addition and it is not certain if this team was an official one or not.

A minute book surviving from this period gives the following information about this season's activities off the field. The Annual General meeting was still held at the Bedford Head Hotel (as it was in the 1880s), this one taking place on 3rd September 1896 which enabled seventeen members to attend and elect the Officers for the forthcoming season. At a Committee meeting held on 20th November, it was decided to appoint a sub-committee to take the necessary steps for entertaining the Monkstown F.C. on 28th November (see earlier). At the same meeting it was proposed and, after a long discussion, agreed that the tour for season 1897/98 should be in the Midlands and that a guarantee of £20 should be asked from each opponent and not less than £15 accepted. As we played Coventry and Leicester, they obviously paid up. It was also proposed that there be no match arranged with Birkenhead Park unless in London or at Birkenhead with a good guarantee. From later meetings it would seem that they offered only £5; we wrote back asking for £20 (we would accept £15 if it was offered), but this proposal obviously did not meet with the approval of our opponents as we did not actually play them again until 1928! It must be added that £20 was quite a sum in these days, our Groundsman was paid only £1 per season and our share of the gate money up to 16th January 1897 only came to just over £17. It is not clear whether such a sum was asked for when the Club no longer wanted to meet a team, perhaps this was the case with Birkenhead Park. A general meeting was held on 20th February for the election of caps. These were awarded to C.B. Gervis and I.S. Thornton (1st XV), F.D. Smith and H.B. Foster ("A" XV) and G. Pritchard (2nd XV). It was proposed by Cipriani, seconded by Norman Hill and passed unanimously that, a hearty vote of congratulations be conveyed to Henry Surtees on the occasion of his marriage and also that he receive the thanks of the Club for his past services (he was still playing for the first team) and their hopes that he would continue in his position as secretary and treasurer. It seems as though our loss of Chiswick Park was quite sudden because, at the Committee meeting on 24th March, the secretary read out correspondence regarding the ground and, after lengthy discussion, it was passed that a sub-committee consisting of Cipriani, Norman Hill and Henry Surtees be appointed "to negotiate for a ground".

During the close season on 3rd June at 35, Bedford Row, another Committee meeting was held purely for the purpose of deciding on a ground for the next season. This resulted in a motion being passed which read "That the Harlequins do not play at the Crystal Palace next season but play at Catford Bridge if possible". Thus our new ground was found but it was only for the next two seasons.

1896/97

260996	OLD MERCHANT TAYLORS	CHISWICK PARK	W	1G(5)-0
031096	KENSINGTON	CHISWICK PARK	W	2G2T(16)-0
101096	RICHMOND	CHISWICK PARK	L	2T(6)-1G1PG2T(14)
171096	ROYAL INDIAN ENGINEERING COLLEGE	COOPER'S HILL	L	0-1T(3)
241096	CAMBRIDGE UNIVERSITY	CAMBRIDGE	L	0-4G4T(32)
311096	ROSSLYN PARK	OLD DEER PARK	W	1T(3)-0
071196	LONDON WELSH	CHISWICK PARK	W	2G2T(16)-1G(5)
211196	OXFORD UNIVERSITY	OXFORD	L	3T(9)-5G2T(31)
281196	MONKSTOWN	CHISWICK PARK	L	1T(3)-1G1T(8)
051296	CROYDON	CHISWICK PARK	W	1T(3)-0
121296	OLD LEYSIANS	STAMFORD BRIDGE	C	
191296	MARLBOROUGH NOMADS	SURBITON	C	
261296	COVENTRY	COVENTRY	W	2T(6)-1PG(3)
281296	LEICESTER	LEICESTER	D	0-0
291296	NORTHAMPTON	NORTHAMPTON	D	2T(6)-2T(6)
020197	BLACKHEATH	CHISWICK PARK	C	
090197	LONDON SCOTTISH	CHISWICK PARK	L	0-1T(3)
160197	GUY'S HOSPITAL	CHISWICK PARK	D	1G1T(8)-1G1T(8)
230197	OLD MERCHANT TAYLORS	OLD DEER PARK	C	
300197	ST.BARTHOLOMEW'S HOSPITAL	CHISWICK PARK	C	
060297	BLACKHEATH	BLACKHEATH	L	1G1T(8)-1G2T(11)
130297	ROSSLYN PARK	CHISWICK PARK	W	2G1PG1T(16)-1G(5)

200297	MARLBOROUGH NOMADS	CHISWICK PARK	W	1G3T(14)-1T(3)
270297	RICHMOND	RICHMOND	D	1G1PG(8)-1G1T(8)
060397	KENSINGTON	WOOD LANE	W	3T(9)-1T(3)
130397	OLD LEYSIANS	CHISWICK PARK	W	3G4T(27)-1G(5)
200397	BIRKENHEAD PARK	CHISWICK PARK	W	1G1T(8)-1G(5)

6

A Problematic Time On and Off the Field 1897-1901

So, it was to Catford that we moved in time to start the 1897/98 season. From the information contained in the fixture card, the ground was located close to Catford Bridge Railway Station.

Cyril Wells resigned the captaincy so it was decided to approach Cipriani and if he declined, John Whittaker would be elected. As history shows, this is what happened and Whittaker became our sixteenth captain in what was to be his final season in the first team. The fourth team (known as "B" XV) actually appears in print this time with two games against Dulwich College 3rd XV. A report in "The Sportsman" on 23rd September 1897 states that "The management of the Sports Company are making good efforts to boom the fixtures and have instituted a season ticket admitting to all matches, at 5s a head". This is believed to be the first example of a season ticket for our games and with fourteen games to see it appears to have been good value for money.

The bulk of the first team remained the same, as twenty four players made appearances this season who played in the last one. Again, as with the previous season we lost some long serving forwards, these were, P.E Bodington (67) who first played for us against Marlborough Nomads on 15th February 1890, Henry Hindley (59) who made his debut in 1888/89 and whose last appearance was against Old Merchant Taylors on 25th September and Henry Surtees (159) who played first against Blackheath on 2nd October 1886. Two notable firsts were R.W. (Robert) Bell, who only made two appearances for us (the other was in the following season) and who went on to gain three caps for England in 1900 when his club was Northern and W.L. Furrell, he debuted against the Royal Indian Engineering College on 16th October and went on to make 101 appearances. An item of interest took place on 2nd October against Kensington when our full back (H.N. Matthews) went off, he was replaced by L. Lindop, who himself went off later. As replacements were not allowed at this point, it must have been an agreement between the two captains which enabled this to happen.

In the game at Cambridge against the University on 23rd October, we were a man short so A. Hacking from Christ's College made up our numbers. He went on to play in the 1898 and 1899 varsity matches. We managed to chalk up fifteen victories in this season. The highs were, achieving our biggest ever win over the R.I.E.C., defeating Dublin Wanderers by a goal to nil despite being a man short throughout, achieving another "double" over London Scottish and gaining a bit of revenge over St. Thomas's Hospital for taking our ground from us with a 19-3 win. The lows were, losing our first home game at Catford to Old Merchant Taylors, only managing to draw with Coventry and lose to Leicester on the Christmas tour and getting well beaten at Cambridge (0-34) and at home to Blackheath

(0-30). Several records were set or equalled this season, Cyril Wells set a new record for conversions by an individual in a season with fifteen and the record for most by the team in a season went with 33 being kicked. The record for most tries by the team, set in 1870/71, was equalled with 60 being scored (G.E. Mortlock top scoring with thirteen). This meant that he shared top points with Wells (he had scored three tries to add to his conversions), both therefore scoring 39. The team points scoring record in a season was smashed by more than sixty, the new figure being set at 249. Mortlock was the sole player to appear in all twenty five games, although Norman Hill and Pank (24), R.W. Hunt and Whittaker (22) and H.M. Cruddas (21) were not far behind.

Several letters were received from various clubs asking for a fixture against us and among those read out at a Committee meeting on 11th November were requests from Bedford and Lennox. Unfortunately, due to the fact that no dates were available both of these had to be declined. We were, however, to play them first in 1908 and 1901 respectively. At this same meeting it was decided that fixtures with Coventry and Leicester should be arranged with guarantees of £25 to be asked for and not less than £20 accepted. The guarantee seems to have risen five pounds in one season for no apparent reason, unless, of course inflation was high at the time! Our entrance into the Surrey County Cup was discussed at the meeting on 16th February and after lengthy discussion it was decided that the Club should not enter for cup ties. Caps for this season were voted for at a general meeting on 10th April and were awarded to N. Miller and H.M. Cruddas.

1897/98

250997	OLD MERCHANT TAYLORS	CATFORD	L	2G(10)-1G1PG3T(17)
021097	KENSINGTON	WOOD LANE	W	2G3T(19)-1T(3)
091097	RICHMOND	RICHMOND	L	2T(6)-1G1T(8)
161097	ROYAL INDIAN ENGINEERING COLLEGE	COOPER'S HILL	W	4G3T(29)-1PG(3)
231097	CAMBRIDGE UNIVERSITY	CAMBRIDGE	L	0-5G3T(34)
301097	LONDON SCOTTISH	CATFORD	W	2G1T(13)-1G(5)
061197	ROSSLYN PARK	OLD DEER PARK	W	2G1T(13)-0
131197	MARLBOROUGH NOMADS	STAMFORD BRIDGE	W	1G(5)-1T(3)
201197	OXFORD UNIVERSITY	OXFORD	L	0-2G(10)
271197	ST.THOMAS'S HOSPITAL	CATFORD	W	2G3T(19)-1T(3)
021297	DUBLIN WANDERERS	CATFORD	W	1G(5)-0
041297	CROYDON	CATFORD	W	1T(3)-0
111297	LONDON SCOTTISH	RICHMOND	W	2G(10)-1T(3)
181297	OLD LEYSIANS	STAMFORD BRIDGE	C	
271297	COVENTRY	COVENTRY	D	1T(3)-1T(3)
271297	PORTSMOUTH	PORTSMOUTH	C	
281297	LEICESTER	LEICESTER	L	1T(3)-1DG1T(7)
010198	KENSINGTON	CATFORD	W	1G2T(11)-0
080198	BLACKHEATH	CATFORD	L	0-3G5T(30)
150198	LONDON WELSH	CATFORD	W	4G(20)-1G(5)
220198	OLD MERCHANT TAYLORS	OLD DEER PARK	W	1G(5)-1T(3)

290198	ST.BARTHOLOMEW'S HOSPITAL	CATFORD	W	3G2T(21)-0
050298	BLACKHEATH	BLACKHEATH	C	
120298	ROSSLYN PARK	CATFORD	L	1G(5)-2G1T(13)
190298	MARLBOROUGH NOMADS	CATFORD	L	0-3T(9)
260298	RICHMOND	CATFORD	W	1G3T(14)-0
050398	NORTHAMPTON	CATFORD	L	1T(3)-1G1DG3T(18)
120398	OLD LEYSIANS	CATFORD	W	4G3T(29)-0

The next season was to prove an absolute disaster and as far as games won, the worst season since 1879/80. Furthering tinkering with the team results in the "A" team disappearing and the 3rd XV coming back. It all started promisingly off the pitch with William Smith becoming President (a position he was to hold until 1914) and R.F. Cumberlege becoming captain for this and the next season. When the matches began, things were immediately starting to fall apart and the first eight games were lost. We had scored just three tries and conceded thirty three, this added up to nine points for and 141 against! In amongst these games was our biggest ever defeat at the hands of Cambridge University (0-43), our only ever defeat by Croydon (0-20) and our first loss to the Marlborough Nomads for seventeen years (0-18). Monkstown came over from Ireland again and used Catford as their practice ground for the tour, we were duly dispatched by a goal and a try to nil to give us that eighth defeat on the trot. We actually won against Rosslyn Park in the next game, scoring three tries to nil. Over the following three months we played twelve matches and won only two, those against St. Thomas's and Richmond. We managed a scoreless draw against the O.M.T.s, but the other nine were nightmares. These included both matches on the Midlands tour against Northampton and Leicester, Blackheath and the return with Rosslyn Park. In that game at Leicester, we had to borrow two men from the home side to make up our numbers and these were among the twenty seven players out of a total used during the season of sixty nine to make only one appearance. Our final tally for the season was played 21, won 3 drawn 1, lost 17, For 54, Against 248.

C.E.L. (Charles) Hammond, a future England international, made his debut in the game against Oxford University and Pank made his last appearance in the match at Leicester. Not surprisingly, this season saw no records set and our meagre total was the last time (excluding the war years) that we failed to score over one hundred points in a season. Out of sixteen tries scored, S. Mason got six and therefore topped the list and with his eighteen points was also top points scorer. The captain managed two of the three conversions kicked. Only W.L. Furrell played in all twenty one games and the nearest to him was H.B. Carslake with sixteen appearances. This lack of a settled side probably accounts for some of the poor results. To end this season on a positive note is difficult but, looking to the future, there was a letter received from Racing Club de France asking for a fixture with us. It was agreed that the game should be fixed subject to the approval of the Rugby Union and it did indeed go ahead in February 1901. B.C. (Bernard) Hartley and J.W. (John) Sagar were two more of our players to go on and gain international honours with other clubs - Hartley in 1901 and 1902 when he played for Blackheath and Sagar in 1901 when he was at Cambridge University.

1898/99

011098	OLD MERCHANT TAYLORS	OLD DEER PARK	L	0-1T(3)
081098	RICHMOND	CATFORD	C	
151098	ROYAL INDIAN ENGINEERING COLLEGE	COOPER'S HILL	L	1T(3)-1G1T(8)

221098	CAMBRIDGE UNIVERSITY	CAMBRIDGE	L	0-5G6T(43)
291098	LONDON SCOTTISH	CATFORD	L	1T(3)-2G1T(13)
051198	CROYDON	CATFORD	L	0-4G(20)
121198	MARLBOROUGH NOMADS	CATFORD	L	0-3G1T(18)
191198	OXFORD UNIVERSITY	OXFORD	L	1T(3)-5G1T(28)
261198	MONKSTOWN	CATFORD	L	0-1G1T(8)
031298	ROSSLYN PARK	CATFORD	W	3T(9)-0
101298	LONDON SCOTTISH	RICHMOND	L	1T(3)-1G(5)
171298	OLD LEYSIANS	CRYSTAL PALACE	L	0-5T(15)
241298	MARLBOROUGH NOMADS	SURBITON	L	0-3G3T(24)
261298	NORTHAMPTON	NORTHAMPTON	L	0-2G1T(13)
271298	LEICESTER	LEICESTER	L	1T(3)-3T(9)
311298	KENSINGTON	WOOD LANE	L	1T(3)-1PG2T(9)
070199	ST.THOMAS'S HOSPITAL	CHISWICK PARK	W	1G2T(11)-0
140199	BLACKHEATH	CATFORD	L	1T(3)-1G3T(14)
210199	OLD MERCHANT TAYLORS	CATFORD	D	0-0
280199	ST.BARTHOLOMEW'S HOSPITAL	CATFORD	C	
040299	BLACKHEATH	BLACKHEATH	C	
110299	ROSSLYN PARK	OLD DEER PARK	L	1T(3)-2G1T(13)
250299	RICHMOND	RICHMOND	W	2G(10)-0
040399	KENSINGTON	CATFORD	L	0-1G(5)
110399	OLD LEYSIANS	CATFORD	C	

The next season saw the turn of the century and us on the move yet again. After our short stay at Catford, Wimbledon Park was to be our new home. It was conveniently situated just three minutes' walk from Southfields Station on the District Railway. The number of teams reduces back to three with the return of the "A" XV and the loss of the 3rd and "B" XVs. At last there is some continuity with the next change coming in 1920/21. Off the field, the financial situation of the Club was becoming worrying and at various Committee meetings it was mentioned. On 24th November, it was agreed that a letter was to go out from the Honorary Treasurer to all members whose subscriptions were unpaid, drawing particular attention to rules 7-10 (these dealt with subscriptions and defaulters), which in future would be strictly adhered to. This was followed on 3rd January when it was proposed by Alfred Eiloart and seconded by Norman Hill that a general meeting be called for some date at the end of January to discuss the position of the Club. This meeting was duly called on Tuesday 30th January 1900 at the Rainbow Tavern, Fleet Street and was attended by forty five members. William Smith and S.B. Peech gave able speeches on the present position of the Club and after a general discussion it was decided to raise a subscription in the room in aid of Club funds, the result of which was that £66 9s 6d was raised. A letter was later sent out to all members requesting a donation towards Club funds and it seems that from this the Club rose out of impending disaster and started on a steady climb out of the depths of gloom it had fallen into.

We somehow doubled the number of wins we had managed in the previous season, although no new scalps were taken and it seemed to be the same old teams were being defeated. The Dublin Wanderers were back again but the game was cancelled, one of six lost this season. The Midlands tour was an even bigger disaster than it had been the year before and after borrowing G. Thorneycroft from Northampton's "A" team to make up our numbers, we were comprehensively beaten 0-35 (this was our heaviest defeat of the season). In the second match at Leicester, we were again soundly beaten by three goals (two dropped) and four tries to a goal and a try. This was to be our last venture to the Midlands for a Christmas tour which had started so promisingly in 1894 yet had seen us lose our last five games, two to Northampton and three to Leicester. In other games, we were to lose to O.M.T.s, Richmond and London Scottish (all twice) and Blackheath, Marlborough Nomads and Oxford and Cambridge Universities. Our win over St. Thomas's Hospital (34-3) was the biggest of the season.

As with the previous season, the lack of continuity seemed to help towards our lack of good results and only W.H. Devonshire (21) and W.L. Furrell (19), who had both been awarded Club caps at the start of the season, played more than fifteen matches. On the try scoring front, Devonshire and C.M. Merritt shared top spot with six each and R.F. Cumberlege kicked nine conversions and got one try for a total of twenty one points. Making his debut on 11th November against Marlborough Nomads was Reginald Curtis-Hayward, he went on to make 105 appearances for the first team over the next seven seasons. Sadly, someone making his last appearance for us before retiring was Cyril Wells. When he played in his final game, on 14th October against the R.I.E.C., it was his seventy first appearance for the first XV. During his career with us he had scored a total of 173 points (30 tries, 1 dropped goal and 39 conversions), this had caused him to be top or joint top try scorer on three occasions and top or joint top points scorer four times. He was to be badly missed over the next few seasons.

1899/1900

300999	OLD MERCHANT TAYLORS	WIMBLEDON PARK	L	1T(3)-5G2T(31)
071099	RICHMOND	RICHMOND	L	1G(5)-5T(15)
141099	ROYAL INDIAN ENGINEERING COLLEGE	COOPER'S HILL	W	2G(10)-3T(9)
211099	CAMBRIDGE UNIVERSITY	CAMBRIDGE	L	0-2G3T(19)
281099	LONDON SCOTTISH	RICHMOND	L	0-3G4T(27)
041199	CROYDON	WIMBLEDON PARK	W	3T(9)-1T(3)
111199	MARLBOROUGH NOMADS	SURBITON	L	1G(5)-3G(15)
181199	OXFORD UNIVERSITY	OXFORD	L	0-4G2T(26)
251199	LONDON WELSH	WIMBLEDON PARK	W	3T(9)-0
301199	DUBLIN WANDERERS	WIMBLEDON PARK	C	
021299	ROSSLYN PARK	WIMBLEDON PARK	L	0-1DG1T(7)
091299	LONDON SCOTTISH	WIMBLEDON PARK	L	0-2T(6)
161299	OLD LEYSIANS	CRYSTAL PALACE	C	
231299	MARLBOROUGH NOMADS	WIMBLEDON PARK	C	
261299	NORTHAMPTON	NORTHAMPTON	L	0-2DG9T(35)
271299	LEICESTER	LEICESTER	L	1G1T(8)-1G2DG4T(25)
301299	KENSINGTON	WIMBLEDON PARK	C	
060100	BLACKHEATH	WIMBLEDON PARK	L	1G1T(8)-1G2T(11)
130100	ST.THOMAS'S HOSPITAL	WIMBLEDON PARK	W	5G3T(34)-1T(3)
200100	OLD MERCHANT TAYLORS	OLD DEER PARK	L	0-5T(15)

270100	GUY'S HOSPITAL	WIMBLEDON PARK	W	1G(5)-1T(3)
030200	BLACKHEATH	BLACKHEATH	C	
100200	ROSSLYN PARK	OLD DEER PARK	C	
170200	ST.BARTHOLOMEW'S HOSPITAL	WIMBLEDON PARK	D	0-0
240200	RICHMOND	WIMBLEDON PARK	L	1G(5)-2G1DG(14)
030300	KENSINGTON	WOOD LANE	L	2T(6)-1G2T(11)
100300	OLD LEYSIANS	WIMBLEDON PARK	W	1G5T(20)-0

For the next season, H.O. Mills was elected captain and only 59 players were used so it looked as though we would have a more regular side and with that might come more victories. The problem was, we had nowhere to play! We had received a "notice to quit" Wimbledon Park and it seemed a bit late trying to organise somewhere for the up-coming season and as a minute book showing a Committee meeting on 12th September shows, we had our eyes set on obtaining a ground for the next season. In the event, we played at three different "home" venues, these were Wimbledon Sports Club (Southfields), Richmond Athletic Enclosure (second ground) and the Finchley Cricket Club enclosure. We played on each ground one, four and three times respectively. After another dreadful start where we lost eight and drew one of the first nine games, we eventually defeated Rosslyn Park at Richmond for our first win. One of those losses was our heaviest defeat by an English side up to this point; it was Oxford University who defeated us by fifty points to nil! After defeating the Park, we managed five wins, a draw and seven losses in the remaining matches. The Racing Club de France were met in Paris on 10th February and the following short report from the "Sporting Life" gives some details about the game.

"Paris Feb. 10. This match, under the Rugby code, was played here today before a gate of about 4000 spectators. Owing to the recent bad weather, the ground was in a very heavy state. Nevertheless, a good game took place, the locals being too fast for the visitors, the game eventually ending in a win for the Racing Club by 16 points to 3".

Our biggest win of the season was our 42-8 drubbing of St. Thomas's Hospital at Chiswick Park. Against London Welsh on 24th November, play did not start until thirty minutes after the advertised time and was therefore restricted to twenty minutes each way due to their late arrival. Mr. H.C. Green, who was due to referee the game at Eltham against the Old Leysians on 15th December, failed to turn up and so one of our players (W.L. Furrell) took charge. He must have been extremely fair because we lost 9-15! The following week when we met Marlborough Nomads, we were two men short and had to use a substitute from Surbiton (who arrived just before half time). This was at the same time as C. Longhurst (our centre three quarter), so our numbers were eventually made up. Imagine playing a game today and only having thirteen men for most of the first half! Of the above mentioned fifty nine players, none managed all twenty three games but Reginald Curtis-Hayward did play in twenty two and R.H. Fox and Mills (the captain) (20), W.H. Devonshire (19) and W.L. Furrell (18) were all thereabouts. Another of our players, full back H.W. Taylor, had left for South Africa on Monday 11th March with The Yeomanry. This, of course, was around the time of the South African War and although it is impossible to say how many players volunteered and went away, the nucleus of the playing side of the Club appears to have stayed more or less the same. Taylor did come back and play in season 1902/03 and was to appear now and again over the next five years. C.M. Merritt scored eleven tries in his thirteen games at half back and these were enough to make him top points scorer with 33. Another name in the series of unknown players was used in the defeat at Oxford, one of our half backs was O.N.E. More! Debuting at half back in the first game of this season against the O.M.T.s was E.W. (Edward) Dillon, who was to gain four England caps (three in 1904 and one in 1905). Another England man to be played for us first at

Northampton on Boxing Day 1900, he was V.H. (Vincent) Cartwright who went on to gain fourteen caps and captain his country on six occasions. Unfortunately, he only played for us eight times in four seasons.

At the Annual General Meeting, held on 11th May 1900 at the Rainbow Tavern, R.F. Cumberlege and R.A. Brandram were both awarded their Club honours caps. Among the Officers elected for the forthcoming season were the following Vice Presidents, H.K. Gow, A.A. Surtees, S.B. Peech, A.B. Cipriani, R.W. Hunt and C.M. Wells.

1900/01

290900	OLD MERCHANT TAYLORS	SOUTHFIELDS(H)	D	1G1T(8)-1G1T(8)
061000	RICHMOND	RICHMOND(H)	L	1G(5)-2G1T(13)
131000	ROYAL INDIAN ENGINEERING COLLEGE	COOPER'S HILL	L	0-2G3T(19)
201000	CAMBRIDGE UNIVERSITY	CAMBRIDGE	L	0-4G4T(32)
271000	LONDON SCOTTISH	RICHMOND(H)	L	1T(3)-2G1T(13)
031100	LONDON IRISH	HERNE HILL	L	0-1G(5)
101100	MARLBOROUGH NOMADS	FINCHLEY(H)	L	1T(3)-3T(9)
171100	OXFORD UNIVERSITY	OXFORD	L	0-4G10T(50)
241100	LONDON WELSH	FINCHLEY(H)	L	0-2G(10)
011200	ROSSLYN PARK	RICHMOND(H)	W	2G1T(13)-1T(3)
081200	LONDON SCOTTISH	RICHMOND	D	1T(3)-1T(3)
151200	OLD LEYSIANS	ELTHAM	L	1G1DG(9)-1G1MG2T(15)
221200	MARLBOROUGH NOMADS	SURBITON	L	0-1T(3)
261200	NORTHAMPTON	NORTHAMPTON	L	1G1T(8)-2G2T(16)
291200	KENSINGTON	WOOD LANE	W	6T(18)-1G(5)
050101	BLACKHEATH	RICHMOND(H)	L	1G(5)-1G2T(11)
120101	LENNOX	STAMFORD BRIDGE	W	1G2T(11)-0
190101	OLD MERCHANT TAYLORS	OLD DEER PARK	L	0-2G(10)
260101	GUY'S HOSPITAL	HONOR OAK PARK	C	
020201	BLACKHEATH	BLACKHEATH	C	
090201	ROSSLYN PARK	OLD DEER PARK	L	1G2T(11)-2G2T(16)
100201	RACING CLUB DE FRANCE	PARIS	L	1T(3)-2G2T(16)
160201	ST.MARY'S HOSPITAL	FINCHLEY(H)	C	
230201	RICHMOND	RICHMOND	W	1G2T(11)-2G(10)
020301	KENSINGTON	WOOD LANE	W	1G1T(8)-1T(3)
090301	OLD LEYSIANS	ELTHAM	C	
160301	ST.THOMAS'S HOSPITAL	CHISWICK PARK	W	6G4T(42)-1G1T(8)

7

The Stoop Era 1901-1914

So, what is arguably one of the finest eras in the history of the Club began with the 1901/02 season. We now played at Wandsworth Common which was seven minutes' walk from Wandsworth Common Station. W.L. Furrell was made captain and Reginald Curtis-Hayward and H.O. Mills received their caps. At a Committee meeting on 23rd October, a proposal was made to try and get Oxford University to play at Wandsworth Common. It was finally agreed that the Club could not in their present position offer a fixed guarantee and so we only met them away, as we had done since 1876. On 5th November, a special general meeting was held at which Norman Hill was elected a Vice President and Charles Hammond was elected to the Committee to fill the vacancy left by Hill's promotion. At this same meeting, a letter was read out from Northampton offering us a guarantee of £15 for a match against them in the next season. This was duly accepted as it would seem that the Club's financial position left them in no position to argue. At further meetings during the season, it was decided first to try and arrange a return match with Northampton and also matches with other provincial clubs (Coventry, Leicester, Moseley and the Old Edwardians were amongst those mentioned) and secondly a subcommittee was appointed to arrange, if possible, a lease from the Cricket Club of the ground at Wandsworth Common at a rent not exceeding £35 a year.

Our first match at Wandsworth (referred to as the Heathfield Cricket and Athletic Club ground, 300 yards from the station (mentioned earlier)) was against Richmond on 5th October 1901. We started well enough with a try by H.T.H. Bond, converted by Vincent Cartwright to lead 5-0 but, by half time Richmond had scored three tries and as they added a fourth in the second half we lost 5-12. Things were going the way of the previous few years as we managed a draw at Cambridge and seven losses in the first eight games. The last of these was at Oxford and this game is worthy of mention as it saw the debut of A.D. (Adrian) Stoop who was not only to change our fortunes over the forthcoming years but also to change the face of the game itself. He was to gain fifteen caps (two as captain) for England and play 182 games for the Quins. In the game, Stoop scored his first and our only try in a 3-27 loss. In the eight matches he played in during this season, we actually won six. All of a sudden, we started winning games, starting with a victory over St. Bartholomew's Hospital (our first at Wandsworth) by a goal and a try to nil. After this, Rosslyn Park, London Scottish and Old Leysians were all dispatched before Northampton defeated us at Christmas.

The Old Alleynians were met and defeated for the first time on 4th January whereas Lennox were met for the second time and lost to for the first time. Blackheath defeated us on 8th February, the day before we were due to travel out to Paris again to play the Racing Club but this game was cancelled and we did not meet them again until 1907. Kensington were played on 1st March and handed us our first defeat at Wandsworth since November, but we did finish with a flourish and scored fifty one points to three in winning our last three games against Guy's Hospital (11-3), Lennox (8-0) and Old Leysians (32-0). No one appeared in all twenty three games but D. Linton came close with twenty two. The captain managed twenty one and Reginald Curtis-Hayward twenty. Apart from these three, there were another seven who appeared in between fifteen and nineteen matches. The only scoring record set this season was the number of penalties scored, T.J. Wheeler kicked three to pass the record set by J.R. Pank in 1896/97. These were in fact the only ones we had scored in that period! The only other item of note in this area was that the 211 points scored was only the second time that two hundred points had been passed.

1901/02

280901	OLD MERCHANT TAYLORS	OLD DEER PARK	L	1G(5)-5G3T(34)
051001	RICHMOND	WANDSWORTH COMMON	L	1G(5)-4T(12)
121001	ROYAL INDIAN ENGINEERING COLLEGE	COOPER'S HILL	L	0-2G3T(19)
191001	CAMBRIDGE UNIVERSITY	CAMBRIDGE	D	2T(6)-2T(6)
261001	LONDON SCOTTISH	WANDSWORTH COMMON	L	0-2G(10)
021101	LONDON IRISH	WANDSWORTH COMMON	L	0-1G1T(8)
091101	MARLBOROUGH NOMADS	WANDSWORTH COMMON	L	2T(6)-1G1T(8)
161101	OXFORD UNIVERSITY	OXFORD	L	1T(3)-3G4T(27)
231101	ST.BARTHOLOMEW'S HOSPITAL	WANDSWORTH COMMON	W	1G1T(8)-0
301101	ROSSLYN PARK	WANDSWORTH COMMON	W	3G2T(21)-2T(6)
071201	LONDON SCOTTISH	RICHMOND	W	2G1PG2T(19)-0
141201	OLD LEYSIANS	WANDSWORTH COMMON	W	2G1PG2T(19)-1T(3)
211201	MARLBOROUGH NOMADS	SURBITON	C	
261201	NORTHAMPTON	NORTHAMPTON	L	0-3G2T(21)
281201	KENSINGTON	WOOD LANE	C	
040102	OLD ALLEYNIANS	WANDSWORTH COMMON	W	2G1T(13)-0
110102	BLACKHEATH	WANDSWORTH COMMON	C	
180102	OLD MERCHANT TAYLORS	WANDSWORTH COMMON	W	2T(6)-1G(5)
250102	ROSSLYN PARK	OLD DEER PARK	W	2G3T(19)-1PG(3)
010202	LENNOX	DULWICH	L	1PG(3)-1G2T(11)
080202	BLACKHEATH	BLACKHEATH	L	0-3T(9)
090202	RACING CLUB DE FRANCE	PARIS	C	
150202	ST.THOMAS'S HOSPITAL	CHISWICK PARK	C	
220202	RICHMOND	RICHMOND	W	3G2T(21)-1G1T(8)
010302	KENSINGTON	WANDSWORTH COMMON	L	2T(6)-1G2T(11)
080302	GUY'S HOSPITAL	WANDSWORTH COMMON	W	1G2T(11)-1T(3)
150302	LENNOX	WANDSWORTH COMMON	W	1G1T(8)-0
220302	OLD LEYSIANS	ELTHAM	W	4G4T(32)-0

In the following season, only nineteen games were played with fourteen being cancelled. Charles Hammond became captain for this and the following three seasons, making him, with A.A. Surtees, the longest serving captain up until now. Somehow we had managed to get a handsome balance in hand which was reported in the balance sheet for the preceding season at the A.G.M. on 11th August. At a Committee meeting on 27th November, a letter from the secretary of the Middlesex County Union, with a copy of a letter from the secretary of the Rugby Union, was read out asking if the Club would be prepared to play a fixture with a New Zealand team in the event that one toured the following season. The Committee decided that the Club would play if a date could be arranged. Alas, this was not to be and the same fate befell arrangements for a match with a Canadian side due to tour at the same time. At a further gathering, letters were received from Devonport Albion and Plymouth offering guarantees of £40 and £35 respectively to play matches against them at Easter 1904. These were duly accepted, but Exeter's offer of two thirds of the gate money for a match on the same tour was declined. Later it was proposed by Plymouth that Redruth be our second opponents and although their guarantee of £20 was not thought sufficient enough, these were the teams we played, of which, more later.

We started our matches off against the O.M.T.s on 27th September 1902 at their ground on the Old Deer Park. This game can best be described as the classic game of two halves as, in the first, the home side leapt into a lead of sixteen points to nil with two goals and two tries only for us to come straight back after the break with exactly the same to tie the scores. In our side that day we had three lieutenants from the Royal Navy, namely L.J.L. Hammond and W. Tomkinson on the wings and G. Wood-Martin in the forwards. Against Cambridge on 18th October, one of the curios of reporting from these earlier days arose, this was the name of the scorer. Our only try (in a 3-32 reverse) is reported as having been scored by Edward Dillon and A.C.T. Veasey who both fell on the ball together. It remains a mystery who was actually awarded the score! Five "Wednesday" games, so called for obvious reasons were arranged to be played this season against first time opponents Catford Bridge, Merchant Taylor School, Old Dunelians and Royal School of Mines (twice). Unfortunately, all but the Catford fixture (won 8-0) were cancelled. Against Marlborough Nomads, we actually loaned the opposition a player (J.H. Witney) and as has been seen this occurrence was usually the other way round! A first appearance for Oxford at Wandsworth Common took place on 15th November and this saw only our second ever win over them by fourteen points to five.

Some strange happenings took place in the second half of this season, first, on 3rd January against Northampton, Stoop was partnered at half back by Hammond (the captain) who was usually a forward. It would appear that positions were not all that specialised in 1903. Secondly, we met Blackheath at Wandsworth and strangely, we didn't lose, a 0-0 draw being the result. Lastly, against Richmond on 28th February, because the Wandsworth Common ground was under water, the teams moved to an enclosure at Richmond and at half time moved to the principal ground which had been occupied by the London Scottish and Irish. It was well worth the effort though as we completed a 26-0 victory. Before the return against Marlborough Nomads on 7th March, it was reported that one of our forwards (A.C.T. Veasey) hurrying to the station en route to Surbiton, had the misfortune to break a rib. At the last minute he was replaced by O.O. Wortham. It would seem they were a lot tougher in those days - he was back playing for us the following week!

Our biggest win of the season came against St. Bartholomew's Hospital (30-0) and our heaviest defeat was with a very weak side against Old Alleynians (0-29). We won seven, drew four and lost eight matches so on the whole not a good season but far better than some of our worst. Our captain was top appearance maker with eighteen and J. Bourdas and D. Linton (17), W.W. Creswell (16) and Reginald Curtis-Hayward, R.H. Fox, W.H. Newton, A.C.T. Veasey and G. Wood-Martin (15) were the most prolific of the other players used. W. Tomkinson scored thirteen tries and these enabled him to be top of the points scoring with 39. The team as a whole scored 46 tries, 18 of which were converted. In the fixture card, a printing error led to the first team being described as "1st XVI"!

1902/03

270902	OLD MERCHANT TAYLORS	OLD DEER PARK	D	2G2T(16)-2G2T(16)
041002	RICHMOND	RICHMOND	D	1G(5)-1G(5)
111002	ROYAL INDIAN ENGINEERING COLLEGE	WANDSWORTH COMMON	L	1G1T(8)-1G2T(11)
181002	CAMBRIDGE UNIVERSITY	CAMBRIDGE	L	1T(3)-2G1PG3T(22)
251002	LENNOX	WANDSWORTH COMMON	C	
291002	ROYAL SCHOOL OF MINES	WANDSWORTH COMMON	C	
011102	LONDON IRISH	STAMFORD BRIDGE	W	1PG1T(6)-1G(5)
081102	MARLBOROUGH NOMADS	WANDSWORTH COMMON	W	3G2T(21)-2T(6)
121102	CATFORD BRIDGE	WANDSWORTH COMMON	W	1G1T(8)-0
151102	OXFORD UNIVERSITY	WANDSWORTH COMMON	W	1G3T(14)-1G(5)
191102	MERCHANT TAYLOR SCHOOL	WANDSWORTH COMMON	C	
221102	ST.BARTHOLOMEW'S HOSPITAL	WANDSWORTH COMMON	W	3G5T(30)-0
291102	ROSSLYN PARK	OLD DEER PARK	W	2G5T(25)-1G(5)
061202	LONDON SCOTTISH	WANDSWORTH COMMON	C	
131202	OLD LEYSIANS	WANDSWORTH COMMON	C	
171202	OLD DUNELIANS	WANDSWORTH COMMON	C	
201202	OLD ALLEYNIANS	WANDSWORTH COMMON	L	0-4G3T(29)
261202	SURBITON	WANDSWORTH COMMON	C	
271202	KENSINGTON	WOOD LANE	C	
030103	NORTHAMPTON	NORTHAMPTON	L	1G(5)-2G1DG1PG2T(23)
100103	BLACKHEATH	WANDSWORTH COMMON	D	0-0
170103	OLD MERCHANT TAYLORS	OLD DEER PARK	C	
210103	ROYAL SCHOOL OF MINES	ACTON	C	
240103	ROSSLYN PARK	WANDSWORTH COMMON	C	
310103	LENNOX	STAMFORD BRIDGE	D	1PG(3)-1T(3)
070203	LONDON WELSH	WANDSWORTH COMMON	L	0-1T(3)
140203	ST.THOMAS'S HOSPITAL	CHISWICK PARK	C	
210203	KENSINGTON	WANDSWORTH COMMON	L	0-1G2T(11)
280203	RICHMOND	RICHMOND	W	1G7T(26)-0
070303	MARLBOROUGH NOMADS	SURBITON	L	1G(5)-2T(6)
140303	LONDON SCOTTISH	RICHMOND	L	1G(5)-1G1DG3T(18)
210303	BLACKHEATH	BLACKHEATH	C	
280303	OLD LEYSIANS	ELTHAM	C	

During the period between seasons, a Committee meeting was held at which Queen's Club proposed in a letter to allow us a tenancy of their ground. As they had already let the ground to London Welsh for most Saturdays in the coming season and they were not prepared to let any but a first team play there, it was decided that their proposals should be no further considered. The Club did give permission for their name to be used as patron of a theatrical benefit for the Bolinbroke Hospital in Balham, South East London.

At the A.G.M. on 15th September 1903, it was noted that H.P. Surtees intended to resign the post of treasurer which he had held for seven years. He was thanked most sincerely for the work he had put in both on and off the field over the previous twelve years (although his playing links with the Club went back seventeen). Rule 4 was amended to expand the size of the Committee from ten to twelve and two new rules (22 and 23) were brought in. Rule 22 stated that "all officers shall resign at the Annual General Meeting, but shall be eligible for re-election" and Rule 23 introduced a Club cap for the 1st, 2nd and "A" teams. According to the fixture card, either the ground had moved or people had become fitter because it was now just four minutes' walk from the Station as opposed to seven when we first played there!

The 1903/04 season promised the most games ever played by the first XV as no less than forty games had been arranged including eleven mid-week matches. Needless to say, fifteen were cancelled and nine of those were mid-week fixtures. Had they not been, such teams as London Hospital (the first time since 1885), Streatham (the first time since 1874), and first timers Dover College, Shandon Athletic and Wembley would have been played. The two games which survived were both disasters as far as we were concerned. The first against Catford Bridge on 11th November saw us field just seven players with eight substitutes from Catford making up the numbers and hardly surprisingly we lost 3-27. Three weeks later at Greenwich, we played against the Royal Naval College and although this time we fielded ten men, the College only supplied two substitutes as they were one short themselves, it made no difference and we lost by five tries to nil. We were now in the middle of a mediocre time as far as results are concerned and after losing our first two games, we defeated London Irish for the first time at Wandsworth by fourteen points to eight.

Oxford University gave us a thrashing (0-33) but the consolation to be drawn from this was that their side contained two current and two future English and three future Scottish internationals. Playing against us were Cartwright and Stoop who were already Quins and J.G. Bussell, Edmund Fearenside and Patrick Munro who were later to play for us. As Cambridge had beaten us earlier by twenty three points to nil, this pointed towards a close Varsity match and so it proved, Oxford winning 18-13. On 19th March a momentous moment arrived, our first victory over Blackheath since the fixture began way back in 1881, a total of one draw and twenty two losses. We began well with tries from Hammond and R.T. Phillips which Edmund Fearenside converted, then Blackheath came back with a try from A.B. "Colorado" converted by B.C. Hartley to which we replied with a try from J.V. Nesbitt. Half time arriving with the score at 13-5 in our favour. H. Mullins got a try and F. Kershaw kicked the extra points to pull Blackheath to within three points but our Oxford man, Fearenside, went over for a try to give us that final score of 16-10. For the record, the team that day was, T.J. Wheeler (full back), J. Bourdas, G.S. Tomkinson, J.V. Nesbitt and R.T. Phillips (three quarters), D. Brewster and C. Longhurst (half backs) and A.C.T. Veasey, D. Linton, R. Curtis-Hayward, C.E.L. Hammond (captain), Roc Ward, E. Fearenside, R. Farrant and A. Ryder (forwards).

As mentioned earlier, April saw our short tour of Devon and Cornwall. On 2nd, we met Plymouth at South Devon Place in a game which kicked off at 11 a.m. We had to borrow three men from our hosts to make up our numbers and by half time we were down by four tries to nil. We had a few chances to score before A.C. Bryson got what was to be our only try and after this Plymouth ran away with the game, scoring thirteen more points for a final score of 3-25. The game at Redruth two days later was almost a repeat of our defeat at Plymouth (we borrowed three men and at one stage were 0-12 down). At half time it was 0-9 and when J.C.J. Teague (one of the substitutes) scored our try, it was 3-14. As in the previous match, our opponents then proceeded to race away and Redruth added a further two goals and two tries to make the final score 3-30. So, our only ever games against these two teams resulted in heavy defeats although, considering we only had twelve regulars in each match, the final scores were probably predictable.

In the games against Marlborough Nomads and Lennox, it was reported that, owing to the attention of the photographer the start was delayed. In the first case the game was limited to two 25's and in the second, Lennox kicked off at twenty minutes to four. How times have changed! Harry Lee played for us against Cambridge University on 17th October, he was to gain one cap for England in 1907 against France when his club was Blackheath. The referee in this game was J.T. Trotman, who played 53 times for us between 1881 and 1885. Making his debut against Guy's Hospital on 20th February was R.O.C. Robert "Roc" Ward. He played for us right up to the First World War and made 234 appearances, setting a new Club appearance record. This season has the distinction of being the one where most players were used, the final total was 103. Only thirty tries were scored during the season with Nesbitt claiming top spot with just three. He shared top points (9) with T.J. Wheeler who got a penalty and three conversions.

1903/04

260903	OLD MERCHANT TAYLORS	OLD DEER PARK	L	1G(5)-1G1T(8)
031003	RICHMOND	WANDSWORTH COMMON	L	1T(3)-2T(6)
101003	LONDON IRISH	WANDSWORTH COMMON	W	1G3T(14)-1G1T(8)
171003	CAMBRIDGE UNIVERSITY	CAMBRIDGE	L	0-4G1T(23)
211003	STREATHAM	WANDSWORTH COMMON	P	
241003	LENNOX	WANDSWORTH COMMON	W	2G(10)-1G1T(8)
281003	ROYAL SCHOOL OF MINES	WANDSWORTH COMMON	C	
311003	RICHMOND	RICHMOND	L	1G(5)-1G4T(17)
041103	HAMPSTEAD WANDERERS	WANDSWORTH COMMON	C	
071103	MARLBOROUGH NOMADS	WANDSWORTH COMMON	W	1G2T(11)-1T(3)
111103	CATFORD BRIDGE	CATFORD	L	1T(3)-3G4T(27)
141103	OXFORD UNIVERSITY	OXFORD	L	0-4G1DG3T(33)
181103	LONDON HOSPITAL	WANDSWORTH COMMON	C	
211103	KENSINGTON	WOOD LANE	W	2DG(8)-1G(5)
251103	STREATHAM	WANDSWORTH COMMON	C	
281103	ROSSLYN PARK	WANDSWORTH COMMON	D	1T(3)-1T(3)
021203	ROYAL NAVAL COLLEGE	GREENWICH	L	0-5T(15)
051203	LONDON SCOTTISH	RICHMOND	C	
091203	DOVER COLLEGE	DOVER	C	
121203	ROYAL INDIAN ENGINEERING COLLEGE	COOPER'S HILL	L	0-1G3T(14)

191203	LONDON WELSH	WANDSWORTH COMMON	L	0-1G3T(14)
261203	KENSINGTON	WANDSWORTH COMMON	W	3G(15)-1G2T(11)
020104	NORTHAMPTON	NORTHAMPTON	C	
070104	SHANDON ATHLETIC	WANDSWORTH COMMON	C	
090104	BLACKHEATH	WANDSWORTH COMMON	L	1T(3)-3T(9)
160104	OLD MERCHANT TAYLORS	WANDSWORTH COMMON	L	1PG(3)-3T(9)
200104	ROYAL SCHOOL OF MINES	ACTON	C	
230104	ROSSLYN PARK	OLD DEER PARK	C	
300104	LONDON SCOTTISH	WANDSWORTH COMMON	C	
030204	WEMBLEY	WANDSWORTH COMMON	C	
060204	LEICESTER	LEICESTER	L	0-1G1T(8)
130204	ST.THOMAS'S HOSPITAL	CHISWICK PARK	C	
170204	SURBITON	WANDSWORTH COMMON	C	
200204	GUY'S HOSPITAL	HONOR OAK PARK	W	3T(9)-1T(3)
270204	OLD ALLEYNIANS	WANDSWORTH COMMON	L	1G(5)-1G1T(8)
050304	MARLBOROUGH NOMADS	SURBITON	W	1T(3)-0
120304	LENNOX	STAMFORD BRIDGE	W	1DG1T(7)-1T(3)
190304	BLACKHEATH	BLACKHEATH	W	2G2T(16)-2G(10)
260304	OLD LEYSIANS	ELTHAM	C	
020404	PLYMOUTH	PLYMOUTH	L	1T(3)-2G5T(25)
040404	REDRUTH	REDRUTH	L	1T(3)-3G5T(30)

At the A.G.M. on 12th September 1904 it was noted that there were still a large number of subscriptions outstanding from the previous season. After this, a motion was passed stating that all subscriptions should be paid promptly as it was impossible to carry on the Club except on a sound financial basis. At the next Committee meeting on 12th October, a letter was received from West Hartlepool asking for a game in the next season and also making a very strong appeal to all London clubs to pay a visit to the district. This question was adjourned until it could be ascertained what the prospects were of getting a team to go and although it was decided at a later meeting to write to them to try and arrange a match with them before Christmas 1905 asking for a guarantee of £50, there was obviously no further progress because we didn't play them until their centenary season of 1981. A long discussion followed on whether or not a letter be sent to the press concerning the circumstances of Edward Dillon's desertion from the Club to Blackheath. It would appear that this was an early example of player poaching although Dillon was not the first (or the last) Quins player to have left and won caps with another club. The slight difference with this case was that he was already an England international, having gained three caps the previous season against Wales, Ireland and Scotland. It was decided that the subject should be dropped but his unpaid subscription should be demanded and his name removed from the Club books. It must have been a sudden departure as he was elected to the Committee for this season and is listed as such in the fixture card.

We started off against O.M.T.s and despite losing 3-15 the game had its highlights for us as it saw the first appearance by H.J.H. (Herbert) Sibree at half back, in partnership with Stoop. He was to gain three caps for England in 1908 and 1909. After drawing at Richmond, we met London Irish at Cricklewood for the only time and, in the process of defeating them by two tries to nil, secured our first victory of the season. For this season, the midweek matches had dwindled to two, one each against Hampstead Wanderers and Royal Naval College. The match against the College was cancelled and the one against Hampstead on 9th November was lost, starting us off on a nine match losing run which, due to seven cancellations went on until 11th February. The matches with Hampstead carried on for a few more seasons but eventually died out. United Services Portsmouth were to have been met for the first time on 29th October but the game was among the cancellations mentioned. Another new team on our fixture list were the University College School Old Boys whom we met home and away, each time the home side prevailed. In the away game on 1st April, we had the services of Harry Alexander, N.H. Dakeyne, F.H. Palmer and F.T. Turner from the Richmond Club. Alexander (who kicked two conversions) and Palmer were both England internationals but we went down by one point (10-11).

Against London Welsh, Sibree had appeared as A.F. Fullbach in the original team selection, this being another in the long list of A.N. Other's. This game, being played on their ground at Queen's Club, saw our heaviest defeat of the season as the Welsh ran in ten tries (four converted) for a final score of 3-38. As well as Sibree, two other players of note making their debuts were Douglas "Daniel" Lambert and Kenneth Powell. Both of them did so in the defeat by the R.I.E.C. and Lambert went on to play for England seven times and set many Quins scoring records while Powell was an Olympic hurdler. This was our last poor season before the First World War, which saw the team score only thirty seven tries (eighteen of which were converted) and 154 points in total. Hammond (the captain) was top try scorer with five while Roc Ward was overall top points scorer with twenty seven (one try and twelve conversions). His brother H.E. Horace "Holly" Ward played his first game for the Club against Richmond on 1st October. Like his brother, he went on to play a large number of times for the Club, his total being 174.

1904/05

240904	OLD MERCHANT TAYLORS	WANDSWORTH COMMON	L	1T(3)-1G1DG1PG1T(15)
011004	RICHMOND	WANDSWORTH COMMON	D	1T(3)-1T(3)
081004	LONDON IRISH	CRICKLEWOOD	W	2T(6)-0
151004	CAMBRIDGE UNIVERSITY	CAMBRIDGE	L	1G1T(8)-2G2T(16)
221004	LENNOX	CRICKLEWOOD	L	1DG1T(7)-2G(10)
291004	UNITED SERVICES PORTSMOUTH	WANDSWORTH COMMON	C	
051104	MARLBOROUGH NOMADS	WANDSWORTH COMMON	W	1G4T(17)-1G3T(14)
091104	HAMPSTEAD WANDERERS	WANDSWORTH COMMON	L	1T(3)-1G1T(8)
121104	OXFORD UNIVERSITY	WANDSWORTH COMMON	L	1PG(3)-3G4T(27)
191104	OLD ALLEYNIANS	WANDSWORTH COMMON	L	2T(6)-2G(10)
261104	ROSSLYN PARK	WANDSWORTH COMMON	C	
301104	ROYAL NAVAL COLLEGE	WANDSWORTH COMMON	C	
031204	LONDON SCOTTISH	WANDSWORTH COMMON	L	1G(5)-2T(6)
101204	ROYAL INDIAN ENGINEERING COLLEGE	WANDSWORTH COMMON	L	0-3G1T(18)
171204	LONDON WELSH	QUEEN'S CLUB	L	1T(3)-4G6T(38)
241204	NORTHAMPTON	NORTHAMPTON	C	
261204	SURBITON	WANDSWORTH COMMON	C	

311204	OLD ALLEYNIANS	WANDSWORTH COMMON	L	1G(5)-2G1T(13)
070105	BLACKHEATH	BLACKHEATH	C	
140105	OLD MERCHANT TAYLORS	OLD DEER PARK	L	0-3G3T(24)
210105	ROSSLYN PARK	OLD DEER PARK	C	
280105	LONDON SCOTTISH	RICHMOND	C	
040205	LEICESTER	WANDSWORTH COMMON	L	0-3T(9)
110205	UNIVERSITY COLLEGE SCHOOL OLD BOYS	WANDSWORTH COMMON	W	3G(15)-1T(3)
180205	GUY'S HOSPITAL	WANDSWORTH COMMON	L	2G1T(13)-1G3T(14)
250205	RICHMOND	RICHMOND	L	1G(5)-1G2T(11)
040305	MARLBOROUGH NOMADS	SURBITON	W	5G2T(31)-1G2T(11)
110305	LENNOX	WANDSWORTH COMMON	W	1T(3)-0
180305	BLACKHEATH	WANDSWORTH COMMON	C	
250305	OLD LEYSIANS	ELTHAM	W	1G1T(8)-1T(3)
010405	UNIVERSITY COLLEGE SCHOOL OLD BOYS	ISLEWORTH	L	2G(10)-1G2T(11)

A letter had been received from the Rugby Union back in January 1905 asking for the Club's views on an alteration in the scoring laws, this had been answered in the negative but, more clubs must have requested a change because at the beginning of the 1905/06 season a change was made. The value of a goal from a mark was reduced from four points to three and this was the only change from the existing values brought in twelve years before. On 25th July 1905, the A.G.M. was held but due to the very small attendance and the very serious deficit shown on the balance sheet it was adjourned until 29th September. After a discussion it was finally resolved that a voluntary subscription should be got up to wipe off the said deficit. The sum of £23 13s 0d was raised in the room and a notice was then sent to all members informing them of the situation and inviting them to subscribe likewise. It was later shown that £48 17s 6d was received in donations and decided that this should be put to one side and used for any further emergencies in the future.

On 15th February 1906, permission was sought to form a club in South Africa bearing the name and wearing the colours of the Harlequin Football Club. It was proposed by Reginald Curtis-Hayward and seconded by O.O. Wortham that the Honorary Secretary should write and give the required permission, hence the Pretoria Harlequins came into being. At the same meeting it was decided that the Ground committee should enter into negotiations for a new lease as the current one expired at the end of the season. It was felt that the Quins should not share the whole of the gate money in addition to paying £35 rent per annum. In future years this appears to have happened as the words "share of" disappear from the balance sheet and it is just presented as "Gate money". An interesting item appears on the balance sheet for this season, namely the purchase of a goal post for £1 4s 6d!

Although season 1905/06 was to be Hammond's last as captain, he went on playing for the first XV until 1910. In his four season tenure, he captained the side on sixty seven occasions and scored fifteen tries. We started the same as the previous eight seasons in failing to win our opening game (we had managed two draws and six defeats in that time). All the games had been against the O.M.T.s and so it was no surprise when we were beaten 8-25. Making his debut in the centre was J.G.G. (John) Birkett, another future England international, he was to gain 21 caps between 1906 and 1912 and make 162 appearances for the Club. With Lambert, Stoop and the brothers Ward also in the team, we were starting to see the makings of the very successful side from this era. A.C. (Alexander) Palmer, another future England man (two caps in 1909) played for us in the last game of the season against Lennox and Harry Alexander appeared again, this time against Hampstead Wanderers. D. Linton made his last appearance against Rosslyn Park (his debut had been against them in 1899) on 20th January after 97 games in seven seasons. After winning just one out of our first five matches, we met United Services Portsmouth for the first time, the venue was Wandsworth Common. Sibree (2), Lambert and A.A. Claxton scored tries and Roc Ward kicked two conversions in a 16-6 victory. This really kick started the season for us and we strung together a run of four victories, including one over Oxford University.

On 23rd December we met the Old Merchistonians from Scotland for the first time. They came down around Christmas for a short tour and we played them five times over the next seven years. On this occasion, we played two current and two future English caps against their three current and one future Scottish caps and came off second best by twenty one points to nil. We were to face six of this side when we met London Scottish on 27th January in what proved to be our first defeat of 1906. In the game against Richmond on 24th February, Lambert equalled the Club scoring record in a match when he scored four tries and four conversions (20 points) in a 29-5 win. Cambridge University were defeated (24-15), but when we met Northampton for the first and what proved to be the only time at Wandsworth, we went down to our seventh straight defeat at their hands (3-18). Our last game against Lennox at Cricklewood (mentioned earlier) saw us fielding thirteen men to their fifteen but, thanks to eleven points from Lambert, we saw them off by 18-10. Having used seventy six players, it was not surprising that no one appeared in all twenty seven matches. Those who managed over twenty were Lambert and Roc Ward with twenty five and Holly Ward with twenty two. On the points scoring side, several records were set with Lambert leading the way. He set new records for conversions (24), tries (28) and points (132). The team followed suit with the same records, scoring 40 conversions, 97 tries and 371 points. This season also saw our best number of wins (14) since 1897/98 (15).

1905/06

300905	OLD MERCHANT TAYLORS	OLD DEER PARK	L	1G1T(8)-2G5T(25)
071005	RICHMOND	WANDSWORTH COMMON	L	1T(3)-3G1T(18)
141005	LONDON SCOTTISH	WANDSWORTH COMMON	L	4T(12)-2G2T(16)
211005	LENNOX	WANDSWORTH COMMON	W	2G3T(19)-0
281005	MARLBOROUGH NOMADS	WANDSWORTH COMMON	L	3T(9)-2G2T(16)
041105	UNITED SERVICES PORTSMOUTH	WANDSWORTH COMMON	W	2G2T(16)-1PG1T(6)
081105	HAMPSTEAD WANDERERS	WANDSWORTH COMMON	W	2G1T(13)-3T(9)
111105	OXFORD UNIVERSITY	OXFORD	W	2G2T(16)-1T(3)
181105	OLD ALLEYNIANS	WANDSWORTH COMMON	W	6G4T(42)-1G(5)
251105	ROSSLYN PARK	WANDSWORTH COMMON	L	3T(9)-3G(15)
291105	ROYAL NAVAL COLLEGE	GREENWICH	W	4G(20)-1G(5)
021205	LONDON IRISH	WANDSWORTH COMMON	C	
091205	LONDON WELSH	WANDSWORTH COMMON	L	1T(3)-1G1T(8)
161205	BLACKHEATH	WANDSWORTH COMMON	L	2T(6)-1DG3T(13)
231205	OLD MERCHISTONIANS	WANDSWORTH COMMON	L	0-3G2T(21)
261205	SURBITON	WANDSWORTH COMMON	W	1G4T(17)-2G(10)

301205	OLD ALLEYNIANS	DULWICH	W	2G2T(16)-1T(3)
060106	UNIVERSITY COLLEGE SCHOOL OLD BOYS	WANDSWORTH COMMON	W	1G5T(20)-1G1T(8)
130106	OLD MERCHANT TAYLORS	WANDSWORTH COMMON	C	
200106	ROSSLYN PARK	OLD DEER PARK	W	1G3T(14)-3T(9)
270106	LONDON SCOTTISH	RICHMOND	L	1T(3)-2T(6)
030206	BLACKHEATH	BLACKHEATH	L	3G(15)-2G3T(19)
100206	LEICESTER	LEICESTER	C	
170206	MARLBOROUGH NOMADS	SURBITON	W	3G3T(24)-0
240206	RICHMOND	RICHMOND	W	4G3T(29)-1G(5)
030306	CAMBRIDGE UNIVERSITY	CAMBRIDGE	W	3G3T(24)-3G(15)
100306	NORTHAMPTON	WANDSWORTH COMMON	L	1T(3)-1G1DG3T(18)
170306	UNIVERSITY COLLEGE SCHOOL OLD BOYS	ISLEWORTH	L	1T(3)-1G3T(14)
240306	OLD LEYSIANS	BURNTWOOD LANE	L	3T(9)-2G2T(16)
310306	LENNOX	CRICKLEWOOD	W	3G1T(18)-2G(10)

At the A.G.M. on 13th September it was hoped by the Honorary Treasurer that the satisfactory state of the balance sheet would not lead to recklessness in the matter of expenses. It appears from this that the Club were now determined not to go down the same road they had been down twice already and find themselves having to rely on the generous help of the membership to bail it out. Adrian Stoop proposed that the rules should be amended to show that the Club now played in white knickerbockers as opposed to dark blue ones. This motion was seconded by Roc Ward and passed unanimously. The members of the Club appeared to be quite outspoken on several subjects, one of which was whether Irish, Scottish and Welsh players should be allowed to play for English Counties. It was decided that the feeling of the meeting was that they should not be allowed to play and it was considered desirable that the County qualifications should be revised. At the next meeting, Heathfield C.C. wanted to purchase an automatic checking turnstile out of the gate money for use on the Football ground, this was affirmed. The balance sheet for the end of 1906/07 showed that the Club had purchased £50 of India 3% stock (which is shown as costing £46 13s 9d) and also some footballs (including new bladders) for £2 12s 3d.

The new season promised so much after all the record setting of the previous year and it got off to a good start when we entertained the O.M.T.s at Wandsworth. Although the first half ended evenly at a try each, we stormed away in the second to win 19-3. Our tries were scored by G.H. Birkett (2), John Birkett (2) and Douglas Lambert with Lambert and T.S. (Thomas) Kelly getting one conversion each. This was Stoop's first game as captain of the Club, a position he was to hold until the outbreak of war in 1914. The game against Marlborough Nomads on 27th October saw us defeat them 39-10 and was remarkable for the fact that Lambert set a new mark for points in a game by scoring no fewer than seven tries and three conversions, making twenty seven points. In the return match in February, he scored only four tries in our 44-3 win but Roc Ward kicked seven conversions to set a new mark for conversions in a game. When we met Oxford University on 10th November, it was not at Wandsworth as scheduled, but on the second pitch at the Richmond Athletic Ground. Our ground was unfit and, as reported at the time, thanks to the good sportsmanship of Richmond, London Scottish and the Richmond Athletic Association, we were permitted to play there. As it turned out, our game was watched by two thirds of the gate, the rest decided to watch

Richmond and London Scottish on the main pitch. The game itself was described as "bright and well-contested" and the superiority in the end of our forwards enabled us to win by nine points to eight. In the space of three weeks we were to meet the very strong Devonport Albion side, at home first on 17th November and then away on 8th December. It turned out that both games (played in terrible conditions) were lost and we failed to register a single point (0-6 and 0-23).

On 13th January we met the Racing Club de France again, this time at Bagatelle and, unlike the first game, we won by eight points to nil. We were due to play Blackheath on 2nd February but, unfortunately, the match was called off on the Saturday morning. One of the newspaper correspondents of the time filed the following report under the heading - "RUGBY MEN AT SOCCER":

"It was not until I got to Clapham Junction on Saturday that I found out Harlequins and Blackheath could not play. Most of the Harlequins team were there, but only one representative of Blackheath, H. Mainprice. I journeyed on to Wandsworth, where the Harlequins had a pick up Soccer match to keep themselves fit. Many of the crowd which had come to see Blackheath and Harlequins play stayed for this improvised Soccer game, and were much amused at the efforts of the Harlequins to dribble a regular Soccer ball. The International J.G.G. Birkett was frequently penalised "for hands"; the Brothers Stoop were always dangerous when they got the ball; J.R. Bond was purely an individualist, as also Roc Ward; Holly Ward put in some big kicking at full back; the Brothers Lambert, especially the International, had great control over the ball; Sibree made a most efficient half-back with Denison and T.L. Pearce; and A.L. Sloper, the well-known referee, kept goal for either side. The game served its purpose of keeping "the boys" fit, and afforded much enjoyment to a really good crowd".

It is interesting to note that Douglas Lambert did, in fact, start life as a Soccer player. He was an inside-right in the Eastbourne College XI of 1899 and moved over, with the rest of the side, to the School First XV when they changed to Rugger in 1900. He joined us on leaving school and was an "A" XV forward until the same trial game in which Sibree was picked out. During this game Stoop, already capped, got something of a shock. In his own words he described how he thought he was going to score a try but suddenly found himself about ten yards over the touch line. When he recovered he asked "What the hell was that?", the answer was that it was Lambert, who plays forward for the "A". Stoop replied saying "Well, now he plays wing three quarter for the First". He was obviously the right man for the position as he played for the Club right up to the War (in which he was killed).

In the game against United Services, Portsmouth on 9th February, Sibree played as a "rover", this appeared to be an experiment in the next three matches and was then dropped, although it did appear again the following season on a couple of occasions. On our seventh visit to Northampton, we had a number of changes to our side and although we still had Lambert, Sibree and Stoop playing, it was widely thought that we were to be on the receiving end of a large score. This looked to be coming true as we trailed 0-16 at half time but, showing determination, we came back at the home side and equalled their score with three tries from Lambert, one from Stoop and two conversions from Roc Ward. Even with our draw, it still meant that in nine meetings going back to 1896, we still had not defeated them. Out of the eighty four players used during the course of twenty three matches, not one was an ever present. Roc Ward only missed one and his brother H.E. and J.H. Denison missed four. W.F. Hill and Sibree (18) and the captain and Douglas Lambert (17) were the only others to play in more than fifteen games. On the points scoring front, Lambert set another record for tries in a season with 32 and the team records for conversions and points (set the previous season) were equalled. During the course of this season, another five England internationals (three already capped and two to become so in the future) played for us. They were Thomas Kelly, G.H. d'O (George) Lyon, S.H. (Sidney) Osborne, G.D. (Geoffrey) Roberts and F.M. (Frederick) "Tim" Stoop.

1906/07

290906	OLD MERCHANT TAYLORS	WANDSWORTH COMMON	W	2G3T(19)-1T(3)
061006	RICHMOND	WANDSWORTH COMMON	W	4G5T(35)-1G1DG(9)
131006	LONDON SCOTTISH	RICHMOND	L	1G(5)-2G1T(13)
201006	LENNOX	CRICKLEWOOD	W	4G3T(29)-2T(6)
271006	MARLBOROUGH NOMADS	WANDSWORTH COMMON	W	3G8T(39)-2G(10)
031106	CAMBRIDGE UNIVERSITY	WANDSWORTH COMMON	W	1G2T(11)-0
071106	HAMPSTEAD WANDERERS	WANDSWORTH COMMON	W	2G1DG3T(23)-3T(9)
101106	OXFORD UNIVERSITY	RICHMOND(H)	W	3T(9)-1G1T(8)
171106	DEVONPORT ALBION	WANDSWORTH COMMON	L	0-2T(6)
241106	ROSSLYN PARK	WANDSWORTH COMMON	L	1T(3)-3T(9)
011206	LONDON IRISH	BLACKHORSE LANE	W	1G2T(11)-1G1T(8)
081206	DEVONPORT ALBION	DEVONPORT	L	0-4G1T(23)
151206	LENNOX	WANDSWORTH COMMON	W	4G3T(29)-0
221206	BLACKHEATH	BLACKHEATH	L	1T(3)-1G2T(11)
261206	SURBITON	WANDSWORTH COMMON	C	
291206	OLD ALLEYNIANS	DULWICH	C	
050107	LEICESTER	LEICESTER	L	0-3T(9)
130107	RACING CLUB DE FRANCE	BAGATELLE	W	(8)-0
190107	ROSSLYN PARK	OLD DEER PARK	L	0-1G3T(14)
260107	LONDON SCOTTISH	WANDSWORTH COMMON	C	
020207	BLACKHEATH	WANDSWORTH COMMON	C	
090207	UNITED SERVICES PORTSMOUTH	WANDSWORTH COMMON	W	3G5T(30)-1G3T(14)
160207	MARLBOROUGH NOMADS	THAMES DITTON	W	7G3T(44)-1T(3)
230207	RICHMOND	RICHMOND	L	2G1T(13)-4G1PG2T(29)
020307	NORTHAMPTON	NORTHAMPTON	D	2G2T(16)-2G2T(16)
090307	OLD ALLEYNIANS	WANDSWORTH COMMON	W	3G6T(33)-1T(3)
160307	UNITED SERVICES PORTSMOUTH	PORTSMOUTH	L	1G2T(11)-2G1DG3T(23)
230307	UNIVERSITY COLLEGE SCHOOL OLD BOYS	ISLEWORTH	C	

The purchase of the India stock was confirmed at the 1907 A.G.M. on 18th September and the treasurer was complimented on the best balance sheet in the history of the Club. A meeting was then held after the A.G.M. where it was felt that we could not drop one of the two fixtures with Rosslyn Park until we had thoroughly defeated them twice in one season. This duly happened in season 1908/09 (36-3 and 16-0) and we didn't play them twice in a season again until 1972/73. It was decided on 17th December that, subject to a member being found to undertake to arrange all the details, the Committee should sanction a Harlequin team going to Frankfurt. At the same meeting it was proposed by W.F. Hill and seconded by Reginald Curtis-Hayward that the Honorary secretary be authorised to write to the Rugby Union with regard to letting the Twickenham ground. This was to prove an inspired piece of forward thinking as will be seen later. In this season's fixture card it was noted that Preece's Riding School (located at 248, Fulham Road) had been engaged on Thursday evenings during the season at 6.30 for training purposes. This seems to have been a short term policy as, although by the following season this had been extended to Tuesdays as well, by 1909/10 it was not mentioned and is assumed to have fallen by the wayside.

In our first game of the 1907/08 season, we played the O.M.T.s at the Old Deer Park in what proved to be an exciting encounter played in beautiful conditions. It was reported in one account that the heat would have been quite sufficient excuse to delay the start half an hour to four o'clock. As it was, Adrian Stoop kicked off at twenty to four from the pagoda end and shortly after Parker got a try for the home side to open the scoring. Sibree, Birkett and Lyon got tries for us, Lambert converted one and although Dellschaft got the Taylors' second, we led 11-6 at the break. The second half was to be nip and tuck all the way with the home side regaining the lead through tries by M.J. Lepingwell and Raphael and a dropped goal from Cockell, we came back though and Birkett, Palmer and Lambert got unconverted tries to give us a four point lead. Although Dellschaft completed his hat trick and R.A. Lepingwell converted both scores, we were able to just keep our noses in front with scores of our own from Lambert and Stoop, with Lambert's conversion of one giving us a narrow 28-26 victory.

After thrashing Richmond 42-0, we had a midweek draw with the Royal Military College at Sandhurst, defeated London Scottish and then met Bath for the first time on 19th October at home. Luckily for Bath, our normal full back (J. Batstone) found at the last minute that he was unable to make the game and so R.E. Hemmingway came in totally unprepared for what was to be his only appearance for the first team. He was described as being a thorough sportsman as he was only intending on being a spectator and as it was he had to borrow a pair of boots which appeared to be a couple of sizes too big! It was his excusable blunders which led to Bath scoring two tries whereas had Batstone played it was reported that the visitors would have been beaten pointless. As it was Adrian Stoop and his three quarters gave a typically Welsh exhibition of passing that had never been equalled at Wandsworth and in scoring eleven tries proceeded to win 49-8. In this game, Lambert set a new record for conversions in a match with eight. Bath did get their revenge in the return game in March to the tune of nine points to eight when it was our turn to be weakened (we had to borrow N.W.A. Henderson from Bath College to make up our numbers).

In our next match against United Services, Portsmouth on 26th October we suffered an unexpected reverse as even the Services had hoped to do little more than hold their own against us. But, to our dismay, we conceded seven tries and lost our captain (Adrian Stoop) with a broken collarbone (he was to be out of action until March), the final score was 0-27. Further defeats were to follow against both Oxford and Cambridge but after this we only lost four games out of eighteen. Although the Leicester and Northampton games were cancelled, we managed victories over, among others, London Irish, Blackheath (twice), Old Merchistonians and Old Alleynians. A side did make it out to Germany at Easter to play against FC 1880 Frankfurt. The match would have been played somewhere around 17th April and a win followed to the tune of 18-0. Adrian Stoop, Roc Ward and V.F. Eberle formed part of our XV.

Out of twenty six matches played, W.F. Hill (24), Holly Ward (23) and Sibree (19) were the top appearance makers. Lambert set more new records for most conversions with forty four and most points (178) with thirty tries added to his conversions. The team set new marks for tries (117), conversions (57) and points (478). This was the first time we had scored over one hundred tries, a feat which has been achieved on numerous occasions since. J.A. (John) Scholfield and F.N. (Francis) Tarr were two new English internationals to play for us alongside eight other cap winners who had appeared before.

1907/08

280907	OLD MERCHANT TAYLORS	OLD DEER PARK	W	2G6T(28)-2G1DG4T(26)
051007	RICHMOND	WANDSWORTH COMMON	W	6G4T(42)-0
091007	ROYAL MILITARY COLLEGE	SANDHURST	D	2G2T(16)-2G2T(16)
121007	LONDON SCOTTISH	WANDSWORTH COMMON	W	2G1T(13)-1MG(3)
191007	BATH	WANDSWORTH COMMON	W	8G3T(49)-1G1T(8)
261007	UNITED SERVICES PORTSMOUTH	PORTSMOUTH	L	0-1G1DG6T(27)
021107	CAMBRIDGE UNIVERSITY	CAMBRIDGE	L	1T(3)-4G2T(26)
061107	HAMPSTEAD WANDERERS	WANDSWORTH COMMON	C	
091107	OXFORD UNIVERSITY	OXFORD	L	1G2T(11)-1G1DG1T(12)
161107	ROSSLYN PARK	WANDSWORTH COMMON	W	2G2T(16)-1T(3)
231107	OLD ALLEYNIANS	WANDSWORTH COMMON	W	4G4T(32)-1T(3)
271107	CHELTENHAM COLLEGE	CHELTENHAM	W	1G1DG1T(12)-2T(6)
301107	LONDON IRISH	WANDSWORTH COMMON	W	5G2T(31)-0
071207	MARLBOROUGH NOMADS	WANDSWORTH COMMON	W	1G6T(23)-1G1T(8)
141207	NORTHAMPTON	WANDSWORTH COMMON	C	
211207	BLACKHEATH	WANDSWORTH COMMON	W	1G1PG1T(11)-0
261207	SURBITON	WANDSWORTH COMMON	W	5G2T(31)-1T(3)
281207	OLD MERCHISTONIANS	WANDSWORTH COMMON	W	3G2T(21)-2G1PG(13)
040108	LEICESTER	WANDSWORTH COMMON	C	
110108	OLD LEYSIANS	BURNTWOOD LANE	C	
180108	ROSSLYN PARK	OLD DEER PARK	W	1PG3T(12)-1G1T(8)
250108	LONDON SCOTTISH	RICHMOND	L	1G(5)-1G1DG2T(15)
010208	BLACKHEATH	BLACKHEATH	W	2G1T(13)-1PG1T(6)
150208	UNITED SERVICES PORTSMOUTH	WANDSWORTH COMMON	L	1T(3)-6T(18)
220208	RICHMOND	RICHMOND	W	1G3T(14)-0
290208	LONDON HOSPITAL	WANDSWORTH COMMON	L	1T(3)-1G5T(20)
070308	OLD ALLEYNIANS	DULWICH	W	3G1PG5T(33)-0
140308	LENNOX	WIMBLEDON	W	5G2T(31)-1T(3)
210308	BATH	BATH	L	1G1T(8)-3T(9)
280308	OLD MERCHANT TAYLORS	WANDSWORTH COMMON	W	1G4T(17)-2G1T(13)
??0408	FC 1880 FRANKFURT	FRANKFURT	W	(18)-0

At the A.G.M. on 16th September, it was decided by a narrow majority to continue the fixture with Leicester. This was fortunate as our first victory over them since 1895 was just around the corner. At a Committee meeting on 11th December, a sub committee consisting of W.F. Hill, Douglas Lambert and Adrian Stoop was appointed to enquire on what terms the Rugby Union were prepared to let the new football ground at Twickenham. This was obviously successful as at a further meeting, the agreement with the R.F.U. was discussed and accepted and the names of Henry Surtees and Adrian Stoop were inserted as lessees. On 10th May 1909, the Honorary Secretary was authorised to extend the season of the Club to 16th April for the purpose of arranging fixtures with Cardiff and

Newport and also to arrange a tour at Easter which should not involve the Club in any expenditure. Finally, it was reported that the fixture with London Hospital was to be scratched due to foul play on the part of A.A. Adams (a member of the Hospital team).

The 1908/09 season was another record breaking one and was to prove the most successful so far as we managed to win no fewer than twenty out of twenty five matches. It all started in amazing fashion as we trounced the O.M.T.s 53-5 (this beat the previous record score in a match), Richmond 39-12 and the Royal Military College 33-0. In the next game, against London Scottish, Stoop broke his collarbone (again) a few minutes into the game and a few minutes from the end Birkett did the same (although this was also reported as a broken bone in his shoulder), we still won the game by thirteen points to nine. Bedford were met for the first time on 17th October and after a scoreless first half, we ran out winners by scoring thirteen unanswered points in the second. The next four games were against some of our strongest opponents (U.S. Portsmouth, Cambridge, Oxford and Northampton) and were all lost. In the game against the United Services (6-16) we were only able to field four of our usual side due to injuries and the London Counties game against the Australian touring side and against Northampton (0-29) at least half of the side were not regular members of the first team. In the other two games we were beaten up forward by Cambridge (5-22) and by superior backs in the Oxford team (8-28). The matches against the two varsities were watched by 3,000 and 5,000 spectators respectively.

From this point on we managed to win fourteen out of fifteen, the two most noteworthy victories being against Surbiton on 26th December and Leicester on 13th March. In the first game we were not at full strength and, like our visitors, played a man short. Even so we managed to increase the Club record score in a match to 74 points. Surbiton were completely outclassed by us and by half time we had amassed thirty three points through tries by F.H.B. Champain (2), G.F. Elmslie, Charles Hammond (2), L.M.B. Salmon (he was Jamie Salmon's Grandfather and he would play for us in the 1980s) and Holly Ward and six conversions from Elmslie. It was even more of a procession in the second half with J. Batstone, B.H. Bonham-Carter, Champain (2), E.S. Holmwood, Salmon (2), Roc Ward and C.H. Wolff adding tries to which Elmslie added seven more conversions to set a Club record of thirteen in a match. Surbiton did manage to score a try reported as being due to a "momentary lapse" on our part, "through having too much of the game". Against Leicester we produced what was described by many of the newspapers at the time as our best performance of the season. Leicester had already taken the scalps of Devonport Albion, London Scottish, Cardiff, Newport and Swansea at home, so it was always going to be a tough game. Leicester did take the lead when H.S.B. Lawrie scored a try and later in the first half he added a penalty but, between these scores, Lambert and R.W. (Ronald) Poulton had scored tries with Lambert kicking both conversions to give us a 10-6 lead at the interval. We effectively won the game with our next scores, H.J. Bulkeley and Lambert crossing for tries, the latter converting both and we led by fourteen points. Leicester did press very hard after this and managed a dropped goal from E.J. Jackett and a goal from a mark by their first half scorer Lawrie. This was not enough and we held on to win 20-13.

Top appearance makers were Roc Ward (22), Douglas Lambert (19) and T. Potter and Holly Ward both with eighteen. Out of the eighty six players used during the course of the twenty five games played, thirty seven only made one appearance. Two more future England internationals to make their debuts were Henry Brougham and Ronald Poulton. Lambert once again proved his prowess at scoring points when he set new records for tries (35), conversions (52) and points (216). To get an idea of how prolific he was it is necessary to mention a few match facts. He equalled his own points in a game record twice with 27 (4 tries, 1 penalty and 6 conversions) against Richmond on 3rd October and with 5 tries and 6 conversions against Rosslyn Park on 21st November then, a week later against London Irish he set a new mark with 31 points (5 tries, 1 dropped goal and 6 conversions). In these three games alone he had kicked eighteen conversions from twenty two tries (fourteen of them his own). The team again set new records for tries (127), conversions (57) and points (536). As in the previous year with tries, this time it was the first time we had scored over five hundred points in a season. A Club record number of wins on the trot was set when twelve matches were won between 21st November and the 20th February. This record was equalled in both 1988/89 and 1996 before being eclipsed in 2005/06.

1908/09

260908	OLD MERCHANT TAYLORS	WANDSWORTH COMMON	W	7G6T(53)-1G(5)
031008	RICHMOND	RICHMOND	W	6G1PG2T(39)-4T(12)
071008	ROYAL MILITARY COLLEGE	SANDHURST	W	3G6T(33)-0
101008	LONDON SCOTTISH	RICHMOND	W	2G1T(13)-1G1DG(9)
141008	ROYAL MILITARY ACADEMY	WOOLWICH	W	2G1T(13)-1G2T(11)
171008	BEDFORD	BEDFORD	W	2G1T(13)-0
241008	UNITED SERVICES PORTSMOUTH	WANDSWORTH COMMON	L	2T(6)-2G2T(16)
311008	CAMBRIDGE UNIVERSITY	WANDSWORTH COMMON	L	1G(5)-2G4T(22)
041108	HAMPSTEAD WANDERERS	WANDSWORTH COMMON	C	
071108	OXFORD UNIVERSITY	WANDSWORTH COMMON	L	1G1T(8)-2G1PG5T(28)
141108	NORTHAMPTON	NORTHAMPTON	L	0-2G1DG5T(29)
211108	ROSSLYN PARK	WANDSWORTH COMMON	W	6G2T(36)-1PG(3)
281108	LONDON IRISH	CATFORD	W	6G1DG(34)-0
051208	MARLBOROUGH NOMADS	WANDSWORTH COMMON	W	4G5T(35)-0
091208	CHELTENHAM COLLEGE	CHELTENHAM	W	1G2T(11)-1G(5)
121208	OLD ALLEYNIANS	DULWICH	C	
191208	BLACKHEATH	BLACKHEATH	W	3G3T(24)-1T(3)
261208	SURBITON	WANDSWORTH COMMON	W	13G3T(74)-1T(3)
020109	OLD MERCHISTONIANS	WANDSWORTH COMMON	C	
090109	OLD LEYSIANS	WANDSWORTH COMMON	C	
160109	ROSSLYN PARK	OLD DEER PARK	W	2G2T(16)-0
230109	LONDON SCOTTISH	WANDSWORTH COMMON	W	1G1T(8)-1G(5)
300109	BLACKHEATH	WANDSWORTH COMMON	W	3G5T(30)-1G1PG(8)
060209	LENNOX	WIMBLEDON	W	4G4T(32)-0
130209	UNITED SERVICES PORTSMOUTH	PORTSMOUTH	W	2G(10)-3T(9)
200209	RICHMOND	WANDSWORTH COMMON	W	1G2T(11)-0
270209	LONDON HOSPITAL	HALE END	L	0-1G1T(8)
060309	COVENTRY	WANDSWORTH COMMON	C	
130309	LEICESTER	LEICESTER	W	4G(20)-1DG1MG1PG1T(13)
270309	OLD MERCHANT TAYLORS	OLD DEER PARK	W	4T(12)-1G1PG1T(11)

The fixture card for the 1909/10 season states that our ground is the Rugby Football Union, Twickenham and so, our long association with the ground as well as the area begins. The prime mover in this scheme to get us to Twickenham was said to have been W. Williams (hence the almost forgotten nickname “Billy Williams's Cabbage Patch”). A new addition to the rules was passed at this year's A.G.M. being that “Each member is entitled to introduce two ladies to the members' enclosure on “A” stand free of charge. At the same time the secretary explained that the Honorary Treasurer had been unable to produce the balance sheet owing to one of his books having been mislaid! The book must eventually have been found as the sheet was produced at a meeting two weeks later and showed a balance in hand of £187. A funny story did emerge from all this as the treasurer explained that since W.F. Hill (the previous holder of that post) was unable to account for £25, he had handed over a cheque for that amount to the Club (did this have something to do with the missing book? Alas, we shall never know!). It was mentioned by the secretary on 15th February that he was proposing to take a team to Frankfurt at Whitsun, drawn from members of the Club and this, as will be seen later, he duly did. So, season 1909/10 proved to be our first at Twickenham and just like the previous one it was to be successful. Although we could not match the twenty wins, we did manage eighteen with one draw and four losses. After opening with a victory over the O.M.T.s, we met Richmond in the first 1st XV game at Twickenham (the “A” XV met Harrow the previous week in the first match and won 41-5) and in a close game ran out winners 14-10. Both sides were said to have been handicapped by the long grass which badly needed cutting, but considering the several days of rain which preceded the contest, the turf stood up well. After G.V. (Gordon) Carey (who later became headmaster at Eastbourne College) had the distinction of being the first person to kick-off at Twickenham, we started well but finished badly (Richmond did the opposite) and had our backs to thank for victory with John Birkett scoring the first try on the new ground and Douglas Lambert and Adrian Stoop adding others for a 9-0 lead at half time. W.B. Odgers went over for the visitors and H.C. Terry added the goal points before Tim Stoop went over for Lambert to convert and we were clear by nine points again. As we tired, Richmond reduced the deficit by another five points through the same combination as before but we had just done enough to hold on. The new arena was described at the time as having covered seating for 9,000 with room for another 11,000. One of the reporters of the time could not imagine a crowd of more than 16,000 being exceeded very often (I wonder what he would have made of the ground today?). He went on to say that the short approach to the ground was very nearly a quagmire and this could be improved by a convenient footpath. He also mentioned that a six penny cab fare would prove popular with those disinclined to walk from the station. The other thing which was not really up to scratch was the train from Waterloo, one instance being complained about was the fact that the 5.12 took nearly an hour to complete a journey of eleven miles and a half. Times have not really changed all that much there!

By the time of our next match against London Scottish one week later, the grass had been trimmed and this seemed to suit us as we ran up forty three points without reply. Our pack ran out of steam again but this did not seem to matter. We managed six wins on the trot before meeting Oxford University at Iffley Road, Oxford. The game ended all square, eight points each and one of the correspondents said the reason for the match not coming up to expectations was our unbeaten record. This leads to “nerves” and “forgetfulness of certain chivalrous instincts common to rugger”. “All this bad football derives from greed of victory” the scribe went on and he further referred to touch judges becoming forgetful of their judicial office and shouting for one side and in their excitement becoming oblivious of the position of the well chalked out touch line. In the match against Rosslyn Park on 20th November, Douglas Lambert set another best for points in a game which still stands today with thirty three (five tries and nine conversions) out of our total of fifty seven (thirteen tries and nine conversions) to nil. The successful run continued and resounding wins over Fettesian-Lorettonians (a Scottish school side on their Christmas tour) (42-0), Old Merchistonians (more Scottish tourists) (32-5) and London Scottish (30-0) followed. Two more victories were achieved but our first fall from grace was just around the corner in the shape of the students from Oxford and it was to be one of our own who proved to be a thorn in our side. After a sensational start when Douglas Lambert scored a try and converted it, we were pegged back to 5-5 at the break when Cunningham did the same as Lambert. When the sides changed over, we apparently looked a beaten team as Oxford now had the use of the wind. It was Ronald Poulton who dropped a goal from our 25 and when Cunningham added a penalty, the students led 12-5 and our first defeat at Twickenham in nine games had become a reality.

On 12th March we met Leicester at home and in a game that was described as "quite the dullest and most uninteresting yet seen at Twickenham", we lost by a try (scored by P.W. Lawrie seven minutes from the end) to nil. The next Saturday we played against Marlborough Nomads and won convincingly by 56-0. They were two men short throughout and this obviously helped our score. Douglas Lambert scored 31 points with five tries and eight conversions. In our last game of the season we travelled to Newport to meet the strongest Welsh side of the year. It had generally been said that we would meet with a heavy defeat but, contrary to this we actually led 15-3 at half time with tries from John Birkett, Adrian Stoop and Douglas Lambert (who converted all three). We failed to score in the second half as Newport added two dropped goals and two tries to their first half effort to win 17-15. At the time it was said that Newport's last try came after time should have expired and that the referee could not let the best Welsh side lose in the last game of the season. All of this of course is just rumour and cannot be substantiated and, as the referee is the sole arbiter of fact, the record must show the try as standing. It was, however, a great performance from us to end the season and it was generally agreed that no better team had been seen in Wales that season. New records were again set by Lambert for tries (41) (which stood for over 65 years until beaten by Colin Lambert in 1975/76), conversions (65) and points (253) while the team set new marks for tries (129) and points (541). G.D. Roberts became the first player to score more than one dropped goal in a season with two. In the first team a total of fifty players were used throughout the season. This was the lowest number since 1897/98 when forty nine appeared. Out of these fifty, Douglas Lambert (22), T. Potter and Adrian Stoop (20) and Sibree (18) were the most regular attenders in the twenty three matches played.

The promised game against Frankfurt (the newspaper appears to have a different way of spelling it!) was played on 18th May 1910 and the following two extracts have been taken from the "Sporting Life". Firstly, from 17th May.

"May 18 has been set apart for the Rugby match between the London Harlequins and the

Frankfort F.C., 1880. The Harlequins are not unknown in Frankfort, as three years ago they beat the F.F.C. by 18 points to 0. The Germans have learnt a good deal since then, for last year they managed to beat the Old Alleynians, and are very keen on playing against the Harlequins".

Then, from 25th May, the following:

"London Harlequins at Frankfort helped to popularise Rugby by their very good display, and Frankfort lost by 15 points to 3". The match referred to three years ago was obviously the one played in 1908. Adrian Stoop led the side which also contained Douglas Lambert and Maxwell-Dove. The match was played as part of a sports exhibition that included cycling and football as well.

The British Lions had an unofficial tour to Argentina in May and June 1910 when they played six matches including one against Argentina. The organisers called the team the 'English Rugby Union team' but in Argentina it was known as the Combined British (there were 16 English and 3 Scottish players). The test match played on 12th June was the first for the Argentinian national team and caps were awarded (unfortunately, no caps were awarded to the tourists). Walter Huntingford, Alexander Palmer, Horace "Holly" Ward, ES Holmwood and Whalley Stranach were in the squad. All games were won and all bar Holmwood played in the test match and Ward scored a try in the 28-3 victory.

1909/10

250909	OLD MERCHANT TAYLORS	OLD DEER PARK	W	2G4T(22)-1G3T(14)
021009	RICHMOND	TWICKENHAM	W	1G3T(14)-2G(10)
091009	LONDON SCOTTISH	TWICKENHAM	W	8G1T(43)-0
161009	BEDFORD	TWICKENHAM	W	1G6T(23)-1PG(3)
231009	UNITED SERVICES PORTSMOUTH	PORTSMOUTH	W	4G(20)-2G(10)
301009	BRISTOL	BRISTOL	W	1G1T(8)-2T(6)
061109	OXFORD UNIVERSITY	OXFORD	D	1G1T(8)-1G1PG(8)
131109	NORTHAMPTON	TWICKENHAM	W	4G1DG1T(27)-1G2T(11)
201109	ROSSLYN PARK	TWICKENHAM	W	9G4T(57)-0
041209	BLACKHEATH	TWICKENHAM	W	2G4T(22)-1PG(3)
111209	OLD ALLEYNIANS	TWICKENHAM	C	
181209	LONDON IRISH	CATFORD	W	4G3T(29)-1G(5)
301209	FETTESIAN-LORETTONIANS	TWICKENHAM	W	6G4T(42)-0
010110	OLD MERCHISTONIANS	TWICKENHAM	W	4G4T(32)-1G(5)
220110	LONDON SCOTTISH	RICHMOND	W	3G5T(30)-0
290110	BLACKHEATH	BLACKHEATH	W	1G6T(23)-1G1T(8)
050210	RICHMOND	RICHMOND	W	4G1DG2T(30)-1T(3)
190210	OXFORD UNIVERSITY	TWICKENHAM	L	1G(5)-1G1DG1PG(12)
260210	UNITED SERVICES PORTSMOUTH	TWICKENHAM	W	2G(10)-2T(6)
050310	COVENTRY	COVENTRY	W	2G2T(16)-2T(6)
120310	LEICESTER	TWICKENHAM	L	0-1T(3)
190310	MARLBOROUGH NOMADS	TWICKENHAM	W	8G1DG4T(56)-0
020410	OLD LEYSIANS	WANDSWORTH COMMON	L	3T(9)-1G4T(17)
090410	NEWPORT	NEWPORT	L	3G(15)-2DG3T(17)
180510	FC 1880 FRANKFURT	FRANKFURT	W	(15)-(3)

The A.G.M. was held at Carr's restaurant on 14th September 1910 and was almost immediately followed by a Committee meeting at which a letter was read out which had been received from Coventry asking for financial assistance. The honorary secretary proposed and the honorary treasurer seconded a resolution that a donation be paid to them out of Club funds, the amount decided on a further resolution (proposed by the treasurer and seconded by J.H. Witney) at ten pounds. At a meeting on 24th October, A.B. Cipriani was unanimously elected a life member for past services and a further donation for ten pounds was made out of Club funds, this time to the Twickenham Hospital (this was repeated in 1912 and 1913). At the meeting on 6th February 1911, it was reported that the Rugby Union were prepared to grant a three year lease on the Twickenham ground at a rental of £200, but at the same time tried to restrict the number of games played on the ground. On 23rd May, it was further reported by the secretary that the Rugby Union were proposing to reserve the ground for their own use only if it was not taken by the Harlequin F.C. It was then decided in view of this, that we should agree to the terms of the Rugby Union. The terms were a rent of £200 and the use of the ground to be limited to twenty or twenty one Saturdays. At the conclusion of this meeting, a silver vase (purchased by subscription from members of the Club) was presented to William Smith (the President) in commemoration of his silver wedding.

By the middle of the next season, after defeating the O.M.T.s for the seventh consecutive time, we had thrashed Richmond at the Athletic Ground 38 (four goals and six tries) to nil, Bedford at Bedford 47 (seven goals and four tries) to 7 (one dropped goal and one try) and Cambridge at Twickenham 36 (four goals, one dropped goal and four tries) to 6 (two tries). It was not all good news as we had lost to London Scottish, United Services Portsmouth, Guy's Hospital and Old Alleynians and drawn with Blackheath. After these setbacks, the Scottish and United Services were both defeated in the return games and Coventry were easily beaten 39-0. On 8th April, we entertained Newport at Twickenham and achieved a respectable 3-3 draw and the following week we travelled down to Wales for our first Easter tour to play Swansea and Cardiff. A 5-5 draw was gained at Swansea on the Saturday but Cardiff edged us out 5-10 on the Monday. Top appearance makers were Roc Ward (28), R.E. Cranfield and Sibree (25), John Birkett and W.M. Dodds (21) and Adrian Stoop (20). Although no records were broken during this season, Douglas Lambert was again top in tries, conversions and points and achieved only our sixth ever goal from a mark in the match against Coventry. G.R. Maxwell-Dove, Geoffrey Roberts and Cornelius Thorne each got one dropped goal and Cranfield, Lambert and Roberts scored one penalty each.

In this season we said goodbye to two forwards, one (J.H. Denison) who had made 91 appearances since his debut against the Royal Naval College on 2nd December 1903 played his last game against Blackheath on 28th January and the other (Charles Hammond) who debuted back in 1898 and had made 97 appearances before his last game against Old Blues on 24th December. A third forward who, unlike the other two, was making his first appearance was K.M. (Ken) Carnduff. After playing against United Services, Portsmouth on 25th February he went on to play 49 times for the first XV between then and the last season before the First World War. One old, one current and one future international played for us in this season. On our tour of Wales at Easter, W.C. (Walter) Wilson made his two appearances for us against Swansea and Cardiff. His two England caps had been won in 1907 when he played for Richmond. Against the Old Blues on 24th December, Patrick Munro the Scottish half back guested for us to make his only appearance in our colours. He had last won a cap against England in 1907 but was about to be recalled to play three more times in 1911, his final total of caps being thirteen. On 7th January we met the Old Leysians and making the first of nine appearances between now and 1920 was J.E. (John) "Jenny" Greenwood (England) who, like Munro was to captain his country. His first cap came against France in 1912 although he is named as playing for Cambridge University and Leicester. He went on to gain a further twelve caps and was captain on four occasions in 1920.

1910/11

240910	OLD MERCHANT TAYLORS	TWICKENHAM	W	1G2T(11)-1G(5)
011010	RICHMOND	RICHMOND	W	4G6T(38)-0
081010	LONDON SCOTTISH	RICHMOND	L	1G(5)-2G2T(16)

151010	BEDFORD	BEDFORD	W	7G4T(47)-1DG1T(7)
221010	UNITED SERVICES PORTSMOUTH	TWICKENHAM	L	0-1G(5)
291010	CAMBRIDGE UNIVERSITY	TWICKENHAM	W	4G1DG4T(36)-2T(6)
051110	OXFORD UNIVERSITY	TWICKENHAM	W	2G1T(13)-0
121110	NORTHAMPTON	NORTHAMPTON	W	3G1T(18)-1G1PG1T(11)
191110	ROSSLYN PARK	OLD DEER PARK	W	4T(12)-1G(5)
261110	GUY'S HOSPITAL	HONOR OAK PARK	L	1T(3)-1G1T(8)
031210	BLACKHEATH	BLACKHEATH	D	1G1PG(8)-1G1T(8)
101210	OLD ALLEYNIANS	DULWICH	L	0-2T(6)
171210	LONDON IRISH	RICHMOND	W	1G1DG3T(18)-0
241210	OLD BLUES	TWICKENHAM	W	1G2T(11)-1DG(4)
311210	OLD MERCHISTONIANS	TWICKENHAM	W	2G7T(31)-1G(5)
070111	OLD LEYSIANS	WANDSWORTH COMMON	W	2T(6)-1G(5)
140111	MARLBOROUGH NOMADS	TWICKENHAM	W	4G1PG2T(29)-1T(3)
210111	LONDON SCOTTISH	TWICKENHAM	W	1G7T(26)-1T(3)
280111	BLACKHEATH	BLACKHEATH	L	1T(3)-2G1DG(14)
040211	RICHMOND	TWICKENHAM	C	
110211	LENNOX	TWICKENHAM	W	5G1PG2T(34)-1G(5)
180211	OXFORD UNIVERSITY	OXFORD	W	2G3T(19)-1G1T(8)
250211	UNITED SERVICES PORTSMOUTH	PORTSMOUTH	W	1G1DG1T(12)-1G2T(11)
040311	COVENTRY	TWICKENHAM	W	3G1MG7T(39)-0
110311	LEICESTER	LEICESTER	L	1G1T(8)-1G2T(11)
250311	OLD MERCHANT TAYLORS	OLD DEER PARK	W	2G1T(13)-1G1T(8)
010411	BRISTOL	TWICKENHAM	W	3G1T(18)-2T(6)
080411	NEWPORT	TWICKENHAM	D	1T(3)-1T(3)
150411	SWANSEA	SWANSEA	D	1G(5)-1G(5)
170411	CARDIFF	CARDIFF	L	1G(5)-2G(10)

At the A.G.M. on 20th September, H. Gardiner was re-elected as auditor at the fee of six guineas. At a meeting on 23rd March 1912 it was unanimously decided to discontinue the fixture with Coventry on account of the reprehensible tactics pursued by that club. It is not known exactly what this was all about but we did not meet them again until 17th April 1937! On 29th July, we were back to asking for a guarantee from the French, this time it was for £100 from Stade Français for the match in Paris on 16th February 1913. The secretary was instructed to call on Oddeninos restaurant offering to pay the account outstanding for the dinner, which took place in 1904. Never let it be said that we do not settle our accounts!

The 1911/12 season proved to be just as successful as 1908/09 on the subject of games won with twenty being the figure obtained. Whereas five games had been lost in that season, this time six were lost and one drawn. So, marginally a poorer season overall, but not by much. We started well with victories over Bedford, Bristol and Richmond (all at Twickenham), notching up 85 points for and only 25 against in the process. Our first away game, in Portsmouth, saw the United Services defeat us 5-14, so any chances of a 100% season had gone after just four games. We soon returned to winning ways though and after defeating both Oxford and Cambridge, we met Northampton at Twickenham on 11th November. This was described as "the finest game seen for years" by one newspaper at the time. It goes on to say that both sets of forwards played a fine game "but behind the scrum there was no sort of comparison between the two sides. Sibree was at his best and Stoop as clever as ever". It finishes by saying that "One's opinion, on leaving the ground, was that England could do no better than play at least four of the Harlequin back division, and Poulton". This they very nearly did and Birkett and Brougham played in all four internationals with Stoop joining them in two. Although Poulton was playing up at Oxford (and played twice for them against us), he still managed three appearances for us later in the season. We did defeat Northampton by thirty two points to nil, a record margin of victory against them which still stands today. The next week, we met Lansdowne from Dublin for the first time. We had been due to play them on 3rd December 1889 but that meeting had been cancelled. With the heavy going and wet conditions taking their toll, we ran them ragged to win easily by twenty seven points to nil. On 30th December, we met one of the three services teams for the first time when we played the Royal Navy at Queen's Club. The game proved to be a 10-10 draw with the Navy equalising with the last kick of the match.

An interesting thing happened against the London Scottish at Richmond on 13th January when, at the request of the England selectors, J.A. (John) Pym of Blackheath (who was going to make his debut against Wales the following week) played with his half back partner Adrian Stoop. Pym did not get on the score sheet in this match but Stoop did get a try in our 22-9 victory. The following week Pym did score as did our winger H. Brougham (also on his debut) in an 8-0 England win. Coventry (in the game that led to our discontinuing fixtures with them, as mentioned earlier) and Leicester were defeated and we ventured into Wales again to play Swansea (5-10) and Newport (5-21) on consecutive Saturdays, but not Cardiff. Our third and final trip to Germany to play against FC 1880 Frankfurt was undertaken and although the date and score are unknown, we did win again. Only one man out of fifty three who were used in the twenty seven games played by the 1st XV appeared in all of them, he was Roc Ward. His brother, Holly Ward (25), Adrian Stoop (21) and John Birkett and Douglas Lambert (19) were the other leading appearance makers. The only record setting was the equalling of the penalty record for the team in a season when three were kicked (two by George Roberts and one by Lambert). Lambert (it almost goes without saying) came top in tries (27) and points (180) for the seventh consecutive season and in conversions (48) for the sixth time out of seven. The only time he was not top was when Roc Ward outscored him 17-14 in 1906/07. As far as the team goes, tries (118), conversions (67) and points (505) were all up on the previous year.

On 15th April 1912, the RMS Titanic sank after colliding with an iceberg on her maiden voyage from Southampton to New York. The Titanic Relief Fund was set up to give aid to relatives of victims of the disaster and the Harlequin F.C. contribution to this was a cricket match played at Twickenham against the Outcasts. We were led by Adrian Stoop and the rest of the team were Rees, Lambert, Roberts, Brougham, the Ward brothers, Maxwell-Dove, Birkett, Speller and Grundy. In the first innings, the Wards took eight wickets and Maxwell-Dove got the other two as the Outcasts scored 118. In our first innings, Birkett top-scored with 24, followed by Lambert and Brougham both with 19; Stoop got a duck (in both innings) but we managed 121. The Outcasts got their act together second time around and scored 109-4 when they declared and when play finished, we had managed 42-7 in reply. J.W. Douglas was top scorer in the second innings with 54 and N.V. Turner managed 46, both were unbeaten. For us, Brougham was unbeaten on 23 as the match ended in a draw.

1911/12

300911	BEDFORD	TWICKENHAM	W	4G3T(29)-3G1DG(19)
071011	BRISTOL	TWICKENHAM	W	3G4T(27)-1PG(3)
141011	RICHMOND	TWICKENHAM	W	4G1PG2T(29)-1T(3)
211011	UNITED SERVICES PORTSMOUTH	PORTSMOUTH	L	1G(5)-2G1DG(14)
281011	CAMBRIDGE UNIVERSITY	CAMBRIDGE	W	1DG1PG2T(13)-2T(6)
041111	OXFORD UNIVERSITY	OXFORD	W	5G1T(28)-1G1PG3T(17)
111111	NORTHAMPTON	TWICKENHAM	W	5G1DG1PG(32)-0
181111	LANSDOWNE	TWICKENHAM	W	3G4T(27)-0
251111	GUY'S HOSPITAL	TWICKENHAM	W	4G5T(35)-1PG3T(12)
021211	ROSSLYN PARK	OLD DEER PARK	W	2G3T(19)-0
091211	BLACKHEATH	TWICKENHAM	L	1T(3)-2T(6)
161211	OLD ALLEYNIANS	DULWICH	W	3G6T(33)-2T(6)
231211	OLD MERCHANT TAYLORS	OLD DEER PARK	L	0-2G2T(16)
301211	ROYAL NAVY	QUEEN'S CLUB	D	2G(10)-2G(10)
010112	OLD MERCHISTONIANS	TWICKENHAM	W	7G1T(38)-3G3T(24)
060112	OLD LEYSIANS	WANDSWORTH COMMON	L	1G2T(11)-1G1DG1PG2T(18)
130112	LONDON SCOTTISH	RICHMOND	W	2G4T(22)-1G1DG(9)
270112	BLACKHEATH	BLACKHEATH	W	1G1T(8)-1PG1T(6)
030212	RICHMOND	RICHMOND	C	
170212	OXFORD UNIVERSITY	TWICKENHAM	W	3G3T(24)-1G3T(14)
240212	UNITED SERVICES PORTSMOUTH	TWICKENHAM	W	3G2T(21)-1T(3)
020312	COVENTRY	COVENTRY	W	1G1T(8)-0
090312	LEICESTER	TWICKENHAM	W	3G1T(18)-2T(6)
160312	OLD BLUES	TWICKENHAM	W	4G3T(29)-0
230312	OLD MERCHANT TAYLORS	TWICKENHAM	W	1G(5)-0
300312	BRISTOL	BRISTOL	W	3G2T(21)-1DG(4)
060412	SWANSEA	SWANSEA	L	1G(5)-1DG1PG1T(10)
130412	NEWPORT	NEWPORT	L	1G(5)-3G2T(21)
????12	FC 1880 FRANKFURT	FRANKFURT	W	

At the A.G.M. on 18th September, the secretary called the attention of the meeting to the severe loss the Club had sustained through the death by drowning of R.W. Evers. He had made 27 appearances as a forward, making his debut on 24th October 1908 against United Services, Portsmouth and playing his last match against Swansea on 6th April 1912. At a further meeting held after this one, 13 shillings was paid to T. Allen for the wreath sent by him to the funeral on behalf of the Club. The balance sheet showed a profit on the season 1911/12 of £299 19s 3d as against £423 13s 8d in 1910/11. The difference was due to the increased rent paid to the Rugby Union and to the new policy of paying the "A" teams' expenses incurred in numerous matches against Public Schools. The balance at the start of the 1912/13 season was £1,163 1s 1d. At a meeting on 4th October, a resolution was passed that season tickets admitting to the ground only be issued at four shillings each and that friends of members could be admitted to the ground and members enclosure on presentation of a fixture card for 1s 6d. A further meeting was held one week later at which it was reported that the R.F.U. had given us permission to sublet the Twickenham ground to the London Authorities for the game against the South African tourists on 16th November. The agreement was confirmed as £25 minimum plus 7.5% of the net takings and 2.5% of such monies as the London Authorities should receive on the division of the pooled takings for the South African tour. The total amount not to exceed 10% of the net takings. The Club was doing quite well at this point as at the meeting on 19th June, the treasurer was instructed to purchase £500 each of Argentinian 5% bonds and Brazilian 5% bonds (new issue).

The 1912/13 season had all possibilities of becoming our most successful so far when, by the first week in January, we had a record of won 12 and lost 2. The most notable victories had been against Bedford (31-3), Bristol (14-3) and Northampton (19-5) all away and Oxford University (26-13) at home. The two defeats had been at the hands of Cambridge University (8-21) at Twickenham and London Scottish (3-35) at Richmond. This last score was the first time we had conceded more than thirty points in a game since the London Welsh had thrashed us 3-38 at Queen's Club in December 1904. Unfortunately, the record evaded us because we managed to lose eight, draw one and win just four of our remaining games. We did beat Stade Français on 16th February by seven points to nil in our first meeting, but the most interesting story to come out of this game was the one involving a member of the team. This version comes from Wakelam's original "Harlequin Story" and was as follows: "We were one short two hours before starting off from Victoria, but one of the administration stepped into the gap, producing a man with a very famous South African Rugby name, and informing all and sundry that this was the famous Springbok cap. He was the life and soul of the party - until we got on the field! Then one almost wondered if he had ever played before. Later it turned out that he was completely bogus, but he certainly got away with a grand weekend". The name of the man in question was Steve Joubert and he would have been the first South African international to play for us. He played at centre in the game in Paris and the following week he was on the wing against U.S. Portsmouth. As Wakelam actually played in the first named match, we must accept his story as an accurate account, however disappointing it may be from an historical point of view.

After this we trounced Oxford on their own patch 38-5, although this was not our biggest win of the season. We achieved this against the Old Alleynians at Dulwich on 18th January, defeating them by forty two points to three. The success story effectively ended with these wins and the rest of the season was a disaster with the only other victory being against the Old Merchant Taylors. We lost up at Leicester, went on tour at Easter (losing to both Swansea and Cardiff) and went down to a dropped goal to nil at home to Newport. In these four games we only managed three points for and conceded thirty eight. Gloucester were met for the first time on 29th March and a draw of eight points each was the result. H.B.T. (Henry) Wakelam (referred to earlier) made his debut against Blackheath on 30th November for the first of 119 appearances between now and 1924 and A.F. (Alfred) Maynard, who went on to gain three caps for England, made the first of his nine appearances against Bristol on 5th October. The top appearance makers were Roc Ward, who played in all 27 matches, Adrian Stoop and Holly Ward (21) and Ken Carnduff and Herbert Sibree (20). With Douglas Lambert playing in only twelve games, the way was left open for some different top scorers. Henry Brougham got the most tries with 13, George Roberts and Adrian Stoop each dropped two goals while Roberts made a new mark for penalties in a season with four and kicked eighteen conversions. He was also top points scorer with one try and one goal from a mark (in addition to those already mentioned) for a total of 62. This season was the first since 1905/06 that Lambert had failed to top score in anything. His limited appearances meant that our overall scoring was down on the previous season and the team managed 88 tries (down 30), 6 dropped goals (a new team record), 5 penalties (also a new record), 41 Conversions (down 26) and 388 points (down 117).

1912/13

280912	BEDFORD	BEDFORD	W	5G2T(31)-1PG(3)
051012	BRISTOL	BRISTOL	W	1G1PG2T(14)-1T(3)
121012	RICHMOND	RICHMOND	W	1PG3T(12)-1PG(3)
191012	UNITED SERVICES PORTSMOUTH	TWICKENHAM	W	2G1MG1T(16)-1T(3)
261012	CAMBRIDGE UNIVERSITY	TWICKENHAM	L	1G1T(8)-3G2T(21)
021112	OXFORD UNIVERSITY	TWICKENHAM	W	4G2T(26)-2G1T(13)
091112	NORTHAMPTON	NORTHAMPTON	W	1DG5T(19)-1G(5)
161112	LONDON SCOTTISH	RICHMOND	L	1T(3)-4G5T(35)
231112	GUY'S HOSPITAL	HONOR OAK PARK	W	1G5T(20)-2T(6)
301112	BLACKHEATH	BLACKHEATH	W	2PG(6)-1T(3)
071212	ROSSLYN PARK	OLD DEER PARK	W	2G2T(16)-0
141212	OLD MERCHANT TAYLORS	TWICKENHAM	W	5G2T(31)-1G1T(8)
211212	ST.THOMAS'S HOSPITAL	TWICKENHAM	C	
281212	BLACKHEATH	TWICKENHAM	W	2G2T(16)-1G1T(8)
010113	ROYAL NAVY	QUEEN'S CLUB	W	3G1DG2T(25)-1G2T(11)
040113	OLD LEYSIANS	WANDSWORTH COMMON	C	
110113	LONDON SCOTTISH	TWICKENHAM	L	2G1T(13)-2G1DG(14)
180113	OLD ALLEYNIANS	DULWICH	W	4G1DG6T(42)-1T(3)
010213	RICHMOND	TWICKENHAM	L	2T(6)-1G1T(8)
080213	OLD BLUES	TWICKENHAM	L	1DG1PG1T(10)-1G2T(11)
160213	STADE FRANÇAIS	PARC DES PRINCES	W	1DG1T(7)-0
220213	UNITED SERVICES PORTSMOUTH	PORTSMOUTH	L	1G(5)-1G1DG1T(12)
010313	OXFORD UNIVERSITY	OXFORD	W	5G1DG3T(38)-1G(5)
080313	LEICESTER	LEICESTER	L	1T(3)-1G4T(17)
220313	SWANSEA	SWANSEA	L	0-3T(9)
240313	CARDIFF	CARDIFF	L	0-1G1T(8)
290313	GLOUCESTER	GLOUCESTER	D	1G1T(8)-1G1T(8)
050413	OLD MERCHANT TAYLORS	OLD DEER PARK	W	2G1T(13)-1PG2T(9)
120413	NEWPORT	TWICKENHAM	L	0-1DG(4)

The balance sheet at the A.G.M. on 17th September 1913 showed a profit of £417 11s 0d for season 1912/13. At a Committee meeting on 21st November, the secretary was instructed to write to the R.U. with a view to renewing the lease on the ground for a further five years. This he obviously did as at a further meeting on 13th January 1914 held at Goldsmith Building, Temple, we find that the R.U. had offered to renew the lease of the ground for three years on the same terms as before, but reserving the monies received for the admission of motor cars. The secretary was instructed to accept this offer if the restriction on the number of Saturdays was removed so that the ground was available on all Saturdays excluding those set aside for trials, internationals and those preceding internationals.

He was also asked to stipulate that members' cars be admitted to the ground free of charge. It appears we drove a hard bargain in those days! It was then unanimously resolved that it is advisable to purchase a ground and a sub committee consisting of Adrian Stoop, Holly Ward and Roc Ward was appointed to make enquiries and report to the Committee. They were to hold a further meeting on 6th July but first we must record the last full season of the Club for five years.

We started well enough with a 51-0 thrashing of Bedford at Twickenham before losing to two dropped goals to nil at the hands of Gloucester. Although Oxford (7-9), Blackheath (3-6), Rosslyn Park (8-10), Cardiff (twice) (5-9 and 0-8), Newport (0-6) and Swansea (0-7) all defeated us, we did do the double over Richmond (11-7 and 16-11), U.S. Portsmouth (18-4 and 26-6) and London Scottish (3-0 and 37-0) as well as beating London Hospital (for the only time in four meetings) (19-11), Oxford (in the return) (35-0), Leicester (15-3) and Bristol (38-4). In the return Portsmouth game, played at Twickenham on 18th April, having been postponed from 24th January, it was noticed that the visitors were fielding sixteen men. Lieutenant Turle had to retire after two minutes play to even up the numbers again. The home game against Cardiff at Twickenham on 21st February was our first meeting with them there and we had to wait until 1933 for the next one. The Bristol game on 28th March was scheduled to kick-off at four o'clock owing to the boat race, but did not do so until ten minutes later. We finished with a record of won 19, drawn 1 and lost 8 from 28 games, comparable to that of the previous season.

Two more England internationals made appearances for us this year, Harry Millett (who was to win his only cap in 1920 when he played for Richmond) against the Royal Navy on 31st December and J.G. (James) Milton (who had won his five caps between 1904 and 1907 when he played for Camborne School of Mines) against U.S. Portsmouth on 18th October. These were just two of a total of thirteen internationals appearing during the season, equalling the record set in 1910/11. Roc Ward was ever present for the third season in a row, John Birkett (26), Douglas Lambert (24), Herbert Sibree and Adrian Stoop (23) and R.M. (Ronnie) Gotch (22) led the appearance figures. Of the fifty five players used in this season, only thirteen were to play for the 1st XV again. On the scoring side of things, Lambert was back in full swing with thirty tries and forty four conversions which, added to his two penalty goals gave him 184 points for the season. As a consequence of Lambert's contribution, tries, conversions and points were all up again but no new records were set. Sadly, Douglas Lambert was one of those who had played his last game. His phenomenal scoring saw him set a Club points record that would last for over sixty years and indeed, the number of tries he scored is still a record and will most probably never be beaten. His full total is 1,462 (253 tries, 1 dropped goal, 1 goal from a mark, 6 penalties and 339 conversions) from at least 180 appearances.

On 6th July and further to the last meeting, three grounds had been looked at. The first, at Sunbury, was rejected because it was felt that the train service was not satisfactory. The second, at Broxbourne, was considered too inaccessible from the point of view of attracting spectators in case the ground should ever be used for first team matches. The third choice at Osterley Park was priced at £2,500 and was ready for football but was without dressing accommodation. The price was considered too great in view of the Club's financial position. Further to this, the secretary was instructed to insert advertisements in the Times, Telegraph, Sportsman and Daily Mail for a ground to hire or purchase. At a meeting ten days later it was proposed by George Rope and seconded by Roc Ward that we have the suggested ground at Osterley valued by a responsible firm of surveyors. The secretary also wrote to the London and South Western Railway Company to ask whether they have any suitable ground they would be prepared to let on a long lease. After all this the Committee decided that, after going in to estimated figures of cost of upkeep that the Club would not be justified in taking any ground unless it could be let to some tennis or cricket club for the summer months. This was the last meeting contained in the minute book and was held at Carr's restaurant and those present were: - W.H. Devonshire (in the chair), G.H. Rope, Roc Ward, H.J.H. Sibree, D. Lambert and the Honorary Secretary (A.D. Stoop). Little could they have known that all the planning for the forthcoming seasons would be overtaken by the tragic events which followed and which, ultimately, led to the outbreak of the First World War on 4th August 1914.

The minute book for season 1914/15 is reported to have just one meeting contained in it. This was held (again at Carr's restaurant) on 17th September 1914. It records the reading of a letter from Mrs. W.A. Smith, sending all good wishes from her husband, but fearing that he could not live many weeks longer. He did, in fact, die very shortly after. We therefore said goodbye not only to our President but a man who had been associated with the Club since 1869. The balance sheet showing a profit of £276 was approved and a resolution that all fixtures should immediately be cancelled was carried unanimously. It was also decided that the Club should forthwith present a sum of £500 to the Prince of Wales's National Relief Fund. Part of this fund was used to build the Star and Garter home for badly disabled servicemen, located on the top of Richmond Hill. After this the members of the Club were scattered far and wide and the Club, as a playing entity, ceased to exist.

As a postscript to this period, it must be stated that during the years 1908-14 we were undoubtedly one of the top two teams in the country (the other being Leicester). In head to head competition with ten of them, we came off best against all except Leicester (we both managed to win three games). In our first five seasons at Twickenham, our record there was quite impressive and it read as follows: P59 W46 D1 L12.

1913/14

270913	BEDFORD	TWICKENHAM	W	6G7T(51)-0
041013	GLOUCESTER	TWICKENHAM	L	0-2DG(8)
111013	RICHMOND	TWICKENHAM	W	1G2T(11)-1DG1T(7)
181013	UNITED SERVICES PORTSMOUTH	PORTSMOUTH	W	3G1T(18)-1DG(4)
251013	CAMBRIDGE UNIVERSITY	CAMBRIDGE	W	2G1DG1T(17)-1DG1PG1T(10)
011113	OXFORD UNIVERSITY	OXFORD	L	1DG1T(7)-1G1DG(9)
081113	NORTHAMPTON	TWICKENHAM	W	3G2T(21)-0
151113	LONDON SCOTTISH	TWICKENHAM	W	1T(3)-0
221113	GUY'S HOSPITAL	HONOR OAK PARK	W	3G(15)-1PG1T(6)
291113	BLACKHEATH	TWICKENHAM	L	1T(3)-2T(6)
061213	ROSSLYN PARK	OLD DEER PARK	L	1G1T(8)-1DG1PG1T(10)
131213	OLD MERCHANT TAYLORS	OLD DEER PARK	D	2G1PG1T(16)-2G2T(16)
201213	OLD ALLEYNIANS	TWICKENHAM	W	2G1DG5T(29)-1G1T(8)
271213	BLACKHEATH	BLACKHEATH	W	1PG2T(9)-2T(6)
311213	ROYAL NAVY	QUEEN'S CLUB	W	1G2T(11)-1G(5)
030114	OLD LEYSIANS	WANDSWORTH COMMON	W	2G4T(22)-1MG1T(6)

100114	LONDON SCOTTISH	RICHMOND	W	5G4T(37)-0
240114	UNITED SERVICES PORTSMOUTH	TWICKENHAM	P	
310114	RICHMOND	RICHMOND	W	2G2T(16)-1G2T(11)
070214	LONDON HOSPITAL	HALE END	W	2G3T(19)-1G2T(11)
210214	CARDIFF	TWICKENHAM	L	1G(5)-3T(9)
280214	OXFORD UNIVERSITY	TWICKENHAM	W	4G1MG1PG3T(35)-0
070314	LEICESTER	TWICKENHAM	W	5T(15)-1T(3)
140314	OLD MERCHANT TAYLORS	TWICKENHAM	W	2G1T(13)-1T(3)
210314	OLD BLUES	TWICKENHAM	C	
280314	BRISTOL	TWICKENHAM	W	4G1PG5T(38)-1DG(4)
040414	NEWPORT	NEWPORT	L	0-2T(6)
110414	SWANSEA	SWANSEA	L	0-1DG1T(7)
130414	CARDIFF	CARDIFF	L	0-1G1T(8)
180414	UNITED SERVICES PORTSMOUTH	TWICKENHAM	W	4G2T(26)-2T(6)

1914/15 (All Games Were Cancelled Due to the First World War)

260914	BEDFORD	BEDFORD
031014	GLOUCESTER	GLOUCESTER
101014	RICHMOND	RICHMOND
241014	CAMBRIDGE UNIVERSITY	TWICKENHAM
311014	OXFORD UNIVERSITY	TWICKENHAM
071114	NEWPORT	TWICKENHAM
211114	GUY'S HOSPITAL	TWICKENHAM
051214	ROSSLYN PARK	OLD DEER PARK
121214	OLD MERCHANT TAYLORS	TWICKENHAM
191214	OLD ALLEYNIANS	DULWICH
020115	LONDON HOSPITAL	HALE END
160115	ROYAL NAVY	TWICKENHAM
060215	NORTHAMPTON	NORTHAMPTON
130215	OLD BLUES	TWICKENHAM
270215	OXFORD UNIVERSITY	OXFORD
060315	LEICESTER	LEICESTER
130315	OLD MERCHANT TAYLORS	OLD DEER PARK
270315	BRISTOL	BRISTOL
030415	SWANSEA	SWANSEA
050415	CARDIFF	CARDIFF
170415	RICHMOND	TWICKENHAM

1915/16 (No Games Due to the First World War)

1916/17 (No Games Due to the First World War)

1917/18 (No Games Due to the First World War)

1918/19 (No Games Due to the First World War)

8

Roll of Honour

In Memory of All Those Who Failed to Return 1914-1919

This is a list of all those who made at least one appearance for the 1st XV and shows the date and place of death or burial/commemoration:

Harry Alexander	17.10.1915	Hulluch
Thomas Allen	26.02.1915	Flanders
George G. Barnes	16.07.1916	Thiepval memorial
George N. Berney	06.11.1917	Beersheba war cemetery
George H. Bickley	04.10.1917	Tyne Cot memorial
Richard C. Blagrove	12.08.1915	Ypres Reservoir cemetery
Edward F. Boyd	20.09.1914	Vailly British cemetery
Frank A. Brock	23.04.1918	Zeebrugge Raid
Henry Brougham	27.09.1918	Vis-en-Artois memorial
John G. Bussell	28.06.1915	Tancrez Farm cemetery
Ken M. Carnduff	12.01.1916	Vermelles British cemetery
George M. Chapman	13.05.1915	Zonnebeke Road, Ypres
Walter M. Dodds	14.10.1918	Poznan Old Garrison cemetery
Errol R. Garnett	18.10.1916	Warlencourt British cemetery
George M.G. Gillett	26.09.1916	Thiepval memorial
Roby M. Gotch	01.07.1916	The Somme
William B. Grandage	14.05.1917	Swan Chateau, Ypres
Arthur C. Hammond	12.01.1916	Guards cemetery, Windy Corner, Cuinchy
Ralph E. Hancock	28.10.1914	Festubert
Norman W.A. Henderson	10.11.1914	Ypres (Menin Gate) Memorial
Arthur H. Hudson	31.07.1917	Hooge Chateau, Ypres
Thomas H. Hudson	13.10.1915	Hulluck
Douglas Lambert	13.10.1915	Loos
Gwion L.B. Lloyd	07.08.1915	Beach A, Sulva Bay, Gallipoli
Alfred F. Maynard	13.11.1916	Beaumont Hamel, The Somme

Ronald W. Poulton	05.05.1915	Ploegsteert
Kenneth Powell	18.02.1915	Ypres
Alan P. Rosling	04.03.1917	Thiepval memorial
Gerald C. Southern	21.07.1915	Maala cemetery
Francis Nathaniel Tarr	18.07.1915	Railway Dugouts Burial Ground (Transport Farm)
Cornelius Thorne	30.09.1916	The Somme
Donald O.H. Tripp	18.08.1916	Thiepval memorial
Robert O.C. Ward	20.11.1917	Flesquiers Ridge

9

We Begin Again
1919-1925

Sadly, as has been shown, our Club, like so many others, had lost so many old and current players in the preceding five years. The war years also meant that any celebration of our fiftieth season was impossible. On the positive side, we still had our Twickenham agreement and a balance of £1,250 in the bank. W.P. Ward, taking on the job of Acting Secretary (as Adrian Stoop was still away on active service), after consultation, called a meeting at London Bridge of those members he had managed to make contact with. The first meeting was duly held in December 1918 and was attended by W.P. Ward (in the chair), John Birkett, Holly Ward (back from four years as a prisoner of war in Germany), E.M.C. Clarke, H. Hughes-Onslow and Henry Wakelam. It was decided at this meeting that an effort must be made to get some kind of a programme going for the 1919/20 season, and the first and most important business was to find players. Further to this, notices were inserted in the Press asking old Harlequins to rally round and it was decided to recruit young hopefuls rather than attempt to recruit known names. The greatest triumph from this policy was Ward's enlisting of a young Royal Air Force officer; his name was William Wavell Wakefield (later to serve as Member of Parliament for Marylebone and later still to sit in the House of Lords as Lord Wakefield of Kendal). It seems that our invitation was just in front of a similar approach from Blackheath. In the autumn of 1919 he was posted to the R.A.F. Depot at Uxbridge. He was trying to build up a team for his service (as well as playing for them), so was unable to play for us all the time.

So, the first season after the war (for us at any rate) was the 1919/20 season and we had a new captain in the shape of N.B. (Noel) Hudson (he later became the Bishop of Newcastle). Our first game was supposed to have been against Gloucester but this was cancelled and so we took the field at Richmond to play the Richmond Club on 11th October. Our team was, R.H. King (full back), W.R. Shirley, J.G.G. Birkett, N.B. Hudson and A.H.F. Luckyn (three quarters), H.A.V. Maynard and R. Berry (half backs) and W.G. Tatham (who was an Olympic hurdler), H.B.T. Wakelam, W.R.F. Collis, J. Hughes, P.W. Adams, W.R. Bion, C.W. Williams and W.W. Wakefield (forwards). All were playing their first games except for Birkett, Hudson, Maynard and Wakelam. We trailed to a try by R. Jones at half time but in the second half, Birkett dropped a goal and we led by a point, only for J.M.S. Gardner to go over for Richmond's second try (converted by C.G. Ainsworth) to leave them winners by eight points to four. We went on from there to lose our next four games to U.S. Portsmouth (0-12), Cambridge (3-43) (our heaviest defeat of the season), Oxford (0-33) and Newport (0-13) before recording our first win. This came against London Scottish at Richmond on 15th November when one of our forwards (J.A.B. Davies) scored a hat-trick of tries in a 20-9 victory.

This was closely followed the next week by our first home victory of the new season against Guy's Hospital. At this time, the Guy's team was full of mature South African players and it was their habit to give their forwards their scrum and line out instructions in Afrikaans, so as to keep their opponents guessing. We managed to get over that difficulty by playing a young South African Gunner subaltern from the Royal Artillery Mess at Woolwich (believed to be D.A. Wolfe) for just this game. It seemed to work and our two tries to their goal gave us a 6-5 win after a scoreless first period. On 24th January, we renewed our acquaintance with St. Bartholomew's Hospital, when we met them for the first time since 1902. The result then had been a win for us by thirty points to nil, this time we were the losing side by eleven points to three. Our first match was played against the Army on 14th February at Twickenham, in which we trailed by eleven points at half time. We did manage a try from G.R. Rougier (converted by Wakelam) but a penalty goal gave the Army a nine point win (5-14). Our biggest win of the season was against Richmond on 10th April by thirty points to three, although it was surrounded by three defeats. Two of those came on the Easter tour to Wales (which had been revived), when both games (against Swansea and Cardiff) were lost by four points. The other was the last match of the season on 24th April (away at Bristol) when we went down 0-8. This was our first defeat by the West Country team in seven attempts dating back to 1909. We finished with a record of P26 W10 L16 and, although not a brilliant season it was a reasonably solid one to get us back on the road to recovery after the five year break.

The leading appearance makers were R.H. (Rex) King and Henry Wakelam (25), Noel Hudson (23) and J. Hughes (22). Out of a total of seventy nine players, 26 made just one appearance (including one by R. le Quinn against Oxford on 28th February and one by R. le Quin against Cardiff on 5th April) and a further 38 made less than ten. This shows how well the team did to win the number of games it did with such an unsettled line up. Not surprisingly, the scoring was well down on the 1913/14 season and the most our top try scorer (John Birkett) could manage was eight while Wakelam managed just twenty conversions and, added to his three tries and single penalty goal, fifty two points. The team managed only forty nine tries, two dropped goals, one penalty goal and twenty one conversions for a total of 200 points. This was our lowest total since 1904/05 when we had scored just 154. We had some ten internationals from three countries in our first team at various stages of the season. From England, John Birkett and Adrian Stoop won their caps before the war, John Greenwood won his last caps during this season, H.L.V. (Harold) Day and Wavell Wakefield won their first caps in this season, whilst V.G. (Vivian) Davies, R.H. (Richard) Hamilton-Wickes and J.R.B. (James) Worton were future cap winners. The remaining two were both future internationals, W.R.F. (William) Collis from Ireland and A.L. (Archibald) Gracie from Scotland. The last mention in this season must be of the number of debutants who went on to make numerous appearances for the Club. They were P.W. (Peter) Adams (200), Rex King (104) and Wavell Wakefield (136) who first played against Richmond on 11th October, A.A. (Arthur) Moller (70), Cambridge University on 25th October, B.L. Jacot (67), Oxford University on 1st November, Vivian Davies (224), London Scottish on 15th November, S.P. Simpson (66), Rosslyn Park on 6th December, James Worton (100), Old Leysians on 20th December, Richard Hamilton-Wickes (126), Royal Navy on 31st December and Archibald Gracie (93), Old Merchant Taylors on 13th March.

1919/20

041019	GLOUCESTER	GLOUCESTER	C	
111019	RICHMOND	RICHMOND	L	1DG(4)-1G1T(8)
181019	UNITED SERVICES PORTSMOUTH	PORTSMOUTH	L	0-4T(12)
251019	CAMBRIDGE UNIVERSITY	TWICKENHAM	L	1T(3)-6G1DG3T(43)

011119	OXFORD UNIVERSITY	TWICKENHAM	L	0-4G1DG1PG2T(33)
081119	NEWPORT	TWICKENHAM	L	0-2G1T(13)
151119	LONDON SCOTTISH	RICHMOND	W	1G5T(20)-3T(9)
221119	GUY'S HOSPITAL	TWICKENHAM	W	2T(6)-1G(5)
291119	BLACKHEATH	BLACKHEATH	L	0-1G1DG2T(15)
061219	ROSSLYN PARK	OLD DEER PARK	W	1G4T(17)-0
131219	OLD MERCHANT TAYLORS	TWICKENHAM	W	1G1PG(8)-1G(5)
201219	OLD LEYSIANS	WANDSWORTH COMMON	W	4G1T(23)-1DG4T(16)
271219	BLACKHEATH	TWICKENHAM	L	0-1G6T(23)
311219	ROYAL NAVY	QUEEN'S CLUB	W	1G2T(11)-1T(3)
030120	LONDON HOSPITAL	HALE END	C	
100120	LONDON SCOTTISH	TWICKENHAM	W	1G(5)-1T(3)
170120	ROYAL NAVY	TWICKENHAM	L	1G(5)-2T(6)
240120	ST.BARTHOLOMEW'S HOSPITAL	WINCHMORE HILL	L	1T(3)-1G2T(11)
310120	OLD ALLEYNIANS	DULWICH	C	
070220	NORTHAMPTON	NORTHAMPTON	L	2G1T(13)-2G4T(22)
140220	ARMY	TWICKENHAM	L	1G(5)-1G1PG2T(14)
210220	UNITED SERVICES PORTSMOUTH	TWICKENHAM	W	1G2T(11)-1G1T(8)
280220	OXFORD UNIVERSITY	OXFORD	L	1G2T(11)-4G3T(29)
060320	LEICESTER	LEICESTER	L	0-1G5T(20)
130320	OLD MERCHANT TAYLORS	OLD DEER PARK	W	2G1T(13)-1G(5)
270320	BRISTOL	BRISTOL	C	
030420	SWANSEA	SWANSEA	L	1DG1T(7)-1G2T(11)
050420	CARDIFF	CARDIFF	L	1G(5)-3T(9)
100420	RICHMOND	TWICKENHAM	W	3G5T(30)-1T(3)
240420	BRISTOL	BRISTOL	L	0-1G1PG(8)

At the A.G.M. on 18th September, a hearty vote of thanks was accorded to the Officers of the Club for the season 1919/20. In particular to Mr. W.P. Ward, Major E.M.C. Clarke and Mr. H. Hughes-Onslow for their invaluable work in restarting the Club at the conclusion of the war. The Chairman announced that there were 140 ordinary playing members, 81 under rule 20 (University, Public School, Hospital and Cadets) and 83 non-playing. The Vice Presidents (as listed in the fixture card) were J.G.G. Birkett, E.M.C. Clarke, C.E.L. Hammond, H. Hughes-Onslow, C.M. Wells, F.C. Stoop and W.P. Ward. What happened to the pre-war ones is not clear, the only survivors on the new list being Birkett and Wells. S.B. Peech, W.H. Devonshire, R.W. Hunt, J.N. Hill, F.W. Burnand, G.H. Rope and the Surtees brothers (A.A. and H.P.) were the names that disappeared. At a Committee meeting on 25th September, it was decided not to issue season tickets for the coming season as it had been found in the past that the demand for them was very small and did not justify the extra trouble involved. On the subject of honorary members, it was decided to restrict the election of these as much as possible and it was defined that such elections should be confined to persons of distinction who would be useful to the Club or to friends of members who have deserved well of the Club and as a special favour to such members. It was also considered that the Club had sufficient numbers of playing members and that the election of these in future should be confined to players of considerable skill. The Committee meeting on 22nd November was held at Mr. W.P. Ward's office, London Bridge, at which it was decided to engage the Riding School at 13, Kenway Road, Earl's Court for the use of members on Tuesday evenings (although this was dropped the following season), the fee was £27 6s 6d. The 2nd XV is replaced by the Extra "A" XV but this wouldn't last long.

For the next season (1920/21), we showed a new captain again, this time it was Wavell Wakefield. This was to be the first of his three stints as captain, a total of five seasons in all spread over the next ten years. Following the death back in 1914 of our President (William Smith), a new one was elected in 1920, he was Adrian Stoop (who was also the secretary). This was a fine accolade to a marvellous player coming to the end of his career who had held nearly every position at the Club at one time or another. We started off on the playing side with a huge win over a very weak Bedford side at Twickenham by seventy six points to nil. In this game, a new record for tries was set when Gracie went over for our seventeenth, beating the old record (set against Surbiton in 1908) by one. For the record, our other try scorers that day were J.C. Connell, Vivian Davies (4), Hamilton-Wickes (3), E.E. Hill (2), Jacot (4), Wakelam and Worton. A new points score was also set, again beating the Surbiton record (74-3). Not surprisingly, this also turned out to be our biggest win of the season. Our heaviest defeat came at the hands of Guy's Hospital at Honor Oak Park on 23rd October. We fielded only six of the side which had beaten Bedford and paid the price with the Hospital scoring eight tries in a thirty six points to nil drubbing. Worse was to come for the Quins players in this game as, during it, a thief had broken into their dressing room and although his financial haul was not thought to have been considerable, he went off with our President's socks, leaving his own in exchange!

We played the Royal Air Force for the first time on 27th December at Queen's Club, a certain Flying Officer Wakefield being among our opponents that day as well as fellow Quins J.E.L. Drabble, S.P. Simpson, E.F. Turner and R.H.C. Usher. We did manage to defeat them reasonably easily by twenty four points to six, after leading 16-0 at the break. We now had regular fixtures with all three services and victories over the Royal Navy on 5th January (15-10) and the Army on 22nd January (21-6) were to follow. On 6th November, we travelled down to Newport a man short and had to borrow Archie Bell (a forward) from the home side, who promptly went on to defeat us 34-6. Following on the Welsh theme, the Easter tour was again undertaken and again we came away with nothing to show for our efforts. Swansea winning on the Saturday (6-17) and Cardiff winning on the Monday (5-8). Our best result after ten tour games was a draw in the first one against Swansea in April 1911, the rest having been lost. In the first half of the season we had won six and lost eight but then the team seemed to gel together and the art of winning was discovered, with eleven games being won to three lost. Among others we lost to Gloucester (8-10) and Blackheath twice (0-22) and (10-12), while victories were achieved over Rosslyn Park (37-4) and Leicester (11-3). H.B. "Pup" Style made his debut against U.S. Portsmouth on 16th October (and went on to make 83 appearances) to become the first of three brothers to appear over the next eight seasons. In this game, the United Services were, it was noted in the press at the time, wearing numbers. This, it would seem, was not a regular occurrence in the twenties. One current and two future internationals appeared for us during this season, A.H. (Alfred) MacIlwaine (who had won five England caps between 1912 and 1920) made his only appearance for us against London Scottish on 2nd April, John Clifford Gibbs (who was to go on and gain seven caps for England) made the first of 169 appearances on 18th December against Richmond and H.L. (Leo) Price (England, four caps) played first against Blackheath on 8th January (this was the first of his 77 appearances for the 1st XV and later he was to become Headmaster of Bishop's Stortford College).

Among other players making their debuts for us were Viscount Encombe (his real name was J. Scott), in the match against Leicester on 5th March (he only made one further appearance), E.H. Fouraker (who made 96 appearances) against Richmond on 9th October and S.H. Townell (58) against Cambridge University on 30th October. In the twenty eight games played, only four out of the eighty players utilised played over twenty times. Vivian Davies and Rex King led the way with twenty four, while Gracie and Wakelam were just one behind on twenty three. Gracie did top the try scorers with twenty and Wakelam got most points, his final total being 111 (9 tries, 2 penalty goals and 39 conversions). The team set a new record for most penalties in a season with seven. Apart from Wakelam's contribution, King got three and V.U. Oldland and H.B. Style one each. No other records were set although the amounts were up on the previous season. The number of tries was 110, conversions came in at 66 and points were up nearly 300 on 483.

1920/21

250920	BEDFORD	TWICKENHAM	W	11G1PG6T(76)-0
021020	GLOUCESTER	TWICKENHAM	L	1G1PG(8)-2G(10)
091020	RICHMOND	TWICKENHAM	W	2G1PG3T(22)-1DG1T(7)
161020	UNITED SERVICES PORTSMOUTH	TWICKENHAM	L	2T(6)-1G4T(17)
231020	GUY'S HOSPITAL	HONOR OAK PARK	L	0-4G1DG4T(36)
301020	CAMBRIDGE UNIVERSITY	TWICKENHAM	W	3G1T(18)-1G1PG2T(14)
061120	NEWPORT	NEWPORT	L	1PG1T(6)-5G3T(34)
131120	LONDON SCOTTISH	RICHMOND	L	1PG1T(6)-2G3T(19)
201120	OXFORD UNIVERSITY	OXFORD	L	2T(6)-1G1PG(8)
271120	BLACKHEATH	TWICKENHAM	L	0-2G1PG3T(22)
041220	ROSSLYN PARK	TWICKENHAM	W	5G4T(37)-1DG(4)
111220	OLD MERCHANT TAYLORS	OLD DEER PARK	W	4G2T(26)-1T(3)
181220	RICHMOND	RICHMOND	L	2G1PG(13)-1G3T(14)
271220	ROYAL AIR FORCE	QUEEN'S CLUB	W	3G3T(24)-2T(6)
010121	LONDON HOSPITAL	HALE END	C	
050121	ROYAL NAVY	TWICKENHAM	W	3G(15)-2G(10)
080121	BLACKHEATH	BLACKHEATH	L	2G(10)-4T(12)
220121	ARMY	TWICKENHAM	W	3G2T(21)-1PG1T(6)
290121	ST.BARTHOLOMEW'S HOSPITAL	TWICKENHAM	W	2G3T(19)-1T(3)
050221	NORTHAMPTON	NORTHAMPTON	W	2G3T(19)-1G(1PT)2T(11)
190221	UNITED SERVICES PORTSMOUTH	PORTSMOUTH	W	2G(10)-1T(3)
260221	OXFORD UNIVERSITY	OXFORD	W	4G1PG1T(26)-0
050321	LEICESTER	TWICKENHAM	W	1G2T(11)-1T(3)
120321	OLD MERCHANT TAYLORS	TWICKENHAM	W	4G2T(26)-1G1T(8)
190321	OLD LEYSIANS	TWICKENHAM	W	5G1T(28)-1G(5)
260321	SWANSEA	SWANSEA	L	2T(6)-2DG3T(17)
280321	CARDIFF	CARDIFF	L	1G(5)-1G1T(8)
020421	LONDON SCOTTISH	TWICKENHAM	W	3G5T(30)-3T(9)
090421	BRISTOL	TWICKENHAM	W	3G(15)-1T(3)

At a Committee meeting on 8th September (the day before the A.G.M.), those present voted 12-2 in favour of issuing season tickets for the coming season. At the same meeting it was proposed by H.E. Hill and seconded by H. Hughes-Onslow that five hundred War Savings Certificates be purchased at a cost of £387 10s 0d and deposited at the bank in the names of H.E. Ward and A.D. Stoop. On the following day, at Carr's restaurant, three out of the four new Vice Presidents added were from the pre-war list mentioned earlier (Devonshire, Hill and H.P. Surtees), the fourth being N.B. Hudson. At a further meeting on 23rd December, the honorary secretary was authorised to search for a site for a new ground with a view to providing playing accommodation for "A" teams and an Old Boys Club to be formed as a subsidiary to the Harlequin Football Club. The Club must now have been on a reasonably sound financial footing as on 22nd February, a further £650 was invested in 7% preference shares of the Shell Trading and Transport Company. At the same meeting, the secretary reported that the silver bowl presented by members of the Harlequin Football Club to the late President, W.A. Smith, on the occasion of his silver wedding, was at present pawned with no hope of redemption by members of his family. The secretary proposed, C.A. Lyon seconded and it was carried unanimously that the bowl be redeemed by the Club and held in trust for Ernest Smith, son of the late President. This gesture was nothing more than the memory of the man known as the "Father of the Club" deserved. At a further meeting on 30th March, the earlier mentioned formation of the Old Boys Club was opposed by E.M.C. Clarke on the ground that it would arouse a storm of adverse criticism in the press and that members of schools other than those from which the suggested Old Boys teams were drawn, would be discouraged from joining the Club by the idea that they would not receive fair treatment. The minute book states further that while the discussion was in progress the number present dwindled to a bare quorum and it was felt that the matter was too important to be dealt with in such a manner. Consequently, it was decided to summon a general meeting of the Club to deal with the question. Further to this at the A.G.M. on 1st August 1922, no seconder was found to the President's motion on the formation of one or more Old Boys Clubs to be formed as subsidiaries to the H.F.C. The matter, therefore, was finished.

As with the last two seasons, we started with a new captain, Henry Wakelam taking over from Wavell Wakefield (who was on a two year R.A.F. course at Cambridge). We started off with a trouncing of London Scottish at Twickenham on 24th September by forty four points to nil. This was our biggest win in a fixture dating back to 1878. Against Newport on 5th November, we managed our first win over our illustrious opponents, but, little did we know that our second victory was another thirty years away! Newport had taken the lead with a penalty by F. Baker, we came back and led 5-3 at half time when I.J. (Jim) Pitman (who became an international when capped later in this season for England against Scotland and was to serve as M.P. for Bath in later years) went over for a try which King converted. Gracie and S.J. Rossdale added further tries in the second half to give us an 11-3 victory. Our biggest win of the season came against the Old Leysians at Wandsworth Common on 21st January. We scored twenty six points in the first half and twenty five in the second, getting thirteen tries in the process. Clifford Gibbs scored five of them and became the first player since Douglas Lambert in 1910 to perform that feat. As the Old Boys failed to score the result was 51-0. The only other Old Boys teams we were due to play this season were the Old Blues and the Old Merchant Taylors (twice). The first was cancelled, while the games against the O.M.T.'s were shared. We won the game at Twickenham 34-0, but lost at the Old Deer Park 0-12. Our heaviest defeat of the season came against Cambridge University at Cambridge on 22nd October. The final score was 39-14 to the students, who won with a little help from some of our own players. Appearing in their line up were A. Carnegie-Brown, A.P.F. Chapman (Cricket captain of Kent and England), Hamilton-Wickes and Wakefield.

On 29th October, Guy's Hospital again beat us scoreless (this time by the reduced margin of fourteen points), two weeks later Adrian Stoop appeared again when he refereed the game against St. Bartholomew's Hospital and two weeks after this, the game at Blackheath was reduced to twenty minutes each way because of fog (each side managing to score a goal and a try in a drawn game of eight points each). In the last week in December we met the three services and lost to them all. On Christmas Eve we met the Royal Navy at Twickenham (15-17), on Boxing Day we met the Royal Air Force at Queen's Club in the last game of rugby to be played there (0-15) and on New Year's Eve we played the Army at Twickenham (8-11). In these three games, no fewer than twelve players opposed us who played for us at some stage in their careers. On 8th January, we were due to meet Olympique in Paris but this game was cancelled. On 25th March, we met the London Welsh for the first time since 1905. One of our half backs was the same in both games. Adrian Stoop made his last but one appearance for the first team in this match, he failed to score and we lost 10-12. Once again we had to borrow a player to make up our numbers when Wakefield missed his train to Bristol on 8th April. J. Hunt from Clifton deputised for him until he arrived at half time. Although both matches on the Easter tour to Wales were again lost, we registered our highest score so far against Cardiff in the 16-20 defeat.

On 22nd April, an interesting event took place when a team from before the war took on the present team in a charity match played at Twickenham. Unfortunately, the afternoon was a wet one and the attendance was quite poor so the purpose of helping King Edwards' Hospital Fund was only partially successful. However, there were several internationals on display and a good game ensued, the present team running out victors by twenty six points to eleven. The past players started well and took the lead when F.M. Stoop went over for an unconverted try before Gracie, Gibbs and Hamilton-Wickes scored tries for the present (the second and third being converted by King and Wakelam respectively) and so they led 13-3 at the break. The present went further ahead in the second half when their stamina and fitness began to tell and Wakelam, S.H. Townell and G.D. Hale got further tries (two of which were converted by Davies and Gracie), this ended their scoring and the last words went, quite fittingly to the past with tries from W.V. Heale (converted by H.G. Howitt) and G.F. Elmslie to give us that final score. The teams were:- Present: R.H. King (full back), J.C. Gibbs, A.L. Gracie, G.D. Hale and R.H. Hamilton-Wickes (three quarters), V.G. Davies and S.H. Townell (half backs) and W.W. Wakefield, J.M. Currie, S.J. Rossdale, R.R. Stokes (later to become M.P. for Ipswich), S.P. Simpson, H.P. Marshall, R.F.G. Adams and H.B.T. Wakelam (forwards) and the Past: G.D. Roberts (who became the Recorder of Bristol) (full back), F.M. Stoop, N.B. Hudson, J.G.G. Birkett and G.F. Elmslie (three quarters), A.D. Stoop and H.J.H. Sibree (half backs) and G.V. Carey, R.W. Ling, H.G. Howitt, G.R. Vick (who became the Recorder of Newcastle), N.M. Benton, W.V. Heale, H.E. Ward and W.G. Hewitt (forwards). Apart from Pitman, the only other "new" international was C.K.T. Faithfull, who was to be first capped by England in 1924. Among players debuting who went on to make a number of first team appearances were H.V. Brodie (98) against Guy's Hospital on 29th October and W.H. Wainwright (72) against the Royal Air Force on 26th December. We played twenty eight games (including the charity match) and the leading appearance makers were King (24), J.M. Currie and Gracie (22) and Rossdale (21). Gracie and Wakelam topped the same scoring tables they had the previous season and the team just managed one hundred tries (just over half being converted) and as everything else also went down, no new records were set.

1921/22

240921	LONDON SCOTTISH	TWICKENHAM	W	7G1PG2T(44)-0
011021	GLOUCESTER	GLOUCESTER	L	0-2T(6)

081021	RICHMOND	RICHMOND	C	
151021	UNITED SERVICES PORTSMOUTH	TWICKENHAM	W	1G2T(11)-1G1T(8)
221021	CAMBRIDGE UNIVERSITY	CAMBRIDGE	L	1G3T(14)-6G3T(39)
291021	GUY'S HOSPITAL	TWICKENHAM	L	0-1G1PG2T(14)
051121	NEWPORT	TWICKENHAM	W	1G2T(11)-1PG(3)
121121	ST.BARTHOLOMEW'S HOSPITAL	WINCHMORE HILL	W	4G1PG2T(29)-2G2T(16)
191121	OXFORD UNIVERSITY	TWICKENHAM	L	1T(3)-1G(5)
261121	BLACKHEATH	BLACKHEATH	D	1G1T(8)-1G1T(8)
031221	ROSSLYN PARK	OLD DEER PARK	W	4G2T(26)-1G2T(11)
101221	OLD MERCHANT TAYLORS	TWICKENHAM	W	5G3T(34)-0
171221	RICHMOND	TWICKENHAM	W	2G2T(16)-2PG2T(12)
241221	ROYAL NAVY	TWICKENHAM	L	3G(15)-1G4T(17)
261221	ROYAL AIR FORCE	QUEEN'S CLUB	L	0-3G(15)
311221	ARMY	TWICKENHAM	L	1G1T(8)-1G2T(11)
080122	OLYMPIQUE	PARIS	C	
140122	BLACKHEATH	TWICKENHAM	W	1G2T(11)-2T(6)
210122	OLD LEYSIANS	WANDSWORTH COMMON	W	6G7T(51)-0
280122	CAMBRIDGE UNIVERSITY	TWICKENHAM	W	2G4T(22)-2T(6)
040222	NORTHAMPTON	TWICKENHAM	W	1T(3)-0
110222	OLD BLUES	TWICKENHAM	C	
180222	UNITED SERVICES PORTSMOUTH	PORTSMOUTH	W	2G2T(16)-1DG(4)
250222	OXFORD UNIVERSITY	OXFORD	C	
040322	LEICESTER	LEICESTER	L	0-1G1T(8)
110322	OLD MERCHANT TAYLORS	OLD DEER PARK	L	0-1G1DG1T(12)
250322	LONDON WELSH	TWICKENHAM	L	2G(10)-1G1DG1T(12)
010422	LONDON SCOTTISH	RICHMOND	W	3T(9)-1T(3)
080422	BRISTOL	BRISTOL	L	2G1T(13)-1G1DG6T(27)
150422	SWANSEA	SWANSEA	L	1T(3)-1G4T(17)
170422	CARDIFF	CARDIFF	L	2G2T(16)-2G1DG2T(20)
220422	PRESENT v PAST	TWICKENHAM	W	4G2T(26)-1G2T(11)

At a Committee meeting on 28th December, it was decided to send a team to play the Rhine Army at Cologne if it proved feasible to do so. Further to this (at a meeting held at the Red House, Bishopsgate, EC3), Mr. Wakelam reported that a match had been provisionally arranged for Saturday 10th February 1923 but that the sanction of the Rugby Football Union had not been obtained (the chairman undertook to apply immediately for the necessary sanction). The expenses of the journey would have to be borne by the Club as the Army could not offer to do more than entertain the team when in Cologne. Mr. Wakelam was authorised, subject to the aforementioned sanction being obtained from the R.F.U., to decide whether the team should travel by air or otherwise and to make all the necessary arrangements for the return journey at a total expense not exceeding £120. To this statement a further note was added saying that from the information by Wakelam it appeared that the cost of sending the team by air might be about £20 more than that of the journey by boat and rail; but in the present condition of affairs in Germany (after the war), it seemed uncertain whether it would be possible to travel by rail from the Dutch frontier to Cologne and back. As will be seen later the trip by air and the game were both successfully undertaken. At a Committee meeting on 17th February, the chairman was requested to convey to Flying Officer J.E.L. Drabble the profound sympathy of the Club in the accident which recently rendered it necessary for him to undergo a serious operation. It does not state exactly what the accident was but it was almost certainly responsible for ending his career (he made the last of his eleven appearances against Oxford University on 18th November). On 27th March, a long discussion took place on the subject of the proposed new ground and it was decided that the possibility of the Club losing its tenancy of Twickenham should not influence the decision as to the proposed new site. It was thought better to purchase rather than rent a ground and so the secretary was instructed to insert adverts in "The Times" setting out the requirements of the Club. At this same meeting the secretary was instructed (by a large majority) that when making the fixtures for the 1924/25 season, he should try and omit the London Welsh, Old Blues and one of the Old Merchant Taylors matches. He managed the first two but we did play the last named on two occasions. It was obviously felt that these teams were no longer up to our standard. The teams are now listed in the fixture card simply as 1st and "A" XV with all games except the firsts in one list.

For the following season (1922/23), we showed yet another new captain, Vivian Davies. He was our fourth captain since the war and was to lead the side for three out of the next four seasons. On the playing side this was to be a season where we never really got going, our longest run of successes being just three games. We started with another victory to nil, our opponents as in the previous season's opener were London Scottish, the score being slightly reduced at 27-0. After this we were quickly brought down to earth by Gloucester at Twickenham by eleven points to nil and any thoughts of an unbeaten season had vanished. In this game, it was mentioned in the press that the Harlequins were numbered, but Gloucester were not, an omission which should be remedied. The roller coaster ride continued into the third week of the season and beyond with a 46-0 win over Rosslyn Park. We had led by nineteen points at half time before seven tries (including four from Gibbs) in the second half blew our visitors away. After this we lost to U.S. Portsmouth (14-16), defeated Cambridge (19-11), but lost to Guy's (5-10) and Newport (3-9). We did not play the Air Force, lost to the Navy (7-12) and beat the Army on our first ever visit to Aldershot (14-8).

As mentioned earlier, we travelled by air to Cologne to play the British Army of the Rhine on 10th February. H. Hughes-Onslow and Wakelam between them had managed to arrange the transportation of fifteen players for £8 a head and so the party left Croydon Airport in two aircraft belonging to Instone Airlines at a quarter to twelve and arrived at Cologne at twenty past three on the Friday afternoon. They had become the first complete Rugby side ever to fly. Only a few of them had ever flown before and one or two of those first chosen had, apparently, been denied parental permission. On the return trip, according to Wakelam, the pilots of the two planes amused themselves by flying side by side and alternately see-sawing up and down. This was not so amusing to the fifteen somewhat jaded occupants, several of whom showed visible signs of distress! The game itself was played in Riehl (a suburb of Cologne) and ended in a handsome win for us by fifty two points to three. We managed thirteen tries, including three a piece for Davies and Gracie (five converted by H.B. Style) and a penalty by Wakelam to a solitary try for the Rhine Army by Lieutenant Maxwell (when we had amassed forty six points). At a Committee meeting on 17th February at Twickenham, the chairman was requested to convey to the committee of the Army of the Rhine the gratitude of the Club for the generous hospitality offered to the team which played at Cologne the week before. This proved to be our biggest win of the season while our heaviest defeat was only 5-18 at the hands of Richmond at Twickenham back on 16th December.

We played Leicester home and away for the first time in a season although, unfortunately, both games were lost. The London Welsh were met at Herne Hill and defeated 20-4 (this was our first win over them since 1899). After the Easter tour (on which we drew with Swansea (3-3) and just lost to Cardiff (6-9)), we finished strongly with victories over Bristol and London Scottish at Twickenham to finish with fifteen wins, two draws and twelve losses from twenty nine games played. Two more future internationals made their debuts for us during this season, they were G.V. (Godfrey) Palmer (who went on to win his three England caps when he played for Richmond in 1928) against, funnily enough, Richmond on 11th November and W.F. (William) "Horsey" Browne (who made twelve appearances for Ireland between 1925 and 1928) against the Old Blues on 17th March. Among the new boys was J.S. Chick, who made the first of his 108 appearances against Guy's Hospital on 28th October. No fewer than ten of the fifty players used managed to play in twenty or more games, the top of which was Wakelam (who appeared in 27) followed by Jacot (26), King (25), J.M. Currie (24), Peter Adams, Davies and S.H. Townell (23), H.P. (Howard) Marshall (21) and Gibbs and Gracie (20). On the scoring side, Gibbs top scored in tries with twenty and points overall with a dropped goal to add to his tries for a total of sixty four, Townell set a new record for dropped goals in a season with three and King kicked seventeen conversions. The team managed 95 tries, 41 conversions, 4 dropped goals, 1 goal from a mark and 6 penalty goals for a total of 404 points in all, whilst conceding 216.

1922/23

230922	LONDON SCOTTISH	RICHMOND	W	4G1DG1T(27)-0
300922	GLOUCESTER	TWICKENHAM	L	0-1G2T(11)
071022	ROSSLYN PARK	TWICKENHAM	W	5G7T(46)-0
141022	UNITED SERVICES PORTSMOUTH	PORTSMOUTH	L	1G3T(14)-2G2T(16)
211022	CAMBRIDGE UNIVERSITY	TWICKENHAM	W	2G3T(19)-1G2T(11)
281022	GUY'S HOSPITAL	HONOR OAK PARK	L	1G(5)-2G(10)
041122	NEWPORT	NEWPORT	L	1T(3)-3T(9)
111122	RICHMOND	RICHMOND	W	4G1T(23)-2T(6)
181122	OXFORD UNIVERSITY	OXFORD	L	1G(5)-1G1T(8)
251122	BLACKHEATH	TWICKENHAM	W	2G3T(19)-1PG(3)
021222	LEICESTER	TWICKENHAM	L	1PG1T(6)-2G(10)
091222	OLD MERCHANT TAYLORS	TEDDINGTON	W	1G2T(11)-1PG(3)
161222	RICHMOND	TWICKENHAM	L	1G(5)-1G1DG3T(18)
231222	ROYAL NAVY	TWICKENHAM	L	1DG1T(7)-1G1DG1T(12)
301222	ARMY	ALDERSHOT	W	1G1PG2T(14)-1G1T(8)
060123	ST.BARTHOLOMEW'S HOSPITAL	WINCHMORE HILL	L	1G4T(17)-1G1DG3T(18)
130123	BLACKHEATH	BLACKHEATH	W	1T(3)-0
200123	OLD LEYSIANS	WANDSWORTH COMMON	C	
270123	CAMBRIDGE UNIVERSITY	CAMBRIDGE	L	1G2T(11)-2DG2T(14)
030223	NORTHAMPTON	NORTHAMPTON	W	2G2T(16)-1T(3)
100223	ARMY OF THE RHINE	COLOGNE(RIEHL)	W	5G1PG8T(52)-1T(3)
170223	OXFORD UNIVERSITY	TWICKENHAM	W	1G1PG3T(17)-1T(3)

240223	UNITED SERVICES PORTSMOUTH	TWICKENHAM	C	
030323	LEICESTER	LEICESTER	L	1DG(4)-1G2T(11)
100323	OLD MERCHANT TAYLORS	TWICKENHAM	W	2G2T(16)-0
170323	OLD BLUES	TWICKENHAM	D	1G(5)-1G(5)
240323	LONDON WELSH	HERNE HILL	W	1G5T(20)-1DG(4)
310323	SWANSEA	SWANSEA	D	1MG(3)-1T(3)
020423	CARDIFF	CARDIFF	L	2T(6)-1G1DG(9)
070423	BRISTOL	TWICKENHAM	W	2G2PG(16)-1DG2T(10)
140423	LONDON SCOTTISH	TWICKENHAM	W	2G1DG(14)-1G1T(8)

At a Committee meeting held at Carr's restaurant at 5 p.m. on 14th September, it was decided to recommend to the General Meeting the purchase of a ground for the "A" XV in Fairfax Road, Teddington. The President then raised the question of electing Irishmen to the Club. It was decided (rather strangely) that in future, candidates for membership must register as English before election! After this meeting (at 6 p.m.), the A.G.M. took place, at which it was indeed decided to purchase the said ground at Teddington at a price of £2,125. The Committee were authorised to sell the Club securities and borrow money for the purpose of buying and equipping the ground. Because of this "Harlequin Estates Limited" was formed and it was further decided to appoint three trustees, these were confirmed at a meeting on 9th October as C.E. Dardier, Adrian Stoop and H.E. Ward. A further Committee meeting was held at the O.M.T.'s ground, Teddington on 26th January at which a letter was read out from the London Welsh asking for the fixture with them to be renewed at Herne Hill next season (see earlier). It was decided that we could not comply with this request and Vivian Davies should discuss the matter with the President of London Welsh and offer them up to £50 to cover any financial loss. On 25th March a letter from A.C. Valentine was read out by the secretary proposing a match against the American Olympic Team on 26th April. Valentine, as it turned out was a member of the team. The Committee decided to offer half the net gate and to invite the U.S. Team to dinner at the expense of the Club. The Treasurer then read out a long list of members whose subs for the current season were unpaid. This list included a large proportion of the 1st XV! On 5th June, it was decided that the Club could afford to spend £3,000 on a pavilion to be built at Fairfax Road with accommodation for the groundsman forming part of the building. It was also decided that the war memorial should be erected as a separate item and it should be placed inside the pavilion.

Vivian Davies captained the Club again for the 1923/24 season which, after the first month began to look like the previous season in its lack of stability. Gloucester had beaten us for the fifth time on the trot (this time at Gloucester) and we had also lost by a point to both London Scottish and Newport at Twickenham. Against the Scots, we had led 8-0 at half time (Rougier getting a try and Hamilton-Wickes converting and adding a penalty) only for them to score a couple of tries and in between kick a penalty for a final score of 8-9 and against the Welsh we had led by a Gibbs try to nil at the break only for them to drop a goal and win by four points to three. We were due to meet both the Royal Military Academy (Woolwich) and Royal Military College (Sandhurst) in this season for the first time since 1908 but, in the event, the match against the first named was cancelled and we only played the College (winning by nine points to nil). Cambridge were our only other scalp in this early part of the season, with two draws following against U.S. Portsmouth (8-8) and Guy's Hospital (3-3). So, things were not looking too good with a record of won two, drawn two and lost three in our first seven games.

After this, we went from strength to strength and had winning runs of six and eight games and finished with twenty two wins to set a new record for wins in a season, passing the mark of twenty set in both 1908/09 and 1911/12. Leicester were beaten at Twickenham (but lost to away) and both the Army and the Royal Navy were defeated. On New Year's Eve we entertained the Fettesian-Lorettonians on the Old Merchant Taylors ground at Teddington. We put out a very much weakened side, showing eleven changes from the 29-10 defeat of the Army only two days earlier and including R.K. Melluish (O.M.T.s) and P.H. Lawless (Richmond) in our line-up. Not surprisingly, we lost by the margin of two goals and two tries (16 points) to nil. Our only other losses were by a point to Oxford at Twickenham (11-12) and, rather surprisingly, the Old Blues, also at Twickenham (8-11). We undertook a short tour to Yorkshire in March when both Headingley on 22nd March and Otley two days later were played. These were both first timers for us and although Headingley have been played a number of times since, Otley have only been met twice. After a scoreless first half against Headingley, Wakelam got a try, H.B. Style converted and Townell dropped a goal for a 9-0 victory. Against Otley (who had F.G.V. Cawdry from Ilkley at full back) it was a much tighter contest and after Townell had dropped another goal to give us a half time lead, J.A. Hall (on the right wing) scored two tries to put the home side two points in front, before H.V. Brodie went over for H.B. Style to convert and give us a 9-6 win.

On our second short tour (this time the regular one to Wales), we finally won both games. On the Saturday we defeated Swansea (11-10) and on the Monday it was Cardiff's turn (14-3). This was our first win over Swansea (in nine attempts) and only our second win over Cardiff (in eighteen attempts). Our last game of the season was against the earlier mentioned United States Olympic Team (from Stanford University, California) and was played at Twickenham on 26th April. Playing for us was W.J.A. (William) Davies (who had won the last of his 22 caps for England in 1923) at fly half. This was the first of his four first team appearances. During the game, J.M. Currie (one of our forwards) had his leg broken in an accident which was to end his career. He had made his debut on 5th November 1921 against Newport and had gone on to make 73 appearances for the first team. We started well and raced into an eleven point lead before the United States got on the board with a try to make it 11-3 at the break. William Davies got our first try of the second half (to add to others scored by T.L. Lowe, Hamilton-Wickes and H.B. Style in the first half) to which Style added the points. Back came the Americans with two tries and a conversion before William Browne went over for our fifth try and Style's conversion sealed the victory by 21-11. The only other new international during this season was a future England player, H.J. (Harold) Kittermaster, who made his debut on 17th November 1923 against Oxford. Other newcomers were C.D. Adams (58) and H.C. Pattison (65), who made the first of their appearances against Gloucester on 29th September and the Royal Navy on 22nd December respectively. This season had turned out to be our most successful so far even though no new records were set as regards scoring. Hamilton-Wickes topped the try scoring chart with twenty to his credit, Townell equalled his own record of three dropped goals and H.B. Style kicked forty two conversions and scored six tries on his way to the top points slot with 102. The team managed 446 points for and conceded 234, scoring 104 tries, 54 conversions, 5 dropped goals and 2 penalty goals in the process. On the appearance front, the following were the most regular, Currie (27), W.H. Wainwright (26), Davies, Lowe and Marshall (25), Brodie (24), H.B. Style (22) and C.D. Adams (20).

1923/24

290923	GLOUCESTER	GLOUCESTER	L	2G(10)-1G3T(14)
031023	ROYAL MILITARY COLLEGE	SANDHURST	W	3T(9)-0
061023	LONDON SCOTTISH	TWICKENHAM	L	1G1PG(8)-1PG2T(9)

131023	UNITED SERVICES PORTSMOUTH	PORTSMOUTH	D	1G1T(8)-1G1PG(8)
201023	CAMBRIDGE UNIVERSITY	CAMBRIDGE	W	4G3T(29)-1G1DG1T(12)
271023	GUY'S HOSPITAL	TWICKENHAM	D	1T(3)-1T(3)
031123	NEWPORT	TWICKENHAM	L	1T(3)-1DG(4)
071123	ROYAL MILITARY ACADEMY	WOOLWICH	C	
101123	RICHMOND	RICHMOND	W	1G1T(8)-0
171123	OXFORD UNIVERSITY	TWICKENHAM	L	1G1PG1T(11)-1G1DG1PG(12)
241123	BLACKHEATH	BLACKHEATH	W	2G4T(22)-1T(3)
011223	LEICESTER	TWICKENHAM	W	2G(10)-1G1PG(8)
081223	OLD MERCHANT TAYLORS	TWICKENHAM	W	2T(6)-1G(5)
151223	RICHMOND	TWICKENHAM	W	1G4T(17)-1G1T(8)
221223	ROYAL NAVY	TWICKENHAM	W	4T(12)-1G(5)
291223	ARMY	TWICKENHAM	W	2G1DG5T(29)-2G(10)
311223	FETTESIAN-LORETTONIANS	TEDDINGTON(OMT)	L	0-2G2T(16)
050124	ST.BARTHOLOMEW'S HOSPITAL	WINCHMORE HILL	C	
120124	BLACKHEATH	TWICKENHAM	W	3G2T(21)-1G1T(8)
190124	LONDON WELSH	TWICKENHAM	W	2G1T(13)-1PG1T(6)
260124	CAMBRIDGE UNIVERSITY	TEDDINGTON(OMT)	W	2G1DG4T(26)-2T(6)
020224	NORTHAMPTON	TWICKENHAM	W	3G2T(21)-2T(6)
090224	OLD BLUES	TWICKENHAM	L	1G1T(8)-1G2T(11)
160224	OXFORD UNIVERSITY	OXFORD	C	
010324	LEICESTER	LEICESTER	L	1G(5)-1G1PG2T(14)
080324	OLD MERCHANT TAYLORS	TEDDINGTON	W	4G2T(26)-1G1PG1T(11)
150324	ROSSLYN PARK	OLD DEER PARK	C	
220324	HEADINGLEY	HEADINGLEY	W	1G1DG(9)-0
240324	OTLEY	OTLEY	W	1G1DG(9)-2T(6)
290324	LONDON SCOTTISH	RICHMOND	W	6G1T(33)-1DG1T(7)
050424	BRISTOL	BRISTOL	W	2G1T(13)-1G1DG1T(12)
120424	UNITED SERVICES PORTSMOUTH	TWICKENHAM	W	5G2T(31)-2T(6)
190424	SWANSEA	SWANSEA	W	1G2T(11)-2G(10)
210424	CARDIFF	CARDIFF	W	2G1DG(14)-1T(3)
260424	UNITED STATES OLYMPIC TEAM	TWICKENHAM	W	3G2T(21)-1G2T(11)

At the A.G.M. on 12th September, it was decided that the tie supplied by Messrs. Lillywhites should be adopted for the Club. The President reported that the Fairfax Road ground would be ready for play by February (so far as the turf was concerned) and that owing to the uncertainty of the renewal of the lease of Twickenham, it had not been possible to decide the form which the pavilion would take. He also referred to the slackness of members in paying their subscriptions. At a Committee meeting held at the Mitre Tavern on 24th October, Hughes-Onslow proposed and Wakelam seconded that the lease of the R.F.U. ground should be extended for a further three years (till the end of the 1927/28 season) at a rental of £300, this was carried unanimously. It was also decided that the pavilion at Fairfax Road should be constructed so that it might form the nucleus of a stand. On 15th December, it was resolved that members be circulated and asked to take up to forty debentures of £100, each bearing 5% interest or 4% interest and life membership, in order to provide the capital necessary for building the pavilion. It was further resolved that the plan submitted by the architect, providing for tiers of seats in the roof at an estimated cost of about £3,700 be adopted.

After the previous season's results (which were always going to be a hard act to follow), we started reasonably well with wins over Richmond (18-9) and the Royal Military College (16-9). We were not helped by the fact that we used twenty more players (seventy seven as opposed to fifty seven, forty of which were different players) than the previous season and this started to show as we won only two out of thirteen games up to the New Year, against U.S. Portsmouth (16-6) and Gloucester (17-6), both at Twickenham. The Royal Military Academy were met with a second strength XV and we were duly defeated by seventeen points to three. In another close encounter with Newport, we went down by just a goal (five points) to nil whilst borrowing J.V. Waite from our opponents to make up our forward numbers (as had happened the previous week when T.W. Meisner had been borrowed from Guy's Hospital). We finally met Moseley for the first time (after the cancelled fixture in 1887) and lost (6-14) and Blackheath beat us at Twickenham (6-15), but we won the return by three points (24-21). In the New Year we did manage to win more games than we lost, but only just. After the second Blackheath game, we lost in quick succession to Cambridge, the Army and Northampton before winning the return with Oxford and doing the double over U.S. Portsmouth but, the following week, Leicester completed the double over us. Out of the last seven games, the only two lost were on the Easter tour. Our biggest win of the season came on 28th March against London Scottish at Richmond when we managed to score forty points without reply, which included ten tries. The heaviest defeat we suffered was against Oxford on 15th November (8-35). Our last game was against Headingley at Twickenham and William Davies (playing his last game for us) was among the try scorers in a 24-8 victory. This enabled us to finish with a record of P29 W12 L17, scoring 385 (93 tries and 46 conversions) points for (our worst since 1919/20) and conceding 388.

Three English international players made their debuts for us during this season, one old and two current. C.A. (Cecil) Kershaw played in the games against Richmond on 8th November and Blackheath on 10th January. He had won the last of his 16 caps in 1923. H.M. (Harold) Locke was a Birkenhead Park man and made his only two appearances for us in games between internationals (Cambridge and the Army on 24th and 31st January). He went on to gain 12 caps between 1923 and 1927. Finally, R.R.F. (Roderick) MacLennan gained three caps in this season and made his only appearance for us in the defeat of London Scottish. The 1st XV lost the services of Wakelam this season and he played his last game on 22nd October against the Royal Military Academy (he did carry on in the seconds for a few seasons). In his playing career (which had lasted since 1912), he had scored 304 points (31 tries, 6 penalty goals and 97 conversions) and had captained the side on twenty occasions. He went on to pursue a successful career in broadcasting and actually gave the first running commentary ever broadcast in Britain, on the England versus Wales game in 1927. He also commentated on Cricket, Football and Lawn Tennis. Debuts were made by P.E. (Philip) Hodge (who went on to make 167 appearances for the first team) against Cambridge on 18th October, M.L.P. Jackson (57) against Gloucester on 29th November and C.G. Stanley (69) against Richmond on 27th September. The top six appearance makers were Howard Marshall (24), Vivian Davies (22), W.H. Wainwright and Wakefield (back as captain again) (21) and Arthur Moller (20). Gibbs topped the try scorers with seventeen and Worton was top points scorer with 65 (nineteen conversions and nine tries).

1924/25

270924	RICHMOND	TWICKENHAM	W	3G1T(18)-1MG1PG1T(9)
011024	ROYAL MILITARY COLLEGE	SANDHURST	W	2G2T(16)-3T(9)
041024	LONDON SCOTTISH	RICHMOND	L	1G1PG1T(11)-2G1T(13)
081024	KING'S COLLEGE HOSPITAL	EAST DULWICH	C	
111024	UNITED SERVICES PORTSMOUTH	TWICKENHAM	W	2G2T(16)-2T(6)
181024	CAMBRIDGE UNIVERSITY	TWICKENHAM	L	1G1T(8)-1G1DG1PG(12)
221024	ROYAL MILITARY ACADEMY	WOOLWICH	L	1T(3)-2G1DG1T(17)
251024	GUY'S HOSPITAL	HONOR OAK PARK	L	1G(5)-2G2T(16)
011124	NEWPORT	NEWPORT	L	0-1G(5)
081124	RICHMOND	RICHMOND	L	1G2T(11)-2G1DG1T(17)
151124	OXFORD UNIVERSITY	OXFORD	L	1G1T(8)-4G5T(35)
221124	BLACKHEATH	TWICKENHAM	L	2T(6)-3G(15)
291124	GLOUCESTER	TWICKENHAM	W	1G4T(17)-2T(6)
061224	LEICESTER	TWICKENHAM	L	1G2T(11)-1G4T(17)
131224	OLD MERCHANT TAYLORS	TEDDINGTON	L	1G3T(14)-3G1DG1PG2T(28)
201224	MOSELEY	MOSELEY	L	2T(6)-1G3T(14)
271224	ROYAL NAVY	TWICKENHAM	C	
030125	ST.BARTHOLOMEW'S HOSPITAL	WINCHMORE HILL	C	
100125	BLACKHEATH	BLACKHEATH	W	3G3T(24)-3G2T(21)
240125	CAMBRIDGE UNIVERSITY	CAMBRIDGE	L	2G1T(13)-2G2T(16)
310125	ARMY	ALDERSHOT	L	0-2T(6)
070225	NORTHAMPTON	NORTHAMPTON	L	1T(3)-2G1DG4T(26)
210225	OXFORD UNIVERSITY	TWICKENHAM	W	3G2T(21)-1G1PG1T(11)
280225	UNITED SERVICES PORTSMOUTH	PORTSMOUTH	W	4G1T(23)-5T(15)
070325	LEICESTER	LEICESTER	L	2G1MG(13)-5G(25)
140325	OLD MERCHANT TAYLORS	TWICKENHAM	W	3G4T(27)-1G(5)
210325	ROSSLYN PARK	OLD DEER PARK	W	4G1T(23)-1G(5)
280325	LONDON SCOTTISH	RICHMOND	W	5G5T(40)-0
040425	BRISTOL	TWICKENHAM	W	1G1T(8)-1DG(4)
110425	SWANSEA	SWANSEA	L	1G2DG(13)-2G3T(19)
130425	CARDIFF	CARDIFF	L	1T(3)-1G1T(8)
180425	HEADINGLEY	TWICKENHAM	W	3G3T(24)-1G1T(8)

10

Consolidation and More Overseas Visitors 1925-1930

After the loss to Newport on 7th November, the Committee issued a statement that they had decided to discontinue the fixtures with Newport, the reason given was the constant infringement of the rules by them during the match. One of our players was quoted as saying that it quickly became evident that the visitors were determined to win, if necessary, by brute force. There were allegations of Quins players being kicked on the ground and obstruction off the ball. Newport put an announcement in the South Wales papers asking to ban us because we refused to discuss the matter or have an investigation. They went so far as to ask all South Wales teams to drop their fixtures with us in protest and refuse to play us if we requested a game – Cardiff and Swansea kept the fixtures going. We did not meet Newport again until April 1929 and it appears that the matter was still rumbling under the surface.

We showed V.G. Davies back as captain again for the 1925/26 season and also a return to winning ways. We started with a run of seven victories which included wins over London Scottish (26-8), U.S. Portsmouth (23-16) and Cambridge University (22-5). Our first loss came against Headingley in an away fixture. We fielded quite a strong side but by half time trailed 3-10, we had managed a try by Wakefield in response to Headingley's try, dropped goal and penalty goal. Worton got a try early in the second half but the home side stretched their lead with a further goal and try to leave us trailing by twelve points. We did score further tries through Wakefield and Hamilton-Wickes (who added one conversion) but we could not close the gap any further, leaving the final score at 14-18. Noel Hudson made the last of his forty five appearances in a career stretching back to 1912 in this game. He had scored four tries and captained the side on twenty three occasions. Further losses followed to Newport (9-10) (the infamous game referred to earlier), Richmond (0-16) and Leicester (9-11) although these were offset by three victories. One of these (over St. Bartholomew's Hospital) started the New Year off nicely and although Blackheath defeated us the following week, we then proceeded to run off ten victories in a row including the games against Northampton (25-10), Oxford University (43-25), Leicester (11-10), London Scottish (our first 1st XV game at Teddington) (41-10), Swansea (8-3) and Cardiff (6-5).

We were then beaten at Bristol before equalling the most wins in a season (22) with a final match victory over U.S. Portsmouth (28-12). Out of the twenty eight games played, only seven players managed twenty or more, these were H.V. Brodie (24), C.G.J. (Jim) Stanley (23), Peter Adams (22), J.S. Chick (21) and Vivian Davies, Philip Hodge and Arthur Moller (20). Two future England internationals made their debuts this season, J.C. (Jack) Hubbard (who gained his only cap against Scotland in 1930 and went on to make 119 appearances for the Club) against

Rosslyn Park on 26th September and H.C.C. (Colin) Laird (who won ten caps between 1927 and 1929 and made 93 appearances for the Club) against the Royal Military Academy on 21st October. Another debutant who was not to be an international was G.B. Coghlan (88 appearances) who first played against Leicester on 5th December. Rex King (our long serving full back) made his last appearance against the Old Merchant Taylors on 13th March, having scored 113 points (one dropped goal, seven penalty goals and forty four conversions) in his seven seasons. Gibbs topped the try scorers again with 21 and Hubbard was top points scorer with 72 (one dropped goal, two penalty goals and thirty one conversions). The team managed 477 points which included 111 tries and 59 conversions (these were all improvements on the previous season although none were Club records).

In 1926, a general revision of the laws of the game took place and several amendments were made to the existing rule book. The following were just some of them. The plan of the field was brought in as Law I and the measurements of the goals were more defined to state that from the top of the bar to the ground should be 10 feet and from inside to inside of the goal posts should be 18 feet 6 inches. The year of 1926 was the first time there had been a definition for "no side" which was described as "the end of the game". Another surprising omission had been how long a game should last. Again, the revision of the laws stated that international matches were to last two periods of forty minutes each and in other matches the duration of play was to be agreed upon by the respective sides. If this was not possible, the referee would fix the time which, in any event, should be exclusive of an interval at half time of no more than five minutes and of any other permitted delay not exceeding three minutes.

1925/26

230925	ROYAL MILITARY COLLEGE	SANDHURST	W	2G1PG2T(19)-1PG1T(6)
260925	ROSSLYN PARK	TWICKENHAM	W	2T(6)-0
031025	LONDON SCOTTISH	RICHMOND	W	4G2T(26)-1G1T(8)
101025	UNITED SERVICES PORTSMOUTH	PORTSMOUTH	W	4G1T(23)-1DG4T(16)
171025	CAMBRIDGE UNIVERSITY	CAMBRIDGE	W	2G4T(22)-1G(5)
211025	ROYAL MILITARY ACADEMY	WOOLWICH	W	4G4T(32)-1T(3)
241025	GUY'S HOSPITAL	TWICKENHAM	W	2G(10)-1PG(3)
311025	HEADINGLEY	HEADINGLEY	L	1G3T(14)-1G1DG1PG2T(18)
071125	NEWPORT	TWICKENHAM	L	3PG(9)-1DG2T(10)
141125	RICHMOND	RICHMOND	L	0-2G2T(16)
211125	OXFORD UNIVERSITY	TWICKENHAM	W	2G4T(22)-3T(9)
281125	BLACKHEATH	BLACKHEATH	C	
051225	LEICESTER	TWICKENHAM	L	1PG2T(9)-1G1PG1T(11)
121225	OLD MERCHANT TAYLORS	TWICKENHAM	W	5G(25)-1T(3)
191225	GLOUCESTER	GLOUCESTER	W	1G3T(14)-2G(10)
020126	ST.BARTHOLOMEW'S HOSPITAL	WINCHMORE HILL	W	1G3T(14)-0
090126	BLACKHEATH	TWICKENHAM	L	1T(3)-2G(10)
160126	RICHMOND	TWICKENHAM	C	
230126	CAMBRIDGE UNIVERSITY	TWICKENHAM	W	2G3T(19)-1G1T(8)
300126	ARMY	TWICKENHAM	W	3G1DG1T(22)-2G2T(16)

060226	NORTHAMPTON	TWICKENHAM	W	3G1DG1PG1T(25)-2G(10)
130226	OLD BLUES	FAIRLOP	W	2G(10)-1G(5)
200226	OXFORD UNIVERSITY	OXFORD	W	8G1T(43)-5G(25)
060326	LEICESTER	LEICESTER	W	1G2T(11)-2G(10)
130326	OLD MERCHANT TAYLORS	TEDDINGTON(A)	W	1G1T(8)-1G(5)
270326	LONDON SCOTTISH	TEDDINGTON	W	4G7T(41)-2G(10)
030426	SWANSEA	SWANSEA	W	1G1T(8)-1T(3)
050426	CARDIFF	CARDIFF	W	2T(6)-1G(5)
100426	BRISTOL	BRISTOL	L	1G1T(8)-1MG1PG3T(15)
170426	UNITED SERVICES PORTSMOUTH	TWICKENHAM	W	5G1T(28)-4T(12)

Howard Marshall took over the captaincy for one season before Wakefield took it back for the next three. Marshall had made his debut in September 1921 against the London Scottish and was to go on to play 116 times for the first team until his last game in September 1928 against Wasps. He became more famous for his work as a journalist and a Cricket commentator on radio. We started well under his captaincy and went one better than the start to the previous season when we posted eight wins on the trot. We played Wasps in our first game on 11th September at Twickenham. This was our first meeting since 10th January 1885 (when we had proved victorious by one goal and one try to one try) and we ran out easy winners in the end by thirty two points to nil. Against U.S. Portsmouth on 9th October, we scored our highest total against them in the thirty one meetings so far (45-3). This was also our biggest win of the season. On 30th October at Twickenham, we met the Maoris, who were actually in Europe at the invitation of the French and consequently they only played France in an international, winning twenty two out of their thirty one matches on tour. By half time we had built a lead of six points to nil with a try by Laird and a penalty by Hubbard. After this, Wakefield added our second try, Hubbard converted and we were home and dry. The Maoris did score a try through A. Falwasser which was converted by D. Pelham but, unfortunately for them, this left us winners by 11-5. In our next match, against Bristol on 6th November, we met with our first defeat. A.T. Hore had scored a try and kicked a penalty for them before half time and in the second half, as all we could muster was a try by E.H. Fouraker and a conversion by Hubbard, we lost by the margin of 5-6. Oxford, Blackheath, Leicester and Gloucester were beaten in the weeks leading up to Christmas. The last named by, what was at the time, a record score for us against them (36-7), including another five try haul for Gibbs and six conversions from H.B. Style.

We got a bit of a shock in the return with Blackheath on 8th January, a thrashing to the tune of thirty one points (five goals and two tries) to nil. As we had three of the England team (Gibbs, Hamilton-Wickes and Laird) to play against Wales at Twickenham the following week in our side, there were some adverse comments from the crowd (this was confirmed to me by Harold Caccia, who played in the centre that day and who went on to become Ambassador to Washington and later, Lord Caccia) and in the press. All the criticism, however, proved to be wrong as Wales were dispatched 11-9. That game at Blackheath, needless to say, was our heaviest defeat of the season and the most points we conceded. After this, we managed six wins out of twelve games, the most notable being away victories over Northampton (6-3) and Oxford University (31-20). Bristol completed the double over us with another one point victory (5-6 again!) at Twickenham and both matches were lost on the Easter tour. No new internationals appeared for us this season although ten did play, six of them current. A.E.C. (Tony) Prescott made his debut on 11th December against the Old Merchant Taylors for the first of his 188 appearances. The top appearance makers this season were Stanley (26), Fouraker, Hamilton-Wickes and Hubbard (24), Davies (22), Laird (21) and Wakefield (20). Hamilton-Wickes grabbed eighteen tries and Hubbard set a new record for penalty goals in a season with five. He just topped the one hundred points in the season by one (with two conversions in the last game against Cardiff), scoring forty one conversions and a dropped goal in addition to his penalties. Overall, the team scoring was just down on the previous year with no new records being set.

The British Lions made the journey to Argentina again in July and August 1927 for a second unofficial tour (the party was made up by players from England, Ireland and Scotland). This time, AD Allen, Granville Coghlan and Roger Wakefield were in the squad and all nine matches were won. Four tests were played against Argentina and Allen appeared in all four while Coghlan played in the second and fourth (he scored a try in the last). Once again, disappointingly, no caps were awarded.

1926/27

110926	WASPS	TWICKENHAM	W	4G4T(32)-0
250926	ROSSLYN PARK	OLD DEER PARK	W	2G3T(19)-1PG(3)
290926	ROYAL MILITARY ACADEMY	WOOLWICH	W	4G4T(32)-2G(10)
021026	LONDON SCOTTISH	TWICKENHAM	W	2G1DG1PG1T(20)-1G2T(11)
091026	UNITED SERVICES PORTSMOUTH	TWICKENHAM	W	6G5T(45)-1T(3)
161026	CAMBRIDGE UNIVERSITY	TWICKENHAM	W	4G1T(23)-1G1T(8)
231026	GUY'S HOSPITAL	HONOR OAK PARK	W	2G2PG2T(22)-2PG(6)
301026	THE MAORIS	TWICKENHAM	W	1G1PG1T(11)-1G(5)
061126	BRISTOL	BRISTOL	L	1G(5)-1PG1T(6)
131126	RICHMOND	RICHMOND	L	1T(3)-1G1T(8)
201126	OXFORD UNIVERSITY	TWICKENHAM	W	1G3T(14)-1G1T(8)
271126	BLACKHEATH	TWICKENHAM	W	1G1T(8)-0
041226	LEICESTER	TWICKENHAM	W	1G(5)-1T(3)
111226	OLD MERCHANT TAYLORS	TEDDINGTON(A)	L	1G(5)-1G1DG1T(12)
181226	GLOUCESTER	TWICKENHAM	W	6G2T(36)-1DG1T(7)
010127	ST.BARTHOLOMEW'S HOSPITAL	WINCHMORE HILL	W	5G1T(28)-1G(5)
080127	BLACKHEATH	BLACKHEATH	L	0-5G2T(31)
220127	CAMBRIDGE UNIVERSITY	CAMBRIDGE	C	
290127	ARMY	ALDERSHOT	W	4G1PG1T(26)-1G3T(14)
050227	NORTHAMPTON	NORTHAMPTON	W	2T(6)-1T(3)
190227	OXFORD UNIVERSITY	OXFORD	W	5G2T(31)-1G5T(20)
260227	UNITED SERVICES PORTSMOUTH	PORTSMOUTH	L	1T(3)-2G(10)
050327	LEICESTER	LEICESTER	L	1T(3)-1G2T(11)
120327	OLD MERCHANT TAYLORS	TWICKENHAM	W	2G4T(22)-1PG(3)
190327	OLD BLUES	TWICKENHAM	W	2G1T(13)-1G(5)
260327	LONDON SCOTTISH	RICHMOND	W	4G2T(26)-1G1T(8)

020427	RICHMOND	TWICKENHAM	L	0-2G1DG(14)
090427	BRISTOL	TWICKENHAM	L	1G(5)-2T(6)
160427	SWANSEA	SWANSEA	L	1PG1T(6)-1DG2T(10)
180427	CARDIFF	CARDIFF	L	2G1T(13)-2G1PG1T(16)

In the period of time from the end of the First World War and up to and including the end of the 1927/28 season, the English national side had an excellent record of P38 W27 D3 L8. In that time, no less than four Grand Slams had been achieved, including back to back successes in 1923 and 1924. The captain from 1920-23 was William Davies (who appeared for us after his international career had finished) and in the eleven matches he played in, ten were won and one was drawn. In 1927/28, the side recorded wins in all five games for the only time in the history of English rugby. Colin Laird (at that time our fly half) played in all five games and Godfrey Palmer (who had played for us earlier in the decade) appeared in the last three. During this time, we regularly supplied three or more players to the side in what was a golden period for the national team.

As mentioned earlier, Wakefield came back to captain the side for the next three seasons. To open the 1927/28 season, once again, we met Wasps at Twickenham and, although we won the match, the result was a lot closer than the previous encounter (8-6). We defeated the Royal Military College (27-10) but then lost to Rosslyn Park (3-6) and the Royal Military Academy (6-11) before seeing off the challenges of London Scottish (this proved to be our biggest win of the season, 27-5) and U.S. Portsmouth (8-6). We shared the spoils with Oxford and Richmond, beat Gloucester but lost twice to Cambridge and Bristol. On 17th December, we had been due to meet Birkenhead Park for the first time since 1897 but the match was cancelled. We were due to play Stade Français at home and away, the home game at Teddington being cancelled, the away game in Paris resulting in an 11-11 draw. Against the Old Blues on 11th February, we had to enlist the services of W.S. Gammell from Rosslyn Park to make up our numbers and he helped himself to a try in our 19-4 victory. We managed to defeat Leicester 3-0 (with a try from Vivian Davies) at Twickenham and draw 18-18 in the return. We lost to Swansea (5-10) and defeated Cardiff (19-11) on the Easter tour before venturing down to Barnstaple on 21st April. With more or less a full strength side, we just managed to beat our hosts (8-3) through tries by Wakefield and Laird (this one converted by Hubbard) to a single try by T. Phillips (which enabled them to lead 3-0 at half time).

Debutants were S.A. Block (who made 54 appearances) against Wasps on 10th September, J.R. (John) Cole (103) and B.J. Collins (54), U.S. Portsmouth on 8th October, D.H. Duder (69), Guy's Hospital 22nd October, C.R. Hinds-Howell (85), Royal Military Academy 28th September, P.W.P. (Peter) Brook (94), Devonport Services 21st January and H.A. Style (76), Leicester 3rd March. New internationals were Brook (three caps for England, one in 1930, 31 and 36 respectively), J.W.R. (John) Swayne (also capped for England, in 1929) who made six appearances for us between 1927 and 1932 and André Verger (seven caps for France, three in 1927 and four in 1928) who made three appearances for us during the season, playing first against Rosslyn Park on 24th September. We ended up with a playing record of sixteen wins, two draws and fourteen losses from thirty two games, with only two of sixty eight players used appearing in more than twenty one of them, these were Davies (24) and Hubbard (22). This had been a disappointing season regarding scoring all round, Gibbs getting eleven tries and Hubbard kicking four penalties and twenty three conversions (to top score with fifty eight points) to end up with the lowest top scores since 1919/20. The team scores were also well down, tries and conversions nose diving to just sixty six and thirty five respectively and these contributed towards the points total of 314.

1927/28

100927	WASPS	TWICKENHAM	W	1G1T(8)-2T(6)
210927	ROYAL MILITARY COLLEGE	SANDHURST	W	(27)-(10)
240927	ROSSLYN PARK	TWICKENHAM	L	1PG(3)-1PG1T(6)
280927	ROYAL MILITARY ACADEMY	WOOLWICH	L	2T(6)-1G1PG1T(11)
011027	LONDON SCOTTISH	RICHMOND	W	4G1DG1T(27)-1G(5)
081027	UNITED SERVICES PORTSMOUTH	TWICKENHAM	W	1G1T(8)-1PG1T(6)
151027	CAMBRIDGE UNIVERSITY	CAMBRIDGE	L	1G1T(8)-1G3T(14)
221027	GUY'S HOSPITAL	HONOR OAK PARK	L	0-1T(3)
291027	GLOUCESTER	GLOUCESTER	W	1G2T(11)-1T(3)
051127	BRISTOL	BRISTOL	L	0-1G(5)
121127	RICHMOND	RICHMOND	W	1G1T(8)-1G(5)
191127	OXFORD UNIVERSITY	TWICKENHAM	L	2T(6)-3T(9)
261127	BLACKHEATH	BLACKHEATH	W	2G1PG(13)-0
031227	LEICESTER	TWICKENHAM	W	1T(3)-0
101227	OLD MERCHANT TAYLORS	TWICKENHAM	W	1G1T(8)-0
171227	BIRKENHEAD PARK	BIRKENHEAD	C	
241227	STADE FRANÇAIS	TEDDINGTON	C	
311227	ARMY	TWICKENHAM	C	
070128	ST.BARTHOLOMEW'S HOSPITAL	WINCHMORE HILL	W	5G1T(28)-1G2T(11)
140128	BLACKHEATH	TWICKENHAM	L	1G2T(11)-2G2T(16)
210128	DEVONPORT SERVICES	TWICKENHAM	W	1G4T(17)-1PG1T(6)
280128	CAMBRIDGE UNIVERSITY	CAMBRIDGE	L	0-7T(21)
040228	NORTHAMPTON	NORTHAMPTON	L	0-1G2T(11)
110228	OLD BLUES	FAIRLOP	W	2G1PG2T(19)-1DG(4)
180228	OXFORD UNIVERSITY	OXFORD	W	2G2T(16)-1G1T(8)
260228	STADE FRANÇAIS	PARIS	D	1G1PG1T(11)-1G2T(11)
030328	LEICESTER	LEICESTER	D	3G1T(18)-3G1PG(18)
100328	OLD MERCHANT TAYLORS	TEDDINGTON(A)	W	2G1T(13)-1G1PG1T(11)
170328	OLD LEYSIANS	TEDDINGTON	L	2G(10)-2G2T(16)
240328	LONDON SCOTTISH	TEDDINGTON	L	1T(3)-1G1DG2T(15)
310328	BRISTOL	TWICKENHAM	L	0-2G(10)
070428	SWANSEA	SWANSEA	L	1G(5)-2G(10)
090428	CARDIFF	CARDIFF	W	2G1PG2T(19)-1G1PG1T(11)
140428	RICHMOND	TWICKENHAM	L	0-2T(6)
210428	BARNSTAPLE	BARNSTAPLE	W	1G1T(8)-1T(3)

After an initial loss of £146 and takings on the gate of £834 in the 1919/20 season, our end of season figures remained in profit throughout the twenties. Our best season for gate money income was in 1926/27 when £3,930 was taken and this was transferred over to an overall profit figure of £588. Our best overall profit during this time came in 1923/24 when £869 was made, the gate receipts being £3,153. Apart from the years mentioned, our gate receipts ranged between £1,451 and £2,874 and our overall profit was between £463 and £851.

After defeating Wasps at Teddington (16-9), we lost to both Rosslyn Park and London Scottish in close games, then we set up an unbeaten run of six matches defeating (among others) Bristol and Oxford University before going down to Blackheath (5-11). We managed to pick ourselves up from this and the next week we defeated Leicester at Twickenham (17-5) and after the cancellation of the previous season's fixture, we actually met Birkenhead Park at Twickenham and beat them 14-5. Gloucester followed the following week and after four years of success, we lost by the only try to nil. Boxing Day saw our first meeting with Woodford (at Woodford) and in a reasonably close game, we ran out winners 16-6. Three days later, we met the Army at Portsmouth (a couple of our own men opposing us) and lost 8-14. We were due to meet the Old Millhillians at Headstone Lane on 19th January, but the match was cancelled, as were the returns with Cambridge, Oxford, U.S. Portsmouth and Leicester. We met London Scottish at Richmond on 23rd March and proceeded to notch up our biggest win of the season. By half time all we had scored was a dropped goal by Hubbard but in the second half tries were added by P.P. Galloway, V.A.C. Bergne, G.J. (Geoffrey) Dean, J.C. Hardy and Leo Price, three of which were converted by Hubbard to leave the final score at 25-0. After this, we completed doubles over Bristol and Richmond, but lost to Cardiff (11-15), Newport (5-19) and Swansea (8-22), the last two being our heaviest defeats of the season. The game against Swansea was supposed to be Gracie's last before retirement but he did appear for us a couple of times in the next two seasons.

Long servers debuting this season were J.S.R. (James) Reeve (who made 76 appearances) against U.S. Portsmouth on 13th October, Geoffrey Dean (100), Northampton on 2nd February and E.A. (Edward) Hamilton-Hill (90), Old Blues on 16th March. More internationals appeared in the shape of Englishmen William Alexander (one cap in 1927) who made four appearances for us, all in this season, Geoffrey Dean (one cap in 1931), Edward Hamilton-Hill (three caps in 1936) and James Reeve (eight caps between 1929 and 1931) and Irish cap J.S. (John) Synge (one cap in 1929) who made his only appearance for us against Leicester on 1st December. In total, fifteen international players appeared for us this season, beating the previous best of fourteen set in 1921/22 (although four only played in the charity match for the past team) and 1924/25. This season was another poor one as regards appearances and scoring. On the appearance front, only five players managed twenty or more games out of twenty seven, Davies was top with twenty three and Chick, Fouraker, Hubbard and L. de M. Thuillier all came next on twenty. John Cole scored the most tries with only seven and Hubbard top scored again, this time with just nineteen conversions and a single dropped goal and penalty goal for a total of forty five points. Overall, points went up to 342 including 81 tries and 38 conversions whilst we conceded 233.

1928/29

150928	WASPS	TEDDINGTON	W	2G2T(16)-1G1DG(9)
290928	ROSSLYN PARK	OLD DEER PARK	L	2T(6)-1G2T(11)
061028	LONDON SCOTTISH	TWICKENHAM	L	1G1T(8)-3G(15)
131028	UNITED SERVICES PORTSMOUTH	PORTSMOUTH	W	2G1PG2T(19)-1G1T(8)
201028	CAMBRIDGE UNIVERSITY	TWICKENHAM	D	1G1PG1T(11)-1G2T(11)
271028	GUY'S HOSPITAL	HONOR OAK PARK	W	2G3T(19)-1G(5)
031128	BRISTOL	TWICKENHAM	W	2G1PG2T(19)-1G(5)

101128	RICHMOND	RICHMOND	W	1G2T(11)-1DG1T(7)
171128	OXFORD UNIVERSITY	TWICKENHAM	W	2G(10)-2T(6)
241128	BLACKHEATH	TWICKENHAM	L	1G(5)-1G2T(11)
011228	LEICESTER	TWICKENHAM	W	1G4T(17)-1G(5)
081228	OLD MERCHANT TAYLORS	TEDDINGTON	W	3G3T(24)-1G(5)
151228	BIRKENHEAD PARK	TWICKENHAM	W	1G3T(14)-1G(5)
221228	GLOUCESTER	TWICKENHAM	L	0-1T(3)
261228	WOODFORD	WOODFORD	W	2G2T(16)-2T(6)
291228	ARMY	PORTSMOUTH	L	1G1T(8)-1G3T(14)
050129	ST.BARTHOLOMEW'S HOSPITAL	WINCHMORE HILL	W	2G3T(19)-2G(10)
120129	BLACKHEATH	BLACKHEATH	W	1G1PG(8)-1G(5)
190129	OLD MILLHILLIANS	HEADSTONE LANE	C	
260129	CAMBRIDGE UNIVERSITY	CAMBRIDGE	C	
020229	NORTHAMPTON	NORTHAMPTON	L	1T(3)1PG2T(9)
160229	OXFORD UNIVERSITY	OXFORD	C	
230229	UNITED SERVICES PORTSMOUTH	TWICKENHAM	C	
020329	LEICESTER	LEICESTER	C	
090329	OLD MERCHANT TAYLORS	TEDDINGTON(A)	W	1G1DG1T(12)-1T(3)
160329	OLD BLUES	FAIRLOP	W	3G2T(21)-1G1T(8)
230329	LONDON SCOTTISH	RICHMOND	W	3G1DG2T(25)-0
300329	SWANSEA	SWANSEA	L	1G1T(8)-2G2PG2T(22)
010429	CARDIFF	CARDIFF	L	1G2T(11)-3G(15)
060429	BRISTOL	BRISTOL	W	3G(15)-1G2T(11)
130429	RICHMOND	TWICKENHAM	W	1PG3T(12)-1G(5)
200429	NEWPORT	NEWPORT	L	1G(5)-3G1DG(19)

It was announced at the A.G.M. on 10th September that a loss of about £450 was made for 1928/29 as opposed to a profit of a similar amount the preceding season. Some of the reasons for this were given as, the United Services match was cancelled owing to weather conditions, a large expenditure had been necessary on the Fairfax Road ground and extra demands by the Revenue authorities. It was stated that there was no immediate cause for alarm, but it might be necessary to encroach to a small extent on the nest egg of National Savings Certificates. The President expressed his regret at having to announce the death of J.N. Hill (who had made 109 appearances for the first team between 1893 and 1898 and had been a Vice President since 1901). First team caps were awarded to J.S. Chick, V.G. Davies, E.H. Fouraker, J.C. Hubbard, H.C.C. Laird, H.L. Price and W.W. Wakefield with new caps going to J.R. Cole, G.A. Rutter and L de M Thuillier. At a Committee meeting held after the A.G.M., it was reported that the St. Thomas's Hospital training hall had been demolished and so was not available for the use of the Club. A further meeting was held at the Metropole Hotel on 9th May where it was decided that the Newport fixture should not be renewed (indeed, after the game in November 1930, we did not play them for twenty years). It was also decided that the use of the Fairfax Road ground be allowed for the Teddington Town Fete, Empire Day and finally, St. Mark's School and a letter was sent to the nephew of the late George Rope (another Vice President, he had joined the Club in 1872) expressing the sense of loss sustained by the Club.

The 1929/30 season started off disappointingly as three out of the first four games (against Wasps, Royal Military College and Royal Military Academy) were cancelled and the only one played (against Rosslyn Park) was lost by two tries to three tries (6-9). Success in the next two games against London Scottish (15-8) and U.S. Portsmouth (8-6) led us on to our heaviest defeat of the season. Our opponents were the students of Cambridge University and, despite playing seven of our past, present or future internationals, they ran out winners by twenty four points to nil. Against Bristol, after a scoreless first half, we were outscored by two tries to one (each side converting one) to lose 5-8. We were, however, handicapped by the loss of one of our centres (Laird) through injury. This was to be the first of seven consecutive losses to our West Country rivals. The first Oxford game was cancelled, after which Blackheath were disposed of 18-9. Newport came to Twickenham on 30th November and again we lost to them, this time by three points (5-8). On 21st December, we travelled up to play Birkenhead Park on their own ground for the first time since 1895 and came away defeated by sixteen points to three after playing the first twenty minutes without the services of Tony Prescott, who arrived late. After beating Woodford and the Army over Christmas, we lost to St. Bartholomew's Hospital (11-25) at Winchmore Hill and drew with Blackheath in the return match (3-3) before starting on our best run in one season since 1908/09. It began with the game against Devonport Services which was played in Plymouth, the result being 8-7 (after we trailed 0-7 at half time). The next game was away to Eastbourne (the first of eight midweek matches against them over the next nine seasons) and this proved to be our biggest win of the season by thirty points to thirteen. Among our other victories were away wins at Northampton (3-0), Oxford (18-8) and Leicester (never an easy place to win) (15-13).

This run lasted until 5th April when Gloucester defeated us by eleven points to eight and with further losses following to Bristol (3-6), Swansea (10-12) and Cardiff (8-20), we ended the season with a run of four defeats. In the Cardiff match, Wavell Wakefield appeared as one of the touch judges. Following on from the previous season, a new record amount of internationals appeared for us, this time it was sixteen. The new ones were Englishmen P.E. (Phillip) Dunkley (who went on to gain six caps for England in, 1931 (two) and 1936 (four) and appear no fewer than 145 times for us) who debuted on 12th October against U.S. Portsmouth and Alan Key who gained two caps (one each in 1931 and 1933) played the first of his two games for us against Oxford on 15th February and Scotsman J.E. (James) Hutton (who won two caps, one each in 1930 and 1931) who debuted for us against Blackheath on 23rd November. K.H. (Ken) Chapman made the first of at least 208 appearances in the Devonport Services match on 18th January while Vivian Davies (who scored 227 points made up of 67 tries, one dropped goal and 11 conversions and captained the side on seventy occasions) and Wavell Wakefield (who scored 184 points made up of 51 tries, one penalty goal and 14 conversions and captained the side on eighty two occasions) made their final appearances against Richmond on 9th November and Cambridge on 25th January respectively. The top try scorer was Gibbs with just seven and, once again, Hubbard topped the points with 68 (one dropped goal, two penalty goals and 29 conversions) while the team managed 316 points for including 69 tries and 39 conversions as opposed to 256 points against. Finally, top appearance makers out of thirty games were Hubbard and Tony Prescott (25), Adams (23), Duder (22), J.C.H. Sears (21) and Fouraker, Laird and D.F. Phillips (20) out of a total of sixty six players used.

The summer of 1930 saw the British Lions on tour to New Zealand and Australia. James Reeve (a wing) was our first member of a Lions party since the 1891 tour to South Africa. He played and scored a try in the first test on 21st June (won by the Lions, 6-3), missed the second through injury and played in the last two and the one in Australia (all of which were lost).

1929/30

140929	WASPS	TEDDINGTON	C	
250929	ROYAL MILITARY COLLEGE	SANDHURST	C	
280929	ROSSLYN PARK	TWICKENHAM	L	2T(6)-3T(9)
021029	ROYAL MILITARY ACADEMY	WOOLWICH	C	
051029	LONDON SCOTTISH	RICHMOND	W	1G1DG1PG1T(15)-1G1T(8)
121029	UNITED SERVICES PORTSMOUTH	TWICKENHAM	W	1G1T(8)-2T(6)
191029	CAMBRIDGE UNIVERSITY	CAMBRIDGE	L	0-4G1DG(24)
261029	GUY'S HOSPITAL	TWICKENHAM	W	3G1T(18)-1T(3)
021129	BRISTOL	BRISTOL	L	1G(5)-1G1T(8)
091129	RICHMOND	TWICKENHAM	W	1G1T(8)-0
161129	OXFORD UNIVERSITY	TWICKENHAM	C	
231129	BLACKHEATH	BLACKHEATH	W	3G1T(18)-1PG2T(9)
301129	NEWPORT	TWICKENHAM	L	1G(5)-1G1T(8)
071229	LEICESTER	TWICKENHAM	D	1G1T(8)-1G1T(8)
141229	OLD MERCHANT TAYLORS	TEDDINGTON(A)	W	2G3T(19)-1PG(3)
211229	BIRKENHEAD PARK	BIRKENHEAD	L	1T(3)-2G2T(16)
261229	WOODFORD	WOODFORD	W	2G1PG(13)-2T(6)
281229	ARMY	TWICKENHAM	W	1G1T(8)-0
040130	ST.BARTHOLOMEW'S HOSPITAL	WINCHMORE HILL	L	1G2T(11)-2G5T(25)
110130	BLACKHEATH	TWICKENHAM	D	1T(3)-1T(3)
180130	DEVONPORT SERVICES	DEVONPORT	W	1G1T(8)-1DG1T(7)
220130	EASTBOURNE	EASTBOURNE	W	4G1DG2T(30)-2G1T(13)
250130	CAMBRIDGE UNIVERSITY	TWICKENHAM	W	2G3T(19)-2G1T(13)
010230	NORTHAMPTON	NORTHAMPTON	W	1T(3)-0
080230	OLD BLUES	FAIRLOP	W	1DG1T(7)-0
150230	OXFORD UNIVERSITY	OXFORD	W	3G1T(18)-1G1T(8)
010330	LEICESTER	LEICESTER	W	3G(15)-2G1T(13)
080330	OLD MERCHANT TAYLORS	TEDDINGTON	W	1G1DG1PG1T(15)-2T(6)
220330	LONDON SCOTTISH	TEDDINGTON	W	1G1PG1T(11)-1G1T(8)
290330	RICHMOND	RICHMOND	W	2G1T(13)-1T(3)
050430	GLOUCESTER	GLOUCESTER	L	1G1PG(8)-1G1PG1T(11)
120430	BRISTOL	TWICKENHAM	L	1T(3)-2T(6)
190430	SWANSEA	SWANSEA	L	2G(10)-1PG3T(12)
210430	CARDIFF	CARDIFF	L	1G1T(8)-4G(20)

11

Sevens in the 1920s
1926-1929

As far back as 28th April 1883, the first Seven-a-side tournament was held at The Greenyards in Melrose, Scotland. In need of funds to stop the Club going under, the idea was put forward by Ned Haig to hold a football tournament. Because having several matches in one day featuring regular sized teams was thought to be impossible, they were reduced to seven men per side. Thus the Melrose Sports began which contained foot races, drop kicks, dribbling races and place kicking as well as the main event for which a trophy was presented by the Ladies of Melrose for the winners. To begin with, each team contained a full back, two quarter-backs and four forwards but as the passing game developed, the forwards were reduced to three and that made room for another back. The game we see today has virtually the same make up but the forwards are now two props and a hooker with a scrum half, fly half, centre and wing. Each game was to be seven minutes each way with a one minute interval except for the final which would be ten minutes each way. In the event of a draw, sudden death extra time of five minutes duration would be played until someone scored.

London had to wait until 1926 when Dr J.A. Russell-Cargill set up the Middlesex Sevens in aid of the King Edward VII Hospital Fund. The first event saw forty nine teams from the Middlesex area enter with fifteen of these passing directly into the second round. This left thirty two sides in a straight knockout. The first two rounds were completed between 15th and 21st April before the finals on 24th April at Twickenham. Even on the 24th, there was not enough time to fit in all the games at the main ground so four third round ties and two quarter finals were played elsewhere. Orleans Park, Twickenham and our ground at Fairfax Road were utilised for this purpose. Both grounds hosted one quarter final with the winner of each travelling to Twickenham for the semi-finals. Quins, Bank of England, Lensbury, Osterley, Richmond and Rosslyn Park entered two sides and the rest of the main London clubs, the Hospital sides and Old Boys' teams made up the entrants. No players had any experience of playing sevens so it was a new and exciting time for everyone. Some of the first matches were played after 6 p.m. on 15th April and featured our 1st VII against Harrow and the 2nd VII were up against Old Millhillians. Both were successfully through on a Wednesday afternoon in front of a hundred or so onlookers and on 21st April, the second side defeated Old Leysians 12-0. On the same day at Fairlop, Old Blues beat Old Cranleighans 21-0 and the following day, there was a clarification of this in the paper. The report stated that the result might have been qualified by a further statement that, for business reasons, three members of the Old Cranleighans team could not reach the ground in time. It is amazing that the four who did get there only conceded five tries! A crowd of 15,000 turned up on finals day where tickets were priced at one shilling each, two shillings for a ringside seat and five shillings in the stands. The second side beat Richmond I in Orleans Park (8-5) before going out in the quarter final to Old Merchant Taylors by 6-8. The firsts did slightly better and saw off King's College Hospital, London Scottish (13-3) and Blackheath (15-5) to reach the final where they outplayed St. Mary's Hospital to the tune of 25-3 to lift a replica of the Kinross Arber Cup. Clifford Gibbs, Hamilton-Wickes, Vivian Davies, John Worton, J.S. Chick, W.F. Browne and Wakefield were the winning team and our second seven were represented by Laird, Hodge, Brodie, Field-Hyde, Stanley, Moller and Faithfull. Just over £1,621 was raised for charity at an event that would grow and remain part of the rugby calendar for over eighty years.

The following year, fifty four sides entered and both of our teams received byes into the second round. On 23rd April, matches following the first two rounds were played. The second VII went out to the Honourable Artillery Company (0-8) and didn't make finals day but the 1st VII once again excelled and beat Twickenham (20-0), Old Millhillians (15-0), Old Blues (10-5) and Richmond (10-0) before meeting Blackheath in the final. Between the second semi-final and the final, there was what was described as the energetic and hilarious Thousand-a-Side Push Ball Match! The ball used was kindly lent by the Daily Mail newspaper. When the crowd had left the pitch, H.C. Pattisson scored the opening try and H.B. Style converted before Bishop got one back. Hamilton-Wickes stretched our lead at half time after Laird made an opening but Pratten got Blackheath back in the game. After this, we ran away with it and added further tries from Hamilton-Wickes (2), W.F. Browne and Pattisson. Style converted all four to make it 28-6 and we had won again. Wavell Wakefield and Chick (two of four survivors from 1926) completed the side. The crowd was approaching 10,000 and the amount raised for charity was £1,065.

On 28th April 1928, the third Middlesex tournament took place and the crowd was nearly 20,000. Gibbs returned to the side as did Davies and Browne, Laird and Wakefield played again. J. S. R. Reeve and Faithfull made up the side (although there are question marks as to whether H.L. Price and H.C. Pattisson played instead of Reeve and Faithfull). Our second side received a bye in the first round, defeated Old Cranleighans (15-14) in the second round but went out in the next round. Once more, the 1st team continued their unbeaten run with victories over Rosslyn Park (13-3), Old Millhillians (15-0) and Edgware in the semi-final by 8-0. Blackheath were once again met in the final and the same end result was achieved. Davies scored tries either side of one by Novis and Price converted the second. Gibbs and Davies added more tries and although Taylor got one for Blackheath, Gibbs secured the title for the third year in a row with his second of the game. A total of £3,194 was raised for charity, the best so far.

In 1929, the number of entrants had grown to 83 and once again, we had two sides out. The second VII failed to qualify and, as had now become a regular occurrence, the first team defeated Old Paulines (13-3), Edgware I (6-5) and Old Merchant Taylors (9-3) before meeting Rosslyn Park in the final. Against Edgware, it was reported that if it hadn't been for the injury to K.H. Chapman (our future President) when he tackled Wakefield, Quins might possibly have lost. As it was, we didn't and in that final, Wakefield, Rylands, Browne and Hardy scored tries (Wakefield converting two) to give us a 16-0 lead. After this, we eased up and Dent dropped a goal for Park (despite wearing Tennis shoes) and Moore converted Hunt's try to bring them up to nine points but it was nowhere near enough to prevent us from making it four in a row and that record would last for over sixty years. Davies, McCreight and Price completed the seven. The amount raised for charity fell to a low of £986 this time. It was clear that sevens were here to stay.

12

The Thirties

1930-1939

At the A.G.M. on 9th September, the President announced the retirements of Wavell Wakefield and Vivian Davies. Wakefield had set a record for England international appearances (31) that was to last for many years. He was described by the President as the greatest player of his generation and an example to all young players. He also stated that a gratifying feature of the past season had been the success of the "A" XVs. They finished with combined records of P58 W44 L14 F1218 A493. He was particularly pleased that old internationals and blues of Oxford and Cambridge did not consider it beneath their dignity to serve the Club by playing in the "A" XVs. New caps were awarded to D.H. Duder, A.E.C. Prescott and J.S.R. Reeve. A sad event took place on Whit Sunday 1931 when William "Horsey" Browne died after being attacked by a fatal and incurable illness. For his last days, he was moved from the Aldershot Military Hospital to Hartley Grange (at the express request of the Stoops) to be among friends. He was only twenty eight years of age.

For this and the next season (1931/32), Peter Adams led the side after Wakefield's departure. Our first match in the 1930/31 season was again against Wasps and was played on 13th September. Unfortunately, we were defeated by eight points to nil, thus suffering our first reverse against them in a fixture dating back to 1872. Against the Royal Military College on 24th September, D.R.S. (Douglas) Bader made his debut, he was to go on and become a famous World War Two fighter pilot and campaigner for the disabled (he lost both of his legs in a flying accident at Woodley Airfield). As a consequence of this, his appearances for the first team were limited to just seventeen and his accident came two days after his last appearance against the Old Merchant Taylors on 12th December 1931. Also appearing in this match were three gentleman cadets who made up our numbers. Despite this, we managed to win 23-14. After defeating Rosslyn Park, we scored our biggest win of the season, against London Scottish (34-0). This included seven tries, with thirteen points coming from the boot of Laird (five conversions and a penalty goal).

Wins over Cambridge University (27-14), Guy's Hospital (24-15), Richmond (23-0) and Blackheath (16-3) followed but, between times, losses were recorded against Bristol (5-12), Oxford University (8-11) and Newport (0-12). The return with Blackheath was cancelled and in the return with Richmond on 31st January, Reeve scored six tries in a 26-9 win. This was the first time anyone had scored six in a first team game, but it was still one short of Douglas Lambert's seven in 1906. We lost by twenty one points to nil at Northampton but worse was to come when we played the return with Leicester, having already beaten them at Twickenham (13-11) on 6th December. Unfortunately, we only had about seven of our first choice players on duty and Leicester showed us no mercy. They ran in six tries (five being converted) and added a dropped goal to our solitary penalty by H.B. Style to win 32-3. This was our heaviest defeat of the season and their biggest points total against us (they were to repeat the score in 1948).

Archibald Gracie appeared (for the final time) as "R. le Quin" in the 15-15 draw with the Old Merchant Taylors on 14th March (in the course of his career he had scored 176 points made up of 54 tries, 2 dropped goals and 3 conversions) and against Oxford we had to borrow three men from their ranks to make up our numbers in a 13-19 defeat. We met the Old Blues on the Christ's Hospital ground at Horsham (for the only time) and won 18-5 before undertaking the now customary Easter tour to Wales. In the first match, at Swansea, we ran up our biggest total against them. Philip Dunkley got twenty points (two tries and seven conversions) and J.R. Cole, D.H. Duder, James Reeve (2) and H.A. Style scored tries in a 35-10 victory. We went down in the Cardiff match (10-19) and also at Bristol (5-16) and at home to Gloucester in the final game of the season (10-13). Our only new international player was D.H. (Denys) Swayne (one cap for England in 1931) who made his debut against U.S. Portsmouth on 28th February. Other newcomers to the first team were Chris Thompson (who went on to make 163 appearances), debuting against Wasps on 13th September and J.D. Ronald (125 appearances) against London Scottish on 28th March.

Unfortunately, we lost a couple of our more experienced players due to their retiring. Colin Laird made his last appearance against U.S. Portsmouth on 28th February having scored 177 points for the Club (38 tries, 4 dropped goals, one goal from a mark, 4 penalty goals and 16 conversions) and H.B. Style finished off against Leicester on 7th March, he had scored 211 points (16 tries, 5 penalty goals and 74 conversions) in his career. James Reeve topped the try scorers with sixteen, Laird equalled the dropped goal record with three and Dunkley got the most points with 63 (2 tries, 3 penalty goals and 24 conversions). The team set a new record for penalty goals in a season with eight, equalled the record for dropped goals with six as well as adding 82 tries and 63 conversions, making a total of 423 points. Out of a total of thirty games played and seventy four players used, the following made the most appearances, Tony Prescott (24), Hodge (23), Adams and Dunkley (22) and Dean and Hinds-Howell (20).

1930/31

130930	WASPS	TEDDINGTON	L	0-1G1T(8)
240930	ROYAL MILITARY COLLEGE	SANDHURST	W	4G1T(23)-1G3T(14)
270930	ROSSLYN PARK	OLD DEER PARK	W	2G1MG1T(16)-1G1T(8)
011030	ROYAL MILITARY ACADEMY	WOOLWICH	C	
041030	LONDON SCOTTISH	TWICKENHAM	W	5G1PG2T(34)-0
111030	UNITED SERVICES PORTSMOUTH	PORTSMOUTH	W	2G1DG3T(23)-1G1T(8)
181030	CAMBRIDGE UNIVERSITY	TWICKENHAM	W	3G4T(27)-1G3T(14)
251030	GUY'S HOSPITAL	HONOR OAK PARK	W	2G2DG1PG1T(24)-3G(15)
011130	BRISTOL	TWICKENHAM	L	1G(5)-1PG3T(12)
081130	RICHMOND	RICHMOND	W	2G1DG2PG1T(23)-0
151130	OXFORD UNIVERSITY	TWICKENHAM	L	1G1T(8)-1G1PG1T(11)
221130	BLACKHEATH	TWICKENHAM	W	2G2T(16)-1T(3)
291130	NEWPORT	NEWPORT	L	0-4T(12)
061230	LEICESTER	TWICKENHAM	W	2G1PG(13)-1G2T(11)
131230	OLD MERCHANT TAYLORS	TEDDINGTON	W	2G1DG(14)-1PG1T(6)

201230	BIRKENHEAD PARK	TWICKENHAM	W	2G1PG2T(19)-1G(5)
271230	ARMY	PORTSMOUTH	W	3G2T(21)-3G(15)
030131	ST.BARTHOLOMEW'S HOSPITAL	WINCHMORE HILL	W	3G2T(21)-0
100131	BLACKHEATH	BLACKHEATH	C	
240131	CAMBRIDGE UNIVERSITY	CAMBRIDGE	L	2G(10)-4T(12)
310131	RICHMOND	TWICKENHAM	W	1G7T(26)-1PG2T(9)
070231	NORTHAMPTON	NORTHAMPTON	L	0-3G2T(21)
180231	EASTBOURNE	EASTBOURNE	P	
210231	OXFORD UNIVERSITY	OXFORD	L	2G1PG(13)-2G3T(19)
280231	UNITED SERVICES PORTSMOUTH	TWICKENHAM	W	2G1DG3T(23)-1PG1T(6)
070331	LEICESTER	LEICESTER	L	1PG(3)-5G1DG1T(32)
110331	EASTBOURNE	EASTBOURNE	C	
140331	OLD MERCHANT TAYLORS	TWICKENHAM	D	3G(15)-3G(15)
210331	OLD BLUES	HORSHAM	W	3G1T(18)-1G(5)
280331	LONDON SCOTTISH	RICHMOND	W	2G1T(13)-1G2T(11)
040431	SWANSEA	SWANSEA	W	7G(35)-1DG1PG1T(10)
060431	CARDIFF	CARDIFF	L	2G(10)-2G3T(19)
110431	BRISTOL	BRISTOL	L	1G(5)-2G2T(16)
180431	GLOUCESTER	TWICKENHAM	L	2G(10)-2G1T(13)

At the A.G.M. on 8th September 1931 the President stated that he hoped the backs would break themselves of the habit of presenting tries to their opponents, which was growing at the end of the previous season. Strong words indeed! New caps were presented to G.B. Coghlan, G.J. Dean, P.E. Dunkley, C.R. Hinds-Howell, P.E. Hodge and J.E. Hutton. On 27th January, it was decided that the fixtures with the Old Blues and Birkenhead Park be discontinued and be replaced by games against Aldershot Services, Cardiff or the Royal Navy. At the committee meeting on 6th July, the subject of redecorating the interior of the pavilion (at Fairfax Road) at an estimated cost of £60 was given the go ahead. When this work had been completed, the actual cost was £40 more than the estimate but the additional cost was approved. The matter of the replacement of defective goal posts was discussed and it was decided that a decision be left to the discretion of the honorary treasurer. Finally, it was decided that presentation caps were to be awarded for season 1931/32 but not purchased out of Club funds.

After disposing of Wasps (in a game which was only twenty five minutes each way) by the margin of eight points to three, we came unstuck against the Royal Military College (7-10). In this game, Irish international E.W.F. de Vere (Edward) Hunt guested for us (he gained five caps between 1930 and 1933) and in the next game (against Rosslyn Park) he opposed us and was on the losing side again (although he converted their only try) by the margin of 19-5. After beating London Scottish (16-3), drawing with U.S. Portsmouth (6-6), losing to Cambridge University (16-26) and defeating Guy's Hospital (20-9), we met Bath on 31st October for the first time since 1908 and in a one sided contest, we won 19-0. In the next match, against Bristol, we suffered our heaviest defeat of the season by twenty eight points to nine. When we played Birkenhead Park on 19th December, to make up our numbers, P.H. (Patrick) Davies from Sale substituted for us (he had won one cap for England in 1927) but did not improve our performance and we lost 3-8. Our two biggest wins of the season came within two weeks of each other, first on 12th December we defeated the O.M.T.s (23-3) then, on 26th December, we met the Army (at Portsmouth once again) and, despite trailing by a dropped goal (by H.J. (Howard) "Jay" Gould) to two tries, we came back to add tries by F.L. Hovde (converted by J.B.D. (Bruce) Chapman), J.A. Baiss, H.C. Pattisson and T.L. Tanner (the last two converted by J.D. Ronald) and a second dropped goal from Gould to finish with a score of 26-6.

On 16th January we did play at Aldershot (against the Aldershot Services not the Army) and managed to win by fourteen points to eight. Cambridge were beaten in the return (11-9) and Northampton were defeated by two Bruce Chapman penalties to nil before we made the trip down to Eastbourne. Although we had quite a reasonable side out, they saw us off by twenty one points to nine. We finally met the Old Millhillians at Headstone Lane on 27th February and managed to win 8-3 despite the fact that R.S. Spong (the England fly half) was playing for them. This game was sandwiched between Oxford University and Leicester completing doubles over us. After this we only had an 8-5 victory over the O.M.T.s to show for our efforts as our last five games were lost. The first four were the two Easter games, Gloucester and Bristol before London Welsh were met (for the first time since 1924) at Twickenham. Despite Hovde putting us into a 3-0 lead with a try, the Welsh came back before half time and got a try from their captain, A.H. Jones, (converted by F. Instone) and that is how it remained. We said goodbye to two long serving members of the first team this season with J.C. Hubbard making his last appearance in the Old Millhillians match (he had scored 386 points in his career, made up of 4 dropped goals, 16 penalty goals and 161 conversions) and Leo Price bowing out against U.S. Portsmouth on 10th October (he had managed 15 tries, 3 dropped goals and 1 conversion, a total of 59 points).

Bruce Chapman made the first of 60 appearances for the Club against Guy's Hospital on 24th October and a week later (against Bath) H.P. Skinner made the first of his 51 appearances. Only six players managed twenty or more appearances out of the thirty one matches played, they were Tony Prescott (27), Adams (25), Dunkley (24), Coghlan and Hinds-Howell (23) and Bruce Chapman (20). On the scoring side of things, F.L. Hovde managed just nine tries to finish top, Chapman kicked five penalties (to equal the record for a season) and Dunkley top scored with thirty eight points (4 tries, 2 penalties and 10 conversions). The team achieved just one new record, this was the ten penalties which were kicked. Other scoring consisted of 74 tries and 30 conversions which, added together, came to 336 points in total.

1931/32

120931	WASPS	TEDDINGTON	W	1G1T(8)-1T(3)
230931	ROYAL MILITARY COLLEGE	SANDHURST	L	1DG1T(7)-2G(10)
260931	ROSSLYN PARK	TWICKENHAM	W	2G1PG2T(19)-1G(5)
031031	LONDON SCOTTISH	RICHMOND	W	2G2T(16)-1T(3)
101031	UNITED SERVICES PORTSMOUTH	TWICKENHAM	D	2T(6)-2T(6)
171031	CAMBRIDGE UNIVERSITY	CAMBRIDGE	L	2G2T(16)-4G2T(26)
241031	GUY'S HOSPITAL	TWICKENHAM	W	4G(20)-3T(9)
311031	BATH	TWICKENHAM	W	2G3T(19)-0
071131	BRISTOL	BRISTOL	L	1PG2T(9)-3G1DG3T(28)

141131	RICHMOND	TWICKENHAM	W	2G1T(13)-1T(3)
211131	OXFORD UNIVERSITY	TWICKENHAM	L	2T(6)-3G1DG(19)
281131	BLACKHEATH	BLACKHEATH	W	1G1PG1T(11)-1G1PG(8)
051231	LEICESTER	LEICESTER	L	0-1G2T(11)
121231	OLD MERCHANT TAYLORS	TEDDINGTON(A)	W	2G1DG3T(23)-1T(3)
191231	BIRKENHEAD PARK	BIRKENHEAD	L	1T(3)-1G1T(8)
261231	ARMY	PORTSMOUTH	W	3G2DG1T(26)-2T(6)
090132	BLACKHEATH	TWICKENHAM	W	2G1DG1T(17)-1G1T(8)
160132	ALDERSHOT SERVICES	ALDERSHOT	W	1G1PG2T(14)-1G1T(8)
230132	CAMBRIDGE UNIVERSITY	TWICKENHAM	W	1G2T(11)-3T(9)
300132	RICHMOND	RICHMOND	L	1T(3)-2G(10)
060232	NORTHAMPTON	TWICKENHAM	W	2PG(6)-0
130232	OLD BLUES	FAIRLOP	C	
170232	EASTBOURNE	EASTBOURNE	L	3T(9)-3G2T(21)
200232	OXFORD UNIVERSITY	OXFORD	L	4T(12)-1G1MG3T(17)
270232	OLD MILLHILLIANS	HEADSTONE LANE	W	1G1PG(8)-1T(3)
050332	LEICESTER	LEICESTER	L	1G2T(11)-1DG3T(13)
120332	OLD MERCHANT TAYLORS	TEDDINGTON	W	1G1PG(8)-1G(5)
260332	SWANSEA	SWANSEA	L	1T(3)-1G5T(20)
280332	CARDIFF	CARDIFF	L	1DG1PG1T(10)-3G1PG2T(24)
020432	GLOUCESTER	GLOUCESTER	L	2G1T(13)-3G1T(18)
090432	BRISTOL	TWICKENHAM	L	1PG1T(6)-1G1DG(9)
160432	LONDON WELSH	TWICKENHAM	L	1T(3)-1G(5)

At the A.G.M. on 8th September, the President referred to the loss sustained to the Club by the death of H. Hughes-Onslow. He had been a most valuable and devoted member of the committee and had been largely responsible for the reconstruction of the Club after the war. The Club also mourned the death of N.E. White, who had been killed while flying. Adrian Stoop (the President) had, by this time, started giving a small speech on the previous season's efforts on the field by both the forwards and backs. According to him, the forwards had given a good account of themselves under the captaincy of Peter Adams, but the backs had shown a lack of intelligence. Their prevailing idea appeared to be whenever possible to throw away a winning lead. Stoop obviously did not believe in pulling his punches! It was decided that every player in an away match should contribute two shillings towards the Club's expenditure on his behalf. S.A. Block was the only person to whom a new cap was awarded. A loss of £526 was reported, this was due to diminished gate receipts and the £100 cost of the upkeep of the Teddington ground. Adrian Stoop was elected to the Presidency of the Rugby Football Union for season 1932/33, becoming the second Harlequin to hold this office (V.H. Cartwright had been the first in 1928/29).

Clifford Gibbs captained the side during the 1932/33 season, his last but one before his retirement. To open the season, we had a game, once again, against Wasps. We played the Chapman brothers in the centre (Bruce and Ken), they were the sons of Herbert Chapman (the famous and successful manager of Arsenal Football Club). Ken was to score ten of our points that day (one try, one penalty and two conversions) in a

19-5 win. This game also saw the last appearance of Peter Adams, he had captained the side on forty eight occasions, scored nine tries and a conversion during his career and had played in thirteen out of the last fourteen seasons. Our next match was at Sandhurst against the R.M.C., we made eleven changes from the Wasps game and duly lost 14-19. This was Gibbs' first game as captain, having missed the Wasps fixture. His second was altogether more successful and he scored a try in a 9-3 win over Rosslyn Park at the Old Deer Park. In a close match with London Scottish at Twickenham on 1st October, we just got home thanks to a dropped goal from Bruce Chapman in the first half. He did the same against Guy's Hospital on 22nd October (this time in the second half) to help us to a 7-6 win. The following week we met Bath on their home patch and six points to each side (us in the first half and them in the second half) saw a drawn game. After we had beaten Richmond (5-0) on 12th November, we went through a bad patch at home, losing three on the trot to Oxford University (5-6), Blackheath (10-18) and Leicester (13-22). The rot was stopped with a victory over Birkenhead Park on 17th December by eighteen points to five.

Over the Christmas and New Year period, Richmond got us back with a narrow win of their own (5-9) and the Army (met at Aldershot) defeated us for the fifth time in thirteen meetings (8-11). This match saw the last appearance of James Worton, he had scored some 121 points (23 tries and 26 conversions) in his career. Blackheath completed the double over us, the Cambridge University return was cancelled and we beat Northampton by thirteen points to seven. At Eastbourne on 15th February, we played four internationals (one old, two current and one future). Hutton was in his last season with us, C.L. (Carlton) Troop was making his only appearance for us (a few days after winning the first of his two England caps), Reginald Bolton (who had made the first of at least 120 appearances for us against Northampton on 4th February and went on to gain five caps for England) and N.F. (Noel) McGrath (who gained one cap for Ireland in 1934) a debutant against U.S. Portsmouth on 8th October. G.B. Coghlan was making the last of his 88 appearances and, along with McGrath, scored a try in a 23-5 win. Incidentally, our touch judge that day was Henry Wakelam and the referee was George Carey (of Twickenham kick-off fame). On 4th March, we went up to Leicester to try and avoid a fifth straight defeat against them. In the first half, Leicester took an early lead through tries by M.P. Crowe and S.H. Saunders (converted by J.H.F. Edmiston) but we came back to lead by half time with tries of our own by Gibbs and Hodge (both converted by Hutton). Bolton put us further ahead with a try, R.A. Buckingham replied in kind for the home side before another try by Hodge and a third conversion from Hutton saw us home 18-11.

The following week saw our biggest win of the season when we played the O.M.T.s at Twickenham. By half time, Brook and H.A. Style had scored tries for us to lead 6-0. After this, five further tries were scored by Gibbs (2), George Gray, Hodge and Thompson (three of which were converted by Style) to leave the final score reading 27-0. After this match (although we defeated the Old Blues (13-11) and Bristol (11-3) our season went downhill in the last few weeks with defeats by London Scottish (5-6), Gloucester (21-28), Swansea (5-15) and Cardiff (9-12). Apart from the three already mentioned, the only other new international in our ranks this season was C.E. St.J. (Charles) Beamish, who gained twelve caps for Ireland between 1933 and 1938 and made the first of his eight appearances for us against London Scottish on 1st October. In the thirty games played by the first team, only forty eight players were used, this was the lowest total since forty three were used in the twenty two matches of the 1896/97 season. The top appearance maker was Tony Prescott with twenty seven, he was five ahead of Hinds-Howell and Hodge on twenty two, Reeve had twenty one and three followed on twenty (Bruce Chapman, McGrath and Skinner). Gibbs proved to be top try scorer with 17 (his one conversion making him top points scorer on 53), Bruce Chapman again equalled the penalties record with five and H.A. Style kicked fifteen conversions. The team set no new records but scored 75 tries, 2 dropped goals, 8 penalties and 39 conversions for a total of 335 points.

1932/33

100932	WASPS	TEDDINGTON	W	2G1PG2T(19)-1G(5)
210932	ROYAL MILITARY COLLEGE	SANDHURST	L	1G1PG2T(14)-2G2PG1T(19)
240932	ROSSLYN PARK	OLD DEER PARK	W	3T(9)-1PG(3)
011032	LONDON SCOTTISH	TWICKENHAM	W	1DG(4)-0
081032	UNITED SERVICES PORTSMOUTH	PORTSMOUTH	W	1PG3T(12)-1T(3)
151032	CAMBRIDGE UNIVERSITY	TWICKENHAM	W	3G1PG(18)-2G1T(13)
221032	GUY'S HOSPITAL	HONOR OAK PARK	W	1DG1T(7)-1PG1T(6)
291032	BATH	BATH	D	1PG1T(6)-2T(6)
051132	BRISTOL	TWICKENHAM	L	0-1T(3)
121132	RICHMOND	RICHMOND	W	1G(5)-0
191132	OXFORD UNIVERSITY	TWICKENHAM	L	1G(5)-2T(6)
261132	BLACKHEATH	TWICKENHAM	L	2G(10)-1G1DG3T(18)
031232	LEICESTER	TWICKENHAM	L	2G1T(13)-2G4T(22)
101232	OLD MERCHANT TAYLORS	TEDDINGTON(A)	W	1G2T(11)-1T(3)
171232	BIRKENHEAD PARK	TWICKENHAM	W	3G1T(18)-1G(5)
241232	RICHMOND	TWICKENHAM	L	1G(5)-3T(9)
311232	ARMY	ALDERSHOT	L	1G1T(8)-1G2T(11)
070133	ST.BARTHOLOMEW'S HOSPITAL	WINCHMORE HILL	W	1G2T(11)-2T(6)
140133	BLACKHEATH	BLACKHEATH	L	1PG1T(6)-2G3T(19)
280133	CAMBRIDGE UNIVERSITY	CAMBRIDGE	C	
040233	NORTHAMPTON	NORTHAMPTON	W	2G1T(13)-1DG1T(7)
150233	EASTBOURNE	EASTBOURNE	W	4G1T(23)-1G(5)
180233	OXFORD UNIVERSITY	OXFORD	W	1PG2T(9)-1G1T(8)
250233	UNITED SERVICES PORTSMOUTH	TWICKENHAM	C	
040333	LEICESTER	LEICESTER	W	3G1T(18)-1G2T(11)
110333	OLD MERCHANT TAYLORS	TWICKENHAM	W	3G4T(27)-0
180333	OLD BLUES	TWICKENHAM	W	2G1T(13)-1G1PG1T(11)
250333	LONDON SCOTTISH	RICHMOND	L	1G(5)-2T(6)
010433	GLOUCESTER	TWICKENHAM	L	3G1PG1T(21)-3G1DG3T(28)
080433	BRISTOL	BRISTOL	W	1G2T(11)-1PG(3)
150433	SWANSEA	SWANSEA	L	1G(5)-1G1DG2T(15)
170433	CARDIFF	CARDIFF	L	3T(9)-1G1DG1T(12)

At the Annual General Meeting on 12th September, the President expressed that the criticism he made regarding the 1931/32 season applied equally to 1932/33 although he did add that some improvement had been made. A loss of £84 12s 1d on the season was reported but good savings had been made with regards to travelling expenses and taxation. It was reported that W.H. Devonshire had passed away (he had made 91 appearances for the Club between 1896 and 1901). New caps were awarded to N.F. McGrath and F.D. Russell-Roberts. On 13th May, a letter from the manager of the Caswall Bay Hotel was read out (enclosing a builder's estimate for repairs) regarding the damage caused by the team during the Easter tour. It was decided that Mr. Wakefield should examine the situation on the spot and report back to the committee after discussion with the hotel manager. This he duly did and reported back (on 4th July) that the damage could be repaired for £7 10s rather than the £35 claimed by the manager. The committee decided that the captain be instructed to write to members of the team with a view to collecting the amount of the damages as estimated by Mr. Wakefield or thereabouts. The said money was eventually collected (but only after some members of the team had been personally interviewed by the captain of the Club) and hopefully the manager of the hotel was happy. From this wholly unacceptable situation stemmed a number of letters criticising the general conduct of the Club. The honorary treasurer wrote in to suggest that all administrative officers of the Club be changed. R.H. Hamilton-Wickes proposed and A.A. Moller seconded that a vote of confidence be taken in the President and honorary secretary, this motion was unanimously passed. The general opinion was that the sort of ailments from which the Club was suffering lay in the fact that there was no esprit de corps and that individual members did not realise that they were personally responsible for the honour and good name of the Club. This matter was to be further raised at the annual general meeting in September 1934 (it would seem that several members felt that the Club had a serious problem with this situation which had arisen from the Caswall Bay Hotel incident).

Philip Dunkley was to captain us for this and the next two seasons. Our first game of the 1933/34 season was not against Wasps, for a change, but against Rosslyn Park because a game scheduled to be played against the Royal Military College was cancelled. They were defeated, at Twickenham, by ten points to nil as were Bath (19-9), U.S. Portsmouth (14-0) and Guy's Hospital (18-9). Between times, London Scottish were beaten at Richmond (21-8) but Cambridge University defeated us at Cambridge (3-14). The 6-6 draw that followed against Richmond was the first in the fixture since 1904. From this point up to Christmas our form fell apart as Oxford University, Blackheath, Leicester and Richmond all beat us pointless. Our only victory came against Cardiff (only our fifth over them), Style (one penalty and one conversion) and Bruce Chapman, T.H. (Humphrey) Tilling and C.L. Sparke with tries were our scorers in a 14-0 final score. We managed to beat the Army (15-8) and Blackheath in the return (13-8) before meeting the Old Millhillians for the second and final time. The result was the same as the first time (although slightly closer), the only score being a dropped goal from J.H.E. (John) Howarth before half time. In the return with Cambridge at Twickenham on 27th January, it looked all over for us at half time when we trailed 8-22 having been outscored by five goals (including one dropped and one penalty) to a goal and a try. The second half was a much better one for us and we came within a whisker of snatching victory. H.A. Style scored a penalty and converted two of our three tries by J.F.G. Dingle, Tilling and F.D. (Douglas) Russell-Roberts but a single try by Johnston and a conversion by Parker gave them victory by 27-24.

Northampton were seen off the following week (21-6) as were Eastbourne (21-7) but the Aldershot Services defeated us 8-14. After these games we fell apart completely and nine successive matches were lost (this was our worst run since nine games were lost in the 1904/05 season), this meant that Oxford, Leicester and Bristol completed doubles over us. The Royal Navy were met on 24th February for the first time since 1923 and they beat us by twenty one points to sixteen. Cardiff got their own back (5-9) and Swansea equalled their biggest win over us from two seasons before (3-20) but we did finish with a win over London Welsh at Twickenham on 21st April by thirteen points to six. New internationals appearing for us during the season were A.G. (Arthur) "Geoff" Butler (who won two England caps in 1937 and went on to make at least 88 appearances for the first team) who made his debut against Eastbourne on 14th February, R.E. (Robin) Prescott (six England caps between 1937 and 1939 and at least 126 appearances) debuted against Rosslyn Park on 23rd September, A.L. (Anthony) Warr (two caps for England in 1934) made the first of his three appearances for us against the Army on 30th December and finally, V.J. (Victor) Lyttle (three caps for Ireland, one in 1938 and two in 1939) making his only appearance for us against Cambridge University on 21st October. Other notable first appearances were John Howarth (who went on to play 57 times for the first XV) against Rosslyn Park on 23rd September and G.E.C. Hudson (82) against Richmond on 23rd December. For any new people, we nearly always have to say goodbye to some of the old ones and this season was no exception. Clifford Gibbs made his last appearance on 18th November against Oxford University and had scored some 481 points in his career with the Club (155 tries, 3 dropped goals and 2 conversions) and Philip Hodge, after scoring 163 points (51 tries and 5 conversions) played for the last time against Bristol on 7th April, he had captained the side on just one occasion (against Blackheath on 25th November 1933). We used fifty six players during the course of thirty one games played in this season with the following making the most appearances Tony Prescott and Chris Thompson (26), Dunkley and Robin Prescott (25), Russell-Roberts (23), Bolton (22), Skinner (21) and Dean and Tilling (20). The joint top try scorers were H.L.V. Faviell, Gibbs and Robin Prescott with just five each (this was the lowest since Charles Hammond got five in the 1904/05 season). H.A. Style set a new record for penalties with six (his one try and eighteen conversions allowed him to top points score as well with 57) while the team only managed 63 tries and 36 conversions to notch up just 290 points (this was our lowest total since 1919/20).

1933/34

200933	ROYAL MILITARY COLLEGE	SANDHURST	C	
230933	ROSSLYN PARK	TWICKENHAM	W	2G(10)-0
300933	BATH	TWICKENHAM	W	2G3T(19)-1PG2T(9)
071033	LONDON SCOTTISH	RICHMOND	W	3G2PG(21)-1G1T(8)
141033	UNITED SERVICES PORTSMOUTH	TWICKENHAM	W	1G3T(14)-0
211033	CAMBRIDGE UNIVERSITY	CAMBRIDGE	L	1PG(3)-1G3T(14)
281033	GUY'S HOSPITAL	TWICKENHAM	W	3G1PG(18)-2PG1T(9)
041133	BRISTOL	BRISTOL	L	1DG1T(7)-1PG2T(9)
111133	RICHMOND	TWICKENHAM	D	2T(6)-2T(6)
181133	OXFORD UNIVERSITY	TWICKENHAM	L	0-1DG3T(13)
251133	BLACKHEATH	BLACKHEATH	L	0-1PG3T(12)
021233	LEICESTER	TWICKENHAM	L	0-1DG(4)
091233	OLD MERCHANT TAYLORS	TEDDINGTON(A)	C	
161233	CARDIFF	TWICKENHAM	W	1G1PG2T(14)-0
231233	RICHMOND	RICHMOND	L	0-3G1T(18)
301233	ARMY	TWICKENHAM	W	3G(15)-1G1T(8)
060134	ST.BARTHOLOMEW'S HOSPITAL	WINCHMORE HILL	L	2G(10)-4T(12)
130134	BLACKHEATH	TWICKENHAM	W	2G1T(13)-1G1T(8)
200134	OLD MILLHILLIANS	HEADSTONE LANE	W	1DG(4)-0

270134	CAMBRIDGE UNIVERSITY	TWICKENHAM	L	3G1PG2T(24)-4G1DG1PG(27)
030234	NORTHAMPTON	TWICKENHAM	W	3G2T(21)-2T(6)
100234	ALDERSHOT SERVICES	ALDERSHOT	L	1G1T(8)-1G3T(14)
140234	EASTBOURNE	EASTBOURNE	W	3G2T(21)-1DG1T(7)
170234	OXFORD UNIVERSITY	OXFORD	L	1T(3)-1MG1PG1T(9)
240234	ROYAL NAVY	PORTSMOUTH	L	2G1PG1T(16)-3G2T(21)
030334	LEICESTER	LEICESTER	L	0-1G1DG1PG1T(15)
100334	OLD MERCHANT TAYLORS	TEDDINGTON(A)	L	1G1T(8)-3G2T(21)
240334	LONDON SCOTTISH	TEDDINGTON	L	2T(6)-2G1T(13)
310334	SWANSEA	SWANSEA	L	1T(3)-2G1DG2T(20)
020434	CARDIFF	CARDIFF	L	1G(5)-1G1DG(9)
070434	BRISTOL	TWICKENHAM	L	1G1T(8)-1G3T(14)
140434	GLOUCESTER	GLOUCESTER	L	0-1G1T(8)
210434	LONDON WELSH	TWICKENHAM	W	2G1T(13)-2T(6)

At the A.G.M. on 10th September, it was announced that A.B. Cipriani (who must have been one of our oldest surviving members) had passed away. In his will he had bequeathed to the Club the sum of £500 and his debenture in Harlequin Estates Limited. It was noted that he had been captain of the Club in seasons 1887/88 and 1893/94 and was vice-captain between 1888 and 1893. The honorary treasurer informed the meeting that he was very dissatisfied with the management and conduct of the Club and by way of bringing matters to a head, he had tendered his resignation. The President apologised to him and appealed for him to withdraw his resignation, this he did to the great satisfaction of all the members present. He then went on to present the accounts, these showed a loss of £429 16s 8d which was said to be due entirely to the great fall in gate receipts. At a Committee meeting on 5th October, it was announced that H. Gardiner (who had been elected in 1905 and had been the auditor since 1910) had died. New caps were awarded to R. Bolton, R.E. Prescott, H.P. Skinner and C. Thompson. On 3rd June, more caps were awarded to P.W.P. Brook, A.G. Butler, K.H. Chapman, B.J. Collins, H.L. Faviell, E.A. Hamilton-Hill, J.H.E. Howarth, G.E.C. Hudson, K.S. Robinson, J.D. Ronald and D.H. Swayne. It was resolved to apply for a licence to sell alcohol at Teddington and Tony Prescott's offer to present a dart board to the Teddington pavilion was gratefully accepted.

We were due to start the 1934/35 season against Wasps (again!) but, the difference this time was that this game was to have been played on their ground at Sudbury. Unfortunately, it was cancelled so we actually started against and defeated Rosslyn Park. This was followed by an away win over Bath (6-0), a home win over London Scottish (17-4) and another away win against U.S. Portsmouth (16-14). In this last game the home side needed a conversion from their last try to tie the scores but, unfortunately for them, Chris Thompson deflected G.M. Sladen's attempt to give us the win. Our unbeaten record fell (as it had the previous season) to Cambridge University. They scored a goal and a dropped goal in the first half while we replied with tries from H.L. Faviell and George Gray (our wingers) but it was not enough and the students triumphed by nine points to six. In the absence of our captain (P.E. Dunkley) against U.S. Portsmouth and Cambridge, Geoffrey Dean captained the side for the only times in his career. On 10th November, we met Richmond at the Athletic Ground and suffered our heaviest defeat of the season. They went into a thirteen point lead by half time and although Brook did score a try for us in the second half we still lost by ten points. This game was sandwiched between a draw with Bristol (11-11) and a loss to Oxford University (6-8) after which we defeated Blackheath (8-6), Leicester (10-4) and O.M.T.s (10-0) before losing to Cardiff at Twickenham on 15th December by nine points to three. Our win over Blackheath was our second in a run of eight consecutive victories over them.

We managed to avoid Richmond completing a double over us by winning 8-3 and saw off the Army at Portsmouth (10-0) before defeating St. Bartholomew's Hospital (16-0). On 12th January, we completed the double over Blackheath with a great comeback. We had trailed 5-9 at half time (each side scoring a goal, Blackheath adding one of the dropped variety) before Ken Chapman kicked a couple of penalties (Blackheath replying with another dropped goal and a try) to leave us trailing 11-16. After this it was left to John Howarth to close the gap to two points with a try and then win the game with a dropped goal (18-16). Oxford and Cambridge Universities were both beaten in return games but Northampton beat us (6-12) and Leicester were drawn with (5-5). On 16th March we met the Aldershot Services for what proved to be the only time at Twickenham and defeated them easily by twenty three points to five. The following week we completed the double over London Scottish before notching up our biggest win of the season. Our visitors were Gloucester who came in the knowledge that we had not beaten them since 1927. Things did not look too good for us as our visitors got a try and a dropped goal for a seven point lead before we started to get our act together. By half time, we led 11-10 with G.E.C. Hudson and B.J. Collins scoring tries and Ken Chapman kicking one conversion and a penalty in reply to which Gloucester had scored their second try. The second half was a totally different story as Geoff Butler (2) and Hudson got further tries, Howarth dropped a goal and Chapman added two conversions and another penalty to leave us victors by a margin of thirty one points to ten. Our now yearly visit to Eastbourne ended in our second defeat at their hands (13-19). A weakened side travelled down on 3rd April (after the match scheduled to take place on 27th February had been postponed), we played Brook and Hamilton-Hill (normally back row forwards) in the centre and on the wing respectively and the only other players in the team from the Gloucester game the previous Saturday were Robin Prescott and B.G. Smith. We ended with a victory over the London Welsh at Twickenham (15-10) and one win and one loss on the Easter tour. Swansea beat us by four points on the Saturday (16-20) and we defeated Cardiff on the Monday (13-3) to give us our twenty first victory in thirty one matches.

We only lost eight games during the course of the season, the smallest amount since six were lost in 1925/26. Only one new international player appeared for us during the course of the season, he was F.J.V. (Frederick) Ford who gained his only cap for Wales in 1939 and appeared for us first against Eastbourne on 3rd April and went on to play ten games in total. The Eastbourne match also saw the sixty ninth and last appearance of D.H. Duder, a forward, who had made his debut in 1927. Also making his last appearance was James Reeve (against Rosslyn Park on 22nd September) who had scored 125 points (41 tries and one conversion) in his career with the Club and who, sadly, was to lose his life in a motor accident shortly after. We did welcome new boy K.S. (Ken) Robinson against London Scottish on 6th October, he went on to make 72 appearances. Of the fifty two players used, the top appearance makers were Hudson (30), Ken Chapman and Tony Prescott (29), Howarth and J.D. Ronald (28) and Robin Prescott (27). On the scoring side of things, Geoff Butler got seventeen tries, Howarth equalled the dropped goal record with three, Ken Chapman set a new mark for penalties with twelve which, when added to his thirty two conversions and two tries, made him the first player since Jack Hubbard in the 1926/27 season to score over one hundred points with 106. As a team, seventy seven tries were scored (thirty nine were converted), the penalty record went with Ken Chapman scoring the only ones, four goals were dropped and in total 361 points were scored.

1934/35

080934	WASPS	SUDBURY	C	
220934	ROSSLYN PARK	TWICKENHAM	W	2G1T(13)-1G1T(8)
290934	BATH	BATH	W	1PG1T(6)-0
061034	LONDON SCOTTISH	TWICKENHAM	W	2G1DG1T(17)-1DG(4)
131034	UNITED SERVICES PORTSMOUTH	PORTSMOUTH	W	2G2T(16)-1G3T(14)
201034	CAMBRIDGE UNIVERSITY	TWICKENHAM	L	2T(6)-1G1DG(9)
271034	GUY'S HOSPITAL	HONOR OAK PARK	W	1DG1PG1T(10)-1G(5)
031134	BRISTOL	TWICKENHAM	D	1G1PG1T(11)-1G2T(11)
101134	RICHMOND	RICHMOND	L	1T(3)-2G1T(13)
171134	OXFORD UNIVERSITY	TWICKENHAM	L	2T(6)-1G1T(8)
241134	BLACKHEATH	TWICKENHAM	W	1G1T(8)-1PG1T(6)
011234	LEICESTER	TWICKENHAM	W	2G(10)-1DG(4)
081234	OLD MERCHANT TAYLORS	TEDDINGTON(A)	W	2G(10)-0
151234	CARDIFF	TWICKENHAM	L	1PG(3)-1G1DG(9)
221234	RICHMOND	TWICKENHAM	W	1G1T(8)-1T(3)
291234	ARMY	PORTSMOUTH	W	2G(10)-0
050135	ST.BARTHOLOMEW'S HOSPITAL	WINCHMORE HILL	W	2G1PG1T(16)-0
120135	BLACKHEATH	BLACKHEATH	W	1G1DG2PG1T(18)-1G2DG1T(16)
260135	CAMBRIDGE UNIVERSITY	CAMBRIDGE	W	2T(6)-1G(5)
020235	NORTHAMPTON	NORTHAMPTON	L	1PG1T(6)-1PG3T(12)
160235	OXFORD UNIVERSITY	OXFORD	W	3T(9)-1G(5)
230235	UNITED SERVICES PORTSMOUTH	TWICKENHAM	W	1G2T(11)-1T(3)
270235	EASTBOURNE	EASTBOURNE	P	
020335	LEICESTER	LEICESTER	D	1G(5)-1G(5)
090335	OLD MERCHANT TAYLORS	TWICKENHAM	W	3G2T(21)-1PG2T(9)
160335	ALDERSHOT SERVICES	TWICKENHAM	W	1G1PG5T(23)-1G(5)
230335	LONDON SCOTTISH	RICHMOND	W	3G(15)-1G(5)
300335	GLOUCESTER	TWICKENHAM	W	3G1DG2PG2T(31)-1DG2T(10)
030435	EASTBOURNE	EASTBOURNE	L	2G1T(13)-2G2PG1T(19)
060435	BRISTOL	BRISTOL	L	1PG1T(6)-1DG1T(7)
130435	LONDON WELSH	TWICKENHAM	W	3G(15)-1DG2T(10)
200435	SWANSEA	SWANSEA	L	2G2T(16)-1G1PG4T(20)
220435	CARDIFF	CARDIFF	W	2G1T(13)-1T(3)

At the A.G.M. on 10th September, a loss of £167 7s 2d was reported, this was a lot less than the previous season so must be looked upon as some sort of success. The President mentioned that congratulations were due to P.E. Dunkley on a most successful and enjoyable season, towards the end of which, some very skilful football had been played and that the Club was greatly indebted to the backs who had given up so many Sundays in the early part of the season to practice (in particular, J.H.E. Howarth). The list of Vice Presidents now read as follows, J.G.G. Birkett, E.M.C. Clarke, H.P. Surtees, Bishop of Labuan, H.B.T. Wakelam, F.M. Stoop, R.H. King,

C.A. Lyon, G.V. Carey, W.W. Wakefield, J.C. Gibbs, V.G. Davies, C.R. Style, P.W. Adams, A.L. Gracie, H.P. Marshall and R.H. Hamilton-Wickes. At a meeting on 11th October, a resolution was carried on the casting vote of the Chairman (Adrian Stoop) that Dunkley and Stoop should be jointly responsible for selection of the team. In the case of a disagreement, Dunkley's opinion would prevail on the forwards and Stoop's on the backs. On 8th November, a sub-committee was appointed to investigate the possibility of buying the O.M.T.s ground at Teddington. On 6th August, a new cap was awarded to P.N. Keymer and a proposal by the President urging that all 1st XV matches be transferred to Fairfax Road received no support. The death of F.S. Schooling was reported - he was one of, if not, the oldest surviving member (he had made his debut against University College on 8th February 1868).

Our first game in the 1935/36 season was against Wasps at Sudbury and this time the game went ahead, on 14th September. We managed a nice win (31-12) with Ken Chapman scoring a try and kicking five conversions and a penalty for a personal haul of sixteen points. It must be noted that at this time, Wasps were not the force they have now become. Our unbeaten record only lasted one more match (when we defeated Rosslyn Park 14-10) before London Scottish defeated us at Richmond on 5th October by thirteen points to eight. The following week we met the Combined Services for the first time, at Twickenham. After a close game, a burst of thirteen points after half time set us up for a 21-16 victory. Our biggest win of the season came against Guy's Hospital on 26th October. We had led 13-0 by half time with tries by G.D.A. Lundon (2) and W.T. Anderson and two conversions from Chapman. In the second half Lundon completed his hat trick, Anderson got his second and Dunkley and Collins added further tries (although Chapman could only add two conversions) and Howarth dropped a goal. Guy's could only manage one try which left us winners by a thirty point margin (33-3). Losses followed to Bristol (3-4), Richmond (8-20) and Oxford University (6-21) before we started to put together a few wins. Blackheath were beaten on their home ground (11-0) and Bath (9-5) and Leicester (11-5) were beaten at Twickenham while Cardiff were met on our "A"XV ground at Teddington and were also defeated (15-6).

Although Richmond and Oxford University (against whom we only had fourteen men for the entire first half) completed doubles over us, we lost only two other games for the rest of the season. We managed doubles over Blackheath and Leicester and other victories followed against Northampton (12-8) and Aldershot Services (13-11). In the Northampton game, J.E. (Jack) Manchester (nine caps) made his only appearance for us. He had led the Third All Blacks on their tour of the four home countries, they defeated Scotland and Ireland and lost to Wales (by one point) and England (0-13). We had Philip Dunkley and Edward Hamilton-Hill in the victorious England side that day, although neither scored. At Eastbourne on 4th March, we had to borrow three players from Eastbourne College to make up our numbers. They were E.I. Davis, R. Gray and B.G. Smith (the last two had played for us before during the season). With a full team, we ran out winners by twenty eight points to seventeen. We finished the season very well by winning our last five games including Bristol (8-0), Swansea (3-0), Cardiff (17-3) (this was to be our last victory over them for some eighteen years) and finally on 18th April, at Gloucester (10-5).

We lost three experienced players at the end of the season, John Cole made his last appearance against London Welsh on 29th February, he had scored 106 points (34 tries and 1 dropped goal) in his career and had captained the side on just one occasion, John Howarth played his last match against Gloucester on 18th April, he had managed thirty seven points (3 tries and 7 dropped goals) and Tony Prescott made his last appearance against the Combined Services on 12th October. Newcomers included M.E. Golding (who went on to make 62 appearances) against Cardiff on 21st December and R.B. Horsley (63) against Richmond on 9th November. Apart from Jack Manchester, our only other new international was W.B. Young, who went on to gain ten Scottish caps between 1937 and 1948 and made his first appearance for us against Rosslyn Park on 28th September. Horsley scored the most tries with 12 and Ken Chapman got the most points with 99 (2 tries, 7 penalties and 36 conversions). The team managed 84 tries and 33 conversions as well as 5 dropped goals and 7 penalties for a total of 359 points. Out of twenty nine games, the top appearance makers were Ken Chapman (28), B.J. Collins (27) and G.E.C. Hudson (25).

The British Lions were off to Argentina again in July and August 1936 for a ten match tour. Charles Beamish, Philip Dunkley, Thomas Huskisson and Robin Prescott made the trip and all except Dunkley made the test side. As usual, no caps were awarded for this but it was another successful tour with all games being won. It was the last time the Lions would tour Argentina.

1935/36

140935	WASPS	SUDBURY	W	5G1PG1T(31)-1G1DG1T(12)
280935	ROSSLYN PARK	TWICKENHAM	W	2G1DG(14)-2G(10)
051035	LONDON SCOTTISH	RICHMOND	L	1G1PG(8)-2G1T(13)
121035	COMBINED SERVICES	TWICKENHAM	W	3G2T(21)-2G2T(16)
191035	CAMBRIDGE UNIVERSITY	TWICKENHAM	W	1G5T(20)-1DG1PG(7)
261035	GUY'S HOSPITAL	TWICKENHAM	W	4G1DG3T(33)-1T(3)
021135	BRISTOL	BRISTOL	L	1T(3)-1DG(4)
091135	RICHMOND	TWICKENHAM	L	1G1T(8)-2G1DG2T(20)
161135	OXFORD UNIVERSITY	TWICKENHAM	L	1PG1T(6)-3G1PG1T(21)
231135	BLACKHEATH	BLACKHEATH	W	1G2T(11)-0
301135	BATH	TWICKENHAM	W	1PG2T(9)-1G(5)
071235	LEICESTER	TWICKENHAM	W	1G2T(11)-1G(5)
141235	OLD MERCHANT TAYLORS	TEDDINGTON(A)	W	1G3T(14)-0
211235	CARDIFF	TEDDINGTON	W	3G(15)-1PG1T(6)
281235	RICHMOND	RICHMOND	L	1PG(3)-1G(5)
110136	BLACKHEATH	TWICKENHAM	W	1G1DG3T(18)-0
180136	ARMY	TEDDINGTON	C	
250136	CAMBRIDGE UNIVERSITY	CAMBRIDGE	C	
010236	NORTHAMPTON	TWICKENHAM	W	1G1DG1T(12)-1G1T(8)
080236	ALDERSHOT SERVICES	ALDERSHOT	W	2G1T(13)-1G2T(11)
150236	OXFORD UNIVERSITY	OXFORD	L	1G1T(8)-3G(15)
220236	UNITED SERVICES PORTSMOUTH	PORTSMOUTH	W	2G1T(13)-1G1T(8)
290236	LONDON WELSH	TWICKENHAM	L	4T(12)-1G2PG1T(14)
040336	EASTBOURNE	EASTBOURNE	W	5G1T(28)-1G4T(17)
070336	LEICESTER	LEICESTER	W	1G3T(14)-1G2T(11)
140336	OLD MERCHANT TAYLORS	TEDDINGTON(A)	L	1T(3)-1G2PG(11)
280336	LONDON SCOTTISH	TEDDINGTON	W	2G1PG(13)-1T(3)
040436	BRISTOL	TWICKENHAM	W	1G1T(8)-0
110436	SWANSEA	SWANSEA	W	1PG(3)-0
130436	CARDIFF	CARDIFF	W	2G1DG1T(17)-1T(3)
180436	GLOUCESTER	GLOUCESTER	W	2G(10)-1G(5)

At the A.G.M. on 15th September, the President referred to the disastrous financial results of the past season in spite of the good football played by the 1st XV and congratulated Philip Dunkley, Peter Brook and Reginald Bolton on regaining their England caps after an interval of several years. At a meeting on 5th October, caps were awarded to P.E. Hodge, D.B. Willis, F.M.H. Taylor, A.M. Paterson (who was to die while serving in the R.A.F. in 1939), B.G. Smith, T.H. Tilling, W.P. Heath, B.D. Napper, C.F. St.J. Briggs and K.B.B. Cross. The honorary treasurer assured the meeting that the Club was rapidly heading towards bankruptcy and urged that immediate steps be taken to bring about a more satisfactory state of affairs (this subject was still not solved when hostilities broke out in 1939). The President then urged the advisability and desirability of completing the proposed stand at Teddington and transferring the 1st XV to that ground. It was recognised that if this was adopted, it would be necessary to discontinue the "A" XV. The following March, the President's proposal of the desirability to transfer 1st XV matches to Teddington was defeated by a large majority. One proposal which did get passed was C.R. Hinds-Howell's (seconded by Ken Chapman) that inquiries be made from St. Mary's Hospital as to whether they would be prepared to lease to the Club a pitch at Udney Park Road when they took over from the Old Merchant Taylors with the idea that dressing accommodation be provided at Fairfax Road for the teams playing at Udney Park Road. Unfortunately, St. Mary's replied that they were unable to provide a pitch on the days when the 1st XV had home matches. Back on 2nd November, a letter was received from W.G. Beauchamp (an old member) in Colombo asking permission for the Harlequin Association Football Club of Colombo to use the colours (jerseys) of the Club, this request was granted. In January 1938, the Ceylon Naval Volunteer Force (CNVF) was created and Commander W.G. Beauchamp was its first Commanding Officer. On 27th July, the auditor sent in a letter which set out the progressive decline in gate receipts and showed a loss on the season's working of probably £370, in spite of the reduction of rent. It was obvious to the Committee that the Club could not carry on for more than three or four seasons under these conditions. It was resolved that it be a recommendation from the Committee to the A.G.M. that the subscription be raised to two guineas and a circular pointing out the reasons for this step should be sent to members with the notice of the general meeting.

Ken Chapman was elected captain of the Club for the 1936/37 season and carried on for the following two until the war. We met Rosslyn Park on 26th September at the Old Deer Park and won by twelve points to nil. In this game Philip Dunkley made the last of his 145 appearances (68 of these had been as captain and he had scored a total of 149 points made up of 18 tries, 5 penalties and 40 conversions) and J.G. Jenkins and Joe Mycock made the first of their 79 and 41 appearances respectively. Our next two games (against London Scottish and United Services Portsmouth) also produced wins but Cambridge University defeated us at Twickenham (11-16). After we had defeated Guy's Hospital at Honor Oak Park (29-10) (in this match B.J. Collins made the last of his 54 appearances), Bath (on 31st October) notched up their first win over us since 1908 by six points to five. Wins followed over Bristol (7-0) and Richmond (12-0) but Oxford University completed the first leg of a double (7-11) before we got back on the winning road against Blackheath (16-0) and Leicester at Twickenham. In the Leicester game, we rattled off twenty four unanswered points, thirteen of which were scored before half time. Ken Chapman scored two tries and kicked three conversions and one penalty to add to tries by K.H. Roscoe, J.R. Rawlence and R.F. Crichton. Leicester's only reply was a try by J.N. McLeod which was converted by N.A. York for a final score of 24-5. We followed this with a one point defeat by the O.M.T.'s (10-11) and a three point loss to Cardiff (11-14) but we did manage to end the year on a high note with a 6-0 victory over Richmond on Boxing Day.

On 2nd January, we met St. Bartholomew's Hospital at Winchmore Hill and drew 3-3. Our first defeat of 1937 came at Portsmouth when the Army overcame us by one point (9-10), this was closely followed by our second at the hands of Oxford. This proved to be our heaviest defeat of the season (3-14). Against U.S. Portsmouth (although some newspapers reported this as the full Royal Navy side as they were playing in blue) on 27th February, neither side managed to score. Our biggest win of the season came against Eastbourne on 3rd March. The game was played at Hampden Park, Eastbourne and in our side we fielded no fewer than four Eastbourne College old boys including the captain, R. Gray. The final margin was twenty one points which meant a score of 27-6. The return with Leicester was won (11-3) and the O.M.T.'s were drawn with (11-11) but the London Scottish avenged their earlier defeat by a margin of ten points to nil. On the Easter tour, we were defeated by Swansea (13-18) and achieved a scoreless draw with Cardiff. Our last three matches produced an away loss at Bristol (0-6), a home win over Gloucester (16-6) and finally, a home defeat against Coventry by the same margin as the earlier game at Bristol. New English internationals appearing during the season were H.D. (Hubert) Freakes (3 caps in 1938 and 1939) who appeared a total of six times for the 1st XV made his debut against Blackheath on 9th January, G.G. (Gordon) Gregory (13 caps between 1931 and 1934) who made the first of his twenty appearances on 12th December against O.M.T.'s, Joe Mycock (5 caps for England in 1947 and 1948) and B.E. (Basil) Nicholson (2 caps in 1938) who made his debut against Cambridge University on 23rd January and went on to make 38 appearances. Geoff Butler topped the try scorers with eleven and Ken Chapman got the most points (66) with 3 tries, 7 penalties and 18 conversions while the team managed to score 301 points (66 tries, 4 dropped goals, 7 penalties and 33 conversions). Out of a total of 29 games played, only five players managed twenty four or more appearances, these were J.G. Jenkins (28), Ken Chapman, Robin Prescott and Cornelius Thorne (26) and Edward Hamilton-Hill (24).

1936/37

260936	ROSSLYN PARK	OLD DEER PARK	W	1G1DG1T(12)-0
031036	LONDON SCOTTISH	TWICKENHAM	W	2G1T(13)-1G(5)
101036	UNITED SERVICES PORTSMOUTH	PORTSMOUTH	W	2G(10)-0
171036	CAMBRIDGE UNIVERSITY	TWICKENHAM	L	1G1PG1T(11)-2G1PG1T(16)
241036	GUY'S HOSPITAL	HONOR OAK PARK	W	4G1PG2T(29)-2G(10)
311036	BATH	BATH	L	1G(5)-1PG1T(6)
071136	BRISTOL	TWICKENHAM	W	1DG1T(7)-0
141136	RICHMOND	RICHMOND	W	1G1DG1T(12)-0
211136	OXFORD UNIVERSITY	TWICKENHAM	L	1DG1PG(7)-1G1PG1T(11)
281136	BLACKHEATH	TWICKENHAM	W	2G2T(16)-0
051236	LEICESTER	TWICKENHAM	W	3G1PG2T(24)-1G(5)
121236	OLD MERCHANT TAYLORS	TEDDINGTON(A)	L	2G(10)-1G2T(11)
191236	CARDIFF	TWICKENHAM	L	1G2PG(11)-1G1PG2T(14)
261236	RICHMOND	TWICKENHAM	W	2T(6)-0
020137	ST.BARTHOLOMEW'S HOSPITAL	WINCHMORE HILL	D	1T(3)-1T(3)
090137	BLACKHEATH	BLACKHEATH	W	3G3T(24)-1PG1T(6)
230137	CAMBRIDGE UNIVERSITY	CAMBRIDGE	W	1G2T(11)-2T(6)
300137	ARMY	PORTSMOUTH	L	3T(9)-2G(10)

060237	NORTHAMPTON	NORTHAMPTON	C	
200237	OXFORD UNIVERSITY	OXFORD	L	1T(3)-2G1DG(14)
270237	UNITED SERVICES PORTSMOUTH	TWICKENHAM	D	0-0
030337	EASTBOURNE	EASTBOURNE	W	3G4T(27)-2T(6)
060337	LEICESTER	LEICESTER	W	1G1PG1T(11)-1T(3)
130337	OLD MERCHANT TAYLORS	TEDDINGTON	D	1G2T(11)-1G2T(11)
200337	LONDON SCOTTISH	RICHMOND	L	0-1DG2T(10)
270337	SWANSEA	SWANSEA	L	2G1T(13)-3G1PG(18)
290337	CARDIFF	CARDIFF	D	0-0
030437	BRISTOL	BRISTOL	L	0-2T(6)
100437	GLOUCESTER	TWICKENHAM	W	2G2T(16)-2PG(6)
170437	COVENTRY	TWICKENHAM	L	0-2T(6)

At the A.G.M. on 14th September, the search for a ground continued and a resolution was carried to instruct the Committee to investigate the possibility of renting Lords as a 1st XV ground (at a further meeting on 1st November a letter from the M.C.C. was read out to the effect that the scheme to play football on the practice ground was impracticable). New caps were awarded to M.P. Brooks, L.R.H. Leach, K.A.W. Goodall, F.P. Dunkley, L.H. Dillon, J.H.P. Gilbey, B. Barlow and R.B. Horsley. On 7th February, Tony Prescott urged that immediate steps should be taken to acquire a new ground and it was resolved that the Committee proceed to obtain full particulars of the ground at East Molesey and that the area on the map to the south-west of London (within thirty minutes train journey from Waterloo and Victoria) be divided up and allocated to various members to be inspected. By 21st March it was being proposed by Rex King and seconded by Ken Chapman and unanimously resolved that 1st XV matches be transferred to Teddington and that necessary alterations to the ground be undertaken forthwith. The full alteration programme was going to cost in the neighbourhood of £12,000 and it was decided on 9th May to carry out the full programme. Later on it was noted by the Committee that it would not be possible to move the 1st XV to Teddington until season 1939/40. Also on 9th May, Colin Laird proposed and Jay Gould seconded that on principle we should apply for a fixture with the Canadian touring team and offer a date of 21st September 1940 (on 18th July this date was confirmed but, alas, it was not to be as thanks to the intervention of the war no tour took place). B.H. Bowring, M.J. Daly, R.B. Horsley and B.E. Nicholson were awarded new caps.

The 1937/38 season started in much the same way as the previous one. We defeated Rosslyn Park (13-0), London Scottish (13-7) and U.S. Portsmouth (21-11) before going down to Cambridge University (15-22). Against Rosslyn Park, M.J. (Maurice) Daly made his debut for us and scored both of our tries. He was to play for us until the 1948/49 season (making at least eighty appearances) and gained his one and only cap for Ireland against England in 1938 (scoring a try in a 14-36 defeat). Against Guy's Hospital at Twickenham on 23rd October we achieved our biggest win of the season, scoring tries through R.B. Horsley (3), J.G. Jenkins, W.S. (Sam) Kemble and M.E. Golding and a penalty each from Ken Chapman and Joe Mycock (who also added a conversion). Guy's could only score a penalty in reply and a 9-3 scoreline at half time had become 26-3 at the final whistle. Our next match saw us gain revenge for our defeat at Bath the previous season with a fourteen points to three win, while against Bristol on 6th November, we had to borrow E. Farmer from them to make up our numbers in the forwards and came away with another victory (14-12). We beat Blackheath by eleven points to three with the help of another hat-trick of tries from Horsley but lost to Leicester for the first time since 1934 (8-11).

The O.M.T.'s had now moved from Teddington to Croxley Green near Watford and we met them there for the first time on 11th December. Another couple of tries from Horsley and one each from Kemble and Hamilton-Hill (two converted by Ken Chapman) in the first half were enough to see us home (despite two tries from the home side in the second half) by the score of 16-6. The following week we met Cardiff at Twickenham and, despite the fact that our soon to be welsh international Frederick Ford got two tries, we still lost, 9-13. Once again, we finished off the year with a victory over Richmond by eight points to three. On New Year's Day, we played the University Vandals (for the only time) at Walton-on-Thames. After going behind to two early tries, we picked ourselves up and replied with seven of our own. Horsley scored three once again, Daly got two and Ford and Fred Dunkley grabbed one each to which Ken Chapman added three conversions and a penalty for a final score of thirty points to eight. This win gave us a record of 12-3 for our first fifteen games of the season but, unfortunately, our second set of fifteen were not nearly as good. We could only manage six wins and a draw against eight defeats. After starting the year off so well against the Vandals, we quickly lost to Blackheath, Coventry and the Army but slightly redeemed ourselves with good wins over Cambridge (10-8) and Northampton (14-8). We then won at Leicester and defeated the O.M.T.'s (6-4) and London Scottish (7-6) which proved to be our last win of the season. We finished off with four tough games and lost them all narrowly. Bristol were met at Twickenham (8-9), Gloucester were met away (13-14) and the two tour matches at Easter were played at Swansea (3-9) and Cardiff (6-13). G.E.C. Hudson made his eighty second and final appearance for the first team against Cardiff having scored twenty two tries.

As well as Maurice Daly, the only other new international to appear for us was R.M. (Robert) Marshall who gained five England caps in 1938 and 1939 although his only appearance for us was against the Army on 29th January. Not surprisingly Horsley was the top try scorer with nineteen, while I.H. (Ian) Watts's three dropped goals equalled the record set by S.H. Townell in 1922/23 and 1923/24 and equalled by Colin Laird (1930/31) and John Howarth (1934/35). Ken Chapman finished top points scorer with 90 (2 tries, 8 penalties and 30 conversions) and the team improved on the previous season with a total of 341 points (76 tries, 4 dropped goals, 11 penalties and 32 conversions). A total of thirty matches were played, the most appearances being made by Ken Chapman (29), Golding (28), Jenkins and Ronald (25) and B.H. Bowring (24).

Basil Nicholson was chosen to go on the 1938 British Lions tour to South Africa. He played in the second of the three tests, the only one being won was the third.

1937/38

250937	ROSSLYN PARK	TWICKENHAM	W	1DG1PG2T(13)-0
021037	LONDON SCOTTISH	RICHMOND	W	2G1T(13)-1DG1T(7)
091037	UNITED SERVICES PORTSMOUTH	TWICKENHAM	W	3G2T(21)-1G2T(11)
161037	CAMBRIDGE UNIVERSITY	CAMBRIDGE	L	3G(15)-3G1DG1PG(22)
231037	GUY'S HOSPITAL	TWICKENHAM	W	1G2PG5T(26)-1PG(3)
301037	BATH	TWICKENHAM	W	1G1PG2T(14)-1PG(3)
061137	BRISTOL	BRISTOL	W	1G3T(14)-4T(12)
131137	RICHMOND	TWICKENHAM	W	2G1PG1T(16)-3T(9)
201137	OXFORD UNIVERSITY	TWICKENHAM	W	3G1T(18)-1G1PG1T(11)
271137	BLACKHEATH	BLACKHEATH	W	1G2T(11)-1PG(3)

041237	LEICESTER	TWICKENHAM	L	1G1T(8)-1G1PG1T(11)
111237	OLD MERCHANT TAYLORS	CROXLEY GREEN	W	2G2T(16)-2T(6)
181237	CARDIFF	TWICKENHAM	L	1PG2T(9)-2G1T(13)
271237	RICHMOND	RICHMOND	W	1G1T(8)-1T(3)
010138	UNIVERSITY VANDALS	WALTON-ON-THAMES	W	3G1PG4T(30)-1G1T(8)
080138	BLACKHEATH	TWICKENHAM	L	1PG(3)-2G1PG(13)
150138	COVENTRY	COVENTRY	L	1G(5)-2G1T(13)
220138	CAMBRIDGE UNIVERSITY	TWICKENHAM	W	1DG1PG1T(10)-1G1T(8)
290138	ARMY	TWICKENHAM	L	1DG(4)-1G(5)
050238	NORTHAMPTON	TWICKENHAM	W	1G3T(14)-1G1T(8)
120238	ALDERSHOT SERVICES	ALDERSHOT	W	2G2T(16)-0
190238	OXFORD UNIVERSITY	OXFORD	L	0-3G1T(18)
260238	ROYAL NAVY	PORTSMOUTH	D	1T(3)-1PG(3)
050338	LEICESTER	LEICESTER	W	1G2T(11)-1PG1T(6)
090338	EASTBOURNE	EASTBOURNE	C	
120338	OLD MERCHANT TAYLORS	TEDDINGTON	W	2T(6)-1DG(4)
260338	LONDON SCOTTISH	RICHMOND	W	1DG1T(7)-1PG1T(6)
020438	BRISTOL	TWICKENHAM	L	1G1T(8)-1G1DG(9)
090438	GLOUCESTER	GLOUCESTER	L	2G1T(13)-1G1PG2T(14)
160438	SWANSEA	SWANSEA	L	1T(3)-1PG2T(9)
180438	CARDIFF	CARDIFF	L	2PG(6)-2G1PG(13)

At the A.G.M. on 13th September, the President referred to the loss to the team by the retirements of Hamilton-Hill and Bolton and mentioned also the retirement of Philip Hodge who had gained his first "A"XV cap in 1923 and played his last game for the 1st XV in 1934. The honorary treasurer presented the accounts for season 1936/37 with the good news that the excess of working expenditure over nominal income had been reduced from £244 to just £1. On 6th February the President announced that a letter had been received from Hamilton, New Zealand asking permission to make use of the name and colours of the Club, permission was granted. On 3rd July new caps were awarded to R.F. Crichton, W.S. Kemble, J. Mycock and O.B. Rooney and the honorary secretary reported that he had received an invitation from Avirons Bayonnais to play two matches - one at Bayonne and the other at Bordeaux or Toulouse. It was decided that in the event of permission being granted for the resumption of matches with French clubs (the French had been banned in February 1937 due to suspicions of professionalism when, in January 1937 ten of the leading French clubs broke away from the FFR to form their own union, with the intention of competing for a separate club championship) possible dates could be 12th and 13th May 1940, but no final decision would be taken until the subject had been discussed with the playing members when the new season started.

We began what was to be our last full season with a full fixture list for seven years with a narrow victory over Rosslyn Park. By half time we had sped into a lead of eighteen points to six with tries from Golding (2) and Horsley (2) and three conversions from Ken Chapman to a try and a penalty for the home side. Three tries and two conversions put the Park into a one point lead before Ken Chapman kicked a penalty to settle the match in our favour 21-19. Our first home game was on 1st October against London Scottish at Twickenham and ended in a drawn game of three points each. This was followed by victories over, among others, Cambridge University (16-15), Bath (13-0) and Bristol (13-8). Our first loss came on 12th November at the Athletic Ground against Richmond (6-18) and this was followed by further defeats at the hands of Blackheath (0-6) and Cardiff (3-21). The loss to Cardiff was our worst defeat by them since the fixture began in 1882. We did beat Oxford University (12-7), Leicester (20-11) and Richmond (22-8) before the end of the year although our chance to get some revenge over Coventry was lost as the game was cancelled.

For our first match of 1939, we played St. Bartholomew's Hospital and despite the fact that we only had thirteen men for the first twenty five minutes (Daly and Watts turning up late), we won 14-6. Our biggest win of the season came in the return with Cambridge on 28th January on their home ground. The university got their only points when T.R. Juckes got a try and K.I. Geddes converted for the first scores of the match. We led by the interval after tries by Bowring and Nicholson had put us 6-5 up. The second half was a one sided romp for us as, first, Ken Chapman put over a penalty and then went on to convert three of our six tries which followed. Kemble got two, Bowring and Nicholson both got their second scores and M.M. "Micky" Walford and Rooney got the others to make the final score 33-5. Defeats followed to Northampton (13-17), Oxford University (7-18), Leicester (3-13) and Eastbourne (5-6). The remarkable thing about the last game was the appearance of Adrian Stoop, seventeen years after his last game (for the Past against the Present in 1922). We won against the O.M.T.'s and the Aldershot Services before losing four on the trot against London Scottish (11-26), Bristol (3-22) (our heaviest defeat of the season), Swansea (12-13) and Cardiff (8-9). The last game of the season was played at Twickenham on 15th April and our visitors were Gloucester. Thanks to a try by Nicholson and a Ken Chapman penalty, we triumphed 6-3 with Gloucester's points coming from a penalty by H. Boughton. Our team that day was B.D. Napper (full back), R.B. Horsley, J.L. Crichton, B.E. Nicholson and M.J. Daly (three quarters), T.G.K. Bishop and N.A. Steel (half backs) and R.E. Prescott, F.P. (Fred) Dunkley, B.H. Bowring, O.B. Rooney, K.H. Chapman, R.F. Crichton, J. Mycock and C.G. Sharpe (forwards).

We lost two experienced players during the season when Edward Hamilton-Hill played the last of his ninety games for the Club, scoring seventy three points (twenty three tries and two conversions) during that time and Cornelius Thorne, who played in 163 games and scored 57 points (nineteen tries) during his career. E.K. (Edward) Scott made his first appearance for us on 29th October against Bath and went on to gain five caps for England in 1947 and 1948 when he played for St. Mary's Hospital and Redruth. R.B. Horsley scored the most tries with ten and Ken Chapman kicked 99 points (24 conversions and 17 penalty goals (a new record)) while the team managed 63 tries, 4 dropped goals, 23 penalty goals (another record) and 30 conversions for a total of 334 points. On the appearance side of things Ken Chapman finished top with 28, Fred Dunkley and J.G. Jenkins managed 26 and B.H. Bowring was next with 23.

1938/39

240938	ROSSLYN PARK	OLD DEER PARK	W	3G1PG1T(21)-2G1PG2T(19)
011038	LONDON SCOTTISH	TWICKENHAM	D	1T(3)-1PG(3)
081038	UNITED SERVICES PORTSMOUTH	PORTSMOUTH	W	1G1PG4T(20)-1DG1T(7)
151038	CAMBRIDGE UNIVERSITY	TWICKENHAM	W	1DG3PG1T(16)-3G(15)
221038	GUY'S HOSPITAL	HONOR OAK PARK	W	2G2PG(16)-1PG(3)
291038	BATH	BATH	W	2G1PG(13)-0

051138	BRISTOL	TWICKENHAM	W	2G1T(13)-1G1T(8)
121138	RICHMOND	RICHMOND	L	2T(6)-3G1T(18)
191138	OXFORD UNIVERSITY	TWICKENHAM	W	3PG1T(12)-1DG1T(7)
261138	BLACKHEATH	TWICKENHAM	L	0-2T(6)
031238	LEICESTER	TWICKENHAM	W	4G(20)-1G2PG(11)
101238	OLD MERCHANT TAYLORS	CROXLEY GREEN	W	1T(3)-0
171238	CARDIFF	TWICKENHAM	L	1T(3)-2G2DG1PG(21)
241238	COVENTRY	TWICKENHAM	C	
311238	RICHMOND	TWICKENHAM	W	2G1PG3T(22)-1G1T(8)
070139	ST.BARTHOLOMEW'S HOSPITAL	CHISLEHURST	W	1G2PG1T(14)-1PG1T(6)
140139	BLACKHEATH	BLACKHEATH	W	1PG3T(12)-1PG(3)
280139	CAMBRIDGE UNIVERSITY	CAMBRIDGE	W	3G1PG5T(33)-1G(5)
040239	NORTHAMPTON	NORTHAMPTON	L	2G1T(13)-1G2PG2T(17)
180239	OXFORD UNIVERSITY	OXFORD	L	1DG1PG(7)-3G1T(18)
250239	ROYAL NAVY	TWICKENHAM	W	1G1PG(8)-2T(6)
040339	LEICESTER	LEICESTER	L	1T(3)-1DG3T(13)
080339	EASTBOURNE	EASTBOURNE	L	1G(5)-1PG1T(6)
110339	OLD MERCHANT TAYLORS	TWICKENHAM	W	1G1DG1PG1T(15)-1T(3)
180339	ALDERSHOT SERVICES	ALDERSHOT	W	2G2T(16)-2G1T(13)
250339	LONDON SCOTTISH	RICHMOND	L	1G2PG(11)-4G2T(26)
010439	BRISTOL	BRISTOL	L	1PG(3)-2G4T(22)
080439	SWANSEA	SWANSEA	L	1G1DG1T(12)-2G1T(13)
100439	CARDIFF	CARDIFF	L	1G1T(8)-3T(9)
150439	GLOUCESTER	TWICKENHAM	W	1PG1T(6)-1PG(3)

13

Sevens in the 1930s

1930-1939

Going back to the start of the decade, the fifth Middlesex tournament took place on 26th April 1930 and we were trying to achieve five successive wins. Our second team scratched against Old Haberdashers so it was left, once again, to the first seven to fly the flag. They beat Westminster Bank (15-3) and Old Cranleighans (10-6) before coming up again London Welsh in the semi-final. In a remarkably fast and determined game, Laird scored a try which was converted before Lewis got one back in the second half. When the Welsh were awarded a penalty for someone lying on the ball, Powell stepped up and slotted the goal to knock us out by a single point (5-6). It was the first time we had ever been defeated in the five years of the event. In the final, our conquerors went on to beat Blackheath II by six points to nil. Even the Graf Zeppelin airship made an appearance when it passed almost overhead. The amount raised for charity this time was £949 and despite a couple of years being lower than this, the 1930s generally produced more than a thousand pounds with a high of £1,921 in 1939.

By 1931, the press still reported that Sevens in England was ordinary rugby played by seven instead of fifteen-a-side. The 1st VII reached the final for the fifth time with victories over Old Blues (13-5), London Irish (8-0) and in the semi-final against Blackheath, P.E. Dunkley scored from the kick-off after a loose Blackheath pass and that proved to be the only score. In the final, London Welsh got a try in the first half and two in the second to lead 9-0 before McCreight scored for us and Dunkley converted to give us a chance. Unfortunately, the Welsh defence held out and we had lost. The rest of the Seven were Reeve, Douglas Bader, Hodge, H.L. Price and Duder. The second side failed to reach the final rounds.

The following year, there was a strange occurrence when the second team reached the final by beating Harrow (25-10), Old Dunstonians (18-5), Old Blues (10-0), Saracens II (23-8), Wasps I (10-6) and Old Cranleighans in the semi-final (11-8). The first Seven came in at the fourth round stage and beat the Honourable Artillery Company (15-8) before going down to Old Merchant Taylors in a shock result (8-10) after leading 8-0 at half time. In the final, Harlequin II played Blackheath I and W. Graham Davies scored our first try which was converted. Approaching half time, Blackheath drew level and then scored another two converted tries in the second half before Ken Chapman got one back for us. Blackheath had the final word with another try to make the final score 10-18. The rest of our team were H.J. Gould, Hodge, E. Monk, R.R. Cooke and Hamilton-Hill.

A year later with 101 teams entering, it was back to business as usual. The second side defeated City of London Police (10-0), Wembley (walk over), St. Bartholomew's Hospital (15-0) and Old Cranleighans II (10-3) before losing

10-15 to our first VII at Teddington (matches were still being played on other grounds, even on finals day). The first team entered in the fourth round again and dispatched Lensbury I (19-0), London Irish I (18-0), Quins II (15-10) and Rosslyn Park 13-0 in the semi-final. Our opponents in that final were Wasps and with Gibbs in a starring role, we won again. He scored two against Park in the semi-final and three against Wasps. Russell-Roberts and Cole got the others and Dunkley took the kicks to make it 23-0. It was said that no one could mark or even touch Gibbs. It is interesting to note that the only side to score against Quins I was Quins II. C. Lionel Sparke, G.J. Dean and C. Thompson were the rest of the winning side (although H.A. Style is also reported as playing).

In 1934, we had our worst year so far because, after beating Streatham I by 8-3, we went down to the Barbarians 3-19 in the fifth round. They went on to win the trophy by beating Richmond I in the final after extra time (6-3). The second team lost to Old Haberdashers in the second round.

We returned the following year with Geoff Butler, G.E.C. Hudson, Cole, Dean, Peter Brook, Dunkley and Hamilton-Hill making up the main team. For the sixth time in ten years, they swept all before them with Gloucester (18-3), Old Cranleighans (9-5) and Richmond (3-0) in the semi-final all falling victim. The Richmond match went to the second period of sudden-death extra time before Cole settled it with a try. Our opponents in the final, London Welsh, agreed to an extra ten minutes' rest to give us a chance to recover from that draining game before. In the first half, the Welsh dominated but could only score one try from Rees-Jones. Into the wind in the second half, we rallied and Cole scored for Dunkley to convert and he did the same with the conversion of Hamilton-Hill's try after a fifty yard dash from a lineout to make the final score 10-3. The second Seven failed to qualify.

The next year, the seconds reached the 6th Round but never won a game because they had a walk over against Midland Bank before losing to Old Cranleighans (5-16). The holders had a team of J.R. Rawlence, Hudson, J.H.E. Howarth, Dean, Dunkley, Thompson and Hamilton-Hill. They entered the competition in the 6th Round and defeated Finchley (24-0), An Army VII (8-0) but went out to London Scottish I by 5-8. Guest side Sale won the trophy after beating Blackheath I by 13-6 in the final.

In 1937, Reg Bolton, Butler, Basil Nicholson, Kenneth Cross, Sam Kemble, Ken Chapman and Hamilton-Hill made up the first choice Seven with the reserves being J.L. Crichton, M.E. Golding, Robin Prescott and Thompson. They beat St. Bartholomew's Hospital (16-0) and Sale (8-0) but lost to London Scottish I again, this time 0-8 in the Eighth Round. The second VII went out to Hendon 0-6 in the 3rd Round (after extra time) and the Scots went on to beat Old Merchant Taylors I in the final (19-3).

On 30th April 1938, our squad contained Hudson, Maurice Daly, T.G.K. Bishop, Dean, Prescott, Chapman and Bolton with reserves named as C.S.M. Quigley, Hamilton-Hill and Thompson. Ultimately, neither of our sides appeared at Twickenham on the day. The number one team beat Unilever (15-8) but went down in the Sixth Round to Old Paulines (0-7) at Orleans Park. The seconds began in Round 1 with a win over Barclays Bank (13-3) and followed by beating Napier II (13-0), Ealing I (13-6) and Saracens I (10-0) before bowing out against Rosslyn Park (0-5). Metropolitan Police won the final against London Scottish (13-3).

The last tournament before the outbreak of World War 2 took place on 22nd April 1939 and once again, it proved to be a fruitless one for us. The first VII were named as Daly, Nicholson, Bishop, R.F. Crichton, Chapman, F.P. Dunkley and Joe Mycock with R.B. Horsley, J.L. Crichton and O.B. Rooney as reserves. They beat Napier (8-0) but went out in the first game of finals day to Metropolitan Police I (0-8). The second VII scratched against Chartered Accountants in the First Round. In the final, Cardiff defeated London Scottish I by eleven points to six. We would not participate again until 1946.

14

The War Years 1939-1945

At the A.G.M. on 12th September the honorary treasurer informed the meeting that the Club was in debt to a very considerable extent. It was considered that in order to provide recreation which was badly needed the Club should carry on if possible. In order to do this it was considered that bond holders should be asked to forego the interest on their debentures. If this was agreed it was estimated that it would cost the Club about £450 a year to keep the ground going. A trial game was held on 23rd September at which nearly half the players were not members of the Club and a number were members of clubs which had closed down. After consulting the meeting (held after the trial game) the President made the following announcement to the players who had taken part in the game:- That the Club proposed to carry on as long as possible to provide games for members and others who were able and wished to play. It would not be possible to pay travelling expenses and it would be necessary to take steps to raise money in view of the fact that it cost over £400 per annum to run the ground. On 24th October, a meeting was held at 4, Serjeant's Inn at which it was resolved that for the duration of hostilities the President and honorary treasurer be authorised to conduct the affairs of the Club and to exercise the powers of the Committee in view of the difficulty of assembling the said Committee.

With the beginning of hostilities, it became obvious that the planned 1939/40 season was not going to be a normal one and, consequently, only our first two fixtures were as planned although the season did start a week late. Robin Prescott was to have been captain of the Club for this season but due to the outbreak of war it appears that he shared the role with Ken Chapman. We started off against Rosslyn Park on 30th September with a match played at the Old Deer Park. Seven of our team were making their 1st XV debuts and after leading 5-0 at half time, we conceded eleven in the second half and so lost by a margin of six points. Against the London Scottish at Richmond a week later it was the same story although we only lost by three points, scoring ten in the first half and conceding thirteen in the second. Our third loss on the trot came against an Army XV at Teddington. During this time there were a lot of services XVs in existence including teams from Australia and New Zealand. Our opponents included players from the following teams, Bedford, Lloyd's Bank, National Provincial Bank, Old Cranleighans, Richmond and Woodford. A Ken Chapman penalty and a Robin Prescott try put us 6-3 up shortly after half time but the Army XV rallied and scored three converted tries to finish winners by eighteen points to six. The following week we gained our first victory of the season by defeating St. George's and Middlesex Hospitals at Wimbledon by nine points to nil. The next two games also produced wins over hospital opposition. First, Guy's (13-0) and then King's College (14-0) which proved to be our biggest win of the season.

On 11th November we met the students from Cambridge University at Cambridge and in a close game we edged them out for a 12-11 win. Our fly half J.R.E. Evans dropped a goal, Reg Bolton got a try and Ken Chapman kicked a penalty and converted the try while two of the home team's tries came from E.R. Knapp, who was to play for us after the war. Beckenham appeared on our fixture list for the first time since 1877 and St. Bartholomew's Hospital were met at Mill Hill, both games being won by margins of 21-9 and 6-3 respectively. For our next match we travelled to Oxford to meet the University and in a game containing ten tries (we scored two!) the students ran out easy winners 37-13. We met the Metropolitan Police for the first time on 9th December at Teddington and lost 3-13 and had some sort of return with an Army XV (although the game was again played at Teddington) on 16th December which ended up with the same result but the score was a lot closer (8-10).

The next six games were cancelled for one reason or another and some interesting fixtures were lost including a return with the Metropolitan Police at Hendon and other matches against a joint London Irish/London Welsh side and a team from the Aldershot Command (both at Teddington). On 10th and 24th February we met Rosslyn Park at the Old Deer Park and, like the first game of the season, both of these were lost. On 2nd March, we met the Old Paulines for the first time since 1873 (at Thames Ditton) just to prove that this season was to be one for renewing very old friendships! On this occasion we were beaten, quite convincingly, by twenty two points to six. Our first and only draw of the season came against St. Mary's Hospital on their ground at Teddington on 9th March when each side scored eight points. The last time we had met Bedford (in 1920), the score had been in our favour by seventy six points to nil, this time it was a lot closer, Bedford winning by the odd point in fifteen. In this game five Bedford men deputised for absent Quins. The ground at Goldington Road, Bedford was used by kind permission of the Civil and Military Authorities concerned (as noted on the front of the match programme). On 23rd March we met Saracens for the first time (although it was to be another forty five years to the day before we met them again) and succeeded in winning narrowly by five points to three. Our last game of this somewhat shortened season was against the Old Blues and was played at Hampton. For us, J.R.E. Evans, P.R.L. Hastings and J.L. Crichton got tries (Crichton converting Evans' effort) to one try for the Old Boys and a final score of 11-3.

Our next two matches against Middlesex Hospital and London Hospital were both cancelled which meant that our next game of Rugby was over three years away! Bruce Chapman made his last appearance in the match against Saracens having scored 103 points (8 tries, 2 dropped goals, 11 penalty goals and 19 conversions) in his career and the only new international player to appear in our colours during the season was T.F. (Thomas) Huskisson who had made eight appearances for England between 1937 and 1939 when his club was the Old Merchant Taylors. Unfortunately, full appearance details are not available for this and most of the next twenty seasons so the information given is as known. Out of the nineteen games played, Norman Steel appeared in eighteen, Ken Chapman in seventeen and J.L. Crichton in sixteen. A.D. Keay got the most tries with eight, Crichton dropped two goals and Ken Chapman kicked ten penalties and fourteen conversions for a top total of 58 points.

1939/40 (Proposed) (All Games Were Cancelled Due to the Second World War)

230939	ROSSLYN PARK	TWICKENHAM
071039	LONDON SCOTTISH	RICHMOND
141039	UNITED SERVICES PORTSMOUTH	TWICKENHAM

211039	CAMBRIDGE UNIVERSITY	CAMBRIDGE
281039	COVENTRY	COVENTRY
041139	BRISTOL	BRISTOL
111139	RICHMOND	TWICKENHAM
181139	OXFORD UNIVERSITY	TWICKENHAM
251139	BLACKHEATH	BLACKHEATH
021239	LEICESTER	TWICKENHAM
091239	OLD MERCHANT TAYLORS	CROXLEY GREEN
231239	RICHMOND	RICHMOND
301239	ARMY	ALDERSHOT
060140	LONDON IRISH	SUNBURY
130140	BLACKHEATH	TWICKENHAM
200140	BEDFORD	BEDFORD
270140	CAMBRIDGE UNIVERSITY	TWICKENHAM
030240	NORTHAMPTON	TWICKENHAM
100240	ALDERSHOT SERVICES	TWICKENHAM
170240	OXFORD UNIVERSITY	OXFORD
240240	ROYAL NAVY	PORTSMOUTH
020340	LEICESTER	LEICESTER
060340	EASTBOURNE	EASTBOURNE
090340	OLD MERCHANT TAYLORS	TEDDINGTON
230340	SWANSEA	SWANSEA
250340	CARDIFF	CARDIFF
300340	LONDON SCOTTISH	TEDDINGTON
060440	BRISTOL	TWICKENHAM
130440	GLOUCESTER	GLOUCESTER
200440	LONDON WELSH	TWICKENHAM

1939/40 (Actual)

300939	ROSSLYN PARK	OLD DEER PARK	L	1G(5)-1G2T(11)
071039	LONDON SCOTTISH	RICHMOND	L	2G(10)-2G1T(13)
141039	ARMY XV	TEDDINGTON	L	1PG1T(6)-3G1T(18)
211039	ST.GEORGE'S AND MIDDLESEX HOSPITALS	WIMBLEDON	W	1G1DG(9)-0
281039	GUY'S HOSPITAL	HONOR OAK PARK	W	2G1T(13)-0
041139	KING'S COLLEGE HOSPITAL	TEDDINGTON	W	1G3T(14)-0
111139	CAMBRIDGE UNIVERSITY	CAMBRIDGE	W	1G1DG1PG(12)-1G2T(11)
181139	BECKENHAM	BECKENHAM	W	3G1PG1T(21)-3T(9)
251139	ST.BARTHOLOMEW'S HOSPITAL	MILL HILL	W	1PG1T(6)-1T(3)
021239	OXFORD UNIVERSITY	OXFORD	L	2G1PG(13)-5G1PG3T(37)

091239	METROPOLITAN POLICE	TEDDINGTON	L	1PG(3)-1DG1PG2T(13)
161239	ARMY XV	TEDDINGTON	L	1G1T(8)-2G(10)
231239	ST.THOMAS'S HOSPITAL	TEDDINGTON	C	
301239	WASPS	SUDBURY	C	
060140	METROPOLITAN POLICE	HENDON	C	
130140	LONDON IRISH/LONDON WELSH	TEDDINGTON	C	
200140	ALDERSHOT COMMAND	TEDDINGTON	C	
270140	GUY'S HOSPITAL	HONOR OAK PARK	C	
100240	ROSSLYN PARK	OLD DEER PARK	L	1PG1T(6)-4G1PG(23)
240240	ROSSLYN PARK	OLD DEER PARK	L	1G1PG1T(11)-3G1T(18)
020340	OLD PAULINES	THAMES DITTON	L	1PG1T(6)-2G2PG2T(22)
090340	ST.MARY'S HOSPITAL	TEDDINGTON(A)	D	1G1PG(8)-1G1PG(8)
160340	BEDFORD	BEDFORD	L	1DG1PG(7)-1G1T(8)
230340	SARACENS	TEDDINGTON	W	1G(5)-1T(3)
300340	OLD BLUES	HAMPTON(H)	W	1G2T(11)-1T(3)
060440	MIDDLESEX HOSPITAL	CHISLEHURST	C	
130440	LONDON HOSPITAL	HALE END	C	

At a meeting held in London on 12th September 1941 at 40, Old Broad Street, it was reported that the income of the Club was insufficient to pay the premium on the redemption policy for the debentures of Harlequin Estates Limited. It was therefore decided to invite all debenture holders to sell their debentures to the company at a price of £80 for each £100 debenture and to offer to holders of 5% debentures the privilege of nominating a life member when activities of the Club resumed. It was further decided to sell sufficient National Savings Certificates to provide for the outstanding liabilities of the Club.

Both the 1940/41 and 1941/42 seasons were completely lost to the war but we were resurrected on 17th April 1943 for a game against Rosslyn Park at the Old Deer Park. Nine of the team had appeared before and one making his only appearance was J.H. (John) Steeds who went on to gain five England caps in 1949 and 1950 when he played for Saracens. One other making his debut was D.K. (David) Brooks who was to go on to become captain and President of the Club and make 161 confirmed appearances for the 1st XV and we said goodbye to Robin Prescott who made his last appearance having made his debut in 1933. Thanks to a try by Maurice Daly and a penalty and conversion from R.E. Bibby in the first half (Park managed two tries in reply in the second half) we ran out winners by eight points to six.

Our second wartime game was again against the men from the Old Deer Park and was played on 10th April 1944 on their home patch. Seven of our team had played in the previous encounter and among those making their debuts was J.R.C. (John) Matthews who went on to win ten England caps between 1949 and 1952 and also captain the Club. The first half ended with just a penalty for the home side from H.G. (Howell) Thomas being scored. In the second half Micky Walford dropped a goal to put us into a lead which we never lost. Ken Chapman kicked a penalty and D.L. Marriott scored two tries, both were converted and we had triumphed by seventeen points to three. As well as Howell Thomas, three other members of the Rosslyn Park team that day (C.D. (Cecil) McIver, H. (Hugh) de Lacy and B.H. McGuirk) became members of the Harlequin Football Club.

The last of the three wartime matches came on 2nd April 1945, again the opponents and venue were the same as was our captain (Ken Chapman). The only thing that changed was the result, the Park winning by eight points to five. M.R. (Michael) "Micky" Steele-Bodger made his first appearance for us and while at Cambridge University won nine English caps in 1947 and 1948 and D.B. (Douglas) Vaughan (who won eight caps for England between 1948 and 1950) also made his debut in this game.

1940/41 (No Games Due to the Second World War)

1941/42 (No Games Due to the Second World War)

1942/43

170443	ROSSLYN PARK	OLD DEER PARK	W	1G1PG(8)-2T(6)

1943/44

100444	ROSSLYN PARK	OLD DEER PARK	W	2G1DG1PG(17)-1PG(3)

1944/45

020445	ROSSLYN PARK	OLD DEER PARK	L	1G(5)-1G1PG(8)

15

Roll of Honour

In Memory of All Those Who Failed to Return 1939-1945

This is a list of all those who made at least one appearance for the 1st XV and shows the date of death:

Francis V. Beamish	28.03.1942
Hugh V. Brodie	06.12.1941
William A.H. Chapman	25.07.1942
John L. Crichton	11.11.1942
Michael B. Crickmay	19.09.1944
Vivian G. Davies	23.12.1941
Edward B. Eason	06.05.1943
Hubert D. Freakes	10.03.1942
Ronald B. Galt	14.07.1941
John L. Gordon	17.06.1940
Cecil W. Haydon	01.06.1942
Francis S. Hodder	06.09.1943
Edward W.F. DeV Hunt	20.12.1941
Frederick R. Ievers	17.09.1943
Maver L.P. Jackson	22.03.1943
Peter H. Lawless	09.03.1945
Gordon D.A. Lundon	04.03.1943
Robert A.P. Macpherson	22.12.1941
Bastian Maitland-Thompson	28.07.1945
Michael C.X. Mack	24.08.1943
Robert M. Marshall	12.05.1945
Donald R. Moffat	08.04.1943
Leslie H. Morrison	14.11.1942
Richard C. Rendle	09.04.1941
Howard P. Skinner	03.10.1942
Charles L. Sparke	11.12.1942

Adrian F. Stoop	09.02.1944
Christopher Thompson	16.06.1943
David K. Warren	25.08.1940

16

Starting Up Again
1945-1950

With the end of the war, the way was clear for a new start in season 1945/46. An emergency meeting was held at St. Stephen's Tavern, Westminster Bridge on 21st June 1945 at which some seventeen members made an appearance. The honorary treasurer stated that the Club held National Savings Certificates to the value of £276 and National War Bonds to the value of £300, our balance in the bank was £380 and the closing of Harlequin Estates should produce a further £25 and that 85-90 members were still paying their subscriptions. The President stated that the ground at Twickenham required considerable repairs before the West stand would be suitable for spectators but that they were able to use the East stand as they had when the West stand was being rebuilt and the R.F.U. were prepared to let the ground for a rent of £100. The pitch at Teddington was reported to be in first class condition but one goal post was broken although the pavilion needed little more than redecoration to bring it up to scratch. At a meeting held on 24th October, A.A. (Arthur) Moller, in the absence of the honorary treasurer laid before the Committee the accounts for the past six years. During this period the Club had received £1,195 1s 0d in subscriptions and the balance sheet at 31st May 1945 showed a surplus of £5,563 7s 11d as against £3,983 8s at 31st May 1939. This meant that it would be far easier starting again this time than it was after the First World War.

At the A.G.M. which followed on from the Committee meeting a proposal to amend rule 21 so as to enable the Committee to elect non-playing members at an annual subscription of three guineas was decided against. At a further Committee meeting held after the A.G.M. it was resolved unanimously to keep alive Harlequin Estates Limited in case it should be necessary to raise further capital even though the original work was now finished. The prices at Twickenham were fixed at Entrance 1s (boys 6d), ringside 6d, ground and stand 2s 6d, stand 1s 6d and car park 2s with programmes selling at 3d. It was also decided to contribute one guinea to the testimonial of C.S. Bongard from the Middlesex Rugby Union but, at the meeting on 18th December, due to the fact that testimonials were prohibited by the rules on professionalism this was annulled. On 27th March a letter was read out from the Twickenham Town Clerk on the subject of the ground at Teddington stating that "the Corporation would wish to acquire the site if there was any possibility of its being used for private development" and asking for an option in that event at a price equal to the value which would be payable if the Corporation exercised compulsory powers i.e. the marked value of the land at 31st March 1939. The honorary secretary was instructed to inform the Town Clerk that the Club had no intention of disposing of the ground, but intended to retain it as a playing field. At a further meeting it was stated that it was hoped to avoid compulsory purchase of the ground.

Ken Chapman was again elected as captain of the 1st XV and he also undertook the work of secretary to that team. The first match of the new post-war era was played on 22nd September and, appropriately, was against Rosslyn Park at the Old Deer Park. Perhaps fittingly, the game ended in a draw of nine points each. The home side had started the better with a try by E.G. McKeown and a penalty from J.M. Reichwald before two penalties by Ken Chapman levelled the scores only for McKeown to score his second try to put Park up by three points at half time. In the second half the only score was a try for us by Micky Steele-Bodger to set up the draw. We only had to wait until the following week for our first win, it came at Teddington where Bath were the visitors and the margin was 11-6. One more week and it was time for our first defeat. Our old rivals London Scottish were responsible for keeping us scoreless whilst getting eight points for themselves. Our first game against Wasps in just over ten years saw them set their biggest winning margin over us in fixtures going back to 1872 with a seventeen point win (5-22). This was to stand until January 1991 when they defeated us 35-3 at Sudbury.

After wins over Cambridge University and Bristol and a loss to Coventry, we drew the second of four games during the season. This was the first game to be played at Twickenham since 1939 and our opponents were a combined Richmond and Blackheath side. The visitors were to score first (a try by J.J. Remlinger) and last (a try by W.O. Chadwick) in the first half with us getting a penalty by Norman Steel and tries from J.A. (Jack) Davies and Douglas Vaughan (who converted Davies' try) for a lead of 11-6. A try right at the start of the second half by J.A. Gregory and a penalty and try from J.G.W. Davies (our reply being a try from R.H.G. (Robert) Weighill) left the visitors ahead by a point, before Geoff Butler scored and Steel converted to give us what looked like a victory. In the very last seconds of the game the Richmond and Blackheath fly half (G.T. Wright) picked up the ball from some loose play and dropped a goal to tie the scores at 19-19. Before Christmas we had good wins over Oxford University (11-8), Leicester (15-4) and Richmond/Blackheath in the return (16-10) but were beaten by Wasps at Sudbury (6-19) and Cardiff (3-23) before finishing the year off with a 30-13 win over the Metropolitan Police at Twickenham.

Our first match against London Irish since 1910 was a victim of the weather as was the game with Bedford. We did manage to defeat Northampton and complete the double over Cambridge but lost to Guy's Hospital and drew 0-0 with the Royal Navy at Portsmouth. After beating Oxford for the second time we drew our fourth game of the season against Leicester (8-8) and won at Teddington against the Old Merchant Taylors and the Royal Marines. In the games against Leicester and the O.M.T.'s we played a man short throughout. The last six games of the season were not nearly as successful with only a good 16-9 win over Swansea on the revived Easter tour to show for our efforts. Defeats were met at the hands of London Scottish (5-27), London Welsh (8-26), Bristol (6-16), Gloucester (5-11) and Cardiff (6-14). Even with these losses we still managed fourteen wins against eleven defeats to go with the four draws already mentioned.

Robert Weighill, who made his debut in the match with United Services, Portsmouth was to win four caps for England, two each in 1947 and 1948. He led the team in his last international against France (lost 0-15). Hugh de Lacy was our other new international player to make his debut this season. He played first against Rosslyn Park on 22nd September and was to win two caps for Ireland in 1948. Among the others playing their first games was A.A. (Alan) Grimsdell (who went on to make at least 161 appearances). Norman Steel (who had been a regular member of the side over the war years) made the last of his 49 confirmed appearances against Cardiff on 22nd April. C.H. Watson was top try scorer with 13, Ken Chapman got 71 points (one try, 8 penalties and 22 conversions) and the team scored 66 tries and 337 points. Top appearance makers were Ken Chapman (21), Geoff Butler and Jack Davies (18) and Norman Steel (16). So ended a reasonably successful season, the first full one for several years.

1945/46

220945	ROSSLYN PARK	OLD DEER PARK	D	2PG1T(9)-1PG2T(9)
290945	BATH	TEDDINGTON	W	1G2T(11)-2T(6)
061045	LONDON SCOTTISH	RICHMOND	L	0-1G1T(8)
131045	WASPS	TEDDINGTON	L	1G(5)-2G2PG2T(22)
201045	CAMBRIDGE UNIVERSITY	CAMBRIDGE	W	1G3T(14)-2G(10)
271045	COVENTRY	COVENTRY	L	1G1T(8)-1G1DG2T(15)
031145	BRISTOL	BRISTOL	W	2T(6)-1G(5)
101145	RICHMOND/BLACKHEATH	TWICKENHAM	D	2G1PG2T(19)-1DG1PG4T(19)
171145	OXFORD UNIVERSITY	TWICKENHAM	W	1G2T(11)-1G1T(8)
241145	WASPS	SUDBURY	L	2PG(6)-3G1DG(19)
011245	LEICESTER	TWICKENHAM	W	3G(15)-1DG(4)
081245	OLD MERCHANT TAYLORS	CROXLEY GREEN	W	(21)-(3)
151245	CARDIFF	TWICKENHAM	L	1T(3)-4G1T(23)
221245	RICHMOND/BLACKHEATH	RICHMOND	W	2G2T(16)-2G(10)
291245	METROPOLITAN POLICE	TWICKENHAM	W	3G5T(30)-2G1T(13)
050146	LONDON IRISH	SUNBURY	C	
120146	GUY'S HOSPITAL	TWICKENHAM	L	1G1T(8)-2G(10)
190146	BEDFORD	BEDFORD	C	
260146	CAMBRIDGE UNIVERSITY	TWICKENHAM	W	2G2PG3T(25)-1G1PG3T(17)
020246	NORTHAMPTON	NORTHAMPTON	W	1G1T(8)-1G(5)
090246	ROYAL NAVY	PORTSMOUTH	D	0-0
160246	OXFORD UNIVERSITY	OXFORD	W	3G3T(24)-2G1PG2T(19)
020346	LEICESTER	LEICESTER	D	1G1T(8)-1G1PG(8)
090346	OLD MERCHANT TAYLORS	TEDDINGTON	W	4G(20)-1G1PG(8)
140346	ROYAL MARINES	TEDDINGTON	W	(24)-(13)
230346	LONDON SCOTTISH	TEDDINGTON	L	1G(5)-3G1PG3T(27)
300346	LONDON WELSH	TWICKENHAM	L	1G1PG(8)-4G2T(26)
060446	BRISTOL	TWICKENHAM	L	1PG1T(6)-2G2T(16)
130446	GLOUCESTER	GLOUCESTER	L	1G(5)-1G1PG1T(11)
200446	SWANSEA	SWANSEA	W	2G1PG1T(16)-1PG2T(9)
220446	CARDIFF	CARDIFF	L	2T(6)-1G3T(14)

At the A.G.M. held at Teddington on 21st September 1946 a loss on the year's working of £120 was made, the takings being £904. The President urged players to do their utmost to avoid incurring penalty kicks and stressed that no one can get more out of anything than he puts into it. On 9th October, Arthur Moller referred to the unselfish devotion to the interests of the Club which had been shown by Adrian Stoop as secretary for the past forty years and the enormous amount of work on the Club's behalf which he had done during that period and he proposed that a formal record of the appreciation and gratitude of the Committee and members of the Club should be made in the minutes. This was seconded by P.W. Adams and carried unanimously. Stoop's replacement as secretary was Ken Chapman who was to hold the post until 1949. The beginnings of the modern press officer were formed when it was decided to appoint a sub-committee to deal with the press, the members being Ken Chapman (Chairman), Maurice Daly and D.B. (Derek) Willis.

The first mention of a supporters' club is made and although discussions were held over, it was finally decided to start one at the beginning of the 1949/50 season with the secretary suggesting organisation and draft rules for the club. On 10th April the subject of the Club's history is mentioned for the first time and eventually culminated in Wakelam's original "Harlequin Story" in 1954. On 13th May at a meeting held at The Green Man on the Strand, John Matthews proposed, Maurice Daly seconded and it was unanimously decided that in view of the Club's association with Mumbles arising out of the Welsh tour that a donation of £26 5s 0d be sent to the Mayor of Swansea's fund for the relatives of those lost in the Mumbles lifeboat disaster. On 17th June new caps were awarded to Jack Davies, Ian Watts, Fred Dunkley and John Matthews while Jack Hubbard was elected as a Vice President. It was noted that Cambridge University had decided to play only one game per season against London clubs and so the gap created by this in our fixture list had been filled by the Royal Air Force.

After feeling our way back the previous year, this season was going to let us know exactly where our playing strength stood in relation to other teams in the country. B.D. (Basil) Napper was elected captain for the season, he had made his debut for the 1st XV back on 3rd November 1934 against Bristol and was one of a number of old players still playing first team rugby. These men, through no fault of their own had lost six of their best rugby playing years and were now in the latter stages of their careers. We started in excellent fashion, winning our first six games (our best start since 1926/27) with victories over, amongst others, London Scottish (17-8), Cambridge University (18-5) and Coventry (14-6). Our first reverse came at Twickenham on 2nd November against Bristol. We failed to get on the scoreboard whilst conceding fourteen points. We sneaked past Richmond (8-0) before Oxford University got their revenge for the previous season's losses with a 24-0 victory. A crowd of some 12,000 witnessed this game and gate receipts totalled £846 (the record in all matches was a crowd of 16,000 and gate receipts of £2,250 when we met the Maoris in 1926). Blackheath were now back to playing as themselves again (as were Richmond) and a draw of six points each was the result. Leicester visited us at Teddington on 7th December and scored a try and dropped a goal for a narrow win. Our next match produced an easy win over the Old Merchant Taylors, we managed to score ten tries but could only convert one for a scoreline of 32-0.

The return with Richmond at Twickenham produced an away win by eleven points to nine and we finally met London Irish on 4th January at Sunbury and proceeded to win 13-6. Bedford won a game containing six penalty goals (which was believed to be, at the time, a record for their ground) by seven points (15-22). After this the big freeze came and two months and eight cancelled games later (including first games against Birkenhead Park in 15 years, Newport in 17 years and the Royal Air Force in 26 years) we met London Scottish at Richmond on 22nd March and outscored them by three tries to one and by fourteen points to six. London Welsh were met the following week and some revenge was gained for our defeat at the same time the previous year when we triumphed by eight points to three. Making his debut for us in this game was B.H. (Basil) "Jika" Travers who, having already won two England caps, went on to win four more (two each in 1948 and 1949). The Easter tour had an additional game this year with a match at Bath on Maundy Thursday, 3rd April. Defeat by one try to nil set the tone for a tour of low scoring games. The Saturday encounter with Swansea saw J.V. Bartlett score a try for us in the first half only for W.G.A. Parkhouse to kick a penalty for the home side in the second to draw the game. Against Cardiff on Easter Monday we trailed by eleven points before Ian Watts dropped a goal to narrow the margin of defeat.

Our last two games meant trips to the West Country on successive Saturdays, the first was to Kingsholm to meet a Gloucester side weakened by calls to the County Championship semi-final. Having said this, Gloucester are never an easy side to defeat on their own patch and so it proved as they gave us a run for our money after E.L. Horsfall (converted by Jack Davies) and Cecil McIver had got tries and Maurice Daly had kicked a penalty to give us a lead of eleven points to nil at the break. D.D. Evans dropped a goal and W. Dix grabbed a try to pull them within four points of our score before renewed pressure enabled Daly to kick another two penalties for a 17-7 victory. On 19th April we travelled to Bristol who, having been the first club to lower our colours, became the last to do so as well in this season. Maurice Daly scored all our points with a converted try and a penalty but Bristol's six unconverted tries left them with a ten point winning margin.

R.M. (Ricky) Bartlett made his debut against Leicester on 7th December and went on to make a confirmed 276 appearances for the 1st XV and win seven caps for England in 1957 and 1958. E.L. (Edward) Horsfall debuted in the same game and appeared at least 48 times and gained a single cap for England in 1949. D.M. (David) Stileman made the first of at least 38 appearances in the match with St. Mary's Hospital on 21st September and J.D. Ronald made his last appearance against London Irish on 4th January having played first in 1931. He scored 74 points (2 dropped goals, 4 penalties and 27 conversions) during the course of his career in the 1st XV. Geoff Butler and Maurice Daly shared top spot for the most tries with eight each, Ian Watts dropped two goals, Jack Davies kicked nine penalty goals and Daly was top points scorer with fifty nine (adding five penalties and ten conversions to his tries). The team scored only 47 tries and 230 points (which was over 100 down on the previous season). Out of a maximum of twenty three appearances, Daly came top with nineteen closely followed by Jack Davies (18) and John Matthews (16).

1946/47

210946	ST.MARY'S HOSPITAL	TWICKENHAM	W	2G1T(13)-1PG2T(9)
280946	ROSSLYN PARK	OLD DEER PARK	W	2G1T(13)-2PG(6)
051046	LONDON SCOTTISH	TWICKENHAM	W	1G4T(17)-1G1PG(8)
121046	UNITED SERVICES PORTSMOUTH	PORTSMOUTH	W	1G1T(8)-1PG(3)
191046	CAMBRIDGE UNIVERSITY	TWICKENHAM	W	3G1PG(18)-1G(5)
261046	COVENTRY	TWICKENHAM	W	1G3T(14)-2T(6)
021146	BRISTOL	TWICKENHAM	L	0-2DG2T(14)
091146	RICHMOND	RICHMOND	W	1G1T(8)-0
161146	OXFORD UNIVERSITY	TWICKENHAM	L	0-3G3T(24)
231146	BLACKHEATH	BLACKHEATH	D	2PG(6)-2T(6)
301146	BATH	BATH	C	
071246	LEICESTER	TEDDINGTON	L	0-1DG1T(7)
141246	OLD MERCHANT TAYLORS	CROXLEY GREEN	W	1G9T(32)-0
211246	CARDIFF	TWICKENHAM	C	
281246	RICHMOND	TWICKENHAM	L	1PG2T(9)-1G1PG1T(11)
040147	LONDON IRISH	SUNBURY	W	2G1PG(13)-2T(6)
110147	BLACKHEATH	TWICKENHAM	L	1DG2T(10)-2G1PG(13)
180147	BEDFORD	BEDFORD	L	4PG1T(15)-2G2PG2T(22)
250147	CAMBRIDGE UNIVERSITY	CAMBRIDGE	C	
010247	NORTHAMPTON	NORTHAMPTON	C	

080247	BIRKENHEAD PARK	BIRKENHEAD	C	
150247	ROYAL AIR FORCE	TEDDINGTON	C	
220247	ROYAL NAVY	PORTSMOUTH	C	
010347	LEICESTER	LEICESTER	C	
080347	WASPS	SUDBURY	C	
150347	NEWPORT	NEWPORT	C	
220347	LONDON SCOTTISH	RICHMOND	W	1G1PG2T(14)-1PG1T(6)
290347	LONDON WELSH	TWICKENHAM	W	1G1PG(8)-1T(3)
030447	BATH	BATH	L	0-1T(3)
050447	SWANSEA	SWANSEA	D	1T(3)-1PG(3)
070447	CARDIFF	CARDIFF	L	1DG(4)-1G2T(11)
120447	GLOUCESTER	GLOUCESTER	W	1G3PG1T(17)-1DG1T(7)
190447	BRISTOL	BRISTOL	L	1G1PG(8)-6T(18)

At the A.G.M. on 16th August a record profit on the year was reported as £1,540 11s 7d (we had actually taken £2,160 in gate money) and a payment was reported on 17th October as having been received on account from the War Damage Commission in respect of the Teddington ground, the amount being £51 19s 4d. On 28th May a letter was read out by the secretary from the Harlequin Club in Victoria, Australia asking whether we would agree to affiliation of that club with our own in England. The secretary was instructed to reply in friendly terms agreeing to the said affiliation.

Because of the large amount of matches cancelled in the previous season it was impossible to fully judge the strength of the 1st XV, this season would show that we lacked strength in depth. We started off well enough under the captaincy of John Matthews with a 23-13 win over St. Mary's Hospital but we lost Geoff Butler who broke a leg in scoring his try and so finished his career after scoring 54 tries. The following week during the twenty four points to three victory over Rosslyn Park at Twickenham, our full back (K.A.W. Oldham) crashed into the seating early in the game, injured his leg and had to leave the field. By the time our third game against London Scottish at Richmond came around, we had lost Edward Horsfall and Thompson "Tom" Danby through injuries as well. We still managed to defeat the Scots with tries from David Stileman, David Brooks, Maurice Daly and Jack Davies (who added the conversion to the second try) to a penalty goal for the home team. When we met United Services, Portsmouth at Twickenham on 11th October, the brilliance of Davies and De Lacy at half back laid the foundations for our victory. They both actually scored, Davies getting two tries and De Lacy one while Daly added two conversions for a 13-0 win. This was to be the last we saw of Davies as, after this match, he turned professional.

Our winning run was about to come to an end with a narrow defeat at Cambridge (8-11). Following on from this we were beaten narrowly away at Coventry (12-16) and Bristol (10-14) and by larger margins at Twickenham by Richmond (9-21) and Oxford University (0-24). The rot was stopped with a draw of eight points each against Blackheath and a narrow win at Bath with a try by Daly in the last thirty seconds (12-9). The following week it was Leicester's turn to visit Twickenham after having lost ten and drawn one of their last eleven games. After a close game the Tigers ran out winners by eleven points to eight. We briefly returned to winning ways against the Old Merchant Taylors at Croxley Green on 13th December, outscoring them by thirteen points to eleven. The following week we met Cardiff at Penarth for the only time. The reasons for this were that the game was originally scheduled to be played at Twickenham but the Final Trial for the England versus Australia game was taking place there, Teddington could not cope with a large gate and Wales were playing Australia at Cardiff Arms Park on the day in question. Penarth and Pontypridd were suggested as possible venues, but finally the first named club was approached and it was willing to help. Both sides were weakened but Cardiff proved too strong and ran out easy winners by 29-8.

After this our decline reached free fall proportions and we managed to lose twelve out of our last fifteen matches. Richmond completed the double over us for the first time in twelve years (and would have to wait until 1972 before doing it again) by beating us 12-3 at the Athletic Ground and the greater speed and deadly tackling of the London Irish allowed them to defeat us by twenty two points to nil at Teddington where we played schoolboy international P. Wilson at fly half. After this we fell to Blackheath (7-14), Cambridge University (3-8), London Scottish (3-26) and Northampton (0-6) before having a respite when our fixture at Newport was cancelled. On 28th February, the Royal Navy were our visitors and it looked as though we might stop the rot when we went into the lead after C.H. Watson grabbed a try and Stileman converted but the Navy came back and by the end of the first half led by a point thanks to two penalties from J.C. Murphy O'Connor. In the second half J. Lindsey-Smith scored an unconverted try to stretch their lead but we were not to be denied and tries from R.D. Austen-Smith and a second from Watson (converted by Stileman) saw us home 13-9.

Unfortunately, with such a strong fixture list another tough game is never far away and a trip to Leicester was our next appointment. By half time we had managed only a penalty from Daly to the home side's two goals and a penalty and things got considerably worse after this with another two goals, two penalties and a try coming for Leicester with nothing from us. This enabled them to run up their highest score of the season and equal their best score against us (3-32) set on the corresponding Saturday seventeen years before. It was also, needless to say, our heaviest defeat of the season. More defeats followed against Bedford, Wasps, Swansea, Cardiff and Gloucester but our last two home games did produce victories over London Welsh and Bristol. In the match against London Welsh we managed to win 3-0 thanks to a try from Watson but the Welsh should and probably would have won had they not missed twelve penalty kicks at goal! Our final playing record for this season was P29 W9 D1 L19. The last time we had failed to win less matches than the nine won this time (excluding the shortened 1939/40 season when eight were won) was the 1904/05 season when we managed just six victories against fifteen losses and a draw.

P.J. Goodman made the first of at least 60 appearances against London Scottish on 4th October but we lost M.E. Golding (64 appearances) who played his last match against Bristol on 1st November, Basil Napper (at least 75) against Richmond on 27th December and Ken Chapman against London Welsh on 3rd April having scored 662 points (18 tries, 1 dropped goal, 72 penalties and 194 conversions) during his career with the Club (he would go on to become President of the Club in due course). David Stileman scored seven tries and also top scored with 58 points (adding seven penalties and eight conversions to his tries) and C.G. Bellamy got two dropped goals. Tries and overall points dropped again, this time down to 44 and 229 respectively, tying in with our dismal playing record. Stileman appeared in the most games (24), the closest to him being Fred Dunkley (19), P.J. Goodman (17) and Hugh De Lacy and John Matthews with sixteen.

1947/48

200947	ST.MARY'S HOSPITAL	TEDDINGTON(A)	W	2G1DG1PG2T(23)-2G1PG(13)
270947	ROSSLYN PARK	TWICKENHAM	W	3G3T(24)-1T(3)
041047	LONDON SCOTTISH	RICHMOND	W	1G3T(14)-1PG(3)

111047	UNITED SERVICES PORTSMOUTH	TWICKENHAM	W	2G1T(13)-0
181047	CAMBRIDGE UNIVERSITY	CAMBRIDGE	L	1G1T(8)-1G2PG(11)
251047	COVENTRY	COVENTRY	L	1PG3T(12)-1DG3PG1T(16)
011147	BRISTOL	BRISTOL	L	2G(10)-1G3T(14)
081147	RICHMOND	TWICKENHAM	L	3PG(9)-3G1PG1T(21)
151147	OXFORD UNIVERSITY	TWICKENHAM	L	0-3G1PG2T(24)
221147	BLACKHEATH	TWICKENHAM	D	1G1PG(8)-1G1PG(8)
291147	BATH	BATH	W	1PG3T(12)-1PG2T(9)
061247	LEICESTER	TWICKENHAM	L	1G(5)-1G2T(11)
131247	OLD MERCHANT TAYLORS	CROXLEY GREEN	W	2G1T(13)-1G2PG(11)
201247	CARDIFF	PENARTH	L	1G1T(8)-4G1PG2T(29)
271247	RICHMOND	RICHMOND	L	1PG(3)-4T(12)
030148	LONDON IRISH	TEDDINGTON	L	0-2G1PG3T(22)
100148	BLACKHEATH	BLACKHEATH	L	1DG1PG(7)-1G3T(14)
240148	CAMBRIDGE UNIVERSITY	TWICKENHAM	L	1PG(3)-1G1T(8)
310148	LONDON SCOTTISH	TEDDINGTON	L	1PG(3)-2G1DG1PG3T(26)
070248	NORTHAMPTON	NORTHAMPTON	L	0-1PG1T(6)
210248	NEWPORT	NEWPORT	C	
280248	ROYAL NAVY	TWICKENHAM	W	2G1T(13)-2PG1T(9)
060348	LEICESTER	LEICESTER	L	1PG(3)-4G3PG1T(32)
130348	BEDFORD	TWICKENHAM	L	0-1G1DG2T(15)
200348	WASPS	SUDBURY	L	1DG2T(10)-1G1PG1T(11)
270348	SWANSEA	SWANSEA	L	1DG1T(7)-3G1PG1T(21)
290348	CARDIFF	CARDIFF	L	1G(5)-5G2T(31)
030448	LONDON WELSH	TEDDINGTON	W	1T(3)-0
100448	GLOUCESTER	GLOUCESTER	L	1PG(3)-1DG2PG2T(16)
170448	BRISTOL	TWICKENHAM	W	2G(10)-1G(5)

At the A.G.M. on 16th July it was reported that a loss on the year of £585 10s 1d had been made, this was quite a shock after the profit of the previous season but the reasons were due to a large reduction in gate receipts (down to £977) attributable partly to the ban on basic petrol which had made attendance at Twickenham much more difficult and also the indifferent playing record of the 1st XV. Arising from this, various points were raised over the lack of playing members of the required standard. It was felt that a crucial point in the history of the Club had been reached and that action had to be taken. On 29th October it was reported that jerseys were in very short supply and John Matthews undertook to try and find out from South Africa whether the Pretoria Harlequins Club could produce sets of jerseys in its colours at a more reasonable figure than had so far been quoted but this idea was later discarded as being impracticable. A number of jerseys were eventually acquired from Lillywhites but the colours were said to have differed somewhat from those previously worn by the side.

The search for a new ground was still on and three games had been arranged to be played at the Oval (home of Surrey County Cricket Club) in season 1949/50 and apart from these, the Club would be staying at Twickenham.

Unfortunately, this was leaked to the press and members of the Committee were urged to keep all matters confidential until the appropriate time. On 7th January G.C. Burgess the "A" team captain made a suggestion to change the name of the 2nd XV from first "A" team to something like the Wanderers or Vandals. This was seen as desirable from the point of view of both esprit de corps and obtaining better fixtures. This would in turn enable players playing in this side to appear for the 1st XV if and when required. The Committee agreed that the various captains should decide on the most popular name and on 28th January it was agreed that the name be changed to Harlequin Wanderers.

A new captain, W.M. (Martin) Jackson, led us for the 1948/49 season and after the disasters of the previous one things surely could only get better. For the most part results did improve slightly although we got off to a none too promising start when St. Mary's Hospital defeated us by five points to three at Twickenham. This was the first season after the dropped goal had been reduced in value from four points to three and a newspaper report on the game stated that this did not deter the two teams from making between them the five worst attempts the reporter hoped to see all season! Our next four matches were won including victories over London Scottish (22-10) and United Services, Portsmouth (29-0) which proved to be our biggest win of the season. Our colours were then lowered by Coventry, Bath and Bristol in successive weeks and on 20th November Oxford University defeated us by the same score for the third consecutive time (0-24).

On 4th December, we met Leicester at Teddington and, after a scoreless first half, the visitors took the lead with a try by D.E.B. Rees. This they held until the final minute when Austen-Smith grabbed a try and Basil Travers kicked the conversion to win the match. The following week we played our first ever game against Heriot's Former Pupils when they came to Twickenham. The visitors took the lead when F.C. Cheshire scored a try and converted it (he added a second try later in the half), we came back to level things at half time with a try from J.R. O'Donnell (converted by Travers) and a dropped goal from C.G. Bellamy. In the second half, despite being trapped in our own twenty five for most of the time, we broke out near the end and Cecil McIver got over for the try that gave us an eleven points to eight victory. Cardiff beat us again the following week by nineteen points to three (we had not now beaten them since the Easter tour of 1936) and we met the London Irish at the Rectory Field, Blackheath for the first time and were duly beaten by seventeen points to nil.

On 8th January, we met Blackheath at Twickenham, the visitors trying to and succeeding in breaking a run of twelve straight defeats by scoring a penalty goal after just four minutes. A week later, Birkenhead Park were met for the first time since 1932 and were defeated by a penalty goal from Alan Grimsdell. Our last victory of the season came at Teddington on 19th February against the Royal Air Force. In the first half honours were even, each side scoring a goal and a try. For us, Danby (who turned professional with Salford in June 1949 having won his only England cap against Wales in January; he would go on to win three caps each for England and Great Britain) and Grimsdell got tries and P.J. Goodman kicked a conversion while for the servicemen two of our own players scored all their points (R.J.H. (Richard) Uprichard (who won two caps for Ireland in 1950) scoring two tries and Edward Horsfall converting one). After the interval we managed to score sixteen more points with two tries by N.T. (Norman) Fryer and a try, two conversions and a penalty from Goodman to leave us winners by 24-8. J.M. (John) Williams made his debut in this game and was to go on and win two England caps in 1951 when he played for Penzance-Newlyn. There cannot have been many sides with a more difficult end to the season than us which left us with seven away trips and just two home games at Twickenham.

The first away day was to Portsmouth to meet the Royal Navy and our cause was not helped by the late arrival of Alan Grimsdell, who took the field after fifteen minutes. With only ten minutes remaining, we trailed by eleven points and staged a recovery which almost gave us victory when J.S. Stones and P.J. Goodman scored tries, Goodman converting his own to add to his first half penalty, but it was not enough and we went down 11-14. Against Leicester, snow fell throughout the game and ruined the spectacle and we came away defeated by a penalty goal and a try to nil. Against Bedford, we almost pulled off a victory when D.A. (Dennis) Barker scored a try shortly after the interval only for Bedford's fly half (R.H. Haynes) to get a penalty goal with just two minutes left to tie the scores. On 26th March, we travelled up to Manchester to meet Sale for the very first time and after a very close game we lost out by six points to five (after leading 5-3 at half time) when the home side kicked a penalty in the second half. Joe Mycock, who had played for us over forty times, appeared in the Sale team. In the game with London Welsh, a draw was reported to have been the best result as neither side deserved to win. We, too often, signalled what we intended to do and were too orthodox and our visitors missed five kicks at goal. Both sides did somehow manage to notch up nine points. On 9th April, we met Gloucester at Twickenham and lost yet again by a narrow margin. After B.K. (Brian) Caughey had scored a try in the second half to put us into the lead, Gloucester replied with a try of their own (right under the posts). The conversion was kicked and the visitors had won 5-3. This was Gloucester's first away victory since their defeat of Richmond back in October.

It is interesting to note that of the last six games we had played, two had been drawn and four had been lost by six points or less so could have gone either way. Next on the agenda was the Easter tour and a couple of tough games against Swansea and Cardiff. In the first match at St. Helens, we actually led for the first forty five minutes, but once the home side levelled with a dropped goal they surged ahead with three converted tries and a penalty goal to win by eighteen points. On Easter Monday and in front of a crowd of some 12,000 we took on a Cardiff side whilst having to borrow Derek Evans (a centre) from Penarth. We found Cardiff's captain (Bleddyn Williams) in brilliant form and he scored four tries to add to others from T. Cook and L. Roberts and one conversion by S. Judd. All we could achieve in reply was a dropped goal from Evans and a try from J.M.H. (John) Roberts which was converted by Goodman to leave Cardiff winners by twenty points to eight. In our final game of the season on 23rd April, we travelled to Bristol and had saved our worst for last. We put out a much weakened side (including J. Woodward from Bristol) and paid dearly for it as the home team scored three tries (two converted) to lead by thirteen points at half time. In the second period it became a complete rout and a dropped goal got them on their way. This was followed by a penalty goal and four converted tries to leave them victors by thirty nine points to nil. This was obviously our heaviest defeat of the season and was the first time we had conceded this many points since Cambridge University defeated us 14-39 in October 1921. We have to go back even further (to October 1919) to find a bigger losing margin. Again it was at the hands of the students from Cambridge, the score was 3-43.

On 5th May, Martin Jackson made a statement to the Committee to explain the poor showing of the 1st XV at Bristol. He said that no less than forty eight players had been invited to play for the Club in this match and had not been able to do so. The younger players who had come in had not been up to the standard of football played by the Bristol team. The President then confirmed that he had written a letter to Bristol explaining that the team was not weakened to allow the 2nd VII to win through the preliminaries of the Middlesex seven-a-sides.

Having reached a low point in the 1947/48 season, the overall tries and points actually went up to 46 and 269 during the 1948/49 season although Norman Fryer, the top try scorer, only scored five. Basil Travers scored 72 points (2 tries, 12 conversions and 14 penalties) and Goodman (25), Martin Jackson (16) and Travers (15) were the top appearance makers. New players included D.A. (Dennis) Barker who made the first of a confirmed 144 appearances against Bedford on 12th March, N.T. (Norman) Fryer (at least 93) against London Scottish on 2nd October, G.J. (Gordon) Weston (at least 67) on 8th January against Blackheath and another future England international M.B. (Murray) Hofmeyr who debuted against Cardiff on 18th December. In the same game, Fred Dunkley played the last of 92 confirmed matches for the Club.

1948/49

180948	ST.MARY'S HOSPITAL	TWICKENHAM	L	1PG(3)-1G(5)
250948	ROSSLYN PARK	OLD DEER PARK	W	2G2PG1T(19)-2G(10)
021048	LONDON SCOTTISH	TWICKENHAM	W	2G1PG3T(22)-2G(10)
091048	UNITED SERVICES PORTSMOUTH	PORTSMOUTH	W	4G1PG2T(29)-0
161048	CAMBRIDGE UNIVERSITY	TWICKENHAM	W	2G2PG1T(19)-2T(6)
231048	COVENTRY	TWICKENHAM	L	2PG(6)-1DG2PG(9)
301048	BATH	BATH	L	2G1T(13)-1DG5T(18)
061148	BRISTOL	TWICKENHAM	L	1PG(3)-2T(6)
131148	RICHMOND	RICHMOND	W	3PG4T(21)-2T(6)
201148	OXFORD UNIVERSITY	TWICKENHAM	L	0-3G3PG(24)
271148	BLACKHEATH	BLACKHEATH	W	2T(6)-1PG(3)
041248	LEICESTER	TEDDINGTON	W	1G(5)-1T(3)
111248	HERIOT'S F.P.	TWICKENHAM	W	1G1DG1T(11)-1G1T(8)
181248	CARDIFF	TWICKENHAM	L	1DG(3)-2G3T(19)
271248	RICHMOND	RICHMOND	W	2G1DG1PG(16)-1DG(3)
010149	LONDON IRISH	BLACKHEATH	L	0-1G1DG3T(17)
080149	BLACKHEATH	TWICKENHAM	L	0-1PG(3)
150149	BIRKENHEAD PARK	BIRKENHEAD	W	1PG(3)-0
220149	OLD MERCHANT TAYLORS	CROXLEY GREEN	W	(15)-(13)
290149	LONDON SCOTTISH	RICHMOND	L	2PG1T(9)-2G4T(22)
050249	NORTHAMPTON	NORTHAMPTON	C	
190249	ROYAL AIR FORCE	TEDDINGTON	W	3G1PG2T(24)-1G1T(8)
260249	ROYAL NAVY	PORTSMOUTH	L	1G1PG1T(11)-1G1PG2T(14)
050349	LEICESTER	LEICESTER	L	0-1PG1T(6)
120349	BEDFORD	BEDFORD	D	1T(3)-1PG(3)
260349	SALE	SALE	L	1G(5)-1PG1T(6)
020449	LONDON WELSH	TWICKENHAM	D	1PG2T(9)-2PG1T(9)
090449	GLOUCESTER	TWICKENHAM	L	1T(3)-1G(5)
160449	SWANSEA	SWANSEA	L	1T(3)-3G1DG1PG(21)
180449	CARDIFF	CARDIFF	L	1G1T(8)-1G5T(20)
230449	BRISTOL	BRISTOL	L	0-6G1DG1PG1T(39)

At the A.G.M. on 30th June, a large majority confirmed the change of name of the "A" XV to Harlequin Wanderers, a name which has pretty much disappeared today. Our takings in 1948/49 were £2,235 which led to a profit of £542 but 1949/50 was not so good as takings only amounted to £995 which, in turn, led to a loss on the year of £1,042. At this time, seasons were often referred to as "on" or "off". This meant that in an "on" season, our gate receipts would be very good as we tended to play the bigger crowd drawing teams such as Cardiff and Coventry at home whereas in an "off" season these games would be away and therefore no gate money would be forthcoming and our takings would be well down. The end of the season saw a few changes off the pitch for the Club as Adrian Stoop did not wish to seek re-election as President (despite all efforts at persuading him otherwise), Holly Ward resigned as Honorary Treasurer, a post he had held since 1912 and Ken Chapman left the post of Honorary Secretary. They were replaced by Sir William Wavell Wakefield, Denys Gardiner and H.J. (Jay) Gould respectively.

The 1949/50 season saw a different captain but not a new one. John Matthews was back again for this and the next two seasons. Our second team is called the Wanderers in print for the first time and there are now two "A" XVs. Our first match, once again, was against St. Mary's Hospital and was played on their ground at Udney Park Road, Teddington. In keeping with the previous season's encounter, this was another tight game and was only decided in the final minute when our scrum half (Austen-Smith) went over for a try to give us an 8-6 victory. We lost him, injured, in our first game at Twickenham against Rosslyn Park and so lost the match, despite making an excellent fist of it, by nine points to nil. After a draw with London Scottish, we defeated U.S. Portsmouth (who became handicapped by an injury to one of their forwards) and lost to Coventry (which was now becoming a bit of a habit). Bath were met at Twickenham on 29th October and after a good performance (we were described in one report as having winged feet and Bath as having lead in their boots) we ran out easy winners 24-6.

We then travelled to Bristol and were again beaten scoreless, but this time the home side only got a penalty goal with ten minutes left. Unfortunately, heavy rain made conditions very difficult and both sides failed to come to terms with them. Making his debut in this game was P.D.F. (Pat) Cleaver, he went on to play at least 66 matches for the 1st XV over the next six seasons. Richmond, Blackheath and Leicester were all beaten but Oxford University defeated us by just a goal to nil before two historic matches were played. The first, on 10th December was our second against Heriot's F.P. but it was the first time we had played in Scotland. The game was played at Goldenacre and we managed to score twice in the first half through B.H. McGuirk and Brian Caughey with both tries being converted by Alan Grimsdell to which Heriot's replied with a penalty kicked by D.E. Muir and a try by J. Thomson. After the break the home side rallied and went into the lead with tries by T.R. Stewart and D.W. Deas (the last one being converted by F.C. Cheshire) and in the remaining ten minutes we could only score a try by J.R. O'Donnell to which Grimsdell could not add the extra points. Time ran out with the score standing at 13-14 to the home side.

The second match was our first meeting with the Paris Université Club from France. N.J.D. (Nick) Williams got the opening score and Grimsdell converted before A. Fremeau grabbed a try to pull back three points before half time. Playing into the wind in the second half, we started badly and F. Gaillard dropped a goal to put the Frenchmen one point ahead. After this the game was won for us by Brian Caughey who forced his way over for a try and dropped a goal just before the end to make the final score eleven points to six in our favour. On Christmas Eve and New Year's Eve we faced both tenants from the Richmond Athletic Ground, defeating Richmond first and then drawing for the second time this season with London Scottish (3-3 again!).

We followed these matches with two trips to Blackheath to meet London Irish and then Blackheath (in the days before the M25 this was not an easy trip to undertake!). We lost to the Irish (6-11) and completed the double over Blackheath (12-3) but our game the following week against Cambridge University was cancelled for the second time in one season. Northampton were met at Teddington and even though they turned up with ten regulars missing (all required for the County Championship semi-final) we only just managed to win by nine points to five. We played Cardiff on 18th February at the Old Deer Park (kindly lent by Rosslyn Park) but a different venue made absolutely no difference to the result and we lost to them for the twelfth consecutive time. On this occasion, we had scored the first eight points and everything was going well until Cardiff scored fourteen of their own. C.G. (Charles) "Peter" Woodruff played the first of his 190 confirmed games for the 1st XV in this match and went on to win four caps for England. Revenge was gained over the Royal Navy (8-6) for the previous season's defeat and we won against Leicester (completing the double in the process) and Bedford before meeting Newport in Wales for the first time since 1930. Peter Woodruff opened our account with a try only for the home side to score three of their own, convert two and add a penalty to win by sixteen points to three. Interestingly, Woodruff (who had attended Newport High School) had played for Newport earlier in the season at the request of the Welsh selectors and our scrum half (Norman Fryer) had also appeared in their colours.

Revenge over Sale followed on 25th March at Teddington when we outscored them by five tries to one for a 21-3 final score. This victory set us in motion for our longest sequence without defeat since 1910. We were to stay undefeated for the remaining five games of this season and the first six of the next. Three of the matches were draws, against London Welsh (8-8) and Cardiff and the return with the Paris Université Club (at the Stade Jean Bouin in Paris) were both 6-6. The two wins were against Swansea on Easter Saturday and Bristol at Twickenham. At Swansea, victory was due mainly to our forwards, who played a great game. Peter Woodruff and Dennis Barker got tries and Alan Grimsdell (who converted Barker's try) added a penalty when Swansea had closed to within two points of our score with a penalty goal and a try. The earlier mentioned draw with Cardiff enabled this to be the first Easter tour since 1936 on which we had remained unbeaten. In the match with Bristol, it was our turn to upset their winning run which had been going since Cardiff defeated them back in the middle of January. This time two Grimsdell penalties were enough to outscore a try by G. Green for the visitors.

R.C.C. (Richard) "Clem" Thomas made his first appearance for us in the Leicester game and was to go on and win 26 caps for Wales. His next (and last two) appearances for us were to be on the tour to Rumania in 1956. This had been our best season since 1938/39 with sixteen wins being registered against five draws and eight defeats. It now appeared that, at last, things were looking up. J.R. O'Donnell scored the most tries (12), Brian Caughey got two dropped goals, N.J.D. (Nick) Williams scored our first goal from a mark since the 1930/31 season and Alan Grimsdell top scored with sixty two points (2 tries, 13 conversions and 10 penalties). Overall, the team scored 50 tries and 252 points, another slight increase in tries but the total number of points was down. Out of a total of 29 games, Alan Grimsdell and Nick Williams appeared in twenty three, Dennis Barker and G.J. Weston in twenty two and these four were closely followed by John Matthews (21), B.H. McGuirk (20) and Norman Fryer (19).

Vic Roberts made the 1950 British Lions tour to New Zealand and Australia but played in none of the test matches. In New Zealand, one was drawn and three were lost while in Australia, both were won.

1949/50

170949	ST.MARY'S HOSPITAL	TEDDINGTON(A)	W	1G1T(8)-2T(6)
240949	ROSSLYN PARK	TWICKENHAM	L	0-1DG2T(9)
011049	LONDON SCOTTISH	RICHMOND	D	1T(3)-1T(3)
081049	UNITED SERVICES PORTSMOUTH	PORTSMOUTH	W	2G1PG2T(19)-1T(3)
151049	CAMBRIDGE UNIVERSITY	CAMBRIDGE	C	
221049	COVENTRY	COVENTRY	L	0-3PG(9)
291049	BATH	TWICKENHAM	W	3G3T(24)-1PG1T(6)
051149	BRISTOL	BRISTOL	L	0-1PG(3)
121149	RICHMOND	TWICKENHAM	W	1G2T(11)-2PG(6)
191149	OXFORD UNIVERSITY	OXFORD	L	0-1G(5)
261149	BLACKHEATH	TWICKENHAM	W	1G2PG1T(14)-0
031249	LEICESTER	TEDDINGTON	W	1G1PG2T(14)-1T(3)
101249	HERIOT'S F.P.	EDINBURGH	L	2G1T(13)-1G1PG2T(14)
171249	PARIS UNIVERSITÉ CLUB	TWICKENHAM	W	1G1DG1T(11)-1DG1T(6)
241249	RICHMOND	RICHMOND	W	2PG1T(9)-2DG(6)
311249	LONDON SCOTTISH	TWICKENHAM	D	1DG(3)-1DG(3)
070150	LONDON IRISH	BLACKHEATH	L	1PG1T(6)-1G1PG1T(11)
140150	BLACKHEATH	BLACKHEATH	W	1PG3T(12)-1PG(3)
280150	CAMBRIDGE UNIVERSITY	CAMBRIDGE	C	
040250	NORTHAMPTON	TEDDINGTON	W	1PG2T(9)-1G(5)
180250	CARDIFF	OLD DEER PARK(H)	L	1G1PG(8)-1G2PG1T(14)
250250	ROYAL NAVY	TWICKENHAM	W	1G1PG(8)-2PG(6)
040350	LEICESTER	LEICESTER	W	1G1PG1T(11)-2PG1T(9)
110350	BEDFORD	TWICKENHAM	W	1G1MG(8)-0
180350	NEWPORT	NEWPORT	L	1T(3)-2G1PG1T(16)
250350	SALE	TEDDINGTON	W	3G2T(21)-1T(3)
010450	LONDON WELSH	HERNE HILL	D	1G1T(8)-1G1T(8)
080450	SWANSEA	SWANSEA	W	1G1PG1T(11)-1PG1T(6)
100450	CARDIFF	CARDIFF	D	2PG(6)-1PG1T(6)
150450	BRISTOL	TWICKENHAM	W	2PG(6)-1T(3)
230450	PARIS UNIVERSITÉ CLUB	STADE JEAN BOUIN	D	2T(6)-1PG1T(6)

17

Sevens in the 1940s

1940-1949

With World War 2 raging all around, the Middlesex Sevens continued unabated except now there were a lot more military sides taking part and finals day was now held at Richmond because of Twickenham being out of action. The 1940 tournament was played on 13th April and St. Mary's Hospital defeated O.C.T.U. Sandhurst (an Army side) in the final by 14-10.

The following year, the holders went out to Guy's Hospital in the Fourth Round after extra time (3-6) and eventually, Cambridge University took the trophy with a win over the Welsh Guards 6-0. The matches were split between Richmond Athletic Ground and Wasps' ground in Sudbury.

For the 1942 event, Richmond was again utilised although the number of teams participating was reduced somewhat. St. Mary's Hospital won again by beating the Royal Air Force 8-6.

The same result in 1943 with St. Mary's Hospital beating Middlesex Hospital 8-3 in the final. There was even a team from the Royal New Zealand Air Force taking part although the losing finalists beat them in the Fifth Round.

St. Mary's completed the hat-trick the following year; the New Zealanders were back again along with such teams as Nottingham, Rosslyn Park, R.A.F. Jurby, Durham Medicals, Twickenham and the Royal Air Force. In the final, the hospital beat Jurby by fifteen points to five.

They couldn't equal our feat in the last of the War tournaments because, although they reached their fourth final in a row, Nottingham won narrowly by 6-3. During these six years, donations to charity amounted to £2,517.

The tournament returned to Twickenham on 27th April 1946 and our 1st VII was represented by C.H. Watson, Daly, J.A. Davies, Norman Steel, Jack Matthews, Gerry Loader and R.L. Hudson; Geoff Butler and David Brooks were reserves. Quins II beat Old Gaytonians (6-0) in Round 2 and H.M.S. Valkyrie (7-3) before succumbing to the New Zealand Army Touring Team (0-24). The firsts defeated Old Blues in Round 5 (10-8) but went out to the eventual winners in the next round (0-14). They were St. Mary's Hospital who won against Cardiff 13-3.

It was noted in the programme for 1947 that over £25,000 had been raised in 21 years and while the Middlesex Hospital had been the main beneficiary, this year the proceeds would be devoted to the War Memorial Appeal of the County Regiment. The seconds reached the latter rounds by beating Napier (10-0), Kodak (18-3), St. Mary's Hospital II (14-5) and London Scottish II (18-0). Maurice Daly captained them and was joined by J.A. Davies, I.H. Watts, Hugh de Lacy, Martin Jackson, Jack Matthews and David Brooks. They went out to Waterloo in Round 5 but our first Seven got revenge. They were represented by David Stileman, A.J. Hockley, Basil Napper (captain),

Ricky Bartlett, George Plumtree, Chris Horner and R.L. Hudson. In their first game, Old Blues I were beaten narrowly (6-3), then Waterloo (11-8) before Richmond proved too strong in the semi-final (8-10). Rosslyn Park I won the final 12-6 for their first win.

On 24th April 1948, as was usual, only our first team made finals day. The second Seven came in at Round 2 and won against U.C.S. Old Boys (16-0) and Old Elizabethans (8-0) before going out to Wasps I (0-11). The team representing our chances was S.G. Fowler, Daly, de Lacy, J.M.H. Roberts, Stileman, E.L. Horsfall and Matthews; M.B. Devine, C.D. McIver and Plumtree were held in reserve. They won against London Irish I (15-3), Rosslyn Park I (3-0) and St. Mary's Hospital I (8-5) before going down to Wasps I in the final by 5-14. The Surrey Sevens started this year and although we didn't even reach the semi-finals in the first two years, we would taste success in the fifties.

By 1949, the Preliminary Rounds were all played on the same day, this time it was 23rd April and the grounds involved were Thames Ditton (Old Paulines), Colindale (Metropolitan Police), Headstone Lane, Pinner (Old Millhillians), Udney Park Road, Teddington (St. Mary's Hospital) and Elmers End (Beckenham). The second Seven played at Headstone Lane and won through to the final rounds the following week with victories over Old Haberdashers I (8-0), Royal Signals (Catterick) II (18-5), Aldershot Services I (8-5), Old Fullerians (13-6) and R.A.F. (Danesfield) (15-13). Representing us on finals day were J.R. O'Donnell, Roberts, F.G.C. Brown, R. Austen-Smith, Devine and B.H. Travers but they came up against guest side Newport and were eliminated by thirteen points to three. Quins I contained. D.A. Barker, T. Norman, Daly, de Lacy, Horsfall, G.J. Weston, and Alan Grimsdell; Norman Fryer and Jackson were in reserve but they too went down in Round 6 albeit narrowly to Wasps I (5-8). The other guest side was Heriot's F.P. and they went on to defeat London Scottish I by 16-6 in the final. In the four years since the end of hostilities, over £11,000 had been raised for the charities.

The Oxfordshire Sevens had started in 1945 and we reached the final in 1949 but lost to Oxford University Greyhounds 0-9.

18

Building Up Our Strength 1950-1956

At a Committee meeting on 19th February the Treasurer pointed out that subscriptions for the season amounted to £532, the highest figure ever known (for 1950/51 this figure rose to £571). It was an "on" year and gate receipts amounted to £2,441 helping the Club to a profit of £490. The Club made an application to the Rugby Football Union to meet the Paris Université Club on 6th May (instead of 29th April), this would have meant playing in the close season and the request was turned down. This meant the team had to fly over to France on the morning following the Middlesex 7-a-sides at Twickenham. At this time, we were paying £300 for the use of Twickenham and £23 for the use of the Old Deer Park. Some other expenses included £6 for membership of the Rugby Union and the various County Unions and £141 for the Easter tour to Wales whereas receipts from the car park amounted to £176.

The first game of the 1950/51 season was, as usual, against St. Mary's Hospital and was played at Twickenham. It was a very impressive start for us and our play was said to have been "as scintillating as our shirts". We had introduced a new concept to English Rugby, a system of coded calls at the lineout. The idea was taken from American Football and worked simply like this: The player throwing the ball in (at this time, wingers tended to do this) would receive a call from the captain (John Matthews) and by deciphering the code he and the rest of the team would know where the ball was going to be thrown whereas the opposition would not. In this game, almost without exception, we won our own lineout. The rest of the game went according to plan as well and we scored three converted tries and a penalty goal to our visitors' solitary penalty goal to win by eighteen points to three. Another hospital side were our next opponents when St. Thomas's were the visitors at Twickenham. This was our first meeting since 1901 because five games in a row had been cancelled and we made light work of them this time, running out easy winners (14-0). H.C. (Hugh) Forbes made his first appearance in our colours in this game and went on to play at least 68 matches for the 1st XV.

Our first away game resulted in a win (over our old rivals Rosslyn Park, 8-0) as did our next three home games against London Scottish, U.S. Portsmouth (48-3, which was our biggest score against them and our biggest win of the season) and Cambridge University. In the United Services match, Dennis Barker got six of our eleven tries and so became the first man since James Reeve in 1931 to score five tries or more in a game. Our first reverse came at Twickenham against (rather predictably) Coventry. At this time, they had one of the most formidable packs in the country and the eventual dominance over our forwards enabled them to win by six points to nil. Against Coventry, Martin Jackson played the last of his 40 confirmed matches for the Club. He had made his debut in February 1939 and, like so many others, had lost his best rugby playing years to the Second World War. For the following two weeks, we returned to winning ways against Bristol (6-5) and Richmond (6-3). Against Richmond we scored the winning try with time running out and with some spectators apparently appealing for a knock-on. We met Leicester at the Old Deer Park on 2nd December and although they became the first team to reach double figures against us during the season, we still managed to defeat them by sixteen points to ten. The following week we received Heriot's F.P. on their second visit to Twickenham and this time they won by a try and a dropped goal to nil. This proved to be our final game of the year as the next three were lost to the weather.

Our first match of 1951 was against the London Irish on their ground at Sunbury and we were beaten by the narrowest of margins (3-0). Things picked up for a while after this and we ran up six wins on the trot including a couple of interesting "firsts". We travelled to Kent on 20th January to play the United Services, Chatham in Gillingham. After the home side had taken the lead with a try, we came back and got tries of our own through Dennis Barker (2), Chris Horner and Norman Fryer which, when added to a conversion by Alan Grimsdell, gave us a 14-3 victory. The following week we travelled down to Devon to play against Paignton. Before the match the two teams were introduced to the Chairman of Paignton Council and afterwards the visiting Quins attended the annual dinner of the Paignton Rugby Supporters' Club. As far as the actual game was concerned, we scored a try after just one minute when Barker went over and the result many people expected appeared to be on the way. They had reckoned without the home side's defence and all we could add was another Barker try, this time converted by Alan Grimsdell, for a final score of eight points to nil. The local newspaper reported that the Quins would be coming again but, alas, it was not to be and this remains the only occasion on which the two sides have met (as was to be the case with U.S. Chatham).

Another Old Deer Park game (the third of nine we would play as the home side) saw us win against the Royal Air Force (6-5) and Leicester gained revenge for their earlier loss with a five-point win at Welford Road (8-3). On 17th March, we achieved what was probably our most amazing result for many a season. Our visitors were Newport and the match was played at Teddington on the morning of the England versus Scotland international. The Welshmen came to us with an unbeaten record stretching back forty matches (when they had been beaten by Cardiff at home on 4th March 1950). Of these, thirty eight had been won and two drawn including twenty seven victories and one draw during the current season. The visitors did have an off day but our defence stood firm and our forwards were outstanding. The decisive point of the match came after just fifteen minutes when one of Newport's forwards (Peter Davies) fell offside and Alan Grimsdell stepped up and kicked the goal to give us a lead which eventually turned into a three point victory. This obviously upset Newport because they were to win the next six games between us (leaving us scoreless in four of these). Funnily enough, our next two matches just happened to be the Easter tour games in Wales against Swansea and Cardiff. We failed to score in either whilst conceding nineteen and three in the respective games. Against Cardiff, in front of a crowd of between 5,000 and 10,000 (three different reports give three different figures!) the conditions were so bad by the end that the referee, unable to distinguish between the two sets of forwards, blew the whistle some seven minutes early.

Following two draws against London Welsh and Gloucester, we again met London Welsh. The first match had been played on their ground at Herne Hill and now we played the return at Twickenham. We fell behind to a penalty kicked by the London Welsh full back (J.D. Marshall) but by half time were in front thanks to tries by Hugh Forbes and R.M. (Ricky) Bartlett and a conversion by Goodman. The only score after this was another try from Bartlett to leave us victors by eleven points to three. Our final game in England this season saw us in the West Country again with a visit to Bristol. When we arrived, we found we were a man short as J.M.H. (John) Roberts had missed the train from Paddington. An SOS went out to Peter Brook (whose last three games for the 1st XV had been in 1937, 1943 and 1944); he was now a master at Clifton College. He rushed to the ground and played in the whole match. We managed two tries by Peter Woodruff to lead 6-3 at half time but the home side scored eight points without reply in the second half to win by eleven points to six. Our final game of the season took place in Paris at Stade Charlety on 29th April against the Paris Université Club. The only score in the match came after 32 minutes when Ricky Bartlett broke away and sent B.H. McGuirk in for a try.

Dennis Barker got sixteen tries and Alan Grimsdell kicked sixty points (15 conversions and 10 penalties). The team scored one more try than the previous season (51) but the number of points scored fell again, this time to 239. Thirty matches were played in this season and the most regular members of the team were Alan Grimsdell with 22 appearances, David Brooks and G.J. Weston (21), P.D. Cleaver, John Roberts and Nick Williams (20), Peter Woodruff (19) and Norman Fryer (18).

1950/51

160950	ST.MARY'S HOSPITAL	TWICKENHAM	W	3G1PG(18)-1PG(3)
230950	ST.THOMAS'S HOSPITAL	TWICKENHAM	W	2G1PG2T(19)-0
300950	ROSSLYN PARK	OLD DEER PARK	W	1G1T(8)-0
071050	LONDON SCOTTISH	TWICKENHAM	W	1G1PG(8)-1T(3)
141050	UNITED SERVICES PORTSMOUTH	TWICKENHAM	W	6G1PG5T(48)-1PG(3)
211050	CAMBRIDGE UNIVERSITY	TWICKENHAM	W	1G(5)-0
281050	COVENTRY	TWICKENHAM	L	0-1DG1PG(6)
041150	BRISTOL	TWICKENHAM	W	1PG1T(6)-1G(5)
111150	RICHMOND	RICHMOND	W	1PG1T(6)-1T(3)
181150	OXFORD UNIVERSITY	TWICKENHAM	L	0-1G1PG(8)
251150	BLACKHEATH	BLACKHEATH	C	
021250	LEICESTER	OLD DEER PARK(H)	W	2G2T(16)-2G(10)
091250	HERIOT'S F.P.	TWICKENHAM	L	0-1DG1T(6)
161250	METROPOLITAN POLICE	IMBER COURT	C	
231250	RICHMOND	TWICKENHAM	C	
301250	BATH	BATH	C	
060151	LONDON IRISH	SUNBURY	L	0-1T(3)
130151	BLACKHEATH	TWICKENHAM	W	1G1DG2PG1T(17)-1DG1PG(6)
200151	UNITED SERVICES CHATHAM	CHATHAM	W	1G3T(14)-1T(3)
270151	PAIGNTON	PAIGNTON	W	1G1T(8)-0
030251	NORTHAMPTON	TWICKENHAM	W	1G3T(14)-1PG(3)
100251	WASPS	SUDBURY	W	1PG(3)-0
170251	ROYAL AIR FORCE	OLD DEER PARK(H)	W	2T(6)-1G(5)
240251	ROYAL NAVY	PORTSMOUTH	D	1PG(3)-1PG(3)
030351	LEICESTER	LEICESTER	L	1PG(3)-1G1PG(8)
100351	BEDFORD	BEDFORD	W	1T(3)-0

170351	NEWPORT	TEDDINGTON	W	1PG(3)-0
240351	SWANSEA	SWANSEA	L	0-2G1PG2T(19)
260351	CARDIFF	CARDIFF	L	0-1T(3)
310351	LONDON WELSH	HERNE HILL	D	1T(3)-1DG(3)
070451	GLOUCESTER	GLOUCESTER	D	1T(3)-1T(3)
140451	LONDON WELSH	TWICKENHAM	W	1G2T(11)-1PG(3)
210451	BRISTOL	BRISTOL	L	2T(6)-1G2T(11)
290451	PARIS UNIVERSITÉ CLUB	PARIS	W	1T(3)-0

At a Committee meeting on 21st March 1952, Ken Chapman outlined plans to open the 1952/53 season with a game against a team of international players (as will be seen later this became Sir Wavell Wakefield's International XV). The idea of this fixture was to try and recoup some of the 1951/52 season's losses (two matches had been cancelled and one had been switched). A letter was received from the Kenya Harlequin F.C. asking for affiliation to our Club. A letter of good wishes was sent back; affiliation was granted and at a later meeting permission was granted for them to use our colours. Honours caps were awarded to Peter Woodruff, Dennis Barker and Hugh Forbes. In the Committee's report on the season several difficulties encountered by the side were mentioned including the tour by South Africa and Middlesex winning the County Championship, which were both a drain on our playing strength. We were only able to play seven out of our twelve Twickenham fixtures and because of this the R.F.U. reduced our rent by £150. We also received a payment of £178 from the Middlesex County R.F.U. for allowing the County Final to be played at Twickenham. It was also reported that subscriptions were the highest on record at £597.

Like the previous season, we began with a run of six unbeaten games (although this time two were drawn). We started with a win over St. Thomas's Hospital at Chiswick by fourteen points to nil, drew with St. Mary's Hospital and Rosslyn Park and defeated London Scottish, United Services, Portsmouth and on 20th October, Moseley. This was Moseley's first visit to Twickenham and only our second game with them. We took the lead with a penalty from Alan Grimsdell which was equalised with a similar kick by D.M. Layton. Just before half time we shot into a 16-3 lead with tries by Norman Fryer, A.E. (Albert) Agar and W.P.C. (Phil) Davies and two conversions from Grimsdell. The game was as good as won now and in the second half we piled on the points with E.L. Horsfall, S.D. Little and Hugh Forbes adding tries (Grimsdell kicking two more conversions) to which the visitors could only reply with two penalty goals from L. Morgan to make the final score 29-9. Agar and Davies had made their first appearances against St. Thomas's Hospital and St. Mary's Hospital respectively and both went on to gain international honours (Agar winning 7 and Davies 11 England caps). Coventry ended our unbeaten run again (0-6) and narrow defeats followed against Bristol (3-6) and Richmond (0-3). It is interesting to note that the game at Coventry was the first football match of any code to be televised in the Midlands. The B.B.C. cameras were there and it was reported that this new innovation did not appear to have adversely affected the attendance.

After the game against Oxford University had been cancelled, we set off on another unbeaten run starting against Blackheath at Twickenham (20-9) and then Leicester at the Old Deer Park by nine points to three. Against Leicester, P.J. Fuller made the first of at least 109 appearances and M.L. (Malcolm) "Micky" Grant appeared for the first of at least 173 occasions (he also went on to win four Scottish caps). On 8th December, we travelled up to Edinburgh to meet Heriot's F.P. and in a dull encounter before a large crowd at Goldenacre neither side was able to score. We met the Metropolitan Police at Imber Court for the first time (the previous season's match was scheduled to have been played there but it was cancelled) and by scoring five tries (one being converted) we won by seventeen points to nil. Revenge was gained over Richmond and Bath were unlucky not to defeat us. Had it not been for the fact that two of their players had to go to hospital, they probably would have done but, as it was, we eventually ended up victors by fourteen points to eight.

We then completed the double over Blackheath and the match against Cambridge University was cancelled. On 2nd February, we travelled to the Midlands again to take on Northampton but the start had to be delayed to give the sun a chance to improve the playing surface. A third of our first choice team was playing for Middlesex but Northampton were at full strength and they eventually scored three unconverted tries to win by nine points to nil. Another of our "one-off" matches took place on 16th February when we met Penzance and Newlyn at the Mennaye Field, Penzance. This was our first visit to Cornwall since the game against Redruth back in 1904. This time the result was a lot different and in a very close, well fought game we just sneaked home by a goal to a penalty goal. We went down by a point to the Royal Navy before our third trip of the season to the Midlands, this time it was the return match with the Tigers of Leicester. J.P. Morris, a Leicester old boy, turned out for us at fly half although we were missing John Matthews and Albert Agar. The game was ten minutes old when Hugh Forbes scored our first try, Alan Grimsdell converted and we were five points up. Cullen kicked two penalties and Beaver got a try for the home side but between these scores Grimsdell and Forbes had scored further tries (the first named converting his own) to give us a lead of thirteen points to nine at half time. It was more of the same after the break when Peter Woodruff got our fourth try and Grimsdell added two penalties to which Leicester's only reply was a penalty by Barrow. This made the final score 22-12 in what was to be our last victory of the season.

We played at Bedford the following week with a weakened side as Middlesex were playing and defeating Lancashire in the County Championship Final at Twickenham. This handicap proved too much against an almost full strength Bedford side and we went down 5-20. Against Newport, we only turned up with fourteen men and were met by a telegram from Gordon Weston (our hooker). It stated "Apologies. Just saw train disappear". Help was at hand and the home side lent us their Welsh international, Ben Edwards (they had intended to rest him) to make up our numbers. This was our fourteenth trip to Rodney Parade and, once again, it was to prove fruitless. We failed to score for the seventh time while Newport got three penalty goals and a dropped goal. We did manage to draw against Wasps and Cardiff (both 3-3) but defeats against Gloucester (5-21), Swansea (5-9) and finally, Bristol (8-16) took some of the gloss off what had been developing into quite a successful season. It was reported that the referee in the Swansea game (Tom J. Howells) was taking charge of his eighth game in eight days and that this feat was a typical example of his fitness as one of the oldest referees on the panel. Alan Grimsdell's brother W.R. (Bill) made his debut in the Bristol game and went on to make at least 64 appearances and D.S. (Dyson) Wilson played his first game against Swansea. He only played 6 times for us but won 8 caps for England between 1953 and 1955. Our last scheduled match in Paris against the Paris Université Club was cancelled. Two other England internationals making their debuts for us during the season were Nigel Gibbs (who went on to win 2 caps) and V.G. (Victor) "Vic" Roberts (who was in the process of winning 16 caps). E.A.J. (Ewen) Fergusson (a future winner of five Scottish caps) also made his first appearance.

W.P.C. (Phil) Davies scored ten tries and once again Alan Grimsdell was top points scorer with 59 (1 try, 16 conversions and 8 penalties). Overall, tries were up (55) as were the total points which went up fifteen on the 1950/51 season to 254. Hugh Forbes appeared in twenty one out of twenty seven matches, Peter Woodruff played in twenty and the best of the rest were David Brooks and Phil Davies (19) and Alan Grimsdell (18).

1951/52

150951	ST.THOMAS'S HOSPITAL	CHISWICK	W	1G1PG2T(14)-0
220951	ST.MARY'S HOSPITAL	TEDDINGTON(A)	D	2PG1T(9)-1DG2PG(9)
290951	ROSSLYN PARK	TWICKENHAM	D	1G1DG(8)-1G1DG(8)
061051	LONDON SCOTTISH	RICHMOND	W	1PG5T(18)-1PG(3)
131051	UNITED SERVICES PORTSMOUTH	TWICKENHAM	W	2G6T(28)-1DG(3)
201051	MOSELEY	TWICKENHAM	W	4G1PG2T(29)-3PG(9)
271051	COVENTRY	COVENTRY	L	0-1DG1T(6)
031151	BRISTOL	TWICKENHAM	L	1T(3)-1PG1T(6)
101151	RICHMOND	RICHMOND	L	0-1T(3)
171151	OXFORD UNIVERSITY	TWICKENHAM	C	
241151	BLACKHEATH	TWICKENHAM	W	1G3PG2T(20)-3PG(9)
011251	LEICESTER	OLD DEER PARK(H)	W	2PG1T(9)-1PG(3)
081251	HERIOT'S F.P.	EDINBURGH	D	0-0
151251	METROPOLITAN POLICE	IMBER COURT	W	1G4T(17)-0
221251	RICHMOND	TWICKENHAM	W	2G1PG1T(16)-1G1T(8)
291251	BATH	BATH	W	1G3T(14)-1G1T(8)
120152	BLACKHEATH	BLACKHEATH	W	1G(5)-1T(3)
260152	CAMBRIDGE UNIVERSITY	CAMBRIDGE	C	
020252	NORTHAMPTON	NORTHAMPTON	L	0-3T(9)
160252	PENZANCE AND NEWLYN	PENZANCE	W	1G(5)-1PG(3)
230252	ROYAL NAVY	TWICKENHAM	L	1G1T(8)-1PG2T(9)
010352	LEICESTER	LEICESTER	W	2G2PG2T(22)-3PG1T(12)
080352	BEDFORD	BEDFORD	L	1G(5)-4G(20)
150352	NEWPORT	NEWPORT	L	0-1DG3PG(12)
220352	WASPS	SUDBURY	D	1T(3)-1T(3)
290352	LONDON SCOTTISH	TWICKENHAM	C	
050452	GLOUCESTER	GLOUCESTER	L	1G(5)-1PG6T(21)
120452	SWANSEA	SWANSEA	L	1G(5)-3PG(9)
140452	CARDIFF	CARDIFF	D	1T(3)-1T(3)
190452	BRISTOL	BRISTOL	L	1G1PG(8)-2G1PG1T(16)
270452	PARIS UNIVERSITÉ CLUB	PARIS	C	

At the A.G.M. on 20th June (held at the Mayfair Hotel, Berkeley Street, London W1) G.E. (Graham) Loader and John Matthews were elected as Vice Presidents. At a Committee meeting on 29th August (held at The Running Horse, Davies Street, London W1) the Secretary outlined plans for floodlighting part of the Teddington ground thus enabling practice and training to take place throughout the season. The cost was estimated at £250, the go ahead given and the scheme was later completed at a cost of only £130. On 7th November a proposal to write a history of the Club was discussed, the main problem was seen as getting enough information about the origins of the

Club and the first four decades of the playing history. It was decided that the Club would bear the cost of research, authorship and publication (to be recouped wholly or in part by sales) and the cost to playing members should not exceed 5s. On 13th December the Secretary reported he had been approached by Rosslyn Park asking whether we would consider becoming co-tenants at the Old Deer Park. It was decided by the Committee that this would not be a good move for the Club. On 10th April it was decided that Mr. H. Linney (groundsman at Teddington since 1925) and his wife were to be retired and a new groundsman was to be employed. The wages would be £7 per week (£1 per week for his wife) and a contributory pension scheme yielding £3 per week would be started. At the end of May it was announced that the new groundsman (Mr. Lewis R. MacDonald) and his wife would commence work on 22nd June 1953. Honours caps were awarded to Albert Agar, Phil Davies and Vic Roberts. In the 1952/53 season our largest gate was for the Oxford University game and our smallest was for the Old Merchant Taylors game when the takings were only £9! Our total gate receipts for the season were £2,583 leading to an overall profit of £1,548.

David Brooks was to be captain for this and the following (1953/54) season. His first game was the special fixture against Sir Wavell Wakefield's International XV at Twickenham on 6th September. We were able to field five internationals from England (plus three future caps) and one from Scotland. One of the future caps making his debut for us was N.A. (Nick) Labuschagne. He was to gain five caps and play at least 55 games for the Club. The Scottish international was also making his debut; J.T. (James) Greenwood only played a confirmed 17 games for us but went on to win 20 caps. The side we faced contained internationals from England (2), France (4), Ireland (1), Scotland (1) and Wales (7). In the first half R. Bienes got a try and J.D. Robins converted to give the invitation side the lead. By half time Phil Davies had scored a try to which Alan Grimsdell added the conversion and a penalty goal to put us three points in front. At this point the International XV lost G. Brum (one of their centres) through injury and played the entire second half with fourteen men. We stretched our lead when Dennis Barker added a try shortly after the break but K.J. Jones scored two tries (both converted by Robins) to undo all our hard work and put the visitors into a lead of four points. This they held until two minutes from the end when Nick Labuschagne went over, Grimsdell converted and we had a one point victory.

Our next two matches were both at Twickenham against hospital opposition (St. Thomas's and St. Mary's), the first being won by thirteen points to three and the second a drawn game of six points each. During the course of the St. Mary's game Alan Grimsdell had struck and laid out one of the opposition. Although this was not reported in the newspapers, the Committee was informed and it was said in Grimsdell's defence that he had committed the foul under the greatest provocation. The outcome was that Grimsdell should write to the captain of St. Mary's and the matter was to be left there. In one report of the match, it was stated "an unusual feature of the game was the continual booing of the Harlequins by their own crowd, who disliked their unnecessary rough play". After Rosslyn Park had been dispatched at the Old Deer Park, we met London Scottish at Twickenham on 4th October (unaware that this would be our last fixture against them at Twickenham for nearly twelve years). The visitors produced their best performance for two seasons to defeat us by five points (11-16). Against Cambridge University, Alan Grimsdell sealed victory for us with a penalty goal from 50 yards to add to a try from Peter Woodruff. Coventry came next and outlasted us at the Old Deer Park; scoring two converted tries in the last 10 minutes for an 18-3 win. After this setback, we won our next six games defeating, amongst others, Northampton (11-0), Oxford University (9-0) and Heriot's F.P. (15-6). Against Oxford, I.H.M. (Ian) Thomson, the Scottish international full back was due to play for us but unfortunately, he was held up by fog and failed to appear in time. Newport were met at Twickenham on 20th December (the same day as the England trial) and a weakened team just lost by a goal and a penalty goal (all scored in the first half) to nil. To end the year Richmond gained revenge for their earlier defeat with a win at the Athletic Ground (described as an hour's fun in the fog) by eight points to three.

We started off the new year with our first win at Bristol since 1945 (16-6) and followed with victories over Blackheath (3-0), Old Merchant Taylors (11-0) and our first match at Twickenham against the Royal Air Force (14-0). K.J.H. (John) Mallett debuted against Bristol in the first of at least 89 games. What followed next was quite amazing as we managed to draw two games in a row (against London Scottish and Northampton) by the scoreline of 0-0. This was the first time this had happened since 1888 and only the eighth time ever. Against St. Mary's Hospital on 14th February, we were forced to make six changes due to travelling difficulties and influenza victims. Hugh Forbes, whose car broke down, had to change in a taxi. He was still in time because the kick-off had been delayed by fifteen minutes. We took the lead when Alan Grimsdell kicked a penalty goal (his only success in six attempts) before G.H. Sullivan got a try for the home side to level things up at the break. The only score of the second half was another try for the Hospital, this time by J.M. Halls, to give them victory by six points to three. Our next two games were both rousing affairs (against the Royal Navy and Leicester) and both ended in draws (3-3 and 6-6 respectively).

After losing at Bedford, we travelled the comparative short distance to Herne Hill to take on the London Welsh. After a very scrappy first half, we scored tries through P.R.Y. Anderson (2) and D.M. Gunson with Alan Grimsdell converting one to run out winners by eleven points to nil. We had now arrived at Easter and it was time to go on tour again, the first stop being Bath on Maundy Thursday. Our hosts were reported to have dropped over £100 on the game due to the downpour which made the ground conditions not very good at all. Despite this and the very greasy ball, our forwards and backs were said to have handled uncommonly well. By half time we led 11-0 with tries from Gunson, Ricky Bartlett and David Brooks, the last being converted by Bill Grimsdell. At the break, Bath lost one of their centres (Wilcox) with concussion and were thus reduced to fourteen men for the rest of the game. We stretched our lead when Albert Agar went over for our fourth try and despite Sidoli getting a try for the home side, our half time lead was not encroached upon. Next to Swansea where the match was voted one of the best of the season by an appreciative crowd. Swansea scored four tries (all unconverted) to our two (one of which was converted) to run out winners by twelve points to eight. In the Monday game against Cardiff we went down without troubling the scoreboard operator (0-15).

It was back to London for our final two games of the season, the first (against London Irish) was played at Blackheath and resulted in a win for us by sixteen points to eight which halted a run of four consecutive defeats at their hands. The second was played at Twickenham on 18th April and our opponents were Gloucester. We notched up our nineteenth win of the season with tries from I. Marshall and E.A. Harris and two conversions and a goal from a mark by Alan Grimsdell to Gloucester's goal, penalty goal and try. We were targeted by some newspapers for placing the seven-a-side game first and putting out a weakened side against Gloucester but, having said that, they still had to praise our play and mention that we deserved to win. Another player appearing for the first time this season was H.G. (Hugh) Greatwood who made the first of 55 confirmed appearances against United Services, Portsmouth on 11th October.

Dennis Barker came out with the most tries (12) and Alan Grimsdell kicked 103 points (2 goals from a mark, 23 conversions and 17 penalty goals). With those two goals from a mark, he set a new Club record for a season. Overall the team managed 58 tries and 281 points, the only new record being Grimsdell's two goals from a mark. Top appearance makers were David Brooks, Alan Grimsdell and Peter Woodruff with 28 followed by Dennis Barker, Phil Davies and Norman Fryer (25) and Hugh Forbes (24).

1952/53

060952	SIR W WAKEFIELD'S INTERNATIONAL XV	TWICKENHAM	W	2G1PG1T(16)-3G(15)
130952	ST.THOMAS'S HOSPITAL	TWICKENHAM	W	2G1PG(13)-1PG(3)
200952	ST.MARY'S HOSPITAL	TWICKENHAM	D	2T(6)-2PG(6)
270952	ROSSLYN PARK	OLD DEER PARK	W	1G2T(11)-0
041052	LONDON SCOTTISH	TWICKENHAM	L	1G2T(11)-2G2T(16)
111052	UNITED SERVICES PORTSMOUTH	TWICKENHAM	W	1G1PG1T(11)-1PG1T(6)
181052	CAMBRIDGE UNIVERSITY	TWICKENHAM	W	1PG1T(6)-0
251052	COVENTRY	OLD DEER PARK(H)	L	1T(3)-3G1T(18)
011152	NORTHAMPTON	TWICKENHAM	W	1G2T(11)-0
081152	RICHMOND	RICHMOND	W	1MG1PG(6)-1DG(3)
151152	OXFORD UNIVERSITY	TWICKENHAM	W	3T(9)-0
221152	BLACKHEATH	BLACKHEATH	W	1G4PG2T(23)-0
291152	BATH	TWICKENHAM	W	2G1PG(13)-1PG1T(6)
061252	LEICESTER	OLD DEER PARK(H)	C	
131252	HERIOT'S F.P.	TWICKENHAM	W	3G(15)-2T(6)
201252	NEWPORT	TWICKENHAM	L	0-1G1PG(8)
271252	RICHMOND	RICHMOND	L	1T(3)-1G1DG(8)
030153	BRISTOL	BRISTOL	W	2G2PG(16)-1PG1T(6)
100153	BLACKHEATH	TWICKENHAM	W	1PG(3)-0
170153	OLD MERCHANT TAYLORS	TEDDINGTON	W	1G2T(11)-0
240153	ROYAL AIR FORCE	TWICKENHAM	W	1G2PG1T(14)-0
310153	LONDON SCOTTISH	RICHMOND	D	0-0
070253	NORTHAMPTON	NORTHAMPTON	D	0-0
140253	ST.MARY'S HOSPITAL	TEDDINGTON(A)	L	1PG(3)-2T(6)
210253	ROYAL NAVY	PORTSMOUTH	D	1T(3)-1PG(3)
070353	LEICESTER	LEICESTER	D	1PG1T(6)-2T(6)
140353	BEDFORD	BEDFORD	L	1G(5)-1G1DG(8)
280353	LONDON WELSH	HERNE HILL	W	1G2T(11)-0
020453	BATH	BATH	W	1G3T(14)-1T(3)
040453	SWANSEA	SWANSEA	L	1G1T(8)-4T(12)
060453	CARDIFF	CARDIFF	L	0-1PG4T(15)
110453	LONDON IRISH	BLACKHEATH	W	2G2T(16)-1G1T(8)
180453	GLOUCESTER	TWICKENHAM	W	2G1MG(13)-1G1PG1T(11)

At a Committee meeting on 31st July a selection committee comprised of the President, Captain and vice-Captain (with the power to co-opt three other members) was formed. An amendment to allow the captain to exercise an overriding decision was defeated by six votes to two. The Rugby Union had decided to allow the Club the use of the Twickenham ground for the next three years at a cost of £30 per match. The normal number of matches would be twelve but if circumstances and weather allowed more games might be permitted. At a Committee meeting on 17th March it was announced that five matches had been arranged at the White City for the next season. Doubts were expressed about the suitability of the ground and the captain was asked to go and inspect the pitch. This was carried out later in company with the Secretary and the site was duly approved. The famous venue was known as the Soulless Stadium, a feeling created by its size. It was originally planned that it would hold 367,000 people all seated! It was built in less than two years for the 1908 Olympics and the capacity was reduced to 130,000 with 60,000 seated. Over the years, many sporting and non-sporting events were held there including American Football, Baseball, Boxing, Cricket, Football, Greyhound Racing, Hockey, Polo, Rugby League, Speedway and Track and Field. The non-sporting events included Billy Graham's London Crusade in 1954. Eventually, it was demolished between October 1984 and March 1985, the land was purchased by the B.B.C. and the Wood Lane studio complex was built. The biggest crowd we were to attract was against Cardiff in October 1954 (18,720) and, in fact, the four other games with an attendance of over 5,000 were all against the Welsh side. Our lowest crowd was a paltry 150 against London Scottish at the end of January 1960.

Invitations were received from Bradford, Gosforth, Saracens and Streatham to play against them but all were refused. The last two owing to the rule that the 1st XV should not play midweek fixtures (although later a midweek fixture was fixed with the Metropolitan Police for the 1954/55 season. Honours caps were awarded to Ricky Bartlett and Nigel Gibbs and our gate receipts amounted to £2,131. The best was against Cardiff when £813 was taken and the worst was the match with Bedford when just £2 was received. The overall picture showed a loss of £159, quite a drop from the previous season. A Colts XV is added to the fixture list although it disappears in 1962/63 and reappears in 1978/79.

We began the 1953/54 season in the same winning mode as we had finished the previous one. Our first match was against St. Thomas's Hospital and was played for the first and only time on their ground at Cobham, Surrey. A half time lead of six points to nil was comfortably converted into a 14-0 win in what proved to be our last meeting with them. Our first visitors to Twickenham were the medics from St. Mary's and, in a game described as "so untidy and so thoroughly uninteresting", we won by three penalty goals (kicked by Albert Agar) and a try (scored by Nigel Gibbs) to nil. Leicester were welcome visitors on 26th September for their first game at Twickenham since December 1947. Despite losing their full back after just ten minutes play and trailing by six points to nil at half time, the Tigers played well in the second half and managed nine points of their own to snatch a win. Three victories followed over London Scottish (18-6), United Services, Portsmouth (14-10) and on 17th October, Waterloo. This was our first meeting with the team from Blundellsands and ten points in the first half were enough to defeat them as all they could score in the second half was a try. A midweek fixture followed on 21st October at Imber Court against the Metropolitan Police and, rather surprisingly, we lost by eleven points to eight.

On the following Saturday, we met Swansea for the thirty third time and for the first time at Twickenham. It was, in fact, the first time we had played them at home. Things did not go according to plan for us to start with as we lost John Boothman (one of our wingers) with a chipped ankle after 20 minutes. Alan Grimsdell moved out to the wing and by half time we led by eight points to nil. We held our own for three quarters of the second half before losing our scrum half (Howard Jones) who was knocked unconscious and carried off to leave us with just thirteen men. Five minutes later Swansea did manage to score a try but it was not enough and we held on for a great win. Bath and Bristol were both beaten at Teddington and we played out a scoreless draw with Richmond at the Athletic Ground during the course of which the home side missed eight penalty kicks and we missed two. Our unbeaten run stretched to six games with victory over Oxford University and on 28th November, a 3-3 draw with Blackheath.

All good things come to an end and, at the Old Deer Park a week later against Rosslyn Park, our unbeaten run did just that. We led 11-3 at the break but the Park came back and won by the odd point in twenty three. Our last two matches in 1953 were against Welsh opposition. The first was against Cardiff (who included 13 of the side which had beaten the New Zealand touring side) in front of nearly 20,000 people. A three point deficit at half time stretched to eleven by the end and we had failed to score for only the second time this season. Our second Welsh opponents came in the shape of Newport at Rodney Parade. Even though the home side were weakened by injuries and international calls (we also put out a weakened XV) they still had enough strength in depth to give us our second heaviest defeat at their hands. A crowd of barely over one hundred (the draw of the Wales v. New Zealand game at Cardiff being televised was the reason for the poorest gate the ground had seen for several years) saw us concede twenty five points and score none to end the year on a disappointing note. During the first half of the season, we had welcomed future England internationals D.L. (Donald) Sanders against St. Mary's Hospital on 19th September and R.W.D. (Reginald) "David" Marques against United Services, Portsmouth on 10th October. They were to win 9 and 23 caps respectively. Other newcomers were J.S. (Jeff) Abbott who made the first of 118 confirmed appearances against Oxford University on 21st November and R.A.M. (Roger) Whyte (189 known appearances) against Newport on 19th December. John Matthews made the last of 120 confirmed appearances against Waterloo on 17th October.

On 2nd January, we travelled down to Bristol for the return game and attempting to complete the double over them for the first time since the 1928/29 season. After twenty minutes and against the run of play, we got a try through Roger Whyte which Alan Grimsdell converted to put us in front. Just before the interval the home side completed the scoring when M. Payton scored an unconverted try. This enabled us to start the New Year with a victory which we added to the following week with another away win, this time over Blackheath. This game was much like the one at Bristol in that we had a lot of defending to do. The sides were level at 8-8 when, just before the end, the Blackheath forwards swept into our half with their backs in support and it looked as though they might score the winning try. Suddenly, they lost the ball, it went to Ricky Bartlett who fed Dennis Barker and he went on a run of some 60 yards which ended with a try between the posts. This was converted and we had won by thirteen points to eight. The following week we travelled to Paris again for a Sunday game with the Paris Université Club. They outscored us by three tries to one and by twelve points to five. Cambridge University defeated us for the first time since 1948 on 23rd January when they held out for a four point win (9-13).

We got back into the winning groove against London Welsh (9-6) and the Royal Navy (16-9) before having a slight blip against Leicester (3-12). Bedford then came to Teddington (for the first time) on 13th March and after an even first half (which finished with a penalty for the visitors to a try for us), we managed three tries against their one to win 14-6. We then travelled to Birmingham to play Moseley at The Reddings for the second time. R.W.W. Dawe and Peter Woodruff had scored tries and Alan Grimsdell had added one conversion before the home side kicked two penalties to narrow the gap at half time. Moseley lost one of their wingers (who had hurt a neck muscle) for most of the second half but they still remained in touch and it took a goal from a mark (35 yards out) from Grimsdell to make sure of victory. I.D.S. (Ian) Beer (another future England international going on to win two caps) made his first appearance in this game. Although there was still over a month of the season left, this proved to be our last victory as we were to record six defeats in a row. It all started with a trip to Edinburgh to play Heriot's F.P. This was our third visit to Goldenacre and we had yet to win, our best being a 0-0 draw in 1951. The home side scored a goal, a penalty goal and a try before half time and we had to wait until they had added another try to get on the scoreboard. Roger Whyte kicked a penalty and scored a try but Heriot's got another two tries before the end to our one from Gunson to run out convincing winners by twenty points to nine. We managed one less point at Coventry (8-20) and went down in a close encounter at Gloucester (8-12). The Easter tour proved to be a disastrous one as regards results. On Maundy Thursday, against Bath, we started off by conceding thirteen points, managed a rally and scored two goals but it was not quite enough. Moving into Wales, we fared no better and lost to both Swansea (3-11) and Cardiff (6-11).

Dennis Barker, John Boothman and R.W.W. Dawe each scored five tries, Alan Grimsdell equalled his own record of two goals from a mark and Nigel Gibbs top scored with 61 points (1 try, 10 penalties and 14 conversions). Once again, tries overall were in the fifties (52) and for the eighth season in a row points were in the two hundreds (279). Time would show this to be the last season in which our points total overall was below 300. Top appearance makers were Nigel Gibbs (23), Alan Grimsdell (22) and David Brooks (20).

1953/54

120953	ST.THOMAS'S HOSPITAL	COBHAM	W	1G1PG2T(14)-0
190953	ST.MARY'S HOSPITAL	TWICKENHAM	W	3PG1T(12)-0
260953	LEICESTER	TWICKENHAM	L	1DG1PG(6)-1PG2T(9)
031053	LONDON SCOTTISH	RICHMOND	W	1PG5T(18)-1PG1T(6)
101053	UNITED SERVICES PORTSMOUTH	TWICKENHAM	W	1G1PG2T(14)-2G(10)
171053	WATERLOO	TWICKENHAM	W	2G(10)-1T(3)
211053	METROPOLITAN POLICE	IMBER COURT	L	(8)-(11)
241053	SWANSEA	TWICKENHAM	W	1G1PG(8)-1T(3)
311053	BATH	TEDDINGTON	W	1G2T(11)-0
071153	BRISTOL	TEDDINGTON	W	2G2T(16)-1G(5)
141153	RICHMOND	RICHMOND	D	0-0
211153	OXFORD UNIVERSITY	TWICKENHAM	W	2G1PG2T(19)-3PG(9)
281153	BLACKHEATH	TWICKENHAM	D	1PG(3)-1PG(3)
051253	ROSSLYN PARK	OLD DEER PARK	L	1G2T(11)-1DG3T(12)
121253	CARDIFF	TWICKENHAM	L	0-1G1PG1T(11)
191253	NEWPORT	NEWPORT	L	0-2G1PG4T(25)
020154	BRISTOL	BRISTOL	W	1G(5)-1T(3)
090154	BLACKHEATH	BLACKHEATH	W	2G1T(13)-1G1T(8)
170154	PARIS UNIVERSITÉ CLUB	PARIS	L	1G(5)-1PG3T(12)
230154	CAMBRIDGE UNIVERSITY	CAMBRIDGE	L	3PG(9)-2G1PG(13)
060254	NORTHAMPTON	TEDDINGTON	C	
200254	LONDON WELSH	TEDDINGTON	W	2PG1T(9)-2PG(6)
270254	ROYAL NAVY	TWICKENHAM	W	2G2PG(16)-2PG1T(9)
060354	LEICESTER	LEICESTER	L	1PG(3)-4T(12)
130354	BEDFORD	TEDDINGTON	W	1G3T(14)-1PG1T(6)
200354	MOSELEY	MOSELEY	W	1G1MG1T(11)-2PG(6)
270354	HERIOT'S F.P.	EDINBURGH	L	1PG2T(9)-1G1PG4T(20)

030454	COVENTRY	COVENTRY	L	1G1T(8)-1G1PG4T(20)
100454	GLOUCESTER	GLOUCESTER	L	1G1T(8)-1PG3T(12)
150454	BATH	BATH	L	2G(10)-2G1T(13)
170454	SWANSEA	SWANSEA	L	1MG(3)-1G2T(11)
190454	CARDIFF	CARDIFF	L	1PG1T(6)-1G1PG1T(11)
240454	LONDON IRISH	TWICKENHAM	C	

It was decided on 23rd July 1954 that there should be a small executive committee to handle the day to day running of the Club. This would consist of the President, the honorary secretary, the honorary treasurer, the captain and six other members of the Committee (David Brooks, Ken Chapman, E.M.C. Clarke, E.A. Harris, John Matthews and Howell Thomas). Four members would constitute a quorum. Concern had been expressed by some members over some of the content of Harlequin Story and that it would not sell to the present generation. By 9th October, this appears to have been proved right as, out of 2,000 copies held by the Club, only between three and four hundred had been sold. At a meeting on 18th October suggestions as to changes in the system of awarding honours and club caps were put forward for consideration by the full Committee. For an honours cap, no one can be eligible unless they have played in not less than two thirds of the 1st XV fixtures for more than one season. The standard required is at least as high as international standard though failure to gain an international cap is not a bar to the award of an honours cap. For a club cap, no one is to be eligible unless they have played at least three seasons for the Club and the cap will be awarded for one of two reasons only. A consistently high standard of play or sound player who has also contributed personally to the success of the Club or a team. These were later approved on 17th December. Honours caps for the season were awarded to D.L. (Donald) Sanders and Roger Whyte. Gate receipts totalled £3,196 with a best of £693 against Richmond and a worst of just £2 against Coventry. When the net proceeds from the floodlit match against Cardiff are taken into account, the figure for gate receipts jumps to a massive £6,091! This all led to a profit of £2,606 which was the best so far in the history of the Club.

Ricky Bartlett was our new captain for the 1954/55 season and was to remain in post until the end of the 1958/59 season. This was to be the longest run since Adrian Stoop in the early part of the century (Ken Chapman's run was interrupted by the Second World War). He started off with a victory in our first ever game against Gosforth. We had a personal contribution from R.I. (Ray) Harrison of twenty points made up of four penalty goals and four conversions of tries by Dennis Barker, Donald Sanders, Jeff Abbott and one of the captain's two. Gosforth could only score three penalties and we came away with a 35-9 victory. Harrison got another thirteen points in our next match against St. Mary's Hospital which was won 28-6 and revenge was gained over the Metropolitan Police at Imber Court (19-11). On 25th September, we met Leicester in our first game at the White City Stadium (Twickenham was not available due to the overhauling of the drainage system). In an exciting game, we led 9-6 at half time thanks to two penalties from Nigel Gibbs and a try for Vic Roberts to two penalties for Leicester by M.R. Channer. After this, Leicester took the lead with Channer's conversion of Bleasdale's try, we retook it with a Sanders try and a third penalty from Gibbs and they took it back again when Channer converted his own try. Peter Woodruff collected his own chip ahead for our third try, J.E. Maynier went over for another and Woodruff grabbed his second to which Gibbs added two conversions and we had won 28-16.

Swansea and United Services, Portsmouth were beaten next and then, on 12th October, we met Cardiff in the first floodlit game of rugby ever played in the South of England. A crowd of 20,000 turned up to watch and at the interval we trailed by a try and a penalty goal to nil. We gradually clawed our way back into the match with Ray

Harrison kicking a penalty immediately after the break. It was mostly Cardiff for the rest of the half until, in the last ten minutes, we camped in their "25". With a couple of minutes left, Ricky Bartlett put in a diagonal punt to the right corner flag and Woodruff got the touchdown. From a wide angle Harrison converted to win the match and give us our first victory over Cardiff since 1936. Unfortunately, Cardiff did not count this game as official for record purposes so presumably, remained unbeaten! Another last minute win was achieved against London Irish and our unbeaten record remained intact against the Paris Université Club (14-9) and at Bath (8-3). On 6th November, we came up against Bristol and all attempts to win our eleventh game in a row evaporated as the home side won by twenty one points to five. The sequence of ten games won at the start of the season was our best ever, the closest to it was at the start of the 1909/10 season when six were won, one drawn and then a further nine were won (although this was a better run overall, the one draw makes the 1954/55 run a better start). Despite the excellent start, our form started to fall away and even though we defeated Richmond and Rosslyn Park, we had lost a further five matches before the end of the year. Both Oxford and Cambridge Universities turned us over at home before Cardiff (with six reserves) also achieved the same as the students, winning by nine points to three (we fielded six internationals). Newport were next on our fixture list and this time we were missing seven of our regulars but could not achieve what Cardiff had and we failed to reply to the visiting side's twenty one points. Our last game of 1954 ended with a visit from Richmond and another loss (6-13).

On New Year's Day 1955 and for the second time this season, we travelled down to the Memorial Ground to meet Bristol. Things did not look good as we had nine players missing through injury and playing in the final England Trial. However, we managed to pull off a major surprise by drawing 3-3. Bristol went into the lead when Cripps kicked a penalty but before half time J.R. (John) Tarry had scored a try for us to level the scores. He had to go off with a knee injury and with twenty minutes left we were down to fourteen men. Our defence was excellent and no further scores came despite repeated Bristol attacks. Defeats followed to Blackheath and the Royal Air Force before we achieved our first win of the year. Our opponents were London Scottish and after trailing by five points at half time, we rallied and scored eleven points without reply in the second half to win 17-11. The next week we were on the receiving end of our heaviest defeat of the season at Northampton (0-24). We played Leicester on 5th March and on a treacherous pitch played the better rugby. The teams were locked at eight points each at the break but two tries for us in the second half from Micky Grant and Peter Woodruff saw us home 14-8 and enabled us to complete the double over the Tigers. The following week we played at Bedford and with a side containing six internationals we were expected to win against the home side who were going through a lean patch. Unfortunately for us the Bedford pack had a storming game and we were confined to our half for most of the afternoon. In the first half our opponents got a penalty goal and a try and that is how it remained. We were well beaten by Coventry at Teddington (6-19) and Gloucester sneaked past us by ten points to five after a scoreless first half.

On 7th April, it was time for the Easter tour again and as it was Maundy Thursday we found ourselves at Bath. The start was delayed by fifteen minutes due to the late arrival of several of our players and we actually began the game with only fourteen men (Peter Woodruff was still changing). The crowd was much reduced because of rain and the pitch was like a glue pot but both teams managed to serve up some exciting rugby. In the first half Bath scored a goal and a dropped goal to lead 8-0 and it was not until late in the game (which was finished by floodlight) that we finally woke up. We had, according to a report on the game, "struck back in traditional Harlequin style of fast, open play". We could not score though and Bath held on for their victory. Against Swansea, we fell behind to a penalty by Alan Prosser-Harries (who was later to become one of our own) but tries from Phil Davies and Dennis Barker enabled us to lead at the interval. Prosser-Harries kicked his second penalty to bring the home side level but

Barker got his second try and we had our first win in five games. The euphoria did not last long as on the Monday we went down to Cardiff in front of 18,000 spectators by six points to nil. On 16th April we made the long journey up to Waterloo (for the first time) and were comprehensively beaten by nineteen points to nil and in our last game of the season we travelled out to Paris on 1st May and were beaten by the Paris Université Club (11-22). John Roberts (74 confirmed appearances) and Nigel Gibbs (at least 62) played their last games during the season and we welcomed the following to our ranks; G.P. (Geoffrey) Vaughan (61), Keith Pontin (64), P.D.F. (Pat) Cleaver (66), A.H.M. (Howard) Hoare (105) and D.R. (David) Thompson (172) (all appearances are as confirmed).

Dennis Barker again topped the try scoring table with fifteen to his name and Ray Harrison managed the most points with 75 (15 penalties and 15 conversions). Overall, tries remained average at 55, a new mark was set for penalty goals (27) and points moved into the three hundreds for the first time since the 1945/46 season with 319. Top appearance makers were Roger Whyte with twenty eight, Ricky Bartlett and Peter Woodruff (24), Dennis Barker (23) and Micky Grant, W.A.J. Leaver and Donald Sanders (21).

In 1955 the British Lions toured South Africa once again and this time we were strongly represented by Phil Davies, James Greenwood (listed as playing for Dunfermline), Clem Thomas (now playing for Swansea), Johnnie Williams (playing for the Old Millhillians and would make his debut for us in 1961) and Dyson Wilson (now playing for the Metropolitan Police). In the four test series, each side won two matches. Greenwood played in all four and scored a try in the first and fourth games, Davies appeared in the first three and Thomas the last two.

1954/55

110954	GOSFORTH	GOSFORTH	W	4G4PG1T(35)-3PG(9)
180954	ST.MARY'S HOSPITAL	TEDDINGTON(A)	W	2G1DG3PG2T(28)-2PG(6)
210954	METROPOLITAN POLICE	IMBER COURT	W	2G1PG2T(19)-1G1PG1T(11)
250954	LEICESTER	WHITE CITY	W	2G3PG3T(28)-2G2PG(16)
021054	SWANSEA	WHITE CITY	W	2G1PG1T(16)-1G1T(8)
091054	UNITED SERVICES PORTSMOUTH	PORTSMOUTH	W	3G1DG2PG3T(33)-2T(6)
121054	CARDIFF	WHITE CITY	W	1G1PG(8)-1PG1T(6)
161054	LONDON IRISH	WHITE CITY	W	3G(15)-1G2PG(11)
231054	PARIS UNIVERSITÉ CLUB	WHITE CITY	W	1G3PG(14)-1PG2T(9)
301054	BATH	BATH	W	1G1T(8)-1T(3)
061154	BRISTOL	BRISTOL	L	1G(5)-3G2T(21)
131154	RICHMOND	RICHMOND	W	3T(9)-2PG(6)
201154	OXFORD UNIVERSITY	TWICKENHAM	L	0-2G1T(13)
271154	CAMBRIDGE UNIVERSITY	TWICKENHAM	L	1G1PG(8)-2G(10)
041254	ROSSLYN PARK	OLD DEER PARK	W	1G2PG(11)-1T(3)
111254	CARDIFF	TWICKENHAM	L	1T(3)-1PG2T(9)
181254	NEWPORT	TWICKENHAM	L	0-3G1DG1T(21)
271254	RICHMOND	TWICKENHAM	L	1PG1T(6)-2G1T(13)
010155	BRISTOL	BRISTOL	D	1T(3)-1PG(3)
080155	BLACKHEATH	TWICKENHAM	L	0-1DG2T(9)
150155	LONDON WELSH	TWICKENHAM	C	

220155	ROYAL AIR FORCE	TWICKENHAM	L	0-1DG2PG1T(12)
290155	LONDON SCOTTISH	RICHMOND	W	1G2PG2T(17)-1G2PG(11)
050255	NORTHAMPTON	NORTHAMPTON	L	0-3G1PG2T(24)
120255	ST.MARY'S HOSPITAL	TEDDINGTON(A)	W	1G1PG(8)-1G(5)
190255	ROYAL NAVY	PORTSMOUTH	C	
050355	LEICESTER	LEICESTER	W	1G3T(14)-1G1PG(8)
120355	BEDFORD	BEDFORD	L	0-1PG1T(6)
260355	COVENTRY	TEDDINGTON	L	2PG(6)-2G1PG2T(19)
020455	GLOUCESTER	GLOUCESTER	L	1G(5)-2G(10)
070455	BATH	BATH	L	0-1G1DG(8)
090455	SWANSEA	SWANSEA	W	3T(9)-2PG(6)
110455	CARDIFF	CARDIFF	L	0-2T(6)
160455	WATERLOO	WATERLOO	L	0-2G1DG2T(19)
010555	PARIS UNIVERSITÉ CLUB	PARIS	L	(11)-(22)

At the Annual General Meeting on 8th July 1955, Graham Loader asked for more support for the 1st XV in away matches. In the last season (1954/55) only three supporters had travelled with the team on its nine away trips. Howell Thomas was elected as assistant honorary team secretary (his job being to assist all the team secretaries) and Derek Whiting was elected as assistant honorary secretary. At a meeting on 18th October it was suggested that some Wanderers fixtures should be changed into 1st XV matches. From this emerged a suggestion that the Club should no longer distinguish between the various teams but all should merely be called "The Harlequins" (like the M.C.C.) or "A Harlequin side". At the next meeting these proposals were rejected. At meetings in January and February it was decided that in view of various considerations no admission fee be charged for the Northampton and Bedford matches at Teddington on 4th February and 10th March. In any event, the first game was cancelled. On 16th February a tour to Romania in May 1956 was outlined as were tours by German and Italian XVs at the start of the 1956/57 season. Honours caps were awarded to Micky Grant and Nick Labuschagne. Gate receipts were £5,427 and a loss of £598 was made on the year. This was due to (amongst other reasons) the generally increased costs of printing stationery, advertising and bill posting and the failure of the floodlit match with Cardiff at the White City due to inclement weather.

Gosforth were again our opponents for our first match, this time beginning the 1955/56 season. Again we travelled up to Newcastle and defeated them, but not by such a large margin as before. Haydn Mainwaring (a future one cap Welsh international) scored two tries, a penalty goal and three conversions to add to a try by Ian Beer to which the home side could only reply with one goal. Our next match was against a touring Rumanian XV at Twickenham. After going into a lead of nine points to nil (tries from Beer and Dennis Barker and a penalty from Mainwaring) we let our visitors back into the game and they scored a penalty before the break and a dropped goal and a try after it to tie the match at 9-9. We were to return the visit in May 1956 and this we will come back to in a while. After defeating St. Mary's Hospital and Leicester, we met London Scottish at the White City on 28th September (a Wednesday evening). The kick-off had been brought forward from 6.15 to 5.30 and this was thought to be the reason for the small crowd. In the event, the match could not start until 5.45 due to the fact there was no ball! It turned out that David Brooks (who was responsible for the ball) had gone to collect it from Stuart Surridge (the Surrey County Cricket captain) and had started to discuss Surrey's fourth Championship win. Haydn Mainwaring scored a try for us in the last five minutes (to add to his first half penalty goal) and although the Scots pulled three points back with a penalty of their own with two minutes left, we held on for a narrow victory.

Three days later, we made our way to Dublin for a game with Lansdowne. This was something of a return as we had played them at Twickenham back in 1911 although the result this time was to be a lot different. We started well enough and Dennis Barker scored a try to put us into the lead. After this though, it was all one way traffic and Lansdowne scored five tries (two being converted) to one for us from Peter Woodruff before half time. Mainwaring kicked a penalty to close the gap but two more tries and one conversion saw the Irishmen home by twenty seven points to nine and our unbeaten record had been smashed. In what was proving to be a tough period for us we next met Cardiff in another floodlit game at the White City. Like the previous year it proved to be a close game and although it rained heavily before the game (but not during it) the play was full of enterprise. It remained scoreless until ten minutes from the end when Donald Sanders went over for a try to give us another narrow win. This set us off on another winning run with victories in our next six matches, the best of which were wins over Waterloo (17-14) and Swansea (16-0). On 19th November, we entertained the students from Oxford University and it looked as though we might extend our winning run when Ian Beer got a try for us after only two minutes. That was, unfortunately, the end of our scoring and as we conceded seventeen points before the end of the game, our visitors ran out easy winners.

The following week we did beat the other participants in the Varsity match (13-10) but went on to chalk up losses against Cardiff and Newport. We completed the double over Richmond on 24th December and ended the year with a game against Birkenhead Park at the White City. The match turned out to be close all the way. Barker put us ahead with a try, K.N. Williams replied in kind for the visitors, Ricky Bartlett kicked a penalty and T. Walsh did the same to tie the scores at half time. Fifteen minutes into the second half D. Thompson put us back in front with a try only for A. Hodgson to level things up again with the fourth try of the match. Bartlett kicked his second penalty to regain the lead and this time the next score was another to us as Micky Grant dropped a goal to give us a 15-9 victory. Three newcomers made their debuts during the first half of the season and each went on to play a large number of games for the 1st XV. V.R. (Vic) Marriott on 31st December against Birkenhead Park appeared at least 179 times (he also won four England caps), J.R. (John) Simons against Cardiff on 5th October played in at least 161 matches and D.J. Pack on 5th November against Bristol played in a confirmed 115.

The new year of 1956 began with a trip to Bristol on 7th January and despite the fact we were missing six men (all playing in the England trial), we played well and only conceded two tries in the last fifteen minutes. A draw with Blackheath followed and on 28th January we met the Royal Air Force at Halton. On this occasion we went down by a try (scored in the first half) to nil. The matches against Northampton, Paris Université Club and the Royal Navy were all cancelled, the only one to survive being the midweek fixture against the Army at Teddington. This was our first meeting since 1938 and we got off to a good start with a goal from a mark by Bill Grimsdell and a try from G. Read. The Army, with four internationals in their side fought back and scored a goal before half time but our lead was four points thanks to a try from M.E. (Maurice) Kershaw. At the start of the second half Grimsdell kicked a penalty followed a while later by a penalty for the Army. Kershaw's second try put us 15-8 in front and that is how it remained. In these years, the services teams were very strong due to the existence of National Service. On 3rd March, we went up to Leicester to try and complete the double over them. We trailed for most of the match with D. St.G. Hazell kicking three penalties and converting M. Lubbock's try to which we replied with tries by Micky Grant and Phil Davies. With 25 minutes remaining we trailed by eight points, Ricky Bartlett scored a try and added a penalty before, with only three minutes to go, Grant dropped a goal to give us the narrowest of wins. Bedford were beaten at Teddington, we lost to London Irish and drew with Heriot's before beginning the Easter tour.

We had not enjoyed a successful tour since 1950 so it was nice when we got off to a winning start against Bath. We outclassed the home side and scored four tries (Barker (2), Grant and Woodruff) and one conversion by Bartlett to nil. Against Swansea we trailed by two goals, two penalty goals and a try to two Bill Grimsdell penalties with time running out. Our enterprise was rewarded when D. Thompson and Grant crossed for tries (both converted by Bartlett) but, as we pressed for the winning score, time ran out and Swansea had won by three points. We kept our open rugby going against Cardiff and, as against Bath, it paid off. At half time it stood 5-3 in the home side's favour but this was not to be for very much longer. Phil Davies and J.R. (John) Simons scored tries (the second being converted by Whyte) and we had won by eleven points to five. We won at Gloucester (8-6) for the first time since 1947 and then on 14th April, we met London Welsh at Twickenham. In the first half Ricky Bartlett had kicked a penalty for us and G. Pym had scored a try for the Welsh. The only score in the second half was a try for us from Bill Grimsdell to give us a record equalling twenty second victory of the season. The previous occasions had been the 1923/24 and 1925/26 seasons. Our attempt at setting a new record fell short at Coventry where the home side won 12-6.

Dennis Barker yet again topped the try scorers with twelve and Haydn Mainwaring got 74 points (5 tries, 9 penalties and 16 conversions). Overall, tries (68) were the best they had been since 1937/38 when 76 were scored and points were twenty up on the previous season (339). Out of 34 games the most consistent players were Ricky Bartlett (32), Peter Woodruff and Roger Whyte (27), Micky Grant (25) and Keith Pontin (24).

1955/56

030955	GOSFORTH	GOSFORTH	W	3G1PG(18)-1G(5)
100955	RUMANIAN XV	TWICKENHAM	D	1PG2T(9)-1DG1PG1T(9)
170955	ST.MARY'S HOSPITAL	TEDDINGTON(A)	W	3G2PG(21)-1PG(3)
240955	LEICESTER	TWICKENHAM	W	2G(10)-1PG1T(6)
280955	LONDON SCOTTISH	WHITE CITY	W	1PG1T(6)-1PG(3)
011055	LANSDOWNE	DUBLIN	L	1PG2T(9)-3G4T(27)
051055	CARDIFF	WHITE CITY	W	1T(3)-0
081055	UNITED SERVICES PORTSMOUTH	WHITE CITY	W	1G1PG4T(20)-1G1T(8)
151055	WATERLOO	TWICKENHAM	W	1G4T(17)-1G1DG1PG1T(14)
221055	SWANSEA	TWICKENHAM	W	2G2T(16)-0
291055	BATH	WHITE CITY	W	1G1PG1T(11)-1PG(3)
051155	BRISTOL	WHITE CITY	W	2G1PG1T(16)-1G(5)
121155	RICHMOND	RICHMOND	W	1G(5)-1PG(3)
191155	OXFORD UNIVERSITY	TWICKENHAM	L	1T(3)-1G3PG1T(17)
261155	CAMBRIDGE UNIVERSITY	TWICKENHAM	W	2G1T(13)-2G(10)
031255	BLACKHEATH	BLACKHEATH	W	2G1PG(13)-0
101255	CARDIFF	TWICKENHAM	L	0-2G1PG(13)
171255	NEWPORT	NEWPORT	L	1T(3)-1G2PG(13)
241255	RICHMOND	TWICKENHAM	W	1G1PG(8)-1DG(3)
311255	BIRKENHEAD PARK	WHITE CITY	W	1DG2PG2T(15)-1PG2T(9)

070156	BRISTOL	BRISTOL	L	0-2T(6)
140156	BLACKHEATH	WHITE CITY	D	2T(6)-2T(6)
280156	ROYAL AIR FORCE	HALTON	L	0-1T(3)
040256	NORTHAMPTON	TEDDINGTON	C	
080256	ARMY	TEDDINGTON	W	1MG1PG3T(15)-1G1PG(8)
190256	PARIS UNIVERSITÉ CLUB	PARIS	C	
250256	ROYAL NAVY	TWICKENHAM	C	
030356	LEICESTER	LEICESTER	W	1DG1PG3T(15)-1G3PG(14)
100356	BEDFORD	TEDDINGTON	W	1G3T(14)-0
170356	LONDON IRISH	TWICKENHAM	L	1PG1T(6)-2G1T(13)
240356	HERIOT'S F.P.	EDINBURGH	D	1DG1T(6)-1PG1T(6)
290356	BATH	BATH	W	1G3T(14)-0
310356	SWANSEA	SWANSEA	L	2G2PG(16)-2G2PG1T(19)
020456	CARDIFF	CARDIFF	W	1G1PG1T(11)-1G(5)
070456	GLOUCESTER	GLOUCESTER	W	1G1PG(8)-1PG1T(6)
140456	LONDON WELSH	TWICKENHAM	W	1PG1T(6)-1T(3)
210456	COVENTRY	COVENTRY	L	2PG(6)-2PG2T(12)

19

The Rumanian Tour
May 1956

We returned the visit from the Rumanians earlier in the year over the period of 7th-14th May (today's spelling of the country is Romania and as this did not come about until around 1975, I have used the spelling in use at the time). As soon as the 1955/56 season had finished, plans were afoot to get the squad ready for the trip. Our full back, John Gardner (who had twisted knee ligaments) was receiving daily treatment at Highbury under the Arsenal Football Club trainer (Billy Milne) so as to get fit in time. Ian McGregor (the Scottish international wing forward) had been invited to play but was ruled out with a broken arm and John Currie (the England second row forward) had turned down an invitation to tour so as to concentrate on Cricket at Oxford University (where he was trying to win a Blue). Ken Chapman was prevented by business commitments from managing the tour and Jay Gould took his place.

The touring party consisted of the following players and officials:- Committee: H.J. Gould (Secretary); D.K. Brooks, A.A. Grimsdell, R.T. Kindred and D.A. Whiting. Players: R.M. Bartlett (captain); P.R.Y. Anderson, T. Bleasdale, W.P.C. Davies, J.J. Gardner, M.L. Grant, W.R. Grimsdell, N.A. Labuschagne, K.J.H. Mallett, V.R. Marriott, K. Pontin, D.L. Sanders, J.R. Simons, R.C.C. Thomas, D.R. Thompson, R.A.M. Whyte and C.G. Woodruff. Referee: Dr. P.F. Cooper; Press representative: Terry O'Connor; Independent Television News cameraman: Len Dudley. Also present and combining our visit with a political mission were:- Sir Wavell Wakefield M.P. (accompanied by Lady Wakefield) and J.P.W. Mallalieu M.P. together with D.B. Willis (who was invited as a guest of the Rumanians).

The players officially gathered at Teddington on Sunday 6th May so as to get an extra period of training in. Spirits were said to have been high and the standard of fitness was good considering the long, hard season which had just finished. The journey began on Monday 7th May with an early flight from London Airport (now Heathrow) to Brussels by British European Airways. Once at Brussels the party transferred to Sabena (Belgian Airlines) bound for Prague from where they were divided into two Russian built Lisunov Li-2 (DC-3/Dakota) aircraft to complete the journey with the longest leg to Bucharest. Differences were noticed between the style and luxury between western and Rumanian airlines such as no seat belts or hostesses. After one refuelling stop at Arrad (just inside the Rumanian border), Bucharest was finally reached in the early evening. After being met by a large reception committee at the airport, the party was transported to the Athenee Palace Hotel in the city centre.

The next day the party had a morning of sightseeing and many of the people encountered were anxious to discuss the state of affairs in the West. As travel between countries was so restricted the party found the locals to be both friendly and inquisitive. In the afternoon the team trained at the Dinamo Stadium where the first match (against Bucharest "B") would take place the following afternoon. The ground was in good condition and a large number of athletes trained on the running track.

Another reason for the tour was so that Wavell Wakefield could compile a complete report on the status of Rumanian rugby after allegations of financial rewards being offered to players if they defeated Cardiff, Swansea or the Harlequins on their tour earlier in the season. As a consequence, the Welsh Rugby Union asked the International Board to give a ruling on future games with them and, as the Board had no evidence to discuss, they sanctioned this tour in the hope they would learn something.

On the morning of the match (Wednesday 9th) the party travelled some 15 or 20 miles from Bucharest to Snazor where a ceremony was held at the graves of 84 airmen from Britain, Australia, Canada and South Africa who had been killed in wartime bombing raids. This coincided with other VE Day commemorations being held throughout Rumania. Those present included more than 100 Rumanian soldiers, a band, high ranking officers and members of the Government, the British minister in Bucharest (Mr. Dermot McDermott) and members of his staff. After the British and Rumanian National Anthems had been played 12 wreaths were laid on behalf of Bucharest factories, trade union movements and local community centres. Our wreath (made up of white lilac, red tulips and white lilies) to commemorate the airmen's sacrifice was laid by Reg Kindred (who was a flying officer during the war and lost a leg when he was shot down in a bomber) and John Simons to represent the Royal Air Force past and present.

The party returned to Bucharest for lunch and a rest before the game which was to kick-off at five o'clock as the heat during the afternoon was higher than anything the Harlequins had experienced during the season just gone. The team was:- Gardner, Woodruff, Simons, Davies, Anderson, Bartlett (captain), Pontin, Sanders, Labuschagne, Whyte, Bleasdale, W.R. Grimsdell, Thomas, Mallett and Thompson.

The crowd was some 35,000 strong, the referee was Dr. Peter Cooper and the first half ended scoreless. By this time we had John Gardner (full back) and Paul Anderson (wing) injured and this meant moving John Mallett from the scrum on to the wing, playing seven forwards and two partially lame full backs. With just eighteen minutes left David Thompson scored a try for us after a break by scrum half Keith Pontin which Ricky Bartlett converted and shortly after, Phil Davies ran 80 yards from an interception to score our second try (again converted by Bartlett) to secure a ten point win.

As a legacy of our victory, we had the injuries mentioned earlier and on top of these, Micky Grant pulled a muscle in training the day before the match. All three were treated at the Rumanian Institute of Sporting Medicine on the Thursday but only Grant was fit enough to play in the second game. Between times, the party were involved in independent sightseeing, conducted tours and training as well as a cocktail party on the Friday evening, given by the British Consul General. The impression was that our visit was a very prestigious one to all concerned.

So, on Saturday 12th May, we met the Bucharest "A" side containing 14 internationals. Terry O'Connor, the only British press representative covering the tour, reported that "as far as the 45,000 spectators expected are concerned this is virtually Rumania versus England". As it was, almost 50,000 people turned up to watch the game in the Republic Stadium and as mentioned earlier, we had to make some changes to our fifteen. Grant came in at full back for Gardner, Derek Whiting played on the wing instead of Anderson and Alan Grimsdell came in for his brother (Bill) in the second row. After his exploits against Bucharest "B", Phil Davies was heavily marked and it was left to John Mallett to open our account when he won the race for a touchdown under the posts which Ricky Bartlett converted. Dobre, one of the Rumanian backs got a try which Peter Woodruff, who was confused by the absence of grass behind the posts (cinders from the athletics track were used instead), might otherwise have prevented and just before half time, Ionescu got a penalty to put the home side 6-5 ahead. Palosanu scored two tries after the break (Ionescu converted the second) to open up a nine point lead although the first should not have been allowed. Bucharest were awarded a penalty 30 yards out and after ordering the touch judges behind the posts for a kick, the referee allowed a short punt while we were still walking back and the try resulted. However, our players admitted afterwards that a dropped goal from Dobre in the first half went through the posts but was not given (so everything evened out in the end). We rallied well but could only manage a John Simons try which was converted by Alan Grimsdell. It was not quite enough and the Rumanians had won by fourteen points to ten. It was felt that Mr. Munteau, the Rumanian referee, started off reasonably well but deteriorated badly in the second half. However, the players considered the refereeing to be no worse than that they had met with in certain parts of England during the 1955/56 season! This second game saw the last appearances in the 1st XV by Alan Grimsdell, who had amassed 335 points during his career (10 tries, 4 goals from a mark, 49 penalties and 74 conversions) and Donald Sanders who had made at least 62 appearances.

On the Sunday, the party were guests of their hosts for a picnic in the mountain district about 80 miles from Bucharest followed by an informal meeting at the Embassy Club. A start was made on the journey home early on Monday morning and after a refuelling stop at Arrad, the party landed at Prague and had a two hour sightseeing tour around the city. From here, the journey home was completed and so, a very eventful and enjoyable first overseas tour had been undertaken.

Rumanian Tour

090556	BUCHAREST B	BUCHAREST	W	2G(10)-0
120556	BUCHAREST A	BUCHAREST	L	2G(10)-1G1PG2T(14)

20

The Loss of a Legend 1956-1961

At the Annual General Meeting on 17th July 1956 (held in the Ballroom Foyer at the Mayfair Hotel, Berkeley Street, London W1) a proposal to increase the subscriptions from two to three guineas was proposed. There were speakers in favour and against the amendment but it was passed in the end by the required two thirds majority. Wavell Wakefield put forward a proposal that, for the forthcoming season the Harlequins announce that they were not proposing to take any place kicks at goal from any penalty awarded to them and they hoped that the sides they played against would be agreeable to do the same. At this time there was a strong feeling in the rugby world that too many games were being spoilt by excessive penalty kicks, and in particular by the scoring of so many penalty goals in a game. After a fairly lengthy discussion, it was decided that no announcement be made and that it be left up to the captain on the field to decide. If he decided to act on the proposal, he should not inform the opposing captain nor ask him to co-operate. The Club captain (Ricky Bartlett) had said that he felt it was a good idea and supported the proposal. We did not convert a penalty until our fourth game of the 1956/57 season. At a meeting on 23rd July it was decided to send a telegram to Donald Sanders wishing him a speedy recovery from the very serious injury sustained during his recent holiday in Yugoslavia.

On 24th January it was recorded that Phoenix House Limited (the printers of Harlequin Story) had written to say that they still held 1,677 copies of the book and had been offered 1s per copy by a remainder merchant. Under the agreement, the Club held the option to take these books at the same price if so desired. The honorary treasurer advised that the Club still held 1,200 copies of its own and these were being disposed of at a very slow rate. In view of this, the Committee decided to allow the printers to dispose of their stock and the assistant secretary would write to Phoenix House to that effect. A new seven year lease had been negotiated with the R.F.U. for the use of Twickenham and a further agreement had been entered into for the use of the White City stadium during season 1957/58. On 11th June, the honorary treasurer said that the final profit figure of £297 was disappointing when gate receipts were the largest so far in the history of the Club (£7,185). The costs of printing and stationery, expenses for the secretary, treasurer, team secretaries and referees, jerseys, footballs, laundry and entertaining visiting teams had all gone up and this had not helped. Five points were put forward for review by the Committee to try and cut costs and to ensure that greater vigilance was shown when the Club's money was being spent.

After our highly successful tour to Rumania (even though only one of the two games had been won) it was soon time to start the activities of the 1956/57 season. Our first match was up in Newcastle against Gosforth. Although they once again cut down on the number of points conceded, we still managed to win by three tries to nil. In the first half Paul Anderson got one and in the second, John Simons added two more. A week later on 8th September, we received some overseas visitors in the shape of a German XV and duly despatched them by twenty six points to eight. Our unbeaten record went unexpectedly against St. Mary's Hospital at Twickenham (6-8) but we came back strongly to see off Leicester (34-11), Bath (17-3) and our second overseas visitors (an Italian XV) by the odd point in 29. We started off well enough against the Italians and M.E. (Maurice) Kershaw (2) and Ricky Bartlett scored tries to put us in a strong position. Lanfranchi pulled back a penalty before half time and Pescetto and Ponchia added tries (one of which was converted by Lanfranchi) to put them two points up. Penalties were then swapped by Bill Grimsdell and Lanfranchi before Hugh Greatwood had the final word with our fourth try. At Twickenham on 20th October, we had our biggest win since 25th September 1920 (when we defeated Bedford 76-0) by beating the Paris Université Club 55-0. We ran in twelve tries with Ricky Bartlett adding eight conversions and Hugh Greatwood kicking a penalty to complete the scoring. This was quickly followed at the White City with a 28-0 win over Rosslyn Park before we were humbled by Cardiff in the floodlit game to the tune of eight points to six.

Our biggest win against Bristol since 1914 came on 3rd November (25-3) and Richmond were also beaten. On 17th November at Twickenham, we were defeated for the third time when Oxford University won by fourteen points to six although we did beat the other varsity side the following week by eight points to five. We scored seventeen points without reply against Blackheath at Twickenham before playing Cardiff (again at the White City) on 8th December. We showed five changes from the floodlit match whereas Cardiff had nine. These changes obviously affected them more than us as we ran out winners 17-11. The following week saw us travel down to Newport for our regular defeat and suffered our seventeenth loss in as many visits (3-8) after playing with fourteen men for most of the first half when D.I. Jones missed his train at Paddington. Roger Whyte (who had kicked a conversion and a penalty and dropped a goal against Cardiff) got our only points with a penalty and he kicked another conversion and a penalty in the return with Richmond. David Thompson, John Simons and Brian Calvert got our tries in a 14-0 win. Our last fixture of 1956 was a game at Twickenham against Coventry. We had not beaten them since 1947 and we got off to a bad start when P.B. Jackson (in the first half) and W.J. Stewart (in the second half) got tries (both converted by G. Cole). Roger Whyte did kick a penalty for us but it was nowhere near enough and the visitors secured their tenth win on the trot over us. Despite those last two defeats, our good form in the early part of the season had seen us to a record of W14 L5 so it was not all gloom and doom. During the first half of the season, we saw the debuts of two more future England internationals. D.G. (David) Perry played the first of his 27 games for us against United Services, Portsmouth on 13th October (although he was to win his 15 caps over the period 1963-66 whilst playing for Bedford) and J.G. (John) Willcox against Richmond on 10th November (the first of at least 85 appearances) who went on to gain 16 caps over the years 1961-64.

We started off 1957 with a trip to Bristol and, despite two tries from Maurice Kershaw, we went down 11-14. Before these losses became the norm, we had to start winning again and our next match on 12th January against Blackheath would give us an opportunity of doing just that. By half time and playing with a bitter wind we had only managed a try by Phil Davies and the inevitable penalty from Roger Whyte. Blackheath had defended desperately in the first 40 minutes and within eight minutes of the restart, they were level with a try from Cowan and a penalty by Sharp. It did not look good for us and another defeat seemed inevitable until Phil Davies stepped up and rallied the troops. His runs tore the Blackheath defence to shreds and these openings enabled Kershaw, Simons, Evans and

Calvert to score tries to which Whyte added the conversion to one. These fourteen points stopped Blackheath in their tracks and a final score of 20-6 in our favour was the result. Back at Twickenham the following week, we managed to defeat London Welsh (12-0) but the Royal Air Force defeated us for the third time running. After trailing 6-17 at half time we managed eight points in the second half but could close the gap no further. We exacted revenge over St. Mary's Hospital for our earlier defeat (5-3) and defeated the other two branches of the Armed Forces but came up against a determined Leicester side on 2nd March and lost by eight points to three. The next week we destroyed Bedford, scoring nine tries in a 37-6 victory before travelling to Paris for our return with the Paris Université Club. This time it was a lot closer and we sneaked home 23-22.

We then had two games in three days over 150 miles apart! First, we travelled up to Waterloo, won a close encounter 11-5 and then made our way down to Bristol for a floodlit match played at Ashton Gate (the home of Bristol City F.C.). Eleven of the team which played against Waterloo appeared on the Monday at Bristol and in an even tighter game we won again. Both sides scored three tries and in the end the difference came down to a single point (a penalty by Ricky Bartlett for us to a conversion for Bristol by L.D. Watts). We came down to earth with a massive bump and were well beaten by London Scottish at Richmond (8-27) despite being level at 8-8 early in the second half. This proved to be our heaviest defeat of the season. In our last home match of the season, we played Gloucester at Twickenham. Gloucester had been having an up and down season with 14 wins, 6 draws and 14 losses. Included in this were wins against Coventry and a double over Newport. We started well enough and were 11-0 up at the break after spending no more than 15 minutes in the visitors half. Roger Whyte had kicked a penalty (as had Micky Grant) and converted Dennis Barker's try. Gloucester came storming out of the blocks and within 10 minutes of the restart were level, scoring a goal, a try and a dropped goal. Another goal saw them in the lead and although John Simons scored a try which Grant converted to level things up again Gloucester had the last word when Lane got their fourth try for a 19-16 victory. Our next scheduled match (against London Irish) was cancelled with the agreement of both clubs as it clashed with the preliminary rounds of the Middlesex 7-a-side tournament.

The last three games of the season comprised the Easter tour. The matches at Bath and Swansea were lost by narrow margins (0-6 and 13-16 respectively) but we proved victorious against Cardiff (8-5) when Peter Woodruff got a try just before the end after an earlier effort by Keith Pontin (converted by Grant) had opened the scoring. This victory enabled a new record to be set as it was our 24th win of the season (out of 37 matches) and beat the previous best of 22 set in the 1955/56 season. This record was to last for some 27 years. During the season, Nick Labuschagne went back to South Africa and Dennis Barker ended his 1st XV career having scored at least 81 tries. J.D. (John) Currie made his debut against Leicester on 2nd March and went on to gain 25 caps for England (being the other half of a double act with David Marques in the second row). He made a confirmed 52 appearances for the first team (playing until 1960 when he moved to Bristol). Another new international appeared for us in the course of the season, he was Guy Stener (France) who won 5 caps but only played 4 games for us. He debuted against Northampton on 2nd February and made his last appearance in the match with Gloucester on 6th April.

Maurice Kershaw scored 21 tries (this was the most by one player in a season since Clifford Gibbs in 1925/26), Ricky Bartlett dropped five goals (a new record) and Roger Whyte got the most points with 76 (1 try, 15 penalties and 14 conversions). The team scored 108 tries (the most since 1926/27), 6 dropped goals (equalling the Club record) and, overall, 551 points. This was the highest number of points ever scored beating the previous total of 541 set by the remarkable side of 1909/10. Most appearances were made by Roger Whyte with 31 followed by D.J. Pack (27), Ricky Bartlett and John Simons (26) and Micky Grant and David Thompson (25).

1956/57

010956	GOSFORTH	GOSFORTH	W	3T(9)-0
080956	GERMAN XV	TWICKENHAM	W	4G2T(26)-1G1T(8)
150956	ST.MARY'S HOSPITAL	TEDDINGTON(A)	L	2T(6)-1G1T(8)
220956	LEICESTER	TWICKENHAM	W	2G1DG1PG6T(34)-1G2T(11)
290956	BATH	WHITE CITY	W	1G1DG3T(17)-1PG(3)
061056	ITALIAN XV	TWICKENHAM	W	1PG4T(15)-1G2PG1T(14)
131056	UNITED SERVICES PORTSMOUTH	WHITE CITY	W	1G1DG3T(17)-2PG(6)
201056	PARIS UNIVERSITÉ CLUB	TWICKENHAM	W	8G1PG4T(55)-0
271056	ROSSLYN PARK	WHITE CITY	W	(28)-0
301056	CARDIFF	WHITE CITY	L	1DG1T(6)-1G1PG(8)
031156	BRISTOL	WHITE CITY	W	2G2PG3T(25)-1PG(3)
101156	RICHMOND	TWICKENHAM	W	3G1PG3T(27)-1PG(3)
171156	OXFORD UNIVERSITY	TWICKENHAM	L	1PG1T(6)-1G1PG2T(14)
241156	CAMBRIDGE UNIVERSITY	TWICKENHAM	W	1G1PG(8)-1G(5)
011256	BLACKHEATH	TWICKENHAM	W	(17)-0
081256	CARDIFF	WHITE CITY	W	1G1DG2PG1T(17)-1G1PG1T(11)
151256	NEWPORT	NEWPORT	L	1PG(3)-1G1T(8)
221256	RICHMOND	RICHMOND	W	1G1PG2T(14)-0
291256	COVENTRY	TWICKENHAM	L	1PG(3)-2G(10)
050157	BRISTOL	BRISTOL	L	1G2T(11)-1G1PG2T(14)
120157	BLACKHEATH	WHITE CITY	W	1G1PG4T(20)-1PG1T(6)
190157	LONDON WELSH	TWICKENHAM	W	3PG1T(12)-0
260157	ROYAL AIR FORCE	TWICKENHAM	L	1G2PG1T(14)-1G3PG1T(17)
020257	NORTHAMPTON	NORTHAMPTON	L	1T(3)-1DG1PG1T(9)
090257	ST.MARY'S HOSPITAL	TEDDINGTON(A)	W	1G(5)-(3)
160257	ROYAL NAVY	PORTSMOUTH	W	2G(10)-1T(3)
200257	ARMY	TEDDINGTON	W	1PG3T(12)-1PG(3)
020357	LEICESTER	LEICESTER	L	1T(3)-1G1T(8)
090357	BEDFORD	BEDFORD	W	5G4T(37)-1PG1T(6)
170357	PARIS UNIVERSITÉ CLUB	PARIS	W	4G1PG(23)-2G1DG2PG1T(22)
230357	WATERLOO	WATERLOO	W	1G2T(11)-1G(5)
250357	BRISTOL	ASHTON GATE	W	1PG3T(12)-1G2T(11)
300357	LONDON SCOTTISH	RICHMOND	L	1G1T(8)-3G1DG2PG1T(27)
060457	GLOUCESTER	TWICKENHAM	L	2G2PG(16)-2G1DG2T(19)
130457	LONDON IRISH	BLACKHEATH	C	
180457	BATH	BATH	L	0-2T(6)
200457	SWANSEA	SWANSEA	L	2G1DG(13)-2G1DG1T(16)
220457	CARDIFF	CARDIFF	W	1G1T(8)-1G(5)

At the Annual General Meeting on 18th July questions were raised as to whether our use of the White City was necessary and whether we could play more fixtures at Twickenham during the early part of the season. It was explained that the White City was a necessity as we would be restricted to twelve matches at Twickenham. The White City did pay (even without including the money spinning floodlit match with Cardiff) and the terms of the lease at Twickenham made it imperative to have a second ground and this appeared to be the best alternative despite the remoteness felt by spectators. It was noted that no honours caps were to be awarded for this season. On 22nd August, it was revealed that we were to undertake a short tour in May 1958 to France to play against Stade Bordelais University and Aviron Bayonnais. On 12th September, a suggestion by Roger Whyte that a high netting fence be put up at Teddington to protect nearby houses and gardens from rugger balls was rejected on the grounds of the heavy cost of erecting and maintaining.

On 27th November, our past President, Adrian Dura Stoop passed away. He had been an influential figure in the Rugby Union since the early part of the century and all club sides had observed a minute's silence before their games on 30th November in memory of a great man. He had served the Club since 1902 and played in one of the best Quins sides ever seen back in the few years before the First World War. He truly was a legend having held every position at the Club and devoted a lot of his life to the sport. A wreath had been sent to his funeral on behalf of the Club and a number of officers had attended. A memorial service had been held at St. Martin's-in-the-Fields in London where a large congregation heard an address given by our President, Wavell Wakefield and the Club had held a minute's silence at their annual dinner on 14th December at the House of Commons.

On 5th February, the Adrian Stoop memorial sub-committee was set up to recommend to the full Committee on the form of a memorial which the Club should erect in his memory. The members of this sub-committee were Ken Chapman (Chairman), Vic Roberts, E.M.C. Clarke and Alan Grimsdell. On 27th March it was reported that the following suggestions had been made - a stained glass window at Rugby School, an annual memorial match and gates and tablets at Twickenham or Teddington. Ken Chapman felt that the Club itself would prefer any memorial to be at Teddington which was not only our home ground but Adrian Stoop had been responsible, far more than anyone else, for it being in existence at all. It was agreed in principle that any memorial should be created at Teddington and that this ground be named the Stoop Memorial Ground. The 1st XV tour to Germany in May 1959 was given the go ahead even though it would probably involve the Club in a certain amount of expense. On 13th June, an invitation was received from Blackheath to share the Rectory Field, this was turned down.

The 1957/58 season saw a different start to the previous three, the Gosforth fixture was dropped and replaced by a short tour to Devon and Cornwall. Our first game was against a combined Penryn and Falmouth XV and was played at the Recreation Ground, Falmouth on 7th September. We put out a very strong team and gave our opponents a lesson in how the handling game should be played. Roger Whyte got two tries in the first ten minutes (he also got our seventh and last) and these were followed by tries from Peter Woodruff, John Simons and Vic Marriott. Ricky Bartlett could only add one conversion and we led 17-3 at half time. Maurice Kershaw added our sixth try in the second half which, when added to Whyte's gave a final score of 23-3. On the following Monday we moved into Devon to play Devonport Services in Plymouth and won with Bartlett's two second half penalties to the home side's goal earlier in the same half. On 14th September, we had our first ever meeting with Llanelly (the Scarlets from Stradey Park). The contest was effectively over after just 20 minutes as Llanelly had lost two of their internationals (centre Cyril Davies and prop Henry Morgan) injured. By this time Bartlett had kicked a penalty and Simons had grabbed two tries, Whyte converted both and our visitors could only reply with a penalty. Before half time Whyte added a penalty and Woodruff scored a try. Llanelly made a real fight of it after this and limited our scoring to tries from P.J. (Peter) Fuller and Woodruff (the latter being converted by J.G. (John) Willcox) and although they only managed another penalty, they had avoided an avalanche of points and in the end only lost 27-6.

Four wins followed in quick succession the picks of which were our biggest win of the season, against United Services, Portsmouth (49-5) and the 19-6 defeat of Leicester. Although our unbeaten record was preserved against Waterloo, we could only achieve a draw and the same occurred in the floodlit fixture with Cardiff. Next up were our third Welsh visitors of the season in the shape of Swansea. A try in each half was enough to deprive us of our unbeaten record stretching back to the last game of the 1956/57 season and comprising eight wins and two draws. Bristol were made to pay for this loss (33-18), although one consolation for them was a 60 yard penalty by Cripps, but it all went wrong against Richmond (0-8). One bright spot in this game was the debut of J.J. (Joseph) "Joe" McPartlin who went on to play in a confirmed 111 matches and win 6 caps for Scotland. His international career lasted between 1960 and 1962. Once again we defeated one university and lost to the other but it was Cambridge who handed us a defeat this time (3-33). At this time, several of our players (current and future) turned out for Oxford and Cambridge and this season turned out to be no exception (the Oxford side contained six and the Cambridge side contained three).

We recovered from the light blue mauling to defeat Bath but suffered reverses against Blackheath and the Combined Services (in our first meeting since October 1935). We did at least secure our first win against Newport since 1951 in the match played at Twickenham on 21st December. Despite Newport being depleted owing to the Welsh trial, they took the lead when C. Lewis went over for a try. This proved to be the end of their scoring and we were level at half time thanks to a try by J. Hancock. In the second half T.D. (Terry) Gathercole got a try and Roger Whyte kicked a penalty to sew the game up. The return with Richmond on 28th December ensured that we ended the year on a high as we outscored them by three tries to two (to go with David Thompson's dropped goal) to win 14-6.

A familiar scene saw us play Bristol on the first weekend of 1958 and, despite missing seven regular first teamers (including Ricky Bartlett and Phil Davies), we made more than a match of it. Against the run of play, Terry Gathercole picked the ball up on the half way line, ran through, put in a short punt and collected it before the defence could cover and he was over for a try to give us the lead at half time. In the second half Bristol were unfortunately reduced to thirteen men through injuries and Gathercole scored his second try (converted by Whyte). The brave 13 played on and near the end got their reward when T.E. Base scored a try which G. Cripps converted. It was not enough and we had won by three points. Gathercole got another two tries the following week to help us defeat Blackheath (9-0) and prevent them from completing the double over us. We followed this with losses to London Irish (10-19) at Blackheath and the Army (in a midweek match at Teddington) by ten points to nil. Against the Royal Navy on 22nd February, as against Bristol, we benefited from our opponents losing men to injuries. This time though, it was only one (their full back) and we managed three tries to nil in a 16-3 win. At this stage of the season we were regularly losing our first team players to either county, inter-service or international duty and so our performances and teams varied from week to week. This was shown against Leicester (when a weakened side lost by three tries to nil) and the following week we were very nearly at full strength for the visit of Bedford. On this occasion it made no difference to the end result and we still lost, but only by the narrow margin of two points (6-8). Micky Grant managed to play in this game even after having thirteen stitches in his head the previous week.

We had now lost four of our last five matches and badly needed a win. Our next game, on 15th March, was at Roehampton against Rosslyn Park. This was our first meeting with them on their new ground (they had played at the Old Deer Park since before the end of the last century). We again suffered as regards team selection and had Bartlett, Currie and Marques in action for England against Scotland at Twickenham. Added to this, Maurice Kershaw failed to turn up and John Hardwicke had to be called from the "A" team at Teddington to play in the second half and make our numbers up to fifteen. By this time, Roger Whyte had been successful with two penalty kicks and John Willcox had converted a try by T.A. (Tom) Mace against Park's one goal and a try. David Thompson scored our second try and Willcox again converted to stretch our lead. The home side got more of the play against our full team than when we were one short but they could only manage one more try to leave us well deserved winners (16-11). After a gap of two years, we once again made the trip up to Edinburgh to meet Heriot's F.P. and, in a game in which Ricky Bartlett was outstanding, we really turned on the style. Bartlett got two of our four tries and dropped two goals as we ran out winners by twenty five points to eight.

On the following Tuesday (25th March) we travelled down to Ashton Gate for our second floodlit game with Bristol. This time they got the better of us by scoring eleven points without reply. At a meeting of the Executive Committee on 18th April, it was announced that Bristol had written a letter of complaint referring to the team we had sent to this game. We had arrived one short and several changes were made to the side advertised. As a result of this, the Secretary was instructed to write a letter of apology to the Bristol Club. We ran up a nice score against London Scottish (33-12) and our win against Bath was to be our only success on the Easter tour. Swansea beat us in a scrappy game (11-3) and a Ken Richards dropped goal with 17 minutes left was enough for Cardiff. Our last game of the domestic season saw us on an away visit to Coventry. At the end of the first half we had scored thirteen points without reply and, as both sides managed a try after this we won 16-3 and handed Coventry their heaviest home defeat of the season. It was our first victory over them since 1946 and our first win at Coventry for 46 years.

Roger Whyte topped the appearance ladder with 33 followed by Ricky Bartlett and David Thompson with 29, Peter Woodruff on 27 and John Simons just behind him on 25. Woodruff scored 12 tries whilst Whyte got the most penalties (21), conversions (24) and subsequently, most points with 120 (three tries making up his total). This was the most points scored by an individual in a season since Douglas Lambert got 184 in 1913/14. Overall, all methods of scoring (except penalties) were down on the previous, record breaking season and consequently our points dropped by over 150. With twenty wins, two draws and twelve defeats the 1957/58 season was still a reasonably successful one. The highlights being the home wins over Llanelly and Bristol and the away win over Coventry.

A short tour to south-west France had been arranged and we were due to play two matches against Stade Bordelais University and Aviron Bayonnais on 11th and 18th May respectively. Unfortunately, no record of the results has been found.

1957/58

070957	PENRYN AND FALMOUTH	FALMOUTH	W	1G6T(23)-1PG(3)
090957	DEVONPORT SERVICES	DEVONPORT	W	2PG(6)-1G(5)
140957	LLANELLY	TWICKENHAM	W	3G2PG2T(27)-2PG(6)
210957	ST.MARY'S HOSPITAL	TWICKENHAM	W	1G2PG2T(17)-1T(3)
280957	LEICESTER	TWICKENHAM	W	2G1PG2T(19)-1PG1T(6)
051057	PARIS UNIVERSITÉ CLUB	WHITE CITY	W	1G1PG(8)-1DG(3)
121057	UNITED SERVICES PORTSMOUTH	WHITE CITY	W	8G3PG(49)-1G(5)
191057	WATERLOO	TWICKENHAM	D	1T(3)-1DG(3)

221057	CARDIFF	WHITE CITY	D	1G(5)-1G(5)
261057	SWANSEA	TWICKENHAM	L	0-2T(6)
021157	BRISTOL	TWICKENHAM	W	3G2PG4T(33)-3G1PG(18)
091157	RICHMOND	RICHMOND	L	0-1G1DG(8)
121157	OXFORD UNIVERSITY	TWICKENHAM	W	2PG(6)-1PG(3)
231157	CAMBRIDGE UNIVERSITY	TWICKENHAM	L	1PG(3)-3G2PG4T(33)
301157	BATH	WHITE CITY	W	2G1PG1T(16)-0
071257	BLACKHEATH	BLACKHEATH	L	1G1T(8)-2G1T(13)
141257	COMBINED SERVICES	TWICKENHAM	L	1PG(3)-1PG1T(6)
211257	NEWPORT	TWICKENHAM	W	1PG2T(9)-1T(3)
281257	RICHMOND	WHITE CITY	W	1G1DG2T(14)-2T(6)
040158	BRISTOL	BRISTOL	W	1G1T(8)-1G(5)
110158	BLACKHEATH	BLACKHEATH	W	3T(9)-0
250158	ROYAL AIR FORCE	WHITE CITY	C	
150258	LONDON IRISH	BLACKHEATH	L	2G(10)-2G2PG1T(19)
190258	ARMY	TEDDINGTON	L	0-2G(10)
220258	ROYAL NAVY	TWICKENHAM	W	2G1PG1T(16)-1PG(3)
010358	LEICESTER	LEICESTER	L	0-3T(9)
080358	BEDFORD	TWICKENHAM	L	2PG(6)-1G1T(8)
150358	ROSSLYN PARK	ROEHAMPTON	W	2G2PG(16)-1G2T(11)
220358	HERIOT'S F.P.	EDINBURGH	W	2G2DG1PG2T(25)–1G1PG(8)
250358	BRISTOL	ASHTON GATE	L	0-1G1PG1T(11)
290358	LONDON SCOTTISH	RICHMOND	W	6G1PG(33)-1DG3T(12)
030458	BATH	BATH	W	1G1DG2T(14)-1PG1T(6)
050458	SWANSEA	SWANSEA	L	1PG(3)-1G1DG1PG(11)
070458	CARDIFF	CARDIFF	L	0-1DG(3)
120458	COVENTRY	COVENTRY	W	2G1PG1T(16)-1T(3)
110558	STADE BORDELAIS UNIVERSITY	BORDEAUX	?	
180558	AVIRON BAYONNAIS	BAYONNE	?	

At the Annual General Meeting on 18th July 1958, it was announced that gate receipts had totalled £6,803 and subscriptions had reached £1,061 (this figure was an all-time high for the Club). This all helped to make a profit of £567. Honours caps were awarded to Hugh Greatwood, John Simons and David Thompson. On 12th September, it was stated that the Stoop memorial match would be played on 5th September 1959 at Twickenham. Later it was suggested that the Barbarians or an international XV raised by Wavell Wakefield would provide our opponents but later still (on 17th November) as the Barbarians had turned us down our opponents would be the Wolfhounds from Ireland. Reg Kindred reported that the B.B.C. were prepared to televise 15 minutes of the forthcoming floodlit match with Cardiff as part of the programme "Sportsview". They would be prepared to pay a fee of about £100 but this was academic as the Club received no benefit from television fees (how times have changed!). A lot of people felt that this fixture had lost its novelty and it had become increasingly difficult to get the press interested and so the idea of holding a seven-a-side tournament early in the season was discussed. On

13th October, there was talk of arranging a floodlit match in 1959/60 between a combined Harlequin/Cardiff XV to play a side drawn from the newly returned British Lions. The International Board were strongly opposed to such fixtures and previous ones had been strongly criticised. In any event, Cardiff replied in the negative and the idea was dropped.

It was announced that Horace "Holly" Ward, who had been a player for 18 years (although the First World War had cut the total of actual seasons he played in to eleven) and treasurer for 31 years (beginning in 1912), had died on 31st May. On 16th December, further to the proposed tour to Germany in 1959, a guarantee of £250 had been received from the German Rugby Federation and the British Army of the Rhine (B.A.O.R.) had said they would like to field a side against us in Berlin or elsewhere. Later, on 21st January 1959, the Secretary reported that unless Reg Kindred could raise £200 from players and supporters to offset the extra cost of a charter flight, we would not be able to play the game against the B.A.O.R. side. On 24th March, a letter was received from the Harlequin Rugby Club of Queensland, Australia asking if they may be accepted as an affiliated club. Unfortunately, this request had to be declined as we had only one affiliated club in any one country of the Commonwealth.

Once again we travelled down to Cornwall to play against a combined Penryn and Falmouth XV and then St. Ives and Hayle. On 6th September, we met the Combined XV (this time at Penryn). With a very strong side, we gave a good performance and after the home side had held their own for a while at the start we scored tries through J.N. Hancock, R.J.N. (Dick) Leonard (2), Ricky Bartlett and Terry Gathercole (John Willcox converting four) to lead 23-0 at the break. It was more of the same after this and further tries came for us from John Simons, D.C. (David) Mills and Willcox (who added his fifth conversion) to leave us winners by 34-0. In this game, J.R.L. (John) Adcock made the first of at least 116 appearances for the 1st XV. On the following Monday, the game against St. Ives and Hayle produced a much closer scoreline but the same result. We were held to 3-3 at half time but three tries in the second half helped us to a 16-3 win. Our season really began now and Saturday 13th September saw Llanelly visit Twickenham. We started well enough and led through a 40 yard penalty by John Willcox after only six minutes. Unfortunately for us, Terry Gathercole injured a leg and had to be stretchered off after 20 minutes which meant we had to play the remaining 50 minutes with only fourteen men (the game was cut by the players to 70 minutes as the sun was too hot and the ground too hard!). By half time the visitors led 9-3 and a goal, a dropped goal and a try later the match was all over except for a consolation try for us by S.C. Coles to make the final scoreline a bit more respectable.

We were back to winning ways the following week against St. Mary's Hospital (35-6) but we could only draw with Leicester in controversial circumstances. They drew level with only two minutes remaining thanks to the conversion of a penalty try awarded after the referee decided one of their wingers had been pushed to the ground when chasing a punt ahead outside our 25 yard line. J.R.C. (John) Young made his debut in this game and went on to make 102 appearances and win 9 England caps and against St. Mary's Hospital, M.S. (Malcolm) Phillips played the first of only five games for us but he had started an international career which would yield 25 England caps. Our highest score against Swansea in 27 years gave us a good victory (playing in blue shirts) by twenty one points to six and then it was time for the now annual floodlit match at the white City against Cardiff. It was very nearly all Cardiff in the first half but they only led 6-5 and in the second they could only manage a penalty goal whereas we scored a try and converted it (as we had in the first half) to win by a single point. After another thrashing of United Services, Portsmouth (29-0), our form took a tumble and we lost four games in a row. This was to be the shape of things to come during the rest of the season. We met Paris Université Club in Paris the day after the U.S.

Portsmouth game and went down by four points (8-12) and the other noteworthy defeat was that at the hands of Lansdowne at Twickenham (8-17).

The last of the four defeats (against Bristol at the White City) saw the debut of Harry Eden. He was to play at least 171 games over the next seven seasons. We briefly returned to winning ways against Richmond and Oxford University but Cambridge University thrashed us again, this time we could not score and they managed 27 points. Against Bath on 29th November, we trailed by four points at the interval but came through strongly and scored thirteen unanswered points in the second half to win 22-13. This was to prove our last victory of 1958 and in three of the remaining four games we failed to score. Against Blackheath and Cardiff we lost after being level at half time, Newport scored nine points in the first half but none in the second against a very weakened side (we had four men playing in the English trial) and against Richmond we actually led at half time with a try from Dick Leonard and a conversion and a penalty by John Willcox to a goal. We suffered a terrible blow when Willcox dislocated his shoulder after 50 minutes (Micky Grant moved from the wing to full back to cover), Richmond gradually took control and two more tries saw them to a thirteen points to eight victory.

Unfortunately, 1959 began where the old year had finished and defeats followed against Bristol (6-19) and the Royal Air Force (3-16). The R.A.F. benefited from the services of Frank Carlton and Austin Rhodes of St. Helens Rugby League Club who were both able to play as they were doing their National Service. After six defeats in a row, we met London Scottish at Richmond on 31st January. At half time neither side had scored in what was a sterile forty minutes. We had looked slow and dispirited but all that changed when John Young scored our first try of the year. Roger Whyte quickly added a penalty and converted a try by Harry Eden before Joe McPartlin got our third and we led 14-0. The Scottish did pull one try back near the end but we had won by a good margin. The following week we went up to Northampton with only one change from the team which had been victorious over London Scottish (Jeff Abbott coming in for Vic Roberts who had made the last of at least 94 appearances in that game). No mercy was shown by the home side and, after a dropped goal and six tries (three converted) had been conceded by us, we had been on the receiving end of our second 27-0 defeat of the season. Another defeat to the London Irish followed before we were successful against the Royal Navy (19-8) and the Army (8-3).

Against Leicester, heavy rain before and during the match turned the Welford Road ground into a quagmire. Even so, both sides handled the ball well and both had scored a penalty goal by half time. Leicester's second penalty was equalised by Jeff Abbott's try five minutes from the end and just when it looked as though a draw would be the result, Horrocks-Taylor went over in the corner for Leicester and our fifteenth defeat of the season became a reality. Victories were becoming few and far between, our next match against Bedford proving no exception. The scoring went in four sections as first, the home side scored two tries and converted one to lead by eight points. We struck back to lead by half time with two John Young tries converted by John Currie and J.S.M. (John) Scott (who was playing the first of a confirmed 55 games having already won his only England cap against France in 1958). Two further penalties by Currie appeared to have put us on the way to victory but the Bedford fly half (A.M. Brannan) had other ideas. He kicked three penalties to put them into a one point lead and converted his own try to seal a 22-16 win. Further wins looked to be in short supply as it was time for the Easter tour.

As an added extra, we played Llanelly at Stradey Park for the first time (to mark the official opening of their new clubhouse). This meant that the game against Bath on 26th March was the first of four hard matches in the space of just five days. We could only score one try (by Harry Eden) in the first half but, as it turned out, this would have been enough to win. For good measure we scored four tries in the second half through McPartlin (converted by Whyte), Woodruff, Eden and Hancock. Bath could not break their duck and we won 17-0. G.C. (Grahame)

Murray made his debut in this game and was to go on and become the Club's leading appearance maker with a confirmed 307 matches played in. After Bath it was on to Wales for the really testing part of the tour, the first match being played on Good Friday at Stradey Park. We failed to score against Llanelly (0-6) and could only manage a try against Swansea (3-21) and Cardiff (3-8) to end a disappointing tour which had started so promisingly. Our last two matches were trips to Liverpool on successive Saturdays. First we met Waterloo and had to borrow J.C. Wright from them as John Young failed to arrive. An early penalty goal miss by Whyte was a chance we should have taken as the only points in the game were five to the home side in the first half when P.H. Thompson scored a try which R. Uren converted. We had a much more successful return trip on 11th April when we met Birkenhead Park. We outscored our hosts by four tries to nil (two in each half) to run out winners by sixteen points to nil. A.J.S. (Tony) Todman played the first of 127 confirmed appearances in this match.

Dick Leonard scored the most tries (12), Roger Whyte kicked nine penalties but John Willcox scored the most points overall (73) with one try, one dropped goal, seven penalties and twenty three conversions. Overall, the points scored by the team dropped another 41 on the previous season and consequently, all methods of scoring were down with only 70 tries being scored. Ricky Bartlett led the overall appearances in his last season as captain with 33 out of a maximum of 35 followed by John Simons (27), A.H.M. (Howard) Hoare (26) and Jeff Abbott (23).

In early May, it was time for another short tour, this time to Germany. The party left Blackbushe Airport on Friday 1st May at 1045am on board a Vickers Viking of Eagle Aviation. One of the party (Peter Woodruff) described this to me as quite an adventure. Reggie Kindred (who had served in the Royal Air Force) had assured everyone of the highest standards of airmanship and a perfect landing but it was a slipshod affair with a series of jack rabbit bounces followed by a tooth jarring bang as the aircraft finally settled on the runway. Pat Meaney (who had heard these tales from Reggie on a number of occasions) declared that's another air force myth exploded! That arrival was at Hanover-Langenhagen Airport at 1.45 p.m. where they were met by the President of the German Rugby Union (Heinz Reinhold) and transported to the venue for the first match. We played a German XV on the ground of SV 1908 Ricklingen in Hanover and won 13-11. A banquet was arranged in Hanover after the game and when the party returned to their accommodation at a sports school in Barsinghausen, the polished tiled flooring proved quite hazardous to most! During the course of the evening, Peter and a group entered a very seedy bar only to find Micky Papernick sat there with what he describes as a bunch of ruffians and he proceeded to introduce one of them as his friend, Wolfgang! They went on to eat salted herring which led to them happily having bigger thirsts to quench.

The following day, the party had been given permission to fly from Hanover to R.A.F. Wildenrath to make it easier to get to our next match against a combined R.A.F. Germany (2nd Tactical Air Force) and British Army of the Rhine (BAOR) XV at R.A.F. Bruggen on 3rd May. On Saturday, the party watched a match against the teams who would form our opposition and were entertained in great style that night in the Officers' Mess at Bruggen. That second game was won but the score remains unknown. Afterwards, the return flight to Blackbushe happened without incident.

On the 1959 British Lions tour to New Zealand, Australia and Canada, we were represented by David Marques and John Young. Two others who later played for us were K.J.F. (Ken) Scotland and W.M. (Bill) Patterson. Young and Patterson played in the second test in New Zealand with the second named scoring a try, Marques played in that match as well as the second test in Australia and Scotland only missed the second test in New Zealand. As far as results went, in New Zealand one was won and three lost while in Australia both were won.

1958/59

060958	PENRYN AND FALMOUTH	PENRYN	W	5G3T(34)-0
080958	ST.IVES AND HAYLE	ST.IVES	W	2G2T(16)-1T(3)
130958	LLANELLY	TWICKENHAM	L	1PG1T(6)-1G2DG3T(20)
200958	ST.MARY'S HOSPITAL	TWICKENHAM	W	4G2PG3T(35)-1PG1T(6)
270958	LEICESTER	TWICKENHAM	D	1G2T(11)-1G2PG(11)
041058	SWANSEA	TWICKENHAM	W	3G2T(21)-1PG1T(6)
081058	CARDIFF	WHITE CITY	W	2G(10)-2PG1T(9)
111058	UNITED SERVICES PORTSMOUTH	WHITE CITY	W	4G3T(29)-0
121058	PARIS UNIVERSITÉ CLUB	PARIS	L	(8)-(12)
181058	ROSSLYN PARK	WHITE CITY	L	1G1T(8)-2DG2PG(12)
251058	LANSDOWNE	TWICKENHAM	L	1G1T(8)-1G1PG3T(17)
011158	BRISTOL	WHITE CITY	L	2T(6)-1G1DG(8)
081158	RICHMOND	WHITE CITY	W	2G1PG(13)-1G1PG(8)
151158	OXFORD UNIVERSITY	TWICKENHAM	W	1G2PG(11)-1G1T(8)
221158	CAMBRIDGE UNIVERSITY	TWICKENHAM	L	0-3G4T(27)
291158	BATH	TWICKENHAM	W	2G3PG1T(22)-2G1PG(13)
061258	BLACKHEATH	WHITE CITY	L	0-2G1DG1PG(16)
131258	CARDIFF	TWICKENHAM	L	0-1T(3)
201258	NEWPORT	WHITE CITY	L	0-2PG1T(13)
271258	RICHMOND	RICHMOND	L	1G1PG(8)-2G1T(13)
030159	BRISTOL	BRISTOL	L	2PG(6)-2G3T(19)
100159	BLACKHEATH	BLACKHEATH	C	
170159	HERIOT'S F.P.	TWICKENHAM	C	
240159	ROYAL AIR FORCE	WHITE CITY	L	1PG(3)-2G2T(16)
310159	LONDON SCOTTISH	RICHMOND	W	1G1PG2T(14)-1T(3)
070259	NORTHAMPTON	NORTHAMPTON	L	0-3G1DG3T(27)
140259	LONDON IRISH	WHITE CITY	L	1DG(3)-1G1DG1PG1T(14)
210259	ROYAL NAVY	PORTSMOUTH	W	2G2PG1T(19)-1G1DG(8)
250259	ARMY	TEDDINGTON	W	1G1PG(8)-1PG(3)
070359	LEICESTER	LEICESTER	L	1PG1T(6)-2PG1T(9)
140359	BEDFORD	BEDFORD	L	2G2PG(16)-2G3PG1T(22)
260359	BATH	BATH	W	1G4T(17)-0
270359	LLANELLY	LLANELLY	L	0-1PG1T(6)
280359	SWANSEA	SWANSEA	L	1T(3)-3G1DG1T(21)
300359	CARDIFF	CARDIFF	L	1T(3)-1G1T(8)
040459	WATERLOO	WATERLOO	L	0-1G(5)
110459	BIRKENHEAD PARK	BIRKENHEAD	W	2G2T(16)-0
010559	GERMAN XV	HANOVER	W	(13)-(11)
030559	RAF GERMANY/BRITISH ARMY OF THE RHINE XV	BRUGGEN	W	

At the A.G.M. on 22nd July 1959 it was reported that annual subscriptions were up again at £1,132 but gate receipts were down over £1,300 to £5,553. The reason for the fall in gate money was down to the relative failure of the floodlit fixture with Cardiff and this eventually led to an overall loss of £202. No honours caps were awarded for the previous season and the honorary treasurer reported that, so far, only £760 had been received from 140 contributors in response to the Stoop Memorial Fund. It was agreed that pre-season training would be held at the Honourable Artillery Company ground, Armoury House, London, EC1. On 29th July, it was noted that an invitation had been received to play Llanelly on Good Friday 1960. In view of the recent experience of playing four games in five days, the invitation was turned down as it was felt this would impose too great a strain on the touring side. At a meeting on 16th September, D.M. Goldstein from the Kenya Harlequin Club said that his club were trying to organise a visit to Kenya by both the London and Pretoria Harlequins in May 1961 so that each club could play the other. The Committee agreed to this in principal on 6th October provided that Pretoria were able to make the trip as well. On 15th January 1960 the confirmation came from South Africa that Pretoria were okay to go and so the date was set. David Marques announced that he was considering what the best method of training for the 1st XV would be and had come up with a monthly session either on a Sunday or weekday evening. In May 1960, the first edition of the new Club newsletter "Harlequinade" appeared. This was run by an editorial team of Howell Thomas, Reg Kindred, Micky Grant and Ray Relf and was to run on and off until 1970 before being resurrected for a short time between 1987 and 1991.

David Marques began his two season reign as captain, but did not play his first game until 31st October against Bath as he had been on the British Lions tour during the summer (it was customary for players who had participated to make a delayed start to the season). With Howard Hoare as captain in the absence of David Marques, the team began the season at Twickenham with the first Stoop memorial match against the Wolfhounds from Ireland. This was their first match outside Ireland and their side contained internationals from France (2), Ireland (7), Scotland (1) and Wales (3). At half time the score looked reasonably respectable with two John Currie penalties for us against two goals and a try for the Wolfhounds. In the second half though, things were totally different and our much fitter and faster opponents outscored us by four goals (one dropped) and four tries to a goal and a try to run out winners 43-14. One newspaper headline summed it up with the words: "Oh, Quins, this was pathetic". After this shocking defeat, we bounced back to record victories over Heriot's F.P. (34-6), St. Mary's Hospital (25-6) and Leicester (18-11). Against London Scottish, we came unstuck and in the end lost quite convincingly (8-23) although it must be said that we did lose C.M. (Colin) Payne and S.C. Coles with eye injuries and finished the match with only 13 men. Our next fixture was a midweek match at the White City against Wasps. We flopped again and went down by eighteen points to three despite scoring first (a penalty by Micky Grant).

We defeated a below strength United Services, Portsmouth team easily enough in the end (19-8) and had another close call against Waterloo before coming good in the last 15 minutes to win 13-9. Our first Welsh visitors of the season came in the shape of Cardiff for the last of the floodlit matches at the White City. As our recent form had shown, we were not playing at our best and duly went down by twelve points to three despite again scoring first. Swansea came to Twickenham the following Saturday and with 12 minutes left, neither side had scored thanks to the strong defences of both teams. Swansea broke the deadlock and got two tries (the first of which was converted), we could only reply right on the stroke of full time when G.N. (Nick) Paterson scored a try which Roger Whyte converted from the touch line and another match had been lost. As mentioned earlier, our new captain took charge of the team on the pitch for the first time the following week when Bath provided the opposition. The return of David Marques coincided with the return to the side of John Currie and, as a result, our line out work was much stronger. In the first half, we were vastly superior and tries from Bob Mustard and C.D.C. Brooks and a conversion and a penalty goal from Roger Whyte gave us a comfortable lead of eleven points. We had, however, lost our hooker (Howard Hoare) with a broken nose and this seemed to disrupt the whole team. In the first 36 minutes of the second half, Bath were right on top and had pulled level with exactly the same scores as us. Then, with only four minutes to go we suddenly attacked, Mustard scored his second try, Whyte converted and the game was as good as won. For good measure and right on the stroke of full time, John Currie added our fourth try (which was again converted by Whyte) and our winning margin had become ten points (21-11).

The next day it was off to Paris again for a match against the Paris Université Club which we won by sixteen points to eleven. Fog ruled out any hopes of our match against Bristol at Twickenham taking place but the following two games against Richmond and Oxford University did go ahead and both were won. Against Oxford, five of the university team were (or became) members of the Club and one of them (John Willcox) scored their penalty goal. Blackheath lost one of their centres after just 17 minutes (when we were already leading 11-0) and finally succumbed 29-3. Following this we had to play two Welsh teams in a row and, as was becoming a regular occurrence, we lost both. Cardiff came to Twickenham and won by fourteen points to five and we travelled to Newport and lost to two tries in the second half. On Boxing Day, we played Richmond in the Twickenham Jubilee match. Just over fifty years after the first meeting at Twickenham and in driving rain, we once again defeated our near neighbours. This time our victory by ten points to nil was completed in an easier fashion than the win in 1909. For the record, Dick Leonard and M.R. Handfield-Jones scored our tries in the first half and Roger Whyte converted both. In the first half of the season we had seen debuts from two future England internationals and the departure of an old one. Colin Payne played the first of at least 248 games for the Club in the Wolfhounds match (he was to win 10 caps between 1964 and 1966) and Jeremy Spencer (who was to win 1 cap in 1966) made his debut against Wasps on 7th October. We said goodbye to Phil Davies who made the last of his at least 120 1st XV appearances against the Wolfhounds.

We lost narrowly to Bristol (11-14) and completed the double over Blackheath by the narrowest of margins (9-8). Our first points came from a twice taken penalty by John Willcox (his first effort had sent the ball wide), Bob Mustard got our try and Whyte kicked another penalty to seal the win. Against the R.A.F., we had a guest at full back playing his only game for us. He was the new Cambridge University captain, K.J.F. (Ken) Scotland. His first cap for Scotland was won in 1957 and he went on to gain a total of 27, the last in 1965. The Racing Club de France had pulled out of their match against Cambridge and this enabled him to appear in our colours. As it turned out, we were extremely glad he played. In the first half, his penalty was cancelled out by a try for the visitors by W. Burgess but in the second, they had no answer and he went on to kick two more penalties and score an excellent try just three minutes from the end to give us a 12-3 win. After this, we played our last three games ever at the White City against London Scottish, Northampton and London Irish. Against the first named, we had lost half of our first choice players to Surrey and went down 6-11, Northampton (even though playing with fourteen men for the second half) outscored us thanks to the kicking of R.W. Hosen (14-24) and finally, the London Irish (who were having an excellent season) outplayed us to win by eleven points to three. In the London Scottish match, Nicholas Silk played the first of a confirmed 62 matches and went on to win 4 England caps in 1965. Our record at the White City stadium (over the last six seasons) had been P40 W26 D2 L12.

We had another close game with the Army at Teddington on 24th February, Harry Eden scored a try in each half, the Army could only score a second half penalty and we won 6-3 (despite having nine regular first team men missing). As the Royal Navy visited Twickenham the following Saturday, we had the chance to register victories against all three services teams. After half an hour, the visitors led by a goal to nil but by half time we had the lead after Nick Paterson and Jim Stolarow had scored tries (one of which Roger Whyte converted). Vic Marriott scored our third try, Whyte converted and we led 13-5 only for the Navy to come back and score two tries (the second with just five minutes remaining) to bring them to within two points of our total. It all hinged on the conversion attempt, it was missed and we had scraped home. Leicester gained revenge for their defeat earlier in the season (6-16) and Bedford defeated us for the third time in a row (8-22). On 19th March, we welcomed Birkenhead Park to Twickenham and set about dismantling their defence. After 30 minutes, we had scored tries from Harry Eden and Dick Leonard (2) and two conversions by Roger Whyte to lead by thirteen points to nil. Then John Scott fractured his collar bone and had to go off (Jeff Abbott moved out of the pack to play at full back). With us down to fourteen men, Birkenhead Park came storming back with two goals to cut our lead to just three points. Leonard completed his hat-trick and all that remained was for Whelan (the visiting scrum half) to drop a goal from 45 yards to end the scoring and we had won 16-13. Against London Welsh, we again suffered injury setbacks. David Thompson (our blind side wing forward) had to leave the field with concussion after just eleven minutes and John Young (on the wing) pulled a hamstring late in the game. Despite this, we pulled back a half time deficit of eight points to tie the scores at 18-18.

On 2nd April, we had our first win over Northampton since 1952 and our first at Northampton since 1946 (14-9) and a Midlands double was notched up when we defeated Coventry the following week by fifteen points to eleven. All that remained of the season was the Easter tour and it began at Bath on Maundy Thursday, 14th April. In an open game, we achieved our highest score and biggest winning margin against them since 1907. Tries for us were scored by Harry Eden (4), Joe McPartlin, Grahame Murray, John Simons and Derek Whiting to which Ricky Bartlett added the conversions to five. Bath could only manage two goals (one dropped) and two tries to make the final score 34-14 in our favour. In the other two games, we defeated Swansea (13-8) but lost to Cardiff (6-17) to round off another up and down season which was almost the exact reverse of the previous one. This time we won 20, drew 1 and lost 15.

Harry Eden and Bob Mustard scored 13 tries each and Roger Whyte kicked his way to the most points (85) with 13 penalties and 23 conversions. Overall, all scoring was up on the previous season with a new Club record of 28 penalty goals being set. The conversion total of 52 was the best since 1930/31. Joint top appearance makers were Ricky Bartlett and D.J. (David) Pack with 31 followed by Harry Eden and Vic Marriott (27), S.C. Coles (26) and Jeff Abbott on 25.

1959/60

050959	WOLFHOUNDS(SMM)	TWICKENHAM	L	1G2PG1T(14)-5G1DG5T(43)
120959	HERIOT'S F.P.	TWICKENHAM	W	5G3T(34)-2T(6)
190959	ST.MARY'S HOSPITAL	TEDDINGTON(A)	W	2G3PG2T(25)-2PG(6)
260959	LEICESTER	TWICKENHAM	W	3G1PG(18)-1G1PG1T(11)
031059	LONDON SCOTTISH	RICHMOND	L	1G1PG(8)-4G1PG(23)
071059	WASPS	WHITE CITY	L	1PG(3)-1DG4PG1T(18)
101059	UNITED SERVICES PORTSMOUTH	PORTSMOUTH	W	2G3T(19)-1G1T(8)
171059	WATERLOO	WATERLOO	W	2G1T(13)-1PG2T(9)
211059	CARDIFF	WHITE CITY	L	1PG(3)-2PG2T(12)

241059	SWANSEA	TWICKENHAM	L	1G(5)-1G1T(8)
311059	BATH	WHITE CITY	W	3G1PG1T(21)-1G1PG1T(11)
011159	PARIS UNIVERSITÉ CLUB	PARIS	W	2G1PG1T(16)-1G1PG1T(11)
071159	BRISTOL	TWICKENHAM	C	
141159	RICHMOND	RICHMOND	W	1G1PG1T(11)-1G1T(8)
211159	OXFORD UNIVERSITY	TWICKENHAM	W	2PG(6)-1PG(3)
281159	CAMBRIDGE UNIVERSITY	TWICKENHAM	L	1G1PG1T(11)-2G2PG1T(19)
051259	BLACKHEATH	WHITE CITY	W	4G1PG2T(29)-1PG(3)
121259	CARDIFF	TWICKENHAM	L	1G(5)-1G1PG2T(14)
191259	NEWPORT	NEWPORT	L	0-2T(6)
261259	RICHMOND	TWICKENHAM	W	2G(10)-0
020160	BRISTOL	BRISTOL	L	1G2T(11)-1G1PG2T(14)
090160	BLACKHEATH	BLACKHEATH	W	2PG1T(9)-1G1PG(8)
230160	ROYAL AIR FORCE	TWICKENHAM	W	3PG1T(12)-1T(3)
300160	LONDON SCOTTISH	WHITE CITY	L	1PG1T(6)-1G1DG1T(11)
060260	NORTHAMPTON	WHITE CITY	L	1G1PG2T(14)-3G3PG(24)
200260	LONDON IRISH	WHITE CITY	L	1PG(3)-1G2DG(11)
240260	ARMY	TEDDINGTON	W	2T(6)-1PG(3)
270260	ROYAL NAVY	TWICKENHAM	W	2G1T(13)-1G2T(11)
050360	LEICESTER	LEICESTER	L	2PG(6)-2G1DG1T(16)
120360	BEDFORD	BEDFORD	L	1G1T(8)-2G1PG3T(22)
190360	BIRKENHEAD PARK	TWICKENHAM	W	2G2T(16)-2G1DG(13)
260360	LONDON WELSH	OLD DEER PARK	D	3G1DG(18)-3G1T(18)
020460	NORTHAMPTON	NORTHAMPTON	W	1G3T(14)-3T(9)
090460	COVENTRY	TWICKENHAM	W	3G(15)-1G1PG1T(11)
140460	BATH	BATH	W	5G3T(34)-1G1DG2T(14)
160460	SWANSEA	SWANSEA	W	2G1PG(13)-1G1PG(8)
180460	CARDIFF	CARDIFF	L	1DG1PG(6)-1G2PG2T(17)

Gate receipts fell to £4,970 and a loss of £889 was reported for the 1959/60 season. A dispute with one of the neighbours at the Teddington ground was reported on 11th January 1961 - a Mr. Weller had declined to return two balls which had been kicked into his garden, Ken Chapman was instructed to write to him and the balls were eventually returned. A letter had been received from the district valuer on 2nd December confirming their interest in the freehold of 0.85 acres of land adjacent to the Teddington ground. The price was £12,000 and it was believed they wanted to build six flats and four homes on the area. It was decided on 8th February that all proceeds from this sale would be put into the Stoop Memorial Fund. A number of bids totalling £80 had been put in for items of furniture (to go in the clubhouse at Teddington) from the S.S. Britannica which was being broken up at Inverkeithing. Unfortunately, they were not high enough and nothing was acquired.

We began the 1960/61 season with a trip to Devon to play a South Devon XV at Torquay as part of the Torquay Rugby Festival. Our hosts were made up of players from Brixham, Newton Abbot, Paignton, Plymouth, St. Luke's College (Exeter), Teignmouth and Torquay. In what was (as far as we were concerned) a high scoring game, we outscored the Festival XV by seven tries to one. B.L. Spencer scored our only try in the first half and this was accompanied by a conversion, two penalties and a dropped goal from the boot of John Willcox which enabled us to lead 14-3. In the second half, Tony Todman, Jeff Abbott, John Simons (2), Harry Eden and Jim Stolarow added tries to which Willcox added the goal points to four. Our opponents could only score a penalty in the first half and a try in the second to leave us winners by forty points to six. Our next fixture was against the Wolfhounds in the second Stoop Memorial match at Twickenham in which we hoped to avoid another drubbing (as received in the first one). In the first half, it looked as though it might happen again as we trailed by eight points at the interval. Despite Harry Eden and M.J. (Mike) Whiteside (who was making his debut) scoring tries, the first of which John Willcox converted, the Wolfhounds had scored three goals (one a penalty) and a try of their own. Early in the second half they lost their full back to injury but still stretched their lead when Tony O'Reilly scored their fourth try. However, we were leaner and fitter than we had been the previous season and Grahame Murray scored a try, Willcox kicked a penalty and further tries from John Young and John Simons saw us home with one point and five minutes to spare.

After St. Mary's Hospital and Leicester had been defeated we came up against Swansea at Twickenham. A dropped goal and three tries for the visitors were enough to take our unbeaten record. Something which was becoming increasingly rare, a 0-0 draw, happened in the match with United Services, Portsmouth and Northampton put on a sparkling exhibition of rugby in defeating us 24-5 despite losing their full back after 15 minutes of the second half. A narrow loss to Llanelly (3-6) at Stradey Park followed in a game which saw the referee (R. McCoy of Cardiff) carried from the field after getting involved amongst the forwards. His place was taken by T. John of Kidwelly who just happened to be watching the game. A brief respite from our run of defeats was gained in the match with Bath when Harry Eden got the only try of the game in the first half. J.L. (John) Bazalgette made the first of at least 90 appearances in this game. Our next match was a trip to Bristol and we suffered our heaviest defeat of the season in going down by twenty eight points to three. One newspaper reported that "a full list of the Harlequins' failings would occupy an unseemly amount of space". This seems to have summed up our results over the last six games and they did not really improve until the end of the year.

A 3-3 draw with Richmond at Teddington saw the debuts of two South Africans, Fred Swart (a prop) and Aubrey Luck (a scrum half). The participants of the varsity match were met on the next two Saturdays and although we defeated Oxford 11-3, we went down by five points to Cambridge (6-11). The first leg of a double was achieved against Blackheath (8-0) but two big tests followed on consecutive weekends against Cardiff and Newport. Against Cardiff, it was close all the way with never more than three points separating the sides. A penalty by A.J. Priday (Cardiff's full back) gave them the lead but we came back strongly with a try from Bill Coutts and a conversion by John Scott. Against the run of play, Priday kicked a second penalty a minute before half time to regain the lead for the visitors. David Perry got our second try at the start of the second half, we were back in front and we continued to lead until fifteen minutes from the end when Priday completed a hat-trick of penalties to give Cardiff the narrowest of victories. The Newport match on 17th December was away and with a side weakened by the final England trial, the subsequent defeat (by seventeen points to three) could probably have been predicted. We finished the year off with a nice trio of away victories (all in London) against Richmond (8-6), Rosslyn Park (20-8) and London Scottish (16-5).

Our second trip of the season to Bristol was more successful than the first and we came away with a victory (14-11) before completing the double over Blackheath. Alan Godson (a Cambridge blue) was making his debut for us on the right wing and it was he who kicked a penalty and scored a great try after a 60 yard run to put us 6-0 up at half time. Two penalties from Blackheath full back M.C. Clarke evened things up but in an amazing last 25 minutes

Godson landed another penalty and then converted tries by John Young, John Simons and Jeff Abbott to make the final score 24-6 in our favour. Our encounter with the Paris Université Club was cancelled as the R.F.U. stated that Twickenham was unplayable. A letter was sent by the Club deploring this decision as only a little rain had fallen and the cancellation created a bad impression with our opponents. The R.A.F. ended our run of five wins with victory at Twickenham by nine points to three. We lost at Northampton (6-11) but defeated London Irish for the first time since 1954 (outscoring them by five tries to one) and in the space of five days lost to the Royal Navy at Portsmouth (3-11) and the Army at Teddington (5-12). Associated Television televised the second half of the Army game for a fee of £75 and, as mentioned earlier, the Club did not really benefit from these arrangements. On this occasion, 75% of the money went to the R.F.U. and only 25% (about £19) was retained by the Club.

We travelled up to Leicester and received our biggest defeat at their hands since 1948 with a try count of 7-2 in their favour. After they had led 16-0 at the interval, we got two tries back to cut the deficit to ten points but conceded another thirteen to lose by twenty nine points to six. Bedford visited us at Teddington on 11th March and, having been unsuccessful in the last three encounters, we needed a win. We began well and R.A. Hewitt got a try for us which John Scott (who was returning from a three month injury lay off) converted for a 5-0 lead at half time. Bedford got a penalty but John Mallett scored our second try (again converted by Scott) to extend our lead. The visitors finally scored a try (when Harry Eden was off the field injured and Hewitt was limping badly) to make the final score 10-6 in our favour. One report of the game mentioned that as this was Teddington, the ball had to be frequently rescued from back gardens and on one occasion from a tree (perhaps Mr. Weller had a point!). This victory spurred us on and a visit to Scotland to play Heriot's F.P. at New Goldenacre in Edinburgh came next. With an excellent display of open rugby from both sides, our backs won the day and tries from D.F.B. (David) Wrench, Harry Eden (2), Joe McPartlin and John Simons (two being converted by John Scott) enabled us to win 19-6.

We then went on the Easter tour and came up against Bath on 30th March. We promptly ran up our third highest score ever with eleven goals (one a penalty) and three tries to two tries, a penalty and a dropped goal or, in other words, 62-12. We had only beaten them 3-0 back in October and they fielded a weakened side this time just as we were starting to put together some excellent rugby. Our tries came from Eden (3), McPartlin (3), Tony Todman (2), Payne, T.I. (Iorrie) Evans, Scott, Marques and B.J. (Brian) Bennett with Whyte providing the kicked points. Swansea and Cardiff were to provide much sterner opposition and the results were a draw with the first named (6-6) whilst a loss was recorded at the latter's ground (3-9). Another trip to the Midlands resulted in an away win at Coventry. Despite trailing by eight points to nil at half time, we rallied strongly and, shortly after the start of the second half, Iorrie Evans went over for our first try which was converted by McPartlin. A Harry Eden double strike (the second being run in from 50 yards out and again converted by McPartlin) put us in command, our final try by John Simons merely confirmed our superiority and although the home side managed one more try, we ran out winners by sixteen points to eleven. We therefore became the first English team to defeat Coventry all season. Our final game provided a victory at Twickenham over Waterloo (11-6). Newcomers making their debuts during the season were R.F. (Robert) "Bob" Read against the Army on 22nd February (who went on to make at least 93 appearances) and future England international David Wrench against the Royal Navy on 18th February (who played in a confirmed 193 games and won two caps in 1964).

Harry Eden got the most tries (18) and Roger Whyte was the top points scorer with 56 (4 penalties and 22 conversions) while overall, points scored fell to 389 and, consequently, tries, penalties and conversions were all down on the previous season. Eden also made the most appearances (29) followed by Jeff Abbott (28), John Simons (27), Ricky Bartlett (26) and John Mallett and David Marques both with 25

1960/61

050960	SOUTH DEVON XV	TORQUAY	W	5G1DG2PG2T(40)-1PG1T(6)
100960	WOLFHOUNDS(SMM)	TWICKENHAM	W	1G1PG4T(20)-2G1PG2T(19)
170960	ST.MARY'S HOSPITAL	TEDDINGTON(A)	W	2G1PG2T(19)-2PG2T(12)
240960	LEICESTER	TWICKENHAM	W	2T(6)-0
011060	SWANSEA	TWICKENHAM	L	0-1DG3T(12)
081060	UNITED SERVICES PORTSMOUTH	PORTSMOUTH	D	0-0
151060	NORTHAMPTON	TWICKENHAM	L	1G(5)-3G3T(24)
221060	LLANELLY	LLANELLY	L	1PG(3)-1PG1T(6)
291060	BATH	TEDDINGTON	W	1T(3)-0
051160	BRISTOL	BRISTOL	L	1T(3)-2G2DG1PG3T(28)
121160	RICHMOND	TEDDINGTON	D	1PG(3)-1T(3)
191160	OXFORD UNIVERSITY	TWICKENHAM	W	1G1PG1T(11)-1T(3)
261160	CAMBRIDGE UNIVERSITY	TEDDINGTON	L	1PG1T(6)-1G2T(11)
031260	BLACKHEATH	BLACKHEATH	W	1G1PG(8)-0
101260	CARDIFF	TWICKENHAM	L	1G1T(8)-3PG(9)
171260	NEWPORT	NEWPORT	L	1T(3)-1G1PG3T(17)
241260	RICHMOND	RICHMOND	W	1G1PG(8)-2T(6)
271260	ROSSLYN PARK	ROEHAMPTON	W	4G(20)-1G1PG(8)
311260	LONDON SCOTTISH	RICHMOND	W	2G1PG1T(16)-1G(5)
070161	BRISTOL	BRISTOL	W	1G3T(14)-1G2T(11)
140161	BLACKHEATH	TWICKENHAM	W	3G2PG1T(24)-2PG(6)
210161	PARIS UNIVERSITÉ CLUB	TWICKENHAM	C	
280161	ROYAL AIR FORCE	TWICKENHAM	L	1T(3)-1PG2T(9)
040261	NORTHAMPTON	NORTHAMPTON	L	2T(6)-1G2T(11)
110261	LONDON IRISH	SUNBURY	W	2G3T(19)-1T(3)
180261	ROYAL NAVY	PORTSMOUTH	L	1T(3)-1G2T(11)
220261	ARMY	TEDDINGTON	L	1G(5)-1PG3T(12)
040361	LEICESTER	LEICESTER	L	2T(6)-4G3T(29)
110361	BEDFORD	TEDDINGTON	W	2G(10)-1PG1T(6)
250361	HERIOT'S F.P.	EDINBURGH	W	2G3T(19)-2PG(6)
300361	BATH	BATH	W	10G1PG3T(62)-1DG1PG2T(12)
010461	SWANSEA	SWANSEA	D	2T(6)-1PG1T(6)
030461	CARDIFF	CARDIFF	L	1T(3)-3T(9)
080461	COVENTRY	COVENTRY	W	2G2T(16)-1G1PG1T(11)
150461	WATERLOO	TWICKENHAM	W	1G1PG1T(11)-2T(6)

21

Sevens in the 1950s

1950-1959

For the first Middlesex tournament of the 1950s, the 1st VII went through to Round 5 and played on the College Ground against St. Mary's Hospital, they lost 3-11 so once again, no appearance at Twickenham. The second Seven went out in the same round against Swansea (3-9) but at least they did win against No.2 District, Metropolitan Police (16-3), Pinner II (13-0), Old Millhillians (13-5) and Old Merchant Taylors I (16-0) at Headstone Lane in the Preliminary Rounds. The holders (Heriot's F.P.) got through to the final again where they lost 0-16 to Rosslyn Park. In the Oxfordshire Sevens, we got to the final again but lost to Oxford University Greyhounds 3-6 after extra time.

On 28th April 1951, H.R.H. Princess Elizabeth visited to present the new Russell-Cargill Memorial Cup to the winners and also to unveil the Rugby Union War Memorial. The new trophy had been given by the Middlesex County Rugby Football Union and the old one (the Kinross Arber Cup) was accepted by the R.F.U. to be retained by them in memory of the 25 previous holders of the title. This time, there were 155 teams competing for the right to be called Middlesex Sevens champions. The first VII again played one match and lost, this time to St. Mary's Hospital II (3-6). The squad was Peter Woodruff, H.C. Forbes, Roberts (captain), Fryer, B.H. McGuirk, G.J. Weston and N.J.D. Williams; Alan Grimsdell and F.G.C. Brown were reserves. The seconds again qualified from Headstone Lane by beating London Fire Brigade I (13-0), Richmond I (13-8), London University (9-0) and Middlesex Hospital (13-8). At Twickenham, their squad was B.M. Prior, Bartlett, P.M. Crawford, F.M. Papernik, P.D. Strang, J. Foreman and David Marques; M.T. Wilford and M.K. Adams were the reserves. In their Round 6 match, they defeated Leicester (8-5) and then London Scottish I (8-3) before losing to Richmond II 0-10 in the semi-final (they went on to win against Wasps by 13-10).

In 1952, the main team qualified at Thames Ditton with wins over Esher II (15-5), Old Cranleighans I (5-0), Old Paulines I (13-0) and Richmond I (10-8) but went down to St. Mary's Hospital I again (3-20). The seconds qualified automatically and beat London Hospital I (6-0) and Saracens I (16-0) before losing narrowly in the semi-final to eventual winners, Wasps (3-6 after extra time). In the final, they won against St. Thomas's Hospital by 12-10. The following made up the first VII; B.M.G. Pryer, Micky Grant (captain), P.N. Wilson, J.P.S. Townend, David Marques, P.J. Fuller and P.D. Strang; D.J. Brown, M.K. Adams and K.T. O'Connor were reserves. The seconds (which looked more like a first string) contained Dennis Barker, Phil Davies, Albert Agar, Forbes, Matthews (captain), Foreman and Alan Grimsdell; reserves were Bartlett, Brooks and Woodruff. In the Surrey Sevens, we had a bye in the first round when the Civil Service failed to show, Esher were beaten 16-0, Guildford by 8-6 and then

Wasps in the semi-final (8-3). In the final, Streatham were beaten 13-5 to give us our first win in the tournament. Our squad was Dennis Barker, Phil Davies, Albert Agar, Norman Fryer, P.D. Strang, M. Forman, P.J. Fuller, Alan Grimsdell and Jack Matthews with Forbes as the reserve.

On 18th April 1953, both our teams attempted to qualify for the finals the following week. The firsts beat Cassiopeians (15-0), St. Thomas's Hospital II (16-0) and St. Mary's Hospital I (13-0) before moving on to the final rounds and winning against London Scottish I (10-5) and Blackheath I (18-0) but going out to London Welsh I (0-6) in the semi-final. The second string had a walk over against Southern Railway but lost to St. Mary's Hospital II (0-8). Barker, Davies, Agar (captain), Bartlett, Ian Beer, Nick Labuschagne and Matthews were supplemented by Forbes and McGuirk in reserve. Richmond I defeated the Welsh 10-3 in the final; it was the first time their 1st VII had won the competition. We won the Surrey Sevens for the second time by beating Streatham again in the final.

In 1954, the finals were on 1st May and both sides qualified. The first VII beat Old Cranleighans II (23-0), Ilford Wanderers (30-0) and London Hospital I (22-5); the seconds had victories over N. Polytechnic (18-0), Imperial College (12-0), London Hospital II (8-3) and Old Wycombiensians (28-3). Unfortunately, our participation was over in the space of forty minutes; the seconds went down to Bridgend (10-11) and the firsts lost to Blackheath I (0-8). Rosslyn Park ended up winning the title by defeating London Scottish I 16-0. R.W.W. Dawe, Davies, Bartlett (captain), L.D. Ashcroft, D.L. Sanders, P.J. Fuller and Roger Whyte represented the senior side with Woodruff and D.M. Gunson as reserves. The second side contained Barker, J.R. Tarry, Grant, D.J. Hardwicke, Jeff Abbott, Foreman and Vic Roberts (captain); Labuschagne and C. Holmes-Smith stood ready to replace any injured. We reached the semi-final of the Oxfordshire Sevens.

Mid-way through the fifties, it was now twenty years since we last won the Middlesex tournament and there was to be no victory celebrations this year either. The firsts were represented by Barker, Bemrose, Grant, Bartlett (captain), Sanders, Whyte and P.J. Stubbs; the reserve list was Vic Roberts, Woodruff, Holmes-Smith and G.P. Vaughan. They qualified for the final rounds on 30th April with wins over Old Colfeians II (23-0), Sidcup II (28-8), R.E.M.E. Arborfield (10-6) and Lloyds Bank I (25-3) but suffered a shock reverse in Round 5 against Old Rutlishians. It was reported that from this day on the Old Rutlishians can speak with pride of when they beat Harlequins and almost beat Llanelly (they went down 6-13). We were three goals down in no time at all after Mills, Robinson and Marshall scored for Standish to convert. The crowd had a reputation for being merciless to the great in distress and roared its approval again and again. We came back to 15-8 but a final try by Mills and another Standish conversion sealed the win. The second Seven didn't qualify because, after defeating Metropolitan Police T.C. (22-0) and Bank of England (11-0), they lost to Lloyds Bank I (5-6). Richmond I went on to beat St. Luke's College, Exeter 5-0 in the final. The Esher tournament started this year and would eventually become the Esher Floodlit Sevens.

Our 1956 campaign was over on 21st April, the day of the Preliminary Rounds! Quins I won against Old Elizabethans II (16-0) and Stonyhurst Wanderers (15-5) but lost to Saracens II (10-13) and Quins II beat Finchley II (8-3) and then lost to London Hospital II (8-11). The trophy was won by London Welsh I who saw off the challenge of Emmanuel College, Cambridge by 24-10. Nearly thirty thousand spectators attended the event which was growing bigger by the year. The Surrey Sevens title was secured with a win over London Scottish.

The next year saw one side get through at Teddington, that was the first Seven represented by M. Kershaw, John Simons, Grant (captain), K. Pontin, Nick Raffle, Fuller and M.R.M. Evans; Whyte, Bartlett and Roberts made up the reserve. They won against Polytechnic I (18-0), National Physical Laboratory (17-0), St. George's Hospital I (11-0) and St. Mary's Hospital I (13-5). In the final rounds, they defeated Old Askeans I (14-3) before going down by a single point to Public School Wanderers (15-16). Quins II managed to get past Charing Cross Hospital (walk over) and Lensbury I (8-3) but lost to Richmond I (3-14). St. Luke's College, Exeter came through the qualifying rounds at Colindale and went on to defeat the holders 18-5 in the final. The Surrey tournament was won again with a victory over London Welsh but we lost in the final of the Berkshire Sevens to Esher (8-11).

Once again, only one of our teams qualified for finals day on 26th April 1958. The first Seven beat Grasshoppers II (36-0), Windsor I (26-0), Osterley I (21-3) and Old Blues (13-5) before winning against Streatham I (16-10) in Round 5. Against London Welsh I, we led all the way (helped by tries from Pontin and Simons), were reduced to six men and conceded two tries in the last two minutes to go out 6-8 after Mainwaring nailed the last conversion. Dick Leonard, Simons, Bartlett (captain), Pontin, Evans, A.H.M. Hoare and J. Hancock made up the side with Fuller and D. Shepherd in reserve. The seconds beat Borderers II (10-5) and Beaconsfield (18-0) but lost to Loughborough College I (5-9). Blackheath knocked the Welsh out and beat Saracens I in the final 16-3. In the Oxfordshire Sevens, we again lost in the final, this time to Wasps (10-25). In the Surrey Sevens, we reached the semi-final and we won the Berkshire tournament, beating Wycombeians in the final.

For the last tournament of the decade, both sides attempted to qualify at Colindale (home of the Metropolitan Police). For a change, they got through! Quins I defeated City of London Police II (30-0), Old Grammarians I (25-0), Metropolitan Police II (15-3) and Saracens II (18-0) while Quins II reached Twickenham with victories over Standard Telephones II (19-0), Mill Hill I (15-8), Old Grammarians II (33-0) and Metropolitan Police I (13-8). Leonard, Bartlett, John Scott, Pontin, J.N. Hancock, Hoare and Colin Payne made up Harlequin I with Yates in reserve; the second side contained G.N. Patterson, W. Coutts, Raffle, Thompson, Adcock, Whyte and Tony Todman. In the event, neither made a lasting impression although Saracens I were defeated (6-3) by the firsts before they lost to Richmond I (5-8); the other side also went out to Richmond I by three points (0-3). Loughborough College won after extra time by scoring the only try of the final against London Welsh (played in continuous rain). The charity donations had by and large gone up throughout the Fifties with something over £48,000 being raised. Sevens was now starting to develop as specialist players and teams began to appear; the first years of the Sixties would see one team dominate. As we did in 1958, we got as far as the semi-final in the Surrey tournament and were runners-up at the Manchester F.C. tournament.

22

The East African Tour May 1961

The touring party consisted of the following players:- R.W.D. Marques (captain); J.D. Currie, H. Eden, M.R.M. Evans, T.I. Evans, T.M. Hall, M. Hardwicke, A. Luck, K.J.H. Mallett, R.B. Marson, G.C. Murray, W.M. Patterson, R.F. Read, F. Swart, M.P. Weston, M. Whiteside, D.A. Whiting, R.A.M. Whyte, D.F.B. Wrench and J.R.C. Young. In addition, N.A. Labuschagne (who was now a dentist in Durban) would be joining the party when they arrived. William "Bill" Patterson and Michael "Mike" Weston were guests from Sale and Richmond respectively and were both England internationals. Patterson had won his only two caps earlier in the year whereas Weston had won the first of his 29 in 1960 and would gain his last in 1968.

The party left London Airport on 3rd May in a De Havilland Comet 4b of East African Airways bound for Entebbe (arriving there the next morning). The day was spent looking around tea plantations, a sugar factory, the town of Kampala and the Nakivubo Stadium (where the players later trained). The following day was spent picnicking on Lennox Island (which is situated on Lake Victoria) and then it was time to start playing some games. We opened the six match tour at the Nakivubo Stadium (in Kampala) against Uganda on Saturday 6th May. One newspaper report on the game stated that it was a football impossibility for Uganda to beat us and so it had proved. By half time we led 21-8 with tries from John Mallett, Harry Eden (2) and Iorrie Evans (2) and three conversions by Roger Whyte. Uganda replied with a goal and a try. The second half was a virtual copy of the first and we ran in further tries through Fred Swart, Eden (completing his hat-trick), Mallett, Aubrey Luck and Bob Read with Whyte converting all but Read's. Uganda managed one goal to make the final score 44-13 in our favour. Nick Labuschagne had met up with the party and played his first game for us since September 1956 (when he had returned to South Africa). He even managed to take three wickets in a cricket match played against Entebbe on the Sunday.

Our second match (our first in Kenya) was played at the Kitale Sports Club on Wednesday 10th May against West Kenya. Enough changes were made from the opening game so as to enable the remainder of the party to play their first game of the tour. We were rocked after just six minutes when the home side took the lead with a try but came back almost immediately when John Young scored an equalising try. John Currie converted this as well as further efforts from the two guest players (Patterson and Weston) to give us a 15-3 lead at half time. The game was being played at altitude (6,500 feet) and this was beginning to tell on our players although Weston did drop a goal to extend our lead. West Kenya completed their scoring with another try before Grahame Murray and Iorrie Evans brought our try tally to five to make the final score 24-6.

The following day, the party moved on to Nairobi (covering the 240 miles in two small coaches) where, over the weekend of 13th and 14th May we would meet the two other Harlequin clubs involved in the tour. On Saturday, we met the Pretoria Harlequins at Ngong Road, Nairobi (home of the Kenya Harlequins). Pretoria had flown three men up (two of them just for this match) to add to the strength of their team. We started well and Whyte kicked a penalty before converting our first try. While Pretoria were watching Young, Read broke through and passed inside to Patterson who scored under the posts. Pretoria scored their first points when D. Holton kicked a penalty before Patterson intercepted a dropped pass and sent Mallett in from 25 yards out for Whyte to again convert. Holton kicked his second penalty to leave the South Africans seven points adrift at the break. In the second half we tired through the effects of the heat and altitude and the play was constantly around our 25 yard line. A few minutes from the end, Groenweld grabbed a try and Holton added the extra points but it was too little too late and we had scraped home 13-11 (although had Holton's late drop goal attempt not bounced back from one of the uprights it might have been a different story!). This match was played in front of the largest crowd ever to watch a rugby game in East Africa and before it, both teams were presented to the Governor of Kenya (Sir Patrick Renison).

The following day it was time to meet the Kenya Harlequins (on the same ground as the previous day's game). Before the match some people had forecast a complete thrashing for the home team and, while they failed to score, the doubters were completely wrong. Dave Wrench gave us the lead with a try in the first five minutes and, shortly afterwards, Young got our second which Whyte converted. Kenya tackled ferociously and these were the only points scored in the first half. Our bad handling coupled with some scrappy play also helped to keep the score down and a try by Eden (converted by Whyte) and a dropped goal from 40 yards by Weston was all we had to show for our efforts in the second half although it did double our margin of victory to sixteen points.

Before our next game, lots of sightseeing was undertaken to such places as the East Africa Breweries at Ruaraka and the local game park. Our hosts had also laid on tennis, golf and swimming so a great time was had by all. On Wednesday 17th May, we met Kenya Central Province (again at Ngong Road). In what proved to be at times a lack-lustre display by us, we were held to a draw by a Province side playing the best rugby by a local XV for many years. Although we were never behind, we could not get more than three points ahead at any stage of the game. Bob Read got a try after six minutes, Province were level after 15 minutes with a penalty by B. Granville-Ross but we led at half time with a try Eden. The scores were level again four minutes into the second half when T. Tory got a try only for Aubrey Luck to put us back in front ten minutes later with an excellent blind side try near the corner flag. The lead was even shorter lived this time and a second penalty by Granville-Ross one minute later levelled things up for the last time.

On the next day, the party set off for Nakuru (the market town for the central highlands) where we would play our final match against Kenya on Saturday 20th May. The party stayed mostly with farmers who were hoping for rain for their recently planted crops. It did come and chose to start just before our final match with a gentle drizzle which quickly turned into a heavy downpour. The drop in temperature definitely helped us and we ran out winners by eight points to nil thanks to another dropped goal from Weston and a try from Patterson (converted by Whyte).

So ended our second tour to another country and a very successful one it was too with the hospitality having been excellent. The party had also visited the Governor of Kenya at Government House in Nairobi.

East African Tour

060561	UGANDA	KAMPALA	W	7G3T(44)-2G1T(13)
100561	WEST KENYA	KITALE	W	3G1DG2T(24)-2T(6)
130561	PRETORIA HARLEQUINS	NAIROBI	W	2G1PG(13)-1G2PG(11)
140561	KENYA HARLEQUINS	NAIROBI	W	2G1DG1T(16)-0
170561	KENYA CENTRAL PROVINCE	NAIROBI	D	3T(9)-2PG1T(9)
200561	KENYA	NAKURU	W	1G1DG(8)-0

23

Success at Home and a New Ground
1961-1966

At the Annual General Meeting on 20th July (held at the Mezzanine Cinema, Shell-Mex House, Strand, London WC2), the accounts showed that gate receipts had fallen just under £3,000 to £2,023 which led to a loss of £663. An honours cap was awarded to John Scott and an increase in non-playing members was averted by a proposal to increase the annual subscriptions. Another problem at this time was the collection of match fees from the players. It was proposed to appoint an "overlord" to collect these from the respective captains. Sam Kemble saw the need for a supporters' club, if only from a financial angle, although he considered that the Club did absolutely nothing for the public who supported our matches regularly. The Stoop Memorial Fund now stood at £2,066 which had been received from 345 subscriptions. Jeff Abbott announced on 24th July that he planned to organise Club training sessions every Tuesday and Thursday starting on 15th August. In addition, there would be a training weekend over the 19th and 20th August for the top 35 players. On 2nd November, a request for affiliation from Boston R.F.C. (USA) was turned down as it appeared they were not sufficiently established. At a Committee meeting on 7th December, Ken Chapman gave full details of the proposed 42 year lease of the Craneford Way sports arena from Twickenham Borough Council. A proposal was suggested by Derek Whiting (seconded by R.L. Hudson) that we should offer the Borough Council £15,000 for the lease and an extra £2,000 annual rental. A letter was received from the Town Clerk on 11th January to confirm that our offer had been accepted and the ground would be ready for use on 1st August 1963. On 3rd May, honours caps were awarded to Jeff Abbott and Howard Hoare.

We began the 1961/62 season with a new captain, Jeff Abbott taking up the post for his final season in the 1st XV. Our first match was again in South Devon and was against a Torquay Festival XV. Despite being held 3-3 at half time, we managed to stretch away in the second half with tries from John Simons, Brian Bennett and Iorrie Evans with Roger Whyte kicking all three conversions to add to his first half penalty goal. The following week, on 9th September, we met the Wolfhounds in the third Stoop Memorial Match at Twickenham. Five changes were made to the side which played in the festival game to take on a team containing nine internationals. As in the previous game it was 3-3 at half time but, unlike the previous game, the opposition went away from us and late in the day we found ourselves 3-16 down. Colin Payne added two tries to an earlier penalty from John Willcox but it was not enough and we lost by seven points. We bounced back quickly and defeated Heriot's F.P. (16-11) but lost to Leicester (6-13). Bath came next having put together a run of fifteen wins after our last win over them in March. Before a record crowd of 4,500 at Bath, we ended their run with a 13-6 victory. The Paris Université Club came to Twickenham on 7th October and were completely outplayed. This was due in no small part to what seemed a reluctance to tackle on their part. After Eden had scored our fifth try, Abbott (our captain) ruled that no attempt be made to convert it such was our domination. Another eight tries followed in the win over United Services, Portsmouth (28-11).

Our next match (the following Thursday) against Coventry, was to commemorate the switching on of their £3,000 floodlights. John Mallett got the first points of the game for us with a try but George Cole equalised this with a penalty. His second success put the home side in front only for Bob Read to pull us level with a penalty. Ten minutes from the end, Cole dropped a goal from 45 yards out to give Coventry their first win over us for nearly five years. Against Waterloo, we achieved both our biggest win and biggest winning margin of the season. Tries in the first half by Brian Bennett, Colin Payne and John Mallett and one conversion from Bob Read saw us 11-0 up. Shortly after half time the visitors got what proved to be their only score when Garner got a try. Unfortunately, they lost two of their forwards (Gosling and Edelstein) to injury and after this it was one way traffic. Bennett had a field day kicking two penalties and two conversions as well as getting his second try to finish with sixteen points. Payne and Thompson scored our fifth and sixth tries to leave the final score at 30-3.

After this we reeled off four more wins in a row, the pick of these being against Swansea (14-3). Cambridge University defeated us as did Blackheath (this was the first of four matches played at the Old Deer Park due to the unavailability of Twickenham) but Cardiff were beaten in a game of under strength XVs. A trip to Newport resulted in two players (Marques and Thompson) missing the train from Paddington and David Brooks (our Chairman) being brought in for his first 1st XV game since 19th February 1958 when he played against the Army. This did prove to be the last of at least 161 appearances. In the event another defeat was suffered but not by as many points as may have been the case (5-14). Richmond gained revenge for our earlier 9-0 win by outscoring us 20-0 at Twickenham. This proved to be our last match of the year as, due to bad weather, the games against Rosslyn Park and London Scottish were cancelled. Players making their debuts during the first half of the season were C.P. (Colin) Simpson against Paris Université Club on 7th October (who went on to gain one England cap in 1965), J.E. John "Johnnie" Williams who won nine caps (also for England) when he played for the Old Millhillians (1954-56) and Sale (1965) against United Services, Portsmouth on 14th October and R.H. (Robert) "Bob" Lloyd on 11th November against Richmond (he won five England caps in 1967 and 1968) which proved to be the first of at least 259 1st XV games in which he played.

For the tenth consecutive season, Bristol were due to be our first opponents of the New Year. This time however, the weather intervened and so our first game was against Blackheath on 13th January. A very low scoring encounter was settled in the first half when Olsen scored a try for Blackheath. We then drew with the Royal Air Force and lost away at Northampton before facing the Army at Teddington on 7th February. The Army scored first with a penalty goal but by half time we were level with a try by our full back N. Clayden. The stalemate continued until, with less than ten minutes left, we suddenly came to life and Brian Bennett was on hand to score a try and convert it. We led 8-3 and Bennett added to his tally with a dropped goal and another try to secure a victory. Making his debut in this game was P.S. (Paul) Parkin who went on to play in a confirmed 140 matches for the 1st XV. We had our best win over the London Irish since 1910 in a match played at the Old Deer Park (18-0), the Royal Navy were beaten in a high scoring game at Twickenham (27-14) which saw us win the try count 7-3 but the match at Leicester was cancelled. Our fourth and last game at the Old Deer Park saw Bedford as our visitors and, as had happened the previous season, they were beaten, this time by fourteen points to nine.

Due to an international being televised, only a small crowd witnessed the game against Coventry at Twickenham. It turned out to be a one man show from Bob Read (on leave from Trinity College, Dublin). By half time he had scored two penalties and converted his own try to enable us to lead 11-8. In the second half, Harry Eden went over for a try and Read added his third penalty to give us a handsome victory. Making his debut against Coventry was J.D. (John) Gibbs (son of Clifford) who went on to play in 118 games for the first team. We were on our travels again the following week with a trip to Liverpool to play Birkenhead Park. Approaching the last ten minutes it was 9-6 in our favour (three penalties from John Willcox to a penalty and a try for the home side) but, suddenly, Grahame Murray, Johnnie Williams and Bob Read went over for tries (Willcox converted two) and we were sitting on a sixteen point lead which we never lost.

Playing at Gloucester is never easy and any victory is always a hard fought one. In what turned out to be a real nip and tuck encounter, we led five times and four times Gloucester managed to reel us back in. With three minutes remaining the score stood at 14-12 to the home team (one goal, two penalties and a try to one penalty and three tries) and it looked as if we may lose for the first time since 3rd February. Right on the stroke of full time, Williams sneaked over from a scrum, Willcox converted and we had our seventh win on the trot. On 7th April we played against Neath at Twickenham. This was the first time the clubs had met even though Neath had been founded in 1871. The result, perhaps fittingly, was a draw (0-0). Micky Grant made his last appearance in this game having scored 106 points (22 tries, 2 dropped goals, 4 penalties and 11 conversions) in his first team career. It was Easter tour time again and we met the usual three teams. Bath were beaten 14-9 on Maundy Thursday, we achieved our biggest win over Swansea since 1931 on the Saturday (22-0) but lost to Cardiff in our last match of the season (3-13). This match was the last appearance of Jeff Abbott who had scored ten tries during his 1st XV career.

Harry Eden was, once again, top try scorer with 16, John Willcox got the most points (60) with 1 try, 1 dropped goal, 12 penalties and 9 conversions and Brian Bennett got most conversions (10). Overall, tries were just up on the previous season (87) as were points (409). Jeff Abbott and Grahame Murray topped the appearances with 30 followed by Eden (28), Colin Payne (25) and David Thompson (23).

In 1962 the British Lions toured South Africa once again and, once again, we had representation (although none were officially listed as playing for us). John Willcox (who played in the first, second and fourth tests and kicked a conversion and a penalty in the fourth) was listed as playing for Oxford University but had made ten appearances for us in the 1961/62 season, Mike Weston (who had appeared for us during the tour of East Africa in 1961 and was now playing for Durham City) played in all four tests and H.J.C. Brown who played in none of the tests, was to play a few games for us in 1963 and 1964 and was currently appearing for Blackheath and the Royal Air Force. The manager of the tour party was Douglas Vaughan who had played for us in 1945. Of the four tests played, the first was drawn, the second and third were lost narrowly and the fourth saw a defeat by twenty points.

1961/62

040961	TORQUAY FESTIVAL XV	TORQUAY	W	3G1PG(18)-1T(3)
090961	WOLFHOUNDS(SMM)	TWICKENHAM	L	1PG2T(9)-2G2T(16)
160961	HERIOT'S F.P.	TWICKENHAM	W	2G2T(16)-1G1DG1PG(11)
230961	LEICESTER	TWICKENHAM	L	1PG1T(6)-2G1PG(13)
300961	BATH	BATH	W	2G1PG(13)-1DG1T(6)
071061	PARIS UNIVERSITÉ CLUB	TWICKENHAM	W	2G1PG3T(22)-1PG(3)
141061	UNITED SERVICES PORTSMOUTH	PORTSMOUTH	W	2G6T(28)-1G2PG(11)

191061	COVENTRY	COVENTRY	L	1PG1T(6)-1DG2PG(9)
211061	WATERLOO	TWICKENHAM	W	3G2PG3T(30)-1T(3)
281061	SWANSEA	TWICKENHAM	W	1G3T(14)-1T(3)
041161	BRISTOL	TWICKENHAM	W	2G2T(16)-1G1DG1PG(11)
111161	RICHMOND	RICHMOND	W	1PG2T(9)-0
181161	OXFORD UNIVERSITY	TWICKENHAM	W	2T(6)-1T(3)
251161	CAMBRIDGE UNIVERSITY	TWICKENHAM	L	1PG1T(6)-2G1DG1T(16)
021261	BLACKHEATH	OLD DEER PARK(H)	L	1G2T(11)-1G1DG1PG1T(14)
091261	CARDIFF	OLD DEER PARK(H)	W	1G3T(14)-1T(3)
161261	NEWPORT	NEWPORT	L	1G(5)-1G3T(14)
231261	RICHMOND	TWICKENHAM	L	0-1G3PG2T(20)
261261	ROSSLYN PARK	ROEHAMPTON	C	
301261	LONDON SCOTTISH	TWICKENHAM	C	
060162	BRISTOL	BRISTOL	C	
130162	BLACKHEATH	BLACKHEATH	L	0-1T(3)
270162	ROYAL AIR FORCE	TWICKENHAM	D	1PG1T(6)-2T(6)
030262	NORTHAMPTON	NORTHAMPTON	L	2PG(6)-1G3PG2T(20)
070262	ARMY	TEDDINGTON	W	1G1DG2T(14)-1PG(3)
170262	LONDON IRISH	OLD DEER PARK(H)	W	3G1T(18)-0
240262	ROYAL NAVY	TWICKENHAM	W	3G4T(27)-1G1PG2T(14)
030362	LEICESTER	LEICESTER	C	
100362	BEDFORD	OLD DEER PARK(H)	W	1G1DG1PG1T(14)-1PG2T(9)
170362	COVENTRY	TWICKENHAM	W	1G3PG1T(17)-1G1PG(8)
240362	BIRKENHEAD PARK	BIRKENHEAD	W	2G3PG1T(22)-1PG1T(6)
310362	GLOUCESTER	GLOUCESTER	W	1G1PG3T(17)-1G2PG1T(14)
070462	NEATH	TWICKENHAM	D	0-0
190462	BATH	BATH	W	1G1PG2T(14)-3T(9)
210462	SWANSEA	SWANSEA	W	2G1PG3T(22)-0
230462	CARDIFF	CARDIFF	L	1PG(3)-2G1PG(13)

At the A.G.M. on 19th July, a break from tradition was proposed by electing up to 50 non-playing members. This was felt to be a necessity for us to survive as our income had shown deficits in three out of the last four seasons. A proposal by Ricky Bartlett (seconded by Ken Chapman) was passed by 42 votes to 15, the Club rules were amended accordingly and the annual fees were set at 4 guineas for playing and 6 guineas for non-playing membership. Gate receipts went up to £3,333 and this led to an overall profit of £481. On 23rd August, Ken Chapman announced that tenders for construction of the new clubhouse at Craneford Way (when approval was given) should be in by 13th September and the building work should be completed within five months. It had also been arranged by Major I. Debenham-Harper for the Club to train at the Duke of York's Regiment Headquarters at Sloane Square on all Wednesday evenings throughout the season for a fee of £2 10s. On 7th December, it was decided to let the fixture with the Wolfhounds lapse. They had refused a proposal to split the next gate 50/50 as they felt they needed to make more money on this fixture in order to finance their tour in Ireland. The current financial arrangement had been a guarantee of £400 and 25% of the net gate. On 6th February, it was agreed that the new ground at Craneford Way should be called the "Stoop Memorial Ground" and honours caps were awarded to Vic Marriott, Colin Payne and Johnnie Williams. On 8th May, a telegram of good luck was sent to Marriott and Bob Read on the eve of their departure with the England touring side to New Zealand. Although Read failed to win a cap, Marriott played in all three tests (two in New Zealand and one in Australia) which were subsequently lost.

The 1962/63 season saw Colin Payne in the first of his three season stint as captain. His first task was to lead the team on our first visit to McCracken Park, Gosforth to play Northern. We began well and by half time had scored nine points without reply with Alan Prosser-Harries (making his debut) kicking a penalty, Bob Read dropping a goal and Bob Lloyd scoring a try. In true Harlequin fashion, we let Northern back into the game and when R.S. Appleby converted a try by J. Rogan, they actually led 11-9 with ten minutes remaining. Then, in an exciting finish, Brian Bennett went over in the corner only for the touch judge to rule the ball in touch before (with only two minutes to go) Roger Whyte stepped up and slotted over a penalty for a final score of 12-11. As already mentioned, our fixture with the Wolfhounds five days later was to be the last. We again led at half time but were outscored in the second half and eventually went down by seven points (12-19). After three defeats on the trot at the hands of Llanelly, we managed a 3-3 draw at Twickenham. This has been one of only two draws in the 63 games played so far. Leicester were our next opponents and came to Twickenham unbeaten in their five matches so far. Alan Prosser-Harries landed two penalties for us in the first ten minutes but the Tigers came back into it and led at half time thanks to tries from D.J. Matthews and N.J. Drake-Lee, the second being converted by Ken Scotland (who had made one appearance for us in 1960). Johnnie Williams was in great form and two brilliant movements inspired by him brought us victory. First, he broke from the scrum and sent a perfectly timed reverse pass to Bob Read who scored and a minute later he again broke and Bob Lloyd reaped the reward as he dived in at the corner after a 40-yard run to leave us winners by twelve points to eight. John Young could have scored another try in the last minute but refused to run in after a knock-on which had been missed by the referee.

Our good run of form was to continue for another seven games, the best wins being over Swansea, Northampton, Lansdowne and Bristol. Oxford University brought our run to an end with help from three of our own men (John Willcox, Joe McPartlin and Nick Silk). In the first half Willcox converted a try by R.M. Wilcock and this proved to be enough as a Prosser-Harries penalty was all we could manage in the second period. Our misery continued against the students from Cambridge and Blackheath and, on 8th December, we played Cardiff at Roehampton (due to the Varsity match at Twickenham the following Tuesday). As Cardiff had misplaced their kit, Rosslyn Park had to lend them some jerseys and a London store had to be hurriedly approached for shorts, socks and boots. So Cardiff played in new kit and while they were still getting used to it, John Young went over for a try. L. Williams equalised in similar fashion after 12 minutes but five minutes before the break John Gibbs laid on a try for Harry Eden which Prosser-Harries converted. In the second half, facing the heavy rain and wind, we appeared to lose all our fire and three unconverted tries from the Welshmen gave them a four point victory. Five losses in a row were avoided with a 3-3 draw at Twickenham against Newport. On 22nd December, we made the short journey to the Athletic Ground to play Richmond. A fog had descended over the pitch but 200 yards away on the main road the sun was shining. The referee (Sir Augustus Walker) decided that the game should go ahead even though the two captains had already agreed that it should be cancelled. Unfortunately, between this and the players changing, the fog returned and after 32 minutes the referee finally called a halt to proceedings with no scores from either side.

The snow and frost descended, the big freeze set in and this was the last taste of rugby for Quins players and supporters until 16th February 1963 when we played at Stradey Park, Llanelly. This meant that nine games had been lost to the weather (three of these were later rearranged). Against Llanelly, we were behind in the first minute to a try but came back and ran riot with moves which involved dozens of pairs of hands and tries followed from Vic Marriott, Bob Lloyd and Harry Eden (this one being converted by Prosser-Harries). Llanelly got a goal of their own between our second and third tries to give a half time score of 13-8. One newspaper report describes the "brilliant handling and intelligent backing up of the Harlequins side". Johnnie Williams stretched our lead and although the home side did get their third try, it was not enough. The game against the Royal Air Force had been lost to the weather back in January but the Army and Royal Navy fixtures survived and were both won. In what was to be our last 1st XV fixture at Fairfax Road, Teddington we met Leicester on 2nd March. This was Leicester's first game since 15th December 1962 and the nearest they had got to action had been the odd excursion into "touch" rugby (according to a report of the match). Although tries from J.T. (John) Cox (who had made the first of 197 confirmed appearances against Llanelly) and Bob Lloyd and one conversion from Alan Prosser-Harries had enabled us to lead during the second half, Leicester dominated proceedings after this and two more goals (to add to one in the first half) saw them win by fifteen points to eight. In the period between 1926 and 1963, the 1st XV had a playing record at Teddington of P56 W36 D2 L18.

The following week we travelled to Bedford who, like Leicester, were reopening their season and playing their first match of 1963. We were outscored by two tries to one in the first half and that was how it remained but we were not helped by losing Vic Marriott with concussion for the last half an hour of the game. Our next two matches were real away days. The first was to Liverpool to play Waterloo. Once again we were simply too good for our opponents and rattled up the points despite losing John Young after 35 minutes with a twisted knee. We did finish the game with one more player than the home team as they lost two men late in the second half. By half time we were on our way thanks to tries from Paul Parkin and Young and penalties from D.R. Trentham and Joe McPartlin. The rout was completed in the second half with tries being added by A.J.S. (Tony) Todman, Johnnie Williams, Trentham and Parkin with McPartlin kicking three conversions for a final tally of thirty points without reply. This proved to be our biggest winning margin of the season even though we did reach the same figure of thirty once more before it ended. The second long trip was up to Edinburgh to play Heriot's F.P. in what was to be our last fixture against them. Thanks to a try from Marriott and a penalty by Prosser-Harries, we led 6-3 at the break. This score was repeated in the second half when Lloyd got our second try and McPartlin kicked a penalty. Heriot's could only manage two penalties in the entire match, one from Blaikie and one from Ken Scotland (playing against us again!).

Originally scheduled to be played on 2nd February, the away game with Northampton was rearranged for 27th March (a Wednesday) and it took place under lights at the British Timken sports ground, Duston. It took just one score to win the game for Northampton, a penalty by R.W. Hosen two minutes from the end. Gloucester were our next opponents at Twickenham on 30th March and, after we had scored tries through Harry Eden (2) and Brian Bennett and a conversion from Alan Prosser-Harries to lead 11-0, we let the visitors back into the game with a penalty and a try. Just before half time Eden and Gilbert-Smith of Gloucester collided and both had to leave the field. In the second half Bennett completed his hat-trick, Tony Todman (taking Eden's place on the wing) added two tries of his own and Bob Lloyd got our eighth (Joe McPartlin and Prosser-Harries kicked one conversion each) to which Gloucester's only reply was a goal to leave us winners by thirty points to eleven. Another rearranged fixture took place on the following Wednesday when we made the short journey to Richmond to play against London Scottish. Even though we lost Todman ten minutes into the second half with a cut head, we held on to win 13-9. Rosslyn Park were defeated in our last home game of the season and then it was Easter and time for the usual three games in five days.

An 18-9 win at Bath on Thursday was followed by Swansea on Saturday. We benefited from the fact they were playing their fifth game in just ten days and we were able to score fourteen points without reply. Against Cardiff, a try from John Cox in the first half and a penalty from Prosser-Harries in the second were enough to see us through to our third success of the tour. This was the first time we had ever won all three games and the first time since 1935/36 (when we only played Swansea and Cardiff) that all matches on the tour had been won. Our fifth game in ten days was played against Richmond at the Athletic Ground and just one goal two minutes from time to the home side was enough to gain them victory (even though we had dominated most of the match and had looked the more capable and constructive side). We took a very weakened side to Birmingham for a match against the Old Edwardians. Roger Whyte kicked a penalty for us in the first half only for the home side to equalise with a try. The only score in the second half was a second try for the Old Boys to give them a narrow victory. Our final game of the season saw us visit Paris on 4th May to play the Paris Université Club. Our hosts led at half time by ten points to three (our score being a try by Brian Bennett). The score remained the same until ten minutes from the end when a scoring blitz of sixteen points saw us come from behind to win by a clear margin. Harry Eden, David Wrench, Bob Lloyd and John Cox scoring our tries.

Newcomers during the season included D.R. (Rhys) Williams who played in the first of his 113 appearances against Lansdowne and R. (Robert) "Bob" Hiller who made his debut against the Army. He was to go on to play in at least 265 games for the 1st XV and win 19 England caps. He also captained Club and Country. Peter Woodruff (having scored 62 tries) appeared for the last time in the game against the Old Edwardians and Howard Hoare was another to finish his first team career during the season.

Bob Lloyd was the top try scorer with 12, Joe McPartlin and Bob Read each dropped two goals and Alan Prosser-Harries got the most points with 95 (17 penalties and 22 conversions). Overall, points dropped by just three to 406 (dropped goals and penalties were up, tries were down and conversions stayed the same). The playing record was P33 W21 D2 L10 (with one game, against Richmond, being abandoned and six cancelled). Colin Payne appeared in 29 out of the 34 games played, J.L. (John) Bazalgette and Bob Lloyd played in 28 closely followed by Johnnie Williams (26).

1962/63

030962	NORTHERN	NEWCASTLE	W	1DG2PG1T(12)-1G2PG(11)
080962	WOLFHOUNDS(SMM)	TWICKENHAM	L	1PG3T(12)-2G1PG2T(19)
150962	LLANELLY	TWICKENHAM	D	1T(3)-1PG(3)
220962	LEICESTER	TWICKENHAM	W	2PG2T(12)-1G1T(8)
290962	BATH	TWICKENHAM	W	4G3T(29)-1T(3)
061062	SWANSEA	TWICKENHAM	W	2G1T(13)-1DG1PG(6)
131062	UNITED SERVICES PORTSMOUTH	PORTSMOUTH	W	3G3T(24)-1G1PG(8)
201062	NORTHAMPTON	TWICKENHAM	W	1G1PG(8)-1PG(3)
271062	LANSDOWNE	TWICKENHAM	W	3PG1T(12)-1G2PG(11)
031162	BRISTOL	BRISTOL	W	1G1PG2T(14)-1PG(3)
101162	RICHMOND	TWICKENHAM	W	3PG4T(21)-1T(3)
171162	OXFORD UNIVERSITY	TWICKENHAM	L	1PG(3)-1G(5)
241162	CAMBRIDGE UNIVERSITY	TWICKENHAM	L	1PG1T(6)-2PG2T(12)
011262	BLACKHEATH	BLACKHEATH	L	0-1G3T(14)
081262	CARDIFF	ROEHAMPTON(H)	L	1G1T(8)-4T(12)
151262	NEWPORT	TWICKENHAM	D	1PG(3)-1PG(3)
221262	RICHMOND	RICHMOND	A	0-0
261262	ROSSLYN PARK	ROEHAMPTON	C	
291262	LONDON SCOTTISH	RICHMOND	P	
050163	BRISTOL	BRISTOL	C	
120163	BLACKHEATH	TWICKENHAM	C	
190163	BIRKENHEAD PARK	TWICKENHAM	C	
260163	ROYAL AIR FORCE	TWICKENHAM	C	
020263	NORTHAMPTON	NORTHAMPTON	P	
090263	LONDON IRISH	SUNBURY	C	
100263	PARIS UNIVERSITÉ CLUB	PARIS	P	
160263	LLANELLY	LLANELLY	W	2G2T(16)-1G2T(11)
200263	ARMY	TEDDINGTON	W	3G1PG1T(21)-1G1T(8)
230263	ROYAL NAVY	PORTSMOUTH	W	3G(15)-0
020363	LEICESTER	TEDDINGTON	L	1G1T(8)-3G(15)
090363	BEDFORD	BEDFORD	L	1T(3)-2T(6)
160363	WATERLOO	WATERLOO	W	3G2PG3T(30)-0
230363	HERIOT'S F.P.	EDINBURGH	W	2PG2T(12)-2PG(6)
270363	NORTHAMPTON	NORTHAMPTON	L	0-1PG(3)
300363	GLOUCESTER	TWICKENHAM	W	3G5T(30)-1G1PG1T(11)
030463	LONDON SCOTTISH	RICHMOND	W	2G1DG(13)-3T(9)

060463	ROSSLYN PARK	TWICKENHAM	W	3G1T(18)-1PG2T(9)
110463	BATH	BATH	W	1DG1PG4T(18)-1PG2T(9)
130463	SWANSEA	SWANSEA	W	1G1DG2PG(14)-0
150463	CARDIFF	CARDIFF	W	1PG1T(6)-0
170463	RICHMOND	RICHMOND	L	0-1G(5)
200463	OLD EDWARDIANS	BIRMINGHAM	L	1PG(3)-2T(6)
040563	PARIS UNIVERSITÉ CLUB	PARIS	W	2G3T(19)-(10)

England undertook their first tour to Australasia in May and June of 1963 and played six matches in just 18 days, three of which were test matches. The first two against New Zealand were lost (11-21 and 6-9) as was the one against Australia (9-18). The non-test matches saw one win and two defeats. Our representation consisted of current players Bob Read and Vic Marriott, former players Malcolm Phillips and David Perry and future Quin Mike Davis. Read got no caps but the others all played in three tests apart from Davis who missed the third one.

At the A.G.M. on 18th July 1963, the annual accounts were presented and a profit of £331 was recorded. Gate receipts fell by over £1,000 to £2,117. The appalling weather was mainly responsible and the surplus was only due to insurance claims being made for the games which had been cancelled. A telegram was received and read out explaining the absence of Paul Anderson, David Marques, R.H.C. Page and John Scott. This was due to their taking part in the preliminary sailing trials of the new 12-metre yacht "Sovereign" in races against the 1958 Americas Cup challenger "Sceptre". The limit of fifty special members was removed as it was felt that this helped to bring in extra money through subscriptions and also valuable help on the administration side of the Club. The Adrian Stoop Memorial Fund now stood at £3,025 but another £1,000 was needed to help finance the new ground at Craneford Way. It was announced that the following old players had passed on, P.W. Adams, E.H. Fouraker, R.H. King, R.H. Hamilton-Wickes, H.J.H. Sibree and H.B.T. Wakelam as well as the honorary secretary of the Harlequin Club of Australia (W.H. Baldwin) and the President of the R.F.U. (F.D. Prentice). At a meeting on 25th July at the East India and Sports Club, St. James's Square, London W1 a tour to South Africa was proposed. The itinerary would be fixed by the Pretoria Harlequins and the tour would take place for two weeks in August 1966 (later changed to May). On 22nd August, other possible tours to Japan and Rumania were discussed although these were later discounted.

The first fixture at the new Stoop Memorial Ground (Teddington would now be let from 1st December to the council) would be an "A" XV match against Thames Valley Grammar School and would be played on 16th November 1963 (this was later changed to a veterans match between Harlequins and a combined Richmond/ London Scottish XV consisting of two twenty minute halves). On 5th September, it was announced that the Club now had £14,688 out of the £15,000 required to pay the premium for the new ground. Further donations were needed and it was considered extremely undesirable to dig into Club funds. When the (west) stand at the Stoop Memorial Ground was originally built, there were only concrete steps to sit on and the Club had to pay out some £650 to have wooden slats put in. Also, in keeping with most rugby grounds at this time, there were no floodlights so this was looked into but it was considered too expensive to have them installed in the immediate future. On 2nd April, preliminary arrangements for our Centenary season (1966/67) were announced. Games would be played against the Barbarians in September and a mid-week match at Rugby School against the Australian touring team (although both came to nothing). Honours caps were awarded to John Willcox and John Young and a request from Nottingham for a fixture on 23rd September 1964 was turned down. A sad note to end on was a report at a Committee meeting on 4th June that M.R. Handfield-Jones (who had made 14 appearances for the 1st XV between 1959 and 1961) had been killed on active service in Aden.

We began the 1963/64 season with a match at Twickenham against Roma F.C. from Italy. They included eleven internationals, we had four (plus three future caps). Despite a rousing finish by our visitors, we ran out narrow winners by sixteen points to fourteen. S.H. (Steve) Wilcock played the first of his 51 games in this match. The following week we played against the R.F.U. President's XV (again at Twickenham). Geoff Butler, the new President, had played for us between 1934 and 1947. Thanks to a hat-trick from A.M. Underwood, the President's XV won by six points (8-14). The following Monday, we travelled up for our fourth visit to Gosforth. This time (unlike the previous three occasions) we lost. The home side scored a goal to our penalty goal kicked by John Willcox. On 14th September, we welcomed Coventry for the fifth and final Stoop Memorial Match. The previous four had been played against the Wolfhounds and this one produced the first draw. Vic Marriott scored a try for us in the first half which John Willcox converted but we trailed by eight points as Coventry had scored two goals and a try. We made a tremendous fight of it in the second half and Marriott got his second try, again converted by Willcox who added a penalty to tie the scores. Flanagan got his hat-trick try for the visitors but Willcox had the final word with a 40-yard penalty to end the scoring. R.P. (Roger) Lewis played the first of at least 76 games for the 1st XV in this one.

A great win over Llanelly followed (22-0) and this has been the only time so far that they have failed to score against us. Oddly for us, another Monday night game was played and it was another long trip, this time up to Leeds to play against Headingley. As with our previous Monday night game we lost a close encounter, this time by four points (12-16). Johnnie Williams made his last appearance for us in what was a memorial game for his brother. D. Saunders (2) and T.M. Boyd (both making their debuts) scored tries for us to add to a Willcox penalty. New experimental laws authorised by the Rugby Union received their first airing at Twickenham on 28th September when Leicester were our opponents. These included the law that backs must lie ten yards back from line outs and scrums. Two tries (one for each side) came directly from infringements of the new laws before we ran out winners 13-6. Our second visit to Dublin to play Lansdowne resulted in another loss (5-22) with both sides reduced to 13 men by the end. Over the next month we defeated Gloucester, Coventry and Richmond but lost to Bristol and Oxford University and drew with Swansea.

The match with Cambridge University is worthy of mention, but not for the result. We failed to score whilst the students got thirteen points. This was the long awaited first match at our new home at Craneford Way, Twickenham. The ground (which was named after Adrian) was the Stoop Memorial Ground and it was to eventually become our real home. We only managed a draw against London Welsh in our second match but it was third time lucky against Blackheath. After three successive defeats against our old rivals, it was nice to achieve our biggest win over them in 82 years of fixtures. Paul Parkin and Mike Whiteside scored tries in the first half to which Bob Hiller added one conversion. He kicked two penalties in the first twenty minutes of the second half to effectively end the game as a contest but it was not until the last fifteen minutes that we cut loose. John Cox, Tony Todman, John Adcock and Parkin with his second took our try total to six and two more conversions from Hiller took the total to 30-0. We ended 1963 with a draw against Cardiff at Twickenham (both sides scoring a penalty in the second half) and a defeat against Richmond at the Stoop by eight points to nil.

We played our last ever game against St. Mary's Hospital (on their home ground at Teddington) on 4th January and won by two goals to one with our winning score coming in the last minute. Against Blackheath, we lost John Young with a broken leg after 68 minutes and, consequently, finished the game with 13 men having lost Vic Marriott early in the first half with a leg injury. Despite leading 11-0 at one stage, our bad luck enabled Blackheath to come back and tie the scores. Two narrow defeats to the Royal Air Force and Northampton were followed by a win over United Services, Portsmouth before Llanelly notched up their first win of 1964 in a Friday night match at Stradey Park. A dropped goal from Prosser-Harries and a try by J. Dougal in the last five minutes helped to seal a 9-3 win over the Royal Navy and Bob Hiller's kicking along with tries from John Bazalgette, Bob Lloyd, Steve Wilcock, Harry Eden and Rhys Williams gave us victory over the Army. London Scottish were beaten for the third time on the trot and we completed the double over Leicester (6-0).

We lost to Bedford at Twickenham (6-9) and then went on the road for six out of our last seven games. Waterloo were our first victims and a try count of 3-1 in our favour ensured a victory by sixteen points to eleven. Yet again, it was Easter tour time and the same three opponents were met on the same three days. On Thursday 26th March, Bath led for 25 minutes through a penalty from Heindorff but during the next 25 we took the game over with tries by Lloyd, Eden and Silk (Hiller converting the last). Frankcom brought Bath some hope with their only try but near the end we were awarded a penalty try when the home side illegally halted what would have been a pushover (to which Hiller added the conversion). Swansea had been reduced to 13 men through injuries and were unlucky to lose to us by a single try to nil. Harry Eden scored it after an excellent run by John Willcox to inflict on the All Whites their first home defeat since mid-December when they had been beaten by the All Blacks. We were unable to secure a second undefeated tour on the trot as we went down by eight points to nil at the Arms Park to Cardiff.

Our last home game of the season brought Bristol to the Stoop. On a miserably wet afternoon, we ran out easy winners by scoring five tries and a penalty goal to nil. John Cox (2), Mike Whiteside, Harry Eden and Bob Lloyd got the tries and Bob Hiller kicked the penalty. It was the first time Bristol had failed to score against us since 1936. The following week we travelled to Coventry for our third match against them this season. Despite leading at half time with tries from Colin Payne and John Cox to one for Coventry by Robbins, we failed to add to our total in the second half. The Midlanders scored two more tries (Cole adding one conversion and a penalty) to run out winners. On 17th May, we played the return game with Roma in the Acquacetosa Stadium, Rome. Both sides scored pretty evenly in each half with us leading 15-9 at half time and converting this into 30-17 by the end. Alan Prosser-Harries converted all six of our tries.

During the second half of the season we said goodbye to five players. John Simons made his final appearance against United Services, Portsmouth on 8th February, Ricky Bartlett made his against the Army on 26th February, David Marques against Cardiff on 30th March and John Mallett and R.B. (Richard) Marson (who was making the last of 44 confirmed appearances) both against Coventry on 11th April.

Harry Eden scored the most tries (9) and Bob Hiller got the most points (78) with 12 penalties, 18 conversions, 1 try and 1 dropped goal. Overall, points dropped by 55 to 351 on the previous season's total which meant that tries, penalties and conversions all dropped as well but dropped goals stayed the same on 4. Grahame Murray played in all but one game (36) and he was well ahead of Colin Payne (30), John Bazalgette (28) and Harry Eden, Bob Lloyd and David Wrench (27).

1963/64

030963	ROMA F.C.	TWICKENHAM	W	2G2T(16)-1G1DG1PG1T(14)
070963	R.F.U. PRESIDENT'S XV	TWICKENHAM	L	1G1T(8)-1G1PG2T(14)
090963	GOSFORTH	GOSFORTH	L	1PG(3)-1G(5)
140963	COVENTRY(SMM)	TWICKENHAM	D	2G2PG(16)-2G2T(16)
210963	LLANELLY	TWICKENHAM	W	2G2DG1PG1T(22)-0
230963	HEADINGLEY	HEADINGLEY	L	1PG3T(12)-2G2PG(16)
280963	LEICESTER	TWICKENHAM	W	2G1PG(13)-2T(6)
051063	LANSDOWNE	DUBLIN	L	1G(5)-2G2PG2T(22)
121063	GLOUCESTER	TWICKENHAM	W	1PG2T(9)-1PG1T(6)
191063	COVENTRY	TWICKENHAM	W	1PG2T(9)-1G1DG(8)
261063	SWANSEA	TWICKENHAM	D	1T(3)-1T(3)
021163	BRISTOL	BRISTOL	L	2T(6)-1G1PG1T(11)
091163	RICHMOND	RICHMOND	W	2G1T(13)-1G1T(8)
161163	OXFORD UNIVERSITY	TWICKENHAM	L	0-1PG1T(6)
231163	CAMBRIDGE UNIVERSITY	STOOP MEMORIAL GROUND	L	0-2G1PG(13)
301163	LONDON WELSH	STOOP MEMORIAL GROUND	D	1PG1T(6)-2PG(6)
071263	BLACKHEATH	STOOP MEMORIAL GROUND	W	3G2PG3T(30)-0
141263	CARDIFF	TWICKENHAM	D	1PG(3)-1PG(3)
211263	NEWPORT	NEWPORT	C	
281263	RICHMOND	STOOP MEMORIAL GROUND	L	0-1G1T(8)
040164	ST.MARY'S HOSPITAL	TEDDINGTON	W	2G(10)-1G(5)
110164	BLACKHEATH	BLACKHEATH	D	1G2PG(11)-1G2PG(11)
180164	BIRKENHEAD PARK	BIRKENHEAD	C	
250164	ROYAL AIR FORCE	TWICKENHAM	L	1G(5)-1G1PG(8)
010264	NORTHAMPTON	NORTHAMPTON	L	2T(6)-2PG1T(9)
080264	UNITED SERVICES PORTSMOUTH	PORTSMOUTH	W	3G1PG2T(24)-1T(3)
150264	LLANELLY	LLANELLY	L	2T(6)-1G1DG1T(11)
220264	ROYAL NAVY	TWICKENHAM	W	1DG2T(9)-1T(3)
260264	ARMY	STOOP MEMORIAL GROUND	W	2G1DG1PG3T(25)-1DG1T(6)
290264	LONDON SCOTTISH	TWICKENHAM	W	2G1PG(13)-1PG2T(9)
070364	LEICESTER	LEICESTER	W	1PG1T(6)-0
140364	BEDFORD	TWICKENHAM	L	1PG1T(6)-3T(9)

210364	WATERLOO	WATERLOO	W	2G1PG1T(16)-1G2PG(11)
260364	BATH	BATH	W	2G2T(16)-1PG1T(6)
280364	SWANSEA	SWANSEA	W	1T(3)-0
300364	CARDIFF	CARDIFF	L	0-1G1T(8)
040464	BRISTOL	STOOP MEMORIAL GROUND	W	1PG5T(18)-0
110464	COVENTRY	COVENTRY	L	2T(6)-1G1PG2T(14)
170564	ROMA F.C.	ROME	W	6G(30)-(17)

At the Annual General Meeting on 16th July 1964, Lord Wakefield of Kendal presented a cheque for £327 and expressed the appreciation of the Club for the unrelenting efforts on behalf of the Club and its members made by Mr and Mrs MacDonald (the Teddington groundsman and his wife) over the last decade. Another deficit in the accounts was mainly due to the fact the Club was running two grounds for most of the season. Gate receipts were £3,256 and Subscriptions were £2,398 leading to a loss of £900. Better results could be expected both in savings in rent at Teddington and additional revenue from running the Stoop for a full season. On 6th August, it was announced that a scoreboard had been erected at the Stoop at a cost of £90 (which had been shared with Twickenham Borough Council). A meeting was held on 19th October solely for the purpose of authorising £1,500 for floodlighting on the training pitch at Craneford Way. It was decided by 13 votes to 4 to look into cheaper schemes for providing our own floodlighting. As already mentioned, the cost of putting floodlighting on the first team pitch was out of the Club's reach at this time. One estimate would have erected four 100 feet high towers (one in each corner of the pitch) at a cost of £12,000. It was decided that, if all the bar lights were switched on, training could just about be carried out on the first team pitch. In the end Harrods pitch was used for training after a request for a fixed weekly training event at the Richmond Athletic Ground was turned down.

On 10th September 1964, we met Bromley R.F.C. in Hayes, Kent. The event was to commemorate the beginning of their 78th season and their change of name from Catford Bridge. We turned up with a very strong team and proceeded to score fourteen tries and ten conversions to record a 62-3 victory. The tries were scored by Harry Eden (5), John Cox (2), Paul Parkin (2), Joe McPartlin, J. Dougal, John Hancock, Steve Wilcock and Tony Todman. Conversions were kicked by Bob Hiller (8), Eden and Dave Wrench. Although this score equalled the number of points we got against Bath in 1961, the margin of victory (59 points) had only before been exceeded in 1908 and 1920. Rosslyn Park were beaten narrowly at Roehampton (16-14) and we met the Old Whitgiftians for the first and, so far, only time. The match was played on their ground at Croham Road, South Croydon to celebrate the opening of the extension to their new clubhouse. After going behind to a try, John Bazalgette equalised in similar fashion before the break and a Prosser-Harries penalty gave us a narrow win.

On 19th September, we met Llanelly at Twickenham. The final score of fifty points to eight in our favour was not too much of a surprise when it was known beforehand that Llanelly had nine men playing for the Western Counties against the Fijians at Stradey Park. By half time we were sixteen points to the good with a John Willcox penalty and tries from McPartlin, Todman and Murray (the last two converted by Willcox). The visitors made a fight of it at the start of the second half and managed a goal and a dropped goal but we were not to be denied our cricket score and further tries followed from Marriott, Jones, Read, Eden, Parkin and Cox (3) with five more conversions by Willcox making up the total. To make matters worse for Llanelly, their right wing (Denman) collided with one of the posts late in the game and had to be taken off with a leg injury. Leicester and Swansea were our next victories before we travelled unbeaten to Gloucester with six wins and 177 points for and just 40 against. Gloucester gave their best performance of the season so far and after an even first half, in which Hiller and Rutherford exchanged penalties, they just led when Ainge dropped a goal. Three goals (one a penalty) for Gloucester to which we replied with just one try from Bob Lloyd meant we trailed by thirteen points with just a few minutes to go. A tremendous late rally from us saw John Hancock and Bob Hiller go over for tries (both converted by the latter) but it was not quite enough and we went down to our first defeat of the season (16-19).

We were soon back to winning ways though and victories followed over Coventry, Waterloo and Cheltenham. This was our first fixture with Cheltenham but it was the last appearance for us by John Willcox. During his Quins career, he had scored 297 points (2 tries, 8 dropped goals, 39 penalties and 75 conversions). In the 45-0 thrashing of Waterloo, the referee (Dai Hughes) gave three penalties against us which were described as "unfair". He admitted afterwards that he would not have given them in the normal way but as they were forty points down, he was feeling soft hearted. Our scrum half (Roger Lewis) queried one of them with the referee making the point that either they were playing rugby or they were not! In any event they were all missed and the report goes on to tell us that the referee went home to Llanelly - who crashed 50-8 to us last month! Bristol defeated us with two dropped goals to nil before we saw off Richmond and Oxford University. We finished the year off with wins over Blackheath and Cardiff but losses against Cambridge University, Newport and Richmond.

Our usual start of the year match with Bristol was now dispensed with and was replaced by a fixture against the Army. The first such game was played on 2nd January at the Stoop and we ran out winners 19-3. Despite us leading 9-0 at half time, Blackheath came back by scoring fourteen points of their own without reply to snatch a win. On the reserve pitch at the Stoop, Birkenhead Park achieved their first victory over us since 1931 by six points to three. The following week, we were again playing on a reserve pitch, this time it was the London Irish second team pitch at Sunbury. Our opponents were the Royal Air Force and we won with ease by scoring eight tries without reply (32-0). We then lost to London Scottish and Northampton defeated us for the eleventh time out of the last fifteen games. Llanelly gained a narrow revenge over us for their mauling back in September (8-14) but we were too good for U.S. Portsmouth (21-6) and the Royal Navy (22-0). On 6th March, we met Leicester at Welford Road. By half time, the Tigers held a six point lead through two goals (one dropped) and a try to a Steve Wilcock try converted by Bob Hiller. During the second half we came back at them and a try by our captain (Colin Payne) converted by Hiller put us to within one point. Hiller had the final say with a penalty and we had sneaked home by two points for our first double of the season.

Our third trip of the season to the Midlands saw us venturing to Bedford aiming to halt a run of three successive defeats at Goldington Road. We began very well with a hat-trick of tries by Paul Parkin (all converted by Hiller) and one from John Adcock to lead 18-0 at half time. Bedford staged something of a revival during the second half and scored four tries of their own but we got two more ourselves through Steve Wilcock (converted by Hiller) and a fourth for Parkin to leave us winners by ten points (26-16). We again managed to stop Waterloo from scoring but could only get a goal and a penalty ourselves but we did achieve our highest winning score against

London Irish in the 24 matches played since 1900 (40-8). We did to Bristol on their ground what they had done to us at Twickenham by beating them by six points (11-5) but Coventry gained revenge for their earlier defeat (14-26). The Easter tour was a partial success with a win over Bath followed by a narrow defeat at Swansea and a draw with Cardiff to end a successful season. Our playing record stood at P36 W23 D1 L12.

During the last two months of the season, we said farewell to a number of players. Against Waterloo on 20th March, Harry Eden played his last game for the 1st XV. During his career he had scored 82 tries and 4 conversions for a points total of 254. David Thompson appeared for the last time against Bristol on 3rd April, he had scored 66 points (21 tries and 1 dropped goal) and Roger Whyte appeared for his final game against Cardiff on 19th April having scored some 427 points (8 tries, 69 penalties and 98 conversions) and appeared in practically every position for the 1st XV. He remains the most versatile player ever to have played for the Quins. Making their first appearances were V.S.J. (Victor) Harding against the Royal Navy on 27th February who went on to appear 23 times for us having won 6 England caps in 1961 and 1962, P.C.R. (Pat) Orr against London Irish on 27th March who played at least 112 times and D.I. (Doug) Yeabsley against Waterloo, he went on to make at least 70 appearances.

Paul Parkin topped the try scorers with 20 and Bob Hiller got the most penalties (15), conversions (47) and, subsequently, points (154) with 5 tries making up the total. The team overall scored some 130 tries which was a new Club record beating the previous highest of 129 set in 1909/10. Penalties and conversions were up on the previous season and a total points haul of 597 was also a new Club record passing the previous best of 551 set in 1956/57. Top appearance maker was Tony Todman with 35 followed by Grahame Murray (32), Bob Hiller (31) and John Cox and Roger Lewis both with 30.

1964/65

100964	BROMLEY	HAYES(KENT)	W	10G4T(62)-1PG(3)
120964	ROSSLYN PARK	ROEHAMPTON	W	2G2T(16)-1G2PG1T(14)
160964	OLD WHITGIFTIANS	CROYDON	W	1PG1T(6)-1T(3)
190964	LLANELLY	TWICKENHAM	W	7G1PG4T(50)-1G1DG(8)
260964	LEICESTER	TWICKENHAM	W	2G3T(19)-1T(3)
031064	SWANSEA	TWICKENHAM	W	3G2PG1T(24)-1PG2T(9)
101064	GLOUCESTER	GLOUCESTER	L	2G1PG1T(16)-2G1DG2PG(19)
171064	COVENTRY	TWICKENHAM	W	1G1DG1PG(11)-1PG2T(9)
241064	WATERLOO	TWICKENHAM	W	3G10T(45)-0
311064	CHELTENHAM	CHELTENHAM	W	2G1DG3T(22)-1G1DG(8)
071164	BRISTOL	TWICKENHAM	L	0-2DG(6)
141164	RICHMOND	TWICKENHAM	W	1T(3)-0
211164	OXFORD UNIVERSITY	TWICKENHAM	W	1G1DG3T(17)-0
281164	CAMBRIDGE UNIVERSITY	TWICKENHAM	L	1G1PG(8)-2G1PG(13)
051264	BLACKHEATH	BLACKHEATH	W	1PG(3)-0
121264	CARDIFF	TWICKENHAM	W	2G1PG(13)-1G2T(11)

191264	NEWPORT	TWICKENHAM	L	0-1G1PG4T(20)
261264	RICHMOND	RICHMOND	L	1PG1T(6)-1G1T(8)
020165	ARMY	STOOP MEMORIAL GROUND	W	2G2PG1T(19)-1T(3)
090165	BLACKHEATH	TWICKENHAM	L	1PG2T(9)-1G2DG1PG(14)
160165	BIRKENHEAD PARK	STOOP MEMORIAL GROUND	L	1PG(3)-1PG1T(6)
230165	ROYAL AIR FORCE	SUNBURY(H)	W	4G4T(32)-0
300165	LONDON SCOTTISH	RICHMOND	L	1DG1PG1T(9)-2G2PG(16)
060265	NORTHAMPTON	NORTHAMPTON	L	0-2G1DG1PG1T(19)
130265	UNITED SERVICES PORTSMOUTH	STOOP MEMORIAL GROUND	W	3G2T(21)-1PG1T(6)
200265	LLANELLY	LLANELLY	L	1G1T(8)-1G2PG1T(14)
270265	ROYAL NAVY	PORTSMOUTH	W	2G4T(22)-0
060365	LEICESTER	LEICESTER	W	2G1PG(13)-1G1DG1T(11)
130365	BEDFORD	BEDFORD	W	4G2T(26)-2G2T(16)
200365	WATERLOO	WATERLOO	W	1G1PG(8)-0
270365	LONDON IRISH	STOOP MEMORIAL GROUND	W	5G1PG4T(40)-1G1T(8)
030465	BRISTOL	BRISTOL	W	1G2T(11)-1T(3)
100465	COVENTRY	COVENTRY	L	1G1PG2T(14)-4G2T(26)
150465	BATH	BATH	W	3T(9)-1PG1T(6)
170465	SWANSEA	SWANSEA	L	3G1PG1T(21)-3G2PG1T(24)
190465	CARDIFF	CARDIFF	D	1G1T(8)-1G1T(8)

At the AGM on 22nd July 1965, a loss of £558 on the season was recorded. Gate receipts totalled £2,616, subscriptions were £2,479 and a record bar profit of £729 was achieved. On 5th August, it was reported that three new shareholders to be appointed in Harlequin Estates should be the Chairman (Reg Kindred), the Secretary (Bill Wiggans) and the captain (Grahame Murray). At a meeting on 2nd September at the Royal Aero Club in Fitzmaurice Place, London, W1, it was announced that thanks to several donations from members, floodlights were to be installed on the second pitch at the Stoop Memorial Ground. The tour to South Africa in May 1966 was formerly announced at a meeting on 4th November as were admission charges at the Stoop. Entrance to the ground would be 3s and transfer to the stand would be 2s. On 25th November, it was noted that we were looking at a fixture with the British Lions when they returned from their Australasian tour (unfortunately, this never really got any further than this). On 3rd February 1966, the Centenary arrangements on the playing side were listed as follows:-

3rd September 1966 v. Jean Prat's XV.

October 1966 - Fixture at Rugby School and a possible fixture against an Invitation XV raised by the manager of the British Lions (neither of these took place).

On the non-playing side there was a Harlequin Ball, the Annual Dinner at the Mansion House in London and a cocktail party at the House of Lords.

Grahame Murray became captain for this (1965/66) and the next (Centenary) Season. His first match was our third (and last) against Roma. Like the first, this one was also played at Twickenham. A haul of sixteen points in the first half proved enough even though we failed to score after this as the Italians could only manage a penalty in the second half. F.G. (Francis) "Gerry" Gilpin played the first of at least 18 games for us in this one. He had won three caps for Ireland in 1962. Our encounter with Rosslyn Park four days later was to be our last against them for seven years. We won through by fourteen points to six despite a violent thunderstorm shortly after the start which saturated the pitch and turned the ball into something resembling a brown bar of soap. Sidcup came to the Stoop on 15th September and were defeated 11-6 before we met Llanelly the following Saturday at Twickenham. Gilpin had a great game and, through his kicking, we wore Llanelly down. We led by nine points at half time thanks to a try from Bob Lloyd and two Bob Hiller penalties. Paul Parkin stretched our lead after the break with our second try and by the time Nick Silk (converted by Hiller) and Steve Wilcock had doubled the try count, Llanelly had only managed a try and a dropped goal to leave us easy winners.

A regular pattern was now emerging with our season as we tended to play nearly all of our home matches at Twickenham before Christmas (when it was least used) and afterwards we were rarely at home. This season was no exception and fifteen out of our last twenty fixtures were scheduled to be away games. Leicester were our next opponents and after Alan Pearson had scored a try for us our play gradually deteriorated which enabled the visitors to score a goal and a penalty to win the game and take our unbeaten record from us. Two good wins over Swansea and Gloucester followed before Coventry lowered our colours for the second time this season (0-6). Another win over Waterloo (leaving them scoreless for the third time in a row) was followed in quick succession by defeats at the hands of London Welsh (3-11) (our first away game of the season), Bristol (8-18) and Richmond (3-13).

We returned to winning ways against the two varsity sides before going off the rails again. Against Oxford, eight of our side were former Oxford Blues and six of their side were Harlequin members. One of these was J.B.H. (John) Coker who was to become the first African to win a Rugby blue. He did eventually make his debut for us but not until the 1966/67 season. Tries from Jeremy Spencer and John Cox were enough to see us home. Against the light blues and despite conceding a try after just 40 seconds, we came through to triumph in the end. We led at half time with tries from Bob Lloyd (converted by John Scott) and John Cox and maintained the five point gap in the second period with further scores from John Young and Cox with his second. Cambridge managed a try and a penalty either side of our scores to leave the final score at 14-9. This was the first time since 1952/53 we had defeated both Oxford and Cambridge in the same season. Blackheath and Cardiff came to us, played and conquered in what turned out to be our last two games of the year as the fixtures with Newport and Richmond were cancelled.

1966 began with an encounter on New Year's Day at the Stoop against the Army. On a quagmire of a pitch, the visitors led by a try to nil at half time scored by T.K. Colgate (a Quin). In the end, our pack out-gunned the Army and tries from Cox (2) and Dave Wrench plus a conversion from Hiller was enough. This game saw the last appearance of Steve Wilcock and the first of T.W. (Tim) Rutter. He was to go on and play in 79 matches for the 1st XV over the next ten years. A win over Blackheath (11-3) was followed by another two cancelled games (Birkenhead Park and the Royal Air Force). A loss to London Scottish (6-16) came at the end of January before we travelled up to play Northampton. Before this match, we had been accused of departing from our traditional style of play and morale was said to have been at a low ebb. Nothing could have prepared anyone for what was to follow as we hit our most impressive form with a scintillating performance. The first half saw us build a nine point lead with tries from

Hiller and Marriott and a dropped goal from McPartlin. Northampton got a try early in the second half but that was as close as they got and we piled on the agony with tries from John Gibbs, Lloyd (2), Cox (2) and Hiller (who added three conversions). The final score of 33-3 was only the second time since our first meeting in 1896 that we had scored over thirty points against them. The previous occasion was a 32-0 whitewash at Twickenham in 1911 during the glory years.

This seemed to spur us on and victories followed over U.S. Portsmouth (22-9), Llanelli (note the change of spelling from Llanelly, apparently to make it sound more Welsh!) (5-3) and the Royal Navy (8-3). A Wednesday evening kick-off on 2nd March at Newport saw us go down 3-13 in terrible conditions which limited the scoreless second half to 30 minutes. Nick Silk made his last appearance against Northampton and M.J. (Mike) Mason played the first of at least 184 games in the Royal Navy fixture. Leicester completed the double over us at Welford Road (3-14) and we defeated Bedford in a dreary game at Twickenham (12-6). Even though there were still another eight games of the season to go, this was our last home fixture. Our away game with Coventry was played on Tuesday 15th March under lights and in what proved to be a very open game, the Coventry pack eventually got on top and enabled them to win 19-8. Waterloo were again defeated away (29-10) with the help of tries from Mike Mason, Bob Lloyd (3), T.K. Colgate, John Cox and John Young and London Irish were thrashed at Sunbury in a game where our score could have been much higher had we taken all of our chances. As it was, we had to settle for thirty one points against five for the Irish. Bob Hiller converted five of our seven tries which had been scored by Lloyd (another hat-trick), Young (2), D.E. Parry and Colgate. This was to be our last win of the season as five tough away games brought us no success.

All five were played in the West Country or Wales, the first was Bristol and three penalties from Hiller and a try by Cox were clearly not enough against three goals and three tries from the home side. Jeremy Spencer made his last appearance for us in this one and in the next game against Bath we said goodbye to John Bazalgette but welcomed J.D. (John) Gronow for the first of 56 first team appearances. The game itself resulted in our first loss against Bath since 1957 (a sequence of fourteen straight wins). All the scoring came in the first half with Bath getting a goal and a penalty while for us Bob Hiller converted his own try. Swansea saw us off (3-13) as did Cardiff (after we had outclassed them) by eight points to six. Our final fixture of the season was at Kingsholm against Gloucester. The final score of 6-3 in favour of the cherry and whites was almost forgotten as Dave Wrench became the first Quins player in the history of the Club to be sent off in a first team fixture. He knocked out Gloucester prop D. Christopher, the referee saw it and ordered him off. Christopher was carried from the field but returned eleven minutes later. In this game, we saw the last appearances of Mike Whiteside and Joe McPartlin, who had scored 120 points in his career (20 tries, 5 dropped goals, 7 penalties and 12 conversions). Despite our terrible finish to the season (which was to be a regular occurrence in the seventies) we still managed to win two more matches than we lost (18-16).

John Cox scored the most tries (18) and Bob Hiller got the most points (129) made up of 6 tries, 19 penalties and 27 conversions. Overall, tries were down by 59 on the previous season to 71 as were conversions (down 35 to 31) but penalties were up by 2 to 23. Our points total of 350 was well down on the 1964/65 total and was our lowest amount since 1955/56. Top appearance maker was John Cox (30) followed by Grahame Murray (28), Bob Lloyd (27) and Pat Orr (26).

1965/66

070965	ROMA F.C.	TWICKENHAM	W	2G1PG1T(16)-1PG(3)
110965	ROSSLYN PARK	TWICKENHAM	W	1G2PG1T(14)-1PG1T(6)
150965	SIDCUP	STOOP MEMORIAL GROUND	W	1G1PG1T(11)-1PG1T(6)
180965	LLANELLY	TWICKENHAM	W	1G2PG3T(20)-1DG1T(6)
250965	LEICESTER	TWICKENHAM	L	1T(3)-1G1PG(8)
021065	SWANSEA	TWICKENHAM	W	2G1PG(13)-1G1T(8)
091065	GLOUCESTER	TWICKENHAM	W	1G1PG2T(14)-1G(5)
161065	COVENTRY	TWICKENHAM	L	0-1PG1T(6)
231065	WATERLOO	TWICKENHAM	W	1G2T(11)-0
301065	LONDON WELSH	OLD DEER PARK	L	1PG(3)-1G2T(11)
061165	BRISTOL	TWICKENHAM	L	1G1PG(8)-3PG3T(24)
131165	RICHMOND	RICHMOND	L	1T(3)-2G1PG(13)
201165	OXFORD UNIVERSITY	TWICKENHAM	W	2T(6)-0
271165	CAMBRIDGE UNIVERSITY	TWICKENHAM	W	1G3T(14)-1PG2T(9)
041265	BLACKHEATH	STOOP MEMORIAL GROUND	L	1PG(3)-1G1PG1T(11)
111265	CARDIFF	TWICKENHAM	L	0-2G2T(16)
181265	NEWPORT	NEWPORT	C	
271265	RICHMOND	TWICKENHAM	C	
010166	ARMY	STOOP MEMORIAL GROUND	W	1G2T(11)-1T(3)
080166	BLACKHEATH	BLACKHEATH	W	1G1PG1T(11)-1PG(3)
150166	BIRKENHEAD PARK	BIRKENHEAD	C	
220166	ROYAL AIR FORCE	TWICKENHAM	C	
290166	LONDON SCOTTISH	TWICKENHAM	L	1PG1T(6)-2G2PG(16)
050266	NORTHAMPTON	NORTHAMPTON	W	3G1DG5T(33)-1T(3)
120266	UNITED SERVICES PORTSMOUTH	PORTSMOUTH	W	2G4T(22)-1PG2T(9)
190266	LLANELLI	LLANELLI	W	1G(5)-1PG(3)
260266	ROYAL NAVY	TWICKENHAM	W	1G1PG(8)-1PG(3)
020366	NEWPORT	NEWPORT	L	1PG(3)-2G1T(13)
050366	LEICESTER	LEICESTER	L	1PG(3)-1G2PG1T(14)
120366	BEDFORD	TWICKENHAM	W	1DG2PG1T(12)-2PG(6)
150366	COVENTRY	COVENTRY	L	1G1PG(8)-2G3PG(19)
190366	WATERLOO	WATERLOO	W	4G3T(29)-2G(10)

Nick Cross

260366	LONDON IRISH	SUNBURY	W	5G2T(31)-1G(5)
020466	BRISTOL	BRISTOL	L	3PG1T(12)-3G3T(24)
070466	BATH	BATH	L	1G(5)-1G1PG(8)
090466	SWANSEA	SWANSEA	L	1T(3)-2G1T(13)
110466	CARDIFF	CARDIFF	L	2T(6)-1G1T(8)
160466	GLOUCESTER	GLOUCESTER	L	1PG(3)-1DG1PG(6)

24

The South African Tour
May 1966

The touring party consisted of the following players:- G.C. Murray (captain); J.R.L. Adcock, R.C. Ashby, J.T. Cox, J.D. Gibbs, F.G. Gilpin, J.N. Hancock, V.S.J. Harding, I.H.P. Laughland, R.H. Lloyd, V.R. Marriott, M.J. Mason, P.C.R. Orr, P.S. Parkin, C.M. Payne, A.S. Pearson, P. Ross, T.W. Rutter, A.J.S. Todman, M.J. Whiteside, D.R. Williams, D.F.B. Wrench and J.R.C. Young. David Brooks was the tour manager ably assisted by Tom Bishop, Philip Dunkley and Derek Whiting. R.C. (Roland) "Clive" Ashby of Wasps (who had won two of his three England caps during the last season) and I.H.P. (Ian) Laughland of London Scottish (who had won the first of his 31 caps for Scotland in 1959) both guested for us. Permission had been granted by their clubs and the R.F.U. in order to boost the strength of the party.

This was yet another "first" for the Harlequin F.C. as it was the first time a club side had toured South Africa. Flying from London (Heathrow) Airport by South African Airways Boeing 707, on Tuesday 3rd May, the party arrived in Johannesburg and were due to play their first match on Saturday 7th against the Quaggas (the South African equivalent of the Barbarians).

The match took place at Ellis Park, Johannesburg in front of a crowd estimated at between 20-25,000. It was a very tough game to open our tour with and, as well as having the altitude to deal with, the Quaggas had six Springboks in their team (although we did have eight internationals in ours). After 20 minutes, we trailed by two goals and a penalty to nil but we never gave up. Bob Lloyd scored two unconverted tries in an eight minute spell but the Quaggas stretched their lead to eighteen points by half time with another goal and two tries. The first score of the second half came for us when Tony Todman went over for John Young to convert but the Quaggas had the last word and their sixth try made the final score 27-11.

Our next game was on the following Wednesday (11th May) at Willowmoore Park, Benoni against an Eastern Transvaal Invitation XV. Three changes were made to the side which lost to the Quaggas which led to us playing what was probably our strongest team. Once again, we tried our hardest to produce running rugby and it paid off even though our pack tired towards the end of the game. By this time we had scored tries through Paul Parkin (converted by John Hancock) and Colin Payne to which the Invitation XV could only reply with a dropped goal leaving us victorious by five points. This time the crowd was one of 10,000.

At Loftus Versfeld on 14th May, we played our third match against a Northern Universities side before a crowd of 17,000. In another good display it was generally felt that we out-thought, out-ran and out-played the students.

Clive Ashby and Ian Laughland both played an important part in our play and we completed our victory with tries from John Cox (who also kicked a conversion and a penalty), Bob Lloyd, Paul Parkin, Rhys Williams and Dave Wrench and a conversion by Gerry Gilpin. The Universities XV could only manage a goal, a penalty and a try in reply and our margin of victory was eleven points (22-11).

On 18th May, we met a Country Districts XV at Witbank with several changes being made to the side which played in the previous game. Gerry Gilpin was moved to his preferred position of fly half, John Young played at full back, John Gibbs came in at centre for his first appearance of the tour and Bob Lloyd played on the right wing. The one problem we did have which could not be easily remedied was the lack of a reliable goal kicker (hence the different kickers used so far). A capacity crowd saw us go into a six point lead with tries from Lloyd and Todman (Young hitting a post with the attempted conversion) before the Country XV got a penalty just before half time. After this, we were handicapped by injuries and a try by the home side enabled them to draw the match.

Our fifth encounter was against one of our own, the Pretoria Harlequins, at Groenkloof. By this stage of the tour, eight out of twenty three players could not be considered due to injuries so our weakest side was put in the field. Pretoria were not having a very good season and had lost most of their games but nothing was taken for granted. Our hosts began the scoring with a dropped goal but we were soon into our stride and by half time we had scored tries through Tony Todman (converted by John Hancock) and Clive Ashby. The home side lost their fly half with over half an hour left, the result of this was that their pack had only seven men in it and tired before the end. They scored their only try midway through the second half and Hancock converted his own try to leave us winners by thirteen points to six.

Our final match was against a Southern Universities XV at Newlands on May 25th. This could perhaps have been considered as one game too far but as it was, we managed to field five internationals. One of these, John Young, was making his final appearance for the 1st XV and had scored some 118 points during his career (34 tries, 2 penalties and 5 conversions). After the Universities XV had missed four penalty attempts, we got what was to be our only score of the game. Just before half time, a mistake by their scrum half led to Murray sending Alan Pearson over for Hancock to convert. The scores were soon tied by the students (but not before they had missed with their fifth penalty attempt) when they scored the first of five tries and converted. Despite Pearson hooking five times against the head during the second half, the Universities still got two goals and two tries to run out winners by twenty one points to five.

This was a sad way to finish the tour but no more could have been asked of our team especially after ending a full domestic season just one month earlier. The party flew home the next day after David Brooks had expressed the team's gratitude for South African rugby hospitality. It was later reported (on 1st September 1966) that a loss of £2 13s 6d had been made on the tour overall.

South African Tour

070566	QUAGGAS	ELLIS PARK, JOHANNESBURG	L	1G2T(11)-3G1PG3T(27)
110566	EASTERN TRANSVAAL INVITATION XV	WILLOWMORE PARK, BENONI	W	1G1T(8)-1DG(3)
140566	NORTHERN UNIVERSITIES	LOFTUS VERSVELD, PRETORIA	W	2G1PG3T(22)-1G1PG1T(11)

180566	COUNTRY DISTRICTS XV	WITBANK, EASTERN TRANSVAAL	D	2T(6)-1PG1T(6)
200566	PRETORIA HARLEQUINS	GROENKLOOF, PRETORIA	W	2G1T(13)-1DG1T(6)
250566	SOUTHERN UNIVERSITIES	NEWLANDS, CAPETOWN	L	1G(5)-3G2T(21)

25

A Centenary to Celebrate

1966-1971

During the summer of 1966, the British Lions toured Australia and New Zealand. Although we had no official representative, one player did tour who was to play some games for us during the 1970/71 season. K.F. (Keith) Savage of Northampton had just started his run of winning 13 English caps which was to end in 1968. He played in none of the test matches (but did win four caps on the 1968 tour of South Africa), of which the two in Australia were won but all four in New Zealand were lost.

On 12th May 1966, a request for affiliation was received from Elizabeth RUFC in South Australia. As we were already affiliated to the Melbourne Harlequins, this request was turned down. Further to this, the Club made a donation of £25 towards the purchase of a new ground for the Melbourne Harlequins. On 16th June, a loss for season 1965/66 of £312 was recorded and it was noted that Flight Lieutenant P.S. Martin had been awarded the D.F.C. (Distinguished Flying Cross) for service in the Far East. At a meeting on 4th August, we agreed to accept an invitation from the Paris Université Club to make an eight day, three match tour to France between 29th April and 4th May 1967. All expenses would be paid although the party of 22 would have to donate £10 each. W.D. & H.O. Wills (a tobacco company) were to sponsor the prestige booklet to commemorate the centenary and 1000 copies were printed at their expense. It was recorded that a loss would be made on the South African tour. On 19th January 1967, a request was received from the London Welsh to play their game against Cardiff on 14th September 1968 at the Stoop. Permission was granted as we had used their ground at the Old Deer Park in the past (during the 1961/62 season). Bob Hiller and Nigel Starmer-Smith went on the England tour to Canada although neither played in the unofficial test match on 30th September. On 18th May, there was the question of a tour to South Africa in 1969 with a general proposal that us and the New Zealand Harlequins would play six matches each and as a finale, both sides would produce a combined side to play a strong South Africa side. This trip never got off the ground but, in any event, sporting links with South Africa were cut soon after anyway. Honours caps were awarded to Bob Hiller and Bob Lloyd and fixtures had been agreed to in principal against Japan in the winter of 1968 and centenary matches with Neath in 1971/72 and Durham City in 1972/73. The only game that went ahead was the one with Durham.

1966/67 was the Club's centenary season and, despite some grand ideas for celebratory matches, the only one to take place was the first of the season (although other games were listed as special events). On 3rd September, we took on Jean Prat's French International XV at Twickenham. Jean Prat had captained his country on 17 occasions out of the 51 times he had played. He won his first cap in 1945 and his last in 1955. The International XV contained five internationals (but seven more were to go on and win caps) whereas our team had just two (plus two future caps). At half time, we trailed by two tries to one (by D.E. (David) Parry). In the second half, the scoring was one-sided and, after a late tackle on John Cox, Hiller kicked a penalty to tie the scores. He also had the last word with the conversion of a try by John Adcock to give us a winning start to our centenary season by eleven points to six. Our unbeaten record was not to last for very long and in our very next game against Wasps at Sudbury, it went. This match (played on Thursday 8th September) was billed as a joint centenary celebration in which we shared the gate proceeds. This was our first meeting since 1959 and our first at Sudbury since 1952. Wasps outscored us by three tries to two on their way to a 14-9 win. Two players making their debuts for us in this match were John Coker (the first of his 50 appearances) and Ian Howard (the first of at least 134 appearances).

The following Saturday saw us visit Northampton for the fifth time in a row. We were ahead within a minute of the kick-off when Tim Rutter went over for a try which Bob Hiller converted and a few minutes later he also kicked a penalty. We spent the rest of the half mainly on the defensive but all the home side could muster was one penalty goal. Further tries followed for us in the second half from Bob Lloyd (2) and Rutter with Hiller converting Lloyd's second. Northampton did manage a goal and a try and could have scored more points had they not played like they had just met up for the first time just before the game (according to one report). Llanelli were beaten for the third time on the trot (9-6) and then we played a touring East African XV at the Stoop on 22nd September. The match turned out to be an easy victory for us with tries coming from Bob Lloyd (6) (the first time since 1951 that a 1st XV player had scored this many), John Coker and Ian Howard as well as four conversions from Hiller. We sneaked home against Leicester in a dreadful game full of errors by eight points to five and defeated Swansea (11-8) with the help of an injury time try by Paul Parkin which Bob Hiller converted (his only success out of eight attempts).

Our next fixture was at Twickenham against another touring side, the Athletic Club from Wellington, New Zealand. This was their first match of a tour which would see them play Moseley, Bristol, Gloucester and Blackheath before departing for Ireland, Hong Kong and Japan. The tourists led at half time with a try (which came from a knock-on at a line out) and extended this lead in the second half with a penalty. All we could manage was a Bob Hiller penalty (his only success out of five attempts) and our second defeat of the season was suffered. During the second half, the referee (M.F. Turner) pulled an Achilles tendon and was replaced by J.V. Rolfe for the remainder of the game. Against Coventry on 15th October, we suffered from injuries caused by boots rather than bad luck. First, John Cox received a boot as he tried to touch down (he had to go off for repairs and returned after half time) and second, Pat Orr received one kick on the head and another behind an ear (which required twelve stitches) and had to go off permanently. At this point in the second half we trailed by three points, Bob Hiller dropping a goal to two tries from Coventry. Our front row was now a makeshift one (as a specialist hooker could not be replaced easily, unlike today when it is compulsory) and Coventry added further points through a goal, a dropped goal and a try. Waterloo were thrashed again (31-3), we drew with London Welsh (8-8) and Richmond (3-3) and lost to Bristol (9-16) before defeating both Oxford and Cambridge Universities. Blackheath (on the day of the centenary dinner at the Mansion House in London) and Cardiff ensured we suffered our fifth and sixth defeats of the season before we finished the year with a trio of victories.

On 17th December, we met Newport at the Stoop and achieved our first victory over them since December 1957. Bob Hiller (luckily for us) had been left out of the final England trial and proceeded to land three penalties to a dropped goal from D. Watkins for a final score of 9-3. An away victory over Richmond followed (6-0) in a game which saw the first of 140 appearances by scrum half N.C. (Nigel) Starmer-Smith (who was to go on and gain seven England caps between 1969 and 1971) and on New Year's Eve, we again played at the Athletic Ground when our opponents were London Scottish. Despite fielding nine reserves (due to the final Scottish trial), the Scots led until three minutes from the end when Hiller kicked a penalty, to add to his conversion of John Adcock's try earlier in the second half, to overhaul two penalties scored in the first half by the home side.

Our first fixture of 1967 was to have been on 7th January at the Stoop against the Army but this was cancelled and it was at Twickenham against Blackheath that we opened our new year programme. We gained revenge for our earlier defeat at the Rectory Field by scoring thirteen points without reply. Birkenhead Park were dispatched the following week (17-5) as were the Royal Air Force (but in strange circumstances). On arriving at the Stoop, it was found to be waterlogged and the venue was changed to the Royal Army Ordnance Corps (RAOC) pitch at Southam Garrison, Feltham, Middlesex (a few miles from the Stoop). The game started some 50 minutes late and each half was limited to 30 minutes. In the first period, a penalty for the R.A.F. was cancelled out by two for us by Hiller before we killed the game off in the second half with tries from Doug Yeabsley and Dave Wrench (converted by Hiller). We then completed the double over Northampton and saw off United Services, Portsmouth (for our eighth win in a row) before making our annual trip to Stradey Park. Unfortunately for us, six of our players were required by Surrey but we held our own in the first half and equalled Llanelli's try and penalty with our own from Doug Yeabsley and John Scott respectively to lead twice. As the weather conditions deteriorated considerably, Llanelli got two more tries to seal the win.

Against the Royal Navy, the lead changed hands no fewer than three times in the first half with the Navy leading by the odd point in nineteen at the break. They failed to score again and we added tries by John Coker (his second) and Grahame Murray (Hiller converting this one to add to his two first half penalties) for a final score of 17-10. This was turning out to be a topsy-turvy period of the season and the victory over the Navy was followed by a loss at Leicester, a win at Bedford and, after ten wins on the trot, our first loss to Waterloo since 1959. We outscored them by three tries to two but, as they converted theirs and a penalty apiece effectively cancelled each other out, they won by a point. Against Bath, Dave Wrench and Doug Yeabsley did not arrive until 15 minutes had passed but even this was not enough to stop us from winning. John Coker and Colin Payne got tries in the first half and Bob Hiller got one in the second (to add to his two conversions) in reply to the first score of the game when Bath got their only points, a goal. In this match, K. Jones made the first of 66 appearances and N.O. (Nick) Martin appeared for the first of at least 170 games. He would go on to captain the Club and win one cap for England when he came on as a replacement against France in 1972. Swansea were also defeated (6-0) but we could only draw with Cardiff (3-3).

Bristol were beaten at the Memorial Ground to gain some revenge for our home defeat earlier in the season and we travelled up to play Glasgow Academicals for the first and, so far, only time on 4th April. On the left wing, P.B. (Peter) Glover made his only appearance for us. He had won one England cap earlier in the season and was to win two more (his club was Bath). We actually led at half time with a try from Payne, a penalty by S. Fraser and a dropped goal from D.A. (David) Snare in reply to a goal by the Scots. A strong rally saw the home side turn around their deficit with three goals (one dropped and one a penalty) to which we could only manage to reply with a try by Murray for a final score of 12-16. At Coventry four days later we suffered our worst defeat of the season. It was also our worst defeat at the hands of Coventry. The game itself was extremely entertaining and at half time there were just two points in it. Bob Read had dropped a goal, Doug Yeabsley had kicked a penalty and John Cox and Tim Rutter had scored tries but Coventry led with a goal, two penalties and a try. The second half by contrast was completely one sided and the home team swept us aside in scoring seven more tries (three of which were converted) whereas we failed to add to our total. Our last game of the season was against Gloucester. They led at the break by a penalty goal to nil and increased their lead with a dropped goal but we came back to level with a Coker try and a

Hiller penalty. The game was won for them by their full back (D. Rutherford) who dropped a goal from 40 yards and kicked a penalty from 50 yards.

A playing record of P37 W22 D3 L12 ended a reasonably satisfactory centenary season. Bob Lloyd got 13 tries, Paul Parkin dropped two goals and Bob Hiller got the most points (120) with 3 tries, 1 dropped goal, 18 penalties and 27 conversions. Overall, tries, dropped goals and penalties were up, conversions stayed the same and points rose slightly to 398. Pat Orr and Colin Payne appeared in 32 out of the 37 matches played followed by John Cox, Bob Hiller and Grahame Murray on 28.

A short tour to France took place at the end of the season involving three matches in a week. The first was played in Guéret (just over 50 miles north-east of Limoges) on Sunday 30th April against Sélection Française. Our team contained seven internationals against nine in the French side. Guy Camberabero put them ahead with a dropped goal after two minutes and after missing two penalties, Hiller brought us level with a try. Just before half time, Rupert scored a try to give the home side a narrow lead. On 46 minutes, Cayrouse scored a try (converted by Camberabero) and two minutes later, Astarie did the same before we came back with our second try converted by Hiller. Yachevilli stretched the lead on 54 minutes with another try and Rougerie scored their fifth three minutes later. With two conversions from Camberabero, the score was 24-8. Back we came again and our third try arrived after 59 minutes, converted by Hiller. Scott got another (converted) and when the fifth was scored, the conversion was missed but we only trailed 24-21 with five minutes left. Unfortunately, the French had the last word and Courtial scored a try for Camberabero to convert and seal the win right at the end.

Four days later, we took on Sélection du Limousin at the Stade Municipal in Brive. In the first half, we scored fourteen points against eight (try by Ruaut, conversion and penalty by Bordas) with the second half producing just one try each (Evans for the French side) to leave us winners by 17-11.

The last game took place on the following Saturday at the Parc des Princes in Paris against Paris Université Club. Unfortunately, no record of the result has been found.

1966/67

030966	J.PRAT'S FRENCH INTERNATIONAL XV	TWICKENHAM	W	1G1PG1T(11)-2T(6)
080966	WASPS	SUDBURY	L	1PG2T(9)-1G1PG2T(14)
100966	NORTHAMPTON	NORTHAMPTON	W	2G1PG2T(19)-1G1PG1T(11)
170966	LLANELLI	TWICKENHAM	W	1DG2T(9)-1DG1T(6)
220966	EAST AFRICAN XV	STOOP MEMORIAL GROUND	W	4G4T(32)-0
240966	LEICESTER	TWICKENHAM	W	1G1T(8)-1G(5)
011066	SWANSEA	TWICKENHAM	W	1G2T(11)-1G1PG(8)
081066	ATHLETIC F.C.	TWICKENHAM	L	1PG(3)-1PG1T(6)
151066	COVENTRY	TWICKENHAM	L	1DG(3)-1G1DG3T(17)
221066	WATERLOO	TWICKENHAM	W	2G2PG5T(31)-1PG(3)
291066	LONDON WELSH	TWICKENHAM	D	1G1T(8)-1G1DG(8)

051166	BRISTOL	TWICKENHAM	L	2PG1T(9)-2G2PG(16)
121166	RICHMOND	STOOP MEMORIAL GROUND	D	1PG(3)-1PG(3)
191166	OXFORD UNIVERSITY	TWICKENHAM	W	2G1T(13)-2T(6)
261166	CAMBRIDGE UNIVERSITY	TWICKENHAM	W	2PG(6)-1PG(3)
031266	BLACKHEATH	BLACKHEATH	L	1G1PG(8)-2G1PG(13)
101266	CARDIFF	TWICKENHAM	L	0-2G1T(13)
171266	NEWPORT	STOOP MEMORIAL GROUND	W	3PG(9)-1DG(3)
241266	RICHMOND	RICHMOND	W	(6)-0
311266	LONDON SCOTTISH	RICHMOND	W	1G1PG(8)-2PG(6)
070167	ARMY	STOOP MEMORIAL GROUND	C	
140167	BLACKHEATH	TWICKENHAM	W	2G1T(13)-0
210167	BIRKENHEAD PARK	TWICKENHAM	W	1G2PG2T(17)-1G(5)
280167	ROYAL AIR FORCE	SOUTHAM GARRISON, FELTHAM	W	1G2PG1T(14)-1PG(3)
040267	NORTHAMPTON	TWICKENHAM	W	1DG1PG2T(12)-1PG1T(6)
110267	UNITED SERVICES PORTSMOUTH	STOOP MEMORIAL GROUND	W	5G1T(28)-2PG2T(12)
180267	LLANELLI	LLANELLI	L	1PG1T(6)-1PG3T(12)
250267	ROYAL NAVY	PORTSMOUTH	W	1G2PG2T(17)-2G(10)
040367	LEICESTER	LEICESTER	L	0-1G3T(14)
110367	BEDFORD	BEDFORD	W	1G1PG3T(17)-1G2PG(11)
180367	WATERLOO	WATERLOO	L	1PG3T(12)-2G1PG(13)
230367	BATH	BATH	W	2G1T(13)-1G(5)
250367	SWANSEA	SWANSEA	W	1PG1T(6)-0
270367	CARDIFF	CARDIFF	D	1T(3)-1PG(3)
010467	BRISTOL	BRISTOL	W	2G(10)-1DG1T(6)
040467	GLASGOW ACADEMICALS	GLASGOW	L	1DG1PG2T(12)-2G1DG1PG(16)
080467	COVENTRY	COVENTRY	L	1DG1PG2T(12)-4G2PG5T(41)
140467	GLOUCESTER	GLOUCESTER	L	1PG1T(6)-2DG2PG(12)
300467	SÉLECTION FRANÇAISE	GUERET	L	(21)-(29)
040567	SÉLECTION DU LIMOUSIN	BRIVE	W	(17)-(11)
060567	PARIS UNIVERSITÉ CLUB	PARC DES PRINCES		

One great flaw in our centenary season was the loss of £1,250 (this did not take into account the contribution of £600 from the 200 Club). The idea of this club was that 200 people subscribe 5s per week. Each week there would be a draw for one prize of £10 and twice a year there would be a draw for either £500 or a car. An amusing note appears in the Committee minutes on 1st August 1967 when a proposed raffle of a colour television set was cancelled as problems had arisen in connection with the reliability of colour television!! On 5th October, there is the first mention of a council proposal to acquire our ground at Fairfax Road, Teddington so that they may build a school on it. On 2nd November, the death was reported of John Birkett (one of our most famous players from the Stoop era). On 7th December, among the Christmas gratuities was one of £1 for MacDonald junior for his very valuable services in returning balls at Twickenham! The Quaggas from South Africa were to tour in 1968/69 and unfortunately, we were unable to accommodate a possible fixture with them. Season tickets for the 1968/69 season were to cost £3 (announced on 6th June 1968). On 8th July, Vic Roberts reported that we had been invited by Richmond to join them in a tour of the USA from 15th May until 1st June 1969. We were to play nine matches in just fourteen days with a squad of 30 players. It was felt however, that similar tours to America had been undertaken so frequently in recent years that there was little to be gained from going on this one and so the invitation was politely declined. A surplus of £566 was achieved for the 1967/68 season.

The 1967/68 Season began with a short tour of the South West with games being played against Torquay, Newton Abbot and Exeter. Leading the team was our new captain, David Wrench. On 1st September, we met Torquay and, in a close contest, we were defeated by the odd point in 27. Fortunes were reversed the next day at Newton Abbot where we won by two tries to a goal. The final game at Exeter saw another close encounter. The scores were level at half time with a try to each side. We got two goals to Exeter's one in the second half to run out victors by thirteen points to eight despite the home side having a monopoly on possession for large parts of the game. Our next match was at the Stoop against Wasps. This ended in defeat by eight points to nil and began our worst run since 1947/48. We desperately needed a coach (according to newspaper reports of the time) to help out David Wrench. Eventually, former players Ricky Bartlett and Vic Roberts stepped in to do the coaching and things were turned around (but not before some bad defeats were suffered). Northampton eased passed us in a game of four penalty goals (3-9), Llanelli (who included a young Phil Bennett in their team) achieved their first victory at Twickenham since 1958 (8-14), we were handicapped by the loss of Tudor Williams (our full back) through injury against Leicester but only went down narrowly (3-8) and against London Welsh we could only manage a penalty from Wrench (3-14).

Swansea came next and handed us our fifth defeat at Twickenham in as many games with a 15-9 victory. Against Gloucester on 14th October, we lost Ed Gould (prop) after just 10 minutes when someone apparently stamped on his face, sending him to hospital - he never played for the 1st XV again. Don Rutherford (Gloucester's full back) was man of the match and landed four penalties to which they added two tries for an easy win by eighteen points to nil. So, we had managed to score just 26 points in our last seven matches and with Coventry next to visit Twickenham, the outlook was bleak as they had beaten us in our last five meetings. At half time, Bob Hiller had kicked a penalty to equalise an earlier dropped goal to leave the sides level at 3-3. Suddenly, however, everything changed and John Coker ran 30 yards to score a great try, Vic Marriott added a second and Tim Rutter got another with Coker adding two more either side of the latter. Hiller added three conversions and Coventry could only manage a try at the end to leave us winners by 24-6. This was an amazing upset but alas, it was not to last long. Against

Waterloo, Bristol and Richmond we returned to losing ways but from then on we managed to win more than two thirds of our remaining games. The first was against Oxford University at Twickenham on 18th November and, after an even first half, we stretched away to win quite easily 14-3. Cambridge University (18-12) and Blackheath (22-3) were added to our victims but then we travelled to Rodney Parade to take on the might of Newport. We started well enough and took the lead when Bob Hiller gathered the ball in his own half, kicked ahead, followed up and scored a try which he converted. Newport then got a goal of their own before Bruce Davies put us in front with our second try and when Jarrett converted the home side's second try, they led by two points. Just before the break, Hiller put over a penalty to put us back in front. After twelve minutes of the second half, Jarrett put over a penalty from 45 yards out and this proved to be the last score of the match.

The following Saturday, we met Richmond at the Stoop and achieved a six point win (19-13). This game will only be remembered for one incident involving our captain (David Wrench) and Brian Stoneman (one of Richmond's props). Wrench apparently knocked Stoneman out, breaking his nose in the process (the incident was missed by the referee but not by several spectators and the press). Due to this, the game lasted some 105 minutes (25 over the scheduled time). After Wrench told one newspaper that it had really been retaliatory, he was asked if he had been struck, his reply was "He tried but he missed". The matter was later dealt with by the Club at a Committee meeting and, after a frank discussion Wrench was told that the Club would not tolerate incidents of this nature in the future and, if there should be a recurrence, he would be relieved of the captaincy. At the East India Club twelve days later, when Wrench attended the meeting of the Committee, two photographers (Joe Bulaitis and Derek Cattani of the Daily Mail) were waiting to get some shots of him. As he left the Gents, they made their move but Wrench knocked one flashgun away and delivered what was described as a fierce Karate chop to the neck of Cattani, causing him to fall and smash the top of his camera. When asked about the incident, a club spokesman stated that the Committee did not see the incident and therefore cannot comment on it. A further meeting of senior club members was held to look into the whole affair and it seems Wrench lost the captaincy because he didn't appear for the rest of the season after the Army game on 6th January.

On Boxing Day we had visitors from South Africa when Pretoria University were our opponents at Twickenham. At half time it was one try each and, in reply to a penalty for the students in the second half, we mustered a dropped goal and a penalty from Hiller and a try by Campbell Hogg (to add to a try from Ian Howard in the first half). Our last match of 1967 was a very high scoring game against London Scottish. We raced into a 16-0 lead with tries from John Cox, John Gronow and Doug Yeabsley (Bob Hiller adding a penalty and two conversions) before the Scots scored with two penalties before half time. In the second half we raced away again with a second try for Gronow and others from John Coker, Ian Howard and David Snare (Hiller converting all four) so that we led 36-6. With all hope gone, London Scottish threw the ball about and closed the gap to fourteen points with four goals (two of which were penalties).

In the first half of the season, we saw five new boys appear who would go on to make 360 first team appearances between them. Against Torquay, Gerry Miller made the first of 60 appearances, A.M. (Mike) Davis appeared first against Llanelli and went on to make 79 appearances for us as well as gaining 16 England caps between 1963 (when he played for Torquay Athletic) and 1970, M.J. (Michael) "Mike" Novak made the first of his 67 appearances against Leicester on 23rd September (he would win 3 England caps in 1970), C.S. (Campbell) Hogg from New Zealand played the first of his 82 matches against Swansea and John Joannou appeared against Richmond on 23rd December for the first of 72 games. John Adcock made his last appearance on 28th October against Waterloo having scored 33 points (11 tries) during his 1st XV career.

The Army achieved what was to be their last win over us on 6th January at the Stoop when they outscored us by two tries and a penalty to one try and a penalty. The matches against Blackheath and Birkenhead Park followed the same fate as the Cardiff game back in December when they were both cancelled. We returned to action (and winning ways) on 27th January when the Royal Air Force were defeated 15-3. Northampton away from home has nearly always been a difficult game for us and this one proved to be no exception. After being level 3-3 (yet again) at half time, we just lost out in the second period when Savage scored for Northampton right on time to give them a victory by three points. A victory over United Services, Portsmouth followed when we were grateful to Paul Parkin for a hat-trick and a conversion by Bruce Davies and then we travelled to Stradey Park (the second of our three trips to Wales during the season) to play Llanelli. We became the first English side to win there during the season with a narrow 5-3 success. Against the Royal Navy, we had John Scott and Doug Yeabsley to thank for victory as both kicked a penalty in reply to one by the Navy. On 2nd March we went up to Leicester to gain some revenge for our defeat at Twickenham earlier in the season. The home side opened the scoring after five minutes with a goal to which we replied in kind after 23 minutes when Tim Rutter touched down for Hiller to convert. Following this, a lot of the play was scrappy and untidy until, after 72 minutes when Bob Lloyd scored for Hiller to again convert and hand us victory. The following week, Bedford came to Twickenham and at half time it was still a close game. We had scored four tries through Paul Parkin (2), Gerry Miller and Bob Lloyd to two for Bedford by Rogers and Philbrook. After this, we continued to score tries and John Cox, Campbell Hogg and John Gibbs all registered scores to which the visitors only reply was a penalty from Philbrook. We ran out winners 21-9 to give us our fourth victory in a row over Bedford and hand them their first defeat of the year. Interestingly, Bob Hiller missed all seven conversions and two penalties (one from 20 yards out in front of the posts). This was also our last home game of the season with over a month remaining.

The first away day out of London was the long trip to Waterloo. They had beaten us earlier in the season at the Stoop and so it was a chance for revenge. The wind was described in one report as "not so much biting as carnivorous" so this gives an idea of how cold it was! We began well with that wind at our backs and by half time had scored eleven points without reply. John Scott and Doug Yeabsley had kicked penalties and Scott also converted a try by John Cox. The scoreline was almost reversed in the second half but Waterloo could only manage two goals and a penalty attempt to win it for the home side with the last kick of the match finished in a hedge. A short journey to the Old Deer Park followed on 23rd March to play London Welsh and our six game winning streak came to an end by nine points to five. The next scheduled match was against Coventry but it was cancelled and so we travelled down to Bristol the following week and, in a rather dull game lost by a penalty and a dropped goal to a penalty (this result enabled Bristol to go through the entire season without losing to a London club).

On 11th April, we began the Easter Tour with a visit to Bath and lost (a sight which was to become all too familiar in the coming years) by twenty one points to eight. Our points came from Bob Hiller converting his own try in the first half and John Coker scoring in the second. Next up were the All Whites of Swansea and, by half time we trailed by five points. Alan Prosser-Harries had kicked us into the lead with a penalty before the home team had replied with a goal and a try. Prosser-Harries got us back into it with his second penalty five minutes into the second half and shortly after this Swansea lost one of their wing forwards (Thomas) with concussion after a collision with John Gronow. A penalty for Swansea put their lead back at five points but within three minutes of this, Bob Lloyd scored our first try of the game, Prosser-Harries converted and the scores were level. Just three minutes from the end, Colin Payne won the ball at the back of a lineout, it went down the line and finally reached Mike Novak who beat off a tackle by Ferguson and scored in the corner to win the match. Bank Holiday Monday meant Cardiff at the Arms Park (as it turned out this was to be the last match played here). It was a match which saw the lead change hands no fewer than six times. We scored first when the hero at Swansea (Mike Novak) went over for a try, Cardiff then scored a goal to go in front, Coker got our second try before a penalty for the home side and a second Novak try made it 9-8 to us at the break. A try in the first minute of the second half put Cardiff in front again and this is how the score remained until 10 minutes from the end of the game. Bob Hiller coolly slotted over a penalty goal and despite some frantic attacking by Cardiff, it was enough to see us home. This was to be our last Easter Tour victory for eight years and our last in Cardiff for fifteen!

No new stalwarts made their debuts in the second half of the season but we said goodbye to John Scott, who had scored 64 points in his career (3 tries, 9 penalties and 14 conversions), against Waterloo, Vic Harding against London Welsh (he had managed just two tries) and Alan Prosser-Harries (who had scored 123 points in just 35 appearances (1 dropped goal, 22 penalties and 27 conversions)) and Tony Todman (he had scored 92 points (24 tries, 4 penalties and 4 conversions) and led the team on one occasion) against Swansea.

John Cox scored 13 tries and Bob Hiller was top points scorer (89) with 2 tries, 3 dropped goals, 10 penalty goals and 22 conversions. Overall, tries, penalties and points were down, dropped goals stayed the same and conversions were up by one on the previous season. Grahame Murray appeared in 29 of 35 matches, Colin Payne (27) and John Cox and Mike Mason (26) and Tim Rutter and Campbell Hogg (25) were the best of the rest.

Another British Lions tour to South Africa in 1968 saw Bob Hiller make the trip but appear in no test matches. Keith Savage (who was playing at Northampton) appeared in all four tests; one was drawn but the first, third and fourth were lost. Bob Lloyd was originally picked to go but was unable to tour due to exams. David Brooks made up the Quins contingent as he was the tour manager.

1967/68

010967	TORQUAY	TORQUAY	L	2G1T(13)-1G3T(14)
020967	NEWTON ABBOT	NEWTON ABBOT	W	2T(6)-1G(5)
040967	EXETER	EXETER	W	2G1T(13)-1G1T(8)
070967	WASPS	STOOP MEMORIAL GROUND	L	0-1G1PG(8)
090967	NORTHAMPTON	TWICKENHAM	L	1PG(3)-3PG(9)
160967	LLANELLI	TWICKENHAM	L	1G1PG(8)-1G1DG2T(14)
230967	LEICESTER	TWICKENHAM	L	1DG(3)-1G1T(8)
300967	LONDON WELSH	TWICKENHAM	L	1PG(3)-1G1PG2T(14)
071067	SWANSEA	TWICKENHAM	L	1PG2T(9)-2PG3T(15)
141067	GLOUCESTER	GLOUCESTER	L	0-4PG2T(18)
211067	COVENTRY	TWICKENHAM	W	3G1PG2T(24)-1DG1T(6)
281067	WATERLOO	STOOP MEMORIAL GROUND	L	1PG(3)-2G1DG1PG(16)
031167	BRISTOL	BRISTOL	L	1T(3)-1G1DG2PG1T(17)
111167	RICHMOND	RICHMOND	L	1PG3T(12)-2G1PG1T(16)
181167	OXFORD UNIVERSITY	TWICKENHAM	W	1G1DG2T(14)-1T(3)

251167	CAMBRIDGE UNIVERSITY	TWICKENHAM	W	1DG1PG4T(18)-1DG2PG1T(12)
021267	BLACKHEATH	STOOP MEMORIAL GROUND	W	2G1PG3T(22)-1T(3)
091267	CARDIFF	STOOP MEMORIAL GROUND	C	
161267	NEWPORT	NEWPORT	L	1G1PG1T(11)-2G1PG(13)
231267	RICHMOND	STOOP MEMORIAL GROUND	W	2G1DG1PG1T(19)-2G1PG(13)
261267	PRETORIA UNIVERSITY	TWICKENHAM	W	1DG1PG2T(12)-1PG1T(6)
301267	LONDON SCOTTISH	TWICKENHAM	W	6G1PG1T(36)-2G4PG(22)
060168	ARMY	STOOP MEMORIAL GROUND	L	1PG1T(6)-1PG2T(9)
130168	BLACKHEATH	BLACKHEATH	C	
200168	BIRKENHEAD PARK	BIRKENHEAD	C	
270168	ROYAL AIR FORCE	TWICKENHAM	W	3G(15)-1PG(3)
030268	NORTHAMPTON	NORTHAMPTON	L	1G2PG(11)-1G2PG1T(14)
100268	UNITED SERVICES PORTSMOUTH	PORTSMOUTH	W	1G2T(11)-0
170268	LLANELLI	LLANELLI	W	1G(5)-1PG(3)
240268	ROYAL NAVY	TWICKENHAM	W	2PG(6)-1PG(3)
020368	LEICESTER	LEICESTER	W	2G(10)-1G(5)
090368	BEDFORD	TWICKENHAM	W	7T(21)-1PG2T(9)
160368	WATERLOO	WATERLOO	W	1G2PG(11)-2G(10)
230368	LONDON WELSH	OLD DEER PARK	L	1G(5)-2PG1T(9)
300368	COVENTRY	COVENTRY	C	
060468	BRISTOL	BRISTOL	L	1PG(3)-1DG1PG(6)
110468	BATH	BATH	L	1G1T(8)-3G2T(21)
130468	SWANSEA	SWANSEA	W	1G2PG1T(14)-1G1PG1T(11)
150468	CARDIFF	CARDIFF	W	1PG3T(12)-1G1PG1T(11)

On 19th September 1968, P.C. Forbes reported that Fritz Grunebaum (a Harlequin member living in America) had contacted him with the offer of a 1st XV tour to America for 12 days involving 6 games. The only cost would be £57 per head for the charter flight to Montreal. Once again, the offer was declined as was one to take part in a Pacific Rugby Carnival in Honolulu in April 1969. Another tour was turned down (this time a lot closer to home) when Camborne RFC offered a trio of three match trips at the start of the 1972, 1973 and 1974 seasons. On 3rd June 1969, the accounts for the 1968/69 season were discussed and it was recorded that a profit of just below £2,000 had been made. On 17th July, it was mentioned that George Palmer (former groundsman at the Stoop) had died. Honours caps were awarded to John Cox and Mike Davis for the season just ended and another possible fixture with the Chicago Lions was turned down as the Club had a rule of not playing any midweek fixtures and a Sunday match was not desirable.

We began the 1968/69 season with a new captain (Bob Hiller) and a trip to Northampton on 14th September. This match was our first in which the new experimental law (later made permanent) where you could only kick directly to touch from inside your own 25 yard line was used. A try put the home side in front, Campbell Hogg dropped a goal to level the scores before a penalty put the Saints back in the lead. We then got two tries through John Cox to lead 9-6 at half time. The game remained close right through the second half, Bob Hiller kicked a penalty for us to which Northampton could only reply in kind to give us a three point victory. Our first home game of the season followed a week later when Llanelli were the visitors in the first of a run for us of eleven consecutive games at Twickenham. We scored seven tries in a 34-12 win before losing our 100% record in a 9-9 draw with Leicester. Swansea were beaten by three points (14-11) and when Gloucester fell on 12th October, our unbeaten record was the only one surviving in senior rugby. The game against Coventry was seen as a kicking duel between our own Bob Hiller and George Cole of Coventry and to a certain extent, it was. Hiller kicked a penalty and two conversions and Cole kicked two penalties and dropped a goal but it was our four tries that swung the match in our favour. Waterloo became cannon fodder and conceded tries by John Cox (2), Paul Harris (2), Paul Parkin, Colin Payne, Nick Martin and Tim Rutter while Bob Hiller kicked five conversions and dropped a goal for a 37-0 scoreline and our biggest win of the season.

On 2nd November, our record was on the line once again, this time against Bristol. By half time we led by eleven points to nil and it looked safe. A miraculous turn around after this saw the visitors outscore us by nineteen points to five and snatch victory by three points. Despite that loss, we still boasted the best first class record in England when we took on Richmond at Twickenham. By half time we led 16-8 through two tries by John Cox (converted by Hiller who added a penalty) and a dropped goal from Nigel Starmer-Smith to a goal and a penalty from Richmond. They doubled their score but a dropped goal from Campbell Hogg kept us in front before tries from Parkin and a third for Cox gave us a well-deserved victory. Good victories followed over the two varsity sides (Oxford 6-3 and Cambridge 19-0) before London Welsh came to Twickenham for a game which was effectively to see who would be the top London club. At half time, a try and a penalty from the Welsh were enough to give them the lead over a Bob Hiller dropped goal in front of a crowd of 10,000. A second penalty from London Welsh full back J.P.R. Williams pushed them three points further in front and they held this lead with just eight minutes remaining. We then came into our own and John Cox scored our first try when he ran through after Hiller had created the overlap. Five minutes later, Bob Lloyd got our second, Hiller converted to put us in front and to cap it all, he picked up a loose ball on the half way line and made it all the way to give us a five point winning margin. Blackheath held us to a draw (9-9) at the Rectory Field and the games against Cardiff and Richmond were cancelled. This meant that our last game of the year was the match squeezed in between against Newport at Twickenham on 21st December. We started having to field eight reserves and things just got worse when our number eight (Roger Hosken) left the field after 30 seconds with a suspected broken jaw (later found to be badly bruised). Not surprisingly, we were well beaten and a half time deficit of eleven points became twenty nine by the end and we failed to score in what was our heaviest defeat of the season.

1969 began with a visit from the Army on 4th January. Once again we were missing players (due to the England trial) but managed to score tries through John Gibbs and Paul Parkin both converted by Campbell Hogg (who also added two penalties) without reply in the first half to lead 16-0. After this we went off the boil as the Army put the pressure on and managed to score a goal and a penalty of their own but it was not enough to prevent us from winning and gaining revenge for our defeat the previous year. P.J. (Paul) Grant made the first of at least 209 appearances for the 1st XV in this match. During the week when playing in a county game, Bob Hiller had the amount of time he spent setting up a place kick called into question by referee Geoff Fenn (who pulled him up twice for time wasting). It was interesting to see that the same referee was to be used in our return game with Blackheath at Twickenham. Although Hiller did take 65 seconds (five more than the time allowed) on one kick, this time Mr. Fenn said nothing. Needless to say, all reports on the game made the most of this but we still managed to win by fourteen points to five (including Hiller's conversion from touch of his own try which bounced on the bar and hit a post before creeping over). Blackheath were not helped when leading 5-3 at half time by losing their full back (Jorden) with a nasty shoulder injury.

Our next match against Birkenhead Park on 18th January and against United Services, Portsmouth on 8th February (both at the Stoop) were cancelled which meant that our next opponents were the Royal Air Force at Twickenham on 25th January. A tight first half saw us lead through a Bob Lloyd try (converted by Hiller) to a penalty goal. The second half was one way traffic and tries followed for us from Pat Orr, Bruce Davies (2), John Cox, Tim Rutter, Mike Novak and Mike Davis with Hiller converting five for a final score of 36-3. Northampton fielded virtually an "A" XV the following week and paid the price as we completed our first double of the season to the tune of seventeen points to eight. Against Llanelli, we lost in the last minute of the game and were outscored by four tries to two (14-16) before defeating the Royal Navy at Portsmouth after trailing by eight points at half time (12-8) and Leicester by again scoring all our points in the second half (11-3). Our third drawn game of the season followed on 8th March at Bedford. We failed to score in the first half for the third match in a row but Bedford could only manage a penalty goal. Bob Hiller levelled with a penalty from almost half way before a try by the home side put them back in front. Mike Novak ran 75 yards for a try which tied the scores and, had he moved in nearer to the posts (which he had time to do), we might well have won the day.

Our second double of the season came on 15th March when we visited Waterloo. A try by Ian Howard in reply to a penalty goal were the only scores in the first half despite Waterloo losing one of their forwards (Mason) with an arm injury. After 11 minutes of the second half, the referee (Mr Devonald) went off feeling unwell and the Waterloo touch judge (Len Reid) took over for the rest of the game. This failed to upset our momentum and tries followed for us from John Cox (2), Paul Grant, Mike Novak, Nigel Starmer-Smith and Colin Payne and with Doug Yeabsley adding just one conversion, our winning margin was restricted to twenty points. The return with London Welsh at the Old Deer Park saw a crowd of 7,000 and another exciting game. Having decided to play against the wind in the first half, we found ourselves trailing by three dropped goals and four penalty goals to just one penalty goal at the break. In a true game of two halves, we started to come back when Novak got a try but the home side got another penalty to restore their lead to eighteen points and this proved to be the crucial score. We managed to score four more tries in the last ten minutes through Payne, Rhys Williams, Hiller and a second from Novak but, as Hiller could only add two conversions to his first half penalty, we lost 22-24. Another victory followed over London Scottish (13-3) but the Easter tour was a total disaster. A defeat at Bath (5-15) was followed by further losses at Swansea (5-17) and Cardiff (15-22). Against Swansea, Doug Yeabsley made his last appearance having scored 47 points in his career (9 tries, 6 penalties and 1 conversion). After this, we did remain undefeated until the end of the season. A good win at Coventry gave us our third double of the season (17-8) and we finished off with only our third ever draw against Bristol in 85 meetings (14-14).

John Cox was again top try scorer (17) and Bob Hiller topped the most points for the sixth successive season with 165 (4 tries, 2 dropped goals, 23 penalties and 39 conversions). His 23 penalties overtook Roger Whyte's record of 21 set in 1957/58 and this led to an overall record of 29 beating the old one set in 1959/60. The dropped goal record was equalled for the fifth time with 6, this was originally set in 1881/82. Tries were up overall by 18 (91), conversions by 14 (46) and points by 100 (470). This season had seen the least amount of losses (seven) since the 1925/26 season (when only six were lost) and of the rest of the games, nineteen were won and four were drawn. Campbell Hogg appeared in all 30 matches and Paul Harris missed just one. The other top appearance makers were David Wrench (27), John Cox and Nigel Starmer-Smith (26) and Colin Payne (25).

1968/69

140968	NORTHAMPTON	NORTHAMPTON	W	1DG1PG2T(12)-2PG1T(9)
210968	LLANELLI	TWICKENHAM	W	5G1PG2T(34)-1PG3T(12)
280968	LEICESTER	TWICKENHAM	D	3PG(9)-3PG(9)
051068	SWANSEA	TWICKENHAM	W	1G2PG1T(14)-1G1DG1PG(11)
121068	GLOUCESTER	TWICKENHAM	W	2G2PG(16)-1T(3)
191068	COVENTRY	TWICKENHAM	W	2G1PG2T(19)-1DG2PG(9)
261068	WATERLOO	TWICKENHAM	W	5G1DG3T(37)-0
021168	BRISTOL	TWICKENHAM	L	2G2PG(16)-2G2DG1PG(19)
091168	RICHMOND	TWICKENHAM	W	2G2DG1PG2T(25)-2G2PG(16)
161168	OXFORD UNIVERSITY	TWICKENHAM	W	2G3T(19)-0
231168	CAMBRIDGE UNIVERSITY	TWICKENHAM	W	1PG1T(6)-1T(3)
301168	LONDON WELSH	TWICKENHAM	W	1G1DG2T(14)-2PG1T(9)
071268	BLACKHEATH	BLACKHEATH	D	3PG(9)-3PG(9)
141268	CARDIFF	TWICKENHAM	C	
211268	NEWPORT	TWICKENHAM	L	0-4G2PG1T(29)
281268	RICHMOND	RICHMOND	C	
040169	ARMY	TWICKENHAM	W	2G2PG(16)-1G1PG(8)
110169	BLACKHEATH	TWICKENHAM	W	1G1DG1PG1T(14)-1G(5)
180169	BIRKENHEAD PARK	STOOP MEMORIAL GROUND	C	
250169	ROYAL AIR FORCE	TWICKENHAM	W	6G2T(36)-1PG(3)
010269	NORTHAMPTON	TWICKENHAM	W	1G1PG3T(17)-1G1PG(8)
080269	UNITED SERVICES PORTSMOUTH	STOOP MEMORIAL GROUND	C	
150269	LLANELLI	LLANELLI	L	1G2PG1T(14)-2G2T(16)

220269	ROYAL NAVY	PORTSMOUTH	W	4T(12)-1G1PG(8)
010369	LEICESTER	LEICESTER	W	1G2T(11)-1PG(3)
080369	BEDFORD	BEDFORD	D	1PG1T(6)-1PG1T(6)
150369	WATERLOO	WATERLOO	W	1G6T(23)-1PG(3)
220369	LONDON WELSH	OLD DEER PARK	L	2G1PG3T(22)-3DG5PG(24)
290369	LONDON SCOTTISH	RICHMOND	W	2G1PG(13)-1T(3)
030469	BATH	BATH	L	1G(5)-2PG3T(15)
050469	SWANSEA	SWANSEA	L	1G(5)-1G4T(17)
070469	CARDIFF	CARDIFF	L	3G(15)-2G2PG2T(22)
120469	COVENTRY	COVENTRY	W	1G1PG3T(17)-1G1PG(8)
190469	BRISTOL	BRISTOL	D	1G2PG1T(14)-1G2PG1T(14)

A proposed tour to Casablanca was discussed on 17th January 1970; it would take place between 12th and 19th May 1970 and three games would be played on 13th, 15th and 17th. The only problem was that it would cost £250 minimum and the financial arrangements were uncertain. It was decided that the availability of players would be ascertained. By 10th February, both this and a tour to France and Spain were dropped because of the unavailability of players. A second tour to South Africa was to be discussed between Lord Wakefield and Danie Craven to see if the climate was right. As our next visit wasn't until 1993, it can safely be assumed that it was decided that the climate was not right! A proposed league was to be discussed at a meeting of gate-taking clubs on 13th February. We did not support the proposal as it was purely for financial reasons and the original idea was to improve the playing standard of the game in England. At a meeting on 10th March, it was decided that, as it was the 50th anniversary of hospitality received from Pennard Golf Club on the Easter tour, a cup would be presented. This would be called the captain's cup and would be played for in the captain's competition; the cost would be in the region of £50. On 10th April it was reported that K. H. Roscoe (our senior Cambridge University representative) had been killed in a car accident. At the Annual General Meeting on 16th July, it was announced that G. V. Carey had passed away; he had kicked off in the first matches at Twickenham and the Stoop. An honours cap was awarded to Mike Novak. The chairman said that the Club was old and ancient in tradition, yet young and vigorous in achievement and it was flourishing. A profit of £1,409 was made on the year. Lady Wakefield had been elected a life member, becoming only the second lady to have the honour bestowed on her; the first had been Audrey Stoop.

Bob Hiller was retained as captain for the last season of the decade and we opened with a 6-6 draw at Twickenham against Northampton on 13th September. After this, we were quickly into our stride and Llanelli were dispatched at Twickenham the following week. Although we did not play well and only led by two penalty goals from Hiller and a try by John Coker to a goal and a try with just 14 minutes remaining, our strength and stamina came through in the end and a try from Ian Howard converted by Hiller (who later added a penalty) made the game safe. It was our captain we had to thank in our next match against Leicester as he proceeded to score all our points. In the first half he kicked two penalties to leave us trailing by two points at half time. He kicked a third to put us in front before A. Chapman got his second for Leicester to snatch the lead back. With just four minutes left, Hiller kicked another penalty and we nosed in front. Then, he intercepted a pass on our 10 yard line and ran 65 yards to seal the game with our first try, the conversion followed to give us a 17-11 victory. Swansea were beaten in a thoroughly distasteful game in which Nick Martin had his nose broken and was also bitten on the arm. This meant we had to play the last fifty minutes with only fourteen men. We won thanks to a penalty and conversion (of a try by Cox) from Hiller to two penalties.

Our first defeat of the season followed swiftly on from this when we visited Kingsholm to take on Gloucester. We did score first and last with tries from Parkin and Davis but fourteen points in between for the home side was enough to take our record. We bounced back with our fourth successive win over Coventry (29-17) and another easy win over Waterloo (30-15) before going down narrowly again to Bristol (21-23). On 8th November, we met Richmond (at the Athletic Ground) for the 150th time and, as on 78 previous occasions, we emerged victorious. By half time, we had scored tries through Lloyd, Novak and Cox with Hiller adding all three conversions and a penalty but we lost Thorniley-Walker to injury and had to play the second half into the wind. Richmond could only manage one try and three penalties to leave us six points in front. Oxford were beaten once again (14-6) as were Cambridge (13-6) although this time the game was played at Cambridge. This was our first game there for 15 years and our first win there since 1945. We met London Welsh on 29th November at Twickenham where the long grass had kept the frost out although snow covered the pitch. We outscored our opponents by five tries to two which helped us to a 21-9 victory. Blackheath were seen off at the Stoop with tries from David Gay, R. Cook, Parkin and Hogg (18-6) and then an "A" XV went to Southend and came away winners by 36-3. This date had become vacant as Cardiff were otherwise engaged.

Our third Welsh visitors of the season were Newport who had consistently been our bogey team since our first meeting in 1883. This time was to prove no exception although we did lead at half time through two penalties from J.M. Wright to a goal. Newport took the lead with their second try before Cox was able to score one for us and restore our advantage. Unfortunately, Gay was penalised by the referee for a deliberate knock on at the back of a line out and the resulting penalty was kicked to give the visitors a two point victory. Our last game of the decade was against Richmond at Twickenham on 27th December. By half time we trailed by five points (6-11), we had managed a Hiller penalty and a try from Lloyd to a goal and two penalties for Richmond. A further penalty for our visitors ended their scoring and by the time Gibbs and Gronow (thanks to an error from a touch judge) had scored and Hiller had added one conversion, we were level at 14-14. At this point, Richmond lost Bucknall (with injuries to both legs) and the game was effectively over as a contest when Hiller kicked a penalty and Hogg dropped a goal. To add insult to injury, Gay and Gronow (converted by Hiller) added tries for a fourteen point winning margin (28-14).

Newcomers during the first half of the season had been D.J. (David) Gay against Northampton (he would go on to gain 4 England caps and score 6 tries for us in 26 appearances in what proved to be his only season), P.J. (Peter) Dixon (the first of 32 appearances against Newport) who was to win 22 caps for England and John Stockdill who appeared for the first of 76 occasions against Richmond on 27th December. We said goodbye to Vic Marriott against Cambridge (he had scored 28 tries during his career for a total of 84 points).

The Army visited Twickenham once again to start the 1970s and were thrashed out of sight. No fewer than nine tries were scored through John Cox (3), Ian Howard (3), Mike Novak (2) and Nick Martin with Bob Hiller landing eight conversions and two penalties to which the solitary reply from the Army was a penalty for a final score of 49-3. Victories followed over Blackheath (19-6) and Birkenhead Park (19-3) before our form took a serious downward spiral. From having a playing record of W14 D1 L3 from eighteen games, we finished with a run-in of just two wins and one draw from our last fourteen matches. A regular occurrence during this decade was the loss of most of the later games in a season. The reasons for this were probably that most of the matches were away from home, a lack of strength in depth existed at the Club and we had the strongest fixture list in the country. The first of the eleven losses was, rather surprisingly against the Royal Air Force at the Stoop. Although we had six men at the England trial we should still have been able to defeat a services side. We were never in front but did manage to level at 3-3 and, in the second half at 8-8 before a final goal and a try saw the R.A.F. pull away. Next up were London Scottish and having to play three quarters of the game with fourteen men after prop John Joannou went off injured did not help our cause and a narrow defeat followed (6-8).

Northampton won by eleven points at Franklin's Gardens (13-24) but we did beat United Services, Portsmouth (9-5) and the Royal Navy (6-3) either side of a single point defeat at Stradey Park to Llanelli (5-6). Bedford came to the Stoop on 14th March for our last home match of the season. We went down by three points (8-11) when Bob Hiller missed a penalty from just outside the 25 yard line nearly in front of the posts right at the end of the game. We couldn't even defeat Waterloo such was our loss of form and, despite leading 8-3 at half time, we allowed them back into the game and they drew level at 8-8. The tour at Easter was, yet again, a disaster and the first match at Bath resulted in our biggest defeat of the season. We did take the lead when Bob Hiller kicked the first of two penalties but didn't get a look in after this as Bath established a lead of six points by half time with a dropped goal, a penalty and a try. It was one way traffic after this and three goals and a try followed for a final score of 6-27. We were unlucky yet again with an injury, this time to Grahame Murray after 24 minutes at Swansea but still managed to lead 6-0 at half time with two penalties from our captain and kicking machine (Hiller) playing at fly half. A goal and a try put the All Whites in front before Novak scored for Hiller to convert only for Swansea to equalise with a penalty. The game was heading for a draw when Mel James got the winning try in the second minute of injury time. In the last match of the tour against Cardiff, the contest was over by half time when we trailed by nineteen points to nil. We won the second half but could only manage two penalties and a conversion of a try by Gibbs from Hiller.

Bristol showed us no mercy and in being outscored by five tries to one (by Bill Petch), we eventually lost by sixteen points (11-27). We travelled to Coundon Road with recent history on our side. We were clearly out fought though and three Hiller penalties were outscored by three goals (including one dropped and one penalty) to give a final score of 9-11 and we had failed to make it five wins out of five against Coventry. Our last match of the season probably couldn't have come soon enough but we still had to travel to the Old Deer Park to play London Welsh where we had registered a draw and three defeats in our previous visits. One newspaper report ranked this loss as our most humiliating defeat of the season as the Welsh played for 45 minutes with 14 men and still dictated play with ease. They scored four tries (two in each half) with one conversion and two penalties completing the rout as we failed to trouble the scoreboard operator for the first time this season.

No significant new players made their debuts in the second part of the season although we did part with a few old friends. Pat Orr made his last appearance against Blackheath on 10th January (having scored two tries in his career), Colin Payne took his bow against Cardiff having scored 29 tries (87 points) and captained the 1st XV on 93 occasions, Roger Lewis said goodbye (with five tries to his name) at Coventry and John Coker (22 tries), Campbell Hogg with 47 points (7 tries, 4 dropped goals, 2 penalty goals and 4 conversions) and David Gay all made their last appearance for us against London Welsh.

The John Cox and Bob Hiller show came top again with 16 tries and 185 points (2 tries, 33 penalties and 40 conversions) respectively. Hiller set another new mark for penalties and overall the record rose to 36. Conversions went up by just two and points and tries were down. The top appearance makers were Bob Lloyd and Campbell Hogg (27 out of 32), John Cox and David Gay (26) and Bob Hiller and John Gibbs (24).

1969/70

130969	NORTHAMPTON	TWICKENHAM	D	1PG1T(6)-2T(6)
200969	LLANELLI	TWICKENHAM	W	1G3PG1T(17)-1G1T(8)
270969	LEICESTER	TWICKENHAM	W	1G4PG(17)-1G2PG(11)
041069	SWANSEA	TWICKENHAM	W	1G1T(8)-2PG(6)
111069	GLOUCESTER	GLOUCESTER	L	2T(6)-1G3PG(14)
181069	COVENTRY	TWICKENHAM	W	4G1PG2T(29)-1G2PG2T(17)
251069	WATERLOO	TWICKENHAM	W	3G1DG2PG2T(30)-1DG4PG(15)
011169	BRISTOL	TWICKENHAM	L	3G1PG1T(21)-1G1DG4PG1T(23)
081169	RICHMOND	RICHMOND	W	3G1PG(18)-3PG1T(12)
151169	OXFORD UNIVERSITY	TWICKENHAM	W	1G1PG2T(14)-2PG(6)
221169	CAMBRIDGE UNIVERSITY	CAMBRIDGE	W	2G1T(13)-1G1PG(8)
291169	LONDON WELSH	TWICKENHAM	W	3G2T(21)-1PG2T(9)
061269	BLACKHEATH	STOOP MEMORIAL GROUND	W	3G1T(18)-2PG(6)
201269	NEWPORT	STOOP MEMORIAL GROUND	L	2PG1T(9)-1G1PG1T(11)
271269	RICHMOND	TWICKENHAM	W	2G1DG2PG3T(28)-1G3PG(14)
030170	ARMY	TWICKENHAM	W	8G2PG1T(49)-1PG(3)
100170	BLACKHEATH	BLACKHEATH	W	2G2PG1T(19)-1PG1T(6)
170170	BIRKENHEAD PARK	BIRKENHEAD	W	2G3T(19)-1DG(3)
240170	ROYAL AIR FORCE	STOOP MEMORIAL GROUND	L	1G1T(8)-2G1PG1T(16)
310170	LONDON SCOTTISH	STOOP MEMORIAL GROUND	L	2PG(6)-1G1T(8)
070270	NORTHAMPTON	NORTHAMPTON	L	2G1T(13)-3G3T(24)
140270	UNITED SERVICES PORTSMOUTH	PORTSMOUTH	W	3T(9)-1G(5)
210270	LLANELLI	LLANELLI	L	1G(5)-1PG1T(6)
280270	ROYAL NAVY	STOOP MEMORIAL GROUND	W	2T(6)-1T(3)
070370	LEICESTER	LEICESTER	C	
140370	BEDFORD	STOOP MEMORIAL GROUND	L	1G1T(8)-1G1PG1T(11)
210370	WATERLOO	WATERLOO	D	1G1T(8)-1G1T(8)
270370	BATH	BATH	L	2PG(6)-3G1DG1PG2T(27)

280370	SWANSEA	SWANSEA	L	1G2PG(11)-1G1PG2T(14)
300370	CARDIFF	CARDIFF	L	1G2PG(11)-2G1DG1PG1T(19)
040470	BRISTOL	BRISTOL	L	1G2PG(11)-3G2PG2T(27)
110470	COVENTRY	COVENTRY	L	3PG(9)-1G1DG1PG(11)
180470	LONDON WELSH	OLD DEER PARK	L	0-1G2PG3T(20)

On 26th August 1970, a touring team from Nova Scotia requested a fixture with us. They were later offered a game against a Wanderers XV but it never took place as there was a change in their charter travel arrangements. At the committee meeting on 22nd September, it was reported that our assistant honorary treasurer (Gordon de Bruyne) had suffered a stroke and, as a result, Clifford Gibbs offered to take on the role which was confirmed on a permanent basis on 27th October. Once again, the difficulties of raising a Quins XV to play midweek was raised and it was decided that the Club should not take on such fixtures. Radio Rentals offered to install a television set rent free in the clubhouse in exchange for a free half page advertisement in the programme from November for the rest of the season. The Club was responsible for loss or damage to the set and it was subsequently insured for 52s 6d. On 20th January 1971, it was advised by G. S. Hamilton that arrangements had to be made to cater with decimalisation as far as the Club's accounts were concerned. This was being brought in during February. On the playing side, the strength of the Club was confirmed at 20 full backs, 25 wingers, 44 centres, 27 fly halves and 33 props (the other positions were not noted). To celebrate the centenary of the Rugby Football Union, there was a proposed match between a Founder Clubs XV and an International XV. This was considered by the committee but such a venture was thought unlikely to be successful.

On 23rd February, Jack Matthews gave a brief outline of a proposed Middlesex Cup competition and the committee considered the proposal at a later date. It was decided that there was little to gain and, subsequently, we did not enter in 1971/72. The new R.F.U. Knockout Cup competition would begin in 1971/72 and it was decided that the gate taking clubs would take part. We would be willing to enter for one season if we were nominated as one of the metropolitan seeds. On 23rd March, a club plaque and a copy of Harlequin Story was to be sent to the Harlequins RFC in Dallas, Texas, USA although affiliation could not be considered yet (this was eventually agreed to some years later). The entry charges for Twickenham and the Stoop had been set for 1971/72 and they were as follows - Ground 20p, Ground and Stand 30p, Vehicles 10p (this was later increased to 15p on 18th August) and Programmes 5p. In the committee report, it was recorded that an honours cap had been awarded to Nigel Starmer-Smith.

A change of captain at the Club saw Bob Lloyd take over for this and the next (1971/72) season. Unfortunately, a change of captain did not ensure a change in fortune on the pitch. Carrying on from where we left off, Northampton were our first visitors to Twickenham on 12th September. There was only ever one team in it and that wasn't us! From the moment they scored their first try in the first minute of the game, it was a question not of who would win but by how many Northampton would win by. As it was, they had managed eleven points by half time and another nineteen in the second half took them to thirty. All we could score were two penalties from Hiller. Far worse was to come in our next match against Llanelli. We were actually leading with a Lloyd try (converted by Hiller) to a penalty when Tony Behn went off with concussion. By half time Llanelli led 14-5 and before we were reduced to 13 (when Mike Novak injured an ankle) they were starting to stretch away at 25-5. The procession got into full swing after this and a further 31 points in 25 minutes completed the rout. This was our heaviest defeat ever, our worst since Oxford University had beaten us 50-0 in November 1900 and a record that would stand for almost 30 years. A Harlequin XV played a midweek match at Ealing on 23rd September and won 24-3, our 1st XV was still without a win though and Leicester were our next opponents. This game was closer than the previous two but we still lost (17-20) and yet again finished a man short. D.M. (David) Coley made the first of 52 appearances for the 1st XV in this match.

Another defeat followed to Swansea (9-19) even though this time they were the team to finish with fourteen players. Against Gloucester on 10th October, our form returned briefly and it was enough to give us victory (despite trailing to two penalties inside five minutes). Hiller kicked two penalties, David Coley dropped a goal and K.F. (Keith) Savage grabbed a try for us to lead 12-6 at half time. Savage was making his team debut and went on to make as many appearances for us as he did for England (13). Keith Jones got a try which Hiller converted and the scoring was complete when he added his third penalty. Gloucester finished with 14 men after lock forward Nick Jackson was sent off. Coventry were narrowly beaten (19-17) and it was like old times when Waterloo were soundly beaten at Twickenham (48-6) in what was to be our biggest win of the season. The try count was 9-0 but it has to be said that injuries and representative calls had taken their toll on Waterloo. Still, the result stood us in good stead for the visit of London Welsh the following week. Disaster struck again after only 13 minutes when Mike Thorniley-Walker went off injured and this set the tone for a nine point defeat (5-14).

Bristol came to visit on 7th November and to the amazement of a lot of people, were out of form and defeated. Hiller was again responsible for most of our points with two penalties and a conversion, our tries being scored by Phil Hayward and Keith Savage while Bristol's reply was a single penalty goal. Richmond (9-3) and Oxford (25-0) were beaten but we could only draw with Cambridge (12-12). This was our first draw with the Light Blues since 1928. A. (Tony) Lewis made the first of 56 appearances in the Richmond match. Blackheath were defeated at the Rectory Field (14-3) with the help of tries from Mike Novak (2) and David Coley but then we faced the might of Cardiff and Newport on successive Saturdays. We were actually leading Cardiff 11-8 at half time but, again we finished with one man short and lost the second half (3-13) and the match. John Cox made his last appearance in this match having scored 105 tries (315 points) and captained the side twice. Against Newport, we fared the same as we always had done at Rodney Parade, we lost. Bob Hiller did kick three penalties at regular intervals but the home side managed four tries (one converted) and a dropped goal (as well as having lock forward L. Martin sent off for kicking an opponent) to run out winners. This was our last match of the year as the return with Richmond was cancelled.

Our expected visit from the Army to the Stoop was cancelled and so our first game of 1971 was the return with Blackheath at Twickenham. Four tries for us in the second half from Hiller, Savage, Novak and Lloyd settled the issue with three penalties from Hiller making absolutely certain of our first double of the season by twenty one points to six. Against Birkenhead Park, we finished with 13 men and went down by the odd point in seventeen before the Royal Air Force came to Twickenham. We exacted revenge for our defeat the previous year with the help of Bob Hiller and his four penalty goals and conversion of a try by Gibbs. The R.A.F. could only manage two penalties and a try in reply. England international C.B. (Claude) "Stack" Stevens made his debut in this game and was to play in eight matches for us (he was in the process of winning 25 England caps). A trip to Richmond to play London Scottish resulted in another victory (12-6) with three Hiller penalties and a try from Lloyd completing our scoring. It was Hiller again (at Northampton) who kicked a penalty and converted a try by Savage. This time though, it was not enough as Northampton had scored twelve points. United Services, Portsmouth were beaten once again and had not tasted victory against us since 1927. John Stockdill (hooker) took over kicking duties in the absence of Bob

Hiller and landed two penalties and a conversion of Mike Mason's try to help us to a win by eleven points to six. E.W. (Earle) Kirton made his first appearance for us in this match. He was to go on and play 69 times having won 13 New Zealand caps.

The following week, we travelled to Llanelli and again, our hooker (this time Gerry Miller) took over kicking duties. He failed to convert tries by Peter Carroll, Nigel Lewis and Mike Mason but did land two important penalties to help us to a four point win (15-11). This victory went some way to repairing the damage caused by their thrashing of us back in September. After nine wins in a row over the Royal Navy, we had a draw at Portsmouth on 27th February. Miller kicked a penalty and Mason scored another try to two tries from the Navy. Savage failed to get on the score sheet to add to his tally of six tries for the Club in his last appearance. At Leicester on the following Saturday, we had a man sent off for only the second time when prop forward Bryce Wilson was dismissed along with Leicester prop J. Dawson near the end for fighting. By this time, the game was over as far as scoring was concerned. Leicester led at the break by a try to nil to which they added a goal and a try in the second half. We could only manage tries from Nick Martin and Mike Mason. On 13th March, we travelled to the Midlands again, this time to Bedford. We were seeking revenge for a defeat at home the previous year and we began well enough so that by half time, we only trailed by three points. Bedford had scored a goal and two dropped goals to tries for us by Earle Kirton (converted by Hiller) and Nigel Starmer-Smith. Midway through the second half, we took control and scored eleven points in a short space of time with tries coming from Novak and Martin and Hiller added one conversion and a penalty. Bedford replied with a penalty and a try but the conversion from the touch line (the last kick of the match) was missed and we had won 19-17.

Our second successive draw at Waterloo was achieved even though we only had 14 men for the last 30 minutes (Nigel Lewis going off injured). Both sides scored two penalties and two tries, ours coming from two Miller penalties and a try each for Martin and Novak. In the return with London Welsh, it looked as though we would be thrashed as they dominated for the first 20 minutes and led 6-0. They became over confident and we cashed in with three tries through Martin, Grant and Lloyd (two converted by Miller) to lead 13-6 at half time. In the second half we failed to score while the home side came back with three tries and two conversions to win by six points. Eight of these points were scored while Mason was off the pitch with badly bruised ribs, so our injury hoodoo had struck again. Another double was completed when we travelled to Coundon Road to take on Coventry on 3rd April. In the first half we outplayed our hosts to a large extent but only led by three tries to two. Another game was ruined by the loss of a player, this time Coventry lost one of their forwards (P. Bryan) with a dislocated shoulder and the result was never in doubt. Charles Bale, Nigel Starmer-Smith and Bob Lloyd added to tries by Lloyd, Phil Hayward and Paul Grant in the first half, John Stockdill converted two and, as Coventry could only reply with a penalty and a try, we ran out easy winners (22-12) to hand them their third defeat in eight days.

The Easter tour followed as did three more defeats. Bath led 17-0 at half time, we were without Nick Martin for the entire second half with a painful ear injury but still managed to score a try (Wilson) and a penalty (Miller) to their single try. Swansea just beat us (11-16) but Cardiff ran away with the game (16-37). Gerry Miller made his last appearance in this game and had scored 48 points in his career (2 tries, 10 penalties and 6 conversions). We then travelled to Bristol for our last match of the season. A close game ensued and two goals for Bristol in the first half were enough to give them the lead over three tries scored by Paul Grant, John Gronow and Mike Novak. We built an unassailable lead in the second half with further tries from Novak (his second) and Tony Lewis and two penalties from Earle Kirton to which Bristol replied with two penalties. This was enough to give us our first double over the West Countrymen since the 1957/58 season. Newcomer D.M. (David) Barry made the first of 91 confirmed appearances in this fixture and came to us from London Irish to get a game as the resident hooker at Sunbury was Ken Kennedy of Ireland.

Mike Novak topped the try scorers with 13 but Bob Hiller retained his crown with 162 points (1 try, 39 penalties and 21 conversions). More penalty records were set as overall the mark rose to 52. Tries (76), points (450) and conversions (30) all fell on the previous year but dropped goals remained the same (2). Out of 32 matches, David Coley missed just two, Bob Lloyd three and Keith Jones, Mike Mason and Gerry Miller made 26 appearances each.

1970/71

120970	NORTHAMPTON	TWICKENHAM	L	2PG(6)-3G3PG2T(30)
190970	LLANELLI	TWICKENHAM	L	1G(5)-7G2PG5T(56)
260970	LEICESTER	TWICKENHAM	L	1G2PG2T(17)-1G3PG2T(20)
031070	SWANSEA	STOOP MEMORIAL GROUND	L	1PG2T(9)-2G3T(19)
101070	GLOUCESTER	STOOP MEMORIAL GROUND	W	1G1DG3PG1T(20)-2PG(6)
171070	COVENTRY	TWICKENHAM	W	2G2PG1T(19)-1G3PG1T(17)
241070	WATERLOO	TWICKENHAM	W	6G1DG2PG3T(48)-2PG(6)
311070	LONDON WELSH	STOOP MEMORIAL GROUND	L	1G(5)-1G1DG2T(14)
071170	BRISTOL	TWICKENHAM	W	1G2PG1T(14)-1PG(3)
141170	RICHMOND	STOOP MEMORIAL GROUND	W	2PG1T(9)-1T(3)
211170	OXFORD UNIVERSITY	TWICKENHAM	W	2G1PG4T(25)-0
281170	CAMBRIDGE UNIVERSITY	TWICKENHAM	D	3PG1T(12)-2PG2T(12)
051270	BLACKHEATH	BLACKHEATH	W	1G1PG2T(14)-1PG(3)
121270	CARDIFF	TWICKENHAM	L	1G3PG(14)-3G1PG1T(21)
191270	NEWPORT	NEWPORT	L	3PG(9)-1G1DG3T(17)
261270	RICHMOND	RICHMOND	C	
020171	ARMY	STOOP MEMORIAL GROUND	C	
090171	BLACKHEATH	TWICKENHAM	W	3PG4T(21)-1PG1T(6)
160171	BIRKENHEAD PARK	TWICKENHAM	L	1G1T(8)-1PG2T(9)
230171	ROYAL AIR FORCE	TWICKENHAM	W	1G4PG(17)-2PG1T(9)
300171	LONDON SCOTTISH	RICHMOND	W	3PG1T(12)-1PG1T(6)
060271	NORTHAMPTON	NORTHAMPTON	L	1G1PG(8)-3PG1T(12)
130271	UNITED SERVICES PORTSMOUTH	STOOP MEMORIAL GROUND	W	1G2PG(11)-1DG1T(6)
200271	LLANELLI	LLANELLI	W	2PG3T(15)-1G1PG1T(11)
270271	ROYAL NAVY	PORTSMOUTH	D	1PG1T(6)-2T(6)
060371	LEICESTER	LEICESTER	L	2T(6)-1G2T(11)

130371	BEDFORD	BEDFORD	W	2G1PG2T(19)-1G2DG1PG1T(17)
200371	WATERLOO	WATERLOO	D	2PG2T(12)-2PG2T(12)
270371	LONDON WELSH	OLD DEER PARK	L	2G1T(13)-2G3T(19)
030471	COVENTRY	COVENTRY	W	2G4T(22)-1PG3T(12)
090471	BATH	BATH	L	1PG1T(6)-1G1DG2PG2T(20)
100471	SWANSEA	SWANSEA	L	1G1PG1T(11)-2G2PG(16)
120471	CARDIFF	CARDIFF	L	2G2PG(16)-5G4T(37)
160471	BRISTOL	BRISTOL	W	2PG5T(21)-2G2PG(16)

26

Sevens in the 1960s

1960-1969

The first and second Seven attempted qualification for the 1960 Middlesex competition but at different grounds (One at Colindale and Two at Thames Ditton). Incredibly, they both claimed a place in the concluding rounds on 30th April. Quins I defeated Vauxhall Motors (14-5), Hendon II (23-0), Old Elizabethans (31-0) and Metropolitan Police I (13-5). The team was John Young, Malcolm Phillips (captain), Joe McPartlin, S.C. Coles, Payne, Fuller and Abbott; Harry Eden, Bill Coutts and Todman were held in reserve. The seconds knocked out R.N.V.R. (5-0), R.M.A. Sandhurst (18-3), Old Rutlishians (8-0) and Rosslyn Park II (13-5) and they were represented by Paterson, Simons, Bob Read, P. Faure, Grahame Murray, Hoare (captain) and Vic Marriott; Bob Mustard, T. Mace and Derek Whiting provided the back up. The previous year's runners-up (London Welsh I) put out the first Seven (3-8) and Richmond I defeated the seconds (9-0) which meant our participation was over by a quarter to two. London Scottish won the trophy by beating the Welsh 16-5.

The following year the first Seven made it again from Colindale by winning against Metropolitan Police II (18-0), Old Hertfordians (14-3), Camelot (6-0) and Saracens I (13-0) but they went out in the first game to London Welsh I (9-13). Young, McPartlin, Simons, M.J. Whiteside, Todman, J.L. Bazalgette and Payne made up the side with G.A.A. Currie, Mallett, Fred Swart and Dave Wrench in reserve. The second Seven tried at Thames Ditton and beat Barclays Bank I (21-0), Streatham I (8-5) and Old Paulines I (13-8) but lost to Oxford (3-6) in the final preliminary round. The holders retained the trophy with a final win over Stewart's College F.P. (20-6). We reached the final of the Esher Sevens by beating (among others) Blundell's Squirrels, St. John's, Cambridge (13-5) and Cambridge University LX (8-5) but lost to Richmond (8-13). Our team was G.A.A. Currie, John Scott, Bill Coutts, P. Faure, Dave Wrench, John Bazalgette and Jeff Abbott. At the Oxfordshire Sevens, we won through the Preliminary rounds, lost in the first round of the finals but went on to defeat Old Colfeians 9-5 in the final of the Plate competition. In the Surrey competition, we beat Camberley (18-0), Wimbledon Athletic Club (10-0) and Old Wandsworthians (11-0) before losing to Voyagers in the semi-final (0-13). We also took part in the Old Gaytonians and Manchester F.C. tournaments and won the Bershire event by beating Oxford in the final.

In 1962, both sides had a change of venue, the firsts were at Beckenham and the seconds at Teddington. Quins I beat Old Shootershillians I (20-5), Old Elthamians (15-0), Maidstone (16-0) and London Scottish II (8-6) but went down to London Irish I in Round 5 (3-6). They were represented by Young (captain), J.D. Gibbs, Read, J.E. Williams, Murray, Bazalgette and Vic Marriott; Abbott and Nick Silk were the reserves. The seconds had a walk over against St. Mary's College but went out in the next round to St. Luke's College, Exeter II (6-8). London Scottish I completed a hat-trick of wins by beating Rosslyn Park I (18-6). They excelled at the Seven-a-Side game and no one came close to causing an upset. The following week, we travelled to France for the Paris Sevens tournament and made the final but London Scottish stood in the way. Williams (2), Read and Young scored tries (Read and Young adding conversions) but the Scots scored 23 points to record another victory. Another semi-final appearance was the best we could do in the Surrey Sevens. We also took part in a Sevens tournament at Bristol in October which was one of the events staged to celebrate Bristol's 75th Anniversary. We were defeated 13-3 by Cheltenham in the opening round and they went on to lose in the final to Bristol. Our squad was Young, Lloyd, Parkin, Coutts, J. E. Williams, Murray, Bazelgette, Wrench, Payne and Marriott.

Both sides tried again in 1963 (at Sunbury) and, although they reached the final rounds, they were unfortunate enough to be drawn against Public School Wanderers and London Scottish I. The first Seven had Harry Eden, Bob Lloyd, McPartlin, Williams (captain), Marriott, Bazalgette and Murray; Read was reserve. They won against National Physical Laboratory II (34-0), Old Beccehamians II (26-0), Honourable Artillery Company I (21-0) and St. Mary's Hospital II (18-5) but the Public School Wanderers proved too strong and ran out 13-10 winners. Our other side (featuring B.J. Bennett, Paul Parkin, Whiteside, J. Spencer, Todman (captain), A.S. Pearson and Adcock with Wrench as a reserve) came through against Metropolitan Police II (6-3), Old Surbitonians I (16-3), St. Thomas's Hospital (11-5) and Oxford (13-3) but the holders continued their run (20-11) and equalled our record with a fourth win on the trot. A record crowd of 40,000 turned up to see them beat Hawick in the final by 15-11. They were seen as the best ever exponents of the shortened version of the game. The Surrey Sevens was a good event for us as we defeated Old Tiffinians (13-3), Merton and Morden (29-3), Old Emanuel (8-5), London Irish (18-0), Rosslyn Park (18-0) and Old Whitgiftians in the final 18-13. The winning team was Paul Parkin, Bob Lloyd, Joe McPartlin, Johnnie Williams (captain), Tony Todman, John Bazalgette and Grahame Murray.

At Sunbury on 18th April 1964, our first Seven beat London French (31-3) and Royal Marines (8-3) but went down to Streatham I after extra time (0-3). The seconds won through against Staines I (15-0), Osterley I (8-5) and Streatham II (11-0). The side, led by Payne and including Cox, Parkin, T.M. Hall, R.P. Lewis, Bazalgette and J.M. Jones, won their first game against London Welsh I (13-8) but Coventry knocked them out (8-11). There was a surprise in the final when Loughborough Colleges I defeated the holders 18-16. The Scottish came within two minutes of a record making fifth title in a row but two late tries saw their hopes dashed. At Sunbury, the venue for the Surrey Sevens, we beat Esher (15-5), Old Wandsworthians (8-0), Wimbledon Athletic Club (15-3), Old Paulines (18-3) and Old Whitgiftians in the final 11-6.

In 1965, the first Seven qualified at Osterley by defeating Polytechnic (36-0), Old Isleworthians (38-0), Borderers (29-5) and St. Luke's College, Exeter II (15-8). The second team were at Beckenham and got through to the last preliminary round where they lost to Old Whitgiftians I (3-8). They won against Park House (17-3), Sevenoaks (18-5) and Sidcup II (11-10). On finals day, Parkin, Lloyd, Bob Hiller, Lewis, Payne, Pat Orr and Todman (captain) beat Melrose (10-8) and St. Luke's College, Exeter I (6-3) but went down to Loughborough Colleges I (6-11). The London Scots were back to winning ways by beating the Students in the final 15-8. We also participated in the Surrey and Berkshire tournaments. In the latter, Quins II defeated Quins I in the final.

The different qualifying grounds in 1966 were Beckenham (firsts) and Southgate (seconds) but only one got through. The main side beat Old Beccehamians I (18-5), Old Brockleians II (37-0), Maidstone (23-0) and Sidcup I (13-3). The second string got past Haringey II (24-3), Northern Polytechnic (13-3), Cambridge (16-3) and Eton Manor (18-10) before going out to Saracens I (5-8). Lloyd, Tim Rutter, Hiller (captain), Whiteside, D. Parry, Orr and J.N. Hancock would try to win with Gibbs, Payne and Todman as reserves. They began well and knocked out Wasps II (29-8), then the holders (15-8) and looked a good side but were disappointing against Northampton in the semi-final and lost narrowly (6-8). The Saints went on to lose 29-10 to Loughborough Colleges I. The crowd of 50,000 had seen the near stranglehold by Scottish broken at last. We took part in the Berkshire Sevens and at the Chiltern Sevens in Amersham we defeated Phoenix I, Old Windsorians I (21-0), Richmond I and Aylesbury II (8-5) to reach the final where London Scottish proved too strong (8-25). In the Surrey Sevens, we triumphed again by beating Sutton (11-0), Old Mid-Whitgiftians (23-5), Streatham/Croydon (8-3), Old Whitgiftians (15-3) and Richmond 26-0 in a one-sided final. In September 1966, we travelled to Cheltenham and got to the final where we lost narrowly to Moseley (10-13).

1967 brought another attempt; the first Seven made it through qualifying at Kidbrooke against Lloyds Bank II (24-0), Old Dunstonians I (18-3), Maidstone (21-0) and Old Askeans I (21-0). The seconds failed at Headstone Lane although they did beat Pinner II (23-0) and London Hospital (21-0) but lost to Streatham/Croydon II (0-10). Bob Lloyd, Tim Rutter, Bob Hiller (captain), Roger Lewis, Mike Mason, Pat Orr and Colin Payne looked a good side and we were due a good run. First up were London Scottish I and we trailed 0-10 at half time before Lloyd and Hiller (2) got tries, the last named converted all three and the game was won. Against Headingley again we trailed with seconds to go by five points but Hiller intercepted and ran 60 yards to score under the posts. His conversion tied it up and after five minutes of extra time, he scored the winning try with a run of 50 yards (16-13). In the semi-final, Northampton held us at 3-3 after the first half but Hiller then kicked a penalty and converted Rutter's and his own try (another long run, this time 75 yards) to take us to 16-3. Although the Saints scored a goal to finish, we were through to the final where we would play Richmond I. Lloyd opened the scoring with a try but Richmond rallied and Stoneman (converted by Moffatt) and Cormack (2) gave them the half time lead. We had been used to coming from behind and this game was to be no exception. Lloyd got his second try (Hiller converted) and our captain added a penalty to make it 11-11. Rutter had the last word with a run in from 30 yards to score the tournament winning try. The crowd of 55,000 (which included our President, Lord Wakefield of Kendal) had seen us lift the trophy for the first time since 1935. At the Surrey Sevens, we won again with a side containing Lloyd, Rutter, Hiller, Mason Orr, Payne and Lewis. They beat Old Haileyburians (walk over), Camberley (44-0), Old Tiffians (19-5), Richmond (8-5), Rosslyn Park (14-0) and Blackheath (13-3). In the first Esher Floodlit competition, we beat London Scottish in the final 9-0 with a team consisting of Lloyd, Rutter, Payne, Hiller, Mason, Lewis and Orr. At the Berkshire tournament, we lost in the final to Oxford Thursday.

Harlequin II attempted to qualify at Osterley in 1968 and beat Woodford (21-0) and Old Isleworthians (19-0) before losing to London Welsh II (0-16). The first Seven were the holders so went through to Round 5 automatically. In that first game, they went out unluckily to London Welsh I. Tim Rutter was off with concussion for five minutes in the first half when a 3-0 lead became a deficit of five points. Back we came to lead 11-8 before another goal sent the Welsh through. John Cox, Lloyd (captain), Nigel Starmer-Smith, Payne, Orr and Mason were the rest of the team with B. Davis in reserve. Our conquerors went on to beat Richmond I in the final 16-3. At Esher, we began our defence of the title in the second round against Rosslyn Park. After beating them 13-0, we accounted for Richmond (18-3) and met Guy's Hospital in the final. Our team was the same as the previous year except for Starmer-Smith and P. Davies for Lewis and Mason respectively. By half time, despite going behind to a try under the posts in the first minute, we were in control thanks to tries from Lloyd (2) and Rutter plus two conversions by Hiller. In the second half, Rutter (2) and Starmer-Smith added more tries which Hiller converted. Guy's did get two tries but we were well clear at the end (28-11). This year also saw the start of our own Sevens tournament but, unlike most other events, this took place in September. The date chosen was 7th September, a week before our opening 1st XV game of the season. There were eight teams in a straight knock-out with the first round losers going into the Plate competition. Bath, Llanelli, North of Ireland, Cardiff, Loughborough Colleges, Blackheath and Melrose were the other seven teams. We beat North of Ireland (11-5) and Llanelli (8-5) but lost to Cardiff in the final by 21-13 (this would be a recurring theme!). In the Plate, Melrose defeated North of Ireland by a single point (16-15). Under the guidance of Howell Thomas and his organising committee, the event would run for over 25 years.

For the last tournament of the decade, both sides attempted to qualify at Osterley and, as usual, only Quins I made it through. They beat Southend II (30-0), Borough Road College (23-5), Ealing I (26-0) and Cambridge (28-3). The seconds won against Hawker Siddeley (26-0), London Transport (16-0) and Borough Road College II (16-0) before succumbing to Oxford I (8-10). The team consisted of Gibbs, Cox, Rutter (captain), John Gronow, P. Harris, Gerry Miller and John Novak with Vic Marriott and Orr in reserve. In the first game, St. Luke's College, Exeter I just sneaked home by 13-10 and went on to beat Edinburgh Wanderers in the final by 21-16. The finals day was regularly attracting over 50,000 spectators and, as a result, the charity donations were on the increase because during the 1960s, over £98,000 was raised. Our fifth win in seven years at the Surrey event was gained by Gerry Miller, P. Harris, Starmer-Smith, Rutter, John Cox, John Novak and John Gibbs. They won against Bec Old Boys (24-3), Voyagers (10-0), Streatham/Croydon (13-5), Blackheath (24-0) and Rosslyn Park (31-10). In our tournament, we lost to Melrose first up and went into the Plate where we defeated Lansdowne in the final. We trailed 0-8 at half time but with help from our captain Bob Hiller (he scored a penalty, two conversions and a 90-yard try) we managed to win 13-11. Llanelli beat Loughborough Colleges 19-11 in the main event.

27

The Knockout Cup and Merit Tables are Introduced 1971-1973

The British Lions went on tour to Australia (two matches against Queensland and New South Wales) and New Zealand in the summer of 1971 and there were three of our men in the squad who became the first (and so far only) Lions to win a series in New Zealand. Bob Hiller didn't get any caps again but played a full part in a very successful trip. "Stack" Stevens joined as a replacement but didn't make the test team whereas Peter Dixon appeared in the first, second and fourth tests and scored the Lions only try in the last. Dave Barry was also a reserve for the tour but was not called upon. The first test was won 9-3, the second lost 12-22, the third won by 13-3 and the fourth was a 14-14 draw.

England made a trip to the Far East in September and October 1971 and Nigel Starmer-Smith, Bob Lloyd and "Stack" Stevens were selected in the party. Lloyd played against Waseda University (captain) (21st September) Japan (24th September), Hong Kong (30th September) and Ceylon (6th and 8th October). Starmer-Smith played against Japan (24th September), Singapore (full back) 3rd October and Ceylon 6th October. As mentioned above, Stevens was called up by the Lions so didn't go on the tour. All seven matches were won although none of the test matches were awarded full status.

On 22nd September, new kit prices were agreed at £1.20 for socks, £2 for shorts and £6 for jerseys. The sad news of the death of Colin Laird was announced on 20th October and the Senior Vice President of the Club Major-General Sir Campbell Clarke also passed away; this being minuted on 24th November. More proposed tours were to Toulouse (playing three matches against Toulouse and District, Arieres and District and Bagniere/Tarbes) between 23rd and 30th April 1972, Algiers in May 1972, United States of America (also in May) and Ceylon. The Ceylon trip was deemed as not viable on 3rd January 1972 as between 70 and 80 people would be required. Coventry had invited us to join them on their American tour but we declined and by February, the French tour was being undertaken by the Bosuns instead of us. There was no more mention of the Algiers tour. It was decided that a major tour should be undertaken as soon as possible. On 23rd February, more deaths were reported; Arthur Moller just before Christmas and Gordon de Bruyne two weeks previously.

At a meeting of London clubs, it was decided that in the R.F.U. Knockout Cup competition in 1972/73

Games should be played by a certain Saturday and not on a fixed Saturday.

All senior clubs would co-operate when two clubs had a game, the other two would play each other.

While a merit table was not favoured, there seemed to be no other method of selection of qualifiers from the south-east. However, it must be on the previous year's results and the major clubs must have six qualifiers from these numbers.

On 15th March, the senior players and senior members of the committee had discussed the current unsatisfactory state of the Club's affairs and came up with a number of proposals. These were accepted with the exception of the first. They were as follows:-

A news-sheet should be distributed once a month to all the membership, giving a resume of all the Club's activities and plans.

The experiment of running an executive committee had hindered communications and should be discontinued forthwith. In future, as in the past, full committee meetings should be held once a month.

Every effort should be made to get greater playing representation on the committee. To secure greater efficiency committee members who either did not attend meetings and/or do their jobs properly should be asked to give up their committee seat forthwith.

The players of the 1st XV and Wanderers to be responsible for putting forward their own nomination for the captain of the Club to the committee. This nomination to be decided at a specially convened players' meeting.

To provide a recognised channel of support, such as the major provincial clubs enjoy with their local clubs, we should tie up with similar clubs in our area (e.g. Esher, Streatham Croydon) who would feed players to us and in reverse absorb our surplus in times of embarrassment. To stimulate recruiting and help the maturing of members joining from school we should endeavour to run an Under-21 XV.

Set up a selection committee composed of the captain of the Club as chairman, the captain of the Wanderers and three others chosen by the Club captain, with the three being prepared to attend matches every Saturday. The captain of the Club, whilst seeking advice in the selection committee, should have the final say on the composition of the 1st XV. With all other XVs a straight vote, where required, would apply. Written or oral reports by other team captains and/or spotters should be made available to the selection committee, but they should not attend selection meetings unless specifically required to do so by the chairman.

The practice of personalised, or named, "A" XVs should be discontinued.

For 1st XV matches at the R.F.U. ground the committee tea-room bar should be closed promptly at 5.30 p.m. The food for the teams would be provided at S.M.G., both steps being designed to encourage players, members, committee and opposition to stay on in our clubhouse.

The facilities, comfort and appearance of the S.M.G. clubhouse to be improved. It was pointed out that plans for this were being drawn up but the go-ahead must await the purchase of the stadium.

The 1st XV Easter tour, with 3 hard matches in 4 days, was proving too onerous and that, therefore, the Bath fixture should be discontinued as soon as possible.

The overall discipline of the Club should be tightened up, and it was the duty of all committee members to give continual support to captains in this regard.

At a players' meeting on 13th April 1972, the following points were made with regard to the principles behind selection for the 1st XV and other XVs:-

The emphasis should be on team building not merely the selection of the best available fifteen players.

A logical progression to the 1st XV should be aimed at and new members as a rule should not go straight into the 1st XV, but should be seen to be joining the Club.

It was important that players in the "A" XVs should be aware that somebody with some influence on selection throughout the Club was watching them.

Every encouragement should be given to young "A" XV players with potential to improve their game and work their way up to the 1st XV.

A system of squad training should be considered.

As a result of these meetings with the players, a playing sub-committee was formed to help with the future development of the playing side of the Club.

It was back to more talk of tours and now we were looking at possibilities in New South Wales, East Africa or Rhodesia in 1973. Requests from Washington and San Francisco for a game in September 1972 were declined. On 17th May, the tour to Australia had reached an advanced stage; it would take place in 1973 or 1974 and six matches would be played. There would be games against the Melbourne Harlequins, a Country XV plus two matches in Brisbane and two in Sydney. The Club would have to finance the travel to Australia only. On 14th June, the admission prices for the forthcoming season were decided at – Ground 30p, Ground and Stand 40p, Vehicles 20p and Season tickets would rise to £4.

The 1971/72 season saw two big changes come in the game. The points value of a try which had been three since the beginning of the 1893/94 season was being increased to four and the Rugby Football Union National Knockout Cup Competition came into being. In the early years, the format was somewhat shoddy as ties were not played on nominated Saturdays but whenever the various clubs could agree to play them, more of which, later. We began with a trip to Harrogate for the start of their centenary season on 4th September. We did not play well and into the second half, we trailed by two goals and three penalty goals to a penalty from Wright, a try by Starmer-Smith and a conversion from Grant. Then, we launched ourselves on a great comeback and J.L. (Jeremy) Cooke and Gibbs got tries to bring us to within four points. Entering the fourth minute of injury time, it looked like we would be defeated but Wilson battered his way over and Wright converted for a two point victory. In our first game under the new scoring system we had benefited as, under the old one, this match would have ended 19-19 instead of 23-21 in our favour.

Northampton defeated us easily (6-20) and one newspaper report suggested it was time we had a regular coach (how things have changed!). We did finish with 13 men but the writing had been on the wall and we never really looked like crossing the Northampton line, Stockdill's two penalties making up our score. We faded against Llanelli to eventually lose by nine points (22-31) but our pack proved too good for Leicester and we outscored them by four tries to one (28-9) for what proved to be our biggest win of the season. Swansea came to Twickenham on 2nd October and we achieved what was to be our last win over them for five years (victories were to be very scarce over the next 25 years) thanks to four John Stockdill penalties and a try from John Joannou to three penalties. Our form was very much up and down and an away trip to Gloucester ended in defeat (4-12) as did a home game against Coventry (4-17) before a respite when Waterloo came to Twickenham. On their eleven previous visits to Twickenham (they had won on their only visit to the Stoop in 1967) they had drawn once and lost the other ten, conceding thirty points or more in six of these. This game was no exception to the "lost" column for Waterloo and three tries in each half from Chris Forth, Bob Lloyd, David Cooke (in the first), Derek Prout, Ian Howard and Earle Kirton (in the second) plus Bob Hiller's conversions of Prout's and Kirton's enabled us to win 28-10. Hiller was playing in his first 1st XV game since returning from the British Lions tour to New Zealand in the summer.

The powerful London Welsh team followed and at half time a Chris Forth try (converted by Hiller) was enough to equal two penalties for the visitors. After 10 minutes of the second half, we lost Bryce Wilson with a suspected broken rib and, although we may still have lost with a full team, we had absolutely no chance with 14 men. It proved to be a complete slaughter and the Welsh ran in eight tries (five converted) in the last 28 minutes for a final score of 6-48. Had the seven British Lions belonging to London Welsh been playing, one can only imagine what the score might have been. The cries for the use of substitutes in club games were now gathering pace although it was to be a few years yet before they were allowed. Bristol gained the first part of what was to be a double revenge for the previous season (10-22) and we drew our only game of the season the following week against Richmond (4-4). Both universities were defeated at Twickenham, Oxford 25-12 and Cambridge 27-9 before an unprecedented weekend on 4th and 5th December.

On Saturday, we met Blackheath at the Stoop and won a ragged encounter 14-6, while on the Sunday at the Athletic Ground, Richmond, we took on London Scottish in the 1st round of the new National Knockout Cup with eleven of the fifteen who had appeared against Blackheath. For the record our team was:- Bob Hiller (full back); Derek Prout, David A. Cooke, Paul Grant and Chris Forth (three quarters); Earle Kirton (fly half) and Nigel Starmer-Smith (scrum half); Grahame Murray, John Stockdill, Peter Johnson, Nick Martin (captain), Maurice Trapp, Ian Howard, Peter Dixon and Mike Mason (forwards). There was a dispute as to when the tie should be played (we did not want to play on a Sunday) and this probably added to the incentive to win. Some of our players played although not fully fit but this was gradually forgotten as we took the lead when Starmer-Smith went over in the corner and Hiller bounced his conversion off the crossbar and kicked a penalty for a 9-0 half time advantage. Ten minutes into the second half, Hiller kicked his second penalty before the Scots scored a try through Patterson to give them some hope. An attempted clearance kick by the Scottish full back enabled Prout and Hiller to send Cooke over for Hiller to convert and we successfully moved into the second round to the tune of eighteen points to four and our cup history had begun.

Despite having the vast majority of possession, we contrived to lose to Cardiff at Twickenham (12-19) before being thrashed at Newport (10-32). On 27th December, we travelled to Northampton for a match which rekindled memories of our first meeting which had been in December 1896. In front of Northampton's biggest crowd for years (7,000), Nick Martin (captaining the side in the absence of Bob Lloyd) roused the forwards for a thrilling second half fight back after we had trailed by a David Cooke try to two tries at half time. Bob Hiller kicked a penalty at the start of the half to cut the lead to one point before Northampton scored their third try to stretch the lead to five. Back we came and when Earle Kirton sold a dummy, Maurice Trapp went with him to score under the posts for Hiller to convert for a 13-12 victory. It would be three years before our next win at Franklin's Gardens.

In the first half of the season, we welcomed M.W. (Maurice) Trapp for his first game against Harrogate (he went on to make at least 75 appearances), D.A. (David) Cooke against Llanelli in the first of 179 confirmed matches (he was to win four England caps) and D.H. (Derek) Prout who only made 8 appearances, his first was against Swansea and his last was against Cardiff (he won two caps for England) and he managed just the one try. Paul Parkin made his last appearance against Leicester having scored 192 points for the Club (61 tries and 3 dropped goals) and "Stack" Stevens appeared for the last time against Oxford University.

The Army visited the Stoop on New Year's Day and, after leading 11-18 at half time, lost by the odd point in 43. The following Saturday saw our 2nd round cup tie against Blackheath (again at the Stoop). We made five changes from the 1st round team and Bob Lloyd was now back as captain. This tie turned into a very poor game in front of a crowd of just 550 (opposed to the 1,600 who saw the London Scottish tie). Blackheath contrived to miss four shots at goal whereas Bob Hiller kicked three (two penalties and the conversion of Paul Grant's try). A half time lead of 9-0 led to a final score of 12-4 and we marched into the quarter finals. A trip to Birkenhead Park on 15th January saw the start of an unbroken ten match winning sequence against the northern side when we escaped with a 13-10 victory. Grant and Hayward scored tries with Stockdill converting one and kicking the winning penalty goal. The R.A.F. were dispatched quite easily at Twickenham (28-10) and London Scottish came looking for revenge after their cup exit on 29th January. In the first half, we trailed by two points as a try by David Coley converted by John

Stockdill (who added a penalty) was not enough to match two tries and a penalty by the Scottish. In the second half, the lead changed hands four more times (added to twice in the first half) and we just edged the scoring 17-16 with tries from Terry Donovan, Mike Bartley and Peter Carroll and one successful conversion and a penalty from Stockdill. This, however, was not quite enough and two goals and a try saw the Scottish home 26-27.

A trip to Sudbury, North London and the home of Wasps was next (this fixture was to become a permanent one from now on). On this occasion we won easily with Hiller kicking three penalties and a conversion and Starmer-Smith and Grant adding tries against a solitary penalty for Wasps. Against United Services, Portsmouth, we lost three men to England but still managed to win 12-0 but the following week at Llanelli we came severely unstuck. We actually led 6-3 at half time and trailed only 12-16 with 10 minutes left but three goals in that time gave the home side a big win. Nigel Starmer-Smith gave an incredible performance of covering and tackling in this game which helped to keep the score down. The Royal Navy were beaten at Twickenham (18-9) but we went down to Leicester at Welford Road (8-15). On 11th March, it was time for the cup quarter final tie against Wilmslow from Cheshire. With five internationals in our side, we were big favourites to make the semi-finals. There was a lot of surface water on the pitch at Twickenham on a dismal day and after just eight minutes we trailed by six points when Wilmslow scored their first try. Hiller kicked a penalty ten minutes before half time but a further goal for the visitors put them 12-3 up. Most of our players had a game they would want to forget but, all credit to Wilmslow as they harried and counter-attacked swiftly. After 66 minutes, the game was won for them when Jones (a centre) dribbled a charged-down kick from Coley some 60 yards for a try. We did finally manage a late consolation try from Peter Dixon but, at 7-16, it was far too little, too late. The victors went on to lose in the semi-finals to Moseley.

We did bounce back to beat Waterloo (16-4) but defeats followed to London Welsh (12-19) and Bath (13-27). The London Welsh match saw the last appearance of Mike Davis who had captained the side on one occasion and scored three tries (10 points) and against Bath we saw the debut of Australian prop J.R. (James) Roxburgh. He played in our last five matches of the season and had gained nine caps for his country. Against Swansea, we were left scoreless after we had lost Murray with a gash beneath his right eye. They scored three goals (including two penalties) and a try after he had left the field. We were not helped by the total failure of four goal kickers who missed seven attempts between them. At Cardiff, we fared slightly better in that we managed one penalty goal from Chris Ryan to the home side's two tries and a penalty to fall to our sixth successive defeat against them. Coventry won a game of ten tries by sixteen points (20-36). We only scored three of them through Ryan, Starmer-Smith and Hiller (who also kicked two penalties and a conversion) before we took on Bristol in our last match of the season on 15th April. This proved to be our sixth successive defeat and we were 0-14 down at half time before scoring a penalty by Hiller and a try from Nigel Lewis. As it was, we lost the second half as well as Bristol managed a goal and a penalty to run out easy winners (7-23). Peter Dixon said farewell in this game after having scored just two tries in his time with the 1st XV. This last defeat meant that our playing record for the season was W17 D1 L18 and for the first time since 1958/59, we had lost more games than we had won.

Paul Grant only scored 9 tries but that was enough to top the list and Bob Hiller yet again got the most points (a lot less than the previous year) with 121 (1 try, 27 penalties and 18 conversions). Tries scored fell again to 73 as did penalties (but only one short of equalling the record total of the previous season). Dropped goals went up by one and conversions by two whereas points shot up by 68 (due to the rise in the value of a try). Paul Grant appeared in 29 of 36 matches, the best of the others being Maurice Trapp (27), David Cooke (26) and Nigel Starmer-Smith (25).

England travelled to South Africa and played a one-off test match in June 1972 which was won. "Stack" Stevens played in the game but our other tourist, Peter Dixon was not in the team.

1971/72

040971	HARROGATE	HARROGATE	W	2G1PG2T(23)-2G3PG(21)
110971	NORTHAMPTON	TWICKENHAM	L	2PG(6)-2G2T(20)
180971	LLANELLI	TWICKENHAM	L	2G2PG1T(22)-2G1PG4T(31)
250971	LEICESTER	TWICKENHAM	W	3G2PG1T(28)-1G1PG(9)
021071	SWANSEA	TWICKENHAM	W	4PG1T(16)-3PG(9)
091071	GLOUCESTER	GLOUCESTER	L	1T(4)-1G2PG(12)
161071	COVENTRY	TWICKENHAM	L	1T(4)-1G1PG2T(17)
231071	WATERLOO	TWICKENHAM	W	2G4T(28)-1G1T(10)
301071	LONDON WELSH	TWICKENHAM	L	1G(6)-5G2PG3T(48)
061171	BRISTOL	TWICKENHAM	L	1G1T(10)-3G1T(22)
131171	RICHMOND	RICHMOND	D	1T(4)-1T(4)
201171	OXFORD UNIVERSITY	TWICKENHAM	W	2G3PG1T(25)-4PG(12)
271171	CAMBRIDGE UNIVERSITY	TWICKENHAM	W	1G1DG2PG3T(27)-1G1PG(9)
041271	BLACKHEATH	STOOP MEMORIAL GROUND	W	2PG2T(14)-1G(6)
051271	LONDON SCOTTISH(RFU1)	RICHMOND	W	2G2PG(18)-1T(4)
111271	CARDIFF	TWICKENHAM	L	1G2PG(12)-2G1DG1T(19)
181271	NEWPORT	NEWPORT	L	2PG1T(10)-3G2DG2T(32)
271271	NORTHAMPTON	NORTHAMPTON	W	1G1PG1T(13)-3T(12)
010172	ARMY	STOOP MEMORIAL GROUND	W	1DG1PG4T(22)-1G1PG3T(21)
080172	BLACKHEATH(RFU2)	STOOP MEMORIAL GROUND	W	1G2PG(12)-1T(4)
150172	BIRKENHEAD PARK	BIRKENHEAD	W	1G1PG1T(13)-1G1T(10)
220172	ROYAL AIR FORCE	TWICKENHAM	W	1G2PG4T(28)-1G1T(10)
290172	LONDON SCOTTISH	TWICKENHAM	L	2G2PG2T(26)-2G1PG3T(27)
050272	WASPS	SUDBURY	W	1G3PG1T(19)-1PG(3)
120272	UNITED SERVICES PORTSMOUTH	PORTSMOUTH	W	1G1DG1PG(12)-0
190272	LLANELLI	LLANELLI	L	1G2PG(12)-4G2PG1T(34)
260272	ROYAL NAVY	TWICKENHAM	W	2G2PG(18)-1G1DG(9)
040372	LEICESTER	LEICESTER	L	2T(8)-2G1PG(15)
110372	WILMSLOW(RFUQF)	TWICKENHAM	L	1PG1T(7)-2G1T(16)
180372	WATERLOO	WATERLOO	W	1G2PG1T(16)-1T(4)
250372	LONDON WELSH	OLD DEER PARK	L	1G2PG(12)-2G1PG1T(19)

310372	BATH	BATH	L	1G1PG1T(13)-2G1PG3T(27)
010472	SWANSEA	SWANSEA	L	0-1G2PG1T(16)
030472	CARDIFF	CARDIFF	L	1PG(3)-1PG2T(11)
080472	COVENTRY	COVENTRY	L	1G2PG2T(20)-1G2PG6T(36)
150472	BRISTOL	BRISTOL	L	1PG1T(7)-2G1PG2T(23)

England undertook a tour to South Africa in May and June and our only representative was Brian "Stack" Stevens and he played in the only test which was won by 18-9. The other games saw five wins and a draw which all added up to a very successful trip.

On 22nd August it was reported that a French team from St. Girons would be coming over to play Richmond on 2nd September and us on 3rd; in the event, the game never took place. On 30th November, two more deaths were reported. Tim Stoop (from 1907-1922) and Fred Dunkley (from 1937-1948) both passed away. On 19th December, a tour was finally decided on which would actually go ahead. The trip to East Africa was set for 3rd to 20th May 1973. On 24th January, another question of affiliation came from the Harlequins RFC from Denver, Colorado, USA. They were told that the Club had to establish itself over several more seasons before it could be considered for affiliation. Proposed visits from Randwick and Northern Suburbs, Sydney were set for 1973/74 and it was decided that we would not be taking part in the Middlesex Cup in that season. On 30th May it was recorded that an honours cap had been awarded to Earle Kirton. The same date saw the admission prices decided for the forthcoming season – Ground 35p, Ground and Stand 50p, Car Park 25p and Season tickets £4.50. On 12th June, the committee heard that the cost of the Australian tour would be between £8,000-9,000; it was now being planned for August 1974.

The sale of Teddington had been ongoing since March 1968 and was finally completed in 1971. It all started when the Council offered to negotiate or enforce a compulsory purchase order as they wanted to build a school on the land. It was decided on 7th March 1968 to sell the ground to the local authority for the highest possible price receivable in cash. Use the smallest possible portion of the net proceeds of the sale necessary to stabilise the rent commitment for the remainder of the licence period of 42 years on the Stoop or, if this cannot be negotiated economically, to obtain a longer term at a flat rent. Invest the remaining capital sum to the best advantage in suitable securities with the object of providing a capital fund to acquire, if necessary, a new ground at the end of the term at the Stoop and to obtain an income on it. Teddington had been purchased in or around October 1923 comprising 9¼ acres. In 1963 two acres had been sold to Twickenham Borough Council for £12,000 and council houses had been built on it. An offer of £185,000 for the purchase of Teddington by the local authority would be put on hold until a price for the freehold for the Stoop could be obtained. In January 1970, it was estimated that it would cost £8,400 per year to run the Stoop but this did not include depreciation or redecoration of the stand, clubhouse or drainage and re-turfing of the pitches. It was also decided that it was imperative that no details of this were given to the press. By 10th March, the Council had decided that they were prepared to sell the Stoop to the Club for £100,000 with an additional £60,000 payable if the ground was sold for redevelopment. An offer was to be made of £85,000 with the further premium to be negotiated. On 6th July, it was decided to sell the freehold on Teddington for £185,000 subject to the purchase of the Stoop for £90,000 with a fee of £100,000 to be paid if redevelopment occurred within 5 years (£75,000 if the ground was redeveloped after this). Approval was agreed in principle for the purchase of a house for the groundsman at the Stoop. On 23rd February 1971, it was anticipated that the sale of Teddington would be complete within the next few weeks. A special committee meeting was called at the East India and Sports Club on 6th April to discuss the proposed purchase and the proceeds from the sale of Teddington (to be completed on 24th March) which would leave £180,000 to invest. The committee report for 1970/71 reported that the sale had gone through. On 7th June, it was reported that after the purchase of the Stoop, there would be £74,000 left for investment. Income was reported to be £7,120 whereas the estimated running costs for the Stoop would be £7,000 which made it a viable option. On 24th November, a 999 year lease on the Stoop with a purely nominal rent was considered but, after all this, the sale of the Stoop to the Club was completed on 18th July 1973.

Earle Kirton became captain for the 1972/73 season but missed the first game where Bob Read led the side in his absence. Again we started with a centenary match, this time in Durham against Durham City. At best it was a half strength team which made the long journey on 2nd September. In the first half, Bob Read went off with a broken arm and in the second Tom Walpole (our hooker) left the pitch with a broken leg. As it was, Durham went on to win by two tries to a goal in a typical early season game. Northampton blew us away in the second half after we had led 15-3 at half time, scoring twenty five points without reply and we went down narrowly to Llanelli (15-20) with Bob Hiller keeping us in touch yet again. This run of defeats was to go on and on to equal our worst ever start to a season (which had happened in 1898/99) with eight defeats in a row. Next up was a visit from Leicester on 23rd September and, as they had already notched up 150 points and four wins out of four, were in no mood to lose their unbeaten record. It was all square at half time, two goals for Leicester were matched by a try from Nigel Lewis and a conversion and two penalties by Bob Hiller. It seemed as though we were relying on him more and more as the games went on. Dave Cooke scored our second try again converted by Hiller but Whibley converted all three Leicester tries in the second half (as he had done with both in the first) to enable them to win by twelve points (18-30).

On 30th September, it was cup time again and a visit to Twickenham by London Welsh. This match was also the first in the new London League which would be used to determine who would qualify for the next season's cup competition. Every match against a team in the league would count although in later years, only one would count and matches were demerited when a team was weakened because of the County Championship. At half time, we trailed by a try from Earle Kirton (converted by Hiller) to two tries and a dropped goal. Unfortunately for us, Paul Grant injured an ankle in the first five minutes and Kirton sustained severe concussion in scoring his try. This meant we were effectively down to 13 men (although Grant stayed on the field) for the entire second half. The tie became a farce as the Welsh ran in seven tries (three converted) to one for us by Chris Forth (converted by Hiller) to leave us trailing by 33 points and dumped out of the cup in the first round. Swansea became our next conquerors, but only by a single point when they kicked a penalty in the 93rd minute of the match (9-10). T.C. Terry Claxton played the first of at least 223 games against Swansea and would go on to become captain of the Club. He was an uncompromising, no nonsense prop forward who took no prisoners. Against a Gloucester side which was being criticised in the press for being blatantly intimidating, we were scoreless for the whole game but a goal, a penalty and a try saw them home. Defeat number eight came in our first meeting with Rosslyn Park since 1965. Things were looking extremely bleak for us now and the closest we got was when Hiller kicked a penalty at the start of the second half to leave us trailing by eight points (3-11). A further two goals and a try for the visitors put the seal on their victory. This was our fourteenth successive defeat (including the last six from the previous season) and was only one short of our all-time run without a win (between October 1876 and March 1877) of 15 matches. This was made up of five defeats, three matches drawn in favour and seven drawn against. It was perhaps lucky for us that Waterloo were our next opponents. A 15-0 half time lead seemed to be enough but we were made to struggle and lost the second half by eighteen points to eight. Hiller was again in form with the boot and kicked three penalties and a conversion to add to tries from Nigel Lewis, Dave Cooke and Nigel Starmer-Smith. Waterloo managed two goals and two penalty goals to give us our first victory since the away win over the same opponents back in March.

Our next test was against Bristol at the Stoop on 4th November. In what was Bristol's worst first half of the season so far, Hiller landed two penalties and a conversion of one of two tries from Grant to a penalty. It looked a bit ominous when Bristol came back to within a point just 14 minutes into the second half but, thankfully, it was only a temporary glitch and further scores from Starmer-Smith and Hiller (who also added a penalty and one conversion) saw us chalk up our biggest win over Bristol since 1964 and our highest score against them in 15 years. This was to be our last win over them for sixteen years, a span of some eighteen games. We lost by a single point in a morning game against Richmond (8-9) and lost to Oxford University for the first time in nine years (16-26 - their highest total against us since November 1939), partly thanks to us losing Tony Lewis (a flanker) for 55 minutes of the match when we led 13-0. Cambridge University finished with 13 men and we won easily enough by twenty points to six before going into a nose dive for most of the rest of the year. Blackheath edged us out by two points (12-14), Cardiff inflicted our heaviest defeat of the season (when we lost four men to the England trial), scoring ten tries to two (8-47), Penryn (another centenary game) beat us by the same score as Blackheath, Richmond completed the double over us (0-22) as did Northampton with a convincing win on Boxing Day (14-29). Our last match of the year was on 30th December at Richmond against London Scottish. We had lost five out of five encounters with London opposition but, with a committed defence, we managed our first win by the narrowest of margins (12-11).

Several new players appeared in the first half of the season including a number of long-termers. C.D. (Chris) "Bootsy" Barrett appeared against London Welsh for the first of at least 119 games, J.H. (John) "Harry" Burroughs (first of at least 61), T.C. (Terry) Claxton (first of a confirmed 223) and R.F. (Roger) Looker (first of at least 87) all made their debuts against Swansea and Maurice Rocks played in the first of a confirmed 78 matches against Oxford University.

In a bright opening to the New Year, the Army found us just too good (despite having to play the entire second half with fourteen men). When they lost one of their centres (Lt. P.M. Davies) at half time, they were trailing by sixteen points to nil. Bob Hiller had converted two of our three tries by Nigel Lewis, Paul Grant and Dave Cooke and he managed the same ratio in the second when Grant and Cooke both got their second and Nigel Starmer-Smith scored our sixth try. In an amazing turnaround, the Army scored 25 points (three goals, one penalty and a try) during the second half and, by the end, had nearly done enough to win the game. Revenge was gained over Blackheath (25-15) and Birkenhead Park were also beaten (23-15). Against the Royal Air Force, a half time lead of twenty points to nil became a rout when another twenty one were added without reply. Harry Burroughs got a hat-trick of tries, Ian Howard got two and the others were scored by Nigel Lewis and Dave Cooke, Bob Hiller kicked three penalties and just two conversions. This was not our biggest win of the season though as this was left for another services team. We were becoming one of the teams to watch and against Wasps (in our first meeting at Twickenham since 1927), we again scored over forty points. They did lose a man injured but a half time lead of just 10-6 had become another easy win by the end. Eight tries in all and four conversions and two penalties gave us a 46-9 victory.

United Services, Portsmouth came to the Stoop on 10th February with a weakened team as the Royal Navy were playing across the road at Twickenham in the Inter Services Championship. By the end, they had been absolutely blitzed, conceding fifteen tries in a seventy six points to nil demolition. This was our highest score of this or any other season since Bedford were beaten by the same score on 25th September 1920 at Twickenham. Our tries came from Dave Cooke (3), Ian Howard (3), Paul Grant (2), Bob Hiller (2) (he also added eight conversions), Nigel

Lewis, Bob Lloyd (2) and Nigel Starmer-Smith (2). Against Llanelli the following week, we found ourselves down by 18 points at the break (4-22). We did rally late in the game and managed four tries to two in the second half but, it was not enough and we lost our first game of 1973 (22-32) after six straight wins. Dave Cooke picked up a dropped ball and ran 45 yards to score our winning try against the Royal Navy at Portsmouth (13-9) and another good game saw Bob Hiller score a try, three penalties and two conversions at Leicester. We trailed by nine points early on but Starmer-Smith scored our first try and Hiller added fourteen points to put us 18-9 up at the break. A goal and two penalties put the home side back in front before Dave Cooke touched down and Hiller kicked his third penalty just before the end to ensure victory (25-21).

Against Bedford, we were dominated in the rucks and mauls but our speed and handling skills shone through for us to record another win (23-16). The Old Deer Park was not becoming a happy hunting ground for us and this is where we went next. We did manage to score the same as in September and reduced the Welsh score to thirty five but it was still a large margin of defeat. Our match with Rosslyn Park at Roehampton on 31st March had become crucial to our chances of qualifying for the following season's knockout cup. This now depended on where you finished in your respective area (we were in the London table of clubs). At half time, we trailed by just three points, Park had scored two goals and we had a penalty from Hiller (who converted a try from Grant). Another Hiller penalty and conversion of a try by Tony Lewis put us six points in front before, in injury time, Park equalised with their third goal. We then got a penalty when the home side were penalised for deliberately knocking the ball into touch and up stepped Hiller to boot it over from 40 yards out and near to touch for a tremendous win to give us four wins from our ten London League matches.

Bristol got revenge for their earlier defeat by twenty two points to ten at the Memorial Ground and our first meeting with the Metropolitan Police since October 1954 led to a 25-10 victory. Bob Hiller, our king of scoring kicked four penalties and a conversion, Earle Kirton dropped a goal and Paul Grant and Mike Novak scored tries. Bath wiped the floor with us in our first Easter tour game (10-37) and our total for all three games would not put us past their total. Our squad on the tour was a depleted one and it was, therefore, hardly surprising that we lost at both Swansea (13-28) and Cardiff (in our last match of the season) (10-28). In this game, Mike Thorniley-Walker (usually a back row man) played on the left wing and Stuart Winship (a scrum half) played at full back. Tony Lewis got our try and Earle Kirton kicked two penalties in reply to two goals and four tries from Cardiff.

In the second half of this season, J.R. (Jonathan) Legg made his debut against U.S. Portsmouth on 10th February (he would go on to make 62 appearances for the 1st XV) and Stuart Winship was playing in the first of 66 matches in the Swansea game. We did bid farewell to a number of old stagers as well. John Joannou appeared in his last match against the R.A.F. (he had scored three tries in his career) and Bob Lloyd (having scored 308 points (99 tries and 1 dropped goal) and captained the side 93 times) and all-time record appearance maker Grahame Murray (at least 301 games (77 as captain) and 24 tries (73 points)) having made his debut back in March 1959 made their last appearances in the Bath game. Rhys Williams finished in the Swansea game (having scored just two tries since making his first appearance in 1962) and Bob Read having scored 78 points (7 tries, 5 dropped goals, 8 penalties and 9 conversions) and captained the team once and Nigel Starmer-Smith (89 points made up of 21 tries and 4 dropped goals) both ended their careers with the 1st XV against Cardiff. Starmer-Smith went on to pursue a successful career as a sports commentator.

Dave Cooke had been in great form and ended up as top try scorer with 17 and Bob Hiller set a new points scoring record with 262 (8 tries, 1 dropped goal, 43 penalties and 49 conversions). He overtook Douglas Lambert's mark set in 1909/10 (253), his forty three penalty goals were also a record. Overall, tries (98) were the best since

1964/65 (130), penalties were again one short of the record, conversions were up by twenty (52) and finally, points were at an all-time high (655) beating the previous best set in 1964/65 of 597. Out of thirty six games (it had been a disappointing season with just fifteen victories), our captain played in 32 as did Mike Mason, Bob Hiller and Paul Grant appeared in thirty, Nigel Lewis and Terry Claxton were seen in 29 and Dave Cooke and Roger Looker (28) and Maurice Trapp (27) were the other front runners.

1972/73

020972	DURHAM CITY	DURHAM	L	1G(6)-2T(8)
090972	NORTHAMPTON	TWICKENHAM	L	2G1PG(15)-2G1DG3PG1T(28)
160972	LLANELLI	TWICKENHAM	L	2G1PG(15)-2G2T(20)
230972	LEICESTER	TWICKENHAM	L	2G2PG(18)-5G(30)
300972	LONDON WELSH(RFU1)	TWICKENHAM	L	2G(12)-3G1DG6T(45)
071072	SWANSEA	TWICKENHAM	L	3PG(9)-2PG1T(10)
141072	GLOUCESTER	TWICKENHAM	L	0-1G1PG1T(13)
211072	ROSSLYN PARK	TWICKENHAM	L	1PG(3)-2G1PG3T(27)
281072	WATERLOO	TWICKENHAM	W	1G3PG2T(23)-2G2PG(18)
041172	BRISTOL	STOOP MEMORIAL GROUND	W	2G3PG2T(29)-2G1PG(15)
111172	RICHMOND	STOOP MEMORIAL GROUND	L	2T(8)-3PG(9)
181172	OXFORD UNIVERSITY	TWICKENHAM	L	4PG1T(16)-2G1DG1PG2T(26)
251172	CAMBRIDGE UNIVERSITY	TWICKENHAM	W	2G2T(20)-1G(6)
021272	BLACKHEATH	BLACKHEATH	L	1G2PG(12)-1G2T(14)
091272	CARDIFF	STOOP MEMORIAL GROUND	L	2T(8)-2G1DG8T(47)
161272	PENRYN	PENRYN	L	4PG(12)-2PG2T(14)
231272	RICHMOND	RICHMOND	L	0-1G4T(22)
261272	NORTHAMPTON	NORTHAMPTON	L	1G2T(14)-2G2DG1PG2T(29)
301272	LONDON SCOTTISH	RICHMOND	W	2G(12)-1PG2T(11)
060173	ARMY	STOOP MEMORIAL GROUND	W	4G2T(32)-3G1PG1T(25)
130173	BLACKHEATH	TWICKENHAM	W	2G3PG1T(25)-2G1PG(15)
200173	BIRKENHEAD PARK	TWICKENHAM	W	2G1PG2T(23)-1PG3T(15)
270173	ROYAL AIR FORCE	TWICKENHAM	W	2G3PG5T(41)-0
030273	WASPS	TWICKENHAM	W	4G2PG4T(46)-1G1PG(9)
100273	UNITED SERVICES PORTSMOUTH	STOOP MEMORIAL GROUND	W	8G7T(76)-0
170273	LLANELLI	LLANELLI	L	1G4T(22)-2G5T(32)
240273	ROYAL NAVY	PORTSMOUTH	W	1G1PG1T(13)-1DG2PG(9)
030373	LEICESTER	LEICESTER	W	2G3PG1T(25)-2G3PG(21)

100373	BEDFORD	BEDFORD	W	2G1PG2T(23)-1G2PG1T(16)
170373	WATERLOO	WATERLOO	C	
240373	LONDON WELSH	OLD DEER PARK	L	1G2PG(12)-4G1DG2T(35)
310373	ROSSLYN PARK	ROEHAMPTON	W	2G3PG(21)-3G(18)
070473	BRISTOL	BRISTOL	L	1DG1PG1T(10)-1G1DG3PG1T(22)
140473	METROPOLITAN POLICE	STOOP MEMORIAL GROUND	W	1G1DG4PG1T(25)-2PG1T(10)
200473	BATH	BATH	L	1G1T(10)-5G1PG1T(37)
210473	SWANSEA	SWANSEA	L	1G1PG1T(13)-2G4PG1T(28)
230473	CARDIFF	CARDIFF	L	2PG1T(10)-2G4T(28)

28

The Second East African Tour
May 1973

The second tour to East Africa had been arranged with just four months preparation and the Four Home Unions had approved it on 23rd February 1973. One of the main reasons for the trip was to celebrate the 21st Anniversary of the Kenya Harlequin Football Club. It took place between 5th and 19th May and the party was made up of the following players:- E.W. Kirton (captain); C.D. Barrett, D.M Barry, J.H. Burroughs, T.C. Claxton, T.J. Donovan, N.H. Drury, C. Forth, P.J. Grant, J.D. Gronow, K.G. Jenkins, J.R. Legg, T.A. Lewis, N.L. Lewis, M.J. Mason, G.C. Nicholls, W.L. Petch, R.F. Read, M. Rocks, T.W. Ross, P.D. Snare, J. Stockdill, M. Thorniley-Walker, J.N. Whipp and D.R. Williams. Vic Roberts was the tour manager, J. Seldon was his assistant, M.J. Hollins was the physio and Dr R. Rossdale was our doctor.

The touring party along with forty supporters flew from London's Heathrow Airport on 3rd May on board a Boeing 747 of British Overseas Airways Corporation (BOAC) to Nairobi and internal flights were by Douglas DC-9 of East African Airways. Otherwise, journeys were made by coach and the combination of narrow roads and local drivers did not help the nerves of the travellers!

In the first match played against Scorpions at Ngong Road, Nairobi on 5th May, it was soon clear that the playing standards in the area had dropped since our last visit. Our pack had plenty of ball and were quicker than the opposition and we were in front when Grant finished off a 60 yard move. Nicholls dropped a goal from the halfway line and the ball went through level with the top of the posts; this was the effects of altitude (here it was 7,400 feet). Mason grabbed another try but Parker pulled one back for the Scorpions which Jones converted. Before half time, Grant got his second for Kirton to convert and we led 17-6. The second period was one way traffic and tries followed through Gronow, Burroughs, Donovan, Barry and Grant (Nicholls converted the second and last) as we got off to a great start with a 41-6 final score.

Next up were West Kenya at Nakuru three days later and this game was limited to 35 minutes each way because three of the opposition (who were travelling over 100 miles through hill country) had a puncture and arrived after the scheduled kick-off time. Of course, the visitors were more than happy to wait and the young Quins side notched another victory. Nigel Lewis on the wing scored five tries with others coming from Read and Ross. John Stockdill kicked a penalty and five conversions and the only response was a try from Barlow to make the final score 41-4.

It was back to Ngong Road on 10th May for our third match against Nairobi Clubs. This was expected to be one of our toughest games but once again, fitness and teamwork told and another big victory followed. We took the lead when Dave Barry got the first try but Evans kicked a penalty to make it 4-3. As the opposition were worn down,

Williams and then Burroughs (from an excellent cross-field kick) got further tries to make it 12-3 at the interval. Barry got two more at the start of the second half followed by Snare (converted by Kirton), Kirton and Barry with his fourth to give us a big lead. A great run by Nigel Lewis was carried on by Barrett and Williams went over in the corner and Nicholls put Grant over for our tenth try. Kirton converted this but eight had been missed and the final score of 44-3 could have been much greater. It is interesting to note that Stockdill (a hooker) was our only recognised goal kicker on tour.

At the Mombasa Sports Ground on 12th May, we met a Mombasa Invitation XV. Torrential rain eventually gave way to continuous drizzle; the ground was soggy and the ball slippery. This match was played at sea level and the humid conditions proved exhausting but another victory was gained. Our traditional running style proved too much for the Invitation side with four tries scored in the first half and five in the second through Snare (2), Thorniley-Walker (2), T. Lewis (2), Ross (2) and Legg. Stockdill kicked a penalty and four conversions to make it 47-0.

The fifth game was played at the Gymkhana Ground in Dar es Salaam, Tanzania three days later and our opponents were another selection side, this time called a Tanzania Invitation XV. Despite losing Chris Forth with sunstroke, we literally ran amok and set a new record score for the Club. The previous best of 76-0 was set in September 1920 against Bedford and equalled a few months before the tour in February against United Services Portsmouth. Our tries came thick and fast from Forth (2), Snare (3), Ross (4), Jenkins, Drury, Williams, Thorniley-Walker (2), Mason, Donovan (2) and Nicholls (who added no fewer than eleven conversions). Although close to a record, Nicholls fell two short of the thirteen kicked by G.F. Elmslie back in December 1908 against Surbiton. The final score of 94-0 would have been even greater had the game not been limited to 30 minutes each way. The total was surpassed on the 1986/87 tour to Australia and South East Asia but the winning margin remains the best ever.

On 17th May, we found ourselves back at Ngong Road to play the Kenya Harlequin team and they had asked that the side played its normal game and requested that Earle Kirton be in the side. At half time, we had moved 26-0 ahead with tries from T. Lewis, Barry, Jenkins, Burroughs and Legg plus three conversions from Nicholls. We continued in the same way after the break and further tries followed from Jenkins, N. Lewis (2), T. Lewis and Burroughs (3). Nicholls and Forth added a conversion each and the hosts managed a try near the end from Bean which was converted by Allison to make it 58-6.

The seventh and final game was played once again at Ngong Road and our opponents were Kenya Clubs. This proved to be the hardest match of the tour and the result was in doubt right to the end. Some of the selected team were not fully fit and this hampered us but we managed to build a lead with a try from Gronow and a conversion and penalty by Read before Kenya Clubs got a try to make it 9-4 at half time. Donovan grabbed a brace but Rowland pulled back three points with a penalty and Kabetu scored a try before Read kicked another penalty to give us a nine point lead. When a maul erupted and the referee was knocked off balance, Terry Claxton was sent off (he had apparently been warned earlier) and we were down to fourteen men. Kenya Clubs ran in a try through Mitchell, didn't bother with the conversion and tried to get the next score to win the game but time ran out and we finished with a 100% record. There was some confusion as to how to deal with the sending off and the case was eventually heard at the House of Lords on return to England. Lord Wakefield of Kendal (President), Earle Kirton (captain), J. Seldon (secretary) and Vic Roberts (tour manager) decided that Terry would be reprimanded by letter and suspended for the first week of the 1973/74 season. This was communicated to the East African Rugby Union who were happy with the decision.

It was noted in the tour manager's report that our hosts were incredibly generous and made the stay a memorable one. Barbeques, discotheques and dances were the order of the day and the Club had given a 21st Anniversary party for the Kenya Harlequins at the golf range (they even took a cake out with them). Because of the political outlook, he notes that future tours looked most unlikely and sadly, that is how it has turned out.

East African Tour

050573	SCORPIONS	NAIROBI	W	3G1DG5T(41)-1G(6)
080573	WEST KENYA	NAKURU	W	5G1PG2T(41)-1T(4)
100573	NAIROBI CLUBS	NAIROBI	W	2G8T(44)-1PG(3)
120573	MOMBASA INVITATION XV	MOMBASA	W	4G1PG5T(47)-0
150573	TANZANIA INVITATION XV	DAR ES SALAAM	W	11G7T(94)-0
170573	KENYA HARLEQUINS	NAIROBI	W	5G7T(58)-1G(6)
190573	KENYA CLUBS	NAIROBI	W	1G2PG2T(20)-1PG3T(15)

29

A Disaster and Two Near Misses in the Cup 1973-1980

England went on a short notice tour to Fiji and New Zealand in August and September after the original tour to Argentina had been cancelled after terrorist threats against the players. Stevens was our only representative again and Nick Martin was inbetween stints with us. Fiji were defeated by a single point (13-12) and three non-test matches in New Zealand were all lost. When the test against the All Blacks came, England remarkably won it by 16-10; their first win over the hosts since 1936.

On 9th August 1973, it was recorded that the Australian tour was still a possibility but it would now take place in May 1974. If this fell by the wayside (which it did due to escalating costs), the next possibility would be South Africa or Rhodesia in 1975 and this should be brought forward by a year. If neither of these came good, a short tour to France would be undertaken. In the event, the short tour to France took place in May 1974. Even after all this, on 20th March 1974, the committee were still investigating the possibilities of tours to Australia, New Zealand and any other places. On 23rd October, a fixture with Paris Université Club on 25th November was noted although this never took place. On 19th December, the floodlights on top of the West stand were approved at a cost of £1,061.60 plus VAT. It was minuted on 15th January 1974 that a new groundsman (Sidney East) had been appointed on a wage of £1,500 per annum. He was trying to find accommodation and his wife was said to be an excellent cook. His search for accommodation failed so a caravan was hired on a temporary basis at a cost of £3,150. On 21st May, the committee were informed that a footbridge was being built over the Chertsey Road during the summer. In the committee report for 1973/74, the death of Howard Marshall (from 1921-1928) was recorded. On 24th July, it was decided that the Club should play the Nippon Iron and Steel Company touring team during 1974/75. Unfortunately, the proposed fixture on 7th April was cancelled.

The 1973/74 season saw Mike Mason take over the captaincy for one season. Bob Hiller was still playing for the 1st XV but he had been appointed Club coach in the close season. We began our home programme, as usual, with a match at Twickenham against Northampton on 8th September. For the fourth time in a row, we suffered a defeat although it was not as heavy as the previous three encounters. We trailed 6-21 at half time and staged a recovery in the second half with Hiller kicking his third and fourth penalties and converting a try from Nigel Lewis to leave us just three points adrift. Against Llanelli the following week, we lost Chris Forth, our right wing, with a leg injury after 20 minutes and, although we only trailed by seven points to nil, the contest had ended. The visitors went on to score three goals, one dropped goal, one penalty goal and a try (in addition to the try and penalty already registered) to two tries for us from Maurice Trapp and Paul Grant (Hiller converting one). The final score of thirty five points to ten was pretty conclusive. If this wasn't bad enough, Leicester came to Twickenham and blew us away by 33-3 and yet again we lost a man injured, this time it was back row forward Steve Godfrey. K.M. (Keith) "Billy" Bushell made his debut in this game at centre and kicked our only points with a penalty. He was to go on and become a prolific scorer in his 214 1st XV appearances. On Wednesday 26th September, we met touring side Northern Suburbs from Sydney, Australia at the Stoop. Both sides scored a goal and a penalty for a 9-9 draw which meant we had avoided defeat for the first time this season.

It was back to normal on the following Saturday when London Welsh came to Twickenham and walloped us (despite leading them by nine points to four at half time). They outscored us 34-10 in the second half, scoring six tries in the process. John Stockdill (2) and Billy Bushell got penalties for us against Swansea at the Stoop but two goals and a try saw us off. David Coley made his last appearance for us in this match having scored 41 points (9 tries and 3 dropped goals). On 13th October, we travelled down to deepest Somerset for a 1st round cup tie against Bridgwater and Albion. Bob Hiller came back into the side after putting Bushell in at full back against Swansea (as he was seen as the natural successor to Hiller). Bushell moved to fly half to form a partnership with Stuart Winship (he was also to become Club coach). In the first half, Winship dropped two goals to give us a narrow lead at the interval. From the first scrum of the second half, Bushell dropped our third goal of the tie and added a penalty between two from Albion full back Vickery. We had more or less constant possession and Bridgwater played their hearts out to contain us but we still won quite a bit easier than the 12-6 score suggests. The next day, twelve out of the fifteen who played in the cup tie appeared against Randwick (another Australian touring side) at the Stoop. Keith Jones played for us for the last time having a total of three tries to his name during his career. At half time, Bushell and K. King (the visiting full back) had each kicked two penalties but into the second half, Hiller and Legg got tries and Bushell added a conversion to which the Aussies replied with a goal of their own. It was not enough and we had won two matches in a row. A third in eight days came against Rosslyn Park who were themselves going for their thirteenth match unbeaten. An even first half saw them lead by the odd point in thirteen but a burst of sixteen unanswered points in the first 24 minutes of the second half made the game safe for us. Park did manage a try but Bushell kicked his second penalty (to add to his own dropped goal and two conversions and tries from Tony Lewis, Roger Bacon and Bob Hiller) to give us an impressive 25-11 victory.

Cardiff came next to Twickenham and despite trailing 6-20 going into the last quarter, we came back to within one point before the referee called a halt. Bristol (10-25) and Richmond both scored victories over us before we in turn accounted for Oxford University (15-9) and Cambridge University (18-17). In these four games, Billy Bushell had scored all but twelve of our points and was quickly becoming as indispensable as Bob Hiller had been. John Gronow appeared for the 1st XV for the last time against Bristol having scored 9 tries and P.R. (Peter) Rawle made the first of 105 appearances in the Cambridge game. The result in this match was probably closer than it would have been as we lost Keith Jenkins from our left wing with concussion after only 20 minutes. We trailed 6-14 midway through the second half when debutant Graham Birkett (who was to go on and make 166 appearances for us and gain a solitary cap for Scotland in 1975) followed up a penalty miss from Bushell to touch down under the bar. Bushell converted, dropped a goal and kicked the winning penalty with only injury time remaining. Blackheath beat us with a penalty in the last minute (11-14) and Bedford got a shock at the Stoop (having led by seven points to nil at half time), losing 9-7. This was to be our last victory of 1973 despite having three home games out of four.

A.J. (Alan) Wordsworth, a Cambridge "blue" made his debut (he had already won his only England cap) in the match with Newport. The second half deteriorated into a mess as both packs came to blows which ultimately ended with Roger Looker (one of our props) having to leave the field with a cut face. Newport ran out winners by twelve points to four. Steve Godfrey went off again after a Richmond boot had cut his head open (a wound which required eleven stitches) after 17 minutes and despite leading 10-9 at half time, we went down 16-23. A trip to Northampton on Boxing Day was spoilt when Maurice Trapp aggravated an old rib injury and left the field after just 15 minutes. We had just gone in front with a try from Mason but eventually lost 13-28. Our other points coming from a try by Peter Rawle, a conversion from Bushell and a dropped goal by Wordsworth. Another disaster befell us against London Scottish when Robin Hammond (on the right wing) suffered a broken nose and a suspected fracture of the cheek bone after a mere 10 minutes. Billy Bushell got a penalty goal for us but this could in no way match six tries (four converted) and a penalty goal for the Scots.

1974 began with a visit to Aldershot to play the Army but, as the stadium was out of action, the match was played on the Queen's Parade Ground (a park). At half time, the Army, playing down the slope and with the wind led by a dropped goal and a try to nil. We got our act together in the second half and tries from John Kirkby, Harry Burroughs and Chris Barrett with two conversions and a penalty supplied by Billy Bushell to a try for the Army gave us victory. The return with Blackheath at the Rectory Field went narrowly in our favour (19-15) after Blackheath lost one of their forwards with a broken arm with 20 minutes gone. Birkenhead Park were played on 19th January and proved to be our third victims of the year. The Park defence was said to be very brittle and even our weakened team seemed to be able to play as they pleased. Bushell contributed two penalties and a conversion to add to tries from Jon Legg, Paul Grant and Chris Forth to give us a 20-6 victory. Playing with the wind in the first half against the R.A.F., we led with two Bushell penalties (the second from 65 yards out) before they got on the scoreboard with a penalty of their own. Two further penalties and a try for the visitors in the second half saw them record a well-deserved win and take from us our unbeaten record in 1974.

Our next three matches were away from home, the first a shortish trip to Sudbury, the home of Wasps. We went down by twenty points to seven (a try and a penalty from Bushell) and lost Terry Claxton midway through the second half. He was sent off for saying too much to the referee. As Terry tells it, this is what happened – Wasps had quickly taken a penalty and he had wrapped his arms around the guy coming with the ball. As they fell over the line, the ball was between them but the referee (H. Stone) gave a try. Terry said "You are some c*** you are" the referee asked him for clarification as to what he had said, Terry provided it and off he went. After the game, Terry went up to him in the bar and said listen here......Mr Stone cut him off and said No, you listen here, I'm a sergeant in the Metropolitan Police. Terry said he must be used to being called that then. The referee continued and explained to Terry that if he had added the word "Sir" to his sentence, he would have remained on the pitch! The reply was "Well you are a f****** c***, Sir"! He was subsequently dropped until his case came up before the disciplinary committee. This caused discontent amongst the players and although he still missed the second round cup tie at Orrell the next week, he was picked for a Wanderers match the same day but it was called off. He was eventually banned for four weeks by the Middlesex disciplinary committee and didn't appear for the first team until the match with Bristol on 6th April. One bright spot in the game was the debut of Fijian international P.B. (Bosco) Tikoisuva who went on to make 56 appearances for the 1st XV. A now infamous comment was made by one of our committee that

Orrell was "a lay-by off the M6" (the motorway can be seen from the ground). This did nothing other than stir up the very proud Lancashire club and, as will be seen, this curse was to last for most of the next 25 years! Back to the cup tie at Edge Hall Road, which was played on a pitch that had taken two days of continuous rain. The home side were superb and a goal and three penalties gave them a 15-0 advantage down slope at half time. Bosco Tikoisuva intercepted and ran in our only try before Orrell scored their second and Bushell kicked a penalty to claw us back into it at 7-19. This was merely an act of defiance from us and before the end, the home side had scored their third try which, like the first, was converted for a final, humiliating score of 25-7. This remains our most embarrassing cup exit closely followed by the defeat to Wilmslow two years earlier. Earle Kirton said farewell in this match having scored 47 points (4 tries, 1 dropped goal, 9 penalties and 1 conversion) and captained the side on 32 occasions (although he did play in one game on the 1980 tour to the USA and got injured in the process). He would return as coach in a few years' time.

We did sneak past U.S. Portsmouth (at Portsmouth) with three John Stockdill penalties and a Billy Bushell try to nil and the Royal Navy back at the Stoop (22-6). Bushell, yet again, was our main scorer with four penalties and a conversion to add to tries by Winship and Tikoisuva. The following week we travelled to Leicester on the first of three consecutive trips to the Midlands. This time it was our opponents who were handicapped by the loss of a player when one of their wing forwards (Forfar) went off after five minutes. S.F. (Steve) Simson, playing in the first of 96 games for the first team, scored a try after ten minutes, Bushell converted and kicked a penalty before the Tigers replied with a penalty to leave us six points up at the break. After this, the fourteen men of Leicester drew level with a goal but Tikoisuva had the last word when he grabbed a try to leave us winners 13-9. We now started on a run which would be our worst end to a season ever. The victory over Leicester was to be our last win and there were still nine games left. Importantly, only one of these was at home and none of them were easy matches. The first was against Bedford on 9th March. Stuart Winship dropped another goal but we still lost (3-13) and against Coventry, we led 11-10 with only a minute left but conceded a try to go down by three points.

More of the same followed as we met our third touring side of the season when Ponsonby (New Zealand) were visitors at the Stoop on Sunday 17th March. Three of the six New Zealand internationals in their team went on to appear in our colours (Andy Haden, Terry Morrison and Peter Whiting). Trailing by ten points at half time, we made a fight of it in the second period and Hammond scored for Bushell to convert before another goal from the visitors sealed their win. Burroughs unluckily had a try disallowed by the referee late on but it would have only altered the scoreboard and nothing more. Against London Welsh on 23rd March, Winship and Bushell each dropped a goal and J.L. (Jeremy) Cooke got a try for Bushell to convert to put us 12-9 ahead after 47 minutes. Both sides were down to fourteen men shortly after when Scaife (one of our wing forwards) was followed off by Clive Rees (left wing). The match was settled by three John Taylor penalties for the Welsh. Mike Mason made his last appearance in this one having scored 8 tries and led the side on 32 occasions.

A short trip to Roehampton to play Rosslyn Park followed and again we lost a man injured when Tikoisuva went off late on. The match had long since slipped from our grasp and an eleven point lead at half time turned into a thirty point demolition by the end and we had failed to score for the first time this season. With only two wins from our ten London League games, it was no surprise that we failed to qualify for the cup in 1974/75. It must be said that Park were preparing to face Coventry in the Cup Final and were a very good side. Paul Grant captained the side at Bristol but three Bushell penalties were nowhere near enough to counter two goals, three penalties and a try from our hosts. Mike Novak made his last appearance in this game having scored 45 tries (139 points) during his time in the first team. The Easter tour was another whitewash and we only managed nineteen points in three games whilst conceding seventy one. The losses were to Bath (6-20), Swansea (3-18) and Cardiff (10-33) to finish the season on a very low note.

The most tries were scored by Jeremy Cooke and Robin Hammond with just four each. Excluding the seasons of 1942/43 and 1943/44 (when only one match was played in each), this was the lowest most tries scored since the 1903/04 season. Stuart Winship set a new record for dropped goals in a season with six. This overhauled Ricky Bartlett's mark of five set in 1956/57. Billy Bushell set a new mark for penalties (44) and subsequently got most points (191) with 2 tries, 5 dropped goals and 18 conversions added on to his penalties. Overall, tries hit a low of 44 which was our least amount scored since 1947/48 (when the same total was recorded). New records were set for dropped goals (13) and penalties (55) (the previous marks were 6 and 52 respectively). The final playing record of W12 D1 L25 saw our heaviest number of defeats ever. Top appearance makers were Billy Bushell (35), Mike Mason (33), Jon Legg (30), Paul Grant and Roger Looker (29) and Stuart Winship (28).

The short tour to France was undertaken between 22nd and 27th May 1974 and two matches were played. The first against Sélection Ariege in Foix was won 18-13 and the second against Stade Toulousain in Toulouse on 27th May was a cracker. We had a number of guest players in our side - Hefin Jenkins, Ray Gravell, Derek Quinnell and Gareth Jenkins from Llanelli and Chris Wardlow from Coventry. We went ahead with tries from Wardlow and Bushell before Massat scored for Toulouse and Fourcade converted. Before half time, Quinnell, Winship and Bushell added more tries and with the last named converting all three, we led 26-6. That became 36-6 with scores from Wardlow and Gravell (Bushell converted one) but Toulouse came back with tries of their own from Tristan, O'Callaghan and Barrère plus a conversion and a penalty from Fourcade to make it 36-23 with fourteen minutes left. That was as near as they got and three more tries followed from Lewis, Birkett and Winship. Bushell added two conversions and it finished 52-23.

We had no representation on the 1974 British Lions tour to South Africa which proved to be the most successful of the 20th century. The first three tests were won and the fourth drawn in controversial circumstances. Fergus Slattery scored a try right at the end of the game but the referee disallowed it. Photographic evidence and Slattery's own account afterwards all pointed towards a try but it ended 13-13. All eighteen of the other matches were won as they returned home unbeaten.

1973/74

080973	NORTHAMPTON	TWICKENHAM	L	1G4PG(18)-2G3PG(21)
150973	LLANELLI	TWICKENHAM	L	1G1T(10)-3G1DG2PG2T(35)
220973	LEICESTER	TWICKENHAM	L	1PG(3)-3G1PG3T(33)
260973	NORTHERN SUBURBS	STOOP MEMORIAL GROUND	D	1G1PG(9)-1G1PG(9)
290973	LONDON WELSH	TWICKENHAM	L	1G1DG2PG1T(19)-5G2T(38)
061073	SWANSEA	STOOP MEMORIAL GROUND	L	3PG(9)-2G1T(16)

131073	BRIDGWATER AND ALBION(RFU1)	BRIDGWATER	W	3DG1PG(12)-2PG(6)
141073	RANDWICK	STOOP MEMORIAL GROUND	W	1G2PG1T(16)-1G2PG(12)
201073	ROSSLYN PARK	TWICKENHAM	W	2G1DG2PG1T(25)-1PG2T(11)
271073	CARDIFF	TWICKENHAM	L	1G1DG2PG1T(19)-1G2PG2T(20)
031173	BRISTOL	TWICKENHAM	L	2PG1T(10)-2G1DG2PG1T(25)
101173	RICHMOND	RICHMOND	L	2PG(6)-1G2PG2T(20)
171173	OXFORD UNIVERSITY	STOOP MEMORIAL GROUND	W	1G3PG(15)-1G1PG(9)
241173	CAMBRIDGE UNIVERSITY	TWICKENHAM	W	1G1DG3PG(18)-1G1PG2T(17)
011273	BLACKHEATH	TWICKENHAM	L	1PG2T(11)-2PG2T(14)
081273	BEDFORD	STOOP MEMORIAL GROUND	W	1G1PG(9)-1DG1T(7)
151273	NEWPORT	TWICKENHAM	L	1T(4)-1G2PG(12)
221273	RICHMOND	STOOP MEMORIAL GROUND	L	1G2PG1T(16)-1G3PG2T(23)
261273	NORTHAMPTON	NORTHAMPTON	L	1G1DG1T(13)-1G2PG4T(28)
291273	LONDON SCOTTISH	TWICKENHAM	L	1PG(3)-4G1PG2T(35)
050174	ARMY	ALDERSHOT	W	2G1PG1T(19)-1DG2T(11)
120174	BLACKHEATH	BLACKHEATH	W	1G3PG1T(19)-1G3PG(15)
190174	BIRKENHEAD PARK	BIRKENHEAD	W	1G2PG2T(20)-1G(6)
260174	ROYAL AIR FORCE	STOOP MEMORIAL GROUND	L	2PG(6)-3PG1T(13)
020274	WASPS	SUDBURY	L	1PG1T(7)-1G2PG2T(20)
090274	ORRELL(RFU2)	ORRELL	L	1PG1T(7)-2G3PG1T(25)
160274	UNITED SERVICES PORTSMOUTH	PORTSMOUTH	W	3PG1T(13)-0
230274	ROYAL NAVY	STOOP MEMORIAL GROUND	W	1G4PG1T(22)-2PG(6)
020374	LEICESTER	LEICESTER	W	1G1PG1T(13)-1G1PG(9)
090374	BEDFORD	BEDFORD	L	1DG(3)-1G1PG1T(13)
160374	COVENTRY	COVENTRY	L	1PG2T(11)-2PG2T(14)
170374	PONSONBY	STOOP MEMORIAL GROUND	L	1G(6)-1G2PG1T(16)
230374	LONDON WELSH	OLD DEER PARK	L	1G2DG(12)-1G4PG(18)
300374	ROSSLYN PARK	ROEHAMPTON	L	0-2G2DG3T(30)
060474	BRISTOL	BRISTOL	L	3PG(9)-2G3PG1T(25)
120474	BATH	BATH	L	1G(6)-2G2T(20)
130474	SWANSEA	SWANSEA	L	1DG(3)-1G3T(18)

150474	CARDIFF	CARDIFF	L	1DG1PG1T(10)-3G1PG3T(33)
??0574	SÉLECTION ARIEGE	FOIX	W	(18)-(13)
270574	TOULOUSE	TOULOUSE	W	6G4T(52)-2G1PG2T(23)

Some of my earliest memories are running into Twickenham Stadium with my Dad through the West car park gate five minutes before kick-off. Always stood there was the same man, always with a smile and a cheery word. Years later, I would work with him on the Ground Committee. That man was John Christy, a real Club stalwart in the truest sense of the word. He passed away on 23rd March 2015 and it is only right that I pay tribute to him here with a brief run down of his life in rugby.

In the early years, his main role was where I used to see him but he would also work the turnstiles and sell programmes when Quins or England played at Twickenham. John made the role his own at the Stoop and when we had relatively small crowds, he would run the day with just six stewards, today it could be close to 200. Over the first 10 years he would be found at the turnstiles in the south-east corner managing his staff. In those days, stewards would have to work the turnstiles and control the crowd. On match days, John would be seen riding his Victorian two-wheeled bike with a basket on the front around the ground. In those amateur days, the payment for working was chilli and a beer in the old West stand. Later, John was co-opted on to the Ground Committee helping other members to redevelop the ground. When more staff were required he had more of an operational role in the Club, but still would be found on match days on a chair by the south-west corner gate. This would be a signature position for many years. John's role as Operations Manager saw him in charge of hospitality, stewards, car park and turnstile staff while still working closely with the RFU. As the game went professional, the Club was forced to move towards licensed safety stewards and in 1997, his company, JAC Events Stewards was set up. By then, the rest of the family was working at the Club (Andy Christy, his son, Deb Christy, his daughter and a number of grandchildren and other family members). JAC was employing in the region of 109 staff. John ran the company up to the day he passed away. The Club was his life, and he had been involved with it for over 60 years. He will be sadly missed by all those who knew him. A funny and true story to end - John was the only man who sold a Quins' programme to a blind man! Wherever he rests in peace, I know that he will always be on the pitch with us.

On 19th November 1974, the death of Bruce Chapman was reported along with a possible trip to Barcelona to celebrate the 75th anniversary of the game in Spain. In February, proposed tours to France, Italy, British Army of the Rhine, Germany and Spain (May 1975), Canada or Boston (1976) and Bermuda (1977) were mentioned. On 17th April, it was decided that an international baseball match between England and West Germany should not be held at the Stoop. On 20th May, it was announced that Sidney East (our groundsman) had told the Club that he had received a better offer and, due to a lack of suitable accommodation, would be leaving. His wages were increased to £32 per week including free accommodation and heating and his wife should take on the catering but his two weeks' notice expired on 23rd May and he was to leave us. The caravan would be sold for around £2,000 but would stay until the bungalow was built and plans for this were proceeding. On 17th June, we offered a fixture to the Marauder Sports Club from New Zealand (on 22nd February 1976) but the game never happened and turned down a fixture with the Dallas Harlequins (on 9th November 1975). The subject of affiliation would be discussed on that date as a form of recompense.

Nick Martin returned after two seasons with Bedford to become Club captain for this and the following two seasons. Northampton were our first opponents on the lush, green turf at Twickenham on 14th September. This game saw the debuts of A.C. (Adrian) Alexander, R.A. (Bob) McLean and G.E. (Gordon) Wood. Alexander made the first of at least 134 appearances, McLean only played nine times for us but won five Australian caps and Wood (a real speedster on the wing) appeared for the first of 78 confirmed games. We had lost eight of our last nine matches against the Saints but came back very well after they had gone into a six point lead after 10 minutes. Billy Bushell got a penalty and in first half injury time Paul Grant got a try for Bushell to convert. After John Kirkby (a New Zealander from Wellington) had scored our second try and Bushell had knocked over a huge penalty from 57 yards out, we led 16-6 just ten minutes into the second half. Then disaster struck midway through the half when Adrian Boulton (a prop from New Zealand) kicked an opposing player on the head at a ruck and was immediately sent off by referee R.F. Johnson (he was subsequently banned for 10 weeks). A penalty try (converted by Raybould) made it 16-12 and right on time Oldham ran over in the corner for the visitors and managed to run round far enough for Raybould to kick the winning conversion.

Against Llanelli, we led with a Bushell penalty and a Wordsworth dropped goal before the same scores brought our opponents level by half time. Two unconverted tries in the second half were enough to hand us our eleventh defeat on the trot. Our first game of the season at the Stoop was against Leicester on 28th September. Our early dominance led to nothing and it was 7-7 after 30 minutes (Wood had scored a try and Bushell had kicked a penalty for us). By half time, Wood had got his second, Bushell converted and landed his second penalty to put us nine points up. We fairly destroyed the Tigers in the second half and a single penalty from them was responded to by us with tries from Hammond (2) and Terry Claxton; two more conversions from Bushell enabled us to win 32-10. Making the first of at least 39 appearances for us in this match was C.R. (Clive) Woodward. He was to gain 21 England caps between 1980-84 whilst playing for Leicester. A sixth successive defeat to Swansea followed (12-20) before we travelled to Lydney on the following Tuesday for a match to commemorate the official opening of their floodlights. Five tries (scored by Birkett (2), Howard, Hammond and Alexander) and a penalty and three conversions from Woodward were enough to see us home by twenty nine points to six but we suffered our heaviest ever defeat to Gloucester at Kingsholm on 12th October (this statistic has been subsequently beaten). We only managed a try by McLean and two penalties from Bushell in answer to thirty three points from Gloucester. Rosslyn Park beat us by sixteen points (13-29) in a game which saw the first of at least 258 appearances by D.H. (David) Cooke. He was to win 12 England caps and was also a future captain of the Club.

Cardiff came to Twickenham with a run of ten consecutive victories over us behind them although we managed to lead 9-0 at half time. Woodward (playing at fly half) had kicked a penalty and converted a try by Grant. Cardiff pulled a penalty back but Woodward dropped a goal and converted a try from centre David A. Cooke. Cardiff replied with a goal of their own but we still won by nine points. Dave Wrench made his last appearance in this game having scored 53 points (15 tries, 2 penalties and 1 conversion) and led the side on 23 occasions during his career. We were not having a good time against most sides and Bristol were no exception. They came to Twickenham and beat us more easily than the 7-19 scoreline suggests. Against Richmond, we led with a try from Hammond (converted by Woodward) after only two minutes. This was the extent of our scoring and twenty four unanswered points later we had been decisively beaten. The Oxford University game at Twickenham was cancelled and we were beaten by Cambridge University at Grange Road (12-31). This was our first loss at Cambridge since 1954 and their first win over us in a decade. They did it with the help of two of our current players and one shortly to make his debut. Gordon Wood grabbed two tries, Alan Wordsworth played at fly half and S.R.R. (Steve) Edlmann would appear in the first of at least 52 games for us at Bedford on 14th December. M.F. Malcolm "Mickey" Claxton (brother of

Terry) made the first of at least 203 appearances against Cambridge. Hammond was on the score sheet again and Woodward converted his try as well as kicking a penalty and dropping a goal. London Welsh won their tenth consecutive match against us when they visited the Stoop on 30th November (7-18). We now had a record of W3 L9 in our first twelve matches and things were not looking good.

A shining light appeared the following week against Blackheath when P.J. (Peter) Whiting (who was in the process of winning 20 New Zealand caps) played in the first of 22 matches for the 1st XV. Woodward had converted his own try but we trailed by a point at the break. Bushell took over the kicking with 20 minutes left and put over two enormous penalties (from 60 and 56 yards respectively) to put us five points in front. Blackheath got their second try to close the gap but a try from David A. Cooke sealed a narrow victory. Against Bedford we started impressively and Woodward dropped his third goal of the season but we trailed off and Bedford led by ten points at the half way point. Peter Whiting got the forwards going and for 30 minutes we hammered away at the Bedford defence. We were rewarded with penalties by Woodward and Bushell and a David A. Cooke try in between to level the scores. After this, Bedford came back to the fore in the last 10 minutes but there was no further scoring. The following week we met Newport at the Stoop and defeated them for only the fifth time. For the second week running Billy Bushell captained the side and became the first player in our history to kick five penalties in a match. We had trailed by a goal to nil at half time but Bushell kicked three penalties before Hiller dropped a goal and the captain went on to complete his record haul to leave us victors by 18-6. This win also brought an end to Newport's twelve match unbeaten run. Our last match of 1974 was on Boxing Day at Franklin's Gardens, Northampton. Bushell again led the side in Nick Martin's absence and was in fine form with the boot; landing two penalties and converting tries from Hammond and David H. Cooke to lead us to an 18-12 victory.

The Army visited the Stoop on 4th January and found themselves eighteen points down in almost even time. Bushell had kicked two penalties and converted tries by Grant and Hammond. In true Harlequin fashion, we went to sleep and when we woke up, the Army had closed the gap to just one point. Grant bulldozed his way through the Army defence for a great try, Bushell converted and Hiller got our fourth although the Army had the final word when they scored a penalty to leave the margin at eight points. In another close game with Blackheath, we completed the double with the help of five Bushell penalties and a try from Gordon Wood (back from Cambridge). Blackheath got three tries of their own but could only improve two. Against Birkenhead Park we played in the quagmire formerly known as the Stoop. The match was scheduled to be played at Twickenham but that pitch was considered unsuitable. By half time David A. Cooke and Ian Burrell had scored tries and Bushell had converted both and kicked a penalty. It looked as though we would romp to victory but the only score in the second half was a try for the visitors. On two occasions, one of our wingers (Tikoisuva) dribbled over the line but due to the small in-goal area at the Stoop (before the removal of the running track) the ball went out of play before he could reach it. The Royal Air Force had Geoff Bond (their number 8) sent off after a late tackle on Bushell and were then reduced to 13 men a few minutes later when centre Peter Williams went off with a hamstring injury. They had led by the odd point in seven at half time but we eventually took the spoils with tries from Grant and Tikoisuva and a conversion and penalty by Bushell. John Stockdill made his last appearance in this match having scored 132 points (32 penalties and 18 conversions) in his career. This was our eighth game unbeaten and was our best since the run of nine games (eight wins and a draw) at the end of 1967/68 and the beginning of 1968/69.

The fixture with Wasps was cancelled so we took our unbeaten run to Stradey Park, Llanelli on 8th February. We actually took the lead when Bushell landed a penalty from inside his own half. A goal and three penalties for the home side and a try for us from Robin Hammond made it 7-15 at half time. Our forwards failed to last the pace and Llanelli were in rampant mood. Andy Hill kicked immaculately for them, landing nine out of nine. He converted all four tries and added a penalty in a totally one sided second half to destroy our run to the tune of forty two points to seven. Mike Luke, the Canadian captain made the first of four appearances for us in this match and was in the process of accumulating 16 caps. Nick Martin returned after an absence of two months in our next game against United Services, Portsmouth at the Stoop. A half time lead of 13-4 became a romp by the end and we won 37-12. We scored seven tries to three with Bushell scoring seventeen points in all. The following week we met eight of the United Services players again when we took on the Royal Navy at Portsmouth. The result this time was altogether different and we trailed by a goal, a penalty and a try to a Bushell penalty at half time. In the second half, we made a great comeback with tries from Grant and a pair from Bushell (who also kicked two conversions) to put us in front. Two penalties from Navy full back Piercy levelled the match at 19-19. We completed the double over Leicester at Welford Road (15-9) after it had remained scoreless at the interval. This was Leicester's fifth successive defeat and we were again indebted to Bushell who converted both tries from Grant and added a penalty.

On 8th March, due to both teams' opponents having cup commitments we welcomed Bradford to the Stoop for our only meeting. Another match spoilt by incessant rain was 0-0 at half time before Bushell kicked us in front with a penalty. Lightowler levelled for Bradford and Tikoisuva was tackled into touch as he dived for the corner right on the final whistle to give us our third draw of the season. Coventry came to the Stoop bristling with internationals and the title of National Knockout Cup Champions for a morning kick-off before England took on Scotland at Twickenham in the afternoon. Playing with the wind, we led by ten points at the break with tries from David A. Cooke and Dave Barry with Bushell adding a conversion and a penalty to a solitary penalty from Coventry. One minute into the second half Preece intercepted a pass from David A. Cooke and raced in from 50 yards out to score under the posts for Rossborough to convert. Despite hardly being out of our half for the rest of the game, the visitors could not add to their score and we ran out narrow but deserving winners 13-9. Sadly, this was to be our last win of the season with seven matches still to come. Six of these were against the same opponents as the previous season, only the last match against London Scottish was different. Against London Welsh at the Old Deer Park, we led with a Bushell try (which he also converted) and actually dominated in every department only for the Welsh to equalise just before the break. A dropped goal and a penalty goal edged the home side in front before they stunned us with three tries in the last nine minutes. We did have the last word when Bushell converted Tikoisuva's try but couldn't stop the Welsh from romping home by twenty six points to twelve.

The Easter tour was worse than usual and we opened at Bath in a driving blizzard. We failed to score and conceded ten points to lose to Bath for the eighth successive time. We did get two Billy Bushell penalties at Swansea to lead 6-3 at half time but were blown away in the second half as the home side scored 25 unanswered points. We saved the biggest disaster of all until the last when we met Cardiff on Easter Monday. We began the match with three props in the front row and were reduced to fourteen men by the end when Jonathan Legg finally left the field suffering from concussion. We did actually lead when Tikoisuva picked up a loose ball and proceeded to run through most of the opposition to score a beautiful try which Bushell converted to add to his earlier penalty. By the interval, three penalties for Cardiff had levelled the scores. Unfortunately, as against Bath and Swansea, we failed to score in the second half. Cardiff got six tries, converted four of them and ran out winners 41-9. The tough matches just kept on coming and a trip down to Bristol was next on the fixture list. We were outscored by four tries to one and went down by twenty six points to ten.

Rosslyn Park showed us no mercy and completed the double over us by converting a 12-9 lead at half time into a 22-12 final score. Bushell kicked four penalties while Park managed two goals, two penalties and a try. Mike Luke made his last appearance in this game and Bob McLean made his in our next game against London Scottish having scored just the one try. This was our final match of the season and it was effectively a cup final. It came down to this game to see who between us and the Scots would play cup rugby in the 1975/76 season. History was on our side as we had won on our five previous visits and had not lost to London Scottish at Richmond since January 1965 (although they had thrashed us in our last meeting at Twickenham). As it turned out, we played some of our worst rugby of the season and were again beaten out of sight. A half time deficit of sixteen points just increased as the game went on and a penalty from Bushell was our only response to eighteen further Scottish points. So, we failed for the second successive season to qualify for the knockout cup. At this time, qualification was based on an unofficial London Clubs table. The top seven teams went into the cup the following season and this operated throughout the country with a certain number going through (depending on how many were in the particular table). The ridiculous situation was that not all teams played each other and it was decided on percentages. This meant you could have a scenario where one team played twelve matches, won half of them and ended with a 50% total and another side having played just seven matches and won only four of them finishing higher up the table by virtue of having a better percentage (57.14). It wasn't until the proper leagues began in 1987/88 that the percentage situation was sorted out.

Paul Grant topped the try scorers with 9, Clive Woodward dropped three goals and Billy Bushell topped the points with 203 (5 tries, 45 penalties and 24 conversions). His 45 penalties surpassed his previous mark from last season by one. Overall, points were up by 30 on 1973/74 to 454, tries rose by ten to 54 and conversions were also up by ten to 32 but dropped goals went down by eight and penalties dropped to 53. Out of 33 possible appearances, Billy Bushell and Paul Grant came top with 29 each with David A. Cooke (27) and Terry Claxton (26) following close behind.

1974/75

140974	NORTHAMPTON	TWICKENHAM	L	1G2PG1T(16)-3G(18)
210974	LLANELLI	TWICKENHAM	L	1DG1PG(6)-1DG1PG2T(14)
280974	LEICESTER	STOOP MEMORIAL GROUND	W	3G2PG2T(32)-2PG1T(10)
051074	SWANSEA	STOOP MEMORIAL GROUND	L	1G2PG(12)-1DG3PG2T(20)
081074	LYDNEY	LYDNEY	W	3G1PG2T(29)-2PG(6)
121074	GLOUCESTER	GLOUCESTER	L	2PG1T(10)-4G3PG(33)
191074	ROSSLYN PARK	TWICKENHAM	L	3PG1T(13)-2G1DG2PG2T(29)

261074	CARDIFF	TWICKENHAM	W	2G1DG1PG(18)-1G1PG(9)
021174	BRISTOL	TWICKENHAM	L	1PG1T(7)-2G1PG1T(19)
091174	RICHMOND	TWICKENHAM	L	1G(6)-2G4PG(24)
161174	OXFORD UNIVERSITY	TWICKENHAM	C	
231174	CAMBRIDGE UNIVERSITY	CAMBRIDGE	L	1G1DG1PG(12)-4G1PG1T(31)
301174	LONDON WELSH	STOOP MEMORIAL GROUND	L	1PG1T(7)-1G3T(18)
071274	BLACKHEATH	BLACKHEATH	W	1G2PG1T(16)-1PG2T(11)
141274	BEDFORD	TWICKENHAM	D	1DG2PG1T(13)-1DG2PG1T(13)
211274	NEWPORT	STOOP MEMORIAL GROUND	W	1DG5PG(18)-1G(6)
261274	NORTHAMPTON	NORTHAMPTON	W	2G2PG(18)-4PG(12)
040175	ARMY	STOOP MEMORIAL GROUND	W	3G2PG1T(28)-4PG2T(20)
110175	BLACKHEATH	TWICKENHAM	W	5PG1T(19)-2G1T(16)
180175	BIRKENHEAD PARK	STOOP MEMORIAL GROUND	W	2G1PG(15)-1T(4)
250175	ROYAL AIR FORCE	STOOP MEMORIAL GROUND	W	1G1PG1T(13)-1T(4)
010275	WASPS	STOOP MEMORIAL GROUND	C	
080275	LLANELLI	LLANELLI	L	1PG1T(7)-3G4PG(42)
150275	UNITED SERVICES PORTSMOUTH	STOOP MEMORIAL GROUND	W	3G1PG4T(37)-3T(12)
220275	ROYAL NAVY	PORTSMOUTH	D	2G1PG1T(19)-1G3PG1T(19)
010375	LEICESTER	LEICESTER	W	2G1PG(15)-1G1PG(9)
080375	BRADFORD	STOOP MEMORIAL GROUND	D	1PG(3)-1PG(3)
150375	COVENTRY	STOOP MEMORIAL GROUND	W	1G1PG1T(13)-1G1PG(9)
220375	LONDON WELSH	OLD DEER PARK	L	2G(12)-2G1DG1PG2T(26)
270375	BATH	BATH	L	0-2PG1T(10)
290375	SWANSEA	SWANSEA	L	2PG(6)-3G2PG1T(28)
310375	CARDIFF	CARDIFF	L	1G1PG(9)-4G3PG2T(41)
050475	BRISTOL	BRISTOL	L	2PG1T(10)-2G2PG2T(26)
120475	ROSSLYN PARK	ROEHAMPTON	L	4PG(12)-2G2PG1T(22)
190475	LONDON SCOTTISH	RICHMOND	L	1PG(3)-3G4PG1T(34)

England went on tour to Australia in May and June and Alan Wordsworth and old boy Peter Dixon made the party (the last named was a replacement). Unfortunately, both tests were lost (9-16 and 21-30) but Wordsworth came on as a replacement in the first one. Of the other games, four were won and two lost for an overall 50% record. A large number of injuries were suffered which didn't help and Mike Burton became the first English player to be sent off in an international when he was dismissed in the second minute of the second test.

At a committee meeting on 16th September 1975, a point was raised dealing with the poaching of Graham Birkett by London Scottish. This was being looked into but the source and nature of the pressure allegedly brought to bear on him was difficult to ascertain (as he was qualified to play for Scotland, they weren't keen that he played for any other club). They had failed to contact us as they should have done when interested in one of our players but it was agreed that to break off relations and fixtures with them (as advocated by H.J. Gould) was too extreme. Instead, we should contact Blackheath (who had themselves lost a number of players to Rosslyn Park and another offending club) with a view to putting forward recommendations to the meeting of London clubs. Further investigation drew no new conclusions and the matter was quietly dropped and in any event, Graham was back with us before the end of the 1976/77 season. On 21st October it was reported that Bert Sibley had become our new groundsman and his wages were £40 per week for a 40 hour week. He didn't last very long as R. Smith (aged 49) had replaced him by the meeting of 18th May 1976; he was to begin work on 1st June). Also, it was minuted that there was a proposed fixture against Eastern Suburbs from Sydney on 3rd November. The venue was to have been Esher but, like so many of these games, it never took place. The short tour to Canada was also mentioned and this was to take place between 16th and 30th August 1976. On 16th December, a visit to Barnstaple for their centenary in 1977/78 was confirmed. At a meeting on 20th January 1976, the Campbelltown Quins from Australia were still anxious to become affiliated to us and an invitation to go to Venice between 15th and 17th May was accepted (although the dates would be changed to the end of that month). An enquiry from the Wanderers to take part in the Middlesex Cup in 1976/77 was not agreed as practical for a variety of reasons (although this would not always be the case) and an honours cap was awarded to Bosco Tikoisuva. At the Annual General Meeting on 23rd July (which took place at the Gloucester Hotel, Harrington Gardens, London SW7), a gold watch was presented to him in appreciation of his three years at the Club. Around this time, Tom Inwood ran the line for the 1st XV for a number of years, resplendent in his blue tracksuit.

Our fixture list had taken on a very familiar look now and fortunately for us, our side was getting stronger and playing with a lot more conviction under the captaincy of Nick Martin and the coaching of Earle Kirton (said by those who played under him to be the best coach ever). Familiar results came in the first two matches as we lost to Northampton (6-16) and Llanelli (10-29). Familiar names were responsible for our points in both matches with Billy Bushell getting two penalties in the first and a conversion in the second to add to tries from Nick Martin and Gordon Wood. Our third game of the season brought the Tigers of Leicester to Twickenham. The visitors played with a gale force wind in the first half but lost one of their wing forwards (Kempin) after just 14 minutes which hampered their progress. By the interval they only led by two points, having scored three penalties and a try against tries from Tim Rutter and Colin Lambert plus a Bushell penalty. When it was our turn to use the wind, we just ran riot. David Cooke, Gordon Wood (2), Bosco Tikoisuva, Paul Grant and Colin Lambert (with his second) ran in tries to which Bushell added the extra points to five to leave us 45-13 ahead with just seconds remaining. Leicester did have the last word with their second try but they had been completely and utterly defeated. This was our biggest win over them in fixtures dating back to 1895. Tim Rutter had returned to the team in this match after an absence of seven years (spent building his medical career).

There had been glimpses of greater things to come and these continued to appear in the Swansea match when we found ourselves trailing by twenty eight points to ten midway through the second half. We proceeded to score three sparkling tries through Wood, Lambert and Cooke but, as all three conversions were missed by Bushell, we lost by six points. Carelessness was costing us too many games and this was responsible for at least twelve of Gloucester's points the following week at the Stoop. Thanks to tries from Lambert and Cooke (the latter converted by Hiller) we actually led for a brief time in the first half but, by half time, Gloucester were back in front. With just minutes left, we trailed 13-18 and attempted to run the ball from our own line only for Cooke to drop a pass and Gloucester's number 8 picked up and scored their third try which, like the previous two was converted. Rosslyn Park had beaten us in our last three meetings and were at the top of their form having reached the final of the knockout cup in 1975, going on to reach it this season as well. Unfortunately for them, they lost both. This was a rip-roaring contest with never more than six points separating the teams. Harry Burroughs scored a try in the first minute, Bushell converted from the touchline and added two penalties to which Park replied with a goal and a dropped goal. Ten minutes into the second half, Bushell got his third penalty before Park hit us with twelve points in as many minutes to lead by six. Near the end, David Cooke went over for Bushell to convert and we had tied the scores at 21-21. At Twickenham on 25th October in front of the touring Australians we managed to subdue Gareth Edwards and defeat Cardiff 32-19. Trailing by five points at half time (7-12), we showed some excellent attacking play and ran in three great tries against one for Cardiff. Billy Bushell had a great game with the boot, kicking four penalties and two conversions to add to tries from Lambert (2), Burroughs and Cooke. This was to be our last win over Cardiff for eight years.

Bristol achieved their sixth successive win over us (3-10) and we just sneaked past Richmond (14-9) before Bushell set a new Club record for penalties in a match when he kicked six against Oxford University at Twickenham on 15th November (Peter Johnson scored our only try in a 22-9 victory). Cambridge were our next victims (30 9) before London Welsh were narrowly beaten with a late Bushell penalty (15-13) for the first time in twelve attempts. We had last beaten them on 29th November 1969 (exactly six years to the day). We really let rip in our next two games, scoring seven tries against both Blackheath (39-17) and Waterloo (38-3). In that game, Mickey Claxton was one of the try scorers and, when the ball was kicked ahead, he looked set for number two. The problem was that he was tugged back and heard his brother (Terry) saying "you're not scoring again". The funny part to this is that when you look at the number of tries scored over their Quins careers, Terry has 13 and Mickey got 12! We travelled down to Newport on a Friday night (the day before Australia met Wales in Cardiff) trying to notch up our seventh win in a row. Yet again we were to be denied at Rodney Parade despite leading with a Bushell penalty at half time. A try and two penalties to one more Bushell effort enabled Newport to win by ten points to six. Eight days later we met Richmond in the return fixture at the Stoop and bounced back from the defeat in Wales in tremendous style. Gordon Wood, David Cooke and Colin Lambert had got tries in the first half (the first two being converted by Bushell) to which Richmond replied with a goal and a penalty to leave the score at 16-9. This is how things remained after 60 minutes when Richmond ran out of steam and the flood gates opened. Cooke and Lambert both got their second tries and further scores came from Nick Martin and Steve Edlmann with the impeccable Bushell converting all four to make the final score 40-9. We were being praised from all quarters for our attacking play which was reminiscent of the great team of the Stoop era. So we finished 1975 on a high note but it was far from the peak of our performances in this season.

During the first half of the season, we saw C.R. (Chris) Kelly make the first of at least 68 appearances and C.W. (Colin) Lambert the first of at least 112 appearances (both against Northampton) whilst we said goodbye to Jon Legg against Richmond having scored 12 points (3 tries) during his career.

The Army met the same force as Richmond had a week before when we met them at Aldershot Military Stadium. Colin Lambert and Gordon Wood (who were having a personal duel on the tries front) scored two apiece, Nick Martin grabbed one as did Billy Bushell (who also kicked four penalties and four conversions). The following week in the return with Blackheath, we matched our total against the Army but Blackheath exceeded the Army's total by six points. Lambert and Wood were in fantastic form and made their mark yet again. By half time, we had run in six tries and Bushell had converted all of them to lead 36-0. When Blackheath had the use of the wind, they outscored us by thirteen points to eight but it was quite clearly not enough. Our tries were scored by Tikoisuva (2), Wood (2), Winship, Lambert, Grant and Alexander. A trip to Birkenhead Park maintained the winning run and four more tries helped us to a 29-9 victory. On 24th January, we welcomed the Royal Air Force to Twickenham for what was to be an amazing game. We hit the peak of our form and completely massacred the military side who must have wondered what had hit them! Inside 20 minutes Colin Lambert had scorched in for four tries before the R.A.F. got their only points with a goal. Bushell landed a penalty and converted tries by Rutter and Grant to leave us 31-6 up at the break. Lambert got his fifth, sixth and seventh, Wood grabbed a couple and Chris Barrett, Terry Claxton and Adrian Alexander all got a piece of the action. Bushell scored a try himself and landed seven more conversions before Lambert put the icing on the cake by scoring his eighth try for Bushell to convert. These eight tries set a new world record for tries in a senior match and eclipsed the previous Club record of seven scored by Douglas Lambert on 27th October 1906 against Marlborough Nomads. He failed by one point to also take Lambert's all time Club points scoring record in a match set in 1909.

This victory set things up very nicely for the visit of London Scottish to Twickenham the following Saturday. All were to be disappointed though as a ground frost meant that, in the opinion of our visitors, the pitch was unplayable. Earle Kirton set up a 20 minute seven-a-side game for the Quins to show that the conditions were acceptable. After all our high scoring deeds over the last couple of months, we came down to earth with a bump at Northampton to lose by six points to four. Two first half penalties were enough for the home side although Stuart Winship (before scoring our try) lost the ball over the line and Paul Grant was brought back by the referee for a supposed knock-on. Before we could get back to winning ways, we went to Stradey Park and were outscored by five tries to two by Llanelli. A deficit of ten points at half time (6-16) had more than doubled by the end (15-37).

A trip to Portsmouth to play United Services resulted in nine more tries and another fifty points to the season's total. Wood grabbed five, Lambert two and Burroughs and Martin one each. Bushell landed seven conversions to make the final score 50-15. Six of the losing side made the trip to the Stoop the following Saturday in the Royal Navy team who were to become our next victims. After Colin Lambert and Stuart Winship had opened our account with tries, the Navy pegged us back with a penalty. Our response to this was tries from Wood (2), David Cooke and Ken Brabbins (Bushell could only convert one of these six tries). The second half was a one way procession with ten more tries coming from Lambert (5), Tikoisuva, Alexander, Wood and Bushell (2). Bushell took his tally for the match to twenty points with five more conversions and, if he had been in his usual kicking form, our score against the R.A.F. would surely have been beaten. As it was, we had to settle for a very healthy 76-3 win. This result meant we had scored 207 points against the three services sides and conceded just 16. These scores effectively dealt a fatal blow to our matches with them and by the 1979/80 season, only the Army remained on our fixture list.

Against Leicester on Friday 5th March, we were attempting to make it five wins on the trot against the Midlands outfit. The match was played on a Friday so as to avoid clashing with an England international on the Saturday. Midway through the first half, Colin Lambert and Terry Claxton scored tries, Bushell improved the first and later added a penalty to make it 13-0 in our favour at the break. A Peter Carroll try, a second penalty from Bushell and another try from Paul Grant stretched our lead by eleven points before Leicester got a goal back only for Lambert to score his second and our fifth try to make the final score 28-6. The second of a trio of trips to the Midlands in successive weeks saw us visit Bedford. Colin Lambert had been showing his try scoring prowess, in this game it was his boot that did the talking. He landed a penalty and converted Tikoisuva's try to give us a 9-7 lead at the interval. A try for the home side put them back in front but Lambert settled the issue with a penalty from 46 yards out with fifteen minutes left.

Our trip to Coventry was not looking good at half time as we trailed by eleven points. Lambert had scored with a penalty and Adrian Alexander got a try but Coventry had scored a goal, a dropped goal and three penalties. We began our comeback five minutes into the second half when Lambert kicked his second penalty and Terry Claxton added a try. When Paul Grant went over, the scores were level and Lambert's conversion nudged us ahead. By this time, Coventry had lost a man injured and had another limping but we paid no attention to this and killed off the home side with further tries from Lambert (who added a conversion and a penalty) and Winship to leave the final score at 33-18 in our favour. A trip to the Old Deer Park proved completely fruitless and London Welsh gained more than ample revenge for their earlier defeat at Twickenham when they raced to a 26-0 win. Bristol led 11-3 at half time, Bushell kicking a penalty for our points. His second effort brought us three points closer before Lambert ran 60 yards for an excellent try to make it 11-10. Bushell's attempted conversion from the touchline in the dying seconds missed narrowly and we had lost. At Roehampton, we made sure of our place at the top of the London Merit Table with a 24-9 victory over Rosslyn Park and a record of P8 W6 D1 L1. The Easter tour began at Bath with our equal worst defeat of the season (9-35), brightened up when we defeated Swansea after eight successive defeats (19-15) but ended in defeat at Cardiff (4-21).

Our final matches of the season were played during a trip to Venice to play Club Treveneto I Dogi (a selection XV from the area) on 27th May and Rovigo two days later. The party travelled from London via Munich and arrived in Venice where it was raining heavily around 2.30 p.m. After getting to the hotel in Treviso around 4 p.m. the party was received by the Mayor one hour later and departed to Padua for the first game after a meal. Some had been travelling since 6 a.m. and kick-off was not until 9.30 p.m. – not exactly ideal preparation. Our opponents were four players short of having the entire Italian national team playing for them and within ten minutes led by a penalty and two tries to nil. Wood scored a try for us and had one disallowed before the home side got another penalty just before half time. They stretched the lead with another penalty before Wood got his second (converted by Lambert) and third to make it 14-17. In the final minute, we were awarded a penalty near the opposition posts and, as there was no scoreboard, our captain (Stuart Winship) asked the referee what the score was. The reply was that he didn't know!! Winship thought we needed five points and elected to take a short penalty from which a try was nearly scored but I Dogi held on for the win in front of between five and six thousand spectators.

In the second game against the current Italian champions, we were well rested and a far different result was seen. Four changes were made and Bosco Tikoisuva was made captain in his last game for the Club before his return to Fiji on 15th July. Rawle put us in front with a try after eight minutes and Carroll converted but two penalties from Rovigo brought them level. Before the break, Wood and Lambert scored unconverted tries to make it 14-6. Into the second half, Rawle went off after 45 minutes and Stuart Winship became the first ever player to come on as a substitute for us. Wood (converted by Lambert) and Simmons added tries before the first named also went off and was replaced by N. Hassall after 65 minutes. Gilbert ran 70 yards for his try and Hassall and Mickey Claxton also scored. Lambert converted the last two to make it a comfortable win (40-6). The crowd of between two and three thousand gave the players a standing ovation at the end.

The following day, the party was entertained to drinks and lunch at Treviso Rugby Club from where they returned to Venice Airport for the flight home to Heathrow where the party dispersed at 6.30 p.m.

Graham Gilbert made his debut against "I Dogi" and went on to play at least 103 times for the 1st XV. Several players made their last appearances during the second half of the season. Tim Rutter had scored 58 points (18 tries) in his career (which had begun on 1st January 1966 against the Army) when he said goodbye in the rout of the Royal Air Force and Maurice Trapp had managed 32 points (8 tries) in his career which ended against Northampton. We also lost John Gibbs against Cardiff (he had scored 40 points (13 tries)) and Tony Lewis (19 points (5 tries)) and Bosco Tikoisuva (71 points (17 tries and 1 dropped goal)) against "I Dogi". One of our most famous players made his last appearance against Bath when Bob Hiller appeared for the final time. He had won us countless games and had scored a Club record 1509 points (36 tries, 9 dropped goals, 245 penalties and 314 conversions). He managed to beat the previous record of Douglas Lambert by a mere forty seven points.

Colin Lambert surpassed Douglas Lambert's record for number of tries in a season set in 1909/10 with 42 and Billy Bushell scored 286 points (5 tries, 44 penalties and 67 conversions) to beat Bob Hiller's all time points in a season record of 262 set in 1972/73. Overall, the points record of 655 (also set in 1972/73) went and was increased to 912. Tries were also at an all-time high of 150 (20 more than in 1964/65), conversions were up by 46 on the previous season but penalties were down by two. A playing record of W21 D1 L13 was achieved and players making the most appearances were Bosco Tikoisuva, who played in all but two of the matches, Chris Barrett and Colin Lambert who missed only three and they were closely followed by Nick Martin (31), Adrian Alexander (30) and Billy Bushell (29).

1975/76

130975	NORTHAMPTON	TWICKENHAM	L	2PG(6)-1DG3PG1T(16)
200975	LLANELLI	TWICKENHAM	L	1G1T(10)-3G1DG2T(29)
270975	LEICESTER	TWICKENHAM	W	5G1PG3T(45)-3PG2T(17)
041075	SWANSEA	TWICKENHAM	L	2PG4T(22)-3G2PG1T(28)
111075	GLOUCESTER	STOOP MEMORIAL GROUND	L	1G1PG1T(13)-3G2PG(24)
181075	ROSSLYN PARK	STOOP MEMORIAL GROUND	D	2G3PG(21)-2G1DG2PG(21)

251075	CARDIFF	TWICKENHAM	W	2G4PG2T(32)-2G1PG1T(19)
011175	BRISTOL	TWICKENHAM	L	1PG(3)-1G1T(10)
081175	RICHMOND	RICHMOND	W	2PG2T(14)-1DG2PG(9)
151175	OXFORD UNIVERSITY	TWICKENHAM	W	6PG1T(22)-1G1PG(9)
221175	CAMBRIDGE UNIVERSITY	TWICKENHAM	W	3G3T(30)-1G1PG(9)
291175	LONDON WELSH	TWICKENHAM	W	1G3PG(15)-3PG1T(13)
061275	BLACKHEATH	STOOP MEMORIAL GROUND	W	4G1PG3T(39)-1G1PG2T(17)
131275	WATERLOO	TWICKENHAM	W	2G2PG5T(38)-1PG(3)
191275	NEWPORT	NEWPORT	L	2PG(6)-2PG1T(10)
271275	RICHMOND	TWICKENHAM	W	6G1T(40)-1G1PG(9)
030176	ARMY	ALDERSHOT	W	4G4PG2T(44)-1PG1T(7)
100176	BLACKHEATH	BLACKHEATH	W	6G2T(44)-3PG1T(13)
170176	BIRKENHEAD PARK	BIRKENHEAD	W	2G3PG2T(29)-3PG(9)
240176	ROYAL AIR FORCE	TWICKENHAM	W	10G1PG6T(87)-1G(6)
310176	LONDON SCOTTISH	TWICKENHAM	C	
070276	NORTHAMPTON	NORTHAMPTON	L	1T(4)-2PG(6)
140276	LLANELLI	LLANELLI	L	2G1PG(15)-4G3PG1T(37)
210276	UNITED SERVICES PORTSMOUTH	PORTSMOUTH	W	7G2T(50)-2G1PG(15)
280276	ROYAL NAVY	STOOP MEMORIAL GROUND	W	6G10T(76)-1PG(3)
050376	LEICESTER	LEICESTER	W	1G2PG4T(28)-1G(6)
130376	BEDFORD	BEDFORD	W	1G2PG(12)-1PG2T(11)
200376	COVENTRY	COVENTRY	W	2G3PG3T(33)-1G1DG3PG(18)
270376	LONDON WELSH	OLD DEER PARK	L	0-2G2PG2T(26)
030476	BRISTOL	BRISTOL	L	2PG1T(10)-1PG2T(11)
100476	ROSSLYN PARK	ROEHAMPTON	W	1G1DG1PG3T(24)-1G1PG(9)
150476	BATH	BATH	L	1G1PG(9)-4G1DG2T(35)
170476	SWANSEA	SWANSEA	W	2G1PG1T(19)-1G1DG2PG(15)
190476	CARDIFF	CARDIFF	L	1T(4)-1G1PG3T(21)
270576	I DOGI	PADUA	L	1G2T(14)-3PG2T(17)
290576	ROVIGO	ROVIGO	W	4G4T(40)-2PG(6)

A tour to Eastern Canada was undertaken between 13th and 30th August 1976. According to the tour brochure, the party consisted of the following players:- M. Bagg, B. Bazell, T.J. Bryan, P.R. Carroll, T.C. Claxton, M.F. Claxton,

D.H. Cooke, G. Gilbert, P.J. Grant, R. Hammond, J.M. Hockley, W. Jenkins, J. Keily, C.W. Lambert, D. Lauffer, R.F. Looker, M. Luke, D. Puddle, T. Sinclair, C.B. Stevens, D.R. Williams (captain), S. Winship and G.E. Wood. The coach was Earle Kirton and the manager was Dr. Leon Walkden.

The party flew on British Airways from Heathrow to Toronto where they were accommodated by the Toronto Nomads Club for the first three days. An unusually wet summer had produced good grounds and apart from the game in Toronto, all were played in warm and humid conditions. Six matches were played and the first of these was against Niagara District at Hamilton on 16th August where a narrow win was achieved (12-6). In the second game two days later against South West Ontario in Sarnia, an easy victory followed (55-14) but we lost the next match to an Ottawa XV in Ottawa by 3-15 in the only Saturday fixture of the tour. One of the home players was sent to hospital by our tour manager with heat exhaustion. Clubs acting as hosts up to this point had been Niagara Wasps, Hamilton, Burlington, Sarnia Saints and the Ottawa Area Rugby Association. Against a Montreal Area XV in Montreal on 24th August, we returned to winning ways by 28-6 and followed this up with a 24-0 defeat of a Quebec Province XV two days later. In Toronto on 29th August, we met an Ontario XV in the final game of the tour and won again by 15-6. Further hosts had been the Montreal Area Rugby Clubs Association and Toronto Scottish. Another successful tour came to an end with the party leaving for home the next day.

Eastern Canada Tour

160876	NIAGARA DISTRICT	HAMILTON	W	(12)-(6)
180876	SOUTH WEST ONTARIO	SARNIA	W	(55)-(14)
210876	OTTAWA XV	OTTAWA	L	(3)-(15)
240876	MONTREAL AREA XV	MONTREAL	W	(28)-(6)
260876	QUEBEC PROVINCE XV	MONTREAL	W	(24)-0
290876	ONTARIO XV	TORONTO	W	(15)-(6)

After being sent off in an alleged case of mistaken identity whilst playing for Middlesex, Terry Claxton was banned until the end of season 1976/77. He appealed against this decision and, consequently, his ban was reduced until 1st April. During July, there was a report that the clubhouse facilities were in need of improvement and the possibilities of having a purpose built clubhouse were being looked at. On 16th August 1977, it was noted that our groundsman had given one month's notice beginning on 29th July. On 31st August, a request had been received from "I Dogi" for a visit in January 1977 (after our trip to Venice in May 1976) when they hoped to be in England.

The long awaited move towards using substitutes in club matches finally arrived with the start of the 1976/77 season (as has been noted already, we actually first used them in the game against Rovigo). The number allowed was two but they were only to be used in case of injury. For the first time, we began our season with a home game at the Stoop. Northampton were our visitors and following our short tour to Canada, we were in good condition. Gordon Wood and Colin Lambert grabbed two tries each and David A. Cooke and Adrian Alexander scored others to which Billy Bushell added a penalty and four conversions. A half time lead of 21-9 turned into an easy 35-16 victory to give us our highest ever score against the Saints. This good form didn't, unfortunately, last more than one match. Our first ever home replacement was used in the Llanelli match on 18th September when Terry Claxton was replaced by David H. Cooke near the end of the first half. We actually led with a Tim Bryan penalty and a try by Peter Rawle to a penalty from Phil Bennett for Llanelli. But, in just four minutes near to half time, we conceded three tries (two converted by Bennett) to leave us trailing by twelve points. A.A. (Andre) Dent scored a try in the first of at least 169 1st XV appearances, Tim Bryan converted and landed his second penalty to leave us trailing by nine points. Llanelli were not to be denied their rout and three more goals took them to a 43-16 victory. We had been defeated by a superb display of running rugby from the Scarlets orchestrated by Phil Bennett (who ended up with one penalty and six conversions).

After five consecutive wins over Leicester, our run came to an abrupt halt despite a Colin Lambert try putting us 4-3 in front just three minutes before half time. Marcus Rose (later to appear in our colours) landed three penalties and converted the last of Leicester's three tries to give them a convincing victory by twenty three points to four. There was no let-up in the star studded teams visiting us and Swansea were our next opponents. We went down by six points (10-16) before travelling down to Gloucester to face the West Country giants who were severely depleted by county calls. Colin Lambert scored three tries, his final score a last ditch seventy yard run with seconds left to snatch victory (14-9). Against Rosslyn Park, we were beaten easily by thirty four points to twelve in a London merit table match. The merit tables were now the qualifying method for the knock out cup (which had become the John Player Cup). Cardiff had one of their props (G. Wallace) sent off for butting in injury time at the end of the game but still managed to win easily (29-11) before we had our second merit table game against London Welsh at Twickenham on 30th October. Against Cardiff, P.D. (Paul) Jackson made the first of at least 140 appearances and the London Welsh game saw the first of at least 109 matches for R.F. (Richard) "Dick" Best. His name was to become part of Harlequin folklore in the years to come when he both captained and coached the team successfully. The Welsh had won all five of their merit games so far but we put them in their place with 21 unanswered points to win 21-13. Bushell kicked four penalties from way out and converted a try from Wordsworth (who added a dropped goal). This season was to be one of inconsistency in which we would not win more than three matches in a row.

A loss to Bristol (10-24) was followed by a merit table win over Richmond (13-9) and a ten try thrashing of Oxford University (50-12). Against Cambridge on 27th November, David Hodgkiss played the first of his 87 matches. Gordon Wood opposed Colin Lambert in this one, Lambert coming out on top by one try to nil. The match result was very different and a six point lead at the interval had become eleven by the end for the light blues (16-27). Our next visitors were the mighty Gloucester in the first round of the John Player Cup. They were back to full strength after our win over them in October and hungry for revenge. We managed to more than hold our own in the first half and three Bushell penalties to a try and a penalty for Gloucester gave us a two point lead at half time. After this, the visiting pack took charge and we were rarely allowed outside our own half. Masaru Fujiwara (the Japanese international winger) was making the first of at least eleven appearances in our colours in this tie, but he and the rest of our men could not change the course of the tide and a goal and a try in the last ten minutes for Gloucester sealed our fate by seventeen points to nine. So, while our return to cup action had been all too brief, it was still promising for the future.

It was back to Twickenham the following week when Cheltenham were the visitors. We had first played them in 1964 but had not met since. On a bitterly cold day, many mistakes were made but we made fewer and scored four tries to nil. All our points came in the first half with Fujiwara, Alexander, David A. Cooke and Lambert getting the tries and Bushell landing three conversions. Cheltenham managed one penalty in the first half (to take the lead) and two in the second but it was far from enough. This was their twenty fifth consecutive defeat and their fifteenth this season. This was to be our final win of 1976 as our last two matches were lost at Bath and Northampton. At the Recreation Ground, hot soup was available at half time it was so cold and we needed it! Gordon Wood got a try for us but ten points from Bath settled it. Franklin's Gardens on 27th December was not the place to be for any Harlequins. We were so short of players that Dick Best (a prop) came on as substitute for Billy Bushell (full back). We had taken the lead with a Bushell penalty but, by the time Tim Bryan got our second penalty, we trailed by more than twenty points. Six tries (half of which were converted) and four penalties helped Northampton to a crushing victory (6-42).

On New Year's Day, we entertained the Army and won narrowly (13-7) before meeting "I Dogi" in the return match (we had met them back in May in Venice) at the Stoop on Sunday 2nd. Robin Hammond made his last appearance against the Italians having scored 12 tries in his career. He failed to get on the score sheet in this one and three Tim Bryan penalties were more than cancelled out by three tries and two conversions enabling our visitors to maintain their unbeaten record. The following weekend, the Stoop was unplayable so our London merit table match with Blackheath was transferred to the Rectory Field. With Barrett, Bushell and Martin all out injured, our chances of victory were slim and so it proved. We were down by twenty four points before Wordsworth and Lambert got tries to which the latter added one conversion before Blackheath kicked their third penalty to seal victory. Birkenhead Park were dispatched quite easily (21-12) and then the R.A.F. came to Twickenham trying to avoid another drubbing like the one suffered the previous season. In the end, they scored the same points as they had done on their last visit but we only managed four penalties from Bushell.

Our fifth merit table match was played at the Athletic Ground against London Scottish. Despite being 7-0 down at the interval, we came back in the second half to lead by two points thanks to a try from David A. Cooke and a conversion and penalty by Bushell. London Scottish had lost their kicker (Wilson) in the first half with a neck injury and Lawson had taken over the kicking duties. He had been unsuccessful with four attempts before getting one over in the last few seconds to secure a narrow one point victory by ten points to nine. Ian Howard played his last first team game against Wasps on 5th February (he had scored 106 points made up of 29 tries). The match was our sixth and final merit table encounter and was played at Sudbury. A strong wind (which always seemed to be present on this ground) blew straight down the pitch and with first use of it, we led 12-0 at half time. Billy Bushell had scored two penalties and converted Fujiwara's try. In the second half, Wasps did pull three points back with a penalty goal but Paul Jackson ran in from 40 yards out after Gilbert and Martin had sorted out the defence to give us our third win in the table and a record of W3 L3 (50%).

We actually led twice at Stradey Park before Llanelli swept us away (as they had done back in September). We managed tries from Graham Gilbert (2) and Dave Barry with two penalties from Bushell but the Scarlets scored nine tries (luckily for us only three were converted) and two penalties to hand us another thrashing. This was not our heaviest defeat of the season (although it was the highest total conceded) as Northampton had beaten us by 36 points in December. Our most surprising result of the season came on 19th February when we travelled to Portsmouth to take on the Royal Navy. Mickey Claxton was sent off after 40 minutes and we slumped to a six try defeat. Their kicker was off target and only managed to land one conversion and a penalty but the total amounted to twenty nine points; we failed to score any. The following week we met Headingley for the first time since 1963. It was also our first meeting at the Stoop. Two tries under the posts by Maxwell for Headingley effectively sealed our fate (both came from charged down kicks) after we had taken the lead with a try from Paul Jackson. We trailed by three points at half time and by nine shortly afterwards when Maxwell got his first. We battled back to 13-13 with a penalty and conversion from Gilbert and a try by Wood before the second gift lost us the game (13-19). Harry Burroughs made his last appearance in this match having scored 20 tries for the first team.

Against Leicester the following week, we were out to get revenge for our defeat at the Stoop back in September. The kick-off was brought forward to noon so as not to clash with televised international matches. Leicester led 12-4 at half time despite us having 80% of the possession; Nick French getting our try in reply to a goal and two penalties. Our forward domination began to turn into points in the second half and Leicester's only score in this half (a try) was the last in the game. In the intervening minutes Colin Lambert and Malcolm Nicholls had kicked penalties, Stuart Winship dropped a goal and Paul Grant (2) and Nicholls (who also added a conversion) scored tries to leave us victors by eleven points. Our next game was our first ever meeting with Esher and we won comfortably enough (20-7) before meeting Coventry at the Stoop on 19th March. A deficit of four points at the break turned into a twelve point victory as we outscored our opponents with tries from David A. Cooke, Stuart Winship, Gordon Wood and Colin Lambert (who added a conversion and a penalty) and two dropped goals by Graham Gilbert to a penalty and three tries.

London Welsh defeated us at the Old Deer Park (0-20) and we ended up at Bristol with 3rd XV shirts due to a blunder by an official. When you added this to the fact we were missing several players due to such reasons as their car broke down, attending a wedding or having a fever, it was just not going to be our day and so it proved. We lost the try count 5-1 and on points 27-6! The Bath match had been dropped from the Easter tour but it made no difference to results and both games were lost by twenty points or more. All we managed was a penalty at Swansea (3-23) and a try at Cardiff (4-26). Our last match of the season was the return with Rosslyn Park and, as they had beaten us easily in the merit table fixture, prospects of a victory for us did not look good. In the first half, Bushell kicked four penalties to one for Park (playing with a slight breeze at our backs). In the second half, Park had some 85% possession but were unable to score more than a try and a penalty and we held on for a miraculous win.

In the last part of the season we lost a number of players. Alan Wordsworth made his last appearance against Esher having scored 28 points (4 dropped goals and 4 tries), Nick Martin appeared for the final time against Swansea, he had scored 68 points (18 tries and 1 penalty) and captained the side on 84 occasions. Chris Barrett had scored four tries before ending his career against Cardiff (he was involved in a car accident) and Masaru Fujiwara made his last appearance against Rosslyn Park with just two tries to his name. Against Bristol, J.H. (John) Macaulay played in the first of 82 confirmed games and was to be the Club's fly half on and off for the next five years.

Colin Lambert got 17 tries, Billy Bushell was again top points scorer (even though his total was way down on his record breaking amount the year before) with 131 (31 penalties and 19 conversions) and Graham Gilbert and Alan Wordsworth each dropped two goals. Not surprisingly, no new records were created, we scored less than half the amount of tries than we got in the previous season (65), penalties were down to 43, conversions slumped to 28 but dropped goals were up to 5. Fortunately, this was to be our worst season for 23 years but, having said that, bad seasons are never ever welcome. This season had been a copy of the last in that we had played thirty four games, but twenty had been lost and fourteen won. Top appearance maker was David A. Cooke with 31, the nearest to him were Colin Lambert (26), Nick Martin (25), David H. Cooke (24), Adrian Alexander (23) and Chris Barrett, Billy Bushell, Mickey Claxton and Peter Rawle who all missed a dozen matches. This last statistic alone is probably a good enough reason to explain why this had been such a poor year. Without a settled side you are never going to see the full potential coming through.

Between 10th May and 19th August 1977, the British Lions went on tour to New Zealand. Once again, we had no representation in the squad but this time, the series was lost narrowly 3-1. The first test was lost 12-16, the second won 13-9, the third lost 7-19 and the fourth also lost but by a single point (9-10). There was a feeling that the Lions should have won it but they conceded points at crucial times and failed to take opportunities. On their way home, they stopped off in Fiji for a one-off test and lost 21-25 to a side captained by Bosco Tikoisuva.

1976/77

110976	NORTHAMPTON	STOOP MEMORIAL GROUND	W	4G1PG2T(35)-1G2PG1T(16)
180976	LLANELLI	STOOP MEMORIAL GROUND	L	1G2PG1T(16)-6G1PG1T(43)
250976	LEICESTER	STOOP MEMORIAL GROUND	L	1T(4)-1G3PG2T(23)
021076	SWANSEA	STOOP MEMORIAL GROUND	L	1G1T(10)-4T(16)
091076	GLOUCESTER	GLOUCESTER	W	1G2T(14)-3PG(9)
161076	ROSSLYN PARK(LMT)	ROEHAMPTON	L	1G2PG(12)-4G1DG1PG1T(34)
231076	CARDIFF	TWICKENHAM	L	1PG2T(11)-1G1PG5T(29)
301076	LONDON WELSH(LMT)	TWICKENHAM	W	1G1DG4PG(21)-3PG1T(13)
061176	BRISTOL	TWICKENHAM	L	1DG1PG1T(10)-2G4PG(24)
131176	RICHMOND(LMT)	TWICKENHAM	W	1G1PG1T(13)-3PG(9)
201176	OXFORD UNIVERSITY	TWICKENHAM	W	5G5T(50)-1G2PG(12)
271176	CAMBRIDGE UNIVERSITY	TWICKENHAM	L	1G2PG1T(16)-3G3PG(27)
041276	GLOUCESTER(JPC1)	STOOP MEMORIAL GROUND	L	3PG(9)-1G1PG2T(17)
111276	CHELTENHAM	TWICKENHAM	W	3G1T(22)-3PG(9)
181276	BATH	BATH	L	1T(4)-1DG1PG1T(10)
271276	NORTHAMPTON	NORTHAMPTON	L	2PG(6)-3G4PG3T(42)
010177	ARMY	STOOP MEMORIAL GROUND	W	(13)-(7)
020177	I DOGI	STOOP MEMORIAL GROUND	L	3PG(9)-2G1T(16)
080177	BLACKHEATH(LMT)	BLACKHEATH	L	1G1T(10)-3G3PG(27)

150177	BIRKENHEAD PARK	STOOP MEMORIAL GROUND	W	1G1PG3T(21)-3T(12)
220177	ROYAL AIR FORCE	TWICKENHAM	W	4PG(12)-2PG(6)
290177	LONDON SCOTTISH(LMT)	RICHMOND	L	1G1PG(9)-2PG1T(10)
050277	WASPS(LMT)	SUDBURY	W	1G2PG1T(16)-1PG(3)
120277	LLANELLI	LLANELLI	L	2PG3T(18)-3G2PG6T(48)
190277	ROYAL NAVY	PORTSMOUTH	L	0-1G1PG5T(29)
260277	HEADINGLEY	STOOP MEMORIAL GROUND	L	1G1PG1T(13)-2G1DG1T(19)
050377	LEICESTER	LEICESTER	W	1G1DG2PG3T(27)-1G2PG1T(16)
120377	ESHER	TWICKENHAM	W	1G2PG2T(20)-1PG1T(7)
190377	COVENTRY	STOOP MEMORIAL GROUND	W	1G2DG1PG3T(27)-1PG3T(15)
260377	LONDON WELSH	OLD DEER PARK	L	0-1G2PG2T(20)
020477	BRISTOL	BRISTOL	L	1G(6)-2G1PG3T(27)
090477	SWANSEA	SWANSEA	L	1PG(3)-5PG2T(23)
110477	CARDIFF	CARDIFF	L	1T(4)-1G5T(26)
160477	ROSSLYN PARK	ROEHAMPTON	W	4PG(12)-2PG1T(10)

On 8th November 1977, it was recommended that Harlequin Estates Limited be put into liquidation as it was serving no purpose and it was costing the Club approximately £45 per annum. The company had been formed in September 1923 in conjunction with the purchase of Teddington. The tour to France in the first week of May 1978 was discussed on 1st February and it was proposed that games be played in Lyon, Dijon and Paris and a request for a game against the National Bank of Argentina was turned down. On 25th April, the Club decided that the London Merit Table should be the only method of entering the John Player Cup and that the Middlesex Cup would not be entered in season 1978/79. The qualification for a Club cap was defined as follows – that a player must have played for at least three seasons and either obtained a high standard of play or be a sound player who has also contributed personally to the success of the Club or a team. In the committee report for 1977/78, it was noted that Dave Barry was off to a new life in Canada. A fixture with Maidstone on 1st September 1979 was given the go-ahead and the new admission prices were set at – Ground 50p, Ground and Stand 80p (a rise of 5p from the previous season) and Car Park 40p.

David A. Cooke was our new captain for this and the next (1978/79) season. We began with a visit to centenary celebrating Barnstaple in Devon. After trailing for more than an hour, we eventually scraped home by four points (16-12). Colin Lambert (2) and Mickey Claxton got our tries and Billy Bushell landed two conversions to overcome the home side's four penalties. In our first home game (against Northampton at the Stoop), we led at half time with a Lambert try and a conversion and penalty from Bushell to a dropped goal and a penalty. The only points in the second half came after only three minutes when Raybould kicked his second penalty to level the scores at 9-9. It was the same old story against Llanelli the following week. We trailed by only ten points at half time but, by the end, this had become twenty five and a final score of 12-37. A try count of 7-1 in favour of the Welshmen said it all really. Against Leicester, our coach Stuart Winship (who was still playing occasionally for the first team) must have been wondering where it was all going wrong as error after error was made. Only the excellent Billy Bushell in defence made it possible for us to hold them to a 7-3 lead at the interval. Bushell added a try and his second penalty at the start of the second half to give us a narrow lead. Thirteen unanswered points for the visitors took them into a ten point lead and although Lambert got a try and Bushell kicked another penalty, a third penalty from Hare for Leicester took them to a six point victory.

Our third defeat in a row came against Swansea in a low scoring affair. The visitors led with a penalty after 22 minutes only for Lambert to put us ahead with a try just before the break. Our lead lasted only a few minutes before a try for Swansea gave them a narrow victory. Billy Bushell had a terrible day with the boot, missing with six penalty attempts and a conversion. Making his debut in this game was E.W. (Everton) Weekes, a Barbadian playing at number 8. He went on to make at least 185 appearances for the 1st XV. Unfortunately, in the Swansea game, he had to go off with a damaged eye. Gloucester came to Twickenham with a side weakened by County championship calls and paid the price. By half time we led by three tries and a penalty to nil but lost our momentum in the second half to run out winners by twenty one points to three. Bushell kicked three penalties and Graham Gilbert, Colin Lambert and Terry Claxton got tries to one penalty for Gloucester. Northern Suburbs from Sydney visited again after a gap of four years and this time in another Wednesday match, we ran out winners (after the previous draw). Playing with not quite a full strength team, we led 13-0 with two tries from Gordon Wood and one conversion and a penalty from John Macaulay. The Aussies won the second half with a goal and a try but a second Macaulay penalty saw us home. Our first London merit table game was next and our opponents were Rosslyn Park at the Stoop. In an exciting contest, there were never more than six points between the teams. Lambert (2) and Gilbert got tries and Bushell kicked one conversion and a penalty to Park's goal, penalty and a try to leave us 17-13 up at half time. A try and a dropped goal gave Park a narrow lead before Bushell got another penalty nine minutes from the end to tie the game.

On 22nd October, Cardiff came to Twickenham and, like our two previous Welsh visitors, went away unbeaten. A six point lead after 40 minutes was not quite enough for us and twelve points without reply enabled them to win by six. A draw with London Welsh (6-6) saw our second merit table game end with the honours even followed by our first victory over Bath since 1967 (14-6) and an eleven point defeat at Richmond on a freezing cold November day (0-11) in a merit table game. A dull encounter with Oxford University saw us eventually victorious (16-6) but Cambridge outscored us by six tries to three and by thirty one points to fourteen. Blackheath were beaten in a merit table fixture at the Rectory Field (25-12) before we met Bedford (one of the strongest sides in the country at this point) at Twickenham. Unfortunately, we were missing five men (required by the selectors at the trials) and Bedford were without four for the same reason. Tries for us from Colin Lambert and Graham Gilbert and a conversion and penalty from Neil Booth saw us home against Bedford's goal and penalty. The following week, we ventured down to Bath for only the third time in December and two reserve sides played out a gripping match on a heavy pitch. In the first half, Neil Booth landed a penalty and converted Gary Senior's try in between two penalties from the home side. Kevin Douglas and Graham Birkett added tries after the break, Booth converted the second and we led 19-6. Bath did manage a goal but the match ended in a victory for us which was marred by violence when first, Stefan Purdy (one of our lock forwards) and then B. Jenkins of Bath were given their marching orders by the referee for punching and retaliating respectively. Purdy was subsequently banned for six weeks.

We were now on something of a roll and the return with Richmond at Twickenham on Christmas Eve came next. We managed to field our strongest side of the season but still trailed by a goal (Wood try, Bushell conversion) to a goal and a penalty at half time. Our captain (David A. Cooke) was replaced by Clive Woodward after 27 minutes when he injured his leg but this had little effect on our play. We slowly took control in the second half and added tries through Gary Senior and Adrian Alexander (Bushell kicking both conversions and two penalties) to which Richmond replied with one goal to make the score 24-15 with five minutes left. Bushell kicked his third penalty and we were now in free scoring mode as tries by Chris Lamden, Paul Jackson and Gordon Wood showed. Billy Bushell brought his tally to nineteen points with two more conversions to leave the final score at 43-15 and give us what was to be our biggest win of the season. On Boxing Day, we travelled to Northampton and although we avoided the thrashing of the previous season, we still lost. After trailing 0-19 at the interval we came back with a Booth penalty and a David H. Cooke try but it was nowhere near enough. We made five changes from two days before and played Peter Rawle (a scrum half) at number 8! As a general rule these fixtures at Christmas time didn't agree with us and we have never really played consistently well in them. Stuart Winship made his final appearance for the 1st XV against Northampton as a replacement hooker. He had scored 49 points (7 tries and 7 dropped goals) in his career. Our final game of 1977 was at Richmond against London Scottish on New Year's Eve and was also an important merit table match. We had won one, drawn two and lost one of our games so far which gave us a 50% record. A niggly game followed and we went down 6-13, our only scores coming from a Wood try and a Bushell conversion. Our qualification for the following season's John Player Cup would come down to the result of the match with Wasps on 4th February at the Stoop.

In our first match of 1978, we visited the Army at Aldershot and came away with a ten point margin of victory (23-13). Our game on 14th January saw the return with Blackheath at the Stoop in a non-merit table encounter. Our captain returned after injury to score a brace of tries which, coupled with further scores from Steve Edlmann and Colin Lambert, gave us victory. Bushell kicked a conversion and a penalty and Gilbert dropped a goal to leave the final score at 24-11. Despite not being allowed to load our kit onto the train at Euston (which caused us to play in borrowed kit), we carried too much weight for Birkenhead Park's liking and ran out easy winners. Bushell led the side and landed a penalty and two conversions to add to tries from Steve Edlmann (2), Gordon Wood (2) and Colin Lambert (2) (who also kicked our last conversion) for a 33-10 scoreline. On 28th January, we visited Portsmouth to play the United Services in the first round of the Cup and outscored our hosts by three tries to one to advance to the second round with a 19-6 win. The following week, the all-important merit table clash against Wasps took place. In a game played in the rain and mud, we had two chances and took them both. At half time, there was no score and we turned to face the wind in the second half. Peter Whiting inspired the pack and soon Peter Rawle had nipped over for a try. Bushell missed the conversion but Gilbert managed to find a patch of dry ground to drop a goal and win us the match, thus enabling us to qualify for the 1978/79 cup competition.

Bad weather curtailed the trips to Llanelli and Headingley which meant our next match was the cup tie with London Irish at Twickenham on 25th February. We began very well and Alexander went over for a try and Bushell landed a penalty from 62 yards. Two more penalties from Bushell took us into a thirteen point lead before McKibbin kicked two for the Irish to leave the score at 13-6 at the interval. More indiscretions by us handed McKibbin three more chances which he took and with fifteen minutes left, we trailed by two points. In a desperate last effort, Alexander and Edlmann counter-attacked from deep inside our 22 and took play to the Irish 22 where Billy Bushell joined the line at speed and threw out a long pass to Lambert who raced over in the corner for the winning score. We travelled to Leicester and won at Welford Road for the sixth consecutive time. Gordon Wood scored two of our four tries and Billy

Bushell landed three conversions for a 22-20 victory. Liverpool were our opponents in the third round of the cup; the tie being played at the Stoop. The reward for the winners would be a place in the semi-finals on 1st April. We began quickly again and Bushell landed a penalty and converted Alexander's try for a 9-0 interval lead. With Liverpool on the attack and looking likely to score, their left winger dropped the ball, Birkett secured it and broke away to give a pass to David A. Cooke who ran in for a try which Bushell converted. Another penalty from him put us eighteen points up and it became too late for the visitors to do anything and their goal only altered the scoreboard and we were into our first semi-final. This was our eighth consecutive victory and we were still unbeaten in 1978.

This run was to come to an abrupt end at Coundon Road, Coventry the following weekend. Steve Simson grabbed a hat-trick of tries but Coventry scored five to run out easy winners (12-27). It was Easter time again and the usual trip to Swansea and Cardiff took place. We took a reasonably strong squad but were no match for either of the Welsh sides. We held Swansea to a lead of seven points at half time (4-11) with Wood scoring our try. Three more unconverted scores in the second half made the game safe for Swansea by twenty three points to four. A similar tale was revealed on Monday as we were outscored by four tries to one. Colin Lambert got ours and Neil Booth converted to leave the final score at 22-6 in favour of Cardiff. On 1st April, we took part in our first ever cup semi-final. The venue was Twickenham and our opponents were the then giants from the West Country, Gloucester. We had first use of the wind and by half time, Billy Bushell had managed to kick two penalties to put us six points up. When Gloucester turned round, their pack took control and two penalties from Butler levelled the scores. With just over ten minutes remaining, Clewes scored a try for Gloucester which Butler converted and we were out, but only by a score of 12-6. Peter Whiting said his farewell in this game having captained the side on three occasions.

A trip to Roehampton saw a tight game with Rosslyn Park. Steve Simson got a try for us in the first half but two for the home side enabled them to lead. A penalty stretched the lead to seven points before David A. Cooke got a try, Bushell converted and Terry Claxton went over for our third to put us three points in front with just three minutes left. Park only needed two of these and their third try secured a one point win. Our last game of the season saw a trip to an unhappy hunting ground for us, the Old Deer Park. We now had a record of D1 L11 on this ground and came with hopes of gaining our first victory. Peter Rawle, Gordon Wood and Billy Bushell got tries for us in the first half but these were matched by the Welsh who added a fourth after the break for a narrow win. Dave Barry appeared for the last time in our colours in this game, having led the team in four matches and scored 20 points (5 tries) during his spell at the Club. After such an impressive run of eight wins at the start of the year, it was disappointing to finish with six defeats.

Colin Lambert got 19 tries, Graham Gilbert dropped 2 goals and Billy Bushell topped the points with 187 (6 tries, 35 penalties and 29 conversions). Overall, tries were up by fourteen on last season to 79, conversions were up seven at 35 but penalties fell by three to 40 and Gilbert's were the only dropped goals scored. Points rose more or less in line with the extra tries scored. Top appearance makers were Graham Birkett and Colin Lambert with 28, followed by Billy Bushell (27), Mickey Claxton (26), Terry Claxton (25) and Adrian Alexander (24).

The next tour was another short one to France in late April and early May 1978. Three matches would be played against Lyon Olympique, Stade Dijonnais and Paris Université Club. Unfortunately, at the last minute, Lyon had to withdraw so a game against Bourgoin-Jallieu, was arranged instead. The party of twenty three players, two committee members and three supporters left the Stoop at 8.30 p.m. on Saturday 29th April and arrived in Dieppe the following morning at 5 a.m. after the crossing from Newhaven. After suffering a burst tyre, they arrived in Bourgoin around 6.30 p.m. and were then faced with having to make their own beds as they were staying in a hostel a few miles outside the town. This was not a good way to start the tour and when the rain came, the pitch resembled something more suited to water polo than rugby in the words of the manager, Howell Thomas. We didn't play well and went down 7-17 but a very good party given by the Bourgoin Club cheered everyone up.

The following day, the journey to Dijon was undertaken where the party stayed before the next match against Stade Dijonnais on 3rd May. The members of the party who hadn't played in the first game all played in this one. This was a much better performance from us and in the first quarter, we led 16-0 but allowed Dijon to come back into it. There was time for us to pick up our game again and ran out 29-21 winners. The following day, the party were guests of the Mayor at the Hotel de Ville and spent the rest of the day sightseeing.

At some point, a stop was made to pick up wine and this led to a fight breaking out on the coach between Adrian Alexander, Terry Claxton and Peter Whiting. The emergency door on the coach flew out on to the road so when Malcolm Hollins (the physio) asked them to close the door, it was too late. What he didn't realise was that Mickey Claxton was filling his pipe up with weed!

On 5th May, the party made the journey to Paris where the rain started again and this would continue until 4 p.m. the following day. The accommodation arranged was not available as a team of Irish rugby players had wrecked the place two days before. Luckily, our hosts managed to secure an alternative venue about a kilometre from Stade Charlety where the match would be played. On Friday evening, a reception was held at the Martini Terrace on the Champs-Élysées for the whole tour party (including some of the wives of the players who had arrived) and some of the Paris Université Club committee. The last match of the tour kicked off on 6th May at 5 p.m. so it didn't clash with the French Championship semi-final on television but even this did not help with the attendance. Both sides were affected by the conditions and the home team ran out narrow winners by seven points to nil. The journey home the following day went smoothly from Paris to Calais and the party arrived back at the Stoop exactly eight days after they left.

1977/78

030977	BARNSTAPLE	BARNSTAPLE	W	2G1T(16)-4PG(12)
100977	NORTHAMPTON	STOOP MEMORIAL GROUND	D	1G1PG(9)-1DG2PG(9)
170977	LLANELLI	TWICKENHAM	L	1G2PG(12)-3G1PG4T(37)
240977	LEICESTER	TWICKENHAM	L	3PG2T(17)-1G3PG2T(23)
011077	SWANSEA	TWICKENHAM	L	1T(4)-1PG1T(7)
081077	GLOUCESTER	TWICKENHAM	W	3PG3T(21)-1PG(3)
121077	NORTHERN SUBURBS	STOOP MEMORIAL GROUND	W	1G2PG1T(16)-1G1T(10)
151077	ROSSLYN PARK(LMT)	STOOP MEMORIAL GROUND	D	1G2PG2T(20)-1G1DG1PG2T(20)
221077	CARDIFF	TWICKENHAM	L	1G2PG1T(16)-1G4PG1T(22)

291077	LONDON WELSH(LMT)	TWICKENHAM	D	1G(6)-2PG(6)
051177	BATH	TWICKENHAM	W	2PG2T(14)-2PG(6)
121177	RICHMOND(LMT)	RICHMOND	L	0-1PG2T(11)
191177	OXFORD UNIVERSITY	TWICKENHAM	W	2G1T(16)-2PG(6)
261177	CAMBRIDGE UNIVERSITY	CAMBRIDGE	L	1G2T(14)-2G1PG4T(31)
031277	BLACKHEATH(LMT)	BLACKHEATH	W	2G3PG1T(25)-(12)
101277	BEDFORD	TWICKENHAM	W	1G1PG1T(13)-1G1PG(9)
171277	BATH	BATH	W	2G1PG1T(19)-1G2PG(12)
241277	RICHMOND	TWICKENHAM	W	5G3PG1T(43)-2G1PG(15)
261277	NORTHAMPTON	NORTHAMPTON	L	1PG1T(7)-2G1PG1T(19)
311277	LONDON SCOTTISH(LMT)	TWICKENHAM	L	1G(6)-1DG2PG1T(13)
070178	ARMY	ALDERSHOT	W	1G3PG2T(23)-(13)
140178	BLACKHEATH	STOOP MEMORIAL GROUND	W	1G1DG1PG3T(24)-1PG2T(11)
210178	BIRKENHEAD PARK	BIRKENHEAD	W	3G1PG3T(33)-2PG1T(10)
280178	UNITED SERVICES PORTSMOUTH(JPC1)	PORTSMOUTH	W	2G1PG1T(19)-2PG(6)
040278	WASPS(LMT)	STOOP MEMORIAL GROUND	W	1DG1T(7)-0
110278	LLANELLI	LLANELLI	C	
180278	HEADINGLEY	HEADINGLEY	C	
250278	LONDON IRISH(JPC2)	TWICKENHAM	W	3PG2T(17)-5PG(15)
040378	LEICESTER	LEICESTER	W	3G1T(22)-2G2T(20)
110378	LIVERPOOL(JPC3)	STOOP MEMORIAL GROUND	W	2G2PG(18)-1G(6)
180378	COVENTRY	COVENTRY	L	3T(12)-2G1PG3T(27)
250378	SWANSEA	SWANSEA	L	1T(4)-1PG5T(23)
270378	CARDIFF	CARDIFF	L	1G(6)-3G1T(22)
010478	GLOUCESTER(JPCSF)	TWICKENHAM	L	2PG(6)-1G2PG(12)
080478	ROSSLYN PARK	ROEHAMPTON	L	1G2T(14)-1PG3T(15)
150478	LONDON WELSH	OLD DEER PARK	L	3T(12)-4T(16)
010578	BOURGOIN	BOURGOIN	L	(7)-(17)
030578	STADE DIJONNAIS	DIJON	W	(29)-(21)
060578	PARIS UNIVERSITÉ CLUB	STADE CHARLETY	L	0-(7)

The ongoing saga of the groundsman continued when the only applicant turned down the Club's offer. It was agreed that a former groundsman's brother should be interviewed for the post and that further advertising should take place, perhaps in Northern Ireland. The post was eventually advertised in the local job centre but, in the meantime, Stan Ashbridge was helping out. By 20th March 1979, George Hawkins had been appointed to the post. Stuart Winship resigned as coach on his move to Canterbury and it was noted that Earle Kirton was the players' choice as successor. For the time being, Grahame Murray was being aided by Don Mackay who was a former All Black three-quarter who had won 5 caps between 1961 and 1963. On 25th April, an invitation to play in an international tournament in Boston, U.S.A. was accepted. This would take place from 22nd-27th May 1980. An invitation to play against Suburbs Club from Auckland on 21st October was declined as we would be involved in the Middlesex Cup! On 21st May, it was announced that an honours cap was to be awarded to David A. Cooke.

For our first match of the 1978/79 season, we welcomed Woodford to the Stoop for our first meeting since Boxing Day 1929. On a rainy Tuesday night, we started in fine style and tries came from Lambert, Woodward and Dent with Bushell adding one conversion and three penalties. We continued our unopposed scoring in the second half and Lambert got his second, third and fourth tries and Edlmann added another to leave us easy winners to the tune of 39-0 (this proved to be our biggest win of the season). I.C. (Ian) Smith made his debut at hooker having joined from Rosslyn Park and went on to appear a total of 45 times. Our fixtures now settled into their usual pattern with a visit from Northampton to Twickenham on 9th September. The grass was always long at this time of year at Twickenham and comments would always be made in the press. This year was no exception and it was described as "terrifically lush grass" by one reporter. We actually led 21-12 at one stage thanks to a brace of tries from Edlmann, one from Woodward and three conversions and a penalty from the ever reliable boot of Bushell. As has so often been the case, we relaxed and three tries were spurned by knock-ons over the line. Northampton never gave up and three unconverted tries (the last by ex-Harlequin Tim Bryan, who intercepted a David A. Cooke pass) saw them home by three points.

During this period, we came to detest the visits by Llanelli and Cardiff as we usually got thrashed. This season proved no exception and we trailed by eighteen points to nil at the break against the Scarlets. We did manage two goals and a try in the second half but Llanelli got three goals to stretch their winning margin to twenty points. Our next visitors were Leicester at Twickenham on 23rd September. The most memorable sight in this match was Steve Edlmann out pacing Paul Dodge over 60 yards for our second try. We eventually scored three tries to win 21-9. Clive Woodward made his last appearance in this game having scored 61 points (3 tries, 3 dropped goals, 8 penalties and 8 conversions) in his first team career. He would go on to join Leicester and become a thorn in our side on more than one occasion. A side weakened by the calls of the London Counties (who were playing Argentina at Twickenham) didn't have a hope against London Welsh in a merit table game (3-35) although T.G. (Terry) Morrison made the first of six appearances for us (he had gained one cap for New Zealand). We led Swansea 15-6 but were destroyed by a four try burst in 12 minutes during the second half for a final score of 15-35 and Gloucester were defeated (20-9) in a match between two depleted sides due to the County Championship.

Rosslyn Park took us to the cleaners (14-34) and then we met Cardiff with another weakened side. This time, the London Counties were playing the touring New Zealanders. For the fifth time in seven weeks we conceded more than thirty points. We only trailed 6-9 at half time but by the end, John Macaulay's four penalties were not enough to dent Cardiff's total of three goals, two penalties and three tries. The following week we met Bath at Twickenham and actually led at half time with a try from Colin Lambert. Our two match winning streak against them was not to stretch to three and three tries and a dropped goal for them in the second half saw us lose for the third match in a row. We played Richmond in our second merit table fixture at Twickenham on 11th November which, if won, would see us with a 50% record. The team printed in the programme saw five changes to it but we still managed to lead at the interval. Gordon Wood grabbed a try and Lambert landed a penalty to one for Richmond. As was now becoming a regular occurrence, we would be very close to our opponents but then a few minutes of madness would see the battle lost. Richmond scored nineteen points in six minutes and that was that. Although David H. Cooke did get our second try, another goal for the visitors left us trailing by seventeen points.

Our four game losing streak was broken with three quick fire victories and a draw. First came the two universities, Bushell got 20 points against Oxford and ten against Cambridge (1 try, 6 penalties and 4 conversions) to which the rest of the team added seven tries to give us wins by 36-21 and 22-9 respectively. Against Blackheath, we desperately needed a win to give us some sort of placing in the London merit table to aid our qualification for the cup. After a scoreless first half Colin Lambert went over to open the scoring but a try for The Club (as Blackheath are known as they are the oldest open rugby club in the World) from one Jamie Salmon (he was to play for us some four years later after playing for New Zealand) and a conversion from Williamson left us two points behind. John Macaulay got our second try after some inept tackling from the home side and Bushell converted for a cushion of four points. Blackheath came back when Crust landed a penalty but it was not enough and our first merit table win was secured. In a dull match against Bedford, we trailed at half time by a penalty from Bushell to a goal, a penalty and a try. We came back superbly in the second half and a try from Wood was converted by Bushell before David H. Cooke scored to level the match. Bushell's attempted conversion from the touchline hit a post and bounced the wrong way to leave matters all square. This proved to be our last crumb of the year as four away trips resulted in four defeats.

At Bath, a quagmire helped nobody and a try count of 4-1 in their favour was reflected in a 10-21 scoreline. Two days before Christmas, we made the short journey to the Athletic Ground to play the return with Richmond. A close game ensued and with 15 minutes left, we led 12-9. For us, Graham Gilbert and Paul Jackson had scored tries with John Macaulay converting both to which Richmond had scored three penalties in reply. A goal and a penalty from the home side put them six points ahead before Steve Simson ran in from 40 yards out to give Bushell the chance to level the scores, he missed and the match was lost. A Boxing Day fixture at Franklin's Gardens proved to be a complete disaster and, with an already weakened side, injuries caused Andy Hickmore (only present to watch brother John play) to make his debut for the 1st XV. Macaulay kicked a penalty but Northampton scored nine tries and three conversions to complete the rout at 42-3. Not surprisingly, although not the most points we would concede in this season, it was our heaviest defeat and proved to be our last visit here on Boxing Day! Roger Looker made his last appearance in this debacle, he was to become Chairman of the Club in 1986 until 1997. Our final game of 1978 was another visit to the Athletic Ground, this time to play London Scottish and we failed to score for the first time this season (0-16). This was our third loss in four London merit table games and our chances of qualification looked slim with only two matches remaining.

1979 began with the cancellation of the games against the Army and Blackheath (both at Twickenham) which meant our first visitors were Birkenhead Park to the Stoop on 20th January. Colin Lambert was again on the score sheet in prolific fashion with four tries and a penalty with further tries being added by Graham Gilbert and Peter Sutton to leave us winners by twenty seven points to four. The following week we were to have met Plymouth Albion (for the first time) at the Stoop in the first round of the cup but bad weather meant a postponement until 10th February. The week after this we met the Wasps at Sudbury in a must win merit table game. In an entertaining encounter, we led when Bushell kicked a penalty only for a Wasps goal to put them in front after just three minutes.

David A. Cooke went over for two tries (the first converted by Bushell) but a penalty and a try for Wasps levelled the scores at 9-9 and 13-13 respectively. By half time Gordon Wood and Colin Lambert had scored tries and when Bushell got our fifth in the second half, the game was safe although Wasps had the final word with a goal to make the score 25-19 in our favour.

The long awaited cup match took place on the new date but the venue changed to Twickenham which had an icy north-east wind swirling around it. In the first half, Albion led with a dropped goal and a penalty before Billy Bushell kicked a penalty and converted Gilbert's try to put us in front only for a second Plymouth penalty to put them level at the break. The second half was one-way traffic as far as scoring was concerned with Lambert grabbing a try which Bushell converted (as well as kicking his second penalty) and Gilbert dropping a goal to put us into the second round to the tune of 21 points to nine. Our reward for all this hard work was a trip to Gosforth. This proved to be our next match as our proposed trip to Headingley was another victim of the weather. At Gosforth in the second round tie, we were distinct underdogs (as they had won the cup in both 1976 and 1977) and found ourselves nine points down within the first 25 minutes when Young landed three penalties. In the second half, Bushell got one back for us and although we really threatened near the end, we just couldn't break through and out we went. Considering a mound of snow had been cleared from the pitch which left a swamp behind, we were unlucky to lose in conditions which completely favoured Gosforth's heavy pack.

After six successive victories at Welford Road, we came down to earth with a big bump on 3rd March when we were beaten by a clear thirty points. The final score was unimaginable at the interval when Bushell kicked a penalty to level the scores at 3-3. After this we conceded five goals to nil and a depressing final score of 33-3 was recorded against us. Due to the continuing presence of Bedford in the cup, we entertained Ebbw Vale for the first time at the Stoop a week later and in a close contest, went down by a try to two tries. Our third trip of the season to the Athletic Ground (our second to play London Scottish) saw a closer contest but the result was the same. This came about because both our opponents (London Welsh) and the Scots' opponents (Moseley) were still in the cup. In the first half Billy Bushell landed a penalty and Mickey Claxton scored a try to leave us trailing by five points. Gordon Wood got our second try but a penalty had made the game safe for the Scots (11-15). After a gap of two years, we met the Royal Navy again (this was our first meeting at Twickenham since 1972) and we gained revenge for our heavy defeat in 1977. Colin Lambert and Graham Birkett (2) got tries and Bushell landed two penalties and a conversion to a goal, a penalty and a try for the Navy which made the final score 20-13. We would not meet them again until December 1995.

On 7th April, we travelled to Bristol and suffered our second heaviest defeat ever at their hands. Lambert kicked a penalty and Andre Dent scored a try for us when Bristol had amassed eighteen and twenty eight points respectively but that was about as good as it got for us. Four more unconverted tries sealed their victory and we had conceded forty four points for the first time in our history. The Easter tour saw both matches lost at Swansea (13-22) and Cardiff (15-21) but we were perhaps a little unlucky to go down in them. The Swansea game saw the debut of John Butcher at full back (although he played most of his 89 confirmed appearances on the wing). The last match of the season was our sixth merit table game but, as it turned out, both us and Rosslyn Park had already qualified for the 1979/80 cup competition. David A. Cooke made his last appearance for us having scored 51 tries (204 points) and captained the side on 48 occasions (he would go on to join Northampton) and Gordon Wood also appeared for the final time having scored 56 tries (224 points) (he was to join London Scottish). We outscored Rosslyn Park by three tries (Adrian Alexander, Graham Gilbert and

Graham Birkett) to one and Billy Bushell landed two penalties to a Park dropped goal and conversion to leave us worthy winners by eighteen points to nine.

Our playing record was W11 D1 L19 so was worse than the previous one and four matches were cancelled (the most since the same number were lost in the 1968/69 season). Colin Lambert topped the try scorers again with 17, Billy Bushell was top of the points scorers with 126 (2 tries, 26 penalties and 20 conversions) and Graham Gilbert dropped the only goal of the season. Top appearance maker was Ian Smith who didn't miss a game followed some distance behind by David A. Cooke, Mickey Claxton and Adrian Alexander (23) and Billy Bushell and Gordon Wood on 22. Overall, tries fell by eleven to 68, penalties rose by two to 42 and conversions dropped to just 26. Points were also down to 453, a drop of 59 on the previous season.

1978/79

050978	WOODFORD	STOOP MEMORIAL GROUND	W	1G3PG6T(39)-0
090978	NORTHAMPTON	TWICKENHAM	L	3G1PG(21)-1G1DG1PG3T(24)
160978	LLANELLI	TWICKENHAM	L	2G1T(16)-5G2PG(36)
230978	LEICESTER	TWICKENHAM	W	3G1PG(21)-1DG2PG(9)
300978	LONDON WELSH(LMT)	STOOP MEMORIAL GROUND	L	1PG(3)-1G3PG5T(35)
071078	SWANSEA	STOOP MEMORIAL GROUND	L	1G3PG(15)-3G3PG2T(35)
141078	GLOUCESTER	GLOUCESTER	W	1G2PG2T(20)-1DG2PG(9)
211078	ROSSLYN PARK	STOOP MEMORIAL GROUND	L	2PG2T(14)-2G1DG1PG4T(34)
281078	CARDIFF	STOOP MEMORIAL GROUND	L	4PG(12)-3G2PG3T(36)
041178	BATH	TWICKENHAM	L	1T(4)-1DG3T(15)
111178	RICHMOND(LMT)	TWICKENHAM	L	1PG2T(11)-3G2PG1T(28)
181178	OXFORD UNIVERSITY	STOOP MEMORIAL GROUND	W	2G4PG3T(36)-1G5PG(21)
251178	CAMBRIDGE UNIVERSITY	STOOP MEMORIAL GROUND	W	2G2PG1T(22)-1G1PG(9)
021278	BLACKHEATH(LMT)	BLACKHEATH	W	1G1T(10)-1G1PG(9)
091278	BEDFORD	STOOP MEMORIAL GROUND	D	1G1PG1T(13)-1G1PG1T(13)
161278	BATH	BATH	L	2PG1T(10)-1G1PG3T(21)
231278	RICHMOND	RICHMOND	L	2G1T(16)-1G4PG(18)
261278	NORTHAMPTON	NORTHAMPTON	L	1PG(3)-3G6T(42)
301278	LONDON SCOTTISH(LMT)	RICHMOND	L	0-1G1DG1PG1T(16)

060179	ARMY	TWICKENHAM	C	
130179	BLACKHEATH	TWICKENHAM	C	
200179	BIRKENHEAD PARK	STOOP MEMORIAL GROUND	W	1PG6T(27)-1T(4)
270179	PLYMOUTH ALBION(JPC1)	STOOP MEMORIAL GROUND	P	
030279	WASPS(LMT)	SUDBURY	W	1G1PG4T(25)-2G1PG1T(19)
100279	PLYMOUTH ALBION(JPC1)	TWICKENHAM	W	2G1DG2PG(21)-1DG2PG(9)
170279	HEADINGLEY	HEADINGLEY	C	
240279	GOSFORTH(JPC2)	GOSFORTH	L	1PG(3)-3PG(9)
030379	LEICESTER	LEICESTER	L	1PG(3)-5G1PG(33)
100379	EBBW VALE	STOOP MEMORIAL GROUND	L	1T(4)-2T(8)
170379	COVENTRY	TWICKENHAM	C	
240379	LONDON SCOTTISH	RICHMOND	L	1PG2T(11)-1G1DG2PG(15)
310379	ROYAL NAVY	TWICKENHAM	W	1G2PG2T(20)-1G1PG1T(13)
070479	BRISTOL	BRISTOL	L	1PG1T(7)-4G5T(44)
140479	SWANSEA	SWANSEA	L	1G1PG1T(13)-2G2PG1T(22)
160479	CARDIFF	CARDIFF	L	2G1PG(15)-1G1PG3T(21)
210479	ROSSLYN PARK(LMT)	ROEHAMPTON	W	2PG3T(18)-1G1DG(9)

In May and June, England went on a tour to Japan, Fiji and Tonga and won all seven matches including tests against the three nations. No caps were awarded and we had no representatives in the playing party.

Adrian Alexander was elected to captain the side for the 1979/80 season and was described in a report of our first match at Northampton on 8th September as a future England number 8. A new concept was introduced at the start of the season, it was the London Senior Clubs Rugby Festival. The trophy at stake was the Charrington Cup and the competition was played at Wembley Stadium. The idea was to have twelve teams divided into four Pools; each team would play two games within the Pool with the winners progressing to the semi-finals and final. It was 15-a-side, each game was played under the normal laws of the game and was of 20 minutes duration (10 minutes each way with a one minute interval). The final was 30 minutes duration (15 minutes each way with a two minute interval). In the event of a drawn match, it was decided on the most tries or five minutes extra time. If there was still no result, the side incurring the least amount of penalties would be the winners. In the semi-finals and final, extra time of five minutes each way would be played until one side scored (the penalty rule would not count). Each club could nominate 18 players in their squad and anyone sent off or replaced through injury could take no further part in the competition.

There was a preliminary round featuring Blackheath against Saracens and Wasps against Metropolitan Police. Saracens and Wasps progressed and joined Pool B and D respectively. We were in Pool A against Stade Toulousain and Rosslyn Park. After Park had beaten Toulouse 4-3, we went down 6-7 to the French and 0-6 to Park and were eliminated. In Pool B, Blackrock lost 0-7 to Saracens and 4-9 to Liverpool and Saracens beat Liverpool 9-4 to progress. Pool C contained Heriot's F.P., London Irish and London Scottish; The Irish beat Heriot's 10-7 and drew with London Scottish 0-0 while Heriot's defeated Scottish 11-4. Because of the marking system in a drawn game, Heriot's progressed to the semi-finals. The same happened in Pool D with Rovigo drawing 0-0 against Wasps and losing 0-22 to Richmond; Wasps beat Richmond 10-0 but the last named went through.

In the semi-finals, Rosslyn Park beat Saracens 4-0 and Heriot's knocked out Richmond 19-4. The Scottish guest side went on to carry off the trophy with a 6-0 win against Rosslyn Park.

Northampton were celebrating their centenary and we had won just three of the previous twenty meetings so the odds were stacked against us getting a victory. With 10 minutes to go, we had slowly built a 12-0 lead through an interception try from Dent (who ran 65 yards) and a conversion and two penalties by Bushell. The Saints did pull a try and a penalty back in time remaining but we had handed them their first loss of the season. The following day a weakened side travelled to Maidstone (who were also celebrating their centenary) and came away with a hard fought victory (15-7). Our recent record against Llanelli was appalling, thirteen straight defeats in which we had only twice scored more than twenty points. Steve Edlmann got a try after Alexander had got past the defence from a scrum, Bushell converted and kicked a penalty and between Llanelli goals, Gilbert dropped a goal from a five yard scrum to level it up at half time. A third goal put Llanelli in front but we came back with a penalty and a try (given even though the ball appeared to be lost over the line) from Bushell before a penalty gave the lead back to the Scarlets once more. In the past this would have been game over as far as we were concerned but back we came and with eight minutes left, Terry Claxton charged over from a few yards out with two Llanelli defenders hanging onto him for the clinching try. Bushell converted to make the final score 25-21 in our favour. Not since 1965/66 had we strung together three wins in a row at the start of a season so things were looking up. The big question was - could we sustain it?

Our next visitors were the cup holders Leicester, complete with Clive Woodward. Missed chances and bad tackling led to our downfall and two penalties from Bushell left us trailing by fifteen points at the end. Our first London merit table fixture was against London Welsh on 29th September at Twickenham. Colin Lambert got our first try which was equalised by the Welsh. Lambert then went off injured and was replaced by R.A. (Ray) Dudman who was making the first of 133 confirmed appearances for the 1st XV after joining us from Twickenham. He grabbed his first try shortly afterwards which Bushell converted and when Graham Birkett got our third before half time victory was in sight. Everton Weekes moved onto the wing (when Dan Lauffer went off injured at half time) and scored a try and Bushell landed a penalty to increase the lead further. Our visitors did score a goal and a penalty but further tries from Dudman and David Hoade saw us win by sixteen points (29-13). Against Swansea, S.P. (Steve) Moriarty made his debut and would go on to make at least 82 appearances over the next seven years and Everton Weekes was actually selected on the wing after his performance against London Welsh. Swansea came to Twickenham unbeaten and had a shock when Bushell landed two penalties and Alexander scored a try in between to give us a ten point lead after only 15 minutes. We held the lead until half time and lost it during a nine minute spell just after the break when a penalty was sandwiched between two tries. At the last gasp, we broke out and had Weekes held a pass from Bushell it might have been our day. As it was, we now entered a run of defeats which carried on right into November.

Harlequin F.C. 1880/81 season. Standing: P.G.C. Burnand, C. Job, A.W. Claremont, C.E. Grasemann, A.J. Waley, J.C. Howe, A.E. Stoddart; Seated: H. Watts, E.H. Coles, A. Tillyer (c), C.E. Macrae, H.L. Stoddart, L. Weber; Front row: E.S. Kell, F.S. Watts, F.W. Burnand

Harlequin F.C. 1891/92 season. Standing: C.E. Wilson, S.B. Peech, C.L. McNab, G.W.T. Pimbury, N.L. Garrett, H.P. Surtees, J.H. Kempson, H.C. Crusoe (hon. sec.), J.C. Wilson, F de W Lushington, W.F. Surtees; Seated: A.E. Earnshaw, F.C. Bree-Frink, R.W. Hunt, A.A. Surtees (c), A.B. Cipriani, F.B. Hannen

The East Stand at Twickenham in 1909. © World Rugby Museum, Twickenham

The Quins team in the first 1st XV match at Twickenham against Richmond in October 1909. Standing: G.R. Maxwell-Dove, J.H. Denison, B.H. Bonham-Carter, G.V. Carey, W.G.S. Beauchamp, T. Potter, R.E. Hancock, R.O.C. Ward; Seated: H.J.H. Sibree, D. Lambert, A.D. Stoop (c), W.A. Smith (president), J.G.G. Birkett, J.G. Bussell, R.W. Poulton; Front row: F.M. Stoop, G.M. Chapman

Action from the match against FC 1880 Frankfurt in 1910

Douglas Lambert, Herbert Sibree and Adrian Stoop against Swansea in April 1911

Action from the game at Twickenham against The Maoris in October 1926

The Middlesex Sevens winners from 1935. Standing: G.E.C. Hudson, E.A. Hamilton-Hill, P.E. Dunkley, P.W.P. Brook, A.G. Butler; Seated: G.J. Dean, J.R. Cole.

Quins *v.* St. Bartholomew's Hospital at Mill Hill in November 1939. Back row: I.L. Gordon, G.L.A. Anthony, P.R. Noakes, R.C. Rendle, E.W.R. Gaff, P.R.L. Hastings; Middle row: A.D. Keay, T.F. Huskisson, J.F. Tiffitt, Mr Golden (referee); Front row: M.B. Crickmay, J.L. Crichton, K.H. Chapman, R. Bolton, G.W. Plumtree; Seated: N.A. Steel.

Harlequin 1st XV 1947-48. Standing: C.H. Gadney (referee), T.H. Pigot, M.B. Devine, D.M. Stileman, P.J. Goodman, R.L. Hudson, J.M.H. Roberts, C.D. McIver, R.H.G. Weighill, E.L. Horsfall; Seated: D.K. Brooks, W.M. Jackson, A.D. Stoop (president), J.R.C. Matthews (c), K.H. Chapman (hon. Sec.), M.J. Daly, F.P. Dunkley; Front row: J.A. Davies, H de Lacy

Harlequin 1st XV 1956-57. Standing: M.E. Kershaw, D.J. Pack, N.C.G. Raffle, H.G. Greatwood, R.W.D. Marques, M.R.M. Evans, G.P. Vaughan, J.R. Simons, B. Calvert; Seated: W.P.C. Davies, M.L. Grant, R.M. Bartlett (c), V.G. Roberts, R.A.M. Whyte; Front row: K.D. Jones, D.R. Thompson

Harlequin 1st XV 1962-63. Standing: J.L. Bazalgette, J.J. McPartlin, A. Prosser-Harries, G.C. Murray, A.J.S. Todman, J.R.L. Adcock, R.B. Marson, J.T. Cox, R.H. Lloyd, D.R. Trentham; Seated: V.R. Marriott, D.K. Brooks (chairman), C.M. Payne (c), W. Wiggans (team sec.), J.E. Williams, D.F.B. Wrench; Front row: B.J. Bennett, R.F. Read

The Stoop Memorial Ground complete with picket fence and running track in 1963

The first game at the Stoop against Cambridge University on 23rd November 1963

The long grass at Twickenham bogged both us and Gloucester down on 13th October and two penalties from Bushell were simply not enough (6-15) as three weren't the following week against centenary celebrating Rosslyn Park in a merit table clash (9-18). We fell to our eighth successive defeat against Cardiff who completely out played us in every department (19-43) and, after leading Bath 17-15 after 51 minutes, we completely collapsed to lose 17-41. Iestyn Thomas had joined from London Welsh and made the first of at least 59 appearances in this game. In the future, he would go on to become Club coach. Our third merit table match was against Richmond at the Athletic Ground and this also resulted in defeat, a penalty from Billy Bushell was all we had to show until very late in the game when Dent went over for a try which Bushell converted (9-24). We returned to winning ways at last against Oxford and Cambridge (this was the first time since 1945/46 that we had played them both away in the same season). Billy Bushell had kicked four penalties and converted a try from Terry Morrison to complete our scoring before Oxford had got on the board but they could only halve our total. Against Cambridge, we trailed by two points at the interval despite tries from Simson and Butcher and a penalty from Bushell. In the second half Butcher scored his second, Alexander and Gilbert added two more, Bushell converted the first two and victory was safe.

On 1st December another merit table fixture was upon us and this time the visitors were Blackheath. Billy Bushell was once again the mainstay of our scoring and converted tries by Gilbert and Chris Kelly as well as kicking two penalties to help us to an 18-3 win. This match proved to be the last for our captain (Adrian Alexander) as the following Friday (7th December) at 1 p.m. he signed for Oldham Rugby League Football Club and turned professional. He had played one reserve team trial for them and the fee was £15,000. Under the rules of the time he was banned for life from playing or coaching rugby union again. He had scored 21 tries (84 points) and captained the side on 13 occasions. He was a great loss and was sadly missed as, without a doubt, he would have won a cap at some stage in the near future. He would go on to play for Leigh, Kent Invicta and Fulham in a long professional career. Terry Claxton took over for the rest of the season as captain and would continue for the following season as well. Our run of close games with Bedford continued when we sneaked home by two points (15-13) and we conceded three tries in ten minutes at the start of the second half at Bath. A deficit of six points had suddenly become twenty and the match was lost (10-27).

The return with Richmond was successful after three straight defeats at their hands with Billy Bushell contributing 14 points (4 penalties and a conversion) to add to tries from Dent and Dudman (22-10). Our last match of the decade was against London Scottish at the Stoop in another merit table game. Bushell put us into the lead with a penalty but Gordon Wood (on his return) twice broke through, once to give a try to Hume and then to touch down himself which helped Scottish to win 17-3. Against Bedford, we said goodbye to Steve Edlmann who had scored 10 tries (40 points) during his 1st XV career and Terry Morrison who had only managed one try during his all too brief stay in London. Against Richmond we welcomed another New Zealand international in the form of the legendary A.M. (Andy) Haden who went on to play just eleven times for us but was amassing some 41 caps for his country.

We were due to play Nottingham for the first time on New Year's Day but the weather put paid to it. However, we did not have to wait long for that first meeting as it turned out. So, our first match of the New Year was a visit to the Army at Aldershot on 5th January. Tries from John Butcher, Chris Pratt and Peter Rawle and a conversion and a penalty by Ray Dudman were good enough to secure victory (17-6). In the return with Blackheath, we went behind to a penalty after seven minutes when Steve Killick was penalised for apparently raking an opponent on the ground. We came back strongly and Billy Bushell and Everton Weekes scored good tries to which Bushell added one conversion. Five minutes before the break, referee Norman Sanson hauled Killick from a ruck by his shirt, immediately pointed to the dressing room and we were down to 14 men. Two goals from the home side put them five points ahead but Steve Simson squeezed in at the corner, Bushell landed the conversion and we had won by a point.

We entered the Middlesex Cup for the first time and defeated Osterley in the 4th round. Our games in this competition never appeared on the 1st XV fixture list and they were counted as matches played by the Wanderers.

Our proposed trip to Birkenhead Park was cancelled so our next fixture was the first round cup-tie against Esher at the Stoop. The tie was effectively over as a contest by half time after Bushell had landed a penalty and converted tries by Rawle and Weekes; Macaulay added a third to Esher's solitary penalty goal. We couldn't quite put them to the sword after this and although Simson did get our fourth try, a second Esher penalty left the final score at 23-6. The following day at the Stoop, we met the Metropolitan Police in a Middlesex Cup quarter final. Bushell put us in front with a penalty before Tansley equalised. We gradually took control and Rawle went over for a try followed by one from Jackson and another from Simson. Bushell converted the second and third before the Police got one back through Patrick but our passage to the semi-final was ensured when Jackson scored our fourth and Bushell converted for a 25-7 victory. The Metropolitan Police visited again the following week in an all-important merit table game, a must win for both sides. Bushell failed to arrive on time so Dudman took his place at full back and got two penalty kicks over to give us a narrow 6-3 lead at half time. In the second half Rawle and Dave Bowman got tries, Dudman converted the first and although the Police got a second penalty, we had qualified for the cup again next year. Against Llanelli, their talisman Phil Bennett came back after five months out after a knee operation to guide them to victory (23-4) and we achieved our first win at Headingley since 1924 (7-3). We had only met them on two occasions since that first meeting though!

Our reward for beating Esher was a second round trip to Beeston to play Nottingham on 23rd February. This was our first meeting and the prize was a place in the quarter finals. Billy Bushell was acting Club captain in the continuing absence of Terry Claxton and three successful penalties by him from 35, 25 and 40 yards put us in the driving seat. Nottingham were not playing well and by the time Holme had got their two penalties, we had added to our tally with tries from Weekes and Cooke. Lambert and Bushell each kicked penalties before the end and we were on a collision course with Gosforth in the quarter final on 8th March. Terry Claxton's other brother (Gary) made the first of 79 appearances in this game and would go on playing in the 1st XV on and off for 10 years. Thirteen of the fifteen who were to take on Gosforth appeared against Leicester and were completely thrashed. Eight tries were conceded and Cusworth (who scored two of them) contributed thirty points in all to make up the Leicester total of 54 which was our highest ever number of points conceded against an English team. We did get two penalties from Dudman and a try from Maurice Rocks to put us on the board but that was all it did do! Colin Lambert made his last appearance in this match having scored 441 points (94 tries, 15 penalties and 10 conversions) in his career.

The following day, we met Wasps at Sudbury in the Middlesex Cup semi-final. Four changes were made to the side after the annihilation at Welford Road and it proved to be a close encounter. Ray Dudman kicked three penalties and converted a try by Pratt but the Wasps reply of a try from Taylor and a conversion and four penalties by Yarrow enabled the home side to edge us out 18-15.

After this match, Graham Gilbert and Colin Lambert walked out in a row over coaching methods and their non-selection for the cup match against Gosforth. Gilbert had expected a recall after helping Surrey reach the semi-final of the County Championship. He issued a "pick me or I quit" ultimatum after the thrashing at Leicester, was supported by Lambert and when neither was picked, they applied to join Richmond. Lambert never returned but Gilbert was back in 1982.

A gale blew down the pitch at the Stoop when we entertained Gosforth in the cup tie and with first use of it, we only led by a Bushell penalty to nil at half time. It might have been so different had Dave Cooke held on to a pass from Jackson as he was going over the line. Jackson himself gave away a needless penalty, Gosforth converted it and the tie was level. Gosforth would now progress to the semi-finals as the away side in a try-less game if the score remained the same. Paul Jackson had other ideas though and with the last move of the match he made a break, moved the ball left and Simson put in a kick ahead. The ball was fumbled twice by Gosforth defenders as it continued on a roll towards their line. Jackson picked it up and scored in the corner, Bushell converted against the wind and the final whistle went. We now had to gather ourselves for a semi-final at Twickenham against Leicester (the cup holders) and try to avoid another fifty point thrashing. Nigel O'Brien (another New Zealander) made his debut in the Gosforth tie; he would go on to play at least 125 games for the 1st XV. The two games (both away) between the cup rounds were lost to Coventry (10-22) and London Welsh (9-21) and our form was not good.

We started poorly in the semi-final and after Bushell had equalised Hare's penalty for the holders, we fell asleep and allowed Dodge in for a try under the posts. As Hare ran up for the simple conversion, a gust of wind blew the ball over and his attempt went under the bar. His second penalty was matched by the same from Bushell and we were just four points down at half time and playing quite well. John Macaulay dropped a goal from 35 yards to bring us to within a point but then disaster struck. Terry Claxton sprung a rib cartilage after 52 minutes and had to leave the field. This gave the Leicester pack the only leeway they needed and our scrummage was disrupted from here on in. Two more penalties from Hare merely put the icing on the cake for the Tigers. Ian Smith appeared for the final time in this match having given sterling service in his two seasons at the Club. There was no chance of us raising ourselves for the Easter tour after the semi-final defeat and both matches were once again lost. An extremely weakened squad were demolished by Swansea (9-49) but were unfortunate to lose narrowly to Cardiff (18-26). Our last game of the season saw the return with Rosslyn Park at Roehampton on 12th April. It was effectively a third-place play off for the cup as both sides had been semi-final losers. After a scoreless first half, Park scored a goal to take the lead before we replied in kind when Ken Granger (an All Black tourist to Argentina in 1976) scored and Bushell converted. Park fly half Ralston dropped the ball in his own in-goal area and Graham Birkett was up to score the crucial try as the only remaining scores were penalties from Bushell and Greenhalgh. Our victory over Rosslyn Park enabled us to have a playing record of W17 L16. A definite turning point had been reached as the new decade would see a gradual improvement in the overall playing standards at the Club.

Steve Simson was top try scorer with just eight touchdowns and Billy Bushell topped the penalties (42), conversions (21) and, subsequently the points with 180 (3 tries making up his total). The number of tries scored fell by twelve to 56 but dropped goals (2), penalties (54) and conversions (28) all rose to leave the overall points total ten higher than 1978/79 on 463. Top appearance maker was Graham Birkett with 27 followed by Billy Bushell and David Cooke (25), Peter Rawle (23), John Macaulay and Steve Simson (22) and Everton Weekes and Paul Jackson on 21.

1979/80

080979	NORTHAMPTON	NORTHAMPTON	W	1G2PG(12)-1PG1T(7)
090979	MAIDSTONE	MAIDSTONE	W	(15)-(7)
150979	LLANELLI	TWICKENHAM	W	2G1DG2PG1T(25)-3G1PG(21)
220979	LEICESTER	TWICKENHAM	L	2PG(6)-3G1PG(21)

290979	LONDON WELSH(LMT)	TWICKENHAM	W	1G1PG5T(29)-1G1PG1T(13)
061079	SWANSEA	TWICKENHAM	L	2PG1T(10)-1PG2T(11)
131079	GLOUCESTER	TWICKENHAM	L	2PG(6)-1G1DG2PG(15)
201079	ROSSLYN PARK(LMT)	TWICKENHAM	L	3PG(9)-1G1DG3PG(18)
271079	CARDIFF	TWICKENHAM	L	1G3PG1T(19)-3G3PG4T(43)
031179	BATH	TWICKENHAM	L	3PG2T(17)-5G1PG2T(41)
101179	RICHMOND(LMT)	RICHMOND	L	1G1PG(9)-2G4PG(24)
171179	OXFORD UNIVERSITY	OXFORD	W	1G4PG(18)-1G1PG(9)
241179	CAMBRIDGE UNIVERSITY	CAMBRIDGE	W	2G1PG3T(27)-3PG1T(13)
011279	BLACKHEATH(LMT)	TWICKENHAM	W	2G2PG(18)-1PG(3)
081279	BEDFORD	STOOP MEMORIAL GROUND	W	2G1PG(15)-1G1PG1T(13)
151279	BATH	BATH	L	1G1T(10)-1G3PG3T(27)
221279	RICHMOND	STOOP MEMORIAL GROUND	W	1G4PG1T(22)-2PG1T(10)
291279	LONDON SCOTTISH(LMT)	STOOP MEMORIAL GROUND	L	1PG(3)-1G1PG2T(17)
010180	NOTTINGHAM	STOOP MEMORIAL GROUND	C	
050180	ARMY	ALDERSHOT	W	1G1PG2T(17)-(6)
120180	BLACKHEATH	BLACKHEATH	W	2G1T(16)-2G1PG(15)
190180	BIRKENHEAD PARK	BIRKENHEAD	C	
260180	ESHER(JPC1)	STOOP MEMORIAL GROUND	W	2G1PG2T(23)-2PG(6)
020280	METROPOLITAN POLICE(LMT)	STOOP MEMORIAL GROUND	W	1G2PG1T(16)-2PG(6)
090280	LLANELLI	LLANELLI	L	1T(4)-2G1PG2T(23)
160280	HEADINGLEY	HEADINGLEY	W	1PG1T(7)-1PG(3)
230280	NOTTINGHAM(JPC2)	NOTTINGHAM	W	5PG2T(23)-2PG(6)
010380	LEICESTER	LEICESTER	L	2PG1T(10)-5G1DG3PG3T(54)
080380	GOSFORTH(JPCQF)	STOOP MEMORIAL GROUND	W	1G1PG(9)-1PG(3)
150380	COVENTRY	COVENTRY	L	1G1T(10)-2G2PG1T(22)
220380	LONDON WELSH	OLD DEER PARK	L	1G1PG(9)-1G1PG3T(21)
290380	LEICESTER(JPCSF)	TWICKENHAM	L	1DG2PG(9)-4PG1T(16)
050480	SWANSEA	SWANSEA	L	1G1PG(9)-7G1PG1T(49)
070480	CARDIFF	CARDIFF	L	2G2PG(18)-2G2PG2T(26)
120480	ROSSLYN PARK	ROEHAMPTON	W	1G1PG1T(13)-1G1PG(9)

In May 1980, the USA tour took place and five matches would be played. According to the tour brochure, the party was made up of the following players:- Dick Best, Graham Birkett, Dave Bowman, John Butcher, Neil Booth, Terry Claxton (captain), David H. Cooke, Andre Dent, Nigel Drury, Malcolm Foulkes-Arnold, Mark Green, Duncan Harris, David Hoade, Jules Hydleman, David Judd, Steve Killick, Rick Lawrence, Phil McLeod, Chris Pratt, Steve Simson, Ian Stoppani, Iestyn Thomas, Everton Weekes and John Whipp. Earle Kirton was the tour manager, Rhys Williams the assistant manager and three members of the committee also travelled (Frank Cottrell, Malcolm Joyner and John Moore-Gillon).

In brief, the party flew into New York on 18th May, travelled to Albany on 19th and played and won a match against Albany Knickerbockers on 21st. It was then on to Boston on 22nd for an international tournament. Matches were played on 25th and 26th against Austin and Boston (both were won). On 29th, another match was played against Old Gold in Boston which produced another victory. The party then travelled to New York on 30th, played against New York RFC the following day and won again before flying home from New York on 1st June. Some of the pitches were no more than local parks and before kick-off, the players had to walk the pitch to remove all manner of debris from the playing area. One repeatable story from the tour goes like this - Andre Dent was taken on a tour of singles bars in New York by Terry Claxton where the prop would proceed to arm wrestle the bouncers (on one occasion, even smoking a cigarette at the same time). He won every one until at last, he was beaten - at that point he said "Denty, we're going home".

USA Tour

210580	ALBANY KNICKERBOCKERS	ALBANY	W	
250580	AUSTIN	BOSTON	W	(26)-(3)
260580	BOSTON	BOSTON	W	(4)-0
290580	OLD GOLD	BOSTON	W	
310580	NEW YORK	NEW YORK	W	

30

Sevens in the 1970s
1970-1979

Both Sevens teams qualified for the Middlesex finals on 2nd May 1970. The firsts beat Woodford (23-3), Guy's Hospital II (35-0), St. Mary's College II (22-0) and London Welsh II (14-5); the seconds defeated Old Blues (6-3), Hayes I (18-0), Old Haberdashers I (8-3), St. Mary's College I (18-0) and U.C.S. Old Boys II (25-0). Lloyd, Rutter, Hiller (captain), Starmer-Smith, Mason, Miller and Novak (reserves were Paul Grant, Orr, Gronow, R. Bell and R. Cook) represented Quins I and P.J. Burgess, Gibbs, C.S. Hogg (captain), Lewis, Peter Dixon, John Stockdill and Mike Davis (reserves were Bill Petch, J. Westwood, Cox, A. Lewis, R. Penn and D. Laundy) represented Quins II. London Welsh I dispensed with our second team 21-0 but the first fared much better. They knocked out Streatham/Croydon I (21-0) and Rosslyn Park I (16-11) before losing to Edinburgh Wanderers (8-20) in the semi-final. They in turn lost to Loughborough Colleges I by 26-11. We reached the final in our own Sevens again only to lose once more. We beat Oxford and Cambridge (14-5) and Cardiff (18-5) before going down to Loughborough Colleges (15-23). In the Plate final, Llanelli beat Oxford and Cambridge by 16-11.

The next year, Quins I qualified at Sunbury by beating Orleans F.P. (14-0), Osterley II (24-0), Staines I (13-11) and Meadhurst (20-6). The seconds won through to the last game but lost to Saracens I (0-24). The first Seven contained Rutter, Lloyd (captain), D. Coley, Gronow, Nick Martin, Stockdill and Mason with Starmer-Smith and P. Hayward as reserves. Sidcup I were our first victims (18-11), then Edinburgh Wanderers (18-10) and Guy's Hospital I by 25-3 in the semi-final. London Welsh I were met in the final and we went down 9-18. Victory was gained in the Esher Floodlit and the Surrey Sevens by beating Rosslyn Park in both finals. To win the Surrey competition, we defeated Warlingham (23-0), Streatham/Croydon (13-8) and Old Whitgiftians (11-3) before facing Park in the final. They took the lead with a goal but Starmer-Smith and Stockdill got tries (the second named converting one) to put us ahead at the break. Coley and Rutter added more in the second half and Stockdill converted both. A penalty and a try followed for Park but we had too much (18-11). The rest of the winning side was Lloyd (captain), Mason and Hayward. In our Sevens, we lost to Heriot's F.P. (6-20) and then also lost in the Plate to Penryn (6-12). St. Luke's College, Exeter won the title by beating Llanelli 27-10 and Cork Constitution won the Plate, defeating Penryn by 23-6.

In 1972, the first Seven had qualified by being runners-up and the second string failed to qualify out of Sunbury. They lost 14-16 to the Royal Marines in Round 4. Our first team consisted of David Cooke, Lloyd (captain), D. Coley, Starmer-Smith, A. Lewis, Barry and Mason (reserves were D. Judd, C. Ryan, M. Bartley and J. Cooke). Old Wandsworthians I were beaten 26-10 but we fell to Public School Wanderers in the next round (6-21).

They lost in the final to London Welsh I (18-22). We retained our Surrey title by beating Esher in the final. We had won against Exiles (22-4) and Old Croydonians but against Esher, we lost Hayward with a suspected fractured ankle after four minutes and would have to play the remaining sixteen minutes with six men. At this stage, we led through a Coley try but when Gronow pushed an Esher player off the ball, they were awarded a penalty try and we trailed 4-6. After an even struggle, Cooke got the ball, went down the touchline, escaped a tackle and managed to reach the line. Coley converted and the final whistle went. The other heroes were Lloyd (captain), Barry and Mason. This year the Quins Sevens changed to a Pool related competition with no Plate element. We beat Moseley (12-6), Gloucester (16-10) and London Irish (18-10) to qualify for the final where our opponents were Rosslyn Park. Chris Forth scored either side of a goal from Park and Cooke added a third, Stockdill converted all of them and we led 18-6 at half time. Unfortunately, Park scored three tries in the second half, converted one and edged us out by two points (18-20).

Both sides played at Osterley on 28th April 1973, the firsts won through against Hayes I (36-0), Ruislip (27-0), Metropolitan Police II (32-4) and U.C.S. Old Boys I (42-6) but the seconds failed to qualify. Lloyd, Rutter, Hiller (captain), Stuart Winship, Novak, Peter Johnson and Maurice Trapp made up the side with Nick Martin as reserve. As it turned out, they only played one game and lost to London Scottish I (10-26). In the final, London Welsh I completed the hat-trick with a 24-22 win over Public School Wanderers. We fell at the semi-final hurdle in the Surrey Sevens but Mason, Barry, Trapp, Starmer-Smith, Hiller, Cooke and Grant won the Esher Floodlit competition by beating Rosslyn Park II (16-6), Wasps (26-6) and Richmond (12-10). In the final, we played Bosuns (a mixture of Bedford and Northampton players) and each time they went in front, we replied. Cooke got our try in the first half (converted by Hiller) to make it 6-6 then Barry scored and Hiller's conversion tied it up again. In the last minute, Paul Grant went over in the corner and that was that. At the Stoop, we failed to win a game but did run the eventual winners close. We started against West of Scotland (6-18), lost by a point to North of Ireland (18-19) and lost another close one to Public School Wanderers (12-18). The Irish side (with Irish and British Lions legend Mike Gibson in the side) went on to beat Neath 28-10 in the final.

The following year, neither side qualified because the seconds beat Windsor (24-6) and Marlow (16-0) but lost to St. Luke's College, Exeter (6-28). The firsts beat Ealing II (48-0) and Cambridge (31-6) before losing to Borough Road College (10-26). They went to Twickenham and lost to a last minute penalty from Saracens (18-19). In the final, Richmond I beat London Welsh I by 34-16. At Esher, we came within a whisker of another title. We beat Metropolitan Police (24-4), Richmond (22-12) and Rosslyn Park (18-10) before coming up against London Welsh in the final. Despite trailing 3-16 at half time, we came storming back to lead 21-20 and almost clinched the match but Davies ran the length of the pitch to win it for the Welsh. Trapp, Grant and Jenkins got tries and Bushell landed three conversions and a penalty. The other members of the team were Stockdill, A. Lewis and Winship. An international Sevens tournament took place in Paris over two days at the end of April and the beginning of May and we took part along with Rosslyn Park, an international selection team (named after Guy Stener who played for us in 1957) and nine French sides. The final was won by the Guy Stener team who beat Stade Bagnérais by 31-16. In our Sevens, Alan Wordsworth, Billy Bushell, David A. Cooke, John Stockdill, Adrian Alexander, Stuart Winship and Nick Martin won through to the final with victories against Public School Wanderers (20-12), Gala (15-14) and Gloucester (12-3). Against Gala, we actually played the entire second half with six men when Stockdill went off with a suspected broken rib. In the final against Bridgend, we led 16-4 at half time thanks to three tries from Cooke and two conversions by Bushell. Four tries for Bridgend in the second half (two of which were converted) took the cup away from us yet again. Dave Barry had replaced Stockdill in that final, our fourth loss in seven years.

Again, Osterley was the ground where our assault on the trophy would begin in 1975. The seconds featured Steve Simson, Bob Hiller, Barney Bazell, Nigel Davis, Miles Hockley and Paul Snare among their ranks and the firsts had Harry Burroughs, Clive Woodward, Billy Bushell, David H. Cooke, Stuart Winship (captain), Graham Birkett, Gordon Wood, Mike Luke, Miles Hockley and T.A. Lewis. Quins I began with an easy win over Old Hamptonians I by 32-0; tries came from Burroughs, Woodward (3), Cooke and Bushell (he also landed four conversions). Windsor fell next by 26-0 (Burroughs (2), Woodward (2) and Winship got the tries with Bushell adding three conversions. Marlow I were seen off by 24-6 with tries from Burroughs, Woodward and Bushell (2) and four conversions from the last named. In the final preliminary round, Purley I fared no better and Burroughs (2), Birkett and Bushell got tries with the usual kicker adding a penalty and three conversions. The second team beat Old Albanian (14-6), Antlers I (20-6) and Hampstead I (16-12) before going out to St. Luke's College, Exeter (10-30). The following week, we began with a win over Saracens (13-7) and edged out Coventry (16-12) with Wood, Burroughs and Bushell (who added two conversions) getting the tries. Against Loughborough Colleges I in the semi-final, Cooke scored for Bushell to convert but we lost 6-16. Richmond proved too strong in the final and ran out winners 24-8. We made the semi-final in the Surrey Sevens but got no further. At Esher, we again reached the final by beating Sidcup (20-12), Wasps (12-4) and Sutton and Epsom (18-12). London Welsh were our opponents and we lost again but this time it was more convincing. Bazell scored our try and Davis converted but the Welsh scored six and J.P.R. Williams added four conversions to make it 32-6. The rest of our side was Steve Simson, Chris Forth (Graham Birkett replaced him in the final), Stuart Winship, David H. Cooke and T.A. Lewis. The first London Floodlit Sevens (organised by Rosslyn Park) took place this year and we defeated Metropolitan Police (24-0) and St. Luke's College, Exeter (16-6) to win the Pool but lost in the semi-final to eventual winners London Scottish (6-12). Our tournament moved to a Sunday for the first time in 1975 and we beat Blackheath (22-6), lost to Bridgend (10-28) and won against Paris Université Club (32-6). It wasn't enough because, in the end, Bridgend scored one more try than us to go through to the final where they lost to Melrose (6-20). Our squad and scorers were Stockdill, Bushell (8 conversions), Winship (1 try), Alexander (2 tries), David A. Cooke (4 tries), Lambert (5 tries) and Martin.

In 1976, the firsts beat Old Hamptonians II (28-0), Marlow II (22-6), Cambridge II (34-6), Orleans F.P. I after extra time (16-12) and London Welsh II (21-14). The seconds almost made it but fell at the final hurdle by losing to London Welsh I (4-40); they had beaten Windsor (16-14), Barclays Bank (16-6) and Purley I (16-6). Colin Lambert, David A. Cooke, Bushell, Winship, Martin (captain), Bosco Tikoisuva and Adrian Alexander made up the 1st VII. We played Richmond II and won comfortably (28-0), Alexander, Cooke, Lambert, Tikoisuva and Bushell (who kicked four conversions) got tries. Next up were Richmond I and tries from Tikoisuva and Cooke (2) plus two conversions from Bushell saw us home 16-4. London Welsh I were dispatched in the semi-final by 22-12; Lambert, Tikoisuva, Cooke and Bushell got the tries and the last named added three conversions. Into the final against Loughborough Colleges I, we took the lead when Tikoisuva scored but Bushell hit the post with his conversion attempt. By half time, we trailed 4-12 with tries by Douglas and Williams (both converted by Glynn) and when he added a penalty and converted a try by Douglas, we were seventeen points adrift. Back we came and scored through Tikoisuva and Lambert (both converted by Bushell) to make it 16-21. With time running out, Lambert went again and was chased all the way by the defender who pushed him wide and he scored right in the south-east corner. Bushell had the conversion to win the title but he just missed to the right and we had lost after looking the best side on the day. As part of the entertainment, a flying demonstration was given by a Royal Navy Wessex helicopter between the semi-finals and the final. In the Surrey tournament, we lost to eventual winners, Blackheath in the second round (18-16). A strong side represented us in our own tournament – David A. Cooke, Nick Martin, Adrian Alexander, Pete Rawle, Dave Barry, Billy Bushell and Colin Lambert. They won the Pool with victories over Nottingham (28-6), St. Giron (28-0) and Voyagers (24-16). In the final against Melrose, Lambert and Rawle got tries and Bushell converted both to give us a 12-0 lead. Melrose scored next through Calder for Wood to convert but Cooke got another and Bushell converted again. Just before the break, Dodds scored and Wood converted. Into the second half, a pass from Lambert went to Robertson who scored for Wood to make it all-square. Cooke went over next, Bushell converted and victory was within our grasp. Right at the end, Wood converted his own try to make it 24-24 and extra time would be required. Bushell was brought down a yard from the line, we were awarded a penalty and Alexander almost got over. Another penalty to us but Calder intercepted and just as it looked as though he would score, Lambert came steaming over to take him down. The ball bounced perfectly for Robertson to kick on and he just beat Cooke to the touchdown – we had lost by 24-28.

As runners-up, the first Seven qualified automatically in 1977 but the seconds lost to Old Wimbledonians II (0-16) in the second game. Streatham/Croydon I were our first opponents and tries from Lambert, Cooke, Graham Gilbert (2) and Bushell (plus four conversions) helped us to a 28-6 win. Against Wasps I, two tries from Lambert and one by Bushell saw us home 12-6 and in the semi-final against Gosforth, Bushell converted two more from Lambert. At that point, we led 12-10 but, in the tenth minute of the second half, Britten crashed into the corner flag and was awarded the try to knock us out. David H. Cooke, Wood, Steve Edlmann and Dave Puddle made up the squad. Gosforth went on to lose 16-26 to Richmond I in the final. We won the Surrey Sevens by beating Old Whitgiftians in the final. At Esher, Lambert, David A. Cooke, Bushell, Winship, Puddle, Barry and Best beat Oxford (12-0), Rosslyn Park (22-0), Leicester (20-6) and Esher (24-12) to take the title again. We drew with Loughborough Colleges (12-12) and defeated Blackheath (18-4) to reach the semi-final in the London Floodlit event having scored one more try than Loughborough (6-5). In the semi-final, we went down to Rosslyn Park 10-16 who then beat London Welsh in the final by 22-6. In our event, named the Jubilee tournament (as everything seemed to be in 1977), we beat Paris Université Club (20-6) but went down to Bedford (6-8) and Bridgend (12-18). That meant elimination but the Pool winners (Bridgend) lost 10-34 to Gosforth in the final.

Qualification from Osterley in 1978 proved beyond the second string again; they did win against Old Isleworthians (20-0) and Old Colfeians (30-14) but Old Thamesians I just edged a close contest (12-18). The firsts breezed through against Ealing II (30-4), Old Blues II (48-0), Civil Service I (44-0) and London Welsh II (16-0) – this side had serious pace and meant business. Wood, Cooke (captain), Gilbert, Chris St.J Lamden, Alexander, Kevin Douglas and Lambert were the men in question with Burroughs, Dick Best and Neil Booth in reserve. To the finals and after we had beaten Maidstone I (26-6) and Hawick (14-6), it was London Welsh I in the semi-final. David Rees scored for them before Wood and Gilbert scored tries and Lambert and Lambden converted before half time. At this point, Mick Jones (the Welsh prop) who had been outstanding, was tackled out of the game and despite Clive Rees scoring for their first try scorer to convert, we went through narrowly (12-10). In the final, we met Rosslyn Park I and by half time, led 24-0. After a small rally to get it back to 24-12 (tries from George and Lloyd both converted by George), Park faded away and we added another sixteen points to set a record score for a final. Tries came from Douglas (2), Wood (2), Lambert, Cooke, Lamden and Gilbert with conversions from Lamden (3) and Lambert to make it 40-12. The trophy was once more in our hands! The Surrey crown was retained with Esher as runners-up as was the Esher Floodlit trophy with Richmond beaten in the final. At the Stoop, we failed again and lost to Hawick (16-26) but won against Rovigo (24-16) and London Irish (18-4). Hawick went on to beat Sale in the final by 32-10.

To end the decade, the seconds tried to join the holders by qualifying at Osterley. They did win against Marlow II (40-0) and Borough Road II (18-10) but went out to London Welsh I (0-28). Against Marlow, tries came from Paul Grant (2), Phil McLeod, Paul Jackson, Dave Puddle and Dave Bowman (2) plus six conversions by Harry Bartlett. In the Borough Road game, Jackson (2) and Bowman got the tries and Bartlett converted all three. The defending champions were Wood, Bushell, Gilbert, Andre Dent, Alexander, Douglas and Lambert (captain); Birkett got injured and Best was the reserve. We beat Blackheath I (10-6) and London Irish I (12-10) but lost to Richmond I in the semi-final 18-6. They went on to defeat London Scottish I by 24-10 to lift the trophy. Somewhere around 60,000 people attended the 1979 tournament as the standard of play on the pitch got better and better. We completed a hat-trick of wins at the Esher Sevens by beating Rosslyn Park in the final. At the London Floodlit tournament, we got through the Pool stages with wins over Metropolitan Police (30-0) and Esher (32-0), beat Richmond in the semi-final (18-0) and finished off a great night with victory against London Welsh (28-18). We even took part in the Raynes Park Sevens but no result is known. Our own Sevens eluded us again following narrow defeats in the Pool against Bath and Heriot's F.P. (both 8-10) but we did beat Blackrock College 24-10 in between. Heriot's went on to beat Bridgend easily in the final by 30-10.

31

Never Mind the Bollocks...Here Come the Harlequins!

Here are a selection of stories and anecdotes from the seventies and eighties. I'll leave it up to the reader to decide whether they are true or not!

When he was captain, Terry Claxton used to bring a bottle of sherry into the changing room before a game to give everyone a shot to get them going.

Harry Bartlett (who was the son of Ricky Bartlett) served in the Royal Marines and says that when he landed on West Falkland in 1982, he remembered what he'd learned from fighting with Adrian and Terry. On one occasion, Terry gave him a "dig" on the bus and broke his ribs!

In 1973, playing against Rosslyn Park, one of their second row forwards had just thumped one of our players. Terry Claxton stepped in to deal with him at the next lineout and as he came down, Terry hit him in the jaw with a right hander. The referee (Johnnie Johnson) saw the incident and said to him "He deserved that Terry"!

The Club had to install a cage around the bar because one thirsty player (Terry Claxton) found it difficult to resist the delights on offer. One of the back row (Everton Weekes) was the man responsible for obtaining cigarettes from the bar to take on away trips.

In the eighties, there was one occasion when, after a training session, cars were raced around the old running track under the lights.

After a tip-off from the groundsman, Mickey Claxton used to bring his truck round to empty it in the skips at the Stoop just before the bin men visited.

One lady from catering used to walk across the pitch during a game when play was at the other end and as she reached Terry Claxton and Mark Green, she would hand them pork chops. When Green asked why Terry got two and he received only one, the answer was simple "because he's the captain".

During another tough encounter with Gloucester, Terry Claxton broke Mike Burton's finger. It was described as being in the shape of the letter Z. When Burton complained, Terry's retort was "Well, you shouldn't stick it in my eye then"!

Another case of "jolly japes" was when Adrian Alexander was talking to a Northampton official about their brand new clock. What he couldn't see and Adrian could was that Mickey Claxton was climbing up to remove the clock from the wall. When the chap turned round to proudly point out the clock, it was gone! The said time piece was returned on this occasion.

Terry Claxton recalls that a letter was sent to his father's house asking Terry not to come back to the Club as he was the wrong sort of person – he was having none of it. When he saw some of the old elitist officials (Jay Gould, Ronnie Hudson and John Seldon) he said he would be captain of this Club one day. They told him if you do, we'll never set foot in this place again! When he became captain, he went up to them and said "I've kept my side of the bargain, now keep yours"!

Terry Claxton was playing for Twickenham, went for a 20 minute training session at Quins, thought no more of it and went on holiday to Spain for three weeks with work colleagues. When he returned, his Mum said that there was some foreigner who kept ringing him up. The phone rings again, Mum answers and says to Terry "It's that foreigner again". When he gets to the phone, a voice says "Terry, it's Earle Kirton at Harlequins, can you come over". He left his dinner and rushed to the Stoop. When he walked in, he could see Bob Hiller, Nigel Starmer-Smith and Mike Novak sitting there and couldn't quite believe it. He said "Claxton's my name, where do I change"? After training they said see you at 1 p.m. at Twickenham. He replied that he hadn't even told them he had left and now Quins were expecting him to play against them. It was pointed out that it was at Twickenham against Swansea. Terry said "What, that bloody great big stadium up the road and who the bloody hell are Swansea"? He soon found out! The speed of the game took him completely by surprise and he was finished after ten minutes. There were 17 minutes of injury time and at the end, he filled up one of the baths with cold water and sat in it for 20 minutes. Mike Mason, the captain, came up to him and told him it wouldn't get any worse than that.

During Adrian Alexander's season of mayhem, on a trip back from a game they'd won against Oxford University, Adrian and Terry Claxton decided not to go back on the team coach but get a lift from another player. Of course they'd had a few jars. On the journey home they got pulled over by the police and their driver was arrested for drink driving. The driver was taken for tests and while Adrian and Terry were waiting they were made to stand with the local delinquents. Terry was 'on form' as usual. Behind the counter was a young country copper who asked where they were from. Quick as a flash Terry told him they were Bodie and Doyle (TV detectives from The Professionals) and that they were undercover looking for problems in the area and asked for his help. The copper agreed to help if he could. There was no organisation in the waiting room whatsoever. Terry told them to get to attention and face the wall and that they hadn't got to move until he said so - he was Inspector Doyle. Adrian was dying to laugh but had to keep a straight face. They all got in a line, faced the wall and it all went very quiet. Terry then asked the constable where he could go to the toilet and was told there wasn't one really but he could try round the back of the building at the social club but he thought it might be closed. Terry said "no problem". Ten minutes later he appeared with a case of beer and proceeded to give cans to the supposed criminals and let them all sit down. Unbeknown to the copper Terry had gone round to the social club which was shut and broken the door down, got a case of beer and left a fiver on the counter. This went on for about 45 minutes and then suddenly right behind the copper stood a bloke with a hat on with all silver braid standing there staring at them. He said "Now, which one of you is Bodie and which one of you is Doyle"? That set Adrian off laughing. With that he said "It's no laughing matter I can do you for impersonating a police officer". "Now" he said "all I can say is your friend has passed the tests so f*** off out of Oxfordshire and don't ever come back". So they scampered out the door never to be seen again.

Adrian Alexander's first game for Harlequins was at Twickenham in September 1974 against Northampton. He played second row and he'd come from Cornwall at the beginning of the summer. He had been down there dossing with a friend, living in a barn and working in a tin mine. He ended up playing for St. Ives Colts but had broken his ankle in a game against Spain playing for Cornwall Colts. He returned to London and his friend Graham Birkett who'd been picked by Harlequins said why don't you come along to Quins and get your body and ankle fit and then go back to Old Thamesians. He worked hard during the training sessions and they did 20 minute training games called 'Chukkas'. Unbeknown to Adrian quite a few of the Quins back row started to get injured. The first thing on the map was the Harlequin Sevens. As Adrian was the last man standing and he had played a lot of sevens with Old Thamesians (who were very good at it), he ended up in the team. It was the first tournament at the beginning of the season and Quins got to the final. Adrian had never known a game played so fast. His mother was sat at home listening to it on the radio, Peter West was doing the commentary and she burst into tears when they mentioned his name. He remembered the game with great pride. The following Saturday Quins had trials for the Northampton game. He was standing next to Mickey Claxton. He was expecting to be in the second team, the names were read out and his name wasn't read out. He was unbelievably disappointed, it all went quiet, everybody gave him the 'tough talk' to keep strong, it will get better. Suddenly, Club captain Nick Martin came up to him and put his arm round him and said "Alex, you're with me in the second row at Twickenham on Saturday". His legs buckled and his throat went dry and Mickey Claxton collapsed laughing. He'd seen his disappointment at first and then his disbelief. Second row at Twickenham against Northampton, his debut, a baptism of fire!

When they went to Lydney on a Wednesday night to open their new floodlights, it was another battle down in the West Country. We were short of a prop so on the way down they went to Oxford University to pick up a Don called Wrench. Adrian Alexander had never heard of him and thought he was an old man in his 40s and he was a typical 'Old School' type. He was to be totally surprised. They got there, the game kicked off and the next thing they knew there was mayhem as Lydney tried to take us apart. Quins fought back and Wrench the Oxford Don, the 'posh' man was right in the front of it shouting and stamping and saying this is the way Harlequins should have always played. Unbelievable, everyone just stood looking at each other. Where had they found this bloke? Then the stories of his past came out, how he had destroyed various props in his day. We won the game and after the game had finished the atmosphere in the clubhouse was horrible. The committee were fine but the players were so nasty. Adrian thought it was going to kick-off again but there wasn't a problem. It was an honour to play with the great Wrench who took no prisoners.

On the way back from games, the players would always stop at a service station. As they were working their way down the self-service counter they would eat the food and when they got to the counter the woman would be waiting for them to pay and someone would say "15 teas please love" and she'd just look at them. There was nothing she could do because they'd eaten all the evidence. One night when they were out in town with Dr Peter Rawle, they ended up at St. Thomas's Hospital because it had a late cafe. As they got to reception there was a caretaker with the thickest glasses you have ever seen and he could hardly see. Terry Claxton went in first covered in tattoos and said "any messages for Dr. Clack"? The bloke looked through all the pigeon holes and said he couldn't find anything for Dr. Clack. They went down to the cafeteria having been out drinking all night in bars in the West End and proceeded to do their normal trick, eating everything before they got to the till. They could see the woman with her arms folded staring at them. "Four teas love" said Terry. She said "You doctors are all the bloody same". At least rugby players weren't the only bad ones in the world!

Adrian Alexander and Chris Butcher jumped into a cab on their way to Bootleggers night club and explained to the cabbie they were stunt men from the new Superman film (they had the jackets on to prove it). As they drove down The

Mall, Chris decide to show off his skills, he went out of the window, across the roof and back in through the opposite window! When they reached their destination, they asked what the price was – the answer, for that display, no charge!

Before Mark Green's first game at Twickenham, he was understandably a bit nervous but Terry Claxton told him to meet up at The Nelson pub in Whitton for a couple of pints to settle him down. Mark ordered an Orange juice, Terry slipped in a vodka and this was repeated on the next round. In the game, Mark was in a ruck and a boot came either side of his face. As he was trying to protect himself, whilst asking himself what the hell he was doing there, the guy suddenly disappeared to be replaced by Terry looking down at him asking if he was okay. He didn't look back from that point on and the story continues at the selection meeting when Geoff Ashby asks who was being selected on Saturday. They said they could play Greenie because he always plays well when Terry plays and the same when Mickey played. Mark knew that whenever there was a punch-up on the pitch, he could count to two and a Claxton would arrive. If there was no Claxton, you were on your own.

When Mark was brought on to the Club committee, at his first meeting, he asked Herridge and Looker what he should do and they said put your hand up when we do – great advice!

At a dinner in a curry house at Hampton Court, Terry Claxton was short of cash at the time and kept his costs down to a minimum. Unfortunately, some others started drinking wine and the bill came to twenty pounds each. When a chap delivered the news to Terry, he felt he had been taken for a ride. He told the spectacle wearing person that he didn't hit people with glasses but would make an exception in his case. He took his glasses off, gave him a tap and as he was lying on the floor, Terry put his glasses back on!

When Joe Sass was preparing to play against Gloucester and Mike Burton, he asked Terry Claxton for advice. He told him that when Burton started to take him down, he was to hit him. That's what he did and Burton was no problem after that. When the game had finished, the Gloucester man came up to Joe and asked him who gave him the advice, when he said Terry, Mike knew he had been stitched up.

Roy Croucher first became involved with the Rugby Union at Twickenham about 1950 (his father was a charge hand there from 1928-52). His jobs were Programme Boy, Cushion seat seller, clearing straw from the pitch (laid to protect it from ice and snow), Steward and Seat washer. He joined Quins in October 1984 and left at the end of the 1998/99 season. He did all aspects of maintenance on both the main and training pitches, maintaining the bars and ordering stock. Being ground manager was never a dull job because he used to deal with situations as they arose, repairs and staffing plus anything else that came up. People used to say that he had the largest back garden in London! Between late May and August there was an extensive workload including rejuvenating pitches and maintenance of the Clubhouse. During the period Roy was at the Club, training was on Monday and Thursday evening with matches played on Saturday and Sunday. There was also Middlesex and England Training and any other club that wanted to hire the pitch when we weren't using it. When he had finished marking the pitches up, Pitch 1 would be J W C and Pitch 2 was M R C – these were the initials of his parents John William Croucher and Margaret Rose Croucher.

When Roy was marking the pitch one Friday before the game the next day, he noticed that there appeared to be water running down the stairs of the old West stand. On closer inspection, a pipe had fractured at some point overnight and the bar was sitting in four inches of water! The only way to clear it was to sweep it through the double doors at the end, down the stairs and out. Not ideal preparation but all was sorted in time for the game.

When we reached our first cup final in 1988, Roy would sell tickets through one of the bedroom windows of his bungalow and this would be repeated for other big games. This was probably our first ticket office! His dog was called Sandy and she was a Lurcher (Alsatian/Collie cross). On one occasion he had a letter from the Chairman because somebody complained Sandy was out of control and it should be corrected. He wrote back to the Chairman and informed him that Sandy's position was to keep undesirable people away from the ground so he assumed the person who wrote the letter was an undesirable person!

32

A Time of Slow and Steady Improvement 1980-1987

It was time for another Lions tour in 1980 and this time it was the turn of South Africa to host the side. Our only representative was Clive Woodward although he was now at Leicester; he played in the second and third tests. The first three were lost narrowly (22-26, 19-26 and 10-12) but the fourth was won (17-13) to salvage a little bit of pride. This tour had been overshadowed by the apartheid question and, rightly or wrongly, the home unions had decided that it should go ahead.

The aforementioned Ken Granger was offered the groundsman's job at the Stoop and stayed with his wife and two sons in the bungalow until the end of this season. On one occasion, the kiwis at the Club decided to show the English boys how to put a Hangi down. They spent ages digging a pit at the north end of the old stand and getting iron bars to put in and heat up as they couldn't find the right stones. They got all the food prepared and put into the ground wrapped in damp sacks. They had everyone mesmerised with this Maori cooking style and they were all happy to pay £2 a head to help cover costs. After some 15 hours in the ground it was time to lift the Hangi. With something like thirty excited guys watching, they brought the food out and to their shock it was only half cooked! They ended up taking it up to the kitchen in the stand and finishing it off there! Meanwhile it cost the poor kiwis a lot of money entertaining the boys with drinks from the bar awaiting their feed! They never lived it down and were reminded of their cooking prowess for the rest of the season!

In the early part of the 1980s, the Club undertook some short pre-season training tours. They were not official tours in the true sense of the word but some hard games resulted. Places visited would be Clermont (1981), San Sebastian and Bayonne (1983) and Valencia (1986). The last one was when the Spanish national side was played.

The London Senior Clubs Rugby Festival returned on 6th September 1980 and this time the venue was Twickenham. The rules remained the same and once again fourteen teams took part. The first round actually took place at the Stoop and saw four matches played. The four winners moved into the second round and the victorious sides from these games progressed to the quarter finals where the remaining six teams entered the competition. At the Stoop, Rosslyn Park went out to London Scottish 0-4, Metropolitan Police defeated Saracens 6-0, Ray Dudman kicked two penalties for us in a 6-4 win against London Welsh and Wasps beat Blackheath 9-0. Moving on to Twickenham, London Scottish defeated the Police 4-0 and Wasps knocked us out 3-0. In the quarter finals, Maidstone drew with Richmond 3-3 after extra time but won on the penalties rule; Heriot's went out 6-0 to London Scottish; Lansdowne drew 4-4 with Wasps (again after extra time) but went out on the penalties rule and Bagnères beat London Irish 6-0 to complete the semi-final line-up. Maidstone's run came to an end against Scottish (0-6) and Wasps beat Bagnères in the other game (9-4) before losing to London Scottish in the final (3-7).

We began the first season of the new decade with a match against centenary celebrating Sutton and Epsom on their ground in Cheam on 10th September. With virtually a full strength 1st XV, we outscored our opponents by forty points to three. Tries came from Steve Moriarty, Duncan Harris, Gary Rudolph, Ray Dudman, Graham Birkett and Billy Bushell (2) - he also added six conversions. Sutton and Epsom's points were from a penalty goal, the first score of the match. This was to be our biggest win of the season. The serious stuff began three days later when Northampton visited Twickenham. Iestyn Thomas led the side in the absence of Terry Claxton who was recovering from an ankle injury. We played well and deserved our victory (19-10) after Harris and Rick Lawrence had got tries and Billy Bushell had kicked three penalties and a conversion. The following Wednesday, we played against the Old Cranleighans at the Stoop. Graham Birkett was captain of a side showing six changes from the Northampton game. Ray Dudman converted all five tries (scored by Steve Simson (3), Lawrence and Harris) for a comfortable win (30-12). John Gilmer (our scrum half) dislocated his shoulder and broke his right wrist and elbow after falling on a loose ball against Llanelli and with him went our chances of a win. We trailed 3-6 at half time after Macaulay had dropped a goal in reply to two Llanelli penalties. A great try from Phil Bennett ten minutes from time and a conversion by John sealed their win, another try shortly before the end merely made the victory margin greater.

For this and the next six seasons, we played a few midweek matches during the early part of the season before the clocks went forward as we had no floodlights. On Tuesday 23rd September, our visitors were Nottingham for a 17.45 kick-off at the Stoop. After trailing by a goal to nil at the break, John Butcher scored a try and Billy Bushell kicked a penalty to put us one point in front with 30 minutes left. We survived 29 of these before allowing Nottingham a penalty which they kicked to go 9-7 up. Bushell had an opportunity to win the game for us but he failed with an attempted penalty from 40 yards out. C.S. (Chris) Butcher (brother of John) made the first of 98 appearances for us in this game, he would win 3 caps for England. Our next match was at Twickenham against Leicester, the three times in-a-row cup winners. With a side containing five internationals (including our own Clive Woodward) to our one, they were in no mood to be defeated. After just 22 minutes, we trailed by 21 points but rallied up to half time with three Bushell penalties and his conversion of Birkett's try. Our scoring ended at this point and three goals and three penalties turned the match into a stroll for the Tigers (15-45). Dusty Hare landed six conversions, three penalties and scored a try for a personal haul of 25 points but this was not to be our heaviest defeat of the season. Swansea defeated us (9-24) and in the process were accused of kicking some of our players on the ground and off the ball, accusations which they denied.

Another midweek match at the Stoop (against Loughborough Students) saw the return of Club captain Terry Claxton for his first match since the semi-final defeat against Leicester. This match was witnessed by our new coach David Rollitt, himself a former Loughborough man (who also played for Bristol and England). We played poorly for most of the game and were pushed to the limit by the students. Tries from Dick Best (2) and Eddie Quist-Arcton (2) plus a conversion from Ray Dudman and a John Macaulay dropped goal saw us home by eight points (21-13). This was our first win in five matches and our last in the month of October as our next three were lost. An away trip to Gloucester resulted in a ten point loss (9-19) and the most interesting part of the Rosslyn Park match the following week was when Terry Claxton's 12½ stone Newfoundland dog (Khan) decided to join his master on the pitch. It didn't help and two penalties were enough to win the match for the visitors. Against Cardiff, it was the usual story, we only trailed 6-11 at half time but conceded another twenty before we scored again. Two minutes from the end, we produced our only good move and Lawrence scored for Bushell to convert (to add to his two early penalties).

This was our tenth successive defeat by Cardiff and it was to be another two and a half years before we tasted success against them again.

After four losses in a row against Bath, it was time to get a win. We actually played well throughout the game and by the interval, were leading by nineteen points to ten. Bushell had kicked a penalty to open the scoring and converted tries from John Butcher and the first of a brace from Quist-Arcton. Butcher's second (again converted by Bushell) effectively sewed the game up but Bath fought back well and did manage a try and two penalties to narrow the victory margin. Our first merit table fixture was at Twickenham against Richmond on 8th November and proved to be a very disappointing affair. Richmond included two of our former stars (Graham Gilbert and Colin Lambert). Bushell gave us the lead with a penalty (but missed with three further attempts) and Lambert equalised in the same fashion (he and Whibley missed another ten kicks between them during the course of the game) before half time. No scores in the second half saw Richmond lose their (up till now) 100% record. Playing in the first of 11 games for the 1st XV against Richmond was Chris Rogers who won four caps for South Africa in 1984, he also played for Rhodesia and Zimbabwe.

Wet and windy conditions prevailed in the game against Oxford University which saw a future Harlequin (centre S.J. (Simon) Halliday) playing for the university. We won this (12-3) and the Cambridge fixture (25-12). Bushell contributed fourteen of those points (4 conversions and 2 penalties), Dave Hodgkiss, Everton Weekes (2) and N.H. (Nick) Allen (2) got tries and Tim Bryan dropped a goal. Allen made his debut against Cambridge on 22nd November and went on to play 9 times for us and twice for New Zealand. Another All Black made his debut the previous week against Oxford in the shape of B.G. (Bernie) Fraser, he only played four times for us but was to win 23 caps for his country. For Cambridge, one of our own appeared against us (Steve Moriarty) and two future Quins also appeared (full back W.M.H. (Marcus) Rose and prop C.J. (John) Kingston). Our sixth match in a row at Twickenham produced a thrilling draw with London Welsh. Playing against a bitter north wind in the first half, we found ourselves trailing by nineteen points to nil after 25 minutes. By half time we had reduced the deficit to thirteen after Ken Granger scored a try which Bushell converted. Fifteen minutes into the second half, we had levelled with tries from Rawle and Hodgkiss and a penalty and conversion from Bushell. The last quarter was untidy and disjointed and no further scores were achieved.

Our first and so far only fixture with Nuneaton was played at the Stoop on 6th December. Ray Dudman booted over two penalties, one dropped goal and the conversion of Granger's try for a 15-3 victory. Bernie Fraser said goodbye to us in this game, unfortunately without a single point to his credit. Bedford were disposed of by five tries (Granger, Simson (2), Best and Weekes) to a penalty goal, Bath got revenge for their earlier defeat (0-16) to give them their sixteenth victory in the last twenty matches between the sides and in our last match of the year on the second team pitch at the Athletic Ground, Richmond were defeated by a Dave Cooke try to nil. Peter Rawle made his last appearance against Bath with 47 points (11 tries and 1 dropped goal) to his name and the earlier mentioned Simon Halliday made his debut in the win over Richmond. He went on to make a further two appearances during the season and another 25 between 1991 and 1992 after a long spell with Bath (he was to win a total of 23 caps for England).

Our first fixture of 1981 saw a visit from Irish side Old Belvedere on New Year's Day. Both sides sported international fly halves; for us, Nick Allen of New Zealand and for them, Ollie Campbell of Ireland. By half time, both teams had managed seven points - ours was made up of a try and a dropped goal, Old Belvedere's a try and a penalty goal and that is how it ended. Against the Army, there were no fewer than eight changes to our team printed in the programme but it didn't affect our ability to score points. John Gilmer made a welcome return to the side after his injury against Llanelli to partner Nick Allen for the first time. The Army opened the scoring with a try but that was the extent of their points. John Butcher and Gary Rudolph went over in the first half and Billy Bushell kicked a penalty after replacing the injured Allen. In the third quarter, we only managed a try from Steve Moriarty to give us a 15-4 lead. In the final twenty minutes the Army were worn down and conceded further scores by Gary Claxton, Nigel O'Brien, Everton Weekes and Billy Bushell (who added two conversions) to leave us handsome winners 35-4.

On 10th January, we played only our second merit table fixture when Blackheath visited the Stoop. In icy conditions, we ran up an eighteen points to nil lead in the first 25 minutes. Geoff Ball grabbed two tries and the Claxton brothers (Terry and Gary) got two more. Billy Bushell got one conversion over and we appeared to be on the way to a massive win. We became bogged down against a mediocre Blackheath side and only had a Simson try (converted by Bushell) two minutes from time to show for our efforts in the final 55 minutes. Blackheath managed a couple of penalties but we won comfortably enough. Chris Rogers made his last appearance in this game and Nick Allen made his in the next against Birkenhead Park (who were disposed of 14-12). While Rogers failed to score, Allen had scored 11 points made up of 2 tries and a dropped goal. After this came a real test against Rosslyn Park in the John Player Cup 3rd round at Twickenham on 24th January. Unfortunately, our cup run was over almost before it had begun as Park surged into a thirteen points to three lead by half time. Ten minutes into the second half, it was all over when Cullen was awarded a try (even though he had lost the ball in the act of scoring) after Greenhalgh had kicked his fourth penalty. We were outplayed in every department and our only consolation was a try in the fifth minute of injury time by Geoff Ball which Bushell converted to add to his earlier penalty. Our only "victory" came in the form of Chris Butcher knocking down future Quins players Paul Ackford and Paul Curtis. Fortunately for Butcher, this was unseen by the referee!

Our next assignment was a merit table game against London Scottish at Richmond. They were sporting a 100% record at the start of the game but had lost it by the end although we couldn't defeat them. Gordon Wood scored a try against us which was converted to leave the Scots six points ahead at the interval before two Ray Dudman penalties levelled matters. Even with eleven minutes of injury time at the end of the game, neither side could produce any further scoring and a run of seven successive defeats against the Scots had been halted. Our first visit to Imber Court to play the Metropolitan Police since 1954 produced another merit table victory. Two Steve Moriarty tries, one from Chris Butcher and two Dudman conversions saw us to a 16-9 win. Six defeats on the trot now followed to make it a miserable period lasting a month. We conceded forty points at Llanelli but tries from Simson (2), Eddie Quist-Arcton and Terry Claxton plus three conversions by Dudman managed to make the score respectable. Dudman landed a penalty for an early lead at Headingley but we then proceeded to concede twenty four points. Yet another future Quin opposed us in this game, a certain P.J. (Peter) Winterbottom. It was to be another seven years and eight months before he would pull on our jersey though.

Our fifth merit table encounter produced our first loss, albeit narrowly, to a reasonable Wasps side. We trailed by sixteen points a little way into the second half but fought back to within two points with scores from Rick Lawrence (2) and Quist-Arcton and a conversion from Bushell. A goal from Wasps stretched the lead to eight points but a penalty try converted by Bushell left the score at 20-22 before a try right at the end confirmed our defeat. Three missed penalties in the first half by Dudman proved very costly indeed. He redeemed himself by landing two against Leicester to give us an early lead before we conceded five tries to lose quite easily (6-29). In the Wasps game, Paul Grant made his final appearance for the first team having captained the side on one occasion and scored 194 points (46 tries, 3 penalties and 4 conversions). After four wins and two draws, Bedford handed us our first loss against them since 1974. It was a game of two halves in the scoring sense as we trailed 0-21 at the break before pulling back tries from Quist-Arcton and Lawrence and a conversion from Dudman in the second half but it was not enough. Another Dudman penalty saw us lead until the last 15 minutes in the wind, mud and rain at Coundon Road but a penalty and a goal gave Coventry victory in a game which ended with both packs swinging fists at each other. M.R. (Malcolm) "Will" Wall made the first of 85 appearances for the 1st XV in this game. He would go on to become Chairman of the Club after finishing his playing career.

These last results didn't give us much confidence when we travelled to the Old Deer Park for another merit table match. We played with the wind in the first half and Will Wall got a try which Dudman converted and also kicked a penalty which took us in front of the goal scored by the Welsh after 14 minutes. The half time score was the final score and it had proved to be fifteenth time lucky at the Old Deer Park. We failed to score for the third time in the season when Bristol rattled up twenty one points at the Memorial Ground on 4th April and we gained revenge for our cup exit by defeating Rosslyn Park at Roehampton by sixteen points to twelve in our final merit table game. The following day, we played against the Pretoria Harlequins behind closed doors at the Stoop. Some of our players couldn't play due to opposition to the apartheid laws in South Africa but we did put out a strong side. Dick Best got a try, Ray Dudman landed a penalty and John Macaulay dropped a goal; the tourists replied with a try and two penalties to tie the game. All that was left in the season was the Easter tour to Wales to play the usual two (Swansea and Cardiff). As had become the normal train of events, both matches were lost. We suffered our heaviest defeat of the season at Swansea and conceded the most points since Llanelli walloped us in 1970. We leaked ten tries, six conversions and a penalty goal but only managed tries by Andre Dent and Ray Dudman (who added both conversions and a penalty) to leave the final score at 15-55. At Cardiff on Easter Monday, half strength sides battled out a close encounter with the home side winning it by six points (13-19).

Our playing record was slightly worse than last year's, ending up as W16 D5 L18. The number of drawn matches was the most since the same number was achieved in 1963/64. Steve Simson was again top try scorer with 8, John Macaulay dropped two goals and Billy Bushell got the most points for the eighth season in succession with 122 (3 tries, 18 penalties and 28 conversions). We used at least 54 players in the 1st XV during the course of the season with no one appearing in more than thirty of the thirty nine games played. Most appearances were by Steve Simson (30) followed by Terry Claxton and Everton Weekes on 26, David Hodgkiss (24) and Dick Best, Ray Dudman and John Dyson with 23. Overall, tries went up to 79 (a rise of 23), dropped goals were the best since the record number in 1973/74 (6) and although penalties fell to their lowest level since 1968/69 (30), conversions went up to their highest since 1975/76 (46). As a result of the rise in the number of tries, points rose by 53 on the previous season to 516.

1980/81

100980	SUTTON AND EPSOM	CHEAM	W	6G1T(40)-1PG(3)
130980	NORTHAMPTON	TWICKENHAM	W	1G3PG1T(19)-2PG1T(10)
170980	OLD CRANLEIGHANS	STOOP MEMORIAL GROUND	W	5G(30)-1G2PG(12)
200980	LLANELLI	TWICKENHAM	L	1DG(3)-1G2PG1T(16)
230980	NOTTINGHAM	STOOP MEMORIAL GROUND	L	1PG1T(7)-1G1PG(9)
270980	LEICESTER	TWICKENHAM	L	1G3PG(15)-6G3PG(45)
041080	SWANSEA	TWICKENHAM	L	1G1PG(9)-2G4PG(24)

081080	LOUGHBOROUGH STUDENTS	STOOP MEMORIAL GROUND	W	1G1DG3T(21)-1G1PG1T(13)
111080	GLOUCESTER	GLOUCESTER	L	1G1PG(9)-1G3PG1T(19)
181080	ROSSLYN PARK	STOOP MEMORIAL GROUND	L	0-2PG(6)
251080	CARDIFF	TWICKENHAM	L	1G2PG(12)-2G1PG4T(31)
011180	BATH	TWICKENHAM	W	3G1PG1T(25)-4PG2T(20)
081180	RICHMOND(LMT)	TWICKENHAM	D	1PG(3)-1PG(3)
151180	OXFORD UNIVERSITY	TWICKENHAM	W	1G1DG1PG(12)-1PG(3)
221180	CAMBRIDGE UNIVERSITY	TWICKENHAM	W	3G1PG1T(25)-1G2PG(12)
291180	LONDON WELSH	TWICKENHAM	D	2G1PG1T(19)-2G1PG1T(19)
061280	NUNEATON	STOOP MEMORIAL GROUND	W	1G1DG2PG(15)-1PG(3)
131280	BEDFORD	TWICKENHAM	W	5T(20)-1PG(3)
201280	BATH	BATH	L	0-1G2PG1T(16)
271280	RICHMOND	RICHMOND	W	1T(4)-0
010181	OLD BELVEDERE	STOOP MEMORIAL GROUND	D	1DG1T(7)-1PG1T(7)
030181	ARMY	STOOP MEMORIAL GROUND	W	2G1PG5T(35)-1T(4)
100181	BLACKHEATH(LMT)	STOOP MEMORIAL GROUND	W	2G3T(24)-2PG(6)
170181	BIRKENHEAD PARK	STOOP MEMORIAL GROUND	W	1G2T(14)-2G(12)
240181	ROSSLYN PARK(JPC3)	TWICKENHAM	L	1G1PG(9)-4PG2T(20)
310181	LONDON SCOTTISH(LMT)	RICHMOND	D	2PG(6)-1G(6)
070281	METROPOLITAN POLICE(LMT)	IMBER COURT	W	2G1T(16)-1G1PG(9)
140281	LLANELLI	LLANELLI	L	3G1T(22)-5G2PG1T(40)
210281	HEADINGLEY	HEADINGLEY	L	1PG(3)-2G4PG(24)
280281	WASPS(LMT)	SUDBURY	L	2G2T(20)-2G2PG2T(26)
070381	LEICESTER	LEICESTER	L	2PG(6)-3G1PG2T(29)
140381	BEDFORD	BEDFORD	L	1G1T(10)-1G1PG3T(21)
210381	COVENTRY	COVENTRY	L	1PG(3)-1G1PG(9)
280381	LONDON WELSH(LMT)	OLD DEER PARK	W	1G1PG(9)-1G(6)
040481	BRISTOL	BRISTOL	L	0-1G1PG3T(21)
110481	ROSSLYN PARK(LMT)	ROEHAMPTON	W	1G2PG1T(16)-1G2PG(12)
120481	PRETORIA HARLEQUINS	STOOP MEMORIAL GROUND	D	1DG1PG1T(10)-2PG1T(10)

180481	SWANSEA	SWANSEA	L	2G1PG(15)-6G1PG4T(55)
200481	CARDIFF	CARDIFF	L	1G1DG1T(13)-2G1PG1T(19)

England managed to get their tour to Argentina in May and June 1981 after the cancellation in 1973. Current player David Cooke and old boy Clive Woodward were our only representatives on a successful trip. Of the seven matches, the five non-test fixtures were all won and of the two tests, the first was drawn (19-19), the second was won 12-6 to give England a series victory. Woodward played in both tests but Cooke only appeared in three of the other matches.

The committee nominated Terry Claxton as Club captain for 1981/82 but this was not accepted at the Annual General Meeting on 17th June 1981. A special general meeting was called on 11th August and the President (Ken Chapman) and 28 members present voted Dick Best in as Club captain (a group of players got together and overturned the Committee's decision). All members were urged to give him their full and active support and Chapman went on to emphasise that the Club would be damaged if the membership became factionalised. They had canvassed him before but his answer was "no thanks" because the support and management team was not a good one. Dick was in Thailand on holiday at the time and the news was broken to him by his father who said he would have to leave the Club if he didn't take it. He wasn't happy and said he'd go to London Welsh (they had already approached him) but decided to think about it. The trip lasted 6-8 weeks so by the time he returned, the next season was almost upon us. When the Committee contacted him, he had decided to accept on certain caveats including that the team travelled the night before big games and were put up in a hotel at the Club's expense – these conditions were accepted and he became captain. The Colts XV disappears again and is replaced by the U19s.

Proposals for London clubs to hold a fifteen-a-side festival at Richmond Athletic Ground during September 1983 were being discussed during July 1982. It was minuted that Gary Rudolph would be leaving at the end of August when his work permit expired. He had been doing the groundsman's job and steps were being taken to find a replacement; it was hoped that another overseas player might do the job. In the committee report for 1981/82, the passing was reported of Audrey Stoop (Adrian's widow) and Sam Kemble (who played between 1936 and 1946). The tragic death was also reported of Alistair Proud in a motor accident. He was a prop forward in his second season with the Colts and had still been at school at Tonbridge.

As mentioned before, a pre-season tour resulted in a game against Clermont on 29th August. Andy Barker recalls this game and at one point there were 36 players fighting as all the subs came on, it was like a Wild West brawl. The referee could be seen crawling away on his hands and knees but not one person was sent off! The crowd loved it, it was probably one of the wildest matches in the Club's history. Of course, everyone shook hands after and a beer was had with the opposing front row. The French loose head was paid to play against him but he paid his own expenses as the Club was very amateur in terms of payment (as the sport was supposed to be). For the record, Birkett and Jackson scored tries which Riley converted to put us 12-0 up after 45 minutes. Clermont came on strong in the final twenty two minutes with tries from Xausa, Droitecourt, Brugiroux and Marocco with all but the first being converted by Aguerre.

As mentioned above, Dick Best took over the captaincy from Terry Claxton for this and the next (1982/83) season. His first match in charge was a trip to Cheltenham on Thursday 3rd September to play in the first game at their new Prince of Wales stadium in Pittville. Their President was a famous Harlequin, Phil Davies, who had appeared in our colours throughout most of the 1950s. Ray Dudman was now the first choice full back and landed two penalties after three and thirty six minutes to give us a narrow lead at half time. A goal for the home side brought the scores level before Geoff Ball was driven over by the pack for the winning try. Six days later, we met touring side Boston (from Massachusetts in the USA) at the Stoop in another evening kick-off. Showing six changes from the Cheltenham game, we were trailing by a try to nil when Steve Moriarty went over to make it level at the break. An injury to Gary Claxton forced Dick Best to move into the front row as our replacement (John Atkin) was a flanker. Further tries from John Gilmer and Steve Brinkley (both converted by Barry Riley) against a solitary penalty for the visitors saw us home by sixteen points to seven.

The following Saturday, we had to field a different captain against Northampton due to Dick Best having his left leg in plaster and Geoff Ball (Vice-captain) also being unfit. Graham Birkett led the side and played a large part in our come back. We trailed 3-18 before Brinkley got his second penalty and converted two tries from Moriarty. Unfortunately, we lost Riley with a badly gashed forehead and went down 18-27. The following day, a large part of this side travelled up to help West Hartlepool in their centenary celebrations and on a windy and rainy Sunday, we suffered another defeat with Brinkley's penalty being our only score (3-18). A midweek match against the Old Cranleighans produced our biggest win of the season. Tries came from Micky Bell (4), Kevin Bennell (3), Everton Weekes (2), Andy Barker, Craig Kersey and Gary Rudolph plus five conversions by Brinkley for a final score of 58-6. Llanelli beat us again (9-16) in a game which saw the end of their real dominance over us and we avenged the defeat of the previous season against Nottingham (20-13).

We were suffering badly with injuries at this point so it was no time to meet a strong Leicester side. We actually led from the first minute (when Dave Wright landed a penalty) until half time after he converted John Butcher's try, Leicester had managed a penalty and a try. A goal took them into the lead for the first time but Wright's second penalty brought it back to 12-13. After this, there was an avalanche of Leicester points as they added six tries, Hare got a penalty and three conversions and Cusworth dropped a goal to leave us trailing way behind at the final whistle (12-49). Dick Best had injured his cruciate ligaments against Boston and would be out for fourteen weeks. One evening after the debacle against Leicester, he arrived at the Stoop for training only to be told by Colin Herridge that Dave Rollitt had resigned as coach. Dick put a plastic bag on his leg to cover his plaster and made his way over to the number two pitch (where the flats are now). He asked Rollitt what was happening, he explained that the Leicester defeat had hurt him and he felt it was getting too much but said he would take this session. Dick didn't agree with this and so began his coaching career that would see him rise to the top of English Rugby and become very successful. He even took the shirts home one night to put them through his washing machine – the result was a broken washing machine and an unhappy wife! Dick remembers Grahame Murray (a really nice man and a great Harlequin) with great fondness as he employed Dick for a short period at his printing company when, because of a strike at ITV, he was unable to work.

Our only victories were coming from midweek matches and another of these was against Guildford and Godalming at the Stoop on 30th September. Swansea saw us off easily enough (14-24), Loughborough Students failed to arrive due to traffic problems and we drew with Gloucester at Twickenham with each side scoring a penalty goal in the second half. We began our merit table matches with a visit from Rosslyn Park. The flag at Twickenham flew at half-mast owing to the death of Audrey Stoop (widow of Adrian) and the sombre mood spread to the pitch as we lost narrowly (6-14).

A try count of 8-3 in favour of Cardiff plus the kicking of Gareth Davies saw them home by a thirty point margin (17-47). On 31st October, we entertained London Welsh at Twickenham in our second merit table game. We again started badly and trailed by nine points after just ten minutes. Billy Bushell appeared at fly half for the second week running and kicked two penalties to leave us trailing by just three points at half time. Tries from Gilmer and Weekes (the latter converted by Bushell) put us in front before a penalty pulled the Welsh back into the game. Bushell's third successful penalty put us more than a score in front and Dave Cooke sealed a fine win with a try in injury time. This was our first win on a Saturday this season, having suffered six losses and gained one draw so far. A morning match at the Stoop against Bath saw another defeat (10-17) before Richmond handed us our second merit defeat and secured their first win (6-28). We finally returned to winning ways against Oxford University thanks to tries from Graham Birkett (3), Nick French (2), Dave Cooke and Ray Dudman (who also kicked a penalty and two conversions). Oxford led at half time by the odd point in twenty three but eventually went down 35-15. At Cambridge the following week, we led 11-3 three minutes into the second half with a penalty from Dudman and tries by Nigel O'Brien and Birkett before we were torn apart by a future Harlequin. Marcus Rose scored a total of twenty three points (1 try, 1 dropped goal, 4 penalties and 2 conversions) to see the university home as they ran up 24 points in the last half an hour (11-27).

Our second Sunday match of the season the following week against Blackheath at the Stoop was to be our last game of the year. Our side was getting back to normal after all the injuries and against Blackheath, some of the promise started to come through. We trailed at half time despite scoring the only tries through John Butcher and Graham Birkett as the visitors had kicked three penalties. It was all change after this as further tries were scored for us by Birkett and Chris Butcher (2). Hugh McHardy kicked a penalty after Dudman had missed four conversions and despite a penalty and a late try from future Harlequin Mickey Skinner, we won comfortably, 23-16. The bad weather set in after this and matches against Bedford (at the Stoop), Bath (at the Rec) and Richmond (at the Stoop) were all cancelled.

During the first half of the season, we said goodbye to Chris Kelly against Guildford and Godalming (he had scored a single try during his first team career) and Billy Bushell against Oxford on 21st November. Billy had scored no fewer than 1437 points (26 tries, 5 dropped goals, 288 penalties and 227 conversions) during his time in the team and was most unlucky in never gaining an England cap during his career. We said hello to J.A. (John) Atkin against Boston when he came on as a replacement for the first of at least 49 appearances, A.M. (Alex) Woodhouse in the first of at least 108 appearances in the first team against his old club, Guildford and Godalming and Richard Riddell (another New Zealander) against Gloucester for the first of 53 matches.

We managed to squeeze one game in at the start of 1982 before bad weather caused more problems. Another Sunday game, this time at Aldershot against the Army gave us our first match for a month. It wasn't long before we got into our rhythm and the Butcher brothers (Chris and John) and Andre Dent got tries but two penalties for the Army cut their deficit to six points at the break. Dudman eventually found his accuracy and kicked a penalty and four conversions during the second half. Tries were scored by Richard Riddell, Graham Birkett, John Butcher and Terry Claxton to leave us winners by thirty nine points to six. Making his debut in this game was lock forward William "Bill" Cuthbertson. He went on to make at least 62 appearances for the first team and gain 21 caps for Scotland. The weather then caused the postponement of the merit table game at Blackheath and the cancellation of our fixture with Birkenhead Park. Our next match was a joint merit table/John Player 3rd round tie against Wasps at the Stoop on 23rd January. Dudman kicked us into a fourth minute lead with a penalty before a try for Wasps put them a point up. Dudman's second success nudged us ahead at half time before Wasps regained the lead in controversial circumstances. A minute into the second half, an attempted dropped goal by Hughes quite clearly went under the crossbar but the referee gave it and we were behind again. Dudman and Stringer exchanged penalties and with ten minutes to go, we trailed by a point. Our progress to the next round was assured when first, Paul Jackson and then Graham Birkett went over for tries and Dudman's conversion of the second merely stretched our winning margin to nine points.

London Scottish were severely depleted due to the calls of the Anglo-Scots and consequently, the game was de-merited. Tries from Best, Cooke, McHardy and Hodgkiss were enough to see us home 21-3. Yet another Sunday match was the one against Metropolitan Police on 7th February at Imber Court, this one was a merit table fixture and proved to be a bruising encounter. The Police lost one of their forwards (J. Hames) with a broken nose, then fly half (M. Williams) with concussion and left wing (R. Williams) with a neck injury and concussion. Graham Gilbert with a dropped goal and Steve Brinkley with two penalties saw us home against a try from the home side. The packs had been involved in brawling for a large part of the match and, after the referee (Colin Little) had given a final warning, Chris Butcher was sent off for punching. The following week, we travelled down to Llanelli and won for the first time at Stradey Park since February 1971. Ray Dudman kicked three penalties and converted his own try and David Hodgkiss ran through from 35 yards out to stretch our unbeaten run to six matches with a final score of 19-8.

We went to Reading on a Tuesday night to play Abbey as part of their 50th Anniversary celebrations and came away with another victory (31-3) before chalking up number eight against Headingley (26-13). Ray Dudman was now in tremendous form with the boot and landed four conversions and a penalty against Abbey and two penalties and two conversions against Headingley. Tries in the first match came from Dave Cooke, David Hodgkiss, Richard Riddell, Kevin Bennell and Guy Merrison and in the second from Graham Birkett (2), Hodgkiss and Andre Dent. On 27th February, we met the Metropolitan Police in the 4th round of the cup at Imber Court. This time both sides behaved themselves and by half time we had started to book our place in the quarter finals. Dudman had kicked three penalties, McHardy had dropped a goal and Moriarty had scored a try; in reply, the Police had managed just a penalty. After this, our domination increased and our reply to the home side's second penalty was emphatic. Tries from Birkett and Hodgkiss both converted by Dudman made the final score 28-6. We gained revenge against Leicester at Welford Road for our earlier thrashing at Twickenham thanks to tries from Dave Cooke and Dick Best and a conversion and a penalty by Ray Dudman. The final score of 13-7 set us up nicely for our quarter final tie against twice winners, Coventry.

We began in excellent fashion and after 15 minutes, we had scored tries through McHardy and Riddell. Dudman landed both conversions but missed two penalties just after (the second hitting an upright). Coventry began their comeback with a try (after a lucky bounce) from Simon Maisey, Marcus Rose converted and kicked a penalty when Dudman had been harshly penalised for a pass after the tackle. Into the second half, Rose levelled with another penalty before referee Alan Welsby awarded Coventry two penalty tries (for a late tackle by Gilbert and against Cooke for impeding the play at a five metre scrum) which, when converted by Rose put the visitors into the semi-finals by twenty four points to twelve. Penalty try controversy was to dog us again the following week when we were the visitors to Coundon Road. Trailing by five points late in the game, Hugh McHardy broke from a ruck and chipped the ball past Coventry's full back who then pulled him down. Dave Cooke won the race for the touchdown to secure the try only for the referee (Ken Harrower) to award us a penalty instead. Dick Best asked how long was left and was told eight minutes. Dudman kicked the penalty and just two minutes later, the referee blew the final whistle. Perhaps it was a confusion of accents as the referee was from Scotland and he said a minute was left! - who knows but, as a result, we had gone down twice to Coventry in the space of eight days.

It seems that the easiest thing to do is slip into a run of defeats and the trip to London Welsh provided our third in a row (9-16). On Wednesday 31st March, we played our postponed merit table fixture at Blackheath where four penalties from Ray Dudman could not help us avoid defeat by seven points. We were simply outplayed by Bristol at the Stoop and their margin of victory was only limited by Dudman's six penalties (equalling Bushell's record from 1975) (18-31). After five successive defeats, we achieved that winning feeling again in the most unlikely surroundings. After eleven losses in a row on the Easter tour to Wales, we finally won at Swansea on 10th April. Andre Dent, Steve Moriarty (2) and David Hodgkiss scored the tries and Ray Dudman added two conversions for a 20-4 victory. We looked good for a win at Cardiff on the Monday as well when we led 9-3 at half time but a rally by the home side in the second half saw them sneak home 18-13. N.A. (Norman) Rowan appeared in both the tour games. He was to gain 13 caps for Scotland but these were to be his only appearances in our colours. Our last game of the season was a visit to Roehampton for the return with Rosslyn Park. A Steve Moriarty try put us in front, Ray Dudman converted but a goal and a penalty for the home side saw them lead by three points. Further tries for us in the second half from Craig Kersey and Andre Dent and a conversion by Dudman gave us a lead of seven points. Near the end, Park did add another goal to their tally but we still won by a single point.

Our playing record at the end of the season was W19 D1 L16. We had won more games than we had lost thanks in large part to the run of ten wins in a row between December and March. Graham Birkett got the most tries with 11 and Ray Dudman was top points scorer for the first time with 177 (3 tries, 37 penalties and 27 conversions). Overall, 93 tries were scored, the most for six seasons, dropped goals fell to just 3 and conversions were down by two (44) but penalties rose by twenty two (52) which enabled the points scored to rise again to 625. Out of 36 matches played, David Hodgkiss missed only five and he was well clear of Andy Barker (26), Craig Kersey (25) and Ray Dudman, Graham Birkett and Dave Cooke on 24.

1981/82

030981	CHELTENHAM	CHELTENHAM	W	2PG1T(10)-1G(6)
090981	BOSTON	STOOP MEMORIAL GROUND	W	2G1T(16)-1PG1T(7)
120981	NORTHAMPTON	NORTHAMPTON	L	2G2PG(18)-1G3PG3T(27)
130981	WEST HARTLEPOOL	WEST HARTLEPOOL	L	1PG(3)-1G4PG(18)
160981	OLD CRANLEIGHANS	STOOP MEMORIAL GROUND	W	5G7T(58)-2PG(6)
190981	LLANELLI	LLANELLI	L	1G1PG(9)-1G2PG1T(16)
220981	NOTTINGHAM	STOOP MEMORIAL GROUND	W	2G2T(20)-1G1PG1T(13)
260981	LEICESTER	TWICKENHAM	L	1G2PG(12)-4G1DG2PG4T(49)
300981	GUILDFORD AND GODALMING	STOOP MEMORIAL GROUND	W	2G1T(16)-1PG(3)
031081	SWANSEA	TWICKENHAM	L	2PG2T(14)-3G2PG(24)
071081	LOUGHBOROUGH STUDENTS	STOOP MEMORIAL GROUND	C	

101081	GLOUCESTER	TWICKENHAM	D	1PG(3)-1PG(3)
171081	ROSSLYN PARK(LMT)	TWICKENHAM	L	2PG(6)-2PG2T(14)
241081	CARDIFF	TWICKENHAM	L	1G1PG2T(17)-6G1PG2T(47)
311081	LONDON WELSH(LMT)	TWICKENHAM	W	1G3PG2T(23)-1G2PG(12)
071181	BATH	STOOP MEMORIAL GROUND	L	2PG1T(10)-3PG2T(17)
141181	RICHMOND(LMT)	RICHMOND	L	1G(6)-2G4PG1T(28)
211181	OXFORD UNIVERSITY	STOOP MEMORIAL GROUND	W	2G1PG5T(35)-1G1DG2PG(15)
281181	CAMBRIDGE UNIVERSITY	CAMBRIDGE	L	1PG2T(11)-2G1DG4PG(27)
061281	BLACKHEATH	STOOP MEMORIAL GROUND	W	1PG5T(23)-4PG1T(16)
121281	BEDFORD	STOOP MEMORIAL GROUND	C	
191281	BATH	BATH	C	
261281	RICHMOND	STOOP MEMORIAL GROUND	C	
030182	ARMY	ALDERSHOT	W	4G1PG3T(39)-2PG(6)
090182	BLACKHEATH(LMT)	BLACKHEATH	P	
160182	BIRKENHEAD PARK	BIRKENHEAD	C	
230182	WASPS(JPC3/LMT)	STOOP MEMORIAL GROUND	W	1G3PG1T(19)-1DG1PG1T(10)
300182	LONDON SCOTTISH	STOOP MEMORIAL GROUND	W	1G1PG3T(21)-1DG(3)
070282	METROPOLITAN POLICE(LMT)	IMBER COURT	W	1DG2PG(9)-1T(4)
130282	LLANELLI	LLANELLI	W	1G3PG1T(19)-2T(8)
160282	ABBEY	READING	W	2G1PG4T(31)-(3)
200282	HEADINGLEY	STOOP MEMORIAL GROUND	W	2G2PG2T(26)-1G1PG1T(13)
270282	METROPOLITAN POLICE(JPC4)	IMBER COURT	W	2G1DG3PG1T(28)-2PG(6)
050382	LEICESTER	LEICESTER	W	1G1PG1T(13)-1PG1T(7)
130382	COVENTRY(JPCQF)	STOOP MEMORIAL GROUND	L	2G(12)-3G2PG(24)
200382	COVENTRY	COVENTRY	L	2PG1T(10)-1G2PG(12)
270382	LONDON WELSH	OLD DEER PARK	L	1G1PG(9)-2G1T(16)
310382	BLACKHEATH(LMT)	BLACKHEATH	L	4PG(12)-1G2DG1PG1T(19)
030482	BRISTOL	STOOP MEMORIAL GROUND	L	6PG(18)-3G3PG1T(31)
100482	SWANSEA	SWANSEA	W	2G2T(20)-1T(4)

120482	CARDIFF	CARDIFF	L	1G1DG1T(13)-2G2PG(18)
170482	ROSSLYN PARK	ROEHAMPTON	W	2G1T(16)-2G1PG(15)

Eight matches were played on the 1982 tour by England to Canada and the United States. Only David Cooke made the party of our current players but Clive Woodward joined him as did future Quins Peter Williams and Peter Winterbottom. Every match was won by a decent margin including the non-cap tests against Canada (43-6) and the USA (59-0). Winterbottom and Woodward both played against the host nations.

The death of Archibald Gracie (whose playing career lasted between 1920 and 1931) was reported on 17th August 1982 and Sir Douglas Bader (1930 to 1931) was not far behind him as he was mentioned at the next committee meeting on 21st September. There was talk of an Australian tour in 1984 and the marking of our 75th anniversary at Twickenham with the additional possibility of a major match thrown in. In December, a short tour to France in May 1983 was discussed but, like so many others, this never materialised. In February, the search for a coach went on and it was mentioned that Dick Best was meeting someone from Sidcup who had expressed an interest in coaching the Club. Ronnie Hudson (1943-1949) passed away before the meeting on 15th March and a proposed tour to South Africa in 1984 was given an airing. Iestyn Thomas was announced as the new coach on 26th April. On 17th May, it was decided that honours caps would be awarded to Dick Best and Dave H. Cooke and the Dallas Harlequins were finally affiliated on 19th July 1983. Proposals from the R.F.U. for the introduction of a National Merit Table saw the start of the long march towards league rugby although the implementation was postponed until season 1984/85.

We started the season on 4th September with our third trip to Maidstone (our first had been just over 100 years before) in which we put out a very strong XV. Simon Cheetham landed a penalty goal in the first minute and although the home side equalised in kind, Cheetham landed another from 50 yards and Alex Woodhouse and Dave Cooke added tries to put us eleven points ahead. Further tries were scored by John Butcher, David Hodgkiss and Steve Moriarty and Cheetham kicked two conversions and a penalty; Maidstone's only reply was a goal to leave us easy winners, 33-9. Making the first of at least 183 appearances in this game was C. J. (Christopher) "John" Olver. He would go on to captain the side from 1987/88 to 1989/90 and would win three caps for England after leaving us to join Northampton. The following Wednesday, we made six changes to the team to play the Old Gaytonians at the Stoop. A try count of 6-0 in our favour said it all and we were fully deserving of our 35-3 win. Against Northampton at Twickenham on 11th September, we were back to full strength and we were very convincing winners again. A narrow half time advantage of two points (11-9) was stretched in the second half to give us our biggest win over the Saints for six years. Nigel O'Brien, Graham Halsey (2) and John Butcher got the tries and Alex Woodhouse (in the absence of Ray Dudman, suffering from a hamstring injury) kicked a conversion and three penalties for a final score of 27-9.

The next day, we travelled to Sidcup in Kent to play a match as part of their centenary season and came away with our fourth win of the season (35-7), before coming down to earth with a bump against Llanelli the following weekend. We trailed by twenty seven points before Dent (converted by Woodhouse) and Gilbert got tries for us late in the game after Llanelli had relaxed somewhat. Our second midweek game of the season was a visit to Guildford and Godalming on 22nd September, this time the home side were celebrating their Diamond Jubilee season and we were again successful, achieving our biggest win of the season by sixty five points to three. Leicester were our next opponents in a game which saw the return of Ray Dudman. He scored a try, kicked three penalties and converted both of John Butcher's tries but still this wasn't enough as the Tigers managed four points more (a try from Les

Cusworth being the difference in the end). A.T. (Adrian) Thompson made the first of at least 140 1st XV appearances in this match. Borough Road College were seen off in midweek, but only by four points (11-7) before Swansea came to Twickenham on 2nd October. Dave Cooke led the side in Dick Best's absence and we found ourselves trailing at half time by two penalties to nil. Two minutes into the second half, Terry Claxton bulldozed his way over for our first try and Dudman added a penalty six minutes later to put us in front. An exchange of penalties between Blyth and Dudman saw us leading by a point with twenty minutes left. A try for Swansea by Dacey, converted by Blyth left the Welshmen five points ahead with only five minutes remaining. Deep into injury time, Geoff Ball ran round the front of a line out and went over in the corner, Dudman converted brilliantly from the touchline and we had our first back to back wins over Swansea since 1968.

Dudman was again on the score sheet against Loughborough Students when he converted four of our five tries to help us to a 28-3 win. We had just completed our first month of the season and had won eight of our ten games. We took a weakened side down to Gloucester due to County calls and duly lost, Ray Dudman landing three penalties which left us seven points adrift of the home side. Three more penalties from Dudman and a try from Andre Dent were not enough to beat Rosslyn Park in a non-merit table game as another weakened team went down fighting gamely (13-27). On 23rd October, we had an anticipated first encounter with Birmingham ruled out by a waterlogged pitch at the Stoop so, it was to Twickenham we went for our next game against London Welsh. Andy Haden made his last appearance in this match but we welcomed another New Zealander to the team. He was J.L.B. (James) "Jamie" Salmon who would go on to appear at least 141 times for the first team having gained three caps for New Zealand. He would also become a double international and win 12 England caps during his time with us. A game full of fighting finished all square, we won the try count 2-1 but London Welsh won the penalty count 5-3. Ray Dudman landed one conversion and got our penalties and Graham Gilbert and Andre Dent scored the tries.

Bath came to the Stoop with a side containing two internationals and six future caps and went away with a win after a poor performance from us for the first half and the last twenty minutes. In the good period, Dudman got a penalty and Adrian Thompson scored a try but Bath managed three tries, two penalties and a dropped goal overall to run out easy winners. The following weekend we had another busy time, on the Saturday we played hosts to Richmond and on Sunday we travelled to Holland to play against Haagsche RFC as part of their 50th anniversary celebrations. Against Richmond, we trailed by a try (scored by Nick French) to a goal and two penalties (by Richmond's full back Colin Green) at half time but came back strongly to run away with the game. Two tries from John Butcher sandwiched efforts from Hodgkiss and Dent, Dudman added four conversions and we had our first win in five matches. In The Hague we defeated the home side by fifteen points to six.

At Oxford, we took the lead against the university when Chris Preston scored a try but, by the time Simon Cheetham added his dropped goal, the students had scored eighteen points and were in control. We rallied well in the second half and captain Dick Best got a try and Dudman kicked a penalty before Geoff Ball scored a try with five minutes to go. Dudman stepped up and struck the ball clean through the posts for another victory. A weakened side took on Cambridge University at the Stoop and thanks yet again to the kicking of Ray Dudman, won the day. He got three penalties and a conversion and John Butcher and John Atkin scored our tries for a 19-4 result. We suffered a shock at the Rectory Field when Blackheath held on despite a late onslaught to sneak home by a point (13-12) and a single penalty was enough to account for us at Bedford. After our earlier loss at home to Bath, we managed a credible draw at the Recreation Ground. Mike Russell and Alex Woodhouse got our tries and Dudman kicked one conversion and a penalty. The home side got a try and three penalties and, had Dudman's second conversion attempt from the touchline not hit a post and stayed out, we may well have won. This was our last match of the year as the away return with Richmond was cancelled by our hosts. John Macaulay made his last appearance in the Bath game having scored a total of 77 points (3 tries, 3 dropped goals, 12 penalties and 10 conversions) and captained the side on one occasion.

We began 1983 in emphatic style with a seven try demolition of the Army at the Stoop on New Year's Day. A 15-0 lead at half time was extended to a winning margin of 36 points thanks to tries from John Butcher (3), Alex Woodhouse (2), John Olver and Everton Weekes and a dropped goal, three penalties and one conversion from Ray Dudman. The Army did manage one goal but the final score of 42-6 was the least we deserved for a rousing display of rugby. Blackheath came next in our first merit table fixture and were safely dispatched (21-7), this time Steve Moriarty got the hat-trick. The following day saw the Wanderers back in the Middlesex Cup and our fourth round opponents were Metropolitan Police. We won the away fixture, but only just by 7-3. The following week, Birkenhead Park were the visitors and were completely destroyed. This time, a total of ten tries were scored by Dick Best (2), Ray Dudman (2), Steve Moriarty (2), John Butcher, Nick Chesworth, Jamie Salmon and Everton Weekes. Dudman only managed one conversion and a dropped goal in addition to his brace of tries so our final tally could have been in excess of sixty points. As it was, we had to settle for a score of 45-3. This was our tenth successive win over them and was to be the last fixture between the clubs.

The next weekend saw us entertain Gosforth in a 3rd round cup tie at the Stoop. We trailed by six points early on when Johnson kicked two penalties for Gosforth but, by half time we led, thanks to two penalties and the conversion of Mickey Claxton's try by Dudman. A dropped goal and two more penalties from Johnson put the visitors three points in front but we were not to be denied our place in the 4th round and tries from Olver and Jackson (both converted by Dudman) saw us home 24-15. London Scottish had ten men missing on 29th January due to the Scottish Inter-District Championship and, as a consequence of this, the match was de-merited. After going behind to a penalty, we rallied strongly and Dudman kicked three penalties to put us ahead at the break. Dave Cooke, Alex Woodhouse and Paul Jackson got tries in the second half, Dudman added the extra points to the second and we had secured our fifth win on the trot. The next day saw the Middlesex Cup quarter final against Orleans F.P. on their home ground at Orleans Park (just off Richmond Road near Marble Hill House). Despite trying to distract the team with their cheerleaders dressed like girls from St. Trinian's, we again progressed by a narrow four point margin (13-9). The Metropolitan Police were played on Sunday 6th February due to the internationals the previous day and we came away with the merit points (16-3) despite trailing at the half way point. This win wasn't without its troubles as we lost Steve Moriarty (winger) and David Hodgkiss (centre) to injuries which meant that Dave Cooke had to play on the wing as the replacement for Moriarty was Chris Field (a prop forward)! Jackson, Gary Claxton and John Butcher went over for tries and Dudman landed two conversions.

We hoped to gain some revenge for our loss at home to Llanelli back in September in our next match but it was not to be. Dudman scored all our points (try, dropped goal and penalty) during a strong second half rally but we conceded two good tries at the start and end of the game and these proved to be the difference (10-21). Graham Gilbert made his final appearance against Llanelli having scored 120 points (22 tries, 9 dropped goals, 1 penalty and 1 conversion) in his first team career. A week before we met Sale at Heywood Road in the next round of the cup, we travelled to Headingley and despite putting out a near full strength XV, we came back without scoring a single point whilst conceding sixteen. On Sunday 20th February, we travelled the short distance to the Athletic Ground to play Richmond in the Middlesex Cup semi-final. This time the ending turned out better than our first effort three years before and we ran out easy winners. Graham Birkett scored our first try and Hugh McHardy converted before Green replied with a penalty to leave us with a narrow 6-3 lead at half time. Steve Simson scored a try, McHardy converted and landed a penalty after Richard Cramb's dropped goal. Simson then grabbed his second to make the final score 22-3. McHardy had a ploy around this time of opting to go for a kick at goal from a penalty, the kick would be missed and one of our backs would sneak up to score a try – it worked against Richmond in the first half!

Our third ever meeting with Sale came on 26th February and what a game it was despite being played in heavy rain on a treacherous surface. Sale had the perfect start when Tony Wright went over for a try in the first minute but we came back strongly and Paul Jackson scored for Dudman to convert. A penalty by Sid Lowdon put the home side ahead by a point but a penalty by Dudman and a try from Moriarty gave us a six point interval lead. Sale came out with all guns blazing at the start of the second half and they were rewarded with a penalty from Lowdon, who also converted Alan Scott's try, to put them 16-13 ahead. The home side were wasting a lot of opportunities and from a penalty, Dudman put up a high kick, Moriarty raced into the in-goal area and scored his second try as Sale hesitated. A spell of pressure saw Gary Claxton go over for the match clinching score which Dudman converted. Lowdon kicked his third penalty but it was too little too late for the home side and we progressed to the quarter finals for the fifth time (23-19). The draw gave us an away trip to Leicester which meant we would play them on the next two Saturdays.

The first game was played on an international day and Leicester had Dodge, Hare and Wheeler missing from their line-up. As it was, we received a boost for the following week, with three Dudman penalties and a Weekes try enough to beat a Cusworth penalty for the Tigers. This game saw the 1st XV debut of a young student who was to win 4 caps for Scotland. He was R. I. (Richard) Cramb who would go on to make at least 100 appearances for the first team (he had appeared for the Wanderers in the semi-final against Richmond two weeks back). The cup tie was not a happy experience for us as, despite putting in our best efforts, two close range tries from Nick Youngs in the second half made the game safe for Leicester. Cusworth had dropped a goal and Hare landed a penalty in the first half before the second named converted both tries to leave us trailing by eighteen points to nil. We did have the very small consolation of scoring the best try of the game through Salmon (after he and John Butcher had shared a 60 yard breakaway). The following week, we welcomed Coventry (who had qualified for the semi-finals) to the Stoop. We had, unfortunately for us, reached our best form a week too late. In a superb display, Coventry were hit for six as we ran in try after try. Dick Best got the first followed by Dave Cooke, Bill Cuthbertson, Mickey Claxton and a brace from Jamie Salmon. Ray Dudman chipped in with three penalties and four conversions to give us our biggest win over them since 1911 (41-13).

The Middlesex Cup reached its conclusion the next day and the Wanderers went to Sudbury to take on the Wasps 1st XV. We opened the scoring after 20 minutes when McHardy was up to his tricks again and a cross-field kick enabled Birkett to score the opening try. Richard Cramb got our second when he pounced on a loose pass by the home side deep inside our half and kicked the ball all the way to the line. Both conversions were missed as was the attempt when Stringer crossed for Wasps to make it 8-4. The cup was won when Everton Weekes went over for McHardy to convert and there was talk of us having two teams in the John Player Cup the following season. Automatic qualification was given to the winners of the County cup but, sadly, the Wanderers never made it.

Our third merit table game was against London Welsh at the Old Deer Park on 26th March which ended in a draw of nine points each despite Jamie Salmon scoring another excellent try. He returned to New Zealand after this match in time for the start of their season but would be back in November. The Easter tour provided one usual and one most unusual result. Against Swansea on the Saturday, we lost narrowly (13-18) despite leading 9-7 at half time.

This match saw another Scottish international make his debut for us. G. M. (Gerald) "Gerry" McGuinness only made three appearances for us and won 7 caps for Scotland. On the Monday, we crushed Cardiff by five tries to one to achieve our first win over them since 1975 (a run of thirteen successive defeats). Both sides were weakened for various reasons but we were the most efficient. Playing with the wind in the first half, we built a lead of twenty two points to nil which, by the end, had become 34-6. Chris Preston (brother of England centre, Nick), John Butcher (who dislocated his shoulder in the process of scoring), Alex Woodhouse (2) and Steve Moriarty got the tries and Dudman added two penalties and four conversions. P. N. (Peter) Williams made the first of six appearances in this game, he was a new recruit for the following season but things would not work out for him (he did go on to gain 4 England caps though). Three days later we met Bristol at the Memorial Ground in a floodlit match. We hadn't won at Bristol since April 1971 so history was not on our side. There were some exciting moments in the game but we were never really in with a shout and were always playing catch-up after Pomphrey had given Bristol the lead after twelve minutes with a try which Barnes converted. A goal, a penalty and a try took Bristol to nineteen points but we ensured a close finish with a penalty and conversion from Ray Dudman, a dropped goal by Richard Cramb and tries from Steve Moriarty and Everton Weekes (after he charged down a clearance kick from Barnes) to make the final score 16-19.

Our fourth match in eight days saw a home game against Racing Club de France at the Stoop to celebrate the centenary of the French Chamber of Commerce. Our previous encounters had resulted in one defeat (1901) and one win (1907). This one saw us edge ahead in the series after an entertaining encounter. For most of the first half the visitors were camped in our territory but this didn't stop us from building a lead of 21-0. Dudman (kicking superbly) landed two penalties, converted tries by Woodhouse and Moriarty and dropped a massive goal. The second half was a different story as the French started to throw the ball about. They scored three goals and a try which, had we not scored again, would have given them a one-point victory. We were secure though as Dudman's boot was as deadly as it had been in the first half and he got another penalty and converted tries scored by Mickey Claxton and Chris Preston for a final score of 36-22. Our last match of the season was a merit table encounter at Roehampton against Rosslyn Park. The pitch resembled a dust bowl (as was usual for this time of year) and we lost narrowly by 15-19. Ray Dudman was again in the points and got a penalty and two conversions of tries from Weekes and Preston). This defeat meant third place in the London merit table for us behind London Scottish and Rosslyn Park. Had we won, we would have finished top.

We managed 23 wins and 3 draws out of 39 games played. This was the most wins since our centenary season of 1966/67 when 22 were achieved. John Butcher was the top try scorer with 16 and Ray Dudman was top points scorer with 263 (4 tries, 4 dropped goals, 47 penalties and 47 conversions). His tally of penalty goals was a new record, beating by two Billy Bushell's mark set in 1974/75. Overall, tries were up 13 at 106 (our best since the 1975/76 season), dropped goals stood at 8 (our best since 1973/74) and penalties (53) and conversions (55) were both better than 1981/82 (these totals do not include the 100 points scored against Sidcup and Guildford and Godalming). Our points total of 817 was our second highest ever total (beaten by 95 points in 1975/76). Top appearance maker was John Olver who appeared in 32 games. He was followed by Ray Dudman (31), John Butcher and David Hodgkiss (30), Dick Best (29), Mickey Claxton (26) and Alex Woodhouse on 25.

New Zealand was the venue for the British Lions tour in 1983 and our representation increased although none of them were current Quins. Clive Woodward (Leicester), Iain Milne (Heriot's F.P.) and Peter Winterbottom (Headingley) all made the party but only the last named won any caps. He played in all four tests and ended up on the losing side every time.

1982/83

040982	MAIDSTONE	MAIDSTONE	W	2G3PG3T(33)-1G1PG(9)
080982	OLD GAYTONIANS	STOOP MEMORIAL GROUND	W	4G1DG2T(35)-1PG(3)
110982	NORTHAMPTON	TWICKENHAM	W	1G3PG3T(27)-1DG2PG(9)
120982	SIDCUP	SIDCUP	W	(35)-(7)
180982	LLANELLI	TWICKENHAM	L	1G1T(10)-2G1PG3T(27)
220982	GUILDFORD AND GODALMING	GUILDFORD	W	(65)-(3)
250982	LEICESTER	TWICKENHAM	L	2G3PG1T(25)-3G1PG2T(29)
290982	BOROUGH ROAD COLLEGE	STOOP MEMORIAL GROUND	W	1DG2T(11)-(7)
021082	SWANSEA	TWICKENHAM	W	1G2PG1T(16)-1G3PG(15)
061082	LOUGHBOROUGH STUDENTS	STOOP MEMORIAL GROUND	W	4G1T(28)-(3)
091082	GLOUCESTER	GLOUCESTER	L	3PG(9)-4PG1T(16)
161082	ROSSLYN PARK	STOOP MEMORIAL GROUND	L	3PG1T(13)-3G3PG(27)
231082	BIRMINGHAM	STOOP MEMORIAL GROUND	C	
301082	LONDON WELSH	TWICKENHAM	D	1G3PG1T(19)-5PG1T(19)
061182	BATH	STOOP MEMORIAL GROUND	L	1PG1T(7)-1DG2PG3T(21)
131182	RICHMOND	STOOP MEMORIAL GROUND	W	4G1T(28)-1G2PG(12)
141182	HAAGSCHE	AMSTERDAM	W	2G1PG(15)-(6)
201182	OXFORD UNIVERSITY	OXFORD	W	1G1DG1PG2T(20)-2G2PG(18)
271182	CAMBRIDGE UNIVERSITY	STOOP MEMORIAL GROUND	W	1G3PG1T(19)-1T(4)
041282	BLACKHEATH	BLACKHEATH	L	2G(12)-1DG2PG1T(13)
111282	BEDFORD	BEDFORD	L	0-1PG(3)
181282	BATH	BATH	D	1G1PG1T(13)-3PG1T(13)
271282	RICHMOND	RICHMOND	C	
010183	ARMY	STOOP MEMORIAL GROUND	W	1G1DG3PG6T(42)-1G(6)
080183	BLACKHEATH(LMT)	STOOP MEMORIAL GROUND	W	1G1PG3T(21)-1PG1T(7)
160183	BIRKENHEAD PARK	STOOP MEMORIAL GROUND	W	1G1DG9T(45)-1PG(3)
220183	GOSFORTH(JPC3)	STOOP MEMORIAL GROUND	W	3G2PG(24)-1DG4PG(15)
290183	LONDON SCOTTISH	RICHMOND	W	1G3PG2T(23)-1PG(3)

060283	METROPOLITAN POLICE(LMT)	STOOP MEMORIAL GROUND	W	2G1T(16)-1PG(3)
120283	LLANELLI	LLANELLI	L	1DG1PG1T(10)-3G1PG(21)
190283	HEADINGLEY	HEADINGLEY	L	0-2G1T(16)
260283	SALE(JPC4)	SALE	W	2G1PG2T(23)-1G3PG1T(19)
050383	LEICESTER	LEICESTER	W	3PG1T(13)-1PG(3)
120383	LEICESTER(JPCQF)	LEICESTER	L	1T(4)-2G1DG1PG(18)
190383	COVENTRY	STOOP MEMORIAL GROUND	W	4G3PG2T(41)-1G1PG1T(13)
260383	LONDON WELSH(LMT)	OLD DEER PARK	D	1G1PG(9)-1G1PG(9)
020483	SWANSEA	SWANSEA	L	1G1PG1T(13)-2PG3T(18)
040483	CARDIFF	CARDIFF	W	4G2PG1T(34)-1G(6)
070483	BRISTOL	BRISTOL	L	1G1DG1PG1T(16)-2G1PG1T(19)
090483	RACING CLUB DE FRANCE	STOOP MEMORIAL GROUND	W	4G1DG3PG(36)-3G1T(22)
160483	ROSSLYN PARK(LMT)	ROEHAMPTON	L	2G1PG(15)-1G1DG2PG1T(19)

On 12th August 1983, the death was reported of Lord Wakefield of Kendal; he was 84 years old. Discussions about the anniversary match at Twickenham had seen the opponents and date decided upon. The match would take place on the first Saturday of the season and the opponents would be the French Barbarians. The actual anniversary of our first Twickenham match was on 14th October 1984 but it was decided that there would be no event to coincide with this. On 20th December, it was proposed that the game could also be the Wavell Wakefield Memorial Match. It was confirmed that the Club had received a warning from Middlesex County RFU disciplinary committee because we had had three members sent off recently. Dave Cooke had issued verbal warnings to the other XVs captains and a letter would also be sent to them. The Club could be banned from playing if anyone else was sent off. On 17th January 1984, a letter had been received from Middlesex following Gary Claxton's disciplinary hearing stating that eleven players had been sent off in recent seasons; seven of those in the last twelve months. Geoff Ashby had been sent off prior to the committee meeting on 29th April and the secretary wrote to Middlesex advising that Ashby had resigned from the captaincy of his "A" XV and had been suspended by the Club for an additional 30 days in addition to the automatic four week ban. The reserve teams were now listed as A1, A2, A3 and U21s but the A3s only lasted a season.

David Cooke became Club captain for this (1983/84) and the following three seasons and, on the whole, it was a reasonably successful period in the Club's history. His first game in charge came on 3rd September against Oxford on the Southern By-pass ground. We paid them the compliment of fielding virtually a first choice team and this showed in the final score of 53-9. We ran in ten tries including six from Chris Preston. He became only the fifth

Harlequin to score this number in a game. The others were scored by Chris Butcher, Graham Birkett, Nigel O'Brien and Bill Cuthbertson. Mark Heeley (on his debut) landed four conversions and Peter Williams chipped in with one conversion and one penalty. Oxford's reply was three penalties from their fly half Barry Abbott. Twelve changes were made for our next game against the Old Gaytonians at the Stoop in a midweek fixture. After they had led by two tries to nil at half time, Ray Dudman landed two penalties and John Atkin got a try to edge us ahead but a third try (this time converted) for the visitors put them in front again. Late in the game, Dudman got his third penalty and John Butcher scored the match winning try to keep up our unbeaten start to the season. David Hodgkiss made his last appearance for the first team in this game having captained the side on one occasion and scored 16 tries and 2 conversions (68 points) during his career. Our undefeated run was only to last for two more days as we travelled to Northampton on the Saturday (10th September). We did take the lead with a Dudman penalty but the Saints scored thirteen unanswered points to lead at half time. Dudman kicked his second penalty and converted a try from Paul Jackson but 12-16 was as close as we got. Two more goals for the home side enabled them to go well clear.

The next day we travelled up to play Bradford Salem and, despite losing our entire front row with injuries, came away with a 12-3 win. A steady performance accounted for Llanelli at Twickenham (11-3) and Maidstone were defeated at the Stoop in midweek (19-3) which meant we faced Leicester with a W4 L1 record. After five minutes, we took the lead when Alex Woodhouse went over for Dudman to convert. Leicester were not going to just lie down and roll over and they came back to score three tries (two being converted) to lead 16-6 early in the second half. It looked as though the Tigers were on their way to another easy win over us but John Butcher had other ideas and two great tries (both converted by Dudman) helped us into an 18-16 lead. However, four minutes into injury time, the visitors controlled a five metre scrum and edged towards our line. Nick Youngs (their scrum half) was able to gather and dive over for the winning score. Had Dudman not missed with a penalty from 35 metres, the conversion of Young's try would have been all important. He did, however, score half of our points (2 penalties and 3 conversions) in an easy victory over West London Institute at the Stoop on 28th September. Tries from Adrian Thompson, Richard Riddell and Richard Cramb completed our total with the Institute getting a couple of penalties in reply. A good performance against Swansea brought our third win in the last four games against them (15-6). This game also saw the last appearance of Peter Williams. He returned up North to play for Orrell having scored just a penalty and a conversion for us.

Flanker Mike Russell was sent off in the midweek fixture against Loughborough Students. S.E. (Stuart) Thresher made the first of at least 151 appearances in this match and landed 4 penalties and a conversion into the bargain. A penalty try was added to with further scores from Geoff Ball and Graham Halsey while Cramb dropped a goal for a final tally of 29-18. Three days later we were back at the Stoop to meet Gloucester. Unfortunately, we lost thirteen of our players to Middlesex and Surrey for County Championship matches which meant Bill Cuthbertson led the side (Gloucester were not as weakened as us as they only lost six men). The only score of the first half was a penalty from Ray Dudman but, this was also to be our only score. The visitors got their act together after this and ran in three tries to help them to a 16-3 win. We played Rosslyn Park in our first London merit table fixture of the season on 16th October and managed to come back from a four point deficit at half time to sneak a win. Mickey Claxton scored a try and Ray Dudman converted to give us the spoils. Back to a weakened side again the following week for the visit of Cardiff and a predictable defeat followed. A Dudman penalty and a try from Rufus Cole on debut just wasn't enough and a try count of 4-1 in favour of our visitors helped them to a 26-7 victory. B.W. (Brett) Codlin made his debut in this game having won 3 caps for New Zealand. He would only make 5 appearances for the 1st XV.

Our second merit table fixture was against London Welsh at Twickenham on 29th October. John Olver went over for a try (which Dudman converted) and, when Mickey Claxton crashed over after a mistake by the Welsh full back, we led 10-0. Two penalties by Avery only altered the score and nothing more. We next met London Irish for the first time since our victory in the cup tie in 1978. This time the venue was the Stoop but the result was the same. In the first half, Nigel O'Brien and Everton Weekes got tries and Dudman converted the latter and added a penalty to a solitary penalty for the visitors. They could only manage a try in the second half but we stretched away to record a comprehensive win. Alex Woodhouse, Adrian Thompson and Richard Riddell scored further tries and Dudman got one more conversion to leave the final score at 27-7. Had our kicker not missed with eight penalty and three conversion attempts, the score might have passed the fifty point mark. We went down to Richmond at the Athletic Ground mainly thanks to the calls of the counties (12-17) but bounced back to knock the stuffing out of Oxford University at the Stoop on 19th November (44-18). A try count of 9-3 in our favour said it all but, for the record, Chris Butcher (2), John Olver, Everton Weekes, Andre Dent, Richard Riddell, Neil Sinclair and Jamie Salmon (on his return to the side) got the tries and Dudman added four conversions. For the Dark Blues, a certain person by the name of Stuart Barnes converted all three of their scores.

Against Cambridge University the following week, we got a bit of a shock despite fielding a weakened side - again! We trailed 6-24 after 50 minutes but rallied strongly with three tries in six minutes (two converted by Dudman) to bring it back to 22-24. A final penalty from Nick Chesworth for the home side saw them home by five points. Brett Codlin played his final game against Blackheath and signed off by kicking a penalty to open our scoring but managed to miss eight other attempts. After trailing 6-12 at half time (Richard Cramb's dropped goal pulling the deficit back), we dominated in the second half and scored tries through Graham Halsey, Alex Woodhouse and Chris Butcher. Two of the Blackheath team would make appearances for us in the future - Laurie Cokell and Mickey Skinner. Our next game against Bedford saw the first of 25 appearances by W.J. William "Willie" Jefferson (he was to win 6 caps for the United States of America between 1985 and 1989). Richard Cramb scored a try for Dudman to convert and we led 6-0 at the break. A goal and a try from Bedford in the second half just gave them enough of a cushion and try as we did, we could only manage a penalty from Dudman in an effort to close the gap. This was our third loss in a row to the Midlands outfit and equalled our worst run against them previously set in the 1940s and late 1950s/early 1960s.

Bath were about to start on their near dominance of the English rugby scene and this is where we travelled to next. Thanks to a good defensive display, we only trailed by four points at the interval. Palmer had landed a conversion and a penalty for Bath to add to tries from Haskin and Gaymond. For us, Dudman got a penalty and converted Cramb's try (an interception and run in from 60 yards out). In the second half, Hugh McHardy dropped an angled goal and Dudman kicked his second penalty to give us a 15-13 advantage. In a frantic last few minutes, Bath missed several try scoring opportunities and Palmer failed with two penalty attempts to leave us winners. Our next fixture was our fourth merit table game against Richmond at the Stoop on Christmas Eve. Our 100% record was kept intact when Everton Weekes scored his second try of the game right on full time for a 14-11 win. Our final game of 1983 came on New Year's Eve against London Scottish (another merit table fixture). The Scottish were never really in the game and after Weekes, Halsey and Salmon had scored tries in the first half, Woodhouse and Dudman (who also got two conversions and a penalty) completed their misery with further efforts to make the final score 27-10.

As usual, we met the Army to kick our New Year matches off. This time it was our turn to travel down the road to Aldershot. As had happened back in 1974, the Stadium was out of use and the match was played on one of the park pitches. Richard Cramb (2) and Jamie Salmon landed penalties to a try for the Army to give us a lead at the interval. Despite the Army putting up stiff resistance, we stretched away in the second half with tries from Steve Simson, Richard Riddell, Graham Halsey and Adrian Thompson and a conversion and penalty from Salmon. The Army did manage a couple of penalties but we still won by a clear twenty points. Steve Simson made his last appearance in this game having scored 104 points (26 tries) in his time in the first team. The defence of the Middlesex Cup began on 8th January when the Wanderers met London New Zealand at the Stoop. Some first team regulars returned to the fold (Chris and John Butcher, Gary Claxton and Nigel O'Brien) and we were too good for our opponents although they did put up a fight. Chesworth gave us the lead with a penalty for a narrow lead at half time. Willie Jefferson ran in two tries (both converted by Chesworth who also added a second penalty) and Wall added a third. The New Zealanders scored a penalty and a try to make the final score 22-7. As was to become a regular occurrence, our form improved after Christmas and, against Bath, we had begun an impressive run which would yield twelve victories from our last eighteen games. On 14th January, it was Blackheath's turn to feel the pressure in our quest for an unbeaten run in the London merit table. We began with a gale at our backs and by half time, the contest was effectively over thanks to Alex Woodhouse (our scrum half). He ran in three tries during the half which Dudman converted before Dent added a fourth for a 22-0 advantage. The Club could only manage four penalties during their turn with the wind advantage and we maintained our domination over the other London sides.

The cancellation of our trip to play Birkenhead Park meant that our next fixture was the 3rd round cup tie against Camborne at the Stoop on 28th January. After only two minutes, we seemed to be on our way when Halsey ran in to score the opening try. We went to sleep after this and allowed Camborne to equalise with a try of their own after our defence failed to deal with a kick ahead. This shock was exactly what we needed and from this point, we didn't look back. Dudman followed up Halsey's break and was rewarded with a try and then converted when Butcher dashed 40 yards down the line for our third try. A dropped goal from Cramb was followed by Halsey's second try for an interval lead of 21-4. We were in full flow now and Salmon, Thompson, Butcher (with his second) and Weekes all got in on the try scoring act. Dudman converted three and landed a penalty to put us into the 4th round to the tune of forty six points to four. After this, the Wanderers played at home to Saracens first team in the Middlesex Cup quarter final on 29th January. In the first twenty minutes, the visitors missed four penalty attempts before Chesworth put us in front with his first effort after 24 minutes. He doubled the lead with another six minutes later and Rick Lawrence added a third on 35 minutes to put us 9-0 up. Before the break, the lead was increased when Atkin and McHardy set up Chesworth for a try that Lawrence converted. Saracens scored all the points in the second half but could only manage a try from Jones and a conversion and penalty from Wright. We won 15-9 but had the visitors kicked more than one of their eight penalty attempts, it could have been different.

The following Sunday, we travelled the shortish distance to Imber Court for our final merit table match. We had to beat the Metropolitan Police to record a 100% record in the London table for the first time ever by any club. We had a good record at Imber Court since our first game there in 1951, winning five and losing just once, so the omens were good although Chris Butcher had been sent off there in 1982. Riddell got two tries in the first 25 minutes with a penalty for the Police coming in between. Dudman converted the second and added a penalty for a half time lead of ten points. With the wind in the second half, Ray Dudman was able to pin the home side back in their own 22 with massive touch kicks. He scored our first try of the half and added two conversions to his points tally and with further tries coming from Dent and Salmon, the final score of 29-3 ensured our place in history.

Stradey Park, Llanelli was our next stop and, despite a Graham Halsey try and a conversion and penalty by Dudman, we went down to our first defeat of the year (9-20). In another Sunday encounter, we played Headingley at the Stoop and ran out 33-21 winners in an exciting game. We had to make five late changes to our starting line-up but this still failed to dampen our enthusiasm. The Headingley XV contained one of our old boys (Tim Sinclair) and one of our future stars (Jon Eagle) and they began well with two penalties by their fly half, Howarth but, by the time he added a third, we were ahead. Halsey scored two tries and Willie Jefferson added a third in the first half but the real star of the game was Rick Lawrence (playing in the centre). He converted all three tries and a penalty to give us a 21-9 advantage we were not to lose. Jefferson got his second try and Lawrence converted but Headingley had started a comeback. Howarth converted their only try and kicked two more penalties to narrow the gap to just six points before Nigel O'Brien scored our fifth try in injury time and, of course, Lawrence added the conversion for a final score of 33-21.

This set us up nicely for our trip to Beacon Park in Plymouth for our 4th round cup tie against Plymouth Albion. This match was to become one of the most dramatic in the history of the competition as Albion played themselves to a standstill. There was never more than six points between the teams throughout the tie and it was the home side who took the lead when Durkin put over a penalty. Dudman levelled in the same fashion and Triggs went over for a try before Dudman got his second penalty and Adrian Thompson scored our first try to give us a slender 10-7 lead at the interval. Into the second half and Dudman completed his hat-trick of penalties before the home side put us into a state of shock. Durkin dropped a goal and kicked a penalty to level the scores before Triggs dropped a goal in the third minute of injury time to put them in front. Two minutes later, Turton had a penalty chance to win the game but put it wide. Our captain, David Cooke, asked the referee (David Hudson of the Manchester Society) how long remained. His answer was "two minutes". Cooke ordered a short sevens-style drop out and Adrian Thompson regained possession and passed to Halsey who took play into the Plymouth 22. From a quickly taken line out, Everton Weekes took the ball with both hands and passed to Geoff Ball who peeled off the front to race over in the corner to put him forever into Quins folklore. Nine minutes of injury time had been played and although Dudman missed the conversion, the tie had been won and we moved into the quarter finals for an away game against Coventry. The following day, the Wanderers continued their pursuit of a second Middlesex Cup trophy against Hendon in the semi-final at the Stoop. In the end, it was an easy win for us with tries coming from Atkin, Lawrence and Preston, a penalty from Lawrence and a dropped goal by Chesworth. Hendon's only response was a penalty from Lavalle to make the final score 18-3.

Leicester was our next port of call and after beginning well with a try from John Olver and rallying with further scores from Jefferson and Olver and a conversion and two penalties by Salmon, we eventually went down 20-35. We conceded six tries in the process and five changes were made to the starting line-up for the quarter final tie in Coventry the following week. Returning to the side were Dudman, Mickey Claxton, Riddell, Cooke and Chris Butcher. Ricky Bartlett (1946-1964) passed away on 6th March and a minute's silence was held before kick-off. We started well and got into our running game which was well suited to our backs, especially our superb wingers Jefferson and Halsey. Against the run of play, Coventry went into a 9-0 lead in 22 minutes; Saunders dropped a goal and Fairn and Thomas got penalties. We came storming back and Jefferson and Butcher scored tries which Dudman converted. A second dropped goal for the home side (this time from Wright) made it all square at half time. Coventry had a giant in the line out by the name of Kidner and we effectively took him out of the game by throwing the ball over him every time. Dudman got his first penalty a minute into the second half to edge us in front before Coventry had a spell of domination and Travers scored from a pushover. We were not to be denied and a brilliant touchline run by Jefferson put Halsey over in the corner, Dudman converted and landed a second penalty to put us out of reach. We had reached our first semi-final since 1980 and a trip to Bristol was our reward. Richard Riddell made his final appearance in the Coventry match having scored 36 points (9 tries) in his career with us.

We were due to play Coventry at Coundon Road again the following Friday night but this was cancelled due to the proximity of the two games. On Sunday 18th March, the Wanderers met Wasps in the Middlesex Cup final at the Stoop. In a repeat of the game almost a year ago to the day, the visitors again played a strong team, this time containing eight 1st XV regulars. Chesworth kicked a penalty and dropped a goal from 42 yards in a tight first half just shaded by Wasps who scored a goal and a penalty by Williams. Haimes charged down an attempted clearance kick by McHardy and fell on the ball to score, Sumner added a third and after Chesworth narrowly missed a dropped goal, McHardy and Ball put Jackson over for our first try to make it 10-17. That was a close as we got and three further tries from Wasps plus a conversion made the final score 10-31 and the cup had been lost.

Our next match was the semi-final at the Memorial Ground, Bristol on 24th March. Once again, we began at breakneck speed and in the first 16 minutes, we had scored two excellent tries to go into a 12-3 lead. Jefferson got the first and Halsey the second, Dudman added both conversions and Barnes got a penalty for Bristol. By half time, ill-discipline by us had enabled Barnes to pot three penalties and it was all square (as it had been against Coventry). For half an hour of the second half, the Bristol pack applied enormous pressure and eventually, we gave way. A collapsed scrum allowed Barnes to kick his fifth penalty and he also converted a pushover try scored by Hesford. We did have the last word when Jefferson scored his second try in the seventh minute of injury time (which Dudman converted) but it was too late and we had lost narrowly (18-21). We suffered for a while after this bitter disappointment and were thrashed at Nottingham after a promising start. We lost Ray Dudman and Gary Claxton to injuries and conceded eight tries to two from Steve Moriarty in a 10-42 result. On 7th April we had a chance of revenge over Bristol as they travelled to the Stoop and we began well with a try from Salmon which Barnes pegged back with a penalty to leave the score at 4-3. Early in the second half, Barnes got his second penalty but when Chris Butcher dived over for our second try, we were back in front. The problem was that our kicker, Nick Chesworth, had missed both conversions and two simple penalty attempts and Bristol remained in contact. Barnes benefited from a fumble by Woodhouse to score, he converted his own try and Bristol had beaten us again, this time by twelve points to eight. This was their fifteenth successive win over us, a run which stretched back to 1973.

We did return to winning ways against Rosslyn Park at Roehampton (26-6) but lost narrowly at Swansea (12-19) in the first match of the Easter tour. P.S. (Paul) Curtis made the first of at least 121 appearances in this match and would go on to play in the following six seasons. Our last match of the season was against Cardiff on 23rd April and would be our last ever here on the tour at Easter. Both sides were weakened but we proved the stronger and tries from Jefferson and Cooke and a conversion and two penalties by Dudman were enough to see us home against a goal and a penalty for Cardiff (16-9). Gerry McGuinness returned to play for us again (he had appeared the previous Easter) as we signed off with only our eleventh tour victory at Cardiff since they began back in 1911.

This had been our best season ever for wins with 25 from the 38 matches played. Indeed, had it not been for the County Championship, this number may have been increased to nearer 30. Graham Halsey scored the most tries (12), Richard Cramb dropped 3 goals and Ray Dudman got the most points with 227 (3 tries, 2 dropped goals, 41 penalties and 43 conversions). Overall, tries rose by four to 110, dropped goals were down to 6, penalties stayed the same (53) and conversions rose to 57 (the highest since 1975/76). The total number of points dropped to 731 after four years of rising. Top appearance maker was Ray Dudman with 30 out of 38 followed by Alex Woodhouse (29), Andre Dent (25) and Nigel O'Brien, Dave Cooke, Richard Cramb, Chris Field and Adrian Thompson all on 24.

1983/84

030983	OXFORD	OXFORD	W	5G1PG5T(53)-3PG(9)
070983	OLD GAYTONIANS	STOOP MEMORIAL GROUND	W	3PG2T(17)-1G2T(14)
100983	NORTHAMPTON	NORTHAMPTON	L	1G2PG(12)-3G2PG1T(28)
110983	BRADFORD SALEM	BRADFORD	W	1G2PG(12)-1PG(3)
170983	LLANELLI	TWICKENHAM	W	1PG2T(11)-1PG(3)
210983	MAIDSTONE	STOOP MEMORIAL GROUND	W	1G1DG2PG1T(19)-1PG(3)
240983	LEICESTER	TWICKENHAM	L	3G(18)-2G2T(20)
280983	WEST LONDON INSTITUTE	STOOP MEMORIAL GROUND	W	3G2PG(24)-2PG(6)
011083	SWANSEA	TWICKENHAM	W	1G3PG(15)-2PG(6)
051083	LOUGHBOROUGH STUDENTS	STOOP MEMORIAL GROUND	W	1G1DG4PG2T(29)-2G2PG(18)
081083	GLOUCESTER	STOOP MEMORIAL GROUND	L	1PG(3)-2G1T(16)
161083	ROSSLYN PARK(LMT)	STOOP MEMORIAL GROUND	W	1G(6)-1T(4)
221083	CARDIFF	TWICKENHAM	L	1PG1T(7)-2G2PG2T(26)
291083	LONDON WELSH(LMT)	TWICKENHAM	W	1G1T(10)-2PG(6)
061183	LONDON IRISH(LMT)	STOOP MEMORIAL GROUND	W	2G1PG3T(27)-1PG1T(7)
121183	RICHMOND	RICHMOND	L	1G2PG(12)-3PG2T(17)
191183	OXFORD UNIVERSITY	STOOP MEMORIAL GROUND	W	4G5T(44)-3G(18)
261183	CAMBRIDGE UNIVERSITY	CAMBRIDGE	L	2G2PG1T(22)-1G3PG3T(27)
031283	BLACKHEATH	STOOP MEMORIAL GROUND	W	1DG1PG3T(18)-1G1DG1PG(12)
101283	BEDFORD	STOOP MEMORIAL GROUND	L	1G1PG(9)-1G1T(10)
171283	BATH	BATH	W	1G1DG2PG(15)-1G1PG1T(13)
241283	RICHMOND(LMT)	STOOP MEMORIAL GROUND	W	1DG1PG2T(14)-1PG2T(11)
311283	LONDON SCOTTISH(LMT)	STOOP MEMORIAL GROUND	W	2G1PG3T(27)-1DG1PG1T(10)
070184	ARMY	ALDERSHOT	W	1G4PG3T(30)-2PG1T(10)
140184	BLACKHEATH(LMT)	BLACKHEATH	W	3G1T(22)-4PG(12)
210184	BIRKENHEAD PARK	BIRKENHEAD	C	
280184	CAMBORNE(JPC3)	STOOP MEMORIAL GROUND	W	4G1DG1PG4T(46)-1T(4)

050284	METROPOLITAN POLICE(LMT)	IMBER COURT	W	3G1PG2T(29)-1PG(3)
110284	LLANELLI	LLANELLI	L	1G1PG(9)-4PG2T(20)
190284	HEADINGLEY	STOOP MEMORIAL GROUND	W	5G1PG(33)-1G5PG(21)
250284	PLYMOUTH ALBION(JPC4)	PLYMOUTH	W	3PG2T(17)-2DG2PG1T(16)
030384	LEICESTER	LEICESTER	L	1G2PG2T(20)-4G1PG2T(35)
100384	COVENTRY(JPCQF)	COVENTRY	W	3G2PG(24)-2DG2PG1T(16)
160384	COVENTRY	COVENTRY	C	
240384	BRISTOL(JPCSF)	BRISTOL	L	3G(18)-1G5PG(21)
310384	NOTTINGHAM	NOTTINGHAM	L	1G1T(10)-5G3T(42)
070484	BRISTOL	STOOP MEMORIAL GROUND	L	2T(8)-1G2PG(12)
140484	ROSSLYN PARK	ROEHAMPTON	W	1G5T(26)-1G(6)
210484	SWANSEA	SWANSEA	L	4PG(12)-2G1PG1T(19)
230484	CARDIFF	CARDIFF	W	1G2PG1T(16)-1G1PG(9)

England toured South Africa in May and June 1984 despite a lot of criticism and behind the scenes political pressure. Chris Butcher was our only current player and Peter Winterbottom from the future made up our total of two representatives. They both played in the two tests which were lost 15-33 and 9-35; the other games returned figures of W4 D1.

Yet another sad loss was reported on 16th October 1984, that of Nick Allen (the former New Zealand fly half) who had played for us during the 1980/81 season. He had died after suffering concussion during what was his retirement game in Australia. More tours were discussed on 18th December – one to France in May 1985 (this was turned down) and one to Spain in August of that year (this was approved but never took place). Matches were proposed against Bayonne on 14th August and in a festival on 16th and 17th. During 1985, the running track would be removed and the 1st XV pitch moved nearer the stand to begin the long term development of the ground (this actually took longer than imagined as the council put up something of a fight). The income from various functions at the ground had risen from around £2,800 to £15,000. This enabled the Club to plan ahead with some confidence as the playing reputation was sufficiently high at the moment.

Dave Cooke was in charge of quite a strong squad which was tested to the full by the French Barbarians in the opening game of the 1984/85 season. The match was billed as the Wavell Wakefield Memorial Match but also celebrated 75 years of rugby at Twickenham of which we had been every bit a part. The French Barbarians included twelve French internationals including Blanco, Sella and Rives just to prove they were taking the fixture seriously. We were never in front but Charles van der Merwe (making his debut, was a Zimbabwe international and would go on to make at least 27 appearances) did get a try after 24 minutes to equalise Blanco's first effort. By half time, we only trailed 4-16 but were blown away in the third quarter. By the end, Dudman and Moriarty (2) had scored tries and the first named added two conversions. The French had run in seven more tries and fly half Lescarboura had banged over five conversions for a final score of 20-42. Lord Wakefield would have loved it even though his Quins had been outclassed. It was back to normality the following week when we welcomed Northampton to Twickenham. W.M.H. (Marcus) Rose made the first of at least 75 appearances for us in this game (he was in the process of collecting 10 England caps) and contributed fully to an excellent performance. His personal haul was 19 points (1 try, 3 penalties and 3 conversions) and by half time, we led 27-0. Jamie Salmon, Will Wall, Steve Moriarty and John Butcher had scored tries and Rose added eleven of his points. Northampton only opened their account after Rose had made it 30-0 when they scored a penalty and a try but it was far too late and a consolation goal came after Gary Claxton went over and Rose completed his tally to make the result 39-13.

The proposed fixture with Old Gaytonians on 10th September was cancelled so our next game was against Llanelli at Twickenham on 15th September. Making his debut in this one was the massive presence of I. G. (Iain) Milne at prop. He went on to play 24 times for us over the next two seasons and won 44 caps for Scotland. Llanelli came and showed their ugly side, employing dirty tactics in the search for victory. It didn't work this time and six penalties from Rose and the conversion of Peter Lillington's try was enough to see off four penalties and a dropped goal from Pearce. Maidstone appeared as our opponents for our first game of the season at the Stoop and were thrashed (53-0). Despite making nine changes from the previous game, we were still far too strong for the visitors from Kent. Ten tries were run in and Dudman added five conversions and a penalty to complete the rout. The road to leagues was now starting to emerge and this season saw the start of the National Merit Tables A and B. We were in A but no one really took it that seriously. To be quite honest, it was never really clear that it was a merit table match! Anyway, we went down in this one to Leicester at Twickenham by ten points (15-25) despite another eleven points from Rose. We had now only won two of the last fourteen meetings between the sides and they were both away.

Next up were London Welsh at the Stoop in a morning kick-off on 29th September and with each side scoring three tries, it came down to place kicks. Rose got three from nine but the Welsh kicker (Price) only missed one of six to give them a narrow win (21-25). Chris Butcher (returning to the team after his extended stay in South Africa), Rose and Dave Cooke got our tries. This was to be our last defeat at their hands; the next six matches would all be won as the London Welsh dropped out of the top echelon. Our inconsistency carried on when West London Institute came to the Stoop in midweek. At half time we trailed by a penalty goal to nil but luckily, two Stuart Thresher efforts were enough to save us from an embarrassing defeat. The trouble with having a strong fixture list is that when you suffer a drop in form, the hard games just keep on coming. Swansea came to Twickenham and went away victorious (10-15). Again Rose missed several attempts at goal, getting just two from eight. The largely makeshift midweek side met Loughborough Students and did suffer the embarrassment of defeat when a try two minutes from the end sealed a narrow win for the visitors (13-16). Our second National Merit Table game was at Kingsholm against Gloucester on 13th October. We had fifteen men missing due to County Championship calls and were never really in with a chance. Stuart Thresher did kick a couple of penalties in the first half but a goal and a try put Gloucester in front by four points. Another goal and a penalty completed their victory and left us with just that narrow win over West London Institute out of our last six games.

With our full side again, we overcame Rosslyn Park at Twickenham with Stuart Thresher getting two penalties and two conversions to add to tries from Willie Jefferson, Iain Milne and Everton Weekes. The final score of 22-12 reflected our superiority. A difficult trip to Cardiff was not helped by County Championship calls but we played very well and were unlucky to go down by six points (19-25). Terry Claxton made his last appearance in this game having scored 13 tries (52 points) and led the side 34 times. A Harlequin XV played against a Spanish XV at the Stoop on 3rd November (the day before the encounter at Sunbury) and won an entertaining game 44-26. We scored six tries through Geoff Ashby, John Butcher, Gary Curtis, Andre Dent and a brace from John Sargent. Ray Dudman added four penalties and four conversions. Our opponents also got six tries through Azkargorta, Longhney, Moreno, Sainza (2) and Tomo and one conversion. Fixtures with London Irish had recently been revived and we made our first appearance at Sunbury since March 1966. This game was doubly important to both sides, as it was a joint London Merit Table/National Merit Table fixture. The Irish were having a terrible start to the season and it looked odds on that we would win easily. Into the second half, Thresher had landed three penalties to a dropped goal and two penalties from O'Donnell for the home side to leave it all square; but we had the last word. The pack drove deep into Irish territory and Milne went over from a five-metre scrum, Thresher converted and that was that.

The County Championship was still extracting a number of our players every other week but Richmond were seen off easily by twenty nine points to four. Stuart Thresher got a try, three penalties and two conversions and Willie Jefferson (2) and Andre Dent completed our scoring with further tries. Against the Universities, we fumbled our way to a win over Oxford (19-12) but went down to Cambridge (3-12) in appalling conditions, which matched our play. In the Oxford game Simon Hunter made the first of at least 47 appearances for the 1st XV. The following week, we travelled to Sudbury to take on Wasps in what was billed as "The championship of London". On a typically rain and wind dominated day in December, our pack was in superb form and despite going behind to two Stringer penalties, we rallied strongly and Chris Butcher scored a pushover try which Marcus Rose converted. Stringer put Wasps back in front with another penalty but Rose dropped a goal to level and got his first penalty to put us in front at half time. Stringer again levelled in similar fashion but when Butcher put Alex Woodhouse in for our second try, Rose's conversion put us six points ahead. Our pack was starting to really dominate possession now and when the final whistle went; we were camped on the Wasps' line trying to score again.

The following week at Bedford, we led at the interval with tries from Steve Moriarty and Everton Weekes and a conversion by Rose to nil. We nodded off in the second half and the home side rallied to draw level. Our fourth National Merit Table "A" game was played the following week against Bath at Twickenham. After going behind to a try, we took the lead when Jamie Salmon raced through, kicked ahead and scored in the corner for Rose to convert. A goal and a try from the visitors put them in control and two penalties from Rose were the best we could manage. A penalty and a try sealed victory for Bath by twenty one points to twelve. Mark Fletcher made his debut in this game and went on to make 65 appearances for the first team during the next six seasons. After two wins out of two in the London Merit Table, we came down to earth with a bump on 22nd December at the Athletic Ground against Richmond. A very poor game resulted in a 13-6 win for the home side. Our final match of the year was on the same ground against the co-tenants, London Scottish. Against a depleted side, we welcomed David Cooke back after an operation to remove a floating bone from his knee. It took us 24 minutes to open the scoring when Willie Jefferson ran onto a chip through by Rose who converted and added a penalty to put us 9-0 up at the break. His second penalty stretched the lead before ex-Quin Nick Chesworth scored a penalty for the Scots. In the last ten minutes, we romped away with further tries from Charlie van der Merwe, Steve Moriarty and Jamie Salmon. Rose converted two to make the final score 28-3.

The Wanderers again took part in the Middlesex Cup and defeated Old Kingsburians at Harrow on 27th January by 23-0 with tries from Simon Hunter (2), John Sargent and Hugh McHardy with Stuart Thresher adding a penalty and two conversions. On 5th January, we met the Army at the Stoop for the final time. The link would be restored in the next century when we would make use of the excellent training facilities at Aldershot. This game would live in the memory not for Willie Jefferson's hat-trick of tries but for the strange goings-on after 30 minutes. John Currie (our Chairman) made his way onto the pitch to talk to the referee (Mr J. Griffiths). After discussing the matter with both captains, it transpired that Gary Rees of Nottingham had withdrawn from the England team to play Romania that afternoon at Twickenham with stomach pains. David Cooke was required to play in his place and left the field to be replaced by Tim Bell. By this time, Cooke had scored a try and Rose had landed two penalty goals. By half time, we led 18-0 after the first two of Jefferson's tries. The Army scored two tries (both converted) but Simon Holland got one in-between and Jefferson completed his hat-trick to leave the final score at 26-12. Although Cooke didn't score, England ran out winners against Romania by twenty two points to fifteen in a match which saw the debuts of, among others, Rob Andrew and Wade Dooley.

The proposed London Merit Table game with Blackheath and the friendly with Birkenhead Park (both at the Stoop) fell foul of the weather and were cancelled. This meant that our next fixture was the 3rd round cup tie against Ealing (also at the Stoop). This was our first meeting with them since 13th January 1883 when we had triumphed by 2 goals and 3 tries to nil at Turnham Green. After Marcus Rose had slotted a penalty to open the scoring, the quality of our all round play told and Mark Fletcher, John Butcher and Alex Woodhouse all stormed over for tries, two of which Rose converted. Ealing full back Steve Foot banged over a penalty on half time and we led 19-3. In the first ten minutes of the second half, John Butcher and Will Wall added tries, Rose converted one and we were into the next round. Ealing were not going out easily though and almost constant pressure from them for the remaining half an hour led to three more penalties from Foot to make the final score 29-12.

The Metropolitan Police came to the Stoop for our fourth London Merit Table match and were eventually comprehensively beaten. At half time, we only led 10-6 with tries from Tim Bell (converted by Rose) and Willie Jefferson to a goal by the visitors. By the time Wiltshire scored their next points with a penalty, we were out of sight. Jamie Salmon, Paul Jackson and Alex Woodhouse had all scored tries, Rose kicked two more conversions and the score was 26-9. John Olver's effort (again converted by Rose) merely altered the winning margin. Paul Ackford appeared against us again in this game (having played for Rosslyn Park before). We were defeating Llanelli more regularly now and travelled to Stradey Park in hope of completing a double over them for the first time since 1965/66. Playing into a biting wind in the first half, we trailed by 10-0 at the interval. Bill Cuthbertson scored ten minutes into the second half after being put through by Chris Butcher, Rose converted and added a penalty from 50 metres with five minutes left. Unfortunately, Llanelli had scored a second try in between which made the final score 14-9 in their favour. This was Willie Jefferson's last game and he had scored 19 tries (76 points) during his time with the Club. Sometime during February, the Wanderers played away against Staines in the Middlesex Cup quarter final and progressed to the semi-final with a 15-9 win.

A trip to Headingley was cancelled so our next fixture was against Lichfield on 23rd February at the Stoop. This was a 4th round cup tie and was to be an exciting game full of nail-biting tension. We started off badly and Lichfield tore into us with all their might and it looked as though they would be added to the names of Wilmslow and Orrell by causing a major upset. Two penalties in the first half by Ian Potter put them ahead and they held this lead until 70 minutes had passed. Marcus Rose landed his first penalty from 55 metres and then levelled matters from much nearer. At this point, Lichfield would still go through as the away side in a drawn game with no tries. With four minutes left, the visitors suffered a cruel blow when their captain, Barry Broad, had to leave the field after being injured making a try saving tackle. From the resulting five metre scrum, Alex Woodhouse plunged over for a try to make it 10-6. With no-one harassing him now, Woodhouse created an opening for Rick Lawrence to add to our total with our second try, Rose converted and we were safely through by 16-6. Some 3,000 supporters who had travelled in 50 coaches from Staffordshire had cheered Lichfield on. They even tried to steal our flag! At the end of the day, it was us who were into the quarter final draw. We were not having a good season really and it felt as though if we came up against a decent team, we would not progress further. As a warm up for the quarter final at Gloucester, we travelled to Leicester and were easily beaten 35-19. We trailed 3-23 at half time before making something of a comeback to win the second half 16-12. Jon Atkin and Alex Woodhouse scored our tries and Rose landed three penalties and a conversion. Making his debut in this game was R. S. (Richard) Langhorn. He only lasted 44 minutes before going off injured but would go on to make at least 132 appearances for the first team until his untimely death in 1994. In the Middlesex Cup semi-final on 3rd March, we played against West London Institute with a side containing a few regular first teamers. Hayward kicked us into an early lead with a penalty before the Institute came back with a try from Short and when Hayward missed with a penalty attempt the students led at half time. Conditions were muddy and the rain didn't help to produce a feast of running rugby but Andre Dent intercepted and scored a try for Hayward to convert. A penalty from Mann reduced our lead to 9-7 but Hayward replied in kind to increase it before Quist-Arcton made a mistake with a loose ball and Gemmell score another try for the visitors. The conversion was missed but when Mann was given a penalty chance from 23 metres, he made no mistake and the students held on for a famous victory by two points (12-14).

In the cup tie at Gloucester, we gave away too many kickable penalties and trailed 6-12 at half time. Rose got two penalties for us; Gloucester's points being made up of a goal and two penalties. Another penalty stretched the lead before Chris Butcher went over from a five metre scrum and Rose converted to narrow the gap to three points. Tim Smith's fourth penalty opened up the six point lead again before we lost our hooker (John Olver) with a strained knee (allegedly through illegal use of the boot). With him went our chances of a semi-final place as our replacement was Will Wall (a lock). Iain Milne tried his best at throwing in but all his efforts were in vain as Gloucester ran in two tries and Smith added another penalty and one conversion for a final score of 31-12. Unfortunately, our squad was just not strong enough on the day although success in the cup was not too far away in the future. Following on from the cup disappointment, we played hosts to Coventry (who had just knocked Leicester out) in our fifth National Merit Table "A" game. We had only won one and were getting desperate as we only had one left after this (at Bristol). Marcus Rose converted three of five penalty chances in the first half to give us a 9-0 lead and Jamie Salmon got two tries in the second to put us seventeen points clear. Coventry gained a consolation try near the end but we had done more than enough to secure our second win in the competition.

We were due to meet London Welsh at the Old Deer Park on 23rd March but they were in the cup semi-final so a game was arranged with Saracens at Southgate. It was exactly 45 years to the day of our only other meeting at Teddington. After an even first half which ended 10-10, we raced away to a convincing win in the second half. Jamie Salmon and Simon Hunter had scored tries in the first half and Marcus Rose added a conversion to which Saracens replied with two penalties and a try. After this, Rose scored a try, a penalty and two conversions to add to tries from Alex Woodhouse, Richard Cramb, Andre Dent and Simon Hunter. Sarries could only manage another try and penalty to leave the final score at 37-17 in our favour. The following week, we met Bristol at the Memorial Ground in our sixth and final merit game. We hadn't won there since April 1971; a run of ten consecutive defeats so the omens were not good. We took the lead in the first minute when Everton Weekes went over from a five metre scrum and Rose converted. This was the extent of our scoring and by half time, we trailed 6-8. By the time the referee abandoned the game after 75 minutes due to the horrendously muddy conditions, the deficit had grown to twenty four points.

The Easter tour saw a new team added to our fixture list in the shape of Bridgend. We still played Swansea on Easter Saturday and indeed, should have come away with a victory. We trailed 0-12 at the interval but came back strongly to lead midway through the second half by 16-15. A penalty try was added to by a brace from Simon Hunter and Rose added a couple of conversions. With two minutes left, the home side scored their third and decisive try to edge them to a 19-16 win. On Monday it was a trip to the Brewery Field, Bridgend for our first ever 15-a-side game (we had met in sevens). The game was played in driving rain and we again trailed at half time. This time though, we had scored and Will Wall's try replied to a goal and a try for Bridgend. Three more tries and a conversion came their way in the second half but we could only get two through Olver and John Butcher (Stuart Thresher converted the first) to leave the final score at 14-24. David Thresher made his debut in this game and went on to play in at least 64 matches for the first team. His brother, Stuart, had already established his place in the first team squad. Our last match of the season was a demerited encounter against Rosslyn Park at Roehampton. Despite leading at half time with a Simon Hunter try, we eventually lost 4-15. Mickey Claxton was sent off for allegedly stamping on someone's head and our future coach, John Kingston (he was also to play for us), appeared at prop for Park, scoring their first try.

After a promising start, this season had been full of ups and downs, the downs just winning out in the end with 17 defeats against 16 wins and a draw. Willie Jefferson got the most tries (10) and Marcus Rose was top points scorer with 184 (3 tries, 1 dropped goal, 37 penalties and 29 conversions). Overall, tries dropped by 21 to 89, dropped goals fell to just 2, conversions were down eleven to 46 but penalties rose by two to 55 (equalling the record set in 1973/74). As a consequence, our points total fell by over a hundred to 619 and things would get worse on this front the following season. Top appearance maker was Everton Weekes with 32 followed by Jamie Salmon on 30 with Malcolm Wall (28) and Adrian Thompson and John Olver on 25. These were the only players to appear in the vast majority of matches.

1984/85

010984	FRENCH BARBARIANS(WMM)	TWICKENHAM	L	2G2T(20)-5G3T(42)
080984	NORTHAMPTON	TWICKENHAM	W	3G3PG3T(39)-1G1PG1T(13)
100984	OLD GAYTONIANS	STOOP MEMORIAL GROUND	C	
150984	LLANELLI	TWICKENHAM	W	1G6PG(24)-1DG4PG(15)
170984	MAIDSTONE	STOOP MEMORIAL GROUND	W	5G1PG5T(53)-0
220984	LEICESTER(NMTA)	TWICKENHAM	L	1G3PG(15)-2G3PG1T(25)
290984	LONDON WELSH	STOOP MEMORIAL GROUND	L	3PG3T(21)-2G3PG1T(25)
031084	WEST LONDON INSTITUTE	STOOP MEMORIAL GROUND	W	2PG(6)-1PG(3)
061084	SWANSEA	TWICKENHAM	L	2PG1T(10)-1G3PG(15)
101084	LOUGHBOROUGH STUDENTS	STOOP MEMORIAL GROUND	L	1G1PG1T(13)-2G1T(16)
131084	GLOUCESTER(NMTA)	GLOUCESTER	L	2PG(6)-2G1PG1T(19)
201084	ROSSLYN PARK	TWICKENHAM	W	2G2PG1T(22)-1G2PG(12)
271084	CARDIFF	CARDIFF	L	2G1PG1T(19)-3G1PG1T(25)
041184	LONDON IRISH(LMT/NMTA)	SUNBURY	W	1G3PG(15)-1DG2PG(9)

101184	RICHMOND	STOOP MEMORIAL GROUND	W	2G3PG2T(29)-1T(4)
171184	OXFORD UNIVERSITY	STOOP MEMORIAL GROUND	W	1G1DG2PG1T(19)-4PG(12)
241184	CAMBRIDGE UNIVERSITY	STOOP MEMORIAL GROUND	L	1PG(3)-1G2PG(12)
011284	WASPS(LMT)	SUDBURY	W	2G1DG1PG(18)-4PG(12)
081284	BEDFORD	BEDFORD	D	1G1T(10)-2PG1T(10)
151284	BATH(NMTA)	TWICKENHAM	L	1G2PG(12)-1G1PG3T(21)
221284	RICHMOND(LMT)	RICHMOND	L	2PG(6)-1G1PG1T(13)
291284	LONDON SCOTTISH	RICHMOND	W	3G2PG1T(28)-1PG(3)
050185	ARMY	STOOP MEMORIAL GROUND	W	2PG5T(26)-2G(12)
120185	BLACKHEATH(LMT)	STOOP MEMORIAL GROUND	C	
190185	BIRKENHEAD PARK	STOOP MEMORIAL GROUND	C	
260185	EALING(JPC3)	STOOP MEMORIAL GROUND	W	3G1PG2T(29)-4PG(12)
030285	METROPOLITAN POLICE(LMT)	STOOP MEMORIAL GROUND	W	4G2T(32)-1G1PG(9)
090285	LLANELLI	LLANELLI	L	1G1PG(9)-2PG2T(14)
160285	HEADINGLEY	HEADINGLEY	C	
230285	LICHFIELD(JPC4)	STOOP MEMORIAL GROUND	W	1G2PG1T(16)-2PG(6)
020385	LEICESTER	LEICESTER	L	1G3PG1T(19)-3G2DG1PG2T(35)
090385	GLOUCESTER(JPCQF)	GLOUCESTER	L	1G2PG(12)-2G5PG1T(31)
170385	COVENTRY(NMTA)	STOOP MEMORIAL GROUND	W	3PG2T(17)-1T(4)
230385	SARACENS	SOUTHGATE	W	3G1PG4T(37)-3PG2T(17)
300385	BRISTOL(NMTA)	BRISTOL	L	1G(6)-3G3T(30)
060485	SWANSEA	SWANSEA	L	2G1T(16)-2G1PG1T(19)
080485	BRIDGEND	BRIDGEND	L	1G2T(14)-2G3T(24)
130485	ROSSLYN PARK	ROEHAMPTON	L	1T(4)-2G1PG(15)

In May and June 1985, England went to New Zealand and played seven matches including two tests. Overall, they had a record of W4 L3 (both tests were included in the losses – the first was a narrow 13-18 defeat but the second finished 15-42). Jamie Salmon and David Cooke were our current players plus Wade Dooley who would be a future Quin. Salmon and Cooke appeared in both tests and Dooley came on as a replacement in the second.

We began the 1985/86 season with a visit to Maidstone on 7th September. Newcomer Simon Cooke opened the scoring with a try which Marcus Rose converted; Rose then added a penalty goal. Maidstone replied with a penalty of their own and we led by six points at half time. The second half was all one-way traffic and John Butcher (he was later sent off), Charlie van der Merwe, Mark Fletcher (he added a conversion), Rose (he added three conversions) and Richard Langhorn all scored tries to leave the final score at 37-3 to give us just the start we needed. Rob Glenister played in the first of 155 matches for the 1st XV in a career which would last for ten seasons. Marcus Rose was back fit again and was in tremendous form against Northampton the following weekend. He scored sixteen of our points with a try, two penalties and three conversions. The last penalty, from the half way line, gave us a last-gasp 24-21 victory. M. G. (Michael) "Mickey" Skinner scored a try on his debut. He was to go on and play at least 110 times for the first team and win 21 caps for England. Our other try came from Stuart Thresher. Although Northampton got four tries, their fly half, Ashley Johnson missed three conversions and two penalty attempts during the game. We were without ten first choice players for the visit of Llanelli and duly paid the price (16-28).

Leicester were next and came to Twickenham on 28th September to play in our first match in the new John Smith's National Merit Table "A". Weakened once again by injuries, we trailed 3-19 at half time but scored the only points in the second half when Mike Summers went in from half way for Fletcher to convert. In our first midweek match of the season, we saw off the students from West London Institute despite trailing 10-13 at the interval. Tries in the second half by Ken Moss, Older and Andre Dent were enough to see us home 22-13. Paul Renucci and Rob Glenister had scored in the first half and Rose had converted one. Swansea were trailing by five Rose penalties to one at half time but when they had use of the wind, they scored three goals and a penalty without reply to run out winners 24-15. Revenge was gained over Loughborough Students for our reverse the previous season (22-6) before the high point of the season was reached far too soon! Gloucester travelled to Twickenham on 12th October for our second John Smith's Merit Table game. Our recent record against the Cherry and White's was not good – one draw and six losses in the last seven encounters. Marcus Rose put us in front after only a minute with a penalty before Dave Cooke, Jamie Salmon and Rob Glenister scored tries; one of which Rose converted. It was unreal, Quins leading Gloucester 17-0 at half time. Things were going to get a hell of a lot worse for the visitors before the end and Mickey Skinner began the second half scoring with a try nine minutes into the third quarter. A quick break by Dent saw Glenister run in for his second try, Rose converted and it was 27-0. A converted penalty try was to be Gloucester's only source of points in the game and we were soon on the front foot again. Attack after attack was made upon Gloucester's line and further tries came from Simon Cooke, Dent and Glenister (completing his hat trick). Rose and Stuart Thresher each kicked a conversion to make the final score 43-6. Not surprisingly, this was our biggest win of the season and our highest score.

Our next game was against Rosslyn Park; it was also our first London Merit Table game of the season. A host of missed chances cost us dear and Park chalked up their eleventh win out of eleven matches played (15-18). Against Cardiff, we led at half time after Rose had kicked two penalties and converted a try by Olver but missed the conversion of Jackson's try. Cardiff managed two penalties and a try to make it 16-10. The second half was a completely different story and four goals and a try and forty minutes later, Cardiff had won by thirty eight points to sixteen! Things were going from bad to worse and we next went down to London Irish at the Stoop in another London Merit Table match. Three penalties from Rose were not enough and thirteen points for the Irish carried the day. It was their first win over us since February 1960. Our next game was yet another London Merit Table fixture and was played at the Athletic Ground against Richmond. This had become a "must win" game and it was extremely close to being another disaster. Rose put us in front with a penalty after five minutes but Richmond scored a try on their first incursion into our territory to go in front. We re-took the lead when Simon Cooke scored a try but when Preston levelled things up after seventeen minutes of the second half, the game was up for grabs. With fifteen minutes left, Paul Jackson went over from close range and we had secured the merit points. In the matches with the Universities of Oxford and Cambridge (both played away), we came through unscathed. Rose scored twelve points at Oxford to help us to a 16-9 win and three conversions at Cambridge after Jackson, Cramb, Simon Cooke, Skinner and Glenister had scored tries to make the final score 26-13.

The London Welsh game on 30th November was another London Merit Table fixture and we were looking for only our second ever win at the Old Deer Park. Micky Bell and Alex Woodhouse (converted by Rose) got tries to give us a 10-0 lead at the break and when Rose landed a penalty after 55 minutes, it was effectively all over. The Welsh did get a try back when Butterworth went over but Micky Bell got his second try which rose converted to give us more merit table points. After a run of four wins, we came down to earth at the Rectory Field against Blackheath. We were missing several men due to the calls of the London Division and three penalties settled the issue. We had failed to score for the first time since 19th February 1983 against Headingley. Against Bedford the following week, the number of players unavailable through injury and Divisional calls ran to twenty one. Dick Best was forced to come out of retirement and play his part in the scrum and Andre Dent captained the side (as he had done against Blackheath) in David Cooke's absence. Stuart Thresher had his kicking boots on and by half time he had been successful with three penalties and the conversion of Micky Bell's try. The visitors only reply was a penalty from Finnie. They did manage a try by Canning in the second half but it was far too little too late as we added to our score with tries from Adrian Thompson and Jon Atkin. Thresher added both conversions and we had achieved our biggest win over Bedford since March 1957 to the tune of twenty seven points to seven. The following week, we played our final game of the year as the fixture with London Scottish on 28th December was cancelled. Bath were our opponents at the Rec and both sides were severely depleted due to Divisional calls. In a close contest we just shaded it 16-7; scoring three tries (Weekes and Micky Bell (2)) to one (Stanley).

During the first half of the season, we had said goodbye to a number of players. Against West London Institute on 2nd October, Mickey Claxton ended his 1st XV career having scored 48 points (12 tries). Jon Atkin had scored 5 tries (20 points) and Dick Best had captained the side 46 times and scored 11 tries (44 points) when they made their final appearances at Bath and Graham Birkett had managed 27 tries (108 points) and captained the side twelve times when he took his final bow against Cardiff (coming on as a replacement).

Our first fixture of 1986 was due to be against Wasps at the Stoop on 4th January but they refused to play; saying that the pitch was frozen. Instead, Blackheath became our first opponents in a London Merit Table fixture at the Rectory Field the following week. This time we had our full side out and Blackheath paid the price. Inside the first three minutes, Munday had kicked two penalties for "The Club" (as they were known) but that was as good as it got for them. Against the wind, we turned round leading 13-6 so it was more or less certain that we would win. As it was, we managed tries through Jackson (2), Weekes, Micky Bell and David Cooke with Rose landing three penalties and two conversions for a final score of 33-6. One report on the game was simply titled "Quintessence!". The next day, the Wanderers opened their Middlesex Cup campaign with a win over Rosslyn Park in the fourth round by 13-3. Saracens visited on Sunday 19th January in our sixth London Merit Table game. After losing the first two, we had now won three on the trot – this was soon to become four. With the strong wind in the first half, we racked up fifteen points without reply before Saracens scored near half time to cut the deficit to 15-6. A single try to the visitors in the second half brought them to within five points but they got no closer.

The following week, we met Headingley at the Stoop in the 3rd round of the John Player Cup and our ability to almost snatch defeat from the jaws of victory appeared again. Headingley had one of their props (Machell) sent off by the referee after throwing a punch and had to play three quarters of the game with only fourteen men. Moran had dropped a goal to put the visitors ahead after five minutes but three penalties from Rose put us on our way but we couldn't kill them off. Worrall got a penalty to make it 9-6 and, with time almost up, Swales had a penalty chance from just outside the 22 to the right of the posts. He struck the ball and it appeared to be right on target. At the last moment, the ball curled just wide, went dead and the referee blew the final whistle. We had survived, but only just, to go into the next round. Jon Eagle and Peter Winterbottom faced us in this game and both would go on to become Quins.

The following day, the Wanderers played at Belfrey Avenue against Uxbridge in the Middlesex Cup quarter final. Our full back, Ray Dudman was on target in the first half with three penalties to give us a lead we never lost. The Uxbridge kicker (Bob Calvert) had missed three so it could have been a lot closer than it was but Dudman was on target with his fourth penalty after 55 minutes and when he converted Simon Cooke's try five minutes later, the tie was won. Calvert did drop a goal but it was too little, too late and we were into the semi-final again. The Metropolitan Police inaugurated their new facilities at Imber Court (including an all-weather pitch) when we met them on 1st February and gave a rousing display. There was never much in it but we should have closed the game down when leading 17-9. We allowed the Police back in and conceded thirteen points without replying to lose by five points (17-22).

Our form was not good and we travelled to Lichfield for our 4th round cup tie with memories of the last encounter with them still fresh in our minds. During the week leading up to the tie, the Lichfield Club had laid 25 tons of straw onto their pitch to keep the frost out – they succeeded and were rewarded with a crowd of 4,000 on a bitterly cold afternoon. This time we made no mistake and steadily built a lead. Marcus Rose kicked a penalty and converted tries from Woodhouse and Jackson to put us 15-0 up at the interval. Lichfield did manage a couple of penalties in the second half but either side of the second one, we added further tries by Thompson and Skinner for a final score of 23-6. For the second year running, our fixture with Headingley fell foul of the weather so, in a desperate attempt to get a game, we travelled down to Beacon Park to take on Plymouth Albion. In another close encounter, we led 7-3 at half time after Graham Halsey had scored a try and Richard Cramb dropped a goal and Butcher had landed a penalty for the home side. They took the lead when they scored a goal at the beginning of the second half before Paul Jackson doubled back to the short side of a scrum and ran 40 yards down the line to edge us in front again. Seven minutes from the end, Butcher kicked his second penalty and Plymouth had exacted sweet revenge for their defeat in the cup by twelve points to eleven. Sometime around this point, the Wanderers played Wasps in the Middlesex Cup semi-final and came off very much second best after suffering a 10-42 reverse.

The match at Leicester was called off due to the inclement weather so our next game was against Waterloo at the Stoop on 8th March. Our record against Waterloo was excellent and in the last ten meetings, we had won eight and drawn two so we were looking good for another victory. Ray Dudman played his first full game for almost two years and did well. He gave us the lead with a penalty, converted a try by Frank Croxford and added a second penalty to leave us 12-0 ahead. Future Quin Mike Molyneux went over for Waterloo, Cotter converted and it was 12-6 at the break. Dudman landed his third penalty and Jackson got a try to put us in the driving seat before King went over for the visitors. A purple patch in the closing minutes led to tries from O'Brien and Salmon; Dudman added both conversions to make the score 31-10. Just before the end, Waterloo lost one of their locks (Wilkinson) who was sent off for punching. We met Coventry at Coundon Road the following week in a John Smith's Merit Table "A" game. Jamie Salmon was playing some of his best rugby but had been dropped by the England selectors. He set up our second try and proved to all watching that his form was still good enough to be considered at international level. Bill Cuthbertson and Micky Bell got our tries, Marcus Rose got two penalties and Richard Cramb dropped a goal. In reply, Coventry could only manage a couple of penalties to leave the score at 17-6 in our favour.

The next fixture was the big one, the cup quarter final against Leicester at the Stoop. In the second minute, Jackson broke from a scrum and passed to Rose who found Dent on the outside to complete the run to the line and put us in front. By the twenty minute mark, Leicester were in front when Cusworth went over for Hare to convert. As the half drew to a close, Jackson scored himself (again from a scrum) to put us 8-6 ahead at half time. Both Rose and Hare were missing kicks and it was the latter who eventually succeeded with a penalty after 57 minutes to put the visitors back in front. Richards had the final word when he scored a try which Hare converted to put Leicester into the semi-final. We had once again just failed to go that one step further. The Easter tour provided two close games with one loss and one win resulting. First it was Swansea who ran out winners by 29-19 on Easter Saturday. We had led 15-6 at half time but three quick tries at the start of the second half effectively won the match. On Easter Monday, we travelled to meet Penarth for the first (and so far only) time. Thanks to tries from Everton Weekes, Simon Cooke and a brace from Simon Hunter plus one conversion by Stuart Thresher, we ran out winners by eighteen points to fourteen.

In our last John Smith's game, we welcomed Bristol to the Stoop. In the words of one report we dominated matters for a mere 45 seconds. In this time, Alex Woodhouse got a try and Rose converted. By half time, Bristol were level through a penalty and a dropped goal and during the second half, they stormed clear scoring a goal and two tries without reply. Their victory by twenty points to six took them clear of any relegation fears they had before the kick-off. We finished in mid-table with a 50% record from our four games. Our final game of the season saw Rosslyn Park complete the double over us by 15-12. Dudman kicked two penalties and converted Dent's try in reply to Park's penalty and three tries. The final part of the season saw us lose three stalwarts. Iain Milne played his last game for us against Bristol, Maurice Rocks appeared for the final time at Roehampton having scored 4 tries (16 points) in his career and our coach Iestyn Thomas made his final appearance at Penarth having scored a single try (4 points) and captained the side on eight occasions.

This season had been slightly better results wise than the previous one but we still lacked players in key areas especially when the first choice was not available. Our final playing record showed eighteen wins and thirteen losses from thirty one matches. Paul Jackson scored the most tries (10) and Marcus Rose was again top of the points with 162 (3 tries, 32 penalties and 27 conversions). Overall, tries (83), dropped goals (1) and penalties (45) all fell and conversions stayed the same on 46. This meant that our points total hit its lowest since 1980/81 with 562. Top appearance maker was Andre Dent on 29 followed by Paul Curtis and John Olver on 25 and David Cooke and Nigel O'Brien with 22. It was no wonder only five players managed 22 or more appearances during the season when you consider that some 58 players were used in the 31 matches played.

1985/86

070985	MAIDSTONE	MAIDSTONE	W	5G1PG1T(37)-1PG(3)
140985	NORTHAMPTON	NORTHAMPTON	W	3G2PG(24)-1G1PG3T(21)
210985	LLANELLI	TWICKENHAM	L	2G1T(16)-1G1DG5PG1T(28)
280985	LEICESTER(JSMTA)	TWICKENHAM	L	1G1PG(9)-2G1PG1T(19)
021085	WEST LONDON INSTITUTE	STOOP MEMORIAL GROUND	W	1G4T(22)-1G1PG1T(13)
051085	SWANSEA	TWICKENHAM	L	5PG(15)-3G2PG(24)
091085	LOUGHBOROUGH STUDENTS	STOOP MEMORIAL GROUND	W	2G2PG1T(22)-1G(6)
121085	GLOUCESTER(JSMTA)	TWICKENHAM	W	4G1PG4T(43)-1G(6)
191085	ROSSLYN PARK(LMT)	TWICKENHAM	L	1G3PG(15)-2G1DG1PG(18)
261085	CARDIFF	TWICKENHAM	L	1G2PG1T(16)-4G2PG2T(38)
021185	LONDON IRISH(LMT)	STOOP MEMORIAL GROUND	L	3PG(9)-3PG1T(13)
091185	RICHMOND(LMT)	RICHMOND	W	1PG2T(11)-1PG1T(7)
161185	OXFORD UNIVERSITY	OXFORD	W	1G2PG1T(16)-1G1PG(9)
231185	CAMBRIDGE UNIVERSITY	CAMBRIDGE	W	3G2T(26)-1G1PG1T(13)
301185	LONDON WELSH(LMT)	OLD DEER PARK	W	2G1PG1T(19)-1T(4)
071285	BLACKHEATH	BLACKHEATH	L	0-3PG(9)
141285	BEDFORD	STOOP MEMORIAL GROUND	W	3G3PG(27)-1PG1T(7)
211285	BATH	BATH	W	2G1T(16)-1DG1T(7)
281285	LONDON SCOTTISH(JSMTA/ LMT)	STOOP MEMORIAL GROUND	C	
040186	WASPS(JSMTA/LMT)	STOOP MEMORIAL GROUND	C	
110186	BLACKHEATH(LMT)	BLACKHEATH	W	2G3PG3T(33)-2PG(6)
190186	SARACENS(LMT)	STOOP MEMORIAL GROUND	W	2G1PG(15)-1G1T(10)
250186	HEADINGLEY(JPC3)	STOOP MEMORIAL GROUND	W	3PG(9)-1DG1PG(6)

010286	METROPOLITAN POLICE(LMT)	IMBER COURT	L	1G1PG2T(17)-2G2PG1T(22)
080286	LICHFIELD(JPC4)	LICHFIELD	W	2G1PG2T(23)-2PG(6)
150286	HEADINGLEY	STOOP MEMORIAL GROUND	C	
220286	PLYMOUTH ALBION	PLYMOUTH	L	1PG2T(11)-1G2PG(12)
010386	LEICESTER	LEICESTER	C	
080386	WATERLOO	STOOP MEMORIAL GROUND	W	3G3PG1T(31)-1G1T(10)
150386	COVENTRY(JSMTA)	COVENTRY	W	1DG2PG2T(17)-2PG(6)
220386	LEICESTER(JPCQF)	STOOP MEMORIAL GROUND	L	2T(8)-2G1PG(15)
290386	SWANSEA	SWANSEA	L	2G1PG1T(19)-3G1PG2T(29)
310386	PENARTH	PENARTH	W	1G3T(18)-(14)
050486	BRISTOL(JSMTA)	STOOP MEMORIAL GROUND	L	1G(6)-1G1DG1PG2T(20)
120486	ROSSLYN PARK	ROEHAMPTON	L	1G2PG(12)-1PG3T(15)

Six years after our last tour, it was time for another and this time we ventured to new locations – Australia and South East Asia. The tour brochure said that the party consisted of the following players:- Martin Birkett, David H. Cooke (captain), Simon Cooke, Frank Croxford, Paul Curtis, Bill Cuthbertson, Andre Dent, Ray Dudman, Mark Fletcher, Rob Glenister, Graham Halsey, Simon Hunter, Paul Jackson, Simon Kift, Richard Langhorn, John Olver, Gary Sharp, Mickey Skinner, Stuart Thresher, Charlie van der Merwe, Malcolm Wall, Everton Weekes and Alex Woodhouse. John Currie was the manager, Dick Best the coach and John Horner the Club physio.

The group left Heathrow on 12th August, flew to Singapore with British Airways and arrived the following day. The first game was on 15th August against Singapore at Singapore Cricket Club. Two free days followed before an evening departure to Sydney where they arrived on Monday 18th August. The second game was played the next day against Eastern Suburbs followed by a day in Sydney and a cocktail party hosted by the Minister for Sport and Recreation (Michael Cleary MP). On Thursday 21st August, we played Manly in the evening. The next two days were taken up with a bush experience and a visit to an old ghost town. From Sydney, they departed to the outback for the fourth match against Dubbo on 25th August. It was back to Sydney and a tour of the harbour before departure to Bangkok on 27th August. A free day was followed by the last game against Thailand on Friday 29th August. This match saw us score the highest number of points in a game in our history although we just missed the magic 100 mark (98-6). The next two days were taken up with sightseeing before departure to London on Tuesday night and the party arrived back on Wednesday 3rd September ready for the start of the 1986/87 season.

Most of the details are unknown for this trip although Ray Dudman scored 1 penalty and 5 conversions against Singapore, 2 penalties and 2 conversions against Eastern Suburbs and 1 penalty against Manly; he played half a game in Bangkok and scored 7 conversions. The tour was not without its problems and some of the the repeatable stories are those about the players revolting over strict training methods and a stand-off, with Dick Best being accused of picking on people. He tried to implement training sessions at 7 a.m. and 4 p.m. with three mile runs included because he saw this as necessary due to the hot and humid conditions and the players were supposed to be building up to start the new season. David Cooke acted as a go-between in a bid to smooth the waters, it was not a happy camp! On arrival from Australia, Everton Weekes was not allowed into Thailand as he had a Barbadian passport so he made his way home from there.

Australia and South East Asia Tour

150886	SINGAPORE	SINGAPORE CRICKET CLUB	W	5G1PG3T(45)-(19)
190886	EASTERN SUBURBS	SYDNEY	W	2G2PG1T(22)-(10)
210886	MANLY	MANLY	L	1PG1T(7)-(24)
250886	DUBBO	DUBBO	W	
290886	THAILAND	ROYAL BANGKOK SPORTS CLUB	W	(98)-(6)

During the 1986/87 season, Simon Cooke put forward a proposal to the Club to improve the facilities and generate some income. His idea was to close the 2nd XV pitch, turn the main pitch through 90 degrees and put a three star hotel on the site. It got no further as there was no interest to develop it. The U21s became the Jaguars and the U19 team returned in addition to the other teams in existence. On 7th May 1987, one of our best supporters passed away, he was Robert "Bob" Wright. He was 79 and had been supporting Quins home and away since he was 17 in 1925. He had seen Wakefield, Gibbs, Hamilton-Wickes and Gracie play and was a most recognisable figure with his shooting stick and black Homburg hat. Back in the days when you could change ends at half time and the sand pit and running track were still in place, many an hour would be spent with him on the touchline discussing the fortunes of Quins. Mention must be made of John Horner who was the Club's physiotherapist for most of the eighties and became indispensable with his knowledge and experience of rugby injuries. He worked at the House of Lords as a Doorkeeper, having served in the Royal Air Force for a number of years before that.

Dick Best replaced Iestyn Thomas as coach (he had gone to London Welsh) and David Cooke began his final season as a player knowing that the Club were on the verge of something special but it was a question of whether the final step could be made. Dick had coached the U21s before moving on to the first team. He also coached the London Division to three Divisional Championships and a victory over Australia in 1988. The spell with us lasted until 1991 when he went to England and stayed there until 1994. He was sacked despite having an excellent record because Jack Rowell (who was then manager) wanted to do that job as well (in truth, the coaches behind the scenes worked the magic and Rowell took the credit). He then came back to Quins from 1994-97 before moving on to London Irish which will be covered later.

A friendly at Bideford in North Devon on 6th September provided a stroll for the XV put out and a 52-0 victory was the result. After the tour of the Far East and Australia, the squad were far fitter and better prepared than in previous seasons and took on Northampton at Twickenham the following weekend in their first serious test. A persistent drizzle fell during the game, the ball was wet and this helped to keep the score at 0-0 at half time. Marcus

Rose landed a 45 yard penalty after 53 minutes to open the scoring after Northampton had missed with three penalty attempts and a dropped goal. Four minutes later, Alex Woodhouse was driven over and Rose converted to put us in the driving seat. The game was put out of Northampton's reach when Graham Halsey scored nine minutes later to make the final score 13-0. Two days later, we met Maidstone at the Stoop in a game which saw the debut of undoubtedly one of the fastest wingers ever seen. His name was A. T. (Andrew) "Andy" Harriman. He went on to play 61 times for the 1st XV and gain a solitary cap for England in 1988. Charles van der Merwe made his last appearance on a cold evening in a team showing eleven changes from the Northampton game. In the end, we managed a win but only by nine points (15-6).

Against Llanelli the following Saturday, we were looking to maintain our winning start to the season. We started well, Marcus Rose landed two penalties before Llanelli equalised when Gravelle converted his own try to leave it even at half time. The visitors came out strongly at the start of the second half and scored a goal and a penalty to give them a lead of nine points. Ray Dudman had come on for the injured Rose and proceeded to kick three penalties out of four attempts to bring the scores level once again. A last effort brought a penalty for the home side just outside the Llanelli 22 and when someone uttered some words to the referee, ten more yards made Dudman's penalty to win the game a formality. We had lost seven games on the trot to Leicester and hadn't beaten them at Twickenham since 1978 so we weren't expected to do much when they visited on 27th September. Charlie Smith made his debut and was to go on and make at least 44 appearances for the 1st XV. In the first half, Marcus Rose kicked two penalties and scored a try when Harriman scorched past England wing Rory Underwood. Leicester actually led, having scored twelve points themselves. In the 35th minute, one of our props, Frank Croxford, was sent off by the referee for stamping and we had to play the remaining 45 minutes with fourteen men. Early in the second half, Mark Fletcher dropped a goal to put us in front, Mickey Skinner got our second try and Rose made the game safe with his third penalty.

We were having our most successful start to a season since 1964/65 and equalled our start of six wins with victory in our next match over West London Institute (29-3). Steve Moriarty appeared for the last time, having scored 35 tries (140 points) in his first XV career but failed to score against the Institute. Tries from Matthew Ebsworth, Paul Jackson (2) and a penalty try helped us to victory and a dropped goal by Fletcher plus two penalties and a conversion by Stuart Thresher cemented the result. We didn't have the best of records against Swansea and our bad run continued at Twickenham despite tries from Jamie Salmon and Mickey Skinner and a penalty and two conversions from Rose as the Welshmen ran out winners by ten points (15-25). This was our first defeat of the season but we had a chance to bounce straight back four days later when we took on Loughborough Students at the Stoop. This match saw the debuts of Martin Hobley (who would go on to play in at least 93 games), E. G. (Everton) Davis (who would play in at least 108 games) and D. S. (David) "Dave" Loveridge of New Zealand All Blacks fame. He had won 24 caps for his country and captained the side as well. He would, sadly, only appear 18 times in our colours. Another debutant was F. Ajia on the right wing and when he got injured, Loveridge came on as his replacement. Stuart Thresher kicked two penalties and Mark Fletcher dropped a goal to put us into a 9-3 lead at the interval before tries from Everton Weekes, Everton Davis, Andre Dent (2) and John Kingston plus three Thresher conversions saw us comfortably home (35-9).

We travelled to Kingsholm for our first John Smith's Merit Table "A" fixture on the back of the roasting we had handed Gloucester on their visit to Twickenham the previous season. We were adding some much needed steel to our play and, by the break, led by three points. Fletcher had dropped another goal and Thresher converted a try by Skinner. Gloucester managed two penalties from Tim Smith. In the second half, Thresher landed a penalty and Morgan got a try for the home side before Dave Cooke sealed victory with our second try. This was the first time we had defeated Gloucester twice in succession since 1962/63. A proposed fixture against Australian tourists Manly the following day at the Stoop was cancelled so our next fixture was against Rosslyn Park at Twickenham on 18th October. A single try from Park could in no way match our fifteen points and we had won nine out of ten. A trip to Cardiff gave us the opportunity of a third win in four visits and the omens looked good when we led 19-7 at the interval. Stuart Thresher had scored a try, kicked a penalty and converted tries from Simon Hunter and Graham Halsey but, crucially as it turned out, Cardiff had got a penalty and a try. In the second half, it was the home side's turn with the wind and they scored in exactly the same way as we had. Those first half points made all the difference in a 19-26 defeat.

On 1st November, we made the short journey to Sunbury to play London Irish in our first London Merit Table fixture. The rain absolutely poured down throughout the match and made the conditions very difficult. The only score of the first half was a penalty for us from 40 metres by Mark Fletcher. He repeated this feat before a series of defensive blunders led to a try and conversion for the Irish to level the scores. It looked as though the match would end in a draw until, in injury time, we were awarded a penalty 45 metres out and just in from touch. The ball sailed between the posts, hit the bar, went over and the referee immediately signalled the end of the game. Mike Wedderburn made the first of at least 76 appearances when he came on for Stuart Thresher in this game. Gosforth were next to visit the Stoop and in a dull encounter, were dispatched by nine points to three. The Universities of Oxford and Cambridge were played next, both at the Stoop. Against Oxford, Jamie Salmon scored twice including a beauty when Weekes, Fletcher and Cooke all handled before passing to Salmon who covered 20 yards, chipped ahead, re-gathered and ran in to score. He was still playing some excellent rugby and it was difficult to see why the England selectors were still ignoring him. Our other tries came from Davis, Halsey, Will Stileman (son of David from the Forties) and a penalty try from a five metre scrum. Marcus Rose added three penalties and three conversions for a final score of 39-14.

The following week against Cambridge, Rose injured his left shoulder two minutes from time after contributing massively to our victory. He had scored a try, a penalty and two conversions to add to tries by Davis, Olver and Langhorn to make the score 23-0. This was the first time we had beaten them scoreless since October 1952. London Welsh were our next opponents at the Stoop in our second London Merit Table fixture and all the headlines were about one man – Everton Davis. Paul Jackson had scored in the first minute and Thresher added a penalty but, in the meantime, the visitors had scored two goals to take the lead. Up stepped Davis and wreaked havoc in the Welsh defence to score a try and make a second for Jackson. Thresher converted this to put us 17-12 ahead at half time. Davis got his second and when Salmon added two more (after mistakes by the Welsh defence), it was all over. Thresher added a conversion and one more goal from the Welsh made the score 31-18 in our favour. It was now time for the Divisional Championship and a weakened side went down meekly to Blackheath at the Rectory Field (9-24) before we pulled ourselves together and defeated Bedford at Goldington Road (22-10) and Bath at the Stoop (25-9). Ebsworth and Thresher (2) got penalties at Blackheath, Smith, Dent and Davis got tries at Bedford (Martin Garrett added two penalties and two conversions) and against Bath Garrett was again prominent. He landed three penalties, scored a try and converted tries from Smith and Dent. Our last game of the year was at the Athletic Ground against Richmond. This was our third London Merit Table game and it was a game we looked like losing as Richmond led 10-0 at half time. Dave Loveridge rescued us with a run, a couple of dummies and a pass to Fletcher who scored in the corner. Rose put over a penalty and then Loveridge sold another dummy from a scrum and dived over in the corner in the closing minutes to seal the merit points.

Wasps were our first visitors of the New Year but the proposed John Smith's fixture had been de-merited owing to the fact that Wasps had seven men on duty in the England trial at Twickenham (we had two). Mark Fletcher got three penalties and converted a try from Charlie Smith to put us on our way but Wasps had scored a try and a penalty to restrict our lead to eight points at half time. A try from Simon Hunter in the second half and a penalty and conversion from Fletcher was replied to by a try from Simmonds but it wasn't enough for the visitors to close the gap and we ran out winners 24-11. The London Merit Table game against Blackheath at the Stoop provided us with revenge for our earlier defeat. On a freezing day, the only things missing were penguins but we did manage to score tries through Wall and Jackson and a couple of penalties from Fletcher for a 14-6 win. Another London Merit game against Saracens was cancelled so our next game was the 3rd round John Player cup tie against Wakefield at College Grove. A closely fought tie went right down to the wire. An even game in all aspects was brought to life when Rose put us in front with a penalty after 55 minutes. Two minutes later, Adamson equalised in similar fashion and that is how it remained. We progressed to a fourth round tie at Orrell by virtue of being the away side in a try less draw.

Our second John Smith's Merit game was played in freezing conditions at the Athletic Ground against London Scottish. Because these tables were still run on percentages, we were top by virtue of having won our only game whereas London Scottish were bottom having lost their only game. At the end of eighty minutes, we had played terribly and lost 11-17 and both sides suddenly had 50% records. Our next game was another London Merit game against the Metropolitan Police at the Stoop. The Police, with Paul Ackford and Simon Dear in their ranks (both future Quins) took a shock lead when O'Reilly got a try which Mercer converted. After 25 minutes, Fletcher pulled three points back with a penalty and then by converting a try scored by Hunter, put us three points ahead. The second half was one-way traffic and we warmed up for the cup tie the following week with further tries through Davis (2), Olver, Cooke and Hunter. Fletcher kicked all five conversions to make the final score 39-6. In this match, W. D. C. (William) "Will" Carling made his debut. He would go on to make 177 appearances for the 1st XV and captain the Club. He would become England captain and gain 72 caps plus one for the British Lions. The next day, the Wanderers met Old Gaytonians at the Stoop in a much delayed Middlesex Cup 4th round tie. The previous week, our opponents had refused to play so we had an impromptu game of eight-a-side for forty minutes to prove the pitch was in a fit state. When the tie did get underway, Wedderburn got the first try and Fletcher converted before Duncan Woods, Wall and Moriarty all scored. Yarrow put over a penalty for the visitors but we had a nice lead at half time. Rees scored a try for Gaytonians early in the second half but Wedderburn went over for our fifth try. Yarrow then kicked two penalties before Wedderburn completed his hat-trick for Sly to convert. Glenister and Cramb rounded things off with more tries to make the final score 40-13 (two more conversions being added along the way).

We appeared at Edge Hall Road almost thirteen years to the day after our shock defeat at Orrell's hands on our only other visit. We held firm against the home side's juggernaut type pack and they failed to cross our line. Mark Fletcher kicked us into an early lead with a penalty and Gary Williams put two over for Orrell before Fletcher evened things up with his second success. Either side of half time, Williams added his third and fourth penalties to put Orrell six points ahead. At the end of the third quarter, Simon Hunter was put in for a try by Charlie Smith but didn't run round far enough and Fletcher missed the conversion. The last 20 minutes were gripping but there was no further scoring and Orrell went through to the quarter finals by the narrowest of margins. Once again we had failed to reach the final but wouldn't have to wait much longer.

After the severe disappointment at Orrell, we had to travel North again the following weekend, this time to Headingley. In a close game, we notched our twenty first victory of the season by thirteen points to seven. C. M. A. (Christopher) "Chris" Sheasby made his debut in this game and would go on to play 188 times for the first team and gain seven England caps. He would have two spells at the Club and his caps would be won whilst at Wasps. The next day, the Wanderers played Richmond in the Middlesex Cup semi-final (it is unclear if there was a quarter final round this year) and won through to their third final. Wedderburn, Everton Davis and Dent scored the tries and Mark Sly added twelve points with the boot for a final score of 24-9. The next week, we were without a game as it was cup quarter finals day so a fixture was arranged with Vale of Lune at the Stoop. This was our first, and so far only, meeting with the team from Lancashire. Mark Fletcher put us in front with a penalty, which Higgin equalised in similar fashion before Fletcher hit his second penalty and converted Skinner's try. This was the extent of our scoring in the first half but our visitors grabbed a try through Nelson, Higgin converted and added two penalties to put them ahead by three points at the interval. A dropped goal from Higgin stretched the lead before Fletcher got another penalty and Dave Cooke went over for a try to put us in front. Fletcher's conversion went narrowly wide but the touch judges' flags went tentatively up and the referee raised his arm. A fourth penalty from Fletcher saw us home by 24-18.

At Leicester on 7th March, we played our third John Smith's merit fixture in icy conditions. At one point snow fell but this gave way to driving sleet as the game progressed. Dave Loveridge was attacked off the field of play and French (one of Leicester's props) was knocked to the ground in a niggly game. After we had led briefly with a try from Simon Hunter, Leicester took the half time lead with a penalty and a goal. John Olver brought us to within one point before another goal and penalty took the home side clear. Our friendly at Waterloo saw us take the field with several men missing through work commitments and playing for Middlesex in the County Championship semi-final against Cornwall. Waterloo were currently top of John Smith's Merit Table "B" and were looking good for promotion into the top division for next season. Will Carling and David Thresher went off injured during the course of the match; Stuart Thresher scored a penalty in the first half and converted a try from Dave Cooke in the second. It wasn't enough though and Waterloo triumphed through two dropped goals, a penalty and two tries (9-17). Will Carling was trying to impress and a quickly taken drop-out resulted in a try for Waterloo! Everton Weekes said goodbye in this game when he replaced David Thresher. He had scored some 41 tries (164 points) during his ten seasons in the 1st XV. On the way back to London, Simon Cooke was asked by Dick Best what he thought of Carling. He told him he should be dropped to the second team for a season to get some experience (thinking he might get some more games that way). Soon after, Will was called into the England squad and the rest is history!

Our next fixture was another John Smith's merit game, this time against Coventry at the Stoop. As the rules dictated that the bottom two teams would be relegated, we desperately needed to win this one to improve our percentage. Marcus Rose put over a penalty but Rowan dropped a goal to make the scores level at half time. Seven minutes into the second half, Chris Sheasby scored a one-handed touchdown and Rose converted to put us into the driving seat. Back came Coventry and, by the time we reached injury time, they were in the lead. First, Hall got a try, Thomas converted and added a penalty. We threw the ball about and Fletcher's long pass found Everton Davis who cut back in from touch just on the Coventry 22, left defenders floundering and threw himself over the line. Rose converted and we had sneaked home by fifteen points to twelve. As things were to turn out, this try was the one which kept us in the first division of English rugby when the leagues proper began the following season. It can't be stressed enough how important this was to the long term future of the Harlequin Football Club. On Sunday

22nd March, the Wanderers played at Wasps in the Middlesex Cup final. In a match described by our coach as best forgotten, we went down 3-31. It was our last fixture in the competition as from 1987/88 with the introduction of leagues, the format was revised and the top clubs no longer took part. We travelled to Beeston to take on Nottingham in our fifth Merit Table "A" game. The pitch was like a quagmire and five penalty goals were the only scores in a tight match. With the scores locked at 6-6 five minutes from the end, a penalty was advanced 10 metres after some perceived dissent by our captain (David Cooke) and Simon Hodgkinson put the ball between the posts to give the home side victory.

Our last Merit Table "A" game was again played in a quagmire, this time at Bristol. Mark Fletcher added a penalty to his two at Nottingham but Bristol scored sixteen points to win the game. From our six fixtures in the John Smith's Merit Table, we had a record of two wins and four defeats which converted into a percentage of 33.33. London Scottish were relegated to the second division and Waterloo were promoted for the 1987/88 season. Against Rosslyn Park, we played our final London Merit Table game of the season. This match saw the final appearance of Dave Loveridge, he had scored one try and had captained the side on one occasion. It was a stroll in the park for us and tries from Mike Wedderburn (2) and Gary Hulls put us on the road to a 23-3 win. The only fixtures left were the two Easter tour matches and this time they were against Swansea and Llanelli. With a heavily weakened squad, we went down in both games. We lost 16-39 at Swansea and 19-38 at Llanelli. Martin Haag made his only appearance for us against Swansea. He scored a try and would win 2 England caps during his lengthy career with Bath. Against Llanelli we said goodbye to two forwards. Nigel O'Brien had scored 9 tries (36 points) and led the side on four occasions. Dave Cooke had played for the last thirteen seasons and had led the side 92 times. He had also been a totally committed captain and club man during his career.

Results wise this had been our best season since 1956/57. We had won twenty four of thirty six matches, drawn one (which was actually won as a cup tie) and lost eleven. Everton Davis and Simon Hunter were equal top try scorers with 9 each, Mark Fletcher dropped 4 goals, Stuart Thresher got the most conversions (15) and Fletcher scored the most points with 106 (1 try, 4 dropped goals, 22 penalties and 12 conversions). Overall, tries fell by three (80), dropped goals rose to 6, penalties went up by 17 to 62 and conversions fell by three to 43. The points total rose by 140 to 702 which was our highest since 1983/84. We used some 62 players in the 1st XV during the course of the season and as a result of this not many players achieved more than twenty five appearances. The top appearance maker was Charlie Smith who played in 30 matches and he was followed by David Cooke and Mark Fletcher on 28 and John Kingston with 25.

The concept of having a Rugby World Cup had been around since the 1950s but it took until 1987 for it to become a reality. The first tournament took place in Australia and New Zealand in May and June and it was to become a massive event over the forthcoming years. Sixteen teams formed four Pools and the top two in each qualified for the quarter finals where the knockout stages would begin. We had three current players representing us, they were Marcus Rose and Jamie Salmon (England) and Richard Cramb (Scotland). Those from the past were Peter Williams (England) and Iain Milne (Scotland) and future Quins were Wade Dooley, Brian Moore and Peter Winterbottom (England), Troy Coker (Australia), Gareth Rees (Canada) and Zinzan Brooke and John Gallagher from New Zealand. The first game on 22 May 1987 saw New Zealand defeat Italy 70-6. England were on the wrong end of some bad decisions from the referee (Keith Lawrence from New Zealand) in their first game against Australia and went down 6-19. They rallied and went on to beat Japan (60-7) and USA (34-6) to finish as runners-up to Australia. In the quarter finals, they went out to Wales in a disappointing game (3-16). New Zealand went on to lift the Webb Ellis Cup after defeating France in the final by a score of 29-9. The Rugby World Cup was here to stay.

1986/87

060986	BIDEFORD	BIDEFORD	W	(52)-0
130986	NORTHAMPTON	TWICKENHAM	W	1G1PG1T(13)-0
150986	MAIDSTONE	STOOP MEMORIAL GROUND	W	1G1DG2PG(15)-2PG(6)
200986	LLANELLI	TWICKENHAM	W	6PG(18)-2G1PG(15)
270986	LEICESTER	TWICKENHAM	W	1DG3PG2T(20)-1G1DG1PG(12)
011086	WEST LONDON INSTITUTE	STOOP MEMORIAL GROUND	W	2G1DG2PG2T(29)-1PG(3)
041086	SWANSEA	TWICKENHAM	L	2G1PG(15)-2G3PG1T(25)
081086	LOUGHBOROUGH STUDENTS	STOOP MEMORIAL GROUND	W	3G1DG2PG2T(35)-1DG2PG(9)
111086	GLOUCESTER(JSMTA)	GLOUCESTER	W	1G1DG1PG1T(16)-2PG1T(10)
121086	MANLY	STOOP MEMORIAL GROUND	C	
181086	ROSSLYN PARK	TWICKENHAM	W	2G1PG(15)-1T(4)
251086	CARDIFF	CARDIFF	L	2G1PG1T(19)-2G2PG2T(26)
011186	LONDON IRISH(LMT)	SUNBURY	W	3PG(9)-1G(6)
081186	GOSFORTH	STOOP MEMORIAL GROUND	W	1G1PG(9)-1PG(3)
151186	OXFORD UNIVERSITY	STOOP MEMORIAL GROUND	W	3G3PG3T(39)-2PG2T(14)
221186	CAMBRIDGE UNIVERSITY	STOOP MEMORIAL GROUND	W	2G1PG2T(23)-0
291186	LONDON WELSH(LMT)	STOOP MEMORIAL GROUND	W	2G1PG4T(31)-3G(18)
061286	BLACKHEATH	BLACKHEATH	L	3PG(9)-1G2PG3T(24)
131286	BEDFORD	BEDFORD	W	2G2PG1T(22)-2PG1T(10)
201286	BATH	STOOP MEMORIAL GROUND	W	2G3PG1T(25)-1G1DG(9)
271286	RICHMOND(LMT)	RICHMOND	W	1PG2T(11)-1DG1PG1T(10)
030187	WASPS	STOOP MEMORIAL GROUND	W	2G4PG(24)-1PG2T(11)

100187	BLACKHEATH(LMT)	STOOP MEMORIAL GROUND	W	2PG2T(14)-2PG(6)
180187	SARACENS(LMT)	SOUTHGATE	C	
240187	WAKEFIELD(JPC3)	WAKEFIELD	D	1PG(3)-1PG(3)
310187	LONDON SCOTTISH(JSMTA)	RICHMOND	L	1PG2T(11)-1G1PG2T(17)
070287	METROPOLITAN POLICE(LMT)	STOOP MEMORIAL GROUND	W	6G1PG(39)-1G(6)
140287	ORRELL(JPC4)	ORRELL	L	2PG1T(10)-4PG(12)
210287	HEADINGLEY	HEADINGLEY	W	1G1PG1T(13)-1PG1T(7)
280287	VALE OF LUNE	STOOP MEMORIAL GROUND	W	2G4PG(24)-1G1DG3PG(18)
070387	LEICESTER(JSMTA)	LEICESTER	L	2T(8)-2G2PG(18)
140387	WATERLOO	WATERLOO	L	1G1PG(9)-2DG1PG2T(17)
210387	COVENTRY(JSMTA)	STOOP MEMORIAL GROUND	W	2G1PG(15)-1G1DG1PG(12)
280387	NOTTINGHAM(JSMTA)	NOTTINGHAM	L	2PG(6)-1DG2PG(9)
040487	BRISTOL(JSMTA)	BRISTOL	L	1PG(3)-1G2PG1T(16)
110487	ROSSLYN PARK(LMT)	ROEHAMPTON	W	1G1DG2PG2T(23)-1PG(3)
180487	SWANSEA	SWANSEA	L	2G1T(16)-4G1PG3T(39)
200487	LLANELLI	LLANELLI	L	1PG4T(19)-5G2T(38)

33

A Trophy at Last and the Arrival of Leagues 1987-1988

Just before the start of the season, Alf Wright passed away. He had worked for over 40 years at Twickenham and had been there when it was a cabbage patch. He had been a long time Quins supporter and was also on the Sevens Committee as well as dealing with season tickets. On 21st October 1987, a decision was taken to extend the membership to include those who, properly proposed and seconded, were able to contribute to the Club in a variety of ways, even by their support. A tour to Canada from 9th to 22nd May 1988 was announced and this would actually take place. On 19th January, an appeal was started to finance floodlights capable of playing night time matches under (although by July, this had only raised £10,000 of the £100,000 required). At this time, we were still only able to kick-off around 6.30 p.m. at the latest and that was at the beginning of the season. A proposal for a new East stand was being prepared although this would only be a temporary measure and would eventually be replaced by the existing structure. At a meeting on 19th April, it was mentioned that the council had tried to ask for £100,000 from the Club to allow us to take up the running track and the planning application for the floodlights was in. On 19th July, it was minuted that there were problems with the running track as the council could effectively leave it lying dormant for all of the 999-year lease and then use it again whenever they wished. Plans for an indoor training facility were being drawn up but the cost would be £80,000 (this never came into being). An invitation to tour New Zealand in 1990 had been received but this too proved to be a non-runner. Honours caps were awarded to John Olver, Jamie Salmon and Mickey Skinner.

We had a new captain for the 1987/88 season; that man was John Olver. He had been a regular member of the 1st XV since 1982 and was one of our longer serving players at this time. This season saw the introduction of a proper league structure. We were in John Courage League Division One along with Bath, Bristol, Coventry, Gloucester, Leicester, Moseley, Nottingham, Orrell, Sale and Waterloo. The London Merit Table had become a thing of the past as qualification for the cup would now be automatic for teams in the top divisions. John Olver's first game in charge came in a one off encounter against Glasgow and District at Twickenham on 5th September. This game saw no fewer than six men making their debuts for us. Laurie Cokell had joined from Blackheath (this would be his only game), Mark Sly and Julian Pike would both make limited contributions in the future. The other three were P.J. (Paul) Ackford from the Metropolitan Police, Jonathan "Jon" Eagle from Headingley and N.G.B. (Neil) Edwards from Rosslyn Park. Ackford would play some 64 times for the 1st XV, win 22 caps for England and also appear in three test matches for the British Lions in 1989. Eagle would appear 64 times and Edwards 82 (as well as winning

5 caps for Scotland). Against Glasgow, we started in great fashion and Pike and Olver scored tries in the first 20 minutes to put us in front. We went to sleep for the second quarter and allowed Glasgow to lead at the interval with a goal and a penalty. A second penalty stretched the lead before we came strongly again and tries from Eagle, Edwards and Eagle again plus three conversions by Fletcher put us fourteen points clear and that should have been that. The visitors were not going down without a fight and two more tries for them and a conversion narrowed our lead to four points. A late tackle on Mark Fletcher allowed him to kick the penalty and take us to a 29-22 victory.

Our unbeaten start didn't last long and we went down at Northampton the next Saturday by fifteen points to four. Our try came from newcomer R.H.Q.B. (Richard) Moon. He had joined from Nottingham and would play 42 games in his Quins career. Llanelli were our next visitors and we were looking for rare back to back victories against them at Twickenham. Making his debut was A.R. (Andrew) "Andy" Mullins. He had been at Durham University with Will Carling and would go on to make 212 appearances for the 1st XV, captain the Club in 1993/94 and win one England cap. For the first time in a number of years, we were in the process of having a team which was capable of winning something and the new recruits among the pack were starting to give the side some backbone. After Stuart Thresher had landed two penalties, Mickey Skinner got a try before Thresher completed his hat-trick. A penalty from Llanelli was cancelled out by Fletcher's dropped goal and we led 16-3 at half time. Llanelli changed kickers and Carwyn Davies had success with two penalties but we scored tries through Richard Moon and Will Carling; Thresher converting the second to put us nearly three scores clear. Llanelli grabbed a consolation score through one of their locks (May) which Davies converted to make the score respectable at 26-15. Afterwards, Phil May said we had the big-game look about us and how nice it was that he was to be proved right!

When Leicester came to Twickenham on 26th September, it was an historic occasion. Not only was it our first league match but it was the first to be played at Twickenham. We had won only two of the last ten meetings but were playing well and we took the lead after only six minutes when Skinner followed up in support of Eagle to go over. Thresher converted from the touchline but went on to miss three penalties. Before half time, Leicester scored a goal of their own and Hare landed a penalty to put them in front. Thresher finally succeeded with a penalty from half way to tie the scores and this is how it remained before a crowd of just over 1,000 until seven minutes into injury time. Thresher, Hunter and Fletcher had all missed dropped goal attempts but Hare didn't. He hit the target from 45 yards and Leicester had stolen the points. There were four points awarded for a win, two for a draw and (to encourage clubs to take the league seriously) one for a defeat. This meant that you got a point for turning up. It was a good thing for rugby to start league competition but it was still not a true league as playing each other home and away was still a few years off. It was back to friendlies now (if games against Swansea can be referred to as such!) for a few weeks. The Swansea fixture at Twickenham was a very close run thing as no-one led by more than three points and the lead changed hands six times. Richard Cramb dropped a goal, Swansea hit back with a penalty and a try, Ray Dudman got a penalty (but missed four others) and Neil Edwards scored a try to give us the interval lead. A goal put the visitors back in front but an Everton Davis try and Dudman conversion put us ahead before Swansea got their third try. Seven minutes from the end Dudman kicked what proved to be the winning penalty (19-17).

In the 36 hours before we were due to take on Gloucester in our second league match, it poured with rain. A decision was taken at 10 a.m. on the Saturday morning to postpone the fixture. The highlights of the game against Rosslyn Park were the sendings off of Paul Curtis (our prop) in the 12th minute for kicking an opponent and Peter Tayler (flanker) of Rosslyn Park near the end for knocking Neil Edwards to the ground with a punch to the jaw. Our fourteen men failed to hold out and went down 7-21. Indeed, Edwards' reward for scoring our try was to receive that punch. Cardiff came next and went away with a 20-12 victory which slightly flattered them. We were suffering something of an injury crisis and Marcus Rose was moved into the fly half position. He played well and continued the following week against London Welsh. We gave one of our best performances of the season so far and ran in tries from Edwards (2), Davis and Salmon in a 26-4 win. Rose was back at full back the next week against London Irish at the Stoop and Cramb filled the fly half berth as the injured players began to return. Despite going behind by seven points as early as the fifth minute, we slowly began to turn the screw. Our place kicking was proving a problem and this game was no exception. Rose could only convert one of our tries in the first half scored by newcomer Dirk Williams (he had made his debut against London Welsh and was from Wellington in New Zealand), Mickey Skinner, Tim Bell and Jay Johnston. We stretched our lead to eighteen points when Johnston got his second as did Skinner (which Rose converted) before Mann got his third penalty for the Irish. After Moon had scored our seventh try, the Irish got a consolation goal shortly after Olver had gone off injured.

On 14th November, we made our first trek to Gosforth since our John Player Cup game in 1979 and came away with a 33-4 victory. Another six tries were added to our tally with Andy Harriman (making his first appearance of the season) getting the first after eleven minutes. By the time Moon, Davis and Edwards had added further scores, Gosforth were well beaten. They did get a try but were finished off by efforts from Salmon and Smith. Rose added a penalty and three conversions to give us our twenty nine point winning margin. The rearranged league game with Gloucester was next and was played at the Stoop. As with our first game against Leicester, this was another close contest. Cramb dropped a goal after eight minutes and Rose doubled the lead with a penalty after 22 minutes. A try from Bennett which Marment converted levelled matters up at half time. Rose managed just one penalty from a further five attempts and we led by three points. In the 46th minute of the second half, Tim Bell strayed offside at a scrum and Hamlin landed the penalty from 40 metres to draw the game. The fixture with Oxford University was moved to the following Tuesday evening to accommodate the Gloucester game and we travelled to Iffley Road and came away with a comfortable win (29-14). It was even more comfortable at Cambridge four days later as we led 28-0 when the game was abandoned after 59 minutes due to fog.

We now moved into the Divisional Championship matches and our weakened team took on Blackheath, Bedford and Rugby. We had a strong squad now and these lesser teams (as they had become in the light of leagues) tended to be put to the sword. Against Blackheath on 5th December at the Stoop, Chris Sheasby scored a hat-trick of tries in a 36-16 win and at home again the following week, Bedford suffered even more. Tim Bell opened the scoring with a try after just 38 seconds and this set the tone for the rest of the match. Thresher converted this, added the next try himself and added the points to a try scored by Chris Sheasby. Seventeen minutes had gone and we led 16-0. Bedford came back into the frame for the rest of the half but couldn't score. Five minutes into the second half Tim Bell got his second try to begin the rout. Everton Davis shook off four tacklers to go in under the posts before Jon Eagle got a brace. Jamie Salmon scored next and from a quickly taken penalty, Paul Ashworth went over for our ninth try. Stuart Thresher got his fifth successful conversion of the half and four minutes into injury time Eagle completed his hat-trick to make the final score 54-0. Paul Jackson made his last appearance in this match having captained the side on one occasion and scored 29 tries (116 points).

The following week we went up to Rugby (again with a weakened side) and nearly lost. Jon Eagle got a try and Rose converted it to give us an early lead. By half time, Howard had kicked three penalties for the home side to put them in front. In a tense second half, the only score was a penalty by Rose eleven minutes from time. Our final game of the year was at the Stoop against Richmond and a glimpse of what was to come later in the season was seen. In a great display of running rugby, we outscored the visitors by eight tries to two. Marcus Rose was in top form and scored a try and seven conversions. Jon Eagle (2), Tim Bell (2), Everton Davis (2) and Adrian Thompson scored the others. After trailing 28-6 at the break, Richmond kept our score down in the second half but still lost 46-20.

In our first game of 1988, we met Wasps at Sudbury in our third league match. The home side lost the toss and had first use of the strong wind. During the course of the first half, they rattled up seventeen unanswered points. Our comeback started immediately when Dirk Williams scored a try two minutes into the second half. Marcus Rose converted, kicked a penalty and the deficit had been more than halved in five minutes. When Neil Edwards was driven over, sixteen minutes remained and only five were left when Rose got his second penalty. That was the end of the scoring and we had only managed sixteen points – one point short of our target. Whilst our league form was not good, our friendly results were excellent. Next up were Saracens and, after a close first half (the only score being a try from Eagle which Rose converted) we ran riot. Tim Bell went over 58 seconds into the second half and he was followed by Eagle (with another three) and Davis plus four conversions from Rose. Saracens managed a goal but went down by thirty four points to six.

On 23rd January we entertained Maidenhead at the Stoop in the John Player Special Cup 3rd round. After Marcus Rose had missed four kicks out of four in the first half (into the driving wind and rain), Jamie Salmon took over and uncovered a facet of his game not seen before. Eagle, Salmon and Moon had got tries to give us a 12-0 interval lead and Maidenhead were on their way out. Salmon landed four out of five conversions of tries from Moon, Eagle, Rose, Mullins and Edwards as we raised our total to forty points. Maidenhead failed to score but went out with their heads held high. The following week a waterlogged pitch at the Stoop meant the cancellation of the London Scottish match. Our next game was another league fixture and a first visit to us by Orrell. The Wigan side had a massive pack and once again gave us a mauling. They scored three tries to which we replied with two penalties from Stuart Thresher. Another narrow loss left us in eleventh place out of twelve teams and staring relegation in the face. We desperately needed a league victory.

On 13th February, we travelled to the Forest of Dean in deepest Gloucestershire to take on Berry Hill in the 4th round of the cup. Memories of New Zealand against Scotland in 1975 came flooding back as a torrential downpour had turned the pitch into a quagmire with surface water everywhere. Rumours abounded that Quins were refusing to play but these were unfounded and the referee decided that the tie would go ahead. In times past, this would have been the tie for the underdog. We came out and tore into the opposition and with the strong wind at our backs, we were soon on the scoreboard. Stuart Thresher kicked a penalty after only three minutes and converted a try from Salmon four minutes later. When Skinner went over in the thirteenth minute, we were well on our way. A minute before half time, Andy Mullins went over from a tapped penalty move and we were 17-0 up. When we faced the wind, we conceded a try to fly half Hoare but that was all and we were into the quarter final draw. In the second half, we changed into Middlesex shirts and we lost Richard Cramb with an injured knee but this was to prove a solvable problem.

Our reward for this win was a home tie against Waterloo and their giant pack of forwards. Before that we had a friendly at the Stoop against Headingley. By this time, our running game was really starting to get going. The visitors were missing a few regulars but they would have been no match for us even if these had played. We got our first try after eleven minutes when Paul Ackford went over. Further scores came from Richard Moon (2) and Richard Langhorn (2). Jamie Salmon and Stuart Thresher each kicked a conversion; Headingley's reply consisted of two penalties but we led at the break by 24-6. We really opened up in the second half and stopped the visitors from scoring. Everton Davis started the ball rolling (he added another with five minutes to go) and his was added to by Will Carling (2), Jon Eagle (3), Moon completed his hat-trick and Neil Edwards got the fourteenth and last. Had Thresher succeeded with more than four conversion in the second period, our score may have taken on record proportions. Although this was our highest score of the season, our biggest win was yet to come. The 68-6 victory was our biggest win over Headingley in thirteen fixtures dating back to 1924.

Waterloo came as favourites to the Stoop on 27th February for a game which doubled as a quarter final tie and a league match. We continued where we had left off against Headingley and quite literally ran the big Waterloo pack off its feet. Adrian Thompson came in at fly half for the injured Richard Cramb and fitted right in with the game plan as he was not renowned for his kicking game. Mickey Skinner got in for the opening try after eight minutes, Thresher converted and Salmon added a penalty to give us the best of starts. When Moon scored from 12 metres out for Salmon to convert, we led 15-0 after 28 minutes and this is how it remained until nine minutes into the second half. It seemed incredible that Waterloo were just not in the game and Salmon added two penalties to put us even further ahead. The visitors did have a ten minute spell after this when they scored a try through Cooley but that was it and we again took control of the tie. John Olver went over after intercepting 30 metres out, Salmon converted this and added a brace of tries and another conversion to make the final score 37-4 in our favour. How Jamie Salmon was not recalled to the England side no-one will ever know as he was playing some of the best rugby of his career. This game also provided us with our first league victory as we began to ease our relegation worries.

Our next league fixture was at the Reddings against Moseley the following Saturday. This was a possible match up for the cup final as we had been drawn against Wasps and Moseley had received a home draw against Bristol after knocking the favourites (Bath) out by four points to three. The referee was delayed in a traffic jam on the motorway so the game kicked off half an hour late. This was our first meeting with Moseley since 1954 when we had won 11-6. The first score came after 20 minutes when Richard Moon scored from a pushover but the home side came back into it, scored a try and a penalty and led 7-4 at half time. They had used both substitutes after losing a lock and a flanker with head injuries. With a magnificent second half performance, we ran in five more tries against one for the home team (scored when they were down to thirteen men). Jamie Salmon got the first followed by Moon, Jay Johnston and a couple of solo efforts from Andy Harriman. Marcus Rose added four conversions and we had secured our first away win in the league (32-11). The home crowd decided that we had played a dirty game (we hadn't) and booed us off the pitch but we had the points and that is what really mattered. Apparently, Dick Best and the Moseley coach even had an altercation in the tunnel after the game. Due to the game with Waterloo being a joint cup and league fixture, the proposed meeting at the Stoop on 12th March was cancelled.

This meant our next game was another trip to the Midlands, this time to play Coventry in another league game. Our running rugby was really paying off now and Harriman was in his element. He got tries after 15 and 48 minutes and Thresher landed a penalty seven minutes after the latter to put us 11-3 ahead. Potter, Coventry's full back converted a try by Parton and landed his second penalty (from 50 metres out) to edge the home side in front with 12 minutes of normal time remaining. We tried and tried but couldn't break through, that is, until into injury time when Harriman kicked ahead and Thresher hacked on to score the match winning try. Our 15-12 win set us up nicely for the cup semi-final against Wasps at Sudbury on 26th March.

Yet again, a strong wind blew down the pitch and we had first use of it. The Wasps team contained Stringer, Smith, Simms, Lozowski, Bailey, Andrew, Rendall and Probyn (all England internationals) whereas we mustered Carling, Salmon and Skinner (although Harriman, Olver, Mullins and Edwards would go on to win caps). After Stringer had missed two early penalties, Salmon put one over after nine minutes and we were in front. He then repeated the feat six minutes later to double our lead. Seven minutes after this, he doubled the lead again with a superb change of direction to touch down near the posts and convert himself. Just before this Harriman had charged down an attempted clearance but knocked on with the line at his mercy. 12-0 is how it stayed until Stringer put over his first penalty after 29 minutes. At half time the discussion was whether we had enough points in the bag with which to face the wind. It was a tremendous cup tie and through our own indiscretions, Stringer managed three penalties in the first 31 minutes of the second half to level the scores at 12-12. With five minutes remaining, Neil Edwards stormed through from 12 metres out to put us in front with our second try. Time was fast running out and we were within sight of the final. A grubber kick by Simms bobbled over our line and Bailey was up to score the equalising try. Stringer had the chance to knock us out but his conversion attempt went across the face of the posts and this meant twenty minutes of extra time. The first ten minutes went by without a scoring incident, the second period was also nearly scoreless. As Wasps attempted to run the ball in the dying seconds, Harriman intercepted and ran back 35 metres, a maul developed, the ball popped out in the Wasps in-goal area and Moon fell on it to send all the Quins players and supporters delirious. It mattered not a jot that Thresher missed the conversion as the final whistle went immediately and we had made the final for the first time. The scoreboard read Wasps 16 Harlequins 20. It was a day to remember and now we had the chance to become the first London club to win the cup. Unfortunately, Dirk Williams returned to New Zealand after this match and the International Rugby Board (IRB) rules stated that there must be a 12 week playing gap for players transferring between two hemispheres. So, even though he was willing and able to play in the final, he was prevented from doing so by red tape.

After all this excitement, there was still the small matter of league games to be sorted out. Our next one was a re-arranged fixture with Nottingham at the Stoop on Good Friday (1st April). Playing with the wind in the first half, we opened up a nine point lead in the first sixteen minutes. Simon Hunter got a try and Stuart Thresher added a penalty and a conversion. In the last fifteen minutes of the half, we got another nineteen points to effectively sew the game up. Thresher got his second penalty, Hunter got his second try and Salmon converted both of Harriman's. This made it 28-0 at half time and despite all of Nottingham's efforts in the second half, they could only manage two tries. We, fittingly, had the last word when Harriman got his hat-trick. He covered 80 metres on his run to the line for a superb score. Salmon again converted and we had achieved our highest score and biggest win over Nottingham (34-8).

A completely different squad undertook what was to be the last ever Easter tour to Wales and, unsurprisingly, went down to Swansea (16-38) and Llanelli (23-44). Our points came from Rob Glenister (2 penalties and 3 conversions), a dropped goal from Mark Sly and tries from Andy Johnson, Martin Hobley, Matthew Hardcastle, Andre Dent and Alex Woodhouse (2). Against Llanelli, Woodhouse played his last game for the 1st XV having scored 163 points (35 tries, 3 penalties and 7 conversions) in his career. The first tour took place in 1911 and we played against Swansea, Cardiff, Bath, Bridgend, Penarth and Llanelli (we first met them before the spelling was changed) during the course of the next 77 years. Our overall record was P159 W38 D9 L112. For the most part we failed to gain a single win, the most successful period being between 1960-68 when the record was W15 D3 L9. Sad though it might have been to drop it from our fixture list, with the inception of Leagues it was no longer practical or even possible to undertake the tour.

Our next league game was at the Recreation Ground, Bath and what a dirty show the home side put on. The referee warned so many of the Bath players it was just amazing how at least four or five were not sent off! Bath were out to prove that their absence from the cup final was an aberration. Neil Edwards was off for fifteen minutes after his nose had been cut open, John Olver had his head split open and Tim Bell went off to have a cut eye bandaged. Bath's captain (Richard Hill) was warned for foul play as were Lee and Chilcott of Bath and Edwards for us. On the playing side, Bath led 7-0 at half time and, despite a penalty and a conversion from Thresher and a try by Charlie Smith, ran out winners by 21-9. In this game, Simon Hunter and Charlie Smith played their last game for the first team. Hunter had scored 19 tries (76 points) and Smith had managed 5 tries (20 points) in their respective careers. The cup final against Bristol would also double up as a league game so the scheduled fixture on 16th April was cancelled. When we took on Sale the following week, they were already relegated and we had moved up into sixth place with just two matches left. We gave a brilliantly display of running rugby and they were never in the game. After Adrian Thompson opened the scoring with a try after just eight minutes, we never looked back. The procession continued with further scores coming from Tim Bell, Andy Harriman (3), Stuart Thresher (2), Richard Cramb (in his first game since the injury at Berry Hill), Everton Davis (2), Jamie Salmon and Chris Butcher. Conversions were made by Thresher (6) and Salmon (3).

All that was left after the 66-0 thrashing was the John Player Special Cup Final against Bristol at Twickenham on 30th April. Our line-up was as follows:- Stuart Thresher (full back); Andy Harriman, Jamie Salmon, Will Carling and Everton Davis (three quarters); Adrian Thompson (fly half) and Richard Moon (scrum half); Paul Curtis, John Olver (captain), Andy Mullins, Neil Edwards, Paul Ackford, Mickey Skinner, Tim Bell and Richard Langhorn (forwards). We hadn't beaten Bristol since 1972, a long run of eighteen games on the trot. We were even drawn as the away side on one of our home grounds! Whereas we had played the vast majority of our starting fifteen the week before, Bristol had rested theirs and this was to prove a massive mistake for them as we raced into an early lead. We ran the ball from the outset and Carling fought his way over after only seven minutes and Thresher converted. In the fifteenth minute, Harriman raced over in the corner, Salmon converted and the lead was doubled. Penalties from Thresher and Salmon made it 18-0 before Jon Webb pulled one back for Bristol right on half time.

They had now caught up with us and their pack started to apply the pressure. Mickey Skinner was playing despite having his nose broken when playing for England against Ireland the previous week – he was having a tremendous game as were Tim Bell and the rest of the team. Webb popped over his second penalty, Duggan got a try and Knibbs dropped a goal to make it 18-13 just thirteen minutes into the second half. Salmon extended the lead with his second penalty and then came the controversial moment. Simon Hogg (Bristol's fly half) dropped a goal which bounced onto the bar and over. The referee (Fred Howard) disallowed it and the eight point gap remained. After we had handled the ball in a scrum on our line, the referee awarded a penalty try which Webb converted to bring the gap down to 21-19 with 15 minutes to go. Bristol were applying unbelievable pressure now and Harding put up another towering kick into our 22. Stuart Thresher caught the ball and passed it to Everton Davis who passed on to Harriman; he made good yardage before passing on to Salmon who fed Will Carling. He had 45 metres to go and covered these in quick time, performed a perfect hand-off of Carr (Bristol's covering winger) and went over in the south-west corner for the match clinching score. It was one of the best tries ever seen at Twickenham. In the last, nervous minutes, Webb pulled back three points with a penalty but Salmon was equal to the task when Bristol were penalised for foul play on the touchline. This came in injury time, Bristol kicked-off, Thompson put the ball into the West stand and the final whistle went. We had won the most thrilling final ever and become the first London club to lift the trophy in the 17 years of its existence by 28-22. It was a day that anyone who was there will never, ever forget. This victory also secured third place in the first season of league competition behind inaugural champions Leicester and runners-up Wasps.

Our final record was P11 W6 D1 L4 F261 A128 Pts30. Our overall record was slightly better than the previous season. We had played three games less but lost only nine, winning twenty one (the abandoned match at Cambridge University would surely have been won had it finished so this would have made 22) and drawing two.

Jon Eagle finished as top try scorer with 18 to his name, Richard Cramb dropped three goals and Stuart Thresher topped the points with 146 (8 tries, 16 penalties and 33 conversions). For the first time in four seasons we topped one hundred tries. In fact, the 144 scored fell just six short of the best set in 1975/76 but the number of conversions was a Club record (82). Penalties dropped by 24 to 38 and dropped goals fell by one to 5. Overall, points were the second highest ever and were 43 short of the best set in 1975/76 (869). Fifty six players were used in the 33 matches with top appearances made by Richard Moon and Adrian Thompson (27) followed by Neil Edwards (26), Andy Mullins (25) and Paul Ackford and Everton Davis both on 23.

1987/88

050987	GLASGOW AND DISTRICT	TWICKENHAM	W	3G1PG2T(29)-2G2PG1T(22)
120987	NORTHAMPTON	NORTHAMPTON	L	1T(4)-1G1DG2PG(15)
190987	LLANELLI	TWICKENHAM	W	1G1DG3PG2T(26)-1G3PG(15)
260987	LEICESTER(JCL1)	TWICKENHAM	L	1G1PG(9)-1G1DG1PG(12)
031087	SWANSEA	TWICKENHAM	W	1G1DG2PG1T(19)-1G1PG2T(17)
101087	GLOUCESTER(JCL1)	TWICKENHAM	P	
171087	ROSSLYN PARK	TWICKENHAM	L	1PG1T(7)-2G3PG(21)
241087	CARDIFF	TWICKENHAM	L	1G2PG(12)-2G2T(20)
311087	LONDON WELSH	OLD DEER PARK	W	2G2PG2T(26)-1T(4)
071187	LONDON IRISH	STOOP MEMORIAL GROUND	W	2G5T(32)-1G3PG1T(19)
141187	GOSFORTH	GOSFORTH	W	3G1PG3T(33)-1T(4)
211187	GLOUCESTER(JCL1)	STOOP MEMORIAL GROUND	D	1DG2PG(9)-1G1PG(9)
241187	OXFORD UNIVERSITY	OXFORD	W	1G1DG5T(29)-2PG2T(14)
281187	CAMBRIDGE UNIVERSITY	CAMBRIDGE	A	4G1T(28)-0
051287	BLACKHEATH	STOOP MEMORIAL GROUND	W	3G2PG3T(36)-2G1T(16)
121287	BEDFORD	STOOP MEMORIAL GROUND	W	7G3T(54)-0
191287	RUGBY	RUGBY	D	1G1PG(9)-3PG(9)
281287	RICHMOND	STOOP MEMORIAL GROUND	W	7G1T(46)-4PG2T(20)
020188	WASPS(JCL1)	SUDBURY	L	1G2PG1T(16)-1G1PG2T(17)
170188	SARACENS	STOOP MEMORIAL GROUND	W	5G1T(34)-1G(6)
230188	MAIDENHEAD(JPC3)	STOOP MEMORIAL GROUND	W	4G4T(40)-0
300188	LONDON SCOTTISH	STOOP MEMORIAL GROUND	C	

070288	ORRELL(JCL1)	STOOP MEMORIAL GROUND	L	2PG(6)-3T(12)
130288	BERRY HILL(JPC4)	BERRY HILL	W	1G1PG2T(17)-1T(4)
200288	HEADINGLEY	STOOP MEMORIAL GROUND	W	6G8T(68)-2PG(6)
270288	WATERLOO(JPCQF/JCL1)	STOOP MEMORIAL GROUND	W	4G3PG1T(37)-1T(4)
050388	MOSELEY(JCL1)	MOSELEY	W	4G2T(32)-1PG2T(11)
120388	WATERLOO(JCL1)	STOOP MEMORIAL GROUND	C	
190388	COVENTRY(JCL1)	COVENTRY	W	1PG3T(15)-1G2PG(12)
260388	WASPS(JPCSF)	SUDBURY	W	1G2PG2T(20)-4PG1T(16)AET
010488	NOTTINGHAM(JCL1)	STOOP MEMORIAL GROUND	W	4G2PG1T(34)-2T(8)
020488	SWANSEA	SWANSEA	L	1G1DG1PG1T(16)-3G5T(38)
040488	LLANELLI	LLANELLI	L	2G1PG2T(23)-4G5T(44)
090488	BATH(JCL1)	BATH	L	1G1PG(9)-1DG2PG3T(21)
160488	BRISTOL(JCL1)	TWICKENHAM	P	
230488	SALE(JCL1)	STOOP MEMORIAL GROUND	W	9G3T(66)-0
300488	BRISTOL(JPCF/JCL1)	TWICKENHAM	W	2G4PG1T(28)-1G1DG3PG1T(22)

34

The Canadian Tour 1988

After the fantastic finish to the season, we undertook what would be the last tour for the Club in the amateur era. The destination was Canada and four matches would be played over eleven days. The touring party is believed to have been made up as follows:- Paul Ashworth, Tim Bell, Paul Brady, Richard Cramb, Paul Curtis, Everton Davis, Andre Dent, Jon Eagle, Neil Edwards, Rob Glenister, Mark Green, Richard Langhorn, Simon Miller, Richard Moon, John Olver (captain), Dave Porritt, Mickey Skinner, Mark Sly, Charlie Smith, Adrian Thompson, Stuart Thresher and Anthony Withers-Green. Dick Best was the coach and Alan Evans was the team secretary. They flew on Wardair out of Gatwick Airport to Vancouver for two weeks of partying. They were successful at this because, as a result, no one can really remember anything about it other than it was a great trip!

The first two matches were played against Tsunami in Port Alberni on 11th May (38-4) and Castaways at Windsor Park, Victoria on 14th May (26-9). At Royal Athletic Park, against Crimson Tide on 18th May, we started well and Jon Eagle scored in the corner after beating three defenders with six minutes gone. Half an hour later, the home side went ahead when Frame scored for Wyatt to convert but we had the lead at the interval when Tim Bell went over from a yard out. In the second half, centre Woods intercepted and ran 60 yards to score despite an excellent chase by Everton Davis. Wyatt again converted but we were level when Anthony Withers-Green scored our third unconverted try. Equality was short lived and Heaman went over for Wyatt to convert and add a penalty at the end of the third quarter to make it 21-12. We came back again and Neil Edwards put Davis over for another try with fifteen minutes to go. The lack of conversions was hurting us and Wyatt put over another penalty to stretch the lead. When he put in a great cross-kick from a penalty, Heaman collected and ran in for his second try and we had suffered our first defeat of the tour by 28-16. The last game was against Red Lions in Vancouver on 21st May and although the game was won, the final score remains elusive.

Canada Tour

110588	TSUNAMI	PORT ALBERNI (NANAIMO)	W	(38)-1T(4)
140588	CASTAWAYS	VICTORIA	W	(26)-(9)
180588	CRIMSON TIDE	VICTORIA	L	4T(16)-3G2PG1T(28)
210588	RED LIONS	VANCOUVER	W	

35

Close Calls and Another Success in the Cup but Nothing to Show for Our Efforts in the League 1988-1992

During May and June, England toured to Australia and Fiji and after losing the tests in Brisbane (16-22) and Sydney (8-28), Fiji were defeated 25-12 (the other matches produced a record of W5 L1). Our representation comprised Will Carling and Mickey Skinner plus Simon Halliday who was inbetween stints, Wade Dooley and Brian Moore who would both appear for us in the future. Carling played in the last two tests, Halliday played in the first and Dooley and Moore appeared in all three.

On 19th September 1988, initial moves towards dropping the Easter tour to Wales were made and, by 21st March 1989, it was announced that the fixtures against Swansea and Llanelli had been got out of, thus ending seventy seven years of touring. On 15th November, it was noted that planning permission for the floodlights had been given although a last minute condition relating to their use had been imposed and this needed to be removed. In March, it was reported that the removal of the running track, moving of pitches, floodlight installation and the erection of the temporary Henley stand were all going ahead. In April, the costings of all this were reported to be £18,000 for the first two items; £55,000 for the floodlights (spread over seven years) and £10,000 for the temporary East stand (this cost would escalate somewhat).

On 27th April, it was announced that Basil Lambert was being brought in to run the Club office which was to be established on the top floor at the Stoop as something more permanent was now required. This was to be on a one day a week basis to begin with. The office has now grown beyond all recognition and around sixty staff run the operation all year round. He was approached by the Chairman and Secretary to become the first paid executive to combine the many administrative responsibilities that had always been carried out by volunteers on the various committees. This would increase the efficiency in all aspects of the Club's operation by introducing the computerisation of accounts, payroll, membership etc. The drawback to this offer was that paid staff were not offered Club membership so he opted to become the Honorary Administrator. His first task was to transfer the 750 strong membership on to a database. Added to this was the secretarial side of handling and dealing with incoming and outgoing mail and preparation of inter-club mailshots. All this was achieved with the assistance of his wife (Madge) and younger daughter (Angela Elliott). Because of the increasing number of spectators at home games it became important to introduce computerised ticket sales and, we were along with Northampton, the only rugby union clubs with this statistical facility. In 1993 he was able, over a period of some months, to convince Rodney Webb of James Gilbert, to manufacture the first ever coloured club rugby ball in Harlequin colours. He was also involved with compiling the annual Membership Book and edited the programme, with the Secretary, until 1995. When the Development Committee was formed to oversee the construction of the East Stand, Basil became its Secretary and kept an eye on progress. Later that year, Angela became Club manager and he took on the role of looking after charitable requests, ground collections, Hall of Fame and archives (which he shared with me until 2015).

In January, there was news of a supporters' club being set up by Malcolm Coombs and Lee Patterson. There had been an initial meeting and this eventually became the Harlequin Supporters' Club. There was a degree of uncertainty within the Club whether this would encourage a hooligan element and there was even a report commissioned but these fears were never founded.

Although the leagues were up and running, friendly fixtures still dominated the list of games played and, as was in the previous season, only eleven league matches were played. Our first game was a friendly at Twickenham against Northampton on 3rd September. All the euphoria from our winning appearance in the final just over four months previously disappeared as Northampton ran out easy winners by nine points (13-22). We would have to pull ourselves together as the following week, we were due to meet Bath at the Stoop in our first league game. In these short seasons, it was important not to lose more than two games in the league as your chances of winning with a worse record than that were remote to say the least. As it was, we played well for 45 minutes but thereafter Bath took control. Stuart Thresher had landed a penalty goal against two from Stuart Barnes to leave us trailing 3-6 at half time. When Andy Harriman went over and Salmon converted to put us 9-6 ahead, an upset looked possible. Unfortunately, Bath scored four tries in the next half an hour and that was that. With a few minutes left, Richard Hill punched Richard Moon as he tried to get the ball to take a quick penalty and was promptly sent off in disgrace. It was a totally unprovoked attack and came after Hill had shown he was still capable of challenging for an England spot with a match winning performance. So, once again, the ugly side of Bath had reared its head and this time at least, the referee had got it spot on by sending Hill off (he later faxed a letter of apology to the Club). The final score of 26-9 reflected the power of Bath's pack in the final reckoning and two pushover tries confirmed this.

Our first Welsh visitors appeared the following weekend when Llanelli came to Twickenham. We were not playing well and it was showing. Just 18 minutes into the game, Jamie Salmon pulled a hamstring and had to leave the field. This didn't help matters and we trailed by five points at half time (10-15). Mark Sly had opened the scoring with a try for us and Stuart Thresher had banged over a couple of penalties but the visitors replied with three penalties by Jonathan Davies who also converted a try by Simon Davies. The second half scoring went in four sections with the Scarlets going into a fourteen point lead when Jonathan Davies converted Morgan's try and added another penalty. We came back with a Thresher penalty and conversion of a try by Edwards before the game was killed off when Ieuan Evans and Morgan got tries and Davies kicked his fifth penalty and one conversion to finish with 21 points. In the final six or so minutes, Edwards and Jay Johnston got tries and Thresher converted the first to leave us eight points behind at full time (29-37).

We had to travel to Sudbury the following week for our second league match against Wasps. Rob Andrew managed a couple of penalties but Marcus Rose had kicked three for us and Cramb had dropped a goal. On top of this, Colin Pinnegar (part of the Wasps second row) had been sent off for head butting Paul Ackford by referee Roger Quittenton in the 23rd minute. When Rose kicked his fourth penalty after 44 minutes it all looked good for our first win of the season. But, as against Bath, we leaked points in the last half an hour and proceeded to lose by eight points (15-23). Our thoroughly miserable start to the season was confirmed when Swansea came to Twickenham and went away with a five point victory (16-21). It must be said that we were missing eight players who were with the London Division in Munster and five others all injured. Andre Dent made his last appearance against Swansea, he had scored 36 tries (144 points) and captained the 1st XV six times during his career. Our next game was a league fixture with Liverpool St. Helens at the Stoop on 8th October and had become a must win game with only nine left to play. In a dour encounter, we picked up our first league points and our first win of the season thanks to a try by Richard Langhorn and three penalties and a conversion from Stuart Thresher. Liverpool managed two penalties in the second half but we were too good for them – just. Right at the end, Will Carling dislocated his left shoulder and as Jamie Salmon had already aggravated his hamstring injury, the victory looked to have been at great cost. Luckily, both were not long term and they were back in action before the end of the month.

Weakened the following week at Cardiff, we went down for the fifth successive time at the Arms Park. We were outscored by eight tries to four; ours being scored by Marcus Rose (2), Jay Johnston and Tim Bell (20-38). We went all the way up to the famous lay-by off the M6 that is Orrell for our next league game and, once again, came away defeated. We lost John Olver with a broken rib after 20 minutes when we were trailing by a penalty to nil. Five minutes later, we were in front when Will Carling shot over for Rose to convert. This lead lasted until four minutes from half time when Cleary scored a try for Ainscough to convert. When Heslop went over on 54 minutes, the game looked to be slipping away from us at 6-13. We came storming back though and Skinner scored four minutes later, Rose converted and added a penalty six minutes after to edge us in front by two points. Four minutes from the end, Harriman was deemed by the referee to have deliberately palmed the ball into touch, Ainscough stepped up, kicked the penalty and the game finished in a one point defeat. The trip back was a long one and not the last we would make from Edge Hall Road after a narrow loss.

On 29th October, we made the short journey to Sunbury to take on London Irish in another friendly. This game saw the debut of P. J. (Peter) Winterbottom, a player who needs no introduction. He went on to play 75 games for the first team, gain a total of 58 caps for England (having already won 29) and add three more to his four caps for the British Isles won whilst at Headingley. He would also captain the Club for three seasons at the beginning of the nineties. He had a quiet start but his presence helped us to a narrow 16-12 win. Thresher kicked two penalties before going off injured at half time, Mark Thomas (son of Clem who went with us on the Romanian Tour in 1956) got two more after this and Moon got the only try of the game. The Irish reply was two penalties and two dropped goals from their fly half, Mullen. The following week when Cambridge University visited the Stoop, Ackford, Harriman and Carling (who was captain) were helping England to defeat Australia at Twickenham. Adrian Thompson was on the bench but, unfortunately, that was as near as he was to get to an England cap. After the cobwebs had been blown away in a morning kick-off, we settled down to run in five tries in a 31-10 romp.

We now had our most intense period of rugby in our history with three league matches on the trot against Bristol (A), Waterloo (H) and Leicester (A). On form, we should have won the first two and lost the third but, as it turned out, the results were the complete opposite. Bristol gained revenge at the Memorial Ground for the cup final defeat and we only had two Thresher penalties to show for our efforts and were probably lucky to lose by twelve points (6-18). Waterloo came to the Stoop having lost all five of their games so far and we were expecting to gain our second victory to ease our relegation worries. In a real nip and tuck encounter, the lead changed hands five times and the biggest gap between the sides was eight points. Thresher kicked two penalties and Salmon scored a try in the first half but Aitchison got two penalties and crucially converted Cooley's try to make it 10-12. When he converted a try by Jenkins as well, things looked gloomy for us but we came back into it. Jay Johnston got over, Thresher got his third penalty and converted another try from Salmon with 15 minutes left. We led 23-18 but it was less than a score in front and we were made to pay for those missed conversions. When Bracegirdle scored a try and Aitchison converted with only four minutes to go, it was enough to send us crashing to a disastrous defeat (23-24). We had only won on three of our last ten visits to Welford Road so the omens were not good. Also, they were in second place, we were in eighth. After just 54 seconds, Cramb had a kick charged down and Dusty Hare scored a try and converted it for a 6-0 lead. We battled back and two minutes later Adrian Thompson scored and Thresher converted to tie the scores. Hare got a penalty and converted a try from Kardooni but Cramb dropped a goal and Thresher's penalty left us three points behind at the break (12-15). We came out in determined mood for the second half and Thresher levelled the scores again with another penalty on 59 minutes before Tony Underwood raced over for Hare to convert and restore the home side's lead. Harriman had been pushed into the advertising hoardings after a tackle and went off with a damaged ankle but we were not to be denied. A tremendous performance by our pack saw them drive right through the heart of the Leicester defence. Paul Ackford, Richard Langhorn and Richard Moon went over for tries, Thresher converted the first two and we had achieved a famous victory by thirty one points to twenty one.

It was back down to earth with a bump and a weakened team the next week at Blackheath when we went down 12-22. Four Marcus Rose penalties were matched by Parker for the home side and beaten by two tries and a conversion. Divisional games really played havoc for this and the next two weeks when we met Bedford at Goldington Road and Rugby at the Stoop. We were simply outplayed by Bedford and could only manage a Glenister try as a consolation against twenty five points conceded. N.J. (Nick) Killick (a hooker) played the first of 87 games against Blackheath and Marcus Rose played his last game at Bedford having scored 569 points (13 tries, 1 dropped goal, 106 penalties and 98 conversions) and captained the side four times (including the Bedford match) during his four years at the Club. C.T. (Craig) Luxton, a scrum half from New Zealand made the first of 72 appearances against Rugby and would be at the Club for the next six years. John Butcher appeared for the final time in this match, he had scored 38 tries (152 points) during his 1st XV career. Against Rugby, we achieved a narrow victory by thirteen points to nine. Mark Thomas got a penalty and converted a try by Adrian Young but missed one after John Butcher had scored. Rugby managed a penalty in the first half and a goal in the second.

Another friendly, this time at the Athletic Ground against Richmond saw us record our sixth win from seventeen games this season. Richmond led briefly twice in the first half with a penalty and a try but we gradually assumed control with tries from Jon Eagle, Rob Glenister and Craig Luxton and a penalty by Mark Thomas. The only score in the second half was Luxton's second try; this was converted by Glenister to leave the final score at 21-7. This was to be our final game of the year as our clash with London Scottish at the same venue was cancelled.

On 7th January, we entertained Wasps at the Stoop in our fifth friendly on the trot. Both sides had lost seven players to the England squad training in Portugal so a lot of the class was missing from this London derby. Craig Luxton had hit the ground running and was proving to be an excellent acquisition. Mark Thomas kicked a penalty to put us in front before a couple of future Quins combined to give the visitors the lead. Alex Tupman got a try and Steve Pilgrim converted before Chris Mantel scored our first try and we held a narrow 7-6 lead at half time. When Young went over for Wasps in the 51st minute, they were back in front, but not for long. As we went for a pushover, the referee awarded a penalty try and this was the beginning of the end for Wasps. Thomas converted and our multi-handling attacks culminated in further tries for Chris Sheasby, Jon Eagle and Craig Luxton. Thomas added two conversions for a final score of 29-10 to give us our biggest win against them for over sixteen years.

Our next game was a league encounter with Rosslyn Park at Roehampton. We both had records of two wins and five defeats but our points difference was better and we started as if we wanted to wipe our twenty point deficit out in the first half. Thresher got a penalty, converted a try by Eagle and added another penalty to put us twelve points up in 25 minutes. In true Quins fashion, we went to sleep and Park came storming back with two penalties and a conversion from Graves and a try by Nelson-Williams. So, after 63 minutes, it was all even and everything to play for but Eagle rescued us when he squeezed over in the corner with eight minutes left to give us a hard earned victory. This sort of game was to dog us for years to come and until these games could be won all the time (and not lost as was all too common), the league title would never come to the Stoop. Against Park, it was like an old boys' reunion as Hugh McHardy (their coach), Alex Woodhouse, Andre Dent and Simon Hunter were all former Quins and Paul Curtis, Neil Edwards, Paul Ackford and Chris Mantel were all former Park players. A friendly against the runaway leaders of the second division, Saracens, at Southgate, was our next encounter and this went to the wire as well. The home side led by a goal and two penalties to a goal and a try when Stuart Thresher scored the match winning try two minutes from the end. The game was played in rain and mud which ruined what had promised to be an open game.

The following week, we travelled to Rugby to open our defence of the cup. New sponsors had come in so it was now called the Pilkington Cup. Rugby felt they had a chance of an upset but failed to break our rhythm from the start and paid the price. Stuart Thresher got penalties either side of his brother, David, scoring our first try which he converted and when Salmon went in after 25 minutes, the tie was as good as over. Howard landed a penalty three minutes from half time for the Lions but that was the extent of their scoring. In the second half, we eased off and another Thresher penalty was all we had to show until Salmon intercepted a pass and ran in for his second try two minutes from time. Thresher converted and we had strolled into the fourth round by 25-3. Our reward was a home tie at the Stoop against division two strugglers London Scottish.

Against London Welsh, we trailed 6-15 at half time but eventually found our running form in the second half and ran in six tries to nil to win 32-15. We used four different goal kickers in this period and, out of Cramb, Moon, Matthew Hardcastle and Sly, only the last named got one over. He converted the last try and it was one of nine attempted kicks. To be fair, we had made fourteen changes to the side which played at Rugby with only Everton Davis surviving.

On 11th February, we entertained London Scottish in the fourth round cup tie and, as against Rugby, we started like a shot out of a gun. Playing with the wind, we scored after eight minutes when Craig Luxton got over for Thresher to convert. By half time, Thresher had added two penalties and Richard Cramb had dropped a goal to which the Scots had replied with a penalty by Grecian. When it was our turn to face the wind, we scored again and killed the game off when David Thresher got our second try. This was followed by his brother kicking his third penalty seven minutes later to put us 22-3 up. The only score to come from the other side was another Grecian penalty as our forwards took control and shut the visitors out.

Headingley had never been an easy venue for us and in our seven games there since 1924, we had won three and lost four. We had a reserve back division but our pack was only two or three players short of being at full strength. In an even first half, Rob Glenister (playing at full back) kicked two penalties and Jon Eagle scored a try against his former club. Headingley scored a goal of their own to leave us four points ahead at the break. Within fifteen minutes of the restart, we held a fourteen point advantage thanks to tries from Luxton and Adam Cleary plus a conversion by Glenister. This should have signalled the start of a romp but the home side were not going down without a fight. They got two penalties and a try to trail by four points and were kept out only by some desperate defending on our part in torrential rain for the last nine minutes. The experience in this weather set us up nicely for our cup quarter final tie against Nottingham at the Stoop on 25th February. A biting wind blew across the pitch and the rain poured down throughout the entire match. It was not a day for the faint hearted! Stuart Thresher got a penalty after seven minutes which Hodgkinson equalised twenty minutes later. This was the score at half time with the only other action being Glenister coming on to replace Adrian Thompson who was injured. Hodgkinson followed Thompson off and was replaced by Worrall before Thresher slotted his second penalty but this was again equalised, this time by Worrall. The crucial moment came after 54 minutes when Glenister chipped through on the blind side, won the race to the ball and scored the only try of the tie. Thresher's conversion put us six points ahead and he stretched the lead with another penalty on 67 minutes. Despite Nottingham's best efforts, they could only manage a penalty from Worrall in the remaining time as our back row of Butcher, Winterbottom and Skinner squeezed the life out of them. The final score of 15-9 ensured our fifth semi-final appearance.

The following week we entertained Gosforth at the Stoop on a Sunday (due to England playing at home in the Five Nations Championship the previous day). Salmon kicked four penalties in the first half before Gosforth got a try after 44 minutes. When Adam Cleary scored and Salmon converted eleven minutes later, we were well clear but the visitors did get a penalty try, a try and a conversion to narrow the gap to four points. Two tries in the last seven minutes from Johnston and Langhorn sealed our eleventh win on the trot. Richard Moon made his last appearance in this game having captained the side five times and scored 15 tries (60 points) during his two seasons at the Club.

When Gloucester came to the Stoop, it was our first league game in nearly two months and our first at home since November. We needed this to be a victory to confirm our place in division one the following season. We began as if our lives depended on it and within thirteen minutes, we were 16-0 ahead. Stuart Thresher got two tries (injuring himself as he scored the second) and converted one; Eagle got our third and Salmon put over another conversion. We failed to score in the next 54 minutes during which time the visitors got two tries and a penalty to bring us back to 16-11. It was merely an illusion though and Salmon scored a try and converted Glenister's try with the last kick of the game to make it 26-11.

A proposed fixture against Coventry was lost to a waterlogged pitch at the Stoop which meant that our next game was the cup semi-final against Leicester (again at the Stoop) on 25th March. For the sixth match in succession, we took the lead. This time it was the boot of Stuart Thresher popping over a penalty after 12 minutes. A minute later however, Dusty Hare collected a kick out to the touchline by Cusworth and went over in the corner to put the Tigers in front by a point. This lead was stretched to seven points by half time when Kardooni ran in under the posts and Hare converted. As we had at the start, we applied pressure at the beginning of the second half and when Hare missed a tackle on Richard Cramb, our fly half was over for a try. Salmon's conversion was wide and, with hindsight, the match was probably lost at that moment. Four minutes later Cusworth dropped a goal and Hare wrapped it up with a penalty three minutes from the end. We had lost the tie mainly through our inconsistent goal kicking; Thresher missed four penalty attempts and Salmon one. Another final appearance would have been fantastic but it was not to be and we still had two league fixtures and two friendlies to play. The first of these was a 7-7 draw with Bristol which proved to be a tedious match all round.

We travelled to Nottingham for our tenth league match and came away without scoring. A goal and two penalties in the second half giving the home side some revenge for their cup exit. The friendly with Rosslyn Park was cancelled and our last game of the season was the home league encounter with Moseley at the Stoop on 22nd April. Dick Best was retiring, this was his last game in charge of the team and Jamie Salmon was supposedly appearing for the last time (he was to come back in the 1990/91 season for a few games). Richard Cramb did appear for the last time, he had scored 13 tries, 14 dropped goals and 5 penalties (109 points) during his time in the 1st XV. We took the lead after only four minutes when Chris Butcher burst over for the opening try which Stuart Thresher converted. Arntzen pulled back three points with a penalty and a goal further increased the Moseley total but, in between, Cleary and Skinner scored tries which Thresher converted for an 18-9 interval lead. More of the same followed in the second half and Eagle, Mullins and Skinner and Cleary (with their second) added to Moseley's woes (Thresher landed two conversions). A consolation score by Charlie Smith (on his return to the Stoop) again converted by Arntzen was nowhere near enough to close the gap and the final score of 38-15 enabled us to finish a disappointing eighth in the table with a record of P11 W5 L6 F194 A184 Pts10.

After the success of the previous season, this had been a poor one even though we had reached the cup semi-finals. Our overall playing record was P31 W17 D1 L13 F566 A495. The points overall had fallen by over 300 and this was obviously reflected in the tries scored. These fell to 78 and conversions went down to 37. These were the lowest totals since the 1979/80 season. Dropped goals fell by one to 4 but penalties rose 18 to 56. Jon Eagle was again top try scorer but his total of seven was the lowest amount to top the list since 1973/74. Richard Cramb dropped all the goals (as he had done the previous year) and Stuart Thresher topped the points scorers with 139 (3 tries, 29 penalties and 20 conversions). Paul Curtis, Everton Davis and David Thresher made the most appearances with 23 and Jon Eagle was the only other player to get to twenty; which he did, just. A total of 54 players were used in the 1st XV and eight of these made only one appearance. The unsettled nature of the side saw seven different scorers with the boot.

1988/89

030988	NORTHAMPTON	TWICKENHAM	L	1G1PG1T(13)-2G2PG1T(22)
100988	BATH(JCL1)	STOOP MEMORIAL GROUND	L	1G1PG(9)-2G2PG2T(26)
170988	LLANELLI	TWICKENHAM	L	2G3PG2T(29)-3G5PG1T(37)
240988	WASPS(JCL1)	SUDBURY	L	1DG4PG(15)-1G3PG2T(23)
011088	SWANSEA	TWICKENHAM	L	1G2PG1T(16)-3G1PG(21)
081088	LIVERPOOL ST.HELENS(JCL1)	STOOP MEMORIAL GROUND	W	1G3PG(15)-2PG(6)
151088	CARDIFF	CARDIFF	L	2G2T(20)-3G5T(38)
221088	ORRELL(JCL1)	ORRELL	L	2G1PG(15)-1G2PG1T(16)
291088	LONDON IRISH	SUNBURY	W	4PG1T(16)-2DG2PG(12)
051188	CAMBRIDGE UNIVERSITY	STOOP MEMORIAL GROUND	W	1G1DG2PG4T(31)-1G1T(10)
121188	BRISTOL(JCL1)	BRISTOL	L	2PG(6)-2G2PG(18)
191188	WATERLOO(JCL1)	STOOP MEMORIAL GROUND	L	1G3PG2T(23)-3G2PG(24)
261188	LEICESTER(JCL1)	LEICESTER	W	3G1DG2PG1T(31)-3G1PG(21)
031288	BLACKHEATH	BLACKHEATH	L	4PG(12)-1G4PG1T(22)
101288	BEDFORD	BEDFORD	L	1T(4)-3G1PG1T(25)
171288	RUGBY	STOOP MEMORIAL GROUND	W	1G1PG1T(13)-1G1PG(9)
271288	RICHMOND	RICHMOND	W	1G1PG3T(21)-1PG1T(7)
311288	LONDON SCOTTISH	RICHMOND	C	
070189	WASPS	STOOP MEMORIAL GROUND	W	3G1PG2T(29)-1G1T(10)

140189	ROSSLYN PARK(JCL1)	ROEHAMPTON	W	1G2PG1T(16)-1G2PG(12)
210189	SARACENS	SOUTHGATE	W	1G2T(14)-1G2PG(12)
280189	RUGBY(PC3)	RUGBY	W	2G3PG1T(25)-1PG(3)
040289	LONDON WELSH	OLD DEER PARK	W	1G2PG5T(32)-2G1PG(15)
110289	LONDON SCOTTISH(PC4)	STOOP MEMORIAL GROUND	W	1G1DG3PG1T(22)-2PG(6)
180289	HEADINGLEY	HEADINGLEY	W	1G2PG2T(20)-1G2PG1T(16)
250289	NOTTINGHAM(PCQF)	STOOP MEMORIAL GROUND	W	1G3PG(15)-3PG(9)
050389	GOSFORTH	STOOP MEMORIAL GROUND	W	1G4PG2T(26)-1G2T(14)
110389	GLOUCESTER(JCL1)	STOOP MEMORIAL GROUND	W	3G2T(26)-1PG2T(11)
180389	COVENTRY	STOOP MEMORIAL GROUND	C	
250389	LEICESTER(PCSF)	STOOP MEMORIAL GROUND	L	1PG1T(7)-1G1DG1PG1T(16)
010489	BRISTOL	STOOP MEMORIAL GROUND	D	1PG1T(7)-1PG1T(7)
080489	NOTTINGHAM(JCL1)	NOTTINGHAM	L	0-1G2PG(12)
150489	ROSSLYN PARK	STOOP MEMORIAL GROUND	C	
220489	MOSELEY(JCL1)	STOOP MEMORIAL GROUND	W	5G2T(38)-2G1PG(15)

In May 1989, England went to Romania to play one test and came away with a resounding 58-3 victory. Paul Ackford and Peter Winterbottom were current and Simon Halliday, Brian Moore and Wade Dooley would play for us in the coming years.

Improvements to the ground for the new season were announced as follows –

a) The pitch had been moved nearer the stand.
b) The running track had gone.
c) The floodlights had been installed.
d) The new East stand was a semi-permanent structure and would cost £43,000 over three years.
e) The main stand had had new seats installed (from the old North stand at Twickenham).
f) Chain link fencing had been erected which enclosed the 1st XV pitch (this was 8' 6" high).
g) Red Star had signed a three year sponsorship deal worth £105,000.

The Lions tour squad to Australia included two of our current players – Paul Ackford and Will Carling. Unfortunately, Carling had to withdraw due to injury but Ackford played in all three test matches. Three future Quins also featured and they were Craig Chalmers (who played in the first test and kicked a penalty and dropped a goal), Wade Dooley (he played in tests two and three) and Brian Moore who, like Ackford appeared in all three. The Lions got off to a bad start and lost the first test 12-30 but came back strongly to take the next two by 19-12 and 19-18. The final test will always be remembered for Campese's blunder which led to a try by Ieuan Evans. The nine non-test fixtures were all won making this team one of the three most successful Lions teams. It was also the first time the Lions had come back to win a series after losing the first test.

Our President passed away on 8th November 1989 aged 81. Ken Chapman had played for us between 1930 and 1948 and had been a Club stalwart for most of his life. His presidency had begun in 1981. David Brooks was to be the new President and this was announced on 17th April 1990. The Harlequin Club shop was set up and this proved to be its first season. The original was run by Derek Wilkins (who also printed the Club programme for a number of years) and was in a lock-up cupboard at the bottom of the stairs in the south corner of the old West stand. Eventually, this was moved into a portakabin next to the fence by the river and now there are two shops in the ground. The number of items has slowly expanded over the years and it now stocks a comprehensive range of goods. At the start of this season, Alex Saward took over as Press Officer from Ken Pragnell (who had done the job since 1979/80) and he would stay in the role until after the game had gone professional. The position became increasingly important and he even got me to star in a programme on Sky Sports! This was to be the first season the club badge had ever been worn on the shirt. It was quite incredible that it had taken over 120 years for this to happen although because of our distinctive colours, it was probably never seen to be needed.

A pre-season tour to Holland over the August Bank Holiday was undertaken and both matches were won against DIOK (39-12) and Kelso (35-3). As with the 1988/89 season, we lost our opening game with Northampton. This time we travelled to Franklin's Gardens with newcomers Mike Molyneux and David Pears in the side. Molyneux would go on to make 55 appearances over the next five seasons and Pears 72 over the next twelve (with large gaps through injury). Pears would also win four caps for England. Geoff Ashby had taken over the coaching reins from Dick Best (who was now concentrating on coaching the London Division and England B). Ashby, like Best, was a former Quins player but made limited 1st XV appearances between 1981 and 1985. Back to the match at Northampton, Pears got his first points with us after only 12 minutes when he kicked a penalty to put us in front. A try from Andy Harriman after 56 minutes was our only other score. This tied the game at 7-7 but another sixteen points for the home side saw them home.

Our first league match was against Bath at the Rec on 9th September and, once again, with only eleven matches to be played, it was important to gain that first win straight away. Bath were the double winners from last season so a sterner test we couldn't have had. After only four minutes, Hall went over for Barnes to convert and we trailed 0-6. We came right back into it when another new boy (Gavin Thompson) scored for Ray Dudman to convert. By the 25th minute, Dudman had landed two penalties to put us 12-6 ahead before two crucial errors effectively cost us the match. First, Thompson froze and missed a fluffed kick-off by Guscott from which Callard scored (Barnes converted) and then Dudman kicked the ball to touch rather than touch down for a 22 drop out. Bath won the lineout and Hoskin scored Bath's third try which Barnes again converted. These mistakes had left us trailing at half time by eighteen points to twelve. A goal and two tries sealed their victory but one rather amusing event followed the last try when Barnes missed the conversion from in front of the posts, the ball going under the crossbar. He complained but the referee had made his decision. Even so, we had been defeated 32-12 and another league title had started to slip from our grasp even at this early stage of the season. The aforementioned Gavin Thompson would go on to play no fewer than 132 times for the first team over the next six seasons.

Two more friendlies followed in quick succession against the Metropolitan Police on Wednesday 13th September and Llanelli three days later. Against the Police at Imber Court, Bill Cuthbertson made his final appearance having scored six tries (24 points) and led the side on five occasions. With nine of the side which lost to Bath, our first victory of the season was achieved against a very lively Police outfit. In the first half, Cleary scored two tries, Dudman converted the second and Pears dropped a goal; the home side scored a goal. Into the second half, Dudman exchanged penalties with the Police fly half before Pears and Alex Tupman got tries to seal the game in our favour. Dudman's conversion of Tupman's try put the icing on the cake before a consolation try for the home side made the final score 26-13. Our fourth away trip in as many starts was a visit to Stradey Park and with eleven men missing on England training, we were expected to lose heavily. This we duly did although we did hold out until the final quarter when the Scarlets piled on the points. Neil Edwards got a try and Rob Glenister kicked two penalties for us against a goal, four penalties and six tries for Llanelli.

A midweek fixture against Maidstone at the Stoop was cancelled so our first home game was the league fixture against Wasps on 23rd September. This was a full-blooded encounter settled entirely by penalty goals. There were several bouts of fisticuffs during the game and these didn't help the spectacle. Thankfully, David Pears got four penalties over against three by Rob Andrew and we had secured our first league points of the season. Increasingly, the friendly fixtures were being used to blood new players including youngsters from Under 21 level with the rest of the team being made up of Wanderers players. Against Loughborough University in another midweek fixture, we won by 19-11. Molyneux and Thompson (2) got our tries and John Marsh got a penalty and two conversions. Our next visitors were London Irish to Twickenham and, as joint leaders of the second division, had high hopes of a first division scalp. In the first half they managed two penalties from their fly half Aitchison but had conceded tries by Glenister, Ackford and Paul Brady with Pears adding a penalty and all three conversions to leave them trailing 21-6. The running rugby continued in the second half on Twickenham's lush pitch and the tries kept on coming. Glenister got his second and Adam Cleary and Gavin Thompson each got a pair before Pears rounded off the scoring with a try of his own. He added another four conversions to give him a total of twenty one points in the match. The Irish did pull six points back with a goal but the final score of 53-12 said it all really. The end of the first month of the season had been reached and we had already played seven matches in 29 days. Will Carling and Andy Mullins were both injured and didn't play for us again until 28th October. This was our biggest ever win over London Irish but a much larger victory (over Bedford) was to come during the season.

Our third Wednesday night game was against West London Institute at the Stoop. Will Wall led the side which contained only Fletcher and Brady from the London Irish game. After Dudman had kicked a penalty to open the scoring, the students took a shock lead when Appleson converted his own try. By half time, Sheasby and Rickerd had scored tries for us and Dudman was successful with one conversion to put us 13-6 up. The second half was more or less one way traffic as our pack took control. The students managed one try but we scored through Bruce Miller (2), Brady and Ben Short plus two more conversions from Dudman for a final tally of 33-10. Swansea came next to Twickenham for our second Welsh clash and, in a niggly (and at times dirty) game, we went down 14-21.

Our first league match at Goldington Road, Bedford (who were quickly becoming the first division whipping boys) was to be a complete annihilation of the home side. After 10 minutes, they took the lead when Harris scored a try and ironically, they also scored the last try of the match when Cullen went over on 85 minutes. Between this, it was a procession of scores throughout our side. David Pears got two tries, a penalty and eight conversions to finish with 27 points; setting a new points in a game league record (beating Jamie Salmon's 23 points against Waterloo in 1987/88). The remainder of our points came from eleven tries scored by Mickey Skinner, Rob Glenister (2),

Craig Luxton (2), Mike Molyneux (2), Richard Langhorn and Mike Wedderburn (3). The final score of 71-8 was our highest since we defeated Thailand in 1986. This victory moved us into second place in division one on points difference.

Our last midweek game was a first ever meeting with Askeans and, after they had taken a twelve point lead in the first 20 minutes, we came back strongly to run out 30-20 winners. Everton Davis returned after injury to score our sixth and final try in a hard earned victory. A game at Twickenham on 21st October against London Scottish was cancelled so our next fixture was our fourth league game (against Orrell at the Stoop). Appearing at scrum half for the visitors was future Harlequin Chris Wright (he would come to us via Wasps). We had first use of an extremely strong wind and during the course of the first half, David Pears kicked five penalties at regular intervals without reply. Try as they did, Orrell just couldn't break through and their three penalties (all in the second half) were not enough to stop us going top of the table. This was our first win over Orrell in five attempts; it was to be nearly five years before our second success! A weakened side was blown away at Cambridge the following week as two penalties from Dudman and a try by Brady were no match for the five tries scored by the light blues in their 34-10 victory.

Our next three games were important league matches against Bristol, Saracens and Leicester and nothing but three wins would do. Against Bristol at the Stoop, we went in front when Luxton went over for Pears to convert after just five minutes. Bristol were in front by half time after Webb kicked a penalty and Harding scored a try (after a 30 metre rolling maul). It was a tight game and just as the Bristol pack looked like it might steamroller us, we came back at them with a Pears penalty and Luxton's second try in a nine minute period midway through the second half. Pears missed the conversion but we had done enough to secure the win (13-7). The journey was then made to Southgate to meet Saracens in a game we had to win to regain our place at the top of the table. We had slipped to second place on points difference with Bath leading the way. Kennedy got a penalty for Saracens after three minutes but we came back with a try from Paul Ackford after eleven minutes which Pears converted. After 23 minutes, Pears dropped a goal to stretch our lead to six points but before half time, the home side got two tries which Kennedy converted to put them six points ahead. In the second half, we applied enormous pressure but a combination of taking the wrong option and poor handling put paid to our chances. There was no further scoring and Saracens had obtained a valuable and unexpected victory by fifteen points to nine. This had effectively killed off our hopes of the league title even though there were still five games to play. The match against Leicester kicked off at noon and was played at the Stoop. John Liley kicked three penalties in the first 26 minutes during which time we had a try from Glenister which Pears converted to show for our efforts. This remained the position until Pears tied the scores with a penalty on 53 minutes. Liley and Pears swapped penalties to leave it at 12-12 as the game entered injury time and Mike Wedderburn was adjudged to have put a foot in touch on his way to score what would have been the match winning try. From this, we won the lineout and ensuing scrum and Pears dropped a goal to send the home fans away happy.

The Divisional Championship was now played in the first three weeks of December which meant that the league programme was stopped until the middle of January. We had outings against Blackheath and Bedford at home and Rugby away during this time but our team was weakened because of the Divisional games. The most notable happening against Blackheath was when the floodlights failed after 74 minutes. We were leading 24-17 and due to a power surge when the Wanderers went for their showers, this remained the final score. Mark Fletcher had helped himself to two penalties and three conversions to add to tries from Brady, Sheasby and Glenister. Bedford were easily beaten (as they had been in the league match) but by a slightly reduced margin. Ten tries were scored and Fletcher converted seven and kicked a penalty. Bedford's reply was two tries and a conversion for a final score of 57-10. Against Rugby, we got a bit of a shock when we relaxed at half time. During the first half, Fletcher was again on the score sheet with three penalties and a conversion which, when added to tries by David Thresher and Andy Mullins, gave us a 19-0 lead. Rugby came out in determined fashion and started to claw back some of our lead as Pell put up some high, hanging kicks to test our defence. They scored nineteen points in exactly the same way we had but Fletcher got his fourth penalty to put us back in front. Not to be denied, Spark went over after Pell's break to score the match winning try. Pell's conversion made the final score 25-22 to the home side. Appearing for Rugby was seventeen year old Mark Mapletoft. He would join us a decade later in the last throes of his career.

Against Richmond in another friendly, we trailed from the sixth minute when Fallon scored a try until the last minute when Fletcher dropped a goal. In between, Radford converted Fallon's try, added two penalties and converted a second half effort by Sole to take Richmond's total to eighteen points. For us, Fletcher kicked a penalty and Eagle scored a try to make it 7-12 at half time. Fletcher then kicked a penalty either side of a try by Edwards to make it 17-18 before his dropped goal ensured a happy Christmas for all at the Stoop. For our final game of the decade, we welcomed Cardiff to the Stoop on 30th December. Richard Langhorn led a side missing ten regulars but you would never have guessed it as they tore into Cardiff. Mark Fletcher was racking up the points and he landed a penalty and a conversion in the first half. Mike Wedderburn, Stuart Thresher and Ian Wood added tries to give us a 17-6 lead at the interval. When David and Stuart Thresher added a try each and Fletcher got a conversion and dropped a goal, Cardiff had only managed two penalties and a dropped goal and trailed by thirty points to nine after 52 minutes. The visitors woke up in the time remaining and scored three goals and a try. Will Carling and Langhorn scored tries for us and Fletcher landed another conversion and a penalty to take his tally to fifteen points. A final try count of 7-4 in our favour said it all as did the final score of 43-31. It was only a twelve point winning margin but it was our highest points total against Cardiff in 107 years of fixtures. It was only our fifth victory against them in the last 35 games.

For our first game of the new decade, we went to Sudbury for our second game of the season against Wasps. We supplied seven and Wasps six men to the England training squad in Lanzarote so both sides were significantly weakened. A pushover try from Ryan and a penalty by Hopley put Wasps in front before Fletcher pulled back a penalty before half time. When Wasps flanker Mark Rigby punched Adrian Young after 38 minutes, he was sent off for foul play and they were down to fourteen men. This became thirteen after 48 minutes when Paddy Dunston (a prop) stamped on Chris Mantel in an attempt to free himself from a tackle. By this time, the game was level at 7-7 after David Thresher had scored from a line out. As the game wore on, it looked as though Wasps might hold out but, Fletcher had other ideas and slotted a penalty after 76 minutes to bring us home in front by a narrow margin.

The league programme returned the following week when Rosslyn Park visited the Stoop on 13th January. Both sides desperately needed the win; us to continue our quest for the title and Park to secure their place in division one. As with our previous match in the league with them, this was another close one. David Pears put us in front after seven minutes with a penalty before old boy Richard Moon scored a try for Graves to convert. By half time Pears and Graves exchanged penalties to leave the visitors three points ahead. Pears levelled four minutes into the second half with his third penalty and Graves edged Park ahead with his second before Will Carling rounded off an attack with our first try to put us back in front. When another ex-Quin (Simon Hunter) put over a dropped goal from 40 metres, it looked as though the visitors would take the spoils. Five minutes from the end, Rob Glenister sneaked over for Pears to convert and the points were in the bag as a final score of 19-15 confirmed.

A friendly with Old Belvedere was played on Friday 19th January and a scheduled match with Saracens two days later was cancelled. This was only our second meeting with the Irish outfit and it proved to be quite an exciting game. The score stood at 9-3 to the visitors when eight floodlights went out after 32 minutes but the light was still sufficient for the game to continue. Mark Fletcher had kicked a penalty for us and when he converted Simon

Newman's try after 36 minutes, the scores were level at the break. In the second half, Craig Luxton and a hat-trick from Mike Molyneux accounted for our tries and three conversions from Fletcher made our total 31. The Irish got two tries in this period but the winning margin was still fourteen points. Ray Dudman played his final game for the first team in this one having scored 890 points (16 tries, 7 dropped goals, 163 penalties and 158 conversions) during his career. He finished in fourth place in the all-time scorers list at the Club.

On 27th January, we made our second trip of the season to Bath; this time it was the 3rd round of the Pilkington Cup. Predictably, the weather was absolutely dreadful; the heavens opened and it rained continuously for hours turning the pitch into a quagmire. We made several changes to the advertised line up and this contributed to our downfall. Glenister was moved from full back to scrum half and Langhorn was played at lock instead of number 8. This meant no place for Luxton and Edwards. We missed both and a crucial error by Stuart Thresher after 34 minutes led to the opening score. Pears had already missed a chance from the opening kick-off when Bath were penalised and this also proved to be crucial. Thresher stepped out of his 22 when he had plenty of time to clear his lines and kicked straight into touch; Bath won the lineout on the 22, drove the ball on and Cronin went over for the try which Barnes converted. The surface was so dodgy that Glenister (a smaller man) would have been far better at full back on the day. In fact, had our original team selection been put out, it is thought that we would have fared much better than we did. A 6-0 half time lead was extended by three points when Barnes kicked a penalty after 50 minutes and that, as conditions deteriorated even more, was that. Both sides changed jerseys after 56 minutes (we returned as Middlesex) and we lost both Wood and Carling with injuries before the final whistle eventually went after 96 minutes of play. We were out and only had ourselves to blame. This was the first time we had exited in the 3rd round since Rosslyn Park knocked us out almost nine years ago to the day. Added to this defeat was the news that Neil Edwards had withdrawn his services until 24th February as he was unhappy at being left out at Bath.

Our fixture with London Welsh was cancelled so our next game was a friendly at the Stoop against London Scottish. A try from Richard Langhorn was all we had to show for a first half against the wind while Gavin Hastings had kicked four penalties and converted a try by left wing Renwick to give the exiles a fourteen point lead. With the strong wind in the second half, David Pears put over five penalties and, although Hastings narrowly missed with one from near the half way line, these were just enough to see us home by 19-18. A visit from Headingley followed the next weekend on Sunday 18th February and the game was sewn up for us by half time. David Pears opened with two penalties and followed this up with conversions of tries by Alex Tupman, Gavin Thompson and Paul Brady. Johnson got a penalty for Headingley but the half time deficit of 24-3 was just too much. We completely took our foot off the pedal after this and a penalty and a try from the visitors were the only scores in the second half. The long trip to Blundellsands to play Waterloo was undertaken next and without our star names, we earned a hard fought victory. Tries from Alex Tupman and Craig Luxton and a conversion by Pears were enough to see off two penalties for the home side. Our fourth friendly on the trot was another long trip; this time to Newcastle to play Gosforth. The home side took the lead when Clark dropped a goal but it didn't take long for us to gain the initiative. By half time, we had scored tries through Everton Davis (2), Neil Edwards, Gavin Thompson and Stuart Thresher and with three conversions by Pears, we led 26-3. The second half was similar to the first except that Gosforth failed to score. Davis completed his hat-trick, Edwards got his second and other tries came from Brady and David Thresher. All four were converted by Pears to make the final score 50-3 in our favour. By the end, the home side were down to thirteen men through injuries.

Against Gloucester, our challenge for the league title was dealt another blow when we went down at Kingsholm. Although we fielded a strong side, we were weakened by the loss of Ackford and Carling who were both rested. In the first half, it was a close contest and three penalties from Pears outscored two for the home side from Smith. Even a change of referee couldn't stop Gloucester's points being accumulated and Smith kicked four more penalties and the conversion of Dunn's try to leave us trailing by fifteen points at the end. With four men missing on international duty, we sent a weakened side to Coundon Road, Coventry for another friendly encounter and to put it mildly, we were slaughtered! We had no answer to Coventry and we only managed to score sixteen points (tries from Davis and Nick Killick plus two penalties and a conversion by Fletcher). Mark Fletcher had scored 238 points (4 tries, 7 dropped goals, 41 penalties and 39 conversions) after making his last appearance for the Club in this match. In reply, the home side ran in eight tries with scrum half Thomas kicking six conversions and a penalty to take their total to 47. This was the most points we had conceded since Cardiff defeated us 47-17 at Twickenham on 24th October 1981.

Our form had taken a real dip now and we were also throwing league points away. This was clearly shown in our last two league matches against Nottingham and Moseley. We began brightly against Nottingham and during the first half, we managed to build a good thirteen point lead. Pears kicked a penalty but couldn't convert any of the tries scored by Gavin Thompson, Stuart Thresher, Everton Davis and Craig Luxton. Sutton landed two penalties for the visitors but we were in command. With eighteen minutes left, we still led despite a try by Hartley and a dropped goal from Sutton because Pears had dropped a goal. Then, we collapsed and Neil Back got two tries, Hartley also went over and Sutton added a conversion to leave the final score at 22-27 to Nottingham. A good, narrow win followed in a friendly at Bristol thanks to a Pears dropped goal and a try from Glenister (7-0). Paul Curtis made his last appearance against Rosslyn Park on 21st April when we fielded a mainly second team and duly paid the price. David Pears kicked a couple of penalties and Jon Eagle grabbed a try but these scores were nowhere near enough to defeat the home side. They had no fewer than five ex-Quins in their side and were helped along with tries from two of them (Moon and Smith). The final score of 26-10 summed up their dominance. Our final game of the season was our eleventh league fixture and it was against Moseley at The Reddings. Moseley were in eleventh place and had only one win from their previous ten matches. We started poorly and during the first half Moseley scored four tries but failed to convert any of them. Pears got a penalty after converting our only try of the half through Duncan Wood and then followed up with the conversion of Tupman's try and two penalties to leave us five points up with fourteen minutes left to play. Three minutes later Moseley got their fifth try and amazingly, Purdy converted it to put them ahead by one point (22-21). The remaining minutes proved scoreless and another defeat was chalked up to leave us with a final record in the league of P11 W6 L5 F218 A180 Pts12. We had improved by one place on the previous season to finish in seventh place but it was just as disappointing. We said goodbye to three men in the Moseley game who had all served us well. Our captain (John Olver) was departing to Northampton where he would win three caps for England. He had captained the side superbly on 56 occasions and scored 64 points (16 tries) during his career. Gary Claxton had scored 5 tries (20 points) and Malcolm "Will" Wall had led the side six times and scored 9 tries (36 points) during their time in the 1st XV.

Our overall record was P35 W22 L13 F761 A614. This had been a poor season by our own high expectations even though we improved slightly in the league. The number of tries scored rose by thirty on last season to 108, dropped goals were up to 7, penalties were back up to record equalling levels at 62 and conversions went up by 24 to 61 and, as a consequence of this, points overall rose by 195. Rob Glenister topped the try scorers with 14, David Pears got the most points with 203 (4 tries, 5 dropped goals, 36 penalties and 32 conversions). Gavin Thompson appeared the most times (27) followed by David Pears (22) and Rob Glenister, Richard Langhorn and Craig Luxton on 21. A total of 58 players were used which was up by four on 1988/89 and no fewer than twelve of these only made one appearance whilst a further seventeen made fewer than ten.

1989/90

020989	NORTHAMPTON	NORTHAMPTON	L	1PG1T(7)-2G1PG2T(23)
090989	BATH(JCL1)	BATH	L	1G2PG(12)-4G2T(32)
130989	METROPOLITAN POLICE	IMBER COURT	W	2G1DG1PG2T(26)-1G1PG1T(13)
160989	LLANELLI	LLANELLI	L	2PG1T(10)-1G4PG6T(42)
200989	MAIDSTONE	STOOP MEMORIAL GROUND	C	
230989	WASPS(JCL1)	STOOP MEMORIAL GROUND	W	4PG(12)-3PG(9)
270989	LOUGHBOROUGH UNIVERSITY	STOOP MEMORIAL GROUND	W	2G1PG1T(19)-1PG2T(11)
300989	LONDON IRISH	TWICKENHAM	W	7G1PG2T(53)-1G2PG(12)
041089	WEST LONDON INSTITUTE	STOOP MEMORIAL GROUND	W	3G1PG3T(33)-1G1T(10)
071089	SWANSEA	TWICKENHAM	L	2PG2T(14)-1G1DG4PG(21)
141089	BEDFORD(JCL1)	BEDFORD	W	8G1PG5T(71)-2T(8)
181089	ASKEANS	STOOP MEMORIAL GROUND	W	3G3T(30)-1G2PG2T(20)
211089	LONDON SCOTTISH	TWICKENHAM	C	
281089	ORRELL(JCL1)	STOOP MEMORIAL GROUND	W	5PG(15)-3PG(9)
041189	CAMBRIDGE UNIVERSITY	CAMBRIDGE	L	2PG1T(10)-4G2PG1T(34)
111189	BRISTOL(JCL1)	STOOP MEMORIAL GROUND	W	1G1PG1T(13)-1PG1T(7)
181189	SARACENS(JCL1)	SOUTHGATE	L	1G1DG(9)-2G1PG(15)
251189	LEICESTER(JCL1)	STOOP MEMORIAL GROUND	W	1G1DG2PG(15)-4PG(12)
021289	BLACKHEATH	STOOP MEMORIAL GROUND	W	3G2PG(24)-1G1DG2T(17)
091289	BEDFORD	STOOP MEMORIAL GROUND	W	7G1PG3T(57)-1G1T(10)
161289	RUGBY	RUGBY	L	1G4PG1T(22)-2G3PG1T(25)
231289	RICHMOND	STOOP MEMORIAL GROUND	W	1DG3PG2T(20)-2G2PG(18)
301289	CARDIFF	STOOP MEMORIAL GROUND	W	3G1DG2PG4T(43)-3G1DG2PG1T(31)
060190	WASPS	SUDBURY	W	2PG1T(10)-1PG1T(7)
130190	ROSSLYN PARK(JCL1)	STOOP MEMORIAL GROUND	W	1G3PG1T(19)-1G1DG2PG(15)
190190	OLD BELVEDERE	STOOP MEMORIAL GROUND	W	4G1PG1T(31)-1G1PG2T(17)

210190	SARACENS	STOOP MEMORIAL GROUND	C	
270190	BATH(PC3)	BATH	L	0-1G1PG(9)
030290	LONDON WELSH	STOOP MEMORIAL GROUND	C	
100290	LONDON SCOTTISH	STOOP MEMORIAL GROUND	W	5PG1T(19)-1G4PG(18)
180290	HEADINGLEY	STOOP MEMORIAL GROUND	W	3G2PG(24)-2PG1T(10)
240290	WATERLOO	WATERLOO	W	1G1T(10)-2PG(6)
030390	GOSFORTH	GOSFORTH	W	7G2T(50)-1DG(3)
100390	GLOUCESTER(JCL1)	GLOUCESTER	L	3PG(9)-1G6PG(24)
170390	COVENTRY	COVENTRY	L	1G2PG1T(16)-6G1PG2T(47)
310390	NOTTINGHAM(JCL1)	STOOP MEMORIAL GROUND	L	1DG1PG4T(22)-1G1DG2PG3T(27)
070490	BRISTOL	BRISTOL	W	1DG1T(7)-0
210490	ROSSLYN PARK	ROEHAMPTON	L	2PG1T(10)-1G1DG3PG2T(26)
280490	MOSELEY(JCL1)	MOSELEY	L	2G3PG(21)-1G4T(22)

In July and August 1990, England toured Argentina and played seven matches. It was not at the best time of year and that showed in the results as a number of regulars decided not to go. Carling, Moore, Olver, Pears, Mickey Skinner, Gavin Thompson and Winterbottom were our current players and Dooley and Jason Leonard were with other clubs. All except Olver, Thompson and Leonard played in both tests (the first was won 25-12 but the second was lost narrowly 13-15). In the other games (all were close contests), England won two but suffered three defeats.

A number of ex-players passed away during this season including John Currie on 8th December (his career lasted between 1957 and 1960), Lord (Harold) Caccia (1925-27), Eric Harriss (1947-54), John O'Donnell (1947-49), Denys Swayne (1931-36) and Humphrey Tilling (1929-39). On 19th September, it was announced that, when planning permission was given, a two storey hospitality building would be put up. The anticipated income from the ground had now risen to £250,000 for the next three years. In 1990/91, income of £65,822 had been surpassed by expenditure of £73,369 to give us a loss of £7,547 (this was £1,856 worse than the previous year). The list of sides at the Club was now 1st XV, Wanderers, Jaguars, A1, Gentlemen and Colts. The seasons leading up to professionalism would see team names such as Astras, Spartans, Emerging Quins and Development XV.

This season saw a new captain (Peter Winterbottom) and a new coach (Mike Davis). Winterbottom would be in charge for this and the following two seasons. Davis had played for us between 1967 and 1972 and took up the position of Director of Coaching and was aided by Dick Best, Geoff Ashby and Mike Mein. We started off with a visit from the Belgian national side at Twickenham on 1st September. Jason Leonard made his debut (having joined from Saracens in the close season) and was to go on to play 278 games for the 1st XV and become England's all-time record cap winner with 114 to his name. He added to this 5 caps for the British Lions and also led the Club for two seasons in the middle of the decade. Our new captain also put in an appearance when he replaced Richard Langhorn in the second half; he didn't actually make his debut as captain until the fifth game of the season against Llanelli. It was all a bit too easy against the Belgians and we proceeded to run in eleven tries through Mike Wedderburn

(3), Alex Tupman (2), Mike Molyneux (2), Adrian Thompson, Jamie Salmon, Rob Glenister and Adam Fox. Stuart Thresher (5), Salmon and Jason Hoad added conversions. The visitors managed a penalty and a try to leave the final score at 58-7.

Our first midweek match of the season was against Askeans at the Stoop. Only six players who had finished the Belgian match appeared in the starting line up with Jamie Salmon leading the side. Richard Banks and Mike Molyneux scored tries and Jason Hoad added a penalty and a conversion. The missed conversion proved all important as Askeans converted both of their tries as well as getting a penalty for a narrow win by two points (13-15). A long trip down to Plymouth was next and again, a weakened side went down to defeat. This was not a narrow loss and Albion ran in five tries; converting three and landing four penalties for a 38-16 victory. We scored through Jon Eagle (a try) and Stuart Thresher (a try, two penalties and a conversion). Back at the Stoop we had another midweek match against the Metropolitan Police and this time the side was strengthened by the return of Andy Harriman after injury. David Pears and Craig Luxton also returned as the half back pairing. After just seven minutes, Harriman scored a try and Pears converted and, although the Police got a goal of their own, a Pears penalty put us 9-6 ahead at the interval. The second half was one-way traffic as far as the scoring went and further tries from Luxton and Molyneux and two conversions and a penalty from Pears gave us a victory by twenty four points to six.

In our next game against Llanelli at Twickenham, we put out our strongest side of the season so far and how it showed. Llanelli had seven internationals in their ranks as well as Tony Copsey (who would have guessed that a decade later he would become our managing director!) and Rupert Moon. Our side contained no fewer than eight internationals including new arrival from Nottingham, B.C. (Brian) Moore. He would play 77 times for the 1st XV, captain the Club in 1994/95 and win a total of 64 England caps. He had already won three British Lions caps in Australia in 1989. Once our forwards had gained control, the points started to flow. By half time, Stuart Thresher had scored a try, three penalties and two conversions to add to tries from Paul Ackford and Rob Glenister and we led 25-6. In the second half, Llanelli added two more tries to their goal and, despite losing Thresher with a cut forehead we still outscored them with tries from Glenister and Salmon (one of which Thresher converted before departing). The full time score of 35-14 was our highest total against the Scarlets since 1964 in what was to be our last scheduled club game at Twickenham (our association would not be ending just yet).

The following Saturday was our opening league fixture against Wasps at the Stoop. Wasps were defending their title and went behind to three Thresher penalties in the first 19 minutes. By half time, Ryan had scored a try and Andrew slotted a penalty to leave a gap of just two points. Andrew scored a try two minutes into the second half before Thresher's fourth success put us back in front by a point. In the last quarter, Wasps took control and a try from Oti and a penalty from Andrew sealed the victory (12-18). We were still reeling from this defeat when Loughborough University came to the Stoop the following Wednesday. They scored two early goals to lead 12-0 before we got into gear. David Pears kicked two penalties and a conversion to add to tries from Harriman and Julian Pike and, despite a penalty from the Students, we led by a point at the break. In the second half, we went into another gear and ran in four further tries through Luxton, Banks (2) and Tim Brentnall. Pears added three conversions for a final score of 38-15. Jamie Salmon made his final appearance in this game, having scored some 273 points (43 tries, 17 penalties and 25 conversions) during his career. This had been the fifteenth time he had led the side.

Two more friendlies followed against London Irish and West London Institute and both resulted in clear wins. Against the Irish, Wedderburn (2), Harriman, Gavin Thompson, Cleary and Glenister got tries and Thresher converted four and added a penalty. The final score of 35-9 was easily exceeded against the Institute the following Wednesday. Gavin Thompson scored a hat-trick of tries with others coming from Adam Fox, Ian Wood, David

Briant, S. Travers, Davis and Cleary. Hoad's seven conversions brought our total to fifty and the visitors' only consolation was a penalty goal.

Against Nottingham at Beeston in our second league game, Troy Coker made his debut. He would make 51 appearances for us over the next four years and gain 27 caps for Australia including a World Cup winners medal in 1991. This was a must win game as defeat would have sent us to the bottom of the division. We played into the strong wind in the first half and only allowed the home side a single try by Potter after 22 minutes which was converted by Hodgkinson. Only two minutes into the second half, Pears broke and linked well to put Adrian Thompson over for our first try. Pears converted this and did the same with a try from Mike Wedderburn ten minutes later. When Harriman went over for our third try, the game was won and a penalty from Pears right on the final whistle merely put the icing on the cake (19-6). After being criticised on England's tour of Argentina, Pears was now coming into his own and the following week against Rosslyn Park, he ran the show. To be fair, it was a turgid game in perfect conditions with not a try in sight. Pears dropped two goals and kicked four penalties to two penalties by Graves for Park. It didn't matter though and we had our second win in the league.

Our next opponents were Saracens, they included our former fly half Mark Fletcher but were struggling in the league and were unfortunate to find us in inspiring form. This was only our second visit to Southgate for a league match and we got off to a good start when Pears slotted over a penalty after only three minutes. Ben Clarke scored a try and Ben Rudling kicked a penalty to put Sarries in front after seventeen minutes but that was the end of their scoring. By half time, Harriman had scored a try and Pears had put over the conversion and two penalties to give us a lead of 15-7. As the Saracens defence tired, we finally took control for the last 30 minutes and ran in three tries through Glenister, Adrian Thompson and Wedderburn. Pears had one of those days to remember with the boot and got all three conversions and two more penalties to finish with 23 points and a 100% success rate (nine out of nine). All this helped our winning margin to increase to thirty two points (39-7).

Our fourth league match in succession brought our fourth win when Liverpool St. Helens visited the Stoop. After just a minute, Troy Coker scored our first try for Pears to convert before the visitors unexpectedly scored nine points to take the lead. A penalty and the conversion of Brian Moore's try by Pears put us into a 15-9 interval lead. A penalty for Liverpool seven minutes into the second half brought them to within three points but that was as near as they got. In the last half an hour (as we had done against Saracens), we opened up and ran in five tries. Harriman (2), Leonard, Gavin Thompson and Thresher all went over and Pears converted three. We did lose Will Carling with an ankle injury but the 41-12 final score took us into first place in the league after five matches. In a morning kick-off against Cambridge University, Rob Glenister had a profitable day, scoring two tries, a penalty and two conversions to finish with fifteen points. Molyneux and Bruce Miller scored our other tries in a 23-6 victory which also saw Jeff Alexander make the first of his 54 appearances for the first team.

The following week, we travelled down to Bath for a top of the table clash minus Paul Ackford. He had been laid out by Federico Mendez whilst playing for England in the international against Argentina and had to serve a mandatory three week break for concussion. After the team coach left the Stoop on Friday, Roy Croucher went to lock the gates to secure the ground and noticed an item of clothing was on top of the fence. It appeared that somebody had tried to get into the ground and it turned out to be Jason Leonard! He was most eager to get to play in the game and the only way he could have done that as Roy explained to him was to get to Richmond, get into London and pick up the train that would take him to Bath. Roy took him to Richmond in his car to help him on his way – he played the next day. After playing well in the first quarter, we made a few mistakes and the game was lost. Barnes kicked a penalty on 20 minutes and by the time half an hour had elapsed, the home side had scored two tries. Adebayo and Haag went over after defensive errors, Barnes converted the first and added a penalty near half time to leave us trailing by sixteen points. Pears got a penalty back for us on 43 minutes but a try by Swift nine minutes later and a Webb penalty near the end left us way behind. We had lost the top spot which we wouldn't be getting back in a hurry.

In our next game against Northampton, we saw the return of John Olver. David Pears was again on target and, in the first half outscored John Steele 2-1 in penalties. The turning point of the game came when we were leading 3-0 and on the attack, Ward of Northampton intercepted a pass and ran 60 yards for a try but the referee recalled him and penalised the visitors. Pears landed the penalty for a 6-0 lead instead of a 3-6 deficit. Steele equalised with his second penalty before our pressure began to tell. This led to three more penalties from Pears to take us clear before Neil Edwards got the only try of the game after 74 minutes. This was converted by Pears to leave the final score at twenty one points to six. It was Pilkington Cup time again the following week and we took on Clifton at the Stoop in the 3rd round. Troy Coker got our first try after six minutes before Clifton equalised two minutes later. By half time, Pears had kicked two penalties and converted Wedderburn's try for a 16-4 lead. We really got down to work in the second half and in 34 minutes we added forty points. Molyneux (2), Wedderburn (2), Banks, Carling and Pears all scored tries and the last named banged over six conversions for a tally of 24 points in the tie. The resulting 56-4 victory proved to be our biggest of the season.

Due to our Divisional and County commitments, it was decided that the away matches against Blackheath, Bedford and Rugby would be cancelled. This meant that our next game was at Richmond on 22nd December. We fielded a largely 2nd XV in this friendly and paid the price (albeit by the narrowest possible margin). The lead changed hands no fewer than five times in an error strewn match with never more than five points between the sides. Rob Glenister (2) and Adam Fox got tries for us and Pears kicked two penalties and a conversion. For Richmond, Livesey got four penalties, a dropped goal and the conversion of Fenn's try to leave the final score at 21-20 to the home side. Our last game of the year was away at Cardiff and, yet again, we fielded a weakened side (this time it was due to England calls). In dreadful conditions, three penalties from Mike Rayer for Cardiff proved to be the only scores. Paul Challinor played the first of 129 games for the 1st XV in this game and would go on to play for most of the next eight seasons.

With six of our men and four Wasps absent in Lanzarote on England training, both sides were weakened for this friendly at Sudbury (we were further troubled because Chris Butcher and Troy Coker were on holiday). As it turned out, Wasps were too strong on the day and ran out easy winners by thirty five points to three. Stuart Thresher got our points with a penalty goal in what was our heaviest defeat by Wasps. On 12th January, the long trek was made up to Orrell for another league game. All of our missing men were back from Lanzarote and a close encounter resulted. In the first half, David Pears exchanged penalties with Martin Strett for a 6-6 scoreline. After 57 minutes Pears dropped a goal to edge us in front before Strett equalised twelve minutes later with his third penalty. In the third minute of injury time, the referee (Ian Bullerwell) penalised Harriman and Davis for an illegal blocking manoeuvre just inside our half. Up stepped Gerry Ainscough to launch the penalty between the posts. The whistle went and disaster had struck us again at Edge Hall Road.

A friendly with Saracens was next in a morning kick-off at the Stoop. Approaching half time, we were trailing 3-13 and looked like going down again when Troy Coker came into his own. Playing in an unaccustomed role at number 6, he drove over from a scrum near the line for Thresher to convert and we only trailed by four points at the break. Glenister levelled matters with another try before Coker scored again from a scrum near the line which Thresher again converted and we led for the first time. All that remained was for Thresher to land his second penalty for a final score of 22-13 in our favour. This match saw the return of Simon Halliday. He had last played for us back in 1980/81 and returned to London after a long and successful time with Bath. Our next game was the all-important cup tie at Kingsholm against Gloucester. We took the field to the boos of the home crowd and proceeded to silence them within the first fifteen minutes. From a lineout, Skinner fed Carling who in turn passed to Thresher. From here the ball went to Harriman who came in off the touchline and went over for the try. Pears converted and it was 6-0 after seven minutes. Smith kicked a penalty for Gloucester four minutes later but, just two minutes after this, Thresher ran 15 yards to the corner for our second try which Pears converted superbly from the touchline. There was no further scoring until Pears put over a penalty on 60 minutes to stretch the lead to 15-3. We had survived tremendous pressure from the home pack with our defence being superb. With nine minutes left, Pears was injured and left the field to be replaced by Luxton. Our pattern went missing for a while and after the referee had missed a knock-on by Teague, Gloucester scored their first try but, crucially, Smith's conversion went wide. We held on desperately until a minute before the end when Marment was first to a chip through by Smith. This time Smith's conversion went in off the post to make the score 15-13 in our favour. There was just time to kick-off before the referee brought this fantastic tie to an end, leaving all the players and supporters emotionally drained.

We met the London Welsh at the Old Deer Park for the first time in two years and with ten of our cup side playing, ran rings around them. Their solitary goal was wiped out by eight tries. Harriman and Chris Butcher each got a brace with the others coming from Carling, Davis, Langhorn and Halliday. A. Hobbs (2) and Challinor put over three of the conversions for a final score of 38-6. This was our highest score against the Welsh since we defeated them 41-0 at Chiswick Park on 10th March 1894. Our next league fixture against Bristol at the Stoop was postponed and the week after that our friendly at home to Headingley was cancelled. This left us with no game for three weeks and our next fixture was the cup quarter final against Rosslyn Park at the Stoop. We had become favourites for the cup and were expected to dispose of Park quite easily. In the first half, we played with a strong wind and after 37 minutes, we only had a Pears penalty and a Stuart Thresher try to show for our efforts. Suddenly, the match was won and lost in the space of four minutes when Harriman and then Skinner stormed over for tries. Pears converted the first and our interval lead was 17-0. A one man scoring effort from John Graves for the visitors produced two penalties, a try and a conversion but Pears kicked his second penalty and Carling killed the tie off with a try eleven minutes from the end. The final score of 24-12 was comfortable enough and it took us through to our sixth semi-final.

The following week, Newcastle Gosforth came to the Stoop and faced a side with just four of the cup side in it. We played quite well in the first half and led 13-6 at the break. Wedderburn and Craig Emmerson had scored tries and Thresher (captain for the day) landed a penalty and a conversion to two penalties from Johnson for the visitors. As the match entered the last fifteen minutes, the visiting team had notched up twelve points without reply to lead 18-13. We tried everything and ran four kickable penalties from which Brady and Davis both nearly scored. A minute from the end, Emmerson scored his second try and with the last kick of the game, Thresher had a conversion attempt to snatch victory by a point. He struck it from near the touchline, it looked on target but struck the post and we had lost by a point instead. Our next fixture should have been an away friendly at St. Helens against Swansea but this was cancelled so we took on Coventry (on the morning of the England v. France grand slam decider at Twickenham) at the Stoop. Despite again having a heavily weakened side, this proved to be an entertaining game with the lead changing hands four times. We fielded five regular first teamers whereas Coventry were at full strength and this showed in the first half. Stuart Thresher got a try after only two minutes and he converted Paul Challinor's try after 28 minutes. Meanwhile, Coventry had been building a lead and they had scored a goal, three penalties and a try to lead by nine points at the break. We came out firing on all cylinders at the start of the second half and ran in two tries through Nick Killick and Mike Molyneux in the first ten minutes; both of which Thresher converted to nudge us three points ahead. Coventry were not going down without a fight and their third try put them back in front by a point before Jeff Alexander and Bruce Miller took the game beyond them with further tries. Neither of these were converted which left the final score at 30-23.

It was back to league action the next weekend and a trip to Welford Road to take on Leicester. We were missing eight of our first choice players (six were playing in the Hong Kong sevens, one was on holiday and one was ineligible) so it looked as though it would be an uphill struggle. As it was, David Pears played a blinder and put us into an early lead when he converted his own try after only four minutes. He then added a penalty but, either side of this, Liley got a penalty and Harris dropped a goal to keep Leicester in touch at half time. Right at the end of the third quarter, Pears got his second penalty but Liley replied with two of his own during the next ten minutes and the scores were level. With four minutes of normal time remaining, Pears completed the scoring with a dropped goal to win the game (as he had done in the previous meeting). Bristol came to the Stoop on 30th March to play the previously postponed fixture to face a side now brimming with confidence. We had started to recapture the 1988 cup winning form and were ripping teams apart with our running rugby. In a tight first half, which we just shaded, Carling and Glenister got tries and Pears a conversion to which Bristol replied with a penalty and a try. The second half saw a try count of 6-1 in our favour as we destroyed the visitors with the pace of Carling and Harriman. Each player completed a hat-trick of tries with the other coming from Glenister. Pears could only convert two so the final winning margin of 38-16 should have been more. Carling was injured when a Bristol defender left his boot in as he scored his third try. The blow to his thigh muscle caused him to depart the field; he was out for three weeks.

On 6th April, it was the cup semi-final against Nottingham at the Stoop. We had first use of a strong, gusting wind and in the first sixteen minutes had almost wrapped the game up. David Pears kicked a penalty in the first minute, converted Glenister's blind side try seven minutes later and added another penalty to take us twelve points clear. Simon Hodgkinson got a penalty back three minutes before the interval to keep Nottingham in the tie. The second half was a reversal of the first as far as the scoreboard was concerned. Hodgkinson kicked his second penalty, Gregory dropped a goal and when Kilford scored a try for Hodgkinson to convert, the visitors led by three points with twelve minutes left. Three minutes later, Pears kicked an unbelievable penalty into the crosswind and guided it over to level the scores. With barely a minute of normal time remaining, Skinner was ruled by the referee (Fred Howard) to have trampled on Gray. This gave Hodgkinson a penalty right in front of the posts and 30 metres out to take his side through to the final. He came up, struck the ball and, as it neared the posts, it cannoned off the right hand upright and Troy Coker carried the ball to safety. The final whistle went and 20 minutes of extra time began. After just two of these, Andy Harriman chipped through and beat three defenders to the touchdown. Pears failed to convert but added another penalty before half time to put us seven points clear. Hodgkinson did get his second penalty in the second half but we played out the remaining minutes of extra time to claim our place in the final after an epic clash no one will ever forget. In the other semi-final, Northampton surprised Orrell 18-10 at Franklin's Gardens to complete the final pairing.

The following Saturday, Moseley came to the Stoop for another league fixture which they had to win to avoid relegation. They started as if they meant business when Arntzen dropped a goal after only three minutes but, by half time, Pears had kicked three penalties and Banks had scored a try to put us 13-3 up. Pears was replaced by

Glenister on 58 minutes but this only spurred us on and Harriman scored a try to increase the lead. Arntzen put over another penalty but in the last thirteen minutes Luxton, Glenister and Harriman all ran in for tries against a dispirited Moseley side. Glenister got two conversions to make the final score 33-6 and condemn Moseley to the second division. Our last friendly match of the season was at Roehampton against Rosslyn Park on 20th April. With snow falling at the beginning and end of the game, the conditions were not perfect by any means. A cracking game resulted and a half time score of 9-7 in our favour ended as a draw of 19-19. We outscored Park by three tries to two but a draw was a fair result. David Pears was again amongst the points and scored a penalty and two conversions. Our tries were scored by Simon Halliday, Wedderburn and Skinner. Our final league fixture was at Gloucester, we decided to send our reserve side down to enable the cup final team to have a week off and this showed in the final score of 38-19 in favour of the home side. Mike Wedderburn got a try as did Mike Molyneux and Jeff Alexander. The last named also scored a penalty and two conversions; the last conversion enabled us to finish in third place in division one by virtue of better points difference than Leicester. Gloucester scored six tries, converted four and added two penalties.

The Cup Final promised to be a good game, we were red hot favourites but, as history shows, favourites don't always come out on top. Our team was as follows:- Stuart Thresher (full back); Andy Harriman, Will Carling, Simon Halliday and Everton Davis (three quarters); David Pears (fly half) and Rob Glenister (scrum half); Jason Leonard, Brian Moore, Andy Mullins, Troy Coker, Paul Ackford, Mickey Skinner, Peter Winterbottom (captain) and Richard Langhorn (forwards). We dominated the first half but only had a penalty from Pears after 27 minutes to show for our efforts. Two penalties from John Steele after 38 and 42 minutes gave the underdogs a three point advantage at half time. Our pressure and possession began to tell and seven minutes into the second half, Richard Langhorn piled over amongst the bodies for Pears to convert and we led 9-6. Just as we were starting to throw the ball about in midfield, a mix up led to the ball being hacked on by Packman and Moss scored the try. Steele got his third penalty and with fourteen minutes left, Northampton led 13-9. Much as we tried, we couldn't find a way through until five minutes from the end. Harriman found space on the right wing and went round Thorneycroft to score in the south-west corner and level the scores. Pears couldn't convert and hit the post with an attempted dropped goal right at the end of normal time which meant that, as with the semi-final, we found ourselves going into extra time. A minute into the first period, Everton Davis charged down a clearance kick by Packman and from this, Halliday took the ball on the burst from a five metre scrum to dive over the line. Pears converted this and five minutes later, Glenister got away after Thresher had wrong-footed the defence and his try sealed the win. Pears converted and with no further scoring, the cup was ours by twenty five points to thirteen. This was a tremendous victory for us but it could so easily have been a disaster. It was to be a long time before any more silverware made its way into our trophy cabinet.

Our overall record during the season was P34 W23 D1 L10 F850 A479. In the league it was P12 W8 L4 F267 A162 Pts16 Pos 3rd. This season had undoubtedly been one of our most successful and almost copied the 1987/88 campaign. Tries scored rose by 19 to 127, dropped goals fell to 5, penalties were down to 57 from 62 but conversions shot up by 17 to 78. The rise in tries and conversions saw the points total go up by eighty nine to 850 (this total was the third highest amount ever). Andy Harriman was the top try scorer with 18, David Pears equalled his five dropped goals from the previous season which helped him to score the most points with 223 (2 tries, 40 penalties and 40 conversions). Andy Mullins appeared in the most games (26) followed by Rob Glenister and Stuart Thresher on 23. These were the only three out of 68 players used in the 1st XV to appear in more than twenty matches. An amazing 44 of these played in less than ten games (15 appeared in only one).

1990/91

010990	BELGIUM	TWICKENHAM	W	7G4T(58)-1PG1T(7)
050990	ASKEANS	STOOP MEMORIAL GROUND	L	1G1PG1T(13)-2G1PG(15)
080990	PLYMOUTH ALBION	PLYMOUTH	L	1G2PG1T(16)-3G4PG2T(38)
120990	METROPOLITAN POLICE	STOOP MEMORIAL GROUND	W	3G2PG(24)-1G(6)
150990	LLANELLI	TWICKENHAM	W	3G3PG2T(35)-1G2T(14)
220990	WASPS(JCL1)	STOOP MEMORIAL GROUND	L	4PG(12)-2PG3T(18)
260990	LOUGHBOROUGH UNIVERSITY	STOOP MEMORIAL GROUND	W	4G2PG2T(38)-2G1PG(15)
290990	LONDON IRISH	SUNBURY	W	4G1PG2T(35)-1G1PG(9)
031090	WEST LONDON INSTITUTE	STOOP MEMORIAL GROUND	W	7G2T(50)-1PG(3)
061090	NOTTINGHAM(JCL1)	NOTTINGHAM	W	2G1PG1T(19)-1G(6)
131090	ROSSLYN PARK(JCL1)	STOOP MEMORIAL GROUND	W	2DG4PG(18)-2PG(6)
201090	SARACENS(JCL1)	SOUTHGATE	W	4G5PG(39)-1PG1T(7)
271090	LIVERPOOL ST.HELENS(JCL1)	STOOP MEMORIAL GROUND	W	5G1PG2T(41)-1G2PG(12)
031190	CAMBRIDGE UNIVERSITY	STOOP MEMORIAL GROUND	W	2G1PG2T(23)-1G(6)
101190	BATH(JCL1)	BATH	L	1PG(3)-1G3PG2T(23)
171190	NORTHAMPTON(JCL1)	STOOP MEMORIAL GROUND	W	1G5PG(21)-2PG(6)
241190	CLIFTON(PC3)	STOOP MEMORIAL GROUND	W	7G2PG2T(56)-1T(4)
011290	BLACKHEATH	BLACKHEATH	C	
081290	BEDFORD	BEDFORD	C	
151290	RUGBY	RUGBY	C	
221290	RICHMOND	RICHMOND	L	1G2PG2T(20)-1G1DG4PG(21)
291290	CARDIFF	CARDIFF	L	0-3PG(9)
050191	WASPS	SUDBURY	L	1PG(3)-4G1PG2T(35)
120191	ORRELL(JCL1)	ORRELL	L	1DG2PG(9)-4PG(12)
190191	SARACENS	STOOP MEMORIAL GROUND	W	2G2PG1T(22)-1G1PG1T(13)
260191	GLOUCESTER(PC4)	GLOUCESTER	W	2G1PG(15)-1G1PG1T(13)
020291	LONDON WELSH	OLD DEER PARK	W	3G5T(38)-1G(6)
090291	BRISTOL(JCL1)	STOOP MEMORIAL GROUND	P	

160291	HEADINGLEY	STOOP MEMORIAL GROUND	C	
230291	ROSSLYN PARK(PCQF)	STOOP MEMORIAL GROUND	W	1G2PG3T(24)-1G2PG(12)
020391	NEWCASTLE GOSFORTH	STOOP MEMORIAL GROUND	L	1G1PG2T(17)-1G1DG3PG(18)
090391	SWANSEA	SWANSEA	C	
160391	COVENTRY	STOOP MEMORIAL GROUND	W	3G3T(30)-1G3PG2T(23)
230391	LEICESTER(JCL1)	LEICESTER	W	1G2DG1PG(15)-1DG3PG(12)
300391	BRISTOL(JCL1)	STOOP MEMORIAL GROUND	W	3G5T(38)-1G2PG1T(16)
060491	NOTTINGHAM(PCSF)	STOOP MEMORIAL GROUND	W	1G4PG1T(22)-1G1DG3PG(18) AET
130491	MOSELEY(JCL1)	STOOP MEMORIAL GROUND	W	2G3PG3T(33)-1DG1PG(6)
200491	ROSSLYN PARK	ROEHAMPTON	D	2G1PG1T(19)-1G1DG2PG1T(19)
270491	GLOUCESTER(JCL1)	GLOUCESTER	L	2G1PG1T(19)-4G2PG2T(38)
040591	NORTHAMPTON(PCF)	TWICKENHAM	W	3G1PG1T(25)-3PG1T(13)AET

England went on tour again to Australia and Fiji in July and played six matches including one test against each nation. Fiji were defeated 28-12 but the usual result was achieved against Australia (15-40) although the other games produced four wins. Will Carling, Jason Leonard, Brian Moore and Mickey Skinner played against Fiji and all apart from the last named appeared against Australia with the addition of Paul Ackford and Peter Winterbottom. Wade Dooley, Simon Halliday, John Olver and David Pears also toured but got no caps.

On 15th August, it was noted that the 125th anniversary book about the Club had been published. It had been written by Philip Warner and 500 copies had been sold prior to publication with a steady stream being sold after it came out. The new building had received planning permission but financing the cost may yet prove a problem. In November, plans for the new building had to be re-thought totally as a sewer had been discovered and the original site was now out of the question. Fresh planning consent might be needed and costs would increase. In April 1992, the committee heard that temporary planning approval had been granted and was for nine hospitality boxes on three levels at the north end of the clubhouse. The cost of erection was £10,000 and projected revenue was £70,000. The Peter Parfitt organisation was supplying the boxes for free. Hugh Forbes (1950-53) had lost his brave battle against cancer on 16th November and the committee was informed the next day. Malcolm Hollins also passed away, he had been the Club physiotherapist for a number of years from the fifties to the seventies. When all the figures had been totted up, a profit of £7,198 had been made for 1991/92.

1991 was a World Cup year and the second event took place in Britain and France during October and November. As a consequence, league fixtures didn't begin until after the final at the end of October. This time we had no fewer than twenty representatives playing in eight of the participating teams. Current players were Troy Coker (Australia), Paul Ackford, Will Carling (who captained the side), Simon Halliday, Jason Leonard, Brian Moore, David Pears (he made no appearances), Mickey Skinner and Peter Winterbottom (England). John Olver was also in the England squad and had recently left us. Future Quins were Gareth Rees and Scott Stewart (Canada), Wade Dooley (England), Laurent Cabannes and Thierry Lacroix (France), Gary Halpin and Jim Staples (Ireland), Massimo Cuttitta (Italy), Zinzan Brooke (New Zealand) and Craig Chalmers (Scotland). In the opening game, England lost narrowly to New Zealand at Twickenham (12-18) but recovered as they had done in 1987 to win their remaining group games against Italy (36-6) and USA (37-9). In a fiery quarter final against France in Paris, Mickey Skinner was at the forefront of the English team as it took on and beat the French 19-10. In the semi-final, England had to travel again, this time to Murrayfield to take on Scotland; again they won, this time by the narrow margin of 9-6 (the Scottish full back Gavin Hastings missed a crucial penalty from almost in front of the posts) and marched into the final against Australia at Twickenham. After playing a forward dominated game for the whole tournament, England reverted to running the ball but it backfired and they lost by twelve points to six despite going back to the forward play in the second half (had they played this way from the start, it is generally felt England would have lifted the trophy). In the final, we were represented by seven Englishmen (Ackford, Carling (captain), Halliday, Leonard, Moore, Skinner and Winterbottom) and one Australian (Coker). It remains a record to this day.

So it was that we began without our international contingent in the first seven matches which were all friendlies. The first of these was at the Stoop against Northampton on 7th September in a re-run of the cup final back in May. John Steele put the Saints ahead with a penalty but, by the time he added a second on the half time whistle, we led by eleven points to six. Mike Molyneux had scored a try and Stuart Thresher had also got a try and a penalty. A quick burst of scoring between the 49th and 54th minutes saw a goal and a dropped goal put the visitors back in front. Mike Wedderburn scored a try three minutes later to equalise which Paul Challinor converted to edge us ahead. We now took control and Langhorn and Killick got further tries and Challinor dropped a goal and added a conversion. The last conversion by Wedderburn left us victorious by 32-15.

Our unbeaten record went in the very next game when Plymouth Albion were the visitors to the Stoop. Stuart Thresher got a penalty and converted Molyneux's try but leads of 3-0 and 9-6 were brushed aside by Plymouth who ran out 21-9 winners. We were missing 17 men (eight with England, one with Australia and eight with London) so this must go down as a major reason for this reverse. The London representatives returned the following week when we travelled down to Stradey Park to take on Llanelli. Mickey Skinner returned to the team from the England World Cup squad and contributed in full to our performance. We went ahead when Paul Challinor scored a try but were caught and overtaken by two goals and a try from Llanelli. Jeff Alexander added a second try, Stuart Thresher converted and also kicked a penalty to leave us trailing 13-16 at the break. Colin Stephens got his second and third tries for the home side to put the Scarlets eleven points ahead before we rallied again. Ian Desmond (on his debut) and Nick Dyte scored tries which Thresher converted and we led by one point. When Stephens dropped a goal it all looked to be going the way of the home side but Desmond's second try gave us a two point victory. It could have been different had a last gasp penalty attempt by Stephens not gone wide.

The following Saturday, we travelled for the first time to Kidbrooke to play Askeans (overall, it was our third meeting). In appalling conditions, we ran out easy winners with tries from Glenister (2), Edwards, Wedderburn and Stuart Thresher (who added a penalty and two conversions). The final score of 27-0 wasn't our biggest win of the season but we matched the winning margin in our next game against London Irish at the Stoop on Friday 25th October. Due to the World Cup, Divisional Championship and County Championship taking place at the same time, we didn't play for the first three weeks of October. Against the Irish, Kent Bray made his debut at fly half. He was to go on and make 51 appearances for the 1st XV over the next three years. He had a reasonably successful night and converted three of our seven tries. In the first half, Glenister and Molyneux got tries, Bray converted the first and the Irish replied with a penalty. They closed the gap to three points with a try after 47 minutes but this is where their scoring ended. Further tries for us came from Steve Shortland, Jon Eagle (2), Neil Edwards and Glenister with his second.

The following Friday, we were away at Cambridge University in a match which was effectively decided in the first half. The students went into a 21-3 lead through three goals and a penalty to a solitary penalty from Stuart Thresher. The second half was tighter but we still lost it. Adrian Davies converted three out of the four further tries scored (Chris Sheasby got one of these as he was now studying at the university). For us, Thresher added a conversion and a penalty and Desmond, Glenister and Molyneux got tries to leave the final score at 20-43. Our seventh friendly was at home against Rugby and provided us with our fifth win. A totally one sided first half saw tries from Edwards, Bray, Glenister and Harriman and two penalties and two conversions by David Pears for a 26-0 lead. Rugby did score first (a goal) and last (a try) in the second half but two goals and a try for us took our winning margin to 42-10. Pears converted those scored by Gavin Thompson and Jeff Alexander with the third coming from Glenister.

On 16th November, we played our first league game of the season at Sudbury against Wasps. We had our chances in this game but for the third time in the league, we came away defeated. Pears missed three penalties and a dropped goal in the first half but we only trailed by six points to nil at the break. Will Carling had departed with blurred vision after 36 minutes and with him went our chances. Three further Wasps tries were added and the conversion of the last left us twenty points down with five minutes of normal time remaining. We did manage a try when Mike Molyneux went over but as Pears converted, the referee blew the final whistle. Nottingham came to the Stoop the next weekend and were promptly dispatched 23-6. They were not having a good time and, after taking the lead, were gradually worn down. David Pears was on the score sheet again and he landed three penalties and converted his own try. Hodgkinson kicked his second penalty for the visitors but late, unconverted tries from Bray and Nick Killick sealed the win.

Our next encounter was the first step in the defence of the Pilkington Cup at Bedford. This one had the potential for a shock but we took an early lead when Pears got a penalty. At the end of the first quarter, Mike Molyneux ran in and Pears converted with the aid of an upright. Seven minutes later, he extended our lead to twelve points with another penalty. Andy Finnie pulled three points back right on half time with a penalty but Bedford would not trouble the scoreboard operator again. Playing down the slope, we never looked like slipping up and Molyneux, Harriman, Pears and Winterbottom added further tries. Pears converted just one but kicked his third penalty for a 33-3 final score. For our third league game, we made the short journey to Roehampton to take on Rosslyn Park. David Pears was in excellent form with the boot and saw us to victory and fourth place in the division. His seven penalty goals from ten attempts set a new Club record in a game and, when added to Kent Bray's dropped goal, helped us to a 24-12 win. Park scored three tries but it was nowhere near enough. Six of the home side had played or would play for us in the future.

The following week, the league game with Saracens at the Stoop was postponed due to fog. This meant that a visit to Sunbury to take on London Irish would be our final game of the year on 21st December. This was the first season for the Irish in the top division and they had a draw and two defeats from their opening three games. We were starting to gel together and looked to be putting in a good winning run. It only took two minutes for the Irish line to be breached when Wedderburn went over. Pears converted this and further efforts from Edwards and Gavin Thompson but couldn't manage to convert his own try. We had played with the gale blowing down the pitch and survived twenty minutes of Irish pressure to turn round 22-0 up. When we faced the wind, nothing really changed and Pears extended the lead with a penalty after 54 minutes. Mullen got a penalty on 66 minutes for the home side but that was as near as they got. One rolling maul went 30 yards and eventually led to Mark Russell going over for our fifth try. In the closing fifteen minutes we added tries through Glenister (converted by Pears) and Challinor. The 39-3 win helped us to jump into second place in the table on points difference and set us up nicely for our next game – Bath at home on 4th January.

The game against Bath was fast becoming the one you had to win to have a chance of lifting the league trophy aloft. We began extremely well and Will Carling went over after only three minutes for Pears to convert. By the 34th minute, Pears had landed two penalties and converted a penalty try (awarded for collapsing a five metre scrum) to put us 18-0 in front and looking good to go top. It then started to go wrong when Simon Halliday was injured by an unintentional flying boot and had to leave the field. Bath then got a penalty try of their own for the same reason as ours and Webb's conversion made it 18-6 at half time. Disaster struck in the 56th minute when Troy Coker saw red, punched someone and was promptly sent off by the referee (David Leslie). It had been a niggly match most of the way through and several other players were lucky to stay on the pitch. We failed to score any more points and Bath gradually nibbled away at our lead. Jon Webb kicked two penalties and, a minute into injury time, Phil de Glanville went over in the corner to make it 18-16. Webb put the conversion over and the match ended all square. This proved to be a nail in the coffin of our league chances and another was added in our next game at Northampton. Carling, Halliday, Leonard and Edwards all pulled out before kick-off and in the first 26 minutes, we had conceded a goal, a dropped goal and a try to trail by thirteen points. Thresher kicked a penalty and Challinor dropped a goal but a Steele penalty made it 16-6 at half time. A try five minutes into the second half by Mike Wedderburn reduced the deficit to six points. A dropped goal by Hunter and a try from Bayfield (converted by Steele) stretched the lead and put paid to our chances. Steve Shortland did score a consolation try but, again, it went unconverted.

Our next game was a morning kick-off against Saracens at Southgate. This was a friendly game as it clashed with an international fixture. Molyneux scored a try to open the scoring and Stuart Thresher added two penalties in the second half, but it was not enough as the home side got two goals, two penalties and a try to run out 22-10 winners. The scheduled fourth round cup game against Wasps at Sudbury was called off at 1.00 on the afternoon of the game due to a frozen pitch. Our next game was another friendly against London Welsh at the Stoop on 1st February. It turned out to be our biggest win and our highest score of the season. Mike Wedderburn became only the sixth Harlequin to score six tries in a game; scoring three in each half. Others were added by Mike Pratley (2), Mark Russell, Gavin Thompson and Kent Bray. Paul Challinor kicked four conversions and a penalty to complete our tally. The Welsh reply was a penalty and a try to make the final score 55-7. This was also our biggest victory over the Welsh in 74 matches. Ronnie Eriksson played in the first of only three games for us in this game but would go on to win 3 caps for Scotland.

The following week, the re-scheduled cup tie with Wasps was played and it proved to be a hard, gruelling encounter. Simon Halliday tweaked a hamstring, Jason Leonard had his right ankle and boot strapped up, David Pears had his nose broken and Mark Russell damaged medial ligaments in his right knee. As it was, Russell scored the opening try and Pears kicked a penalty before Clough scored a try for Wasps which Davies converted. At this point (30 minutes into the game) we lost Halliday and Russell who were replaced by Craig Luxton and Martin Hobley respectively. Before half time, Pears had added his second and third penalties to put us 13-6 ahead. Davies reduced the gap with a penalty but a dropped goal by Challinor and a late try from Langhorn sent us into the quarter finals. As the Five Nations Championship was still ongoing another friendly was played the following weekend; this time we had a trip to Headingley. Despite missing our internationals, we managed another victory; running in six tries to one in a 33-7 rout. Shortland and Alex Tupman went over in the first half when the home side's reply was a penalty goal and Jon Eagle (2), Molyneux and Luxton scored in the second period. Stuart Thresher kicked a penalty and three conversions to complete our scoring with Headingley adding their try.

On 22nd February, we again made the short journey to Roehampton to play Rosslyn Park. This time the prize was a place in the cup semi-finals. Before a crowd of 5,000 (said to have been the largest ever at Roehampton) an enthralling tie took place which was eventually decided just after 60 minutes. Up to that point, we had always been in front but two quick tries from Andy Harriman took us clear at 28-12. Harriman had started the scoring with a try after seven minutes and by half time, Glenister and Gavin Thompson had added others. Thresher kicked a penalty and a conversion. Park replied with a goal and a penalty by Graves to make it 17-9. He kicked his second penalty to reduce the deficit to five points but a penalty and conversion from Thresher and a second try by Glenister (added to those scores from Harriman) gave us a 34-12 win and a home semi against Leicester.

Since the Bath draw, our league form had started to slide and this was confirmed with a totally pointless trip to Bristol. The only score of the first half was a try by Davis for Bristol. In the second half Tainton converted both of Stiff's efforts and we had lost by sixteen points to nil.

A local derby against London Scottish at the Athletic Ground the following week ended in a 17-17 draw. David Currie, Ben Short and Chris Sheasby got our tries and Glenister kicked a penalty and a conversion. The Scots scored in identical fashion. Against Wakefield (in another friendly), we outscored our visitors by six tries to one but only managed to win by four points. A certain Rob Liley landed seven penalties and John Sleightholme scored their try. Challinor couldn't match the kicking prowess of Liley as he only managed a penalty and one conversion. He did score one of our tries though with others coming from Shortland, Adam Fox, Eagle, Wedderburn and Killick. This was Jon Eagle's final game for the 1st XV, having scored 34 tries (136 points) during his four and a half years at the Club. Ronnie Eriksson also made his final appearance, he would go on to join London Scottish. The league game with Saracens originally scheduled for 14th December was eventually played on 21st March and it proved to be another fruitless experience for us. We were missing seven men and were simply outplayed by the visitors. Pears kept us in front during the first half with a penalty and conversions of tries by Wedderburn and Fox. Saracens had scored a goal, a penalty and a try to trail 15-13 at half time. During a twenty minute spell in the second half, the Sarries scored twenty four unanswered points (three goals and two penalties) to put them 15-37 ahead. The game had been lost and Glenister's try (converted by Pears) was not even a consolation score. This defeat saw us drop to eighth place in the table and still not entirely safe from relegation (although we only needed one more win to be safe).

We would be playing Leicester two weeks in a row with the league fixture being followed by the semi-final clash. We outplayed the Tigers in the league game and led from the 20th minute onwards. They had opened the scoring with a penalty by Wills but tries from Sheasby and Pears (who converted his and added a penalty) left us 13-3 ahead at the half way point. Pears put over a second penalty before Thompson went over for our third try to kill the game off at 20-3 after 62 minutes. We then went to sleep allowing Leicester a goal and a try in the final 15 minutes to reduce the margin of victory. In the semi-final, David Pears was again a thorn in Leicester's side and scored all of our points. He was winning the penalty duel with John Liley by three to one when he received the ball from Winterbottom straight from a line out 20 metres from the Leicester line. As the defence came up to mark the centres, Pears dummied and was through to score by the posts. His conversion made it 15-3 at half time. The only score after this was a try from John Liley which he converted himself. He also missed a penalty with just a few minutes left and we spent the remaining time in the Tigers half of the field to book our place in the final against Bath.

In between, we had the small matter of league fixtures against Rugby (A) and Orrell and Gloucester (both at home). We started extremely well at Rugby and Pears kicked two penalties and converted Carling's try to put us 12-0 up after 21 minutes. Rugby pulled a try and a penalty back through Eddie Saunders and Mark Mapletoft (he would play for us some years later). Thompson and Pears added tries before the break and it looked good for us at 20-7. Unfortunately, we went to sleep and Mapletoft came into his own. We failed to score any more points whereas Rugby managed twenty two. Mapletoft scored a try and kicked a penalty, dropped a goal and added the conversions of a penalty try and one from M. Charles to leave the score at 29-20 to the home side. This win effectively secured Rugby's place in the top division for the following season.

On Easter Monday (20th April), we met Orrell at the Stoop and again suffered a defeat. Despite being totally dominated in the first half, we only trailed by a penalty goal to nil. Stuart Thresher levelled matters with a penalty but more Orrell pressure saw them score another penalty and a try. We did score the best try of the day when Thresher broke from deep and Halliday and Wedderburn exchanged passes along the touchline for the England centre to go over. Thresher missed the conversion and 7-10 is how it remained until the end of the game.

In our final league game against Gloucester, David Pears had kicked three penalties in the first 33 minutes and we were going along very nicely. Six minutes later, our chances not only in this game but in the cup final the following week were dealt an almost fatal blow when the referee (Steve Griffiths) sent off both Richard Langhorn and Mickey Skinner for allegedly stamping on Gloucester scrum half Marcus Hannaford. From the resultant penalty, Smith reduced the deficit to six points at half time. In the first half an hour of the second half, Gloucester gradually caught and passed our total with a goal and three more penalties. With the score at 9-18 and just ten minutes to go, we opened up with all guns blazing and first Challinor and then Carling went over for tries which Pears converted to put us 21-18 ahead. He then missed a penalty from in front of the posts and into the wind but the final whistle went and we had triumphed in the most extraordinary circumstances. If we had played like this all season, who knows what might have happened! Mickey Skinner played his final game for us in this one having led the side on eight occasions and scored 21 tries (84 points) during his career. The Middlesex disciplinary committee expedited the hearings for the two sent off and banned them both for a month.

And so, it all came down to the final game of the season, the Pilkington Cup Final at Twickenham on 2nd May against Bath; the holders against the only other side to have won the cup since 1984. To sort out our problems caused by losing Langhorn and Skinner, Dick Best managed to talk Paul Ackford out of retirement for one last fling. It would also be Simon Halliday's last game in our colours. Ackford had scored 5 tries (20 points) and Halliday 4 tries (16 points). As we had done in all our previous cup ties this season, we opened the scoring when Pears kicked a penalty after only two minutes. He then extended our lead by converting Winterbottom's try on 31 minutes. Webb pulled back three points with a penalty of his own before Pears got his second to stretch the lead to 12-3 at half time. We were playing out of our skins and Bath were worried. Webb pulled back another three points with his second penalty and then came a turning point when Fallon (on the wing for Bath) knocked-on in his own 22 but was allowed to continue almost up to our line. This came at a time when we were exerting a lot of pressure on Bath. From his run, de Glanville eventually crossed for Webb to add the conversion and tie the scores with ten minutes left. We applied the pressure in extra time but both Pears and Challinor crucially missed two dropped goal attempts each. Had Luxton (at scrum half) dummied from the base of the ruck, the whole Bath team would have charged offside and Pears would have kicked the winning penalty. But, unfortunately for us, he didn't. Bath cleared their lines, Wedderburn put in a bad defensive kick and the line out went to Bath. It was won by Redman and, as the ball came out to Stuart Barnes, he swung his leg and the ball wobbled over from 40 metres out. We had been beaten by a dropped goal with ten seconds remaining. The final whistle went and our cup dream was over. It had been a tremendous final and we had come so near yet ended up so far from retaining the trophy. When all is said and done, if those dropped goals from Pears and Challinor had gone over, it might have been so different. If only........

Our overall playing record was P29 W17 D2 L10 F664 A456 and in the league it was P12 W5 D1 L6 F213 A207 Pts11 Pos 8th. We had equalled our worst finishing position in the league but reached the cup final which meant that it was one of those "nearly successful" seasons. Tries scored fell by 25 to 102, dropped goals stayed the same (5), penalties fell by eight to 49 and conversions dropped sharply to 47 from 78. As a result of these reduced amounts, our points total was down by 186 to 664. Mike Wedderburn finished with the most tries (12), Paul Challinor dropped 4 goals and David Pears scored the most points with 172 (6 tries, 34 penalties and 23 conversions). Andy Mullins appeared in the most games again (22) and he was followed by Rob Glenister (19), Martin Hobley on 18 and Neil Edwards, Mike Molyneux, Steve Shortland and Gavin Thompson who all played in 17.

1991/92

070991	NORTHAMPTON	STOOP MEMORIAL GROUND	W	3G1DG1PG2T(32)-1G1DG2PG(15)
140991	PLYMOUTH ALBION	STOOP MEMORIAL GROUND	L	1G1PG(9)-2G3PG(21)
210991	LLANELLI	LLANELLI	W	3G1PG2T(29)-2G1DG3T(27)
280991	ASKEANS	KIDBROOKE	W	2G1PG3T(27)-0
251091	LONDON IRISH	STOOP MEMORIAL GROUND	W	3G4T(34)-1PG1T(7)
011191	CAMBRIDGE UNIVERSITY	CAMBRIDGE	L	1G2PG2T(20)-6G1PG1T(43)
091191	RUGBY	STOOP MEMORIAL GROUND	W	4G2PG3T(42)-1G1T(10)
161191	WASPS(JCL1)	SUDBURY	L	1G(6)-2G2T(20)
231191	NOTTINGHAM(JCL1)	STOOP MEMORIAL GROUND	W	1G3PG2T(23)-2PG(6)
301191	BEDFORD(PC3)	BEDFORD	W	2G3PG3T(33)-1PG(3)
071291	ROSSLYN PARK(JCL1)	ROEHAMPTON	W	1DG7PG(24)-3T(12)
141291	SARACENS(JCL1)	STOOP MEMORIAL GROUND	P	
211291	LONDON IRISH(JCL1)	SUNBURY	W	4G1PG3T(39)-1PG(3)
040192	BATH(JCL1)	STOOP MEMORIAL GROUND	D	2G2T(18)-2G2T(18)
110192	NORTHAMPTON(JCL1)	NORTHAMPTON	L	1DG1PG2T(14)-2G2DG1PG1T(25)
180192	SARACENS	SOUTHGATE	L	2PG1T(10)-2G2PG1T(22)
250192	WASPS(PC4)	SUDBURY	P	
010292	LONDON WELSH	STOOP MEMORIAL GROUND	W	4G1PG7T(55)-1PG1T(7)
080292	WASPS(PC4)	SUDBURY	W	1DG3PG2T(20)-1G1PG(9)

150292	HEADINGLEY	HEADINGLEY	W	3G1PG3T(33)-1PG1T(7)
220292	ROSSLYN PARK(PCQF)	ROEHAMPTON	W	2G2PG4T(34)-1G2PG(12)
290292	BRISTOL(JCL1)	BRISTOL	L	0-2G1T(16)
070392	LONDON SCOTTISH	RICHMOND	D	1G1PG2T(17)-1G1PG2T(17)
140392	WAKEFIELD	STOOP MEMORIAL GROUND	W	1G1DG5T(29)-7PG1T(25)
210392	SARACENS(JCL1)	STOOP MEMORIAL GROUND	L	3G1PG(21)-4G3PG1T(37)
280392	LEICESTER(JCL1)	STOOP MEMORIAL GROUND	W	1G2PG2T(20)-1G1PG1T(13)
040492	LEICESTER(PCSF)	STOOP MEMORIAL GROUND	W	1G3PG(15)-1G1PG(9)
110492	RUGBY(JCL1)	RUGBY	L	1G2PG2T(20)-2G1DG2PG2T(29)
200492	ORRELL(JCL1)	STOOP MEMORIAL GROUND	L	1PG1T(7)-2PG1T(10)
250492	GLOUCESTER(JCL1)	STOOP MEMORIAL GROUND	W	2G3PG(21)-1G4PG(18)
020592	BATH(PCF)	TWICKENHAM	L	1G2PG(12)-1G1DG2PG(15)AET

36

Sevens in the 1980s - Multi-coloured Magic!

1980-1989

The eighties were probably the most prolific period for Sevens when the number of tournaments was at an all-time high. We probably played in at least ten a year and won a large number of them during the glory years in the second part of the decade.

Both sides attempted to qualify for the Middlesex competition at Osterley again in 1980, the first Seven beat Shene Old Grammarians (36-3), Windsor (40-6), Old Walcountians I (12-6), Civil Service I (36-6) and London Welsh II (12-0) whereas the seconds won against Old Windsorians I (34-0) and Old Blues II (34-0) before going out to Old Whitgiftians I (10-12). Making up the Seven who got through were Everton Weekes (3 tries), Chris Pratt, Paul Jackson (7 tries), Chris St. J Lamden (1 try, 2 conversions), Graham Birkett (1 try), Billy Bushell (captain) (6 tries, 20 conversions) and Steve Simson (5 tries); Rick Lawrence was the reserve. In the next round a week later, we met Wasps I and despite tries from Lamden, Weekes and Jackson plus two conversions by Bushell, the final score was 16-24. Richmond I held on to their title with a 34-18 win over Rosslyn Park I in the final. We made the semi-final in the London Floodlit Sevens by beating London Scottish (28-0) and Fullerians (18-12) but went out to Rosslyn Park (6-8). Richmond had too much for Park in the final and won 30-18. In the Surrey Sevens, we reached the semi-final but won the Esher event for the fourth time in a row, beating London Welsh in the final. We started well in our own Sevens and beat Lansdowne (18-6) but lost to Stade Bagnérais (14-16) before managing to get through by winning against Orrell (28-4). We ended with eleven tries to their eight and met Heriot's F.P. in the final. They were the holders but we took the lead when Birkett scored for Lawrence to convert. Lawson went over for Heriot's and Yuille converted to make it 6-6 at half time. Stevens got another and when Pratt made a mistake, Marshall scored for Yuille to convert. Pratt did score and Lawrence converted but it was too late and we had lost in the final for the sixth time (12-16).

1981 saw us at the Old Paulines ground at Thames Ditton and Quins I saw off Wimbledon I (34-0), Sutton and Epsom I (16-3), Old Emanuel I (16-6) and Old Cranleighans I (34-0) to reach Twickenham. The second string fell at the last hurdle against Rosslyn Park II (12-13) after beating Bec Old Boys I (36-0), Old Wimbledonians II and Old Emanuel II. Dick Best led the side and was joined by Pratt, Weekes, Lawrence, Simon Halliday, Steve Moriarty and Dave Hodgkiss but they didn't score a point and went out to Blackheath I (0-10). Rosslyn Park I won the trophy by beating London Welsh I 16-14 in the final. In the Surrey Sevens, we beat Old Walcountians (12-0), Guildford and Godalming (16-0) and Shirley Wanderers (34-0) but lost to Rosslyn Park in the semi-final (0-18). London

Welsh beat us in the final at Esher to stop our winning run. At the London Floodlit tournament, our Seven was Pratt, Thomas, Best (captain), Brinkley, Lawrence, Halliday and John Butcher and they beat Rosslyn Park in the semi-final before going down to Wasps by 18-22 despite leading 14-4 at the interval. At the Stoop, it was business as usual in the losing stakes. We lost to Bridgend (0-34), Wasps (8-24) and Lord's Taverners (who were now involved in the event) 10-34. Bridgend went through from our Pool but lost to Rosslyn Park (18-28).

Both teams got through the following year with Quins I beating Richmond Thamesians I (26-0), Maidenhead (30-14), Reading (34-0) and West London Institute I (18-0). The seconds overcame Ealing I (14-0), West London Institute II (34-8), London Welsh II after extra time (14-10) and St. Mary's College I (22-0). Simson, R. Cheal, R. George, Hugh McHardy, Nick Ebel (captain), John Atkin and Geoff Ashby represented Quins II. They went down in their first game against Richmond I (10-20) with Atkin and McHardy scoring tries and the second named adding a conversion. The first Seven contained Best (captain), Iestyn Thomas, Birkett, Lawrence, Gilbert, Andre Dent and Moriarty. They beat Streatham/Croydon (36-6) with two tries each from Dent, Birkett and Lawrence (he also kicked all the conversions). In the next match, Swansea were beaten (16-12) with tries from Gilbert, Dent and Lawrence (who also converted twice). In the semi-final, Richmond I led 12-0 at half time before we rallied and got one back through Gilbert which Lawrence converted. It was not enough and they went on to lose against Stewart's Melville F.P. by 34-12. Our 1st VII reached the semi-final of the Surrey Sevens by beating Old Caterhamians (40-0), Metropolitan Police (28-10) and Richmond I (24-10) but lost to Blackheath (12-18). The second team went one better, beating Sutton and Epsom I (14-9), Old Reigatians, Kingston II (18-10) and Rosslyn Park (24-12) but also fell to Blackheath (18-22). Our Sevens was another good tournament and we did well in the Pool by beating Lansdowne (26-0), drawing with Newport (10-10) and winning against Moseley (30-12) to qualify for the final. Blackheath won the other Pool and went on to beat us by 22-12 just to confirm that they were a thorn in our side in 1982.

Osterley had become our regular ground for qualification now and the first Seven made it through by winning against St. Mary's Hospital II (36-6), Bracknell (28-0), Old Freemen's I (28-6) and London Welsh II (12-9). The second team defeated Southall College of Technology (34-0) but went out by a point to Oxford Old Boys I (19-20). Our squad on 7th May at Twickenham was Jackson, Alex Woodhouse, Birkett, Hodgkiss, Lawrence, Adrian Thompson (captain) and Chris Preston with Weekes and Dent as reserves. We easily beat Wasps I (22-4) and the holders (18-10) but went out in the semi-final again against London Welsh I (4-16). Richmond I grabbed their sixth win in ten years with a 20-13 win over the Welsh. We won the London Floodlit by beating Rosslyn Park in the final (18-12) and did the same at Surrey, Blackheath the beaten side. In our Sevens, Graham Birkett, Alex Woodhouse, Paul Jackson, Hugh McHardy, Rick Lawrence, Andre Dent and Chris Preston got off to a great start with wins over Waterloo (16-6), Heriot's F.P. (40-12) and Mont de Marsan (26-6) to reach the final against Cardiff. Lawrence scored two tries and converted them as well as others from Woodhouse and McHardy; Cardiff's response was a try and conversion by Ring. At last, we had done it and won the Wavell Wakefield Trophy. Sadly, Wavell (who became the Club's Patron in 1981) had died the month before.

At the Centaurs ground, Osterley on 28th April 1984, Woodhouse, Lawrence, Graham Halsey, Thompson, McHardy, Weekes and Jackson (with Atkin as reserve) represented Quins I. Rick Lawrence was a fantastic sevens player who frequently turned defence into attack (and tries) with his lazy kick over the advancing opponents. This was the beginning of a great era of sevens at the Club as the team was successful more often than not. They played Old Isleworthians and Halsey got the first try to give us a narrow lead at half time. In the second half, Lawrence (2) and Halsey got tries and McHardy added two conversions to make it 20-0. Old Blues II came next and Woodhouse, McHardy and Thompson took us clear. Lawrence converted all three as well as those from Jackson and Halsey. The Old Blues did get two converted tries back but we were comfortable winners (30-12). Uxbridge I went the same way as the tries kept coming through Weekes, Halsey and Woodhouse (Lawrence and McHardy (2) kicked the goals). Despite conceding a try after the break, further scores came from Halsey and Jackson. Both were converted by Lawrence to make the final score 30-4. Against R.E.M.E. Arborfield I, Woodhouse (2), Jackson, Lawrence, Halsey (2) and Atkin got tries and McHardy and Lawrence kicked two goals each to make it 36-0. Westminster Hospital blocked our path to the final rounds and they were also beaten easily. Halsey (2), Lawrence and Jackson got tries and Woodhouse, McHardy and Lawrence (2) kicked the goals in a 24-10 victory. The seconds were David Cooke, Haywood, Nick Chesworth, John Olver, Willie Jefferson, Peter Lillington and Dent and they started against Richmond Thamesians. Jefferson (2), Cooke, Dent and Chesworth got tries and Haywood (2) and Chesworth kicked the conversions (26-0). Rather confusingly, the two kickers both wore the number 15 on their shirts! A narrow victory followed against Uxbridge II and, despite going behind to a try, we rallied and a Jefferson double (both converted by Haywood) saw us through (12-4). Centaurs I held us at half time but we got the only scores afterwards to go through to the final game. Dent and Olver got two of the three tries and Haywood kicked all the conversions in an 18-6 win. In the last qualifying round, we met London Welsh II and, after they had taken a ten point lead, Jefferson scored to make it 4-10 at the break. A penalty by the Welsh kept them in front even though Jefferson got another for Haywood to convert. The last score was another try for the Welsh to knock us out (10-17). In the finals, Atkin was scheduled to come in for Halsey but we didn't get past the first game because Blackheath I knocked us out (0-10). It was a victory for London Welsh I over Heriot's F.P. in the final at the end of an exciting day of sevens (34-18). At Hersham, we almost defended the Surrey title with wins over John Fisher Old Boys (18-0), Old Rutlishians I (40-0), London Irish (22-0) and Rosslyn Park (18-10). In the final, we met Blackheath for the third year in a row but went down 12-22. Our second team scratched to give Sutton and Epsom II a walk over. We reached the quarter final at the Old Belvedere Sevens but won the Sevenoaks, London Floodlit (30-12 against Cambridge University) and Kilmarnock tournaments. We competed at the Richmond Invitation Sevens but lost to Blackheath (12-22) in our first game before winning against West London Institute (22-16) and St. Mary's Hospital (30-0). It wasn't enough to qualify because Blackheath won all their games. The Sunshine Sevens at East Grinstead and the Haig International tournament were also visited. As holders, we put up a poor defence at the Stoop and lost all three games to Ballymena (12-22), Orrell (16-18) and Swansea (12-17). In the final, Bridgend won easily against Swansea by 44-16.

At Osterley in 1985, Quins II were in the top half of the draw and were represented by Knight, Thomas, Lillington, Stuart Thresher, Cook, Quist-Arcton and Haywood. They defeated Kingston Polytechnic I (24-0), Old Blues II (22-4) and Richmond Thamesians I (30-0) before going out to West London Institute I (6-14). The scorers were Knight (3 tries), Thomas (1 try), Lillington (1 try), Stuart Thresher (1 try, 11 conversions), Cook (2 tries), Quist-Arcton (6 tries) and Haywood (1 try). Quins I featured Jackson, Hunter, Dent, Woodhouse, Olver, Chris Preston and Lawrence and they walked through the qualifying by winning against Old Haileyburians II (48-0), Kingston Polytechnic I (24-6), R.E.M.E. Arborfield I (22-6) and Centaurs II (24-6). Their points were scored by Jackson (1 try), Hunter (9 tries), Dent (2 tries), Woodhouse (4 tries, 1 conversion), Olver (1 try), Chris Preston (3 tries), Lawrence (1 try, 17 conversions) and 1 penalty try. For the final rounds, Thompson replaced Preston and all was going well because we knocked out the holders with three tries from Hunter (12-4) and West London Institute I (32-4) as the tries continued to flow; there were six from Hunter (2), Olver (2), Dent and Lawrence (who kicked four conversions) before coming up against Nottingham in the semi-final. Hunter scored another and Lawrence converted but the guest side were 10-6 up by half time. A try from Olver (again converted by Lawrence) looked to be enough but Moon scored near the end and we had failed again. Wasps won the final 25-6 but a multi-coloured wind was about to blow at the Middlesex tournament and what a great time it would be! Some of the other tournaments we entered did produce trophies as we won at Old Belvedere and Sevenoaks but lost in the final to London Irish at Surrey and in the first round at Esher. At the Stoop, our Sevens took place on 1st September and Andre Dent, Marcus Rose, Hugh McHardy, Rick Lawrence, Adrian Thompson, John Olver and Alex Woodhouse made up the team. They beat the U.S. Cougars with tries from Thompson, Lawrence, McHardy and Olver plus a conversion by Rose (18-0) and followed this up with one over Saltires. Thompson and Olver (2) produced the tries and Rose added two more conversions. Saltires did pull six points back but we were comfortable enough. Nottingham were next and Lawrence, Woodhouse (2), McHardy and Rose (2) got the tries with Rose kicking two more conversions (28-0). In the final, we met Kelso from Scotland and this turned out to be a tight affair. Woodhouse opened the scoring, Rose converted and we were on our way. Hogarth and Tait (converted by Brown) scored either side of one by Dent to leave it all square at half time. Olver regained the lead for Rose to convert before Jeffrey grabbed two unconverted tries to put Kelso in front with time almost up. From the restart, Thompson burst through to score the match winning try (20-18).

By 1986, the number of teams entering the Middlesex competition was 290 and we took our place in the preliminary rounds. The second Seven lost in Round 5 to London Welsh I (12-20) but the firsts did get through at the expense of Hampstead I (36-0), Civil Service I (34-0), Hammersmith and Fulham (24-6) and London Welsh II ((22-4). The side was Mickey Skinner, John Olver, Andre Dent, Alex Woodhouse, Rick Lawrence (captain), Adrian Thompson and Simon Hunter and they started off well with a win over Wasps II (22-0). Olver, Woodhouse, Thompson and Lawrence got the tries with the last named also converting three. In the next round we faced the holders Wasps I and with tries from Dent and Thompson (2) and three more conversions from Lawrence, it was enough to see us through (18-10). In the semi-final, we met Saracens I and Olver, Thompson and Hunter scored tries (Lawrence converted two) in a 16-4 victory. In the final, we met Nottingham and, after Hartley opened the scoring, Dent scored for Lawrence to convert and we led at half time. As we took control, Woodhouse and Hunter added tries and Lawrence converted both before Moon scored for Hodgkinson to convert. Time expired and we had won our first Middlesex tournament for eight years. At Sevenoaks, we beat Blackheath in the final 24-3, in Dublin at the Old Belvedere Sevens, Greystones were also beaten in the final (16-14) and at the Surrey finals, we beat Sutton and Epsom II (24-6), Rosslyn Park II (18-10), Old Blues (20-6) and London Welsh (36-6) to reach the final. London Irish led 10-0 but we came storming back to win 24-16. Lawrence kicked 19 conversions and scored a try with the other tries coming from Hunter (7), Woodhouse (6), Salmon (3), Hodgkiss (3) and Dent. The other members of the squad were Thomas, Abibuah and Stork. The defence of our own Sevens was in the hands of Everton Davis, Mickey Skinner, John Olver, Andre Dent, Marcus Rose, Adrian Thompson, Simon Hunter and Graham Halsey. In their first game against Sale, Thompson got the first try followed by more from Hunter (2) and Rose (who also kicked three conversions) (22-0). It was tighter against Paris Université Club and although we took the lead with another try from Hunter (converted by Rose), the French were in front 10-6 at the break. Olver scored and Rose converted but the French scored again and it took a last minute 80 yard run from Hunter to get us home (16-14). It was easy against Selkirk with tries from Olver, Davis, Thompson and Rose (he converted two) making it 20-0. In the final, we met the Lord's Taverners and took the lead with a try from Thompson which Rose converted. The Taverners came back with two goals to lead at half time. The second half belonged entirely to us and Hunter, Davis and Dent saw us home with Rose supplying two more conversions (22-12).

With only one team needing to qualify the following year, our second Seven went to Sunbury and beat Guy's Hospital II (24-0) before going out after extra time to London Irish I (10-13). Simon Cooke, David Thresher, Stuart Thresher, Mark Sly, Rob Glenister, Everton Davis and Jim McCall made up the side and Paul Jackson replaced David Thresher in the second game. Stuart Thresher kicked four conversions and Glenister one; tries came from Davis (5) and Glenister. This was the first year for live television coverage of the Middlesex Sevens and the crowd of 55,000 were as enthusiastic as ever. Quins I were Skinner, Olver, Dent, Woodhouse, Thompson, Hunter and Harriman (Cramb replaced him in the final). This seven was becoming known as the Designer Seven because of their trendy hair, collars tucked in their shirts, pre-match meditation huddles and Caribbean-style hand-slapping. They were a fantastic outfit with a team spirit and pace to burn. Andrew Harriman was now without doubt the fastest man ever seen on a rugby pitch and the others fitted in wherever they played. Their first match in defence was against Richmond I and that ended 22-0. Blackheath I led 10-6 at the break but were blown away in the end and couldn't add to their score; we scored twenty four points in the second half. The semi-final brought Wakefield and after we had taken a 16-0 lead in the first half, they came back to tie it up right on the final whistle; sudden-death extra time followed and with a kick and chase, Dent was over in the corner and we were through to the final again. Rosslyn Park II provided the opposition and during a physical game, Harriman and Martin Offiah (the two flyers) were both injured and got carried off, the crowd started singing "Swing Low, Sweet Chariot" (thought by some to be an old slavery song) and the rest, as they say, is history. There are other stories of how this song has been sung for years in relation to rugby but this was definitely the beginning of the modern trend of singing it at Twickenham. Back to the final, we led 6-0 at half time, Park pegged us back but the power came through and three tries took us to a 22-6 win and our tenth title. Tries in the four games came from Skinner (2), Olver, Dent, Woodhouse (2), Thompson (3), Hunter (3), Harriman (4) and Hunter added 13 conversions. With Twickenham bringing the curtain down on the Sevens season, we had entered seven other tournaments and won the lot! An unprecedented run of ten consecutive Sevens titles (if you include our own back in September 1986). There was the Old Belvedere over in Dublin where we beat Wanderers (24-0), Old Wesley (22-6) and Bective Rangers (10-6) to reach the final. There we met Lansdowne and took the lead with a try from Woodhouse, converted by Lawrence. The Irish side came back with two unconverted tries but Lawrence converted his own score to make it 12-8 at half time. Hunter added a third and converted Woodhouse's second to take us clear. A goal for Lansdowne made the final score 22-14. It was our third win on the trot and fifth in total at the event. The place where it all started was Melrose and we made our first appearance this year. Harriman, McCall, Hunter, Glenister, Skinner, Woodhouse and David Thresher represented us and won against Stewart's-Melville (24-6), Hawick (30-0) and Jedforest (10-4) before meeting Melrose in the final. Harriman scorched over for two tries from his own half, McLeish pulled one back but Hunter (2) and Woodhouse made the game safe. Glenister added four conversions and a late try from Ramsay made it 28-8. At Roehampton, the London Floodlit Sevens was always hotly contested and we qualified for the semi-final with wins over London Irish (22-12) and Saracens (34-6). Against Park in that semi, we won 16-10 before meeting London Scottish in the final. Hunter opened the scoring, McCall added a second and Glenister converted both. The response was an unconverted try and it came far too late to cause any damage. The squad was Simon Cooke, Hunter, Sheasby, Harriman, Glenister, Thompson, Stuart Thresher, Olver, McCall and Skinner. At Esher, we defeated Rosslyn Park with a last second Glenister try and conversion from the touchline by Thresher (18-16). We beat Glamorgan Wanderers at the Berkshire Sevens (16-8) and retained the Sevenoaks title by beating Blackheath 16-10. At Sunbury, we won against St. Thomas's Hospital (22-6), Worthing (16-6), scored twenty four points against Old Reedonians and were on our way early in the final against Rosslyn Park when Brady scored for Thresher to convert.

Park equalised but Davis went the length of the pitch to score under the posts, Jackson added another and Thresher (who converted the first two) scored himself to make it 22-6. Davis, Thompson, Andy Johnson, Woodhouse, McCall, Brady and Skinner travelled to Selkirk in August and beat Jedforest (18-16), Kilmarnock (28-6) and Kelso (18-12). In the final, they met Wakefield (who were still smarting from the defeat at Twickenham back in May) and it was all-square at the break. Thompson scored and Johnson converted after Rawnsley (converted by Adamson) had put Wakefield ahead. Woodhouse put us ahead but Scully scored in the corner and Adamson converted to send us to defeat (10-12). A week later, they were guests at our Sevens and proceeded to beat us again. This time it was a pool match (0-10) and although we beat Saracens (12-0) and Newport (28-6), they won all three and went on to beat Lansdowne in the final (24-6).

A week after the fantastic John Player Special Cup win over Bristol, we returned to Twickenham to defend the Sevens title. Obviously Quins I had qualified and Quins II also got through by beating Bank of England I (24-6), Lensbury I (36-0), Sutton and Epsom II (26-4) and Esher I (30-6). The crowd of 65,000 saw a great competition (if you were a Quins fan!). The second string came on first and beat Worthing I 22-10; the firsts then defeated London Irish I 20-0. The two then met in the 7th Round and I beat II in a tight contest by 16-4 (the seconds wore Middlesex shirts to avoid confusion). Cork Constitution were demolished 32-0 and that set up a repeat of the cup final against Bristol. As had happened the previous week, we shot out of the blocks and led 16-0 at half time. Bristol came back to 16-12 before Woodhouse broke clear for the winning score and a late goal for the guest side only altered the final score (20-18). The winning Seven were Olver, Dent (captain), Woodhouse, Richard Moon, Hunter, Harriman and Davis. It would have been interesting to see what would have happened if the two Sevens hadn't been on a collision course. We did win the Surrey Sevens by beating Blackheath in the final. At the Stoop, we beat U.S. Cougars (18-12), Stade Toulousain (18-12) and Hawick (22-8) before meeting Llanelli in the final. Eagle scored two tries (Cramb converted one) to put us 10-0 up but the Scarlets rattled up 21 points to a try from Johnson to run out winners (14-21). The rest of our Seven was Thomas, Brady, Dent (captain) and Moon.

In the last tournament of the decade, the second Seven failed at the last to qualify when they lost to Rosslyn Park II (10-12). The all-conquering 1st VII was becoming a shoe-in for the last game of Round 6 at 2.50 p.m. This time, the team was Sheasby, Peter Winterbottom, Glenister, Stuart Thresher, Jon Eagle (captain), Jay Johnston and Thompson. Because of injuries, unavailability and leavers, none of last year's winning Seven were in the side. In fact, Dent, Hunter and Woodhouse were all playing for Rosslyn Park I. The first match was against West London Institute and, after being held to 12-10 just after half time, we stretched away to double our score with no response from the students. Against Wasps I it was tighter and the score was 10-10 until Eagle scored to take us through (16-10). In the semi-final against the favourites London Scottish I, we left it very late. At half time it was 6-6, the Scots scored again and converted whereas when Johnston scored, the conversion was missed. With a minute left, we were two points down. Sheasby was on our line and he fed Eagle who made it to the Scottish 22, as he was tackled, his pass inside found Sheasby and he went under the posts for the winning score (16-12). We had made our fourth final in a row and who would we meet? Rosslyn Park I of course with their ex-Quins contingent. Sheasby opened the scoring and Thresher converted before Jermyn scored and converted his own score to make it all-square at the interval. This was the point where the crowd sang Auld Lang Syne to the soon to be demolished North stand. When play resumed, Glenister and Eagle scored for Thresher to convert and we were clear. Wyles did score the last try, Jermyn converted, the final whistle went and we had equalled the achievements of Quins I way back in 1926-29 and London Scottish from 1960-63. Our try scorers on the day were Sheasby (4), Johnston (4), Eagle (3), Glenister and Thresher (who kicked eleven conversions).

Could we achieve the impossible dream in 1990 of five on the trot? The Old Belvedere tournament was won again with a different team to what we had become accustomed to (M. Cass, A. Clayton, Sheasby, C. McGlue, Thresher, A. Ward and A. Hunn). They defeated University College Dublin (18-12), Old Belvedere (22-0) and squeezed past Wanderers 6-4 in the semi-final. In the final, London Irish were the opponents and Geoghegan opened the scoring for Mullin to convert before Andy Clayton and Sheasby got tries for us (Thresher converted both) to make it 12-6 at the half way point. Alex Hunn and Thresher (who converted both) got further tries and 24-6 was the final score. The Wang National Sevens took place for the first time at Richmond Athletic Ground, bringing together the top sides in England in a straight knockout. We had a strong side out - Sheasby, Luxton, Thresher, Moon (captain), Adam Cleary, Carling, Eagle, Davis and Winterbottom. We played in the first game against Coventry and Luxton got the first try (converted by Thresher) before they got a try. A two try burst from Eagle (both converted by Thresher) took us clear and a goal from Coventry did nothing to stop our progress (18-10). Saracens were beaten next and Cleary (2), Luxton and Davis supplied the tries, Thresher converted three and Sarries scored the same as our previous opponents had (22-10). In the semi-final, Sheasby and Luxton scored in the first half (Thresher again on target) and even though Bristol scored two tries, Davis scored in between and Thresher's conversion ensured another final appearance (18-10). In that final, we met old rivals Wasps and no one could have predicted what would happen next. It was a procession of multi-coloured tries as Moon, Davis, Moon and Thresher crossed the line. Thresher converted all four and it was 24-0 at the break. Nothing changed in the second half and Sheasby, Moon, Thresher, Eagle (2) and Sheasby again added tries. Thresher converted three of them to end the massacre with the scoreboard showing Quins 54 Wasps 0! In our Sevens, another failure. We beat Melrose 34-0 but lost to Bridgend (10-20) and Nottingham (12-18) and the Welsh side went on to beat Bristol 24-16 in the final.

37

Another Cup Final but No Success on Either Front 1992-1996

Following on from Red Star, it was announced on 15th September that Whitbread had signed a sponsorship deal worth £50,000 per annum over four years. New computer ticketing arrangements were in place for all home games and the privilege of members to bring a guest into a home game free of charge was withdrawn. Membership was now approaching the 2000 mark thanks to the opening up of the Club. On 17th November, more ground development projects being looked at were listed as follows:–

a) Developing the back of the present clubhouse.
b) Building a stand on the east side of the pitch with additional facilities incorporated.
c) A super stadium similar to Celtic Stadium.
d) Comprehensive development of the whole ground including a supermarket, cinema, petrol station, bowling alley etc.

On 16th February, it was announced that Ray Harrison (1954-55) had died the previous week from cancer. Peter Brook (1928-51), Bob Crichton (1936-40) and Micky Grant (1951-62) also passed away during the season. On 18th May, the ground development budget for 1993/94 was revealed. The main refurbishment and extension of the clubhouse £250,000, external works £48,450 and a new telephone system, camera platform and commentary box £15,000. A very small surplus of £856 was made in 1992/93.

After the bitter disappointment of the defeat in the cup final, we were looking for a good start to Peter Winterbottom's final season of captaincy. At Northampton on 5th September in a friendly, two Stuart Thresher penalties were not enough to stop us trailing by seven points at half time. John Steele had kicked a couple of penalties and converted a try by Rob McNaughton. In the second half, Northampton scored first and last (a try from Pask and a penalty by Steele) but in between, we just failed to do enough to secure victory. Stuart Thresher put a penalty over and converted a Chris Sheasby try to leave us trailing by five points at the end (16-21). This game saw the first played by us where the points for a try had been increased to five from four (the four point try having lasted for some twenty one seasons). As it was, it made no difference to the result except to make the margin of defeat one point more.

Against Askeans at the Stoop the following Wednesday, we welcomed Alex Snow for the first of 95 appearances in the first team. We were still missing our England internationals but most of them would return the following

Saturday against Plymouth Albion. It was a procession of tries against Askeans with a total of fourteen being scored. Stuart Thresher got a try, a penalty and six conversions to finish with 20 points. The other tries were scored by Paul Challinor, Everton Davis (2), Simon Dear, Adam Fox (2), Andy Harriman (2), Mark Russell (2), Alex Snow, Steve Thompson and a penalty try. Askeans managed twelve points in reply but the final score read 85-12. This was our highest score at home since the Royal Air Force had been thrashed at Twickenham on 24th January 1976.

The trip to Plymouth saw seven changes from the Askeans game; among the incoming were Will Carling, Brian Moore and Chris Sheasby. This proved to be another try scoring feast from us and another ten were registered through Simon Dear, Andy Harriman (3), Rob Jardine-Brown (2), David Pears, Mark Russell, Stuart Thresher and Mike Wedderburn. Thresher added two conversions and two penalties and Pears and Challinor each got a conversion to make the final score 64-6. For Albion, Andy Berry dropped two goals in the first half.

Our new coach was Bob Templeton who had coached the Australian national side and was currently assistant coach to Bob Dwyer. He returned from helping to prepare them for their tour of Britain and was straight into our first league match of the season against Bath at the Recreation Ground. Once again, we did not play well and, after taking an early lead with a Pears penalty after three minutes, we faded and paid the price. Jon Webb had landed two penalties for Bath when disaster struck after 20 minutes. Carling sent a hospital pass to Pears who had his jaw fractured in three places by the resulting tackle. After this, Pears never regained his form and his career went into a downward spiral. In fact, he didn't play again until the following season. Webb added another penalty before half time and a fourth three minutes into the second half before Challinor pulled three points back with his only penalty success. A minute later, Guscott got a try for Bath which Webb converted. He followed this up with his fifth penalty after 56 minutes to wrap up the points as no further scoring ensued. We did slightly better in our next game against Wasps at the Stoop but still ended up losing. Peter Winterbottom made his first appearance of the season to become our fourth captain (the others had been Adam Fox, Andy Mullins and Brian Moore). Once again, an injury didn't help us when Paul Challinor broke his nose in a collision with Winterbottom after just five minutes. We were trailing 5-0 at this point but by half time, Stuart Thresher had landed two penalties to put us one point ahead. With twelve minutes left, Dean Ryan had put Simon Dear out of the game with an elbow in the face, Emeruwa had scored a try and Buzza had converted and landed a penalty to put Wasps 15-6 ahead. With enough possession to have won, we could only manage one try by Mark Evans which Thresher converted with the last kick of the game to put us within two points but it wasn't enough.

We next faced the long trip to newcomers West Hartlepool at Brierton Lane (they had also suffered two defeats, against Wasps and Bristol). We were not playing well and it took four penalties from Paul Challinor to take us to our first points of the season. Stabler kicked three for the home side but referee Steve Lander denied them a victory at the last. He penalised their winger Dave Cooke for a double movement in the act of scoring and we survived. London Scottish (the other newcomers) were our next opponents at the Stoop. We exploded from the blocks and Will Carling was the recipient of a pass from Mark Evans (after he had broken through the defence) to score a try after only 29 seconds. Thresher added a penalty with the wind on 15 minutes before the Scots pulled three points back with a penalty of their own. We looked to have sewn the game up with further tries from Sheasby and Wedderburn (both converted by Thresher) to give us a 22-3 lead at the interval. The Scots never gave up and crept back into it with a try and a penalty before we lost Neil Edwards with a shoulder injury after 66 minutes. When White got their second try with ten minutes left, the alarm bells started ringing but we still couldn't finish them off. Grecian landed two penalties (the second with the last kick of the game) to hand the visitors a deserved draw at 22-22. Yet again, we had thrown away a handsome interval lead to give our opponents at least a share of the spoils. With only eight league matches left, our chances of recording our first title win were already looking slim.

England met Canada the next weekend and so it was deemed as a non-league weekend. Bedford from division two were our visitors and a close game was produced. We were forced to make eleven changes from the team which faced London Scottish due to the England game and also the London Division meeting Ulster. Johannes Roux made his debut at scrum half and would go on to win eleven caps for South Africa whilst making only five appearances for us. After Stuart Thresher had landed a penalty, Gavin Thompson powered over from 15 metres out and Adam Fox also scored after a multi-handling movement. Bedford had scored two penalties and a try themselves to leave the score at 13-11 to us at the break. The first 20 minutes of the second half saw Bedford's forwards start to dominate and this led to them scoring two goals to lead by twelve points. We came storming back with tries of our own through Fox and Sheasby which Thresher converted to put us 27-25 ahead but, in injury time we allowed Chandler on the right wing to fly hack ahead and score the match winning try for the visitors. This was our fourth defeat in eight matches this season and with four sides being relegated, our league form needed to improve drastically.

Our chance came on 24th October when we visited Southgate to take on Saracens. In the home side were three future Quins; Daren O'Leary, Justyn Cassell and Tony Diprose. Paul Challinor gave an excellent performance and his tactical kicking gained good yardage. In the first seventeen minutes we scored a penalty by Stuart Thresher and a try from Rob Glenister (converted by Thresher). The only other score was a penalty for the home side by Rudling. A downpour at the start of the second half slowed things down a bit but our domination was confirmed with a penalty and a try by Thresher to make the final score 18-3.

Our next visitors were London Irish and they were weakened by the loss of five players on international duty. Challinor was again in top form and he got on the score sheet with our first try. Will Carling added a second but the rest of our twenty three points in the half came from the boot of Stuart Thresher (three penalties and two conversions). Mike Corcoran (another future Quin) landed a penalty after 12 minutes to get the exiles on the board. Within eleven minutes of the restart, Glenister scored a try, Thresher converted and Harriman got another try to put us 35-3 ahead. Corcoran got a quick-fire hat-trick of penalties but Glenister scored his second try, Thresher again converted as well as scoring our sixth try. This gave him a personal haul of twenty two points and at 47-12 the game was over. A late rally by the Irish gave them a goal and a try to leave us winners by 23 clear points.

Our following two games were friendlies against Cambridge University and Nottingham, both at the Stoop. Despite missing four key players on international duty, we came through both games with flying colours. In the first, Challinor (2), Gavin Thompson (2), Harriman, Snow and Kent Bray got tries and the last named also kicked three conversions. The reply from the Students ran to a try and two penalties. Against Nottingham, we trailed 5-13 at half time but rallied in the second half to run out 27-16 winners. Tries from Mark Russell, Andy Parton and Nick Killick (2) plus two conversions and a penalty by Bray saw us home. The following week it was back to league action when Northampton were the visitors. We were in sixth place with the Saints just one place ahead of us and they stayed in front after winning a close encounter. They led 6-0 at half time with two penalties from John Steele with all the remaining scores coming in the first twelve minutes of the second half. Paul Challinor got a try and Thresher converted to edge us one point ahead. Steele kicked his third penalty after 51 minutes and two minutes later Matt Dawson dropped a goal. Had we taken our chances in the first 25 minutes, the result could have been so different but, as it was, we had suffered our third league defeat of the season.

On 29th November, we started our bid for a third successive cup final when we met Blackheath at the Stoop in the third round. For all Blackheath's efforts, they couldn't match our overall strength and our biggest ever victory in the cup was on the cards. After only four minutes, Rob Glenister got the first of his two first half tries, Thresher converted and Andy Mullins (converted by Thresher), Dear, and Glenister again took us into a 24-3 lead. Eagle kicked a penalty for Blackheath but it was already far too late for them to retrieve the game. A second half stroll in the park led to eight more tries through Harriman, Thompson, Edwards, Parton, Russell, Challinor, Glenister and Winterbottom. Thresher's four conversions left the final score at 72-3 and we had achieved our best ever total in the cup.

Our final game of the year was a local derby with Richmond on 28th December at the Stoop. A total of twelve changes were made from the side which ended the Blackheath cup tie but it made no difference to the end result. We started off well and were 15-0 up in 25 minutes before Richmond staged a fight back to lead at half time. Jeff Alexander and Richard Goodwin got tries and Stuart Thresher got one conversion and a penalty. For Richmond, Lamb, Cooper and Morris got tries and Elliott converted one to make it 15-17. They stretched the lead to seven points when Hutton scored a try on 43 minutes but we came back with tries from Jerry Simpson-Kent and Mike Wedderburn and a conversion by Thresher to lead 27-22 after 64 minutes. It was end to end stuff and the hectic pace continued as Morris kicked a penalty for the visitors with eight minutes left but Osman scored our fifth try for Thresher to convert three minutes later to put us clear. Richmond did have the last word with Greenwood getting their fifth try but we held out to win 34-30. Neil Edwards made his last appearance in this game and had scored 25 tries (101 points) and captained the side in three games during his five and a half seasons at the Club.

The first scheduled game of 1993 was at Webb Ellis Road against Rugby but the fixture was cancelled and so it was to Edge Hall Road we travelled on 9th January to take on the might of Orrell. This was our fifth visit to the ground and we still had to achieve anything but losses. Things looked good when Stuart Thresher got a try after only four minutes but Challinor was off target with his conversion attempt. Taberner equalised for the home side eleven minutes later but Challinor slotted over a couple of penalties either side of a Mike Wedderburn try. Once again the conversion was missed which left us 16-5 up at half time. Will Carling had twisted an ankle and left the field to be replaced by Kent Bray and Thresher was injured trying to prevent Cleary from scoring their second try and he was replaced by hooker Nick Killick. The home side's kicker (Ainscough) was not having a good time, he had missed both conversions and completely squandered two golden opportunities to score tries. He did eventually put over a penalty and chipped to the corner for Hamer to score the winning try with eleven minutes left. Another league defeat had been suffered when the points had been in the bag at half time.

The following week a friendly with Saracens at the Stoop produced four penalties for Bray and a try for Wedderburn but the result was a draw (17-17). Wakefield travelled South for a fourth round cup tie and went away with their tails between their legs. It was effectively all over after just 24 minutes as we led 21-0. Bray and Challinor had scored tries as we ripped into the Yorkshire outfit with a vengeance. Challinor put over a conversion and three penalties and before half time also converted Sheasby's try. Future Harlequin Rob Liley pulled back three points with a penalty but at 28-3 we could afford to ease up. Liley's second penalty six minutes into the second half woke us up and we replied with tries from Winterbottom and Thompson and another conversion from Challinor. A goal and a try made the scoreline a bit more respectable but Challinor converted his own try to make it 47-18 and bring his tally to 27 points (a record score for a Quins player in the cup). The previous high was twenty four by David Pears against Clifton in 1990.

A mass brawl near the end of the friendly with London Irish at Sunbury saw Verling sent off for the home side but, with twenty players taking part in the punch-up, it was amazing no-one else followed him. As it was, three Challinor penalties and a Wedderburn try saw us home 14-6. After building a nice 22-0 lead at Blackheath with only 15 minutes left, we nearly blew it again (Jeff Alexander, David Thresher, Mike Molyneux and Gavin Thompson got tries and Kent Bray added one conversion) as the home side conjured two tries (both converted) and a penalty but we just held on. In our next game, Bristol visited the Stoop for a league encounter. We dominated proceedings but could only manage a dropped goal and a penalty from Challinor in the first half. Will Carling scored a try eleven minutes after the break but it wasn't until Sheasby went over near the end that the points were safe. This win eased our relegation worries but we still required one win from our last three matches to make sure of survival.

Headingley had now merged with Roundhay to become Leeds and they came to the Stoop for a friendly on 20th February. Rather like the Askeans game, this turned into a complete romp for us and we registered twelve tries. Leeds had several men playing for Yorkshire in the County Championship whereas we had made thirteen changes from the Bristol line up. Andy Harriman led the way with five tries in his final first team game (he had scored 51 tries (217 points) during his career) followed by Ben Kefford (2), Will Kefford (2), Gavin Thompson, David Thresher and David Dix and Stuart Thresher finished with 23 points (ten conversions and a penalty). Leeds managed a goal and a try to make the final score 83-12 but they had been well and truly beaten.

The long trip to Blundellsands in the cup quarter finals to play Waterloo was undertaken on 27th February and a good tie it turned out to be. Waterloo had beaten Lichfield (39-8), and amazingly Bath (9-8) and Orrell (8-3) in previous rounds so it wasn't going to be easy. The home side dominated the early exchanges and went ahead on 13 minutes when their scrum half (Saverimutto) touched down as the ball reached the line in our scrum (he had earlier hit the crossbar with a dropped goal attempt). The conversion was missed and Challinor nudged us ahead with two penalties before Swindells got one for Waterloo. Right on half time Wedderburn ran in from 40 metres out, Challinor converted and we led by five points. A Challinor penalty after 54 minutes stretched the lead before Handley pulled back another three points in similar fashion. While this was going on, four of our forwards (Leonard, Moore, Mullins and Snow) had to change their boots or studs. Waterloo complained about the length of our studs in an effort to disrupt our scrummage (as they had done against Orrell). A blizzard then blew up but nothing was going to stop us from reaching our eighth semi-final. Jason Leonard began a counter attack; the ball was passed onto Russell, Roux (making his final appearance before returning to South Africa), Challinor, Sheasby and Thompson before Bray went over for our second try. Handley landed his second penalty with ten minutes to go but excellent defence kept the home side at bay and we progressed by twenty one points to fourteen. Afterwards, with Waterloo still complaining about an injury to Swindells, it was revealed that Richard Langhorn had a fractured cheekbone and Winterbottom and Mullins required stitches. It was a tough cup tie and we had deservedly knocked out the giant killers.

On Saturday 6th March, a Quins XV took on Hindu from Argentina who were on a pre-season tour. With England playing in the afternoon, this one was a morning kick-off so it didn't clash. The first score came after 30 minutes when Steve Thompson ran through for a try and added another before the break. Early in the second half, Phil Osman added a third and converted as he did with a fourth scored by Julian Bailey. Hindu came back into it, scored two tries and converted one before laying siege to our line for the last ten minutes. They couldn't score again and we had won by 24-12.

Our next two matches were in South Africa of all places as we had been invited to take part in the MNET Nite Series featuring Eastern Province, Namibia, Northern Transvaal, Orange Free State, Rest of South Africa, South African Barbarians and Transvaal. Our first game was against Orange Free State at Ellis Park, Johannesburg on 9th March. Appearing as a guest for us in this match was England international Wade Dooley. The Free State squandered four try scoring opportunities and their fly half missed three out of five penalty attempts. In contrast,

Paul Challinor had a great game and kicked three penalties, dropped a goal and converted a try by Dooley eight minutes from the end. We moved into the semi-finals to play Transvaal two days later and in the first eight minutes, Challinor missed two penalties and a dropped goal. After this, Transvaal took control against our weakened side (four of our internationals had come back to England early) but we did put in a brave performance. Challinor scored all our points with two penalties and another dropped goal but Transvaal turned a 22-6 half time advantage into a 36-9 victory to move into the final. Dooley eventually gained 55 caps for England and made his second and final appearance in this game.

Our scheduled game with Wakefield on 13th March had been cancelled due to our South African commitment so our next game was against Coventry in a morning kick-off at the Stoop. We achieved our highest ever score against them in fixtures dating back to 1894 whilst passing the fifty point mark for the fifth time this season. Mike Wedderburn and Jeff Alexander both crossed three times with Dear and Dix getting the others. Stuart Thresher landed four conversions and two penalties to leave the final score at 54-18. Our tenth league match was at Welford Road against Leicester and what a miserable afternoon it turned out to be. We had won four out of the five league meetings between the sides but trailed in this one at half time to a Harris dropped goal and a Liley penalty. In the second half we still couldn't get on the scoreboard and seventeen more points for the Tigers took them to a 23-0 victory.

We still needed that one win and as our next opponents (Rugby) were already relegated, surely it must come against them. We started well enough and Jeff Alexander opened the scoring after nine minutes with a try which Challinor converted. He repeated the feat five minutes later and, although Challinor failed to convert, he did add a penalty after half an hour. The fifteen point lead at half time went to eighteen with Challinor's second penalty before Rugby opened their account with a goal. A brace of tries from Peter Winterbottom (on his last appearance as captain at the Stoop) and one from Challinor (who also landed one conversion) took us to safety at 35-7. Seven minutes from the end the visitors got their second goal to pull seven points back but we were home and dry and another season of top division rugby was assured.

The following week was the cup semi-final against London rivals Wasps at Sudbury. This was the fourth time we had met in the cup and we had yet to lose. In a tie which moved from end to end, the first half an hour passed without any score although Bray had made a try saving tackle early on. On 32 minutes, Paul Challinor edged us in front with a dropped goal and this is how it remained at half time. This lead lasted a minute into the second half because Chris Oti got a try after getting past three defenders, Rob Andrew converted and it was 7-3 to Wasps. He stretched this lead with a penalty eleven minutes later before Rob Glenister dropped a goal from the back of a maul 30 yards out. Andrew then cancelled this out with his second penalty and with just over twenty minutes remaining, we trailed by seven points. Paul Challinor got a penalty at last (after four misses) and the gap was down to just four points. After 75 minutes, we won a maul and spread the ball wide to Chris Madderson who ran straight and enabled Gavin Thompson to loop round on the outside and take the pass for a try in the corner. Challinor's conversion hit an upright and bounced out but at least we were in front again. In the next seven minutes, we managed to hold out but, in the 83rd minute, Peter Winterbottom gave away a penalty for being offside on the half way line. Up stepped Rob Andrew to try and put Wasps into the final but his kick went straight instead of curling and it also dropped short. One of our men fielded the ball, kicked it to touch and the referee blew the final whistle. We had reached our third successive cup final where we would meet Leicester on 1st May.

Nine changes were made for the visit to Rosslyn Park where an exciting game was in store. We opened the scoring when Gavin Thompson got a try but by half time, Park had scored a goal and a try to lead 12-5. We came storming out in the second half and a try by David Dix and a penalty from Challinor took us into the lead by a single point. Thompson dropped a goal but the home side retook the lead with a penalty and a goal. With just a few minutes left, Alexander scored in the corner and Challinor had a kick to win the game. His conversion was good and we went away with another single point victory (23-22). Our last league game of the season was at Kingsholm against Gloucester but it turned out to be a disappointing match. Mike Wedderburn opened and completed our scoring after 25 minutes when he went through the Gloucester defence to score a try. By half time the home side had gone into the lead with a try by Morris and a conversion from Smith. In the second half, Gloucester scored again through Fowke and Smith (who also kicked two penalties and a conversion) to run out 25-5 winners. Stuart Thresher made his final appearance for the 1st XV in this one having scored 887 points (33 tries, 164 penalties and 129 conversions) and captained the side 17 times during his ten season career. His points total put him in fifth place in the all-time scorers list at the Club. Also saying goodbye was Mike Wedderburn who had scored 185 points (43 tries and 1 conversion) in his first team spell which ran through seven seasons. Seven of the side we put out against Gloucester would appear in the cup final the following week so our morale was not at a high level.

So it was to Twickenham that we travelled for the last game of the season, the Pilkington Cup Final against Leicester. As with our three previous final appearances, we scored first when Rob Glenister scored a try for Paul Challinor to convert after ten minutes against the run of play. On 20 minutes, the scores were level when Stuart Potter went over for John Liley to convert. After this, the game went quiet until half time with Jez Harris squeezing a dropped goal between two Challinor penalties to leave us in front by thirteen points to ten. Liley levelled the scores again after 44 minutes and when Martin Johnson crashed over from a tapped penalty move, Liley's conversion made the lead seven points and the cup was slipping away. Challinor did pull another penalty back after 71 minutes but we couldn't find a way through to get an all-important second try. Two minutes from the end, Liley landed his second penalty and the Tigers were home by twenty three points to sixteen. This had been our worst performance in a cup final and to lose by a small margin was no crumb of comfort.

Two days after the final saw a new competition appear – the Worthington National Tens at Kingsholm (replacing the National Sevens). Basically, each side would contain five forwards and five backs from a squad of twelve. Once a team had been eliminated, their players could be borrowed for teams still in the competition as injury replacements. Each match up to the final would be ten minutes each way with a two minute interval; the final would be twelve minutes each way with a three minute interval. Like Sevens, any match ending level would go to sudden death extra time, each period to last five minutes. The top sixteen league clubs in England competed in a straight knock-out and we played in the last match against Nottingham. This turned out to be an easy 38-5 win and we followed up with victory over Orrell (35-12). In the semi-final, Saracens were dispatched 26-12 but we came a cropper in the final against Gloucester (0-29).

Our league record of P12 W5 D1 L6 F197 A187 Pts11 Pos 8th was, once again, disappointing. It equalled our worst finishing position of 1988/89 and 1991/92 which meant we had had a marginally less successful season than last year as the cup had been lost by a slightly bigger margin. Overall, we had performed better with twenty wins from our thirty two matches. The record was P32 W20 D2 L10 F902 A521. The points total for of 902 was a new Club record in a regular season, overtaking the mark of 869 set in 1987/88 but not quite enough to get ahead of 1975/76 (which included two tour matches). Andy Harriman topped the try scorers with 13, Paul Challinor dropped four goals and kicked 29 penalties but Stuart Thresher scored the most conversions (43) and points (168). He completed his total with 5 tries and 19 penalties. Overall, tries rose by 18 on the previous season to 120, dropped goals went up one to 6 and penalties and conversions rose to 54 and 61 respectively. All these added up to 238 more points being scored than in 1991/92. Mark Russell appeared in 26 games, Paul Challinor, Rob Glenister and Gavin Thompson in 25 and Andy Mullins (23).

1992/93

050992	NORTHAMPTON	NORTHAMPTON	L	1G3PG(16)-1G3PG1T(21)
090992	ASKEANS	STOOP MEMORIAL GROUND	W	6G1PG8T(85)-(12)
120992	PLYMOUTH ALBION	PLYMOUTH	W	4G2PG6T(64)-2DG(6)
190992	BATH(JCL1)	BATH	L	2PG(6)-1G5PG(22)
260992	WASPS(JCL1)	STOOP MEMORIAL GROUND	L	1G2PG(13)-1G1PG1T(15)
031092	WEST HARTLEPOOL(JCL1)	WEST HARTLEPOOL	W	4PG(12)-3PG(9)
101092	LONDON SCOTTISH(JCL1)	STOOP MEMORIAL GROUND	D	2G1PG1T(22)-4PG2T(22)
171092	BEDFORD	STOOP MEMORIAL GROUND	L	2G1PG2T(27)-2G2PG2T(30)
241092	SARACENS(JCL1)	SOUTHGATE	W	1G2PG1T(18)-1PG(3)
311092	LONDON IRISH(JCL1)	STOOP MEMORIAL GROUND	W	4G3PG2T(47)-1G4PG1T(24)
071192	CAMBRIDGE UNIVERSITY	STOOP MEMORIAL GROUND	W	3G4T(41)-2PG1T(11)
141192	NOTTINGHAM	STOOP MEMORIAL GROUND	W	2G1PG2T(27)-(16)
211192	NORTHAMPTON(JCL1)	STOOP MEMORIAL GROUND	L	1G(7)-1DG3PG(12)
291192	BLACKHEATH(PC3)	STOOP MEMORIAL GROUND	W	6G6T(72)-1PG(3)
281292	RICHMOND	STOOP MEMORIAL GROUND	W	3G1PG2T(34)-1G1PG4T(30)
020193	RUGBY	RUGBY	C	
090193	ORRELL(JCL1)	ORRELL	L	2PG2T(16)-1PG3T(18)
160193	SARACENS	STOOP MEMORIAL GROUND	D	4PG1T(17)-2G1PG(17)
230193	WAKEFIELD(PC4)	STOOP MEMORIAL GROUND	W	4G3PG2T(47)-1G2PG1T(18)
300193	LONDON IRISH	SUNBURY	W	3PG1T(14)-2PG(6)
060293	BLACKHEATH	BLACKHEATH	W	1G3T(22)-2G1PG(17)
130293	BRISTOL(JCL1)	STOOP MEMORIAL GROUND	W	1DG1PG2T(16)-0

200293	LEEDS	STOOP MEMORIAL GROUND	W	10G1PG2T(83)-1G1T(12)
270293	WATERLOO(PCQF)	WATERLOO	W	1G3PG1T(21)-3PG1T(14)
090393	ORANGE FREE STATE(MNETNS)	ELLIS PARK	W	1G1DG3PG(19)-(9)
110393	TRANSVAAL(MNETNS)	ELLIS PARK	L	1DG2PG(9)-(36)
130393	WAKEFIELD	WAKEFIELD	C	
200393	COVENTRY	STOOP MEMORIAL GROUND	W	4G2PG4T(54)-(18)
270393	LEICESTER(JCL1)	LEICESTER	L	0-2G1DG2PG(23)
030493	RUGBY(JCL1)	STOOP MEMORIAL GROUND	W	2G2PG3T(35)-2G(14)
100493	WASPS(PCSF)	SUDBURY	W	2DG1PG1T(14)-1G2PG(13)
170493	ROSSLYN PARK	ROEHAMPTON	W	1G1DG1PG2T(23)-2G1PG1T(22)
240493	GLOUCESTER(JCL1)	GLOUCESTER	L	1T(5)-2G2PG1T(25)
010593	LEICESTER(PCF)	TWICKENHAM	L	1G3PG(16)-2G1DG2PG(23)

For the tour to Canada in May and June 1993, England sent a weakened side due to the British Lions tour going on at the same time. No caps were awarded for the test series which ended 1-1 (the first was lost 12-15, the second won by 19-14); the other three games were all won. Paul Challinor, Richard Langhorn (a replacement during the tour), David Pears and Alex Snow were from our current squad and John Olver was now at Northampton. Pears, Challinor and Olver (who captained the side) played in both tests.

The Lions tour to New Zealand in 1993 saw no fewer than four current Quins in the squad (Will Carling, Jason Leonard, Brian Moore and Peter Winterbottom) plus Wade Dooley who had recently played a couple of games for us in South Africa. Dick Best continued his development as assistant coach to Ian McGeechan. Carling played in the first test, Leonard and Moore played in the second and third and Winterbottom appeared in all three. Dooley had to leave the party to go home due to the sudden death of his father. The first test was lost 18-20 in controversial circumstances; New Zealand were awarded a dubious try to start with and the match winning penalty decision was also a wrong one. In between, the referee made other mistakes but the result stood. The Lions levelled the series by winning the second (20-7) but lost the third by a margin of seventeen points (13-30). The other games produced a record of W6 L4 to leave the overall record at W7 L6.

In November 1993, the Harlequin Hotline was introduced to keep supporters up to date with tickets, fixtures, team news, match reports and travel arrangements to away games. The annual subscriptions were amended for this season to the following – Full playing £25, full non-playing £60, lady £40, over 60 £35, junior/student £15 and overseas £23. In March 1994, it was announced that there would be a special general meeting on 19th April to secure registration of the Club as an industrial and provident society under section 2 of the Industrial and Provident Society Act 1965. On 3rd May, the Club was registered as an industrial and friendly society (registration number 27980R). On 12th April more new proposals for the development of the Stoop were put forward. They included the new covered East stand with seating for 4,800 and hospitality boxes. The building work was provisionally set for Spring to September 1995 and the projected cost was £2 million. Geoff Morey took over as honorary secretary from the outgoing Colin

Herridge who had resigned. Bob Read also left the role of 1st XV fixtures secretary. He had taken over from Jay Gould back in 1979/80. On 4th July, the planning review committee set out the strategic objectives for the Club.

1) To win the Courage League within the next three years.
2) To consistently be in the top three in the Courage League.
3) To change the culture of the Club to a winning one.

They considered that the Club was still coming across as an elitist, gentlemanly club and that Quins were not hard-nosed enough. Winning the Pilkington Cup was not considered to be a strategic objective. It was hoped that this would send a signal to all players and members of the Club that the league and consistency within it was the top priority. Strengths were seen as location, management and structure of the Club, commercial development and international players. Weaknesses were perceived to be spectator facilities, lack of pitches, marketing of the Club to the local area and club culture. Threats were identified as departure of the general manager, competition increasing (no soft games), financially overstretching the Club (the new stand was cited as an example). Opportunities were listed as the local residents, improved facilities, generation of income, increase the pro-activity on public relations, capitalise on the membership, merchandising and player recruitment. It was agreed that the Club would proceed with the fund raising for the new stand even though planning permission had not been granted. On the merchandising side, Cotton Traders reported that it had sold 8,500 shirts in the current year and this was expected to treble next year.

It was recorded in the Annual Report that following a note sent to all 2,500 members requesting information about the Club's history, only one person had replied (someone's father had supplied a press cutting)! During the season, we said farewell to old boys Martin Jackson (1939-50) and James Worton (1919-32) who both died. Income and expenditure was slowly rising and this year, the figures were £605,798 and £596,313 which resulted in a profit of £3,918 for 1993/94.

Taking over from Peter Winterbottom as captain was Andy Mullins. His term was to be only a single season and proved to be quite successful. We began with a short tour to Ireland to play two matches. This was our first visit for a fifteen-a-side game since 5th October 1963 when we lost to Lansdowne (5-22). As it turned out, our opponents were Lansdowne again on 1st September but this time the scores were a lot closer. Eric Elwood put Lansdowne in front with a penalty before Paul Challinor kicked two in reply and added a dropped goal to put us 9-3 ahead after 20 minutes. Before half time, Glennon got a try which Elwood converted and the home side led by a point at the break. Just after the restart, Kent Bray burst through for an unconverted score and we were back in front. We controlled most of the second half but our hosts were not dead and buried. Elwood missed two penalties and when Glennon sliced through our defence near the end, it looked all over. Fortunately for us the try was disallowed for a forward pass and we had prevailed 14-10. Daren O'Leary made the first of 186 appearances in this game having joined from Saracens and would go on to be a regular first team member for the next eight seasons. Our next stop was Blackrock College three days later and another close game ensued. In the first half, David Pears landed two penalties to which the College replied in kind to leave it all square. Fifteen minutes into the second half the Irish took the lead with a try before Pears landed his third penalty. A dropped goal and a try sealed victory for the home side before Gavin Thompson got a consolation try in injury time to leave us trailing by five points at the end.

The following Saturday, we had our first league match of the season against London Irish at the Stoop. The league now consisted of just ten teams but each would play the others on a home and away basis making a total of eighteen games. Consequently, this was the most competitive season in the history of English rugby. London Irish fielded no fewer than four future Quins in their line up (Jim Staples, Michael Corcoran, Paul Burke and Gary Halpin) but they were to have a bad day. Paul Challinor ran the show in the first half and with eight minutes gone, he scored and converted his own try and although he couldn't add the points to Daren O'Leary's first try for the Club, he did land a penalty after 31 minutes to give us a 15-0 lead at the break. We continued as we had left off in the second half and O'Leary and Glenister added tries. Challinor converted the second and we were strolling away at 27-0 with a quarter of an hour left to play. In typical Quins fashion, we applied the brakes and let the visitors in for three tries in nine minutes before Challinor got his second penalty in injury time to seal the win. It was a winning start but a lot less comfortable than it should have been.

On 18th September, we visited Sudbury to take on Wasps and quickly lost our 100% league record. Playing with the wind in the first half, we played terribly and allowed Wasps to score fifteen points. We did have a try disallowed when we were trailing by only three points, Rob Glenister securing the touchdown but an intervention by one of the touch judges ended with Brian Moore being lectured about illegal use of the boot by referee Tony Spreadbury. The second half was a different story as Wasps went downhill and we came out fighting. Jason Leonard got a try before Andrew slotted a penalty to put the home side 18-5 ahead. Kent Bray eventually succeeded with a penalty and Rob Glenister got our second try which Bray converted to close the gap to just three points with twelve minutes left. Right near the end, O'Leary narrowly failed to get to a chip ahead which would have given us victory.

Disaster was just around the corner when we contrived to throw our next game away against Bristol at home. Kent Bray had kicked five penalties in the first half to give us a comfortable lead but then things started to go wrong. Rob Kitchin (who would make his debut for us at the start of the 1994/95 season) came on at the end of the first half for Kyran Bracken. Tainton kicked two penalties in the opening nine minutes of the second half and when Eves got a try for Tainton to convert, the gap was only two points. This is how it remained until injury time when we had a scrum in Bristol's half. All our scrum half (Ben Short) had to do was put the ball into touch and the final whistle would have gone. Instead, his kick was charged down, Bristol won the ball, attacked and Wring sent Saverimutto in for the winning score. Tainton's conversion made the final score 20-15 and we slipped from fourth to seventh place in the table.

A long trip to Newcastle was next and this had become a must win game already. The home side made a lot of errors and we led 14-0 at half time. Kent Bray (2) and Paul Challinor got penalties and Alex Snow went over for a try. Daren O'Leary got our second try after 48 minutes before Newcastle Gosforth opened their scoring with a penalty three minutes later. Bray wrapped the game up right on the final whistle with another penalty and our roller-coaster season had taken an upturn. The following week against Northampton at the Stoop, we trailed by only seven points at half time when playing against a strong wind. The Saints failed to score after this, Kent Bray had his kicking boots on and put over five penalties in 24 minutes to give us a 15-7 victory. This second win in a row put us into third place behind Bath and Leicester.

A break of four weeks from league action followed and we visited Saracens at Southgate on 16th October. Only one player survived from the Northampton game and that was Peter Thresher (who replaced Cassell in the first half of the league game). It was 0-0 at half time; the home side opened the scoring after 47 minutes with a try but we came back and a penalty from Richard Butland and a try by Cameron Short put us ahead. A penalty and two dropped goals for Sarries saw them home to a 14-8 victory. It was a different story against London Scottish at the Stoop and Butland put them in their place with four penalties and a conversion to add to a try and a conversion from Gavin Thompson and tries by Jeff Alexander, David Thresher (2) and Mark Russell. Quins old boy Richard Cramb got a penalty and converted Wichary's try to leave the final score at 41-10. At Webb Ellis Road, we outscored Rugby by three tries to two on our way to a 20-10 victory. Butland was again on form against Cambridge University at Grange Road; this time getting a try, four penalties and three conversions to finish with 23 points. Tries from Ben Short (2) and Simon Dear just added to the misery for the home side and, although they scored a goal, a penalty and a try, we won easily (38-15). Jason Keyter made the first of 112 appearances in this game and Everton Davis took his final bow having scored 33 tries (134 points).

On 13th November, we travelled to Welford Road to take on Leicester in the mud and rain and a close encounter was produced. John Liley opened the scoring after 29 minutes when he kicked a penalty but within four minutes, we had the lead. A pass from Jez Harris was kicked ahead by O'Leary from our 22 and he won the race for the touchdown against Tony Underwood. Liley missed five kicks in the game and when he missed a Challinor up and under, Carling was up to pick up and dive over. Despite having tremendous pressure in the last ten minutes, the Tigers just couldn't break through and we had our fourth league win.

Our next trip was to our least favourite venue, Edge Hall Road, Orrell. This was our sixth visit (our fourth in the league) and we had lost every time. As was now becoming the norm, a close game was played out in front of a very partisan crowd. Ainscough put the home side in front after eleven minutes with a penalty and on 25 minutes, Kent Bray replied in kind to level the scores. A try from Dave Cleary and a conversion and a penalty by Ainscough gave Orrell a 13-3 lead just after the half hour mark. We came back immediately and within 60 seconds Jeff Alexander charged down Taberner's clearance kick and Paul Challinor was there to scoop the ball up and score for Bray to convert. After pulling to within three points, we let our concentration slip again when O'Leary missed touch with a kick, Orrell attacked and Dewi Morris went over in the corner to make the half time score 18-10. An Ainscough penalty after 55 minutes all but sewed the game up as we had been hampered by the loss of Langhorn and Snow (both injured in the first half). Bray got a penalty back, O'Leary sped in for an excellent try from 40 metres out for Bray to convert and, all of a sudden, the gap was a single point with eight minutes left. But, try as we did, we couldn't manage to get another score to snatch victory and the Edge Hall Road hoodoo continued. Richard Langhorn made his last appearance in this game having scored 16 tries (64 points) during the ten seasons he played in the 1st XV.

It was all change the following week when second division Moseley visited the Stoop. Only David Thresher (who came on as a replacement at Orrell) appeared this time as most of the first team were taking the week off before playing Bath (Will Carling, Jason Leonard and Brian Moore were helping England defeat New Zealand at Twickenham). Against Moseley, we actually trailed when Hamlin put over a penalty after 20 minutes before Butland equalised after 40 minutes to leave it all square at half time. Hamlin nudged Moseley ahead with his second penalty four minutes into the second half but Butland soon equalised as he had done in the first half. On 59 minutes, we got our first try when Ben Short went over for Butland to convert but Hamlin made it a hat-trick of penalties to keep it close after 66 minutes. However, our superior fitness began to tell and in the last twenty minutes we added tries through Butland, Jason Murley and Peter Thresher to leave us as comfortable winners. Richard Butland got two more conversions to finish with 17 points and a final score of 32-9 was registered.

Despite our three league defeats, we were still in third place but the game against Bath at the Stoop was a chance to close the gap between us to two points. It was another close game and in the first half, Robinson got a try for the visitors and Barnes kicked a penalty to which Bray replied with two penalties of his own. We huffed and we puffed in the second half but we couldn't get that elusive try despite putting Bath under pressure. There were four penalties scored in the following order; Barnes, Bray, Catt, Bray and this meant the final score was: Quins 12 Bath 14. In these days, we didn't even get a bonus point!

On 11th December, we travelled to the West Country to take on Gloucester without Carling, Leonard, Moore and Coker. We played well despite these handicaps and scored tries through Rob Jardine-Brown and Jason Keyter and a penalty and conversion by Bray in the first half to two tries for the home side to lead 15-10. It all went wrong after this and Gloucester scored two goals in the space of four minutes to sew the game up. Bray did get a try back but the final twenty minutes remained scoreless. Halfway through the league season, our chances of the title had effectively gone; we couldn't afford to lose one more game but in reality, this wasn't going to happen (and it didn't!).

The following week, it was on to cup action and we had a visit from Basingstoke in a fourth round tie. They were in Division 5 South and how it showed despite brave resistance and a large amount of support. During the first half, we coasted away with tries from Troy Coker, Chris Sheasby, Daren O'Leary (2), Simon Dear and Andy Mullins. Bray got a penalty and Challinor added one conversion to leave the half time score at 35-0. After Gavin Thompson had made it 40-0 with our seventh try, Rowledge kicked a penalty to open Basingstoke's account. This was their only score and Challinor and O'Leary (with his third) took the try count to nine and Bray managed one more conversion to make the final score 52-3.

Our final game of 1993 was at the Athletic Ground against Richmond on 27th December with our second string once again taking centre stage. Our hosts were currently in second place in League Three and were more than a match for us. Rob Leach (2), Jardine-Brown and Keyter scored tries and Madderson added a couple of conversions to take our points to 24. Richmond had exceeded this total by half time and proceeded to run in six tries with Hoad adding nineteen points with his boot. All this meant they had achieved their highest points total against us in fixtures dating back to 1869. The final score of 24-49 was the most points conceded during the season but wasn't our heaviest defeat. David Thresher made his last appearance against Richmond and had scored 11 tries (48 points) during his ten season career.

Our first attempt at a game in the New Year was a failure (as it had been in 1993); Blackheath were due to visit the Stoop but the fixture was cancelled. Our next game was a league match against London Irish at Sunbury. Will Carling made his first appearance since the Leicester game back in November and produced an outstanding display of centre skills. He took the Irish to the cleaners, providing opportunities for other members of the team to score the points. Irish still had four future Quins in their line up but Rory Jenkins made up the number instead of Mike Corcoran. Kent Bray was on target with two penalties before a goal put the home side in front after 17 minutes play. By half time, we had regained the lead with a try by Mark Russell being added to by another Bray penalty. The Irish had given their all in the first half but had so little to show for it and when we turned up the heat after the break, they had no answer. Rob Glenister and Daren O'Leary (2) got the tries and Bray added a couple of conversions to make the final score 33-7.

As the return matches were played in the same order, the next one up was Wasps at the Stoop. We had just one win in seven meetings against the men from Sudbury and we desperately needed a win in this one. Kent Bray got us off to a good start with his now customary penalties. He beat Rob Andrew 4-2 in the first half and with Challinor dropping a goal right on half time, we led 15-6. Andrew's third success narrowed the gap before disaster struck the visitors after 57 minutes. Gavin Thompson chipped over the defence and as Buzza ran back to touch down safely, his feet slipped and the ball spun out of his reach. O'Leary followed up for an easy score, Bray converted and the match had turned in our favour again. Wasps had played most of the rugby and we led against the run of play. We defended resolutely in the last ten minutes but couldn't prevent Oti scoring a try and Andrew getting another penalty. This only brought them to within five points and we held on for a fantastic victory.

Our reward for defeating Basingstoke back in December was a home draw against West Hartlepool who were riding high as leaders of the Second Division. This tie was not going to be a walk over and so it proved as we went behind after seven minutes when Oliphant kicked a penalty. Twenty four minutes later, Dear scored a try to put us in front but Bray missed the conversion and three penalty attempts. Challinor was handed the kicking duties and succeeded with two penalties to put us 11-3 up at the interval. West Hartlepool had a massive pack and this was proving difficult to move around but the tie was won for us in the space of two minutes when Mark Russell and Jeff Alexander got tries. Challinor converted one and it was suddenly 23-3 after 60 minutes. The visitors came storming back in the final twenty minutes (fifteen of normal time and five of injury time). Hodder scored for Oliphant to convert and Mick Watson (another future Quin) got another with six minutes to go. Had Oliphant converted this, it might have been a close call but, he missed and we were safe (23-15). The match will be remembered for one incident in particular when Mick Watson thumped Will Carling (who threw a punch in anger as he turned round) and was then punched by Troy Coker. Afterwards Watson explained that he thought Carling had elbowed one of the West Hartlepool players. Simon Mitchell played at hooker for the visitors and would also play for us in the future.

We had lost fourteen of our last fifteen matches at Bristol (including both league visits). On a muddy pitch with wind and rain added in, it could only be the West Country and this was to be our undoing. Bristol led 8-3 at half time, Bray's penalty being sandwiched between Tainton's penalty and John's try. Early in the second half, Glenister got over in the corner only for Blackmore to do the same before Bray got another penalty to bring us to within a couple of points. On 63 minutes, Glenister took a quick throw ten metres inside our half and found his man beautifully. Unfortunately, this turned out to be Barrow of Bristol and in the blink of an eye, Knibbs was diving over the line for a try which, with Tainton's conversion meant we had a mountain to climb. Alex Snow scored our second try but the kicking failures continued and, although we threw everything at Bristol, we couldn't pull the game out of the fire. Over the years, these narrow defeats would become increasingly annoying and disastrous to our league championship winning credentials.

On 5th February, we travelled up to Beeston to play Nottingham and in the first 25 minutes, we had leaked points at the rate of nearly one a minute to trail 0-24. By half time this had increased to 5-31 after Butland had scored our try in reply to four from Nottingham. Butland did kick two penalties in the third quarter but two more tries for the home side sealed their win by forty three points to eleven. This was our heaviest defeat of the season and ranked alongside the Richmond game as our worst performance. It has to be said that in both of these fixtures, our entire 2nd XV had been put out.

On 12th February, we entertained the bottom side, Newcastle Gosforth at the Stoop. They had just a single point from eleven games and were staring relegation in the face. We were expected to win easily but it didn't turn out like that. In what turned out to be a terribly niggly encounter, Johnson gave them the lead after 24 minutes with a penalty. Challinor got two for us before Johnson levelled the scores at the break with his second success. At half time, Peter Winterbottom came on for Chris Sheasby to make his final appearance for the 1st XV. He had scored 6 tries (28 points) in his six seasons at the Club and had captained the side in 47 matches. He showed that he still had it during his one half performance but was adamant that this was the end. He was to be sorely missed. Five minutes into the second half, Alex Snow was sent off after repeated warnings for foul play by the referee. We only just managed to survive thanks to two more Challinor penalties in a mostly forgettable game which ended 12-6. David Pears returned to the side against Newcastle Gosforth but left the field during the next game against West London Institute at the Stoop the following Saturday. It was his first appearance since the game against Blackrock

College on the short tour of Ireland back in September. We now had quite a strong squad and our largely second choice team wiped the floor with the Students. By half time, we had notched up six tries and by the end had added another seven. Ben Richardson (2), Mark Russell (2), David Dix (2), Craig Luxton (2), David Currie (2), David Pears (2) and Jason Keyter got the tries and Richard Butland (4) and Rob Glenister (3) put over the conversions. The Students did score two tries when the score stood at 74-0 but they were never in with a chance. The final score of 79-10 was our biggest win of the season.

On 26th February, we welcomed Sale to the Stoop for the Pilkington Cup quarter final. They were not a bad outfit and currently stood two points behind West Hartlepool in Division 2 but came in the belief that we were slow starters. They didn't get off too quickly themselves and this effectively cost them a place in the semi-finals. After only six minutes, Paul Challinor scored the opening try after our pack had ripped into their opponents. Eleven minutes later, Gavin Thompson went in for our second blind side try and although Challinor missed both conversions, he did add a penalty six minutes later to put us 13-0 ahead. Paul Turner (playing with a cracked cheek bone) kicked a penalty before Pears dropped a goal to restore our thirteen point cushion. It was starting to look bad for Sale but a minute before the break, Erskine went over for Turner to convert and they only trailed by six points. Turner was put out of the game after a knock to his face and his replacement (Jee) landed a penalty to narrow the gap to just three points. During the third quarter, Sale started to dominate but we scored the only points with a Challinor penalty. Eventually, the situation was reached whereby Sale had to score from their own in-goal area to win the game. As they moved the ball, Jee gave a loose pass and Carling was on hand to fall on it and seal the win. Challinor's conversion made it 26-13, ended Sale's hopes and ended the tie.

The following week, we travelled up to Wakefield for another friendly (due to the Five Nations Championship) and came away with a victory. An exciting game saw each side score four tries with the difference coming in the kicking. Glenister and Butland each dropped a goal and landed a penalty and a conversion to add to tries from Jardine-Brown (2), Keyter and Ian Desmond and the score was comfortable enough in the end (36-27). We now went through a disastrous run in which we lost seven games in a row. The first of these was at Northampton in the league; we were in fourth and the Saints were fifth at the start of play and they needed one more win to make sure of first division rugby next season. John Pearson became the first English referee to be wired for sound when he took charge of this match. Challinor kicked a penalty at the end of the first quarter but, after 50 minutes, we trailed 3-15. The fight back started in the 53rd minute when Daren O'Leary got in for a try and Challinor kicked two penalties (the second after 75 minutes). We attacked again and just before the final whistle, Challinor put a dropped goal attempt narrowly wide and we had lost at the Gardens for the fifth successive time. Three of the side went to Coventry on the following Friday evening and went down by seventeen points (13-30). Butland kicked two penalties in the first half and Glenister converted Martin Pepper's try in the second half.

Leicester came next and were challenging Bath for the title. Jason Leonard and Chris Sheasby both went off to play in the Hong Kong Tens and Sevens tournaments respectively but replacements were found in Simon Brown and Troy Coker. Yet again, our failings in the league had begun to show and the Tigers raced into a seventeen point lead after 28 minutes. Back and Potter scored tries, Harris converted both and added a penalty and it looked as though a thrashing was on the cards. We fought back gamely and actually managed to outscore the visitors in the remaining time. Keyter scored a try and Challinor got two penalties and a conversion. Harris added his second penalty and Richards scored from a rolling maul a minute from the end to sew it up (13-25). This was the beginning of a five game losing streak against the Tigers but we had more important matters on our minds as we took on the most successful team in the history of the knock out cup the following week in the shape of Bath.

On 2nd April, one of the most dramatic matches ever seen at the Stoop unfolded and there was even a hailstorm in the second half! We got off to an absolute nightmare and a move which involved thirteen Bath players ended with a try for Swift after only three minutes. Ten minutes later, Robinson charged down Challinor's kick, Barnes picked the ball up and ran 60 metres for their second try which Callard converted. Bath were in total command and the tie looked to have been decided when Catt sent Callard in for a third try after 22 minutes. He also converted this one and it was 19-0 to the visitors. There was no further scoring in the first half but we were further disrupted by the loss of Sheasby (dislocated knee) and Thompson (damaged ankle). Cassell and Alexander came on as replacements and with them came a change in our fortunes. We were playing with the strong wind and on 49 minutes Challinor opened our account with a penalty. Bray set up Pepper for our first try and when Challinor charged down Catt's attempted clearance, the Bath defence panicked. He hacked on and, as the ball bobbled towards the posts, Callard brought him down from behind. The referee (Brian Campsall) gave a penalty try and Challinor's conversion made it 15-19. We were now on a roll and the crowd went wild when a close quarter passing movement saw Cassell score in the south-west corner for Challinor to convert. When the hail came, Challinor dropped a goal and we led by six points with only eight minutes to go. As Bath looked for the winning score, they drove deep into our 22 and, as the ball came out to Ben Clarke, he dropped the ball and it bounced forward. The referee ruled that it was not a knock-on, the ball was moved out to Swift and he ran through Bray's attempted tackle to score. Callard put the conversion over and Bath were back in front by a single point. For the remaining three minutes, the visitors kept the ball to hold on to their 26-25 advantage. This had been one hell of a cup tie and it was a shame that someone had to lose but we were out and that was that. Bath then went on to beat Leicester in the final.

With three league matches and one friendly to go, we had literally nothing to play for except a mid-table position and pride. Against Orrell, the sides were locked at 13-13 with a minute to go when, for some inexplicable reason, we tried a quick throw in. The ball failed to go five metres and it was snapped up by Johnson who went on to score a try which was converted. Yet again, we had hit the self-destruct button in a league match. Against Rosslyn Park in a friendly on 16th April, Butland kicked five penalties in the first half to give us a 15-12 advantage. In the opening ten minutes of the second half, we leaked seventeen points and, despite Mark Taylor getting a try which Butland converted, another loss was added to our tally (22-29). Mike Molyneux appeared for the final time against Park having scored 25 tries (101 points) during his Quins career.

We had now slipped to sixth position in the league and our penultimate game was the return with Bath. Richard Hill was playing in his final home match and a win for them would mean four league titles in a row. We had no heart for the fight and a 15-3 half time advantage was transferred into a 32-13 victory for Bath. Kent Bray got a couple of penalties and converted Thompson's try near the end. Callard kicked two penalties and three conversions to add to tries by Clark, de Glanville, Hall and Hilton for Bath. Our last game of the season was a home fixture against Gloucester. In a totally meaningless game for both sides, we produced some lovely running rugby. Bray put us in front with a penalty before Tim Smith equalised in similar fashion for the visitors. O'Leary got our first try after 35 minutes, Bray converted and added a penalty near half time to put us 13-3 ahead. Early in the second half, Cassell broke through and Carling finished the move off for Bray to convert. The Gloucester pack took charge for a while and Windo and Kearsey got pushover tries before we put them in their place. Bray landed his third and fourth penalties and Keyter sandwiched a try in between before Ian Smith got Gloucester's third try which Beech converted. Right at the end, O'Leary scored his second and our fourth try, Bray converted and we had our highest league score of the season (38-20) to finish off on a positive note.

Two days later, it was down to Gloucester for the second Worthington National Tens. This time fourteen English teams were joined by Melrose and Cardiff in the same knockout format. We played in the first match against Moseley and disappointingly, we lost 12-19. There was to be no repeat of last year's run. Bristol and Gloucester got through to the final where the holders lost 26-5. This proved to be the last running of this event as the game moved towards professionalism.

Our league record was P18 W8 L10 F333 A287 Pts16 Pos 6th. Again, too many matches had been lost when the points should have been in the bag. The ongoing question was why can we do it in the cup but not in the league? Overall, our playing record was P35 W18 L17 F811 A619; this was not as good as last year and although our league position improved by two places, we lost in the cup semi-final to make it a slightly worse season. Daren O'Leary topped the try scorers with 14, Kent Bray got the most points with 153 (2 tries, 39 penalties and 13 conversions) although Paul Challinor scored the most dropped goals (3) and Richard Butland shared the most conversions with Bray. Overall, tries dropped by thirty to 90 (the lowest total since 1988/89), dropped goals stayed the same on 6, penalties rose by thirty to 84 and conversions dropped to just 43 from 61 (again the lowest since 1988/89). Our points total fell by over a hundred to 806. The top appearance maker was Gavin Thompson with 27 and he was followed by Andy Mullins (25), Daren O'Leary (24), Paul Challinor (23), Mark Russell (22), Kent Bray (21) and Jeff Alexander and Simon Dear with 20.

1993/94

010993	LANSDOWNE	DUBLIN	W	1DG2PG1T(14)-1G1PG(10)
040993	BLACKROCK COLLEGE	BLACKROCK	L	3PG1T(14)-1DG2PG2T(19)
110993	LONDON IRISH(JCL1)	STOOP MEMORIAL GROUND	W	2G2PG2T(30)-3T(15)
180993	WASPS(JCL1)	SUDBURY	L	1G1PG1T(15)-1G2PG1T(18)
250993	BRISTOL(JCL1)	STOOP MEMORIAL GROUND	L	5PG(15)-2G2PG(20)
021093	NEWCASTLE GOSFORTH(JCL1)	NEWCASTLE	W	4PG2T(22)-1PG(3)
091093	NORTHAMPTON(JCL1)	STOOP MEMORIAL GROUND	W	5PG(15)-1G(7)
161093	SARACENS	SOUTHGATE	L	1PG1T(8)-2DG1PG1T(14)
231093	LONDON SCOTTISH	STOOP MEMORIAL GROUND	W	2G4PG3T(41)-1G1PG(10)
301093	RUGBY	RUGBY	W	1G1PG2T(20)-2T(10)
061193	CAMBRIDGE UNIVERSITY	CAMBRIDGE	W	3G4PG1T(38)-1G1PG1T(15)
131193	LEICESTER(JCL1)	LEICESTER	W	2T(10)-1PG(3)
201193	ORRELL(JCL1)	ORRELL	L	2G2PG(20)-1G3PG1T(21)
271193	MOSELEY	STOOP MEMORIAL GROUND	W	3G2PG1T(32)-3PG(9)
041293	BATH(JCL1)	STOOP MEMORIAL GROUND	L	4PG(12)-3PG1T(14)
111293	GLOUCESTER(JCL1)	GLOUCESTER	L	1G1PG2T(20)-2G2T(24)

181293	BASINGSTOKE(PC4)	STOOP MEMORIAL GROUND	W	2G1PG7T(52)-1PG(3)
271293	RICHMOND	RICHMOND	L	2G2T(24)-5G1DG2PG1T(49)
010194	BLACKHEATH	STOOP MEMORIAL GROUND	C	
080194	LONDON IRISH(JCL1)	SUNBURY	W	2G3PG2T(33)-1G(7)
150194	WASPS(JCL1)	STOOP MEMORIAL GROUND	W	1G1DG4PG(22)-4PG1T(17)
220194	WEST HARTLEPOOL(PC5)	STOOP MEMORIAL GROUND	W	1G2PG2T(23)-1G1PG1T(15)
290194	BRISTOL(JCL1)	BRISTOL	L	2PG2T(16)-1G1PG2T(20)
050294	NOTTINGHAM	NOTTINGHAM	L	2PG1T(11)-5G1PG1T(43)
120294	NEWCASTLE GOSFORTH(JCL1)	STOOP MEMORIAL GROUND	W	4PG(12)-2PG(6)
190294	WEST LONDON INSTITUTE	STOOP MEMORIAL GROUND	W	7G6T(79)-2T(10)
260294	SALE(PCQF)	STOOP MEMORIAL GROUND	W	1G1DG2PG2T(26)-1G2PG(13)
050394	WAKEFIELD	WAKEFIELD	W	2G2DG2PG2T(36)-(27)
120394	NORTHAMPTON(JCL1)	NORTHAMPTON	L	3PG1T(14)-1G1PG1T(15)
180394	COVENTRY	COVENTRY	L	1G2PG(13)-2G2PG2T(30)
260394	LEICESTER(JCL1)	STOOP MEMORIAL GROUND	L	1G2PG(13)-2G2PG1T(25)
020494	BATH(PCSF)	STOOP MEMORIAL GROUND	L	2G1DG1PG1T(25)-3G1T(26)
090494	ORRELL(JCL1)	STOOP MEMORIAL GROUND	L	1G2PG(13)-2G2PG(20)
160494	ROSSLYN PARK	STOOP MEMORIAL GROUND	L	1G5PG(22)-3G1PG1T(29)
230494	BATH(JCL1)	BATH	L	1G2PG(13)-3G2PG1T(32)
300494	GLOUCESTER(JCL1)	STOOP MEMORIAL GROUND	W	3G4PG1T(38)-1G1PG2T(20)

It was back to South Africa for England in May and June 1994 and an eight match tour. Two tests were played, the first was a convincing win for England by 32-15, the second for South Africa (9-27). In the other games, the tourists didn't do well and posted a record of W2 L4. Will Carling was captain and played in both tests as did Jason Leonard and Brian Moore. David Pears also made the party but got no caps.

The 1994/95 season was totally over shadowed by the death on 25th November of Richard Langhorn. He had gone into hospital for a routine back operation and suffered a heart attack on the operating table. His 1st XV career had lasted from 1985-93 and he would be sadly missed. During the season, we also lost John Crouch (who ran the line for the 1st XV for a number of years) and Maurice Daly (1937-49). The design of the East stand was virtually complete but the cost of building had risen from £2.5 million to £2.7 million. The building work would commence in May 1996 and be finished during the 1996/97 season. For 1994/95, income once again outweighed expenditure and a profit of £8,295 was achieved. Two clubs in Poverty Bay, New Zealand were to merge and become the Harlequin Football Club and they wanted to become affiliated to us. The committee decided that only one club per country could be so affiliated so the answer to this request was no.

Keith Richardson joined us as our new coach from Gloucester for the 1994/95 season and the team began with another short tour to Ireland. We met the same two teams as before (Lansdowne and Blackrock College) but this time we came away with two victories instead of one. Five of the team were making their debuts against Lansdowne on 1st September including William "Bill" Davison (the first of 191 appearances), Rory Jenkins (the first of 185), Peter Mensah (the first of 98) and Chris Wright (the first of 78). Nick Killick made his final appearance having scored 8 tries (35 points) during his career with us. Brian Moore had taken over the captaincy from Andy Mullins but didn't appear in either of the matches in Ireland. Rob Kitchin (who was the fifth man playing his first game) led the side but went off and was replaced by Wright. The first match was played on the Lansdowne Road back pitch on a Thursday evening and we were never behind. A 21-14 half time score was increased to 36-27 by full time. Chris Madderson, Killick, Mensah and Wright got tries and Paul Challinor kicked two conversions, two penalties and dropped two goals to finish with sixteen points. At Stradbrook two days later, revenge was gained over Blackrock College in emphatic fashion. Nine changes were made (one positional) to the team and David Pears was back (although he didn't last the game out). Other familiar names coming into the side were Jason Leonard and Troy Coker. Pears got a penalty and that was our only successful kick of the day. All seven of our tries having been scored by Coker, Jim Hamilton-Smith, Wright, Gavin Thompson, Davison, Madderson and Daren O'Leary went unconverted. In reply, the college managed a single try (again unconverted).

The league remained in the same format for this season with a total of eighteen games being played. Our first was on 10th September at newly promoted Sale and we shot out of the blocks when we turned our hosts over at a maul and Carling and Mensah put O'Leary over after just two minutes. Six minutes later, Sheasby scored after another mistake by Sale, Bray added a penalty and when Carling battered his way over, Bray's conversion made it 20-0 at half time. This last kick proved crucial because Sale came thundering back and scored three tries of their own. Paul Turner converted two but we held out for a one point win to get our league programme off to the best of starts. Martin Hobley played his last game for the 1st XV at Brooklands after making his debut in 1986 and scoring one try (4 points) during his career. Our next game against Wasps at the Stoop began well enough and, despite leaking two tries (one from old boy Simon Hunter), we led comfortably at the break (21-12). Challinor had scored a try (as had Moore) and kicked three penalties and a conversion. No one present could have imagined what happened next or that our next try (from Chris Sheasby) would come in the 81st minute! Wasps came out firing on all cylinders and Hunter scored his second try (the first of their seven in the second half). Nick Greenstock got a brace at the end (he would go on to join us five years later) and Rob Andrew got two conversions, a penalty and a dropped goal to leave the final score at 26-57. We had totally capitulated in the second half and our tackling had been non-existent; the prospects of any honours this season were not good. Keith Richardson had left at half time and when he asked his taxi driver the score later, he must have thought there was some mistake – alas, there was no mistake!

Our next fixture was an away trip to Bristol and yet again we came away with no points. We were outplayed by the home side although we did lead by a point at the break (11-10). Jason Keyter had scored a try and Paul Challinor added a penalty and dropped a goal. His second penalty took us four points clear but Tainton landed three penalties in the second half and Bristol were home by five points. We were now languishing in ninth place with just two points from our opening three games and the only team below us were Northampton who had no points. West Hartlepool came to the Stoop on 1st October for a game which saw the first appearance of Will Greenwood. He would go on to make 156 appearances, gain 55 England caps and also play for the British and Irish Lions and win 2 caps. He played as full back and it would be a while before he would play in his England position of centre. West had defeated Wasps the week before and were not going to be an easy team to beat. Our captain was happier with the tackling and Challinor landed five penalties from eight attempts which, when added to Cassell's try in the 58th minute, took us to victory. The visitors did score a goal and a penalty, it was not enough and a 9-0 half time score had been transformed into a 20-10 one at full time.

At Franklin's Gardens (rarely a happy venue for us), we met Northampton who were reeling from the loss of their first four league games and were firmly rooted to the bottom of the table. Paul Challinor kicked us into the lead with a penalty after eight minutes but Northampton rallied and came back with Paul Grayson's boot levelling the scores with a penalty before he converted Hunter's try to put them in front. Then, as Hunter put in a clearance kick on his own 22, Justyn Cassell not only charged it down but actually caught the ball in the same instant and ran on through the defence to score. Challinor converted and Gavin Thompson added our second try to leave us in front at half time despite a dropped goal from Grayson. We lost Challinor with concussion just before the break and young Will Greenwood took over the kicking duties. He slotted a penalty over a minute into the second half but Grayson pulled the Saints to within a couple of points on 59 minutes. Twelve minutes from the end, the Northampton defence was split again and Thompson grabbed his second try to seal the win by twenty three points to sixteen. Our sixteenth victory at the Gardens in 59 attempts took us up to fourth place in the table.

Our next test came in the shape of unbeaten Leicester at the Stoop on 15th October. Jez Harris dropped a goal after just 54 seconds to open the scoring before Will Greenwood (playing at fly half in the absence of Challinor) put over two penalties in the 3rd and 28th minutes to give us the lead. Harris replied with two of his own before half time and we lost our captain with a muscle tear after 34 minutes to add to our problems. The second half (yet again) was a non-event as far as we were concerned and Thompson's late try was converted by Greenwood but, by this time, Leicester's total had reached forty! Four tries were scored by the visitors (mainly thanks to our generosity in turnovers), Harris converted them all and also kicked his third penalty. The plan had been that if Moore was injured, Leonard would lead the pack and Carling the backs. Instead, the coach said afterwards that we had about nine captains on the field – this said it all!! Once again, at the start of the season, the players and coach had said this would be the season when things changed – yet again they were proving themselves wrong and our performances were getting worse.

Orrell visited the following weekend and went away with the points. Greenwood (back at full back) put over a penalty after four minutes but a disaster before half time cost us the match. A sudden downpour combined with strong winds turned the playing conditions into a nightmare and when Jeff Alexander tried to clear his lines, he dropped the ball in our in-goal area and Dewi Morris was up as quick as a flash to gain the try and put Orrell in front. Langford got a penalty after 61 minutes to stretch the lead and all we could manage in reply was Greenwood's second penalty seven minutes later. A narrow 6-8 defeat was made worse by injuries to Carling and Keyter. A trip to the Rec in league competition had so far produced five defeats and, by half time, this was destined to be stretched to six. Challinor (on return from injury) dropped a goal just two minutes into the game to give us the lead and kicked a penalty after 24 minutes to level the scores after we had lost it. Jonathan Callard put over four penalties and converted Geoghegan's try (a gift from us but he still had to run 60 metres) to give Bath a 19-6 lead at the break.

Challinor went off with a rib injury after 47 minutes and Craig Luxton came out of retirement to play his last game for the 1st XV (having scored 18 tries (74 points) in his seven seasons). Callard put over his fifth penalty, we had the final word when Greenwood scored a try three minutes from the end but our place kicking had contributed in no small manner to our defeat. Between them, Challinor and Greenwood missed a dropped goal, four penalties and a conversion.

Our final league match before the Christmas and New Year break was at home to Gloucester in what had become a must win fixture. We started well enough and Andy Pinnock got over after a couple of near misses (actually dropping the ball over the line on one occasion) for Bray to convert. The visitors then took charge for the rest of the half and future Quin Mark Mapletoft (he would come to us six years later) put Holford in for a try which Osbourne converted to leave it all square at the interval. Bray popped over a penalty fourteen minutes from the end but a quick tap penalty from a mark by Mapletoft saw him go on a run which ended with the Holford/Osbourne combination putting Gloucester in front with eight minutes remaining. Five minutes from time, we had a penalty 15 yards from the Gloucester line and Moore and Bray seemed to have an altercation over what was going to be done. Eventually, Bray put the ball into touch; nothing came from it and we slipped to another defeat. We had now fallen down to eighth place just two points ahead of the relegation place. Kent Bray appeared in his last game having scored 266 points (8 tries, 1 dropped goal, 46 penalties and 24 conversions) during his spell in the first team as did Troy Coker. The big Australian had scored 6 tries (26 points) in his five seasons at the Club. Desperate times called for desperate measures and Dick Best returned to take up the post of Director of Rugby from 1st December. Was he perhaps the only person who could save us from relegation? Only time would tell and the answer would come in the final game of the season at Kingsholm against Gloucester. Best became aware that job interviews in the financial sector could be arranged for players via contacts. This made Quins a more attractive proposition for those wanting to move to London.

Our next fixture was a friendly against Cambridge University at the Stoop on 12th November. Twelve changes were made to the league side and Martin Pepper was made captain. After falling behind to a penalty, David Currie (son of John) replied in kind to equalise and Bill Davison, Russell Osman and Pepper scored tries to help us into an 18-3 lead at half time. Mark Russell got another which Thompson converted before a spirited fight back from the students saw Reynolds run in two tries. We put them in their place after this and further scores came from Adam Jones, Thompson and Hamilton-Smith. With a penalty and six conversion attempts being missed, the 40-13 margin of victory should have been much larger.

Due to the Divisional Championship, we didn't play again until 10th December; our opponents were London Scottish and a complete walk over followed. Tries came from Jeff Alexander (making his last appearance after scoring 68 points (13 tries, 1 penalty and 2 conversions) during his career), Paul Challinor (2), Bill Davison, Will Greenwood, Matt Holmes, Daren O'Leary (2), Chris Sheasby and Gavin Thompson. Greenwood added a conversion and Challinor got five and a penalty to make the final score 65-26. When Alexander eventually left the Club, he was apparently forced to hand over all his Quins supplied kit and turned up quite dishevelled at his new club Esher. He arrived in a t-shirt, scruffy shorts and barefoot – times were indeed changing. Against West London Institute on 14th December, Steve White-Cooper made his debut and scored a try. He would go on to make 104 appearances and gain 2 England caps before retiring to concentrate on his career in the city in 2002. In another thrashing of the opposition, other tries came from Simon Brown, Rob Glenister (2), Will Greenwood, Jim Hamilton-Smith, Barry O'Sullivan (2) and Gavin Thompson (2). Greenwood weighed in with two penalties and seven conversions to finish with 25 points. Final score 70-25.

Three days later we played Saracens at the Stoop in the fourth round of the Pilkington Cup. This would not be easy because we were not playing well and Saracens were starting to stretch away at the top of the second division with eight wins from their nine games. Against the wind in the first half, Paul Challinor succeeded with two penalties to give us a 6-0 lead. On 64 minutes he stretched this to 9-0 with a penalty from the half way line. Sarries did get a consolation of scoring the only try of the tie but it came in the final move and, with the missed conversion, it made the score 9-5. Had their kicker (Tunningley) not missed four kicks, the result might have been different. On a brighter note, Jim Staples (the Irish full back) had served the required 120 day re-qualification period and played the first of 53 games for us. He was in the process of winning 26 caps for his country. In the Saracens team was Tony Diprose and their coach was a certain Mark Evans – both would come to us in 2001 and 2000 respectively. Our last game of a largely forgettable first half of the season was a friendly at the Stoop against Richmond. Chris Madderson landed a penalty and Rob Glenister scored a try, converted it and also added a penalty in a 13-18 defeat.

Our first game of 1995 was meant to be a visit to Roehampton to take on Rosslyn Park but this was cancelled. Instead, we met Sale in a league game at the Stoop. It was their first league fixture here in almost seven years and they certainly did better this time! For once, our goal kicking went reasonably well and Challinor banged over five penalties from seven attempts. Sale got a try in each half, one from Fowler and one from Baxendell; although the referee missed an obvious knock-on for the second. Turner added a conversion and a penalty (after Rory Jenkins had been caught offside) to level the scores at 15-15. Still, as Brian Moore said afterwards one point was a plus. This game saw the debut of red and yellow cards but they were not used. The trip to Sudbury on 14th January was made in the hope that we would avoid another drubbing against an in-form Wasps side. We managed that but a try from Mensah which Staples converted was all we had to show for our efforts. Twenty five points for the home side took them to a double over us with Nick Greenstock again scoring two of their tries. Rob Glenister appeared for the last time in this game having scored 354 points (65 tries, 3 dropped goals, 11 penalties and 19 conversions) during his ten seasons in the first team.

A friendly at home to Blackheath the following week was cancelled so we were straight into the 5th round cup tie at Sunbury against London Irish. The Irish were currently fifth in division two and were not expected to give us a severe test. Paul Challinor gave us an early lead with two penalties before the Irish came back with ten points in five minutes to lead 10-6. This woke us up and by half time Greenwood, Spencer Bromley and Sheasby had scored tries and Challinor added one conversion for a thirteen point lead. The tie was wrapped up in an eleven minute spell beginning five minutes into the second half. Challinor got his third penalty and Bromley and Staples scored tries which Challinor converted to take us thirty points clear. The home side did have the final word when Hennessy scored a try but the remaining fourteen minutes stayed scoreless and we were in the quarter finals.

In a friendly against Nottingham at the Stoop, Mick Watson (from West Hartlepool) made his debut and scored a hat-trick of tries in a match reduced to 30 minutes each way. As it was, kick-off was delayed for 45 minutes because the Nottingham coach was delayed in traffic and the game had to finish in time for the kick-off in the international taking place at Twickenham between England and France. After Watson's opening try, Gallagher kicked a penalty for Nottingham's only points. By the interval, Davison, Watson and Neil Collins had added tries (two of which Challinor converted) for a 24-3 lead. Challinor, Watson and Chris Wright scored in the second half with two more conversions from our fly half to take the final score to 43-3. It was back to league action the following week when Bristol visited the Stoop. In the first 17 minutes, Bristol led by ten points to nil and all was gloom and doom for us. Challinor landed three penalties between the 49th and 63rd minutes to bring us to within a point as we took control of the game. Unfortunately, he let the pressure get to him and missed two later kicks which would have brought two much needed points. Altan Ozdemir made his league debut for Bristol in this game and would join us the following season.

A friendly at the Stoop against Rugby was cancelled so our next game was the cup quarter final (also at home) against Wakefield and a very tense tie it turned out to be. With just six league games left, we had slipped to ninth place on the same points as West Hartlepool and three in front of Northampton. These were dreadfully disappointing times for all those connected with Quins – the players were just not performing on the pitch. Andy Mullins (who withdrew on the Saturday morning) and Jason Leonard were both missing from our pack which meant that Brian Moore had Simon Brown and Ian Desmond either side of him. Desmond hadn't played prop for two years so it would be a major test for him especially (Mark Green was even called from a session in the gym to sit on the bench). The visitors took the lead after four minutes when their captain (Mike Jackson) kicked a penalty. We had to wait until the fifth minute of injury time before Will Greenwood scored in the north-west corner to give us the lead. He then took the opportunity to drop a goal from 35 metres out (after Crawford Henderson had taken a quick throw-in) and when Paul Challinor scored our second try with 68 minutes gone, we led 13-3. Wakefield now decided on all-out attack and were rewarded when Thompson scored in the first minute of second half injury time. Then, in the final minute, Wakefield's fly half made a break, ran deep into our territory and the tie was there for the taking. Fortunately for us, the opportunity was missed thanks to poor passing and a lack of vision and we moved into our fifth successive semi-final. Mark Russell became the first Harlequin to be booked when he tripped Jackson and was probably lucky to stay on the pitch.

Before that, we had two massive league games against West Hartlepool (A) and Northampton (H) to deal with as well as a couple of friendlies. First up it was West Hartlepool at Brierton Lane on 4th March and if we were to avoid relegation this or the Northampton match would have to be won. Paul Challinor kicked a penalty to put us in front after 3 minutes and Peter Mensah added a try after 28 minutes to stretch the lead to 8-0 playing with the wind. Right on half time, Sheasby and Bromley allowed Brown through to score a try and there were now only three points in it. In the second half, our captain decided that the pack were going to keep the ball and they did just that for most of it. Scrums and rolling mauls frustrated West and their supporters but, we lost the ball right near the end, the home side drove up the pitch, Stimpson chipped into the corner and Jones got the touchdown. Well, the referee (Tony Rossall) gave the try but there was considerable doubt as to whether or not he had grounded the ball legally. As it was, the try stood and we had lost by ten points to eight. To make matters worse, Northampton had beaten Bristol at the Memorial Ground to move to within one point of us.

On a lovely sunny day at Sunbury, we took on London Irish in a friendly match which produced no fewer than 77 points. The final try count was 6-4 in our favour and was reflected in a final score of 47-30 (after the Irish had led 18-11 at half time). For us, Paul Challinor kicked three penalties and four conversions of tries from Henderson (2), O'Leary, Greenwood, Watson and O'Neill. Mike Corcoran got exactly half of the Irish points with a try, two penalties and two conversions. Seven changes had been made from the team defeated at West Hartlepool with some of the Wanderers coming in and a further six changes were made from the team which defeated the Irish to that which played Coventry at the Stoop on 18th March in another friendly. Our fly half this time was Jerome Riondet and he converted three of our four tries and landed a penalty. The tries (which took us to a 29-15 victory) were scored by Henderson, Mensah and Watson (2). Gavin Thompson made his last appearance for the Club in this game having scored 210 points (45 tries, 1 dropped goal and 2 conversions) during his six season spell in the first team.

The real relegation battle followed and Northampton led at half time with a Paul Grayson penalty after 28 minutes to nil. Rob Kitchin edged us ahead four minutes into the second half when he burrowed over from a ruck but Grayson kicked two more penalties to leave us trailing 5-9 with half an hour left. After 58 minutes Kitchin and Sheasby executed a perfect move for Staples to run in from an unmarked position and we were ahead again, this time for good as we ground out the remaining time. The rugby had been error filled and our kicking had been appalling (Greenwood missing two of two and Challinor missing four of four) but we had grabbed two absolutely priceless points in our quest for survival. The next visitors to the Stoop were Bath in the cup semi-final and any hopes of a repeat of the thriller from last year were dashed in the second half. Jim Staples got a try and a penalty for us in the first half but Callard had equalled him with two penalties and the conversion of de Glanville's try to take Bath five points clear at the interval. In the second half, Bath were just too good for us and stretched away to 8-31 before Challinor got a try five minutes from time. This had been our worst cup defeat for ten years and, with hindsight, should probably have been expected.

The season now ended with a run of four league games and our England trio of Carling, Leonard and Moore would be restricted to playing in just two of them because of the forthcoming World Cup in South Africa. As things stood, three wins out of four (however unlikely) would mean that Northampton or West Hartlepool would go down. Against Leicester at Welford Road, the England contingent were left out, we played terribly and lost again. Leicester's winning margin of 22-8 did not reflect the amount of possession and chances they actually had. John Liley landed a dropped goal, four penalties and converted Tony Underwood's try and all we could manage in reply was a penalty from Challinor, a try by Wright and a yellow card for Mick Watson for his part in a fight with Matt Poole! Northampton had beaten Orrell and West Hartlepool had lost to Bath so it was now back to a one point margin – three games left and all to play for. Our next one was at Orrell of all places. Our four previous league games at Edge Hall Road had produced no points at all so it didn't look good but we did have our England boys back. Jim Staples also returned from Ireland training duty to strengthen the line-up and his 80 yard run for a try in the second half after an interception by Carling was something to savour. We had led by only a Challinor penalty to nil at half time but had stretched this with two more penalties from him and a try by Mensah. In reply, Ainscough had kicked a penalty for the home side but Orrell were well on the way to defeat. Challinor converted the try by Staples and also Peter Thresher's effort to put us 28-3 ahead before a goal at the end brought Orrell a bit closer. West Hartlepool had beaten Sale and Northampton had lost to Gloucester so this meant we had to win one of our last two games to send one of the other two down.

At the Stoop against Bath, Greenwood, Brown and Hamilton-Smith replaced the England trio as the only changes from the side which defeated Orrell. Bath fielded a dozen of the side which had finished the semi-final and were looking to keep the pressure on Leicester at the top to take the title race into the last weekend of games. Knowing that a win would keep us up, we shot out of the blocks and a Challinor penalty after only two minutes got us going. Then, Chris Sheasby charged down a kick by ex-Quin Richard Butland, recovered the ball and raced 50 metres to score. Butland pulled back a penalty for the visitors but Greenwood got our second try and Challinor added two further penalties to give us a massive 19-3 advantage at half time. We were completely outplaying Bath but the second half would show why we were near the bottom and they were near the top of the table. With only 25 minutes remaining, we still led 19-3 but, in the space of just nine minutes, our lead had disappeared. Guscott, Yates and Sleightholme grabbed tries, Butland put over two conversions and the score read 19-22 to the visitors. Try as we did, we couldn't score again and Butland's penalty a minute from the end sealed the victory by six points. We had thrown it away and lost our eighth game in a row against Bath. We hadn't beaten them since 1986; the draw in

1992 being our only plus since then. Wasps had done us no favours by losing to Northampton and West Hartlepool defeated Bristol to scramble to safety.

After such a long season, it all came down to the last game. We travelled to Kingsholm and Northampton went to West Hartlepool. It was simple – if Northampton won and we lost, we would be relegated. Any other combination would see us safe and the Saints relegated. Osborne put Gloucester in front with a penalty but Crawford Henderson raced over for a try which Challinor couldn't convert. He had already missed two penalties and Brian Moore decided enough was enough and switched kickers to Jim Staples. He was immediately successful with a penalty and the conversion of a penalty try when Carling was brought down by Gloucester's captain Deacon to give us a 15-3 lead at half time. A Cornwell try converted by Osborne at the start of the second half was repeated at the end to give the Cherry and Whites seventeen points. We were never headed though and Staples kicked a penalty, dropped a goal and converted Mensah's try to take us to twenty eight points. So, we had survived but this time, it was as close as it could be. Northampton defeated West Hartlepool 21-12 and finished one point behind them, us and Gloucester. It was said that relegation would have cost the Club somewhere in the region of £500,000. Brian Moore announced his retirement after this game although he came back for seven more appearances at the start of the following season.

Our league record was P18 W6 D1 L11 F275 A348 Pts13 Pos8th. Some severe questions needed to be asked about the commitment of the players after this very poor season of results. Unfortunately, these bad seasons were becoming the rule rather than the exception and this needed to be addressed accordingly. Overall, our playing record was P31 W17 D1 L13 F731 A569. Despite another cup semi-final, our league position had dropped back to that which was occupied in 1991/92 and 1992/93. Gavin Thompson was top try scorer with the lowest number since 1988/89 (8) and Paul Challinor topped the other scoring with 206 points (6 tries, 4 dropped goals, 40 penalties and 22 conversions). Overall, tries went up by two to 92, dropped goals stayed on 6 (for the third season running), there was a big drop in penalties (from 84 to 57) and a smaller one in conversions (down by two to 41). As a result, our overall points total fell to 731. Out of 65 players used in the first team throughout the season, only half a dozen played in twenty or more games. Chris Sheasby appeared in 24, Rob Kitchin was one behind, Paul Challinor finished on 22, Gavin Thompson had 21 and Bill Davison and Rory Jenkins both managed 20.

1994/95

010994	LANSDOWNE	DUBLIN	W	2G2DG2PG2T(36)-1G1DG4PG1T(27)
030994	BLACKROCK COLLEGE	BLACKROCK	W	1PG7T(38)-1T(5)
100994	SALE(JCL1)	SALE	W	1G1PG2T(20)-2G1T(19)
170994	WASPS(JCL1)	STOOP MEMORIAL GROUND	L	1G3PG2T(26)-3G1DG1PG6T(57)
240994	BRISTOL(JCL1)	BRISTOL	L	1DG2PG1T(14)-1G4PG(19)
011094	WEST HARTLEPOOL(JCL1)	STOOP MEMORIAL GROUND	W	5PG1T(20)-1G1PG(10)
081094	NORTHAMPTON(JCL1)	NORTHAMPTON	W	1G2PG2T(23)-1G1DG2PG(16)
151094	LEICESTER(JCL1)	STOOP MEMORIAL GROUND	L	1G2PG(13)-4G1DG3PG(40)

221094	ORRELL(JCL1)	STOOP MEMORIAL GROUND	L	2PG(6)-1PG1T(8)
291094	BATH(JCL1)	BATH	L	1DG1PG1T(11)-1G5PG(22)
051194	GLOUCESTER(JCL1)	STOOP MEMORIAL GROUND	L	1G1PG(10)-2G(14)
121194	CAMBRIDGE UNIVERSITY	STOOP MEMORIAL GROUND	W	1G1PG6T(40)-1PG2T(13)
101294	LONDON SCOTTISH	STOOP MEMORIAL GROUND	W	6G1PG4T(65)-(26)
141294	WEST LONDON INSTITUTE	STOOP MEMORIAL GROUND	W	7G2PG3T(70)-(25)
171294	SARACENS(PC4)	STOOP MEMORIAL GROUND	W	3PG(9)-1T(5)
271294	RICHMOND	STOOP MEMORIAL GROUND	L	1G2PG(13)-(18)
020195	ROSSLYN PARK	ROEHAMPTON	C	
070195	SALE(JCL1)	STOOP MEMORIAL GROUND	D	5PG(15)-1G1PG1T(15)
140195	WASPS(JCL1)	SUDBURY	L	1G(7)-2G2PG1T(25)
210195	BLACKHEATH	STOOP MEMORIAL GROUND	C	
280195	LONDON IRISH(PC5)	SUNBURY	W	3G3PG2T(40)-1G1PG1T(15)
040295	NOTTINGHAM	STOOP MEMORIAL GROUND	W	4G3T(43)-1PG(3)
110295	BRISTOL(JCL1)	STOOP MEMORIAL GROUND	L	3PG(9)-1G1PG(10)
180295	RUGBY LIONS	STOOP MEMORIAL GROUND	C	
250295	WAKEFIELD(PCQF)	STOOP MEMORIAL GROUND	W	1DG2T(13)-1PG1T(8)
040395	WEST HARTLEPOOL(JCL1)	WEST HARTLEPOOL	L	1PG1T(8)-2T(10)
110395	LONDON IRISH	SUNBURY	W	4G3PG2T(47)-2G2PG2T(30)
180395	COVENTRY	STOOP MEMORIAL GROUND	W	3G1PG1T(29)-(15)
250395	NORTHAMPTON(JCL1)	STOOP MEMORIAL GROUND	W	2T(10)-3PG(9)
010495	BATH(PCSF)	STOOP MEMORIAL GROUND	L	1PG2T(13)-2G1DG3PG1T(31)
080495	LEICESTER(JCL1)	LEICESTER	L	1PG1T(8)-1G1DG4PG(22)
150495	ORRELL(JCL1)	ORRELL	W	2G3PG1T(28)-1G1PG(10)

220495	BATH(JCL1)	STOOP MEMORIAL GROUND	L	3PG2T(19)-2G2PG1T(25)
290495	GLOUCESTER(JCL1)	GLOUCESTER	W	2G1DG2PG1T(28)-2G1PG(17)

The 1995 Rugby World Cup took place in South Africa during May and June and this time we had twenty two players representing eleven countries. Only four were current – Will Carling (captain), Jason Leonard and Brian Moore (England) and Jim Staples (Ireland). Troy Coker (who didn't play because of injury) (Australia) and Johannes Roux (South Africa) had played for us and the rest were future Quins. David Wilson (Australia), Gareth Rees (captain) and Scott Stewart (Canada), Laurent Bénézech, Laurent Cabannes and Thierry Lacroix (France), Paul Burke, Gary Halpin and Keith Wood (Ireland), Massimo Cuttitta (captain) (Italy), Zinzan Brooke and Andrew Mehrtens (New Zealand), George Harder (Western Samoa), Craig Chalmers and Eric Peters (Scotland) and Gareth Llewellyn (Wales). England won narrowly against Argentina (24-18) and Italy (27-20) before scoring over forty points against Western Samoa (44-22) to finish top of the Pool. The quarter final saw a meeting with Australia and with the scores locked at 22-22, Rob Andrew dropped a goal from 45 metres to knock the holders out. Against New Zealand in the semi-final, tackling let the side down and Jonah Lomu literally walked over some of the players as his side ran out 45-29 winners. To be fair to England, they did come back from a 0-35 deficit but the gap was just too much. The play-off for third place against France was a game too far and England lost again by a score of 9-19. It was the first time the French had beaten them since 1988. In the final, South Africa beat New Zealand 15-12 after extra time.

On 12th November 1995, it was reported that the long-time chairman of the ground committee had passed away. John Moore-Gillon was a well-respected officer of the Club and he was another who would be sorely missed. The application for planning consent was being supported by council officials and permission was expected to be granted subject to a number of conditions. There was to be a binding agreement to provide and maintain the link road from the council depot to the Chertsey Road. Consent, once given, would not commit the Club to the development as it would be available to be taken up for a period of five years. It would, however, be necessary to use the consent before the end of three years or be faced with the prospect of losing the income which would be generated by the hospitality boxes.

The new European rugby competition began this season and was named after its sponsors, Heineken. The Five Nations Committee initiated it so there would be a level of competition between domestic leagues and test rugby. The first season saw twelve sides taking part representing France, Ireland, Italy, Romania and Wales. They competed in four Pools of three with the group winners going directly into the semi-finals. The first game saw Toulouse defeat Farul Constanţa in Romania 54–10. The French side went on to beat Cardiff in the final 21-18 after extra time at Cardiff Arms Park to become the first Heineken European Cup winners. The crowd of 21,800 was a good start and these would increase massively over the coming years. Clubs from England and Scotland joined the competition in 1996/97 and that same season saw the further expansion of rugby on the continent with the introduction of the European Challenge Cup for teams that did not qualify for the Heineken Cup.

At the end of March 1995, Rupert Murdoch's News Corporation launched an attempt to sever the links holding rugby league players to the Australian Rugby League's competition currently broadcast by Kerry Packer's organisation. It was to be known as Super League and this led to fears that a huge number of the top rugby union players would defect because of the huge sums of money available (given that Union was still an amateur game). Of course, many players were getting paid for playing but it was highly controversial and could lead to them being banned for life from the sport if they got found out. Over the following five months, a group called the World Rugby Corporation (WRC) (formed by Geoff Levy and Ross Turnbull) took on and nearly defeated most of the Rugby Unions around the World. They wanted a professional rugby competition covering the whole planet and at one point had signed up the majority of top players in Australia, France, New Zealand and South Africa. Some were fully committed and others had signed without making a definite decision. Some of the England squad had signed but they got absolutely nowhere with Ireland. What the players liked about the WRC proposal was that they were included whereas the Unions always seemed to ignore their wishes. The three main Southern Hemisphere Unions got together, founded SANZAR and proposed a provincial competition featuring teams from all three countries (this eventually became Super 12 (a revamp of the Super 10), then Super 14 and now Super Rugby). In the end, the pressure told on the South Africans and they signed with their Union and slowly but surely, the others followed suit and the Rugby War was over. The Unions had refused to believe that WRC could be a threat to them and almost lost the players as a result. Some even resorted to threats of a lifetime ban from international rugby if players signed with WRC. Both sides settled their differences and on 27th August 1995, the International Rugby Board (IRB) announced after a meeting in Paris that Rugby Union would turn professional. The RFU imposed a moratorium until the start of the 1996/97 season on the introduction of professionalism in English rugby below international level to try and avoided wholesale bankruptcy of clubs; it was impossible to put it off any longer than that. For an in-depth view of this important period in rugby, I can thoroughly recommend The Rugby War by Peter Fitzsimons which paints the whole picture.

For the first time, income passed the one million pounds mark (£1,013,792) but, because of the huge increase in marketing, playing and administration costs, a loss of £476,416 was recorded. Later, it was explained that a loss of £150,000 had been expected and the extras were made up by £111,000 loyalty payments to the players for staying with the Club during the 95/96 season when they could have left; £103,000 of professional fees for converting the Club from an Industrial and Provident Society to a limited company and £89,000 in the extra six weeks after the normal end of year (this reflected the general overheads and costs of extra staff hired for the professional era in a close season period with no income). Professionalism was not going to be cheap and this would be seen over the next twenty years.

When professionalism came in, Dick Best did a lot of work researching how other professional sports were financed and how they worked their budgets. He decided, with a budget of £2.5 million, it would work like this:-

If you were an England international, your wage would be £50,000 a year
If you were a top international for any of the other big countries, you would get £35,000 a year
If you were an A/B international, it would be £20,000 a year
If you were a non-international, it would be £10-15,000 a year
If you got into the match day squad, you would receive a bonus of £500
If the team won, you would receive a bonus of £1,000

This was all approved by the Board and was fine until Colin Herridge allegedly got involved with Will Carling's agent (John Holmes) and came back to say that he would be on roughly three times the normal amount for an England international.

There was no time for a pre-season tour this time and it was straight up to Orrell on 9th September for our first league game. Jason Leonard was made captain for this and the following season but didn't make an appearance until the end of October at Gloucester after recovering from a shoulder injury. We made only five changes to the side which played at Gloucester in the last game of the previous season; David Pears was the significant "new" player. It made such a difference when a side had a decent kicker and Pears was such a player. He dropped a goal, kicked a penalty and converted one of our two tries (scored by Simon Mitchell and Rob Kitchin) to give us an interval lead of 18-0 before Orrell started a comeback with three penalties from Simon Mason. It was short lived though and Daren O'Leary finally killed them off with our third try to give us a winning start to the campaign. A midweek fixture with London Irish gave the youngsters and other members of the three main squads a chance to shine and although the wet conditions led to poor handling, a narrow victory was gained. Dan Sibson and Ben Maslen scored tries, Mark Wadforth landed a conversion and Chris Wright added a penalty to turn round a 7-13 deficit at the break. Jamie Williams made his debut in this game and went on to play 72 times for the 1st XV. Unfortunately, due to some serious injuries, his career would never take off in the way it promised to.

We hoped to gain some revenge over Wasps for the double defeat last season when they visited the Stoop on 16th September. Rob Andrew put them in front after four minutes when he landed a penalty but we were quickly back in the game with a Spencer Bromley try and a conversion and a penalty from David Pears. Two penalties from Andrew brought the deficit down to just one point at the half way mark. Their hooker, Kevin Dunn, was shown a yellow card for use of the boot at a ruck when not going for the ball (some thought it should have been red). Chris Sheasby got our second try six minutes into the second half, Pears converted and sandwiched a penalty goal between two from Andrew to leave us 20-15 in front with fifteen minutes remaining. Pears then took centre stage (he was out-playing Andrew) and dropped three goals in the last seven minutes and even though Dunston got a try after the second one, we won 29-20. This was the first time we had won our opening two games in nine seasons of league rugby. The kick-off had been moved to 5 p.m. to fit in with Sky TV who were broadcasting the game live. This was a situation which would not improve and gradually, the regular Saturday 3 p.m. start for all games would become a thing of the past. The following Wednesday, it was another friendly, this time at home against near neighbours, Richmond. After a slow performance in the first half, we went on to record an emphatic victory by seven tries to nil. Spencer Copp, Tom Smith (2), Gareth Allison (3) and Jamie Williams got the tries and Challinor made up the points with four conversions. Richmond managed three penalties but we had achieved our biggest win over them since 1910.

Our third league game saw us travel to Bristol to try and win our first league match at the Memorial Ground in five attempts. After Bristol had taken an early ten point lead, Daren O'Leary went over in the corner to open our scoring. Tainton and Pears exchanged penalties and we trailed by five points going into the second half. Will Carling opened up the defence and Greenwood scored for Pears to convert and we led for the first time. A goal edged the home side back in front before a period of pressure led to two Pears penalties and a try from Spencer Bromley to give us a 26-20 lead. With less than ten minutes left, Pears missed a penalty which Paul Hull ran back and, after a series of attacking rucks and mauls, he finished the move off with a try. Tainton's attempted conversion to put them back in front missed and right on time, O'Leary intercepted a pass and ran back 70 metres for the match clinching try. He suffered from cramp for the last half of the run, but there was no one to chase him and we had another victory.

A friendly against London Scottish at the Stoop was cancelled so our next outing was again at home, this time against West Hartlepool. It became known before the kick-off that Will Carling had split from his wife amid rumours of a friendship with Princess Diana and this led to hundreds of journalists and photographers camping at the Stoop to get shots of the England captain (there was even a massive Police presence). Roy Croucher (the Groundsman) was approached to see if he could get Will into the ground without harassment from them. A diversion was created for about an hour and a half where the press were led to believe Will was coming in one of three entrances by the stewards and by word of mouth. When Will came close to the Stoop, he let them know on his mobile where he was and all stewards were moved to a gate which he had no intention of coming in. The plan worked successfully and Carling was greeted by enormous cheers from Quins supporters and these cheers got even louder when he scored a try after 31 minutes. By this time, Pears had opened the scoring with a dropped goal and West had replied with a penalty and a try. Our fly half converted Carling's try but couldn't do the same with Chris Sheasby's effort. A second penalty for the visitors made it 15-11 at the break before Kitchin got over for a try a couple of minutes into the second half. Pears converted but Stimpson got a try and converted it to bring the visitors back to 22-18. In the last quarter of an hour, we moved smartly away with tries from Simon Brown and Spencer Bromley and a third conversion by Pears to leave the final score at 34-18. This win left us in second place in the table behind Bath and West Hartlepool rooted to the bottom with no wins from four games played.

Our next game was another friendly at the Stoop against Brunel University (formerly West London Institute). The entire team was changed from the West Hartlepool game but they were still far too good for the students. Paul Challinor got 21 of our 88 points with a try and eight conversions. The remainder of our fourteen tries were scored by Jamie Williams (2), Rhodri Davies (2), Richard Francis (3), Chris Wright (who added a conversion), Martin Pepper, Matt Wynn, Mick Watson (2) and a penalty try. The first half brought a score of 38-7 and the second was 50-10 to give a final score of 88-17. Back to the 1st XV for the visit of Saracens and the pressure of our unbeaten record was starting to tell. The first half saw just two penalties scored; one from David Pears after only two minutes and the other from Andy Lee for the visitors eight minutes before the break. Pears regained the lead for us with another penalty and converted Gareth Allison's try after 65 minutes. In between, Saracens had scored a goal of their own and led again when Lee went over for a try with ten minutes left. Pears created the space for Staples to send O'Leary over, converted and dropped a goal to hand us an eight point margin of victory.

Our ninth win of the season came in a midweek friendly against Exeter University. Another ten tries were notched up and were scored by Mark Wadforth (3), Adam Jones, Pepper, Adam Jackson, Ian Pickup and Chris Wright (3). Successful kicks were made by Richard Bailey (2 conversions) and Wright (2 penalties and 4 conversions). The students scored a goal but the final score of 68-7 told the story.

All was going well until, after that ninth win, Dick was called to a meeting with the Board and asked what was going on and the team had to stop winning. He asked why and the reply was that the Finance Director (Guy Williams) had only budgeted for the team to win 50% of its matches! Dick said he was employed to win and that is what he did. He asked if they were not happy with the performance but the answer was that the Club was running out of money. His answer was to say that they had better go out and get some more money as they had approved the budget and said go and get on with it. He was then told to go back (as Director of Rugby) and tell the players that their bonuses were being halved. Obviously, they all had contracts so when an emergency meeting was called to announce the cut, people wanted to leave, agents were calling up and contracts were being waved. Dick had to say that the decision had come from above and he was passing on the message. If they didn't accept it, the Club would go under and then no one has a job. After this, four out of the next five matches were lost! Before you know it, there is an emergency Board meeting asking what's going on? We've lost four out of five, the players aren't playing well and they look demotivated…..!

Our tenth game was our sixth league game and was a tricky encounter at Heywood Road against Sale. The home side hadn't won since the opening game of the season and we had every reason to believe we would remain unbeaten. The trouble was, we played dreadfully and, although we remained in with a chance into the second half, a gift wrapped pass to Sale's flanker (Ashurst) killed us off. Sale's other try also led directly from an intercepted pass and with Rob Liley (who would join us two seasons later) adding nineteen points with the boot, we were well beaten. Pears scored with two penalties in the first half and a late try from Jim Staples only altered the margin of defeat. In this game, Andy Mullins became the first player to reach the milestone of 100 league appearances. Our 100% league and season records had gone and with this defeat, we slipped down to third place behind Bath and Leicester.

Our next four matches were league games against Bath (H), Gloucester (A), Leicester (H) and Orrell (H) and our league title winning chances would rest on the results of these. Bath had won all six of their matches so far and came to the Stoop with a league record of W3 D1 in their previous visits. Pears put us in front with a penalty before ten points in 18 minutes put them in the lead. After 31 minutes, O'Leary finished off a move with a try which Pears converted to leave it all square at the interval. Bath were all over us but we had a ten minute period of pressure at the start of the second half when the match might have been won. It wasn't and three Callard penalties took them clear. Pears did drop a goal before he and Catt wrote each other off when Catt tried to charge down a kick from Pears but there was no further scoring and we had lost our second game (13-19).

Jason Leonard made his first appearance as captain in the game at Kingsholm and Challinor replaced the injured Pears. Within the first five minutes, Jim Staples had raced over after a blind side break from Rob Kitchin and Bromley scored our second try from Gloucester's restart. We then went to sleep, Challinor missed five goal attempts (including both conversions) and Wright sent one wide from 15 metres out. Gloucester came back at us and with ten minutes left, we trailed 10-13. Luckily, we gathered ourselves for a final effort and Wright and Challinor scored tries for Staples to convert and we were home and dry.

Leicester visited next in a game we had to win to keep in touch with them and Bath at the top. John Liley kicked four penalties during the first half but Sheasby got a try between his first and second efforts, Challinor converted and also landed a penalty right on half time. We went in front for the second time when Mensah scored two minutes into the second period but the lead only lasted five minutes. Rory Underwood scored Leicester's first try and a penalty try took them further away (Liley's conversion made the gap eleven points). We weren't completely finished and O'Leary scored for Challinor to convert and there were still over twenty minutes left. The only other scores were penalties exchanged by Liley and Challinor to leave the final score at 25-29. Yet again we had made far too many mistakes and lost a game we should really have won – we had a lot to learn about how to win the league championship.

Orrell were on a revenge mission after losing the last two fixtures with us and they had to try and improve their current league position of seventh. It all began well for us when Kitchin scored under the posts after four minutes. Pears converted and we were on our way to victory – or were we? Our kicker then went on a wayward trip with the boot and missed seven out of ten penalty attempts whereas Mason landed five out of six for Orrell. He also scored a try in the first half and they led 14-10. Pears and Mason shared four penalties and when Taberner went over after 73 minutes, they led by nine points. With eight minutes to go, Mensah scored but Pears missed the conversion and our title hopes had again almost completely gone (21-25). Brian Moore finally made his last appearance for us against Orrell, he had scored just two tries (9 points) and captained the side 19 times during his five and a bit seasons at the Club.

A series of friendlies followed because of an international and the Divisional Championship. The first, at Cambridge against the university was cancelled so we took on London Irish at the Stoop on 2nd December. Mullins, Russell and Wright were the only survivors from the Orrell game but it made little difference against an Irish side missing men who were appearing in an Irish exiles match. In the first half, Andy Mullins, Jamie Williams and Adam Jones scored tries and Wright kicked two penalties and a conversion against three penalties for the visitors which completed their scoring. It was all one-way traffic after the break and Mark Russell, Jamie Canham, Williams, Glenn Harrison and Wright (who added three more conversions) got further tries. Wright finished with nineteen of our fifty four points. Nick Walshe made his debut in this game and would go on to appear 57 times during the next four seasons.

John Gallagher (who had won 18 caps for New Zealand) made his one and only appearance for us against Rosslyn Park the following week and was to become our Director of Rugby in 1998. He had a field day and ended up with a try and six conversions in our total of seventy four. Rosslyn Park scored two goals, a penalty and a try but our seven goals and five tries easily outscored them. Nick Walshe, Altan Ozdemir, Bromley (3), Wright (4) (and one conversion), Rhodri Davies and O'Leary crossed the line in an easy victory.

The Royal Navy visited us for the first time since 1979 and were sent away with another defeat. After taking an early lead with a penalty, Simon Mitchell and Harrison scored tries, Wright converted one and we were on our way. A second penalty reduced our lead to six points but further tries from Watson, Bromley and Brown (plus two more conversions by Wright) took us 31-6 clear at half time. An early rally by the Navy at the start of the half led to two goals and the gap was worryingly down to just eleven points. In the remaining time, we outscored them by three tries to two. Wright converted Watson's effort but the attempts to improve Kitchin's double failed. The final score of 48-30 was a fair result in an entertaining game.

Our fourth round cup tie at Orrell was played in freezing conditions - was it to be third time lucky in the cup at Edge Hall Road? An early penalty by Jim Staples put us on the road but two goals for Orrell in the 8th and 27th minutes put us eleven points in arrears. We rallied in the last ten minutes of the half and O'Leary and Carling scored unconverted efforts. The second half produced two penalties for Challinor and one by Mason for the home side. This had happened by the 52nd minute and all that took place in the final, frantic last half an hour was a booking for Cusani of Orrell and our own Mick Watson and a missed attempt at a dropped goal from both sides. This proved to be the last game of the year as our scheduled league game at Sudbury against Wasps was a victim of the weather.

Our first match of 1996 was the home league encounter with Bristol. We were third and they were sixth, just two points behind. We tried Wright, Carling and Challinor as place kickers in this game but the only success was a Carling penalty to give us the lead after 13 minutes. Watson, Bromley and Kitchin scored tries in a twelve minute spell near half time to put us 18-0 ahead. A 20 minute period of severe pressure for the visitors only led to a dropped goal from Thomas as our defence stood firm in a superb display. The game was now won and two late tries by Kitchin to complete his hat-trick against his former club gave us our biggest winning margin against Bristol since 1914. A quickly arranged fixture against Loughborough University (after our original opponents (Nottingham) had to play a re-arranged league fixture) enabled us to put out a reasonably strong side and it showed against the students. Glenn Harrison opened our account with a try, Mensah, O'Leary with two and Wright added others and Gareth Allison converted three to put us 31-0 ahead. The gap was narrowed by three points at half time when the visitors kicked a penalty. We eased off in the second half and only unconverted tries by Walshe and Bromley were added to our total. A goal and a try from Loughborough enabled them to outscore us in this period but the final score was 41-15 in our favour.

The weather now intervened and a friendly at Blackheath was cancelled and our 5th round cup tie at Newcastle was postponed. This was re-scheduled for 10th February but our next game was a noon kick-off on 3rd February against Rugby Lions at the Stoop. Our XV was only missing Greenwood, Leonard, Mitchell and Mullins from the cup line up and the Lions would pay the price. Twelve tries were run in but Allison converted only four of them;

otherwise the margin of victory could have been much wider. Staples, O'Leary (2), Harrison (2), Wright, Bromley (2), Challinor, Russell, Watson and Allison got those tries and 24 points for the visitors turned it into something slightly less than a one-sided encounter. Newcastle Gosforth had been purchased by Sir John Hall (the owner of Newcastle United Football Club) and had effectively become England's first professional rugby union team. This had forced the hand of all the other top teams and the R.F.U. to turn the sport into a professional one. Rob Andrew had joined from Wasps and several other internationals had followed him. These had defected from other clubs, most notably Wasps. One of our old boys now played for them, he was Richard Cramb. Newcastle were looking forward to taking a first division scalp but we had the better start and Will Greenwood got our first try after two minutes. Challinor converted and added a penalty on six minutes before Newcastle got on the scoreboard. McLennan went over for a try as the home side took control and Rob Andrew added a conversion and three penalties in the next twelve minutes before O'Leary got our second try to make it 15-16 at half time. The gulf in class began to show in the second half and O'Leary scored his second after twelve minutes. Challinor converted this and Mensah's effort four minutes later. Two more Andrew penalties left the score at 29-22 in our favour entering the final quarter. In the last ten minutes, O'Leary scored a hat-trick of tries to set up a new cup record of five tries in a match. The final score of 44-22 was a nice way to put Newcastle in their place and we moved into the quarter finals to face a difficult away trip to Leicester.

Our twelfth league match was an away trip to Bramley Road, Southgate to take on Saracens. A disappointing game saw Challinor and Lee share four penalties before the turning point came after 60 minutes. Mensah charged down an attempted kick from their fly half (Lee) near the half way line, gathered the lovely bounce and strode away unopposed to score under the posts for Challinor to convert. With no more scoring, we had achieved our eighth league win in those twelve outings. Our trip to Welford Road in the cup quarter finals came on 24th February and we were eventually destroyed by the big Leicester pack. Our only hope was for a dry day to try and nullify that pack but, a heavy downpour an hour before kick-off ensured that, as the game wore on, they took control. Liley had opened the scoring with a penalty after 18 minutes but Challinor levelled matters in similar fashion two minutes later. That was the half time score and three more Liley penalties took Leicester into a 12-3 lead. Challinor pulled back two penalties but sandwiched in between was a try by Kardooni (converted by Liley). We were surviving on scraps and when Garforth was pushed over from a line out, we were out.

Another friendly, this time against Richmond at the Athletic Ground supplied some 67 points. As was usual, our 2nd XV took the field and took part in a see-saw encounter with our near-neighbours and third division high flyers. Chris Wright (2) and James Storey scored our first half tries and we just led against Richmond's goal and three penalties. Two more goals from the home side in the second half took then thirteen points ahead and despite Ian Pickup scoring our fourth try for Phil Osman to convert, a fourth penalty by Roblin for Richmond left them 31-22 ahead with only six minutes remaining. We suddenly found some rhythm and Glenn Harrison and Jamie Williams (with virtually the last move of the match) got tries. Osman converted both and we had snatched a most unlikely victory. Former Moseley lock Steve Lloyd made his debut in this game but, due to disintegrating discs in his back, he would be forced to retire at the end of the season after only four appearances.

On 9th March, we went to Sudbury for the re-arranged league fixture against Wasps. We had lost on all of our five previous leagues visits so were looking to lay another hoodoo to rest. Gregory put Wasps in front with a penalty but that proved to be as far as they would go and we took command. Spencer Bromley went over for a try and Challinor kicked three penalties and dropped a goal to take us to 17-3 with eight minutes left. Wasps were a shadow of their former selves and tries from O'Leary (2) and Challinor and a conversion by Nick Walshe left us easy winners by thirty four points to three. This was not only our first league win at Sudbury, it was our biggest league win over them and their heaviest defeat both in the league and of the season. To be fair to them, the departure of Rob Andrew and several key players to Newcastle didn't help matters but, had Paul Challinor not missed six kicks at goal, the score may well have been higher.

Glenn Harrison was the only remaining member of the victorious side who travelled to Coventry on 16th March for a morning kick-off. This was to prove our last fixture against Coventry for nearly ten years as increased league games and other demands on players would lead to there being no room in the fixture list for friendly matches during the season. Against a stronger side, it was no good sending a team of youngsters as they just became cannon fodder. This was to be the case on this occasion and a small return of two tries (by Russell Osman and Mark Calverley) was cancelled by the home side's tally of forty four points (two goals and six tries).

Around this time it was announced that timekeepers were to be introduced for Courage League games after questions had been raised about the accuracy of timekeeping by referees. A klaxon and stopwatch was provided to each club and a pitchside location would be provided for the said timekeeper. The watch was stopped for injuries and 40 seconds after a player had indicated his intention to kick at goal; it was restarted when he kicked the ball. When 40 minutes had elapsed in each half, the klaxon was sounded and the referee blew his whistle for half time or no side the next time the ball became dead.

Almost everyone returned the following week for the long journey to West Hartlepool. Our hosts were holding up the table with no wins from eleven outings and would almost certainly have gone down but, as the league was being increased in size to twelve teams in 1996/97, there was to be no relegation. With revenge in mind for the narrow defeat of last season, we shot out of the blocks and had scored eight tries by half time. West managed two penalties but Challinor had added a penalty and four conversions to take us to 51 points. Three unconverted scores for the home side gave them a mediocre return for their efforts while we ran in another six tries which, with five more Challinor conversions took our tally to 91. Our try scorers were Allison (2), Challinor (who finished with 26 points), Watson (2) (who received his third yellow card of the season), Staples (2), Greenwood (2), Mullins, O'Leary (2) and Bromley (2). This score eclipsed the previous highest score in the league (Bath's 76-0 demolition of Bedford in 1990) and was our third highest score ever (after the 98-6 and 94-0 thrashings of Thailand and Tanzania in 1986 and 1973 respectively).

We had hit a rich vein of form now and a home game against Sale brought another avalanche of points. After our first defeat of the season at Sale back in October, we were on another revenge mission and wasted no time at all in putting our marker down. In the first 25 minutes, Staples scored two tries and dropped a goal and O'Leary went over for another try. Challinor's penalty took the half time score to 21-0. There was to be no let-up in this one way traffic in the second half and, as we piled on the pressure, Sale collapsed as they had done in 1988. Challinor dropped a goal and landed three conversions of tries scored by Watson (2) and Bromley (3) to give us a final score of 55-0.

On 6th April, we visited the Rec to try and make it a hat-trick of paybacks against Bath. We had now moved up to second spot just two points behind Bath but both they and Leicester had two games in hand over us. We started with ferocious determination and self-belief and were rewarded with tries by Kitchin and Challinor in the first fourteen minutes. Challinor converted the first and added a penalty just before half time to leave us 15-9 ahead. Callard had kicked three penalties for Bath and continued with two more to level the scores after 56 minutes. After this, the Bath juggernaut took control and we were blown away with an avalanche of 26 points in the last half an hour. Sleightholme, de Glanville and Guscott got tries, Callard added his sixth penalty and one conversion and Catt and Nicol each dropped a goal. The final score of 41-15 didn't really do us justice for our efforts but summed up Bath's ability to kill a team off if you let them take control.

Gloucester had beaten Bath in midweek and were said to be suffering something of a hangover but the game was far from a stroll for us. The first half only produced a penalty and a try from Challinor and a penalty in reply from Smith to leave the score at 8-3 in our favour. In the first five minutes of the second half, we blew them away with Challinor adding to his tally with a dropped goal and a conversion and Staples and O'Leary getting tries. Gloucester couldn't recover from this and, although they outscored us by 16-10 in the remaining time, tries from Greenwood and O'Leary were enough to see us comfortably home by 33-19. This win guaranteed us a top-three finish and would at least equal our third place in 1990/91. We also qualified for the Heineken European Cup the following season whereby the top four in the league would make up England's representatives. This game was chosen as the date for the first Ladies' day in the history of rugby union. The Harlequin Ladies played a Ladies Invitation side, there was a champagne and Pimm's tent, cosmetics, colour analysis, Cabouchon Jewellery and wine tasting. After the main game, there was a Summertime Fashion Show featuring some of the players in the President's Marquee (presented by Dickins & Jones department store and sponsored by the Evening Standard newspaper). This was followed by a Masquerade Ball to round off proceedings. It was a glimpse into the future of match day entertainment and would be repeated for a number of years.

Our final friendly of the season against London Scottish at the Athletic Ground was cancelled so our last game was the league trip to Leicester. With one game left, we were confirmed in third place and, unless Leicester defeated us and Bath didn't win, Bath would be champions. After only a minute, Daren O'Leary completed a good move from a lineout to score the opening try. Challinor missed the conversion and two penalties from Liley put Leicester in front before our second try arrived after an interception. O'Leary and Greenwood enabled Mensah to cross and Challinor's conversion gave us a six point cushion. Liley's try was replied to by Challinor with a dropped goal and we led deservedly by four points at the interval. Mick Watson dropped the ball as he was about to score before Challinor found the target with his first penalty success after 56 minutes. Liley responded with a penalty six minutes later and when Back went over from a rolling maul, the Tigers led by a point with eleven minutes left. We attacked and from a five metre scrum, Challinor got the ball, swivelled and dropped a goal; four minutes remained. Then, deep into injury time, Liley had the chance to win the game with a penalty from 35 metres out. Fortunately for us it was his sixth miss of the day and the referee's whistle sounded the end of the game. As it turned out, Bath drew with Sale so Liley's kick would have won not only the match but the league title as well! And so it was that our last game of the amateur days was a victory at Welford Road.

We took part in the Pulse Appeal Tens at Richmond with a very experimental side and lost to Italy (the eventual winners) by 5-17 and London Scottish (5-10) before defeating London Welsh (26-12). As was the case with Sevens, the Club now had no real appetite for the reduced forms of the game.

Our league record was P18 W13 L5 F524 A314 Pts26 Pos3rd. This was our best league season ever based on the amount of games played and, if it hadn't been for the loss of four games in five weeks during October and November, the league championship may well have been ours. Overall, our record was P32 W25 L7 F1141 A598 and was one of our most successful seasons ever. The best number of wins from 1983/84 was equalled (although six more games were played in that season). Daren O'Leary was the top try scorer with 25. This was the most scored since Colin Lambert's record breaking 42 in 1975/76. David Pears set an all-time record of 7 dropped goals (beating Stuart Winship's 6 in 1973/74) and Paul Challinor was top points scorer with 170 (7 tries, 5 dropped goals, 18 penalties and 33 conversions). Overall, a massive total of 165 tries were scored. This surpassed by 21 the record total of 1987/88. The number of dropped goals rose to 13 and this was an all-time record equalling number (the previous best being in 1973/74). Penalties fell by 18 to 39 and conversions went up by 39 to 80 (this was only two short of the record set in 1987/88). As a result of all these improvements, the overall points total was an all-time record as well. The total was 1141 which was over 200 more than the previous record set in 1975/76. Had our place kicking been better, it is certain that records would have been set in all areas. In the 32 games played, 71 players were used and only twenty of these made double figures. Spencer Bromley and Daren O'Leary came top with 23 appearances each and they were followed by Rory Jenkins, Andy Mullins, Alex Snow, Mick Watson and Chris Wright all on 22.

1995/96

090995	ORRELL(JCL1)	ORRELL	W	1G1DG1PG2T(23)-3PG(9)
120995	LONDON IRISH	STOOP MEMORIAL GROUND	W	1G1PG1T(15)-1G2PG(13)
160995	WASPS(JCL1)	STOOP MEMORIAL GROUND	W	2G3DG2PG(29)-5PG1T(20)
200995	RICHMOND	STOOP MEMORIAL GROUND	W	4G3T(43)-3PG(9)
230995	BRISTOL(JCL1)	BRISTOL	W	1G3PG3T(31)-2G2PG1T(25)
270995	LONDON SCOTTISH	STOOP MEMORIAL GROUND	C	
300995	WEST HARTLEPOOL(JCL1)	STOOP MEMORIAL GROUND	W	3G1DG2T(34)-1G2PG1T(18)
041095	BRUNEL UNIVERSITY	STOOP MEMORIAL GROUND	W	9G5T(88)-1G2T(17)
071095	SARACENS(JCL1)	STOOP MEMORIAL GROUND	W	2G1DG2PG(23)-1G1PG1T(15)
111095	EXETER UNIVERSITY	STOOP MEMORIAL GROUND	W	6G2PG4T(68)-1G(7)
141095	SALE(JCL1)	SALE	L	2PG1T(11)-2G5PG(29)
211095	BATH(JCL1)	STOOP MEMORIAL GROUND	L	1G1DG1PG(13)-1G4PG(19)
281095	GLOUCESTER(JCL1)	GLOUCESTER	W	2G2T(24)-1G2PG(13)
041195	LEICESTER(JCL1)	STOOP MEMORIAL GROUND	L	2G2PG1T(25)-2G5PG(29)
111195	ORRELL(JCL1)	STOOP MEMORIAL GROUND	L	1G3PG1T(21)-5PG2T(25)
171195	CAMBRIDGE UNIVERSITY	CAMBRIDGE	C	
021295	LONDON IRISH	STOOP MEMORIAL GROUND	W	4G2PG4T(54)-3PG(9)
091295	ROSSLYN PARK	STOOP MEMORIAL GROUND	W	7G5T(74)-2G1PG1T(22)

161295	ROYAL NAVY	STOOP MEMORIAL GROUND	W	4G4T(48)-2G2PG2T(30)
231295	ORRELL(PC4)	ORRELL	W	3PG2T(19)-2G1PG(17)
301295	WASPS(JCL1)	SUDBURY	P	
060196	BRISTOL(JCL1)	STOOP MEMORIAL GROUND	W	1PG5T(28)-1DG(3)
130196	LOUGHBOROUGH UNIVERSITY	STOOP MEMORIAL GROUND	W	3G4T(41)-1G1PG1T(15)
200196	BLACKHEATH	BLACKHEATH	C	
270196	NEWCASTLE GOSFORTH(PC5)	NEWCASTLE	P	
030296	RUGBY LIONS	STOOP MEMORIAL GROUND	W	4G8T(68)-1G1DG3PG1T(24)
100296	NEWCASTLE GOSFORTH(PC5)	NEWCASTLE	W	3G1PG4T(44)-1G5PG(22)
170296	SARACENS(JCL1)	SOUTHGATE	W	1G2PG(13)-2PG(6)
240296	LEICESTER(PCQF)	LEICESTER	L	3PG(9)-1G4PG1T(24)
020396	RICHMOND	RICHMOND	W	3G3T(36)-2G4PG1T(31)
090396	WASPS(JCL1)	SUDBURY	W	1G1DG3PG3T(34)-1PG(3)
160396	COVENTRY	COVENTRY	L	2T(10)-2G6T(44)
230396	WEST HARTLEPOOL(JCL1)	WEST HARTLEPOOL	W	9G1PG5T(91)-2PG3T(21)
300396	SALE(JCL1)	STOOP MEMORIAL GROUND	W	3G2DG1PG5T(55)-0
060496	BATH(JCL1)	BATH	L	1G1PG1T(15)-1G2DG6PG2T(41)
130496	GLOUCESTER(JCL1)	STOOP MEMORIAL GROUND	W	1G1DG1PG4T(33)-3PG2T(19)
200496	LONDON SCOTTISH	RICHMOND	C	
270496	LEICESTER(JCL1)	LEICESTER	W	1G2DG1PG1T(21)-3PG2T(19)

38

Professionalism Becomes a Reality 1996-2000

On Thursday 16th May 1996, the announcement came that the Club had effectively been sold to Riverside Sports plc (a health and sports club group) owned by Peter and John Beckwith. They were to buy a 40% stake and it would cost them £3 million. The investment was primarily for the redevelopment of the Stoop and would come in mighty handy now that professionalism had arrived. The brothers were said to be worth around £82 million and this placed them 180th in the Sunday Times rich list for 1996. John Beckwith and Mark Johnson were to join the Quins board as the two representatives from Riverside, Roger Looker (he would also be the Chairman), Colin Herridge and Donald Kerr would be Directors. All this was dependent on the Harlequin F.C. becoming a limited company and this was finally ratified by members at an Extraordinary Meeting at The Friends House, Euston Road, London on 28th May 1996. Prior to all this happening, a proposal had been sent to all members setting out how senior officials at the Club saw the future and what needed to be done to ensure the Quins remained at the forefront of World club rugby. Several clubs had already secured substantial investments including Newcastle, Northampton, Richmond and Saracens so it was imperative to go down this route. It was a fundamental element of the proposals that the trustees would keep control of the company and the Harlequin Trust would retain a Special Share which would give the Trustees the power of veto over major changes and enable them to preserve the objects of the Club irrespective of what the future held. It stated that the proposed investment would not give the investors control of the Club – how wrong this statement proved to be! At the same meeting was former captain David H. Cooke with Robert Bourne and his brother Graham. They had a company called Ex-lands that developed golf courses and offered £1.5 million. Cooke's idea was to build a retail park and hotel next to the A316 and the Club and pitch would be relocated to the Council depot at the back of the Stoop. However, they were outbid and the die had been cast.

In 1994, Dick Best and Bob Catcher had a meeting with a sponsorship agency at Canary Wharf as they had a company that was interested in doing a long term deal with an English rugby club. At that point, Whitbread were paying £50,000 per year so, after discussion, Dick and Bob decided that they would ask for £500,000 per year for three years. The man on the other side of the table didn't bat an eyelid and the deal was done. The company turned out to be NEC Corporation (a Japanese multi-national provider of information technology services and products). Although with all the perks offered by the Club, it turned out to be around £1.2 million but still a significant increase on the current deal. So it was that our sponsors for this inaugural season of professionalism would be NEC. They initially signed up for those three years although the partnership ended up lasting eleven. As part of the package, the name of the Club was changed to The NEC Harlequins of London. There had been talk of a deal with media company, Flextech. Our Chairman, Roger Looker was quoted as saying that in no way will a deal alter the name of the Club – another statement that was proved to be wrong! For the year ending 31st May 1997, the Club made a loss of £1,740,923 and the wage bill was now £2,053,585.

A massive change had taken place in the game and Jason Leonard would be our first captain of the professional era. Each member of the squad had a unique number and their name on the back of their shirt (although some numbers were only used by players who were not members of the main squad). This was an excellent idea as it was easy to see who was playing (especially with so many new faces!). It was frowned upon by a lot of people however and only lasted for two seasons before uniform numbering was adopted. Of the 43 players who appeared during this season, twenty were new to the Club (including eight Union and two League internationals). Our biggest playing loss was Will Greenwood; he departed to Leicester mainly due to a lack of effort to keep him but would return in August 2000. As well as the Heineken Cup, a new competition was introduced – this was the Anglo-Welsh League. The idea was that teams from England would play teams from Wales on a home and away basis. We had Cardiff, Llanelli and Swansea in our group but eventually, the competition faded away and most games were never played.

In our first match against Gloucester, we fielded the following newcomers: Laurent Bénézech (who would make 27 appearances and had won 15 caps for France), Laurent Cabannes (58 appearances and 49 caps for France), Gareth Llewellyn (108 appearances and 92 caps for Wales), Keith Wood (115 appearances, 58 caps for Ireland and would go on to win 5 for the British and Irish Lions) as well as Steve Pilgrim (who would only make a handful of appearances throughout the season). The Gloucester coach (Richard Hill) had come up with an idea of targeting the matches he thought they needed to win to ensure survival and fielded more or less his reserve side. This was a massive mistake and how they paid for it – the biggest score conceded by the Cherry and Whites in 105 years and over 4,000 matches! We hit the ground running and with our new kicker (a certain Will Carling) in good form, the score quickly mounted. In the first quarter, Carling landed two penalties and converted a penalty try (after Bromley had been impeded) and an effort from O'Leary. A try from Mensah was not improved but it meant we led by 25-0. Gloucester's scores were few and far between and their first was a try and conversion from Osborne. By half time, it was already one way traffic and O'Leary, Snow and Staples scored tries all of which Carling converted. Lloyd got Gloucester's second try but at 46-12, the result was a formality. Five minutes into the second half, we passed the fifty point mark when Bénézech scored his first try for the Club. Bromley, Cabannes and O'Leary got further tries and Carling added one more conversion before the visitors scored their second goal. All that remained was for O'Leary to score his fourth try which Carling again converted to make the final score 75-19. The new East Stand was nearing completion and the first seats would be used in October. The final cost was £5 million but it was a fantastic improvement on what we had before. After the game, O'Leary attended his sister's wedding. Before professionalism, he would not have played against Gloucester but with the new contracts in place, he had to appear so he hired a helicopter to whisk him away to attend the event in Orsett, Essex after the final whistle.

We became the early pace setters and had a chance to cement first place with games coming up against West Hartlepool (A), London Irish (H) and Bristol (A). Another new player appeared against West Hartlepool – his name was Dan Luger and he would go on to appear 89 times for the 1st XV, win 27 caps for England and go on tour with the British and Irish Lions (although injury would prevent him from winning any caps). Injury would hamper him for a number of years which cut down both his number of Quins appearances and England caps. He grabbed a brace of tries in the second half after Challinor (2) and Mensah had got us off to a good start. Carling (again the kicker) ended with a penalty and four conversions with our sixth try coming from Nick Walshe. West had only managed three penalties in response before a rally in the final twelve minutes brought them from 9-41 down to 21-41 at the end. We were playing some outstanding rugby and reaping the rewards. The following Wednesday should have seen us playing at Cardiff in the newly formed Anglo-Welsh League but this was postponed until 9th October.

London Irish had been promoted and were the next side to be taken to the cleaners by us. Gary Connolly (from Wigan RLFC and a Great Britain international) made the first of 14 appearances and, after an initial nervous period, found his feet and even scored a try himself after 71 minutes. Glyn Llewellyn (Gareth's brother) made the first of 17 appearances (he had won 9 caps for Wales) and Huw Harries (another Welshman) appeared in the first of 96 1st XV games. Mike Corcoran (a former professional footballer with Chelsea) converted his own try to open the scoring after seven minutes and landed a penalty after Keith Wood's unconverted double to put us 20-0 ahead after 26 minutes play. The Irish (who included two future Quins in their line up (Gary Halpin and Niall Woods)) managed a goal soon after Corcoran's penalty but that was all. The second half was a procession of tries for us with eight being scored (including Connolly's) in another festival of running rugby. Carling got only three conversions over from tries by Rory Jenkins (2), Staples (2), O'Leary and two more for Corcoran (who finished with twenty points). At this stage, only us and Wasps were unbeaten with three wins out of three.

A trip to Bristol is never easy and, as leaders, a hostile reception was inevitable. After 20 minutes, we trailed by ten points but, such was our confidence, we had turned this around by half time. Staples scored on 23 minutes and a penalty try (both converted by Carling) took us to 14-10. Five minutes into the second half, Keith Wood scored and Carling again converted as he did when O'Leary went over after 53 minutes. Between these two scores, Paul Burke had been replaced by Mark Tainton for Bristol and he had converted Corry's try to make the score 28-17 in our favour. Connolly scored our fifth try, Corcoran converted and we were safe. A late try for the home side made the final margin 35-24 as we became the only side to have passed the 200 points mark. Our second rugby league player made his debut in the next match at Franklin's Gardens against Northampton but, as with Gary Connolly, we never really saw enough of Robbie Paul. He came from Bradford Bulls RLFC and made only a dozen appearances for us (he went on to win 28 caps for the New Zealand Rugby League side between 1997 and 2006). Connolly played at centre and Paul was on the left wing (although the preferred option for the latter was fly half). After all the excitement of tries galore, this was a return to forward dominated rugby. It made little difference and we still won as our all-round power proved just too much for the Saints (another newly promoted side). We trailed to a goal before a Staples try and a penalty from Carling enabled us to lead at half time by a single point. Carling then converted his own try before Harries scored another between Beal's try and Grayson's penalty for the home side to leave us winners by five points (20-15).

On 2nd October, we travelled to St. Helens to meet Swansea for the first time since 1988. Because of the introduction of leagues, we hadn't played them at all since October 1989 so this match was a welcome return to the good old days. The reserve portion of our squad was utilised in this game (Paul was the only one remaining from the Northampton game) but it made no difference to our outstanding start to the season. Lee Davies put the All Whites ahead with two penalties and converted a try from Charvis to ensure they led at half time. Nick Walshe got over for us and Steve Pilgrim added a penalty to his conversion. Robbie Paul was in great form and, although he didn't score, he made more than one excellent break to open up the home defence. Into the second half, Mick Watson and Dominic Chapman (making his debut and although he would only appear four times for us, he did get an England cap in 1998) got tries and Pilgrim put over one conversion to give us a nine point lead. Swansea fought back and scored twelve points of their own to re-take the lead. We were not to be denied and Chapman's second try (converted by Pilgrim) and one for Jason Keyter (making his first appearance since returning from Bristol) took us clear. Swansea's fourth try from Harris came too late and we had won again.

Everyone returned for the visit of Orrell to the Stoop as they became another side to go away without any league points. They had lost some sixteen players in the close season and had failed to secure the required finances to attract the better players. This week, Connolly and Paul were paired in the centre and Carling (after his successful debut in the centre) was again at fly half. Orrell were rooted to the bottom of the table with five defeats from as many games whereas we were the exact opposite. After Strett had put the visitors ahead with a penalty after seven minutes, our machine got going. Strett did get a second penalty over but we had scored 39 points. Harries, Paul, Connolly, Bromley, Bénézech and Carling scored tries and the last named added a penalty and three conversions in a dazzling display. A goal at the start of the second half and a try at the end took the visiting side's total to eighteen points but, by then, we were eyeing up a three figure score. Bill Davison, Harries (completing his hat-trick), Watson, Bromley, Paul, Connolly and a penalty try took our number to fourteen. Carling converted another five to finish with twenty four points to make the final score 89-18. This was our biggest winning margin in league competition passing our previous best of 70 set against West Hartlepool during the previous season. Our fifty second half points were scored in half an hour so we really should have posted our first ever score in excess of 100 and indeed, had all the conversions gone over, we would have done just that.

The following Wednesday, we travelled down to Cardiff for our second Anglo-Welsh fixture with five men from the Orrell victory still in the side (including Challinor who had been a temporary replacement). Andy Mullins captained (as he had at Swansea) in the absence of Leonard and led the side to an impressive victory. This was our first visit to Cardiff for six years to a ground where we had won only two of our last twenty matches. Corcoran was the nominated kicker in this game and he put us in front with a penalty before Jarvis equalised for the home side in similar fashion. After Corcoran had landed his second penalty, we exploded with four tries in a 20 minute spell to take a 34-3 lead into the break. Challinor, Mensah, Keyter and Corcoran (who converted all four) got the tries. Cardiff did rally in the second half and scored three close range tries which Jarvis converted but they never came closer than fourteen points. Mensah ran 50 metres for his second try before Connolly and Kitchin completed the rout. Two more conversions from Corcoran took his tally of points to 23. We had now scored 62 tries in eight unbeaten matches.

Our next game was an away trip to Ravenhill in Belfast to take on Ulster in our first pool match in the Heineken European Cup. Both Gary Connolly and Robbie Paul had been brought in for our assault on this trophy and they played against Ulster along with seven other internationals. David Humphreys at fly half was one of four internationals in the home side's line up and it was he who put the Irishmen in front with a penalty after 12 minutes. Mick Watson replied with a try two minutes later, Carling converted and added a penalty just after Humphreys had dropped a goal. Two more penalties from the Irish fly half gave them a two point advantage at half time and a shock was on the cards. Will Carling was not having a good night and missed four out of seven penalty attempts. He did get two in the 52nd and 54th minutes to give us the lead but Humphreys was again successful with a penalty to bring the score back to 16-15 in our favour. In the 75th minute, he had the chance to put the home side in front but his penalty attempt from 35 metres drifted past the right hand upright. Three minutes later, O'Leary went past two defenders to score in the corner and seal our victory by twenty one points to fifteen and give us our first victory in the European Cup at our first attempt. The league had taken a break until the end of the month and we had three more pool games to come against Neath (H), Brive (A) and Caledonia Reds (H). As it was, the competition was set up without home and away fixtures in the pool matches and we probably had our two most difficult games away from home.

Our only previous meeting with Neath came at Twickenham in April 1962 when neither side had scored. This time it was a lot different and Peter Mensah opened the scoring after only one minute of play when he completed a six man move. Carling converted but it would be one of only two successful kicks out of nine attempts during the game. A Geraint Davies penalty brought Neath their first points but by half time, we had moved away. O'Leary scored two tries, Cabannes one and Carling converted the last to give us a 24-3 advantage. A try from Steve Williams reduced the half time deficit to sixteen points. In the third quarter, Jamie Williams scored a brace of tries and Cabannes got his second to sew the game up. Had Carling converted any of these, we would have been approaching the fifty point mark for the fifth time this season. As we relaxed, Neath came back with two goals in the last ten minutes but a hat-trick try from Williams made sure of victory by 44-22. This was our tenth win of the season and our twelfth on the trot which equalled the all-time record number of wins set in 1908/09 and 1988/89.

What looked like the Pool decider came next when we travelled to France to take on Brive on Sunday 27th October. It all started well enough when Carling kicked a penalty and converted a try from Challinor to take us into a ten point lead. Slowly but surely, the home side came into the game being roared on by the 15,000 crowd (complete with drums and firecrackers). A succession of kicks from Brive (two penalties and two dropped goals) gave them the lead at half time and two more penalties stretched this to 18-10 with half an hour to go. We threw everything we had at them but try as we did, we just couldn't break through although Jamie Williams had a try disallowed and Robbie Paul missed a glaring overlap with a few minutes to go. In injury time, Carrat was sent away by Lamaison and proceeded to run 90 metres, beating four defenders on the way, to touch down for the match clinching try. We had fallen to our first defeat of the season and once again, the thirteenth successive victory had proved a game too far.

On the following Wednesday, we went up to Manchester to meet Sale in a league game and slipped to another defeat. Simon Mannix (three penalties) and Dewi Morris (two tries) did the damage with Charlie Vyvyan scoring their other try. For us, Mike Corcoran had opened the scoring with a penalty, Nick Walshe's try had put us temporarily in front (8-6) and Gary Connolly's try came right at the end of the game to make the final score 13-24. If we were to win the league, we had to win games like this one after a testing encounter in France.

Our third game in seven days came at the Stoop against the Caledonia Reds – it was our final pool match and a win would take us into a quarter final at Leicester (if Brive didn't lose to Ulster). Jamie Williams started us off with a try and before half time had bagged his second. Staples got another and Carling added a penalty and a conversion but regular scoring from the Scots including a try from David Officer (who would join us at the start of the 1998/99 season) kept them in the game just four points behind. Staples completed his hat-trick and O'Leary added another (which Carling converted) but the Reds had got a goal and a try of their own to leave the score at 37-28 to us. It was time to move up another gear now and Challinor and Paul scored further tries and when O'Leary got our ninth, we were clear winners. Carling had added two conversions and the visitors had scored another goal but the final score of 56-35 said it all. Ulster had been beaten at home by Brive so it was up the M1 to Leicester we would go on 16th November for a quarter final tie.

Before that, we had our fourth match in eleven days when Llanelli visited the Stoop for an Anglo-Welsh League fixture. The games against Cardiff and Swansea proved to be just warm-ups for this one as our second string ran riot against the reserve team from Stradey Park. Llanelli got a penalty in the first half and a goal in the second to finish with ten points. We had surpassed this total after just 16 minutes as our strength in depth began to show.

Steve Pilgrim put over three conversions of the five tries scored in the first half by Bromley, Wright, Kitchin, Jenkins and Watson to give us a 31-3 lead. The second half was another display of attacking rugby and seven more tries followed. Simon Owen, Jason Keyter (3), Dan Luger, Pilgrim (plus three more conversions) and Corcoran (who also got three conversions) got the tries to make the final score 78-10. This was our biggest ever win over Llanelli and our highest ever score against Welsh opposition. Our next scheduled game was against Saracens in the league but this was postponed and would be played in April.

On 16th November, we met Leicester in the European Cup quarter final at Welford Road on a freezing cold day. For the first 45 minutes, we had Leicester's defence in serious trouble and should have been well clear by half time. All we had to show was a try from Dan Luger after six minutes as Connolly (wasting a four on two overlap) and Staples and O'Leary (somehow contriving to mess up another opportunity near the Leicester line) let the side down. Rob Liley had missed a couple of penalties but finally got one over after 40 minutes. A minute into the second half, Carling scored our second try but another missed conversion kept the Tigers in the game. Just after this came the turning point of the tie. Laurent Cabannes was in our 22 with the ball and eventually decided to dither for so long that his pass to Challinor went to ground first and his attempted clearance kick (which just made touch) ended with a penalty to Leicester for offside. From the penalty, the ball was kicked into the corner by Healey and from the lineout, Cockerill was driven over for the try, Liley converted and it was 10-10. The crowd, which had been silent, erupted into life and we were in real trouble. Two more penalties from Liley to one from Challinor with nine minutes left made it 16-13 to the home side. Two minutes after his success, Challinor had a penalty chance from 40 metres to level the scores. His kick cannoned back off the right hand upright and our chance had gone. With time running out, Liley sneaked through from a line out to score under the posts as Challinor and Carling collided. His conversion made the final score 23-13 to Leicester. We were out and they went on to defeat Toulouse in the semi-final before losing to Brive in the final.

A break of three weeks ended with a trip to Bath and we desperately needed a win. After Callard had put Bath in front with a penalty, we took charge and ran Bath ragged. Challinor equalised with a penalty and converted his own try as well as one from Harries as we raced into a 17-3 lead after 24 minutes. Had Challinor not missed a simple dropped goal and if Catt had not tap-tackled Mensah when he had half the pitch and no defenders in front of him, we would have been completely clear. As it turned out, this lead was nowhere near enough and Bath came out in the second half a totally different side. As they had done in the league game at the Stoop in April 1995, Bath came back and wiped out our lead by the 67th minute. Guscott led the fight back with a try in the first minute of the half, Callard converted and kicked two penalties but one from Challinor briefly kept us in front. When Thomas went over, we trailed by one point and from here on in, it was all Bath. Adebayo and Guscott got further tries which Callard converted and we had suffered our second league defeat of the season. A big blow was an injury to Jim Staples who fractured a cheekbone in a clash of heads with Adebayo. He was potentially out for up to eight weeks but, as it turned out, he returned after five.

It was cup time again on 21st December and we took on Cheltenham at the Stoop in a fifth round tie. A very strong side was fielded against what turned out to be a very gritty visiting side. With an arctic wind howling down the pitch, we played with it at our backs in the first half and ran up a 27-3 lead. At times, we over-elaborated and many passes were dropped due to cold hands. Pilgrim, Connolly (2), Paul and O'Leary got tries but the first named could only convert one. The visitors managed a penalty after 35 minutes and another nine minutes later but that was as close as they got. O'Leary scored another three tries and Luger completed the scoring with our ninth try but no more conversion attempts were successful. Mudway went over for a well-deserved try for Cheltenham but the final score of 47-11 was a fair reflection of the play. For the first time, the new East Stand was fully operational for this game. The lack of kicking success was starting to have an effect and more games would be lost if we couldn't find a kicker who would put over a high percentage of his kicks – this situation was to change in the new year when someone arrived who was capable of doing just that.

Our last fixture of the year was a home league game against Leicester. We desperately needed to gain some revenge for the European Cup defeat to get our league title aspirations back on track. We made four changes from the team defeated at Welford Road in November, the Tigers made three. We had slipped to third place and Leicester were now top, just two points ahead of us. In the first half, Pilgrim and Challinor kicked penalties for us but the visitors got tries from Rory Underwood and John Liley (who added two penalties and a conversion) to lead 18-6. The second half was no better and we simply had no answer to the pace and running of Leicester's backs. Liley added two more penalties and Underwood and Will Greenwood (on his return to the Stoop) scored further tries. In reply, Harries got a pair of tries and Challinor's single conversion reduced the deficit to sixteen points. Our third league defeat dropped us into fourth place behind Leicester, Wasps and Bath and, after such a promising start, the doubts were starting to creep in again. But, with thirteen games to play there was still time to turn things round.

A difficult trip to Loftus Road to play Wasps at their new home (they now had a ground share with Queen's Park Rangers Football Club) was next on the agenda. The move towards ground sharing in the future would see more games played on a Sunday; it seemed like only yesterday when Sunday matches were a rarity and the entrance fee could only be charged by putting the programme price up. The kicker we had so desperately craved finally arrived in the shape of Thierry Lacroix. He was in the process of winning 43 French caps and would go on to make 64 1st XV appearances. Gary Connolly made his farewell appearance after having scored 9 tries (45 points) in his 14 appearances. He went back to Wigan and his first choice sport. Wasps fielded Gareth Rees and Nick Greenstock (both future Quins) and Simon Mitchell and Chris Sheasby (both ex-Quins although both would return). It took some getting used to playing on the narrow confines of the Loftus Road pitch with its much reduced in-goal area and we were quickly in arrears. Damian Cronin scored a try after 5 minutes before Lacroix was successful with his first penalty attempt from the Wasps 22 metre line. Rees added two penalties for the home side before Lacroix made it 6-11 at the break with another penalty. When Rees completed his hat-trick after 47 minutes, we looked to be heading for another loss but Lacroix and Cabannes had other ideas. Cabannes was all over the field and helped to get our driving play going. Gary Connolly signed off in spectacular fashion as he cut and swerved his way in under the posts to make Lacroix's conversion after 55 minutes a formality. Two minutes later, we were in front when Lacroix got his third penalty and when he got his fourth on 64 minutes, we led by five points. King dropped a goal for Wasps but missed a last, desperate attempt just after Rees had failed with a penalty from half way and the points were in the bag. A new confidence had been found from Lacroix's 100% kicking debut.

The following week, Bath visited us for a must win game which saw Robbie Paul make his final appearance before returning to Bradford. He had scored 4 tries (20 points) in his (like Gary Connolly) all too brief foray into rugby union. In the first half, Callard twice put Bath in front with penalties but both times Lacroix pegged them back with penalties of his own. His third and fourth successes put us in front and his dropped goal made the lead nine points. As our forwards took control, Bath started to crumble and the pressure finally told when Paul put Jim Staples over for a try which Lacroix converted to take us to a famous 22-6 victory. It was our first over Bath since

December 1986 – a run of one draw and sixteen defeats. It was also their worst ever league defeat and enabled us to jump into second place.

Another ground sharing club were our next opponents on Sunday 19th January when we travelled to Enfield to take on Saracens. They had also spent well in the summer and three of their signings played in this game. Michael Lynagh, Philippe Sella and Francois Pienaar all made telling contributions. Adrian Olver, Tony Copsey and Tony Diprose were also against us and the last two named scored tries which finally killed off our challenge. Lynagh dropped a goal and landed two penalties to give them a 9-6 lead (Lacroix had put over two penalties for us) at half time. In the second half, Sella scored for Lynagh to convert before we rallied and O'Leary and Cabannes got tries which Lacroix converted to put us 20-16 ahead with most of the final quarter remaining. Lynagh converted one of those last two tries and we had lost again, this time by 20-28.

The return with Cardiff in the Anglo-Welsh League was cancelled so our next game was the 6th round cup tie at Clifton Lane against ambitious Division 2 club Rotherham. A crowd of 4,000 was squeezed into the ground and a double decker bus was used as the press area! Dean Lax put the home side in front on 6 minutes but a twenty two point burst in fourteen minutes put us into a great position. Thierry Lacroix kicked a penalty and converted two of our three tries scored by O'Leary (2) and Luger. Lax got two more penalties before the interval but another penalty from our French fly half and the conversion of O'Leary's third try took us to 32-9 and the game was reasonably safe. Miller and Binns scored tries in a fifteen minute spell of pressure from our never say die opponents which Lax converted but Lacroix added the killer blows with another penalty and the conversion of Luger's second try to put us into the quarter finals again.

Sale were swiftly replacing Orrell as our bogey side and had won two of the last three meetings but had yet to win at the Stoop. Lacroix was yet again on target in this game and it was his boot alone that kept us in the hunt. He had landed one penalty but Sale had scored fifteen points at the end of the first quarter. We awoke from our slumber and two Lacroix penalties and a try from Gareth Llewellyn brought us to within a point at the interval. Lacroix kicked two penalties and converted a try from Huw Harries but the visitors had scored two tries and a penalty and still led by that single point as normal time expired. Enter Chris Yates (the Sale centre) into a maul from an offside position, a penalty to us, Lacroix's boot again and we were in front. From the restart, Sale regained possession, the ball was flung back to Yates and he dropped a goal from 40 metres to win the game 31-30. Villain to hero in less than a minute! We only had ourselves to blame and our chances of the title were quickly disappearing down the drain.

A break from league action brought the Auckland Blues to the Stoop for a friendly fixture. The 130th anniversary challenge was supposed to become an annual fixture but, until now, it has remained a one-off. The mud, wind and rain provided conditions which ensured that there was only one way of playing the game and it wasn't with the ball in hand as the Blues tried to do in the first half. After the visitors had taken the lead with a try, the floodgates opened from an unexpected source. Dominic Chapman, Peter Mensah and Gareth Llewellyn scored for us and Lacroix added a penalty and two conversions to give us a 22-5 lead. A goal right on half time reduced the deficit and after 54 minutes, we trailed 22-25 after two tries and a penalty from the New Zealanders. Nick Walshe scored our fourth try and Corcoran converted to restore our lead but could we hold on for over thirty minutes? Due to the upcoming cup quarter final, we had made six changes at half time and this didn't help our chances although the newcomers tried their best. On 67 minutes, Robin Brooke got their fifth try and Cashmore landed a penalty out of the quagmire just before full time to snatch the game away from us. In this game, Tom Billups (25 appearances and 44 caps for the United States of America) and Luke Gross (21 appearances and 62 caps for the United States of America) made their debuts for the 1st XV.

The following Sunday, 23rd February, was the quarter final tie against Saracens at the mud bath formerly known as the Stoop. We had to win this one because the cup had become our only realistic chance of winning a trophy this season. We played with the strong wind in the first half and, after a sixth successive scrum broke up near the Saracens line, referee Steve Lander awarded us a penalty try which Thierry Lacroix converted. He landed two penalties in time remaining in the first half but a penalty from Lynagh and a try by Sella made Saracens the favourites with the wind in their favour in the second half. We came out fighting and Cabannes had another tremendous game. Within two minutes of the re-start, Carling had scored a try and when O'Leary added another after 59 minutes, we led 23-11. Lynagh had kicked his second penalty but then joined Pienaar off the field before Diprose scored for Lee to convert and the gap had narrowed. Keyter then sent Carling through on a clear run to the line and we were into the semi-finals despite a late penalty from Lee.

Orrell, our next opponents, were bottom of the table with just one win from their twelve games so far and were odds-on to go down. In less than a minute, Naylor had gifted a try to Dominic Chapman and we never looked back. McCarthy, at fly half for Orrell, did land two penalties and convert his own try but, by this time, Lacroix had also kicked two penalties and converted tries by O'Leary and Chapman. Into the second half, he converted his own score and added the points to Mensah's effort. Between these, Chapman had raced 65 metres for the second time to complete his hat-trick and, with 15 minutes left, Taberner scored for our hosts for McCarthy to convert. At 44-20, the game was safe and we rounded things off in style with further tries from Davison and O'Leary plus another conversion by Lacroix to take his total to 21 and ours to 56.

Our next game was also against a side who were struggling and that was West Hartlepool. In the first seven minutes, we raced into a 17-0 lead and a very big win was a distinct possibility. However, we made too many errors and tried to over complicate moves when simplicity would have done and, as a consequence, we only led 29-0 at the break. Thierry Lacroix was again on target and kicked a penalty after only a minute as well as converting three of the four tries scored by Jason Keyter, Daren O'Leary and a couple from Michael Corcoran. By the time 63 minutes had passed, our lead had reached 43-0 and a whitewash looked on the cards. Walshe had grabbed two tries and Lacroix had slotted his fourth and fifth conversions. West rallied and scored a couple of tries but Walshe completed his hat-trick (the tenth of the season for the 1st XV squad) and a rather disappointing 48-10 victory was attained against a very poor West Hartlepool side.

On 29th March, we made the long trek to Heywood Road to play Sale in the Pilkington Cup semi-final. We struggled to deal with Sale's all round pace from the word go and, after Mannix and Lacroix had exchanged penalties, O'Grady went over for the first try from a quickly taken penalty which Mannix converted. Lacroix got his second penalty and then came the turning point of the tie. After 34 minutes, Lacroix split the defence open and passed to Carling who drew the last defender and shipped the ball on to Mensah with the line at his mercy. Somehow, unbelievably, he dropped the ball and our chance had gone. Just two minutes later, Sale won the ball in midfield and Mallinder galloped in from 50 metres out for their second try. Mannix failed to convert but added a penalty right on half time to stretch the lead to 18-6. Lacroix's third penalty gave us some hope but Mannix put over his third and then Tom Beim ran the ball back 65 metres to score in the corner after Challinor had failed to gather a pass. At 26-9, we had to score at least three times to secure our place in the final and this, unsurprisingly proved too much of a hurdle to clear. After making four changes, Gareth Llewellyn did eventually score a try which Lacroix converted but the final score of 26-16 was no more than Sale deserved. The following Wednesday, we were due to meet Swansea at the Stoop in the return Anglo-Welsh League match but, like the return with Cardiff, this was cancelled.

Against London Irish in our sixteenth league game, we raced into a thirteen point lead in the first 15 minutes with a dropped goal, a penalty and a conversion from Lacroix and a 90 metre try from Chapman (after an interception by Cabannes). We then nodded off for the rest of the half and Humphreys kicked two penalties and converted a try from Walsh to leave it all-square at the interval. Two more penalties from Lacroix (although he had missed three others) gave us a six point lead with time running out. The Irish made one last effort and Humphreys broke through for O'Shea to score near the posts. Humphreys put the conversion over and we didn't have enough time to score again. Our sixth league defeat dropped us into fifth place and only a miracle would see us lift the trophy at the end of the season.

Our re-arranged fixture with Saracens was played on 9th April at the Stoop and a hard earned victory was eventually secured. Saracens were just too generous and missed three penalties and a try scoring chance due to a knock-on in the first half alone. We only managed an O'Leary try which Lacroix converted. Keith Wood had returned to the starting line-up for the first time since 11th January due to a shoulder injury and lasted for 64 minutes. As the mistakes continued to mount up from both sides, Lacroix kicked two penalties to put us 13-0 ahead with nine minutes remaining. Jim Staples and Peter Mensah wrapped things up with late tries which were both converted by Lacroix. The final score of 27-0 took us into fourth place in the table. The following Tuesday, we met Bristol at the Stoop and this time gained an easy victory. Paul Burke landed two penalties for Bristol in the first half but a brace of tries by Keith Wood after Lacroix's penalty put us in front. Bristol failed to score in the second half whereas we added to our total with two penalties and a dropped goal from Lacroix. He also added the conversion to O'Leary's late try to make the final score 29-6. A top four place would ensure qualification for the European Cup in 1997/98 – we were currently fifth. With four games left, Leicester, Bath, Sale and Quins were separated by two points. Wasps needed four points from their final three games to win the title.

Four days after the Bristol game, we travelled to Kingsholm for the return with Gloucester. Lacroix and Wood both had an outstanding game and we showed a touch of steel to take Gloucester's seven month unbeaten home record. Our French fly half landed two penalties, one either side of a try and a penalty for Gloucester but his conversion of a try from Jamie Williams ensured our lead at the interval. Mapletoft's second penalty reduced the arrears to two points but we raced away with tries from Lacroix and O'Leary. Two conversions from the metronomic boot of Lacroix took the final margin to 27-11 and the European spot was within our grasp.

Our last Anglo-Welsh League fixture at Llanelli on 23rd April was cancelled as the competition faded into obscurity so our next match was an away trip to Leicester. It was second against fifth and we now knew that if we won our last three matches, we would get into a European Cup spot. Two early penalties from Joel Stransky gave Leicester the lead before Lacroix outscored John Liley two penalties to one to make it 9-6 after 35 minutes. Then, as Staples made a powerful run, O'Leary came off his wing to go over the line with two men hanging onto him. Lacroix put the conversion over before John Liley got his second penalty to make it 13-12 to us at half time. In the second half, John Liley missed two penalties and his brother (Rob) missed with a dropped goal after some intense Leicester pressure. We managed to negotiate the remaining five minutes of injury time to move up into third place. After taking Gloucester's home record, we now took Leicester's and ensured that one more win would take us into Europe.

Our next opponents were Northampton at the Stoop and, despite taking the lead with a Lacroix penalty, we soon found ourselves behind. Alastair Hepher kicked two penalties and converted his own try in a ten minute spell before Keith Wood dragged us back into the game with a try. Lacroix converted both this and O'Leary's effort to give us a 17-13 lead at the break. Hepher's dropped goal proved to be Northampton's last score as we began to run away with the game. Mensah (2) and Mullins scored further tries with Lacroix adding two conversions to take us into Europe with a 36-16 victory. Alex Snow made his last appearance in this match having led the side on two occasions and scored 5 tries (25 points) in his five season career.

In our final game of the season, Wasps came to the Stoop as Champions and paraded the trophy at the end of the match. They proved to be too good for us on the day as we fielded a disrupted side due to injuries. Rees, Greenstock, Mitchell and Sheasby appeared in their starting line-up (all had or would have connections with Quins). After going into an eight point lead, we pegged them back and were in front by half time with Lacroix getting a penalty and converting Allison's try just after the half hour mark. This lead was blown away with a three try blast in a ten minute spell to leave us seventeen points behind. Although Rees got another penalty, tries from Cabannes and Keyter plus a conversion from Corcoran kept us in the hunt with five minutes left. The visitors would not be denied and another twelve points sewed the game up at 42-22 to leave them six points clear at the top of the table. Laurent Bénézech made his last appearance in this game having scored just two tries (10 points) during his season at the Club.

This had been another successful league season as we ended up with a record of P22 W15 L7 F745 A416 Pts30 Pos 3rd. It should really have been a championship winning year but a series of losses at the wrong time (as had happened the previous season) put paid to our chances. It only proved that we still didn't really have that killer instinct which all champion teams possess. Overall, we had a playing record of P35 W24 L11 F1216 A712. Daren O'Leary was again top try scorer with 28 beating his total in the previous season by three and Thierry Lacroix top scored in the other sections. He totalled 219 points in just 17 appearances (2 tries, 3 dropped goals, 42 penalties and 37 conversions). Overall, the record number of tries was equalled (165), dropped goals fell to just 3, penalties rose up to 62 and conversions went up to 98. This was an all-time record, beating the previous best of 82 set in 1987/88. Overall, the total number of points scored (1216) was another all-time record and surpassed the previous record set the season before of 1141. The previously mentioned 43 players were used during the 35 matches and this was the lowest since 1972/73 when 39 were utilised. Bill Davison made the most appearances with 32 closely followed by Laurent Cabannes on 31; he was followed by Will Carling and Jason Leonard (29), Daren O'Leary (28) and Laurent Bénézech, Rory Jenkins and Gareth Llewellyn on 27.

1996/97

310896	GLOUCESTER(JCL1)	STOOP MEMORIAL GROUND	W	7G2PG4T(75)-2G1T(19)
070996	WEST HARTLEPOOL(JCL1)	WEST HARTLEPOOL	W	4G1PG2T(41)-1G3PG1T(21)
110996	CARDIFF(AWL)	CARDIFF	P	
140996	LONDON IRISH(JCL1)	STOOP MEMORIAL GROUND	W	4G1PG7T(66)-1G(7)
210996	BRISTOL(JCL1)	BRISTOL	W	5G(35)-2G2T(24)
280996	NORTHAMPTON(JCL1)	NORTHAMPTON	W	1G1PG2T(20)-1G1PG1T(15)

021096	SWANSEA(AWL)	SWANSEA	W	3G1PG2T(34)-2G2PG2T(30)
051096	ORRELL(JCL1)	STOOP MEMORIAL GROUND	W	8G1PG6T(89)-1G2PG1T(18)
091096	CARDIFF(AWL)	CARDIFF	W	6G2PG1T(53)-3G1PG(24)
161096	ULSTER(HECP)	RAVENHILL	W	1G3PG1T(21)-1DG4PG(15)
191096	NEATH(HECP)	STOOP MEMORIAL GROUND	W	2G6T(44)-2G1PG1T(22)
271096	BRIVE(HECP)	BRIVE	L	1G1PG(10)-2DG4PG1T(23)
301096	SALE(JCL1)	SALE	L	1PG2T(13)-3PG3T(24)
021196	CALEDONIA REDS(HECP)	STOOP MEMORIAL GROUND	W	4G1PG5T(56)-3G3PG1T(35)
061196	LLANELLI(AWL)	STOOP MEMORIAL GROUND	W	9G3T(78)-1G1PG(10)
091196	SARACENS(JCL1)	STOOP MEMORIAL GROUND	P	
161196	LEICESTER(HECQF)	LEICESTER	L	1PG2T(13)-2G3PG(23)
071296	BATH(JCL1)	BATH	L	2G2PG(20)-3G3PG1T(35)
211296	CHELTENHAM(PC5)	STOOP MEMORIAL GROUND	W	1G8T(47)-2PG1T(11)
281296	LEICESTER(JCL1)	STOOP MEMORIAL GROUND	L	1G2PG1T(18)-1G4PG3T(34)
050197	WASPS(JCL1)	LOFTUS ROAD	W	1G4PG(19)-1DG3PG1T(17)
110197	BATH(JCL1)	STOOP MEMORIAL GROUND	W	1G1DG4PG(22)-2PG(6)
190197	SARACENS(JCL1)	ENFIELD	L	2G2PG(20)-2G1DG2PG1T(28)
220197	CARDIFF(AWL)	STOOP MEMORIAL GROUND	C	
250197	ROTHERHAM(PC6)	ROTHERHAM	W	4G3PG1T(42)-2G3PG(23)
080297	SALE(JCL1)	STOOP MEMORIAL GROUND	L	1G6PG1T(30)-1G1DG2PG3T(31)
180297	AUCKLAND BLUES	STOOP MEMORIAL GROUND	L	3G1PG1T(29)-1G2PG4T(33)
230297	SARACENS(PCQF)	STOOP MEMORIAL GROUND	W	1G2PG3T(28)-1G3PG1T(21)
080397	ORRELL(JCL1)	ORRELL	W	5G2PG3T(56)-2G2PG(20)
220397	WEST HARTLEPOOL(JCL1)	STOOP MEMORIAL GROUND	W	5G1PG2T(48)-2T(10)
290397	SALE(PCSF)	SALE	L	1G3PG(16)-1G3PG2T(26)
020497	SWANSEA(AWL)	STOOP MEMORIAL GROUND	C	
050497	LONDON IRISH(JCL1)	SUNBURY	L	1G1DG3PG(19)-2G2PG(20)

090497	SARACENS(JCL1)	STOOP MEMORIAL GROUND	W	3G2PG(27)-0
150497	BRISTOL(JCL1)	STOOP MEMORIAL GROUND	W	1G1DG3PG2T(29)-2PG(6)
190497	GLOUCESTER(JCL1)	GLOUCESTER	W	3G2PG(27)-2PG1T(11)
230497	LLANELLI(AWL)	LLANELLI	C	
260497	LEICESTER(JCL1)	LEICESTER	W	1G2PG(13)-4PG(12)
300497	NORTHAMPTON(JCL1)	STOOP MEMORIAL GROUND	W	4G1PG1T(36)-1G1DG2PG(16)
030597	WASPS(JCL1)	STOOP MEMORIAL GROUND	L	2G1PG1T(22)-3G2PG3T(42)

It was time for another British Lions tour, this time to South Africa. The trip lasted from late May to early July and would contain thirteen matches. Jason Leonard and Keith Wood were our only current players to make the squad with Will Greenwood and Tony Diprose (who was called up as a sub) among the others. The Lions won the first two test matches 25-16 and 18-15 (a dropped goal from Guscott winning the series) and lost the third (16-35) but it mattered not a jot. Of the other games, a record of W9 L1 was recorded to complete a successful tour.

England also toured in May and June to Argentina and played a one-off test against Australia in July. We had two current players (Rory Jenkins and Daren O'Leary) as well as a number of old and future Quins. Tony Diprose, Andy Gomarsall, Nick Greenstock, Martin Haag, Mark Mapletoft and Chris Sheasby all played in at least one of the three test matches. In Argentina, the series finished 1-1; England won the first 46-20 but lost the second 13-33 and won the other four games. The test in Sydney was lost 6-25 to continue the losing streak in that country.

On Tuesday 13 May 1997, it was announced that Dick Best had been sacked and although it was denied by senior Quins executives, it was said to be down to an outbreak of player discontent. Players such as Will Carling had complained that Best tried too hard to live up to his nickname of "Sulphuric" and another unnamed made the point that as it was the awards dinner this evening, they had something else to celebrate. The newspaper blamed the Board for being far more poisonous than anything Best could have inflicted on the squad. Indeed, it seems that his main crime was insisting on daytime training and those with lucrative jobs in the City didn't like it. Some players even made up excuses not to do training with one player going to five funerals in a year! The statement from the Club read: "Best's position has been terminated as a result of differences over playing policies". The conclusion was that there had been an abuse of power by Dick and a case of player power; the reasons for him leaving fell somewhere between the two. As part of his terms for stepping aside, he wasn't allowed to comment on the matter and this could be understood because it was speculated that there would be a lucrative pay-off to cover the remainder of his ten year rolling contract. It was thought to be the best ever in any code of the football game when finalised last year.

As a confirmation to all this and what was to follow regarding the near disappearance of our famous club, Simon Halliday put the following section in his memoirs entitled City Centre - High Ball to High Finance and I repeat it here with his permission. Simon picks up the story...

Harlequins – Up for Auction, Going, Going, Gone (1997)

When professionalism took hold in the mid '90s, you could see that this was going to be a particular challenge for the multi-coloured Harlequins rugby team. By now, well retired, I was coaching the Quins backs after the three-year spell (1992-95) spent coaching Esher. But this was short-lived since a full time job and daytime training were hardly compatible. I stood down from the role with great reluctance, not surprisingly, given the emergence of a young Will Greenwood in the centre who was a joy to coach. I went on record as saying that pound for pound he was the most talented midfielder in the country, and that was in 1996. Unfortunately he did not last very long, departing to Leicester shortly afterwards. It was the first sign that rugby clubs had to change their attitude towards their best players. Will was employed by HSBC in the City. Rather like myself, some years earlier, he was having to rely on the goodwill of his employers to train during the day. You can hardly blame the clubs for jumping at the opportunity to train in daylight after years and years of running around under floodlights, but it wasn't so easy for the players. Will went to Dick Best and explained the problem, seeking some flexibility, but Dick was having none of it, and insisted on full attendance. This just pushed Will into the willing arms of Leicester who needed midfield players and could see Will's potential. The first I heard of anything was when Dick called me to try to persuade Will not to leave. I couldn't believe that we had allowed such a talented player to slip through our hands, and he became a major component of Leicester's success over the next few years. This was followed shortly afterwards by the club having to pay a significant amount of money to stop Jason Leonard going off to join Saracens. The stakes were rising sharply, and a period of exaggerated excess was just commencing. Quite simply, the clubs and the union did not see it coming, but situations like these were becoming more common. Every club was embracing the new regime in different ways, while the Rugby Union was still resolutely in denial. Why else would they not have contracted the England players, allowing the clubs to take ownership of players' financial lives? Quins made Dick Best Director of Rugby and invited the Beckwith Brothers, who were major names in the property world and responsible for the 'Riverside' chain of sports/leisure clubs, in as investors. At the same time a number of trustees were appointed to look after the 'golden share'. This was a way of protecting the membership from predatory behaviour, i.e. a takeover of the club against the members' will, or any action which prevented rugby being played at the Stoop Memorial Ground. So, shortly after my retirement as coach, I took a call from Colin Herridge, the secretary (and a member of the RFU). He proposed that Peter Winterbottom and I should become trustees, as well known ex-players and in honorary positions only. It seemed harmless enough, even if there were papers to sign and the odd meeting to attend. Little did I know that I was to become embroiled in two major scandals, one of which has never seen the light of day, until now. Dick Best was at the centre of one of them. Somehow, professionalism had brought the worst out of him; I think that even he would admit that now. His relationship with the players, now as their employer, inevitably plummeted. He would accuse certain people of not trying, threatening to impact their wages, with obvious consequences for key issues such as mortgage payments. This maverick behaviour eventually impacted on the long-term health of the club. Life was a series of confrontations, upsets and generally amateurish behaviour. I was taking an increasing number of complaints from the players who were desperate for change, threatening to leave the club if nothing happened. Eventually matters were brought to a head, and at a team meeting the chairman Roger Looker surveyed a vote of no confidence. A show of hands, and Dick's career at Harlequins was effectively over. At the time, it was suggested that this was a personal issue between Dick Best and Will Carling, and that Will was pursuing a vendetta. Certainly, they had long since fallen out. But this move had nothing to do with Will; it was simply fashionable, and expedient for the media and Will's detractors to suggest it. I was hopelessly compromised, as a personal friend and colleague of the Harlequins' coach. Knowledge of the squad's intention was a difficult and invidious fact of life. But the events played out and in time Dick bowed out, settling his contract on the steps of the court. None of the players wanted to testify, despite their views. You can understand the choice between keeping your own counsel and refraining from public criticism of your coach, versus the club putting its hand in the pocket to make the problem go away. Dick went on to be the successful coach of London Irish for a number of years. He is now an agent in rugby's professional game, and an occasional TV pundit. Dick Best may have outlived his usefulness at the Quins, and perhaps familiarity bred contempt, but his contribution to Harlequins, England and the game of rugby in general can hardly be overstated. He was a giant in every sense, and his team talks are still comfortably the best I have heard, bar none!

While all this was going on, a far more sinister development was overtaking the club. It was becoming clear that the overwhelming financial burden of early professionalism was taking its toll. The whole viability of the business model was based on the effective sale of debentures to finance the new East stand. Harlequins took a very amateurish approach to this critical piece of the jigsaw. The marketing initiative was under-funded and amateurish. My former playing colleague Jamie Salmon got involved for a while and was one of a number of people who was eventually shown the door. A similar situation was occurring down the road at Bath as most former players seemed to be finding some sort of employment. After a time the club faced a stark truth: it was running out of money.

The trustees had a series of grim-faced meetings, mainly around the fact that the Beckwith Brothers were unprepared to underwrite the club with the bankers. Instead they were ready to assume a majority holding in the event of the Harlequin club effectively going under. At this stage I started to panic. Apart from the fact that the trustees were mandated through the golden share to ensure that rugby was played at the Stoop Memorial Ground, we would be seen to be selling the club down the proverbial river. I was not ready to be associated with the demise of a household name in rugby circles. Visions of Beckwith leisure developments all over the famous old ground danced around in my head. Finally it was crunch time. Our backs were up against the wall; we did not even have enough money to pay our caterers. The banks were sympathetic, but unyielding. The unpalatable was about to happen, and a weekend was set for a series of meetings with the Beckwiths to discuss a transfer of the golden share.

We had no option. On the Thursday night, I was at the UBS offices in the city and due to go out for the evening. A great friend and colleague was about to take up a post in South Africa, and we were giving him a good send-off in the bar under the building, the Brasserie Rocque. By mid-evening, I was ready to spill the beans. The unfortunate recipient of the story was a colleague on the corporate side, David Wilson. As I revealed, in somewhat garbled fashion, that the Harlequins was on the cusp of bankruptcy, he suddenly took an interest. "So, how much money do you actually need?" "Oh, probably £2m," I muttered dejectedly. He mused, "I think I might know someone who would be interested. His name is Duncan Saville, a multi-millionaire from Australia. He is a rugby nut and he would jump at an opportunity like this". I gaped at him and laughed sceptically but David was insistent. "Look," I said, "I am not fooling around here. We are going under in three days, and there is no time for speculation". We had moved all of a sudden into business mode. "I might be able to contact him; he is in Australia, I'll be back". He returned swiftly to his office, while I staggered on through the emotional send-off for our colleague, Johnny Sutton, a Scot and a true rugby fan. We had often bantered over the years; not only was I half Scottish, but I had played the Scots a grand total of seven times in my career. As we became awash with alcohol, back came David Wilson; he had made contact and Duncan Saville was coming over on the next plane. I sobered up pretty quickly at this piece of news and the next morning I called Edwin Glasgow, our senior trustee. He took some convincing that this was not a tall story. But finally, he gathered together Roger Looker, the chairman, and Colin Herridge, a fellow trustee and Harlequin. I do not profess to know all the details of the ensuing events, but Saville arrived at Heathrow, was taken to the ground, took one look and shook hands subject to the usual due diligence. Put simply, the Beckwith Brothers realised the game was up, and sold out to Saville. I am of the opinion that they would have closed down the rugby club over time and turned the whole area into hotels (a leisure centre), corporate development, and no doubt the trustees would have been held liable by the club. As my employers at the time had no idea I was even involved, I knew I was breaching stock exchange rules over 'conflicts of interest' so I heaved a huge sigh of relief that not only a famous rugby club was snatched from the jaws of insolvency, but I was off a potential hook. Duncan Saville and his right-hand man, Charles Jillings, even came to UBS to meet me in order to get a different perspective on the background to the whole situation. These days I often laugh about the whole episode with David Wilson; funny to think that the future of the Harlequins had hinged on one phone call to the other side of the world. This spelled the end of my involvement with the Harlequins at all levels. Not because of any falling out, but because the fight for professional survival was well and truly under way. You cannot play around in the face of such a challenge, and I had neither the time, nor frankly, the inclination.

So, there you have it, the Harlequin Football Club came within a whisker of going under after 130 years! It is a great shame that the Club hasn't recognised the contribution of both Simon Halliday and David Wilson because, if that phone call hadn't been made, there would have been no Club.

Quins had moved from an amateur rugby club to a small company employing 40-odd players and twenty staff so a part-time CEO (Donald Kerr) was brought in. At one meeting with Dick Best, he had received a letter of complaint from the father of a Quins hopeful about Dick's treatment of his son. The story goes that Dick had given him a Quins' car so that he could travel to and from Loughborough for training. He had gone on holiday, left the car in a car park for three weeks and it had been trashed by the time he returned. The car was taken off him. Kerr wondered what to do and started to build a portfolio of complaints against the Director of Rugby. Dick saw them as complaints only because Kerr was taking notice of them. Later, at another meeting, Kerr announced to Dick that the Club had terminated his employment. He refused to take that decision from Kerr and so it was left to Roger Looker to tell him. Looker and Best had played together and were friends but, although Looker said he was sorry and actually broke down when he sacked Dick, there was no U-turn and the player revolt described by Simon Halliday above had won the day. Best replied that we both know what's happened and if you don't get it yet, you will do eventually. Later in life, Looker came up to Dick in a restaurant and said that they got it horribly wrong and he was really, really, sorry.

A solicitor was brought on board via Kerr to deal with Dick's claim for unfair dismissal. Why had he been sacked? Apparently for breach of implied and expressed terms of his contract; basically put, he was not doing his job properly. The trouble was that Quins were third in the league and had done pretty well over the last two seasons. After being offered a sum to settle, Dick went to get his own experienced employment litigation expert and the talks went on for months and months as the Quins dragged out proceedings. He couldn't work as he was under stress fighting the case and his legal bill eventually climbed to some £27,000. He had to prove unfair dismissal and this was done, there was then a long discussion about money but both sides were poles apart. Dick instructed his solicitor to stick at it because he knew the Club would not want to go to court. A day before the scheduled court appearance, Dick's solicitor phoned him to say the Club had made a very good offer, his reply was that she should go for the jugular, the Club will back down. They did and agreed to the terms. Dick's family went through hell during this time and it is hardly surprising that he has never forgiven or forgotten! He didn't go back for a long time but had to when the ground share was in place as he was Director of Rugby at London Irish.

Eventually, around 9th October 1997, it was reported that we had lost our original "fat cats" after only one season and Duncan Saville had bought them out. The Beckwiths retained a 10% interest and Saville now owned

39% having invested an extra £1 million with the remaining 51% in the hands of the trustees. The Club made a loss of £2,989,972 for the year ending 31st May 1998. Beckwith, Johnson and Looker all resigned as Directors and they were replaced by Christopher Haines, Charles Jillings, Huw Morgan, Malcolm Wall and Peter Winterbottom. D Huw Morgan would be appointed as the Club's first Chief Executive Officer in March 1998 and would be in post for just over two years. John Courage ended their sponsorship of the league and Allied Dunbar replaced them. The word 'Premiership' appeared for the first time and would be used from here on. The new sponsors would be around for three seasons but there were no problem getting one signed up as professional rugby was here to stay.

The London Broncos Rugby League team shared the Stoop with us for this and the following season. They reached the Challenge Cup final at Wembley in 1999 but lost to Leeds Rhinos (16-52) in what was the last game of Rugby League played at the old stadium. They would return to the Stoop in 2006 for a longer stay.

We had a new captain and coach for the 1997/98 season. Keith Wood took over from Jason Leonard and Andy Keast carried on where Dick Best left off. Our first game for this very early start to the season on 23rd August was an away trip to Northampton. We had three new boys making their debuts: Rob Liley played in the first of 49 games having joined from Leicester, Massimo Cuttitta appeared as a substitute for the first of only 18 games (he was in the process of winning 69 Italian caps) and Johnny Ngauamo (a centre) appeared for the first of 25 matches. He was a Tongan international and would win 6 caps. Thankfully, Thierry Lacroix retained his magnificent kicking ability and he converted Carling's try after four minutes. In the act of scoring, Carling sustained a calf muscle injury and was replaced by Stuart Power. The Saints came back into the game and scored eleven unanswered points before Lacroix hit another penalty between the posts to make it 10-11 at the interval. We took control in the first 15 minutes of the second half and Lacroix kicked three penalties and converted O'Leary's 50 metre try to put us 26-11 ahead. We failed to kill the game off and Dawson ran in Northampton's second try but Townsend couldn't convert. When Tatupu scored, Dawson converted (as Townsend had missed five kicks at goal). In the last four minutes, the Saints scrum half missed two kickable penalties and we escaped with the victory. This was our fifth successive win over Northampton, the longest run of wins we'd had in fixtures dating back to 1896.

A stiff test awaited us in our next game when Bath came to the Stoop. This was a terrible game (even after you took out all of the dropped passes) and was decided in the end by the award of a penalty try. Jamie Williams and Johnny Ngauamo scored our tries and Lacroix converted both and added a couple of penalty goals. In reply, Richard Butland kicked five penalties, converted the penalty try and scored one of his own a minute from the end to leave Bath winners by 27-20. We had led until injury time but in truth, neither side deserved to win.

Our next assault on the European Cup began with a home game against Munster. This was another match littered with mistakes which we should have won easily. Lacroix kicked two penalties before going off injured, Nick Walshe scored a try (Carling converted) as did Laurent Belligoi. Rob Liley kicked the conversion to give us a 20-3 lead after 18 minutes. The Irishmen scored a goal, two penalties and a try to get back into the game but Liley kicked a penalty and converted his own try to take us twelve points clear at the interval. Sloppy defending allowed Munster to come back to 30-30 before we stretched away again with tries from Jamie Williams (2) and Huw Harries and a penalty from Liley. A penalty from O'Gara and a late goal with the last move of the match wasn't enough to stop us from winning by eight points. A punch from Mick Galwey put Keith Wood out of the game (but he was back the following week); he only received a yellow card when it should have been red. Glyn Llewellyn made his final appearance having scored 6 tries (30 points) in his short spell with us. If we could hold on to those loose passes and tighten up the defence, there was no reason why we couldn't have a fantastic season.

In our next pool match against Bourgoin at the Stoop, they did us the favour of travelling over on the morning of the game and, consequently, were thrashed out of sight. The French side were just blown away by our teamwork and we were quickly into a clear lead. Thierry Lacroix kicked five penalties before Bourgoin replied with a goal but his sixth penalty and the conversion of a try from Jamie Williams killed them off. Just before half time, Ngauamo went over and we were 30-7 in front. By the end, this had become 45-7 with Lacroix adding his seventh penalty (equalling the record set by David Pears in December 1991) and converting Ngauamo's second try. After 75 minutes, Keith Wood put the icing on the cake with our fourth try. The French had learnt a valuable lesson about preparation for a European match!

Our away trip to Cardiff produced a fantastic performance to record the home side's first defeat at the Arms Park in three seasons of European Cup competition. Three early penalty chances were taken by Lee Jarvis and we were 9-0 down after 17 minutes but our attacking rugby was not to be denied. In seven minutes, Lacroix kicked a penalty and converted tries by Williams and Wood to give us the lead and, despite Jarvis getting his fourth and fifth kicks over, Lacroix's second penalty ensured we led at half time. In the third quarter, Jarvis got two more penalties to give Cardiff a one point lead but, in the 72nd minute, Belligoi latched on to Lacroix's kick ahead and ran on to score. A third penalty three minutes later from our kicking machine took us to a vital away win. After three games, we were top of the Pool and looking good for a home draw in the quarter finals with the other three teams on one win and two losses. The following week, we travelled to France to play Bourgoin and, yet again, our attacking play carried all before it. Bourgoin could only manage penalties like Cardiff before them with their full back (Geany) kicking three in each half. They did lead 15-14 after 53 minutes but ultimately it was all in vain. O'Leary and Cabannes went over for excellently worked tries in the first half with Lacroix's conversions enabling us to lead by five points. Lacroix kicked his first penalty to give us back the lead and then added two more after converting a second try from Cabannes to fire us to a twelve point win.

With all the pool matches being played in a straight run of six weeks, our next encounter was the home return with Cardiff and victory would assure us of a home draw in the quarter finals. Cardiff knew they had to win to keep their chances of qualifying for the knock-out stages alive. After just 26 seconds, Lee Jarvis dropped a goal to put the visitors in front and when he converted Howley's try, we were ten points down in four minutes. Lacroix did get three penalty kicks over but Cardiff had scored another seventeen points to put them almost out of sight at the interval. We slowly began to play like we knew we could and Lacroix put over a penalty and Belligoi scored a try to reduce the deficit to only ten points with just under half an hour remaining. When O'Leary scored and Lacroix converted, there were over fifteen minutes remaining. Booth scored Cardiff's fourth try before Belligoi burst through and scored under the posts for Lacroix to convert. The score stood at 31-32 and there were two minutes of normal time remaining. When we were awarded a penalty on the 22 metre line and fifteen metres in from touch, Lacroix lined up the match winning penalty. Alas, his non-kicking foot appeared to slip as he took the kick and the attempt drifted wide. There were no further opportunities in the four minutes of injury time and we had suffered our first home defeat in five European Cup games.

We now knew that a draw against Munster at Thomond Park, Limerick would be enough to take us through as Pool winners. A defeat would most likely leave us facing a tough away draw if Cardiff defeated Bourgoin at home. We went into a lead of 8-0 after only seven minutes with a try from O'Leary and a penalty from Lacroix but conceded a penalty and two goals in fourteen minutes to trail 8-17 with 24 minutes gone. On the half hour mark, Williams got our second try and just after the break, Lacroix put over his second penalty to bring us to within a point of Munster's score. Two penalties from fly half Keane were enough for the Irishmen to preserve their unbeaten home record in the Heineken Cup and we had blown our chances of a home tie in the next round. Cardiff defeated Bourgoin, we won the Pool but finished fifth out of the five winners and so faced a massive away trip to Toulouse on 8th November. Daniel Rouse made the first of just 4 appearances for us against Munster when he came on as a sub for Massimo Cuttitta and would win 20 caps for Fiji.

It was back to league action on 18th October and the short trip to newly promoted Richmond. Tulsen Tollett (who toured Papua New Guinea, Fiji and New Zealand with the Great Britain rugby league team in 1996 but won no caps and would play for us 15 times) made his debut in this game when he came on at half time for Will Carling. This was our first league meeting with our near neighbours and it all started brightly for us as we took a 16-3 lead at the interval. Richmond were not playing well and Liley banged over three penalties and converted a try by new-comer Scott Stewart to one penalty from Va'a for the home side. Stewart would only make 18 appearances for us but would win 54 caps for Canada. Our other new boy in this game was Adam Leach. The Australian (who had been recruited after contacting the Supporters' club web site) went on to play 67 times for the 1st XV. The second half was a totally different story to the first and we just didn't get a look in (despite a couple of scoring chances). Bateman set up Martin for Richmond's first score then ex-Quin Dominic Chapman ran in followed by Bateman and Quinnell. With Va'a kicking all the conversions and two penalties, the final score read as a home win by 37-16 and our season was in danger of collapsing around us.

A visit from Sale gave us a look at two future signings – Matt Moore and Pat Sanderson (both would score tries in this fixture). This was an incredible game and was only won in the last few minutes. Our attacking qualities were there to be admired but our defence was almost as bad as these were good. The big news was that Will Carling had been asked to take his place on the bench and our coach (Andy Keast) declined to use the words dropped or axed. He was one of four players omitted from the starting line-up after the defeat at Richmond but, with a squad of over forty players, he would never be expected to start every game. Our defensive frailties were exposed by Beim after ten minutes when he rounded off an attack after Rob Liley had missed a penalty. Howarth converted this and added a penalty and another conversion of a try from Yates. Between times, Jenkins and O'Leary (2) had scored tries for us and Liley had converted all of these to nudge us ahead. By half time, the game should have been sewn up with further tries from Adam Leach and Spencer Bromley again converted by Liley to put us 35-17 ahead. When O'Leary dropped a goal two minutes into the second half, we looked set for a big win. Unfortunately, we just couldn't stop any of Sale's attacks and Moore scored their third try, Howarth converted and kicked a penalty to reduce the gap. On 70 minutes, Wood scored to take us over forty points but Sale wouldn't lie down and tries from Pat Sanderson and Ellis (both converted by Howarth took them over forty as well. Between these two scores, Tulsen Tollett got our seventh try and Liley put over his seventh conversion. There was no more scoring in the last seven minutes and this extraordinary match finished 52-41 in our favour. With this victory, we stood in seventh place in the table with a 50% record from our four games.

A visit to Kingsholm produced a close encounter and a morale boosting victory just six days before our European Cup quarter final in Toulouse. Williams put us in front after ten minutes for Lacroix to convert before Fanolua got a try for Mapletoft to convert. Lacroix and Mapletoft then exchanged penalties to make it 10-10 at the break. Two penalties by the Gloucester fly half after 45 and 63 minutes put them in the ascendancy but, on 72 minutes after a period of pressure, Gareth Llewellyn got over the line and Lacroix's conversion from the touchline handed us victory by one point. He could even afford to miss a penalty after this and we had our sixth win in a row over Gloucester.

In the Toulouse Football Stadium on 8th November, we suffered our worst ever defeat at the hands of French opposition. Things went from bad to worse as Ntamack scored after just two minutes, Ougier landed three penalties and Lapoutge got their second try. Lacroix's penalty after eight minutes made the score 3-24 at half time. It might have been totally different had the referee (Derek Bevan) spotted an offside (in front of the kicker) after 32 seconds. This would have given us a penalty near the half way line which Lacroix may well have kicked. The second half produced four more tries for the French which helped their total to 51. Lacroix converted his own late try to make it 10-51 but the score didn't really reflect the balance of play. The home side's second and fifth tries should have been ruled out due to forward passes and we had a lot of chances which we failed to take due to taking the wrong option, dropped passes and good Toulouse defending. But, the bottom line was that we had been beaten out of sight and had failed in the quarter finals again. This was the furthest we would get in the European Cup for some time.

Our next league game at home to Wasps didn't take place until 13th December so we had a long time to dwell on our European Cup exit. After only 36 seconds, Lacroix dropped a goal but from the restart, our defence disappeared and allowed the ball to bobble into our in-goal area; Ions was up to score and Rees put the conversion over to give them the lead. It was the Thierry Lacroix show from now on and before the half was over, he dropped a goal, landed three penalties and converted O'Leary's try. The Wasps reply was a penalty from Rees to leave us 22-10 ahead. Jamie Williams scored five minutes into the second half and then Lacroix converted a penalty try awarded after Logan had failed to release the ball in the tackle. Every time the Frenchman scored, there was a chorus of the "Cancan" – this was the seventh time – there would be two more! Wasps got a penalty try of their own for a collapsed scrum which Rees converted and that was the end of their scoring. After 72 minutes, Lacroix converted his own try and left the field suffering from a stomach bug having contributed 26 points. As Rees attempted a huge American Football style pass, it was read perfectly by Tollett who picked it off and ran in under the posts. Challinor had replaced Lacroix and he converted but couldn't do the same with O'Leary's second three minutes later and the final score of 53-17 was complete revenge for our defeat in the last game of the previous season. We now moved up to third place behind Saracens and Newcastle and Wasps were in trouble down in tenth place (on the same points as the bottom two). Dan Rouse made his last appearance in this game as he had to return home due to family circumstances – it was a sad end to his promising Quins career.

On the last Saturday before Christmas, we went to Leicester and found them in a less than charitable mood. Horak put them in front with a penalty after six minutes but Lacroix equalised in kind eleven minutes later. A penalty try for a collapsed ruck and Serevi's conversion put the Tiger's 10-3 up at half time. In the second half, we could make no impression on the home side and they gradually pulled away. Will Greenwood's excellent try was the highlight of an otherwise dull encounter and we finally went down by twenty seven points to three. Andy Mullins came out of retirement to play in this one after Dan Rouse had failed a late fitness test. It was his final appearance having led the side on forty occasions and scored 9 tries (41 points) during his eleven season career. This was to be a dreadful period for us and the second half of the season would be the shape of things to come.

On 27th December, London Irish visited the Stoop, were currently in eleventh place and were not expected to cause us much trouble. That was the theory but, in practice, they caused us a whole lot of trouble. After only two minutes, Ricky Nebbett came up with the ball after good work by Jenkins to open the scoring and Lacroix converted to make it 7-0. The Irish response was amazing; a penalty from Woods and conversions of tries by O'Shea (2) and Bishop to take them to twenty four points. Lacroix kicked four penalties and we trailed 19-24 with 24 minutes left. We couldn't make any headway until, deep into injury time, we were awarded a penalty 15 metres from the Irish line. Huw Harries tapped and went, Jenkins took it on and passed to Tollett who was stopped. The ball flew back and acting captain Bill Davison caught it and charged through to score. This levelled the scores, Lacroix converted and we had sneaked home 26-24.

Our last game of the year was at home to bottom of the table Bristol. We were in fifth and looking to maintain our loose grip on the coat tails of the leaders. We began as if our lives depended on winning and, apart from a Paul Burke penalty, we ran riot in the opening thirteen minutes. Keyter, Liley and Challinor scored tries and the second named added all three conversions. As was to become an all too familiar failing, we fell asleep and when we woke up, we trailed by nine points. Burke led the way with a try, two penalties and three conversions. Lewsey and Brownrigg scored the other tries and four minutes into the second half it was 30-21 to the visitors. We were unbelievably bad and Lacroix was brought on to try and turn the tide back in our favour. Ngauamo scored in the corner but Bristol had their tails up and Burke brought his tally to 25 points with a penalty and the conversion of Tuieti's try. With nine minutes remaining, we needed something special to close a gap of fourteen points and Lacroix seemed to be the man for the job. First, he made the space for Keyter to go over under the posts and then drop-kicked the conversion to save time. The final six minutes (including four minutes of injury time) produced our sixth try when Walshe sent Luger in. The conversion was given to Rob Liley (even Andy Keast couldn't understand why Lacroix hadn't attempted it!!) and he, not surprisingly, missed it. Final score: Quins 38 Bristol 40. Keast said afterwards that the players were arrogant and threatened to put several of them up for sale. The truth was that we were absolutely pathetic and worse still this would happen time and time again over the coming seasons. Until we learnt that the basic idea of professional sport is to win, we would never attain the status of league champions.

1998 began with a testing trip to Loftus Road to play Wasps in the newly named Tetley's Bitter Cup 4th round. In four previous meetings, we had won every time (three of them on Wasps territory). This time, we faced the gale force wind first and went into the lead when Lacroix landed a penalty after 12 minutes. A fifteen point haul in 15 minutes took Wasps into a lead they held until half time. Rees kicked a penalty right on the whistle but Lacroix had got his second over and Williams had scored our first try. Into the second half, Lacroix hit a post with an attempted dropped goal from half way and hit the crossbar with the conversion of Scott Stewart's try after 43 minutes. Rees kicked his third penalty nine minutes later before Williams got his second try but, again, Lacroix could not convert. The scores were locked at 21-21 with just under half an hour left. Rees (whose kicking had been almost immaculate both with and against the strong wind) got his fourth penalty and converted White's try in the 63rd minute to take the home side ten points clear. Ozdemir was booked for infringing at a scrum as we tried our hardest to break out. When we finally managed it, Williams completed his hat-trick but, as Lacroix again failed to add the two points, we went away disappointed and out of the cup. This was our first defeat in the starting round since 1990 and was another game we should have won quite easily. On 9th January, Will Carling announced his retirement from the game, he didn't want to go but it had been rumoured that he had fallen out with Andy Keast and he seemed to confirm this when he spoke of relationships becoming strained of late. He had been linked with a move to Wasps but he insisted that despite being flattered by the interest from other clubs, Quins was where he would end his playing days. This last part was quite correct but it wasn't just yet; he would come out of retirement the following year for one last hurrah.

Saracens had moved from Enfield to another ground share agreement, this time with Watford Football Club at Vicarage Road and it was here we met on 11th January. We had major injury problems and were missing six key players but we did compete for most of the game and almost pulled off a shock victory. The boot of Lynagh slowly put paid to us and his sixth penalty five minutes from the end drove the final nail into our coffin. He had also converted their penalty try (awarded by Brian Campsall after we had collapsed a rapidly retreating scrum on our line). We had actually led three times but couldn't find that last score to take us clean away. Lacroix landed three penalties in the first half (which ended 9-9) and converted Luger's 60 metre sprint to put us 16-9 up before Lynagh completed his day's work. This defeat left us in sixth place – eight points behind the joint leaders (Newcastle and Saracens). The Saracens line up contained two future Quins – Brendon Daniel and Tony Diprose and of course, their Director of Rugby, Mark Evans.

Our first home game of the year was against Northampton and had become a must win situation. Another loss at this stage would almost certainly leave us with no chance of catching the leaders and if we weren't careful, relegation might still become an issue. Playing with the strong wind at our backs, we somehow managed to concede eleven points in the first half without scoring any ourselves. Nine minutes into the second half, Wood and Challinor set up Tollett for what proved to be a consolation score. A kick to the corner by Grayson caught our defence totally out of position and Sleightholme scored and a pass directly to Allen by one of our players handed him their fourth try and an easy victory for the Saints (30-5). This defeat dropped us another place to seventh and we had to use the four week break from league action to get some togetherness in our play. The fact that we were hopeless was of no consolation to the Quins supporters who left in droves before the end of the game. Staying to support your team through thick and thin must remain a priority at all times! Paul Challinor's eight season career came to an end against Northampton. He had scored some 750 points (38 tries, 20 dropped goals, 111 penalties and 86 conversions) in that time and remains our all-time top scorer of dropped goals. He was in sixth place on the all-time list of points scorers at the Club and finished as top points scorer in two seasons.

A friendly was arranged on 1st February against touring South African side the Gauteng Falcons. In a match littered with fights, we were made to struggle for our first victory of the year. In the first half, Leonard and Luger scored tries and Liley converted one in reply to three penalties by van Straaten for the visitors. A try by Viljoen early in the second half restored the lead but we hit back with further tries from Mensah and Gross. Liley kicked the first conversion and was then replaced by Lacroix who got the second to put us twelve points ahead. With ten minutes left, our defence failed again and Lourens scored for van Straaten to convert but we had the final word when Luger set up a score for Stewart. At last we had won a game but, there were no league points on offer and our next trip was to Newcastle (still the joint leaders with Saracens). The Falcons were a more complete team than when we had knocked them out of the cup just over two years before and they took the lead after 19 minutes when Naylor scored for Andrew to convert. A Rob Liley penalty eight minutes later got us on the scoreboard before lapses in concentration cost us dearly. Andrew stretched the lead with a penalty and then a three try blitz in seven minutes before half time took them to 31-3 at the break. The game was over and it just remained to see how many points we would concede. Within five minutes of the restart, the gap had grown with Tony Underwood's score. Andrew converted for the fifth time before we decided to make a fight of it and tries from O'Leary and Luger in a three minute spell restored some respectability. Liley could only convert one and the home side had the last laugh when Shaw scored their sixth try to make the winning margin twenty eight points. Jim Staples made his final appearance in this game having scored 138 points (22 tries, 2 dropped goals, 4 penalties and 5 conversions) during his all too brief four seasons with us. Back in October, he had told one newspaper how he was finding it difficult to fit in a full time job as a stockbrocker and train with Quins. He was forced to go back to pre-professional methods by doing it at night. This wasn't acceptable to him and he eventually came to the conclusion that something had to give and he retired from the sport.

We had fallen from fifth to ninth in the space of four matches and there was to be no respite as we were on the road to Bath two weeks later. Our hosts were the new European Champions and had scored over forty points in defeating both Gloucester and Wasps. We began well enough in trying to avoid a record fifth league defeat in a row and Liley kicked two penalties in the first four minutes. The lead lasted eight minutes before Ubogu scored and

Callard converted but, when Luger intercepted a Callard pass and ran 50 metres to score, Liley's conversion put us six points ahead. By half time, Bath had regained a lead they would not lose with a Callard penalty and conversion of Earnshaw's try. The second half saw us in disarray again and twenty two more points for the home side turned our nightmare of five successive league defeats into a reality. The Bath line up contained Eric Peters and he would play a handful of games for us in 2000/01 after returning from having testicular cancer.

Our fourteenth league match was the home return against Richmond. Thierry Lacroix was back again after recovering from a hamstring injury and Chris Sheasby returned from his spell at Wasps. The Richmond coach was John Kingston (he had played for us back in 1986/87 and would become our coach in 2001/02) and his side had won just a single league game in their last six matches (after starting out with four wins in their first seven). We played with the strong wind in our favour and destroyed the visitors as they had done to us in the second half of the first game. Daren O'Leary got a try at each end of the first half and, in between, Davison and Lacroix scored two more. Lacroix's boot accounted for our other points with a penalty and four conversions. A rally by the visitors in the third quarter saw them score a goal and a try but the final quarter belonged to us and Mensah scored our fifth try and Lacroix completed his 21 point haul with another penalty and a conversion.

A brief jump up to seventh place made us feel a bit dizzy and we dropped down to a more comfortable ninth after our fourth defeat in a row at Sale (three league games and one cup tie). After 33 seconds, we trailed when O'Cuinneagain ran in after a mistake by Luger. He made amends for this when he scored on eight minutes; Lacroix converted and added another penalty to his opener after three minutes to give us a 13-5 advantage. Lacroix became the first Harlequin to be sin binned when he was singled out after persistent infringement after 25 minutes. Howarth kicked the resultant penalty but we were still ahead at half time. This lead lasted only two minutes into the second half when another try brought Sale level. Howarth put them in front with his second penalty and when Quins old boy Duncan Bell got their third try, Howarth's conversion made the gap ten points. Try as we did, there was no further scoring even when Sale had a man sin binned after 65 minutes. Lacroix put one penalty against a post and mistake after mistake cost us dearly. After that good win against Richmond, it was back to the drawing board yet again. Luke Gross made his last appearance against Sale having scored just one try (5 points) during his short stay and Tulsen Tollett did the same (although he had managed 3 tries (15points)) during an equally short career with us.

Three days before our next game at home to Gloucester, Zinzan Brooke was elevated to Head Coach for the remainder of the season. His stint at the Club would ultimately prove disastrous. Against Gloucester, we continued where we had left off against Sale and all we had to show in the first half was a penalty by Rob Liley. Mapletoft had kicked two penalties and converted a penalty try awarded for collapsing a scrum on the line (but, he also missed two penalties and two dropped goal attempts). Gareth Llewellyn scored a try after 53 minutes but Mapletoft landed his third penalty to leave the visitors eight points in front. We began to gather ourselves for a final assault and when Walshe scored for Liley to convert, we trailed 15-16 with ten minutes of normal time remaining. What happened next was totally out of context with the previous 73 minutes – we ran riot. In the final eleven minutes, Sheasby, O'Leary and Mensah scored tries which Liley converted and a possible loss had been turned into a 36-16 victory. Back up to seventh we went and it now looked possible that we would avoid a play-off to stay in the top division. Massimo Cuttitta played his last game for us against the Cherry and Whites after a relatively short time with the Club.

Our next game was an away trip to Loftus Road to take on Wasps. Gareth Rees was again in top form with the boot and landed three penalties and the conversion to our record making sixth penalty try conceded during this season. The referee decided prematurely that we had collapsed a maul after seven minutes. Liley converted his own try after 21 minutes but we trailed 7-16 at the break. Two minutes into the second half, Rees stretched the home lead to 19-7 with his fourth penalty before we sprang into life. Nick Walshe went over from close range, Ngauamo finished off a move by O'Leary and Stewart and Luger scored after a scintillating break by Ngauamo had been carried on by Mensah. Liley converted the last two and we led 26-19 with over half an hour still left to play. However, we couldn't finish the game off and the spectre of defeat loomed again when Rees got his fifth penalty on 72 minutes. With two minutes of normal time remaining, Green was shoved over from a ruck, Rees converted and we had lost again despite outscoring our hosts by four tries to two.

We played well in parts against the Tigers and took the lead when Jason Keyter got a try after four minutes which Liley converted. Joel Stransky brought the visitors level when he converted his own try and his penalty after 32 minutes gave them the lead at the half way stage. Bill Davison was sin binned in the 35th minute but Leicester failed to score during this period. Stransky added a penalty soon after half time but when Leach charged down an attempted clearance kick by him, kicked on and scored, Liley's conversion gave us a one point lead with twelve minutes remaining. An unlikely victory was taken away from us when Stransky dropped a goal and converted Lloyd's try right on the final whistle. Lacking a kicker of Stransky's ability (when Lacroix was not playing) was costing us in too many matches and worse was still to come.

At Sunbury against London Irish, we again came into contact with our old boss Dick Best. After two penalties from Niall Woods, we were awarded a penalty try when O'Leary was impeded and Lacroix put us in front with the conversion. This was the high point for us as, by half time, the Irish were 27-7 ahead. Woods had converted all three of their tries including the one he had scored. The second half produced an exhilarating performance by Best's new team against a pathetic, totally unprofessional one by us. Keyter scored for Walshe to convert (Lacroix had departed injured) but the home side ran in five more tries. Woods got another and put over all the conversions to finish with 32 points. Our capitulation was a disgrace and the 14-62 scoreline was our biggest ever league defeat, the most points we had ever conceded and our heaviest defeat since our loss to Llanelli in 1970. It was made all the worse in that we conceded 28 points in the final fourteen minutes. All Brooke could say was that the only thing which could be done was maintenance until the end of the season. The question that needed answering was why the players only seemed to play decently when it suited them? Best was never happier than when beating Quins and said to Mark Evans afterwards that he would have to have his smile surgically removed!

While Dick was at Irish, he worked with Ged Glynn (one of his coaches) and he, in turn, was close to John Wells (they were both involved with England A). Glynn told Wells (as a wind up) that the Irish used razor blades to make cuts to players to enable blood substitutions. Wells went back to Leicester and told Dean Richards. When Tigers visited Irish, Dean and Wells came over to talk to Dick and Glynn and Dean said that he hoped they didn't start any of their razor blade stuff today! If he saw someone cutting players, he would complain. Glynn shrugged his shoulders and Wells chuckled away – the problem was that Dick didn't have a clue what was going on. Dick's reply was that Dean shouldn't come on to his patch and start telling him what to do (in no uncertain terms). Afterwards, Glynn admitted what he'd done. When the events unfolded some years later, it was quite amusing for our ex-Director of Rugby.

Second placed Saracens visited the Stoop on 29th April and another heavy defeat looked to be on the cards. But, again we saw the "other" Quins in the second half. The first half produced three penalties from Lacroix in response to thirteen points for the visitors. Tim Collier was booked for a stamp after only 37 seconds but this was an isolated incident. Six changes were made from the starting line-up against London Irish and these started to produce results in the second period. Lacroix added a penalty and converted his own try and one by Jamie Williams to send us into a 26-16 lead with twenty minutes left. Sarries were trying for a league and cup double and fought their way back into contention with a try from Tony Copsey. With four minutes left, Reidy forced himself over and Johnson's conversion gave them a two point lead. With time up, Jamie Williams attempted to run in from 40 yards out but Johnson was equal to the task and put him into touch by the corner flag. The final whistle went and the Saracens were back at the top of the table. We now dropped down to tenth place and had to win one of our remaining two matches to avoid a possible play-off.

Four days after the Sarries match, we headed to Bristol for a crunch game. The home side were already resigned to finishing bottom but played with fire and passion to lead 16-6 after 45 minutes (O'Leary had charged down a conversion attempt by Lewsey from in front of the posts). Thierry Lacroix got our points with two penalties and when Cabannes was sin binned for preventing a penalty from being taken quickly by Robert Jones, the signs were not good. However, Keith Wood came on after Bristol's second try and had an immediate impact. Lacroix got his third penalty and converted when our captain charged over to level the scores. Hull landed a penalty to edge Bristol ahead but Luger's try a minute later put us back in front. Our French fly half converted and kicked another penalty on 69 minutes to kill the game off. There was no further scoring although Gareth Llewellyn was booked two minutes into injury time. Tom Billups made his final appearance in this one to end another short staying player's career. The 26-19 victory gave us our third win on the trot at the Memorial Ground and secured our place in the top division for another season.

This was just as well because Newcastle came to the Stoop for the final game of the season needing a win to secure the league title. We needed to start solidly if we were to have any chance of avenging the defeat we had suffered back in February at Kingston Park. We didn't and within 19 minutes, the visiting Falcons were seventeen points ahead. Lacroix's two penalties were then cancelled out by Popplewell's try to make it 6-22 at half time. We played well in patches but a try and conversion from Rob Andrew on 48 minutes started the second half stroll for the new champions. Harries and Luger got tries and Lacroix finished the game with his second conversion but, in between these tries, fifteen more points swelled Newcastle's total to 44. Laurent Cabannes made his farewell appearance in this game having scored 7 tries (35 points) during his two seasons at the Club. For the second season running, the league trophy was paraded around the Stoop after the final game but it wasn't us celebrating.

Our season had been a disappointing one and in the league, our final record was P22 W8 L14 F516 A645 Pts 16 Pos 10th. This was our lowest ever finish and several games had been lost when a win was more or less in the bag. Our overall record was P31 W13 L18 F781 A889. Daren O'Leary and Jamie Williams finished as joint top try scorers with 12 each and Thierry Lacroix was again top points scorer in all other aspects and overall with 268 (4 tries, 2 dropped goals, 56 penalties and 37 conversions). His 56 penalty goals were a new all-time record surpassing the previous best of 47 by Ray Dudman in 1982/83. His points total only fell eighteen short of Billy Bushell's all-time record of points in a season set in 1975/76. Overall, tries fell by a massive 76 to 89 and the lowest total since 1988/89, dropped goals remained on 3, penalties rose by three to 65 and conversions fell by 32 to 66 (as a direct result of the try count falling). Our overall points total of 781 (a fall of 435) was the lowest total since 1994/95 and it was the first time since 1980/81 that we had conceded more points than we had scored. Again, 43 players were utilised with the top appearance makers being Bill Davison and Rory Jenkins who missed just one game each. They were followed by Gareth Llewellyn (28), Laurent Cabannes (27), Huw Harries (26) and Daren O'Leary with 25.

1997/98

230897	NORTHAMPTON(ADP1)	NORTHAMPTON	W	2G4PG(26)-1G2PG2T(23)
300897	BATH(ADP1)	STOOP MEMORIAL GROUND	L	2G2PG(20)-1G5PG1T(27)
070997	MUNSTER(HECP)	STOOP MEMORIAL GROUND	W	3G4PG3T(48)-3G3PG2T(40)
130997	BOURGOIN(HECP)	STOOP MEMORIAL GROUND	W	2G7PG2T(45)-1G(7)
210997	CARDIFF(HECP)	CARDIFF	W	2G3PG1T(28)-7PG(21)
270997	BOURGOIN(HECP)	BOURGOIN	W	3G3PG(30)-6PG(18)
041097	CARDIFF(HECP)	STOOP MEMORIAL GROUND	L	2G4PG1T(31)-3G1DG1PG1T(32)
121097	MUNSTER(HECP)	THOMOND PARK, LIMERICK	L	2PG2T(16)-2G3PG(23)
181097	RICHMOND(ADP1)	RICHMOND	L	1G3PG(16)-4G3PG(37)
251097	SALE(ADP1)	STOOP MEMORIAL GROUND	W	7G1DG(52)-5G2PG(41)
021197	GLOUCESTER(ADP1)	GLOUCESTER	W	2G1PG(17)-1G3PG(16)
081197	TOULOUSE(HECQF)	TOULOUSE	L	1G1PG(10)-3G5PG3T(51)
131297	WASPS(ADP1)	STOOP MEMORIAL GROUND	W	4G2DG3PG2T(53)-2G1PG(17)
201297	LEICESTER(ADP1)	LEICESTER	L	1PG(3)-3G2PG(27)
271297	LONDON IRISH(ADP1)	STOOP MEMORIAL GROUND	W	2G4PG(26)-3G1PG(24)
311297	BRISTOL(ADP1)	STOOP MEMORIAL GROUND	L	4G2T(38)-4G4PG(40)
040198	WASPS(TBC4)	LOFTUS ROAD	L	2PG4T(26)-2G4PG1T(31)
110198	SARACENS(ADP1)	VICARAGE ROAD	L	1G3PG(16)-1G6PG(25)
180198	NORTHAMPTON(ADP1)	STOOP MEMORIAL GROUND	L	1T(5)-2G2PG2T(30)
010298	GAUTENG FALCONS	STOOP MEMORIAL GROUND	W	3G2T(31)-1G3PG1T(21)
150298	NEWCASTLE(ADP1)	NEWCASTLE	L	1G1PG1T(15)-5G1PG1T(43)
280298	BATH(ADP1)	BATH	L	1G2PG(13)-3G1PG3T(39)
070398	RICHMOND(ADP1)	STOOP MEMORIAL GROUND	W	5G2PG(41)-1G1T(12)
140398	SALE(ADP1)	SALE	L	1G2PG(13)-1G2PG2T(23)
290398	GLOUCESTER(ADP1)	STOOP MEMORIAL GROUND	W	4G1PG1T(36)-1G3PG(16)
120498	WASPS(ADP1)	LOFTUS ROAD	L	3G1T(26)-2G5PG(29)

180498	LEICESTER(ADP1)	STOOP MEMORIAL GROUND	L	2G(14)-2G1DG2PG(23)
250498	LONDON IRISH(ADP1)	SUNBURY	L	2G(14)-8G2PG(62)
290498	SARACENS(ADP1)	STOOP MEMORIAL GROUND	L	2G4PG(26)-2G3PG1T(28)
030598	BRISTOL(ADP1)	BRISTOL	W	2G4PG(26)-3PG2T(19)
170598	NEWCASTLE(ADP1)	STOOP MEMORIAL GROUND	L	2G2PG(20)-4G2PG2T(44)

In June and July 1998, England went on what was labelled the Tour from Hell. A weakened side was handed a crazy itinerary and got thumped by Australia (0-76) and New Zealand twice (22-64 and 10-40) before also going down to South Africa (0-18). In fact, they lost every game because the three non-test matches also produced defeats. We had no current players in the party but others who had or would wear our colours were Duncan Bell, Dominic Chapman, Tony Diprose, Matt Moore, Peter Richards and Pat Sanderson. Chapman (came on as a replacement) and Diprose (who captained the side) played against Australia; Sanderson played in the other three and Diprose joined him in the last two.

At the end of May 1998, Chris Sheasby made the centre pages of The Sun newspaper for all the wrong reasons. It appears he had been cheating on his girlfriend with two other women and the two "other women" told how they lured him to a nightclub where they poured buckets of ice cold water over him. Sensational stuff indeed! Andy Keast was shown the door after a bad run from the turn of the year; the writing had been on the wall when he was moved into a player recruitment role when Brooke became head coach. It seemed no one was able to turn us into a winning side and this was set to continue for some time to come. The Club made a loss of £2,150,522 at year end 31st May 1999 and the Directors continued to change; David Richards joined and Winterbottom resigned. An U21 League had been introduced by the professional body as clubs tried to develop youngsters.

For the new season, Zinzan Brooke was appointed captain and John Gallagher became Director of Rugby. Brooke was reportedly on a salary of around £200,000 per year so a lot was expected of him. We had a tough start at Leicester but had strengthened the squad with several international players and five of these made their debuts at Welford Road on 5th September. Zinzan Brooke had won 58 caps for New Zealand and played in the first of 43 matches, Vaughn Going (nephew of All Black legend Sid Going), appeared in the first of only five games (he won 19 caps for Hong Kong between 1994 and 1998), Gary Halpin had won 11 caps for Ireland and made 26 appearances for us, Garrick Morgan (24 Australian caps) began an 88 game career and John Schuster (41 appearances) was a double international and had gained caps for New Zealand (10) and Samoa (3). He had also won 2 rugby league caps for Samoa. David Officer had joined from Currie and would appear 43 times for the 1st XV. A new arrangement concerning shirt numbering had been brought in for the start of the season whereby all teams would wear 1-15 and the seven replacements 16-22. Typically, we made a mockery of this from the start when our wingers (O'Leary and Luger) both wore 14 and number eight (Guy Bibby) appeared as 22! Leicester had been forced by this decision to abandon a 72 year old tradition of wearing letters instead of numbers. The question beforehand was whether Brooke could change our fortunes around – the answer was swift; he had a lot of work to do. John Schuster was the only man to emerge with any credit on our side. He landed five penalties but Leicester scored seven tries to nil in a 49-15 romp. John Gallagher summed it all up when he said there are no excuses, we were awful. The difference was that Leicester played as a team and we didn't. Stransky added two penalties and four conversions to the tries and we returned to London with our tails between our legs. With no relegation last season, Premiership 1 had been increased to fourteen teams with the addition of Bedford and London Scottish.

Our second away game was at Northampton and, after Schuster had given us the lead with a penalty after 18 minutes, disaster struck. Jason Leonard was sent off for stamping on Budge Pountney's head at a ruck by the referee (Robin Goodliffe) and missed the next four games. David Barnes (who had joined from Newcastle) came on as Jason Keyter was sacrificed because of the sending off. He went on to appear in 45 games during this and the following season. The Saints got two tries in each half with our reply coming in the shape of a second Schuster penalty. The final score of 25-6 left us rooted to the bottom of the table. In the absence of any European competition (the English clubs had decided to boycott the European Cup this year which meant Bath didn't get the chance to defend their title), we were due to play a series of Anglo-Welsh friendlies against Cardiff and Swansea. The first of these brought Cardiff to the Stoop on 19th September. A number of different faces appeared in this one but it brought another defeat. Each side scored and converted three tries with Jarvis just outscoring Schuster by two penalties to one. O'Leary, Colin Ridgway and Garrick Morgan got our scores with the last two coming after we had trailed 10-27. Schuster's three conversions took him to thirty points in three games and this was twice the total from the rest of the side.

A visit to Manchester Sale produced a bumper number of points but alas, no league points for us again. John Schuster kept us in touch with his kicking as he converted Ridgway's try after 5 minutes and put over three penalties. The problem was that Sale were scoring tries and our defence was breached four times in the first half. Stuart Power gifted Beim a try in first half injury time to send them in 29-16 ahead. In the first seven minutes of the second half, Dan Luger raced in twice for tries, Schuster converted the second and the league points were up for grabs. No more tries came despite both sides trying their utmost and Howarth (3) and Schuster (2) exchanged penalties to leave us trailing by four points. We were camped on Sale's line and, as we attempted a pushover for the third time, one of our front row was penalised for collapsing the scrum and our chance had gone. During six minutes of injury time, Howarth popped over two more penalties to make the final margin of victory ten points.

As West Hartlepool had lost their opening three matches as well, they took over as the bottom placed team as their points difference was worse than ours. Thierry Lacroix led the side in the absence of Zinzan Brooke; the first of a number of occasions on which he would deputise. John Schuster was proving to be something of a kicking machine and against London Scottish on 3rd October, he added another five penalties and a conversion to his total. Dan Luger got our only try after 16 minutes before we almost let the Scots off the hook (as we had done in their previous league visit to the Stoop in 1992). McAusland got five penalties of his own but couldn't convert a try from Jones with six minutes to go. A narrow victory but at least it was something to build on as we leapfrogged the Scots into twelfth position.

A trip to Bedford saw us start and finish badly with another nightmare performance. In just 12 minutes, we trailed 0-13 with the home side scoring a goal and two penalties before Schuster came to the rescue to fire us ahead by half time. He converted his own try and one from Rory Jenkins before adding a couple of penalties but Yapp dropped a goal to open Bedford's scoring in the second half and our lead was four points. Luger then ran 50 metres to score our third try and the conversion and two more penalties from Schuster put us well clear as the game went into injury time. Bedford had scored and converted their second try between Schuster's penalties but still trailed by ten points. Just into time added on, Ewens scored a try but the conversion was missed and we were still in front. With four added minutes played, O'Mahony was put in by Forster and he ran in beneath the posts for Howard to convert and we had somehow contrived to lose the match after controlling most of the possession (33-35).

When Saracens came to the Stoop on 17th October, they had played and won all four of their matches and we were odds-on for a thrashing. Practically no one gave us a hope of getting anything from this one but we came out fighting, scored seventeen points in the first nine minutes and blew our unbeaten visitors out of the water. Tries from Jamie Williams, Rory Jenkins and Keith Wood and three penalties and two conversions by Schuster gave us a 28-0 lead. Brendon Daniel did get a try back which Penaud converted to narrow the gap at half time. When Jenkins was sent to the sin bin, Sarries took advantage and scored fourteen points without reply. Schuster steadied the ship with two more penalties (one when Wallace was sent to the bin for upending Morgan at a lineout) and then converted O'Leary's try to put us 41-21 up with just eight minutes left. Our visitors scored their fourth goal and O'Leary went into the bin for dissent but we had achieved a major shock and proved just what we were capable of (which made it all the more frustrating when we didn't do it).

The following Tuesday, Gloucester visited the Stoop as we looked to improve on the Saracens result. Gloucester made mistakes, Schuster punished them and kicked three penalties to give us a 9-0 lead after 27 minutes. Five minutes later, O'Leary intercepted a pass and ran in from half way to make it 14-0 at the interval. As the visitors rang the changes, our lead increased. Schuster got another penalty, Chris Wright scored a try and Schuster converted Luger's effort to make it 27-0 after 71 minutes. Gloucester were awarded a penalty try which Mannix converted but Schuster put an end to any lingering hopes of a revival with his fifth penalty and the conversion of O'Leary's second try to make it 39-7. John Schuster had now scored 129 points in just eight matches and was challenging all scoring records in the league as well as Club ones.

Against West Hartlepool (again at the Stoop), the match was ruined as a spectacle by the torrential wind and rain which fell for most of the game. When we faced the elements in the second half, our lead stood at 25-3. Schuster had kicked two penalties and converted tries by Ngauamo and Luger. Huw Harries had scored our first try after Vile had levelled matters with a penalty. Connolly scored a try which Vile converted after 58 minutes but we held out comfortably to move into eighth place with our third league win in the space of eight days. At last, we were starting to show our potential and this would be tested on our visit to Loftus Road to play fourth placed Wasps. The first half saw a kicking duel between John Schuster and Kenny Logan - each being successful with three penalties and a conversion. David Officer got our try and Scrase got one for Wasps. We led 10-3 and trailed 10-16 but Schuster brought us back to level pegging by half time. At the end of the third quarter, Schuster kicked another penalty and dropped a goal in the 76th minute before Greenstock got over for a Wasps try after 82 minutes. Logan had gone off injured and it fell to Ufton to attempt the touchline conversion to win the match. He missed and we had our first away win after four successive defeats.

A visit from Newcastle started the same way as our three previous home games and we raced into a sixteen point lead after just 14 minutes. Schuster was on target yet again and he kicked three penalties and converted Luger's try after a 75 metre passage of play. The reigning champions came back with a try and a penalty to halve our lead by the interval. Schuster put us 19-8 ahead with his third penalty before tries from Massey and Armstrong and a conversion by Wilkinson put the visitors ahead for the first time by a single point; there were thirteen minutes of normal time remaining. In the 72nd and 75th minutes, Schuster confidently stroked penalties between the posts to give him a success rate of seven out of eight. Wilkinson, for Newcastle, had just two from six and this proved to be their undoing. For the final six minutes, Newcastle were camped on our line trying to hammer their way over for a match clinching score and even when Zinzan Brooke was sent to the sin bin for killing the ball, we still held out for a fantastic win. Such were the big hits being put in that Leonard finished with a suspected broken hand and Archer ended up with a neck strain. These were just two of a number of injuries during the course of the match.

A trip to Reading to play Richmond was postponed due to the ground being used for football so we received Bath on 21st November in our next fixture. John Schuster's boot was in good order again and he kicked four penalties and converted his own try right on half time. He couldn't convert Jason Keyter's try after 19 minutes but we led 24-9 at the interval. Preston and Callard (2) got penalties for the visitors. When Schuster scored his second try and converted it, we led by 22 points and victory seemed assured but, you can never write Bath off. They came storming back with tries from Regan, Nicol and Balshaw and a penalty and two conversions from Callard. Keyter scored his second try which Schuster converted but we now only led by seven points with a minute of normal time left. In another attack, Garrick Morgan crossed for our fifth try and the remaining three minutes of injury time passed without incident. John Schuster's 28 points was the highest number scored by any Harlequin in a league game and surpassed by one point the record of David Pears set in 1989 at Bedford. It was also the highest number of points in any game since Colin Lambert's 32 in 1976 against the Royal Air Force. Scott Stewart made his final appearance in this game having scored 15 points (3 tries) during his year at the Club. Our sixth league victory in a row was our best run since 1996 and was a major change from the start of the season. John Gallagher was full of praise for the side and how they deserved it! It was now important for us to knuckle down and extend this run into double figures.

Our next game was an Anglo-Welsh friendly against Swansea at St. Helens and again we got off to a good start with a try from Dan Luger; Rob Liley converted and added two penalties. Gary Halpin's try went unconverted and half time was reached with the teams level at 18-18. Arwel Thomas had already kicked a couple of penalties and converted one of two tries by Richard Rees. In the second half, Thomas put over two more penalties and dropped a goal to open up a nine point gap and Robinson sealed the win with a try one minute from time. Johnny Ngauamo made his last appearance at Swansea having scored 35 points (7 tries) during his one and a half season stint with us. Adam Leach led the side in the absence of both Brooke and Lacroix.

We ended the year with two league games against London Irish at Sunbury and Manchester Sale at the Stoop. After suffering the enormous defeat back in April, we needed a win to maintain our climb up the table. A bad start produced ten points for the Irish before we got our act together. Schuster kicked a penalty on 35 minutes and then converted Keith Wood's try three minutes later to tie the scores. In the first sixteen minutes of the second half, Schuster knocked over two more penalties to give us a six point advantage before disaster struck. The referee awarded a penalty try after O'Kelly was impeded near our line, Cunningham converted and with the final quarter to come, we trailed 16-17. Mistakes began to creep into our game and a final penalty ten minutes from the end sealed a narrow win for the Irish. Once again, we had proved that we were not yet good enough to win the league title – these were the matches you had to win to stand a chance.

On 27th December, we welcomed Manchester Sale to the Stoop for what tuned out to be a close encounter. The first half contained three penalties for Schuster and one for Howarth. When Jamie Williams scored a minute into the second half and Schuster landed his fourth penalty after 57 minutes, it looked like we were on our way to a clear victory. In the space of four minutes, Yates and Hanley scored tries but Howarth could only convert the second. In the final ten minutes, Howarth missed two penalties to win the game so we had our eighth victory from thirteen matches.

A promising second half of the season lay ahead and it all began with the away league game against London Scottish. This was played at the Stoop as they were our tenants for the season. In the first half, John Schuster out-scored McAusland by four penalties to three to give us the lead. A half time hailstorm held up the restart but two more Schuster strikes and a try from Harries took us fourteen points clear before the Scots scored a try and a penalty to keep the game alive. When Zinzan Brooke went over for his first try for us and Schuster converted, only eight minutes remained. As normal time expired, Hunter scored for the Scots, Forrest converted and our lead was down to six points. As we hammered away at our opponents line, Gary Halpin barged over for the match clinching score a minute from the end to complete the double over them.

The following week, we met Esher at the Stoop in the Tetley's Bitter Cup 4th round. This came almost 19 years to the day of our previous meeting, also in the cup. Tom Murphy became our fourth captain of the season and was booked to give him something to remember the day by. Esher came with a number of ex-Quins in their squad and all seven of them played some part. They were Jeff Alexander, Paul Brady, Michael Corcoran, Richard Goodwin, Jonathan Gregory, Simon Owen and Justin Towns. Their coach (Hugh McHardy) was also one of our old boys having played for us between 1981 and 1985. With a three-quarter strength side, we took the lead after nine minutes when Daren O'Leary scored a try which Schuster converted. On 20 minutes, Gregory put Esher on the scoreboard with a penalty before Jenkins got our second try which Schuster converted before adding a penalty to put us 17-3 ahead at the break. Although we weren't playing particularly well, we gradually extended our lead with tries at regular intervals from Jamie Williams (2) and O'Leary (2). Rob Liley could only convert one so it was like a return to the dreadful kicking of the past few seasons without John Schuster. At 39-3, Esher made a determined effort to grab a try and they duly did when Bird scored after 79 minutes. Gregory converted but we had the last word when Lacroix scored our seventh try which Liley managed to convert with the last kick of the game. The final score of 46-10 set us up for a fifth round meeting with London Scottish although we would be the away side.

Before that, we had two massive league meetings with Northampton and London Irish at the Stoop. We were in seventh place and Northampton were second to Leicester on points difference. We began well when Luger made 50 yards and set up O'Leary who recycled the ball for Jason Keyter to send John Schuster through a gap for the opening score. He duly added the conversion before Grayson opened the Saints account with a penalty. On 32 minutes, we were awarded a penalty try after five attempts at a pushover. Schuster converted and with the visitors down to 14 men, it looked good for us. However, mistakes from the kick-off and missed tackles enabled Grayson to score a try. He converted and when Schuster missed two penalties late in the half, the match was evenly poised. Thierry Lacroix was unlucky to have been adjudged offside (when Brooke charged down Beal's attempted clearance) as he sped towards the posts but when Keith Wood dropped a goal from 22 metres, we led by seven points. Within ten minutes, Northampton were level as Pagel scored for Grayson to convert and as the Saints pack applied the pressure, we spent more and more time in our 22. With time running out, Pat Lam went over from a five metre scrum, Grayson again converted and we had lost our first home league match of the season.

Dick Best and Andy Keast were now the coaching team at London Irish and they came to the Stoop on 23rd January trying to make it a hat-trick of league wins over us. The Irish line up contained ex-Quin Ryan Strudwick and future Quins Nick Burrows, Peter Richards and Niall Woods. John Schuster fired us into the lead after 32 minutes with a penalty but we had already lost our captain (Brooke) and Harries to injuries. O'Shea ran in the first of his two tries which Woods converted to give the visitors the half time lead. Daren O'Leary went over on 56 minutes and Schuster converted to give us back the lead which lasted only three minutes. The O'Shea/Woods combination left us trailing and when Woods added a penalty and Bishop completed a move set up by Woods, it was 10-22. Although

12 minutes of normal time remained, it took us another seven minutes of injury time to get our second try. Mensah scored for Schuster to narrow the gap but we ran out of time and slumped to another home defeat.

We were going through a bad patch and London Scottish shocked us in the cup tie after Schuster had put us in front with a penalty and O'Leary had added a try. Jannie de Beer got them going with a penalty before converting his own try. He then kicked another penalty and converted Fenn's try scored when Bill Davison was in the sin bin for a late and high tackle on former team mate Mick Watson. Another one of our former players was Rhodri Davies who appeared in the centre. Peter Mensah got a try for Schuster to convert on half time to make it 15-20. Just as Davison was coming back from the bin, Holmes scored another try for the Scots which de Beer converted for a twelve point lead. We had to wake ourselves up, we duly did and Mensah notched up his second try after 47 minutes. Schuster's groin had started to hinder him so Rob Liley took over the kicking duties. In the space of fourteen minutes, Liley converted Mensah's try, his own effort and added a penalty to give us the lead again. When Schuster grabbed our fifth try after 63 minutes, we led by ten points and the former All Black was within striking distance of the all-time points scoring record in a season set by Billy Bushell in 1975/76. His fifth try of the season took him to 280 points in just nineteen games. There were still almost twenty minutes to go and de Beer put over two more penalties in the 68th and 71st minutes to narrow the gap to just four points. We held on and progressed to the quarter finals with a 37-33 victory.

Will Carling had been coaxed out of retirement and became a full time player until the end of the season. David Pears also came back but he was only on loan from Jewson League One side Wharfedale. He had last played for us in November 1995 at the Stoop against Orrell. Neither player let the side down although Carling only came on for the last eight minutes. Leicester were two points clear at the top of the table and we were ten points behind in eighth place. We desperately needed a win to get our league challenge back on course and Schuster banged over two penalties to put us six points ahead after 21 minutes. A goal and a penalty gave the Tigers a four point advantage before Schuster became the record points holder when he put over his third penalty a minute before half time. It took him to 289 points; Bushell's record had been equalled with his second penalty. We never got any closer and a storming four try performance in the second half took Leicester clean away to victory by thirty four points to nine.

Two visits in a row to Kingsholm to play Gloucester meant a league match and a cup tie. On 13th February, we met in the league and produced a good, solid performance to register our ninth successive win over the Cherry and Whites. Mark Mapletoft helped them to a ten point lead in the first ten minutes when he kicked a penalty and converted Beim's try. We came back and took a brief lead with two penalties and a conversion from Schuster and a try from O'Leary. A penalty try for collapsing a scrum was converted by Mapletoft and we trailed at the half way point. Chris Wright darted over for a try, Schuster added the conversion and a penalty but Mapletoft's penalty in reply made it 23-20 to us with most of the final quarter remaining. Keith Wood then made a break and set up Gareth Llewellyn for our third try and Schuster's fourth penalty made the final margin of victory eleven points. Vaughn Going came on for O'Leary near the end for his last appearance in a Quins shirt.

Our third cup visit to Kingsholm came on 27th February and should have ended in our second win. In the first half, Mapletoft outscored Schuster 2-1 in penalties before Huw Harries scored eleven minutes into the second half. Schuster converted and exchanged penalties with Mapletoft to make it 13-9 with twelve minutes of normal time remaining. Four minutes later, the Gloucester fly half put over another penalty and the lead was one point. Disaster struck five minutes into injury time when Chris Sheasby was adjudged by the referee not to have released the ball in the tackle; Mapletoft scored from in front of the posts and we trailed for the third time. We had controlled large periods of the game but a last chance went awry when Keyter's long pass to Luger lacked the accuracy to give him a run to the line. At the end of ten minutes of injury time, we were out in the cruellest of fashions. Richard Hill had been sacked as Gloucester's coach after our league visit and had been replaced by Philippe Saint-André – he had a winning start!

Our next game was again an away day; another Anglo-Welsh friendly against Cardiff. Our starting line-up contained only seven of the side which finished the game at Gloucester but both teams were weakened as we were in the middle of the Five Nations Championship. Adam Leach scored a try after 14 minutes, Liley converted and added two penalties to give us a narrow lead at the interval. Cardiff scored a goal and a try before the floodgates opened in the second half. Before Lacroix got our second try which Liley converted, the home side had added twenty nine points to their half time score. Robert Jones got their seventh try and Rayer his second conversion (after he had replaced Jarvis) in injury time and we had conceded over forty points for the third time this season.

A second friendly fixture in seven days saw us take on French side Biarritz Olympique at the Stoop on Friday 19th March. Chris Sheasby gave us the perfect start with a try after only five minutes. Thierry Lacroix was our kicker for the night (until he handed over to Liley) and he converted and added a penalty. Biarritz came back into the game and unconverted tries either side of Lacroix's penalty tied the scores before Sheasby and Stuart Power crossed for tries to give us a nice lead at half time. A third unconverted score for the visitors cut our lead in half but we soon stretched away again when Leach scored for Liley to convert. A series of changes in a dozen minutes upset our rhythm but we finished with a flourish and Wright and Lacroix scored tries. Liley put over another conversion to make the final score 39-15.

We now finished the season with a run of eight consecutive league matches as the proposed Anglo-Welsh friendly at home against Swansea on 1st May was cancelled. The first of these was a home fixture against Richmond on 27th March. They were three points and one place behind us in the table and victory was increasingly essential in the scramble for a top six European Cup qualifying spot. Thierry Lacroix had now started to recover his best form at fly half and it was his try after seven minutes which opened the scoring. Schuster converted, couldn't convert Halpin's effort but added a penalty to give us an interval lead. A penalty and a try enabled the visitors to turn around only seven points down and they had drawn level just six minutes into the second half. Va'a converted his own try and his penalty gave them the lead. Lacroix got his second try which Schuster converted but Clarke went over for Richmond and Va'a's conversion made it 25-22 to Richmond. In the space of four minutes with just under twenty minutes to go, Schuster kicked a penalty and converted his own try to give us the lead again. His try took him to 294 league points for the season and this surpassed the 291 scored by Gareth Rees for Wasps in 1996/97. Our defence was breached again when Dixon got Richmond's fourth try, Va'a converted and the scores were again level. In the closing moments, Lacroix, Schuster (twice) and Carling all missed dropped goals in an attempt to break the deadlock. Perhaps the 32-32 draw was a fair result on the play although it helped neither side all that much.

Bedford visited on 17th April and were currently in 13th place with only five wins from their twenty one games played so far. This game was one of our worst performances of the season although we managed to dig in and escape with a victory in the end against the strugglers. John Schuster was still going strong and put over three penalties to two from Yapp for the visitors in the first half. Our narrow lead was short lived as Rory Underwood scored a try which Yapp converted five minutes into the second half. With the introduction of Wood and Brooke, we started to gather ourselves for the final quarter. Dan Luger scored a try but Yapp got another penalty and Bedford still led with twelve minutes to go. In the last ten minutes of normal and injury time, the visitors made mistakes which led to their downfall. Schuster got his fourth penalty and one conversion and Daren O'Leary and Jamie Williams each scored a try to make it 29-16.

On 21st April, we made the long trek up to West Hartlepool to face the bottom placed side. This was an extraordinary match which was only settled in the closing minutes. Rob Liley scored for us first and, during the first half, Jenkins and Luger added further tries. Schuster was on target with two penalties and three conversions. West had scored in exactly the same fashion and the scores were level at the break (27-27). O'Leary put us back in front with our fourth try which Schuster converted but Vile slotted his third penalty and converted Hyde's try to give the lead back to West. Three minutes after this try, Schuster levelled with a penalty before Peter Mensah scored the match winning try. Schuster's conversion and fourth penalty success merely underlined our superiority and gave him a return of twenty two points. This was to be our highest score of the season, surpassing the biggest winning margin against Esher by one point.

For our third game in nine days, we travelled to Vicarage Road to take on Saracens. As the matches came thick and fast, the whole squad needed to play to their potential and John Gallagher had set them a target of five wins from the last six games. The first had been won at Brierton Lane and we had an excellent first half against Saracens. Rob Liley kicked two penalties before the home side scored ten points. Luger, O'Leary and Murphy got tries and two conversions from Liley gave us a 25-10 lead at the interval. Johnson kicked two penalties and converted a try by Daniel but they couldn't catch us. Lacroix had come on for Liley and he added a couple of penalties before Chris Sheasby ran in from a scrum on the 22. Lacroix's conversion put us in the clear and all that Sarries could muster in reply was a penalty try which Johnson converted.

Richmond had already been deducted two points for the postponement of our next fixture back in November and another defeat would knock them out of contention for a European Cup place. Thierry Lacroix was again in superb form and scored twelve points in the first half. He started the scoring after six minutes with a penalty, converted his own try (when he reacted quicker than anyone else to a badly thrown lineout) and Garrick Morgan's when he had set up a lineout close to the Richmond line with a beautiful kick. When Walne went over for Richmond's third try (Bateman and Clarke had scored the others) they held a one point lead at half time. Va'a had landed a penalty but couldn't convert any of the tries. Bateman added his second try soon after the restart but when Lacroix had finished, we had won again. He dropped a goal from 42 yards out, converted Keyter's try and added a penalty. This win put us into fourth place and we only needed to win at Bath five days later to claim our place in the European Cup next season.

To put this into perspective, we hadn't won at the Recreation Ground on our last ten visits. These were all games in league and cup; our last victory had been in a friendly on 21st December 1985. The first quarter belonged to Bath with Perry kicking two penalties and converting Earnshaw's try. Our only reply was a try by Luger before we really came back into contention when Mensah charged down Balshaw's attempted clearance and ran in under the posts from 35 yards out. Schuster's conversion made it 12-13 at half time. Lacroix had missed an attempted dropped goal and Schuster had failed with a long range penalty but Perry's two failures affected Bath more than us. We tackled like demons throughout the second half and when Mensah set up Williams for a run in from near the half way line, we led 17-13 with ten minutes of normal time remaining. Bath camped on our line for most of the seven minutes of injury time but they couldn't get the winning try and we had achieved a famous victory.

Our penultimate game was on the following Tuesday at Newcastle and another high scoring midweek game resulted. Will Carling, Jamie Williams and Thierry Lacroix set up Jason Keyter for our first try which Lacroix converted before adding a couple of penalties. Despite all this, the Falcons led at the break with two tries from Tuigamala and a penalty and the conversions by Wilkinson. When Williams scored for Lacroix to convert after 52 minutes, we were back in front and another victory looked a possibility. Our final score was a dropped goal from Lacroix but, this only brought us level as Wilkinson had kicked two penalties to take the lead away from us. In the last ten minutes, Newcastle had too much power for us and Wilkinson added a penalty to the conversion of Cartmell's try to make the final score 33-23 in their favour.

After nine months of intense rugby, we came to our last game of the season, a home encounter against Wasps. A win would guarantee us a top four finish as our opponents were in third place but on the same points as us. Rob Henderson burst through to open the scoring with a try on 22 minutes; Rees converted and added a penalty five minutes later to put Wasps on their way. Lacroix had missed two attempted dropped goals but made no mistake with a penalty three minutes before half time. A seventeen points scoring spree between the 46th and 58th minutes gave us a 20-10 lead as we changed beyond recognition from the team which played in the first half. Lacroix dropped a goal and converted tries from Harries and himself. Wasps came storming back and Rees converted his own try and kicked his second penalty to tie the scores. Ten minutes after this penalty, Sheasby was driven over from a rolling maul, Lacroix converted and we moved into third place. Saracens beat Newcastle in their final game and we had to settle for fourth position but it had been a tremendous effort by the whole squad. Gary Halpin played his last game against Wasps having scored 3 tries (15 points) during his one season stop at the Club as did Thierry Lacroix. The Frenchman had led the side fifteen times and scored 575 points (13 tries, 8 dropped goals, 106 penalties and 84 conversions) during his two and a half season career. Dan Luger also left to join Saracens but would return to us in 2001.

Our playing record in the league was P26 W16 D1 L9 F690 A653 Pts 33 Pos 4th. This had been our highest number of wins ever and with seven wins, a draw and just one defeat from our last nine league games, it just proved that we were capable of sustaining a challenge for the title. We just needed to eradicate the silly losses like those to Sale and Bedford (away), London Irish (twice) and Northampton at the Stoop. Our overall record was P32 W18 D1 L13 F887 A833. Daren O'Leary was top try scorer on his own again with 13 and Thierry Lacroix got the most dropped goals with 3. John Schuster broke the Club scoring records for penalties and overall. His 83 penalties surpassed Lacroix's mark of 56 set in 1997/98 and his final points total of 368 (6 tries, 1 dropped goal, 83 penalties and 43 conversions) totally eclipsed Billy Bushell's 23 year old record of 286. Overall, tries rose by just one to 90, dropped goals were up by two to 5 and penalties reached a new record mark of 98. These were up by 33 on the previous season and by 14 on the old record set in 1993/94. Conversions fell by two to 64 but the increase in penalty goals enabled the overall points to rise by over a hundred to 887. Only 40 players were used in the 33 matches with Adam Leach appearing in 31 of them. Rory Jenkins (30), Gareth Llewellyn and Daren O'Leary (29), Dan Luger and John Schuster (27), Gary Halpin and Garrick Morgan on 26 and Bill Davison with 25 were the best of the rest.

1998/99

050998	LEICESTER(ADP1)	LEICESTER	L	5PG(15)-4G2PG3T(49)
120998	NORTHAMPTON(ADP1)	NORTHAMPTON	L	2PG(6)-1G1PG3T(25)
190998	CARDIFF(AWF)	STOOP MEMORIAL GROUND	L	3G1PG(24)-3G2PG(27)
260998	MANCHESTER SALE(ADP1)	SALE	L	2G5PG1T(34)-3G6PG1T(44)

031098	LONDON SCOTTISH(ADP1)	STOOP MEMORIAL GROUND	W	1G5PG(22)-5PG1T(20)
101098	BEDFORD(ADP1)	BEDFORD	L	3G4PG(33)-3G1DG2PG1T(35)
171098	SARACENS(ADP1)	STOOP MEMORIAL GROUND	W	3G5PG1T(41)-4G(28)
201098	GLOUCESTER(ADP1)	STOOP MEMORIAL GROUND	W	2G5PG2T(39)-1G(7)
241098	WEST HARTLEPOOL(ADP1)	STOOP MEMORIAL GROUND	W	2G2PG1T(25)-1G1PG(10)
011198	WASPS(ADP1)	LOFTUS ROAD	W	1G1DG4PG(22)-1G3PG1T(21)
071198	NEWCASTLE(ADP1)	STOOP MEMORIAL GROUND	W	1G6PG(25)-1G1PG2T(20)
151198	RICHMOND(ADP1)	READING	P	
211198	BATH(ADP1)	STOOP MEMORIAL GROUND	W	3G4PG2T(43)-2G4PG1T(31)
121298	SWANSEA(AWF)	SWANSEA	L	1G2PG1T(18)-1G1DG4PG2T(32)
191298	LONDON IRISH(ADP1)	SUNBURY	L	1G3PG(16)-2G2PG(20)
271298	MANCHESTER SALE(ADP1)	STOOP MEMORIAL GROUND	W	4PG1T(17)-1G1PG1T(15)
020199	LONDON SCOTTISH(ADP1)	STOOP MEMORIAL GROUND(A)	W	1G6PG2T(35)-1G4PG1T(24)
090199	ESHER(TBC4)	STOOP MEMORIAL GROUND	W	4G1PG3T(46)-1G1PG(10)
160199	NORTHAMPTON(ADP1)	STOOP MEMORIAL GROUND	L	2G1DG(17)-3G1PG(24)
230199	LONDON IRISH(ADP1)	STOOP MEMORIAL GROUND	L	2G1PG(17)-2G1PG1T(22)
300199	LONDON SCOTTISH(TBC5)	STOOP MEMORIAL GROUND(A)	W	3G2PG2T(37)-3G4PG(33)
060299	LEICESTER(ADP1)	STOOP MEMORIAL GROUND	L	3PG(9)-3G1PG2T(34)
130299	GLOUCESTER(ADP1)	GLOUCESTER	W	2G4PG1T(31)-2G2PG(20)
270299	GLOUCESTER(TBCQF)	GLOUCESTER	L	1G2PG(13)-5PG(15)
130399	CARDIFF(AWF)	CARDIFF	L	2G2PG(20)-5G1PG2T(48)
190399	BIARRITZ OLYMPIQUE	STOOP MEMORIAL GROUND	W	3G1PG3T(39)-3T(15)
270399	RICHMOND(ADP1)	STOOP MEMORIAL GROUND	D	3G2PG1T(32)-3G2PG1T(32)
170499	BEDFORD(ADP1)	STOOP MEMORIAL GROUND	W	1G4PG2T(29)-1G3PG(16)

210499	WEST HARTLEPOOL(ADP1)	WEST HARTLEPOOL	W	5G4PG(47)-4G3PG(37)
250499	SARACENS(ADP1)	VICARAGE ROAD	W	3G4PG1T(38)-3G3PG(30)
010599	SWANSEA(AWF)	STOOP MEMORIAL GROUND	C	
030599	RICHMOND(ADP1)	READING	W	3G1DG2PG(30)-1PG4T(23)
080599	BATH(ADP1)	BATH	W	1G2T(17)-1G2PG(13)
110599	NEWCASTLE(ADP1)	NEWCASTLE	L	2G1DG2PG(23)-3G4PG(33)
190599	WASPS(ADP1)	STOOP MEMORIAL GROUND	W	3G1DG1PG(27)-2G2PG(20)

In June 1999, England went on a two match short tour to Australia and after winning the warm-up game, they lost again to the hosts by 15-22. Jason Leonard and Dan Luger (who was on the verge of going to Saracens) were the only Quins in the side.

It was announced in the first programme of the new season that testimonials were being introduced to reward long standing players for their service to the Club. The first recipients of this would be Peter Mensah and Chris Wright. In the same edition, the new website was announced with the chance for supporters to vote for one of three designs. In the accounts for year ending 31st May 2000, another loss was reported, this time it was £1,681,758. Kerr, Morgan and Wall resigned as Directors and Andrew Vander Meersch joined the Board. The fixture card carried team information and this included a statement that the Wanderers would play games on an ad hoc basis.

The World Cup was held in Wales in October and November 1999 with matches also taking place in England, France, Scotland and Ireland. Once again, we were well represented with nineteen players representing eleven nations but only two were current; they were Will Greenwood and Jason Leonard. Dan Luger (England) and Keith Wood (Ireland) had played before but would return to us and the rest would all be seen in the future; David Wilson (Australia), Gareth Rees (captain) and Scott Stewart (Canada), Dan Rouse and Viliame Satala (Fiji), Andrew Mehrtens (New Zealand), Opeta Palepoi and Steve So'oialo (Samoa), Andre Vos (South Africa), Epi Taione and Josh Taumalolo (Tonga), Tom Billups and Luke Gross (USA) and Dafydd James and Gareth Llewellyn (Wales). England got off to a flying start with a big win over Italy (67-7) before going down to New Zealand (16-30) and annihilating Tonga to the tune of 101-10. They were then involved in a play-off against Fiji for a quarter final place. Clive Woodward rested a number of first choice players ahead of the following weekend's test against South Africa (assuming victory would follow). In the end, a comfortable enough win was attained by 45-24. At the Stade de France in Paris, England's fourth attempt to become World Champions came to an end when Jannie de Beer produced five dropped goals and 34 points in total to take the Springboks to a 44-21 victory. Australia lifted the trophy for the second time by defeating France 35-12 in the final at the Millenium Stadium, Cardiff.

This season saw the beginning of a ground share agreement with London Irish. It was initially for two seasons but in the end only lasted one. Apparently, during the ground share, some Quins fans were watching all the home games at the Stoop and never travelling to away games, this meant watching the Irish instead but that didn't seem to bother them as our support fell away.

A short tour was undertaken to South Africa and two matches were played against Namibia, the first was a practice game and was won 29-17. The second was played on 20th August at Tygerburg RFC in Cape Town and produced another win. After a tough opening 20 minutes, David Officer scored the opening try followed by others from Huw Harries and Adam Leach (one of which was converted). The Namibians came back into it with twelve points but David Pears landed a penalty and Zinzan Brooke dropped a goal from 40 yards out to make the final score 23-12. Nick Greenstock made his debut in this one having joined us from Wasps. He had won four England caps and would go on to make 85 appearances. Brendon Daniel also appeared for the first time, he would play in 31 games having joined from Saracens.

After Will Carling had been tempted out of retirement for the last part of the previous season, he was made captain for the end of millennium season. This proved to be a mistake as he was in nowhere near his England form and only made fifteen appearances before finally calling it a day before the end of the season. In the first game, we met Manchester Sale at Heywood Road in a friendly. This was to be our only non-competition match in what was to prove a very frustrating season. We had lost on our five previous visits and were looking for a good start. We were behind for most of the first half after Matt Moore had scored for Davidson to convert (it would be two years before Moore joined us). We led at the break after Brendon Daniel grabbed two tries but trailed after a second goal from the home side five minutes before the end after a mistake by another new boy, Peter Richards. Deep into injury time, Jason Keyter got the ball deep in our half, gained 20 metres and then kicked ahead. As he followed up, the bounce deceived the Sale defender and he proceeded to exchange passes twice with David Officer before scoring under the posts for the winning score. Liley's conversion was the last kick of the game and gave us our first win at Sale since 1994. Richards joined from London Irish and went on to make 39 appearances and Pat Sanderson came from Sale. He went on to win 6 England caps and make 108 appearances for the 1st XV.

Our first league match was at the Stoop against Bath and would be a good pointer as to how far we had come – the answer was not very far! We were dreadful and neither Carling (in his first match as Club captain) or Brooke impressed. One newspaper said that eighty minutes into the season we looked a "tired, uninterested rabble". David Pears had returned but this turned out to be a very brief resurrection of his Quins career. His kicking was not as good as in his prime but he did land a penalty right on half time after the visitors had gone into an eight point lead. The second half produced three more Bath tries with our only reply coming from Keyter after 78 minutes which Liley converted. The final score of 10-30 told us more than we needed to know about the state of our league title prospects after only one game.

Saracens visited us the following week and for the second season running went away pointless. The exodus from us to Sarries had seen Bill Davison, Thierry Lacroix, Dan Luger and Nick Walshe join them. Future Quins in their squad were Jon Dawson, Tony Diprose, Mark Mapletoft, Adam Jones and Matt Powell. Brendon Daniel had come in our direction but wasn't amongst our try scorers on this occasion. In fact, all of Saracens points were scored by ex or future Quins. Diprose, Powell and Jones scored tries and Lacroix added a penalty and all three conversions. We led comfortably at half time with tries from Sanderson, Brooke and Jenkins (all of which Liley converted). When Keyter scored after 53 minutes, it was 26-10 and when Sanderson got his second at the end of normal time, Wright converted to make it 33-17. The consolation try from Jones brought them a little closer but we had our first victory.

At Franklin's Gardens on 2nd October, we met Northampton and, despite starting badly, led 10-0 through tries by Richards and Keyter. Despite Liley adding a penalty, we trailed by half time because the Saints got two goals. The first was a penalty try harshly awarded against Richards (he was adjudged by referee Stewart Piercy to have tripped Sleightholme). By the time Liley converted his own try after 54 minutes, the home side's lead had been stretched by twelve more points. Hepher kicked what proved to be the match winning penalty after 64 minutes and Daniel's injury time try which Liley converted made the losing margin just two points. This proved to be the last appearance for Tim Collier and Ricky Nebbett. Both were sentenced in October to nine months in Wandsworth prison for an assault on a man (Malcolm McDouall) in Whitton High Street on 19th November 1998. Recorder Amelia Page QC (after an attempt by the Club to sentence them to a probation programme) said they were not repentant enough for their "reprehensible, despicable, brutish, loutish, thuggery". He was left with two black eyes, a fractured leg, cuts and bruises and a swollen jaw and they were convicted on a charge of causing grievous bodily harm and subsequently sacked by the Club although Nebbett was employed by Leicester on his release and returned to us at the start of the 2005/06 season; Collier went on to play for Worcester. As a result, the Club introduced anger management courses and mental winding-down lessons for the players.

A Sunday match against Manchester Sale provided some of the worst rugby seen at the Stoop in all the years we have played there. The first half remained scoreless as pass after pass was dropped. Rob Liley missed four penalties during the first hour's play before Sale scored a try with one of their rare forays into our half. After Greenstock had dropped the ball with the line at his mercy, Tinnock scored in the 64th minute for Shaw to convert. Liley finally got a penalty over from 10 metres in front of the posts after 71 minutes but Shaw kicked one five minutes later to send us to another defeat. We were in ninth place out of twelve teams with one win from our opening four games. This match saw the last appearance of David Pears. He had scored 721 points (15 tries, 18 dropped goals, 130 penalties and 107 conversions) during his eleven season career and finished as our top points scorer in the league. He had 434 points in just 43 league appearances. He had been unlucky with injuries and had not really been given a fair crack of the whip on his return to once again prove himself.

With the World Cup taking place, we played our next two matches on a Friday and Thursday night respectively. The first of these was a visit to Gloucester where, although we lost in the cup in February, we hadn't been beaten in a league match since December 1993. We made a bad start and Gloucester went into a 13-0 lead after 24 minutes before Keyter opened our account with a try. Liley converted but Gloucester's second try of the game in first half injury time gave them a comfortable lead. Liley kicked two penalties but when Barnes was sin binned for a late tackle, Mannix sent the home side into the last ten minutes with an eight point cushion. Our fight back continued when Liley got another penalty and was complete when he converted O'Leary's try right at the end of normal time. We led 23-21 but, as had happened in the cup, a late, late penalty for the home side condemned us to defeat. As a result of this, we had dropped a place and were only above winless Bedford and Newcastle.

Bristol came to the Stoop on 28th October in second place and were favourites to continue their good start to the season. In a tight first half, we scored the only try through Daniel to lead by a point. Liley converted the try and added a penalty in response to three penalties from Vile for the visitors. Just two minutes into the second half, Vile put over his fourth penalty to give Bristol the lead but disaster struck soon afterwards. First Archer (for punching) then Nabaro (for a high tackle) were sent to the sin bin and Bristol were down to thirteen men at one point. During this twenty minute period, Liley kicked a penalty and converted Ridgway's try. He missed the extra points to Morgan's try but we led 25-12 by the time the visitors were back to full strength. Vile slotted his fifth penalty but Liley replied in kind with his third and fourth efforts. Nabaro went through some weak tackling to register Bristol's first try but debutant Matt Dallow (who turned up at the Stoop looking for a game whilst on holiday) went over for our fourth to make the final score 36-20.

Against our tenants in their home game, we got off to a good start with two Rob Liley penalties in the first seven minutes. The London Irish then took charge and Cunningham equalised with two penalties of his own before he converted O'Shea's try. On 31 minutes, his third penalty gave them a ten point lead but Liley pulled three points back by half time with his third penalty success. Eight minutes into the second half, Liley put another penalty between the uprights and it was game on. After an infringement on the half way line, we put the resultant penalty kick into the corner to go for a try to win the game. It was now three minutes into injury time and Chris Sheasby was driven over for the try. There was still time left for O'Shea to attempt a dropped goal to snatch victory for the visitors; his effort ended up nearer the corner flag than the posts and we had another victory. With this win, we had moved up to eighth place in the table just four points behind the leaders, Saracens. Gareth Rees came on as a substitute for Matt Dallow after 74 minutes to make the first of 21 appearances. He had won 55 caps for Canada and had also captained his country on 25 occasions.

Bedford had ex-Quins Ronnie Eriksson, Ryan O'Neill (who was between stints) and Scott Stewart in their side as well as future Quins Adrian Olver and Roy Winters. They were rooted to the bottom of the table with no wins from five games but we would struggle against them in both home and away fixtures. Ben Gollings came on as a substitute for Will Carling at half time for the first of at 81 appearances. In another dreadful game containing a small amount of skill from both sides, we led at half time by a try from Sanderson and a penalty from Liley in the first quarter to a try from O'Neill and a conversion from Stewart in the second quarter. The second half remained scoreless until Stewart put the visitors in front with a penalty a minute from the end of normal time. Two minutes later, Gareth Rees banged a penalty over from 40 metres and we held a slender lead of eleven points to ten. In the tenth minute of injury time, Bedford were awarded a penalty in front of the posts but, as Stewart lined up the chance, the touch judge finally drew the referee's attention to a stamping incident by one of Bedford's props. The decision was reversed, the ball cleared and the final whistle went. We had survived the sin binning of Nepia to record our fourth league victory and move up to seventh place still four points behind the leaders who were now Bath. From now on, each league victory would be worth three points as the World Cup had finished; this was done to appease those teams supplying a lot of players.

The following Friday (19th November), we began our assault on the Heineken European Cup with a visit to Cardiff. The home side got off to a flyer and were sixteen points up in the first 26 minutes. Neil Jenkins kicked three penalties and converted a try by Hill before we began a fight back. Pat Sanderson and Zinzan Brooke both went over for tries from lineout possession won by Gareth Llewellyn. Rees converted both but another Jenkins penalty saw Cardiff lead at half time. The second half was a real ding-dong affair and became a kicking duel between Rees and Jenkins with our man just shading it. Two penalties by Rees gave us the lead for the first time but it was short lived as Jenkins dropped a goal. A penalty try was awarded to the home side after a collapsed scrum which Jenkins converted to make it 29-20 with just twelve minutes left. Gareth Rees was showing all his kicking skills and converted two more penalties and dropped a goal to bring the scores level in a four minute spell. Three minutes from the end, Jenkins kicked his fifth penalty but Rees had the last, dramatic, word when he dropped a goal from 40 yards (having just missed one from 45 yards) 23 seconds into stoppage time. This was a good start to our campaign and if we could get three home wins, progress to the quarter finals might be achieved.

The following week we played host to Italian side Benetton Treviso in our second pool match. We began well and controlled the first half with Rees kicking us into a good lead. He landed three penalties and converted Morgan's try to add to Liley's dropped goal on 15 minutes with the only reply from the Italians being a penalty from their fly half, Benade. In the second half, we made mistake after mistake including a pass from Will Carling which was intercepted by Benade. He ran the ball in for a try and when Pilat converted to add to his penalty, our lead had shrunk to just six points (19-13) with the last quarter still to go. We had gone to sleep, the visitors had the upper hand and, in a seven minute spell, we conceded two penalties and a dropped goal to fall behind with five minutes left. Rees had another dropped goal attempt in injury time but this time, it didn't come off and we slipped to a terrible defeat.

A trip to Newcastle came next and the whole team put in a superb performance. Our defence resisted the attacks of the home side but a dropped goal from Rees was all we could manage in the first half in reply to three Wilkinson penalties. Rees continued to be our only source of points, he got his first penalty after 43 minutes and then converted his own try when he ran in from 12 yards out. Wilkinson then outscored Rees 2-1 in penalties but we held on for another one point win. The following day, our former coach Bob Templeton passed away after suffering a heart attack in a Brisbane hospital where he was undergoing knee replacement surgery.

Pool favourites AS Montferrand travelled to the Stoop on 11th December and returned home in shock. A lot of mistakes were made by both sides but when Merceron allowed the ball to bobble into the path of O'Leary (after he had knocked on), he hacked on for Harries to score the softest of tries. Rees had missed a penalty and the conversion so we changed kickers to John Schuster who promptly put over a couple of penalties before the break to give us an 11-0 lead. Playing against the wind in the second period, we performed a rear-guard action for most of the time as Montferrand crept closer and closer to our score. Merceron landed a penalty and dropped a goal and when Viars also dropped one over, eight minutes of normal time remained. With just a couple of minutes to go, Sanderson charged down Merceron's attempt at another dropped goal and the match had been won.

Seven days later, we had to go to Montferrand for the return and we fared worse than our hosts had at the Stoop. Schuster got two penalties in the first half and one in the second but it was nowhere near enough. The closest we got was 6-10 and by the end, the gap had grown to 9-32. The try count of 4-0 in favour of the French summed up our lack of attacking success and left our future participation in the competition hanging by the thinnest of threads going into the Christmas and New Year break.

Our last home game of the century was on 23rd December against Wasps and they were out to gain revenge for the two defeats last season. Things began well enough for us when Schuster kicked a penalty after just six minutes but, by the time Rees dropped a goal and put over a penalty, we had conceded seventeen points. Brooke got our only try after 74 minutes which Schuster converted but we were never in the hunt in the second half. Wasps scored almost at will and ran in five tries to take their total to eight in the match. Kenny Logan converted six of them to hand us our worst ever home league margin of defeat (16-52). By the end of the season, even this record would have fallen again.

At Leicester six days later, we kept up with the Tigers for the first quarter but gradually faded away as they scored twenty one unanswered points. Schuster kicked a penalty and the referee awarded us a penalty try (which Schuster converted) when Leicester brought a maul down to give us a 10-8 lead after 20 minutes. After ending the first half with a deficit of 10-23, we did well to outscore the Tigers 7-6 in the second half. Garrick Morgan grabbed a try for Schuster to convert but penalties from Stimpson and Murphy had already sealed our fate. We finished the year in eighth place in the league and our prospects for the second half of the season were not good.

We did at least begin with a victory when we hosted Thurrock on 3rd January in the fourth round of the cup. This was our 81st cup tie and provided us with our biggest ever cup win. We fielded a weakened team which contained four players from the U21 side but it seemed to make little difference from the moment Peter Mensah scored our first try after five minutes. It was a procession of scores with further tries coming from Chris Wright, Daren O'Leary (4) and Nick Greenstock. John Schuster and Rob Liley each landed two conversions to take the first half total to 43 points. At half time, the referee (N Fisher) was replaced by Ashley Rowden before the one-way traffic resumed. Richard Nias, Steve White-Cooper (2), David Officer, Nick Greenstock and Ed Smith (2) took our try tally to 14 and Liley's five further conversions made the final score 88-0. Hika Reid, the former New Zealand hooker came on as a replacement for Thurrock. He was currently our forwards coach and his team were sufficiently fired up when he came on that, for eleven minutes, we failed to score and this almost certainly prevented us from reaching the magical 100-point mark for the first time ever. This was our third highest ever biggest winning margin after the 94-0 victory over the Tanzania Invitation XV back in 1973 and the 98-6 win over Thailand in 1986.

It set us up nicely for our trip to Treviso for our penultimate European Cup pool match which we had to win to maintain our very slim hopes of qualifying for the quarter finals. After Gareth Rees had kicked a penalty to put us into a second minute lead, we slipped back into our usual form and allowed the Italians to take an 18-6 advantage after 36 minutes. Rees had been successful with a second penalty before we made something of a comeback with another Rees penalty and a try from Carling (converted by Rees). Try as we might, we just couldn't score in normal time during the second half whereas the home side added a couple of penalties to their total. We had made too many mistakes at crucial times so, when Daren O'Leary scored for Rees to convert, the match had already been lost. This result ensured our exit from the competition and our last pool encounter against Cardiff became a meaningless one from our point of view.

We only had pride to play for but that didn't seem to make any difference to us as we slipped behind by seventeen points to nil in the first ten minutes. We were unlucky though, the referee (Ian Ramage from Scotland) decided that Chris Wright had felled Liam Botham with a high tackle and awarded a penalty try after only two minutes. Photographic and video evidence afterwards confirmed that he had made a big mistake. Neil Jenkins stretched the lead to twenty points with his second penalty before we finally found a way through. O'Leary raced through just before the break for Rees to convert and we were in with a slight chance. We came out firing on all cylinders and within twelve minutes of the restart, Cardiff's lead had been wiped out. Rees had kicked two penalties and converted Keyter's try and when he put over his third penalty after 65 minutes, we actually led 23-20. A goal from the visitors gave them the lead again before Rees unluckily hit a post with a perfectly struck penalty although he succeeded with one two minutes later. Keyter had earlier been denied a try by the referee (again, television evidence showed an error) and when Jenkins put over another penalty, we were beaten again.

It was back to league action on 22nd January and a visit from Newcastle. Our injury crisis had become so bad that John Rudd (an 18 year old ex Saracens academy player) came on as a replacement for Huw Harries; he had only been accredited to us 48 hours earlier. This was another awful game and we somehow contrived to lose it. Harries opened the scoring with a try after 26 minutes but Cartmell equalised for Newcastle ten minutes later. When Garrick Morgan and Graham (for Newcastle) were spending ten minutes cooling off in the sin bin, Tuigamala scored a try which Wilkinson converted. This lead was extended when he added a penalty on 63 minutes; our reply (a try from Chris Sheasby converted by Rees) was not enough to stop us from registering our seventh league defeat in twelve games.

Three days later, we went to Goldington Road to play the bottom side Bedford. They had played and lost all ten of their matches so far but we were susceptible to defeat. It looked as though a massive win was on the cards when we leapt into a 21-0 lead after 21 minutes. David Officer, Adam Leach and Huw Harries went over for tries and Gareth Rees converted all of them. Once again, we went to sleep and allowed Bedford right back into the game. In the fifteen minutes before half time, they scored a penalty and two goals to make it 21-17. For most of this period, Morgan was in the sin bin for a professional foul and, by the 70th minute, Bedford were in the lead after another penalty from Thompson and a try by Banks. Zinzan Brooke came on in the 76th minute and proceeded to score the winning try from close range after 84minutes. Gareth Rees converted to seal our third away win of the season. It was to be over a year before we tasted away success in the Premiership again.

The following Sunday, we entertained Darlington Mowden Park in the 5th round of the cup looking to progress to our 19th quarter final. We trailed to a penalty after 31 minutes by Oliphant but got going sufficiently enough to score three tries in the next fifteen minutes to open up a gap which would take us to victory. Leach, Officer and O'Leary were the scorers and Rees landed two conversions. The gritty minnows gave it their best shot and reduced the deficit when Kent scored a try three minutes into the second half. Harries and Greenstock eventually extended our lead with unconverted tries but the final score of 29-8 was not very impressive. We had made extremely hard work of winning this tie and it wouldn't get any easier in the quarter final against Bristol.

John Gallagher had been so impressed by Darlington's full back (Nopera Stewart) that he signed him on a week's loan and played him for the whole game against London Irish on 12th February. This was our home game and Stewart was one of our better players. Peter Mensah suffered a cruciate ligament injury which brought an end to his career. He had scored 155 points (31 tries) during his six seasons in the first team. Adam Leach scored a try in the first half which Rees converted but the Irish had scored 15 points of their own. In the first half an hour of the second half, we conceded a goal and a penalty and trailed by eighteen points. Greenstock went over after an excellent break by Ed Smith, Rees converted and there was still time to pull the game out of the fire. But, in the last five minutes of injury time, we hit the self-destruct button and conceded two tries. O'Shea converted both but the 39-14 scoreline flattered the Irish.

Against Bristol in the cup quarter final two weeks later, we faced a stiff wind in the first half. Honiball put Bristol ahead after just a minute with a penalty but we held out for another 30 minutes before he doubled the lead. Two minutes later, Brendon Daniel chipped over the full back, scored in the corner and when Rees added the conversion, we led by a point. We were in control at this stage and this score at the interval would have been a great achievement. However, Schuster knocked-on a kick through and Honiball scored from the resulting scrum. His conversion gave the home side a 13-7 lead against the run of play. In the opening nine minutes of the second half, Daniel again scored in the corner, Rees converted and kicked a penalty with the wind to give us the lead once more. This lasted barely two minutes before Johnstone scored a try, Honiball converted again and when Simone scored on 68 minutes the tie was over. We just couldn't score and, as time ran out, our desperation increased and the mistakes became more regular. Will Carling came on with normal time virtually up and this proved to be his final appearance for the Club. He had scored 251 points (33 tries, 11 penalties and 35 conversions) and led the side on 16 occasions. He had become a shadow of the player he had been and it was sad to see him carrying on for longer than he should have done.

A gap of two weeks saw us re-visit the scene of our cup defeat for our fifteenth league fixture. This game at the Memorial Stadium turned out to be something of a classic containing no fewer than eighty one points. Guillaume Delmotte made the first of five appearances and lasted all of eight minutes before he succumbed to injury. In that time, he had helped to set up John Schuster for the opening try which Gareth Rees converted. He had won two caps for France and looked to have a lot of promise. Throughout the first period, there were never more than eight points between the sides and it was the home side who were in front at the end of it. Honiball kicked three penalties and converted two of their three tries scored by Short, Dewdney and Brown. For us, Rees kicked two penalties and converted our second try from Jamie Williams. He had replaced Delmotte but was injured himself and was in turn replaced by Liley. Daniel got on the score sheet as did Officer and Morgan and with Rees converting twice more, we sailed into a nice lead of 39-28 with under twenty minutes remaining. Between the 72nd and 74th minutes, we leaked two more tries (both converted by Honiball) and were unable to come back again so another unlikely defeat had been suffered.

We were heading for a mighty fall and it was only a question of when and where it would happen. Our next league game was at home against Gloucester on 25th March. They were fighting for the title, we were more or less playing only for pride down in ninth place. The management were threatening a massive clear-out in the summer so the whole squad was under close scrutiny. We fought well in the first 40 minutes and only trailed by a point thanks to tries from Officer and Leach and a conversion by Rees. The self-destruct button was pressed yet again and we conceded 17 points between the 49th and 59th minutes. Another defeat loomed and although Nepia and Brooke scored tries and Rees got another conversion, Gloucester added a penalty and a try to run out easy winners by thirty eight points to twenty four. Chris Wright made his last appearance in this game having scored 160 points (23 tries, 5 penalties and 15 conversions) and led the side 5 times during his six season career.

Manchester Sale had lost their last six league matches and were in a run of eight consecutive losses when we visited them on 8th April. The first half was littered with mistakes and we trailed 13-16 at the end of it. Schuster had converted Daniel's try and landed a penalty as had Liley to which Sale had replied with three penalties and the conversion of Mather's try by Little. When Gareth Llewellyn was sin binned on 44 minutes for deliberate offside, the score remained the same. When he returned after 57 minutes, we trailed 13-36! Our defence had just capitulated and the whole team played disgracefully in the last 25 minutes. Daniel did go over for his second try which Rees converted with the last kick of the game but the damage had already been done and we had lost our fifth game in a row.

Eleven days later, we met treble chasing Northampton at the Stoop in a match no-one expected us to do well in. The only score in the first half was an Adam Leach touchdown on 27 minutes. We extended this lead to 26-0 with tries from Officer and Gollings (2) plus three conversions from Liley. Leach and Dom Malone were sent to the bin after the Saints had started a rally (they managed to score a goal and two tries in time remaining) but Liley's penalty after 81 minutes made the game safe.

On Easter Monday (24th April), we made the relatively short journey to Watford to face Saracens who were still smarting from three successive defeats at our hands. This was to be the start of the most humiliating thirteen days in the history of the Harlequin Football Club. To say that we were completely thrashed would be understating the defeat. After forty minutes, we had conceded three tries and trailed by 22-0 and, after 62 minutes, this had grown to 50 after another four tries had been scored. Jason Keyter had spent ten minutes in the sin bin and it was something of a surprise when we scored two tries in the last ten minutes through Daniel and Barnes. David Officer appeared for the last time in this game having scored 35 points (7 tries) during his two seasons with us.

If this wasn't bad enough, our next away day to Bath provided the result which had been coming for some time. This was annihilation with a capital A! We went behind to a penalty after a minute but were still in contention with tries from Daniel and Gollings (both converted by Rees) after 30 minutes. In the final five minutes of the half, Bath scored 17 points with a little help from the referee (Robin Goodliffe) to go in 34-14 ahead. Daren O'Leary scored our third try on 48 minutes but that was as close as we got. In an amazing 26 minute spell (50th-75th minute), we conceded 43 points to suffer the worst defeat in our 134 year history. The final score of 77-19 was made even more embarrassing by a try count of 10-3 in favour of the home side.

If things could get any worse, they probably would because our next game was against league leaders Leicester on 6th May. We just capitulated again and rarely looked like scoring although Rob Liley got over after 65 minutes to register our only points of the game. In the meantime, the Tigers had ripped us apart and run in eight tries, four in each half. Stimpson landed seven conversions and, for the third game in a row, we had conceded fifty points or more! This was our heaviest margin of defeat at home in the league and was our worst loss at home since Llanelli had beaten us 56-5 in 1970. The final score of 54-5 took our for and against totals in the last three matches to 34-181. Colin Ridgway made his last appearance in this match having scored 15 points (3 tries) and captained the side on a single occasion. John Schuster with 409 points (7 tries, 1 dropped goal, 91 penalties and 49 conversions) and Chris Sheasby with 161 points (35 tries) (during his two spells over the last fourteen seasons) also played their last matches for the Club.

Thankfully, we had only the away game with Wasps left and we travelled to Loftus Road in tenth place. In an amazing first quarter, we quite literally raced into a twenty two point lead with tries from Gollings, Morgan and Delmotte, two conversions from Rees and a dropped goal by Richards. Everything we tried came off and after Wasps had scored ten points of their own, Delmotte went in again for Rees to convert and add a penalty to make it 32-10. A goal right on half time cut the deficit to fifteen points and, as the home side started to get on top of us, we began to leak points again. King kicked a penalty, Worsley scored a try and when King converted Henderson's try on 72 minutes, the scores were level at 32-32. In a frantic finale, King missed one penalty before succeeding with a second to put Wasps in front for the first time with three minutes of injury time remaining. With the last move of the match, Zinzan Brooke opted to go for a dropped goal when running the ball was perhaps the better option. His effort sailed wide and fell short and just about summed up most of the previous nine months of rugby played by us.

No fewer than ten players made their final appearances in this game. They were David Barnes 5 points (1 try), Zinzan Brooke 30 points (6 tries plus 10 games as captain) he would stay on as coach, Guillaime Delmotte 10 points (2 tries), Huw Harries 90 points (18 tries) in his four season career, Jason Keyter 140 points (28 tries) in his two stints over the last seven seasons, Adam Leach 45 points (9 tries plus one game as captain), Rob Liley 250 points (7 tries, 1 dropped goal, 32 penalties and 58 conversions) in his three seasons, Gareth Llewellyn 30 points (6 tries and 14 appearances as captain) during his four seasons, Simon Mitchell 10 points (2 tries) in his two spells over the last six seasons and, finally, Gareth Rees 145 points (1 try, 4 dropped goals, 22 penalties and 31 conversions).

Our playing record in the league was P22 W7 L15 F441 A687 Pts 18 Pos 10th. Overall, our record was P32 W11 D1 L20 F712 A883. Brendon Daniel scored the most tries with 11 and Gareth Rees was top in everything else with 145 points (1 try, 4 dropped goals, 22 penalties and 31 conversions).

Overall, the team scored 86 tries which was a drop of four on the previous year. Dropped goals went up by one to six, penalties dropped by 51 to just 47 and conversions dropped by five to 59. The total number of points was down by four to 883. Garrick Morgan appeared in every game, Jason Keyter was three behind on 29, Pat Sanderson and Chris Sheasby followed with 28 and David Barnes, Colin Ridgway and Steve White-Cooper all played in 25.

1999/2000

200899	NAMIBIA	TYGERBURG	W	1G1DG1PG2T(23)-(12)
040999	MANCHESTER SALE	SALE	W	1G2T(17)-2G(14)
110999	BATH(ADP1)	STOOP MEMORIAL GROUND	L	1G1PG(10)-2G2PG2T(30)
250999	SARACENS(ADP1)	STOOP MEMORIAL GROUND	W	4G1T(33)-3G1PG(24)

021099	NORTHAMPTON(ADP1)	NORTHAMPTON	L	2G1PG2T(27)-3G1PG1T(29)
101099	MANCHESTER SALE(ADP1)	STOOP MEMORIAL GROUND	L	1PG(3)-1G1PG(10)
151099	GLOUCESTER(ADP1)	GLOUCESTER	L	2G3PG(23)-1G4PG1T(24)
281099	BRISTOL(ADP1)	STOOP MEMORIAL GROUND	W	2G4PG2T(36)-5PG1T(20)
071199	LONDON IRISH(ADP1)	STOOP MEMORIAL GROUND(A)	W	4PG1T(17)-1G3PG(16)
131199	BEDFORD(ADP1)	STOOP MEMORIAL GROUND	W	2PG1T(11)-1G1PG(10)
191199	CARDIFF(HECP)	CARDIFF	D	2G2DG4PG(32)-2G1DG5PG(32)
271199	BENETTON TREVISO(HECP)	STOOP MEMORIAL GROUND	L	1G1DG3PG(19)-1G1DG4PG(22)
051299	NEWCASTLE(ADP1)	NEWCASTLE	W	1G1DG2PG(16)-5PG(15)
111299	A S MONTFERRAND(HECP)	STOOP MEMORIAL GROUND	W	2PG1T(11)-2DG1PG(9)
181299	A S MONTFERRAND(HECP)	MONTFERRAND	L	3PG(9)-3G1DG1PG1T(32)
231299	WASPS(ADP1)	STOOP MEMORIAL GROUND	L	1G1DG2PG(16)-6G2T(52)
291299	LEICESTER(ADP1)	LEICESTER	L	2G1PG(17)-1G1DG3PG2T(29)
030100	THURROCK(TBC4)	STOOP MEMORIAL GROUND	W	9G5T(88)-0
080100	BENETTON TREVISO(HECP)	TREVISO	L	2G3PG(23)-1G4PG1T(24)
160100	CARDIFF(HECP)	STOOP MEMORIAL GROUND	L	2G4PG(26)-3G3PG(30)
220100	NEWCASTLE(ADP1)	STOOP MEMORIAL GROUND	L	1G1T(12)-1G1PG1T(15)
250100	BEDFORD(ADP1)	BEDFORD	W	4G(28)-2G2PG1T(25)
300100	DARLINGTON MOWDEN PARK(TBC5)	STOOP MEMORIAL GROUND	W	2G3T(29)-1PG1T(8)
120200	LONDON IRISH(ADP1)	STOOP MEMORIAL GROUND	L	2G(14)-4G2PG1T(39)
260200	BRISTOL(TBCQF)	BRISTOL	L	2G1PG(17)-2G2PG1T(25)
110300	BRISTOL(ADP1)	BRISTOL	L	4G2PG1T(39)-4G3PG1T(42)
250300	GLOUCESTER(ADP1)	STOOP MEMORIAL GROUND	L	2G2T(24)-3G4PG1T(38)
080400	MANCHESTER SALE(ADP1)	SALE	L	2G2PG(20)-3G1DG4PG(36)
190400	NORTHAMPTON(ADP1)	STOOP MEMORIAL GROUND	W	3G1PG1T(29)-1G2T(17)
240400	SARACENS(ADP1)	VICARAGE ROAD	L	2T(10)-6G1PG1T(50)

290400	BATH(ADP1)	BATH	L	2G1T(19)-9G3PG1T(77)
060500	LEICESTER(ADP1)	STOOP MEMORIAL GROUND	L	1T(5)-7G1T(54)
210500	WASPS(ADP1)	LOFTUS ROAD	L	3G1DG1PG1T(32)-3G3PG1T(35)

39

Sevens in the 1990s

1990-1999

With the increased commitment required in the fifteen-a-side game and the gradual move towards professionalism, the top sides slowly but surely reduced their involvement in Sevens competitions. When we did take part after 1992, a side containing youngsters was quite often put out.

The boys were back in town for the 1990 Middlesex Sevens in a bid to set a record that would never be beaten. After the drunken antics of recent years (it was turning nasty unlike in the seventies and most of the eighties when there was absolutely no trouble at all), it had been decided to make it a soft drink and low alcohol zone. Winterbottom captained the side and was joined by Craig Luxton, Stuart Thresher, Glenister, Davis, Will Carling and Thompson. The seconds also qualified and their team was Sheasby, Chris Mantel (captain), Richard Langhorn, Richard Goodwin, David Pears, Adam Cleary, Alex Tupman with N. Foote replacing Goodwin in the game against Rosslyn Park I. They had beaten Old Wimbledonians I (14-4), Old Emanuel I (24-4) and Esher I (14-6). Despite going behind early to London Scottish I, they rallied and scored three tries to win 16-6. Against Rosslyn Park I, it was nip and tuck in the first half with Quins just shading it 10-8. Park scored first after the break, Pears kicked a penalty to make it 13-12 but a final converted score for Park saw them through (13-18). The holders progressed serenely with victories over Richmond II (22-4), West London Institute of Higher Education (34-6) and Loughborough Students I (20-10). They had never looked in any sort of danger and had scored fourteen tries to get to the final. Davis had got four of them with others coming from Luxton (3), Glenister, Carling (3) and Thresher (3); the last named also kicked nine conversions and Glenister got one. For the third time in five years, we met Rosslyn Park (this time it was their first team) and there were five ex-Quins in the Seven. Carling got over the line but was held by Woodhouse as he cut in. Hunter joined in and they carried him out of play; you could feel Carling's embarrassment all around the ground. He soon made amends and Davis got another before Moon replied to make it 8-4 at half time. Thompson scored from the kick-off (although he lost the ball as he touched down – nowadays, the TMO would have disallowed it!) followed by Thresher and Carling (all three were converted by Thresher). At 26-4, it was all over but Park did get one more through Chesworth and Woodhouse converted. The final whistle brought glory, the record had gone – FIVE IN A ROW! UNBELIEVABLE! It truly was a magnificent achievement. There was even talk of them representing England in the Hong Kong Sevens but it never came off. In the Old Belvedere Sevens, we lost to Lansdowne in the first round (14-20) and suffered the same fate against Bulldogs (10-30) at Esher. We won at Sevenoaks, beating London Scottish (30-4) in the semi-final and Rosslyn Park (28-16) in the final. At Melrose, we beat Boroughmuir (28-10) but went out to a last minute penalty to the host (12-15). In the London Floodlit, we won against Blackheath in the semi-final (16-10) but lost a close final to London Scottish (8-10). In the Joshua Tetley Sevens at Headingley, we conceded just six points in our group games, beat Sheffield in the semi-final (26-8) and Headingley in the final (40-0). With some little known players in the squad (A. Atta, Bruce Miller, D. Baileyns and C. Tweed), Eagle, Winterbottom, David Thresher and Glenister provide the experience. At the Courage National Sevens we were represented by Stuart Thresher, Mantel, Sheasby, Gavin Thompson, Davis, Eagle and Luxton and we beat Coventry (22-4) and Nottingham (24-10) before falling to Rosslyn Park in the semi-final (0-14). They in turn lost 0-30 to Northampton. The Surrey Sevens were played at Dorking and our team consisted of Eagle, Mantel, Glenister, Miller, Pears, Sheasby, Davis and Jason Aldridge. After receiving a walk over against Old Guildfordians, we defeated Old Whitgiftians (12-0), Esher I (22-6) and Richmond I (30-12). In the final we thrashed Rosslyn Park II (36-4). The toughest game we had was the first one where we failed to score in the second half. Our scorers were Eagle (2 tries and 2 conversions), Glenister (1 try and 12 conversions), Pears (1 try and two conversions), Sheasby (1 try), Davis (5 tries), Aldridge (6 tries) and a penalty try. On 19th May, we travelled to Mazamet in France to take part in the First Pavois du Tarn international Sevens Tournament. Unfortunately, there is no record of what happened. At the Stoop, we entered a good team (Mike Wedderburn, Alex Tupman, Eagle, Carling, Glenister, Skinner, Luxton and Winterbottom) and won for the fourth time. Victories over Paris Universite Club (30-0), Orrell (26-6) and Northampton (16-4) propelled us into the final against Bridgend. They didn't know what hit them and in the first three minutes, we had scored through Glenister and Carling. By half time, Glenister had scored again, Eagle got a fourth and Glenister's conversions made it 24-0. The second half scoring was more even and although Bridgend scored two goals, Skinner, Wedderburn and Glenister scored tries for us and with two more conversions from the same source, the final score was an emphatic 40-12.

On 11th May 1991, both teams appeared for the finals and the seconds had beaten Old Pauline I (18-0), Old Freemens (24-6), Twickenham (30-6) and Metropolitan Police (18-6) to get through. The side who were going for the sixth win on the bounce were Sheasby, Luxton, Winterbottom (captain), Glenister, Carling, Harriman and Davis; for the seconds it was A. Hunn, Jeff Alexander, Pears, Goodwin, Paul Brady, Mantel and Bruce Miller. Against Guildford and Godalming, Quins II went through easily with tries from Alexander (3), Hunn and Goodwin plus four conversions from Pears without reply. The holders disposed of Richmond II by 30-8 despite going behind and it being close into the second half. The seconds were no match for the power of Quins I and were 28-0 down before Miller scored for Pears to convert. The final score of 32-6 propelled them into the semi-final against guest side Edinburgh Academicals. More tries scored and no points conceded meant a 26-0 win and into the final we went. London Scottish I provided the opposition and it all started well when Harriman scored for Glenister to convert. Troupe got one for the Scots but Davis went over and Glenister converted before Harrold made it 12-8 at the interval. Walker scored for Appleson to convert and we were behind but Sheasby ran in to grab the lead back again. In a dramatic finale, Troupe dodged a tackle and was in under the posts. Appleson converted and there was no time to restart. Up to the final, we had scored 88 points made up of tries from Sheasby (2), Winterbottom, Carling (3), Harriman (6) and Davis (4) plus twelve conversions by Glenister. Our great run of twenty seven wins in a row had come to an end and so too with the increasing demands on players had the golden era of Sevens. In the Old Belvedere Sevens, we beat University College Dublin (22-12) but lost to Wanderers (0-30). We entered the Caldy tournament and went out to Swansea in the quarter final (12-20) and at Headingley, we won again by beating Halifax (36-6), Morpeth (36-3), Sheffield (16-0) and Headingley (24-20). At the National Sevens (now held at Bath and sponsored by Worthington), we beat Gloucester (24-6) and Saracens (16-12) but went out to Bath in the semi-final 0-10. They went on to beat Leicester by 24-10 to take the title. The London Floodlit was a repeat of the 1990 final but this time London Scottish won by a larger margin (0-18). We won the Sevenoaks title again by beating Rosslyn Park 12-10 and we won the Surrey Sevens at University Vandals ground in Walton-on-Thames. Kingston Polytechnic were beaten 28-0, followed by Old Midwhitgiftians (14-0), Westminster/Charing Cross Hospital (24-6) and Worthing I (18-10) before a 36-10 win in the final against Richmond I. It was our eighteenth title out of twenty one finals, a very impressive record. In our Sevens, we had a scratch side out (Jeff Alexander, Kent Bray, Wedderburn, Eagle, Brady, Richard Langhorn and Glenister) but they did well in the opening game against Kelso. They scored four tries (three converted) for an easy win and then drew 18-18 with Wakefield. In the final pool match, they beat Old Belvedere and ran in six tries in the process. All were converted to make the final score 36-0. Wakefield needed to score a hatful of tries against Kelso but they didn't and we went through to face Newport in the final. Alexander scored a try but Newport had already amassed 36 points and we had failed in the final for the ninth time.

From 1992 onwards, we no longer had a second Seven and we took part as Harlequins because now a certain number of team from the top league qualified automatically. We still had a decent side out – Sheasby, Luxton, Winterbottom (captain), Glenister, Eagle, Alexander and Harriman and romped through against Gloucester (26-4). Glenister scored three tries and also converted them with others coming from Alexander and Harriman. Rosslyn Park put up a fight and each time Harriman scored for Glenister to convert, they equalised. The tie went to sudden death extra time and it was Glenister who put us through by 16-12. Against Western Samoa in the semi-final, we were 0-12 down in no time but Alexander got a try which Glenister converted to get us back in it. The Samoans scored a third converted try in the second half and although Harriman scored (Glenister again converting), there wasn't enough time to get another and we were out. They went on to thrash Scottish 30-6 to win the trophy. A plate competition had been introduced this year involving those losing in the first round and Gloucester were the first winners. The National Sevens now had a Divisional qualifying round because all thirty nine clubs in the National Divisions could qualify for the finals at Bath. The London Qualifying Tournament took place at the Stoop and we qualified after beating Richmond (18-4) and London Irish (38-0). In the finals, we beat Morley (20-12) but lost to Bristol (6-34) to end our interest. London Scottish won the title with a 38-0 win over Leicester in the final. In the Quins Sevens, we lost to Richmond (0-29), Newport (21-33) and Northampton (12-24) in one of our worst performances at our own tournament. In the end, England beat Newport 38-14 in the final.

Our side in 1993 was Sheasby, Brady, Troy Coker, Glenister, Kent Bray, Alexander and Davis and we got off to a flyer against Reading. Tries from Sheasby, Coker (2), Glenister, Bray (plus four conversions), Alexander and Davis (2) took us to a 48-0 win. We were fourteen points down against Saracens but halved the deficit by half time (Glenister try and Bray conversion) and went past them in the second half. Brady and Alexander got tries and Bray kicked the goals (21-14). In the semi-final, Northampton led 14-0 at half time, Mark Evans replaced Bray but we could only manage a try from Glenister in the second half. They scored two more tries to run out 26-5 winners. In the final, Wasps came back from 5-24 down to win 26-24; Richmond won the plate. This was the last proper year of our own Sevens although it carried on for two more as an Under-21 competition. The title was won by a Welsh Exiles team.

From 1994 onwards, we started playing scratch teams and, as a result did very poorly by comparison with a few years before. We had a Seven of Justyn Cassell, Martin Pepper, David Currie, Glenister, Bray (captain), Daren O'Leary and Davis. In the first round, they beat Richmond 19-12. O'Leary and Glenister got tries and Bray converted both before Richmond scored two tries after the interval. Currie got one in between to secure the win. Rosslyn Park proved too strong and we could only manage a try at the end of each half (Bray and O'Leary) to three goals (10-21). Bath went on to win the title by overcoming Orrell 19-12 and Northampton beat Wasps 22-12 in the

Plate final. Crowds were now starting to dwindle, it was not the same without the smaller teams and a lot of the sides now just appeared to be going through the motions because they had to be there.

1995 was not a good year for us at the Middlesex Sevens - Chris Wright, Rob Kitchin, Glenister, Steve White-Cooper, O'Leary, Mick Watson and Adam Jones made up the side. We did win against London Scottish (19-14) but went out to Ithuba from South Africa (7-28). Wright scored the try and Glenister converted. Leicester beat Ithuba quite convincingly in the final (38-19) and Orrell saw off Reading in the Plate (15-12).

Because we didn't qualify automatically in the league, we had to go through the preliminary rounds in 1996 and manged to get through at Upper Clapton with a squad of Gareth Allison, Jim Staples, Pepper, Nick Walshe, Wright (captain), O'Leary, Jamie Williams, James Storey, Russell Osman and Richard Francis. We beat Romford and Gidea Park (41-7), Basildon (52-0), Diss (44-0), Cheshunt (47-7) and Bishop's Stortford (27-5). We racked up no fewer than 35 tries only eighteen of which were converted. Allison got three, Staples (7), Pepper (2), Walshe (one and 9 conversions), Wright (four and 7 conversions), O'Leary (9 and one conversion), Williams (6 and one conversion) and Storey (3).In our first match, we trounced Gloucester 36-5 before going down to Wigan Rugby League (24-36) (now the game had gone professional, anything was possible!). They went on to beat Wasps in the final by 38-15 and Wakefield defeated Richmond in the Plate 31-12. We reached the semi-final of the London Floodlit by beating Malaysia (56-0) and London Irish (31-5) but lost to Richmond after extra time (19-24). At the Henley Sevens, we were defeated by London Scottish (26-28) but won against Millfield Old Boys (64-0) and Coventry (38-5). We ended up in the Plate competition and got to the final by beating Bath (24-17) and Bristol (54-10) before losing to Orrell by 19-29. The Development Squad did win the Sunshine Sevens at East Grinstead by beating Chichester College after extra time.

The following year, Ian Pickup, Allison, Michael Corcoran, Richard Sharples, Gareth Llewellyn, Stuart Power, Jamie Williams, Jason Keyter, Simon Owen, Dinos Alexopolous and Matt Allnut made up the squad. They played Oxford University and won 26-14 (tries from Allison, Williams (2) and Keyter plus conversions by Allnut (2) and Williams). The South American Barbarians proved far too strong and tries from Sharples and Owen (both converted by Allnut) were no answer to the thirty three points scored by them. The Barbarians beat Saracens in the final by a country mile (55-5) and Wasps thrashed Oxford University 45-12 in the Plate.

Our squad for 1998 was Allison (captain), Laurent Belligoi, Spencer Bromley, J. Bull, Rob Hitchmough, J. Kindon, Adam Leach, Emmanuel Palladino, Ian Pickup and Danny Smaje. Against Northampton, Leach and Hitchmough (converted by himself) got tries but the Saints hit back with two of their own to lead at half time. In the second half, Belligoi got two and Hitchmough converted both for a 26-14 victory. In the next round, we took on the Barbarians and lost 17-38. Bromley, Palladino and Bull got our tries. The Barbarians won again, this time it was Leicester in the final (38-28) and London Welsh beat Rosslyn Park 21-12 in the Plate.

The next year, we had to qualify again and managed that successfully at Thames Ditton with wins over Old Reedonians (40-0), Lensbury (29-0), K.C.S. Old Boys (34-7) and Rosslyn Park (28-12). Our squad was Sheasby (captain), Richard Nias, White-Cooper, Walshe, Ben Gollings, Wright, O'Leary, Keyter, Rory Jenkins and Bill Davison. We started with a good win over Bath (34-7) but lost to Penguins (12-28) in the next round. They went on to beat Saracens in the final by 40-35 and the Plate was shared by London Welsh and Wasps because a thunderstorm prevented the final being played.

40

Success in Europe but We Are Robbed at Home 2000-2001

June 2000 saw England embark on a tour to South Africa to play two tests and three other matches. Overall, it was reasonably successful with all games being won except the first test which was lost narrowly (13-18). Revenge was gained with a 27-22 win in the second. Leonard was the only current Harlequin while former or future ones were Will Greenwood, Dan Luger, Paul Volley, Nick Walshe and Roy Winters. Luger played in the first test and Leonard appeared in both.

It was all change off the field as Mark Evans arrived as the new CEO at the tail end of the previous season after being released by Saracens. He actually started on 8th May and replaced D Huw Morgan who left to take up a role with the Arrows Formula One team. He would be a great asset to the Club and would prove to be successful at building the attendances at the Stoop and steering us on to the right road after reaching the lows of the previous season. There would be more low points and great highs but more of that later. Tony Copsey came in as managing director, Mike Scott became Team manager and Richard Hill was the new backs coach. Training facilities had been secured at the Military Stadium, Aldershot while at the Stoop, the floodlights and posts had been painted in Quins colours. For the year ending 30th June 2001, the losses went up to £4,974,355 and our new CEO became a Director and the Board would remain the same until 2004/05.

Evans quickly saw that the fan base was pitiful and there were no player development programmes in place and even though Brooke and Gallagher had identified ten players, none really came through. He could see that the fans were actually laughing at the team, it was a type of gallows humour; he knew that we were in trouble but this was bad. We had to build a crowd and improve the stadium so Mark agreed with the owners that things would be tight on the playing side for three to four years and they were fully aware that relegation was a possibility.

In the Zurich Premiership (new sponsors had appeared), a new method of awarding points in matches was to be introduced. For a win four points would be awarded and, if a team scored four tries or more, they would be given a try bonus point making a total of five points. In the event of a defeat, no points would be given unless you finished within seven points or less of the opposing side or you scored four or more tries. Two points would be awarded for a drawn game but the try bonus point could still be achieved.

After the massive exodus at the end of 1999/2000, a number of new players were required to take us, hopefully, to new heights. Nick Burrows (centre), Alex Codling (second row), Jon Dawson (prop), Tani Fuga (hooker) and Mark Mapletoft (fly half) all joined. On top of these, Will Greenwood returned from Leicester, Ryan O'Neill returned from Bedford and Keith Wood came back after one season with Munster.

After a week of intensive training in Brecon, our first two games were played on a short tour to Wales. Ebbw Vale and Pontypridd would provide the opposition and we were to prove victorious in both. Against Ebbw Vale on 10th August, Keith Wood led the side and opened our account with a try after seven minutes. Will Greenwood, Ben Gollings and Nick Greenstock added further tries before half time and, with Paul Burke kicking all four conversions and a penalty, we led 31-0. Ten changes were made at the interval and we quickly conceded points. Two converted tries for the home side reduced the deficit but we steadied the ship and Ryan O'Neill, Rory Jenkins and Brendon Daniel took our try count to seven. Mark Mapletoft converted all three before one more try for Vale made it 52-19 at the end. Paul Burke made his debut in this one, he would make 98 appearances over the next four seasons and was in the process of winning 13 caps for Ireland. Bruce Starr also played his first game, he would make 69 appearances as did Mark Mapletoft (24 appearances) - he had won one England cap in 1997.

Five days later, we made the journey to Sardis Road for our first ever fixture against Pontypridd. This was a much closer contest and we fell behind after seven minutes to a try. On 25 minutes, Garrick Morgan took four defenders over with him to level the scores and Paul Burke's conversion put us in front. The lead was snatched back before the break when Jarvis kicked a penalty. Danny Badham ran in to score our second try after a break by Peter Richards, Steve White-Cooper and Mapletoft and Ben Gollings got a penalty between two from Davey for the home side; this proved to be the final score (15-14).

After this, the really serious part of the season began with a visit from London Irish in the first Zurich Premiership match on 19th August. After Burke had put us in front with a penalty, Garrick Morgan was sent to the sin bin for a foul on Chris Sheasby. Cunningham levelled with the resulting penalty and put the Irish ahead with another one. Burke brought us back again and made it 9-9 at half time with a dropped goal after Cunningham had kicked his third penalty. Into the second half, Cunningham got his fourth and fifth penalties and converted a try in between to leave us trailing 9-22 with four minutes to go. Right at the death, Will Greenwood scored for Burke to convert but it was too little too late although we did get a losing bonus point. This was seen as sweet revenge for Irish as Quins had allegedly evicted them from the Stoop with a year left on their ground share agreement but in truth, the Irish had inserted a get out clause which Quins took up. Making their debuts in this game were Alex Codling who came on as a sub (62 appearances) and would win one England cap in 2002, Jon Dawson (133 appearances) and Matt Powell (another sub) who would make 66 appearances.

Our next visitors were Premiership newcomers Rotherham. We had started badly against London Irish and continued in that vein of form against the northerners. Fortunately for us, they were not up to it and tries from White-Cooper, O'Leary, Greenwood and Greenstock (plus three conversions from Burke) gave us victory and a try bonus point (26-13). Nick Burrows appeared for the first time when he came on as a substitute and would go on to make 43 appearances.

Moving into September, a visit to Bath was our next encounter and it was the same old story. There were only five survivors from the drubbing we had received in April which showed just what a turnover in players we had gone through. Burke kicked four penalties and Greenwood scored a brace of tries but yellow cards for Andy Dawling and White-Cooper ultimately cost us. Bath scored seventeen points during these 20 minutes and ran out 38-22 winners. After only three matches, we already trailed the leaders, Leicester, by seven points.

It meant we had a must win game at Northampton the following Wednesday to stay in the hunt. We shot out of the blocks after falling behind to a Grayson penalty after seven minutes. First, Burke chipped ahead in his own half, recovered and the ball went to Gollings from Burrows. The left winger then chipped over the defence from 50 metres out and won the race for the touchdown to put us ahead. Then, three minutes later, Richards went over after a run by Greenwood. Burke converted both and the home crowd had been silenced. As is so often the case, the killer instinct was lacking and the Saints were back in front by half time. Pountney scored a try and Grayson added a conversion and two penalties. The second half saw Burke and Grayson share four penalties but a try for the home side saw them win by 27 to 20 but at least we had another bonus point.

We had slipped to tenth place and Wasps visited on 9th September to send us to our second home defeat in three games. Although Greenwood opened the scoring with a try and Gollings scored a second, Wasps got three tries and led 23-10 at the break. Bruce Starr spent ten minutes in the sin bin and, although Wasps scored during this time, Gollings got our third try just before Starr returned. Gollings then landed a penalty on 55 minutes but a fourth try and a third penalty for the visitors saw them home. Tani Fuga made his debut in this one, he came on as a sub would go on to play 232 times; he would also win 11 caps for Samoa between 1999 and 2007 as well as 2 for the Pacific Islanders in 2008.

After four defeats in five games, we desperately awaited the debut of our captain for 2000/01. David Wilson, the Australian international captain, was to make his first appearance for us in the home game against Bristol on 16th September. He would only play in 29 matches but his influence was to prove decisive (he had won 79 caps between 1992 and 2000). Wood stayed on as captain until Wilson settled in but it was the Aussie who stood out in a poor game. Wilson had the ability to turn ball over and convince referees it was the opposition committing fouls in rucks. This would prove invaluable to us in our bids for survival and cup glory both at home and in Europe. In the first half, Gollings landed three penalties but we trailed by four points; Bristol having scored a goal and two penalties. It might have been worse had Ryan O'Neill not put his body on the line to stop lock forward Andrew Sheridan from scoring. A 40 metre break from Richards led to a Garrick Morgan try, Gollings couldn't convert but put over a penalty to give us a 17-13 lead. Keith Wood went through to score with a typically rampaging run and Daniel went in from 35 metres to leave us 31-13 ahead after Gollings had converted both. With victory assured, we took our foot off the pedal and Bristol came back to score two tries in the final seven minutes to narrow the gap to six points.

A visit to Kingsholm is never easy but we had won five of our last seven league encounters there. Once again, we began well when Burke kicked us into a third minute lead with a penalty. A minute later, Greenwood passed to O'Neill who charged up field, linked with Gollings and Wilson before Greenwood got the ball back and scored – this was from our 22! Burke converted but two Mannix penalties made it 10-6 after 26 minutes. Five minutes later, Wood put Burrows in for our second try and Burke's conversion gave us an eleven point lead. By half time, he had kicked his second penalty and Mannix got his third and fourth to make it 20-12 but we still looked well set for an away win. Gloucester were down to fourteen men either side of the interval but the only score was another penalty from Mannix. A sixth was replied to by Burke and we were still in front with 16 minutes of normal time left. During the course of the next ten minutes, Burkes missed a penalty, Mannix kicked three and we were behind for the first time in the game. We failed to add any more points to our total and went down to another defeat. Luckily, the bonus points were just keeping us away from the real trouble area at the bottom.

Newcastle visited the Stoop on 30th September with Jonny Wilkinson in the team. He was to prove the difference between the sides. The first half was dour to say the least and all we had to show was a penalty from Paul Burke after three minutes of added time. The Falcons had a goal and a penalty. We woke up in the second half and four minutes in, Steve White-Cooper grabbed a try before Stephenson went over for Newcastle for Wilkinson to convert.

A Burke penalty made it 11-17 and when O'Neill scored, Burke's conversion put us in front by a single point. There were eight minutes left including added time. With just two minutes to go, Tani Fuga (our hooker) amazingly went offside at a ruck and Wilkinson kicked the match winning penalty. Roy Winters made the first of 105 appearances in this one and would go on to win 2 England caps in 2007.

The following weekend, it was hoped that a change of competition would bring a change in our fortunes as we met Perigueux in our first European Shield pool game. Our Pool consisted of four teams playing each other on a home and away basis with the Pool winner progressing to the quarter-finals. Ex-London Broncos Rugby League player Ed Jennings made the first of his 22 appearances in this one at the Stoop when he came on as a substitute for Nick Burrows just seven minutes into the game. He had a hand in all three of our tries scored by Fuga, Jamie Williams and Winters and also kicked a penalty after 64 minutes to seal a 23-16 victory. Ben Gollings kicked our other penalty and converted the first try. Perigueux scored a goal and three penalties in David Wilson's first game as captain.

An away fixture at Ebbw Vale was our second pool game and we were looking for another victory at Eugene Cross Park to go with our friendly win back in August. Richard Hill had joined us from Ebbw Vale so it was a return for him to a place which held fond memories. At this point, we had an injury list containing fourteen names (including four kickers). The weather was not good, mist and drizzle making conditions difficult. Nigel Matthews (on trial as a back-up hooker) went over after a minute to put us ahead but Vale came back with a dropped goal before Jennings landed a penalty. A similar effort from the home side reduced the gap to 8-6 at the interval. Matthews almost scored his second try and Vale had a dropped goal disallowed before Greenstock made a 35 yard dash, drew the cover and gave Greenwood a clear run to the posts. Jennings converted and added a penalty near the end for an 18-6 victory.

Dax, our next opponents, had also won their first two pool games so this was an important one to win. Paul Burke returned in superb form with the boot and kicked us to victory. He landed three penalties in the first half to one from Dax fly half Fauque and three in the first 22 minutes of the second to put us 18-3 ahead. Three minutes from the end, Greenstock and Williams combined to send Greenwood over the line for a try which Burke converted to give us some confidence for the return in France a week later.

At the Stade Maurice Boyau, we put out a strong side to try and stay clear at the top of the group. A victory would almost certainly put us into the quarter finals but a heavy defeat would probably put us out of the competition. Burke had put us in front with a penalty before breaking his arm in an accidental collision in midfield. In that time, we had conceded a goal and a penalty to trail 10-3. We were in some disarray and went further behind when Fauque landed another penalty. A mistake by Dax let in Greenwood and he sent Greenstock in under the posts for Jennings to convert. A dropped goal from Laharrague made the score 16-10 at half time to Dax. We made an excellent start to the second half and regained the lead when Greenstock (returning the earlier favour) sent Greenwood in under the posts for Jennings to again convert. He then missed two penalty chances and the French went back in front when Dourthe scored for Fauque to convert. Niall Woods came on for his debut after having recovered from a serious knee injury (he would make only 12 appearances for us and had won 8 caps for Ireland between 1994 and 1999). He replaced Jennings with 13 minutes left and, shortly after, Keith Wood was sin binned (after Grau had been for Dax) and we were down to fourteen men. We came storming back and Woods broke through, passed to O'Neill and he fed Morgan who went over in the corner. Woods just shaved the wrong side of the post with his conversion attempt and we ended one point short at 22-23. We remained at the top of the Pool equal on points and tries with Dax but the match aggregate between us was in our favour.

The following week, we travelled down to Plymouth for a fourth round Tetley's Bitter Cup tie against Albion at Beacon Park. Memories came flooding back of our famous win in 1984 when Geoff Ball went over deep into injury time. A lot had changed in the intervening years, professionalism had made Albion's task almost impossible but they were hopefully on a long road to greater things under the coaching of ex-Bath hooker Graham Dawe. Woods was on target straight away with a penalty after only two minutes and he converted tries by Richards and Williams (2) after we had finally broken through some defiant Plymouth defending. At 24-0 after 37 minutes, the tie was effectively over but Albion kept fighting and were rewarded with a penalty just before half time and a try after 55 minutes. By this time, O'Leary and Woods had scored our fourth and fifth tries to take the score to 36-8. In the remaining 35 minutes, we couldn't add to our total but we moved smoothly into the fifth round and a tie at home to Manchester the following week.

This tie was played in driving rain with a swirling wind and the visitors took the lead with a Swindells penalty after four minutes from 49 yards. We were not playing well and made a host of handling errors but were still more than a match for Manchester. Tries from Greenstock (2) and Woods (who converted all three) saw us into a 21-3 lead at the break. During the second half, both sides had two men sin binned and, with a host of replacements, the game became very disjointed. Rory Jenkins, Jamie Williams and Woods scored evenly spaced tries for us; Manchester's reply was a single try to leave the final score at 38-8. This was our 60th win in cup ties going back to 1971.

The fly half position was quickly becoming a jinx for us and, after signing Shaun Connor from Ebbw Vale as cover, he promptly broke a cheek bone in training and his Quins career was over before he made an appearance. Matt Powell came in as emergency cover and played against Perigueux, Ebbw Vale, Plymouth and Manchester and went on to fill the gap until another replacement was found. He was Alex Lawson from Llanelli.

It was back to league action and a visit to Reading to play London Irish. Woods hit the bar with a penalty attempt but Barry Everitt was on form for the Irish. 3-1 in penalties made the half time score 9-3 in their favour but we took the lead when Greenstock went through four challenges to score a try which Woods converted. With ten minutes left, Everitt had outscored Woods 3-2 in penalties so the Irish lead was just two points. Everitt landed his seventh successful kick with three minutes left and, try as we did, we just couldn't get that match winning score. Adrian Olver played the first of 39 games in this one.

Alex Lawson's short loan spell ended with the visit of Leicester to the Stoop and he had another impressive outing. After seven successive home league defeats at their hands, we desperately needed a win to move us up the table and, for a long time it looked as though we would get it. Niall Woods got a penalty after 9 minutes and converted David Wilson's try on 22 minutes. This had been set up by Lawson who ran through the Leicester defence from near half way. Into the second half, Woods got his second penalty on 47 minutes to push us out to 13-0. Lawson was replaced after 73 minutes by our new signing to cover the fly half position. Craig Chalmers (60 caps for Scotland and 1 for the British Lions) came on for the first of 11 appearances. He was in the twilight of his career but we were in desperate need of an experienced number ten. Tim Stimpson had banged over penalties on 58, 69 and 74 minutes and our lead was down to four points. The introduction of Andy Goode and Pat Howard proved crucial and these two combined to send Stimpson over for the match winning score. His conversion made it 13-16 and all we had was another losing bonus point.

After 10 matches, we were in tenth place in the Premiership with 15 points (seven were bonus points) and were grateful to Rotherham for their poor showing (6 points from nine matches). In the short term, it didn't look like getting any better and the month of December would see league games against Manchester Sale (A), Saracens (A) and (H), Northampton (H) and Newcastle (A). Zinzan Brooke appeared to be saying the same things after every game and it couldn't be long before patience ran out.

The first of these came on 2nd December at Heywood Road and, in the first 42 minutes, we competed well. Joe Powell scored a try and Woods added a conversion and a penalty. Hodgson had kicked two penalties and Robinson scored a try to give the home side a one point lead. We had wasted a number of chances and these came back to haunt us in the second half when the errors started creeping in. These enabled Sale to score four unanswered tries to run away with the game by thirty five points to ten. We dropped one place to eleventh as Bristol moved above us with a victory.

It was a return to cup action on 9th December with a quarter final tie against Northampton. Whilst historically our league form has always been inconsistent, our cup form has generally been good. This was only our second cup meeting with Northampton; the first being the 1991 cup final. Paul Grayson kicked the Saints into the lead with a penalty after 11 minutes but Woods replied in kind five minutes later. Rory Jenkins spent ten minutes in the sin bin during which Grayson put Northampton in front with his second penalty. Grayson missed a straightforward penalty eight minutes into the second half from just outside the 22 as the tie remained tight. On 50 minutes, Woods equalised with his second penalty and it was all to play for. After 69 minutes, Matt Powell, Morgan and Greenstock combined to send White-Cooper over for a try in the north-east corner to make it 11-6. Woods missed the conversion, Northampton threw everything at us in the remaining time and they even spurned some kicks at goal in going for the equalising try. This proved to be a big mistake and the final whistle brought joy for the home supporters. Eric Peters came on as a substitute for the first of only 5 appearances. He had recovered from a shattered kneecap and testicular cancer in the previous 18 months and it was fantastic to see him back playing again (he had won 29 caps for Scotland between 1995 and 1999).

At Vicarage Road against Saracens, we lost Jamie Williams after half an hour when he crashed into an advertising hoarding, broke a bone in his shin and dislocated his ankle. He was trying to stop ex-Quin Dan Luger from scoring the first try of the game. It was a cruel blow for Williams from which he never really recovered and he never again achieved the standard he had displayed before this accident. This try left us trailing 6-14 and, by half time, this had moved on to 9-17 (although the gap was still eight points). Niall Woods kicked a total of six penalties for us and, with 11 minutes left, we only trailed by two points. However, Sorrell kicked two more penalties to take his total to seven to deny us victory as well as a bonus point.

If it wasn't bad enough playing the second placed team in the Premiership, the following week, we had to play the third placed side as well. Northampton would be gunning for revenge after their cup defeat earlier in the month and we were on a run of six consecutive league defeats. In the second minute, Woods put us in front with a penalty, kicked another on 27 minutes but missed two more. We trailed by eleven points at the break because Northampton had scored tries through Hepher and Cohen (a 60 metre run to the line) and two conversions and a penalty from Dawson. When Martin scored for Dawson to convert three minutes into the second half, it looked all over but we fought our way back into the game and Stewart and Cohen were sin binned. During this 20 minute spell, Jennings (converted by Woods) and Daniel (converted by Chalmers) grabbed tries and the gap was down to four points with ten minutes of normal time remaining. But, as soon as the Saints were back to full strength, we leaked a fourth try. Hepher's second was converted by Dawson and it was his penalty after three minutes of seven in injury time which robbed us of any points, despite Gollings having narrowed the gap with our third try.

On 27th December, our final game of 2000 (as the proposed New Year's Eve meeting at Newcastle was postponed due to bad weather) was the return with Saracens at the Stoop. This was our worst display of the season and a real low point. Kevin Sorrell gave them the lead with a penalty before Niall Woods equalised in kind. He did kick a second after 38 minutes but the half time score was 25-6 to the visitors. Three tries to nil wasn't a fair reflection as we were unlucky not to get a penalty try when Dan Luger pulled Ben Gollings back as he went for a cross-kick by Greenwood. The trouble is when the luck goes against you, there's not a lot you can do about it. In the first ten minutes of the second half, Woods kicked his third penalty and Daniel scored a try but that was as close as we got. A fourth Saracens try by Luger made the final score 14-30.

This defeat signalled the end of Zinzan Brooke's reign as coach. He failed to achieve anything at the Club and his record of P92 W39 D2 L51 speaks volumes. He also presided over some of the heaviest defeats in the history of the Club. Some of the blame must be laid at the door of the players but, ultimately, the coach is the one who pays when things go wrong. Mark Evans and Richard Hill took over the coaching role until the end of the season; Evans retaining the position of Chief Executive. We would soon see the improvement in the playing side he demanded.

Our first game of 2001 came at the Stoop on 6th January and it couldn't have been a harder one. Our visitors were Leicester in the Tetley's Bitter Cup semi-final. The Tigers were the outstanding side in the country with a five point lead in the Premiership and a game in hand (we trailed them by 35 points) as well as being well placed in their European Cup Pool. They had won the last seven encounters and had not lost at the Stoop since 1992. In short, no one gave us a hope! A shock was on the cards when, after 8 minutes, Will Greenwood set up Keith Wood for a bullocking run to the line for a great try. Chalmers missed a simple conversion (he had already hit the post with a penalty attempt) but we were 5-0 up. We held the lead for ten minutes but Leicester suddenly cranked up a few gears and Murphy and Goode charged in for tries when our defence went missing. Stimpson converted the second and we trailed 5-12 after 22 minutes. Chalmers missed two more penalties but succeeded with a third attempt from 35 metres after 37 minutes; Stimpson replied with one of his own and we still trailed by seven points. Right on half time, we exploded back into contention when O'Neill fed Greenwood with a nice inside pass and the England centre went over behind the posts. Chalmers couldn't miss this one and it was 15-15 at half time. As the Leicester scrum and lineout went to pot, we got more and more fired up. Four minutes into the second half, Greenwood put Nick Burrows away and, as he was dragged down a couple of metres short, he managed to offload to David Wilson and he got over with a defender on top of him. Chalmers converted again and we had a seven point cushion. With 17 minutes of normal time remaining, Stimpson landed his second penalty to make it 22-18 but, by this time, the Tigers were dropping most things and we were running down the clock. The writing was on the wall when Healey fumbled an attempt at a quickly taken penalty. Chalmers even had time to miss another penalty which Niall Woods (who was on as a substitute) should have taken before the final whistle went and the Stoop exploded.

Our opponents in the final would be the Newcastle Falcons who had overcome Manchester Sale 37-25 in the other semi-final. If this performance could be replicated for the rest of the season, we should have no problems avoiding the threat of relegation.

The following Saturday, we travelled to France for our return Pool 5 fixture with Perigueux. In the second minute, Lagarde kicked a penalty for the home side before Woods kicked two for us to give us a lead we never lost. Before half time, Wood and Matt Powell had scored tries and Woods added a conversion and two more penalties for a 24-3 lead. The second half became a procession and Greenwood, O'Neill, Wood, Friday and Daniel all grabbed tries; Woods and Gollings (2) landed conversions to take our total to 55. Astruc got a try (converted by Lagarde) for the French to make it 36-10 but they had one of their props (Chouly) sent off for foul play at a ruck which summed up their day. We were now within one win of a place in the quarter finals. Niall Woods made his last appearance in this game having scored 115 points (3 tries, 24 penalties and 14 conversions) in just 12 appearances. His recurring knee problems had finally taken their toll.

Our chance came on 20th January when Ebbw Vale visited the Stoop. A power cut in the Twickenham area meant that the game finished in near darkness. However, it couldn't dampen our re-found form and we took the lead with a Ben Gollings penalty after five minutes. With Vale's fly half being sin binned for a deliberate knock-on after 15 minutes, we made our move. First, Pat Sanderson (from close range) and then Nick Greenstock (after good work from Powell, Wilson and O'Neill) scored tries. Gollings converted both for a 17-0 lead. This became 24-0 at half time when he added the extra points to a try from Burrows. Burrows and Sanderson got their second tries and, with Gollings kicking both conversions, we were 38-0 up. A mini revival saw the visitors run in tries from T. Morris, Matthews and Wagstaff with one conversion from Connor. There were still 12 minutes left but all that remained was a try from Greenstock, a conversion from Burke and a consolation score from Hawker for Vale. The final score of 45-22 sealed our place in the quarter finals.

The season had been constructed in such a way that our quarter final tie would come next and so it was that we travelled to Brive on Sunday 28th January for a very tough contest. This would not be an easy place to win at and it was a one-off game as well. Steve White-Cooper was put through by Greenwood for the opening score after 5 minutes which was converted by Burke. After this, the home side took control and Burton landed a penalty and converted a try by Christophers before getting a second penalty just a minute before the break to give Brive a 13-7 lead. We had lost Garrick Morgan injured after only 13 minutes and this had enabled the French pack to disrupt in the loose. We weathered the storm at the start of the second half and Burke got his first penalty of the day to close the gap to just three points. Then, after 63 minutes, came the turning point of the tie. Will Greenwood took the ball deep in his own 22 and began running. He kept on going and, with a collection of audacious dummies, he pinned his ears back with 40 yards to go and scored in the right hand corner. Burke converted this amazing solo effort and added a penalty a minute from the end to seal a famous win. We became the first English side to win at the Parc Municipal des Sports in European competition. The 20-13 final score could have been more had Powell got to his charge down of an attempted clearance but, nevertheless, we moved into the semi-finals against Newcastle. Eric Peters made his final appearance in this game but he had played his part even though his time with us had been so short.

Nine days later, we were back to Premiership action against Gloucester at the Stoop. Our last win in the league had been at home to Bristol on 16th September. Rotherham had moved to within five points of us during our cup exploits and we desperately needed a win. We started well and Sanderson scored a try after 90 seconds which Paul Burke converted. Rob Jewell made his debut when he came on as a temporary replacement for Ryan O'Neill. He would go on to make 56 appearances for the 1st XV. After 5 minutes, Hayward kicked a penalty for Gloucester but our lead was nine points when Gollings got over on 14 minutes. But, as had happened so many times in the past, we lost our way and the visitors scored ten points before the interval; we had Wilson and Burrows sin binned and trailed 12-13. We were back to 14 men when Burke put us back in front with a penalty and his dropped goal on 56 minutes stretched our lead to 18-13. The procession of substitutes ensued over the next 23 minutes with no fewer than seven permanent and one temporary taking place. In that time, Simon Mannix (who had broken us earlier in the season with his nine penalties) had come on and pulled three points back within five minutes. As the clock ticked down, Gloucester were awarded a penalty right in front of the posts; Mannix put it over and we trailed by a point. Immediately after the restart, Gloucester were penalised for crossing and Burke had the chance to win the game from 30 metres out five minutes into injury time. He was ice cool, the ball went straight through the posts and the final whistle went to signal our victory. This moved us nine points clear of Rotherham with seven games remaining. Peter Richards played his last game having scored 18 points (3 tries and a dropped goal) during his time with us.

Five days after this, we travelled to Bristol for our sixteenth Premiership game. Bristol were in ninth place but a good thirteen points ahead of us. Jason Leonard and Keith Wood were on the bench and Will Greenwood led the side. We started with a missed penalty by Burke before Johnstone scored a try after 14 minutes which Contepomi converted. Greenwood dropped a goal but two more Contepomi penalties meant the home side led 13-3 at the break. Crucially, Burke had missed two more penalties and a defensive hand prevented Burrows going in under the posts. By the 55th minute, both Leonard and Wood were brought on and we started to claw our way back with a Burke penalty. Contepomi had started missing shots and Burke landed his third penalty with 90 seconds of normal time left. There were four minutes of injury time but we couldn't get the winning score and our first defeat of 2001 followed. This was a poor game and another we should have won.

A two week gap before our next game gave the team a chance to regroup. That game was the Tetley's Bitter Cup Final against Newcastle at Twickenham on 24th February. This was our first appearance in a final since 1993 and our fifth overall. We lined up as follows: Ryan O'Neill; Nick Greenstock, Will Greenwood, Nick Burrows and Brendon Daniel; Paul Burke and Matthew Powell; Jason Leonard, Keith Wood and Jon Dawson; Garrick Morgan and Steve White-Cooper; Pat Sanderson, David Wilson (captain) and Roy Winters. We started well but it was Newcastle who took the lead when May went over from close range after eight minutes; Wilkinson converted to make it 7-0. We came back with a vengeance and Paul Burke landed two penalties either side of Greenwood putting Wilson over for our first try. Wilkinson and Burke exchanged penalties to make it 14-10 to us at the interval. The score could have been more in our favour as O'Neill was prevented from touching down by Gary Armstrong, Wood was stopped just short (if only he'd passed to the support) and the pack were unable to ground the ball after driving over.

Three minutes into the second half, Burke got his fourth penalty, Wilkinson replied three minutes later to which Burke countered on 61 minutes. A minute later, we lost our captain when he was finally forced to give in to the calf injury he had been carrying throughout (he was replaced by Rory Jenkins). He had played magnificently but, after his departure, the Falcons began to come back into the game. May grabbed his second try on 64 minutes but Wilkinson missed the conversion and we still led. After this, Bruce Starr and Ben Gollings replaced Dawson and Daniel respectively before we stretched our lead to nine points with ten minutes remaining. Gollings, Greenwood, White-Cooper and Powell were involved in the build-up before Wood linked up with Burke to send him in for our second try. His conversion gave him a record haul in a cup final of 22 points. Tuigamala drove towards our line and Jenner finished it off with a try in the corner but Wilkinson failed to convert and we led 27-23 with four minutes of normal time remaining. Alex Codling replaced Morgan two minutes later and we had to play out five minutes of stoppage time. We negotiated four of these but that's when the controversy started.

The Falcons had a big overlap on the left side but our defence got across and Burke and O'Neill bundled their prop forward Peel into touch near the line. To the absolute astonishment of everyone in the ground, the touch judge, Steve Lander, ruled it to be a Falcons throw in. The referee (Ed Morrison) asked him to confirm which he did. He said that the ball had come out of Peel's hand and had touched a Quins player before going into touch. Television replays showed this to be a howler of the first degree. The decision was a disgrace and only Lander can know why he gave the throw-in to Newcastle (perhaps one for his memoirs?). Anyway, what happened next was a Newcastle lineout, they got possession, the ball went down the line and Walder darted through a gap to score the winning try. Wilkinson converted and the final whistle went. We had lost 27-30 and the sense of injustice felt then against THAT decision still burns bright today. We had played fantastically well and to be undone by an official's decision was terrible. All of the Quins interviewed afterwards right up to and including Mark Evans felt the same.

A chance for some sort of revenge came quickly as our postponed Premiership game with the Falcons had been re-scheduled for Tuesday 6th March. Paul Burke was on target with a penalty after 6 minutes before Walder equalised in similar fashion. Burke and Greenwood sent O'Neill in for a try which Burke converted and, after a couple of near misses from Gollings, David Wilson was put over by Burke, Sanderson and Morgan. The ball blew over as Burke attempted the conversion but a penalty eight minutes later put us 18-3 ahead. A minute later, Newcastle pulled seven points back to leave the score at 18-10 at half time. Walder and Burke exchanged penalties and our eight point lead was still intact with 27 minutes left. This all changed with successful Walder penalties on 56, 66 and 76 minutes; time was running out and we trailed 21-22. In the final minute, more drama as O'Leary was tackled without the ball and Paul Burke stepped up to knock the ball over and we had our revenge but this didn't bring with it a trophy. This was our first away win in the league in thirteen attempts and we now needed 17 points from our five remaining games to be absolutely sure of staying up. The side had developed something of a backbone since Brooke's departure and this was now beginning to show.

After Bath, our next game was at Rotherham so that was probably going to be the game that decided the relegation battle once and for all. Bath came to the Stoop in third place with an outside chance of winning the title (a complete collapse by Leicester would be required). They had won the last three encounters but we were in confident mood. Matt Perry landed two penalties in the first half and Daren O'Leary sandwiched a try between them after 20 minutes to leave it evenly poised at half time. In the first thirteen minutes of the second half, Voyce scored a try and Perry converted and kicked another penalty. Suddenly, we trailed 5-16 and looked in trouble. Enter Paul Burke with his unfailing boot; three penalties on 55, 61 and 68 minutes brought us back into contention. Perry did get his fourth and fifth penalties but, in between, Greenwood charged down an attempted clearance by Catt, gathered and dived over for our second try. Burke converted to put us in front for a brief period. A minute after Perry's fifth success, Burke got his fourth and we ran the clock down for the remaining nine minutes to put the seal on a well-deserved victory.

Rotherham were not a good side and with only two wins from 17 games, their position said it all. After the previous week's results, it came down to this scenario. Rotherham had to win or draw; if they didn't, they would be relegated. From needing 17 points at the start of the Bath game, we now needed just four; such was the swing in one week. With a strong wind blowing straight down the Clifton Lane pitch and the temperature dropping during the course of the game, this would be a good one to win. We were against the elements in the first half but started excellently with two scores in the fourth minute. First, Paul Burke dropped a goal and then, a cross-field kick from our fly half enabled O'Leary to run in from 20 yards out. Rotherham came into the game and three penalties from Umaga saw them take a 9-8 lead which lasted ten minutes. Keith Wood powered over from Matt Powell's pass, Burke converted and we had a 15-9 lead. Burke and Umaga exchanged penalties in the first 23 minutes of the second period before tries from Rob Jewell and David Wilson (both converted by Craig Chalmers) brought a bonus point win.

Rotherham's fate was sealed and they now had to wait and see if it was to be straight relegation or a play-off against the National Division 1 winners. There was even a possibility that the Premiership would be expanded and they would survive.

Like Bath, Sale Sharks had won the last three meetings with us but we were looking to finish our home campaign with another victory. We were starting to develop something of a running game but this was to be a flash in the pan as future years would prove. At the start of play, we trailed Sale and Bristol by five points so we had something to aim at; perhaps a ninth or tenth place finish? We were all over the Sharks from the word go and Morgan scored after 4 minutes which Burke converted. Hodgson pulled back three points with a penalty before we stretched our lead to 19-3 at the interval with four Burke penalties. O'Leary and Wilson added unconverted tries in the 44th and 53rd minutes before the visitors got a try from Baldwin (converted by Little) after 75 minutes. With the last move of the match, O'Neill charged down an attempted clearance by Robinson and O'Leary ran in for the bonus point score. Burke's conversion made the final score 36-10 and we moved above Sale into tenth place on 38 points. By the end of this game, owing to injuries, Winters and Jenkins made up the second row and Fuga and Chalmers were in the back row.

We now had a ten day rest before our next game, a visit to Loftus Road to play Wasps on Tuesday 10th April. With our European Shield semi-final on 22nd April, the last things we needed were away games against two of the top three sides in the country in the space of five days. Anyway, needless to say, we lost both by a combined score of 24-75. Against Wasps, we were 26-0 down after half an hour before tries from Morgan (converted by Burke) and Adrian Olver cut the deficit at the break. Gollings got a try which Burke converted after 76 minutes but Wasps had added another twelve points to their total by that point. Karl Rudzki came on as a substitute for his debut, it was the first of 54 appearances.

On the day that Leicester paraded the Zurich Premiership trophy, we only gained an injury nightmare before our trip to Headingley. Fuga had injured his ankle at Wasps and Wood popped a rib in the Leicester game. The replacements were Johnny Roddham (he wasn't registered for the European Shield competition) and Andy Dawling (he was suspended after being sent off playing for the Army). Our two other hookers had both left during the season. Mark Evans said that if we couldn't register someone, we couldn't play and the European Shield organisers had said they wouldn't bend the rules. As it turned out, Fuga played and got through the match.

The Leicester game itself was a no-contest; by half time Leicester were 25-0 up and this became 37-0 after 76 minutes. It looked good for a shut-out but Rob Jewell managed to squeeze over on 82 minutes after prolonged pressure on the Tigers line. The conversion was missed and the referee called time a minute later. Our finishing place was confirmed as 11th, some 26 points ahead of Rotherham.

Now the Premiership was out of the way, we could concentrate 100% on making this season something of a success (if only in Europe). Sunday 22nd April was the day, Headingley was the neutral venue and Newcastle were our opponents in the European Shield semi-final. A poor start by both sides saw just a penalty from Wilkinson (after 2 minutes) scored in the first half an hour. Craig Chalmers missed a couple of penalties before Wilkinson stretched the lead after 36 minutes. Two minutes later, Chalmers was successful and it was 6-3. David Wilson and Doddie Weir were sent to the sin bin for fighting so both captains were off for ten minutes. At half time, Ed Jennings came on for Nick Greenstock and Chalmers carried on with his one man show into the second half. In the first five minutes after half time, he dropped a goal from 30 metres and then scored right in the corner after good work by Greenwood. We were defending well whilst our score was growing and Chalmers kicked his second penalty on 58 minutes. Roy Winters became our second player to visit the sin bin and, during his time off the field, Wilkinson out-scored Chalmers 2-1 in penalties. When Winters returned, we led 17-12 with five minutes left (plus five of injury time). Jonny Wilkinson had been tackled out of the game and he departed with four minutes to go. There were to be no dodgy calls in this one and we were through to the final. Chalmers made his last appearance having scored 30 points (1 try, 1 dropped goal, 4 penalties and 5 conversions) in his limited number of games with us.

We had a four week break until that game and, very sensibly, the decision was taken to take the squad down to Launceston to play Cornwall on 7th May. As could have been predicted, this turned into something of a romp for us and points came at regular intervals. O'Leary, Jewell (2), Leonard, Jennings and White-Cooper got tries in the first half with Gollings only missing the first and fourth conversions to make it 38-0. In the second half, Jenkins,

Chris Bell (making the first of 50 appearances), Sanderson, Powell, Jim Evans and Gollings added further tries with Gollings converting the last three. Larkin got a consolation score for Cornwall after our tenth try with the final score reading 74-5.

So it was that our final game of the 2000/01 season was at the Madejski Stadium in Reading. The European Shield Final against Narbonne on 20th May was to be a fantastic spectacle full of running rugby. It was Narbonne who took the lead after 6 minutes when Quesada kicked a penalty. A minute later and we were in front after Ben Gollings roared home after a pass from Greenwood. Burke converted (he would not miss a kick all day) and landed a couple of penalties either side of Quesada's for Narbonne. We led 13-6 at the end of the first quarter and were looking good although the French would be no walkover. Suddenly, Quesada dropped a goal, converted a try from Corletto and added a penalty. In the space of seventeen minutes, we had leaked 13 points but Burke managed to kick another penalty to reduce the deficit to three points at the break. Ben Gollings had limped off and was replaced by Ed Jennings after 32 minutes. Into the second half, Burke set up and converted a try by Pat Sanderson and we were back in front. Matt Powell had a try disallowed for a forward pass before Sudre (their scrum half) was sin binned for stamping. We couldn't turn this to our advantage but we did score again when he returned. Paul Burke knocked over his fourth penalty going into the last ten minutes of normal time to give us a 26-19 lead. At that point, Morgan and Winters were replaced by Alex Codling and Rory Jenkins. With just five minutes remaining, Narbonne equalised with a try from Ledesma converted by Quesada. Jon Dawson was replaced by Bruce Starr with a minute to go and, after a couple of minutes of injury time, the referee called a halt to proceedings. It would be 30 minutes of extra time to decide the winners. Three minutes into extra time, O'Leary crashed over under the posts from Greenwood's pass, Burke converted and added a penalty five minutes later to put us 36-26 ahead. Two minutes before Burke's penalty, our skipper David Wilson was carried off after crumpling to the ground as his right cruciate ligament gave way (he was replaced by Fuga). It was to end his career and he did not play for us again (even though officially he remained captain for the 2001/02 season). He scored 30 points (6 tries) and captained the side on 26 occasions. The true effect on losing him at this stage of his Quins career will never be fully realised and it cannot be underestimated what he achieved during his short time with us. One of his most important attributes was the ability to be all over the pitch throughout the eighty minutes. A try from Reid for Narbonne converted by Quesada made it a three point game at the end of the first period of extra time. As both teams tired, it was Paul Burke who stepped up to put the final nails in the Narbonne coffin. He landed his sixth penalty on 116 minutes and, two minutes later, dropped a superb goal. The 10 year wait for a trophy was over and how we deserved it! Rory Jenkins 55 points (11 tries) and 7 seasons with the Club and Daren O'Leary 573 points (114 tries and 1 dropped goal) and 8 seasons with the Club made their last appearances for us in the final.

Our playing record in the league was P22 W7 L15 F440 A538 Pts 38 (BP 10) Pos 11th. This had been our worst finishing position in the fourteen seasons of league rugby. Overall, our record was P39 W22 L17 F982 A784 which added up to our best season since 1996/97. Will Greenwood got the most tries with 13 and Paul Burke topped all the others with 230 points (1 try, 4 dropped goals, 51 penalties and 30 conversions). Overall, the team scored 110 tries which was up by 24 on the previous year and the first time since 1996/97 that we had scored over the hundred mark. Dropped goals were the same as last season (6), penalties almost doubled to 90 and conversions rose by 13 to 72. The total number of points was up by 99 to 982. Matt Powell appeared in 35 of the 37 matches played and he was followed by Rory Jenkins and Steve White-Cooper on 33, Nick Greenstock and Garrick Morgan (31) and Will Greenwood and Bruce Starr (30).

2000/01

100800	EBBW VALE	EBBW VALE	W	7G1PG(52)-2G1T(19)
150800	PONTYPRIDD	PONTYPRIDD	W	1G1PG1T(15)-3PG1T(14)
190800	LONDON IRISH(ZP)	STOOP MEMORIAL GROUND	L	1G1DG2PG(16)-1G5PG(22)
260800	ROTHERHAM(ZP)	STOOP MEMORIAL GROUND	W	3G1T(26)-1G2PG(13)
020900	BATH(ZP)	BATH	L	4PG2T(22)-3G4PG1T(38)
060900	NORTHAMPTON(ZP)	NORTHAMPTON	L	2G2PG(20)-1G5PG1T(27)
090900	LONDON WASPS(ZP)	STOOP MEMORIAL GROUND	L	1PG3T(18)-1G3PG3T(31)
160900	BRISTOL(ZP)	STOOP MEMORIAL GROUND	W	2G4PG1T(31)-2G2PG1T(25)
230900	GLOUCESTER(ZP)	GLOUCESTER	L	2G3PG(23)-9PG(27)
300900	NEWCASTLE(ZP)	STOOP MEMORIAL GROUND	L	1G2PG1T(18)-2G2PG(20)
071000	PERIGUEUX(ESP)	STOOP MEMORIAL GROUND	W	1G2PG2T(23)-1G3PG(16)
141000	EBBW VALE(ESP)	EBBW VALE	W	1G2PG1T(18)-1DG1PG(6)
211000	DAX(ESP)	STOOP MEMORIAL GROUND	W	1G6PG(25)-1PG(3)
281000	DAX(ESP)	DAX	L	2G1PG1T(22)-2G1DG2PG(23)
041100	PLYMOUTH ALBION(TBC4)	PLYMOUTH	W	4G1PG1T(36)-1PG1T(8)
111100	MANCHESTER(TBC5)	STOOP MEMORIAL GROUND	W	4G2T(38)-1PG1T(8)
191100	LONDON IRISH(ZP)	READING	L	1G3PG(16)-7PG(21)
241100	LEICESTER(ZP)	STOOP MEMORIAL GROUND	L	1G2PG(13)-1G3PG(16)
021200	MANCHESTER SALE(ZP)	SALE	L	1G1PG(10)-2G2PG3T(35)
091200	NORTHAMPTON(TBCQF)	STOOP MEMORIAL GROUND	W	2PG1T(11)-2PG(6)
171200	SARACENS(ZP)	VICARAGE ROAD	L	6PG(18)-7PG1T(26)
231200	NORTHAMPTON(ZP)	STOOP MEMORIAL GROUND	L	2G2PG1T(25)-4G2PG(34)

271200	SARACENS(ZP)	STOOP MEMORIAL GROUND	L	3PG1T(14)-2G2PG2T(30)
311200	NEWCASTLE(ZP)	NEWCASTLE	P	
060101	LEICESTER(TBCSF)	STOOP MEMORIAL GROUND	W	2G1PG1T(22)-1G2PG1T(18)
130101	PERIGUEUX(ESP)	PERIGUEUX	W	4G4PG3T(55)-1G1PG(10)
200101	EBBW VALE(ESP)	STOOP MEMORIAL GROUND	W	6G1PG(45)-1G3T(22)
280101	BRIVE(ESQF)	BRIVE	W	2G2PG(20)-1G2PG(13)
060201	GLOUCESTER(ZP)	STOOP MEMORIAL GROUND	W	1G1DG2PG1T(21)-1G4PG(19)
110201	BRISTOL(ZP)	BRISTOL	L	1DG2PG(9)-1G2PG(13)
240201	NEWCASTLE(TBCF)	TWICKENHAM	L	1G5PG1T(27)-2G2PG2T(30)
060301	NEWCASTLE(ZP)	NEWCASTLE	W	1G4PG1T(24)-1G5PG(22)
100301	BATH(ZP)	STOOP MEMORIAL GROUND	W	1G4PG1T(24)-1G5PG(22)
170301	ROTHERHAM(ZP)	ROTHERHAM	W	3G1DG1PG1T(32)-4PG(12)
310301	MANCHESTER SALE(ZP)	STOOP MEMORIAL GROUND	W	2G4PG2T(36)-1G1PG(10)
100401	LONDON WASPS(ZP)	LOFTUS ROAD	L	2G1T(19)-4G2T(38)
140401	LEICESTER(ZP)	LEICESTER	L	1T(5)-3G2PG2T(37)
220401	NEWCASTLE(ESSF)	HEADINGLEY	W	1DG3PG1T(17)-4PG(12)
070501	CORNWALL	LAUNCESTON	W	7G5T(74)-1T(5)
200501	NARBONNE(ESF)	READING	W	3G1DG6PG(42)-3G1DG3PG(33)AET

41

Rebuilding for a Brighter Future 2001-2004

In June 2001, England went on a short tour to Canada and the United States and this time all five matches were won including the tests, two against Canada (22-10 and 59-20) and one against the USA (48-19). Pat Sanderson played in all three and Steve White-Cooper missed just the first against Canada. Ricky Nebbett, Paul Sackey and Nick Walshe made the party but played in non-tests only.

On 30th December 2001, our President, David Brooks passed away, he was 77; he was just four months short of completing sixty years of involvement with the Club. He would be succeeded by another legend, Bob Hiller. For the year ending 30th June 2002, another loss was posted, this time it was £1,299,591. The Club started an Academy under the direction of Tony Russ (with support from Collin Osbourne and Tony Diprose) and included in the first intake of eleven youngsters were Chris Robshaw and George Robson. The second year, the only one was Jordan Turner-Hall and in year three, another four or five were taken on. The way it worked was that the Club would be watching 200 U14s, then 100 U15s, 60 U16s, 30 U17s and 20 U18s. Four or five would reach the Academy and would be in for two years with the possibility of a further year extension. It cannot be stressed just how much the Club owes to Tony Russ for his work in those early years as more and more young talent is now uncovered. Those following in the years to come would include Nick Duncombe, Chris Bell, Ugo Monye, Tom Williams, Mike Brown and Anthony Allen (allegedly, Gloucester offered him three times as much as we were paying and so he went to Kingsholm).

For just over a month in June and July 2001, the newly renamed British and Irish Lions toured Australia and played ten matches. We had three current players in the squad (Will Greenwood, Jason Leonard and Keith Wood), one who now played for Saracens (Dan Luger) and one future Quin who played for Llanelli (Dafydd James). Wood played in all three tests, Leonard came on as a substitute in the first two, James also played in all three and scored a try in the first; Luger got injured and Greenwood missed out on a cap again. After the Lions won the first test (29-13), the Aussies came back and won the next two by 35-14 and 29-23 to take the series. In the non-test matches, the Lions had a record of W6 L1.

On 5th April 2002, the Club lost an off the field legend when Dr Richard Rossdale died suddenly. He was 78 and suffered a heart attack while on holiday in Switzerland. He had been a member of the Club since 1947, becoming Honorary Medical Officer in 1979 and carrying on until 1998. He also served on the committee from 1974 for a number of years, became a Vice President in 1988 and was responsible for the development of the Club's medical facilities. He will always be remembered running on to the pitch to attend to an injured player wearing a suit and pullover even in the harshest of winters.

The turnover of players at most clubs was gradually increasing every season as contracts were drawn up for one or two years although in some cases, three or four year deals would be signed. Among the newcomers during the course of 2001/02 were Bill Davison and Dan Luger who both returned from Saracens. John Kingston came in as Head Coach and Richard Hill became Assistant Coach; it was hoped that together they would combine to enable us to challenge for the top honours. After winning the European Shield in May, we gained automatic entry to the Heineken European Cup for the 2001/02 season. From the low at the end of the year 2000, we had slowly begun to climb back towards the status the Club deserved but, there was a very long way to go yet.

To start with, we had two pre-season friendlies against Bedford (A) and London Welsh (H). The first of these was played on 18th August (the Premiership started two weeks later than last season) and we fielded a strong side although none of our Lions played. Bill Davison led the side in the absence of David Wilson. Our attacking intentions were clear from the start and we were soon in front with a try by Pat Sanderson which Paul Burke converted. In better than even time, this lead became 33-0 with tries from Jewell (2), Sanderson and Matt Moore with three conversions from Burke. Bedford did pull a try back but the second half gave us an opportunity to try out some defensive work. Bell, Jennings and Bell again finally got tries with Burke converting the first and Mapletoft (coming back after injury) the other two. Full time was sixty one points to five and a great start to John Kingston's reign as head coach. Among the players making their debuts were Scott Bemand (he would go on to make 57 appearances for the 1st XV), Anthony James "Tony" Diprose (he would make 137 appearances and had already won 10 England caps and, as already mentioned, went on the 1997 British Lions tour to South Africa) and Matt Moore (62 appearances).

The following Friday, we met London Welsh at the Stoop in what proved to be another nine try annihilation of the opposition. Garrick Morgan was captain this time and would lead the side in most of the remaining games. Ben Gollings and Adrian Olver got early scores before Dan Luger scorched in from 55 yards for the third try of the night. Mapletoft converted the first and third and then his own after Burrows had added the fourth. A good half time lead was slowly built on as Greenstock, Sanderson, Moore and Mapletoft scored more tries; the last named converted the second and third to finish with twenty points and the final margin of victory was 55-0.

Our first real test came on 1st September when London Irish visited the Stoop for the first Premiership game of the season. We got off to a flyer with a penalty from Paul Burke after 2 minutes but, after that, we were inept and gave the Irish fly half (Barry Everitt) kicking practice. Although Burke put his second over, Everitt landed five and converted Worsley's try (he would join us in 2003). At half time, we trailed 6-22 and were staring down the barrel yet again. So much expectation had been blown away in just 40 minutes. John Kingston blew his top at the break and we came out fighting. Burke kicked five penalties in the first 23 minutes of the half to equal the record of David Pears for penalties in a game set in December 1991. We were only a point behind but, sloppy defending allowed Everitt to cross-kick for Cunningham to catch and go over unopposed. Everitt converted and dropped a goal with four minutes left to kill us off.

A week later, our second home game was against Bristol and this had already become a must win fixture. We steadily built a nice lead with Paul Burke kicking two penalties either side of his try which he also converted. Bristol got a goal and a penalty back but when Luger went over for Burke to convert, it was 20-10 at half time and things were looking up. The third quarter was an absolute disaster for us as we gave away twenty points including an interception try and one where Gollings let the ball bounce after a speculative chip from Drahm who was able to collect and put Little over for their third try. Greenstock went over for us but Drahm kicked his fourth penalty and Salter scored another try to leave us thirteen points behind with 12 minutes left. Scott Bemand did get our fourth try on his debut and Burke converted but it was too late and we were in trouble again.

On Sunday 16th September, the long trek was made to Newcastle. There were not a massive amount of changes from the previous week although Bell came in for Greenstock and White-Cooper and Tamarua (playing the first of 19 games; he would win one cap for the Pacific Islanders in 2004) joined Winters in the back row. To be honest, this was a terrible game and came nowhere near the standards set the previous season in the encounters between us. Suffice to say, Wilkinson put Newcastle in front with a penalty after four minutes, Burke equalised in similar fashion six minutes later before the England fly half got his second two minutes before half time. The second half petered out and was coming to a close when, after a period of sustained pressure, Burke dropped a wobbly goal a minute from the end of normal time to hand us a draw.

It was time for the visit of Wasps to the Stoop on 22nd September, a match that is always keenly anticipated. At this stage, Wasps had 4 points from three games and we had the same but had better points difference than them. We were in ninth, they were eleventh. Burke was again in form and punished every indiscretion by Wasps. After 24 minutes, he had kicked five penalties to put us 15-0 up. Leek went to the sin bin for killing the ball and it was left to Sampson to get Wasps first points with a penalty on 37 minutes. Two minutes later, Luger sent Matt Moore in for his first league try and we were seventeen points clear at the interval. Early in the second half, Luger spent ten minutes in the bin for illegally stopping a move and Leek slotted the resultant penalty. On 50 minutes, Joe Worsley suffered a terrible injury when a stray boot in a ruck ripped his scrotum open; one can only imagine the pain he must have been in! He was rushed to hospital leaving his team mates to their fate. Burke equalled the penalty record again with two in nine minutes before the visitors got their first seven pointer with a Lewsey/Leek combination. We had the final word when Mapletoft scored for Burke to convert to make it 33-13 and give us our first win over Wasps in five attempts.

After missing the competition for a season, we played Bridgend in our first Heineken European Cup pool match at the Brewery Field on 29th September. Quite what we would have done without Paul Burke is anyone's guess; he was playing superbly. This game wasn't any different and, after Cerith Rees had put the home side in front with a penalty after 11 minutes, he popped up to score after all the hard work had been done by Keith Wood. He converted and replied to a second Rees penalty with one of his own. The first quarter had passed and we were in front by four points. Rees put over his third penalty but our half time lead was assured when Bemand sent Tu Tamarua in behind the posts. Burke converted and kicked a penalty to put us 20-9 up. Old boy Huw Harries kicked ahead for Durston to score before Burke exchanged penalties with Rees as the third quarter ended. On 63 minutes, Luger got the clinching score for Burke to convert which was crucial as Bridgend added a goal to their total right near the end. A case of mistaken identity saw Pat Sanderson sin binned less than two minutes after coming on as a substitute but it didn't affect the result.

We were finding some sort of form but the question was, how long would it last? Our next opponents were Munster at the Stoop and this would be a stiff test. When Dan Luger scored a try after 14 minutes, we were in control but, after a series of errors including one by Mapletoft that led to a try, we trailed 13-5 at half time. We played poorly in the second half, Munster took a grip on proceedings and O'Gara steered them to victory. We only had a Burke penalty to show for our efforts against eleven points for the visitors. We had somehow saved our worst form for our home European Cup games and worse was to follow in the next one on 28th October.

It was back to domestic competition with a trip to Gloucester where we were soundly beaten. We conceded a penalty try after just 34 seconds when Luger was adjudged to have deliberately knocked on under his own posts but responded with a try from Will Greenwood six minutes later which Mapletoft converted. Diego Albanese scored with a solo effort but was sent off after 35 minutes when he head butted Mapletoft. A seven point deficit against 14 men should have been turned into our second Premiership win of the campaign. Alas, it was not and we capitulated, conceding nineteen unanswered points in a 33-7 drubbing. Following this, the team were called in for training at 9 a.m. on Sunday by John Kingston as punishment – perhaps this would do the trick!

Back on home soil, we entertained Bath in a dour encounter but managed to grind them down to come out on top 15-8. They fielded virtually a 2nd XV and we were missing Wood, Luger, Greenwood and Leonard. Burke was on target with four penalties and Mark Mapletoft got the other against Bath's penalty and try. We were now in eighth place while Wasps were bottom. Solomona Asora Adrian "Ace" Tiatia made his debut when he came on as a sub and would go on to make 80 appearances; he had won 7 caps for Samoa in the summer of 2001 but would gain no more.

Castres Olympique came to the Stoop and it was quite simple, we had to win to stand any chance of qualifying for the cup quarter finals. After Townsend had kicked a penalty for the visitors after 2 minutes, Dan Luger ran in from 65 yards out to score the first try. Mapletoft converted and we led 7-3. Townsend exchanged penalties with Mapletoft and 10-6 was as good as it got for us. Our error strewn game returned and, by half time, we were fourteen points behind. By the time Castres had scored their fourth try, it was 36-10 and a complete thrashing was on the cards. However, we managed to restore a little pride when Steve White-Cooper went over after 73 minutes. Mapletoft converted but Townsend had the last word with his fifth penalty.

We now had to travel to the South of France for the return pool fixture with Castres and, as our away form tended to be poor in Europe especially, another heavy defeat was a realistic possibility. However, David Slemen (son of Mike, the England wing from the 1970s and 80s) made his debut at fly half and had a great game. He was on trial until the end of November and put a marker down in the first minute with a penalty. After the French had gone in front with a converted try, Keith Wood went over for us and Slemen got his second penalty to give us an 11-7 lead after 15 minutes. After several missed opportunities on both sides, a second goal from Castres put them ahead at the interval. Ten points after the break left us even further behind but Will Greenwood scored our second try which Slemen converted and we were back in it. Ben Gollings had a chance to steal an unlikely victory but put a foot in touch and we had lost again. Bruce Douglas came on as a sub for his debut and would go on to win 43 caps for Scotland but only played seven games for us.

Due to the autumn international series, the next three Premiership weekends would be played on Friday nights. The first of these was on 9th November at Franklin's Gardens against Northampton. There were a number of men missing from both sides because of those internationals but, it was the same for each side and we had to live with that and try to get some points out of these Friday games. After only two minutes, the first scrum erupted in a brawl and Ace Tiatia was singled out for a yellow card. Two minutes later, we were down to thirteen when Bill Davison was harshly shown a yellow for a disputed tackle on Matt Dawson. Due to the touch judge not attracting the referee's attention, Tiatia stayed off thirteen minutes and Davison eleven. However, we survived and took the lead when Gollings flew over for Burke to convert. Hepher then traded penalties with Burke and we were seven points up at the break. Our fly half extended the lead with another penalty after 54 minutes before the Saints started to claw their way back into it. Both hookers had difficulty finding their men in what was becoming a disjointed game. Hepher landed his second penalty and four minutes later he scored in the corner and converted from wide out. Both sides had further, kickable chances to take all four points but 13-13 was how it stayed.

By the time we met Saracens at the Stoop on 16th November, we had dropped to ninth place. In the first 20 minutes, we made all the running but the scores were level at 6-6. Smith and Burke had twice exchanged penalties then came the turning point. Sorrell was shown a yellow card for throwing a punch and we took control. Tu Tamarua got our first try and Paul Burke converted as well as adding a penalty to make it 16-6 at half time. The

Burke show continued unabated and he kicked two more penalties and converted Matt Moore's try after 50 minutes. Ten minutes later, Tamarua and Moore sent Burke scampering over 40 yards for another try which he again converted. Saracens just couldn't get back into it and Adrian Olver was sent clear by Bemand and Mapletoft for the bonus point try. Burke's conversion gave him 28 points in the match and a 100% success rate – nine out of nine. The final score of 43-6 was our highest score and biggest winning margin against Saracens and it temporarily put us in sixth place in the Premiership.

Leicester is not a place many people win at and our last success had come in 1997.We had seven men missing through international call-ups and injuries; they had twelve. We wouldn't have a better chance to end their 44 match unbeaten home run in the league. Paul Burke got a penalty after two minutes to give us the lead but Stimpson got one back on four minutes and converted his own try after 31 minutes to put the Tigers in front. Two Burke penalties in the last ten minutes of the half reduced the gap to just one point with all to play for (although had he kicked either of the simple ones he missed earlier, we would have led). We were conceding too many turnovers and, from one of these, Stimpson got his second try, converted it and responded to Burke's penalty after 49 minutes with his second to put the score at 20-12 in Leicester's favour. Halfway through the second half, Burke got his fifth penalty to narrow the gap but Stimpson's reply on 76 minutes (after Manson-Bishop had spent ten minutes in the sin bin) from inside his own half, maintained the eight point cushion. A dropped goal from our fly half again took us to within striking distance but, despite camping in the Leicester 22 for almost all of the seven minutes of injury time, we only ended up with a losing bonus point.

Our sixth home Premiership match saw a visit from third placed Sale Sharks. The first quarter belonged to the visitors with thirteen unanswered points including a try from Jason Robinson. We rallied strongly and Jason Leonard was driven over for a try and Paul Burke added eight points with the boot (a conversion and two penalties). In the second half, we let it slip and Hodgson got a second penalty and converted when Hanley out-paced Jamie Williams and Pat Sanderson over 20 yards. There were 23 minutes to go but all we managed was another penalty from Burke. Our third losing bonus point of the season was secured. A future Quin appeared as a replacement for Sale in the second half; he was centre Mel Deane. We dropped to seventh place and our next fixture was with the side in bottom place, Leeds Tykes.

We desperately needed a return to winning ways after two narrow defeats. At Headingley on 9th December, we scored after three minutes when Dan Luger ran in for the opening try. Will Greenwood (who led the side) was sin binned for preventing a quickly taken penalty and we leaked ten points in the time he was off. Our opponents had just signed Braam van Straaten who was renowned for his kicking ability. His first penalty attempt missed but his second (after a terrible attempt at catching a high ball by Jamie Williams had led to us conceding a penalty from which Greenwood was shown a yellow card) went over and our lead was cut. A kick ahead (after an unspotted forward pass) led to Dan Scarborough going over after he out-ran Bemand and Williams. Van Straaten converted and then stretched the lead on 33 minutes with another penalty. Burke reduced this with his first penalty to make it 13-8 at half time. He exchanged penalties with van Straaten so the home side's lead was still five points. After 59 minutes, disaster struck when Scarborough was allowed to kick ahead three times to score by the posts, van Straaten converted and time was running out. Jamie Williams had limped off and this would be his final Quins appearance. He had scored 180 points (36 tries) in his seven season career although he had been dreadfully unlucky with injuries and had never regained his form of a few years earlier. We had five good chances in the last ten minutes but could only increase our total with a try from Luger (converted by Burke) with three minutes of injury time left. Another losing bonus point and the same score as against Leicester left us in the same position as we were at the start of play.

It was Powergen Cup time the following week and we had a very difficult tie ahead of us. We had won on only one of our previous eight visits to Heywood Road and that was a friendly fixture. A disastrous start saw Deane going over under the posts in the second minute (memories of our cup tie here in 1983 came flooding back!) for Hodgson to convert. And, just as in that game, we steadied the ship and came out fighting. Paul Burke got two penalties before Hodgson got two of his own. After 35 minutes, Will Greenwood and Tony Diprose enabled Matt Moore to score in the corner and an excellent conversion from Burke tied the scores. Seven minutes into the second half, Tamarua went to the sin bin but we lost no ground as Hodgson's dropped goal was cancelled out by a Burke penalty. It was nip and tuck as the minutes ticked away; Hodgson gave Sale the lead with a penalty, Burke replied in kind and dropped a goal with 14 minutes of normal time remaining to edge us ahead. With two minutes left, Burke missed with a dropped goal attempt to seal victory and it was left to Hodgson to drop a goal from 45 metres with the final kick of added time to tie the scores at 22-22. Ten minutes each way extra time would decide this sixth round tie. A driving maul set up a try for Ryan O'Neill two minutes into extra time which Burke converted and, before the end of the first period, Hodgson landed a penalty in reply and Burke took his match tally to 22 points with his fifth. Despite best efforts, neither side troubled the scoreboard again and we had a famous victory by thirty two points to twenty five.

It was back to Premiership action the following week for the visit of Leicester. This proved too much for us as our league form continued to get worse and worse and a full strength Tigers side took us apart in the second half. The first half was a different story altogether after Murphy had opened the scoring with a try after just 28 seconds which Stimpson converted. Paul Burke scored a try of his own and kicked three penalties to put us in front before a penalty from Murphy narrowed the gap at the break to four points. Three goals in a fifteen minute spell afterwards sealed our fate but Bemand did pull a try back which Burke converted. Leicester had the last word when Martin Johnson ran in from the 22 metre line and side-stepped around O'Neill. A final score of 21-38 would not be our worst defeat of the season but it was a bitter pill to swallow.

Eight days later, we travelled to Vicarage Road for the return with Saracens in our final fixture of 2001. Once again, we conceded a very early try when Horan scored after only 48 seconds (this was becoming too much of a regular pattern). We actually fought back to lead with a dropped goal and penalty from the boot of Burke. A penalty from de Beer put Saracens back in front and two goals and a try before half time sent them clean away. Penalties from Burke made it 9-15 and 12-27 (at half time) before he reduced the arrears further with two more. However, Bracken (converted by de Beer) and Cole added their fifth and sixth tries before Greenwood intercepted a pass and ran in our only try of the game which Burke converted. A 39-25 defeat sent us spiralling down the table into tenth place and only three points above Wasps and Leeds. We were in desperate trouble after our fifth consecutive Premiership defeat.

A dramatic improvement was required if we were to compete with Munster at Thomond Park on 5th January as we played our fifth of six pool matches in the Heineken Cup. We were only playing for pride as there was not even a mathematical chance of us qualifying for the quarter finals. To be fair, we did compete for the first 50 minutes but lost out big time in the final half an hour. The one bright spark was the debut of Nick Duncombe at scrum half; his speed of pass and deed was something we hadn't seen at the Stoop for some years. He went on to gain two England caps and make 20 appearances for the 1st XV. It was a terrible loss when he was taken from us at such an early age. He scored one of our two tries with the other coming from Tony Diprose. Paul Burke converted both but the nearest we got was 3-5. By the time Tamarua was sin binned, the game was long gone. Munster scored six tries (three converted) and five penalties from O'Gara to make the final score 51-17 in their favour. In mitigation, we did have eleven men missing and John Kingston did take Morgan, Burke, Burrows and White-Cooper off to save them for the cup and league games to come. The sooner our European Cup games came to an end the better. This hadn't been our worst performance in the competition but it wasn't far off!

Bridgend came to the Stoop a week later for the wooden spoon game. It was a simple equation, if we lost, we would occupy bottom spot in the Pool. Our opponents had not won a game in their five matches so far whereas our only win had come at the Brewery Field back in September. Mark Mapletoft was at fly half for the rested Paul Burke and it was he who opened the scoring after three minutes with a penalty. Rees replied in kind before two tries in ten minutes saw us surge ahead. First, Rob Jewell beat two men to score and then David Slemen picked up a Diprose tap down from Mapletoft's high kick to run into the corner. Bridgend came back strongly and scored tries through Ma'ama Molitika (who would have a short spell with us in 2005) and Gareth Thomas. Rees converted both and, when Mapletoft missed a couple of penalties, we trailed 13-17 at the interval. After a powerful run by Garrick Morgan, Matt Moore was able to put Chris Bell in for our third try; no conversion but at least we were back in front. This was a highly entertaining game and the tide turned again when Rees went over and added a 40 metre dropped goal on 56 minutes to put the visitors seven points clear. Mapletoft landed a penalty before putting in a long kick for Moore to chase. He powered down the right wing and beat the defender to the ball before kicking on and diving on it over the line. Mapletoft added his third penalty on 76 minutes but we had to defend desperately for the final six minutes to hold on to our lead. At least the 29-25 victory gave us some confidence ahead of our 21st cup quarter final against Leicester the following week.

As with the semi-final the previous season, Leicester came to the Stoop as clear leaders in the Premiership and overwhelming favourites to march on to the next round. We welcomed back Greenwood, Burke, Leonard, Fuga, Tamarua and Nick Duncombe (who started at scrum half). We played against a strong wind in the first half and fell behind after three minutes when Goode put over a penalty. Five minutes later, Paul Burke replied and put us in the lead after 32 minutes with his second. His out of hand kicking had been excellent and time and again, he drove the Tigers back. At half time, a lead of three points with the wind in our favour in the second half was an excellent position to be in but the hard work still had to be done. Leicester brought on Martin Johnson and Neil Back during the break and, during Tamarua's visit to the sin bin, Ollie Smith went outside Greenwood for a try which Goode converted. Just as Tamarua was preparing to come back, Kafer was sin binned for an offside offence and Burke kicked the penalty. Three minutes later, Diprose, Duncombe and Burke enabled Burrows to go over for our only try of the tie. Burke's conversion gave us a six point advantage. Kafer returned to the fray and, six minutes later he got over in the corner and Goode slotted an excellent conversion to put the visitors back in front. Eight minutes remained but, when Goode put over his second penalty, only four were left. Just before this, Burrows was sent to the sin bin and we had to try and win with fourteen men. Burke got three points back with another penalty; it was 19-20 and there were two minutes to go. As time was about to expire, Tony Diprose put in a chip ahead, Neil Back obstructed him and Tony Spreadbury awarded us a penalty. Up stepped Paul Burke to line up a 52 metre penalty more or less in midfield. He struck the ball beautifully towards the north end, it clipped the right hand post and went over. It was a magnificent kick and the Tigers hearts had been broken again! We played out the remaining two minutes of injury time to go into the semi-finals. Why we can conjure up this sort of performance in the cup and not in the league, no one has ever worked out but, perhaps we should treat every game like a cup tie?

We played Northampton in a Premiership fixture on 26th January and it was to be a losing return to league rugby. In atrocious conditions at the Stoop, Burke kicked three penalties in the first half but Paul Grayson got one and converted Smith's try to give the Saints a one point lead. Grayson spent ten minutes in the bin but it was

Northampton who stretched their lead when Ben Cohen went over for a try. Before their fly half returned, we were in front when a superb 40 yard break by Duncombe set up Chris Bell for a try which Burke converted. We couldn't build on this and Grayson returned to give the visitors all the points. He put over two penalties and a dropped goal to deny us a bonus point. The final score of 24-16 dropped us into eleventh place. We were three points ahead of Leeds but they had two games in hand.

On 5th February, we had a visit from the Natal Sharks who were continuing their build up to the Super 12 competition. We did well up to half time and actually led 6-3 (two Mapletoft penalties to one from Du Toit) before a host of changes weakened the side and the Sharks took command. Karl Rudzki went to the sin bin and when he returned, we trailed 6-17 (tries from Snyman and Sowerby and conversions from Du Toit). Our chance had gone and two more goals (tries from Delport and Snyman and conversions from Du Toit) put the Sharks well ahead before Mark Mapletoft scored a try and added the extra points for a final score of 13-31. With over twenty replacements being made, the game descended into a disjointed farce by the end. Dave von Hoesslin appeared for the Sharks; he would spend a brief time with us in 2005. However, with a crowd of 8,344, it was a considerable success and would be repeated again but perhaps it came at the wrong time of year for us. Luke Sherriff made his debut in this game and went on to make 85 appearances for the 1st XV and Ed Jennings made his last appearance having scored 27 points (2 tries, 3 penalties and 4 conversions) during his 1st XV career. Ryan O'Neill also appeared for the final time; he had scored 25 points (5 tries) over his two spells with us.

Four days later, we went to the Rec to take on a Bath side with only one more point than us. As so often happens at Bath, we leaked early points and Burke's penalty was sandwiched between two Bath tries. First Mike Catt and then Dan Lyle went over. Barkley could only convert the first but we had been sloppy and paid the price. We steadied ourselves but Perry dropped a goal on 37 minutes and Ace Tiatia was sent to the bin after a disagreement with Grewcock. Bath couldn't add to their tally and Burke was gradually nibbling away at their lead; he kicked a penalty and dropped a goal in the third quarter. The turning point came when he missed a kickable one with 17 minutes left and Barkley got one over a few minutes later. At 18-9, we couldn't raise our game and another defeat followed. Luckily for us, Leeds also kept losing and we remained three points ahead.

We hit a new low against Gloucester on a freezing day at the Stoop two weeks later. Burke got our only points with two penalties to give us leads of 3-0 and 6-3 but again we made mistakes at crucial times. Newcomer Nick Duncombe ran a penalty instead of letting Burke put us 9-3 up and then his pass was intercepted in the second half which eventually ended with Azam going in under the posts to kill the game off. Albanese had scored their first try but we failed to capitalise on a sin binning when Pucciariello was sent off for stamping. Mercier converted Azam's try and slotted a penalty to set the final margin at twelve points. To top it all off, Leeds won at Saracens and we went bottom.

Our cup semi-final against London Irish would provide a week off from the disaster that was our Premiership campaign. Mark Evans announced that he was to take a leading role in coaching the Club for the foreseeable future with John Kingston taking control of the forwards. Perhaps this was what we needed but only time and results would tell. Playing into a gusting breeze in the first half, we leaked points at an alarming rate and just couldn't get on the board. All was even for the first five minutes but the boot of Barry Everitt soon came into play. He kicked two penalties, converted a try by Venter, put over another two penalties and converted Horak's try and we were twenty six points down at home after 30 minutes play. To say that we were rubbish would be an understatement. The Irish played well but we just kept coughing the ball up, dropping it, our hooker even kept throwing the ball to a green shirt and every error seemed to be punished with points. Eventually, we woke up and Alex Codling scored our first try on our first visit to the Irish 22. Burke converted and added a penalty just before half time. A sixteen point deficit could be overturned with the breeze, indeed it had to be if we were to reach our sixth cup final. Burke kicked a penalty three minutes into the second half and, just as the Irish looked vulnerable after making three substitutions, we went to sleep again and started giving away penalties in crucial attacking positions. Our pack was starting to take control and, eventually, Ace Tiatia was put over by Diprose and Leonard after Codling had won the ball at a lineout. Burke converted and when Diprose drove over with ten minutes left, Burke's conversion made the score 27-26 in our favour. The comeback was to be ultimately unsuccessful as Everitt slotted two penalties for offside (one in normal time and one in injury time) to send them into their first final for 22 years where they would beat Northampton quite easily. Mark Evans questioned why so little injury time had been played after Slemen and Luger clashed heads. Slemen was out cold for over five minutes before being stretchered off but the referee (Steve Leyshon) only played around five minutes in total. The real reason we lost was our absolutely horrendous start in the first half an hour, of which the Irish took full advantage. Nick Burrows played his final game for the 1st XV in this one having scored 30 points (6 tries) during his time at the Club.

Being out of the cup meant our sole aim was to avoid finishing in last place and getting relegated from the Premiership (although the annual saga of whether it would actually happen was still dragging on). The weather could best be described as horrible; rain, wind and a falling temperature didn't bode well for a decent match when the Newcastle Falcons came calling on 16th March. Both teams contrived to produce a hard, gruelling encounter where running rugby was produced in terrible conditions. Keith Wood returned for his first match since the cup win at Sale and was immediately put in as captain for this important game. A Paul Burke penalty and his conversion of Adrian Olver's touchdown gave us an early ten point lead before Jonny Wilkinson began to turn the screw. He set up a Stephenson try, converted it and dropped a goal and, inside a five minute spell, it was 10-10. Burke and Wilkinson exchanged penalties and a period of twenty minutes remained scoreless until Steve White-Cooper benefited from an accurate cross-kick to jog in for a try which Burke converted. Wilkinson dropped another goal but Bell intercepted a pass on his own 22 and ran in for what proved to be the match clinching try. Burke couldn't convert but exchanged penalties with Wilkinson. Into the final quarter, a rolling maul was driven over the Newcastle line for Luke Sherriff to get our fourth try and a vital bonus point. Although Leeds lost and didn't pick up a point, they had won six matches to our four so we stayed bottom (points difference no longer counted above matches won when teams were level on points). Tu Tamarua appeared for the final time after a short spell with us, he had scored 5 points (1 try) and been to the sin bin on three occasions.

We had a two week gap before travelling to the Memorial Stadium to take on Bristol. These fixtures have regularly produced high scoring games and this was no exception. It was another awful performance from us and by half time, we were 8-17 behind. Burke had got a penalty and Greenstock scored a try. Contepomi had converted a try by Christophers, kicked a penalty and then converted his own try. Greenstock's second try and Burke's conversion brought us within two points of Bristol's lead but that was as close as it got. White-Cooper went to the bin and we conceded a try during that time. During a bizarre ten minute spell, the Shoguns added 21 points and that was that (fourteen of those came when they had a player in the sin bin!). In the remaining seven minutes, as is so often the case, we came on strong and Keith Wood scored our third try before a penalty try was awarded by Tony Spreadbury as Bristol defended illegally. Burke converted to make it 27-43 but at least we had a four try bonus point.

Two weeks later on 14th April, we were back down the M4 at the Madejeski Stadium, Reading. All that happened in the first 30 minutes were two Burke penalties followed by one from Brown for the Irish. In first half injury time, Ezulike scored for Brown to convert (after Burke had hit an upright with a long range penalty attempt). At half time, he was replaced by David Slemen due to an ongoing ankle injury. In the third quarter, Slemen and Everitt (who had replaced Brown) exchanged penalties. Ours came after Gustard had been binned for persistent infringement. Slemen dropped a goal from 40 metres two minutes after Everitt's penalty and, seventeen minutes later, he added another from 45 metres to put us in front. When Ben Gollings dropped our third goal five minutes into injury time, we looked to have done enough. We contrived to mess up the restart and, finally, Horak went over in the corner for the equalising try eight minutes into stoppage time. The result rested on the conversion by Everitt. As he ran up, Dan Luger exploded off the goal line and blocked the attempt. The final whistle went and it finished all square at 18 points each. With three matches left, we were two points ahead of Leeds.

On Friday 26th April, we went to Loftus Road to take on Wasps. A win in this one would help us enormously in our quest to avoid relegation. David Slemen put us ahead with a penalty after nine minutes but we were behind at the interval after a Logan penalty and a King dropped goal. This was an error strewn affair and there was no scoring in the second period until Slemen knocked over his second penalty with eleven minutes left. Earlier, Diprose and Gollings had somehow managed to get in each other's way when Greenwood chipped through and there wasn't a Wasps player in sight. All one of them had to do was touch the ball down! With two minutes left, King dropped a goal and we were behind. With time running out, we had a penalty and, amid confusion on the pitch, the decision from the dugout was to go for goal. Obviously the wrong one as Slemen wasn't kicking well. He missed and Wasps cleared deep into our half and, as Greenwood launched our last attack, he had his pass intercepted by Roiser who went in under the posts for King to convert. Final score 16-6 and no points again.

Our last home game was effectively the relegation play off against Leeds. The nerves were jangling but Burke settled the side with a penalty after three minutes. Leeds came back and two from van Straaten edged them ahead. Burke equalised then van Straaten dropped a goal. A minute later, Greenwood punted across for Matt Moore to collect and scorch over and we had the lead again. On 37 minutes, Burke dropped a goal and then converted Greenwood's try right on half time to give us a 21-9 lead. Keith Wood scored eight minutes after the break when he charged through and Burke converted. As the substitutes starting coming on, Benton scored a try for the Tykes which van Straaten converted to give them some hope. This was extinguished when Greenstock latched onto a Matt Powell cross-kick to grab the four try bonus point. With 14 minutes playing time left, Wood sealed victory after blocking a clearance kick, re-gathering and running in unopposed. Burke converted to make it 40-16 and move us seven points away from Leeds. Garrick Morgan made his last appearance in this one having scored 65 points (13 tries) during his Quins career, he had captained the side 24 times and received seven yellow cards. Adrian Olver also ended his time at the Club having scored 20 points (4 tries) during the last two seasons.

Luckily, by the time our final game was played at Heywood Road, Leeds had lost again so we were safe. While we had nothing to play for, Sale were after second place and had to pick up the try bonus and win to make sure; this was bad news for us. After a near scoreless first quarter, Burke slotted a penalty on 18 minutes to put us ahead. Sale's first try followed a minute later when Cueto went over for Hodgson to convert. If the second quarter was uneventful, the second half was all action. Mel Deane scored for Hodgson to convert before Mapletoft got a penalty and Moore scored a try to make it 14-11 to Sale. We then descended into farce and conceded tries from Cueto and Hodgson (he converted both) in just over 10 minutes. In four minutes of injury time, we leaked another twelve points to finish our season with an 11-40 defeat and in ninth place. Three players made their last appearances in this game, Bruce Douglas, Mark Mapletoft (coming on as a substitute) who had scored 66 points

(4 tries, 8 penalties and 11 conversions) and Steve White-Cooper who had scored 50 points (10 tries) in his career which had begun as far back as the 1994/95 season (he had also received one yellow card and one visit to the sin bin). As it turned out, Leeds finished bottom but, as Rotherham were not allowed to come up from National League Division 1, they survived.

Our playing record in the league was P22 W5 D3 L14 F434 A507 Pts 35 (BP 9 - 5TB 4LB) Pos 9th. This had been a disaster of a season and questions had to be asked about the commitment of the team by the players themselves. How could such a talented squad allow themselves to be in relegation trouble almost down to the final game? However, for all our troubles, we did improve our finishing position by two places on last year. Our overall playing record was P34 W11 D3 L20 F763 A807. Matt Moore ended with the most tries (8) and Paul Burke again headed all the other sections with a total of 351 points (4 tries, 5 dropped goals, 80 penalties and 38 conversions). Overall, only 72 tries were scored and that was our worst total since 1979/80 when only 56 were registered. Dropped goals rose by 2 to 8, penalties were also up to 93 from 90 but conversions consequently dropped to 50 (the worst since 1994/95). Our total points dropped by over 200 to 763. Tony Diprose and Garrick Morgan appeared in 32 out of 34 matches with Matt Moore on 30 the only other player to get into the thirties.

2001/02

180801	BEDFORD	BEDFORD	W	8G1T(61)-1T(5)
240801	LONDON WELSH	STOOP MEMORIAL GROUND	W	5G4T(55)-0
010901	LONDON IRISH(ZP)	STOOP MEMORIAL GROUND	L	7PG(21)-2G1DG5PG(32)
080901	BRISTOL(ZP)	STOOP MEMORIAL GROUND	L	3G2PG1T(32)-3G4PG1T(38)
160901	NEWCASTLE(ZP)	NEWCASTLE	D	1DG1PG(6)-2PG(6)
220901	LONDON WASPS(ZP)	STOOP MEMORIAL GROUND	W	1G7PG1T(33)-1G2PG(13)
290901	BRIDGEND(HECP)	BRIDGEND	W	3G3PG(30)-1G4PG1T(24)
061001	MUNSTER(HECP)	STOOP MEMORIAL GROUND	L	1PG1T(8)-1G2DG2PG1T(24)
131001	GLOUCESTER(ZP)	GLOUCESTER	L	1G(7)-3G1DG3PG(33)
201001	BATH(ZP)	STOOP MEMORIAL GROUND	W	5PG(15)-1PG1T(8)
281001	CASTRES OLYMPIQUE(HECP)	STOOP MEMORIAL GROUND	L	2G1PG(17)-2G5PG2T(39)
031101	CASTRES OLYMPIQUE(HECP)	CASTRES	L	1G2PG1T(18)-3G1PG(24)
091101	NORTHAMPTON(ZP)	NORTHAMPTON	D	1G2PG(13)-1G2PG(13)
161101	SARACENS(ZP)	STOOP MEMORIAL GROUND	W	4G5PG(43)-2PG(6)
231101	LEICESTER(ZP)	LEICESTER	L	1DG5PG(18)-2G3PG(23)

011201	MANCHESTER SALE(ZP)	STOOP MEMORIAL GROUND	L	1G3PG(16)-2G3PG(23)
091201	LEEDS(ZP)	HEADINGLEY	L	1G2PG1T(18)-2G3PG(23)
151201	MANCHESTER SALE(PC6)	SALE	W	2G1DG5PG(32)-1G2DG4PG(25)
221201	LEICESTER(ZP)	STOOP MEMORIAL GROUND	L	1G3PG1T(21)-5G1PG(38)
301201	SARACENS(ZP)	VICARAGE ROAD	L	1G1DG5PG(25)-3G1PG3T(39)
050102	MUNSTER(HECP)	THOMOND PARK, LIMERICK	L	2G1PG(17)-3G5PG3T(51)
120102	BRIDGEND(HECP)	STOOP MEMORIAL GROUND	W	3PG4T(29)-2G1DG1PG1T(25)
190102	LEICESTER(PCQF)	STOOP MEMORIAL GROUND	W	1G5PG(22)-2G2PG(20)
260102	NORTHAMPTON(ZP)	STOOP MEMORIAL GROUND	L	1G3PG(16)-1G1DG3PG1T(24)
050202	NATAL SHARKS	STOOP MEMORIAL GROUND	L	1G2PG(13)-4G1PG(31)
090202	BATH(ZP)	BATH	L	1DG2PG(9)-1G1DG1PG1T(18)
230202	GLOUCESTER(ZP)	STOOP MEMORIAL GROUND	L	2PG(6)-1G2PG1T(18)
090302	LONDON IRISH(PCSF)	STOOP MEMORIAL GROUND	L	3G2PG(27)-2G6PG(32)
160302	NEWCASTLE(ZP)	STOOP MEMORIAL GROUND	W	2G3PG2T(33)-1G2DG2PG(19)
310302	BRISTOL(ZP)	BRISTOL	L	2G1PG2T(27)-5G1PG1T(43)
140402	LONDON IRISH(ZP)	READING	D	3DG3PG(18)-1G2PG1T(18)
260402	LONDON WASPS(ZP)	LOFTUS ROAD	L	2PG(6)-1G2DG1PG(16)
030502	LEEDS(ZP)	STOOP MEMORIAL GROUND	W	3G1DG2PG2T(40)-1G1DG2PG(16)
120502	MANCHESTER SALE(ZP)	SALE	L	2PG1T(11)-5G1T(40)

England were back in Argentina in June 2002 for a very short tour with a match against Argentina A and one test against the Pumas. The warm-up was lost but the one that counted was won by 26-18. Our current player in the side was Alex Codling, Nick Walshe had played for us and Andy Gomarsall would join us in the future.

It had been decided to introduce a Harlequin Hall of Fame and the Commission who would decide who got in comprised Chris Wright, Colin Herridge and Andy Mullins. They had a set of criteria which stated that you had to have played over a certain number of games, scored over so many points, gained an international cap and so on. The trouble was that certain players were admitted when they didn't meet the criteria and so, the whole scheme was immediately devalued as a concept. The insistence on having an international cap was a big flaw as this should not apply to a club hall of fame. It should be about rewarding real servants of the Club. Generally, every two years new players were inducted although this hasn't happened since 2012. The complete list so far is as follows:-

2002
John Birkett, Bob Hiller, Adrian Stoop, Wavell Wakefield and Peter Winterbottom
2004
Ricky Bartlett, Douglas Lambert, David Marques and Brian Moore
2006
David H. Cooke, Clifford Gibbs and Colin Payne
2008
Jason Leonard and Grahame Murray
2010
Will Carling, Earle Kirton and Ronald Poulton
2012
Arthur Cipriani, Will Greenwood and Bob Lloyd

Richard Hill left for Newport-Gwent Dragons where he would take charge of coaching the backs. He resumed his partnership with Leigh Jones, who had been appointed the Welsh club's head coach. They had spent two successful years together at Ebbw Vale. Paul Turner came in to replace him from Gloucester. John Kingston had a blood clot removed from his brain at the beginning of August. He remained in post, visited pre-season training and thankfully went on to make a full recovery. The year end accounts for 30th June 2003 revealed a loss of £964,390 and the company changed its name to Blue Sky Leisure Limited on 6th November 2002. We had a new captain, he was Andre Vos from South Africa but he wouldn't arrive until November. In the meantime, Jason Leonard would act as interim captain.

At the beginning of the season, we again chose to play two friendly fixtures. This time we had Glasgow Warriors on 9th August and Beziers five days later. Both matches were away; one was won and one was lost. In the first, newcomer Nathan Williams scored our first points of the season with a try after seven minutes. Next Matt Powell ran through unopposed after good work from Diprose and with Burke continuing his good form from the previous two seasons, we led 14-0. After the break, Tiatia went over for Slemen to convert before Williams produced an excellent run out of defence followed by a nice chip ahead for Moore to kick on over the line and score. The home side did get a goal near the end but 26-7 was a good start. Notable new arrivals making their debuts in this one were Pablo Cardinali who would make just 8 appearances and was in the process of winning 5 caps for Argentina, Laurent Gomez (48 appearances), Simon Miall (110), Ugo Monye who would make 256 1st XV appearances, win 14 England caps and 2 for the British and Irish Lions and Nathan Williams who would make 32 appearances.

At Beziers, we competed for the Bacchus Trophy D'Or on Wednesday 14th August. Paul Burke and Quesada exchanged penalties before Nathan Williams went over for a try. Quesada landed a couple of penalties but Greenwood gathered a lob from Burke to score under the posts (Burke converted) and we led 15-9. Right on half time, Escalle got over after a run from Mignoni and Quesada's conversion gave the home side a one point lead at the break. Shvelidze and Aue (after intercepting Kai Horstmann's pass) got further tries and the boot of Quesada added seven points (he added a penalty earlier in the half) to kill the game. We did get a late penalty try which Ben Gollings converted but it was too late to alter the outcome.

Our first outing in the Premiership was at home against Gloucester on 31st August. We began brightly and Powell and Burke combined to send Moore over after 10 minutes. Burke converted and added a penalty after Gloucester's Mark Cornwell had been sin binned for killing the ball. We failed to capitalise on this and didn't score again until a Burke penalty two minutes into the second half. In the intervening period, Henry Paul kicked a penalty and converted tries from Garvey and Paramore. We fought back and a Burke penalty (67 minutes) and dropped goal (75 minutes) gave us a 19-18 lead. Disaster came in the shape of Woodman as he ran 20 metres to go under the posts after weak tackling from Gomez and Bemand. Mercier added the conversion and, despite five minutes of injury time, we couldn't regain the lead.

Leicester came next and we were on the road up the M1 to one of our least successful venues. A couple of Slemen penalties in the first half completed our scoring for the entire game. The Champions managed two Stimpson penalties and a Back try which Stimpson converted. Slemen missed two penalties and Gollings missed with a couple of dropped goal attempts. These had to go over if we were to win at Welford Road. We had a period of 20 minutes where we were on top but couldn't score any points. Leicester came back strongly and Booth, Hamilton (converted by Stimpson) and Stimpson added tries to leave us trailing 6-30 at the end. It was getting to be a familiar story now; two defeats in two games and we were in bottom place with one point. Making their debuts in this game were Viliame Satala who came on as a sub and would play 20 times (he was on his way to gaining 29 caps for Fiji) and Marco Caputo (he had won his 5 Australian caps back in 1996 and 1997); he came off the bench for his only appearance for us.

Rejuvenated Leeds visited the Stoop next (they had already beaten Leicester) and it was nip and tuck for the first 77 minutes. Burke got us in front with a penalty, converted Viliame Satala's try and dropped a goal. Between his first penalty and the try, Leeds scored ten points to leave it close at the half way stage. The Tykes went back in front when their second group of ten points was exactly the same as the first (Scarborough try, van Straaten conversion and a real monster penalty from 60 metres). Burke and van Straaten exchanged penalties and, when Greenwood got our second try, Burke's conversion tied it up at 23-23 with ten minutes to go. Van Straaten kicked his fourth penalty with three minutes left and then our scrum completely disintegrated which enabled Mather to crash over for van Straaten to convert. We were in shock for the five minutes of injury time. Although not quite a crisis, the ease with which we had conceded late tries in our two home games was extremely disturbing.

London Irish were our next opponents at the Stoop and surely we wouldn't lose again, would we? On the Thursday before, Will Greenwood's baby son Frederick had sadly passed away and Nick Greenstock (who had gone part time to concentrate on his job outside rugby) had been called into the side. Paul Burke was again in great form and three penalties from him in the first half and a try from Moore enabled us to turn around with a 14-6 advantage. Everitt landed his third penalty five minutes into the second half but Ben Gollings got a try and Slemen dropped a goal (after replacing Burke). Everitt plugged away and a fourth success made it 22-12 but the turning point came when Greenstock intercepted his chip to the corner and ran 80 metres for the match clinching score. Slemen converted and, although the Irish pulled seven points back, we were pressing for the four try bonus at the end. We couldn't get it and had to settle for four points but it was our first Premiership win of the season. As a result of this, we moved into tenth place above Newcastle and Bristol.

For our final game in September, we travelled to Heywood Road for a Friday night fixture against the Sharks. The only worry we had was that when Paul Burke didn't play, who was going to kick the goals? Pat Sanderson opened the scoring when Gollings put him over for a try after 6 minutes. Hodgson got a penalty but a dropped goal from Nathan Williams and a penalty by Slemen gave us a lead at half time. On 35 minutes, Ace Tiatia was sent to the bin following a late tackle on the Sale fly half and just before he returned, Hodgson went over and converted his own try to cut the deficit to one point. After a number of replacements had been made, Cueto charged over to give the home side the lead for the first time. Hodgson converted and there were fifteen minutes to go. Luke Sherriff came on to replace Tani Fuga and quickly scored from a forward drive. We were already four minutes into injury time; it all rested on the conversion. It was given to Slemen (who had already missed three out of four) and he failed miserably. There was still time for Hodgson to drop a goal but we still had a losing bonus point. This was another game we should have wrapped up long before the end and it took our games without a win on the road to 15 (12 losses and 3 draws).

The following week, the Falcons came to the Stoop and we welcomed Greenwood, Duncombe and Codling back to the side. Right from the start, Leonard recovered Slemen's kick-off and the fly half's chip to the corner ended with Sanderson scoring after just 41 seconds after Newcastle had fumbled. Slemen and Wilkinson twice exchanged penalties before Gomez was driven over following a rare mistake from the Falcons fly half. Slemen converted this and added a penalty to make it 21-6 and we were in charge. A minute into the second half, the now customary trip to the bin for Tiatia allowed the Falcons to add seven points to their total. The difference here was that when Newcastle lost Vyvyan to the bin, we ran amok. Diprose, Greenwood and Duncombe got tries and Nathan Williams added a couple of conversions to take us to forty points. Near the end, Noon went over for Wilkinson to convert but Fuga scored our sixth try and Gollings ensured the gap stayed at 24 points with the conversion.

Our visit to Caerphilly in the first round, first leg of the Parker Pen Challenge Cup saw us post our highest score of the season. Caerphilly took the lead after two minutes when Richards kicked a penalty. Once we had taken the lead from them when Nathan Williams went through a minute later, that was effectively that. Williams converted his and further efforts from Moore, Duncombe, Jim Evans and Moore again to take us to 35 before the break. Caerphilly had managed ten more points but they were well behind. The second period was pretty much a copy of the first and tries came at regular intervals through Jewell, Sherriff, Duncombe, Gollings, a penalty try and Miall (Williams converted all but the first and last to take his tally to 23 points). In reply, the Welsh got a try from Howells which Richards converted. At 73-20, this was our biggest ever win in Wales and we had one foot in the next round.

The 2nd leg was played the following week and, although the score was a lot closer, we still ran out winners. Ben Gollings started us off with a try on 80 seconds which Williams converted before Gareth Jones got one for the visitors. Seb Fitzgerald and Gollings with his second (both converted by Williams) scored either side of a second one for Jones and on 35 minutes, Rouse got their third which Chiltern converted. It was 21-17 at the break and, when Williams scored a minute into the second period, Caerphilly actually led on the day. Jim Evans regained the lead for us, Williams converted and added a penalty to take us clear although Vunipola scored near the end to make it 31-27. We progressed through to the second round with an aggregate of 104-47.

Adverse weather conditions forced the postponement of our Premiership clash with Bristol at the Memorial Stadium so our next game was a home league encounter with Bath on 2nd November. Andre Vos finally arrived to take his place in the team (although Leonard was still captain) and Will Greenwood played at fly half due to injuries. He had last played there eight seasons before. In extremely wet conditions, neither side performed well and we had Bill Davison sent to the sin bin after 15 minutes. Barkley landed a penalty before Davison came back but when Bath lost Emms to the bin, Greenwood, (converted by Williams) and Moore ran in tries to give us a nice lead.

Barkley nibbled away at that with two penalties in the third quarter but Williams got one of his own and finished Bath off with another three minuted from the end of normal time. Nick Duncombe was starting to really impress, he already had two England caps and was looking good to be our number one scrum half for a very long time as he was still only 20 years old. Vos had captained South Africa and won 33 caps between 1999 and 2001, he would play at least 139 times for us.

At Vicarage Road, we were looking to improve our record of one win in five visits against Saracens. It didn't look good as we leaked points in the first quarter of an hour. Andy Goode kicked two penalties and converted a try from Bracken (he failed with Horan's) to leave us 18-0 down. Nathan Williams got a penalty back before Ben Gollings was wrongly adjudged to have jumped at Winnan when going for a high ball. It was a terrible decision by the touch judge and it cost us another eight points. When Gollings returned it was 3-26 but Matt Moore (put in by Satala) closed the gap into injury time. Flatman was put in the bin two minutes after the interval and, during his stay, Andre Vos got his first try for the Club which Williams converted. Nick Duncombe went over, Williams converted but Goode kept Sarries in front with another penalty. Moore got his second and, although Williams couldn't convert, he landed a penalty with four minutes remaining to put us, incredibly, in front by one point (30-29). Into injury time, Kershaw went over after a run by Horan and Goode converted to take the spoils. At four tries apiece, we did take two points but it should have been five.

Wasps came to the Stoop on 17th November in fourth place and eight points ahead of us. We welcomed back Paul Burke after injury and his boot was quickly showing us what we had missed. Although King had put the visitors in front on four minutes with a penalty, Burke soon equalised, put us in front with his second, converted Nick Greenstock's try and dropped a goal. We even survived Scott Bemand being sin binned without conceding any points. He had replaced Duncombe after only four minutes when the youngster had injured a hamstring. King nailed two penalties in the third quarter but Burke crucially got one and when Greening went over in the corner, it was 19-14 to us with 18 minutes to go. Four minutes later, Burke got his fourth penalty and, deep into injury time charged down Abbott's attempted clearance to score a try. We had survived Fuga's ten minute spell in the bin as well to run out 27-14 winners. We were starting to play a decent brand of rugby but we needed to start winning some away games. We would not qualify for the play-offs if we didn't. This was Greenstock's final appearance for us, he had scored 95 points (19 tries) during his time at the Club.

A good place to start would be Franklin's Gardens. After Grayson had opened the scoring with a penalty, Tony Diprose was driven over from a five metre line out and Burke converted. From this point a series of bad decisions and sloppy play by the team cost us dearly and we were well beaten by the end. Grayson landed a couple of penalties and Reihana and Sturgess (converted by Grayson) crossed for tries. In the second period, Beal scored at the start and end and Grayson converted both to make it 35-7.

The return with Saracens came only three weeks after our first meeting and proved to be just as exciting and high scoring as that one. Burke was influential as usual and he exchanged two penalties and a conversion with Goode. Haughton got the Sarries try and Fuga scored ours to leave the teams locked at 13-13. We appeared to have taken control in the third quarter when Burke kicked a penalty and converted a great try from Nathan Williams after he combined in a 50 metre move with Vos. Goode then converted his own try but another Burke penalty and the conversion of Matt Moore's 45 metre interception score put us 33-20 ahead. Leonard was put in the bin and we tried to hit the self-destruct button. Castaignede scored for Goode to convert but a minute after Leonard's return, Burke got his fifth penalty to give us a 36-27 lead with four minutes of injury time to go. A minute later we gifted

Goode a try but he couldn't convert and we held on. This was our sixth home win on the trot in all competitions which set us up nicely for the visit of Stade Français in the Parker Pen Challenge Cup second round, first leg.

On an absolutely freezing afternoon, we were well on top for the first 29 minutes and looked like taking the lead when Will Greenwood broke through. The wrong option was taken, the ball went loose and was hacked upfield by Stade and eventually, Gomes went over for the first score. Dominguez converted and added a penalty right on half time. When Liebenberg thundered over four minutes into the second half, Dominguez converted and it was 17-0 to the visitors. Playing into the gale, we had no chance and the only further scores were penalties from Liebenberg and Dominguez. This was the first time we had failed to score since March 1993 and the first time at home since October 1980.

Given our away form, it was a foregone conclusion that we would be going out the following week in Paris...... and so it proved. Burke came back into the team and kicked two penalties in each half. Tiatia visited the bin for stamping and Dominguez kicked five penalties and converted tries by Lombard and Moni. A half time score of 16-6 had become 29-12 by the end to make the aggregate total 12-55 against us.

On 21st December, we entertained Leeds Tykes at the Stoop in the 6th round of the Powergen Cup. Braam van Straaten was back again and he put over two penalties in the first ten minutes to open up a lead. Paul Burke pulled three points back but Scarborough ran 45 metres for the first try of the tie; van Straaten converted and we were ten points down. A minute into injury time, Burke got his second penalty and his third arrived fifteen minutes after the break. Four minutes later, Mark Evans made five changes and brought on Keith Wood, Jon Dawson, Jim Evans, Ace Tiatia and Rob Jewell. This tactic proved crucial and, after Burke had cut the deficit to one point with his fourth penalty, eight minutes remained. As time expired, Wood won a loose ball, Tiatia drove on, the ball was passed along the line and Greenwood released Gollings for a clear run to the corner. Five minutes of injury time followed but we had done enough. This was Wood's final appearance having scored 113 points (22 tries and 1 dropped goal); he had captained the side 41 times, made 14 appearances off the bench and also received one yellow card.

Our final game of the year was a visit to Bath. We had to start winning some away Premiership games as this would hit us hard eventually if we didn't. Another poor start and, after Barkley and Burke had kicked penalties, Maggs got a try and Barkley added the conversion and two more penalties to send Bath in at the interval with a lead of 16-3. Neither side was in particularly impressive form and two more penalties from Burke gave us hope before Tindall got a try (which Barkley converted) with 13 minutes playing time left. We played most of these in the Bath half but couldn't get anywhere even when Voyce was sin binned late on.

We began 2003 in seventh place with a more or less 50% record – W5 L6. More importantly, we were nine points clear of the relegation spot. Paul Burke started us off against Bristol with a penalty either side of a David Rees try before Ben Gollings was put over by Burke who converted. Our lead was cut to one point when Gibson went over for Contepomi to convert after 50 minutes. Burke's third penalty stretched the lead to four points but a second try from Rees gave our visitors the lead for the first time. Burke had kicked us back in front by the time Greenwood pounced after Daniel failed to tidy up his chip and chase. Burke converted and 26-17 was a fair result. Unbeknown to everyone, Nick Duncombe had appeared in his last game of rugby. He had scored 20 points (4 tries) in his tragically short career. We had a three week break until our next game as our involvement in European competition had been cut short by Stade Français.

The Powergen Cup draw had, for the third year in a row paired us with Leicester. As with 2002, we met in the quarter finals and, as in all three, the tie was played at the Stoop. This time, there was to be no fairy tale ending although Burke's four penalties kept us in it. Moody and Tiatia each spent time in the bin for different offences but it was tries by Murphy and Moody that eventually proved the difference. Stimpson landed a penalty in the first half to help the Tigers to a 13-9 lead. In the second, he added two more with the second coming a minute from the end. Although we were never beaten until then, crucial mistakes cost us dearly. Leicester did have another try disallowed when Tournaire got penalised for foul play but, in the end, it was the Tigers who marched on.

The return with Newcastle was seen as an opportunity for us to cement our position in the playoff places. Jonny Wilkinson gave Newcastle the lead after 12 minutes with his first penalty but Burke replied immediately. Wilkinson's second on 26 minutes began a funny five minute spell which saw Fuga (converted by Burke) for us and Grimes (converted by Wilkinson) for the Falcons get tries. There was no further scoring in the first half but, when play resumed, Newcastle scored two tries in the third quarter and a third after 74 minutes to kill us off. Vyvyan, Noon and Stephenson scored them and Wilkinson converted the first two. Our usual charge at the end saw Fuga go over for his and our second try which Williams converted to make it 17-32. Newcastle stayed bottom but they were now only two points behind Bath.

Three days later, we had our second fixture with the Natal Sharks. The injury situation meant that Mark Evans was unable to pick seventeen of the squad. Even so, we gave the Sharks a game for seventy minutes. After going behind to a Terblanche dropped goal on 8 minutes, Tani Fuga chipped over the defence for Sherriff to score and, just before the break, Williams ran 60 metres to score our second try. He converted (as he had Sheriff's) and we were 14-3 ahead and looking good. This increased by five points when Williams scored again on 56 minutes. Slowly, the Sharks came back and tries followed from Terblanche, James and van Biljon (plus a conversion from Terblanche) to take them into a 20-19 lead. Loubscher added another two before the end and a conversion of the first by Kruger left the final margin at thirteen points. James Hayter made his debut as a sub, he would make 55 appearances. David Slemen played for the last time having scored 57 points (1 try, 3 dropped goals, 11 penalties and 5 conversions).

Against the Sharks from Manchester four days later, we bizarrely decided to narrow the pitch by twelve feet to try and contain their backs. If it worked, it's a good job because, as it was, we conceded 45 points! We were never in it as Sale slowly built their lead. Thirteen points in the first half became twenty three after 54 minutes. We then made four substitutions but the Sharks added another fifteen points. When Tiatia made his now almost weekly visit to the bin, Hanley scored Sale's fifth try which former Quin Nick Walshe converted to complete the scoring. Mark Evans stated afterwards that, if we played like that for the rest of the season, we wouldn't win a game and would go down.

We now had a three week break until our re-arranged visit to Bristol so the squad was allowed to get away. Nathan Williams and Nick Duncombe headed to Lanzarote for a week's training. Sadly, Nick contracted sepsis (a form of blood poisoning), was rushed to hospital in Puerto del Carmen and died from cardiac and respiratory failure on 15th February. He was only 21 years old and it was so tragic for him to leave us without really confirming his massive potential. The hole he left may never be filled. He had joined us from RGS High Wycombe in the summer of 2001 and made his England debut against Scotland on 2nd February 2002 when he replaced Bracken. He also competed in the Commonwealth games sevens squad and had represented England at U16 and U19 level. Remarkably, he had survived a broken neck whilst representing England schools in April 2000. As a mark of respect, the number 9 jersey was retired for the rest of the season. All shirts had the name Duncombe on them (for the Bristol game) and a small ND logo on the front to commemorate young Nick. A statue of him now stands in the north-west corner at the Stoop in his memory.

It was a terribly sombre squad that took the field at the Memorial Stadium where a minute's silence was held. For the fifth time in the last eight visits to Bristol, the game saw more than fifty points scored. Pichot got the scoreboard moving with a try after two minutes which Contepomi converted. Contepomi kicked three penalties and Nelson and Brown scored tries to take them to twenty nine. Burke had landed a penalty and converted Luger's try so we had ten. Jamie Williams had gifted Luger his try and Higgins volleyed the ball between his own posts into the arms of Will Greenwood who scored. Burke converted but any thoughts of a comeback were shattered when Gibson scored a brace of tries (the first converted by Contepomi) to make it 41-17 after 55 minutes. We were assured of a try bonus point when Diprose and Gollings scored for Burke to convert. A defensive error contributed to Pichot's second try which Contepomi converted before a last, desperate effort saw Nathan Williams get our fifth try. Burke converted and landed a penalty with the last kick of the game to get us our losing bonus point as well. A game that contained 89 points ended 48-41 to the Shoguns. With these two points, we were five points clear of the relegation spot and our next game at the Madejski Stadium would go a long way to deciding our fate with six matches left. Ceri Jones came on as a sub for the first of 252 appearances and would be a real stalwart over this and the following eight seasons; he would also win 2 caps for Wales in 2007. Mel Deane also appeared for the first of 102 games. Ending their Quins careers were Pablo Cardinali and Alex Codling (he had scored 5 points (1 try) and made 22 appearances as a substitute).

On 16th March, a record crowd for London Irish of 18,585 turned up to see who would still be in relegation trouble afterwards. This was a nervous encounter and our lineout was a disaster at the beginning and when Everitt put the Irish in front after nine minutes with a penalty, we needed to keep calm. Ceri Jones and Jon Dawson sorted the scrum out and our pack started to gain the upper hand. On 27 minutes, when a planned move went wrong, Will Greenwood found himself in front of the posts with two men to beat, he did and we were in front. Burke's conversion ensured a 7-3 lead at half time. Nothing was going right for the Irish and they were making mistakes costlier than ours. Burke injured his leg and left the field just after Williams had stretched our lead with a penalty. When he repeated the feat fourteen minutes later, we were ten points up and starting to believe. Mapletoft pulled a penalty back for the Irish but Williams slotted his third penalty at the end of six minutes of injury time to give us a 16-6 victory. It was our first away win in the league since 17th March 2001 – almost two years to the day. As a result, we moved nine points clear of the Irish in bottom spot with five games left.

The matches were not coming thick and fast and we had a three week wait for our trip to Headingley. This proved to be another tight evening which was decided at the death. In the first half, van Straaten and Burke each landed two penalties with the difference being a try by Hill (converted by van Straaten). We came back strongly and Luger got a try, Burke converted and added two penalties to put us six points up with half an hour to play. Van Straaten got his third penalty but Burke dropped a goal from the 22 to restore our six point advantage. The turning point of the match came when Luger was controversially sin binned on 81 minutes for offside. Leeds attacked again and Albanese was put away by Davies for a try just 20 seconds from the end. Van Straaten slotted the conversion and we had gone down by one point (22-23). At least it moved us nearer safety and we were now eight points clear of bottom club Bath.

Our nineteenth Premiership clash was against Leicester at the Stoop and finally, the real Quins turned up. The first half saw Stimpson kick three penalties against a try from Ben Gollings. Paul Burke landed a penalty and there was a point in it. On 56 minutes, yes, you've guessed it "Dusty" was in the bin again (Tiatia was now being compared to the star of an old ITV programme called 3-2-1; he was a dustbin called Dusty Bin). When would this guy ever learn? Luckily, the Tigers could not capitalise on this and the next score came from Burke's boot to put us in front. We had built up a real head of steam and for once we were taking the Tigers apart. We had the wind in our favour and Burke used it to put over another penalty and, a minute later, he settled it with a dropped goal. Full time

17-9 and it looked like we were finally safe and heading into the play-offs. After nine successive home defeats in the league, we had finally beaten Leicester. At the bottom, Bristol were now in the relegation spot.

At Gloucester the following week, we were back to our old selves. In the first half, Burke got two penalties and in the second, Fuga grabbed a late try but we were well beaten again. Gloucester had scored four tries in a 29-11 victory and, in the process had claimed the top spot. They would now play the winners of the second and third place play-off. Viliame Satala came off the bench for his final appearance having scored 5 points (1 try) during his short spell at the Club.

Our last home game in the regular season was against Northampton on Friday 2nd May. Yet again, we relied on Paul Burke's kicking to keep us in touch and he did a first class job. He got two penalties in the first half but Grayson got one and Dawson converted a penalty try to give the Saints a four point lead. Sturgess and Beal grabbed tries either side of another Burke penalty and with Dawson converting both, we now trailed by fifteen points. When we were awarded a penalty try (converted by Burke) and the fly half added a dropped goal, it was 19-24 and four of the eight minutes of extra time had elapsed. Right at the end, Mark Tucker went over in the corner to deny us a bonus point and Dawson's fourth conversion made it worse. Tucker would do much worse to us in 2005. Bruce Starr came on as a sub for his final appearance, he had made 27 appearances off the bench and received one yellow card.

Going into the last round of matches, we had a trip to Adams Park to play second placed Wasps. Bath were bottom but it was so tight, any one of Saracens, Bristol, London Irish or Bath could go down. We had to concentrate on winning to guarantee our play-off place. Burke put us in front with a penalty before Dowd scored a try and King converted for Wasps. Chris Bell went to the sin bin for kicking the ball out of a ruck and King put over the penalty. Then, Ugo Monye latched onto Burke's kick and went round Logan and van Gisbergen to score our first try. Waters then did the same to Monye and Logan scored to give the home side a 15-8 advantage at the break. King stretched the Wasps lead with a penalty but we were not to be denied and Fuga and Monye sent Powell over before Monye again collected a Burke cross-kick and scooted over. Both conversions from Burke put us four points ahead. King pulled three points back with another penalty but Burke dropped a goal to give us a 25-21 win. It was their first defeat in twelve matches and our second double of the season. Bristol finished bottom and were relegated to National Division 1.

Our opponents in the play-off semi-final would be Leicester (who finished fourth). The first leg was played at the Stoop on Wednesday 14th May. We carried on where we had left off on 19th April after a penalty from Stimpson had put the Tigers in front after 20 minutes. Straight away, Fuga scored a try and Mel Deane got another on 26 minutes. Burke converted both and slotted a penalty to put us into a commanding lead of 17-3 at the break. Burke then put over a penalty and dropped a goal either side of Stimpson's second penalty and our lead had grown to 23-6. At this point, West, Garforth and Johnson came on for Leicester and the tide began to turn. Murphy went over for Stimpson to convert and they were back in it. Burke's third penalty gave us hope but eight points in the last nine minutes pulled Leicester to within three points and, with a trip to Welford Road to follow, we were as good as out. Unfortunately, we had blown it, the Tigers had been there for the taking at 23-6 and another score then would probably have sealed our passage to the final. As it was, we would have to try and defend our slim three point advantage.

For the fifth time in one season, we met Leicester and we started well enough the following Sunday but eventually ran out of steam. Burke got a penalty and Monye scorched in on an arcing 65 metre run for a try which Burke converted to put us 10-3 up after 25 minutes. We had already lost Andre Vos with a shoulder injury but when Rudzki injured his ankle in the second half, with him went our chances. At that stage, we were 21-10 down but Paul Burke got a penalty to narrow the aggregate gap to just five points. A late try from Skinner helped the home side to a 51-39 overall win. Our season was over. Making their final appearances in this one were Ben Gollings (as a sub for the fourteenth time), he had scored 178 points (23 tries, 1 dropped goal, 8 penalties and 18 conversions), received one yellow card and made two trips to the sin bin, Dan Luger who had scored 185 points (37 tries), Matt Powell who had scored 20 points (4 tries) and suffered two sin-binnings (one of which was rescinded) and Nathan Williams who had scored 104 points (7 tries, 1 dropped goal, 8 penalties and 21 conversions).

This had been the saddest season ever and the team had done well to get through it all. However, we still performed badly for most of the time and a vast improvement would be needed in 2003/04. Our playing record in the league (including play-off games) was P24 W10 L14 F500 A611 Pts42 (BP – 1TB 5LB) Pos 7th. We had improved our position by two places and had won twice as many games as the previous season. Overall, our record was P33 W14 L19 F712 A827. Again, an improvement on 2001/02 but that wasn't really difficult. Matt Moore again finished top of the tries with 9 and Paul Burke headed the rest for the third season in a row with 257 points (1 try, 8 dropped goals, 58 penalties, 27 conversions). Tony Diprose and Nathan Williams only missed one game of the 33 played, Bill Davison appeared in 30 and Tani Fuga came in next on 28.

2002/03

090802	GLASGOW WARRIORS	GLASGOW	W	3G1T(26)-1G(7)
140802	BEZIERS	BEZIERS	L	2G1PG1T(22)-3G4PG(33)
310802	GLOUCESTER(ZP)	STOOP MEMORIAL GROUND	L	1G1DG3PG(19)-2G2PG1T(25)
070902	LEICESTER(ZP)	LEICESTER	L	2PG(6)-2G2PG2T(30)
140902	LEEDS(ZP)	STOOP MEMORIAL GROUND	L	2G1DG2PG(23)-3G4PG(33)
210902	LONDON IRISH(ZP)	STOOP MEMORIAL GROUND	W	1G1DG3PG2T(29)-1G4PG(19)
270902	SHARKS(ZP)	SALE	L	1DG1PG2T(16)-2G1DG1PG(20)
051002	NEWCASTLE(ZP)	STOOP MEMORIAL GROUND	W	4G3PG2T(47)-2G3PG(23)
121002	CAERPHILLY(PPCC1R1L)	CAERPHILLY	W	9G2T(73)-2G2PG(20)
191002	CAERPHILLY(PPCC1R2L) (AGG 104-47)	STOOP MEMORIAL GROUND	W	4G1PG(31)-1G4T(27)
271002	BRISTOL(ZP)	BRISTOL	P	
021102	BATH(ZP)	STOOP MEMORIAL GROUND	W	1G2PG1T(18)-3PG(9)
101102	SARACENS(ZP)	VICARAGE ROAD	L	2G2PG2T(30)-2G4PG2T(36)

171102	LONDON WASPS(ZP)	STOOP MEMORIAL GROUND	W	1G1DG4PG1T(27)-3PG1T(14)
231102	NORTHAMPTON(ZP)	NORTHAMPTON	L	1G(7)-3G3PG1T(35)
301102	SARACENS(ZP)	STOOP MEMORIAL GROUND	W	3G5PG(36)-3G2PG1T(32)
071202	STADE FRANÇAIS(PPCC2R1L)	STOOP MEMORIAL GROUND	L	0-2G4PG(26)
141202	STADE FRANÇAIS(PPCC2R2L) (AGG 12-55)	PARIS	L	4PG(12)-2G5PG(29)
211202	LEEDS(PC6)	STOOP MEMORIAL GROUND	W	4PG1T(17)-1G2PG(13)
281202	BATH(ZP)	BATH	L	3PG(9)-2G3PG(23)
040103	BRISTOL(ZP)	STOOP MEMORIAL GROUND	W	2G4PG(26)-1G2T(17)
250103	LEICESTER(PCQF)	STOOP MEMORIAL GROUND	L	4PG(12)-3PG2T(19)
010203	NEWCASTLE(ZP)	NEWCASTLE	L	2G1PG(17)-3G2PG1T(32)
040203	NATAL SHARKS	STOOP MEMORIAL GROUND	L	2G1T(19)-2G1DG3T(32)
080203	SHARKS(ZP)	STOOP MEMORIAL GROUND	L	0-4G4PG1T(45)
020303	BRISTOL(ZP)	BRISTOL	L	5G2PG(41)-3G4PG3T(48)
160303	LONDON IRISH(ZP)	READING	W	1G3PG(16)-2PG(6)
040403	LEEDS(ZP)	HEADINGLEY	L	1G1DG4PG(22)-2G3PG(23)
190403	LEICESTER(ZP)	STOOP MEMORIAL GROUND	W	1DG3PG1T(17)-3PG(9)
260403	GLOUCESTER(ZP)	GLOUCESTER	L	2PG1T(11)-3G1PG1T(29)
020503	NORTHAMPTON(ZP)	STOOP MEMORIAL GROUND	L	1G1DG3PG(19)-4G1PG(31)
100503	WASPS(ZP)	ADAMS PARK	W	2G1DG1PG1T(25)-1G3PG1T(21)
140503	LEICESTER(ZWCSF1L)	STOOP MEMORIAL GROUND	W	2G1DG3PG(26)-2G3PG(23)
180503	LEICESTER(ZWCSF2L) (AGG 39-51)	LEICESTER	L	1G2PG(13)-2G3PG1T(28)

Before the World Cup, England ventured down under for a three match short tour to New Zealand and Australia in June 2003. They played the New Zealand Maori and won (23-9), then took on New Zealand in

Wellington and made the famous goal line stand with 13 men before notching up a famous victory by two points (15-13). Against Australia, it was a lot clearer as the future World Champions stormed to a 24-15 win. Greenwood and Leonard appeared in both tests, Gomarsall was a sub against New Zealand and Luger did the same against the Wallabies. Future Quins Stuart Abbott, Paul Volley and Mike Worsley were also in the party.

In the accounts for year ending 30th June 2004, it was revealed that a loss of just £487,219 had been made. It looked as though things were on the up but would the trend continue? On 14th November 2003, the Stoop had been revalued and instead of a valuation of £105,238, the new one was £4.35 million.

The 2003 World Cup in Australia during October and November provided a great chance for Clive Woodward's England to prove that they were the best. We had eighteen players this time representing ten countries but only Will Greenwood and Jason Leonard from England were current. Dan Luger (England), Norman Ligairi (Fiji) (he had made some second team appearances for us back in the 2001/02 season), Keith Wood (Ireland), Bruce Douglas (Scotland), Johnny Ngauamo (Tonga), Luke Gross and Jason Keyter (USA) and Gareth Llewellyn (Wales) had all left us, The remainder would appear over the coming years; Pablo Bouza (Argentina), Stuart Abbott and Andy Gomarsall (England), Maurie Fa'asavalu, Opeta Palepoi and Steve So'oialo (Samoa), De Wet Barry (South Africa) and Adam Jones (Wales). Despite the taunts from the Aussies about being a team of old men and other attempts at derailing the preparations, England got off to a great start with an 84-6 thrashing of Georgia followed by a crucial 25-6 win against South Africa. After a fright against Samoa, they recovered to win 35-22 and then scored over a hundred in the final pool match against Uruguay (111-13). Against Wales in the quarter final, England got off to a disastrous start and trailed 3-10 at half time. Woodward brought Catt on and he steadied the ship as the discipline of Wales let them down badly and Wilkinson kicked England back into the tie. Will Greenwood grabbed a try in the 28-17 win and they marched into the semi-final against France. In that game, the French scored the only try but Wilkinson kicked 24 points as the rain poured down to put England into the final. The host nation awaited and what a tense game it turned out to be. After an early try by Tuqiri, England came back and three Wilkinson penalties and a try by Robinson made it 14-5 at half time. As the England scrum was increasingly penalised by the referee (Andre Watson), Flatley put over three penalties to tie it up at 14-14 at the end of normal time. Jason Leonard came on and the penalties stopped. Wilkinson and Flatley exchanged penalties in extra time before Jonny Wilkinson delivered World Cup glory for England with a last minute dropped goal to make it 20-17. At long last, England were on top of the World!

Andre Vos would captain the side again this season and we hoped for an improvement on last year. We began with three friendlies this time against French, Welsh and English opposition. On 12th August, the team actually left for France and played two halves of forty minutes each against Montpellier and Beziers. Overall, the game (played on 13th) went in our favour 34-17 but is not counted in our official records for obvious reasons. On 19th August we travelled to play Castres Olympique in Millau. The Irish contingent was noticeable and Gavin Duffy (108 appearances and 10 Ireland caps between 2004 and 2009), Mel Deane, Andy Dunne (43) and Ben Willis (23) all started (all except Deane were making their debuts). Dunne got us off to a good start with a penalty and also got a second but Castres had got four themselves as well as a converted try to lead 19-6 at half time (despite Dourthe being sin binned for throwing a punch at Mel Deane). The only score in the second period was a Jon Dawson try which Dunne converted. Also appearing for the first time were George Harder who would go on to make 63 appearances (he had won his 4 Samoan caps back in 1995), Josh Taumalolo (14 appearances and was in the process of winning 26 caps for Tonga) and Mike Worsley who would appear 58 times and win 3 England caps.

Back in the UK, we then went to play Newport Gwent Dragons at Rodney Parade, Newport on 25th August. Matt Moore quickly got us on the scoreboard with a try before Lee Jarvis kicked three penalties for the home side to give them an interval lead. Simon Miall went to the sin bin but we came back strongly and Burke got two penalties to put us back in front. With Burke outscoring the home side's kicker 2-1 in penalties and converting Moore's second try, we came away with a 24-12 victory. This was our first ever victory at Rodney Parade; we had been trying on and off since 1883! Another Irishman made his debut in this one, he was Simon Keogh who would make 140 appearances over the next five seasons.

On 5th September, we played our only home friendly against Saracens. Paul Burke was proving again what a fantastic kicker he was and, in the first quarter, he put over two penalties and converted George Harder's try after eighteen minutes. Goode converted his own try for the visitors but it was all Quins as Monye went over, Burke landed another penalty and converted Harder's second. Goode closed the gap after four minutes of injury time to 28-10 with a penalty. The second half proved scoreless for us and, as Saracens only scored ten points, we ran out 28-20 winners. Overall, we had done well in our friendly fixtures and we now needed to transfer that form to our Premiership matches.

We couldn't have had a more difficult game to start with as the champions (Wasps) came to the Stoop. They quickly got into their stride when Voyce scored for van Gisbergen to convert after three minutes. Burke kicked a penalty and dropped a goal but van Gisbergen got four penalties between the ninth and thirty second minutes to leave us trailing 6-19. The Video Referee had been brought in this season for all televised matches and the first instance of its use was when Brian Campsall didn't allow an effort from Greening after 25 minutes. Of course, Tiatia went to the bin after 17 minutes and it looked like it was to be the same old story. Suddenly, in first half injury time, Burke slotted a penalty and Monye went in for Burke to convert. We were back in it and when Dunne finished off a breakout, Burke's conversion gave us the lead. Roiser restored the Wasps lead with another try but it only lasted four minutes. Burke was again on target with a penalty and when Monye (after an excellent chip by Burke and a good run from Reay) ran in, Burke's conversion took us nine points clear with eight minutes remaining. Eight minutes of injury time were played and the two noteworthy happenings were Luke Sherriff going to the sin bin and van Gisbergen getting his fifth penalty to earn Wasps a losing bonus point.

The Rotherham Titans were next at Millmoor. They were using the football ground as their ground at Clifton Lane was not up to Premiership status. They were the newly promoted team from National Division 1 and made a strong start when Lewis crashed over after 42 seconds but it took the video referee three minutes to decide it was a try. Strange converted and one of our old boys joined the fray when Jason Keyter came on as a replacement winger after eight minutes. We got on the board when Burke kicked a penalty on 12 minutes before we exploded into action with two tries in six minutes from Ugo Monye. Burke missed both conversions but succeeded with the next two when Harder and Tiatia scored within three minutes of each other near the end of the half. There was time for Strange to get a penalty but a healthy lead of 27-10 was our reward for some attacking play. Burke added a couple of penalties and Johnson sandwiched a try between to make the gap eighteen points. In the final ten minutes, Andy Dunne got a penalty and converted when Monye completed his hat-trick. Rotherham were in disarray and we were top of the Premiership after two games.

Our second home game was the visit of London Irish. This was a tight encounter which was decided not so much by a score but by a nice piece of gamesmanship by Ben Willis. Burke had kicked four penalties and Josh Taumalolo had dropped a goal to one penalty from Everitt so we led 15-3 after 66 minutes. Ryan Strudwick the Irish captain had broken through and was looking for support to finish the move off. When he heard shouts of

"Strudders, I'm inside you" he naturally assumed it to be one of his own so he passed. Imagine how he felt when Willis caught the ball and kicked it into touch! Some inside knowledge had helped us to our third straight victory (Willis knew Bob Casey of London Irish and he was always talking about Strudwick using his nickname). Thrower did score for Everitt to convert but it came too late and we played out the remaining eleven minutes to win 15-10. The biggest blow for us was the loss of Simon Miall after 22 minutes with ruptured knee ligaments – his season was over.

On 5th October, we went to Vicarage Road to play Saracens where we had lost narrowly on our last visit. Ceri Jones drove over after four minutes and Burke converted for a 7-0 lead. Andy Goode always seemed to reserve his best for us and he dropped a goal, kicked two penalties and converted Castaignede's try to make it 16-7. Haughton then went to the sin bin for killing the ball and Burke reduced the gap with a penalty. Goode and Burke then landed one each to make it 19-13 at the interval. Another burst of points from Saracens saw us fall nineteen points adrift. Goode kicked another two penalties and converted Haughton's try before converting Randell's after Burke had got his third penalty. At 39-16 with eighteen minutes left, it looked a lost cause but, we were not finished yet. The home side went down to fourteen men when Kershaw was sin binned and we were awarded a penalty try which Dunne converted on 76 minutes. When Chesney was also sent to the bin, we capitalised with a Keogh special converted by Dunne. Backchat caused the referee to award us a penalty on the half way line after the conversion and Dunne put the ball down and knocked it straight between the posts. Try as we might in the remaining two minutes, we couldn't get the winning score and had to settle for a losing bonus point (33-39). As a result, we dropped to second place behind Bath.

The visit of Newcastle to the Stoop was not a good game. It was mistake ridden and littered with penalties. Luckily for us, Paul Burke kicked six out of eight attempts (three in each half). Ben Gollings was the Falcons kicker and he got one in each half and went over for the only try of the game just before his captain (Mark Andrews) was sent off for a knee to the head of Pat Sanderson. With him went any chance Newcastle had of causing an upset of current form.

Our second home game out of a run of three was against Gloucester. In the first half an hour, we lost Fuga and Monye with knee injuries before Paul added to our woes with a penalty on 37 minutes. He doubled the lead (51 minutes) and made it 9-0 with 70 minutes gone. When Burke was replaced by Dunne, any chance of coming back seemed to go with him and so it proved. Dunne had a pass intercepted by Todd two minutes into injury time and Paul's conversion made it 16-0.

The Sharks visited on 25th October with Leeds old boy Braam van Straaten in their line-up and how we were glad to see him again......not! Paul Burke got three penalties in the first three quarters, van Straaten only put one over but converted tries from Cairns, Hanley and Cueto to leave us trailing 9-24. Our defence had crumbled and some inept tackling had contributed enormously to that. Bill Davison went to the sin bin but no points were scored during his time off the field. When he came back, van Straaten quickly added two penalties before Dunne (who had replaced Burke) lit up proceedings. He started moving the ball at pace and Simon Keogh and Andy Reay broke through for tries in the last five minutes. Dunne could only convert the first so we finished with no points for the second week running. In the space of four games we had gone from first to sixth place, nine points off the pace being set by Bath.

A trip up to Headingley to play Leeds on Friday 31st October was a must win after three defeats in four games. Andy Dunne started in place of Paul Burke and put over three penalties but three from Hodge made the scores level at the break. After Christophers went over for Hodge to convert, we scored twice in four minutes to go back in front.

First Dunne went in after selling the defence a dummy 15 metres out and then Bell kicked on from the half way line after Christophers had dropped a pass from Hodge. Dunne converted both and, right at the end of five minutes of injury time, Keogh intercepted a Dan Scarborough pass to run home from 60 metres out. Burke converted this after replacing Dunne and victory was ours.

Northampton came to the Stoop in good form and in second place; we were still sixth. This was a totally one-sided encounter for as long as it mattered. We literally blew the Saints away in the first half with tries from Monye, Sanderson and Fuga. Burke converted the first and last as well as adding three penalties to make it 28-0. Northampton pulled seven points back right on half time with Diprose in the sin bin but still made three changes at the break. It had little effect and Keogh got a brace of tries, Burke got another penalty and Dunne converted the second try. At 43-7 after 65 minutes, we could relax – but not too much. Fuga went to the bin and the Saints ran in two late tries which were converted by Drahm. With this big win, we shot back up into second place behind Bath.

It was up to Leeds again for another Friday fixture but this time, it was the Powergen Cup 6th round. On a wet and windy night, a crowd of just 1,238 saw us put in our worst performance of the season so far. Referee Wayne Barnes awarded the home side a penalty try after only five minutes when he deemed one of our players had deliberately obstructed a scoring pass from an offside position. This was converted, we came back strongly and Monye was denied a try by the referee deciding that crossing had taken place in the final build up. Leeds lost Ponton to the sin bin during a period of pressure on their line and Tony Diprose was penalised when a try seemed likely. Earlier in the second half, Monye had a try disallowed for a forward pass, Ross knocked over a penalty to make it 10-0 and we were in trouble. Burke and Ross exchanged penalties before another penalty on 74 minutes (this time by Dunne) turned out to be the last score of the tie. Deane and Taumalolo had chances to score but an inability to catch the ball cost us dearly. The final score of 13-6 put us out at the first stage for the first time since 1998.

On 22nd November, we went to Bath to play in a top two clash; we were eight points behind them. This game was a case of after the Lord Mayor's Show; how could it possibly compete with the events earlier in the day when Jonny Wilkinson had won the World Cup for England? After Barkley had put Bath in front with his first penalty, Pat Sanderson went over after a lineout move for Burke to convert. Two more Barkley penalties came either side of Lipman being sent off for kicking Sanderson after 33 minutes. In the second half, we couldn't make our advantage count and Barkley out-gunned Dunne 3-1 in the penalty stakes. It was so tight in the top half that this one loss sent us from second to sixth spot.

Our third meeting with Leeds in thirty days brought them to the Stoop for the return Premiership fixture. This was another dour game punctuated by penalties. In the first half, Dunne got two to one by Ross for the visitors. At half time, Clive Woodward (the victorious England coach) walked on to the pitch to rapturous applause. Back to business and Ross brought Leeds level with his second penalty before converting his own try after Rees had forced Duffy to fumble the ball. At this point, World Cup winner Jason Leonard came on for Jon Dawson – it was the biggest cheer of the day. Dunne and Ross had an exchange of penalties and we put enormous pressure on the Tykes line for most of the eight minutes of injury time. Although we probably might have had a penalty try on another day, this day was to be lost 9-16. At least we earned a losing bonus point. The three games against Leeds had seen them win two but the points for and against were even at 45 each.

Our European adventure for this season was in the Parker Pen Challenge Cup, our first round opponents were Spanish side Cetransa UEMC and Luke Sherriff captained the side in both legs. We played the first leg in the Pepe Rojo Stadium in Valladolid on Sunday 7th December. In the first half, we made light work of the Spanish with tries from Ceri Jones (2) and Kai Horstmann. Andy Dunne converted two and the only reply from Cetransa was a penalty from fly half Roque. The third quarter belonged entirely to the home side. Revilla got a try and Roque kicked a penalty and converted a penalty try to make it 19-18. Seven minutes later, the reinforcements came on in the shape of all seven of our replacements. Davison went to the sin bin after being on for a very short time but, when we were back to full strength, Bell (converted by Dunne) and Fuga wrapped things up to give us a thirteen point cushion for the return leg the following Saturday.

There was a little doubt about the result when Cetransa took the lead at the Stoop with a penalty by Roque. We struck back when James Hayter scored after 8 minutes to put us in front but we had to wait until the 29th minute for our next score. Tiatia put Harder over (this was his first game after the injury at Rotherham) and three more tries followed in quick succession after Garcia had been sin binned. Horstmann, Jewell and Keogh scoring, Dunne could only convert two of the five and we led 29-3. The second half was a procession of tries for us as the Spanish failed to register another point. Chris Bell, Andy Dunne, Gavin Duffy (2), Bell again and Ceri Jones got tries and Dunne converted two to make it 63-3 on the day and 94-21 on aggregate. We would now play one of the "lucky losers" in the 2nd round in January.

Six days before Christmas we played the Sharks at their new home, Edgeley Park in Stockport. Ceri Jones gave us an early lead with a try after three minutes; Andy Dunne converted and put over a penalty. Tony Diprose and Jon Dawson were both sent to the bin but, amazingly, Sale couldn't score during this spell. Baxendell got a try on 37 minutes that van Straaten converted but we had the final say in the first half with a great try. Will Greenwood put in a kick, the ball deflected off a Sharks player which put Jim Evans on side. The Sharks stopped and allowed Evans to pick up the ball and stride over from 25 metres out. Dunne converted to put us 17-7 ahead. Cueto scored for van Straaten to convert and when he added a penalty after 58 minutes, the scores were level. Dunne put Keogh in and converted before exchanging penalties with van Straaten to leave us seven points clear with eleven minutes to go. Right at the end of normal time, Cueto dived over in the corner and van Straaten's touchline conversion made it 27-27. It was rough justice on us after an excellent away performance.

A trip to Kingsholm on 27th December had to be won if we weren't to drop out of the top six. There was no score until 26 minutes when Will Greenwood scored for Dunne to convert. Simpson-Daniel got a try for Gloucester to make it 7-5 at half time. When Ceri Jones got our second and Dunne converted eight minutes in, it looked as though we were on our way to another win. Henry Paul landed two penalties before Jim Evans and Chris Forty were sent off for fighting. Woodman got Gloucester's second try on 65 minutes and Paul's conversion proved to be the difference as we could only manage three points through a Dunne penalty in time remaining. Gloucester went above us and we finished the year in seventh position.

A trip to the North East began our league campaign in 2004 and we were well placed to achieve a Heineken Cup spot for 2004/05 through our Premiership position or by winning the Parker Pen Challenge Cup. After Walder had got a penalty, Monye and Duffy scored tries to ease us into a nice lead. The Falcons came back and Noon scored for Walder to convert. However, Dunne had converted Duffy's try and his penalty enabled us to go in with a five point lead. Jim Evans stretched our lead with another try which Dunne converted before Taione (converted by Walder) and Stephenson got tries to make it 22-22 with twelve minutes left. Five minutes into injury time, Walder dropped a goal and the Falcons thought they had done enough. Four minutes later, Ceri Jones was driven over for the match winner and the conversion by substitute Adrian Jarvis put the icing on the cake of a five point victory (he was making the first of at least 79 appearances).

The win at Newcastle set us up nicely for our two leg 2nd round Parker Pen Challenge Cup tie against Montauban. The first leg was played away at the Parc de Sport de Sapiac. Montauban were struggling this season in the French Championship but they still had to be beaten. Paul Burke returned from injury in top form and he started the ball rolling with a penalty. Ace Tiatia scored our first try which Burke converted before the French got on the scoreboard with a penalty. Ugo Monye then struck a double blow and Greenwood added a fourth after 38 minutes. Burke put over the conversion to Monye's tries and we were coasting at 29-3. Mel Deane was in on the action and when Burke added his fifth conversion to Sanderson's try, we had a lead we surely couldn't lose in the second leg. A late try from Beyret narrowed the gap to 35 points.

As with the first round, the 2nd leg was played immediately. Ten of our first choice team were rested in readiness for the expected quarter final tie the following weekend. The decision by Mark Evans was spot on as we continued where we left off. Burke got his customary penalty to start with and converted tries by Hayter (25 minutes) and Moore (40 minutes) to give us a half time lead of 17-10. Montauban didn't score again until injury time when Sieurac scored for Vermis to convert. In the meantime, we had added tries through Roy Winters, Moore and Willis with Burke converting the first two for a final score of 36-17. Our aggregate score of 79-25 took us into a two legged quarter final tie against Brive.

The first leg would be played at the Stoop on 24th January. Brive were on the back foot from the start and George Harder burst over after a mere 45 seconds. Burke couldn't convert but added a penalty and dropped a goal in the first 15 minutes. Tiatia went to the bin and was followed eight minutes later by Bonvoisin. Eight minutes after that, Bassoul also went. The difference was that Brive scored nothing and we scored ten points; Burke with a penalty and the conversion to Harder's second try. Laloo did get a penalty right on half time to open their account and make the score 21-3. Our third try came when Burke put Fuga through after 54 minutes. Burke converted after Worsley, Davison and Diprose had come on only for Vos to become the fourth player to go to the bin. Burke added a penalty and finally Brive took advantage of our player shortage with a try from Naves. It went unconverted and we finished the stronger with a Burke penalty and his conversion of a beautiful solo effort from Keogh who ran 45 metres to score. When the final whistle sounded, the score stood at 41-8; no-one could have dreamt that we would be taking a 33 point advantage to the Parc Municipal.

Between the two Brive games came our third match with the Natal Sharks. Only Andre Vos was left from the starting XV against Brive and it didn't look too good when the Sharks scored three tries in the first half an hour to lead 19-0. James Hayter did open our account in injury time but Dunne couldn't convert. We certainly made a game of it in the second period and Hayter scored his second for Dunne to convert. After we had been called back for a marginal forward pass, the Sharks got away with a massive one and ran the ball in to stretch the lead to 26-12. We would not give up and were now looking more and more likely to get a result when Matt Moore (converted by Dunne) and Rob Jewell scored tries. Dunne's failure to convert this one meant we trailed by two points but he did make amends with four minutes to go by dropping a goal to put us in front. With injury time almost up, Townsend had a penalty chance to win it for Natal which he took to make the final score 27-29. Tom Williams played the first of 231 games against the Sharks, he was to be a regular over the next twelve seasons – he would make headline news later in his career for all the wrong reasons!

At Brive on 1st February, the home side made eleven changes to their starting line up to show they meant business. Paul Burke started the scoring with a penalty, Laharrague dropped a goal and Harder went over for an unconverted try to give us an 8-3 lead on the day. A try from Djoudi evened it up and, despite Burke penalties in the 23rd and 34th minutes, Brive started to get a grip. Donguy and Courrent (2) got tries and the second named converted all three to make it 29-14 in favour of the French. They were only eighteen points behind on the aggregate score but Burke came good and slotted two more penalties before they scored in injury time. Donguy getting his second try after Chinarro had been binned for stamping on Vos and Welborn (a replacement lock) had been shown a red card for repeated stamping. The referee (Gregg Davies from Scotland) had to be escorted from the pitch by security guards after these incidents. The final score on the day was 20-36 but, on aggregate, it was 61-44 in our favour. We were in the semi-final against Connacht to be played over two legs in April.

Back to the more mundane matter of Premiership matches, we welcomed Saracens to the Stoop and another tight game between the sides ensued. To be honest, it was a scrappy encounter and four Burke penalties in the first half were ultimately enough for victory. Sarries managed a try from Broster and a conversion and penalty from Kydd. Castaignede had a long range attempt to drop a goal in the dying seconds but it never seriously threatened to go over. The only worry in this one was an injury to Paul Burke after a collision with Richard Hill early in the second half. He was taken to hospital with a suspected broken neck but was later diagnosed with severe bruising only.

The original date for our fixture at Leicester was 14th February but this had been changed to 19th March so our next game was a visit to the Causeway Stadium to play Wasps. In the second minute, Keogh put Monye in for the softest of tries which Dunne converted. Van Gisbergen pulled a penalty back but Sanderson was over at the beginning of the second quarter for Dunne to again convert. Then came the first of a series of contentious decisions from referee Chris White. He sin binned Rudzki for what he said was his fourth infringement and this enabled Wasps to take the lead with tries from Skivington and van Gisbergen who converted his own. Right from the kick-off, Sanderson was over again after Wasps had failed to deal with the ball. Dunne's conversion took us six points clear. A penalty count of 15-2 against us and the sin binning of Laurent Gomez finally enabled Erinle to score seven minutes into injury time. Van Gisbergen stepped up to slot the conversion and Wasps had stolen it at the end; it was a travesty of justice but the result stood. We were now fifth and handily placed to reach the play-offs. Our next game was at Leicester but not for four weeks.

So, on Friday 19th March, we played at Welford Road and it was time to face Andy Goode again (he had rejoined from Saracens). After two minutes he was kicking his first penalty and after 21 he was converting Leicester's second try by Gibson. Van der Westhuizen had got the first and the score was 17-0 (both tries had been scored while Fuga was in the bin). Two Andy Dunne penalties in the 24th and 35th minutes gave us some hope and when Duffy scored after the interval, Dunne's conversion brought us right back into it. Goode weighed in with two more penalties but we weren't finished yet and Dunne got a penalty and Taumalolo went over in the corner after a mistake by Booth. Dunne crucially missed the conversion to tie the scores and though we tried to win the game, van der Westhuizen got his second try and Goode converted to send the Leicester fans home happy. We were still in sixth place and Leicester stayed in ninth as a result of this match with five games to be played by each team.

It was Leicester again the following week in our home game. When Monye cut the Tigers defence open with a 60 metre run, Willis took the scoring pass and with Dunne converting to add to his penalty (after 7 minutes), we led 10-0. Once again, crucial mistakes were made and a further Dunne penalty in amongst eighteen points for Leicester left us trailing at the break. An anxious second half for both sides saw Deacon sin binned early on before Deane scored our second try for Dunne to convert and we led 20-18 with over half an hour to go. On 67 minutes, Ellis broke clear and Healey finished off to regain the lead for the visitors. We attacked until the end but a bungled lineout call accounted for our last chance.

At the Madejski on 4th April, ourselves and Irish played out a mid-table draw. Everitt was once again the home team's hero with five penalties (the last one four minutes into injury time at the end). Dunne had kicked a penalty in the first half to leave us 3-9 behind but tries from Willis and Keogh and one conversion from Dunne had given us the lead right at the end of normal time. Dunne had missed the first conversion and two long range penalties afterwards. The first hit the right hand upright, the second just went the wrong side of the left hand post. Again our season was full of nearlies!

Irish province Connacht came to the Stoop for the first leg of the Parker Pen Challenge Cup semi-final. This was another great chance to get into a European final for us and we needed to grab the chance with both hands. Connacht would not be a pushover and so it proved. McHugh kicked them into the lead after two minutes with a penalty before the fit again Paul Burke brought us level with a penalty and dropped a goal to give us the lead. Ten minutes later, Mel Deane scored the first try of the semi-final but Burke couldn't convert. Right on half time, Lacey scored after we had been pushed over our line; Elwood converted and there was a point in it. George Harder was fit again and Burke converted his try ten minutes into the second half. Elwood kicked a penalty before and two after Monye's try but when he got his fourth with six minutes to go, for all our possession and a 3-1 try count, we only led 26-22. Crucially, McCarthy was sin binned two minutes later and, from the penalty we kicked to the corner. The ball was won at the lineout and when it reached Greenwood, he stretched over to score our fourth try. Burke was unable to convert this but we had a precious nine point lead to take to Galway in two weeks' time.

Rotherham visited for Round 19 of the Premiership having been relegated as far back as February. As early as the second minute the writing was on the wall for Rotherham's twentieth defeat in a row. Gavin Duffy ran in from 65 metres out after Harder and Greenwood had set him up. Dunne converted and put over a penalty then Jones pulled a penalty back and converted a try from Pritchard. Either side of this try, Ugo Monye and Ceri Jones had scored and, with Dunne's conversion, we led 24-10. The second half was no better for the visitors although they did get the first (Benson penalty) and last points (Wood try, Benson conversion). In the ensuing minutes, Dunne, Jones (converted) and Duffy (converted) completed the six try rout and Mark Evans had the luxury of sending on five replacements at once with more than 20 minutes left. The final score of 43-20 moved us up into fifth place in the table. Josh Taumalolo made his last appearance having scored 8 points (1 try and a dropped goal), he came on for his twelfth appearance as a sub.

At the Sportsground, Galway on 25th April, the 2nd leg of the semi-final with Connacht took place. A capacity crowd of 6,000 saw us take the lead with a penalty from Paul Burke. McHugh replied in kind before Burke darted through and converted his own try after 18 minutes. At this point, we led by 16 points on aggregate and were looking good. Suddenly, that all changed when Yapp went over for McHugh to convert and at half time, it was even on the day. Into the second period, Elwood dropped a goal and McHugh got his second penalty. When Elwood sold a dummy and went over under the posts, Connacht led for only the second time in the tie overall. McHugh's conversion put their aggregate lead at 45-41. We weren't to be denied and after a strong drive by the pack, Greenwood stretched over for our second try to reclaim the overall lead. We defended like dervishes and ensured that Connacht had no try scoring opportunities. Right on 80 minutes Burke kicked his second penalty to narrow the gap on the day to five points. That's the way it stayed and a final kick to touch from Connacht brought an end to a titanic struggle. The aggregate score of 49-45 in our favour ensured a meeting with AS Montferrand in Reading in May.

Before that, we had the small matter of our last two Premiership games. Bath came to the Stoop looking for a victory to make sure of top spot and avoiding the play-off to get into the Championship final. Bath were awarded a penalty try when Matt Moore tried to intercept Malone's pass. It was a debatable decision but it stood and Malone converted. Burke kicked three penalties before the break but these were punctuated by Bath scores. Malone got a penalty and converted Fleck's score but Perry's went unconverted. At this point, it was 22-9 to the visitors and we looked all but finished. It all changed after the break as Burke started to eat into the lead. He was successful with two penalties but missed three others (as he was struggling with a groin injury) before Dunne took over the kicking duties. He was successful with a penalty with five minutes of normal time remaining to make it 22-18 after Beattie had been binned. Our pressure was beginning to tell, Duffy went close and we were denied a penalty try when Bath collapsed a maul five metres from the line. Then, in the eighth minute of injury time, we made one final attack and Dunne fed Keogh who cut inside to score the match winning try among a heap of bodies. Dunne nailed the conversion and we had pulled off a remarkable win. Moore made his final appearance having scored 110 points (22 tries) during his three seasons at the Club as did Rob Jewell who had scored 50 points (10 tries) and came off the bench for his eighteenth appearance as a sub.

For our last league game, we travelled to Northampton on 8th May. It was a simple equation, if we won, we would have a home wild card semi-final against either Leicester or the Sharks. If we lost, we would be away but there were a number of permutations. Northampton had to win to make sure of a play-off spot and they started well with two Drahm penalties and a 35 metre run by Fox to make it 11-0. Within 20 seconds of the restart, Jim Evans charged down Drahm's kick and fell on the ball for our first points. Drahm's conversion of a penalty try proved decisive as we got two tries in the final minutes. Gavin Duffy (78 minutes) and George Harder eight minutes into injury time were the scorers and, had Dunne not just converted Harder's we would have sneaked home. As it was, our bonus point ensured an away wild card play-off semi-final at Welford Road of all places. At least we had the satisfaction of being the only team in the Premiership not to concede a four try bonus point. Chris Bell made his last appearance having scored 50 points (10 tries) and visited the bin on one occasion.

The following Saturday we went to Leicester with our strongest team (except for the injured Paul Burke). We didn't have the bounce of the ball in our favour and it didn't take long for us to go behind. A Goode penalty after six minutes set Leicester on their way and a try was added by van der Westhuizen. Goode converted this, added two penalties and converted a penalty try awarded after a scrum close to our line near half time. Andy Dunne scored a try and converted it before Andre Vos was binned after the penalty try. Before he returned after eight minutes of the second period, Leicester had added twelve points to lead 35-7. This game was over and although we rallied as both sides made changes, we were well beaten. Ellis got their fifth try before Dunne got his second and converted it. Monye and Greenwood (converted by Jarvis) took us to four tries before van der Westhuizen had the final say with a dropped goal in injury time. The final score of 43-26 was insignificant as all eyes now turned to the Madjeski Stadium and the challenge of AS Montferrand in seven days' time. Laurent Gomez finished his Quins career as a sub having scored 5 points (1 try), he made 21 appearances off the bench and visited the bin once.

On a lovely sunny afternoon, a crowd of 13,121 (mostly Quins' supporters) took their seats for what would be an epic encounter with an amazing finish. When Paul Burke kicked a penalty after 12 minutes, we were on our way. Floch replied for the French four minutes later before the first try duly arrived. Will Greenwood put in a diagonal kick from 10 metres inside Montferrand's half and, as their left winger turned to gather, Gavin Duffy zipped in to take the ball and score. Burke missed the conversion and within ten minutes, our lead had gone. Azam crashed over under the posts and, after the referee had consulted the video official, the try was awarded. Floch converted; Raynaud was dispatched to the sin bin for dissent and Merceron dropped a goal. Burke got our noses back in front with two penalties but Floch had the final say in first half injury time with his second penalty to make it 16-14. Montferrand were slowly tightening their grip on the final but we stuck gainfully to our task. Burke put us back in the lead with his fourth penalty but Mel Deane had to leave the field; enter Simon Keogh. Three minutes later, Mignoni went over after peeling off a maul and Floch converted to make it 23-17 with eighteen minutes to go plus injury time. Three minutes later, Burke left the field after missing a simple penalty; enter Andy Dunne. He was immediately called upon to narrow the gap with a penalty when Chanal was sent to the bin for a punch on Fuga. He duly did but Floch replied in kind on 70 minutes. With time running out, Davison came on for Evans and Leonard came on for Dawson. The clock ticked down and down and down, Montferrand were camped in our 22 and we couldn't get the ball. Seven minutes into injury time, Leonard leaned across to try and get the ball at a ruck and Chanal decided to start punching him. This was right in front of the referee (Nigel Whitehouse) and the touch judge. Chanal's second yellow card equalling a red card was a formality and we had a penalty. The ball was dispatched by Dunne down the line for our lineout. From this, the ball came back, Greenwood, Vos and Jones drove it forward and when it reached Harder, he burst up the right. When tackled, he flipped the ball to Monye and his pass found Keogh who needed no second invitation. He was off like a hare, the final Montferrand defences were breached and, in a flash, Keogh was touching down behind the posts. Time was up, there would be one last kick in the 2004 Parker Pen Challenge Cup Final and Andy Dunne had the responsibility of putting the ball between the posts from right in front. He did – game over! Once again, we had won a European trophy and qualified for the Heineken Cup in 2004/05. The Montferrand players would have looked at the scoreboard in disbelief; it read MONTFERRAND 26 HARLEQUINS 27. Five of our more notable players made their final appearances in this game, they were Scott Bemand who had scored 15 points (3 tries), made 23 appearances as a sub and been to the bin once; Bill Davison who had scored 40 points (8 tries), captained the side nine times, made 37 appearances off the bench, been booked once and visited the bin five times; Pat Sanderson had scored 95 points (19 tries), come off the bench 15 times and was sent to the bin once; Paul Burke, our talismanic kicker who had scored 1092 points (7 tries, 21 dropped goals, 250 penalties and 122 conversions) and led the team on one occasion was off to Munster (he would be sadly missed and this decision would come back to haunt us although he had been offered two years by them and we could only offer one so he might not have stayed anyway) and finally, Jason Leonard, a legend in the game who had been in the 1st XV for fourteen seasons and achieved everything in the game (he had scored 24 points (5 tries), captained the side 52 times, made 20 appearances off the bench, been sent off once and was sent to the bin once as well. He too would be sorely missed.

Our overall playing record was P37 W19 D2 L16 F936 A746 and in the league it was P22 W10 D2 L10 F502 A449 Pts 54 (BP 10 – TB 4 LB 6) Pos 6th. This season had been a great improvement on last year with a trophy and a top six finish in the Premiership and the increase in points reflected this. The additional 224 points meant that tries increased by 32 to 104, penalties went up by 15 to 87 and conversions reached 70 (an increase of 17). Dropped goals fell to half of their 2002/03 total (5). Ugo Monye topped the try scorers with 14, Andy Dunne got the most conversions (41) and Paul Burke scored the most points again with 254 (1 try, 3 dropped goals, 62 penalties and 27 conversions). As a result, he also scored the most dropped goals and penalties. Ceri Jones only missed two of the 37 matches, Bill Davison, Tony Diprose and Gavin Duffy appeared in 34 and Jon Dawson, Simon Keogh and Andre Vos ended with 33.

2003/04

190803	CASTRES OLYMPIQUE	MILLAU	L	1G2PG(13)-1G4PG(19)
250803	NEWPORT GWENT DRAGONS	NEWPORT	W	1G4PG1T(24)-4PG(12)
050903	SARACENS	STOOP MEMORIAL GROUND	W	2G3PG1T(28)-2G2PG(20)

130903	LONDON WASPS(ZP)	STOOP MEMORIAL GROUND	W	3G1DG3PG(33)-1G5PG1T(27)
200903	ROTHERHAM(ZP)	ROTHERHAM	W	3G4PG2T(43)-1G1PG1T(15)
270903	LONDON IRISH(ZP)	STOOP MEMORIAL GROUND	W	1DG4PG(15)-1G1PG(10)
051003	SARACENS(ZP)	VICARAGE ROAD	L	3G4PG(33)-3G1DG5PG(39)
111003	NEWCASTLE(ZP)	STOOP MEMORIAL GROUND	W	6PG(18)-2PG1T(11)
181003	GLOUCESTER(ZP)	STOOP MEMORIAL GROUND	L	0-1G3PG(16)
251003	SHARKS(ZP)	STOOP MEMORIAL GROUND	L	1G3PG1T(21)-3G3PG(30)
311003	LEEDS(ZP)	HEADINGLEY	W	3G3PG(30)-1G3PG(16)
081103	NORTHAMPTON(ZP)	STOOP MEMORIAL GROUND	W	3G4PG2T(43)-3G(21)
141103	LEEDS(PC6)	HEADINGLEY	L	2PG(6)-1G2PG(13)
221103	BATH(ZP)	BATH	L	1G1PG(10)-6PG(18)
291103	LEEDS(ZP)	STOOP MEMORIAL GROUND	L	3PG(9)-1G3PG(16)
071203	CETRANSA UEMC(PPCC1R1L)	VALLADOLID	W	3G2T(31)-1G2PG1T(18)
131203	CETRANSA UEMC(PPCC1R2L) (AGG 94-21)	STOOP MEMORIAL GROUND	W	4G7T(63)-1PG(3)
191203	SHARKS(ZP)	EDGELEY PARK	D	3G2PG(27)-3G2PG(27)
271203	GLOUCESTER(ZP)	GLOUCESTER	L	2G1PG(17)-1G2PG1T(18)
040104	NEWCASTLE(ZP)	NEWCASTLE	W	3G1PG1T(29)-2G1DG1PG1T(25)
100104	MONTAUBAN(PPCC 2R1L)	MONTAUBAN	W	5G1PG1T(43)-1PG1T(8)
170104	MONTAUBAN(PPCC 2R2L) (AGG 79-25)	STOOP MEMORIAL GROUND	W	4G1PG1T(36)-2G1PG(17)
240104	BRIVE(PPCCQF1L)	STOOP MEMORIAL GROUND	W	3G1DG4PG1T(41)-1PG1T(8)
270104	NATAL SHARKS	STOOP MEMORIAL GROUND	L	2G1DG2T(27)-3G1PG1T(29)
010204	BRIVE(PPCCQF2L) (AGG 61-44)	BRIVE	L	5PG1T(20)-4G1DG1T(36)
070204	SARACENS(ZP)	STOOP MEMORIAL GROUND	W	4PG(12)-1G1PG(10)
140204	LEICESTER(ZP)	LEICESTER	P	
220204	LONDON WASPS(ZP)	ADAMS PARK	L	3G(21)-2G1PG1T(22)
190304	LEICESTER(ZP)	LEICESTER	L	1G3PG1T(21)-3G3PG(30)

270304	LEICESTER(ZP)	STOOP MEMORIAL GROUND	L	2G2PG(20)-1G2PG2T(23)
040404	LONDON IRISH(ZP)	READING	D	1G1PG1T(15)-5PG(15)
110404	CONNACHT(PPCCSF1L)	STOOP MEMORIAL GROUND	W	1G1DG2PG3T(31)-1G5PG(22)
160404	ROTHERHAM(ZP)	STOOP MEMORIAL GROUND	W	5G1PG1T(43)-2G2PG(20)
250404	CONNACHT(PPCCSF2L) (AGG 49-45)	GALWAY	L	1G2PG1T(18)-2G1DG2PG(23)
020504	BATH(ZP)	STOOP MEMORIAL GROUND	W	1G6PG(25)-2G1PG1T(22)
080504	NORTHAMPTON(ZP)	NORTHAMPTON	L	1G2T(17)-1G2PG1T(18)
150504	LEICESTER(ZWCSF)	LEICESTER	L	3G1T(26)-3G1DG3PG2T(43)
220504	AS MONTFERRAND(PPCCF)	READING	W	1G5PG1T(27)-2G1DG3PG(26)

42

Relegation Becomes a Reality 2004-2005

As World Champions, England returned to New Zealand and Australia in June 2004 at the end of an exhausting year of test match rugby. Stuart Abbott, Gomarsall and Mike Worsley all appeared in at least one of the games but the team was clearly defeated in all three. New Zealand won 36-3 and 36-12 and Australia handed out another thrashing (51-15).

In March 2005, one of the more bizarre stories appeared in the newspapers. James Hayter was employed as a bouncer at the Biggest Ever Filthy Rich Orgy organised by Fever Parties that took place in a former ambassadorial residence opposite BBC Radio One's offices in London's Portland Place. The two undercover reporters from the Sunday Mirror stated that he became overwhelmed with lust, stripped off and joined in the night's action along with three hundred others!

Blue Sky Leisure Limited had arranged a loan facility of £6 million with Allied Irish Bank to finance the new West stand and consolidate the existing debt with Royal Bank of Scotland. The North stand was replaced and Harlequin Estates (Twickenham) Ltd sold land behind the East stand for a residential development; the £3 million proceeds were used to pay for the West stand. The accounts for year ending 30th June 2005 showed a loss of £2,075,696. Haines resigned as a Director with Herridge and Looker returning to the Board and this would remain constant until 2008/09.

Andre Vos was now in the third year of his four year stint as Club captain. The 2004/05 season was eagerly anticipated because of our dramatic victory against Montferrand putting us into the Heineken Cup. We started with two friendly games against Grafton Belfast Harlequins at Deramore Park on 17th August and Ulster three days later at Ravenhill. Mike Brown (making the first of at least 277 appearances for us and would go on to win at least 52 England caps) was to become the best full back in World rugby, Mark Lambert (the first of at least 205 appearances), Steve So'oialo (the first of 102 appearances, he would also gain 38 caps for Samoa and 3 for the Pacific Islanders) and Jeremy Staunton (who would make 27 appearances and was in the process of winning 5 caps for Ireland) all made their debuts in that first match. Brown and Lambert would have long and successful careers at the Club. The starting XV contained several players who would be considered to be in our 1st XV when the Premiership got underway three weeks later. On a windy night, the home side had first use of the wind and went in front when Humphreys put over a penalty after 25 minutes. In first half injury time, Andre Vos got a try and Andy Dunne converted. The second half belonged entirely to us and we added tries through Tiatia, So'oialo, Tiaita again, Deane, Diprose, Tiatia (completing his hat-trick), So'oialo again and Tiatia with his fourth. Dunne kicked all eight conversions to leave the final score at 63-3.

In the Ulster game, nine changes were made to the starting line-up and we didn't make the best of starts when the home side scored tries from Best and Maxwell (both converted by Wallace) to open up a 14-0 lead after just 13 minutes. By half time, we had narrowed that gap to just two points with tries from Ceri Jones and So'oialo (converted by Dunne). Staunton missed a penalty (this was to become a regular occurrence during the season) but converted Andy Reay's try to put us ahead for the first time. When Ward scored for Ulster, there were 12 minutes left and the scores were tied at 19-19. We finished with 14 men when Ma'ama Molitika was shown yellow with three minutes to go (he was making his debut and would make just 5 appearances but was in the process of winning 18 caps for Tonga and 3 for the Pacific Islanders). However, deep into injury time, Sherriff collected his own chip ahead to score our fourth try, Staunton converted and the final whistle went to end a very successful short tour to Ireland.

Our proposed third friendly at home to Saracens on 27th August was cancelled so our next match was the inaugural Twickenham Double Header against London Irish on 4th September. This was a new concept whereby there would be back-to-back matches involving us, London Irish, Saracens and London Wasps. This was to be effectively an away game for us but nice and local for the fans. This was a very disappointing game and the heat contributed towards the many dropped passes and turnovers. Everitt put the Exiles in front before Dunne levelled but we trailed at the break when he got his second penalty. He went to the bin early in the second half for a high tackle on Dunne but it was Irish who scored the only points during those ten minutes when Appleford scored a try which Catt converted. Staunton did pull six points back with two penalties in the 70th and 75th minutes but Sackey got over for the decisive score with two minutes to go. At 9-18, Staunton's penalty six minutes into injury time only secured us a bonus point. After one round, we were in ninth place in the table and things would go downhill rapidly from this point.

The following Saturday, we entertained Northampton at the Stoop. They had beaten Bath on the opening weekend and were occupying top spot. The only positive from this day for us was the opening of the new North Stand. When the game started, Will Greenwood scored a try after six minutes to put us in front. That was about the extent of our joy because, by half time, the Saints had run in four tries through Sealy, Howard, Cohen and Rudd plus three conversions and a penalty from Grayson to lead 29-8 (Dunne had kicked a penalty for us). Things got no better after the break and another two tries (Tucker and Fox) plus a penalty by Drahm put the visitors well clear. Monye got a try five minutes from the end to make it 13-42 before Drahm added another penalty. We dropped to 11th place with only Bath below us.

A Sunday trip up to unbeaten Newcastle followed and this proved to be a very tight contest. After Wilkinson kicked a penalty after 15 minutes, Staunton replied in similar fashion and converted a try from George Harder. He then exchanged penalties with Wilkinson before Luke Sherriff was sin binned for killing the ball. Wilkinson landed the resulting penalty to make it 13-9 at half time. Staunton broke through at the start of the second period and sent Duffy in for our second try. Shortly after Sherriff returned, Miall was binned for persistent offside. Wilkinson put over another penalty and converted a penalty try awarded for killing the ball once again. As time drifted away, Staunton missed a penalty, Wilkinson landed one, Staunton kicked his third and then had two chances in injury time to win the game. First, a long range penalty and then a last-ditch dropped goal attempt - both of which went wide. Wilkinson asked both referee and touch judge if he put the ball out from a 22 drop out the game would end, they said yes so he put it out on the full. The referee then gave us a scrum on the 22! Afterwards they admitted to their mistake (had he bounced the ball out, the game would have ended) but it gave us a chance to snatch the win. Instead of the dropped goal attempt right away, we ran it from the base of the scrum, lost 20 yards and Staunton's attempt was a hit and hope rather than a real chance. The final score of 21-22 sent Newcastle top and us tumbling to the bottom of the table. Afterwards Rob Andrew (Newcastle's Director of Rugby) launched a tirade about our cynical play and how we had killed the ball at the breakdown for the entire game. As it was, Newcastle had McCarthy binned as well so perhaps they were not that innocent after all!

Against Bath on 25th September at the Stoop, we took part in the 1,000th Premiership match. It had taken seven and a bit seasons to reach this number. In the match day programme, there was an all-time Premiership table and of the ten ever present teams in this incarnation of league rugby, we were tenth! Of course, this did not take in to account the seasons from 1987/88 to 1996/97. At this stage, there were only five ever present teams including us (Bath, Gloucester, Leicester and Wasps being the others). We were still missing Will Greenwood (who had been side lined with concussion sustained during the Northampton match) and, although Barkley kicked a penalty after 5 minutes, we came back strongly. Staunton equalised with a penalty four minutes later and Simon Keogh went over for a try after 22 minutes which Staunton converted. Before half time, Lewitt got five points back for Bath to give us a two point advantage at the interval. The second half was a disaster for us as we just didn't turn up. Bath scored with a Chris Malone dropped goal (he would play for us some years later), Higgins scored a try and Barkley converted. The last 20 minutes remained scoreless but we had lost again, this time by 10-18. Our head coach (Mark Evans) was lost for words to describe our second half lack of performance but there was no getting away from it, we were in deep trouble although we gained a place as Worcester went bottom. At this stage, we were already fifteen points adrift of the top side Sale Sharks. Dafydd James came on for his debut in this one and would go on to make 22 appearances (he was in the process of gaining 48 caps for Wales and had won 3 caps for the British Lions during the 2001 tour of Australia).

On 2nd October, it was the battle of the basement at Sixways against Worcester. Even at this early point in the season, games like this were starting to be labelled "must win". The problem was that we were not playing well and we continued to leak points. Our old captain, Pat Sanderson, scored a try after 10 minutes to give Worcester the lead which they never lost. Brown converted (as he did with three of their four other tries) and we were sent packing again. After Hinshelwood had scored their second, Luke Sherriff went over for us on 20 minutes for Staunton to convert. That was the half time score, we failed to trouble the scoreboard after that and Vaili, Fortey and Brown made sure that the home side got the try bonus point with one each. As well as Sanderson, the Warriors side contained no fewer than three other old boys (Ben Gollings, Matt Powell and Tim Collier). Even Mark Evans was talking of a crisis and his decision to release Paul Burke at the end of the last season was coming back to haunt him. After five matches, we were the only side not to have won and now trailed Worcester by five points. Nick Easter came on as a temporary replacement in this game and he would prove to be a real stalwart of the Club over a number of years (he would go on to make 291 appearances and win 54 England caps). Also making the first of just 2 appearances, both as a substitute, was Opeta Palepoi (he was in the process of winning 43 caps for Samoa).

There are no easy games when you are at the bottom and they don't come much tougher than Gloucester away. That is where we travelled on 9th October. Slight changes were made to a side that started with the likes of Duffy, Harder, Greenwood, James, Monye, Jones, Easter and Vos in it. Once again, we started well enough and went into a ten point lead when Staunton added the conversion to Duffy's try after he had kicked a penalty. Gloucester woke up and Paul landed a penalty and Simpson-Daniel grabbed a cross-field kick to score in the corner. Despite another Staunton penalty, we trailed at the break because Paul converted his own try after 37 minutes. Two minutes into the second half, Fanolua scored his first try and Paul converted before Greenwood scored under the posts after Easter had taken a quick free-kick. Staunton converted to close the gap to two points. Unfortunately, Fanolua scored right from the kick-off for Paul to convert. Missed penalties from both Staunton and Paul kept the score the same until our fly half put one over with the last kick of the game to earn us a losing bonus point (23-29). This had been a much better performance but the bottom line was that we were 0-6 for the season. Australian scrum half, Matt Henjak played the first of 2 games for us in this one (he was in the middle of winning 4 caps for his country).

The following week, Leicester Tigers came to the Stoop. The big news was that we had signed Geo Cronje (a South African lock with 3 caps) - alas, injury meant that he would never play a 1st XV game. The match itself turned into a penalty shoot-out between Staunton and Goode. It was a dire contest and, in the first ten minutes, it was Goode 2 Staunton 1. The rest of the half was 2-2 so Leicester led 12-9 at the break. Neil Back spent the last ten minutes of the half in the sin bin but we couldn't get a try. The only score in the second half was Goode's fifth penalty to send us to our seventh defeat in a row. This was Matt Henjak's final game after his very short spell with us. Worcester were keeping pace with our losing bonus points so we still trailed by five points.

Our next two games were in the Heineken Cup and first we travelled to Thomond Park to play Munster. They had never lost a European Cup game there and we were not expected to end the run. We did play well in very difficult conditions and we actually led after nine minutes when Staunton put over a penalty. Unfortunately, Horgan had a clear run to the corner five minutes later and we were behind. By this point, the referee (Hugh Watkins) had sin binned props Maurice Fitz Gerald and Marcus Horan because he believed they were causing all the problems in the scrums. We went down to 13 men when Staunton saw yellow for a deliberate knock-on and Munster took full advantage to stretch their lead when Williams scored for O'Gara to convert. He also landed a penalty on 39 minutes for a 15-3 lead at half time. We had the use of the strong wind in the second period and Staunton put over penalties on 45 and 68 minutes to bring us within six points. Ace Tiatia went to the bin for a high tackle after 58 minutes but we survived this and pressed for an unlikely victory. Right near the end, Staunton was on his way to the line when the referee blew his whistle for what he deemed to be a knock-on; it wasn't but our last chance had gone (Staunton would have been in under the posts and the conversion a game winning one). Had we not had three men in the bin, the result may have been different. Opeta Palepoi made his second and final appearance in this match as a substitute.

Next up were Castres Olympique in our second Heineken Cup game on 30th October and our first at the Stoop since January 2002. Castres had beaten Neath-Swansea Ospreys at home in their first game (38-17) so came to us full of confidence. Paul Volley was in their team and he would be our captain a few years later. As was becoming a regular occurrence, we started well and in the first 22 minutes, we ran up a 13-3 lead. Dafydd James got a try which Staunton converted and then added two penalties after Dourthe had opened the scoring for the visitors with a penalty. He put over two more before half time to close the gap. We lost Andre Vos just before the break with a back injury and he was replaced by Luke Sherriff. Staunton's fourth penalty took us into a seven point lead but two penalties from Dourthe in three minutes brought Castres right up to us. A great flick pass from Greenwood enabled James to get his second try which Staunton converted. There was over half an hour to play but we were looking good for our first serious victory of the season. Fleming scored for Castres almost immediately and Dourthe's sixth penalty brought the scores level at 23-23. Volley went to the bin with 15 minutes to go but all we managed were two penalty misses by Staunton from 40 and 35 metres. These proved crucial and we had to settle for two points.

An away trip to Adams Park to play London Wasps in the Zurich Premiership on Friday 5th November was our next task. We could not have made a worse start. Literally straight from the kick-off, Greenwood dropped the ball in the 22, it was picked up and Voyce was driven over. Van Gisbergen converted and the fastest ever try scored in British top-class rugby had helped to give Wasps a 7-0 lead (it was timed at 9.63 seconds!). We did rally from this point and actually led after 40 minutes. Staunton kicked two penalties and converted Greenwood's try (after a great run from Keogh). Shaw had been in the bin for all but three of those points and when he came back, we lost Vos to the bin (Harder would make the same trip after 60 minutes). Van Gisbergen slotted penalties on 32, 48 and 61 minutes to move the home side ahead but Staunton dropped a goal on 66 minutes to level it up. Three minutes later, van Gisbergen put over his fourth penalty to leave the final score at 16-19. Simon Maling came on as a substitute to play the first of 13 games for the 1st XV (he had just finished his international career with 11 caps for New Zealand). Another losing bonus point was gained but we were still four points behind Worcester and 26 behind Sale at the top.

Saracens were up next for another Friday night fixture which provided another record. Mel Deane scored the second fastest try ever in British top-class rugby when he picked up a loose ball 15 metres out and, after just 18 seconds, we were 5-0 up. Staunton converted and he was to have a lot of practice. Nick Easter, Tom Williams and Mike Worsley got us to the try bonus point in a record 13 minutes 45 seconds. Staunton converted the first two and we led 26-0. By half time, it was 33 when Easter got his second for Staunton to convert. By general consensus, Saracens had played the worst half of rugby ever seen in the Premiership. The rout continued into the second half when Roy Winters went over for Staunton to convert. At 40-0 after just 47 minutes, we began to make changes and this allowed the visitors to run in tries through Randell and Bailey. The second, right near the end was, like the first, unconverted and we had our first victory! This win catapulted us above Worcester into eleventh place.

The Friday night games came thick and fast during England's Autumn International Series and the third one saw us travel to Edgeley Park, Stockport to play Sale Sharks. The Sharks line up was depleted due to international calls so it was an ideal opportunity for us to grab our second win. Keogh went over after four minutes and Staunton converted before Hayward pulled three points back for Sale with a penalty. Staunton restored our lead with another penalty before Vos and Staunton had overlapping spells in the bin. This enabled Sale to draw level with a Todd try converted by Hayward before Staunton nudged us ahead with a penalty right on half time. His third stretched the lead, Hayward got his second (but missed three others) before Staunton's fourth eight minutes from time gave us that all important second victory (Anglesea went to the sin bin just before this). This was our first away league win over Sale since 10th September 1994 and our first away league win since 4th January 2004 against Newcastle. We were now sandwiched between Worcester and Northampton at the bottom but a lot more points were needed yet if we were to survive.

Leeds Tykes were the visitors on Sunday 28th November for another must win fixture as they were six points ahead of us. We opened the scoring when Harder went round the Leeds full back and gave Tani Fuga the scoring pass. After Stimpson and Staunton had traded penalties, Leeds went in front when Rees scored in the left hand corner for Stimpson to convert. However, a tight first half ended with a successful penalty from Staunton to give us a narrow lead. The second half almost entirely belonged to us and a procession of points followed - Staunton penalty, So'oialo try, Staunton conversion and penalty. This took the score to 24-10 and when we drove a lineout 40 metres to the try line for Easter to score, Andy Dunne's conversion sealed the win. Leeds did get the consolation of a try by ex-Quin Chris Bell after a good break by Christophers (he would come back to haunt us later in the season). Stimpson converted to make it 31-17. Our 100% record during the internationals moved us up to tenth spot with 18 points. Worcester had 17 and Northampton 14. We had a break from league action now until we visited Saracens on Boxing Day.

Our next two fixtures were back to back Heineken Cup matches against Neath-Swansea Ospreys. The first was played at St Helens, Swansea. This was the last Heineken Cup match to be played at the famous old ground as the Ospreys were off to a new stadium the following season. We had a great start when Dafydd James crash tackled the ball out of the hands of Henson, Tom Williams fly-hacked on, charged down the attempted clearance and scored under the posts. 57 seconds had passed and Staunton's conversion put us into a 7-0 lead. As the game progressed,

Easter was sin binned at the end of the first quarter and Henson landed two penalties during the ten minutes. By half time, the Ospreys led 12-7 with two more Henson penalties. The second half was a replica of the first as far as their scoring went. Four Henson penalties put us out of our misery. We just couldn't get any foot hold in their territory and the 24-7 scoreline reflected this. We were all but out of the 2004/05 Heineken Cup competition after just three games.

Jeremy Staunton missed the return game with a knee injury which gave promising young fly half Adrian Jarvis his first start of the season. He banged over two penalties to give us a 6-0 lead and we had a man advantage as Spice had been binned. The lead changed hands five times before the break with the Ospreys leading 22-16. For us, Jarvis got his third penalty and converted a try from Greenwood. Our visitors had scored a try from Terblanche and a penalty by Henson (who also converted his own try and that of Ryan Jones). Having been in charge for 20 minutes, we were starting to fade away and Sherriff (47 minutes), Rudzki (57 minutes) and Tiatia (69 minutes) were all sin binned in what turned into a completely shambolic performance. Henson and Jarvis exchanged penalties and that was as good as it got for us. Henson took control and seemed to be able to wander through our defence at will. He converted his second try and those scored by Shane Williams and Matthew Jones to make it 19-46 at the end. If anyone thought we were improving, this match told everyone that we were most certainly not. We had an annoying habit of playing well for the first quarter and then fading away.

This proved to be an accurate description of our Powergen Cup 6th round tie at the Recreation Ground, Bath on 18th December. After 18 minutes, Staunton intercepted a pass by Chris Malone to score and convert. The Quins' supporters could have got up and left at this point to go and do some Christmas shopping because we didn't score again. By the interval, Barkley had kicked a penalty and converted a try by Higgins to give them the lead. The try by Higgins had a bit of farce about it. Barkley put in a cross-field kick from well inside his own half, Williams dithered and Higgins raced past him to touch down. A succession of Barkley penalties made it 19-7 with 14 minutes to go. Steve So'oialo became another one of our now regular visitors to the sin bin after 64 minutes and by the time he returned, we had leaked thirteen points (Barkley converting a try by Mears to add to his penalties). With the final move, Cheeseman scored Bath's third try and Barkley's conversion made it 7-33. For the first time in the history of the knock-out cup competition, we had lost three ties in a row. It was also our heaviest domestic cup defeat since 30 September 1972 when London Welsh had thrashed us in a first round tie. These were sad times at the Club and 2004 couldn't end quickly enough.

The last game of the year was a trip to Vicarage Road, Watford to play Saracens on 26th December. The home side dominated the first half mainly due to the fact that our hooker, Ace Tiatia, had been concussed for most of it and was throwing line out ball to anyone but his own team mates. He thought he was fine but eventually, he was replaced by James Hayter (this took the best part of 40 minutes to sort out). All Saracens could score was a Jackson penalty, we had zero to show for our efforts. This was another lamentable performance from us although Duffy slid over after 60 minutes and when Staunton dropped a goal eight minutes later, we led 8-3. Now all we had to do was cling on for a win. There was no chance of this and Haughton scored in the corner to tie it up. Jackson's conversion attempt bounced off the crossbar to just about sum up a dreadful game. It was now just over half way in the Premiership season and we had accumulated just 20 points from a possible 60. We ended the year in 10th place.

We now knew that we were out of both domestic and European Cup competitions. We had ten Premiership, two Heineken Cup and one friendly fixture remaining and the emphasis quite clearly had to be on those league games. Our first match of 2005 was a home fixture against London Wasps on 2nd January. We had dropped to the bottom again as both Northampton and Worcester had won the day before. Wasps were in second and some 18 points ahead of us. Instead of our usual good start, we found ourselves behind by fifteen points (Dawson try, van Gisbergen conversion and penalty and Lewsey try) before Staunton landed a penalty right on half time. Almost from the kick-off at the start of the second half, van Gisbergen got another try for the visitors and added the conversion. When Andy Dunne replaced Staunton, he injected some pace and Keogh finished off his quick break with a try. Dawson ensured the try bonus point for Wasps and Harder's try (converted by Dunne) came so late it was a pure consolation. We had been outplayed again and Mark Evans predicted the relegation battle would go to the last game – how right he was!! After this game, the old stand at the Stoop started being demolished to make way for the £8 million new stand which would increase the ground capacity to 12,500.

The following Saturday, we travelled to Castres for a meaningless fixture (as far as we were concerned). We actually led with an Andy Dunne penalty after 17 minutes but by half time, a Marticorena penalty and a try from Capo-Ortega had given Castres the lead. Marticorena stretched this with another penalty after 38 minutes but Gavin Duffy scored a try on 49 minutes to reduce the lead to just three points (8-11). What happened next can only be described as the flood gates opening as Castres powered their way to victory. Vigneaux, Albouy, Froment, Capo-Ortega, Froment (again), Bernad and Mola all crossed for tries with the conversions being added by Marticorena to all but the first. Sherriff did get a second try for us to make it 13-37 but we had been annihilated (13-58). It was our heaviest defeat in European competition since the 10-51 quarter final loss at Toulouse in 1997. Rudzki and Duffy both spent 10 minutes in the bin which hindered us even more. Ma'ama Molitika played his last game for us as his brief spell at the Club came to an end. After all was said and done, the result mattered only in the history books as did the following game against Munster.

Because of the reduced capacity at the Stoop, it was decided to play this one at Twickenham. The crowd of 33,883 was a record for a Heineken Cup pool match. Munster only had to win to secure a quarter final spot but Dunne slotted a penalty to put us in front on two minutes. Five minutes later, Horgan scored a try for Paul Burke to convert (he had become a folk hero during his four seasons at Quins and how we could have done with him now in our hour of need). As Munster looked to be almost certain to score again twenty minutes later, Ugo Monye intercepted and raced 80 metres to score. Dunne converted and we were back in front. Four minutes before the break, So'oialo went to the bin and Munster took the opportunity to go back in front when Leamy scored their second try. The visitors starved us of possession in the second half and Paul Burke's penalties after 51 and 66 minutes secured the victory although Cullen had to make a try saving tackle on Monye with six minutes left to deny us at least a bonus point. Andy Dunne played his last game for us having scored 228 points (6 tries, 1 dropped goal, 29 penalties and 54 conversions).

Our last game in January was at Welford Road, home of Leicester Tigers. They held an eight point lead at the top of the table so we couldn't really be going to a tougher place. We took a shock lead after just 68 seconds when Jon Dawson burrowed over for a try, Staunton converted and added a penalty after Goode had opened the home side's account with a penalty. Two more Goode penalties brought the scores almost level but Monye (after an inside pass from Easter) shot over for Staunton to convert. Twenty one minutes had gone and we led 17-9. By the interval, Goode had kicked his fourth penalty and converted Healey's try to make it a two point game in favour of the home side. Our cause wasn't helped when Easter went to the bin for 10 minutes during which Goode added two more penalties. Despite our best efforts, the only further scores were a try from Henry Tuilagi and a conversion from Goode who finished with 22 points in a 32-17 victory. To be honest, we didn't play that badly but, as Mark Evans said, at a place like Leicester, you need to take all of your chances and make no mistakes. We did neither and paid the price. A losing bonus point would have been a fair reward but it wasn't to be. After Round 14 of 22, the bottom of the table read as follows: Quins 20pts, Worcester 21, Northampton 22 and Leeds 25. All four were in deep trouble.

At the start of the season, we had a run of ten games without a win, we were now in a run of eight games without a win. This had to change and fifth placed Gloucester were our visitors on 5th February. Jeremy Staunton was successful with a penalty after 3 minutes and Tom Williams added a try on 10 minutes. Paul pulled back six points with two penalties before Balding was sin binned. Six minutes later, Ace Tiatia swung a punch which floored Sigley (one of Gloucester's props) and referee Ashley Rowden had no option but to show red. When Paul kicked the resultant penalty, we were 8-9 behind and had to play the remaining 47 minutes with fourteen men. Easter was sacrificed because we had to bring James Hayter (the replacement hooker) on. With Balding still in the bin, the sides were even and Staunton kicked two penalties for a 14-9 lead at the interval. Something amazing happened during the break because we came out as an inspired team. In the first 25 minutes of the second half, we scored 17 unanswered points. Staunton put over his fourth penalty, Mike Worsley's brilliant offload sent Simon Keogh over and then Keogh intercepted a pass by Simpson-Daniel to run in from his own 22. Staunton converted both and the only unanswered question was – could we get the try bonus point? We had to wait until the fourth minute of injury time for the answer. Hayter went over to drag us off the bottom of the table. Staunton's conversion made it 38-9 and we had stopped a run of seven successive defeats by the Cherry and Whites. Northampton dropped to twelfth spot and we went eleventh.

An unhelpful interlude (owing to the severity of the situation) came on 10th February when the Natal Sharks appeared for the fourth year in succession. As had happened in the previous meetings, we lost. Immelman and Ndungane got tries (both converted by Barnard) before Dave Harvey (on loan from Newbury) kicked our only points of the night with a penalty. During the second half, we made a larger than normal amount of substitutions and this helped to disrupt the side even more. The Sharks took full advantage and scored tries through Halstead and Russell. Barnard converted both and to prove they were clinical to the end, Schutte added a penalty to make the final score 31-3. Tajik "Tosh" Masson played the first of 56 games for the 1st XV in this one and Dave von Hoesslin made the first of 2 appearances (the second being as a substitute against Newcastle on 13th March), he had won 5 caps for South Africa in 1999 and Karl Rudzki made the last of 54. He had made 28 appearances as a sub and been sin-binned 5 times.

Nine days later, it was the first of a run of seven Premiership games and Worcester were the visitors to the Stoop. This time, Daren O'Leary was in their starting line up to make four ex-Quins in the side. This was a very tense affair and no-one wanted to make a mistake. Brown kicked Worcester into an early lead with his first penalty but Staunton, with use of the strong wind, got two of his own to give us a half time lead. Gavin Duffy was just short of scoring a try and Tani Fuga knocked-on with a big overlap on his left. These were crucial moments and, as the Worcester pack scrummaged us out of the game, Brown kicked four more penalties at regular intervals to leave the visitors ahead by nine points with fourteen minutes left including injury time. The referee was our old friend Chris White and the crowd got more annoyed and frustrated each and every time he penalised us. Worcester did come close twice to scoring a try and Hayes missed with a long range kick at goal. Right on the final whistle in the seventh minute of injury time, Staunton added another penalty to give us our sixth losing bonus point of the season. Northampton were still bottom and this point put us three ahead of them. Mark Evans then made the statement that helped to seal our fate; he said "There are a lot of critical games to go and if we can get 11 points from our last six matches we should be alright". So, the CEO and Head Coach had stated that 37 points would mean safety.

At Bath, where we had won just one out of fifteen previous league matches, we were not expected to get any points. The home side were missing 23 men through injury and international duty but this didn't prevent them from leading 15-3 at the break. Staunton had put us in front with a penalty but Fidler and Mears got tries and Malone converted the first and put over a penalty between the tries. During the interval Evans ordered the team to stop conceding penalties as they had been and this had the desired effect. Four minutes in, Monye was put in at the corner after good work from the forwards and slick handling by Deane and James. Staunton converted to bring us within five and when Maddock's chip went straight to Harder, he fed Dafydd James who cantered home from 35 yards out. Staunton converted and we held Bath at bay for the remaining sixteen minutes. A famous win took us into tenth place on 30 points. Northampton were one below on 27 and Leeds were now occupying the relegation spot with just 26.

Newcastle Falcons were in seventh place and Jonny Wilkinson made his first appearance for two months. He only lasted 34 minutes but had caused us problems during that time. Staunton scored first with a penalty and then got outscored 2-1 by Wilkinson. A mistake by Newcastle in front of their posts enabled Vos to put Harder over before Setiti pulled the Falcons back into it with a try. Staunton and Wilkinson converted the respective scores but we finished the half strongly and Jim Evans grabbed our second try, Staunton converted and added another penalty to give us a healthy lead (23-13). A couple of minutes after the interval, Mayerhofler scored a try and Walder converted but Fuga scored for us before Walder landed a penalty on 52 minutes. When Long went to the bin, Staunton kicked his fourth penalty and Tom Williams got the bonus point try six minutes later. Our fly half couldn't convert that but his fifth penalty just extended the victory margin to 39-23. We were quite literally zooming up the table; 35 points and eighth place was a great feeling especially given that Leeds were nine points behind. Northampton, Worcester and London Irish were also now below us. Former Wales international fly half, Arwel Thomas had joined us and made the first of 4 appearances when he came on for Staunton. He won 23 caps between 1996 and 2000.

So, four matches left and only two points needed according to our CEO. However, this was not the way it read from a mathematical point of view if Leeds started winning. It could still be a different story and it seemed that the crunch would come at Headingley on 17th April. Arwel Thomas started at Northampton on 26th March (because Jeremy Staunton pulled a muscle in training during the week) and put us in front with a penalty after 7 minutes. His second came after Drahm had landed two for the Saints. The first quarter ended all square before Drahm got his third to nudge the home side ahead when Thomas was spending ten minutes in the bin. When he returned, our three-quarter line came to life and Harder crashed over for Arwel to convert. Our interval lead was stretched by another seven points when Thomas intercepted Stcherbina's pass and went 70 yards to score and convert. There were 38 minutes including injury time to play and we were looking good. With 25 minutes left Drahm put over a penalty. We were still holding on and when Tom Williams was also put in the bin, there were just fourteen minutes to go. Drahm got his fifth penalty just before injury time to make it 20-15. When a scrum was called some five minutes later, only ten seconds remained. From this, Drahm found a gap on the blind side and his pass sent Tucker over in the corner. From a tight angle, he added the conversion to give Northampton a 22-20 victory. We had thrown it away and with Leeds winning remarkably at home to Leicester (23-22) and Worcester picking up a losing bonus point, it was getting tighter at the bottom although we still held eighth place.

Two weeks later on 9th April, London Irish visited and, as they were still not safe, it promised to be another tight game and so it proved. As seemed to happen more often than not, we began with a penalty when Thomas was successful after 11 minutes. The Irish came back and went ahead when Everitt kicked a penalty and the conversion of Delon Armitage's try after 26 minutes. In the final ten minutes of the half, Thomas got two more penalties and we trailed 9-10. His fourth edged us ahead but Casey scored a try which Everitt converted as the pendulum swung back in favour of the visitors. Ugo Monye's try brought us level but it came from a forward pass although it was missed by the officials. As the final quarter began, Everitt put the Exiles back in front with his second penalty and when Thomas replied in kind, there were 12 minutes to go and the scores were level at 20-20. However, So'oialo was in the bin at this stage and, just before he was due back on, Reid went over from a scrum to score the match winning try. Yet another losing bonus point was little consolation as news came through that Leeds had won 33-15 at Gloucester. This defeat had dropped us to tenth on 37 points (Mark Evans's target for safety!), Northampton and Leeds were on 35 with the same wins and just four points separating them in the for and against columns. We now knew exactly what we had to do – win at Leeds in our next game on 17 April and deny them a bonus point.

Because Leeds had reached the Powergen Cup Final at Twickenham against Bath on 16th April (which they went on to win 20-12), our fixture, due to take place on Sunday 17th April, had to be moved and that is why we ended up playing in the evening on Tuesday 26th April. Those not able to travel up could watch the drama unfold on SKY TV as they very helpfully covered the match. After a scoreless first quarter, Staunton put us ahead with a penalty on 28 minutes. Snyman went over for a Leeds score (it took the video referee (David Matthews) three minutes to confirm the try) and Ross converted for a 7-3 half time lead. Just after the break, Staunton intercepted a Ross pass and sprinted in from half way to put us back in front. His conversion gave us a three point advantage. Unfortunately, it didn't last and, when we got to 65 minutes, the Tykes broke out from their 22 and Christophers took the scoring pass from Biggs to knock the stuffing out of us. With 12 minutes left, Snyman got his second and, as Ross put over both conversions, the home side led 21-10 and were on the verge of getting a bonus point. They would have got it as well if Regan had not blown an overlap. We couldn't respond and there was no more scoring. As this had been the last game of Round 21, we already knew that Northampton had won, London Irish lost but picked up a losing bonus point and Worcester lost. Simon Maling made his last appearance against Leeds before departing to Japan. Arwel Thomas also finished his short spell with us having scored 30 points (1 try, 7 penalties and 2 conversions) when he came on as a substitute as did Ace Tiatia. He had scored 40 points (8 tries) and had been sin binned 12 times during his 1st XV career.

So, we approached our date with destiny – 30th April 2005. It was just a coincidence that this was 17 years to the day when we had beaten Bristol 28-22 in the John Player Special Cup Final at Twickenham. Any of the bottom five teams could go down and this was how it looked on the final morning of the Premiership regular season.

Position	Team	Won	Drawn	Lost	Points	Points difference
8	London Irish	8		13	39	-36
9	Leeds	8		13	39	-55
10	Northampton	8		13	39	-61
11	Worcester	8		13	38	-130
12	Harlequins	6	1	14	37	-42

One headline said it all, it read simply – "Harlequins staring into the abyss" – indeed we were! The fixtures were Bath *v* Leeds, Gloucester *v* Saracens, Harlequins *v* Sale, Leicester *v* Wasps, Newcastle *v* London Irish and

Worcester *v* Northampton. The scenarios were too numerous to mention but, barring a miracle four try a piece draw between Worcester and Northampton, a win would see us to safety. All six matches kicked off at 3 p.m., the TV cameras were at Worcester with live updates coming from the Stoop, Bath and Newcastle. The atmosphere at the Stoop was a nervous one but we made a great start. Staunton went over for a try on 5 minutes and converted but, crucially, he couldn't do the same with James Hayter's try after 16 minutes (from an easy position). In the second quarter, Sale came back with Hanley scoring a try and Hodgson converting and adding a penalty. In first half injury time, Duffy scored and Staunton converted for a 19-10 lead. It all changed in the second half as Sale started to get closer to us. Hodgson got two penalties but Staunton sandwiched one between to make it 22-16 with eighteen minutes left. Then, with nine minutes of normal time remaining, disaster! Cueto weaved past Greenwood, Keogh and Duffy to score under the posts for Hodgson to convert – Quins 22 Sale 23. If it stayed like this, we were down. In the last minute of normal time, Sale gave away a penalty 41 metres out and in front of the posts. Up came Jeremy Staunton, he took his time and lined up the kick…it was on its way…it was on target and going over…but, it drifted wide of the left hand upright at the northern end of the ground. In time remaining, we huffed and puffed but couldn't get in a decent position for even a dropped goal attempt. The final whistle went after 97 minutes running time and we were relegated to National League 1. The sky had fallen in on the most famous club side in the World. In the games that mattered to relegation, Leeds won at Bath 10-6, London Irish lost at Newcastle 16-23 and Worcester beat Northampton 21-19. The bottom of the final table read as follows:-

Position	Team	Won	Drawn	Lost	Points	Points difference
8	Leeds	9		13	43	-51
9	Worcester	9		13	42	-128
10	London Irish	8		14	40	-43
11	Northampton	8		14	40	-63
12	Harlequins	6	1	15	38	-43

Some said it all came down to Jeremy Staunton's missed penalty (labelled as the most expensive kick in British Rugby history) but, at the end of the day, there were so many ifs and buts, it would be a shame to pin it on one man. However, would Paul Burke have missed so many crucial kicks during the season? Probably not but our fate was almost certainly settled by the absolutely appalling start we made with eight losses on the trot. Despite all that had gone before, it did all come down to that last game and our lack of killer instinct ultimately cost us. If we'd had it, Sale would not have come back like they did and we would have survived. The Quins team was Gavin Duffy, George Harder, Will Greenwood, Mel Deane, Simon Keogh, Jeremy Staunton, Steve So'oialo, Mike Worsley, James Hayter, Jon Dawson, Roy Winters, Simon Miall, Nick Easter, Andre Vos (captain) and Tony Diprose. Substitutes were Ace Tiatia (not used), Ceri Jones (replaced Worsley), Jim Evans (replaced Miall), Luke Sherriff (replaced Easter), Dafydd James (replaced Keogh), Arwel Thomas (not used) and Tom Williams (replaced Duffy).

Right away the Club believed they could bounce straight back. We would get a £1.5 million parachute payment from Premier Rugby Ltd. There was talk of up to 30 job losses (this never happened) and some said the Club might not even survive but this was never an option as the owners had put too much money into the projects at Quins. One columnist accused Evans & Co of treating the sport purely as business but the squad we had were easily capable of staying up and crucial mistakes throughout the whole season contributed to our relegation. The only regret Mark Evans has during this period is that he spread himself too thinly. He was trying to save money and get us bankable so we could borrow money by doing the coaching as well but by 2005, the Club was a lot bigger. Ironically, the following season would have seen the start of the money being spent on players.

In that fateful game, we said goodbye to four players; Dafydd James came on as a sub and had scored 15 points (3 tries) during his brief time with us, Jeremy Staunton had scored 221 points (3 tries, 2 dropped goals, 46 penalties and 31 conversions), Jon Dawson (10 points (2 tries)) and Roy Winters (15 points (3 tries) who was yellow carded on one occasion.

Evans said there was nothing good about relegation and players (including some legends of the Club) came to see him and said they were going. Unfortunately for them, there were contracts in place to give the Club an option of keeping them and that is what happened. He says we were relegated because of our start (0-8) and it put the Club back 18 months growth and financial wise. The following season would be one of damage limitation.

Our playing record was P32 W8 D2 L22 F596 A729 and in the League it was P22 W6 D1 L15 F416 A459 Pts 38 (BP12– TB 3 LB 9) Pos 12th. Obviously, this was our worst ever season because of relegation. Out of 32 matches played, Jones, Keogh and Miall only missed one game, Diprose and So'oialo played in 29 and Vos in 28. Top try scorers were Duffy, Keogh and Monye on just 5 each. Staunton got the most points with 221 (3 tries, 2 dropped goals, 46 penalties and 31 conversions) and subsequently was top for dropped goals, penalties and conversions. Overall, our points total was our worst since 1988/89 and all scoring dropped to reflect our worst number of wins since 1939/40 when the same number were won (but only 19 matches were played). Tries dropped by over 40 to 62, dropped goals by 3 to 2, penalties were down by 25 to 62 and conversions fell from 70 to 47.

2004/05

170804	GRAFTON BELFAST HARLEQUINS	BELFAST	W	9G(63)-1PG(3)
200804	ULSTER	RAVENHILL	W	3G1T(26)-2G1T(19)
270804	SARACENS	STOOP MEMORIAL GROUND	C	
040904	LONDON IRISH(ZP)	TWICKENHAM(A)	L	4PG(12)-1G2PG1T(18)
110904	NORTHAMPTON(ZP)	STOOP MEMORIAL GROUND	L	1PG2T(13)-3G3PG3T(45)
190904	NEWCASTLE(ZP)	NEWCASTLE	L	1G3PG1T(21)-1G5PG(22)
250904	BATH(ZP)	STOOP MEMORIAL GROUND	L	1G1PG(10)-1G1DG1PG1T(18)
021004	WORCESTER(ZP)	WORCESTER	L	1G(7)-4G1T(33)
091004	GLOUCESTER(ZP)	GLOUCESTER	L	2G3PG(23)-3G1PG1T(29)

161004	LEICESTER(ZP)	STOOP MEMORIAL GROUND	L	3PG(9)-5PG(15)
231004	MUNSTER(HECP)	THOMOND PARK, LIMERICK	L	3PG(9)-1G1PG1T(15)
301004	CASTRES OLYMPIQUE(HECP)	STOOP MEMORIAL GROUND	D	2G3PG(23)-6PG1T(23)
051104	LONDON WASPS(ZP)	ADAMS PARK	L	1G1DG2PG(16)-1G4PG(19)
121104	SARACENS(ZP)	STOOP MEMORIAL GROUND	W	5G1T(40)-2T(10)
191104	SHARKS(ZP)	EDGELEY PARK	W	1G4PG(19)-1G2PG(13)
281104	LEEDS(ZP)	STOOP MEMORIAL GROUND	W	2G4PG1T(31)-2G1PG(17)
051204	NEATH-SWANSEA OSPREYS(HECP)	SWANSEA	L	1G(7)-8PG(24)
111204	NEATH-SWANSEA OSPREYS(HECP)	STOOP MEMORIAL GROUND	L	1G4PG(19)-5G2PG1T(46)
181204	BATH(PC6)	BATH	L	1G(7)-3G4PG(33)
261204	SARACENS(ZP)	VICARAGE ROAD	D	1DG1T(8)-1PG1T(8)
020105	LONDON WASPS(ZP)	STOOP MEMORIAL GROUND	L	1G1PG1T(15)-2G1PG2T(27)
080105	CASTRES OLYMPIQUE(HECP)	CASTRES	L	1PG2T(13)-6G2PG2T(58)
150105	MUNSTER(HECP)	TWICKENHAM	L	1G1PG(10)-1G2PG1T(18)
290105	LEICESTER(ZP)	LEICESTER	L	2G1PG(17)-2G6PG(32)
050205	GLOUCESTER(ZP)	STOOP MEMORIAL GROUND	W	3G4PG1T(38)-3PG(9)
100205	NATAL SHARKS	STOOP MEMORIAL GROUND	L	1PG(3)-4G1PG(31)
190205	WORCESTER(ZP)	STOOP MEMORIAL GROUND	L	3PG(9)-5PG(15)
260205	BATH(ZP)	BATH	W	2G1PG(17)-1G1PG1T(15)
130305	NEWCASTLE(ZP)	STOOP MEMORIAL GROUND	W	2G5PG2T(39)-2G3PG(23)
260305	NORTHAMPTON(ZP)	NORTHAMPTON	L	2G2PG(20)-1G5PG(22)
090405	LONDON IRISH(ZP)	STOOP MEMORIAL GROUND	L	5PG1T(20)-2G2PG1T(25)

260405	LEEDS(ZP)	HEADINGLEY	L	1G1PG(10)-3G(21)
300405	SHARKS(ZP)	STOOP MEMORIAL GROUND	L	2G1PG1T(22)-2G3PG(23)

43

Survival, Promotion and Stability 2005-2009

The British and Irish Lions went to New Zealand for their 2005 tour to play eleven matches between 4th June and 9th July. In addition, they played a warm up game against Argentina on 23rd May in Cardiff. Sir Clive Woodward was the coach and he picked a larger than normal squad to cope with the extra demands of the modern game and the higher rate of injuries. In the end, this attracted a lot of criticism when the test series was lost 3-0 (they also drew with Argentina 25-25) but Woodward didn't really deserve this. In the first test, the Lions captain (Brian O'Driscoll) was put out of the tour by a dangerous tackle by Mealamu and Umaga after only a few minutes. This went totally unpunished and the Lions lost 3-21. The other two were lost 18-48 and 19-38 and in the other games, the record was W7 L1. Will Greenwood finally got his caps when he came on as a sub in the first test and started in the third. Our only other representative was future Quin Ollie Smith (he played against Argentina and scored a try).

On 30th June 2006, the whole of the Stoop Stadium was revalued and this time the figure was £20.8 million. The reported loss in the accounts was £641,049. The Stoop Memorial Ground was re-named the Twickenham Stoop to give some local identity to where the ground was actually located. Training facilities were to be used at Richardson Evans playing fields in Roehampton Vale (just off the A3 road out of London). We would stay here until 2010. NEC pledged their support for another two years and, as well as the parachute payment, we had £85,000 for playing in the lower division. It was announced that most of the squad would be retained which was a strong case for our immediate return to the Premiership. The best announcement of all was that Dean Richards would become our new Director of Rugby on a three year contract. Dean had played for Leicester, England and the British Lions during his career and then coached Leicester (very successfully) and Grenoble. He was just the right man to bring us back from the depths of despair. He came onto the radar and was highly recommended by Will Greenwood and Tony Russ. Andy Friend also arrived on a three year contract as Head Coach. He had been involved previously with Australia at U21 level and 7s, Waratahs and Suntory (Japan). An alliance was set up with London Broncos Rugby League team and they were to be re-named Harlequins Rugby League.

Those who did not stay included Dafydd James who went to Llanelli, Andy Dunne to Bath, Jeremy Staunton to Wasps, Roy Winters and Andy Reay to Bristol and Jon Dawson to Wasps.

Andre Vos went into his fourth year of captaincy, a year that was probably the most important so far in the history of the Club. We had to win promotion back to the Premiership in April – Failure was not an option!

Three friendlies had been set up against London Irish, Bristol and Saracens. We, of course, were now the minnows and would face Premiership clubs gearing up for a long season of domestic and European rugby. We only had the domestic league and cup to worry about and we would travel to practically every part of the country during the season. On 12th August, we met London Irish at the newly renamed Twickenham Stoop. Our biggest signing was Andrew Mehrtens, the New Zealand fly half who had won 70 caps between 1995 and 2004. He made the first of 39 appearances in this match when he came on as a substitute. Pablo Bouza was in the process of winning 39 Argentinian caps; he would make 17 appearances during his stay and also came on as a substitute. The third newcomer was Aston Croall. He would make 54 appearances over the following 7 seasons. George Robson made the first of 214 appearances when he too came on as a sub. This game was contested over three 30 minute periods and the Irish led after 26 minutes when Bishop got over in the corner for Everitt to convert. Mehrtens came on at the start of the second period and, in the first nine minutes, Mike Brown and Mehrtens grabbed tries which the latter named converted. It was 14-14 when Dawson scored for Everitt to convert and it was all to play for in the final session. The remaining scores came in the first ten minutes of the third period. Unfortunately, all from the visitors and tries from Laidlaw and Danaher both converted by the former made it 14-28 at the end.

Our second friendly was against the side who replaced us in the Premiership, Bristol. This was played at the Memorial Stadium on 20th August and saw the debut of three more young players who would form the backbone of the Club in the years to come. Chris Robshaw would go on to play at least 235 games and captain the Club in 2010-14 and England from 2012-15 (he would win at least 51 caps), Jordan Turner-Hall would make at least 190 appearances and win two England caps and Tom Guest would appear 223 times. All of them came on as subs and played their part in an excellent win. Tom Williams opened the scoring with a try after 35 minutes when he broke through the defence to score under the posts. Mehrtens converted as he did when he set up Monye for a long run in. After 47 minutes, our advantage went up to 21 points when Guest scored under the posts for Mehrtens to add the simple conversion. As the final quarter approached, the home side got their first points when Nelson scored a try and Gray converted; their second try by Robinson (also converted by Gray) came after Charlie Amesbury (another new boy) had scored our fourth. By this time, Adrian Jarvis had taken over the kicking duties and he added the conversion. He then scored in the corner after Brown, Turner-Hall and Harder had done the hard work. His final act of scoring was to add the points to Brown's try. Final score 40-14.

A week later, our third and final friendly took place at Harpenden RFC against Saracens. This was a close game all the way through and, after Jackson kicked a penalty for Sarries, Mehrtens created an overlap for Monye to score in the corner. Seymour scored, Jackson converted and added a penalty to make it 13-5 to the home side. Lorne Ward was bundled over and Mehrtens converted to narrow the lead to just one point at the break. A number of changes disrupted our play and Sanderson scored a try which Jackson failed to convert. We started to dominate and Steve So'oialo darted over for Mehrtens to convert and give us a one point advantage. When Monye got his second, it was 24-18 and we were on the verge of another win. As it was, we couldn't hold on and Jackson converted his own try to give the Premiership side victory by a single point with the last kick of the game.

Now it was down to the serious business of regaining our Premiership status and our first trip was to Solihull to play Pertemps Bees on 3rd September in National League 1. This was the first of 26 league games we would play and it would be like old times meeting sides like Coventry, London Welsh and Nottingham. The facilities at a lot of the grounds were basic but this was all part of life outside the top division and we had to get used to it. At Sharmans Cross Road, just before 3 p.m. Andre Vos led the team out into the unfamiliar surroundings and a crowd of 3,000. In the first 14 minutes, Monye and Harder scored tries which Andrew Mehrtens converted. Walsh replied with a penalty for the Bees after half an hour. His dropped goal four minutes into the second half was as close as the home side got. Tom Williams scored our third and Monye ran in the bonus point try (Mehrtens converted both) after Lamb had kicked a penalty for the Bees. Two minutes from time, Harder's second was converted by Jarvis to leave us winners by 35 points to 9. We ran into old friend Tu Tamarua here who had played for us back in 2001/02. After one round, we were top with Plymouth Albion, Cornish Pirates and Nottingham being the other bonus point winners.

Our first visit to Otley since March 1924 was our next task and this would be no easy game (the All Blacks had been beaten by The North at Cross Green back in 1979). This was a tough game and Otley played it as though it was a cup tie. Mehrtens kicked us ahead with a penalty after 29 minutes but a try by Whatmuff eight minutes later enabled Otley to lead at the interval. They extended this to 12-3 after 51 minutes when Luffman got over for Binns to convert. A Mehrtens penalty at the end of the third quarter was cancelled out by Binns three minutes later. Mel Deane came on for Greenwood fifteen minutes from the end as we desperately tried to avoid defeat. Andre Vos was driven over from a lineout, the conversion was missed but the gap was down to four points. As normal time ran out and five minutes of injury time followed, we made one last attempt. Evans and Vos drove forward and Mehrtens passed to Deane who crashed through the Otley defence to score by the posts. Mehrtens converted to make it 18-15 and the final whistle went immediately. Nottingham had a second bonus point win so we were second to them along with the Cornish Pirates on nine points.

Our first home league match of the season (because of the building works) saw Newbury visit on 17th September. It was the day chosen for the official opening of the Lexus Stand. The first half was a close affair, Mehrtens kicked a penalty and converted a try by Alex Rogers but Feeney had kicked two for Newbury in between and he converted Cracknell's try to give the visitor's a 13-10 lead at half time (despite having Cracknell in the bin for ten minutes). No one could have predicted what happened next. In the third quarter, Easter and Ian Vass scored and Mehrtens converted. The last 20 minutes saw us score no fewer than 28 points. Easter got his second and Amesbury, Keogh and Deane took our try tally to seven. Mehrtens and Jarvis (who had replaced the New Zealander) added two conversions each. Full time 52-13 and back to the top we went in front of Cornish Pirates on points difference. Newbury boasted no fewer than four players with Quins experience; Neil Collins (1993-95) and Mark Ireland (2002) had played for the 1st XV and Chris Cracknell and Isoa Damudamu had made appearances in lower teams.

Nottingham were met at Ireland Avenue, Beeston on 24th September. It had been over ten years since our last meeting and 15 years since our last win at Beeston. Andrew Mehrtens banged over five penalties in the first 22 minutes, Warnock pulled one back but Mehrtens was successful again when Duffey was sin binned for punching Vass. The home side scored just after the break when Arnold scored for Warnock to convert. When Jarvis replaced Mehrtens (who was injured), he immediately missed a penalty but made no mistake when Monye touched down under the posts. With Arnold in the bin, we were camped in Nottingham's 22 and Simon Keogh went over for our second try of the day for Jarvis to convert. The 32-10 victory wasn't enough to keep us on top because the Pirates had won with a bonus point as we moved into October.

At the Twickenham Stoop on 1st October, Doncaster were our opponents and they had another two ex-Quins in their squad, Rob Liley (1997-2000) and Johnny Roddam (2001-02) (Liley didn't play against us but Roddam did). When Simon Keogh ran in after just 107 seconds, it looked like we might continue where we had left off in our previous home game but Duffy's try after 16 minutes was our only other score in the first half. Jarvis had an off day with the boot and missed both conversions. Doncaster made it 10-7 at the break when Hunt scored for Benson to convert. Ten minutes into the second period, Rogers crashed over, Jarvis converted and we were on our way to our fifth win. With 12 minutes to go, Tosh Masson scored the bonus point try and Mike Brown put the icing on the cake at the end of normal time. Jarvis again missed both conversions to leave it at 27-7. Back to the top we went by one point from Bedford Blues (22) and Cornish Pirates (19) as the gaps started to appear in the table.

Coventry were another club we used to play on a regular basis. Our last meeting with them had been in March 1996 when they had beaten us 44-10. Instead of Coundon Road, they now played at the Butts Park Arena so another new venue for us to visit. Heavy rain hampered both teams but Coventry began well and scored a try after just 101 seconds through their prop Pulu. Mehrtens got a penalty and converted a try from Ceri Jones but Moore landed a penalty for the home side in between and kicked another when Mike Brown was sin binned (although this was later rescinded at a disciplinary hearing). So'oialo scored for Mehrtens to convert to ensure that we led at half time. Our wet weather game was going well and Keogh had an easy run into the corner to stretch the lead. Gulliver was sent to the bin for ten minutes and Jim Evans was the man to get the fourth try. Mehrtens converted and did the same to Keogh's second before a consolation for Coventry from Higgins (converted by Moore) made it 36-18. Because of our fourth try bonus point of the season, we were now two points ahead of Bedford, four ahead of Cornish Pirates and eight clear of Newbury. It seemed that we would explode against someone and run in a hatful of tries.

Our next opponents were Exeter Chiefs at the Stoop on 22nd October. We had met only once before, back in September 1967 at Exeter when a narrow 13-8 scoreline had gone in our favour on a pre-season tour. This time, there was no chance of a close contest as Evans, Monye and Fuga scored tries in the first 18 minutes to put us on track. In first half injury time, further scores from Easter and Duffy (converted by Mehrtens) made it 27-0. The procession continued after the break and before the 60 minute mark, Monye completed his hat-trick, Sherriff, Keogh and Masson added others and Mehrtens converted all but Monye's second and Keogh's. This made it 58-0 but we weren't quite finished yet and Monye was put in twice in five minutes near the end by Masson and then Brown to become the first Quins player to score 5 tries in a game since Daren O'Leary against Newcastle Gosforth in February 1996. Jarvis converted the first of his brace to take us to the seventy point mark but our line was breached a minute from time when Fatialofa got a try. We now led the table by three points from Bedford with Cornish Pirates on 29. Newbury were fourth with 20 points and it seemed, even at this early stage, that anyone below this was out of the running.

Our fourth visit to Rotherham saw our third visit to Clifton Lane. This time, the ground had been renamed as the Earth Arena and the team name changed to Earth Titans. Two of the home side would join us the following season – Chris Hala'ufia and David Strettle. A good start put us 8-0 up in seven minutes (Mehrtens with a penalty and a Masson try) after which, the Titans came into the game and stopped us from scoring for over forty minutes. When the breakthrough came it was Nick Easter who scored for Mehrtens to add the two points. The Titans scored their only points when Mitchell burst through our defence to score, Strauss converted to make it 15-7. Easter's second try (converted by Mehrtens) with 17 minutes to go including injury time gave us the opportunity to go for the bonus point. Brown did get over in the corner with the last move of the match but the referee ruled it out for a forward pass. At the top of the table, it was now a three horse race for the title. We had 37 points, Bedford 35 and Cornish Pirates were just behind on 34.

Our next two fixtures were away at the same venue – Sedgley Park in Whitefield, Manchester. The first was in the 5th round of the Powergen National Trophy. The second tier domestic competition was another result of our relegation. The home side had a dream start when De Jager kicked a penalty and converted a try by Woof (after he had charged down an attempted clearance by Mehrtens). A few minutes later, we got our act together and Kevin Burke scored a brace in five minutes followed by a penalty try from a five metre scrum. Mehrtens converted all three (the last two had been scored while Ponton had been in the bin) and when De Jager got his second penalty, it was

21-13 at the interval. Sedgley failed to add to their tally after this but we piled on the points. In the third quarter, tries from Williams, Harder, Guest and Keogh (all but the last converted by Mehrtens) made it 47-13. Mehrtens was replaced by Duffy so Tom Williams took over the kicking duties and landed the conversions of our last two tries scored by Keogh and Greenwood. The full time score of 61-13 sent us through to the sixth round.

Six days later on Saturday 12th November we met again, this time in a league fixture. We had a good start when So'oialo scored after five minutes and Rowe was sent to the sin bin two minutes later. During his time off the field, Evans got our second which Mehrtens converted. Sedgley Park started to dominate and Woof got a try and Jones converted. In the last five minutes before the break, each side scored a try. Miall got ours (converted by Mehrtens) and Hall scored for the Tigers. Ugo Monye secured our fourth try ten minutes into the second half, Jones pulled three points back with a penalty but Gavin Duffy scored with 15 minutes to go to make it 29-15. At this point, we got sloppy and allowed our opponents back into it. They could only score one try through Voortman for De Jager to convert and give them a losing bonus point. Afterwards, our captain and Director of Rugby slammed our sloppy play for allowing three tries. On the balance of play, we could not have argued if Sedgley Park had tied the game at the end. We remained in first place (42pts) but Cornish Pirates (39pts) leap-frogged Bedford (35pts) into second because they didn't play.

The first big game of the season took place at the Stoop on 20th November against Cornish Pirates before a record National League 1 crowd of 10,843. In a former guise of Penzance and Newlyn, we had met down in Penzance just the once when we emerged 5-3 winners in February 1952. The Pirates had promised us a tough game and the first half proved to be exactly that. Andrew Mehrtens outscored Barlow 4-2 in penalties to leave the score at 12-6 at the break. Unfortunately, we lost Mel Deane who was stretchered off after lying prone on the turf for five minutes – he was out for just over a month with a head injury. A fifth penalty from Mehrtens started us off in the second period and when Senekal was sin binned after 57 minutes, we took full advantage. Sherriff and Easter went over, Mehrtens converted both and we were well clear at 29-6. In the last ten minutes, Williams, Monye and Greenwood added further scores (Mehrtens converted the first two and Jarvis the last) to take us to fifty. Another bonus point took us eight clear of the Pirates and eleven ahead of Bedford.

Our next match was a friendly against Manu Samoa on 23rd November at the Stoop. Steve So'oialo was called into the Samoa team at the last minute to play against us. James Hayter was named as captain in the absence of Andre Vos, the only time he would get the honour. Jarvis started for Mehrtens and kicked four penalties in the first half. Lui scored a penalty and converted an excellent try from Salima to keep Samoa in touch. So'oialo came on after 44 minutes and scored the final try of the game eight minutes from time. In the intervening period, Jarvis got his fifth penalty and Kerslake was sent off for stamping on Charlie Amesbury at a ruck. Three minutes later, Rogers scored our first try and four minutes after that, George Robson was driven over to seal the win. Jarvis added both conversions to make the final score 29-15.

Against Bridgwater and Albion, it was back to cup action and the Powergen National Trophy 6th round. Thirty two years before (October 1973), we had met in Bridgwater in the first round of the RFU Knock-out Competition. We had edged a close tie by twelve points to six. It was highly unlikely that the scoreline would be anything like that this time as they were four levels below us in the league structure. The tie was all but over in the first sixteen minutes as we ran in tries through Jordan Turner-Hall, Luke Sherriff (both converted by Mehrtens) and Andre Vos. Mike Worsley suffered a career ending injury after 19 minutes when he broke one of his legs. He had scored one try (5 points) during his three season stint at the Club. Before the interval, Monye scored two tries. The first when Hastie was in the sin bin, the second after Hastie had received his second yellow (equalling a red card) to reduce Albion to fourteen men. Four changes were made by Dean Richards at half time – Burke, Robshaw, Jarvis and Amesbury replacing Miall, Vos, Mehrtens and Monye respectively. This took the edge off our play and, after Williams scored our sixth try, we had to wait another 24 minutes for the seventh to arrive. Burke scored it and Ian Vass added another before the end, Jarvis converted both and we were in the quarter finals with an easy 48-0 victory. This was our thirteenth win on the trot and broke the Club record of twelve that had been in existence since February 1909 (it had been equalled in 1988/89 and 1996).

Another crunch game followed on Saturday 3rd December at Goldington Road, Bedford. Another old foe against who we had last played in a pre-season friendly in August 2001; the result was a 61-5 victory for us. This would be a hard fought fixture as Bedford had a strong squad with a lot of experience. Future Quins scrum half Karl Dickson was part of that squad although he didn't make an appearance against us. We had a dream start and led 13-0 after only eleven minutes. Mehrtens kicked a penalty either side of a Simon Keogh try that he converted. Harris grabbed three points with a penalty for the Blues but losing Staten to the bin enabled us to score a try by Tom Williams. Mehrtens added the two points to make it 20-3 at half time. Bedford came out firing on all cylinders and Moir scored followed nine minutes later by Phillips (both converted by Harris). In between, Vos went to the bin and Mehrtens kicked a penalty. When Vos returned, Phillips went the other way when he prevented So'oialo from taking a quick penalty and Mehrtens kicked the goal at the end of the third quarter. Harris did get his second penalty three minutes from time but we held on for a 26-20 victory to maintain our eight point advantage at the top and pass 50 points. We were now 14 points ahead of Bedford and had effectively put them out of contention as well.

A trip down to Devon to play Plymouth Albion on 10th December was our last away game of the year. They would visit us on 7th January in the Powergen National Trophy quarter final. We were grateful to the goal kicking of Andrew Mehrtens in this one as his two penalties gave us an early lead. Plymouth hit back and Saumi scored a try and landed two penalties to give them the lead. Easter levelled the scores with a try before Tooala put the home side back in front with their second try. Saumi again missed the conversion and half time came with the score at 11-16. The second period saw us dominate possession and Mehrtens kicked four penalties to put us in front by seven. Easter was sin binned near the end and Albion attacked to try and draw the game but our defence held firm. Plymouth lost their fly half (Barnes) to the bin for an offence at the death and our lead at the top remained the same.

On Boxing Day, London Welsh were the visitors at the Stoop and they hadn't played us since August 2001 when we had won easily by 55-0. Tom Williams opened the scoring after 11 minutes with a try and Mehrtens drop-goaled the conversion before Cholewa opened the account for the visitors with a penalty. Harder scored our second and when Hannon went to the bin, Easter, Keogh and Sherriff added tries to see us to the try bonus point. Mehrtens converted all but the last and the game was over at 33-3. In the second half, we switched off and the Welsh scored tries through Chiltern and Swords. Fortunately, the conversions were missed and Williams grabbed his second for Mehrtens to convert. After 60 minutes, five substitutions were made and we conceded another two tries by Swales and Hannon. Again the extra points were missed otherwise it could have been a lot closer. We had enough in reserve and Gavin Duffy scored try number seven with the last move of the game and Jarvis converted for a final score of 47-23.

The new year of 2006 began with a home game against Pertemps Bees. We produced a brilliant first half display and ran in five tries through Brown, Robshaw, Miall, Robshaw again and Jones. Mehrtens converted all five and all the Bees could offer in reply was a penalty by Walsh that briefly made the score 14-3. They lost Orgee to the bin which further hampered them but, at 35-3, there was no way back. The second half was very scrappy and the only scores were a second try from Jones which Brown converted. A succession of substitutions further disrupted the play and it finished 42-3. The table now read Quins 65 points, Pirates 56, Blues 56 and we had all played 14 matches.

The Powergen National Trophy quarter final was played against Plymouth Albion. On their only previous visit to the Stoop they had proved victorious by 21-9 in September 1991. This was our fourth cup meeting and we had yet to lose. Judging by the league fixture four weeks ago, this would be no walk over. Saumi opened the scoring with a penalty for the visitors but a minute later, Ceri Jones put us in front with a try. Saumi kicked his second penalty and converted a try by Rice but, in between, Fuga and Jarvis scored tries (Jarvis converted his own) and we led at the interval by 17-13. Saumi opened the scoring in the second half as he had done in the first but this was as close as Albion would get. Jarvis dropped a goal and converted a second try from Jones before Saumi knocked over another penalty as the tie entered the last ten minutes of normal time. With five to go, Jarvis landed his first penalty of the game before Dawe scored Plymouth's second try a minute from the end. As the visitors tried to run from deep, Harder put in a massive tackle to dislodge the ball, Greenwood kicked the ball forward and kept it in play with an expert flick and Harder was on hand to finish off. Jarvis converted with the last kick of the game and we were into the semi-final by 37 points to 24.

Otley visited next and it was back to league action as we looked to maintain our lead at the top. At various points, Otley had Shuttleworth, Luffman and Fullman in the sin bin and were down to 13 men for a brief period in the second half. We scored first with Ceri Jones getting a try after 15 minutes for Jarvis to convert, Shuttleworth pulled back a penalty before Jarvis got a penalty and Amesbury scored a try just before half time. A penalty try came eight minutes into the second half, Jarvis converted and Shuttleworth went to the bin for questioning the referee's decision. Keogh scored a minute later, Jarvis added a fifth and Amesbury went over to take us over forty points again. Jarvis got all three conversions to leave the final score at 43-3. This win took us to seventy points, a nine point advantage over the Pirates and the Blues.

The trip to Monks Lane to play Newbury was, apart from London Welsh, our nearest away game. Another excellent first half performance from us saw Tani Fuga score after only 74 seconds (Newbury had bungled our kick-off), Mehrtens added a second five minutes later, converted it and Fuga scored his second five minutes after that. Carter got a try for Newbury but Easter scored the bonus point try after only 22 minutes which Mehrtens converted. We still weren't finished and So'oialo and Keogh took our tally to six, Mehrtens added the extras to both and a penalty by Rogers in between made the score 38-8 at the interval. In the first twenty minutes after half time, Brown, Keogh and Easter all scored (Mehrtens converted the first and last). Bingham scored for the home side after Keogh's try but, at 13-57, it was all too late. Bell went to the sin bin for Newbury and we lost Miall and Evans the same way. As we played the last six minutes with fourteen men, the Blues took full advantage and scored tries through Hart (converted by Roberts) and Bell to claim the try bonus point and make the final score 57-25. With ten league fixtures left, we were still nine points clear of Bedford.

Nottingham visited next and they would be our semi-final opponents in the Powergen National Trophy in five weeks' time. As against Newbury, we came out firing on all cylinders and, despite playing against the wind, we were 14-0 up in twelve minutes. Duffy and Guest got tries and Jarvis converted both before Nottingham pulled back three points with a penalty from Stenhouse. Guest got his second (again converted by Jarvis), Arnold scored for the visitors, Stenhouse converted and kicked another penalty after Jarvis had landed one for us. After the break, Stenhouse kicked his third penalty and the visitors were playing well. Despite losing Cook and Chesworth to the bin, they managed to hold out with 13 men and we were still searching for our fourth try going into the final 13 minutes. After 74 minutes, Duffy made a break that enabled us to reach the

Nottingham line where Jim Evans forced his way over for the try. Jarvis converted to ensure our seventeenth straight league win.

Two weeks later, we travelled to Doncaster and totally destroyed them in the first half. After 15 minutes, there was a mass brawl and Miall for us and Cook for Doncaster were sent to cool off for ten minutes. At this point, we led 10-0 (Jarvis had kicked a penalty and the conversion of a try by Tom Williams) and by the time they came back, Jarvis had converted his own try and one from Evans. A minute before the break, Ugo Monye made it another bonus point game when he got over for Jarvis to convert – 31-0. Two minutes into the second half, Guest got number five for Jarvis to again convert. A whole host of substitutions were then made and Doncaster had a lot of possession and territory in our half. However, excellent defence prevented them from scoring and Simon Keogh intercepted a pass and ran over 70 metres to score under the posts. Jarvis was down injured so Will Greenwood stepped up to put over the conversion. There was no more scoring and the 45-0 win was our second biggest winning margin of the season so far. With 85 points, we were now thirteen ahead of Bedford and nineteen in front of Cornish Pirates (they had both lost games recently).

Coventry were in 7th place and trailed us by some 46 points when they came to the Stoop on 18th February. Straight from the kick-off, Guest, Greenwood and Duffy put Monye over in the corner after just 13 seconds and a good run bagged him his second on 16 minutes. Stewart scored for Coventry but a brace from Ceri Jones (both converted by Jarvis) took us well clear by half time. With yet another bonus point secured, Duffy scored at the half way point of the second half for Jarvis to convert. Moore converted his own try but Easter quickly snuffed out any thoughts of a comeback. The conversion by Jarvis took the score to 38-12 and when he was replaced by the newly-wed Andrew Mehrtens, Easter and Tom Williams scored tries near the end for him to convert and take us past the fifty point mark for the sixth time this season in 26 matches. This was our 23rd consecutive victory and surpassed a run of 22 matches unbeaten between 28th November 1874 and 29th January 1876.

Against Exeter Chiefs at the County Ground, we played against a strong wind in the first half and held on for 24 minutes when Yapp put over a penalty. Mehrtens missed a similar attempt four minutes later and when Lorne Ward went off for ten minutes for foul play, Yapp doubled the lead. Six minutes before the interval, Keogh scored in the left hand corner but Mehrtens was again off target with the conversion. At half time, it was 6-5 to the home side. After 52 minutes Luff broke through and scored a try, Yapp converted and we trailed by eight points. Mehrtens missed another two penalties but finally got one with six minutes left to set up a tight finish. Despite having Hanks in the bin during the last quarter, the Mehrtens penalty was all we could muster and thanks to some excellent defence, the Chiefs held out for a famous victory. Our losing bonus point maintained our lead at the top as Bedford went down at home to Nottingham.

On 5th March, we travelled to Nottingham for the Powergen National Trophy semi-final at Ireland Avenue, Beeston. The pressure on us to reach our first Twickenham Final since February 2001 was immense and this would be a tense affair. When we were caught offside after two minutes, Stenhouse opened the scoring with a penalty but we were in front six minutes later when Nick Easter ran in for Jarvis to convert. Four minutes after this, Fitisemanu scored for Nottingham and Stenhouse converted but Duffy put us back in front on 26 minutes. Jarvis converted and added a penalty to open up a seven point gap at half time. There was no scoring in the third quarter but the home side had a period of pressure in our twenty two. Our defence was excellent and when George Harder came on, he set up Easter for his second try. The conversion by Jarvis took us two scores clear, there was no way back for Nottingham and we had reached the final where we would meet Bedford.

The Earth Titans were next on the fixture list and arrived at the Stoop in fifth place. There were now only three teams who had a mathematical chance of winning the league – us, Bedford and Cornish Pirates. Every point we picked up now would ease us back into the Premiership so we still had to keep winning. Titans took the lead through a Whitehead penalty after two minutes but by the time he converted a try by Strauss, we were in front. Jarvis kicked a penalty and converted tries from So'oialo and Tom Williams. When he converted his own try after 33 minutes, we were 24-10 up and looking good to secure another try bonus point. That duly arrived seven minutes into the second half when Tony Diprose scored for Jarvis to convert. The Titans failed to add to their ten points as we scored three more tries in the final 30 minutes. Harder, Easter and Keogh all went over, Jarvis converted the second and Mehrtens the last to make the final score 50-10. A loss for the Pirates knocked them out of contention so we now knew that, at this point, we needed just 13 points to finish top and gain an immediate return to the Premiership.

Two weeks later, the long trip to Truro was made for the return fixture against Cornish Pirates. A hostile crowd filled the Kenwyn Rugby Club ground to capacity with wind and driving rain adding to the difficulties. With 8 minutes on the clock, Williams burst through and sent Monye over near the posts for Jarvis to convert. He added a penalty nine minutes later but the Pirates came back and Cattle got over the line and Lee Jarvis added a penalty. Three minutes later, Williams received the scoring pass after a good run by Keogh and Jarvis made it a nine point lead at half time. Our third try came 11 minutes into the second half when Keogh had an unopposed run in after a Pirates knock-on. Jarvis again converted and five minutes after the home side had made four substitutions, we killed the game off. Gavin Duffy spotted Guest on the right wing and put in a cross-field kick. It was perfect, he flipped the ball back as he was tackled and Will Greenwood dribbled it slowly over the line and touched down for another five-pointer. Mehrtens failed with the conversion and 29-8 was how it finished. Bedford were now in the position that, if they lost a game and we won with a bonus point, that would be the end of their hopes. As it was, this victory had taken us to 101 points.

Our next game was against Sedgley Park Tigers at the Stoop on 1st April. They were in 13th spot and trailed us by some 67 points! The Tigers took the lead after nine minutes when Albinson went over for a try. A minute later, Skurr was sin-binned for a dangerous tackle and by the time he returned, we were well in front. Fuga, Monye and Guest scored tries (all converted by Jarvis) and Jones got a penalty for the visitors. It got worse for Sedgley Park as we piled on the points before half time. Greenwood, Williams (converted by Jarvis) and Duffy all went over to give us a 30 point lead at the interval (38-8). Another five tries followed to complete the rout with Brown, Easter, Keogh (converted by Mehrtens), Miall and Easter again all crossing the line. The final score of 65-8 meant that if Bedford lost at Exeter, we were up. As the result was announced, those who stayed behind were rewarded for their patience; Exeter 26 Bedford 23! We were Champions and would be returning to the Premiership in September.

This left us in buoyant mood for our next fixture. It was the Powergen National Trophy Final at Twickenham on Sunday 9th April against Bedford Blues. For much of the game it was nip and tuck with little to choose between the sides. The lead changed hands no fewer than five times in the first half after Hepher had opened the scoring with a penalty for Bedford ten minutes in. Fuga's pass sent Williams over to give us the lead but Miall was sin-binned for pulling down his opposite number at a lineout. The Blues made the extra man count and were awarded a penalty try which Hepher converted before Greenwood got our second try for Jarvis to convert and edge us back in front. The lead lasted three minutes until Kettle went over and Hepher converted. We were back to full strength but Bedford lost Malone to the bin as he failed to retreat ten metres at a quickly taken penalty. In the five minutes leading up to the break, Jarvis slotted two penalties to put us in front 18-17 with all to play for in the second half. Bedford were briefly down to 13 men when Brady saw yellow for a dangerous challenge on Fuga and Jarvis stretched the lead by kicking the penalty. Jarvis twice exchanged penalties with Hepher to leave the score at 27-23 to us with eight minutes of normal time remaining. With two minutes left, Easter broke from a scrum and sent Keogh racing over for our third try and Bedford were almost beaten. We continued to attack and, six minutes into injury time, Easter powered over from a tap penalty. Jarvis added the points and we had won our first cup final at Twickenham since 1991 by 39-23. It was fitting that the top two in the league had battled it out in a great final.

Our away game against London Welsh had been switched by them from the Old Deer Park to the Stoop. It had been thought that this would be the promotion winning game and the expected bumper crowd would bring them some much needed cash. As it was, the crowd of 5,120 was over 4,000 above their average home attendance. After Keogh and Brown scored tries in the first quarter and repeated the feat in reverse order in the second quarter, the try bonus point was secure once again. The home side got two of their own between the two batches of scores through Holgate (converted by Cannon) and Ritchie. Jarvis converted all four of ours so we led 28-12 at the interval. Ricky Nebbett went to cool off for ten minutes as a scrappy start to the second half continued. We failed to score again but the Welsh had a long period of pressure and dominated towards the end. They could, however, only score one more try by Swales to give us another win. After the game, Andre Vos was presented with the National League One trophy amid wild celebrations.

As we had started with two away games because of the building works, we finished with two home games and the first of these was against Bedford Blues. Continuing where we had left off in the Powergen National Trophy Final, another high scoring game ensued. Jarvis and Hepher exchanged penalties and then Ugo Monye and his replacement, Mike Brown went over for tries. Jarvis converted the second as well as Easter's effort after Page had scored for Bedford (Hepher converted). Harding got their second and before Hepher converted, Nebbett went to the bin again for throwing a punch. By half time and before our prop came back, Williams scored our fourth try, Jarvis converted and added a penalty to make it 32-17. Eight minutes into the second period, Jarvis put over his third penalty and ten minutes later, got his fourth. In between these, Brady went over for the Blues for Hepher to convert. When Dickson went to the sin bin, it took us eight minutes of it to add to our total. Will Greenwood was put over by Williams and Jarvis converted to give us a 21 point lead with 20 minutes to go including injury time. Bedford would not give up and they scored two tries in the last six minutes. First Roberts and then Allen (converted by Lewis) made the final score 45-36.

Pablo Bouza, Tony Diprose and Will Greenwood all made their final appearances in the last match of the season against Plymouth Albion on 29th April. Pablo had scored 5 points (1 try) during his time in the 1st XV, Tony had played for five seasons, scored 40 points (8 tries), captained the side on seven occasions and been sin-binned twice and Will had played for a total of eight seasons (either side of a four season spell at Leicester), scored 312 points (52 tries, 2 dropped goals, 8 penalties, 11 conversions), been captain on two occasions and had just one visit to the bin. Having been part of the World Cup winning England side in 2003, Will had achieved just about everything there was to in the game. He would be sorely missed.

The only question remaining was whether we could pass 1000 league points for the season. Before the start of play, we had 962 points for and only 322 against. Andrew Mehrtens started for the first time since the Exeter game on 25th February and was on target after 10 minutes with a penalty. At the end of the first quarter, Albion took the lead when Rice got a try, Mehrtens then exchanged penalties with Barnes and converted So'oialo's try on 31 minutes. Our narrow half time lead of 13-8 was stretched when Rouse was sin-binned; So'oialo and Guest scored tries and Mehrtens added the extras. Plymouth were awarded a penalty try when Mike Brown was adjudged to have deliberately knocked-on a scoring pass near our line and Barnes converted. Thomas became Plymouth's second player in the bin and we closed out the game while he was off. Pablo Bouza went over for our fourth try (our 20th try bonus point) for Jarvis to convert. As the game went into injury time, Brown chipped ahead and Tom Williams just won the race to touch down our 137th league try to take us to 1001 league points for the season. Will Greenwood took the conversion attempt but was unsuccessful. He was then replaced by Mel Deane and left the field to a standing ovation. He had been a truly great servant to the Club. The final whistle went three minutes later to bring down the curtain on our National League One adventure. Full time - Quins 39 Plymouth Albion 15. Out of the nightmare of relegation, we had triumphed to make an immediate return to the big time. There was no other option and it was too scary to even contemplate the consequences had we not gone straight back up.

Our overall playing record was P35 W32 D0 L3 F1317 A489, in the league it was P26 W25 D0 L1 F1001 A337 Pts 121 (BP 21– TB 20 LB 1) Pos 1st. Simon Miall only missed one game and he was two ahead of Easter and Keogh (32) with Duffy and Ward a further one behind on 31. Keogh and Monye were joint top try scorers with 21 each and these were the most scored since 1996/97 when Daren O'Leary managed 28. Andrew Mehrtens got the most points with 229 (2 tries, 29 penalties and 66 conversions) and subsequently, the most penalties and conversions; Jarvis dropped the only goal. Overall, a stark contrast was seen from the relegation season, probably due to the inferior opposition but, this is put into perspective by the fact that our squad was not as strong as it would have been had we stayed up. Our points total was the highest ever and topped 1996/97 by over 100. Of course it was also the highest number of tries, beating the records of 1995/96 and 1996/97 by 15 and we topped 100 conversions for the first time as well beating the previous best of 98 in 1996/97 by 34. Because of the amount of tries, not surprisingly, dropped goals fell to just one and penalties dropped to just 50 from 62 the previous season. The total number of wins (32) was another all-time record and beat the previous best of 25 from 32 matches in 1995/96. Three losses also set a record beating 1909/10 when four games were lost out of 23.

2005/06

120805	LONDON IRISH	TWICKENHAM STOOP	L	2G(14)-4G(28)
200805	BRISTOL	BRISTOL	W	5G1T(40)-2G(14)
270805	SARACENS	HARPENDEN	L	2G2T(24)-2G2PG1T(25)
030905	PERTEMPS BEES(NL1)	SOLIHULL	W	5G(35)-1DG1PG(9)
100905	OTLEY(NL1)	OTLEY	W	1G2PG1T(18)-1G1PG1T(15)
170905	NEWBURY(NL1)	TWICKENHAM STOOP	W	7G1PG(52)-1G2PG(13)
240905	NOTTINGHAM(NL1)	NOTTINGHAM	W	2G6PG(32)-1G1PG(10)
011005	DONCASTER(NL1)	TWICKENHAM STOOP	W	1G4T(27)-1G(7)
081005	COVENTRY(NL1)	COVENTRY	W	4G1PG1T(36)-1G2PG1T(18)
221005	EXETER(NL1)	TWICKENHAM STOOP	W	5G7T(70)-1T(5)

291005	EARTH TITANS(NL1)	ROTHERHAM	W	2G1PG1T(22)-1G(7)
061105	SEDGLEY PARK(PT5)	SEDGLEY PARK	W	8G1T(61)-1G2PG(13)
121105	SEDGLEY PARK(NL1)	SEDGLEY PARK	W	2G3T(29)-2G1PG1T(22)
201105	CORNISH PIRATES(NL1)	TWICKENHAM STOOP	W	5G5PG(50)-2PG(6)
231105	MANU SAMOA	TWICKENHAM STOOP	W	2G5PG(29)-1G1PG1T(15)
261105	BRIDGWATER & ALBION(PT6)	BRIDGWATER	W	4G4T(48)-0
031205	BEDFORD(NL1)	BEDFORD	W	2G4PG(26)-2G2PG(20)
101205	PLYMOUTH ALBION(NL1)	PLYMOUTH	W	6PG1T(23)-2PG2T(16)
261205	LONDON WELSH(NL1)	TWICKENHAM STOOP	W	6G1T(47)-1PG4T(23)
020106	PERTEMPS BEES (NL1)	TWICKENHAM STOOP	W	6G(42)-1PG(3)
070106	PLYMOUTH ALBION(PTQF)	TWICKENHAM STOOP	W	3G1DG1PG2T(37)-1G4PG1T(24)
140106	OTLEY(NL1)	TWICKENHAM STOOP	W	5G1PG1T(43)-1PG(3)
210106	NEWBURY(NL1)	NEWBURY	W	6G3T(57)-1G1PG3T(25)
280106	NOTTINGHAM(NL1)	TWICKENHAM STOOP	W	4G1PG(31)-1G3PG(16)
120206	DONCASTER(NL1)	DONCASTER	W	6G1PG(45)-0
180206	COVENTRY(NL1)	TWICKENHAM STOOP	W	6G2T(52)-1G1T(12)
250206	EXETER(NL1)	EXETER	L	1PG1T(8)-1G2PG(13)
050306	NOTTINGHAM(PTSF)	NOTTINGHAM	W	3G1PG(24)-1G1PG(10)
110306	EARTH TITANS(NL1)	TWICKENHAM STOOP	W	6G1PG1T(50)-1G1PG(10)
260306	CORNISH PIRATES(NL1)	TRURO	W	3G1PG1T(29)-1PG1T(8)
010406	SEDGLEY PARK(NL1)	TWICKENHAM STOOP	W	5G6T(65)-1PG1T(8)
090406	BEDFORD(PTF)	TWICKENHAM	W	2G5PG2T(39)-2G3PG(23)
150406	LONDON WELSH(NL1)	TWICKENHAM STOOP(A)	W	4G(28)-1G2T(17)
220406	BEDFORD(NL1)	TWICKENHAM STOOP	W	4G4PG1T(45)-4G1PG1T(36)
290406	PLYMOUTH ALBION(NL1)	TWICKENHAM STOOP	W	4G2PG1T(39)-1G1PG1T(15)

In June 2006, it was the same old story in the two test series in Australia as England went through a bad patch. As we were doing the same, we had no current representatives, just a host of former and future Quins. Stuart Abbott, Duncan Bell, Scott Bemand, Peter Richards, Pat Sanderson (who was captain in both) and Nick Walshe. Richards, Sanderson and Walshe played in both matches, the last named as a sub and Abbott was a sub in the second test. The Wallabies ran away with both games by 34-3 and 43-18 respectively.

In the accounts for year ending 30th June 2007, the loss was £1,090,425. It seemed to be a never ending cycle of doom and gloom with the finances but it was hoped that the Club would become financially stable eventually. This season would see a lot more money being put into the team, training ground and support staff. There would be a business case for the stadium build and a proper development programme for the future.

Back in July 2005, as already mentioned, it was announced that the London Broncos Rugby League side would change their name to Harlequins Rugby League. They would also ground share with us from 2006 and wear our colours. Mark Evans said that there was an opportunity in the coming years to build Harlequins into a powerhouse in both codes. The Broncos stressed that this was not a merger or a takeover and both clubs remained separate entities. Sadly, the dream never became a reality, crowds were disappointing and Harlequins Rugby League finished 7th, 9th, 9th, 11th, 13th and 12th in the years 2006-2011 before the venture ended and the team was back to being called London Broncos again. It had certainly been worth trying to make a success of it but, in truth, it had been a disaster.

A huge number of new players joined during the close season and one of them, Paul Volley, was named as the man to succeed Andre Vos as Club captain and lead us back into the Premiership. Three friendly games had been arranged; two in France and one in Wales. For those who didn't travel, their first glimpse of the side would be in the London Double Header at Twickenham on 2nd September against London Irish in the Guinness Premiership (the title sponsor had changed during our absence). We travelled to Issoire in France to play ASM Clermont Auvergne on 6th August as part of our build up to that game. After Malzieu scored a try to give Clermont the lead on 4 minutes, Jarvis put over a penalty to open our account. Good work by Brown, Jarvis and Strettle enabled Robson to score next to the posts to make it a simple two points for Jarvis. Our try scorer then went to the bin for deliberately killing the ball and that enabled our opponents to add seven points to their total to lead 12-10 at the half time. Tosh Masson was adjudged to have made a dangerous tackle and off he went for ten minutes. Before we scored again through Jones for Jarvis to convert, the French side had added two goals to make the final score 17-26. New boys in this game were Danny Care, a young scrum half who made the first of at least 218 appearances and would go on to win at least 62 caps for England, Ollie Kohn (came on as a substitute) who would make 150 appearances and win 1 cap for Wales, Mike Ross (another substitute) who would make 89 appearances and win at least 61 caps for Ireland, Will Skinner who would make at least 147 appearances and David Strettle would go on to make 85 appearances and win 14 caps for England.

Our next game was at the same venue against Bourgoin five days later. A penalty opened the scoring against us then Ollie Kohn was sent to the bin but we took the lead when Care raced over for Mehrtens to convert. Simon Miall was next to anger the referee and he was off to the bin. Then, when a scrum collapsed 25 metres from our line, the referee decided to award a penalty try which was converted for a 10-7 interval lead to Bourgoin. After Mehrtens had twice exchanged penalties with the French, a dropped goal gave Bourgoin a 19-13 victory. Five more new players of note appeared for the first time in this game; they were Stuart Abbott who had won 9 England caps and would make 17 appearances for us, Chris Hala'ufia who came on as a sub and would appear 40 times as well as winning 24 caps for Tonga, Haldane Luscombe who would make 37 appearances and win 16 caps for Wales, Nicolas Spanghero who would appear 44 times and Paul Volley our captain for this and the next season. He would go on to make 43 appearances for the 1st XV. Unfortunately, both Abbott and Luscombe would have their time with us cut short through injury.

Our third friendly turned into a bad tempered affair at the Liberty Stadium, Swansea against the Ospreys. Their flanker, Filo Tiatia was first to be shown a yellow card before Jimmy Richards was driven over to open the scoring. Mehrtens converted but Henson pulled three points back with a penalty. So'oialo went to the bin, Hook scored after collecting his own kick ahead, Henson converted and Byrne scored another try soon after. Henson's conversion made it 17-7 before James and Spanghero went off to cool down for stamping and punching respectively. The Osprey's third try came from Vaughton and was converted by Hool but we did score a consolation when Monye gathered a chip through from Jarvis who converted. The final quarter remained scoreless mainly due to heavy rain and we ended up on the losing side again by 14-24.

So, the friendlies were over and now it was time for the talking to stop. We would find out whether we could compete with the big boys again after a year away. An away game at Twickenham against London Irish on 2nd September formed part of the London Double header event and we kicked off first at 2 p.m. The attendance was given as 51,960 although this reflected ticket sales for both games. In the first ten minutes, Jarvis landed two penalties but we lost Abbott to the bin for a dangerous tackle and Flutey kicked the penalty. Ojo got over after a mistake by Brown but we went back in front when Jarvis kicked his third penalty after Leguizamon had been binned. The second half saw us stretch the lead with a fourth penalty for Jarvis eleven minutes in. Then Irish took control and, in a ten minute spell, Flutey landed two penalties and dropped a goal to put them 17-12 ahead with 20 minutes to go. They held this lead for the next thirteen until Ceri Jones was driven over from a lineout, Jarvis converted and we were close to an opening victory. After Flutey missed a long range penalty two minutes from time, he was given another chance from 45 metres right on the final whistle which he took to give Irish a 20-19 win. A bad ending to a game we should have won but a point was better than nothing.

A week later, Gloucester made the trip to the Stoop in good spirits after an opening victory over Bath. After Walker had put them in front with a penalty on 6 minutes, we fought our way back and two Mehrtens penalties and a conversion of Jones's try saw us into a 13-3 lead after 32 minutes. Walker and Mehrtens exchanged penalties before the break but there was no sign of what was to come next. It was all Gloucester and lacklustre tackling enabled them to rack up the points. Walker got a penalty four minutes into the half and converted a try from former Quin Peter Richards who ran 60 metres through our non-existent defence. After his fourth penalty, Walker couldn't convert Azam's try but did add the extras to one from Forrester 15 minutes from the end. We were fifteen points behind but could only manage a try from Simon Keogh with seven minutes left. The attempted conversion by Mehrtens hit the post and dropped in front of the bar to leave the final score at 21-31. Our slide down the table put us in eleventh spot just ahead of Worcester on points difference.

The games would not get any easier and a trip to Adams Park to take on London Wasps was not the best fixture we could have had at this stage. Jarvis missed his first penalty attempt but was successful with his second to put us in front. Wasps began to dominate (as they would for most of the game) and Leo scored for Walder to convert. Straight away, we attacked when Voyce knocked on and quick ball produced a try in the corner for Monye. Our narrow lead lasted eight minutes until Walder put over a penalty. We lost Vos to the bin and Hart scored, Walder converted and then exchanged penalties with Jarvis before our man came back on. As Walder had ended the first half scoring, he began the second half scoring the same way. His three points came as a result of Volley going off for ten minutes. Sackey scored another Wasps try, Walder converted and when Volley returned, we trailed 11-30. We were up to full strength for a couple of minutes and then Luscombe went the same way as Vos and Volley for a professional foul. To have any chance whatsoever of competing with Wasps, we had to keep fifteen men on the pitch!! We quite clearly didn't do this and paid the price. Sackey's second (converted by King) killed the game but we fought to the end and Easter ran 60 yards after intercepting a Staunton pass (remember him?) and Luscombe went over after Bracken had scored the home side's fifth try. Jarvis was lucky at the third attempt with the conversion to make it 23-42. After all our efforts, we got no points but, as Worcester lost as well, we stayed eleventh.

Steve Edlmann, Adrian Alexander, Mickey Claxton, Peter Whiting and Terry Claxton take on Gloucester in the John Player Cup semi-final in 1978. © Colorsport

The first Quins winners of our own Sevens in 1983. Standing: Rick Lawrence, Hugh McHardy, Paul Jackson, Chris Preston; Front row: Alex Woodhouse, Graham Birkett (c), Andre Dent

Willie Jefferson runs in our third try against Bristol in the cup semi-final in 1984, much to the delight of the travelling fans. © Colorsport

Will Carling scores his first try in the cup final against Bristol in 1988. © Colorsport

An elated John Olver lifts the John Player Special Cup after the 28-22 win over Bristol. © Colorsport

Andy Mullins, Brian Moore and Jason Leonard prepare to engage in the 1990s. © Joe McCabe

Will Greenwood carries the attack to London Irish also in the 1990s. © Joe McCabe

The new East Stand at the Stoop in 1997

Victory at Bath in May 1999. © Joe McCabe

Tom Williams winks as he leaves the pitch with Steph Brennan during the infamous game against Leinster in April 2009. Image courtesy of Sky Sports

The Twickenham Stoop as seen in June 2010. The flats to the left are where the second pitch used to be. © Nick Cross

Gonzalo Camacho about to score that dramatic try in the Amlin Cup Final in 2011. © Colorsport

Twickenham as it is today, a far cry from the early days. © World Rugby Museum, Twickenham

Quins programmes through the years. © Nick Cross

Leicester came to the Stoop on 23rd September only four places above us. Just 35 seconds into the game, Varndell ran in a try for the visitors but we rallied and good work from the pack enabled Jarvis to kick three penalties in the first half to give us the lead. Paul Burke returned as a Leicester player and landed a penalty eleven minutes into the second half before Will Skinner tackled him late. He didn't even bother to look at the referee (Chris White) as he departed for ten minutes. This proved to be the turning point of the match. Another ex-Quin (Scott Bemand) scored and Burke converted to give the Tigers a lead they wouldn't lose. There was still over half an hour to play including injury time but we couldn't get closer than three points. Jarvis exchanged penalties with Burke twice and future Quin Ollie Smith was denied a try by the video referee to leave us six points adrift at 15-21. A very silly mistake, a schoolboy error, had cost us three points and our first win of the season. As it was, Worcester got a point as well so it stayed the same at the bottom of the table.

The Powergen Cup had been replaced by the Anglo-Welsh Cup (known as the EDF Energy Cup). Basically, the twelve Premiership teams and four Welsh sides would be in four Pools of four teams. The Pool winners would meet in semi-finals and the winners of those would progress to a one-off final. Each side would play three games – some had two home games, others just the one. It was not embraced by all teams but Dean Richards noted in the match programme that we were taking it seriously. However, only four first team regulars were named in our starting line-up at Stradey Park where we took on Llanelli Scarlets. We were penalised no fewer than six times in the opening 12 minutes and found ourselves 12-0 down inside the first quarter. Daniel and Afeaki scored tries and Stephen Jones converted the second one. Monye did score for us while Mel Deane was in the bin and Jarvis's conversion left us five points behind at the break. Two more tries for the Scarlets from Davies and Nathan Thomas gave them a bonus point; Jones converted both. The full time score of 7-26 was a bigger margin than we deserved but we had to somehow stop all the yellow cards we were getting and start taking the try scoring opportunities we were creating. If we didn't, our stay in the Premiership would only last one season. Andy Gomarsall made his debut in this game when he came on as a sub. He would go on to make 52 appearances and was in the process of winning 35 caps for England in an international career that started as far back as 1996. He had been offered a lifeline by Dean Richards after Worcester had let him go one year into a three year deal – he expressed his gratitude for this by playing some of his best rugby and staying for three seasons. George Harder made his final appearance in this one having scored 95 points (19 tries) during his three and a bit seasons with us. Injuries had finally taken their toll on the Samoan who we saw only too briefly in the twilight of his career.

The following week Sale Sharks came to the Stoop for our second EDF Energy Cup game. They were the Premiership Champions during our absence and would be a tough team to beat as we knew to our considerable cost in our most recent encounter prior to this one. Craig McMullen (a late replacement for Stuart Abbott) got us off to a flying start when he went over after three minutes. Jarvis converted but the sides were level just three minutes later when Cox scored for Larrechea to convert. David Strettle got over in the corner but Larrechea kicked a penalty, Jarvis got one for us and the Sale kicker replied in kind to leave the score evenly poised at 15-13 after 27 minutes. Before half time, we lost Strettle to a knee injury and our lead to a Ripol try again converted by Larrechea. The deficit was wiped out by Monye's try and a conversion from Jarvis nine minutes into the second half. It remained like this until eight minutes from the end of normal time (although Monye was unlucky not to have scored his second – he was tackled into touch right on the goal line) when Larrechea landed his third penalty to sneak the visitors ahead for only the second time. Right at the end of normal time, Martens got Sale's third try but the conversion attempt by Lee Thomas hit the post and we were still in with a chance at 22-28. As we threw everything at Sale, Cueto stopped Jim Evans on the line before Tom Williams was worked over in the corner. It all came down to Adrian Jarvis and his conversion attempt. He missed and the final whistle went along with our domestic cup hopes for another year.

It was a trip down the M4 to Bristol as the Guinness Premiership matches made a brief one week return before the European competitions got underway. After four matches, Bristol were top of the league and looking to consolidate that position. As was becoming an annoying habit with us, another sin binning was notched up when Hala'ufia went off after only five minutes after tackling Bristol's scrum half instead of retreating ten metres from a penalty. It set the tone of the game and when he came back on, we trailed 3-14. A penalty by Jarvis was sandwiched between tries by Perry and Clarke (conversions by Strange). After Strange was binned for deliberate offside, Monye just reached a kick through by Tom Williams to bring us briefly back into it. Even with fourteen men, our scrum was destroyed and a penalty try was the result. Taumalolo converted (he along with Roy Winters were the ex-Quins on display for Bristol) and it was 8-21 at half time. This became 8-33 during the third quarter as Lemi got a brace, Strange converting the second. The home side proceeded to bring on their replacements and went off the boil. In the last ten minutes, Vos and Fuga got over (Jarvis converting the first) and Easter went to the bin between the tries. All these late scores did was to keep us off the bottom on points difference.

A trip to Galway took us to play Connacht in our first European Challenge Cup pool match. Our losing streak was now at ten in all competitions. This needed to end now otherwise we would be headed in the wrong direction in this cup as well. We were in a Pool alongside our opponents on the Friday (20th October), Montpellier and Bath. Connacht started well and scored through Hearty after 13 minutes but, by half time, Jarvis had landed three penalties to give us the lead. It was only one point though because Warwick got a penalty three minutes into injury time. Three minutes after the break, Warwick knocked on and from the scrum, Jarvis put in a cross-field kick, Tom Williams got a nice bounce and ran in for Jarvis to convert. Warwick narrowed the gap to five points a couple of minutes later and when Rigney scored for Warwick to convert with seven minutes to go, we were heading for our eleventh defeat in a row. One minute into injury time, the home side were penalised for taking out our jumper at a lineout and Jarvis stepped up to slot the penalty through the posts. Connacht made a last desperate attempt to break through and Mike Brown saved a try with a superb tackle on Ofisa. After this, the Irish were penalised and Jarvis put the ball into touch to give us our first win of the season by a single point (19-18) and no yellow cards had been issued!!

The confidence gained from that win was immeasurable and when Montpellier came to the Stoop, they were in for a shock. Brown got our first try which Jarvis converted on 10 minutes. He then added a penalty and converted further tries from Care, Fuga and Kohn before Durand put the visitors on the scoreboard with a try. The one-way traffic continued after the break when Tom Williams scored and Jarvis converted. Mercier made it 38-10 when he got Montpellier's second try but, in the final ten minutes, Tom Guest and Brown (twice) took our try tally to eight. Brown took over the goal kicking duties and converted the first two. The final score was 57-10 and this was good enough to take us to the top of the Pool but Bath had won both games as well.

As we moved into November, the Premiership action returned for four weeks and Northampton were our first visitors. It was nice to get two wins in the European Challenge Cup but we desperately needed our first in the league. Jarvis and Spencer exchanged penalties, Keogh scored from a Jarvis cross-field kick (converted by Jarvis) and Spencer and Jarvis exchanged penalties in a largely forgettable first half. We produced a great second half performance and in the third quarter, Andy Gomarsall and Simon Keogh enabled Jarvis to add four points to his tally. Northampton's only response was a penalty from Spencer between the tries. When Jarvis went through a gap to score and convert the bonus point try, we relaxed and allowed Lamont and Robinson to score tries in the last five minutes to make it 34-19. Although we stayed in eleventh place, crucially, we opened up a five point gap between us and Worcester.

A Friday night trip to Newcastle is never easy so we needed to put in a good performance to have any chance at all. After Burke put the Falcons ahead after two minutes with a penalty, we stopped them from adding to that score for the rest of the game. Tries from David Strettle and Nick Easter (both converted by Jarvis) in the first half saw us to victory. We played much of the game in the home side's half which suited us and this win shot us up to ninth place above Bath, Newcastle and Worcester.

A crucial game the following Friday at the Stoop against Worcester was, even at this stage of the season, a must win fixture. As already mentioned, Andy Gomarsall had been rescued by Dean Richards after he had been badly treated by Worcester so this was a chance for a bit of revenge for him. Jarvis put a delicate chip into the corner which Strettle got to first and he converted and sandwiched a penalty between two from Drahm to make it 10-6 to us at the break. The turning point came 18 minutes into the second half when Horsman saw yellow after a stamp on Keogh. Jarvis kicked the penalty and converted Luscombe's try as Horsman was about to come back on. The remaining time produced no more scoring, we were up to seventh and now 12 points ahead of Worcester at the bottom.

Our third Friday night fixture on the trot meant another long journey, this time to Edgeley Park, Stockport to play the Champions, Sale Sharks. Jarvis gave us the lead on 8 minutes with a penalty but Larrechea dropped a goal and kicked penalties either side of Lund's try for a 14-3 lead. As Sale lost their way, we came back into it with Jarvis penalties on 47, 57 and 71 minutes to narrow the gap to just two points. Five minutes from the end, Larrechea put over his third penalty to seal the win and we had to be satisfied with a losing bonus point.

Our next fixture was a meaningless one for us; our last EDF Energy Cup pool game. It was another trip to Newcastle, this time on a Sunday. The Falcons still had an outside chance of qualifying but first, they had to win and score at least four tries. Andrew Mehrtens made his first start since the Gloucester game on 9th September and it was his penalty that put us in front. Adam Thompstone then scored our first try and Mehrtens converted to give us a 10-0 lead after only 6 minutes. Newcastle came into the game and tries from Visser and Oakes (both converted by Flood) saw them go in front. The lead was short lived as Thompstone got his second to edge us ahead by a point at the break (15-14). Mehrtens landed another penalty but Rudd got the home side's third try again converted by Flood with 17 minutes left. Our fly half attempted a penalty from just inside our half to level the scores but it was not to be. Even if the Falcons had scored a fourth try, it was not enough because Sale defeated Llanelli Scarlets 21-5 to progress to the semi-finals. We finished bottom of the Pool with just three points. Luke Sherriff made his last appearance in this game having scored 55 points (11 tries) during his career and captained the side on nine occasions.

Our attention moved back to the European Challenge Cup for the next two weeks and this would decide our fate as we had back to back games against Bath. We were at home first but, even though Maddock went to the bin for a spear tackle on Strettle after 5 minutes, we trailed by the time he came back. Abendanon scored a try and Barkley kicked a penalty goal to leave us eight points behind. Jarvis did kick three penalties in the second quarter but Abendanon's second try and another penalty from Barkley left the visitors 16-9 in front at half time. However, Strettle went to the bin for a dangerous tackle on Maddock and Volley followed him for committing a professional foul. During this period, we actually outscored Bath 9-3 with Jarvis adding his fourth, fifth and sixth penalties. The last one put us in front albeit for two minutes before Barkley put one over on 56 minutes. Jarvis then missed a penalty from 30 metres with 12 minutes left and Maddock sealed the win with a try in the last minute of injury time. Bath climbed above us with 12 points to our 10. The away game became all important.

On 16th December, we met at the Rec and Abendanon continued where he had left off the previous week. He scored a try after just two minutes which was converted by Barkley. Jarvis kicked a penalty and when Short was binned for dangerous use of the boot, we had to take advantage. Basically, we didn't and Barkley's penalty was the only score while he was off. In first half injury time, Berne crashed over and Barkley converted for a 17-3 lead. He missed a penalty early in the second half before Jarvis slotted one over. However, Luscombe dropped the ball with the line at his mercy and Jarvis missed a long range penalty before Barkley made it 20-6 with a successful attempt. At this stage, there were only four minutes of normal time remaining. Mehrtens had replaced Jarvis and he put Tom Williams over and kicked a penalty with three minutes of injury time remaining. Unfortunately, the score stayed at 20-14 to Bath and we would now struggle to qualify for the quarter finals.

Saracens visited on 22nd December on a foggy night as heavy traffic caused a ten minute delay to kick-off. We seemed to have stayed in the changing rooms as Castaignede touched down with 37 seconds on the clock. Jackson converted and on 5 minutes, Ratuvou got another try to give Sarries a twelve point lead. We slowly recovered and two Jarvis penalties halved the deficit by half time. In the third quarter, Jarvis pulled another three points back with a successful penalty, Brown went to the bin for a professional foul and Jackson kicked the resulting penalty to restore the six point lead. Jarvis had missed three penalties and one dropped goal attempt and was replaced by Mehrtens with 20 minutes to go. We actually went in front when Brown got over for Mehrtens to convert with 12 minutes left. The lead lasted eight minutes until Saracens broke and Skirving had an unopposed run into the corner. This was our fifth defeat in a row (including two Premiership losses).

The next game was an away trip to Sixways to play bottom side Worcester Warriors on 27th December. Mehrtens put us ahead with a penalty after one minute but Brown landed two for Worcester before we took hold of the game. Mike Brown hacked on and touched down after Delport had lost the ball and then, seven minutes later, Strettle wriggled out of a tackle to score our second try. Mehrtens converted both although Brown kicked two more penalties to make it 17-12 to us at the interval. Ollie Kohn was binned for a professional foul but, amazingly, we outscored the Warriors during the time he was off. Brown slotted his fifth penalty before Keogh gathered when Delport spilt the ball and ran 60 metres to score. Mehrtens again converted and added another penalty to take us 12 points clear. When Quinnell was driven over for a try, there were 16 minutes including injury time to go. We held on and would have denied Worcester a bonus point had Mehrtens landed a last minute penalty. As it was, we had to be pleased with a 27-20 victory which took us nine points clear of the bottom placed side.

We began 2007 with a home Premiership fixture against Newcastle Falcons at the Stoop on New Year's Day. Mehrtens kicked us into an eighth minute lead with a penalty and converted Aston Croall's try just after Flood had been sent to the bin for a professional foul. When he returned, the Falcons scored two tries in three minutes to take the lead. May and Winter got them and Flood converted the second before replying to a Mehrtens penalty to give his side a 15-13 lead at the break. The second half was a totally different story as we took command. Strettle recovered a kick ahead by Abbott and broke through a couple of attempted tackles to score under the posts. Mehrtens converted and dropped a goal and when Strettle got his second try, we led 28-15. There were still over 25 minutes left and it took nine of these for Mike Brown to get the bonus point score. Jarvis had come on for Mehrtens and he slotted the conversion to this and Strettle's hat-trick try two minutes from the end. The extra point edged us to 13 points ahead of Worcester and we were now in 8th place.

The match against Bath at the Stoop on 6th January was played in appalling conditions and it was time to bring out our wet weather game. Jarvis kicked two penalties in the first forty minutes and our only change in the entire game was made during the break when Monye came on for Strettle. Barkley pulled three points back with a penalty but when Barnes was yellow carded for bringing down a maul, Jarvis restored the six point gap with his third penalty. The clock was successfully run down and when Spanghero stole a Bath lineout in the dying minutes, that was that. We climbed a place into seventh and the gap over Worcester was growing all the time.

It was back to European action for the next two weeks and the first of these was an away trip to Montpellier. It was a simple equation for us, we had to win both games and get the maximum points whilst hoping that Newcastle slipped up somewhere. The other teams in contention for a runners-up quarter final berth had easy fixtures and were ahead of us because of our defeats to Bath. We began well in the Stade Sabathe and Jarvis booted over two penalties to give us an early lead. Trinh Duc got one back but when Kuzbik was sin binned, Croall was driven over by the pack for the opening try converted by Jarvis. Trinh Duc landed his second penalty to make our lead 13-6 at the halfway stage. Into the second half, a clearance kick was charged down and Will Skinner picked up and scored under the posts for Jarvis to convert. After this, Montpellier staged a comeback and Boussuge scored in the left corner and Sarramea added another with a great solo run from half way. In between, Monye had been yellow carded and Trinh Duc's conversion brought the scores level. The see-saw scoring carried on as Jarvis scored under the posts and converted but we were pegged back when Kuzbik dived over for Trinh Duc to make it all square at 27-27 with five minutes to go. We were awarded a penalty in front of the posts after a good break by Strettle and Gavin Duffy slotted the kick before we grabbed the bonus point in injury time. Miall stole possession with Montpellier on the attack, fed Strettle and he ran in for our fourth try. Duffy added the two points to make it 37-27 and keep our slim chances alive. This was to be his last appearance in our colours; he had scored 110 points (21 tries, one penalty and one conversion) during his career.

Unfortunately, Newcastle also won so it came down to the last game at the Stoop against Connacht. The problem was that the Falcons were playing Petrarca and that result was a bit of a formality as they had beaten them 50-5 at home in Round One. It proved to be so and a 50-6 victory took their points to 21 and try count to 29-11. All this meant that we had to score no fewer than 21 tries to go through, an all but impossible task. In the first half, Luscombe, Brown and Abbott got tries (Jarvis converting the last two) and McHugh kicked a penalty to briefly make the score 5-3. Incredibly, the second half was even with a goal apiece. Connacht scored through O'Loughlin (converted by Durcan) and Hala'ufia got the bonus point try six minutes from time which Jarvis converted to make it 26-10. It was far too little to send us through but it did show the difference that being in a group with a poor side could make to your qualification chances.

The Premiership return with Bath came only three weeks after the first meeting. After a Jarvis penalty put us in front, Borthwick was driven over for Barkley to convert and Nick Easter went to the bin for a professional foul. Barkley kicked a penalty and Maddock and Scaysbrook scored further tries which Barkley converted. Jarvis did get a penalty between the tries but at 6-24, we were in trouble. In the third quarter, we began something of a fight back with a Jarvis penalty and a Mike Brown try (converted by Jarvis). With the score at 16-24, Fuimaono-Sapolu added Bath's fourth try and Barkley kicked the conversion but we wouldn't give in. Easter went over from close range, Jarvis converted and when Skinner got over five minutes from time, it looked as though we might pull off a shock victory. Sadly, he was penalised for a double movement and when Easter questioned the decision with referee Rob Debney, he was shown his second yellow equalling a red card and off he went. He was the first Quins player to be sent off since Ace Tiatia against Gloucester on 5th December 2005. Abendanon was sent to the bin after Easter's try but we couldn't make any gain and fell to our first defeat in six matches.

London Irish, Newcastle, Northampton and Worcester were separated by eleven points and the side to be relegated looked like it would come from these four. On 17th February, we travelled to Franklin's Gardens to take on Northampton Saints. Our last win at the Gardens was on 23rd August 1997 so we were long overdue another. The unlucky Stuart Abbott was knocked out of the game in the second minute by Cohen and Tupai and Luscombe came on to replace him. After 6 minutes, Andy Gomarsall charged down Spencer's clearance kick to score the first points. Jarvis converted and we were on our way. As tempers frayed, Volley and Short went to the bin to cool down and Tupai scored a try to open the home side's account. The first half had a running time of 52 minutes and we seemed to have needed more of a rest as Cohen went through weak tackling to run 75 metres and score under the posts early in the second half. Reihana converted but, four minutes later, Strettle brought the scores level with a try. After Fox became the second Saint to become a sinner, Jarvis put over two penalties before he came back and matched Reihana's penalty to leave us six points ahead with eleven minutes to go including injury time. Deane broke deep into Saints territory, Strettle took play to the line and Steve So'oialo dived over on the blind side of the ruck for our third try. Jarvis banged over a superb touchline conversion and the final whistle left the score at 28-15. Northampton were in trouble as Worcester closed the gap at the bottom to just three points. The Saints did have a game in hand and that might still prove decisive. We on the other hand could almost start thinking of a top 6, Heineken Cup qualifying, finish.

Bristol came to the Stoop in second place and looking to go top of the tree. Jarvis landed penalties at the start and end of the first half; in between, Strange kicked a penalty and Lemi ran 75 metres to score an interception try. Jarvis kept knocking over the penalties after the interval and three more successes took us to victory. El Abd spent ten minutes in the bin and that led to one of our fly half's penalties. A final score of 15-8 took us into sixth place with a shot at the Heineken Cup qualifying places. A top four finish was probably a step too far but with six games left, anything was possible.

On 3rd March, we made the trek up the M1 to Leicester to play the league leaders. We had lost on our last ten visits to Welford Road and this time would be no different. Jarvis landed penalties either side of two by Goode who then slotted a third to give the home side a narrow lead at the break. After this, the scoring remained pretty equal with Rabeni scoring for Leicester, Jordan Turner-Hall for us (Jarvis converted) then Hipkiss for Leicester (Goode converted). Jarvis then outscored Goode 2-1 in penalties and in between, Mike Brown went to the bin. The game was evenly poised at 19-24 with the final quarter to come. We conceded a penalty deep in our half that Goode converted and, with the last kick of the game (having missed a dropped goal a little earlier) Jarvis banged over a long range penalty to gain us a losing bonus point. We slipped one place to seventh on games won; London Irish overtaking us.

Fourth placed London Wasps came to the Stoop the following week and we played well for the first 40 minutes. Jarvis penalties either side of Simon Keogh's try (also converted by Jarvis) gave us a 13-0 lead; Wasps only answer was a penalty from van Gisbergen. Slowly but surely, Wasps came back into it and van Gisbergen kicked two penalties and converted Haskell's try. Erinle was in the sin bin for a punch on Volley and Abbott was sent there for foul play (the actual culprit was Fuga). This was one of several errors by referee Martin Fox – most went against us. With 15 minutes to go, Bishay had a clear run in and van Gisbergen converted for a ten point lead. With only five minutes left, Jarvis salvaged another losing bonus point for us with his third penalty. This was definitely a case of three points lost. The 23-16 victory was Wasps first away league win of the season. We stayed in seventh but, at the bottom, Worcester were only a point behind Northampton and it now appeared to be a two horse race for the relegation spot as Newcastle and Sale were eight and nine points clear of Northampton respectively.

For us, a trip to Kingsholm to face a Gloucester side in need of points to secure a top four finish was not ideal considering we had lost on our last seven visits. Our defence was breached after just five minutes when Fuga overthrew a lineout and Wood trundled over. Walker converted, kicked a penalty and converted Bailey's try to make it 17-0 in 15 minutes. Although Jarvis got our first points with a penalty after 32 minutes and Keogh added a try a minute later, Gloucester scored their third try after 38 minutes through Forrester which Walker converted. The deficit of 8-24 was cut when Tom Williams went over a couple of minutes into the second half. The game was ended as a contest when Fuga was binned for a dangerous tackle and the home side scored ten points in three minutes immediately following his departure. Walker landed the penalty and converted Foster's try. We did play until the end and two late tries from Fuga and Brown (from the final play which Mehrtens converted) gained us a bonus point in a 25-34 defeat. Our chances of a top six finish were drifting away whilst at the bottom, Northampton were a point adrift of Worcester. Leicester led the way at the top on 62 points followed by Gloucester, Bristol and Saracens.

London Irish came to the Stoop on 7th April one place and six points ahead of us so it was imperative that we produced a good performance. Mehrtens started with an exchange of penalties with Everitt before adding a second after 13 minutes. As we put the pressure on, Evans and Brown scored tries and Mehrtens converted both for a 20-3 lead. Flutey got over for the visitors and Everitt converted to end the first half scoring. Three minutes after the break, Strettle scored our third and four minutes later we had the bonus point when Mehrtens put Abbott over. Two conversions from Mehrtens made it 34-10 with still over forty minutes including ten minutes of injury time to go. We did lose Evans for ten minutes (for bringing down his opposite number at a lineout) and the Irish dominated but, their only further points came a couple of minutes from the end when Roche scored for future Quin Nils Mordt to convert. This game proved to be the last for Stuart Abbott, he had scored 10 points (2 tries) during his injury hampered time with us. We stayed in 7th but the gap was only a point and the situation at the top was the same. At the bottom, Northampton were now two points behind Worcester with a game in hand.

There were now only two games left in our season and the first of these was an away trip to Vicarage Road to play fourth placed Saracens. On our last six visits to Watford, our record was one draw and five losses; our last win was in 1999. Jackson began with two penalties either side of a Chesney try but Mel Deane scored for Mehrtens to convert and Williams got our second just before half time after Jackson's third penalty. The second half belonged almost entirely to the home side and tries from Castaignede (47 mins), Scarborough (69 mins) and Jackson (77 mins) put us completely out of it. Jackson added conversions to the first two before Brown scored our third try and when Mehrtens converted, the final whistle went to leave the score at 19-33. We were still in 7th place and our Heineken Cup hopes would rely on the result of the last league fixture and the final of the European Challenge Cup between Bath and Clermont Auvergne.

Sale Sharks visited the Stoop on 28th April still with an outside chance of Heineken Cup rugby in 2007/08. This was no longer a possibility after the first 40 minutes. Andrew Mehrtens gave a fly half masterclass in his final game for the Club. His penalty after 6 minutes started us off, Brown got our first try that Mehrtens converted and he followed this with another penalty and then a dropped goal. After 26 minutes, it was 16-0 but there was no scoring for 20 minutes when Brown got his second and Mehrtens again converted. Three minutes into the second half, Deane (another making his final appearance) scored the third and Mehrtens the bonus point try. He converted both and with 36 minutes still to play, it was just a case of how many we would get. In the event, it was a brace from Ceri Jones, the first converted by Mehrtens but he failed with the second which meant that we just failed to reach the fifty point mark. The 49-0 victory was our biggest winning margin of the season. Five players made their last appearances in this game, they were Mel Deane who had scored 50 points (10 tries) during his five seasons, James Hayter scored 30 points (6 tries) and captained the side on one occasion, Andrew Mehrtens scored 332 points (3 tries, 2 dropped goals, 45 penalties and 88 conversions), Simon Miall had got 20 points (4 tries) and visited the sin bin on seven occasions and Andre Vos who had scored 25 points (5 tries), been to the sin bin six times and captained the side in no fewer than 111 matches (this put him fourth in the all-time list behind Harlequin greats Ricky Bartlett (151), Adrian Stoop (143) and Ken Chapman (118)). The five points ensured our finish in seventh place with 51 points. At the top, Gloucester, Leicester, Bristol and Saracens claimed the top four places with Leicester beating Gloucester in the final. At the bottom, Worcester and Northampton both won their final games so the Saints went down with 33 points, just a point behind the Warriors. To qualify for the Heineken Cup, we needed a French victory at the Stoop on 19th May - the final score was Clermont Auvergne 22 Bath 16 - A great result!!

The greatest thing about this season was that we had survived back in the Premiership. Our overall playing record was P34 W14 D0 L20 F770 A689, in the league it was P22 W10 D0 L12 F503 A438 Pts 51 (BP 11 – TB 5 LB 6) Pos 7th. Out of 34 matches played, Ollie Kohn topped the appearances with 29, Jim Evans, Mike Ross and Andre Vos were one behind with Mike Brown and Adrian Jarvis on 27. Top try scorer was Mike Brown with 13 and Adrian Jarvis topped the points scoring with 273 (2 tries, 63 penalties and 37 conversions). He also got the most penalties and conversions although Mehrtens dropped the only two goals. Not surprisingly, the total points were down on 2005/06 by a long way (1317 to 770) as were tries (180 to 80) and conversions (132 to 62). However, there was a rise in dropped goals from one to two and penalties by 30 to 80.

2006/07

060806	ASM CLERMONT AUVERGNE	ISSOIRE	L	2G1PG(17)-3G1T(26)
110806	BOURGOIN	ISSOIRE	L	1G2PG(13)-1G1DG3PG(19)
250806	OSPREYS	SWANSEA	L	2G(14)-3G1PG(24)
020906	LONDON IRISH(GP)	TWICKENHAM(A)	L	1G4PG(19)-1DG4PG1T(20)
090906	GLOUCESTER(GP)	TWICKENHAM STOOP	L	1G3PG1T(21)-2G4PG1T(31)
170906	LONDON WASPS(GP)	ADAMS PARK	L	1G2PG2T(23)-4G3PG1T(42)
230906	LEICESTER(GP)	TWICKENHAM STOOP	L	5PG(15)-1G3PG1T(21)
011006	LLANELLI SCARLETS(EDFECGP)	LLANELLI	L	1G(7)-3G1T(26)
071006	SHARKS(EDFECGP)	TWICKENHAM STOOP	L	2G1PG2T(27)-2G3PG1T(28)
151006	BRISTOL(GP)	BRISTOL	L	1G1PG2T(20)-4G1T(33)
201006	CONNACHT(ECCP)	GALWAY	W	1G4PG(19)-1G2PG1T(18)
281006	MONTPELLIER(ECCP)	TWICKENHAM STOOP	W	7G1PG1T(57)-2T(10)
041106	NORTHAMPTON(GP)	TWICKENHAM STOOP	W	4G2PG(34)-3PG2T(19)
101106	NEWCASTLE(GP)	NEWCASTLE	W	2G(14)-1PG(3)
171106	WORCESTER(GP)	TWICKENHAM STOOP	W	2G2PG(20)-2PG(6)

241106	SHARKS(GP)	EDGELEY PARK	L	4PG(12)-1DG3PG1T(17)
021206	NEWCASTLE(EDFECGP)	NEWCASTLE	L	1G2PG1T(18)-3G(21)
091206	BATH(ECCP)	TWICKENHAM STOOP	L	6PG(18)-3PG3T(24)
161206	BATH(ECCP)	BATH	L	3PG1T(14)-2G2PG(20)
221206	SARACENS(GP)	TWICKENHAM STOOP	L	1G3PG(16)-1G1PG2T(20)
271206	WORCESTER(GP)	WORCESTER	W	3G2PG(27)-5PG1T(20)
010107	NEWCASTLE(GP)	TWICKENHAM STOOP	W	4G1DG2PG1T(42)-1G1PG1T(15)
060107	BATH(GP)	TWICKENHAM STOOP	W	3PG(9)-1PG(3)
120107	MONTPELLIER(ECCP)	MONTPELLIER	W	4G3PG(37)-3G2PG(27)
200107	CONNACHT(ECCP)	TWICKENHAM STOOP	W	3G1T(26)-1G1PG(10)
270107	BATH(GP)	BATH	L	2G3PG(23)-4G1PG(31)
170207	NORTHAMPTON(GP)	NORTHAMPTON	W	2G3PG1T(28)-1G1PG1T(15)
240207	BRISTOL(GP)	TWICKENHAM STOOP	W	5PG(15)-1PG1T(8)
030307	LEICESTER(GP)	LEICESTER	L	1G5PG(22)-1G5PG1T(27)
100307	LONDON WASPS(GP)	TWICKENHAM STOOP	L	1G3PG(16)-2G3PG(23)
170307	GLOUCESTER(GP)	GLOUCESTER	L	1G1PG3T(25)-4G2PG(34)
070407	LONDON IRISH(GP)	TWICKENHAM STOOP	W	4G2PG(34)-2G1PG(17)
150407	SARACENS(GP)	VICARAGE ROAD	L	2G1T(19)-2G3PG2T(33)
280407	SHARKS(GP)	TWICKENHAM STOOP	W	5G1DG2PG1T(49)-0

In May and June 2007, England played two tests in South Africa and because the squad was weakened by injuries, they were thrashed in both (58-10 and 55-22). Mike Brown, Nick Easter and Andy Gomarsall played in each match, future Quin Matt Cairns came on as a sub in the first and old boy Roy Winters came on as a sub in the first (as did Pat Sanderson) and played in the second.

NEC finished as our main sponsors and a new three year deal was signed with Etihad Airways (from United Arab Emirates). It was a seven figure deal, the biggest in the Club's history and was announced on 31st July. They would eventually be with us for seven years and we even painted the roof of both the East and North stands so that everyone arriving at Heathrow Airport would see Etihad Airways advertised. The accounts for the year ending 30th June 2008 showed a loss of £1,121,488. We became Harlequin F.C. again and someone who was pleased was Mark Evans. He hated the name change and couldn't wait to get it back to the way it had been since 1870.

The 2007 World Cup took place in France in September and October (although four matches were played in Cardiff and two in Edinburgh) and England were looking to be the first side to successfully defend the title. We had nineteen players involved representing ten nations and four of them were current; Nick Easter and Andy Gomarsall

(England) and Tani Fuga and Steve So'oialo (Samoa). Six had finished their Quins careers; Peter Richards (England), Norman Ligairi (Fiji), Gavin Duffy (Ireland), Ma'ama Molitika (Tonga), Luke Gross (USA) and Dafydd James (Wales). The remaining nine would appear for us in the future; Gonzalo Tiesi (Argentina), Paul Sackey (England), Waisea Luveniyali and Netani Talei (Fiji), Nick Evans (New Zealand), Junior Poluleuligaga (Samoa), Gary Botha (South Africa), Epi Taione (Tonga) and Adam Jones (Wales). After beating the USA in their first game (28-10), England suffered a humiliating loss to South Africa six days later. They failed to score a point and conceded thirty six – all was not well in the camp. The fixture with Samoa became a must win and they did enough to qualify for the quarter finals by virtue of a 44-22 win before seeing off Tonga 36-20. In the first knockout round, Australia were seen off by two points (12-10) as the English pack took control and forced mistakes from their opponents. The hosts were met in the Stade de France in the semi-final and another close match followed. The French led 6-5 at half time but Wilkinson put England into their third final with two penalties and a late dropped goal to make the final score 14-9. In the final, South Africa would be England's opponents - the heavy defeat in the Pool stages was a distant memory as the holders had found some sort of form at just the right time. In a tight game, South Africa led 9-3 at the break before Cueto had a try disallowed when the TMO decided his foot had touched the side line as he scored – it was the closest of decisions and a cruel blow. Wilkinson slotted a penalty but two more for the Springboks proved too much and they had their second World Cup victory. England had dominated both territory and possession but too many errors and no guaranteed ball at the lineout led to their downfall.

Paul Volley continued as captain and with four friendly fixtures lined up, our season began on Friday 17th August with a visit from Manu Samoa who were using the game as part of their World Cup warm up. After Luscombe and Guest scored tries (both converted by Jewell) in the first eleven minutes it looked good for an opening win. But, three converted tries from the visitors after 35, 55 and 63 minutes left us trailing by seven. A try by newcomer John Brooks set up a finale and, with the last kick of the game, Mike Brown put over a penalty to give us a 22-21 victory. Chris Brooker made the first of 87 appearances in this game, his career with us would be cut short by a bad knee injury.

At Northampton eight days later, Amesbury, Brown and Stegmann (2) got tries and Care landed a conversion but five tries and two conversions by the Saints saw them home by 29-22. James Percival appeared for the first of 60 games for the 1st XV and would be part of the set up for three seasons.

Bristol visited on 1st September and even at this early stage, we had a number of injuries. Care, Monye and a penalty try represented our try scoring and Seb Jewell added a penalty and two conversions. But, as against Northampton, it wasn't enough because the visitors scored three tries, converted them all and added two penalties to run out 27-22 winners.

For our fourth and final friendly, Connacht came to the Stoop six days later and were easily beaten. Care, Stegmann and Volley grabbed the tries with Brown getting a conversion and debutant Chris Malone gave an assured display at fly half. He kicked four penalties and a conversion to leave the final score at 31-8. Connacht's penalty and try were scant consolation. Malone would go on to make 41 appearances over the next two seasons.

The real season started on 15th September with the London Double Header at Twickenham. This counted as our home game so it was vital to grab a win. Our opponents again were London Irish and Malone put us in front with a penalty after 12 minutes before Paice was sent to the bin six minutes later. When he returned, we led 8-3 after Kohn's try was replied to by Staunton with a penalty. Jordan Turner-Hall scored a great try which Malone converted; again, Staunton replied with a penalty to make it 15-6 at half time. Tom Williams got our third try at the start of the second half and Malone converted for a 16 point lead. Paice added a try for Staunton to convert but a ten point burst in eight minutes swung it our way. Malone kicked a penalty and converted Luscombe's try. Between two converted tries for Irish, Malone got his third penalty to deny them any points from the game. We got all five and were in fourth place after round one.

The following Saturday, newly promoted Leeds Carnegie were the visitors to the Stoop. After 10 minutes, Malone slotted a penalty to put us in front before a penalty try was awarded after a five metre scrum. Malone converted and added a second penalty before Hinton got the only points for Leeds in the first half with a penalty. In the second period, Leeds scored tries by Oakley (converted by Welding) and Ma'asi but these were small responses to tries from Guest (converted by Malone) and Turner-Hall and then Malone converted his own as well as Keogh's to give us another five point haul in a 39-15 win. Tom Guest went to the bin but we were 32-10 ahead at that point. We were second to Gloucester by the narrowest of margins – they had scored 12 tries to our 9 and 87 points to 74.

Our next port of call was Newcastle to take on the Falcons. The first half an hour saw two Malone penalties and a trip to the bin for Jim Evans. Two tries in four minutes from Parling and May (both converted by Burke) gave the home side an eight point lead at the break. We put the pressure on and two Malone penalties brought us close. His third attempt was missed and when the Falcons got their third try from Burke with fourteen minutes left, it proved to be the final score. A losing bonus point was gained but the Tigers overtook us to go second.

Bristol came to the Stoop on 6th October for the second of five fixtures during the season (they were also in our Heineken Cup Pool). Josh Taumalolo and Roy Winters were returning ex Quins and this theme would increase over the years as more and more players moved between clubs instead of staying at one for their entire career or a large part of it. Chris Malone had started his Quins career well and converted our opening try by So'oialo (on his return from World Cup duty with Samoa) and Keogh's after 29 minutes. His dropped goal five minutes later put us 17-5 up. Lemi had scored for Bristol to make it 7-5 and Hill put over a penalty to make it a nine point gap at half time. After Strange had kicked a penalty, So'oialo got his second try after a break by Turner-Hall which Malone converted. With 16 minutes left, Bristol trailed by thirteen points and, although they managed a try by Arscott (converted by Strange) to get a bonus point, we held on for our third league win of the season. We went back up to second, three points behind leaders Gloucester.

A trip to Bath followed and given that we had won on only two of our previous twenty visits to the Rec, the omens were not good. After Malone missed with two penalty attempts, Bath took the lead when Berne put one over. He then converted Short's try and when Stephenson got their second on 36 minutes, we were in trouble. So'oialo stopped the rot with his third try in two games and Malone converted to narrow the gap. Seven minutes into the second half, Malone put over a penalty but that was as close as we got and, despite several changes of personnel, Bath's lead was fifteen points (Berne put over another penalty and converted his own try after a mistake by Malone). After this defeat, we dropped to fourth spot.

Ninth placed Wasps were up next at the Stoop and we made a good start with Masson scoring after 4 minutes for Malone to convert. He got a penalty at the end of the first quarter and dropped a goal on 27 minutes but Wasps scored two tries of their own (Reddan and Waters), Flutey dropped a goal and Cipriani converted the second try for a narrow lead. Malone restored the lead with two penalties, Waters got his second try and Cipriani converted to snatch it back for the visitors. Towards the end of the third quarter, Malone and Cipriani exchanged penalties to leave Wasps six points clear. When they took a scrum down under pressure, Malone gave us a one point advantage with the conversion of the resultant penalty try. He then missed a simple penalty chance before Walder failed with a last minute dropped goal attempt and we stayed in fourth. During the game, both scrum halves were sent to the bin (Care in the first half and Reddan in the second) with us shading the scoring 13-10 in that time.

It was EDF Energy Cup action eight days later when we travelled to the Madejski Stadium to take on London Irish. Stuart Abbott had announced his retirement in the week before due to a persistent shoulder injury and a replacement centre made his debut against the Irish. He was De Wet Barry from South Africa. He had won 39 caps for his country and would go on to make 42 appearances for us. Dean Richards made seven changes to the starting XV but insisted we were taking the competition seriously. Irish took the lead after 20 minutes when Murphy scored a try but Chris Hala'ufia brought us level and Adrian Jarvis put us ahead 12 minutes later. Delon Armitage restored their lead with a penalty on 38 minutes but Jarvis got one for us just on half time. The second half remained scoreless and we had a win to start with. The Ospreys topped Pool C having obtained a bonus point win and we were second.

The following week, we entertained Worcester in another EDF Energy Cup game. After Talei had opened the scoring with a try, 12 minutes had passed. We came back strongly and Monye scored for Malone to convert and he added a penalty to make it 10-5 after 22 minutes. Five minutes later, Hala'ufia saw yellow and we conceded ten points during his time off the field. Brown landed a penalty and Crichton converted a try from Lutui. When we were back to full strength, Monye got his second try and Malone added the extras. It wasn't enough for the half way lead because Crichton put over a penalty on 40 minutes. It remained a one point game and when Garvey was binned, we took the lead with a try from Mike Brown. Unfortunately, an old boy came back to haunt us and Pat Sanderson got what proved to be the winning try with eight minutes left. We did have a chance to win it at the end but wrong options were taken and we failed to capitalise. We remained second in the Pool but nothing less than a huge five point win against the Ospreys at the beginning of December would do – it looked like we were out.

The Heineken Cup took centre stage now and we travelled to play Stade Français in Paris at Stade Jean Bouin for our first match in Pool 3. After 7 minutes, Malone put us in front with a penalty to which Skrela replied in kind eight minutes later. Liebenberg and Dominici added tries and Skrela converted both for a 17-3 half time lead. We had played quite well but Stade Français had scored from turnovers and taught us a lesson in how to finish. We did score first and last in the second half with tries from Monye (converted by Malone) and De Wet Barry (converted by Jarvis) but in between, Skrela kicked two penalties and Liebenberg converted tries by Saubade and Mirco Bergamasco. The final score of 37-17 meant that our next game at home to Cardiff Blues was a must win if we were to progress to the quarter finals. Nick Easter and Andy Gomarsall returned from World Cup duty in this one.

On 17th November, we welcomed the Blues from Cardiff for our 129th meeting. In a largely forgettable game, Malone put us in front with a penalty after 6 minutes, Blair equalised on 27 minutes but Easter's try and Malone's conversion gave us the interval lead. For all our dominance in the first quarter, it was amazing that Cardiff were still in it. As it was, Blair got his second penalty and converted a try by Spice to put them in front with 20 minutes left. Malone drew us level with a penalty three minutes later and with time running out we had the chance for a dropped goal attempt by Malone. He had already missed three and perhaps this influenced Gomarsall's decision not to pass to him instead opting to try and make more ground. It didn't come off and the match ended 13-13; the eleventh draw in the history of fixtures between us and the highest scoring. As a result of this, we were bottom of the Pool and five points behind leaders Cardiff. The back-to-back games against Bristol would decide our fate.

The Guinness Premiership returned on 24th November with a visit to Kingsholm to play Gloucester. It was first against fourth and a win would put us on equal points with them. We shot out of the blocks and in the first 33 minutes had the try bonus point. Gloucester simply had no answer to David Strettle playing in the outside centre role. Time and again he made good ground enabling us to build a very handy lead. Malone opened with a penalty before Keogh and Monye went over for tries. Malone wasn't able to convert either but he did manage to with his own try scored after Vainikolo had gone over for Gloucester. Paterson converted and added two penalties either side of

Keogh's second which gave us a 25-13 lead at the break. Hazell had been binned for a high tackle and our third and fourth tries had been scored during the fourteen man period. Could this be our first win at Kingsholm in the 21st century? The home side emerged from the changing room in a different mood and pulled back seven points within 5 minutes when Tindall scored for Paterson to convert. Then, during a spell of intense pressure, referee David Rose sent Gomarsall (offside) and Jones (killing the ball) to the sin bin (there was some doubt whether either of them were yellow cards). We survived for four minutes with 13 men before Vainikolo got his second and Paterson converted for the lead. Back to a full complement, we worked our way upfield and Malone had a great opportunity to drop a goal for the win but he missed to the right and the final whistle went leaving the score 25-27. We were now four games without a win and dropped to fifth in the table. There were glimpses in this match of the capabilities of the team and only time would tell if it would ever reach its full potential.

Our final EDF Energy Cup pool game was on 2nd December at the Stoop against the Ospreys. To qualify for the knock-out stages, we needed five points whilst denying them any at all. Jarvis put us in front with a penalty but Henson landed two for the Ospreys. Just before the break, no fewer than three Ospreys went to the bin for various offences and for a brief period they were down to 12 men. The problem was that we could not score anything until they were back to 14 after half time. Barry grabbed a try to put us in front and that was as good as it got because Henson got his third and fourth penalties and converted his own try a minute from time when our try scorer was in the bin. We finished bottom of the Pool with just the opening win over London Irish to show for our efforts. South African international hooker Gary Botha made the first of 42 appearances for us when he came on as a substitute. He had won 12 caps for his country.

Our form was not good going into the Heineken Cup double header against Bristol. We were at home first and anything but a win would mean an exit from the competition. In the first half we played with the driving wind and rain but only had a Danny Care dropped goal to show in reply to tries from To'oalo and Lemi plus a conversion by Hill. The second resulted from a long pass by Barry and Lemi intercepted and ran 60 yards to score. A third try from Arscott two minutes after the break proved to be the last score. Losing Kohn for ten minutes didn't help the cause and we couldn't take advantage when Crompton suffered the same fate. Dean Richards said afterwards that it was our worst performance since he arrived at the Club. We were now seven points behind Pool leaders Stade Français and although not mathematically out, realistically, on current form, we were not going to win away at Bristol and Cardiff let alone against the leaders even though we would be at home.

At the Memorial Stadium the following Sunday, Richards rang the changes and only five of the previous week's starting XV remained. The first half ended 0-0 and while Care was in the bin for the first ten minutes of the second half, Lemi and Tom Williams scored tries and because Jarvis converted, we led 7-5. Bristol took their chances and Blaney got a try, Hill kicked a penalty and, right at the end, Strange converted Clarke's try to make it 7-20. Whatever thin hopes we had at the start had now gone and we were out of the Heineken Cup at the Pool stages again.

Three Guinness Premiership matches followed now and it didn't get any easier with a visit by third placed Saracens. Both halves began in the same way, Jarvis kicked a penalty and Saracens responded with a penalty by Jackson and a goal (De Kock and Russell tries both converted by Jackson) to put them 20-6 ahead with 32 minutes left including injury time. Six minutes later, Fuga went over for Jarvis to convert but Penny scored for Jackson to convert and the gap stayed at fourteen points. When Ugo Monye got our second try, Jarvis slotted the extras to give us a losing bonus point and that was as close as we got. This was our eighth game without a win and we slipped to sixth place in the table as a result.

Our last game of 2007 was an away fixture at Worcester on 29th December. They were bottom with only five points from eight matches so on paper, we should have won. We did get two tries in the first half through Chris

Robshaw and Gary Botha. Malone missed both conversions and a penalty from in front of the posts. This was a worrying trend that would continue. Two minutes from the end Crichton scored and converted for the home side but it was too little, too late and we held on for our first win since 28th October. We ended the year in sixth spot and ten points behind leaders Gloucester.

Fifth placed Leicester came to the Stoop on 6th January. Could we continue our winning form from Sixways? In the first quarter, it looked good and we led 6-0 through two Malone penalties. By half time the lead had gone because Goode kicked a penalty and converted Varndell's try. No one could explain what happened during the break but we just went to pieces and conceded a dropped goal (Murphy) and a penalty (Goode) plus four tries (two each for Croft and Varndell). With Goode converting the second and third efforts, we trailed 6-42. The Tigers had quite simply destroyed us and Strettle's late score converted by Jarvis was absolutely no consolation whatsoever. If anything, it confirmed that we had some way to go before we challenged for the Premiership title. We did remain in sixth place but this form could not continue if we were to get a Heineken Cup spot in 2008/09.

The set up of the season dictated that the final two rounds of Heineken Cup Pools came next and we had a trip to Cardiff to play the Blues. The game was talked up by the coaches and players as one to win but invariably, when one team has all to play for and the other only pride, there is only one outcome. Friday 11th January was the date for this one and the first half provided us with no points. Cardiff got ten through a Blair penalty and his conversion of Hewitt's try. Hal Luscombe got over for us and Malone reduced the deficit to three points but Blair added two more penalties (the second after Barry had gone off for ten minutes). No less than five substitutes came on with eight minutes left but the Blues sealed the win with a try from Shanklin converted by Blair. Mike Brown's late try took us into double figures but we had lost again (12-23).

Our final pool match was the home game against Stade Français. They were still in with a shout of qualification if Cardiff lost at Bristol and they repeated their bonus point win from November. Seven changes were made by Richards but the same scenario remained from last week, we were only playing for pride. Stade played a pretty much full strength side but we took the lead with a Jarvis penalty after three minutes. Despite playing poorly, Stade managed to rack up seventeen points after our penalty. Szarzewski and Arias got the tries and Skrela sandwiched a penalty between both conversions. After the interval, Stade scored the two further tries they required through Skrela and Corleto (Skrela converted both) but this wasn't the full story. Roncero went to the bin and three times the referee checked with the television match official (TMO) and three times we were denied a try. We did cross late in the game through Keogh (converted by Jarvis) but the score of 10-31 ensured we ended our campaign in the Heineken Cup with one draw and five defeats from our six matches. Ricky Nebbett played his last game in this one having scored just 5 points (one try), he had been to the sin bin on two occasions. As Cardiff won at Bristol, Stade also didn't qualify. We had now failed to win any of our last twelve matches in the competition.

Because we had not reached any knockout phases, it was now a run of twelve Premiership matches over the next three and a half months to see if we could make the end of season play-offs. A trip to Edgeley Park to play fifth placed Sale Sharks in a Friday night fixture was our next attempt to get a win in 2008. After an early try for the hosts by Jones that was converted by Hodgson, we were outplayed for most of the first half. We did stick to the task and two Jarvis penalties in the last ten minutes made it a single point deficit. The third quarter belonged to Sale with a McAllister penalty and a try from Ripol (converted by Hodgson). Our scrum had come off second best all night but Fuga scored with 13 minutes to go and the conversion by Jarvis meant a try would bring us an unlikely victory. Sadly, Hodgson landed a last minute penalty to make it 13-20. We had lost again but a bonus point maintained our three point lead over seventh spot.

The return with Worcester at the Stoop followed on 16th February. They were down in eleventh so an ideal opportunity for us to get some points. We started well enough when Care supplied Skinner who chipped over Worcester's full back to put us in front with the first try. Jarvis converted but couldn't manage to do the same with Luscombe's effort four minutes later and would miss four penalties before we scored again. Brown got a penalty for the visitors and Gear scored a try to leave it close at the break. All the rest of the action happened in the final quarter. Worcester lost Hickey to the bin and Jarvis kicked a penalty and converted So'oialo's try to make it 22-8. Hickey came back only for Tuitupou to go the same way and Masson grabbed the bonus point score for Jarvis to convert. Brown then converted his own try but Williams sealed Worcester's fate with our fifth and the conversion by Jarvis gave the final score a bit of gloss (36-15). Paul Volley made his final appearance for us when he came on as a substitute. He had scored just 5 points (one try), captained the side on 39 occasions and visited the sin bin three times. At this stage, anyone down to tenth placed Bristol had a shot at a top four spot so it was still all to play for.

Our next game was an away trip to play fourth placed Saracens at Vicarage Road. We hadn't beaten them since November 2004 so a win was long overdue (for an away win, you had to go back to April 1999). This was being shown live on TV and the kick-off was at a non-standard time of 6.05 p.m. on Sunday 24th February. Ross put Saracens in front after 5 minutes before Jarvis levelled twelve minutes later. Then, we turned the game in our favour; a long lineout throw by Fuga to Guest at the tail, he fed Danny Care and our scrum half erupted through the gap in the middle of the lineout before passing to Chris Robshaw who completed the 20 metres to the line. Care would become synonymous with these breaks and they would bring him more than one try in the future. Sarries just couldn't take any of the chances that came their way and Care executed a cross-field kick for Ugo Monye to go over. Jarvis converted for a 15-3 lead. Ross landed a second penalty for Saracens but that was as close as they got. We defended well and even survived the sin-binning of Hala'ufia for the last three minutes. We remained in sixth place but the gap to second team Leicester was only six points and we had a game in hand on them.

Gloucester were still heading the table and were eleven points ahead of us. Their visit to the Stoop was a must win for us in the race for a top four finish. Back in November, seven tries were scored and it was no different this time. Another excellent game was produced and, as in November, the result was in doubt until the end. Jarvis kicked us into the lead after a quarter of an hour, Adams scored for the visitors, Ceri Jones got our first try and Jarvis converted for a 10-5 lead. Back came Gloucester and Balshaw scored to level matters. Walker converted and kicked a penalty, Allen made the lead ten points with their third try but Brown scored for us right on half time and Jarvis reduced the deficit to three points with the extras. In the third quarter, Jarvis landed a penalty and Simpson-Daniel ensured Gloucester would take away at least a point with another try. After a high tackle on Danny Care, Jarvis kicked his third penalty and George Robson forced his way over through a gap in the visiting defence for the winning try. Malone had come on for Jarvis and he added the conversion for a 30-25 win. We moved above Saracens into fifth place – nine points behind Gloucester who remained top.

After winning on our first visit to Adams Park in 2003, our next three trips had all resulted in losses. If we could make this our fourth win on the trot, a top four finish was a very real possibility. Ibanez got Wasps off to a good start with a try after four minutes, Walder converted and Jarvis opened our account with a penalty three minutes later. Walder added a penalty after 26 minutes but when Luscombe went over, Jarvis converted to level matters. In a disastrous spell seven minutes before the break, Walder kicked a penalty, Waldouck scored a try (converted by Walder) and then Walder dropped a goal. Trailing 23-10, we had not done ourselves any favours and it eventually proved to be too big a margin to make up. Jarvis landed his second penalty and Monye ran in from our 10 metre line but Walder added penalties either side of this score. With ten minutes left, Tom Guest went over for our third try (converted by Malone) to leave us four points behind. We went for broke and put two kickable penalties into the corner but to no avail. Haldane Luscombe made his final appearance for us having scored 40 points (8 tries) with one visit to the sin bin. We dropped one place to sixth as a result of this defeat (25-29) but it was all still to play for.

The following Sunday, we welcomed Bath to the Stoop. They were in second place so it was an ideal opportunity to close the gap on them. In a tight first half when we decided to play against the strong wind, Barkley twice put the visitors in front only for Jarvis to level. We did lose Fuga to the bin on 27 minutes and when the first scrum after this occurred after 33 minutes, Gary Botha replaced left wing Charlie Amesbury. Into the second half, Jarvis and Barkley again exchanged penalties. Jarvis put over his fourth but the next score was not a Barkley penalty in response but the first try of the match. Keogh put in a kick and Care picked up at pace to score. Jarvis converted and his penalty in the ninetieth minute of game running time sealed the win. Right at the end, Claassens scored under the posts and Barkley's conversion gave them a losing bonus point (22-16). Back we went to fifth with ten points separating the top five. Gloucester led the way followed by Leicester, Bath and Sale. Our next three games were against the ninth, tenth and twelfth placed sides so it was odds-on we would get three wins even though two were away.

Bristol had not been a happy hunting ground for us over the years and our only win since 1998 was a pre-season friendly in 2005. With only us and Bath of the top six involved in games this weekend, it meant that a win would take us into the top four. It all began well when Amesbury got a try after six minutes but it was all even at the break as Barnes put over a penalty and Tom Arscott added a try for Bristol; Jarvis responded with a penalty to make it 8-8. In the third quarter, Jarvis went to the bin and Bristol were awarded a penalty try (converted by Barnes). Malone kicked a penalty on 54 minutes to bring us within four points and our final quarter performance was a marker for the future as we outscored our hosts 17-0. Brown (converted by Jarvis), Botha and Robson got the tries to give us a 28-15 bonus point victory. This put us in fourth and, with five matches left, the top of the table was as follows; Bath 55pts, Gloucester 55, Leicester 52 and Quins 50. Sale were in fifth on 46 but they had a game in hand. If we kept winning, we would be in the play-offs for the first time.

It was wet and windy on 29th March when the Falcons came to town. After Wilkinson had opened the scoring with a penalty, Jarvis levelled, Care dropped a goal and Jarvis completed his hat-trick either side of Wilkinson's second to give us the interval lead. After this, in a match which never improved because of the conditions, Jarvis stretched our lead before the one talking point in the match reared its head. On 59 minutes, De Wet Barry was late and high with his shoulder on Matthew Tait. The referee brandished a red card and we had to play the last 21 minutes with fourteen men. Barry was later cleared and the dismissal rescinded at a disciplinary hearing. After several minutes, Tait walked off the pitch holding his jaw. When the game restarted, Wilkinson added his third penalty but we held on for a 15-9 win. Chris Hala'ufia appeared for the final time having scored 10 points (2 tries) during his time in the 1st XV. We climbed to third place just three behind the leaders Gloucester.

Our visit to Leeds on 13th April (we had the previous week off because it was Heineken Cup quarter finals weekend) gave us a great opportunity to cement our place in the top four. The pitch had survived two inspections in the morning and the conditions were atrocious. However, we managed to pretty much control the game all the way through. Jarvis started us off with a penalty and Brown added a try; di Bernardo got a penalty back for Leeds and Jarvis replied in kind for an 11-3 lead at the half-way stage (this was our only score during Ma'asi's trip to the bin). Di Bernardo narrowed the gap to 11-6 with another penalty but Care scored for Jarvis to convert eight minutes later and with 15 minutes left, Jim Evans went over and Jarvis again converted. Four minutes from time, David Strettle was clean through with only one man to beat. He just had to draw him and pass to De Wet Barry for the run in and a bonus point victory. Unfortunately, he got it all wrong and passed at least three yards forward. With the final play of the game, George Robson made 50 metres but was hauled down just short of the line. The ball was recycled quickly and Will Skinner dived over. The conversion from Jarvis made the final score 32-6 and we moved into second place. We dropped back to third before our next game because Bath beat Leicester on the following Tuesday. The top four were now Gloucester 61, Bath 59, Quins 59 and Wasps 55.

With seven wins from our last eight games, we travelled to Reading full of confidence. Despite being on the back foot for most of the first half, we led through a penalty from Jarvis after 35 minutes. The score remained the same until Brown was sent to the bin for offside. While he was off Hickey kicked two penalties and converted Ojo's try (replacement referee Sean Davey who came on for Chris White at half time missed the forward pass that made it). Brown came back and Casey went off to sit in the bin. There was only a minute or so left and just enough time for Jarvis to slot a penalty to give us a losing bonus point. We were now fourth but, given that our remaining games were against fifth placed Sale and sixth placed Leicester, we knew that wins in both would see us finish in a play-off place.

Sunday 4th May saw us play Sale at the Stoop. There were only two games left in our season. Would there be more? The first quarter belonged to us as Williams scored a try after 4 minutes and Jarvis banged over two penalties. The second belonged to the visitors. Wigglesworth scored a try and Hodgson converted. We then lost Fuga who was stretchered off and we leaked 13 points in the last ten minutes of the half. Hodgson got a penalty either side of Viik's try which he converted. At 11-20, we were in trouble against a very strong Sale side. We never gave up even though Hodgson landed his third penalty. Sheridan and Lobbe went to cool off for ten minutes but we could only muster a try from Care. We had lost again but, as against the Irish, we gained a bonus point (16-23). We still held fourth place because Newcastle had beaten Leicester and Wasps lost to Gloucester but any of the teams in third to sixth could still get a play-off spot (Gloucester and Bath were safely in). This proved to be the last time Adrian Jarvis would play for us having scored 638 points (7 tries, 1 dropped goal, 118 penalties and 123 conversions) during his four and a half seasons in the 1st XV; he made 20 appearances as a sub and went to the bin only once.

By the time we travelled to Welford Road to play Leicester on 10th May, we had dropped to fifth because Wasps had achieved a bonus point win at Newcastle on Wednesday night. Basically, we needed to win with a bonus point to give ourselves the best possible chance and hope the key game went our way. Sale were at home to London Irish and if Sale got no points, a regular win would be enough for us. We had lost eleven games on the trot at Leicester and our last win had been in 1997. We played a brand of running rugby which used to be our game and was slowly but surely coming back. Brown got our first try after just three minutes and Malone converted but Leicester came back and Herring and Varndell scored (Goode converting the second). We had the upper hand and, before the interval, Skinner and Tom Williams scored for Malone to convert. Robshaw was sent to the bin before our third try and we nearly held out but Murphy scored Leicester's third try two minutes into the second half. Back to full strength and Williams got his second and our fourth try on 61 minutes. Malone converted and we led 28-17 with nineteen minutes to go. When Crane got Leicester a bonus point, there were fifteen minutes left. It was a fast and furious pace and kicks had been missed and clear cut tries not scored. Eventually, two minutes into time added on, Varndell chipped ahead with nothing much on, the ball bounced kindly for him and he scored for Goode to add the extras. We had somehow contrived again to lose a game we should undoubtedly have won. Dean Richards bemoaned the inconsistent refereeing and that four of the home side's tries were questionable but the record books show that we went down 28-31. What made the loss worse was that Sale had lost at home to London Irish 7-17 and the Tigers had leap-frogged both of us into a play-off spot. Simon Keogh played for the final time having scored 240 points (48 tries) during his five seasons with us. His last ditch try against Montferrand in the 2004 Parker Pen Challenge Cup Final would be remembered for a long time. We ended up sixth and would have to rely on Worcester not winning the European Challenge Cup to claim the last Heineken Cup place. On 25th May at Kingsholm, Bath beat Worcester 24-16 so we would see Heineken Cup rugby at the Stoop in 2008/09. The first piece in the jigsaw of fate had been placed.

This season could have been so different. If only one of our losing bonus points could have been turned into a win. That was the fine line between success and failure in the professional game. It was clear that this was developing into something of a golden era for Quins but it would need to be seen if the team could fulfil its potential. Overall, our playing record was P35 W15 D1 L19 F679 A716, in the league it was P22 W12 D0 L10 F480 A440 Pts 63 (BP 15 – TB 7 LB 8) Pos 6th. Of the 35 matches played, Mike Brown came top (missing just two), Ceri Jones was one behind and Mike Ross appeared in 31. These were the only three to play in over 30 matches. Top try scorer this time was Ugo Monye with 8, Chris Malone had the most points with 143 (2 tries, 2 dropped goals, 25 penalties and 26 conversions). He was our lowest top points scorer since Stuart Thresher managed 139 in 1988/89. He did get the most conversions and shared the dropped goals with Danny Care but Adrian Jarvis had the most penalties with 30. Overall, points dropped again, this time by less than a hundred (770 to 679). As a result, tries dropped by two to 78, penalties were way down (80 to 57) and conversions were also down from 62 to 53 but dropped goals went up by two to 4.

2007/08

170807	MANU SAMOA	TWICKENHAM STOOP	W	2G1PG1T(22)-3G(21)
250807	NORTHAMPTON	NORTHAMPTON	L	1G3T(22)-2G3T(29)
010907	BRISTOL	TWICKENHAM STOOP	L	2G1PG1T(22)-3G2PG(27)
070907	CONNACHT	TWICKENHAM STOOP	W	2G4PG1T(31)-1PG1T(8)
150907	LONDON IRISH(GP)	TWICKENHAM(H)	W	3G3PG1T(35)-3G2PG(27)
220907	LEEDS CARNEGIE(GP)	TWICKENHAM STOOP	W	4G2PG1T(39)-1G1PG1T(15)
290907	NEWCASTLE(GP)	NEWCASTLE	L	4PG(12)-2G1T(19)
061007	BRISTOL(GP)	TWICKENHAM STOOP	W	3G1DG(24)-1G2PG1T(18)
131007	BATH(GP)	BATH	L	1G1PG(10)-2G2PG1T(25)
201007	LONDON WASPS(GP)	TWICKENHAM STOOP	W	2G1DG3PG(26)-2G1DG1PG1T(25)
281007	LONDON IRISH(EDFECGP)	READING	W	1G1PG(10)-1PG1T(8)
031107	WORCESTER(EDFECGP)	TWICKENHAM STOOP	L	2G1PG1T(22)-1G2PG2T(23)
101107	STADE FRANÇAIS(HECP)	PARIS	L	2G1PG(17)-4G3PG(37)

171107	CARDIFF BLUES(HECP)	TWICKENHAM STOOP	D	1G2PG(13)-1G2PG(13)
241107	GLOUCESTER(GP)	GLOUCESTER	L	1G1PG3T(25)-3G2PG(27)
021207	OSPREYS(EDFECGP)	TWICKENHAM STOOP	L	1PG1T(8)-1G4PG(19)
081207	BRISTOL(HECP)	TWICKENHAM STOOP	L	1DG(3)-1G2T(17)
161207	BRISTOL(HECP)	BRISTOL	L	1G(7)-1G1PG2T(20)
221207	SARACENS(GP)	TWICKENHAM STOOP	L	2G2PG(20)-3G2PG(27)
291207	WORCESTER(GP)	WORCESTER	W	2T(10)-1G(7)
060108	LEICESTER(GP)	TWICKENHAM STOOP	L	1G2PG(13)-4G1DG2PG1T(42)
110108	CARDIFF BLUES(HECP)	CARDIFF	L	1G1T(12)-2G3PG(23)
200108	STADE FRANÇAIS(HECP)	TWICKENHAM STOOP	L	1G1PG(10)-4G1PG(31)
250108	SHARKS(GP)	EDGELEY PARK	L	1G2PG(13)-2G2PG(20)
160208	WORCESTER(GP)	TWICKENHAM STOOP	W	4G1PG1T(36)-1G1PG1T(15)
240208	SARACENS(GP)	VICARAGE ROAD	W	1G1PG1T(15)-2PG(6)
010308	GLOUCESTER(GP)	TWICKENHAM STOOP	W	3G3PG(30)-1G1PG3T(25)
090308	LONDON WASPS(GP)	ADAMS PARK	L	2G2PG1T(25)-2G1DG4PG(29)
160308	BATH(GP)	TWICKENHAM STOOP	W	1G5PG(22)-1G3PG(16)
230308	BRISTOL(GP)	BRISTOL	W	1G2PG3T(28)-1G1PG1T(15)
290308	NEWCASTLE(GP)	TWICKENHAM STOOP	W	1DG4PG(15)-2PG(9)
130408	LEEDS CARNEGIE(GP)	HEADINGLEY	W	3G2PG1T(32)-2PG(6)
190408	LONDON IRISH(GP)	READING	L	2PG(6)-1G2PG(13)
040508	SHARKS(GP)	TWICKENHAM STOOP	L	2PG2T(16)-2G3PG(23)
100508	LEICESTER(GP)	LEICESTER	L	4G(28)-3G2T(31)

England went to New Zealand in June 2008 and received another beating in both test matches. They went down 20-37 and 12-44 and after the first defeat, there was an incident with an 18 year old waitress involving Mike Brown and Topsy Ojo. They were both investigated and found guilty of misconduct, Brown was fined £1,000 and Ojo £500. His Honour Judge Jeff Blackett (the RFU Disciplinary Officer) concluded his report by stating that Brown stayed out all night during an England rugby tour and was thereby late for a physiotherapist appointment. In addition he put himself in a position where allegations could be made against him and he warned him to be careful in the future not to put himself in any compromising situations which may lead him to bringing the game into disrepute. Brown and David Strettle played in the first test, Care came on as a sub and in the second, Care started and former Quin Peter Richards came on as a sub.

The IRB announced in May 2008 that it had approved a global trial of a number of Experimental Law Variations (ELVs). They were as follows:-

Assistant Referees

Assistant Referees can assist referees in any manner required when appointed by a match organiser.

Posts and Flags around the field

The corner posts are no longer considered to be in touch-in-goal, except when a ball is grounded against the post.

Lineout and throw

If a team puts the ball back into their own 22 and the ball is subsequently kicked directly into touch there is no gain of ground.

A quick throw may be thrown in straight or towards the throwing team's own goal line.

There is no restriction on the number of players who can participate in the lineout from either side (but with a minimum of two).

The receiver in a lineout must stand two metres back from a lineout.

The player who is in opposition to the player throwing in the ball must stand in the area between the five-metre line and touch line, but must be two metres away from the lineout.

Lineout players may pre-grip a jumper before the ball is thrown in.

The lifting of lineout jumpers is permitted.

The Maul

Players are able to defend a maul by pulling it down.

The reference in Law that heads and shoulders should not be lower than the hips is to be removed.

The Scrum

Introduction of an offside line five metres behind the hindmost feet of the scrum.

Offside rules relating to the scrum half state that the player must be in close proximity to the scrum as in present Law or that they must retreat five metres.

In November 2008, they were reviewed by the IRB Council and in March 2009, it was decided that all would be accepted into full Law except the one concerning numbers in the lineout and the two relating to the maul.

On 26th August, Mark Evans announced the creation of the Big Game. This would be played between Christmas and New Year at Twickenham and would be a Premiership fixture. The accounts revealed another loss for the year ending 30th June 2009; this time it was £2,358,564. Our official sponsors were LV=, Norton Rose, Greene King and Eteach. Sean Fitzpatrick, the ex-New Zealand captain joined the Board as a Director and Wall returned to join him.

Andy Friend had gone after getting the Head Coach role at ACT Brumbies and as a result, there was a restructuring of the set-up. John Kingston became Head Coach, Collin Osbourne was promoted to Assistant Coach from Academy Manager and Tony Diprose moved up to replace him.

Will Skinner became our captain for this and next season following the retirement of Paul Volley. He was in his third season at the Club and continued the long line of back row captains. We had only three friendly fixtures this time, the first was in Galway against Connacht. In torrential rain and with a gale blowing, we played with the wind in the first half and won it 8-3. Keatley slotted a penalty, Nick Evans (making his debut) brought the scores level and Tom Williams raced on to a chip to touch down. Half time saw some changes to our line up as was always the case in friendlies. The rain eased off but the wind remained the same and our lead was gone by the end of the third quarter. Keatley added another penalty and converted a try from Matthews. At one stage, Care tried a box kick but the wind blew the ball back over his head! Keatley dropped two goals to make it 19-8 before Muldoon got the final score with a try. Gavin Duffy, Mel Deane and Andy Dunne all appeared at some point for Connacht. Quins old boys were spread far and wide. Nick Evans had won 16 caps for New Zealand and would go on to become the most prolific scorer in the history of the Club. He would make at least 201 appearances and score at least 2171 points (30 tries, 7 dropped goals, 456 penalties and 316 conversions). Also making his debut in this game as a substitute was a young centre called George Lowe, he would go on to make at least 146 appearances although this total would have been a lot more had it not been for a career threatening neck injury. Another youngster in his first match also coming on as a sub was Sam Smith (his father Simon had been an England international). He would go on to make 83 appearances over the next 6 seasons.

The following week, London Irish came to the Stoop and a close match ensued. Monye ran in from almost half way to open the scoring but the visitors equalised almost immediately when Thorpe crossed. Waisea Luveniyali scored but missed the conversion, Hewat kicked two penalties for the Irish and Luveniyali's penalty with the last kick of the half ensured we had the lead (13-11). After a clearance kick was charged down, McMillan got to it first and Luveniyali added another two points. Within minutes, the lead had been lost because Hewat got a penalty and converted Gower's try. There was still half an hour to play but within ten minutes, Nick Evans replaced Luveniyali and promptly scored a try which he converted. Hewat brought the exiles to within three points with his fourth penalty but subsequently missed two long range efforts in the closing minutes and we held on for the win. Luveniyali appeared for the first time in this one, he would go on to make 17 appearances and was in the process of winning 18 caps for Fiji. Two more capped players made their debuts against the Irish, they were Epi Taione (back row) and Gonzalo Tiesi (centre). Taione was in the process of winning 18 caps for Tonga and 6 for the Pacific Islanders; he would only make 7 appearances for us. Tiesi was an Argentinian and was still a regular in the test team and would win 37 caps; he would make 42 appearances for the 1st XV.

Italian side Overmach Parma visited on 30th August on a gloriously sunny day. We started with fourteen of the fifteen who would begin the following week against Saracens so it was expected that Parma would be put to the sword. It took us just five minutes to open the scoring. Monye grabbing the try but a penalty by Irving pegged us back three minutes later. That only spurred us on and Gonzalo Tiesi, Guest, Jones and Guest again scored tries (Evans converted all but the second) to make it 31-3 at half time. The second half continued in the same vein and Jones and Monye (converted by Luveniyali) scored tries before Mazzariol dropped a goal. Monye completed his hat-trick and Strettle and Skinner made it ten. Luveniyali added all three conversions to leave the final score at 64-6.

The London Double Header at Twickenham meant the start of the 2008/09 Guinness Premiership and this time we played Saracens. Nick Easter came in for Tom Guest as the only change to the starting line up from last week. Jackson fumbled the kick-off from Nick Evans and from the scrum, Care put Strettle over for a try after just 51 seconds. The rest of the half only produced three penalties with Evans getting one in between two from Jackson. We lost the lead on 43 minutes when Powell went over but the response was fantastic. Care got the ball from a lineout and passed to Monye who went straight through the middle and scored under the posts. Evans converted, landed a penalty and dropped a goal to give us a 21-11 lead. Just after De Kock scored for Saracens, Evans went off with a knee injury – he would be out until November. Jackson converted but Luveniyali kept the scoreboard ticking over with a penalty just after replacing Evans. Jackson replied but we held on for the win. We ended the first round in sixth place having had the narrowest victory of the five other winning teams.

Bristol were bottom and we were full of confidence after beating Saracens. Their visit to the Stoop got off to a bad start when good pressure on the Bristol full back (Luke Arscott) resulted in tries from Jordan Turner-Hall and Mike Brown. Luveniyali converted the second but hit the post with the first and missed three penalty attempts. Adrian Jarvis (who had joined from us over the summer) landed two penalties to make it 12-6 at the interval. Monye went to the bin just before the second (right on half time) but there were no further scores until Sidoli went the same way. Tries came from Care and Guest during the sin bin, Luveniyali added the extras to the second and then also to Tiesi's. In the few minutes remaining, Lemi scored a solo try for Luke Arscott to convert but the 31-13 defeat left them at the bottom and catapulted us to the top.

Away at Gloucester on 20th September, we began well and tries from Brown and Care were our reward. Morgan got one back for the home side before Malone put over a penalty for the lead at the break. During the interval, Dean Ryan (Gloucester Head Coach) lambasted the referee (Rob Debney) according to Dean Richards and a penalty count of 7-3 in our favour in the first half changed to one of 8-0 against us afterwards. Ryan insisted he was asking for clarity on the referee's interpretation of the ruck law; Richards was not impressed. In the third quarter, Walker put three kicks over to put Gloucester in front (a dropped goal sandwiched between two penalties). Strokosch ran in from 50 yards out, Walker converted but Malone converted his own score on 62 minutes and the gap was a single point. Barkley's penalty with eight minutes left made the final score 24-20. We had a bonus point but we dropped to third.

London Irish were next on the fixture list and they came to the Stoop in eighth spot but only four points behind us. In a cracking first half, we played some excellent rugby although the Irish scored first (Hewat penalty) and last (Delon Armitage try). Between these scores, we were building a very handy lead with Malone kicking a penalty to level matters, converting Monye's try, putting over his second penalty and improving Guest's score. At 20-8, it was looking good for a home win. The second half was more or less the reverse of the first. We dropped off the pace and let the Irish back into it with all the scoring being contained in the final quarter. Hewat landed a penalty and converted Armitage's second score (there was some doubt as to whether he had gone over the dead ball line before touching down) to make it a two point game. When Hewat intercepted Robshaw's pass and ran 60 metres to score, we were behind and when he added a penalty to the conversion six minutes later, we were in trouble. A late rally saw Care go over for Luveniyali to convert but it was too little, too late. Another losing bonus point saw us drop to seventh, eight points behind leaders Bath.

Only five days later, the first section of the Premiership was brought to a close when we visited Worcester. After Jones had dropped a goal, Monye recovered Malone's chip ahead to register our first points, Care put Tiesi in under the posts (converted by Malone) and Brown scored our third try in six minutes virtually from the kick-off. At 17-3, we had once again built up a decent lead. The question was – could we keep it? With Jones single-handedly reducing the deficit with a penalty and the conversion of his own try, it looked as though we couldn't! However, we woke up and Monye scored the bonus point try and Malone converted for a fourteen point lead at the break. A try from Benjamin early on (converted by Jones) was replied to by Malone with a penalty six minutes later. Worcester's only reply was another Jones penalty on 76 minutes just after Guest had gone to the bin to make the final score 30-23. We were now fourth but on the same points as the second and third placed sides.

Our next Guinness Premiership game was not until 16th November as we now had a mixture of EDF Energy Cup and Heineken Cup matches. The first of these was a trip to the Liberty Stadium, Swansea to play the Ospreys. As it was an EDF Energy Cup match, Richards made a host of changes to the team and only Chris Robshaw remained in the starting line-up. The Osprey's were virtually at full strength and Hook kicked them into a 6-0 lead with two penalties in the first quarter. Luveniyali got one of his own before Hook put over another and Williams grabbed a try. Epi Taione went to the bin for the last part of the first half and the first seven minutes of the second and we somehow managed to score the only points (Barry scored a try for Luveniyali to convert). When Fuga scored, Luveniyali's conversion and penalty gave us a six point lead against a side containing thirteen internationals. Hook got his fourth penalty and after Ryan Jones went to the bin, Luveniyali restored the lead with his third. Two minutes into injury time, the Ospreys attacked and Byrne chipped through to the line where Charlie Amesbury gathered the ball. As Byrne tackled him, the ball spilled over the line and Bowe pounced to score a try. Hook's conversion sent us to defeat by a single point (23-24). This left us in third place in the Pool with games against London Irish and Worcester to follow after two Heineken Cup games.

Our seventh attempt to win the Heineken Cup began at Stradey Park against the Scarlets. This was the last European tie to be played at the famous old ground as a new location would be moved to in November. It was our 29th visit and our record was a poor one - W6 L22. We didn't turn up for the first half and were punished accordingly. A bad clearance from the kick-off saw Stoddart score with only 32 seconds gone. After 9 minutes Mark Jones went over and we were in total disarray. Malone got a penalty for us but three from Stephen Jones gave the hosts a commanding 19-3 lead at the break. Had they not squandered three great scoring opportunities, the score would have been even worse for us (Mike Brown did make two last-gasp tackles to save certain tries). During the interval, John Kingston delivered a tirade and we came out a different team. Malone (he had played dreadfully before half time) kicked two penalties to one from Stephen Jones but we still trailed 9-22. On 55 minutes, Richards brought on Fuga, Robson and Easter and slowly the tide turned in our favour. Care went over from a tap-penalty, Malone converted and landed his fourth penalty. Rees went to the bin just before the penalty and during this time, Monye collected a cross-kick from Malone and scored in the corner for the provider to convert and we led 26-22. With the last kick of the match, Malone slotted another penalty and the comeback was complete. The Scarlets must have wondered how they lost. We were second in the Pool to Stade Français who had beaten our next opponents Ulster.

At the Stoop on 18th October, the Irish province visited for the first time, both previous fixtures had been played at Ravenhill. We went behind when Nagusa scored after three minutes. O'Connor converted but it proved to be a false impression of how the match would develop. With Ulster conceding penalties, Malone kicked one and Turner-Hall scored our first try. McCullough went to the bin and quickly the margin increased by twelve points as Williams and Care got tries, the second being converted by Malone. After McCullough returned, we were awarded a penalty try when Cave body-checked Monye to stop him from scoring. Malone's conversion made it 27-7 and the try bonus point was already in the bag. Mike Brown got the fifth for Malone to convert but when Care went to the bin for obstruction on his opposite number, Ulster made something of a comeback as we went to sleep. Wallace and Trimble got tries (O'Connor converted both) and it suddenly became 34-21 with 23 minutes to go. We woke up and Malone cross-kicked for Williams to score before Care came back. In the remaining quarter, both sides made six substitutions but Malone stuck around long enough to slot his second penalty to make the final score 42-21. We were joint top with Stade Français so the head to head fixtures in December would provide some idea as to how this Pool would end up if one side managed to win both.

Back to the EDF Energy Cup the following week and London Irish came to the Stoop and we had to win to maintain any hope of a semi-final spot. Only two players survived from the previous week's starting XV but we got off to a good start and Phil Davies and Charlie Amesbury got tries and Seb Jewell converted the second for a 12-0 lead after 13 minutes. Thorpe got one back four minutes before the break but our lead became twelve again when McMillan scored our third try on 46 minutes. But then, the Irish came back as they had done almost a month ago. Hewat was again on the list of scorers and he converted his own try but the next two from Thompstone and Bailey were missed. We had conceded 17 points in nine minutes and when Ignacio Elosu (our replacement hooker) went to the bin, Geraghty added a penalty. With time running out, Hewat got his second try and Hickey converted for a final score of 32-17. We were out and our visit to Worcester was a dead rubber as far as we were concerned.

Once again, over two thirds of the side changed (this time, we were almost at full strength) and we got off to an excellent start. Robshaw scored a try after ten minutes, Malone converted and added a penalty before Abbott scored for Worcester for Jones to convert. In the second quarter we reversed our scoring, Malone got the penalty and converted Stegmann's try to give us a nice lead at the half way stage. Our old captain Pat Sanderson came off the bench for the Warriors and scored (Jones converted) and we saw Nick Evans make his return from injury when he too came on. There were no further scores (despite Worcester spending most of the final quarter in our 22) until the final seconds when Tosh Masson intercepted and Brown ran away to score in the right corner. Evans converted with the final kick of the game to make it 27-14. We finished in third place in the Pool just ahead of Worcester.

After a week off, it was back to the Premiership with a visit from Wasps to the Stoop on 16th November. Since the turn of the Century, we had only won a third of the fifteen matches played between the clubs. In a blistering start, Malone dropped a goal from 45 metres after only 19 seconds when Lewsey's clearance went straight to him, Guest scored a try, Evans converted and added a penalty. Eight minutes gone, 13-0 to us. Staunton got a penalty back but Evans landed three more penalties and went through for a try (after the first of the penalties) to make it 27-3 at the interval. Robshaw added a third try but we were unable to get the bonus point. Walder converted Simpson's consolation score with 13 minutes to go but the final score of 32-10 said it all. We moved up to second spot, three points behind leaders Bath after six rounds. London Irish and Leicester (our next opponents) were hot on our heels. Augusitino Junior Poluleuligaga made the first of only 8 appearances in this one when he came on as a sub. He was a scrum half, had won 2 caps for the Pacific Islanders, was a current Samoan international and would go on to win 21 caps for his country.

Welford Road is the hardest place in England to win away at and we certainly piled the pressure on ourselves. In just over a minute, Leicester scored a try through Johne Murphy which Hougaard converted. He and Evans took it in turns to slot two penalties each until Hougaard broke the sequence with a try and conversion. A third penalty from Evans made it 9-20 at half time. This quickly became 9-27 when Matt Smith went over on 44 minutes. Hougaard's conversion made the game safe and although we competed until the end, we only had Brooker's try after 77 minutes to show for it. It was important for the team to play better than this if a top four finish was to be attained. Everyone knew they were capable of doing it. We slipped to sixth with this defeat and Leicester went above us although their position didn't change. They were in fourth at the start of the day. We had 20 points and a narrow gap of four points separated us from seventh placed Saracens.

Leaders Bath came to the Stoop on 30th November and a win was vital going into the two Heineken Cup games against Stade Français. The first half ended all square at 9-9 with Evans and James sharing six penalties. James put Bath in front but there was never more than three points in it. Browne got a try for the visitors on 50 minutes to which Turner-Hall replied thirteen minutes later; all-square again as the kickers missed. With eleven minutes to go, Andy Gomarsall disguised an inside pass to Ceri Jones and the prop went through the gap to score the match winning try. Evans converted to make it 21-14. Despite Bath trying to level matters for a fifth time, we held on for victory which took us up to fifth place.

The trip to the Stade de France to play Stade Français Paris on 6th December was a real test for our young side. Before a Pool record crowd of 76,569 the entertainment had been laid on with girls from the Moulin Rouge, jousting knights, chariot racing, a medieval parade and two eagles. Add to this the fireworks at the end and the scene was set. We tore into our opponents who were unbeaten in 17 Heineken Cup games at home and had lost only once in 32 matches in the same competition in Paris since 1998. After 13 minutes, Care chipped the ball into the home 22, the two defenders got in a muddle and the ball ricocheted around until Tom Williams picked it up and scored the opening points with a try. Evans converted and we were on our way. We were under pressure and when Mike Brown put in a long clearance kick from his own in-goal area, nothing looked on. The Stade full back, Camara, collected the ball and James Percival, the ball popped out and Jordan Turner-Hall grabbed it and ran 40 metres to score our second try. Evans couldn't convert this one and we gave the home side a lifeline when Care was offside and got sent to the bin either side of half time. Hernandez landed a penalty to open Stade's account but we still held a nice lead at the break. With Care still off, Leguizamon scored under the posts, Hernandez converted and suddenly the lead was just two points. Against the run of play, we got a penalty near the Stade 22 and Evans put it over to make the lead five points. Our defence was superb and we repelled every attack the French could muster. With a minute to go and Stade camped on our line, we were awarded a penalty, Care goaded Leguizamon and referee (Alun Lewis) ensured the penalty was reversed. As Stade had to go for the try, they called a scrum which we managed to defend yet again and the game was won 15-10. We had maintained top spot in the Pool; we just had to do it all again the following week back at the Stoop.

The rain poured down, there was a pitch inspection 90 minutes before kick-off but the game went ahead. Evans got the first points after two minutes with a penalty but Stade scored a try through Oelschig who also landed penalties either side of it to leave us trailing 3-11. Back we came through an Evans penalty and when he converted Turner-Hall's try, we were back in front. By the interval though, Oelschig had put over his third penalty and we trailed by a single point (13-14). Into the second half, Evans got his third penalty to inch us ahead but when Hernandez dropped a goal with eight minutes to go, the Pool was wide open. Hernandez missed another and, with time rapidly running out, we restarted from our 22. We marched up the pitch sometimes only going inches, Evans ran once then a second time into the Stade 22 after his option for the dropped goal had been closed down. Turner-Hall almost knocked-on but the ball was eventually set up for Care to pass back to Evans. This time he took the shot from 25 metres out, the ball wobbled out of the mud and went over with inches to spare (the referee Nigel Owens had to get the TMO to confirm it had gone over). In the still pouring rain, Owens put his arm up to signal success and immediately blew the final whistle. We had retained the ball through 29 phases of play which took over four and a half minutes in atrocious conditions – it was last-ditch attacking rugby at its best. Over 60,000 fewer spectators had seen another compelling match without the razzmatazz but with the same result. The score of 19-17 sent us six points clear of Stade Français in second. One more win would ensure our first quarter final since 1997.

On 20th December, we visited Franklin's Gardens to play the tenth placed Saints. They were unbeaten at home so it would be no walkover and in a niggly first 40 minutes it remained tight. Myler and Evans exchanged penalties in the first ten minutes before Myler put Northampton ahead with another. From Gomarsall's pop pass, Monye scored under the posts and Evans put over the conversion and a penalty to give us a seven point lead. Just after the break, Clarke got a try and Myler levelled the scores. The referee Chris White then got his yellow card out and showed it to Gomarsall (for a late tackle) and when he came back on, Fuga got one for a trip. In the first ten minutes, Myler got a penalty but in the second, Downey went over under the posts for Myler to convert. In the last 18 minutes, we had two penalty chances but Evans sent both of them wide. There was no more scoring even though Fernandez Lobbe spent the last five minutes in the bin. This defeat enabled Leicester to sneak past us into fifth place and we dropped to sixth.

Our last game of 2008 was the eagerly awaited Big Game against Leicester at Twickenham. The game was played on 27th December and hoped to attract extra fans because of the Christmas holidays. Unfortunately, due to major rail works, the ground capacity was set at 50,000 and that was easily achieved by the commercial team. The match day entertainment would increase over the years as the Big Game became a permanent fixture in the Christmas sporting calendar. The game itself kicked-off at 4 p.m. and was shown live on Sky Sports. This was our 57th meeting at Twickenham, the first coming on 12th March 1910 and resulted in a narrow win for the Tigers by a single try to nil. Nick Evans began the scoring with a penalty after two minutes and kicked two more after Flood had brought the scores level. In the last ten minutes of the half, Leicester scored thirteen unanswered points. Flood kicked two more penalties and converted Johne Murphy's try after Monye's attempt to smother Dupuy's fly-hack resulted in the ball bouncing off his knee and into Murphy's path. This all happened while Skinner was spending ten minutes in the bin. Ten minutes into the second half, Croft got Leicester's second try and Flood's conversion took them fourteen points clear. A mistake by Flood eventually led to a try by Brown which Evans converted but Flood made amends with his fourth penalty to make it 16-26 with 8 minutes left. Evans put over his fourth penalty from 38 metres on 76 minutes as we went for broke to try and draw level. Moody went to the bin with two minutes left and from Dupuy's poor clearance, we attacked. Tom Williams broke away and this set up a chance for Monye to atone for his earlier error which he duly did. From the touchline with 29 seconds on the clock, Evans stroked the ball between the posts to make it 26-26. A fantastic way to end although both sides could feel unhappy about the failure to win. Our position stayed the same and we were eight points behind the leaders Bath with 12 rounds to go.

Our first game of 2009 was at Adams Park against Wasps. They started in tenth place but it seemed as though places were reversed as in the first 22 minutes they ran up sixteen points. Cipriani kicked three penalties and converted a penalty try awarded after too many scrum infringements. Evans got a penalty but we were too sloppy and Bishay went over in the corner to make it an eighteen point advantage at half way (the TMO awarded the score but there was doubt as to whether he had control of the ball as it touched the ground). Croall went to the bin for ten minutes eight minutes before the break but there was no scoring during his time off. We got a penalty try after 53 minutes from a scrum and Evans converted. When Shaw was binned, we took advantage and Care broke away, chipped over Flutey and raced on to re-gather and score. The conversion was missed so when Walder put over a penalty with five minutes left, we were 15-24 down. Malone kicked a penalty with a minute to go and we went through 19 phases of play from the restart but couldn't get out of our 22. At this point, Care was instructed by the management to put the ball out and so it ended. We stayed in sixth but the gap was now eleven points between us and the leaders who were now London Irish.

On 10th January, we were scheduled to meet Worcester Warriors in Round 12 of the Premiership but due to a frozen pitch, the game was postponed. The referee, Wayne Barnes, inspected the pitch at 4.30 p.m. on Friday afternoon and deemed it unsafe for play despite the ground staff putting on double covers and using hot air blowers. It was the first home game we had lost to the weather since 9th November 1996 when a fixture against Saracens was postponed. As a result of not playing, we dropped to seventh place.

After the enforced break, we travelled to Ravenhill to take on Ulster in Round 5 of the Heineken Cup Pool matches. Unbeaten so far, we were playing into a gale in the first half (an arctic wind was blowing coupled with freezing rain) and we held Ulster to a sixteen point lead even though we lost Care to the bin. Cave scored a try inside the first minute, Humphreys converted and added three penalties. When the sides turned round, Evans put over a penalty and when Care came back on, we had a penalty try within ten minutes. The conversion by Evans made it 16-10 with twenty minutes left. On 73 minutes, we had a penalty on the 22 and five metres to the right of the posts. On the touchline, Dean Richards indicated to thc fourth official that we wanted to replace Evans with Malone. The referee insisted the change was made immediately – Richards was fuming. Malone promptly missed the kick and when his clearance kick was charged down with three minutes left, Best scored to seal the win. With the winds reaching 75mph, one stand was evacuated for safety reasons and two of our players had to be wrapped in survival blankets! Even though we lost, the Scarlets won against Stade Français so we had qualified for the quarter finals. The final pool game against the Welsh side on 24th January would decide whether we were at home or away. Epi Taione made his last appearance for us having come on as a substitute; he went to the bin once.

The weather improved 100% on the previous week for the visit of the Scarlets and they took the lead with a penalty by Stephen Jones after 11 minutes. After this, it was one-way traffic for the next forty in our favour. Nick Evans brought us level with a penalty, Robshaw and Robson went over for tries and Evans converted the second for an interval lead of 15-3. When Percival scored our third on 53 minutes, the conversion by Evans looked to have put the game to bed. However, we fell asleep and gave the visitors a chance. They took it with both hands and tries from Stoddart and Rees (both converted by Jones) reduced our lead to just five points with the final quarter to go. Tom Guest came on for Robshaw and promptly broke from a scrum to send Tom Williams in for the bonus point score. Evans again converted but the final score went to the visitors when Evans grabbed a try with the final move of the game. The conversion from Jones gave them a losing bonus point. We now had to wait on results elsewhere to see if we would get a home or away quarter final. The answer came quickly as Leicester lost at the Ospreys and by the end of the weekend, we were confirmed as number three seeds. The quarter final line up would be as follows:-

1 Cardiff Blues	*v*	Toulouse	8
2 Munster	*v*	Ospreys	7
3 Harlequins	*v*	Leinster	6
4 Leicester	*v*	Bath	5

We now had a run of nine Guinness Premiership matches before this game in April. The date with destiny was fast approaching and that final try against the Scarlets had become the second piece of the jigsaw of fate.

The first of these was against Northampton on 31st January at the Stoop. David Strettle returned from injury with his first game for four months and he played a full part. From the kick-off, we kept the ball for three minutes until Botha scored the opening try. Evans converted and added two penalties to give us a 13-0 lead at the break. Into the second half, this became 20-0 when we were awarded a penalty try as the Saints scrum went backwards towards their line. Evans converted before Myler landed two penalties but we were still two scores ahead going into the final quarter. The only further scoring was a Jim Evans try converted by Nick Evans to make it 27-6 at the end. We moved back up to sixth place on 32 points – nine behind leaders Gloucester.

Two weeks later, we made the short trip to Reading to take on second placed London Irish. Hewat opened the scoring with a penalty before Evans equalised in similar fashion. The game changed on 22 minutes when Irish hooker Paice was shown yellow for fighting. He decided to dispute the decision and the referee (Tim Wigglesworth) changed it to red – he was off for the rest of the match. Immediately, Evans slotted a penalty to put us in front but Hewat equalised to keep it level at half time. On 43 minutes, Lalanne put the Irish in front with a penalty but the lead only lasted six minutes because Ceri Jones scored a try that went unconverted. It remained tighter than it should have against fourteen men and when Evans stretched the lead with three minutes to go with his third penalty, it seemed we had done enough. In the final minute, Gower was stopped on the line and we survived but only just. We moved up to fifth and were five points adrift of Bath in fourth but they had a game in hand.

As with the previous season, Gloucester came to the Stoop at the top of the table. After 7 minutes, we attacked from a quick throw and when the ball reached Nick Evans 70 metres out, he stepped out of Lawson's tackle on half way and threw a dummy the way of Balshaw; he was through and had a clear run to the line. It was the sort of try we were capable of producing as the team grew in confidence and our crop of English youngsters played together more often. After Evans had converted, Barkley landed two penalties before the break and one after to erase our lead. Malone replaced Evans at the break and missed two late penalties to win it. He did put in a high kick which the Gloucester defence couldn't deal with (Lawson put it out on the full to hand us an attacking line out). There was some thought that the high kick had gone forward off a Quins hand but the officials didn't call it. From the lineout, we set up a series of drives and eventually, Tom Williams dived over under the posts. Malone's conversions made it 14-9 and we played out the remaining minutes and stayed in fifth as a result. The gap between us and the leaders was now only seven points.

Our next opponents were Bristol and although our record at the Memorial Stadium was not brilliant, they were rooted to the bottom of the table and looked almost certain to go down. They had also lost their coach Richard Hill during the week. After 18 minutes, Neil Brew put them ahead and Barnes (who had replaced our old boy Adrian Jarvis after only four minutes) added the extras. Eight minutes later, Gary Botha scored for us so we only trailed by two points with half the game to go. Strettle grabbed a second two minutes into the second period and before the next scores Crompton and Jones saw yellow at the same time. When referee Chris White adjudged that Lemi had been pushed to prevent him from gathering a bouncing ball in the in-goal area, he awarded a penalty try which Barnes converted. There were eleven minutes to go and we eventually worked an overlap for Monye to run in our third try. Malone converted this one and we had just done enough to win. We now moved into fourth spot. The top four were Gloucester 51pts, Sale 46, London Irish 45 and Quins 43. Below us, Leicester also had 43 and we were above them by virtue of a single point in the for and against column. Bath had 42 points so our top four spot was by no means guaranteed.

Our sixteenth Premiership match was a home game against Saracens. They were going through internal turmoil with a lot of players being asked to leave with a lot of time left on contracts and a new consortium from South Africa taking over. Evans put us in front with a penalty before Saracens hit back with a penalty from Jackson who also converted van Heerden's try. Their lead was short-lived and by the interval, we were back in front. Evans got another penalty and converted a try from Ceri Jones. When Evans completed his hat-trick we had a six point lead but Haughton scored a try to make it 16-15. With eleven minutes left, Care dived over and we had our tenth league win of the season. We moved up to third on points difference (second to fifth were all on 47 points).

A trip to Newcastle the following Sunday (15th March) was an important one to win as a loss at this stage could easily see us drop out of the top four. They were thirteen points behind us and in eighth place but it would not be easy. Two penalties from Evans set us on our way but a penalty by May and Visser's try nudged the Falcons ahead. Evans and May exchanged penalties in the last four minutes of the half to leave the home side in front by two points (9-11). May added a third two minutes after the restart and the only item of note until the final five minutes was the referee (Martin Fox) going off injured after 56 minutes and being replaced by Wayne Barnes. Into those last five minutes, May knocked over his fourth penalty before Mike Brown wriggled over with 50 seconds left. Malone's conversion gave us a sniff but, as we tried to keep the ball alive, it fell loose and May picked it up and ran in from 25 metres out. His conversion ensured no points for us from our toil in the North East. As a result of this, we dropped to fifth and we still had to play Sale twice and Bath (the teams either side of us). The gap to Gloucester at the top was eight points. Crucially, Nick Evans sprained an ankle and would be out for three weeks, it would be tight but hopefully he would be fit for the Heineken Cup quarter final against Leinster on 12th April.

The first Sale game was next and we had the home advantage first. Because of the injury to Evans, Chris Malone started at 10 and just over 90 seconds in put over his first penalty. Hodgson replied for the Sharks, Malone kicked two more, Hodgson replied in kind, Malone got another and Hodgson levelled to make it 12-12 at the break. Keil went to the bin a minute before half time and just before he came back on, Botha scored our first try for Malone to convert. Hodgson got his fifth penalty before launching a clearance some 80 metres. Unfortunately for him, it went dead and from the scrum way back in Sale's territory, Stegmann scored another try. When Tom Guest added a third, there were 17 minutes left. Malone converted that as well as Barry's bonus point clinching effort on 73 minutes. Hodgson scored a consolation try for the visitors near the end but we had an important victory. We moved back into the top four by virtue of winning one more game than Bath. Junior Poluleuligaga appeared for the final time, coming on as a substitute.

Next was the rearranged game against Worcester at the Stoop. A Wednesday evening fixture on 1st April proved to be very entertaining. Worcester travelled with an inexperienced XV due to injuries and having to play three games in seven days. After only four minutes, they lost Fortey to the bin and we seized the opportunity. Tani Fuga opened the scoring with a try and Malone converted. The next score came from the visitors on 27 minutes when Fellows scored and Carlisle converted. In the remaining time before the break, Care scored, Malone converted and Robshaw added a third to put us 19-7 up. Worcester came back at us and Ruwers scored a try which Crichton converted but our reply was swift. Jordan Turner-Hall secured the bonus point and Monye took the score to 29-14. After Kitchener went the same way as Fortey earlier, Brown stretched the lead to twenty points but again the conversion was missed. As Worcester tired, we ran riot in the final twelve minutes and Nick Easter scored a hat-trick of tries in that time. Luveniyali converted all of them but failed with the ninth scored by Tom Williams. This victory catapulted us to the top of the Premiership table for the first time since 2003. We were on the same points (57) as Leicester and Bath, Gloucester had 56, London Irish 55 and Sale 51.

Against Bath at the Rec three days later, we put in a tremendous performance and annihilated the home scrum and that doesn't happen very often. Malone put us in front with a penalty after 8 minutes and when the Bath scrum disintegrated near their line, Dave Pearson (the referee) had no option but to go under the posts. The conversion of the penalty try was a formality for Malone but James pulled three points back with a penalty just before half time. After Malone had stretched our lead with another penalty, Mike Ross went to the bin but it made no difference. Our grip on the game would not be loosened and Care dropped a goal just after Ross had returned. In the final minute, Malone added his third penalty to make it 19-3. It was our biggest winning margin over them since January 1997 and our biggest at Bath since the fifty point thrashing back in March 1961. Leicester got a bonus point win so we dropped to second and with two matches of the regular season left, any of the top six teams could still make the play-offs.

On Sunday 12th April, Leinster came to the Stoop for the Heineken Cup quarter final. It was our first home quarter final and our third overall (the first since 1997). From the very start, you could sense that this was a big step up from anything we had experienced before. This was the big time and we would need to be at our best to make the semi-finals for the first time. The first half was tight and full of blood and guts with both sides hammering away to try and gain advantage. After 6 minutes, Evans missed a penalty from 33 metres to the left of the posts but Contepomi made no mistake with his from 41 metres to put Leinster in front. When Easter was sent to the bin for a deliberate knock-on after O'Driscoll had been brilliantly brought down by Strettle, Contepomi doubled the lead with another penalty. Half time came and at the moment Easter came back on, Contepomi was heading off for ten minutes after a trip on Robshaw. Evans was replaced by Malone and Leinster almost scored a try; only a forward pass by Contepomi prevented Nacewa putting Kearney over in the south-west corner. Immediately after this, Kearney tried a dropped goal after Malone's clearance kick. His attempt from 42 metres almost shaved the left post and luckily for us, it went the wrong side. Crucially, during Contepomi's time off the field, we had scored nothing. We piled on the pressure and Care raced through, put in a chip ahead and was only just beaten to the ball by the covering Fitzgerald. From the five metre scrum, we spent 6 minutes camped on the Leinster line. Gary Botha got over the line but the TMO ruled he had put the ball down on someone's boot. Eventually, Malone put Mike Brown over for a try but his conversion attempt drifted across the face of the posts and we trailed by a single point with 15 minutes to go. On 69 minutes, Malone went down injured and had to be replaced by Tom Williams. When we were awarded a penalty 54 metres out two minutes later, we were down to third choice kicker Mike Brown. His attempt was short and to the left, we were still a point down. Leinster had been defending for most of the half, it had been a fantastic effort but could they survive the final five minutes? Suddenly, Williams had blood coming from his mouth and, as Evans had been tactically replaced, he was eligible to come on as a blood replacement. The referee (Nigel Owens) checked with the fourth official and he was allowed on despite protests from Leinster's support staff that they could see no blood. As Williams left the pitch he winked and spat out a lot of blood. The problem was how had he cut his mouth when he had not been in contact with anyone since he came on? The game restarted with the clock reading 75.06 and we eventually worked Evans into a position to drop for goal. He was 40 metres out to the right of the posts and there were 45 seconds left. He pulled it to the left of the posts and, after a frantic passage of play during which the visitors almost scored, a knock-on brought proceedings to an end after 81 minutes and 16 seconds. Even though we had been defeated and only eleven points scored, it had been an enthralling encounter. If only we had someone who could have kicked the ball between the posts, we would have won, it was that simple. Afterwards, it became clear that there was a suspicion of foul play and an investigation was launched by ERC (the governing body for the Heineken Cup) just before we played Sale. The fall out would rock the Club and the entire world of rugby. The season had ended before the hearings took place and that will be covered in the next chapter. The term "Bloodgate" would be forever linked to the Harlequin Football Club. Malone never played for us again as he left at the end of the season to go and play for London Irish. He scored 257 points (3 tries, 3 dropped goals, 47 penalties and 46 conversions) and captained the side twice.

Five days later it was back to the Guinness Premiership and our attempt to get a play-off spot. Sale Sharks were in sixth place and had an outside chance of reaching the top four. If we won, we were more or less there. If not, it would go down to the last round the following week. As both Evans and Malone were out (the second named for the rest of the season), Waisea Luveniyali played at fly half. After missing with his first attempt, he put us ahead after 17 minutes. Having lost Monye in the pre-match warm up, Strettle went off with a foot injury and was replaced by Care. We were slowly falling apart under the weight of too many injuries. When Ross was sin binned after 38 minutes, Sale were awarded a penalty try shortly afterwards. Hodgson converted to make it 7-3 at the break. Chabal scored for Hodgson to convert but there were no further scores until Andy Gomarsall put over a penalty. With Care playing at fly half, we had more attacking options but something had to give and it was our defence. Keil got a third try and Wigglesworth finished off a 70-yard counter attack. Hodgson got both conversions, the second being the last kick of the game. The final score of 28-6 was our heaviest defeat of the season. By the end of the weekend's fixtures, we were still in second place level on 61 points with Bath and London Irish. We had thirteen wins against 12 and 11 respectively. Sale moved into fifth and any of the top six could still grab a top four finish going into the final weekend of matches. For us, we had to go for a bonus point victory and if we got it, we would finish no worse than second.

The return with Newcastle was played on Sunday 25th April and we knew what had to be done. The Falcons had nothing to play for and we ripped into them from the word go. In the first quarter, Easter (2) and Fuga scored tries, Luveniyali put over two conversions (he missed the second of Easter's brace) and we were 19-0 up. The second quarter belonged to us as well with Care rampant in the loose. Brown got the bonus point try (Luveniyali converted) and Monye a fifth after Parling scored for the visitors and May converted. The interval score of 31-7 was surely enough to see us home and so it proved. Jones went to the bin on 59 minutes but we couldn't add to our score. In fact, the only points in the second half came with four minutes left when Charlton went over to make it 31-12. Our highest ever league finish earned us a home semi-final against third placed London Irish at the Stoop on 9th May. Leicester had finished top with 71 points, Quins second on 66 points (14 wins), London Irish third also on 66 (12 wins) and Bath in fourth with 65 points. Sale and Gloucester took the remaining Heineken Cup places.

Our injuries were mounting but the week off gave us some chance to repair a few of the walking wounded. The Irish came for a fight and offence after offence went unpunished by referee Chris White. Finally, when Tagicakibau tripped Care, he saw yellow. By then, a clearly unfit and struggling Nick Evans had missed two penalty attempts as had Brown. The Irish had missed two kicks as well and the man who was binned dropped the ball over the line. After all this, there was no score at the break and all to play for. In the second half, the visitors began to accumulate points. Delon Armitage knocked over a penalty and converted Hudson's try. We were regularly on the back foot and couldn't get anywhere, the Irish had us penned in and, with five minutes to go, Catt intercepted Gomarsall's pass and jogged the 20 metres to the posts. Armitage added the conversion and we were out (0-17). It was the first time we had failed to score since 18th October 2003 when Gloucester beat us by sixteen points. In the final on 16th May, the Irish lost to Leicester by a single point (9-10). We said goodbye to three players in this one, De Wet Barry, Andy Gomarsall (substitute) and Mike Ross. Barry had captained the side once, was sent off once and put in the bin twice; he scored 20 points (4 tries). Gomarsall had scored 13 points (2 tries and a single penalty), captained the side once and been to the bin twice. Ross was coming into his prime so it was sad to lose him but this was becoming a regular occurrence now. He had visited the bin twice during his all too short three seasons with us.

The 2008/09 season would ultimately be remembered for the event that took place after 75 minutes of the Heineken Cup quarter final against Leinster at the Stoop on 12th April. The fallout from it was catastrophic for the Club and would put us back somewhere in the region of three years. It would prove the downfall of Dean Richards and several others. If anything, we over achieved in this season and ultimately ended with nothing after looking at one point as if we might do the Heineken Cup/Premiership double. The injuries stacked up against us and by the end of the semi-final against London Irish, we looked a very tired outfit.

Our playing record overall was P36 W22 D1 L13 F834 A649 and in the league (not including the play-off) it was P22 W14 D1 L7 F519 A387 Pts 66 (BP 8 – TB 5 LB 3) Pos 2nd. No one played in all 36 matches but Ceri Jones, Chris Robshaw and George Robson only missed two, Jordan Turner-Hall played in 32 and Mike Brown, Jim

Evans, Tom Guest, Mike Ross, Will Skinner and Tom Williams were two behind him. Ugo Monye got the most tries (14) and Nick Evans scored the most points 143 (3 tries, 2 dropped goals, 37 penalties and 23 conversions). As a result, he was also top of dropped goals, penalties and conversions. Overall, we scored 100 tries (up by 22), dropped goals stayed the same on 4 and both penalties and conversions were up on 2007/08 (from 57 to 66 and 53 to 62 respectively).

2008/09

160808	CONNACHT	GALWAY	L	1PG1T(8)-1G2DG2PG1T(24)
230808	LONDON IRISH	TWICKENHAM STOOP	W	2G1PG2T(27)-1G4PG1T(24)
300808	OVERMACH PARMA	TWICKENHAM STOOP	W	7G3T(64)-1DG1PG(6)
060908	SARACENS(GP)	TWICKENHAM(A)	W	1G1DG3PG1T(24)-1G3PG1T(21)
130908	BRISTOL(GP)	TWICKENHAM STOOP	W	3G2T(31)-1G2PG(13)
200908	GLOUCESTER(GP)	GLOUCESTER	L	1G1PG2T(20)-1G1DG3PG1T(24)
270908	LONDON IRISH(GP)	TWICKENHAM STOOP	L	3G2PG(27)-2G3PG1T(28)
021008	WORCESTER(GP)	WORCESTER	W	2G2PG2T(30)-2G1DG2PG(23)
051008	OSPREYS(EDFECGP)	LIBERTY STADIUM	L	2G3PG(23)-1G4PG1T(24)
111008	SCARLETS(HECP)	LLANELLI	W	2G5PG(29)-4PG2T(22)
181008	ULSTER(HECP)	TWICKENHAM STOOP	W	3G2PG3T(42)-3G(21)
251008	LONDON IRISH(EDFECGP)	TWICKENHAM STOOP	L	1G2T(17)-2G1PG3T(32)
021108	WORCESTER(EDFECGP)	WORCESTER	W	3G2PG(27)-2G(14)
161108	LONDON WASPS(GP)	TWICKENHAM STOOP	W	1G1DG4PG2T(32)-1G1PG(10)
221108	LEICESTER(GP)	LEICESTER	L	3PG1T(14)-3G2PG(27)
301108	BATH(GP)	TWICKENHAM STOOP	W	1G3PG1T(21)-3PG1T(14)
061208	STADE FRANÇAIS PARIS(HECP)	STADE DE FRANCE	W	1G1PG1T(15)-1G1PG(10)
131208	STADE FRANÇAIS PARIS(HECP)	TWICKENHAM STOOP	W	1G1DG3PG(19)-1DG3PG1T(17)
201208	NORTHAMPTON(GP)	NORTHAMPTON	L	1G2PG(13)-2G3PG(23)
271208	LEICESTER(GP)	TWICKENHAM	D	2G4PG(26)-2G4PG(26)
040109	LONDON WASPS(GP)	ADAMS PARK	L	1G2PG1T(18)-1G4PG1T(24)
100109	WORCESTER(GP)	TWICKENHAM STOOP	P	
170109	ULSTER(HECP)	ULSTER	L	1G1PG(10)-1G3PG1T(21)

240109	SCARLETS(HECP)	TWICKENHAM STOOP	W	3G1PG1T(29)-3G1PG(24)
310109	NORTHAMPTON(GP)	TWICKENHAM STOOP	W	3G2PG(27)-2PG(6)
140209	LONDON IRISH(GP)	READING	W	3PG1T(14)-3PG(9)
210209	GLOUCESTER(GP)	TWICKENHAM STOOP	W	2G(14)-3PG(9)
010309	BRISTOL(GP)	BRISTOL	W	1G2T(17)-2G(14)
070309	SARACENS(GP)	TWICKENHAM STOOP	W	1G1T3PG(21)-1G1PG1T(15)
150309	NEWCASTLE(GP)	NEWCASTLE	L	1G3PG(16)-1G4PG1T(24)
220309	SHARKS(GP)	TWICKENHAM STOOP	W	3G4PG1T(38)-5PG1T(20)
010409	WORCESTER(GP)	TWICKENHAM STOOP	W	5G5T(60)-2G(14)
040409	BATH(GP)	BATH	W	1G1DG3PG(19)-1PG(3)
120409	LEINSTER(HECQF)	TWICKENHAM STOOP	L	1T(5)-2PG(6)
170409	SHARKS(GP)	EDGELEY PARK	L	2PG(6)-4G(28)
250409	NEWCASTLE(GP)	TWICKENHAM STOOP	W	3G2T(31)-1G1T(12)
090509	LONDON IRISH(GPSF)	TWICKENHAM STOOP	L	0-2G1PG(17)

44

"Bloodgate" and the Case of the Multi-coloured Winker 2009

Even before the quarter final against Leinster had finished, trouble was brewing and it didn't take long for ERC to launch an investigation into the alleged use of fake blood in the substitution of Nick Evans for Tom Williams after 75 minutes. In fact, it began on 17th April and the hearing was set for 2nd and 3rd July in London before an independent disciplinary committee. In the chair was Robert HP Williams from Wales and alongside him were Pat Barriscale (Ireland) and Dr Stuart Reary (Scotland). Mr Williams confirmed that the Committee was convened by Professor Lorne De Crera (Chairman of the ERC Discipline Panel) pursuant to the disciplinary rules of ERC in respect of a misconduct complaint dated 11th May 2009 and made by Roger O'Connor (ERC Disciplinary Officer). The complaint concerned the substitution of Tom Williams and it was alleged that the Club (and/or others) had, by some means, fabricated a wound or blood injury to the player in order to allow Nick Evans (who started the match but who had been substituted or replaced in the 47th minute by Chris Malone) to return to the field of play for the final few minutes of the match pursuant to Law 3.12 (Exception 1) of the IRB's Laws of the Game which reads as follows:-

3.12 Substituted Players Rejoining the Match

If a player is substituted, that player must not return and play in that match even to replace an injured player

Exception 1: a substituted player may replace a player with a bleeding or open wound

Present at the hearing on 2nd July were:-

Mr Roger O'Connor (ERC Disciplinary Officer)
Mr Max Duthie (Partner, Bird and Bird solicitors – he was presenting the case on behalf of the ERC Disciplinary Officer)
Mr Jamie Herbert (Solicitor, Bird and Bird – acting as assistant to Max Duthie)
Mr Mark Evans (Chief Executive Officer, Harlequin FC)
Mr Dean Richards (Director of Rugby, Harlequin FC)
Mr Tom Williams (player, Harlequin FC)
Mr Steph Brennan (physiotherapist, Harlequin FC)

Mr Oliver Glasgow (Counsel representing Harlequin FC)
Mr Stephen Hornsby (Davenport Lyons – solicitors representing Harlequin FC)
Dr Wendy Chapman (Club doctor, Harlequin FC)
Ms Mary O'Rourke QC (Counsel representing Dr Chapman)
Mr Charles Dewhurst (Medical Defence Union – representing Dr Chapman)
Ms Jennifer Nicol (Harper McLeod solicitors – acting as Clerk to the Disciplinary Committee)

After the Chairman had confirmed the identities and role in the proceedings of everyone, Oliver Glasgow proceeded to give his oral submissions. He took issue with a lot of what was to be produced as evidence against Quins such as sample blood capsules, newspaper reports, witnesses and even tried to argue that there was a breach of both human rights legislation and a constitutional right under Irish law not to be assaulted against Tom Williams when Kevin Stewart (the fifth official) took a sample of the "blood" from his leg in the treatment room. Max Duthie argued against and basically, the committee agreed with him.

The complaints were put to the defendants and pleas were recorded as follows:-

1– The misconduct complaint against the Club was that any of Williams, Richards, Brennan and Chapman had fabricated a wound or blood injury to Williams to allow Nick Evans to return to the field of play. The plea was not guilty.
2– The misconduct complaint against the Player was that he fabricated a wound or blood injury, by some means, to allow Nick Evans to return to the field of play. The plea was not guilty.
3– The misconduct complaint against Dean Richards was that he knew of and/or organised or coordinated the fabrication of a wound or blood injury to Williams to allow Nick Evans to return to the field of play. The plea was not guilty.
4– The misconduct complaint against Wendy Chapman was that she knew of and/or organised and/or assisted in the fabrication of a wound or blood injury to Williams to allow Nick Evans to return to the field of play. The plea was not guilty.
5– The misconduct complaint against Steph Brennan was that he knew of and/or organised and/or assisted in the fabrication of a wound or blood injury to Williams to allow Nick Evans to return to the field of play. The plea was not guilty.

Max Duthie proceeded to present the Disciplinary Officer's case and reminded the committee that the standard proof was based on the balance of probabilities, that the Club is vicariously liable for the acts of employees and that the behaviour of the defendants was misconduct either because it is unsporting behaviour or because it is conduct in connection with match officiating. He made it clear that the rules about blood injuries did not allow injured players to come on for such events. There was a potential reward of €300,000 if a club progressed to the final of the competition so the quarter final match carried tremendous importance. When Nick Evans had come off, the substitute's card was originally marked "injured" and then altered. He said that when Chris Malone (our only recognised goal kicker on the pitch) was injured, Williams went on and the only way Nick Evans could get back on would be because of a blood injury and only then if he had been taken off as a tactical substitution. Evans is seen on a bike with his knee strapped up, Williams goes down, there are tell-tale movements with his hand and Brennan gets him to his feet. As he leaves the field, he is seen by the referee and winks at a colleague. Three people had come forward to state that the substance on his face was not blood. When the Leinster doctor tries to get a better look, someone from Quins shouts to get Williams out of the medical room and the doctor's request to examine him is refused. Evans tried the dropped goal to win the game but missed. Had it been successful, Duthie submitted that the reputation of the tournament would have been in tatters.

He then went on to produce evidence from the fifth official, the match director, a consultant orthopaedic surgeon (Richard Evans), Professor Arthur Tanner (Leinster's doctor), Gonzalo Tiesi and Nick Evans plus visual evidence and specimen blood capsule samples. His video evidence showed (in his opinion) that Evans was clearly injured when he came off and Richard Evans stated that the treatment provided to our fly half was not appropriate. Professor Tanner agreed with this and stated that the substance coming from Williams's mouth was not blood. The video evidence also showed Brennan going on to the pitch when there seems no reason for him to do so and consults with Williams. He argues that Williams can be seen putting something into his sock, runs around for a few minutes, has a minor collision with Nick Easter but sustains no identifiable blow to his mouth. With five minutes to go, he runs to the middle of the pitch, is seen touching his right sock and it looks like he has dropped something on the ground. He is then seen touching his mouth again before Tiesi runs over but does not raise any alarm about an injury. Brennan then runs towards him, does not examine him but gets him to his feet and aids his walk about 20 yards to where the referee is standing. The referee looks at him, Williams starts to leave the pitch and inexplicably winks at a colleague. His mouth is now surrounded by a bright red substance and he is allowed to leave the field. At this point, Tanner, Cebenka and Stewart follow him into the medical room and Stewart takes the liquid sample from his leg – this is clearly not blood.

Richard Evans, Cebenka, Stewart and Tanner all gave evidence about the injury to Nick Evans and the substance found on Williams. Oliver Glasgow tried to prove that they were wrong or had no valid reason for being in the room where he was taken but the evidence was building against Quins and the whole thing looked and sounded dodgy.

At the start of day two, counsel for Wendy Chapman tried to argue that there was no case against her but it was decided to proceed with the witnesses and make a decision later. Nick Evans gave evidence and said that he had been taken off because he couldn't kick but his knee was not painful when he was on the bike. He was unaware of any blood injury but was told he was going back on and tried to do his job of winning the game. Max Duthie said that from the video evidence it appeared that Evans knew he was going back on before Brennan had reached Williams. It was later revealed that Evans had a fracture and was out for 2-3 weeks. Because of the strapping, Evans stated that apart from his kicking, he felt he could have carried on (this seems odd because why bring someone on to supposedly drop a goal when he can't kick?).

There then followed a demonstration of biting into a theatrical blood capsule from Jamie Herbert so that the committee could see the effect of the product appearing on his lips and trickling down the side of his mouth. He then gave a second demonstration of biting into the capsule, consuming some Gatorade and then spewing it out so that the committee could see what it looked like when diluted and the marks it would leave around the chin.

The case was closed but Max Duthie could call Wendy Chapman as a witness later on subject to the outcome of any submission of no case to answer. Her counsel argued that because ERC had specifically stated that her misconduct charge related to bringing Nick Evans back on to the pitch and not covering up afterwards, the committee had to decide on that basis only. In winding up, she stated on behalf of Wendy Chapman that the doctor completely denied there was a cover up.

After hearing from Max Duthie in reply, the committee retired to consider the application in private. When they returned, they decided that there was no case for Dr Chapman to answer because the complaint against her was that she had been involved in returning Nick Evans to the field of play. Because the ERC disciplinary proceedings had to remain credible, no amendment would be permitted to the original charge. She was then called as a witness by Duthie as part of the ERC case against Quins and stated that she did not remember seeing blood around the mouth of Tom Williams but examined him and found a wobbly tooth but couldn't see the source of bleeding for the amount of blood. Williams said it hurt, was taken through to the other room to get some water, his mouth was washed, the source of the bleeding was found and she put some gauze on it. When asked if the substance coming out of the mouth was blood, she replied that "there was bleeding" and "it was watery - down to the drink". She couldn't really remember a fuss being made or any mention of fabrication of the injury.

After this, the case for the defence was opened by Oliver Glasgow who called Dean Richards to give evidence. His reply to the allegation that he had in some way been involved in Brennan taking a blood capsule on to the pitch and passing it to Williams and that the plot had been hatched by the 47th minute when Nick Evans came off was "Not at all. It's ridiculous". He said that Evans was injured with a hyper extension in his right knee and he had spoken to him at half time and it had been established that he could run and tackle "okay" but could not kick. Richards confirmed it was a tactical substitution and the officials were made aware of that although initially, they might have thought it was through an injury. He further stated that "In no way, shape or form was there any chat on faking a blood injury". Williams had gone on to play number 10 but he was then asked to swap with Strettle as he had played 10 and Williams went to the wing. When he became aware of the cut to Williams, he advised Evans to get ready to go back on. He wasn't putting Evans back on to attempt a drop kick as that was the very reason why he was brought off (he couldn't kick). He said that Leinster didn't know the rules when they objected to Evans coming back on and it was only after that their complaints turned to it not being blood. Nigel Owens (the referee) was only concerned whether Evans had gone off as a tactical substitution and once that had been sorted out, he was happy. He had a grumble about Stewart and Cebenka having access all areas passes and said this wasn't right because there had to be patient confidentiality and confirmed that Stewart had shown him his finger in the car park and asked him if this was blood. Richards refused to discuss it as he didn't see it as important at that time. He concluded by saying that Brennan and Williams didn't have it in their nature to set up a conspiracy. When being cross-examined by Duthie, Richards stated he had never fabricated a blood injury and had never heard of any player doing it either. He added that fair play was one of the things he expected from his staff.

As proceedings came to an end, the Chairman directed that the DVD of the game made by Quins should be available to the disciplinary officer by close of business on 10th July 2009 and the meeting would be re-convened at 8 a.m. on Monday 20th July at the offices of Bird and Bird, 15 Fetter Lane, London.

Tom Williams was called by Oliver Glasgow and proceeded to give his evidence. He said there was no truth in the allegations brought against him and he definitely wouldn't have done it. It is an honourable thing to be part of a team and he had never seen a blood capsule until the day of the hearing. He then described how he had injured his teeth before and went on to say how Dean had sent him to a pre-season training camp with the rugby league boys after he had stayed down with a dead-leg against Plymouth some years before to make the point that he expected his players to carry on unless there was no other option. He was then asked about winking as he left the pitch but he didn't remember doing it although his girlfriend had mentioned it later because she thought it was strange. He reiterated there was no connection between the blood capsule and the wink and he was told later it was probably directed at Jim Evans who was asking if he was okay. When questioned about the alleged incident of his hand going from his sock and up to his mouth, he thought it could have been his gum shield and he says he was looking for the other physio as he felt unwell. He denied he was part of a conspiracy and was surprised and shocked at being accused of cheating; he wanted to play the game to the best of his ability and within the stated parameters.

When Max Duthie cross examines him, he raises the point that there is no head contact with Easter and no obvious signs of an injury to the mouth. Williams confirms that this is the only incident when he would have had contact. He could not remember or be sure if his mouth was filling with blood then nor if he is feeling dazed. He couldn't remember how he felt or if he had blood on his hands. He didn't tell anyone when he went down injured and could not recollect tasting any blood. He was not aware at the time that it was said to be a fake blood injury and could give no reason as to why Cebanka, Stewart and Tanner would lie (in fact, for someone who hadn't had a blow to the head, he couldn't really remember much at all!). He was asked why he did not have any dental treatment for the loose tooth to which he replied that the pain subsided and he didn't want a dentist saying he couldn't play. He accepted that it was highly irregular behaviour to put a gum guard into your mouth when there is an injury and it is bleeding.

Steph Brennan was next up and before the Leinster game, he had accepted a position with the RFU so no longer worked at Quins. He also denied there was any truth in the allegation of conspiracy to cheat. He confirmed that the injury to Nick Evans was not deemed bad enough to stop him from playing. He was asked if he has seen blood capsules before and his response was "only in Halloween parties". He himself had never used one. He said that he first realised Williams had a blood injury as he approached him. He said he looked weird and his eyes were dazed. He could see a dental injury and saw blood. He decided to get him to the referee because of the combination of all three things. He didn't see Williams winking because he was concentrating on his job. He took a picture of the injury in the treatment room to show the laceration and cover his back. Pat Barriscale then put the following to Brennan – that he did not know at the time when he went on to Williams that there was a blood injury; Brennan confirmed this. Barriscale went on to say that no other person would have known there was a blood injury at that time; again confirmed by Brennan. He finished with – Nick Evans would not have known there was a blood injury. Nick Evans is getting ready to come on but he couldn't have come on unless there was a blood injury. Unless there was a blood injury, there was no place for Nick Evans to come back on; Brennan did not answer.

Oliver Glasgow confirmed that no further witnesses would be called for the defence.

Max Duthie began his closing submissions at 1.05 p.m. and said there were five stages which the committee should look at, these were about the treatment of the injury to Nick Evans; Steph Brennan talking to Tom Williams on the pitch; the injury suffered by Williams; Williams putting something in his mouth and Evans appearing to know he was coming on before a blood injury had been ascertained; Williams in the medical room. Duthie left the committee to consider what would have happened if Evans had succeeded with the drop at goal.

Oliver Glasgow submitted that there was absolutely no evidence that a blood capsule was ever handed by Steph Brennan to Williams and there is absolutely no evidence that Williams put a blood capsule into his mouth, there were inferences only. The committee had to be satisfied that the incident was more likely than not to have occurred (that it was more likely than not that the blood capsule was taken on to the field). He said that they should not ignore the tear on the player's lip, they should not start with the conclusion that it occurred and work backwards, that the starting point is that they are not cheats. He said Duthie's submission and approach was wrong because he had gone down that road. He went on to say that Dean Richards would have needed a crystal ball to see that Evans would get injured in the 47th minute and why put him back on when he couldn't kick. He then takes issue with the evidence given by Stewart, Cebenka, Tanner and Richard Evans basically saying that they had all erred in one way or another. Regarding Nick Evans, he says the conspiracy could only work for him if he could kick and it doesn't work if the means by how it is to be carried out doesn't exist. Regarding Wendy Chapman, he says he was absolutely stunned that one minute she was a defendant and the next minute ERC wanted to call her as a witness. She had found a laceration to the inside of the mouth of Williams and a bleeding tooth and it may be he had a blow to the head. He says that the injury proves the allegations are wrong

And asked "What are we doing here?" He then deals with the DVD footage saying it proves nothing and emphasises that no blood capsule can be seen. Among other things, he says the wink is a genuine response to a question; asks what the defendants had to lose for so little gain; suggested that the idea Dean Richards would stoop to such a level is so unlikely to be laughable; states that Williams was young, keen to impress and eager to do the right thing, he was certainly not willing to cheat, he is genuinely offended given his love of the game. He adds that the reaction of Williams was still one of shock, upset and almost horror. He goes on to ask why Brennan would risk 15 years of his career to pass a blood capsule to Williams; that the evidence is genuine, compelling and honest. There is no evidence that Brennan gave Williams a blood capsule and no evidence that the player put a blood capsule in his mouth.

The committee considered the evidence against each of the defendants individually and delivered their decisions starting with Tom Williams. They decided that the conversation between Williams and Brennan was not evidence against the player; the video evidence was not clear enough regarding something passing between Brennan and Williams and when Williams moves his hand to his sock (but they decided that his explanation was not credible); the same decision (lack of credibility) was made regarding the incident where Williams says he got the injury and when he was under the posts; they were not impressed with Tiesi's evidence and concluded that he did not help the case of Williams; they found that the referee would not have thought of challenging as genuine what he saw on the mouth and face; regarding the wink, they concluded that it conveyed an impression that he had got away with something and referred to the player himself volunteering the information that his own girlfriend thought it was a strange thing to do; after the blood capsule demonstration, the committee decided that the colour and effect of the substances on the lips, mouth and chin were the same as they had seen on the face of the player; they regarded Professor Tanner as a credible witness as he was the only person giving evidence who could be considered as an expert in blood; in relation to the evidence of Stewart, they felt that despite deciding that the substance swiped from the player's leg might not have come from his mouth, his evidence about what he saw was not weakened and with Cebanka, the committee felt that he neither assisted nor detracted from the case of either of the parties; the committee accepted that Dr Chapman saw an injury, blood and a wobbly tooth and because of this, one member of the committee concluded that as there was evidence of a laceration and blood, the case was not made out whatever substance may or may not have been present at the relevant time; two members concluded that what they saw on the face of the player as he was leaving the pitch was not genuine blood and irrespective as to whether or not there was (coincidently) a genuine blood injury, the fabrication charge had been made out.

The Committee concluded by a majority of 2:1 that Tom Williams had been guilty of the complaint in that he fabricated a wound or blood injury, by some means, in order to allow Nick Evans to return to the field of play in the 75th minute of the match, pursuant to Law 3.12 (Exception 1) of the IRB's Laws of the Game.

The Committee then considered the case of Steph Brennan, they noted that Nick Evans had been happy with his treatment (he was a qualified physiotherapist) and felt it was significant that one of ERC's own witnesses was contradicting the ERC case. They also felt it was significant that at no stage was it ever suggested that Evans was implicated in the conspiracy. They decided the video evidence was not conclusive enough of Brennan passing a blood capsule to Williams and debated whether he should have realised the substance coming from his mouth was not wholly genuine blood; before deciding that this was insufficient to satisfy the Committee on the test of the balance of probabilities that he was part of a "master plan" as alleged in the ERC complaint. They concluded unanimously that the complaint had not been proved against him.

The case of Dean Richards was considered next and because ERC did not produce any evidence linking him to the blood fabrication, it would not be appropriate to find someone guilty because it was felt that "he must have been involved". The Committee concluded unanimously that the complaint had not been proved against him.

Regarding Wendy Chapman, the Committee came to the conclusion that there had been no *prima facie* case for her to answer.

Next, they turned their attention to the Club and because under the Disciplinary Rules the Club is responsible and accountable for not only its own conduct, but also for the conduct of each of its players and other persons in connection with the tournament, once any of the defendants has been found guilty the Club would inevitably be found guilty because of the provisions contained in Rule 2.2 as follows –

> Without prejudice to the personal responsibility of each Person for his own conduct and the conduct of his own agents and representatives, each Club is responsible and accountable for its own conduct and for the conduct of each of its Players and other Persons in connection with the Tournament. In addition, each Club is also responsible and accountable for the conduct of supporters of the Club.

In conclusion, the Committee unanimously decided that the charge against the Club had been proved, the dissenting number of the Committee accepted that once the charge against the Player had been upheld, the Club was vicariously liable.

The Disciplinary Committee reconvened and the Chairman announced the decisions that:-

1. The charge against the Player had been upheld.
2. The charge against Steph Brennan had not been upheld.
3. The charge against Dean Richards had not been upheld.
4. By reason of the Player being found guilty, the charge against the Club was upheld.

When asked to identify which, if any, of the particular part or parts of the charge were made out, the Committee identified parts (a) and (c) – in so far as part (a) was concerned, the Committee were referring to "the act of the Player fabricating a blood injury and not any other named persons".

This referred to the full charge which read as follows:-

> The misconduct complaint against the Club is that it (a) through the acts of one or more of the Player, Messrs Richards and Brennan and Ms Chapman, fabricated a wound or blood injury to the Player, by some means, in order to allow Nick Evans to return to the field of play in the 75th minute of the match, pursuant to Law 3.12 (Exception 1) of the IRB's Laws of the Game; and/or (b) did not exercise appropriate control over those individuals in respect of such acts; and/or (c) in respect of such acts did not instil in those individuals a sufficient degree of respect for the Laws of the Game, the disciplinary authority of ERC and/or the Participation Agreement.

This led to the sanction and before this was announced, the Committee heard submissions from the legal representatives. Among theirs, ERC reminded the Committee of the principles of "the Charter" which stated "Players should be prepared in a manner which ensures compliance with the laws of the game and is in accordance with safe practices and the game at every level is to be conducted in accordance with discipline and sporting behaviour"; they stated that although it was for the Committee to decide the sanction, they would not be seeking an expulsion of Harlequins from the competition as the 2009/10 fixtures had already been announced and logistically, it would be very difficult to re-arrange the fixtures and Pools (points deduction would also alter the balance of the Pools).

For Tom Williams, his representative argued that to suspend him from all games would deprive him of his livelihood and the Committee was invited to consider a fine as opposed to ban or suspension.

In answer to questions raised by the Committee, they were informed that Harlequins had not made any profits, had significant debts, their income from ERC was difficult to calculate, but the differential income generated to the Club by playing in ERC games was quantified and noted. With regard to the ability to pay a fine, they were advised that if the fine were in the region of £100,000 they would raise it within 28 days.

The Committee considered its verdict firstly on Tom Williams and taking everything into account concluded that a one year ban was appropriate.

With regard to the Club, they reluctantly accepted ERC's own submission that a ban should not be imposed nor points deducted. They concluded that a substantial and meaningful fine was necessary to show the seriousness in which they viewed the offence and for there to be a significant deterrent against any similar behaviour in the future. The Committee decided that this would be €250,000 (approximately £215,000) with 50% suspended on terms.

The disciplinary meeting reconvened and the Chairman announced:-

1) That the Player, Tom Williams, would be suspended from playing rugby for twelve months commencing 20th July 2009 expiring midnight 19th July 2010.
2) The Club would be fined €250,000, 50% of which would be paid within 28 days and 50% would be suspended, but in the event of the Harlequins Rugby Football Club being found guilty of committing any act of misconduct in any ERC competition within two years, the suspended sanction shall automatically take effect. The triggering of the suspension shall be without prejudice to any additional penalties which may be imposed for such further act of misconduct.

Regarding costs, after hearing submissions and retiring to consider their decision, the Chairman announced that:-

1) Club and the Player would pay 40% of the ERC costs on a joint and several basis.
2) There would be no other order as to costs, save that the Committee was reserving its position with regard to any application made on behalf of Dr Chapman.

The Chairman reminded all parties of their right to appeal and that the time limit for their appeals would not commence until delivery of the written judgment.

So, it was found that Tom Williams had contrived to cheat in the Leinster game but did he act alone and if he didn't, who helped him if it wasn't Richards, Brennan or Chapman? What followed would rock the Club to its core and expose the whole scandal to the World. On 8th August it was announced that Tom Williams had appealed against the sanction imposed on him; and ERC Disciplinary Officer Roger O'Connor had appealed the level of sanction imposed on the Club and the decision of the Committee to dismiss Misconduct Complaints against the three Club officials.

Williams gave the following specific grounds of appeal:-

(a) The Player was charged with Misconduct in that "he fabricated a wound or blood injury, by some means, in order to allow Nick Evans to return to the field of play in the 75th minute of the Match, pursuant to law 3.12 (Exception 1) of the IRB's Laws of the Game".

(b) The Player denied the charges and gave evidence by statement and in person at the hearing on 20th July 2009.

(c) The Player did not receive independent legal advice prior to signing his statement or giving evidence at the hearing on 20th July 2009.

(d) The Player gave evidence by statement and in person at the hearing on 20th July 2009 under duress and/ or as a result of actions on the part of Mr Dean Richards that caused him to act otherwise than of his own will.

(e) The Player wished to recant the evidence he gave by statement and in person at the hearing on 20th July 2009.

(f) The Player will adduce new evidence as to what occurred during and immediately after the match on 12th April 2009.

(g) The new evidence is materially different to the evidence which formed the basis of the judgment dated 5th August 2009.

(h) The judgment dated 5th August 2009 is wrong in fact as it was based on inaccurate evidence and should therefore be set aside.

(i) The Player sought a de novo hearing on appeal and the admission of new evidence submitted by the Player in the form of an affidavit and a statement. The Player sought a variation in the sanction imposed by the Committee; in particular a reduction in the length of the period of suspension.

As part of his appeal above, Williams decided to give new evidence; in effect, he decided to spill the beans and tell the whole story about the saga now known as "Bloodgate". The entire document is repeated below so as to give the full story to the reader. It starts with a short introduction and from paragraph one, he begins to reveal all.

The Player's new evidence was contained in his affidavit and the supplemental statement. The following numbered paragraphs are taken verbatim from these documents. Dean Richards, Steph Brennan and the Club were each given an opportunity to comment on this new evidence and to make it clear where their position was different from that of the Player. The Club accepted as factually accurate the whole of the new evidence of the Player. In the case of Dean Richards and Steph Brennan where there was a material difference between their versions of events and that of the Player this is noted and discussed in italics. Dr Wendy Chapman has not yet had an opportunity to respond to the new evidence of the Player and accordingly no findings are made by the Appeal Committee with respect to the allegation made by the Player that she cut his lip after the match following his request that she do so.

1. As I will explain below, I did not give a true account of the relevant matters to the Disciplinary Committee. This is a cause of great regret to me and I apologise unreservedly for it. I pride myself on my honesty and integrity, and I am extremely disappointed that I allowed myself to get caught up in the events which I describe below.
2. At the Disciplinary Committee hearing I was represented by the Club's lawyers and did not have any independent advice, legal or otherwise. It was only after the decision that I took independent advice for the first time, first of all from the Professional Rugby Players' Association ("PRA") and then on their advice from independent lawyers. With their assistance, and subsequently the assistance of the ERC Disciplinary Officers, I realised that I had to come clean about what had really happened and cooperate with the ERC. I hope the Appeal Committee will understand the pressures I was under and how painful this choice was for me. Although I desperately wanted to explain the full facts for my own sake, I was fully aware, and constantly reminded by various of the affected parties, that by doing so I would jeopardise the prospects of my Club, my team-mates and the professional futures of a number of individuals whom I like and respect. Despite this, I realise that I must tell the truth, and do so in full.

My Life and Rugby

3. I first started playing rugby aged 5 when I was living in Hong Kong with my family. I have always enjoyed the game, and the values it stands for - in particular working towards a common goal as part of a team and playing with and for your friends. I carried these values throughout my early experiences at local club and school level. My family encouraged and supported me throughout this period and, to an extent, supporting me has provided my family with a focus.

Harlequins RFC ("Harlequins"/the "Club")

4. Throughout my time at school, playing sports was my passion - and rugby stood out above everything else. As I approached the end of my studies I had offers from a number of universities. However, one of my teachers saw some promise in me and put me in touch with one of his contacts, the former England and New Zealand international Jamie Salmon. Jamie helped me to get offers from two rugby clubs - Harlequins and Bristol. For me the choice was easy - I wanted to be a professional rugby player, and I wanted to play for Harlequins.
5. It did not take long for me to agree terms with the Club. At the time, the Head Coach and Chief Executive was Mark Evans. I was signed as a back, and the intention was that I would play as a full-back as my career developed. I started playing in the Club's under21 and reserve teams. I was already dreaming of playing for England.

   There was no paragraph 6.
7. In 2004 I made my debut for the Harlequins first team against Natal Sharks. This was a huge breakthrough, and gave me the chance to demonstrate my abilities against top quality opposition. This was the platform that I needed to establish myself in the first team set-up. I began to make more regular appearances and to develop my reputation as an exciting attacking player who was capable of changing a game. I have gone on to make more than 100 first team appearances for the Club to date.

Dean Richards

8. At the end of the 2004/2005 season, the Club was relegated to Division 1. This was a massive blow to the Club and to me personally. It is fair to say that Harlequins' reputation was not particularly positive at this time - we were seen as a 'soft' London club, and as easy to turn over.
9. In 2005, Dean Richards joined Harlequins as Director of Rugby. His reputation was world famous. He was known as a hard, no-nonsense and extremely competitive player. He immediately set about introducing these qualities to the Club. In his first season in charge, we won all but one of our league and cup fixtures and were promoted as champions.
10. All matters relating to rugby at the Club were controlled by Dean. There was no doubt that he was the boss and that he ran the show. He did not discuss his decisions with me. He gave directions, and these were followed. There were occasions when I disagreed with his decisions. However, I did not feel able to challenge his authority. I do not think that I have ever seen another player challenge Dean's authority.
11. An example of Dean's management style occurred after I was injured in a game in Division 1 against Plymouth. I suffered from a haematoma on my leg and went down while play was continuing. The injury resulted in me being on crutches after the game. In my mid-season appraisal Dean criticised my going down injured during play and ordered me to attend a camp with the Harlequins rugby league side to harden me up. There was no discussion or seeking of my views. That was his decision and there was no debate about it. [This was disputed by Dean Richards who denied that he had criticised the Player in this way and that this was the reason the Player had attended the camp. Dean Richards contended that the camp was a great opportunity for the Player to develop his skills and that the Player attended willingly. A resolution of this dispute would not have assisted in the determination of the appeal so no decision was made on which version was preferred].

The 2008/2009 Season

12. The 2008/2009 season was by far and away my most successful at Harlequins. I played more games than ever, and as a team we found ourselves competing for both the Premiership and the Heineken Cup. As a group of players we are extremely close. We are friends, we socialised together and I could see my career unfolding as I had hoped. I have been told by Dean that I was on the fringes of the England international set-up, and things were really beginning to take-off for me. [The assertion regarding being told he was on the fringes of the England set-up was denied by Dean Richards].
13. The Club's progress in the Heineken Cup was somewhat unexpected. We had been drawn in a difficult group which included Stade Français ("Stade") - one of the favourites for the tournament. We were underdogs. Despite this tag, we managed to beat Stade both home and away. Our victory at home was as dramatic as it could have been, with our fly-half Nick Evans scoring a last-gasp drop goal. I was involved in the move which led to the drop goal, and in the process I suffered an injury to my teeth (one was broken, and others were forced back). I was proud of the part that I played in this win.

The Heineken Cup Quarter Final, Harlequins v. Leinster – 12th April 2009

14. The current controversy concerns the game between Harlequins and Leinster on 12th April 2009, which took place at The Twickenham Stoop (the Club's home ground). It was the quarter-final of the Heineken Cup - the most prestigious European competition in rugby union. The stakes could not have been higher.
15. A few days before the match, the team was announced and I learned that I would not be starting. I was disappointed at this, but I had a place on the bench and hoped to play some part in the game.
16. The atmosphere building up to the match was incredible. There was a real sense of anticipation and excitement around the Club. We were the under-dogs once again, but we all believed that we could cause an upset. We had already done it against Stade, so what was to stop us doing it again? We were also playing at home, which gave us a huge advantage.
17. As the game began, I sat on the bench with the other players who had not made the starting line-up. By half time, we were trailing 6-0, and the game was hanging in the balance. As normal, the team split between forwards and backs for the half-time briefing. There was no mention of me coming on at this stage.
18. I was aware that Nick Evans was receiving treatment from a team physio. However, we had Chris Malone on the bench who provided direct cover for Nick. In the event that Nick would be coming off, Chris would replace him. Shortly after half-time, Nick Evans was substituted for Chris Malone.

Injury to Chris Malone and my introduction to the game

19. With just over ten minutes of the game remaining, Chris Malone picked up a serious hamstring injury. This was without warning, and Dean Richards called me over. I realised that I was potentially about to be brought on, and I was pumping with adrenaline. At the same time, I was anxious. Chris Malone was playing at fly-half, and I have very little experience playing in this crucial position. With ten minutes left and the score standing at 6-5 to Leinster, the pressure would be immense. Dean told me to tell Steph Brennan, one of the Club's physios, that I would be coming off for blood.
20. At the time I was not sure exactly what to make of this. I have no previous experience of faking blood injuries. I had never previously been asked to cheat or do anything dishonest by Dean as far as I can recall. I understood from what Dean said that I would be coming off at some point before the end of the match with a fake injury, but I had no idea how this would work. I can remember telling Steph that I would be coming off for blood as Dean had instructed, but I have no other recollections of this exchange. Given my relationship with Dean Richards it did not occur to me that this was something to discuss, let alone challenge. [The sequence of events and the details of the exchanges set out in paragraphs 19 and 20 are disputed by Dean Richards and Steph Brennan. They say that the decision to fabricate a blood injury to the Player was not made until after the Player had entered the field of play and that the Player had not been told he was coming off for blood until Dean Richards had asked Steph Brennan whether there were in fact any blood injuries to any of the players then on the field of play, including the Player, and Steph Brennan had advised Dean Richards that there were none. Their position was that it was only at that stage that Dean Richards told Steph Brennan that the Player was to come off for blood and Steph Brennan had then gone on to the field of play advised the Player that this was to happen and had given the fake blood capsule to the Player. Steph Brennan had such a capsule in his bag from previous occasions on which blood injuries had been fabricated, he having purchased a quantity of such capsules from a joke shop at Clapham Junction on the

directions of Dean Richards for use as and when required by Dean Richards in faking blood injuries during matches. Steph Brennan's evidence was that there had been four previous occasions on which he had faked blood injuries on the direction of Dean Richards. None of these had been in ERC competitions. Dean Richards advised that he could recollect two or three such occasions. On balance the Appeal Committee preferred the version of events spoken to by Dean Richards and Steph Brennan. It appeared to the Appeal Committee that their version was more consistent with the surrounding circumstances. If the decision to fabricate a blood injury to the Player had been taken before the Player entered the field of play then the logical time to give the Player the capsule was at that time and not in full view of the cameras on the field. In any event a resolution of this difference in the evidence was not material in a determination of the appeal since it mattered little in terms of culpability on the part of those involved when precisely the decision to cheat was taken and when the Player was asked to and agreed to cheat].

Playing Time

21. It is very difficult for me to remember the details of the time I spent on the pitch against Leinster. To a large extent, these events have been overtaken in my mind by the "blood" incident, but I have reviewed a range of footage which records the relevant events.
22. When I first came on for Chris Malone, I started playing at fly-half. As I recall, we won a penalty shortly after my introduction. Whilst Mike Brown was taking the penalty, Steph came onto the pitch and told me to change positions with David Strettle, so that he would be moved to fly-half and I would be moved to the wing. At this point, Steph handed me a blood capsule. I can't remember the full detail of this exchange, but I remember him saying something along the lines of "do the right thing". By this, I understood that he meant I should use the blood capsule to fake an injury, which was the right thing for the team. I instinctively placed the capsule in my sock as there was nowhere else to put it. I have no idea where Steph got the blood capsule. I had never seen one before this incident.
23. I would like to say that I was presented with a huge dilemma when I was handed the blood capsule. However, in reality I was so programmed to Dean's authority and focused on the game that there were no such considerations. Given what Dean had said to me before I came on, it did not come as a shock to be handed the capsule. I have gone over these events in my mind many times now. I had no real choice in the matter. In hindsight, if I had refused to bite the capsule Dean would have seen that I had disobeyed him and might refuse to play me again. This could have spelled the end of my career at Harlequins and how would I face my team mates if my refusal to come off was blamed by Dean for us losing the game?

The "Blood" Injury

24. No one had told me when to fake the injury, but I understood that I should go down once I was involved in some contact. At one stage, Leinster put up a high ball, and I caught it with my back facing the opposition. Nick Easter then came in to secure the ball, and I believe that two Leinster players hit me and Nick from behind. This was my only physical contact since I had been handed the blood capsule, and it was therefore my opportunity to fake the injury. To be clear, I did not sustain any injuries from this collision.

25. Having reviewed the footage, it is clear that shortly after this incident I returned to the full back position and knelt down on one knee to bite the blood capsule. I removed it from my sock and placed it in my mouth. I can't recall whether my mouth guard was in at the time. Although I had not seen or used one before, I assumed all you had to do was bite down. On the first attempt, the blood capsule fell from my mouth. I picked it up and bit it once again.
26. Not only is this aspect of the episode shameful, it is also very embarrassing. However, it is a good indication that I was not thinking about what I was doing. I could not have picked a more exposed position on the pitch to take the capsule. The way I removed it from my sock and dropped it from my mouth was ridiculous. I was not thinking straight, and my execution of the fake injury was completely unplanned.
27. After I had bitten the capsule successfully, I put my hand to my head and laid down on my side to get the attention of the physio. However, I was not injured. It appears from the footage that another player, Gonzalo Tiesi, approached me around this time. It is possible that Gonzalo said something to me, but I do not recall this.
28. Steph Brennan then came over to me on the pitch, but I can't remember what he said to me. We walked towards the touchline together, and Steph took me towards the referee and inspected my mouth, asking me where it hurt. I pointed to my mouth. At least for my part, this move was not planned.
29. I have also been asked to clarify whether I drank purple Gatorade as I left the pitch. I have no idea. I don't fill the water bottles myself. As I understand it, they always contain either Gatorade or water. If it was Gatorade, it could have been one of a number of colours, including purple.
30. I also winked as I left the pitch. This was not a signal or sign to anyone regarding the fake injury, as has been suggested. Instead, I was simply responding to one of my teammates, Jim Evans, who suggested that I should "tough it out" as there were only a few minutes left until the end of the game. My only intention would have been to reassure him that I had to come off.

The Aftermath

31. As I left the pitch, I did not speak to Dean or anyone else as far as I can recall. I headed for the tunnel, and heard loud protestations from the Leinster bench. These protests were along the lines of "that's not real blood". This made me more anxious, and I began to realise that the situation could escalate further.
32. I knew that I was headed for the physio or medical room - this is standard when you leave the pitch with a blood injury. I cannot recall for certain, but I think that Dr Wendy Chapman (one of the Club's match day doctors) met me at the tunnel and escorted me into the Club's medical room. As Chris Malone was being examined on the bed, we moved into the physio room. I understood that we were being followed.
33. I lay down on the examination bed and Wendy started examining my mouth. At this time I heard other voices in the room. I assumed that these individuals were from Leinster given the protests that had been made as I left the pitch. I now understand that the individuals in question were Kevin Stewart (the fifth official) and Yvan Cebenka (the ERC Match Director). A real sense of panic now began to set in and it seemed to me that Wendy was also growing increasingly anxious. I remember that Wendy was touching my tooth and saying that it was wobbly. I think I replied something along the lines of, "well, stop wobbling it then". As far as I am aware, my tooth was not wobbly and I understood her comments to be a panicked response to the presence of other people in the room.

34. I then felt someone wipe their finger across my leg. I now understand that this was the fifth official. I guessed he was wiping what he thought was fake blood from me to examine it. As he removed the substance from my leg, he said that it was not blood. This increased the sense of panic in the room.
35. After this comment, I believe that Wendy and I were left in the room together with Ian Bell. Ian works with the Club, though I am not sure of his exact role. I needed to wash my mouth out, so moved to our changing rooms. I realised that there was a risk that someone would return to inspect my mouth. If they did, it would have been clear that I had not suffered an injury. In the circumstances, it seemed to me that the only solution was to cut my lip. I believe it was at this point that I asked Wendy to make the cut. I cannot recall exactly what was said, but I do remember that she was not happy about it. We were both anxious, and the atmosphere was extremely tense. I believe that Wendy pulled down my lip and attempted to cut it with a scalpel. I think she may have had to leave the room to get the scalpel. I believe that I had rinsed my mouth out before she cut it. Wendy was initially too gentle, and needed to try again to open a cut. When she was successful, there was no need for stitches as it was a clean cut. She put gauze on it and told me to apply pressure to the cut. It took a long time for the bleeding to stop. [Doctor Chapman's evidence at the Disciplinary Hearing was not consistent with this version of events and she was not present at the Appeal Hearing and has not had the opportunity of responding to the Player's allegations regarding the cutting of his lip].
36. I would like to emphasise that, as far as I am concerned, Wendy was as much a victim in these matters as me. I do not believe that she had any prior knowledge that the fake injury was going to take place, and she was put in an extremely hostile and tense environment alongside me in the physio room. She did not want to hurt me at all, and was clearly uncomfortable at opening a cut on my lip. My sense is that she also felt she had no choice in the matter, and if she had been given more time it is entirely possible that she would have behaved differently. We both acted regrettably in the heat of the moment.
37. After the game, I remember that Steph took a photo of the inside of my mouth as evidence. I cannot recall who suggested this, but it was not me.
38. It did not take long for news to filter through that we had lost the game 6-5. I was devastated. I also grew increasingly angry about what had happened to me. I had hoped for an opportunity to make a positive impression on the match and to help my Club win a famous victory. Instead, I had been required to cheat and had been placed in an impossible position.
39. I was due to make an appearance in the corporate box after the game. However, I felt so disappointed that I decided to drop out. I did attend the post-match dinner and sought my family and friends.
40. As far as I can recall, Dean Richards did not speak to me about the incident during this time.

Media Reports and Intervention of the Club

41. In the days following the match, the incident began to receive attention in the media and rumours were circulating that the blood injury had been fabricated.
42. In a meeting with me and Nick Evans, and I think Steph Brennan, Dean Richards provided us with completed statements to read and sign. He said that the ERC wanted a written statement about what had happened from us. I do not know if Dean drafted the various statements himself. He asked us to check it which I understood to be a formality. The way in which Dean presented it to me made it very clear that I had no real choice in the matter, and that I was expected to sign the statement and to toe the Club's line.

[Dean Richards denied that the Player had no choice but to sign this statement although he accepted that he had prepared the statement for the Player to sign and had, in typing up the version for signature by the Player, altered an earlier version which had been prepared by Steph Brennan by hand. He made these alterations in order to ensure that the Player's statement would be consistent with the statements of others. Dean Richards contended that all involved in the cover up had been willing participants].

43. In that meeting and in other brief discussions with him over the following weeks he reassured me that everything would be ok. He told me that all the statements would tie together, and that this would be in everyone's best interests. On one occasion, I remember that Dean asked me whether I was "alright". I responded that this was not why I played sport. My respect for Dean was quickly beginning to fall away.
44. Over this period of weeks I discussed the situation from time to time with Nick Evans, Steph and Wendy. We were all unhappy. Nick described the Club's actions with respect to these statements as "bullsh*t".
45. Throughout this period, I had no understanding that charges had been brought against me personally. The Club did not provide me with copies of the correspondence it exchanged with the ERC at any stage and I believed that this was a problem for the Club alone. I assumed at this point that I was simply a witness. I was completely reliant on the Club to look after my interests. At no stage was I offered independent legal advice, and I basically did what I was told by Dean.
46. I subsequently learned that the ERC was going to investigate the incident further by holding a hearing. I was told that I would have to turn up but I was not told that I had been charged personally. I was told that I would have some questions to answer. I only learned this about seven days prior to the hearing. I was growing increasingly nervous, but I was reassured by Dean that I would not be "hung out to dry" and that I would be the last person to be in trouble.
47. In the week leading up to the hearing, I approached Mark Evans for a copy of the video footage of the Leinster match. I wanted to make sure I had seen this as I guessed that I would be asked about it at the hearing. I went into Mark's office and asked him if he knew exactly what had happened. He said that he had read the statements. By the way he said this I took it to mean that he did not want to discuss the details with me. I do not know if Mark was aware of what had taken place regarding the faked blood injury at this stage.
48. I continued to receive reassurances from Dean that, so long as I went along with the story, we would be ok. He also gave me advice on giving evidence, and told me that I should appear indignant at any suggestions of Misconduct.
49. One day before the Tribunal, a meeting was held with Mark Evans, Dean, Steph, Nick Evans, Ian Bell and me, together with the lawyers who were going to appear at the hearing - Oliver Glasgow and Stephen Hornsby. The meeting took place at the offices of Davenport Lyons (Stephen Hornsby's firm). This was my first meeting with the lawyers. Dean had confirmed to me in advance of this meeting that I should not tell Oliver or Stephen what had really happened, as this might compromise their presentation of the defence.
50. At the meeting, Oliver asked me a few direct questions to prepare for the hearing, such as "what were you taking from your sock?" He told me to be decisive when I gave my answers. He explained that if I did not know the answers, I should state this. I do not recall any suggestion by Oliver or Stephen that I should consider seeking independent counsel. [The Player confirmed that he had continued the cover up at the meeting with his lawyers and had not told them the version of events set out in his new evidence. The version of events which he disclosed to his lawyers was consistent with the untruthful version which he subsequently gave at the Disciplinary Hearing].

The Hearing

51. By the day of the hearing I was feeling ill. This was a combination of nerves and stress. I was growing increasingly anxious at the prospect of lying to the Tribunal. However, at the time I genuinely did not consider that I had a choice. Dean had directed a course and my job was to follow him, not challenge him. I of course wanted the best for the Club and my team mates, and I didn't realise the personal ramifications for myself in following the Club's directions.
52. The Tribunal was initially due to last for two days. As a result of timing issues, the hearing had to be extended by a further day which could not take place for a few weeks. I was to give evidence on the third day, and this delay was difficult to cope with.
53. A further meeting with the lawyers took place the day before the hearing was reconvened at the Twickenham Stoop. Once again, Oliver Glasgow advised me on my delivery.
54. When I came to give evidence at the hearing, I was feeling terrible. I don't like lying, and I am poor at it. I think this came across clearly and I struggled with my answers. Despite my performance, I was still hopeful that everything would be ok. I asked Oliver and Stephen how they thought it was going. They told me that the case could go either way.
55. When the judgment was announced orally on the same day and I learned that I had been suspended for 12 months, I was devastated. For one thing, I had not appreciated that I was potentially exposed to a ban of this nature. The Club had always indicated that the worst possible outcome was a fine, which it would cover. Secondly, I could not understand how I alone could have been found guilty of Misconduct. It must have been obvious that I was not acting alone, and I had no motive for faking a blood injury personally. I felt badly let down by the Club, but Mark Evans specifically reassured me that they would appeal.
56. Shortly after the hearing, the PRA advised me to seek independent counsel and recommended Lewis Silkin.

Decision to Appeal

[The events following the hearing before the Committee can have played no part in the Committee's decisions on the Misconduct complaints concerning the Player and are not the subject of separate Misconduct complaints by the Disciplinary Officer. Accordingly they were not taken account of by the Appeal Committee in reaching its decisions in relation to the Player's Appeal].

57. I realised immediately that I would need to appeal the decision to ban me for 12 months. At this stage of my career, sitting on the side lines for a year could have a catastrophic impact on my progress as a player. I feel that I am on the verge of making the breakthrough to the next level. Facing a lengthy ban will mean that my current momentum is lost, and when I return to the game aged 26 it is certainly possible that my opportunity to step up will be lost. I might even struggle to retain my current status at the Club.
58. The day after the hearing, I went to see Dean with my agent, Christian Abt. Dean assured me that the Club would appeal, and that I would still be paid for the period of my ban. He also went on to criticise the delivery of my evidence and the clothes I had been wearing at the hearing. He told me that I would be better coached for the appeal. On 22nd July I received a voicemail from Dean suggesting someone who could train me to give evidence.

59. I met with the PRA and Owen Eastwood from Lewis Silkin on Thursday 23rd July and we discussed my options. The advice I received confirmed my own view that I should tell the truth and give myself the best chance of reducing my suspension.
60. On 31st July, myself and Damian Hopley, Chief Executive of the PRA, met with Mark Evans at Caffè Nero in Twickenham. In that meeting Mark was friendly but outlined the consequences of my appealing on a full disclosure basis. He told me this route could result in the Club being expelled from the Heineken Cup, they would lose sponsors, that Wendy and Steph could be struck off for life and would in turn sue the Club. He said it would be worse than relegation. I assumed he was speaking in a financial sense.
61. Mark Evans' suggestion that I pursue a limited type of appeal was contrary to my own feelings and my advice. I now had a dilemma and it weighed heavily on my mind. The Club preferred that I should appeal on much more limited grounds, which focused on the length of my ban. This would minimise the Club's exposure. I had no desire to harm the Club, but at the same time I wanted the truth to be told. I had lied so far on the Club's directions, and this approach had resulted in a 12 month ban. I decided that I would not allow the Club to make me lie again.
62. Around this time I instructed my solicitors to speak to the ERC to explore providing substantial assistance in the context of my appeal.
63. On Monday 3rd August, I received a voicemail from Dean in which he apologised to me.
64. On Wednesday 5th August at 9am, myself and Damian Hopley met with Charles Jillings (the Chairman of the Club) at the PRA's offices. My solicitor, Owen Eastwood of Lewis Silkin, joined us later. At 9am Owen was in a meeting in a separate room at the PRA's offices with Mark Evans and Oliver Glasgow. These meetings had been requested by the Club the previous day.
65. In my meeting with Charles, he started by apologising to me for the position I had been placed in. I am sure he was sincere. Charles then laid out a compensation offer to me. This consisted of payment of my salary while I was suspended, an assurance that I would be selected for the team on merit once my suspension ended, a two year contract extension, a testimonial, a three year employment opportunity with the Club after I retired from playing, and an assurance that he would take a direct interest in my post-rugby career. He asked me what I was planning to do in relation to an appeal. Damian Hopley replied that I was appealing on a full disclosure basis. Charles told me that he thought I should appeal, but that it should be on a limited basis focusing on the sanction and not the findings of fact. He told me that the appeal could be dealt with in writing without a personal hearing. Charles said that if the ERC decided to convene a personal hearing and questions were asked of me that might incriminate the other parties I could simply refuse to answer those questions. At the end of the meeting, I agreed to consider what he had said.
66. After this meeting Owen informed me about his meeting with Mark Evans and Oliver Glasgow. I understand that Mark had asked him if my decision to appeal on a full disclosure basis was final and that when Owen had told him that it was, Mark apparently replied that I was making a mistake and that the consequences of undertaking an appeal with full disclosure would be that the Club would likely be expelled from the Heineken Cup, that this would result in substantial loss of income, that sponsors would withdraw, that the playing budget would be reduced by two million pounds, that the bank would seek repayment of loans, that there would be redundancies in the office and that the Club would likely be relegated. I understand that Mark then said that this would be my responsibility, that I would be regarded by others as the person responsible and that it would be extremely difficult for me at the Club should I choose this course of action.

67. I also met with a number of the Club's senior players in the afternoon of Wednesday 5th August. It was clear that they had been speaking with the Club's management as they spoke to me about the basis of my appeal. They told me that the team was behind me 100%. They also encouraged me to appeal, but on the limited basis proposed by the Club. I can only assume that Mark Evans had told them that I should follow this course of action. I have no doubt that the players were trying to act in my best interests. However, this meeting made me doubt my own legal advice as to how I should proceed.
68. By the morning of Friday 7th August, I was feeling under intense pressure from the Club not to appeal on a full disclosure basis. My agent had also telephoned me the previous evening saying that he thought appealing on a full disclosure basis was a mistake. I began to waiver from my previous decision to appeal on a full disclosure basis. Later that morning, I instructed Owen to respond to the Club's offer and to propose what I regarded as adequate compensation for their breach of my employment contract and the reputational damage and emotional injury that had caused me. It also reflected the reality that by not exercising my full appeal rights, as they had requested of me, I would in all possibility be sitting out a season of rugby. After having discussed this with my girlfriend, I took the view that adequate compensation for all of this would be the Club apologising to me, extending my contract on improved terms and paying off the mortgage on the house I own with my girlfriend. The Club had previously stated that it wanted to give me long-term security. My proposals were intended to achieve this. Had I accepted a 12 month ban, without this level of compensation there was a real chance that my career would come to a premature end and I would be left with no security, and limited prospects of making a good living outside the game.
69. The Club rejected my proposal but made a counter-offer which I accepted. The terms of settlement of my breach of contract claim included an apology from the Club (which I am yet to receive), a new four-year playing contract and extra holidays. The Club's solicitor, Stephen Hornsby, stated in his letter to my solicitors that "the Club accepts that through its servants or agents it has damaged Tom and we share your legal analysis [the assertion that the Club has breached its duties of trust and confidence to me]".
70. This letter expressly stated that the Club's offer was made on the basis of damage caused to me by the Club, and was not conditional on whether or how I would appeal against the disciplinary panel's decision.
71. Around 6.30 p.m. on Friday 7th August, Owen received an email from Max Duthie on behalf of the ERC asking a number of specific questions of me. Mr Duthie requested responses by 8 p.m. that evening and warned that if I failed to respond, I could face separate charges of Misconduct. I forwarded this email to Mark Evans as a courtesy. I learned that Mark was in fact at the house of one of the Club's directors, Roger Looker, together with Charles Jillings, Colin Herridge (another of the Club's directors) and Oliver Glasgow. It was agreed that I would meet with them at Roger's house with my girlfriend and Will Skinner (the Club's captain). We arrived at around 9.30 p.m. From my point of view, the purpose of the meeting was to attempt to repair the damage that had been done, and to explain that I was caught between a rock and a hard place. Of course I did not want to cause harm to the Club, but at the same time I needed to tell the truth. Charles, Roger and Mark maintained that it would do no harm for me to appeal on a limited basis. However, they were unable to convince me and the meeting ended on that basis.
72. On the morning of Saturday 8th August, I received a call from Charles Jillings. He told me that Dean Richards would resign and that the Club would support me in disclosing everything.
73. On Wednesday 13th August 2009, I met with the ERC's Disciplinary Officers and lawyers and they interviewed me for approximately 4 hours. I explained the full background as set out above.

Conclusion

74. I hope that now that the true facts are explained, the Appeal Panel will accept that I was not the driving force behind the events which I have described, but rather that I was placed under enormous pressure to go along with a scheme which was not devised by me. I accept that the right thing was nonetheless to stand up to this pressure and I apologise for my failure to do so at the time. However, I have now done so and have cooperated with the ERC to the fullest extent possible.
75. Playing rugby is my life. I find it impossible to imagine a scenario in which I cannot play. A ban for twelve months at this stage of my rugby career will be devastating and something I may never recover from. Even worse than that, such a long ban labels me as the mastermind of this shameful episode. That is just not fair. Although I accept that I should have stood up to it, this was not my scheme. I feel that I have been as much a victim of it as anyone else.
76. When I was debating how to deal with this appeal, I thought about how I would feel when I looked back over my career in 10 or 20 years' time. I realised that if I failed to tell the truth, the permanent stain on my record caused by this affair would be far bigger. I can only hope that by coming clean, future players will realise that they need to stand up for themselves, and to challenge the decisions being made around them.

Supplemental Statement of The Player Dated 14th August 2009

"I have been asked to provide more detail regarding my conversations with Dr Wendy Chapman. I had a conversation with Wendy before the Disciplinary Committee hearing took place. It is possible that we spoke on more than one occasion, but I believe we only spoke once. Given the length of time that has now passed, I cannot be sure exactly when this took place. I am also unsure who instigated this discussion. I do recall that Wendy felt she had been placed in a very difficult position by the Club. She also expressed her concern at the potential impact on her career if it came out that she had cut my lip. In order to protect her, we agreed that in the event the story of the fake injury was exposed, I would say that I had cut my own lip. I believe this is the "understanding" referred to in Wendy's voicemail to me on Monday 10th August. Now that I have had a further chance to reflect on what happened and an opportunity to take independent advice, I realise that I need to tell the full truth about what took place. I received two voicemails from Wendy after the hearing, the first on Sunday 9th August, and the second on Monday 10th August. Transcripts of these recordings have been disclosed. I sent Wendy a text message on 10th August to confirm that I would call her back after training. When we subsequently spoke on 10th August, Wendy reiterated the potential damage to her career that would be caused if it was revealed that she had cut my lip. She also mentioned that the Club had sent a letter to the ERC which stated that she had cut my lip. She seemed upset and asked me what I was going to say. I told her that I would be speaking to my lawyers to discuss my options. On a separate matter, I would also like to clarify one point regarding Paragraph 71 of my Affidavit. Although Oliver Glasgow was at Roger Looker's house when I arrived on the evening of Friday 7th August, at no stage was he present when the discussions detailed at Paragraph 71 of my Affidavit took place" [For the reasons given above Dr Chapman has not had an opportunity of responding to these allegations which are inconsistent with her evidence at the Disciplinary Hearing].

As Charles Jillings had said to Tom Williams, the resignation of Dean Richards was announced on 8th August. Sadly for him, his position had become untenable in the light of Williams appealing and coming clean.

On 17th August 2009, the ERC Appeal Committee sat in the Radisson SAS Hotel in Glasgow to decide what they were going to do after Williams had blown the whole affair wide apart. Even though Richards had left the Club, he still had to appear and was left with no option but to tell the whole truth. His evidence to the Committee went like this:-

Mr Gay asked Mr Richards to give his version of events to the Appeal Committee followed by any comments on the areas of Mr Williams' affidavit with which he disagreed. Mr Richards told the Appeal Committee that the Club were playing Leinster in a quarter-final of the Heineken Cup. He proceeded to apologise for the "sorry situation" he had created. Shortly after kick-off, Nick Evans received an injury to his leg and contrary to expert advice, Mr Richards' opinion was that he could play but couldn't kick. Mr Brennan assessed Nick Evans' leg at half time and strapped his leg. It was agreed between Mr Richards, Mr Brennan and Nick Evans that they would give him another ten minutes to see if the strapping helped the injury. Mr Richards advised the Appeal Committee he was aware of the blood substitution regulations both in the Laws and those specific to the Heineken Cup and had advised team managers in the past to carry a copy of the rules just in case the referee or anybody else involved in the game did not know the rules. Mr Richards recalled that not long after Chris Malone came onto the pitch he tore his hamstring off the bone and was replaced by Mr Williams. At this point he advised Nick Evans that he may be going back on the pitch. Mr Richards noted that the Club were due to play Sale the following Friday.

He advised the Appeal Committee that he did not tell Mr Williams that he was going to be coming off for blood and the only instruction he gave Mr Williams was that he was to go to number 10. Over a very short period of time he drew the conclusion that Mr Williams was not in the right position and thought that David Strettle was a better number 10 as he has "turned a game for the team". Mr Richards asked Mr Brennan to inform Mr Williams to swap places with David Strettle and also to give Mr Williams a blood capsule. Prior to this Mr Richards had asked Mr Brennan to find out if there were any blood injuries on the back line. There were no blood injuries on the back line. Mr Richards had told Mr Brennan to put the blood capsule in his bag "just in case". By telling Mr Brennan to give Mr Williams a blood capsule he intended and Mr Brennan knew he intended, that Mr Williams should fake a blood injury so that he could be substituted under the blood injury rules. Mr Richards told the Appeal Committee that he had faked or attempted to fake blood injuries a few times before. The Chairman asked if this had "worked" on previous occasions. Mr Richards advised the Chairman that it had worked once but not on the other occasions. A player had swallowed the capsule on one occasion and the other had dropped it from his mouth. Mr Richards thought blood capsules may have been used two or three times in the past but could not remember in which games they were used or the players concerned. Mr Richards was "pretty sure" that Mr Brennan had been involved in all of these occasions. He then said it was definitely Mr Brennan who assisted him. Mr Richards advised the Appeal Committee that Mr Brennan passed the capsule to Mr Williams when Mike Brown was taking a kick. The next minute Mr Williams was lying under the post and there was an "unrealistic amount of blood coming from his mouth". He said it looked like something out of the circus and remembered thinking there would be something said about this afterwards.

Mr Richards also remembered seeing Mr Brennan take Mr Williams in front of the Referee at which point the Referee instructed that it was blood and Mr Williams could leave the field. Mr Richards had made a decision two years ago that players who were brought off injured but may be able to go back on are marked as a tactical substitution rather than an injury substitution. Mr Richards recalled the remonstrations from the other side. He told the Appeal Committee that Don Shaw, the Team Manager, had signed the substitution card and was positive that Don Shaw did not know it was a fake blood injury when he filled in the form. Mr Richards admitted that when he instructed Don Shaw to fill in the form as a blood injury he [Mr Richards] knew the blood injury was not real. He said the match then continued with Nick Evans on the pitch for Mr Williams and acknowledged the fact that Nick Evans did attempt a drop goal in the last few minutes of the game. "He didn't kick it very well and missed". In the dressing room immediately after the game Mr Richards was focused on putting the game behind the team and concentrating on the game the following Friday against Sale. He said he was unaware at this point that Mr Williams had sustained a cut to his lip. After the post-match team talk Mr Richards did the usual press, TV and radio interviews. By the time he returned to the dressing room all the players had showered and gone home. He showered and went across to the eating house at this point. Mr Richards said he was made aware of Mr Williams' cut lip by Mr Brennan. Mr Brennan suggested to him that he should advise the Referee that Mr Williams had a cut and ask if he wanted to check it. Mr Richards proceeded to ask Kevin Stewart if he would like to see Mr Williams' cut but was advised there was no need. Mr Richards said he knew in the back of his mind that something was going to happen but he was not sure in what context.

He said the following few days were very intense due to the preparation for the game against Sale, he was leaving the house at 7am and returning at 10 p.m. He "parked everything from Sunday" until after Friday's game. The Club played against Sale on the Friday and lost. Mr Richards received an email from Mr Evans advising that the ERC Disciplinary Officer was investigating the incident and had requested statements from Nick Evans, Mr Brennan, Mr Williams and Dr Chapman. Later that day Mr Williams had come in to Mr Richards' office and explained what had happened post-match. This included telling Mr Richards that he [Mr Williams] had asked Dr Chapman to cut his lip in the changing room and that she had done so. Mr Richards consulted with Mr Williams about the content of the statements and he [Mr Richards] took the decision that they should not do anything in terms of coming clean and admitting what had happened. Mr Richards said Mr Williams and Mr Brennan were both in agreement with this decision. Mr Richards stated he was concerned about the seriousness of the allegations for those involved and the consequences it could have, in particular for Dr Chapman. Mr Richards said he was not responsible for writing these statements. He handed out the questions received from the Disciplinary Officer and then typed up the hand written responses which he received. Dr Chapman came into Mr Richards' office on the Tuesday to discuss matters. He was aware that the consequences of the allegation against Dr Chapman were huge. If there was not a cut in Mr Williams' mouth he said he would probably have held his hands up. The Chairman asked Mr Richards who first told him of the mechanisms of Mr Williams' cut. He said it was Mr Williams during their meeting on the Monday. Professor Crerar suggested to Mr Richards that he would be experienced in preparing witness statements as a result of his time in the police. Mr Richards said it was a "different format" and advised the Appeal Committee that he simply got the answers and then converted them into formal statements. "I typed them up into answers". Mr Richards said he made no changes to Nick Evans's statement but "tweaked" Mr Williams' statement and Mr Brennan's statement when he typed them up to ensure consistency. Dr Chapman was very upset when Mr Richards met with her on the Tuesday due to personal issues. He advised the Appeal Committee that he had only heard from Mr Williams about how the cut came about.

The Chairman suggested this was to be expected considering only two people were present at the time. Ms O'Rourke advised that Ian Bell was also present in the room at the time when the cut is claimed to have been administered. Mr Richards advised that Ian Bell is a Management Consultant within the Club. Mr Richards described the layout of the medical, physio and dressing rooms and explained that Mr Williams and Dr Chapman were in a room, entry to which was gained from a door in the room where Chris Malone was being treated. Mr Richards' understanding was that Mr Williams was initially in the physio room and was then taken to the changing room by Dr Chapman. Mr Richards said everyone had the opportunity to read and change their statements before they were signed and sent to the Disciplinary Officer. He said that if someone had been totally adverse to the statement then maybe a different path would have been taken. Mr Richards conceded "it was probably the wrong decision" to have submitted the signed statements to the Disciplinary Officer when they were known by all concerned to be untrue. The Chairman asked if apart from Mr Williams, Dr Chapman, Mr Brennan and Nick Evans anyone else knew the truth about what happened. Mr Richards said he was not sure if Nick Evans did know the truth. He admitted he had ample opportunity to tell Mr. Mark Evans in the build up to the Disciplinary Hearing and any time he was asked he vehemently denied the allegations. Mr Richards was unsure if Mr Evans spoke directly to Mr Williams, Mr Brennan and Dr Chapman. Mr Richards was adamant that he told Mr Evans only the untruthful version of events given at the Disciplinary Hearing and that he did not disclose the truth to Mr Evans and through him to the other Directors of Harlequins until after the Disciplinary Hearing. Mr Richards recalled giving his evidence on 3rd July, the second day of the Disciplinary Hearing. He noted that Mr Williams had to wait until 20th July to give his evidence. He met with Mr Williams at the training ground primarily to discuss what Mr Williams was going to say in his evidence and to prepare him to give evidence. The meeting lasted for 20 minutes and Mr Williams' attitude was "bullish" according to Mr Richards. He said Mr Williams was very confident about giving his evidence. Mr Richards also recalled that when Mr Williams was leaving the training ground he said "you should know it wasn't Wendy, it was me". Mr Richards knew that Mr Williams was, like Mr Richards, going to deliberately give an untruthful version of events at the Disciplinary Hearing. Mr Richards said Mr Williams had two rehearsals with Mr Oliver Glasgow and Mr Hornsby before giving his evidence. Mr Richards told the Appeal Committee that at no point did Mr Williams say he was uncomfortable. Mr Richards only had the one meeting with Mr Williams on Friday 17th July; he did not meet with him prior to the Disciplinary Hearing on 2nd and 3rd July. He admitted that he did say to Mr Williams that it would not be in Dr Chapman's best interest to tell Stephen and Ollie.

The Chairman confirmed with Mr Richards that he knew from his time in the police that if a lawyer knew his client was lying when he gave his evidence he could not represent him. Mr Richards acknowledged that the legal team appointed to represent himself, Mr Williams, Mr Brennan and the Club were told the same deliberately untruthful versions of events as had been included by Mr Richards in the statements sent to the Disciplinary Officer and which were given orally at the Disciplinary Hearing. The Chairman asked why Mr Richards was so interested in protecting Dr Chapman. He said that Dr Chapman would only have made the cut at Mr Williams' extreme insistence or if she was under huge pressure which would have been as a result of the situation he [Mr Richards] had personally created. Mr Richards would have been very surprised if Dr Chapman had cut Mr Williams. Professor Crerar asked Mr Richards if he had instructed Mr Brennan to carry blood capsules in his bag specifically for the quarter final game. Mr Richards said he was "not sure" but he "wouldn't expect Steph to carry them in his bag ordinarily". He admitted he knew there would have been some blood capsules in the dressing or physio room: He said he had been asked in the past if he would ever consider cutting players and he said he would never do this. Mr Richards said at the time of Mr Williams' entry onto the pitch he [Mr Richards] fully anticipated that Mr Williams would remain on the pitch for the rest of the game. He said he always gives his players a chance to prove themselves. Mr Richards said "I don't think I would have told Mr Williams instantly that he was going to be coming off but it didn't take long to realise he wasn't coping with playing at number 10". Mr Richards admitted that David Strettle should have moved to number 10 at the time of Mr Williams' entry onto the pitch. At the time when Mike Brown was taking a kick, Mr Richards asked Mr Brennan to give Mr Williams a blood capsule and to instruct him to swap positions with David Strettle. He advised the Appeal Committee that the reason he wanted Nick Evans back on the pitch was not down to his ability to kick it was "because of his ability to organise players and control the game". Mr Richards confirmed he asked Mr Brennan over the radio if he had any blood capsules and also instructed one to be given to Mr Williams.

Professor Crerar asked Mr Richards how he anticipated the incident to happen. Mr Richards was not sure. Professor Crerar also asked if he thought David Strettle would not be amenable to do this and why did Mr Richards select Mr Williams. Mr Richards said David Strettle was more comfortable in number 10. Mr Richards assured the Appeal Committee that it was only himself and Mr Brennan that knew blood capsules were kept in a cupboard at the Club. Professor Crerar questioned Mr Richards about his "consultation" with Mr Williams and asked him if he usually adopted a consultative approach with his players. Mr Richards said "I consulted with Mr Williams about his statement although if he was uncomfortable with this we would have taken another route". He advised Professor Crerar that the consultation "was to protect Wendy". Mr Richards acknowledged that he "shouldn't have put anyone in this position". Mr Richards was particularly upset on the day of the judgment. He was upset because of the 12 month ban given to Mr Williams but at the same time pleased for Mr Brennan and Dr Chapman. He said he felt very guilty. He went in to see Mr Evans and told him everything and that he thought he [Mr Richards] should resign. Mr Richards said Mr Evans suggested that he would resign as well. Mr Richards thought this was a ridiculous suggestion. This meeting was on 21st July 2009. He did not admit to Mr Evans at this point what had happened but just explained that "the incident happened under his watch and I felt I should resign". Mr Richards felt that the sanction given to Mr Williams was disproportionate. Mr Evans told Mr Richards to wait until the written judgment was issued before he made a decision. He said he went down to the pre-season camp on 23rd July 2009 and there was not much interaction between himself and Mr Williams. He attended the Club board meeting the following week but chose not to say anything other than to express how disappointed he was and that he felt he carried the can and wanted to resign. Richards finally disclosed to Mr Evans the true version of events on 3rd August. This included the details of the original fabricated blood injury, the subsequent cover up and the deliberate untruths told to the Committee.

An emergency board meeting was held and Mr Richards was asked to consider his position after Mr Evans was told the truth. He [Mr Richards] said he did not want to wait until the written decision of the Committee to resign. Mr Gay said there were some issues with the duress Mr Richards is alleged to have placed upon Mr Williams. Mr Richards proceeded to point out to the Appeal Committee the areas of Mr Williams' affidavit which he disagreed with. In relation to page 5 of the affidavit, Mr Richards did not agree with the comment, "Dean told me to tell Mr Brennan, one of the Club's physios, that I would be coming off for blood". Mr Richards said he gave the message to Mr Brennan. Mr Richards also disagreed with Mr Williams' comment in paragraph 10 of his affidavit, "I did not feel able to challenge his authority. I do not think that I have ever seen another player challenge Dean's authority". Mr Richards said "if he didn't want to do it, I would have no issue". Mark McParland asked how the players were supposed to know when he would have no issue. Mr Richards said at the time it happened nobody took any issue. Mr Richards referred to Mr Williams' comments in paragraph 11 of his affidavit where he said "In my mid-season appraisal Dean criticised my going down injured during play and ordered me to attend a camp with the Harlequins rugby league side to harden me up". Mr Richards said this was part of the development programme and was a great opportunity for a player to have a different experience and learn new skills. He also disagreed that he suggested to Mr Williams that he was on the fringe of the international setup.

Cross Examination by Mr Duthie on Behalf of the Disciplinary Officer

Mr Richards thought he had told Mr Brennan to put the blood capsule in his bag but was not certain. Mr Duthie asked what was so special about this game. Mr Richards said it was a quarter final and desire to win sometimes affects a person's judgment. Mr Duthie found it difficult to believe that Mr Richards had made an assessment within three minutes of Mr Williams coming on the field that he was not playing well. Mr Richards responded advising that he wanted someone who could win the game for the team. Mr Duthie asked Mr Richards if Mr Williams was someone he had used before to fake a blood injury. Mr Richards said he was not. He said he first became aware of the use of fake blood in rugby when he was in Grenoble. Mr Richards confirmed that he was lying during the Disciplinary Hearing when he said he had never come across the problem before. He said he had never instructed players to be cut before as this would be "tantamount to GBH".

Mr Richards confirmed he gave the instruction to Mr Brennan to give Mr Williams the blood capsule over the radio and that a number of people could hear the radio communications. Mr Duthie asked if anyone else heard the conversation in question. Mr Richards said there could have been but whether or not someone would understand is a different matter. Mr Richards said there was a possibility that Richard Bamford may have heard but was certain he would not have understood the message. Mr Richards reiterated to Mr Duthie that between the Disciplinary Hearing and the Appeal Hearing he had vehemently denied the allegations to the Club. He said he quite openly lied to Mr Evans. He denied everything to everyone at the Club apart from Mr Williams, Mr Brennan and Dr Chapman the whole way through until 3rd August 2009. The Chairman questioned why the Club believed Mr Richards. He said it must be remembered that he had four very good seasons with the Club and held a reasonable position with the Club. The Chairman questioned whether Mr Richards had asked Ian Bell what happened in the dressing room. He did not think he had. Mr Richards told Mr Duthie that he had not seen a copy of a Participation Agreement at his time with Leicester either.

Mr Withey on behalf of Mr Brennan and Mr Hornsby for the Club had no questions.

Cross Examination by Mr Hunter on Behalf of Mr Williams

Mr Richards confirmed he knew that the only way Nick Evans could come back on the pitch was for a blood injury. Mr Hunter suggested that as soon as Chris Malone came off, Mr Richards began to organise a blood injury and that he did tell Mr Williams before going on that he would be coming off for blood. Mr Richards confirmed that the only reason he typed up the written statements and made alterations to Mr Williams' statement from the version written up by Mr Brennan was to ensure all the statements were consistent with each other and so make the lies more believable.

Evidence of Mr Brennan

Mr Brennan apologised to Roger O'Connor, Mr Duthie, the Disciplinary Committee and the Appeal Committee for his behaviour. Mr Brennan said there was no plan hatched at the beginning of the match to have a blood capsule in his bag. There was already a blood capsule in his bag from a previous cheating incident. Mr Brennan recalled telling Mr Richards that he thought the strapping he put on Nick Evans' leg at half time "may be inhibiting his knee". Mr Brennan's recollection of events is that Mr Richards asked over the radio, "does anyone have any blood?" Mr Brennan said that it was not uncommon for Mr Richards to make such an enquiry and that he knew Mr Richards was asking did any player have a blood injury which would allow that player to be substituted by a player who had previously been substituted. Mr Brennan told him that no player had any blood injury. Mr Richards then told Mr Brennan that Mr Williams was to come off for a blood injury. Mr Brennan knew that he was being told to fake a blood injury to Mr Williams. Mr Brennan passed the blood capsule to Mr Williams whilst Mike Brown was taking a penalty for the Club. Mr Brennan told Mr Williams to "do the right thing". Mr Brennan admitted that he meant Mr Williams should use the blood capsule. Mr Brennan said that Mr Williams was very annoyed at the prospect of coming off with a fake blood injury. He was annoyed that Mr Richards wanted him off when he had only just got onto the pitch.

The next thing Mr Brennan knew Mr Williams was lying underneath the cross bar holding his head. Mr Brennan thought Mr Williams did look dazed prior to coming off the pitch and thought to himself "how ironic if this guy is actually injured now". Mr Brennan took Mr Williams in front of the referee although Mr Brennan's belief by this point was that Mr Williams had taken the blood capsule and the fabrication was underway. Mr Brennan advised the Appeal Committee that he briefly examined Mr Williams' mouth on the pitch. Mr Brennan noted that Mr Williams' mouth was not cut at this time and he did not think there was any blood coming from his teeth. At no point did Mr Williams say he had a real blood injury but he was doing a fairly convincing job of faking one. Mr Brennan told the Appeal Committee that he left Mr Williams at the door of the medical room but could not remember if Dr Chapman was there at that point. Mr Brennan presumed she must have been as he would not leave a patient without assistance. Mr Brennan said he could not believe Mr Richards brought Nick Evans back on the pitch when he could not kick. Mr Brennan prayed that the Club did not win the match as he knew what they had done was wrong. Mr Brennan admitted that he took the photograph of Mr Williams' mouth and noted that "the laceration wasn't spectacular". Mr Brennan could not remember whether he asked Mr Williams how he got the cut. Mr Brennan said the reason he took the photograph was "to cover their behinds". He got home and told his wife what had happened and read an allegation of cheating on teletext. Mr Brennan told his mate all about what happened. Mr Brennan could not remember exactly when he filled in the statements of himself, Mr Williams and Nick Evans. He advised the Appeal Committee that he was told by Mr Richards to assist Mr Williams and Nick Evans with their statements. He [Mr Brennan] knew this was to ensure there was consistency between the statements. Mr Brennan said he filled in all three statements at the same time. The Chairman reviewed the originals and noted that all three statements had been completed in a black biro. Mr Brennan thought the players handed their own statements back to Mr Richards afterwards but could not be sure. Mr Brennan could not remember but thought he had partially filled in Mr Williams' statement and then consulted with him about the remaining questions. He doubted that he would have filled in the whole statement without consulting Mr Williams. However, he acknowledged that all the handwriting on the statements of Mr Williams, Nick Evans and himself was his and that he knew much of what was said in the statements was untruthful.

Mr Brennan advised the Appeal Committee that another of the Club's players had told him the next day in the physiotherapy room that the Doctor had cut Mr Williams' lip. Mr Brennan could not remember which player told him this. The Chairman advised Mr Brennan that he found this very hard to believe. Mr Brennan told the Appeal Committee that he did not think the incident was "the talk of the Club". Mr Brennan was offered his new job with the RFU on the Monday prior to the Match. The Chairman suggested to Brennan that it should therefore have been easier to refuse Richards' instructions if this was the case since he was already going to a new job. Mr Brennan said he "got caught up in the heat of the moment". Mr Brennan could not remember if he spoke with Dr Chapman after the Match. The Chairman advised Mr Brennan that he refused to believe he could not remember. Mr Brennan then admitted he had spoken to Dr Chapman several times following the Match. Mr Brennan informed the Appeal Committee that Dr Chapman had told him that she had intentionally cut Mr Williams' lip. Dr Chapman had, he claimed, told Mr Brennan that the Player had pleaded with her to cut his lip and she had done so. Mr Brennan said Mr Richards was leading the whole situation. Mr Richards instructed all the false statements. Mr Brennan acknowledged that he knew his task was to ensure that all the statements from himself, Mr Williams and Nick Evans were consistent. He knew the statements contained multiple untruths. Mr Brennan admitted that blood capsules had been used on previous occasions in the 2008/09 season.

Mr Brennan recalled a player [name supplied] taking a blood capsule and was almost sure that this occurred in a Premiership game. Mr Brennan could remember five occasions in total when Mr Richards instructed a blood injury to be fabricated. Mr Brennan advised Professor Crerar that Mr Williams would not have known how to ingest a blood capsule. Mr Brennan said it was very rare in his experience at the Club for players to say no to Mr Richards. Mr Brennan explained that this was how he felt when he was asked to carry a blood capsule onto the pitch by Mr Richards. Mr Brennan explained that the reason [name supplied] was given a blood capsule was down to a "player welfare injury". The Chairman explained to Mr Brennan that the team did not need to fake a blood injury to get an injured player off the pitch. Mr Brennan admitted to the Appeal Committee that there was a packet of blood capsules kept in the changing room which contained 6-8 capsules. Mr Brennan told the Appeal Committee that he had purchased these and had bought two packets in total during his two years with the Club. Mr Richards told Mr Brennan to buy these.

The Chairman asked Mr Brennan to reveal the identities of the 4 players other than Mr Williams he could remember faking a blood injury. Mr Brennan said he could not remember these off the top of his head and advised the Appeal Committee he had given a list to the Club as part of their internal enquiry. The Chairman instructed the Club to send a copy of this documentation to the clerk first thing on Tuesday morning with the originals to follow by post. Mr Evans on behalf of the Club undertook to do so. The Chairman put it to Mr Brennan that he [Mr Brennan] did recall the names and he should disclose them now. Mr Brennan then stated that [name supplied] was asked to use a blood capsule in the season before getting promoted to the Premier Division. [name supplied] in the 2007/08 season and also [name supplied] in the same season. None of these fabricated blood injuries occurred in ERC tournaments. Mr Brennan then apologised for all the trouble he had caused. The Chairman advised that he had difficulty in accepting that Mr Brennan could not remember the identity of the person who told him that Dr Chapman had cut Mr Williams' lip. The Chairman advised Mr Brennan that the person who told him about Dr Chapman cutting Mr Williams' lip would not be subject to disciplinary action just because he had been told what had allegedly happened and asked if this helped him remember the identity of the player concerned. Mr Brennan then said he thought it was a player called [name supplied].

Cross Examination by Mr Duthie on Behalf of the Disciplinary Officer

Mr Brennan explained to Mr Duthie that it was just by chance that there was a blood capsule in his bag. Mr Brennan also explained that he did not empty his bag after the end of each game and instead topped it up in advance of each game. Mr Brennan advised Mr Duthie that there was a single blood capsule in his bag and it had been there since the [name supplied] incident which occurred a few months prior to the game in question. Mr Brennan told Mr

Duthie that he had purchased the blood capsules in a joke store for £3.95 at Clapham Junction. Mr Brennan could not remember whether he put these on an expense form to the Club or not. Mr Duthie asked Mr Brennan why he filled in the statements of Mr Williams and Nick Evans and suggested that the only reason he did this was because he had been told to do so by Mr Richards so as to keep the statements consistent. Mr Brennan advised Mr Duthie that he thought part of the reason he was asked to do this was due to the medical nature of some of the questions posed. Mr Duthie said this was ridiculous and the questions certainly did not require to be answered by a medical expert. Mr Duthie could not see any question that would require a degree of medical knowledge. Mr Brennan acknowledged that Mr Duthie's point was well made and that he had all along been acting on Mr Richards' instructions to ensure the statements were consistent with each other.

Mr Williams was asked regarding these statements at this point and he advised that he could not remember Mr Brennan discussing the questions and answers with him. Mr Brennan advised the Appeal Committee that his motivations in assisting with the cover up were to protect himself, Dr Chapman and Mr Williams.

Mr Brennan undertook to make himself available to the ERC for further questioning in relation to the previous fabricated blood injury incidents. Mr Brennan confirmed that on all the other occasions where a blood capsule was used it was on Mr Richards' instructions. Mr Brennan asked him to stop using blood capsules but three months later he received another message on his radio asking for a blood injury to be fabricated and the same thing happened again. Mr Brennan told the Appeal Committee that sometimes he had used fake blood from a bottle on a piece of gauze and then applied to the player's body rather than use a fake blood capsule. Mr Duthie asked if Mr Brennan was telling the truth earlier when he said he had never seen a copy of the Participation Agreement. Mr Brennan confirmed he was telling the truth.

Cross Examination by Mr Hunter on Behalf of Mr Williams

Mr Brennan advised Mr Hunter that he could not remember speaking with Mr Williams prior to him going onto the pitch.

Neither Mr Gay nor Mr Hornsby had any questions for Mr Brennan.

At this point the Chairman asked Mr Richards about Mr Richards' knowledge of the identity of the players involved in previous fabricated blood injuries. The Chairman advised that he found it hard to believe that Mr Richards could not remember the names of those players and advised that if Mr Richards was not disclosing this information rather than stating he could not remember the names of those involved then he should make his position clear. Mr Richards advised the Chairman that he did not want to disclose this information and would not do so rather than that he did not know the identities. Mr Richards neither confirmed nor denied the identities given by Mr Brennan but he did acknowledge that there had been 4 previous occasions on which blood injuries had been fabricated and that none of these were in ERC tournaments.

Oral Evidence of Mr Williams

Mr Williams was adamant that he told Mr Brennan as he came off the pitch with Chris Malone that Mr Richards said he was to come off for blood. Mr Williams did not say anything to Mr Richards when he was told he was to come off for blood.

Cross Examination by Mr Duthie on Behalf of the Disciplinary Officer

Mr Duthie asked why the Appeal Committee should believe his evidence after he lied to the Committee below. Mr Williams said he had regrettably lied in the build up to and during the Disciplinary Hearing and he was very disappointed in his 12 month ban. He found it hard to believe that the Committee genuinely believed he had concocted the whole fabrication on his own. This was not why Mr Williams participated in the sport. During the aftermath of the Disciplinary Hearing Mr Williams had decided to stand up for himself and for others in the sport. He also hoped to secure a reduction in his period of suspension. Mr Williams was absolutely certain about the evidence in his affidavit regarding the cut to his lip. He also added that Ian Bell did not cut his lip. The Chairman advised that the Appeal Committee would not make a factual finding as to whether Dr Chapman made a cut to Mr Williams' lip; however, the allegation would be reported in the written Decision.

Cross Examination by Mr Gay on Behalf of Mr Richards

Mr Gay asked only one question to confirm with Mr Williams that Mr Richards did not ask anyone to cut Mr Williams' lip. Mr Williams agreed that this was the case. Neither Mr Withey for Mr Brennan or Mr Hornsby for the Club had any questions for Mr Williams.

Points of Clarification from Appeal Committee

Mark McParland asked Mr Williams who else knew about the fabrication of the blood injury. Mr Williams responded advising that there was knowledge around the Club but he could not say exactly who knew. Mr Williams was almost sure Ian Bell was aware of what happened as he would have heard Dr Chapman being asked to cut Mr Williams. Mr Williams advised that he was aware of one previous faked blood injury at the Club. Professor Crerar asked Mr Williams if there was a senior player system at the Club. Mr Williams said there was and he regrettably chose not to make use of it. The Chairman asked Mr Williams at what point Nick Evans knew about the fabrication of the blood injury. Mr Williams said he would have known when they were signing their statements. Mr Williams noted that the statements had all been signed in the same room at the same time.

Determinations by Appeal Committee of Disputed Issues as Between Mr Williams, Mr Richards and Mr Brennan

a) At the 11th numbered paragraph quoted from Mr Williams' affidavit above he complains of Mr Richards' response to him having been injured during a game and of his being required to attend a camp with the Harlequins Rugby League side. The version of events given by Mr Williams was disputed by Mr Richards who denied that he had criticised Mr Williams in the way that was alleged or that the reason given by Mr Williams for his having attended the Rugby League Camp was correct. Mr Richards contended the camp was a great opportunity for Mr Williams to develop his skills and that Mr Williams did so willingly. A resolution of this dispute would not have assisted in a determination of the Appeal so no decision was made as to which version was preferred.

b) At the section of Mr Williams' affidavit quoted at paragraph 12 Mr Williams claims that Mr Richards advised him that he was on the fringe of the England International set up. Mr Richards denies having said this to Mr Williams but again a resolution of this dispute was not necessary for the purposes for the determination of the Appeal.

c) There was a significant dispute between Mr Williams on the one hand and Mr Richards and Mr Brennan on the other regarding the sequence of events and exchanges described at the 19th and 20th numbered paragraphs of the text taken from Mr Williams' affidavit. In essence Mr Williams contends that Mr Richards told him that he would be coming off for blood even before he entered the field of play and that it was he [Mr Williams] who had been required to tell Mr Brennan that a blood injury was to be faked and that he [Mr Williams] was to come off for the fake blood injury. Mr Richards and Mr Brennan both say that a decision to fabricate a blood injury to Mr Williams was not made until after Mr Williams had entered the field of play and that Mr Williams had not been told that he was coming off for blood until Mr Richards had asked Mr Brennan whether there were in fact any blood injuries to any of the players then on the field of play, including Mr Williams. According to Mr Richards and Mr Brennan, he [Mr Brennan] had advised Mr Richards that there were no such actual blood injuries. The position of Mr Richards and Mr Brennan was that it was only at that stage that Mr Richards had told Mr Brennan that Mr Williams was to come off for blood that Mr Brennan had then gone onto the field of play and had advised Mr Williams that this was to happen. He had then given the fake blood capsule to Mr Williams and had told him to use it all under the direction of Mr Richards. On balance the Appeal Committee preferred the version of events by Mr Richards and Mr Brennan. It appeared to the Appeal Committee that their version was more consistent with the circumstances. If the decision to fabricate a blood injury to Mr Williams had been taken before Mr Williams had entered the field of play then the logical time to give Mr Williams the capsule was at that time and not in full view of the cameras and supporters on the field once he had been substituted on. In any event, the resolution of this difference in the evidence was not material in the determination of the appeal or the sanctions ultimately imposed. It mattered little in terms of the culpability of those involved i.e. Mr Richards, Mr Brennan and Mr Williams, when precisely the decision to cheat was taken and when Mr Williams was asked to and agreed to cheat.

d) In his affidavit at paragraph 42 of the quoted text, Mr Williams suggests that he had no real choice in whether to sign the statement put in front of him and that he was expected to sign the statement and to "toe the Club's line". Mr Richards denies that Mr Williams had no choice but to sign the statement although he accepted he had prepared the statement for Mr Williams to sign and had, in typing up the version presented to Mr Williams, altered an earlier version which had been prepared by Mr Brennan by hand. He made these alterations in order to ensure that Mr Williams' statement would be consistent with the statements of others. Mr Richards contended that all involved in the cover up had been willing participants. There is no doubt that Mr Williams could have, at any stage in the process, refused either to take part in the fabrication of an injury or to participate in the cover up. However, the Appeal Committee was satisfied that there was considerable effective pressure put on Mr Williams by Mr Richards, and to a lesser extent Mr Brennan, to participate in the fabrication of the blood injury and in the resulting cover up. We did not believe Mr Brennan when he said that he had consulted with Mr Williams on the content of the handwritten statement. There is nothing in the statement that required any kind of detailed medical knowledge which was the explanation given by Mr Brennan as to why he thought he would have discussed some part of the handwritten statement with Mr Williams. We consider that Mr Brennan was told by Mr Richards to compile the handwritten statements. We did not believe Mr Richards when he said that it was not apparent to him [Mr Richards] that the same handwriting had been used to complete each of the statements of Mr Brennan, Mr Williams and Nick Evans. It was quite apparent from even the most casual reading that the same handwriting was used to complete all three statements. The Appeal Committee considered that Mr Brennan had been tasked by Mr Richards with compiling his statement and those of Mr Williams and Nick Evans in order to ensure that they were consistent. Mr Brennan had then given all three handwritten statements to Mr Richards who had in turn made further changes to that of Mr Williams in the typing up process. The Appeal Committee considered that by the time the typed statement was presented by Mr Richards to Mr Williams it was as close to a fait accompli as made little difference. Any attempt by Mr Williams to extricate himself from the cover up at that stage would have appeared to Mr Williams as being disloyal to the instigator of the cover up, Mr Richards, and would in his mind have put in jeopardy the professional positions of Mr Brennan and Dr Chapman. It would have appeared to Mr Williams that he was expected by Mr Richards to sign the statement which a combination of Mr Richards and Mr Brennan had prepared for him and that he was to "toe the Club's line". At no time was it suggested that Mr Williams had been advised to get independent advice or counselling.

Closing Submissions in Relation to Mr Richards and Mr Brennan

Mr Duthie on Behalf of the ERC Disciplinary Officer

Mr Duthie referred to the document bundle. Mr Duthie was loathe to spend too much time discussing this as the Chairman had previously advised him that "little could be learnt from other sports". Mr Duthie advised the Appeal Committee that this bundle contained a list of analogous incidents provided by the ERC. There was nothing really similar but may be of some assistance to the Appeal Committee. Mr Duthie advised the Appeal Committee that he was not going to advocate any particular sanction in terms of DR 8.5.1 as he accepted these were confined to players. He noted that there was no real equivalent in terms of non-playing staff and accepted the Appeal Committee had a very wide discretion as regards the nature of the sanctions and level of sanctions to be imposed. Mr Duthie submitted that the sensible approach would be to look at analogous foul play cases and then to identify any aggravating or mitigating features. He said there must be some deterrent effect in the sanction given. The sanction also needs to be proportionate. The Appeal Committee should also consider the fact that Mr Richards organised the witness statements to ensure consistency. It was Mr Williams' understanding that he could not change his statement. Mr Williams said he was coached by Mr Richards to lie. Mr Richards repeatedly lied to the Disciplinary Officer and the Disciplinary Committee. Mr Duthie conceded that the issues to consider in relation to Mr Brennan's sanction are less complex.

Mr Gay on Behalf of Mr Richards

Mr Gay advised the Appeal Committee that they must take into consideration the fact that Mr Richards is based in the UK and is currently out of a job. He also urged the Appeal Committee to take into account the fact that Mr Richards' natural employer would be someone within the Heineken Cup. Mr Gay submitted that Mr Richards had now told the untarnished truth and only wanted to protect Dr Chapman's position. Mr Richards admitted his own misjudgement and took full responsibility for orchestrating the incident and the subsequent cover up. He denied imposing any duress on Mr Williams to cooperate. Mr Richards did not force anyone to sign their witness statements. It was not a terribly well organised plot. There have only been five occasions where fabricating blood injuries were pursued. In terms of pre-meditation the use of a blood capsule on this occasion was "impulsive". The cheating was unsuccessful. The Chairman noted that it got a "better" player on the pitch. Mr Gay conceded it was a "minor benefit rather than a major benefit". Mr Gay argued that abusing blood injuries is common place in the game as noted in Lawrence Dallaglio's book. Mr Richards' participation did not embrace any form of cutting. Mr Richards contemplated only the use of a blood capsule. "It was a pretty amateur foul" said Mr Gay. Mr Gay advised the Appeal Committee that this incident will have an incredible impact on Mr Richards' career and noted he had been capped 48 times for England. The consequences of taking responsibility are huge for Mr Richards. His reputation has been "burnt to a cinder". This incident was the only time a blood capsule had been used in the Heineken Cup tournament. The fact that Mr Richards disclosed other incidents displays candour on his part. Mr Gay noted that Mr Richards had a very minor disciplinary record and that he is not someone "who would send his friends to the wolves". Mr Gay meant candour in relation to his own behaviour and also by the fact he did not want anyone else to get into trouble. This is a mark of someone who is loyal and protective towards his colleagues.

Submissions by Mr Withey on Behalf of Mr Brennan

Mr Withey noted that Mr Brennan's position was "largely on all fours" with that of Mr Williams' evidence and also Mr Richards' evidence in relation to Mr Brennan's role. Mr Brennan provided the blood capsule to Mr Williams in the course of the game and Mr Richards has accepted responsibility for the whole thing. Mr Brennan accepted he played a significant role in the incident and he was aware of the consequences almost immediately. Once the incident occurred he did not want the Club to win the game. Mr Brennan has been caught up in an episode that has gained momentum of its own. Mr Brennan had no intention of coming to the Appeal Hearing and being anything but entirely frank with the Appeal Committee. Mr Brennan is dedicated to player welfare. He is full of remorse for his actions and until now has been a respected physiotherapist. He is very proud of achieving the job with the RFU and the senior England team. Mr Withey accepted that there was no doubt that Mr Brennan's employment with the RFU was at risk whatever the sanction given by the Appeal Committee and also the sanction imposed by his professional body. Mr Brennan acknowledges that what happened on the day was an attempt to cheat. He has cooperated with the Appeal Committee and in the internal enquiry conducted by the Club. He has been candid not because he wanted to apportion the blame on others but because he has answered the questions put to him. He acknowledged he had made a grave error of both professional and personal misjudgement. Mr Brennan was entirely uncomfortable in behaving in this manner. He risked his career and compromised his position. He brought the Club, the game and the profession into disrepute and his actions amounted to no more than cheating. Mr Richards has accepted that he orchestrated the events after the game.

Mr Brennan conceded that he was the instigator of the photo of Mr Williams' cut lip. Mr Brennan was entirely candid with the Appeal Committee that it was not the first time blood capsules were used at the Club. The ramifications for Mr Brennan are going to be significant insofar as he anticipates losing his career with the RFU. Mr Brennan's skills are peculiar to sports medicine and he has no intention of working anywhere else but the UK. There is no realistic possibility of him moving away to another jurisdiction. Mr Withey advised the Appeal

Committee that they had significant flexibility in terms of sanctioning a non-player. Mr Withey suggested that the sanction the Appeal Committee impose be limited to pitch side activity which would therefore allow him to continue working in sports medicine albeit probably not with the RFU. Mr Withey explained that Mr Brennan was one of the RFU's senior physios and was contracted to work full time with the England senior squad. This involved attending both home and international games and monitoring and treating England players whilst with their clubs. Mr Withey noted that DR 8.5.3 entitled the Appeal Committee to suspend the person from any aspect of rugby union in relation to the tournament. Mr Withey said the provision does not entitle the Appeal Committee to prevent Mr Brennan earning a living. The Chairman noted that it would be unlikely that the Appeal Committee would seek to impose a sanction which would deny Mr Brennan of earning a living as a physiotherapist. Mr Withey said that Mr Brennan was someone who was very highly respected and if time had permitted, testimonials would have been organised.

Closing Submissions in Relation to The Club

Submissions by Mr Duthie on Behalf of the Disciplinary Officer

Mr Duthie argued on behalf of the ERC that the sanction given by the Disciplinary Committee was low in any event. The Committee below even said itself that it was minded to impose a ban from the tournament. The ERC now considered the Club should be banned from the tournament. Mr Duthie said it was a question of proportionality in terms of balancing the inconvenience for the ERC in having to replace the Club at this late stage with the gravity of the offence. In light of the change of circumstances and the new evidence, the ERC can cope with the obstacles it has to clear in order to exclude the Club from the tournament. The introduction of the new evidence reveals that it was not just Mr Williams that was involved in fabricating a blood injury but instead it was a conspiracy with a number of people after the match who knew what had happened but did not come forward. This has aggravated the Club's offence. We now also know that this was the last incident in a pattern of offending of this nature which puts the Club's conduct in a more revealing light. The Club issued unsigned statements to Roger O'Connor despite having been specifically asked for the statements to be full and frank but instead they were short and initially prepared by Mr Brennan. The response was orchestrated by Mr Richards. Mr Williams felt like he had no opportunity to amend his statement. The Club threw every single possible obstacle at the Disciplinary Committee including arguing against the inclusion of sample blood capsules as evidence, the evidence of Professor Arthur Tanner, Richard Evans, Yvan Cebenka and Kevin Stewart. Mr Duthie reminded the Appeal Committee that this was not the first time the Club had attempted to fake a blood injury and referred to the four other occasions. Mr Duthie said there was a clear desire from the Club not to know the truth. At least three people came before the Disciplinary Hearing and lied. They all knew the incident had been orchestrated. Mr Duthie claimed Nick Evans also knew the truth prior to giving evidence at the Disciplinary Hearing. Mr Duthie emphasised that there was absolutely no question of the Club having provided substantial assistance in advance of the Appeal Hearing. They have not. The Club waited and waited and then at the eleventh hour came clean when they knew they had no choice. He also noted that nobody has yet received a copy of the Club's claimed internal review. Mr Duthie said the Club either demonstrated a clear determination to lie or decided to bury its collective head in the sand. He recommended that the Club be banned from the ERC tournament, the length of which ban was at the discretion of the Appeal Committee. Mr Duthie was not inviting the Appeal Committee to make a points deduction and claimed that if the Committee had been trying to replicate something similar to a ban in its fine then it had failed quite significantly. If the Disciplinary Officer had been aware of Mr Williams' evidence at the Disciplinary Hearing then he would have recommended that the Club should be banned and not just fined.

Submissions on Behalf of the Club by Mr Hornsby

Mr Hornsby advised the Appeal Committee that this was Mr Duthie's appeal and the burden of proof in showing that the Disciplinary Committee was in error rested on him. Mr Hornsby assured the Appeal Committee that this sort of incident was never going to happen again at the Club and that it welcomed a sanction based on proportionality. Mr Hornsby noted that the Club were perfectly entitled to make any preliminary submissions that it thought appropriate to the Committee below and that it should not be penalised for having done so. In support of the submissions which Mr Hornsby made on behalf of the Club he referred to three authorities. The first, Mcinnes v Onslow Fane and another [1978] 3 AllER 211 was, he submitted, authority for the proposition that where a very serious sanction or penalty was under consideration care had to be taken to ensure that the circumstances justified such a penalty. He submitted that the Appeal Committee had to act proportionately and treat like cases alike as regards penalty.

The second case concerned a 1989 world soccer championship qualifying event which could have resulted in a tournament ban. The conduct in that case had involved collective action by the whole team unlike the circumstances of the present case where only specific individuals were involved. In the third case, Sheffield United Football Club Limited v Football Association Premier League Limited IS.L.R. SLR77, an Arbitration Panel had reviewed the decision of a disciplinary body which had held that it would not be appropriate to deduct points inter alia because of the effect that that would have had in relegating the club concerned and that a substantial number of innocent persons would thereby have suffered a serious detriment in terms of possible redundancy and financial consequences. The Arbitration Panel reviewing the decision held that the decision of the disciplinary body not to deduct points had made the decision which had been open to the disciplinary body in question. Mr Hornsby said it would be a slap in the face to those who are innocent at the Club if the Club was banned from the tournament. He argued that the faults were at the playing side and not with the financial and corporate management of the Club. Mr Hornsby said it would be grossly unfair if the Club had to "carry the can" for the wrongdoing of the Director of Rugby.

Mr Jillings, Chairman of Club

Mr Jillings intended to have an open and frank discussion on the matter and apologised in advance for his lack of legal jargon. Mr Jillings accepted that the Club had failed to control some of their employees. Mr Jillings told the Appeal Committee that Mr Richards was considered to be the best coach in Europe and definitely in the UK and that the Club had no reason to doubt him. He thought this kind of incident only happens in books. The Club were not aware of the whole facts until Mr Williams came forward. The incident had taken its toll on everyone involved. Mr Jillings said he had asked Malcolm Wall to conduct a formal enquiry at the Club and also asked him to look at the structures and procedures. As a result, he hoped that the Club would now be the cleanest and most open team in Europe. Mr Jillings said the Club have already apologised to Leinster and their fans. Their focus is to stay in the European Cup. The Club currently have a turnover of £11 million but make no profit. The decision of the Appeal Hearing could mean redundancies within the Club and that the sanction would fall disproportionately on innocent members of staff. Mr Jillings reminded the Appeal Committee that the Club have now lost their Director of Rugby and their reputation has been tarnished. He said the Club were going to be honest and truthful and will be the better for this, as will the European Cup.

Mr Evans, Chief Executive of Club

Mr Evans emphasised to the Appeal Committee the significance of the Club not being in Europe. Should the team be expelled from Europe they stand to lose £900,000 (including contract with main partner £60,000, box holders pro rata return £108,000, refund to season ticket holders £360,000, the incremental losses £350,000). Mr Evans advised that they had a sponsor about to sign for £90,000 and this could be threatened by expulsion from ERC tournaments. Mr Evans repeated the turnover of the Club and said that although they have never made a profit the losses have reduced. The cost of being banned from Europe could easily amount to 15% of the turnover. This would be equivalent to a £25 million fine to Manchester United. Mr Evans said the Club's aim was to break even. He said a ban would cause the most extraordinary financial pressure and he could not see how this could be survived. Mr Evans highlighted to the Appeal Committee that this was the first disciplinary body the Club had been before in ten years except for foul play cases. They have had the lowest number of yellow cards in the past few years. Mr Evans was making this point in order to demonstrate that the Club are not pushing at every boundary. Mr Evans questioned the extent to which the board of the Club could be held totally accountable when they were unaware of what had happened until Mr Richards' and Mr Williams' revelations after the Disciplinary Hearing. He said the Club was heavily reliant on private investment and vicarious liability taken to this degree would make things very difficult for the Club. These hearings have been unbelievably damaging and upsetting internally at the Club. Mr Richards tendered his resignation on 3rd August 2009 when he told Mr Evans that he had fabricated a blood injury and had orchestrated the whole incident. Mr Evans rang the board and Mr Jillings was abroad at the time. He also spoke with Roger Looker a Director of the Club and a former barrister. Mr Jillings added that he was shattered by these events and by the breach of trust he had put in people. Mark McParland sought confirmation of the position held by Ian Bell at the Club. Mr Evans said Ian Bell helped Mr Richards look at the various structures and processes. He looked at how meetings were conducted etc. He reported to Mr Richards. He is a consultant and is paid under a contract for services.

Mr Jillings highlighted that the Club had no whistle blowing policy. He presumed that no other clubs would have had one either but presumably will do now. It was accepted that they have got some fundamental things wrong and will change these over time. Mr Jillings accepted they require much better HR and that they need to improve the ability of staff to come clean and give them the opportunity to do so.

After almost 14 hours of hearings the Independent Appeal Committee, chaired by Rod McKenzie (Scotland) and also comprising Professor Lorne D Crerar (Scotland) and Mark McParland (Ireland), issued the following decisions.

DECISIONS OF APPEAL COMMITTEE

Mr Williams

Following the introduction of new evidence by Mr Williams where he admitted his guilt in the Misconduct and where he explained the part played by Mr Richards and Mr Brennan in fabricating the wound or blood injury, as well as disclosing full details of the steps taken by those involved to cover up what had happened in the period following the match, the Committee upheld the appeal and reduced the sanction to a suspension of four (4) months up-to and including 19th November 2009.

Mr Brennan
The decision of the Committee was recalled following a finding of the Misconduct complaint being accepted by Mr Brennan in light of the new evidence provided by Mr Williams. For the Misconduct now admitted the Appeal Committee imposed a period of suspension of two years from participation in any capacity in the Heineken Cup (which will automatically be extended to all other ERC tournaments) and requests that other tournaments and Governing Bodies give effect to this suspension in their tournaments. The Appeal Committee's rationale for this decision was that Mr Brennan acted as a "willing lieutenant" to Mr Richards. Mr Brennan played a crucial role in the fabrication of the blood injury and had previously assisted Mr Richards in four other cases. In making their decision the Appeal Committee took into consideration the fact that Mr Brennan had personally procured the blood capsule used to fabricate the injury together with the fact he was intimately involved in the cover-up which ensued and had lied to the Disciplinary Officer, his lawyers and to the Disciplinary Committee. Mr Brennan instigated the taking of the photograph of Mr Williams' lip as part of the cover-up. The crucial difference between the involvement of Mr Williams in the fabrication of the blood injury and that of Mr Brennan was that Mr Brennan's involvement was premeditated. It was he, under the instructions of Mr Richards, who had sourced the blood capsule. He kept a blood capsule in his bag ready for use on Mr Richards' instructions.

He had ample opportunity over the months to consider his actions in relation to the fabrication of blood injuries and to decide that he would no longer take part in such conduct. It cannot be said he was caught up in the heat of the moment or had done something without an opportunity for reflection. This was compounded by the consideration that he had already secured a new job with the RFU and was leaving the Club in any event. He can therefore not have felt any influence in the form of employer-employee pressure to commit the act of cheating which he was instrumental in procuring. His involvement in the cover up of events after the match was integral. In initiating the taking of the photograph he must have known that he was photographing an injury which had been inflicted after and not during the match. He was intent on improving the evidentiary basis for the cover-up which was to follow. He wrote out the statements for himself, Mr Williams and Nick Evans without, in the determination of the Appeal Committee, any reference to either Mr Williams or Nick Evans. Mr Brennan was wholly disinterested in the truth of what happened and was intent only in ensuring that the statements were compiled in such a way as to be consistent one with the other. He gets no credit for having changed his plea of guilty only at the stage of the Appeal Hearing and that after having challenged the disciplinary jurisdiction of the ERC. He was effectively compelled into telling the truth by the actions of Mr Williams in disclosing how the fabricated blood injury had happened and the cover-up which followed the match. If Mr Williams had not come forward and given the true version of what had happened then Mr Brennan, like Mr Richards, would never have told the truth and admitted his involvement in the fabrication of the blood injury and the subsequent cover up.

During the course of the hearing it was disclosed that there had been four previous occasions in non-ERC tournaments in which Mr Richards and Mr Brennan had fabricated a wound or blood injury. Details of these incidents will be passed on to the relevant tournaments' organiser.

Mr Richards
The decision of the Committee was recalled following the Misconduct complaint being admitted by Mr Richards in light of the new evidence provided by Mr Williams. The Appeal Committee imposed a period of suspension of 3 years from participation in any capacity in the Heineken Cup (which will automatically be extended to all other ERC tournaments) and requests that all other tournaments and governing bodies give effect of this suspension in

their tournaments. Mr Richards was the directing mind and had central control over everything that happened in relation to the fabrication of the blood injury on the pitch and the cover up in the days after the match. The only aspect of the matter in which the Appeal Committee determined he did not have direct involvement was the alleged cutting of Mr Williams' lip by Dr Chapman. It was Mr Richards who had instigated and directed arrangements which enabled the fabrication of blood injuries as and when that was convenient and would assist the Club during matches. He had instructed Mr Brennan to obtain the necessary blood capsules and had taken steps to ensure that the necessary "equipment" would be available as and when required. In one of the highest profile matches in which the Club had ever been involved he was prepared to try to cheat Leinster out of a victory by bringing on a player at a crucial stage in the match when that player was not entitled to return to the field of play. He was quite disinterested in the consideration that by acting the way that he did the Club which deserved to win the match might be deprived of its victory. He had long since recruited Mr Brennan as his willing lieutenant in such activities and in identifying Mr Williams as the person who would fake the blood injury he had selected a player who he thought could be suborned into cheating.

His was the dominant personality and influence on affairs. He knew or ought to have known that players such as Mr Williams would likely obey his directions whether it meant cheating or not.

Suspicions having been aroused by the amateur theatrics of the blood capsule and Mr Williams' attempts to appear injured, he [Mr Richards] then set about ensuring that those who needed to lie to protect his position did so. He instigated the cover up to the extent of requiring Mr Brennan to fabricate statements and then refining the fabrications to ensure that all statements were consistent. We did not believe Mr Richards when he said that the prime driving force in the cover up was the protection of the professional position of Dr Chapman. We considered the primary interest of Mr Richards was in preventing his own role in events being discovered. Mr Richards arranged matters so that those who were charged with Misconduct complaints would lie to the legal team and would then lie to the Disciplinary Hearing. If Mr Williams' allegation regarding the cut to his lip by Dr Chapman is correct then Mr Richards was responsible for the situation in which those in the physio's room and dressing room found themselves after Mr Williams' substitution. He had created the situation where intense pressure was brought to bear on individuals to cover up for Mr Richards' instructions that the blood injury be fabricated. If individuals went further in this fabrication than he had specifically instructed they were doing so in order to bolster and maintain the lie which Mr Richards had been responsible for creating. Mr Richards was by far and away the most experienced and senior individual involved. It was open to him at any stage to have said that "enough is enough" and that the reputation of Rugby and Harlequins had been sufficiently damaged. If he had admitted at any stage prior to the conclusion of the Disciplinary Hearing the truth of what had happened then the damage to individuals, the Club and the game of Rugby Union would have been very much reduced. It was not until Mr Williams, a relatively junior member of the playing staff, took independent legal advice, effectively breaking the hold which Mr Richards had over him that Mr Richards felt compelled to tell Mr Evans on 3rd August the truth of what had occurred. By this time it must have been apparent to him that the truth was shortly going to emerge and that continuing attempts to cover up the fabrication of the blood injury would be in vain. He was still not prepared to be fully candid even at the Appeal Hearing. He first stated that he could not recollect the identity of the players who had been involved in previous incidents of fabricating blood injuries at the Club and then, only after Mr Brennan had given their identities, acknowledging that he did know the identities but was not willing to confirm them to the Appeal Committee.

The Club

The Decision of the Committee in relation to sanction in respect of the Club was based on the Club being vicariously liable for the conduct of one of their employees, Mr Williams, who had been found guilty of Misconduct. Misconduct complaints have now been established against three of the Clubs' employees, Mr Richards, Mr Brennan and Mr Williams and it therefore follows that the sanction imposed by the Committee requires to be varied and increased. In the submissions made to the Committee Mr Duthie is recorded as having said:-

- Mr Williams was put firmly in the frame;
- with regard to the physiotherapist [Mr Brennan] he was part of the treatment process and therefore part of a conspiracy;
- with regard to Mr Richards he was the one in control and it would be inconceivable that the plan could be effected without him. He [Mr Richards] overrode Don Shaw concerning the marking of the substitution card and that he had told Nick Evans to get ready before they would have to know the player had a blood injury;
- with regard to the Club, they are liable under the Disciplinary Rules for the actions of their players and staff. There was a concerted plan for the benefit of the Club. They were vicariously liable for the actions of their players and staff under DR 2.2 and had breached other of the Misconduct Rules. The Disciplinary Officer's position before the Committee was therefore that Mr Williams, Mr Brennan and Mr Richards had been acting together to fabricate the blood injury and then to cover up matters subsequently, and the Club was responsible because the plan benefited the Club and, in any event, vicarious liability applied. The position of the Disciplinary Officer at the time of the Disciplinary Hearing was therefore not materially different from the position which was advanced on his behalf before the Appeal Committee. It is true that the Disciplinary Officer now has a far greater appreciation of the actual events because of the availability of the new evidence from Mr Williams which has, in turn, led to the evidence of Mr Richards and Mr Brennan given at the Appeal Hearing. Nonetheless, the fundamentals of the position have not changed so far as the Disciplinary Officer and the culpability of Harlequins is concerned.

We now have full details of the cover up which followed the Match but there are no separate complaints before the Appeal Committee in relation to the conduct of individuals during this period and, in any event, so far as the Club is concerned, there is no evidence that any of the Directors of the Club, including the Chief Executive, Mr Evans, knew of the truth of the events on the field of play or the cover up until Mr Williams approached them after the Disciplinary Hearing and Mr Richards confessed to the truth of events on 3rd August 2009. The Appeal Committee, therefore, found it difficult to understand the logical basis on which the position of the ERC had altered, such that before the Committee the Club should not be banned from the Tournament because it would cause too much disruption and deduction of points in the 2009/2010 season would not be appropriate since it would distort the Pools in the competition but that now the Club should be banned from the Heineken Cup, notwithstanding that weeks had passed and presumably the disruption would be greater, and a deduction of points was still not appropriate. The Disciplinary Officer's position before the Committee was that a senior officer of the Club had orchestrated the fabrication of the blood injury and the events which followed. Notwithstanding there is now a much greater body of evidence to confirm that proposition, the availability of such evidence does not alter the substance of what the Disciplinary Officer submitted to the Committee at the Hearing. We recognise that the position might be different if there was evidence that the directors of the Club had known the truth of what had occurred at the Match and/or they had been party to the cover up before the Committee below. However, all the evidence that we heard was to the opposite effect. Indeed, it was not suggested by Mr Duthie that the Club, in the sense of the Directors and the controlling mind of the Club, had been party to the fabrication of the blood injury at the Match or the subsequent cover up.

There is no doubt that the Club were at fault for allowing Mr Richards far too great a degree of unfettered control over matters within the Rugby Department. There was no whistle blowing policy in place and it would appear that little effective control was exercised over his actions. The Club ought not to have allowed Mr Richards to have control over responding to the Disciplinary Officer's investigations after the Match and certainly should not have allowed Mr Richards and Mr Brennan to orchestrate matters in relation to responding to the Disciplinary Officer's requirements as regards statements. The Club were also at fault in allowing Mr Richards to co-ordinate the instructions given to the joint legal team. However, these are all errors of omission rather than commission. In relation to the Misconduct complaints which were before the Committee and which are the subject of this appeal the Club is vicariously responsible for the acts of others. The Club was as much covered up to in relation to the fabrication of the blood injury and the events which followed as was the Disciplinary Officer, the respondents' joint legal team and the Committee.

We accept the thrust of the proposition on behalf of the Club was that to ban the Club from ERC Tournaments would, in effect, impose a penalty on many at the Club who were innocent of any wrongdoing. We agree that the financial implications of the Club from being banned from ERC Tournaments would be very substantial and in our opinion this would represent a disproportionate burden and penalty on the Club, its staff and players given the extent of the Club's culpability in relation to the actions of Mr Richards, Mr Brennan and Mr Williams. However, the extent of that vicarious responsibility on the part of the Club is significantly increased by the Misconduct complaints having now been established as against Mr Richards and Mr Brennan, particularly in the circumstances that the blood injury was a premeditated fabrication and in light of the cover up of events prior to and at the Disciplinary Hearing. In these circumstances, we have substantially increased the sanction imposed by the Committee by increasing the fine from €250,000 to €300,000. It is not appropriate that any part of this fine should be suspended and it must all be paid, in two equal instalments. The first half of the €300,000 fine is payable to the ERC within 28 days of the date of the Appeal Hearing and the remaining €150,000 is payable to the ERC by not later than 1st December 2009. The level of the fine which the Club must now pay reflects the consideration that it was Mr Richards the most senior member of staff in the playing department of the Club that was the instigator of the fabrication of the blood injury and the co-ordinator of the cover up which followed. The practical effect of this variation in sanction is that the amount which the Club must pay as a fine to the ERC for the Misconduct established against it rises by €175,000 from €125,000 to €300,000.

Dr Wendy Chapman

The Appeal Committee dismissed the ERC Disciplinary Officer's appeal on grounds that the Appeal Committee lacked jurisdiction under the Disciplinary Rules in this particular case.

After those damning decisions, it still wasn't over and although ERC reserved its position regarding Wendy Chapman, the General Medical Council had contacted them seeking information regarding Dr Chapman's involvement in the disciplinary process. ERC did confirm on 8th September that the Board believed that the ERC Disciplinary Officer had brought the misconduct charges as far as was feasible in these cases. They had received confirmation from the RFU that they would consider whether or not there were grounds for an investigation into any aspects not dealt with by either the original or appeal committees. Charles Jillings, the Chairman of the Club, resigned on 28th August to become the latest victim of the saga. His main reason was because of the failure of the Board to control Dean Richards, the Club cheated. Ultimately this happened on his watch and the failure to control must fall at his door. He went on to say that he had tried to seek a solution and the offer from the Club to Tom Williams had been for damage to his career and was not a bribe or threat to the player.

His Honour Judge Jeff Blackett (the RFU Disciplinary Officer) carried out his consideration as to whether there were any other matters beyond those which ERC have already ruled on which merited further investigation and possible sanction.

He went on to say:-

In particular I have considered whether any of Harlequins senior officials (other than those already sanctioned):

- knew that fake blood had been used in the match against Leinster on 12 April and/or participated in the subsequent cover up before the initial hearing;
- attempted to interfere with or deceive the ERC disciplinary process;
- pressurised Tom Williams into either lying or hiding the truth from ERC; or
- undertook any other conduct which was prejudicial to the interests of the Rugby Football Union or the Game.

I have decided that there would be no merit in further investigation and there is insufficient evidence to support a case of misconduct by the Club or any of its senior officials which has not already been considered by ERC. There will, therefore, be no further misconduct proceedings against Harlequins or any of its senior officials in relation to the use of fake blood, or any related activities up to the final ERC Appeal hearing. As far as the RFU is concerned the matter is now closed.

I have taken this decision because:

- there is no evidence that anyone senior within the Club, other than those already sanctioned, knew about the cheating on 12 April or the subsequent cover up;
- there is no evidence that anyone within the Club, other than those already sanctioned, attempted to interfere with or deceive the ERC disciplinary process;
- there is no evidence that there was any attempt to induce Tom Williams to lie to ERC;
- when the evidence is considered as a whole and all the various written and oral communications put into context, it is clear that any actions by Harlequins which could be classified as misconduct were not sufficiently serious to merit further significant sanction;

- Harlequins have been sufficiently punished for their misconduct; and
- there has been considerable and damaging media speculation about this case and further investigation would take considerable time during which that would continue. In my judgement such further delay and speculation would cause increasing damage to the image and reputation of the game in England and elsewhere which would be disproportionate to any advantage gained by instituting disciplinary proceedings. In short it is not in the interests of the Rugby Football Union or the Game to proceed any further.

My Full Reasons for this Decision Are Given Below

My Investigation

1. I have read the following documents provided to me by ERC and Harlequins:

    - The judgments of the first instance and appeal hearings (including the affidavit provided by Tom Williams)
    - The transcript of a meeting between Roger O'Connor, Max Duthie (ERC) and Tom Williams and Owen Eastwood (legal representative) on Wednesday 13th August 2009
    - Transcripts of telephone messages between various parties to the proceedings
    - Copies of letters and emails between parties
    - Various other documents prepared by ERC in advance of the Appeal Hearing

2. I have also interviewed Tom Williams, Owen Eastwood (solicitor representing Williams), Damian Hopley (PRA), Mark Evans (CEO Harlequins) and Oliver Glasgow (counsel representing Harlequins). I have previously spoken to Charles Jillings.

Narrative

3. The following narrative has been compiled from the documents provided by ERC and evidence from those I interviewed. Before publication of this statement those parties were given the option to amend the narrative. The following is an agreed version of events.
4. Before the first hearing started in early July there is no evidence that Mark Evans or any of the Board at Harlequins knew what had actually occurred. The lawyers acting for the Club had clear instructions that the "blood injury" had not been faked and that the allegations were not true. Those instructions never changed. Evans himself accepts that he should have paid closer attention, perhaps by conducting an internal investigation, but he accepted the version of events which Dean Richards said he would put before the initial hearing. There has been some speculation that he is the sort of "hands-on" CEO who must have known, and that this speculation is corroborated by Tom Williams affidavit in which he described a conversation with Evans in the week leading up to the original hearing where Williams said: "by the way he said [that he had read the statements] I took it to mean that he did not want to discuss the details with me. I did not know whether Mark was aware of what had taken place regarding the fake blood at this stage". Both Williams and Evans told me that this was a very short conversation en passant which had no significance. I accept that this speculation has no basis in fact and that Evans did not know what had occurred.

5. During this period Dean Richards told Williams that he would support an appeal. On 22nd July he left a voice mail on Williams' phone telling him that he could arrange for someone to coach him on giving evidence. On 3rd August he left a message apologising for what had happened. Williams said that the press reports of Richards being a bully were widely exaggerated - he had a robust style of management and made all of the rugby decisions in the Club. Williams did not have a particularly close relationship with him and lost respect for him through this process.
6. Evans said that he became increasingly concerned during the initial hearing as the evidence unfolded. He said that it did not sound entirely credible. Media commentary, his own reflections and the immediate reaction to the announcement of the first hearing's findings increased his concerns over the next few days. At the end of the hearing he told Williams that the Club would support his appeal (a further indication that he had not known before the hearing about the fabrication).

20th July

7. The final date of the initial hearing at which Williams was suspended for 12 months.

21st July

8. On the day after the initial hearing Richards tendered his resignation to Evans. He did not admit the fabrication but suggested he had to go because he had ultimate responsibility for what had occurred. On the same day Williams contacted Damian Hopley (PRA) to set up a meeting.

23rd July

9. Williams met Hopley and Mr Eastwood and when Williams disclosed the full facts he received unequivocal advice to "tell the truth". As a result of this meeting, Williams instructed Mr Eastwood to act on his behalf and Mr Eastwood subsequently (exact date not agreed, but between 24th and 28th July) contacted Max Duthie (ERC) to inform him, without prejudice, that Williams was considering an appeal by telling the truth about the original fabrication and subsequent events, and asking whether Mr Duthie would support his appeal for a significantly reduced sanction, based on the legal principle of "substantial assistance".

29th July

10. Hopley contacted Evans to set up a meeting, but they were unable to meet until 29th July for personal (holiday) reasons. On that date Hopley, Mr Eastwood and Evans met and Evans was informed of the fabrication and subsequent cover up. Evans said that this disclosure of the full facts surrounding the fake blood substitution and subsequent cover up was the first time that any of the senior officials at the Club had been told what had happened. I am satisfied that this was the first time that Evans knew for certain what actually happened on 12th April and subsequently. At the meeting Mr Eastwood suggested that Williams had two options (described as "a binary decision") either to appeal and tell the appeal panel the complete truth or not to appeal. Evans suggested that there was a third option to appeal on the limited basis of papers only

against the severity of sanction. Evans said that from this point onwards he felt that Richards' position at the Club was no longer tenable.

31st July

11. Two days later Hopley, Williams and Evans met at the Caffè Nero in Twickenham. At that meeting Evans again suggested that there was a third option for Williams, that being an appeal on the papers against severity of sanction. There was no discussion of compensation at this meeting and the three attendees told me that this meeting was to explore options. Evans brought with him a draft email relating to the resignation of Richards which he briefly mentioned to Hopley and Williams, but it had no real significance in relation to their discussions. Williams believed that Richards should resign. Following this meeting Evans spoke to Mr Glasgow and advised him of the change to Williams' account. This was the first time that any of the lawyers acting for the Club were privy to this information.

3rd August

12. Richards met with Evans and told him the full extent of the fabrication and subsequent cover up (which Evans already knew). Subsequently (see 6th August entry below) the Harlequins Board decided that Richards should not resign until the written decision of the initial hearing was published, although Evans himself argued that Richards should resign.
13. Between 31st July and 5th August Williams continued to train at the Club and had a number of meetings with his lawyer. He felt increasingly stressed by the situation and became quite ill. The Club management, his legal adviser, PRA and his colleagues became more and more worried about his emotional wellbeing. He was completely undecided as to whether to appeal or not for much of the period, was worried about the future and, at his lowest thought he should retire from the game. During this period he lost 7 to 8 kg in weight and, he said, felt worse than he had ever felt in his life (even when suffering from food poisoning). However, on 4th August Williams reaffirmed that he wished to appeal on a full disclosure basis and Mr Eastwood informed Evans of this.

5th August

14. There were two separate meetings which occurred almost simultaneously in the PRA offices. Mr Eastwood met with Evans and Mr Glasgow while Charles Jillings met with Williams and Hopley. Evans' meeting with Mr Eastwood covered the same ground as before - that being to discuss options for Williams' appeal. There was no mention of compensation. Mr Eastwood disagreed that the limited appeal option was realistic explaining that in his view the appeal panel would inevitably require Williams to attend a personal hearing and answer questions about what had occurred. Evans said that if the full facts were exposed to the appeal panel and the Club was expelled from ERC next season the financial damage to the Club would be significant. Evans never suggested that Williams should lie and he received legal advice that it was not improper to discuss all possible options with Williams' representatives. The advice also suggested that once Williams decided to appeal no further discussions of that nature should take place. Mr Eastwood said, and

Evans agreed, that Evans was quite animated and at times forceful in this meeting, but he said that Evans was not trying to intimidate Williams.

15. In the other meeting Hopley made it clear at the outset that Williams intended to appeal and make a full disclosure of all the events relating to the cover up. Jillings agreed that he should appeal but suggested that he should consider the other option of a limited appeal on the papers. Williams said that he felt under some emotional pressure during this meeting because he was aware of the potential ramifications for other people at Harlequins, not least the physiotherapist and doctor who had been involved on 12th April. However, he did not deviate from his decision. Jillings also accepted that the Club had effectively breached Williams' contract of employment by asking him to fake an injury and then subsequently lie. He told Williams that the Club would compensate him for having put him in that position and outlined items that a compensation package could include (including an extended player contract and employment beyond the end of his playing career).
16. Club officials from Harlequins assert that this offer of compensation was not connected to Williams' decision to appeal. They are clear on that point: Evans said that Jillings was adamant about that when discussing the issue with the Board. Mr Eastwood said that it was perceived that the offer of compensation and the limited appeal option were linked, but this was never expressly stated. Williams now accepts that Jillings did not intend to link them and that Jillings acted entirely properly. Jillings accepted in his open resignation letter that the link may have been perceived when he said: "With hindsight my judgement can be called into question by the proximity of my suggestion of limited disclosure by Tom Williams on the one hand and a financial package proposal on the other". The parties all now agree that there was no link between compensation and the type of appeal.

6th August

17. Richards formally offered Evans his resignation. Evans believed that it should be announced immediately and he rang all Board members. Some of them asked the announcement to be delayed so that they had a chance to be fully briefed and give the matter due consideration.
18. Evans telephoned Williams and left a message asking him to meet to clarify the situation and apologising for what had occurred. During the morning some senior players at Harlequins approached Evans on the training ground to find out what was happening to Williams. They expressed concern about his state of health. Evans told them in broad terms what was happening and the options in relation to an appeal. He expressed concern that Williams was distancing himself from the Club and asked them to see if they could get him to speak to someone.
19. Later that day seven of the players met Williams in a pub in central London. Williams said that they were very supportive and did not, as has been inferred in some press reports, apply any pressure on him. He said that at this time he was reconsidering and had genuinely not decided whether or not to appeal - the players all said they would support him whatever his decision, but they also said if it were them then they would appeal on the papers against sanction only.
20. Williams said, and Mr Eastwood confirmed, that this meeting, more than any other, affected Williams. He said he was fully aware of the potential difficulties for the Club, particularly the possibility of being expelled from ERC, and he understood that the players did not want this to happen. However, he is adamant that they did not apply any undue pressure.

21. That evening Williams' agent telephoned him and suggested that it would be best for him, given his state of health, not to put himself through a full appeal hearing. Evans had spoken to the agent to try to open up channels of communication between the Club and Williams because they were rapidly breaking down. However, Evans said he had not asked his agent to intervene and Williams confirmed that this was the case. This communication further increased the pressure felt by Williams.

7th August

22. By now Williams and Mr Eastwood had discussed the possibility that Williams might leave the Club and sue for constructive dismissal. Having discussed his options with his girlfriend and family members Williams instructed Mr Eastwood to make a counter offer to Mr Jillings' oral offer of 5th August. Mr Eastwood sent an email at 1055 to Evans in which he stated that the option of "a clean written appeal" was unrealistic. He said that Williams had "a binary" decision to make - he either appeals on the basis that he is prepared to answer any questions put to him or he reconciles himself to missing the season. He said that Williams was prepared to sacrifice his appeal on the basis of 12 conditions relating to an apology, security of tenure, payment of legal fees, increases in salary and a net compensation payment of £390,000. This was not open to negotiation and he required an agreement by 1700, the time Williams had set himself as the deadline for an appeal, although the actual deadline was 1225 on 8th August.
23. Mr Eastwood said that he considered the ethics of this offer very carefully. He said that the Club accepted that they had breached Williams' employment contract and had made a compensation proposal. This letter was a response both to that offer of compensation and the Club's stated preference that he did not appeal on a full disclosure basis. Williams was under no obligation to appeal and was not asking for compensation to tell lies or fabricate evidence. Mr Eastwood expressly stated in his letter that Williams would not lie again. Williams said that in retrospect he regrets instructing Mr Eastwood to send this letter, but he was in a highly anxious state and confused as to how best to proceed in light of the conflicting advice he was receiving.
24. Later that day Stephen Hornsby, Harlequins solicitor, replied by email saying that the Club "cannot make payments to [Williams] that are conditional on him not exercising his legal rights. The exorbitant level of payments you outlined in your email would be equivalent to buying his silence and this is something the Board cannot countenance. The Club continues to believe very strongly that Tom should appeal against the severity of his sanction.....Having said that the Club accepts that through its servants or agents it has damaged Tom and we share your legal analysis. In the circumstances the Club believes that it is not only appropriate but necessary to make some proportionate compensation payments to Tom and undertake some further steps".
25. Evans said that Harlequins' Board discussed this matter and Jillings was absolutely adamant that there could be no compensation, however large or small, in exchange for no appeal. By this stage he, Evans, was of the opinion that a full appeal was the only appropriate way forward.
26. The Club made proposals in relation to salary, payment of legal fees and security of tenure and concluded:

"For the avoidance of doubt if Tom accepts it then he is entirely free to make an appeal in any form he wishes based on the considered advice of your firm. The Club would only ask that it be given a copy of any appeal several hours before ERC receives it".

27. At about 1830 Mr Duthie sent an email to Mr Eastwood stating that ERC was considering an appeal in relation to Richards, Brennan and Dr Chapman and asked Williams to provide answers to questions about events on 12th April. It required answers by 2000 and reminded Williams that failure or refusal to provide assistance to ERC would constitute misconduct under ERC's Disciplinary Rules. As a result of this communication Williams went to meet members of Harlequins Board at a private residence. He was accompanied by his girlfriend and met Roger Looker (his residence), Charles Jillings, Colin Herridge, Mark Evans and Will Skinner. Mr Glasgow was at the residence but left the room before the meeting started and took no part in the discussion that ensued. Williams said that he was in a complete quandary as to what to do and the discussion again went round and round in circles. Finally after about two hours he resolved that he would appeal on a full disclosure basis.

8th August

28. Jillings telephoned Williams to inform him that Richards would resign and the Club would support him in disclosing everything. Later he left a further voice mail message suggesting that there might be a "cleaner route". Evans said that this meant that Harlequins was prepared to approach ERC to disclose everything so as to protect Williams from the further emotional pressure of attending a further hearing and being subject to robust questioning.
29. The Club issued a press release accepting the verdicts and sanctions of the initial hearing and announcing Richards' resignation. At about the same time Williams and ERC both issued notices of appeal.

12th August

30. A meeting was arranged with ERC and on 12th August. Williams, accompanied by Mr Eastwood, was interviewed at length by Mr Duthie and Roger O'Connor. Another solicitor from Mr Duthie's firm was also in attendance. This was a long interview which provided ERC with the evidence against Richards, Brennan and Dr Chapman. Williams was asked about all aspects of the case including whether he had been pressurised into not appealing by officials from the Club. He, on advice from Mr Eastwood, declined to answer some of those questions on the basis that discussions and correspondence with Harlequins were privileged because they related to breach of contract and potential constructive dismissal. Subsequently Williams prepared an affidavit for the appeal hearing in which ERC required him to include details of his discussions with Club officials in advance of him submitting his notice of appeal. He has been concerned that some of the parts of that evidence have been taken out of context in the media.

17th August

31. The appeal hearing took place.

Conclusions From the Evidence

32. It is clear that senior officials of Harlequins were very concerned that the Club might be expelled from ERC competition if the full facts relating to the fake blood and subsequent cover up were exposed to an ERC appeal panel. They believed that the best interests of the Club would be served by Williams appealing on a limited papers basis and without a hearing against the severity of sanction. Their concern related both to the financial effects on the Club, which they estimated to be extremely damaging, and to the professional integrity of Mr Brennan (physiotherapist) and Dr Chapman (doctor).
33. It is also clear that Williams was very upset that he had lied to the initial hearing, felt let down by the Club and, as time progressed, felt increasingly stressed to the extent that he became ill. Pressure came from his own conscience that he knew he had acted out of character, from his worry about the effect on the Club and peoples' employment if he appealed and latterly from ERC in the form of an email from Mr Duthie. In retrospect he is extremely apologetic for his part in this affair.
34. Williams has admitted lying to the initial hearing and was prepared to consider not appealing so that the truth would remain suppressed. Although this raised questions about his credibility - and certainly that would be an issue if he were to give evidence in a hearing on this matter - I found him to be open and honest with me. He is ashamed of his actions, which were out of character, and has learned a hard lesson.
35. Evans has admitted that he should have paid closer attention to the process when the complaint was first made and that once his suspicions were aroused he should have conducted a rigorous review and reported the results to ERC. Harlequins' Board have criticised Evans for these failures and he accepts that criticism. However the Board have also passed a vote of confidence in Evans to continue as their CEO.
36. The communication between Club officials and Williams was undertaken with lawyers or CEO PRA in attendance. The Club certainly wanted Williams to limit the extent of his appeal, and they asked him on a number of occasions to consider that option. However, after a number of days of negotiation the Club agreed that an appeal on the full facts was appropriate. All of the negotiations in relation to compensation were undertaken through lawyers and was not expressly linked to Williams' appeal even though Williams and Mr Eastwood thought there was a link during the negotiations. The letter from Mr Hornsby to Mr Eastwood on 7th August made this point explicitly.

Decision on Whether to Bring Proceedings

37. I have to consider whether any of the conduct described above is prejudicial to the interests of the Union and the Game, and if it is whether it is sufficiently serious to merit disciplinary proceedings.
38. This whole affair has been particularly unedifying and there is no doubt that the whole episode has brought the game into disrepute. Once Evans discovered the full facts of what occurred on 29th July Harlequins

should have taken immediate action against Richards and informed ERC and the RFU. Instead it took them nine days to reach that correct decision. This delay was fuelled to a certain extent by Williams' prevarication about whether or not to appeal.

39. These negotiations and the ensuing delay could be classified as prejudicial conduct but in the context of the whole affair they are relatively minor because Williams and the Club made the right decision in the end.
40. Mr Jillings, in his resignation statement, accepted responsibility for his Club's failings and acted honourably and with integrity in taking that responsibility. Further disciplinary action against him for his part in the negotiations, when set against the sanction on the Club and his resignation, would be oppressive.
41. Mr Williams has suffered enough already in terms of damage to his health and reputation. Further action against him for asking the Club to pay a large sum as compensation for not appealing the original sanction would also be oppressive. He said, and I accept, that this offer was made when he was not acting entirely rationally and he now regrets it.
42. Mr Evans believes that he acted in the best interests of all the employees in the Club and was desperate to limit the damage to them and the Club. He never threatened Williams but he did ask him on a number of occasions to consider limiting his appeal. He can be criticised for not disclosing the facts to ERC and the RFU as soon as they came to his attention and this was an error of judgement. However, bringing disciplinary proceedings against him for this conduct, particularly when set against the sanction imposed on the Club, would also be oppressive.
43. The Club has already lost its Director of Rugby to a three-year suspension and Chairman who has resigned. Additionally they have been fined €300,000 and have yet to pay the full costs of the hearing (likely to be several hundred thousand Euros). The reputation of the Club has also been tarnished. That seems to me to be a proportionate sanction for all that has occurred.

Final Comments

44. I make no criticism of the lawyers involved in this case or of the role of PRA. There was no obligation on Williams to appeal and it was perfectly proper for his and Harlequins' legal adviser to enter negotiations in relation to breach of contract following the initial hearing. Similarly the CEO of PRA's consistent advice to Williams was that he should appeal on a full facts basis and he provided pastoral support for Williams when he needed it.
45. There will be some in the Game who will consider that further action should be taken against Harlequins and senior officials and that my decision has undermined the integrity of the sport. I disagree. This whole saga has lasted for far too long already and a line needs to be drawn so that reputations and the image of the Game may be restored. I have no doubt that everyone involved now understands the importance of telling the truth at the earliest possible opportunity and that in itself will send a powerful message to the rest of the Game.
46. Finally I would like to thank ERC for their determination in seeking out the truth and exposing issues which can now be taken forward in other fora.

Even now, there were still the matters of Brennan and Chapman to be resolved. In the case of Chapman, she was let off with a warning from the GMC after admitting cutting the lip of Tom Williams. After the disciplinary hearing, they announced on 1st September 2010 that her fitness to practise was not impaired despite her actions. Brennan was not as lucky because two weeks later, he was struck off by the Health Professions Council for misconduct after a two day hearing. He had lost his England job because of the ban from rugby and now stood to lose his livelihood as well. Later in the year, he appealed the ban to the High Court and won the day. Mr Justice Ouseley quashed the decision to strike him off and ordered them to reconsider the case. This they did on 18th May 2011 and, as part of its decision, The Panel was satisfied that, in the light of everything which has now been said about, and by, Mr Brennan at this hearing today, a striking off order is no longer a necessary or proportionate response to his misconduct. Instead, it was decided that the Registrar be directed to annotate the registration of Stephen Brennan with a caution order for a period of five years.

The murkiest chapter in the history of the Harlequin Football Club had finally come to an end although their legal bill was expected to be in excess of £450,000.

45

Sevens in the 2000s
2000-2009

From the start of the new millennium, the Middlesex Sevens moved to the start of the season in August rather than its traditional April or May date. Gone too were the qualifying rounds, it was now just sixteen teams in a straight knockout with the first round losers progressing to the Plate competition. Our squad was Ed Jennings, Matthew Powell (captain), Phil Davies, Danny Badham, Ryan O'Neill, Anthony Morris, Richard Nias, Ben Gollings and Brendon Daniel. Another disastrous tournament unfolded as we lost 14-24 to Bristol and then in the Plate to London Welsh (12-24). Penguins beat Saracens 47-19 in the main competition while London Irish took the Plate against the British Army (19-14). It really was a sign of the times when teams were understandably reluctant to play any of their star players for fear of them missing the whole season through injury. In the London Floodlit tournament, we lost to Oxford University in the final (17-34) after fielding a strong team which included Daniel, Keyter, Sanderson and Sheasby.

On 18th August 2001, our squad was another weak and inexperienced one; David Slemen, Rob Hunt, Darryl Griffin, Jim Evans, Karl Rudzki, Ugo Monye, Tim Barlow, Alex Mockford, Ollie Phillips and Nick Duncombe were charged with bringing something back to the Stoop. In the first game, they lost to London Irish and entered the Plate. They defeated Worcester (17-15) and Bristol (26-12) before meeting Blackheath in the final. By half time, Barlow and Duncombe had scored tries, both converted by Slemen and although Blackheath came back with a try by Hammond, Slemen ran 80 metres for the winning score. His conversion made the result 21-5 and an unexpected trophy was collected. The British Army won the main event with a 45-21 win against Newcastle. The crowd this time was a pitiful 17,261 but that is what you get if you play in the middle of the summer holidays.

The following year, another experimental squad containing Jim Evans, Villiame Satala, Rob Jewell, Luke Sherriff, Chris Bell, Nick Duncombe, Scott Bemand, Ben Gollings, Ugo Monye and Nathan Williams went out to Gloucester in the first game (7-21). Owing to the fact we only scored one try, we didn't even get into the Plate! Bradford Rugby League won the main competition with a 42-14 win over Wasps while Newcastle defeated Princess of Wales Royal Regiment in the Plate (26-7).

2003 saw a squad containing Pat Sanderson, Tom Guest, Luke Sherriff, Chris Cracknell, Adrian Jarvis, Max Evans, Ugo Monye, Henry Barrett, Tom Williams, Tom Allen and Andy Reay lose 15-19 to Leeds Tykes and fail again to get into the Plate. Northampton beat Newcastle (31-5) to win the cup and Gloucester were too strong for Rotherham in the Plate (26-5).

Cracknell, Jarvis, Monye, Reay, Sherriff (captain) and Williams all appeared again in 2004 along with Jim Evans, Kai Horstmann, Duncan James and Joe Mbu. Again they fell at the first hurdle and this time, they didn't even score a point in losing to London Irish (0-17). The British Army won 43-24 against Gloucester in the cup final and Newcastle won the Plate this time by beating Loughborough University 33-15. To be honest, it wasn't worth the effort turning up if this was all we could manage.

In 2005, we did do much better with a 43-0 thrashing of Blackheath and a closer win against Bath (22-15) but Gloucester just shaded the semi-final (7-14) and they went on to beat Wasps in the final by 35-26. In the Plate, Newcastle won again by defeating Worcester 14-5.

The 2006 tournament went to Pools instead of a straight knockout and our squad was a mix of youth and experience. It contained Will Skinner (captain), Tom Guest, Phil Burgess, George Robson, Chris Robshaw, Steve So'oialo, David Strettle, Tom Williams, Josh Moore, Adam Thompstone, Mike Brown and Jordan Turner-Hall. We were in Pool 2 with Gloucester and Sale; we beat Gloucester 19-5, Gloucester beat Sale 29-21 and we won against Sale 26-17 to progress to the quarter finals. We proceeded to demolish Bath 42-17 but went out to Wasps in a close game (19-26). They in turn went on to beat Leicester in the final by 29-10.

It was back to recent normality in 2007 with two straight losses. Against Sale, Amesbury (2) and Rhodes got tries and Amesbury also got one conversion (17-21) and we were never in it against Newcastle and a solitary try from Mike Worrincy (converted by Aldique) was all we could manage (7-40). The Falcons went on to defeat Worcester by a single point to claim the title (20-19). We did win the London Floodlit Sevens at Rosslyn Park but these were about the only competitions we entered now.

On 16th August 2008, it was back to the old style – straight knockout. We had a decent squad featuring Epi Taione, Tom Guest, Chris Robshaw, Nick Easter, Mike Worrincy, Gonzalo Tiesi, Rhys Howells, Mike Brown, Ollie Lindsay-Hague, Waisea Luveniyali and David Strettle (captain). Strettle and Guest scored two tries each and Brown got one in the 27-0 victory over Leeds Carnegie to get us off to a winning start. Strettle, Tiesi and Brown followed up with more against Sale to see us through 21-12. Against the holders in the semi-final, Strettle got another two tries with Robshaw, Taione and Worrincy adding others to see us through 29-14. In the final, we met the British Army and started well with tries from Brown and Taione but the Army struck back with a goal and a try to lead at the break. Brown scored again to restore the lead and Strettle rounded it off with our fourth try. There were so many conversions missed because the rules had been changed so that all kicks at goal had to be drop-kicks. The side scoring also kicked off so there was less chance of dominance but it didn't always work like that. This victory was our fourteenth title in twenty finals. In the Plate, Saracens beat Northampton 26-7.

As holders, we put in a reasonable squad for the defence of the title – Jonno Ross, Ollie Richards, Johnny Hampsey, Seb Jewell, Chris Robshaw (captain), Luke Wallace, Karl Dickson, Calum Macrae, Sam Stewart, Waisea Luveniyali, Gareth Williams and Ollie Lindsay-Hague. In the first game, we went out to Kukri White Hart Marauders (17-22). Stewart scored two tries, Lindsay-Hague one and Luveniyali converted the first. We moved into the Plate where we beat Worcester (40-0) and Bath (22-0) before succumbing to Sale in the final by 12-24. Tries came from Lindsay-Hague (7), Williams (2), Hampsey, Luveniyali and Richards; Dickson landed four conversions and Luveniyali got three. London Irish won the main event by beating ULR Samurai 26-19.

46

Recovery

2009-2011

The British and Irish Lions went to South Africa from the end of May until 4th July 2009 to play a total of ten games. Only Ugo Monye made the squad but two future Quins were also there – Adam Jones and Jamie Roberts. Monye played in the first and third tests (he was unjustly criticised for not scoring in the first test and was dropped but scored a 70 metre interception try in the third to make amends); Jones came on as a sub in the first and started in the second whereas Roberts played in the first two. The Lions were unlucky but just made too many mistakes at the wrong times and lost the first two test by 21-26 and 25-28. The third was won 28-9 but, as in 1997 when the Lions lost the last test, it mattered not because the series had already gone. The seven other games produced six wins and a draw for the Lions.

Will Skinner led the side as we tried to recover from the "Bloodgate" debacle. There was a lot of rebuilding to be done both on and off the pitch as a lot of people thought we had not only let ourselves down but had also let the sport of Rugby Union down. As part of the fallout, Jillings resigned from the Board and David Morgan came in as a Director (he would be the new Chairman). Sandra Pope also came in as a Director. The accounts showed another loss for the year ending 30th June 2010 of £1,595,568. There was now a staff of 92 and the wage bill was a staggering £5,601,310. The new South stand was ready for use at the start of the new season as the capacity of the Stoop rose to 14,870. Our official sponsors this season were still LV=, Norton Rose and Greene King with Wynnwith Group being added. Season tickets sales went up to 6,284 but extra ticket sales from the increased capacity didn't materialise. The stadium was revalued and once again, it went up; this time it was £27,190,500.

We started with three friendlies, two at the Stoop and one away in between. On Friday 14th August, Connacht came to visit and they took the lead after 6 minutes with a penalty by Nikora. George Lowe responded with a try seven minutes later and Rory Clegg converted. After this, Nikora kicked a penalty either side of one by Clegg and we led 10-9 at half time. The second half saw fifteen replacements (we used six and Connacht nine) and the game remained tight. Clegg landed a second penalty on 45 minutes but Tuohy scored a try for the visitors. The conversion was missed so we still led by a single point (15-14). The remaining half an hour produced no points and we were off to a winning start. No fewer than five notable new faces made their debuts in this game. They were prop Jon Andress (came on as a substitute), winger/full back Ross Chisholm, fly half Rory Clegg, scrum half Karl Dickson (came on as a substitute) and winger/full back Ollie Lindsay-Hague. Andress would go on to make 44 appearances, Chisholm at least 74, Clegg 62, Dickson at least 155 and Lindsay-Hague at least 63.

A trip up to Myrefield to play Edinburgh at the home of Old Watsonians came eight days later and most of the first team squad had a run out. In an error strewn first half, Robson scored a try for us against three penalties by Paterson. Five minutes into the third quarter, Nick Easter scored, Evans converted and we had the lead. Despite having made a number of substitutions at half time, Houston scored and Laidlaw converted to regain the lead for the home side. The same combination scored and converted our third try (Easter and Evans) and with 23 minutes left, we led 19-16; Tiesi extended this with another try converted by Evans. Right at the end, Sam Smith dived over in the corner for Evans to again convert. The final margin of 33-16 at least proved we were on the right track with the start of the Premiership programme only two weeks away. This game saw debuts of one current and one future international; they were Gonzalo Camacho of Argentina and Joseph "Joe" Marler (came on as a substitute) who would go on to represent England. Camacho would win at least 24 caps and make 34 appearances for the 1st XV; Marler would gain at least 42 caps and make at least 139 appearances for us.

Our final friendly was on 29th August against Cornish Pirates at the Stoop. We began with a XV that could have started the following week in the Premiership so it was a bit of a shock when the Pirates wing Havili intercepted a pass on their 22 and ran in for the try (despite Monye's best efforts at bringing him down). Bentley converted but the lead was short-lived as Tiesi went over five minutes later, Evans converted to tie it up and Camacho scored our second. Bentley's penalty reduced the deficit after half an hour but in time remaining, Strettle and Tiesi added tries and Evans converted both to make it 26-10. We made two changes during half time and another five on 55 minutes so we lost a bit of continuity but, as the third quarter began, Fuga struck for Clegg to convert. The Pirates did get another score (Bentley converting his own try) but by then, Strettle had added a sixth for us which Clegg converted. A minute after Bentley's try, Sam Smith went over after a cross-kick by Clegg (who converted). The final score of 47-17 was a good way to bring our pre-season to a close.

With Dean Richards resigning, John Kingston stepped into the breach until the new Director of Rugby was announced later in the season. Tom Williams would be unavailable until November because of his four month ban. The Premiership season started with the London Double Header at Twickenham against Wasps. As usual, this was an away game for us and, after less than 40 seconds, it all turned sour. George Robson head butted Simpson (the Wasps scrum half) and a brawl ensued. When all was calmed down, the referee consulted his assistants and brandished a red card at Robson. Even though we now faced an entire game one man short, the message from Kingston was to go for the win. After 13 minutes, Monye opened the scoring with a try and when Varndell equalised, Camacho put us in front again. Evans converted and kicked a penalty in between two from van Gisbergen. Varndell's second try gave Wasps a one point lead at the break (16-15). The third quarter remained scoreless but, on 61 minutes, van Gisbergen slotted another penalty and then converted a penalty try with five minutes left (awarded for pulling down a driving maul). If Evans had not missed two kickable penalties, the result might have been different. In the final minute, Turner-Hall went to the bin and that was how it ended. The final score of 15-26 left us in eleventh place with only Bath below us. As a result of his misdemeanour, Robson was banned for six weeks and would be out until 24th October.

The following week, we met Leicester at the Stoop. Like us, they had been beaten in their first match so a win was needed by both teams. It turned out to be a tight game that could have gone either way. After 11 minutes, Evans put us in front with a penalty but returning old boy Jeremy Staunton levelled seven minutes later. The next score was another Staunton penalty two minutes into the second half. From a cross-kick by Evans after a good run by George Lowe, Strettle was wrap-tackled in the air by Crane who was yellow carded. His intervention almost certainly saved a try so perhaps we should have seen the referee award a penalty try but he didn't. Another scoring opportunity was lost when Lowe dropped the final pass but Evans levelled the scores with a penalty on 55 minutes. When Crane came back on, Evans put us ahead after another Leicester infringement. The Tigers controlled the last quarter and three Staunton penalties saw them home. It was quickly becoming obvious that everyone was against us and only time would tell how long it would last.

Saracens had won both their matches so far and were starting to recover from their recent woes. In the first quarter, Nick Evans kicked two penalties but the visitors were level by half time because Hougaard dropped a goal and put over a penalty. Four minutes into the second half, Monye (playing at full back) dropped a high ball from Hougaard and Ratuvou was put over for the try. Hougaard's conversion made it a seven point lead, Evans replied with another penalty but Hougaard dropped a massive goal from five metres inside his own half a minute later. Wyles went to the bin but we couldn't score a single point during his time off the field. When Jim Evans went the same way Hougaard put us away with two more penalties. The 22-9 scoreline left us adrift at the bottom with three defeats and a single point. The leaders were Wasps and they had already accumulated twelve points.

We travelled to Kingston Park for a Friday night game against Newcastle. After Evans had kicked us into a fifth minute lead with a penalty, the Falcons responded with tries from Tu'ipulotu and Swinson (both converted by Gopperth) to surge ahead. After the break, Evans got another penalty and Monye scored a try but when Camacho fouled Tu'ipulotu, Gopperth made it a six point lead with 26 minutes to go. Evans put over a third penalty and when Vickers was sent to the bin with five minutes left, he added a fourth to tie the game and stop our run of defeats. As a result of two points gained, we jumped over Leeds Carnegie into eleventh place.

For the last in a batch of five Premiership games, Bath were the visitors to the Stoop on 3rd October. In the first ten minutes, Little kicked Bath into a 6-0 lead with two penalties and Evans replied with one of his own after 16 minutes. In a largely forgettable encounter, there was no further scoring until Evans put over his second penalty with six minutes left. Then the excitement began – Hape went through the defence to put Bath five points clear but crucially, the conversion was missed so we still had a chance. Tom Guest was clean through but Clegg dropped the scoring pass. Then, as we attacked in wave after wave, Skirving went to the bin for persistent infringement and Nick Easter drove over. Wayne Barnes (the referee) went to the TMO for clarification, the decision was made and Wayne's arm was raised to signal the try. Evans converted with the final kick of the match (in running time, it was the fifteenth minute of time added on) and we had our first league win of the season; the crowd's thunderous response said it all! We moved up one place to tenth spot above Newcastle and Leeds Carnegie but were now 13 points behind leaders Saracens. Gary Botha made his farewell appearance before he returned to South Africa, he had captained the side once and scored 25 points (5 tries) during his time with us. Prop forward James Johnston came on as a sub to make the first of 105 appearances. He was in the process of winning at least 16 caps for Samoa.

As ERC had decided not to hand us a competition ban, we took our place in Pool 5 of the Heineken Cup alongside Cardiff Blues, Sale Sharks and Toulouse. Our first game was at Cardiff City Stadium the following Saturday. Because of the elite player agreement with England, we decided to rest Care, Easter and Monye and this cost us. They had to miss one game between weeks 4 and 7 and, as the week 7 fixture was Toulouse at the Stoop, there was no other option (given that our Premiership form had not been the best). The first half saw just three penalties; Nick Evans slotting one between two from Blair for the hosts. Three minutes into the third quarter, Blair hit the post with a penalty attempt from his own half and from our clearance, he began a counter-attack from which James was put over for the first try. Blair converted but Evans pulled us to within seven points with his second penalty. There were sixteen minutes left and most of these saw us constantly threatening the Cardiff line. Mike Brown dropped the ball (after a poor pass from Masson) with the line at his mercy and when we were penalised for holding on right on the line with a couple of minutes left (in the Premiership, Cardiff replacement second row Jones would have been yellow carded for going off his feet but this was Europe and the decision went against us), our chance had gone. To compound this, Jones then booted the ball into open space after an Evans kick and Halfpenny outpaced Brown to score. Blair converted again and we left with no points and were bottom of the Pool.

The Toulouse game on 17th October kicked off at 6 p.m. to suit the television company and we started well. Evans put over the customary penalty after seven minutes and doubled the lead on 21 minutes. Then, Ugo Monye shredded the Toulouse defence with his strength and acceleration to score a try after which Evans struck a post with his attempt to convert. He made up for that with his third penalty and, had Care been able to touch down his own chip ahead, our 14-0 lead at the break would have been more. The French side came out a totally different outfit in the second half and within eight minutes they were level. Monye fumbled a chip and Donguy gathered to score. He then punched the ball into touch to stop Clerc scoring but Sowerby was shoved over from a driving maul shortly afterwards. Both conversions were successfully kicked by Elissalde. When Monye gathered Brown's grubber kick and scored his second try, we were back in front but Evans again missed the conversion. Elissalde kicked a penalty at the end of the third quarter and Michalak added another to nudge Toulouse ahead. Try as we did, there was no way through and with three minutes left, Fritz put over a third from just inside his own half to make it 19-23. Another defeat but we did have a losing bonus point and if it hadn't been for costly mistakes, we could and should have won. After nine years, Jim Evans made his final appearance against Toulouse. He had captained the side once, scored 75 points (15 tries), been sent off once and put in the bin on four occasions; he made no fewer than 67 appearances as a substitute.

It was back to the Premiership the following week with a visit to Worcester. They were three points and four places above us so we had to start taking these opportunities to put some wins on the board. After Evans had missed a third minute penalty, Care dived over from a ruck to open the scoring and our fly half converted. Walker pulled back three points before Evans restored the gap. Walker and Evans exchanged penalties again before Walker dropped a goal right on half time (the last two scores coming while Ceri Jones was spending ten minutes in the bin for bringing down a maul). Walker got his third penalty but Clegg replaced Evans and immediately kicked a penalty and converted Brown's try (after he gathered Monye's kick) to make it 23-12. Another penalty exchange between Walker and Clegg made the game safe for us but the Warriors grabbed a losing bonus point with a try from Black and Walker's conversion. We climbed to eighth place, level on points with Worcester but still 13 points behind Saracens who led the way.

London Irish were second in the table so this was very much a golden opportunity to close the gap on at least one side in the top four. A record crowd of 14,282 squeezed into the Stoop on the last day of October to watch a close encounter with no tries. Clegg put us in front after three minutes, Lamb equalised and put Irish in front before Clegg got the fourth penalty of the half. There were more substitutions than points in the second 40 minutes with Hewat getting a penalty with eight minutes left and Clegg replying from 42 metres as time expired. We remained in eighth place but lost ground to Saracens as a result of the draw.

We had started interviewing for the Director of Rugby role vacated by Dean Richards and a lot of the top coaches in World rugby had been linked with the job. The latest being Ian McGeechan who had been interviewed on the day before the Irish game and was at the Stoop on the day. Mark Evans stated that a decision would be a while yet and it would take as long as it takes.

The Scarlets were our next opponents in the LV= Cup (LV= Insurance had taken over as sponsors from EDF Energy) and they came to the Stoop on 8th November. David Strettle got us off to a flying start but injured himself in the act of scoring. Rory Clegg converted but the Scarlets came back and led by half time. Priestland kicked a penalty and converted Maule's try for a 10-7 lead. We had lost Mordt as well as Strettle through injury and when Guest was sin-binned for killing the ball just before the break, we were struggling. Before Guest came back, Fenby went over for another try but we struck back with a Clegg penalty and a try from George Robson. Clegg missed the conversion and a penalty with five minutes left but the final chance of the game fell to Stoddart (the visiting full back). With the last touch of the match, he knocked-on as he tried to touch the ball down behind our goal line. As everyone else in our Pool (Worcester, Wasps and Cardiff) won, we were bottom. Hooker Matt Cairns made his debut as a sub in this one. He had won a solitary England cap and would go on to appear 33 times for us.

Our next opponents were Newcastle in another LV= Cup game and we needed to win to maintain some hope of qualifying for the semi-finals. Rory Clegg returned to his former club and promptly kicked a penalty into touch and smashed one of the floodlights! He did manage to put two penalties between the posts before Miller replied for the Falcons. Sam Smith put in a hopeful kick ahead, the back three hesitated and he managed to score the try which Clegg converted. In the second half, Newcastle's sloppy handling cost them and they failed to add to their total until a late score from Tait. Before this, Clegg had kicked two penalties from four attempts to give us a 19-8 win. As a result, we were second in the Pool behind Wasps who had 8 points to our 6. Worcester and Cardiff were a point behind us. Two young players making their debuts against the Falcons were second row Charlie Matthews (who came on as a sub) and back row Luke Wallace. They would go on to become regulars in the 1st XV and make at least 117 and 131 appearances respectively.

The Premiership returned for three weeks and we visited Franklin's Gardens to take on Northampton. This game was significant as it saw the return to action of Tom Williams after his "Bloodgate" ban. A try from Reihana and two penalties by Myler put the Saints 11-0 up after 32 minutes. Then Best was sent to the bin after an illegal challenge on Guest and Evans reduced the lead with the resulting penalty. We then managed to butcher two try scoring chances with a bad pass from Brown to Williams and a forward pass from Strettle to Williams. A punch by Percival led to a kickable penalty being reversed so we trailed by eight points at the break. Before Best came back on, Myler completed his hat-trick of penalties. Just before Kruger added a try for the home side, there was the comical sight of blood streaming from the nose of Tom Williams. However ironic it seemed, poor Tom had a suspected broken nose. On 69 minutes, Drauninui crossed for a try which Evans converted but Tonga'uiha's try sealed the match for the Saints with a couple of minutes left. Myler converted and there was just enough time for Drauninui to get another, this was converted by Mike Brown. The final score of 26-17 left us with no points and we slipped down to tenth as a result. As well as being nineteen points behind Saracens, crucially we were now nine points adrift of fourth place.

Against Gloucester at the Stoop, we fell behind to a Burns penalty and a try from Delve in the first 15 minutes. George Lowe crossed for us (Evans converted) before Sharples went over for Gloucester. Two Evans penalties brought the scores level but Burns restored the lead with his second. Evans ended the half with a lovely solo try but he failed to convert. Six minutes into the second half, Easter went over behind the posts from a clever inside pass by Care and Evans converted (as he did with Lowe's second try a few minutes later). Robinson landed a penalty to make it 32-19 and when Percival was binned for killing the ball, Sharples scored for Robinson to convert. With eleven minutes left Evans scored his third penalty and Gloucester's only response was another penalty from Robinson. The 35-29 bonus point victory put us in 7th place still eight points adrift of a play-off spot.

As we moved into December, so we reached a critical point in our season. We would play two Premiership games either side of a Heineken Cup double header with Sale Sharks. First we had a trip to Headingley to play the bottom side, Leeds Carnegie. After going behind to an early try from Welding (converted by Ford), we came back strongly and an Evans penalty was followed by a Robshaw try converted by Evans. Ford put over a penalty but a defensive lapse saw George Lowe collect a bouncing ball and run in for the easiest of scores. Evans converted and ten minutes later, Care was sent to the bin for a late tackle on Oakley. Ford got another penalty but we outscored them during the sin-binning when Robshaw scored our third try for Evans to convert. Our eleven point lead at half time increased when Evans landed a penalty after six minutes of the second half. Leeds rallied strongly and Myall was driven over and Ford converted. After Evans kicked another penalty, Denton scored for the hosts and Ford converted to make it 30-27. There were still 22 minutes left but amazingly, there were no further scores and we had our fourth league win of the season. We moved up to sixth place and the gap to fourth placed Leicester was down to just five points.

We had home advantage first against Sale in round 3 of the Heineken Cup Pool stage. It had been a longer break than normal since the Friday game at Leeds because this one was scheduled for Sunday 13th December. No team had ever qualified for the quarter finals after losing their opening two pool games and one thing was certain, if we lost, there was virtually no chance of qualification. In the first 21 minutes, Sale scored at a point a minute thanks to a rash of generosity from us. Peel, Macleod and Seymour benefited and Hodgson converted all three. Evans converted his try after 18 minutes to make it 7-14 and Strettle grabbed a second but Hodgson's penalty made it 12-24 at the interval. Four minutes into the third quarter, Easter atoned for gifting Seymour his try by reducing the deficit with our third try. Evans converted and we were back in it. Cohen got a fourth try for Sale on 51 minutes and they withstood a late onslaught from us as we tried in vain to get our first win of the campaign. It finished 19-29 and yet another Heineken Cup competition had passed us by. We were languishing at the bottom of the Pool with just a single point from our three matches. With a gap of nine points to leaders Toulouse, we were not going to make it except for a mathematical miracle. Basically, we needed three bonus point wins and for the other three teams to beat each other with no bonus points being scored on either side.

On 16th December, it was announced that Conor O'Shea would be the new Director of Rugby, succeeding Dean Richards. He was currently the National Director of the English Institute of Sport and would start his new role on 15th March 2010. With the squad assembled by Dean, exciting times lay ahead if Conor could carry them forward.

The following Sunday in driving snow and at times blizzard conditions, we played the return with Sale at Edgeley Park, Stockport. Volunteers were required to clear the pitch before the start and during the second half, the lines were swept twice to allow the game to continue. The second occasion came after 69 minutes when referee George Clancy considered calling a halt. After input from players, coaches and officials, he allowed it to finish. Up to that point, Koyamaibole had put Sale in front with a try after 3 minutes before Evans converted his own try and Aston Croall's to give us a nice lead after 30 minutes. Hodgson kicked a penalty either side of the break and the conversion of a try from Roberts to put the hosts back in front. Evans made it a one point game with a penalty but Hodgson put over his third and that was that. We had given it a go but ultimately we had failed. We were definitely out, there was no way we could reach the quarter finals now with just two points from our four matches so far. Toulouse led the way on 14 points with Sale second on 13 and Cardiff with 9.

Our final game of the year was Big Game 2 against Wasps at Twickenham on 27th December. A Guinness Premiership record crowd (outside of the final) of 76,716 turned up to smash the previous mark of 50,000. The match ball was delivered from high up via the stands by a Sea Eagle and the entertainment was provided by three X-Factor television programme finalists (Jamie Archer, Lucie Jones and Olly Murs), ABBA tribute band 1974 and singing quartet Figaro. Wasps were ahead when Simpson scored a try after two minutes before Evans and Cipriani landed two penalties each to make it 6-5 to us and then 6-11 to Wasps at the break. Cipriani missed four other kicks and Evans two. When Walder replaced Cipriani, he put over a penalty but Care scored for Evans to convert and we were back in it again. With six minutes left, Hart scored and Walder's conversion gave the visitors an all-important eight point lead which meant that Strettle's last minute score only troubled the scoreboard. Evans converted but we ended up one point behind (20-21). Two Big Games and no wins but it looked as though this Christmas fixture would be around for a few years yet. We ended the year in sixth place on 23 points, sixteen behind leaders Saracens and nine back from fourth placed Leicester. It would be an uphill struggle if we were to make the play-offs for a second successive year.

On New Year's Day 2010, we travelled up to Stockport for our third game against Sale in the last twenty days. The pitch was only passed fit an hour before kick-off after sub-zero temperatures had left some frozen patches in the corners. The first quarter was scoreless and Evans opened our account with a penalty after 21 minutes. Hodgson then kicked two for Sale and Evans put over his second in between. Right on half time, Sale burst through and Gaskell galloped home from 40 metres out. Hodgson converted and we trailed despite having the best of the half. Evans traded penalties with Hodgson and when Cohen scored a try on 56 minutes, it looked like we were heading to defeat again. Tom Guest forced his way over and Clegg converted to give us hope and, as we piled on the pressure in the final five minutes, Monye had a chance right at the end. He dived for the corner and looked to have made it but the TMO noticed Hodgson had managed to get his left foot in touch and that was that. The 21-16 defeat signalled our fourth on the trot and the losing bonus point couldn't prevent us from dropping to seventh. Tosh Masson appeared for the last time in this one. He had scored 25 points (5 tries) and appeared as a sub 13 times.

The following week, we were due to play Leeds Carnegie at the Stoop. The cold conditions were not going away and the game was postponed because of the icy condition of the stadium concourse and surrounding area; the pitch itself was playable.

On 17th January, we played the away fixture with Toulouse. After a series of missed kicks, Elissalde put the hosts in front with a penalty but we hit back on 23 minutes with a try from Brown converted by Evans. Elissalde put over two more penalties and Fritz went over under the posts for Elissalde to convert for a half time lead of 16-7. In the third quarter, Toulouse added two more tries (Bouilhou and Heymans, Elissalde converted the first) and when Medard got the bonus point score with fifteen minutes left, it was 33-7. The last two had been conceded while Jones was in the bin but we never gave up and Monye got two tries in the last six minutes (one a superb solo effort) which Evans converted to make the scoreboard a bit more presentable.

Against Cardiff Blues the following Sunday, we were at the Stoop for the first time in six weeks. Half a dozen changes had been made to our starting line-up because it was now more important for us to concentrate on other competitions. Due to a rule change, Cardiff could finish as one of the three Pool runners-up who would now qualify for the quarter finals of the Amlin Challenge Cup. They were level on 13 points with Sale so, it was likely a bonus point win would be enough because the Sharks were at home to Toulouse. It was all Quins in the first eleven minutes and after just 70 seconds, Lowe was in and we led 5-0. Clegg added a penalty but after this, we went to sleep. Gareth Thomas and Blair scored tries in a six minute spell, Blair got both conversions and Cardiff led. Easter got five points back for us but was sin-binned after Sweeney had scored Cardiff's third try. Rush got the bonus point score shortly after and Blair got his fourth conversion before Care scored the seventh try of the half for Clegg to convert. At half time, it was 28-20 to the Blues. When Easter came back on, we started leaking points as our defence went missing again. Roberts burst through to score under the posts to make the conversion easy for Blair who added a penalty. With eight minutes to go, Roberts was put away by Powell and Blair added the extras again to make it 45-20. A bitterly disappointing Heineken Cup campaign had finally ended. It was the first time we had lost all of our six pool games. Cardiff made it into the Amlin Cup because Sale could only pick up a losing bonus point against Toulouse; they went on to defeat Toulon in the final (28-21).

We now had two weeks of LV= Cup matches, the first of which was an away fixture against London Irish on 31st January. We put out a strong team as the LV= Cup was a trophy we could win. During the first half, we slowly built a lead with Nick Evans being the chief architect. He booted over two penalties in the first quarter and converted a try by Sam Smith who intercepted a pass in our 22 and sprinted 85 metres to score. After Turner-Hall went to the bin for a late challenge on Lamb, Evans extended the lead to 16-0 with his third penalty. In first half injury time, Lamb put the Irish on the board with a penalty. Into the second half, Joseph grabbed a try after 55 minutes but even when Croall was sin-binned with five minutes left, the Irish couldn't get into a winning position. In the final minute Joseph got his second but Lamb failed with the conversion (as he had with the first and two penalty attempts). The 16-13 win had put us in with a shout of a semi-final spot, we just had to do better than Cardiff Blues and London Wasps in the last round of matches. The Pool situation was Cardiff and Quins 10 points, Wasps 9 and Worcester 5. Tomas Vallejos Cinalli made the first of 60 appearances when he came on as a substitute. He would go on to win at least 6 caps for Argentina.

By the time we kicked-off against Gloucester at the Stoop the following Sunday, Cardiff had beaten the Scarlets 38-23 to take their points total to 15. We had to beat Gloucester by a big margin and score eleven tries to get through; the odds were against us. We started really well and Evans kicked us in front after 5 minutes with a penalty. He then converted a try by James Percival and added two of his own but was unable to convert either. We led 20-0 but the Cherry and Whites came back to cut the lead to just six points by half time. Simpson-Daniel and Taylor scored tries and Taylor converted both. Evans got his kicking off to a good start again and landed two penalties in the third quarter to put us 26-14 up with 22 minutes remaining. Even when Vallejos Cinalli went to the bin for ten minutes between penalties, Gloucester couldn't score but Simpson-Daniel eventually got his second to give them some hope. With ten minutes to go, Evans banged over his fourth penalty to give us a ten point advantage. Future Quin Tim Molenaar scored Gloucester's fourth try to earn a bonus point and unbelievably, Voyce went over from close range to make it 29-29. With the last kick of the match, Taylor successfully converted and we had thrown it away. Gloucester on the other hand won their Pool as a result of this dramatic win. In the end, we finished behind Cardiff and Wasps in our Pool – a very disappointing end to another competition for us. Waisea Luveniyali played his last game for us in this one, coming on as a sub. He had scored 57 points (1 try, 6 penalties and 17 conversions) during his two seasons with us.

It was Gloucester again the next week as we travelled to Kingsholm for a Guinness Premiership match. We now had a run of ten league games in the race for a play-off spot. After Robinson had put Gloucester in front with a couple of penalties, he converted Vainikolo's try before Evans put us on the board with two penalties of his own. Before the break, Molenaar went over as well to make it 18-6. Before the hour mark, Simpson-Daniel and Voyce had scored and with Robinson's conversions, they were out of sight. We completely lost the plot and in the final five minutes, the free-flowing play of Gloucester rubbed our noses in it. Simpson-Daniel completed his hat-trick and Taylor converted both to make the final score 46-6. This was the first time Gloucester had scored over forty points against us in fixtures going back to 1913. Needless to say it was their biggest winning margin against us beating the previous best of 26 points (7-33 on 13th October 2001). Having gone through the whole of the previous season and up to Christmas without conceding forty points, we had now done so twice in four games. We now dropped to ninth place and would need to win practically every game to stand a chance of reaching the play-offs. We trailed Leicester by 21 points and fourth placed London Irish by 13 points.

Northampton came to the Stoop on 20th February in third place. Five changes were made to the starting line-up and although both sides were missing international players, there was still a lot of talent on show. The first quarter belonged entirely to us and after Nick Evans had put over two penalties, Mike Brown went over for what proved to be the only try of the game. Evans converted and our 13-0 lead remained until six minutes into the second half when Myler popped over a penalty for the Saints. Ten minutes later, he repeated the feat but that was as close as they got. The visitors missed four penalties and Evans failed with one but we had an excellent win against the form side in the Premiership. As a result, we moved into seventh place but still eleven points off a play-off spot. The best we could hope for realistically was a place in the Heineken Cup next season as our form was just not good enough.

Just under a month after our LV= Cup win, we returned to Reading to meet London Irish in the Premiership. The Irish President (Mary McAleese) was at the game and both teams were presented to her before kick-off. After Homer had opened the scoring with a penalty, we had a period of pressure that resulted in a penalty try being awarded and Evans converted to put us in front. By half time, the Irish had opened up a twelve point lead (Homer kicked three penalties and converted Armitage's try). The second half began the same way and Homer's fifth penalty was followed by his conversion of future Quin Nick Kennedy's try (our old fly half Chris Malone was also in the Irish side). After a host of chances on both sides, George Lowe scored in the corner for Evans to convert but sadly for us, that was the end of the scoring. The 29-14 defeat dropped us to eighth place and we were now only five points above Leeds Carnegie in twelfth position. Steve So'oialo came on to make his final appearance for us in what was his 34th as a substitute. He had scored 80 points (16 tries) and visited the bin three times.

Next up were Worcester Warriors at the Stoop on 6th March. They were in tenth but only a single point above the relegation spot. With Nick Evans failing a late fitness test on his knee, Rory Clegg started for only the second time in a Premiership game. After Brown had put us in front with a try after seven minutes, Benjamin equalised in similar fashion three minutes later. Into the second half, Worcester took the lead with a penalty from Jones, Clegg brought us level and this was repeated to make it 11-11 with fifteen minutes to go. Four minutes later, Clegg put over his third penalty, this time from 50 metres to nudge us ahead and we held on for a narrow win. We stayed in eighth place, nine points above Sale who were now bottom and eleven adrift of Wasps in fourth.

Because of the LV= Cup semi-finals and final, our next game at the Rec against Bath would not take place until 27th March. Conor O'Shea was at Bath to watch the game and to get an idea of the task he faced. Barkley put Bath in front with a penalty after 5 minutes and converted his own try twenty minutes later. After Claassens was binned for a high and early tackle on Strettle, Evans put us on the board with two penalties before the break. He then missed one at the start of the second half and with Bath back to full strength, Bell and Maddock scored tries within four minutes of each other and Barkley's conversions took them clear. A late try from Tom Williams which Evans converted made it 24-13. O'Shea said afterwards that the team could have thrown in the towel but didn't and that told him something about his players. We stayed in eighth, Worcester were now bottom and we trailed the leaders Leicester by a massive 26 points with five games left.

The following Saturday, Newcastle came to the Stoop level on points with us after a midweek win over Gloucester. Gopperth put the Falcons in front with a penalty but then went to the bin for a spear tackle. During his absence, Evans stole the show with a penalty and a side-stepping run to the posts from the touch line for our first try. His conversion made it 10-3 and Gopperth returned to cut the deficit to four points with a penalty on 36 minutes. When Walker went over, the visitors led by a point but Evans quickly restored our advantage with two penalties.

Gopperth made it a tight finish with his third but Evans saw us home when he finished off a move and converted to deny Newcastle any points. This win more or less guaranteed our survival in the Premiership but it looked unlikely we would get anything else.

Just over three months later than planned, Leeds Carnegie came to the Stoop on 10th April only three points above Worcester at the foot of the table. We got off to a solid start and Evans landed penalties either side of a Tom Williams try (which he also converted). Thomas got a penalty back for Leeds to make it 13-3 at half time. Brown scored a try (converted by Evans) and Thomas got his second penalty in the third quarter before the turning point came on 62 minutes. Leeds flanker Clark was binned for a late tackle on Evans and the floodgates opened. During his time off, Lowe, Brooker, Brown and Strettle ran in tries. Evans converted the first and third and Clegg got the last. When Clark returned, it was 46-6 and although the visitors scored last with a try from To'oala, they had been thrashed. Luckily for them, Worcester failed to get any points so they remained bottom. We moved into seventh just one point behind Bath. There were three matches left but two of them were away to Saracens and Leicester and they would dictate if we were in the Heineken Cup next season.

At Wembley the following week, we met third placed Saracens. In front of 47,106 spectators, we failed to turn up and our defence was repeatedly opened up. Nick Evans had been a late withdrawal with a hamstring injury and that certainly didn't help. Hougaard opened the scoring with a penalty and Clegg equalised before Saull scored a brace of tries in as many minutes. Hougaard converted the second and added a second penalty after Brooker had scored for us but we trailed by ten points at the break. Brits got a third try for Saracens, Jackson converted and when Brown went to the bin, Tagicakibau secured the bonus point (the TMO had just denied Burger a try). Brown returned but Saracens just kept scoring and Joubert got their fifth try which Jackson converted to make it 37-8. In the last three minutes, we scored twice through Monye and Chris York; neither try was converted and it finished 37-18. We stayed in seventh but our qualification chances for the Heineken Cup had all but disappeared. Bath were ten points clear and they would need to lose both remaining games while we won both and secured bonus points. Gonzalo Tiesi made his last appearance for us against Saracens and his only one as a sub; he had scored 30 points (6 tries).

At Welford Road on 24th April, Leicester needed to win to secure a home semi-final in the play-offs. They were in their usual situation near the top of the table and we effectively had little to play for. After only four minutes, Flood scored the opening try, converted it and then added a penalty to put the Tigers on their way. Care, whose pass was intercepted on half way by Flood for his try made amends by scoring one of his own after ten minutes. Clegg converted but Flood stretched the lead with two penalties. We came back strongly and Strettle and Care put Lowe in for a try which Clegg converted. He then dropped a goal to give us a narrow 17-16 lead at the break. As had happened against Leeds, a sin-binning turned the tide but this time, Robshaw went off and Leicester scored seventeen unanswered points before he came back. Flood kicked a penalty and converted tries from Smith and Youngs. The bonus point try came by way of a penalty try which Flood converted. We did get into Leicester territory long enough for Marler to score our third try but it only affected the final score (22-40). This was the fourteenth game on the trot without a win over Tigers. The only time we had avoided defeat since May 2003 was in Big Game 1. Hooker Rob Buchanan made his debut as a substitute and would go on to make at least 89 appearances. Gloucester over took us so we dropped back to eighth in the table. It seemed this was the best we could hope for and victory in our final match of the season at home to Sale Sharks would make sure it got no worse.

On 8th May, the season ended for us and a long and gruelling marathon ultimately brought nothing. Worcester had already been relegated because even a five point win would only bring them level on points but

Sale had a superior number of wins. After only four minutes, James Percival was stretchered off to be replaced by Vallejos Cinalli. Almost immediately, Lowe was through to open the scoring. Evans missed the conversion but did add the extras to Strettle's try on seven minutes. Hodgson opened Sale's account with a penalty but was then replaced before Tait scored after Vallejos Cinalli was binned for deliberate obstruction. Thomas converted to make it a two point game at half time (12-10). We trailed briefly when Thomas dropped a goal but Clegg (who had replaced Evans) quickly put over a penalty and Easter scored our third try at the end of the third quarter. Clegg landed another penalty but Sale were not finished and Koyamaibole scored for Thomas to convert and it was all to play for with nine minutes left. In the last six minutes, we crossed for two more scores. First, Turner-Hall secured the bonus point (Clegg converted) and with the final move of the match, Tom Williams ran in. Tani Fuga (in his last match for the Club) attempted the conversion but missed and the season ended with a 35-20 victory. With all stoppages included, this game ran for 101 minutes and this was the shape of things to come. We did finish eighth which, after all the troubles caused by "Bloodgate", whilst disappointing was not the end of the world. We said goodbye to two other players in addition to Fuga, they were James Percival and David Strettle. Fuga came on for his 63rd appearance as a sub; he had scored 130 points (26 tries) and been sin-binned seven times. Percival had scored 10 points (2 tries) and had been to the bin twice. Strettle had scored 105 points (21 tries) and been to the bin on one occasion.

The overall playing record was P35 W14 D3 L18 F696 A769. In the league it was P22 W9 D2 L11 F420 A484 Pts 46 (BP 6 – TB 3 LB 3) Pos 8th. Once again, no one appeared in all 35 matches. Tom Guest missed just one, George Lowe played in all but two and Ceri Jones (31) and David Strettle (30) were next. No one else managed to reach thirty appearances although Andress and Stevenson got to 29. George Lowe got the most tries (9) and Nick Evans scored the most points with 266 (7 tries, 51 penalties and 39 conversions). As a result, he finished top of the penalties and conversions. Rory Clegg dropped the only goal. Overall, we scored 76 tries (down by 24), dropped goals fell by three to only one, penalties rose by three to 69 but conversions dropped from 62 to 53. As a result, total points were down by 138 to 696.

2009/10

140809	CONNACHT	TWICKENHAM STOOP	W	1G1PG1T(15)-3PG1T(14)
220809	EDINBURGH	EDINBURGH	W	4G1T(33)-1G3PG(16)
290809	CORNISH PIRATES	TWICKENHAM STOOP	W	6G1T(47)-2G1PG(17)
050909	LONDON WASPS(GP)	TWICKENHAM(A)	L	1G1PG1T(15)-1G3PG2T(26)
120909	LEICESTER(GP)	TWICKENHAM STOOP	L	3PG(9)-5PG(15)
190909	SARACENS(GP)	TWICKENHAM STOOP	L	3PG(9)-1G2DG3PG(22)
250909	NEWCASTLE(GP)	NEWCASTLE	D	4PG1T(17)-2G1PG(17)
031009	BATH(GP)	TWICKENHAM STOOP	W	1G2PG(13)-2PG1T(11)
101009	CARDIFF BLUES(HECP)	CARDIFF	L	2PG(6)-2G2PG(20)
171009	TOULOUSE(HECP)	TWICKENHAM STOOP	L	3PG2T(19)-2G3PG(23)
241009	WORCESTER(GP)	WORCESTER	W	2G4PG(26)-1G1DG4PG(22)

311009	LONDON IRISH(GP)	TWICKENHAM STOOP	D	3PG(9)-3PG(9)
081109	SCARLETS(LVCGP)	TWICKENHAM STOOP	D	1G1PG1T(15)-1G1PG1T(15)
151109	NEWCASTLE(LVCGP)	NEWCASTLE	W	1G4PG(19)-1PG1T(8)
211109	NORTHAMPTON(GP)	NORTHAMPTON	L	2G1PG(17)-1G3PG2T(26)
281109	GLOUCESTER(GP)	TWICKENHAM STOOP	W	3G3PG1T(35)-1G4PG2T(29)
061209	LEEDS CARNEGIE(GP)	HEADINGLEY	W	3G3PG(30)-3G2PG(27)
131209	SALE SHARKS(HECP)	TWICKENHAM STOOP	L	2G1T(19)-3G1PG1T(29)
201209	SALE SHARKS(HECP)	EDGELEY PARK	L	2G1PG(17)-1G3PG1T(21)
271209	LONDON WASPS(GP)	TWICKENHAM	L	2G2PG(20)-1G3PG1T(21)
010110	SALE SHARKS(GP)	EDGELEY PARK	L	1G3PG(16)-1G3PG1T(21)
090110	LEEDS CARNEGIE(GP)	TWICKENHAM STOOP	P	
170110	TOULOUSE(HECP)	TOULOUSE	L	3G(21)-2G3PG2T(33)
240110	CARDIFF BLUES(HECP)	TWICKENHAM STOOP	L	1G1PG2T(20)-6G1PG(45)
310110	LONDON IRISH(LVCGP)	READING	W	1G3PG(16)-1PG2T(13)
070210	GLOUCESTER(LVCGP)	TWICKENHAM STOOP	L	1G4PG2T(29)-3G2T(31)
130210	GLOUCESTER(GP)	GLOUCESTER	L	2PG(6)-5G2PG1T(46)
200210	NORTHAMPTON(GP)	TWICKENHAM STOOP	W	1G2PG(13)-2PG(6)
280210	LONDON IRISH(GP)	READING	L	2G(14)-2G5PG(29)
060310	WORCESTER(GP)	TWICKENHAM STOOP	W	3PG1T(14)-2PG1T(11)
270310	BATH(GP)	BATH	L	1G2PG(13)-3G1PG(24)
030410	NEWCASTLE(GP)	TWICKENHAM STOOP	W	2G3PG(23)-3PG1T(14)
100410	LEEDS CARNEGIE(GP)	TWICKENHAM STOOP	W	5G2PG1T(46)-2PG1T(11)
170410	SARACENS(GP)	WEMBLEY	L	1PG3T(18)-3G2PG2T(37)
240410	LEICESTER(GP)	LEICESTER	L	2G1DG1T(22)-4G4PG(40)
080510	SALE SHARKS(GP)	TWICKENHAM STOOP	W	2G2PG3T(35)-2G1DG1PG(20)

In June 2010, England returned to Australia and New Zealand for a five match tour. They played two tests against Australia and tied the series. After losing the first 17-27, they sneaked home by a single point in the second (21-20). The other three games produced a win and a draw with the Australian Barbarians and a loss to the New Zealand

Maori. Care and Easter played in both tests, Care coming on as a sub in the second. Ugo Monye, Chris Robshaw, former Quin Strettle and future player Paul Doran-Jones appeared in some of the other games.

From June 2010, we had an agreement with the University of Surrey to use their new state of the art facilities at the Surrey Sports Park near Guildford. This was to be the best training base we have ever had, enabling everything to be located in one spot and we would be investing over £500,000 into the site.

It was announced on 25th November 2010 that our Chief Executive had resigned and would leave his job at the end of February 2011. Mark Evans had survived the "Bloodgate" scandal and started to set the Club back on to the right track. He would set up a sports consultancy business and then go on to become the CEO of Melbourne Storm Rugby League Club in Australia. He said that when he joined, we were a tiny club with a fantastic history and tradition and he was leaving it in good hands with a great fan base and attendance figures. David Morgan would step into his shoes until a replacement had been found. The accounts revealed yet another loss for year ending 30th June 2011 of £1,890,775; it was proving impossible to get anywhere near a break even figure. Evans, Herridge and Looker all resigned as Directors and Paul Brewer and Andy Mullins came in.

Will Skinner's two season term as captain came to an end and Chris Robshaw was announced on 22nd July 2010 as the next one. Chris was seen by Conor O'Shea as a star in the making and so it proved. The season started with three friendly fixtures, the first of which was a testimonial for our long serving hooker Tani Fuga on 6th August at the Stoop. Our opponents were billed as a Southern Hemisphere All Stars XV but they were no match for a well drilled Quins team. In the first eight minutes, Camacho, Williams and Skinner scored tries and Evans converted them all for a 21-0 lead. When one of the All Stars was binned for a high tackle on Williams, three more tries followed. James Johnston, Lowe and Brown were the scorers and as Evans only missed the conversion of Lowe's try, we led 40-0 at half time. The All Stars were making changes on a rolling basis and many were also made during the interval. Two thirds of our starting XV changed and this altered the game completely and the scoring dried up. Joe Gray went over on 50 minutes, Clegg converted and did the same to the first of a brace from Wallace (scored when a second All Star was in the bin). The final try (Wallace's second) was the last act in the game and made the final score 59-0. Tom Casson (a centre) made his first appearance when he came on as a sub and would go on to make at least 65 appearances. Joe Gray (hooker) also appeared as a sub in his first game and would make at least 123 appearances and win 1 England cap and Ollie Smith was another making his debut (again as a sub), he was a centre who had won 5 England caps and one for the British Lions against Argentina in 2005. Unfortunately, his career with us would be cut short through injury and he would only make 14 appearances.

After a week's training in Ireland, we played Connacht on 13th August at the Sportsground and another victory was secured. Jordan Turner-Hall got the first try after 14 minutes and we followed that with further efforts from Cairns and Brown. Evans converted all three but our lead at the break was only fourteen points because O'Loughlin scored for Connacht and Keatley converted. After the usual raft of changes at half time, we grabbed three tries in ten minutes to make the result a formality. Williams, Jones and Camacho provided them and Clegg put over two conversions for a 40-7 scoreline.

Our final friendly was a Saturday game on 21st August against Ulster at the Stoop. Chris Robshaw made his first start as Club captain as we attempted to continue our winning start. After 15 minutes, Danny Care got our first try which Evans converted. Our fly half then added a penalty and converted Monye's try right on half time. Despite a good lead, we were making a lot of errors. Six changes were made by us after 52 minutes but a score was not forthcoming until half way through the final quarter. Joe Marler was one of the substitutes and scored our third try for Clegg to convert. That made the final score 24-0 and we would go into the Premiership opener at Twickenham on

4th September against Wasps in good stead. Benjamin Urdapilleta was a fly half/centre from Argentina who was in the process of winning 10 caps; he came on as a sub and would go on to make 18 appearances for us.

Guinness had ended their sponsorship of the Premiership and they were succeeded by Aviva. So, it all began again with the London Double Header being rounded off by us and Wasps; an exciting game ensued. After only two minutes, Evans opened up the Wasps defence to send Easter over for a try which he converted. Van Gisbergen and Evans then exchanged penalties twice before Powell and Varndell went over for tries. Van Gisbergen converted both to wipe out our lead. On 31 minutes, Worsley went to the bin for playing the ball in an offside position but another exchange of penalties between the two kickers were the only points scored until the break. During the third quarter, Evans landed penalties either side of a van Gisbergen effort and when he converted Mike Brown's try, we led 29-26 with 13 minutes left. Unfortunately, we couldn't close it out and van Gisbergen had one last chance and he converted his fifth penalty on 74 minutes to make the final result a 29-29 draw. After only one round, we were in seventh place with London Irish the early pace setters.

When Northampton came to town a week later, they established a nice lead in the first half. Geraghty landed two penalties and converted Ashton's try before Evans put over a penalty after 40 minutes. He then slotted two more and converted Lowe's try to put us ahead after 56 minutes. We held the lead for thirteen minutes until Hartley scored for Geraghty to add the extras. With seven minutes to go, Evans missed a penalty in front of the posts and despite last-ditch efforts from Marler and Care, Northampton held on and we went down by four points (16-20). We slipped to tenth place, two points above Leeds Carnegie in twelfth and six behind leaders Bath.

At Edgeley Park, Stockport on 11th September, we met Sale Sharks and after five successive defeats there, we needed a win. It all began so well when Lowe scored after five minutes, Evans converted and despite two penalties from Macleod, we had a healthy lead at the break because Evans put over a penalty and converted Turner-Hall's try. The third quarter remained scoreless but we lost Ollie Smith to the bin. When Vallejos Cinalli followed him after 63 minutes, it all proved too much. Cueto scored almost immediately and when Tonetti scored eight minutes later, Macleod's conversion put Sale ahead. When we were back to full strength, Macleod popped over another penalty and we were left ruing our indiscipline. A furious Conor O'Shea could hardly contain himself afterwards but it mattered not, we were still searching for a first Premiership win of the season. Although, had Evans not been hauled down just short of the line it might have been different. We needed to learn how to close games out and until we did this, trophies would not come easily or frequently. We dropped to 11th, three points above Leeds Carnegie. Northampton were nine points ahead so we needed to get our act together quickly before it was too late.

New boys Exeter Chiefs visited on 25th September for what had become a must win game for us. Two penalties from Evans in the opening eight minutes were cancelled out by two from Steenson for the Chiefs. In the last quarter of an hour of the first half, Evans got another penalty and converted a try from Nick Easter. The game was ended as a contest when Exeter suffered two sin-bins between 50th and 69th minutes for not retreating ten metres at a penalty. Thomas and Hanks went off and they were briefly down to 13 men. During that time, Evans kicked a penalty and converted Camacho's try and a penalty try to make it 33-6. Tom Guest secured the bonus point after 76 minutes before Foster got Exeter's first try right on full time. Evans and Davis converted their respective tries and we had our first win. The five points catapulted us into seventh place.

The last game in the first batch of Premiership fixtures was against Newcastle Falcons on 2nd October at the Stoop. In the first half, Evans got us off to a good start with a penalty and then replied each time to Gopperth's penalties to leave us 9-6 ahead. After we had a try turned down by the TMO, Golding was binned after a succession of problem scrums (he had only been on for three minutes). After this, the referee awarded us a penalty try and

Evans converted for a 16-6 lead. After 50 and 53 minutes, Gopperth put over penalties and the match was in the balance until Guest went over from a five metre scrum for Evans to convert. We stayed in seventh but were level on match points with Gloucester and Leicester above us. London Irish led the way on 20 points but at least we were now in the mix.

Our failure to qualify for the Heineken Cup meant we were in the Amlin Challenge Cup. We occupied Pool 1 along with Bayonne, I Cavalieri Prato and Connacht. Our first match was away in Bayonne and torrential rain had turned the pitch into a lake. The game went ahead in farcical conditions and Evans put over a penalty after three minutes to nudge us ahead. Bayonne replied with a try from Pietersen that went unconverted due to the strengthening wind. It was in our favour and Evans slotted another penalty from 55 metres to regain the lead. His third and fourth efforts stretched it to seven points (the first of these came after Mazars had been binned for a late tackle on Care). Boyet made up for earlier misses by slotting a penalty after 33 minutes. Four minutes into the second half, the ball was hacked through and, as Mike Brown went to collect, it stopped dead in its tracks in a pool of water, Brown overshot and Gerber kicked on to score the try. After Boyet and Evans had each missed shots at goal, Robshaw was binned for a late tackle and Garcia put over the penalty. Right at the end, we were camped on the Bayonne line but got penalised and we had been beaten 16-12.

Six days later on 16th October, Italian side I Cavalieri Prato from Tuscany visited the Stoop. Ten changes were made to the starting line up from the Bayonne game to cope with the perceived weaker side we were playing. In the first ten minutes, Clegg and Wakarua-Noema exchanged penalties and that was as close as it got. Tom Williams scored the first try after 11 minutes and this was followed at regular intervals by tries from Ross Chisholm, Lowe, a penalty try and Chisholm's second. Clegg converted all but the first to leave us 36-3 ahead at the break. The second half was closer and Cavalieri scored first and last. Majstorovic went over for Wakarua-Noema to convert as he did when Lewis-Pratt scored a minute from time. In between, Williams completed his hat-trick either side of Sam Smith's effort. Rory Clegg converted the second and third as we stormed to the top of the Pool (55-17).

It was back to Aviva Premiership action the following Saturday with a visit to Gloucester. After Robinson had kicked a penalty to put the home side ahead, we responded with a try from Care. Evans converted and added a penalty after Lewis went over and Robinson converted. In seven minutes around the half hour mark, Gloucester scored thirteen points (two penalties from Robinson who converted a try by Sharples) to which our only reply was a penalty from Evans. When Robinson put over his fourth penalty on 43 minutes, it looked all over. When future Quin Paul Doran-Jones was binned, Evans converted his own try and added a penalty when Wood went the same way. The home side were down to 13 for a brief time but when they were back to 15, Evans levelled the scores with his fourth penalty. Deacon went over with three minutes to go, Robinson converted and as we pressed for the opportunity to make it a draw, Robshaw went over right at the end. The referee (Tim Wigglesworth) decided that he didn't make it and without a TMO to check, that was the end of the game. The farce of only televised matches having a TMO would be addressed in the future so that all games whether broadcast live or not would have a TMO present and available to the referee. Once again, we stayed in seventh by virtue of our losing bonus point.

Bath were one point ahead of us when they visited the Stoop on 31st October. After 5 minutes, Bath flanker Lewis Moody left the pitch with blood pouring from a head wound and returned ten minutes later with as many stitches inserted. During that time, Barkley had put Bath ahead with a penalty and this proved to be the only score in an error strewn first forty. After 45 minutes, he repeated the feat but Evans was equal to it and his came after 59 and 63 minutes. Unfortunately, the second half had been as bad as the first regarding errors and a draw was probably a fair result. Both sides increased their points by two and stayed in sixth and seventh (as they had been at the start of play).

The LV= Cup took pride of place for two weeks now and our first fixture was at Leicester on Friday 5th November. Of course, both sides were shorn of most of their current international players because of the autumn internationals. We were in Pool 4 alongside Exeter, Bath and Ospreys but, as was usual, we would not play any of them. In a first half dominated by penalty kicks, we got off to a good start when Evans kicked his first after only two minutes. Twelvetrees replied after four minutes but Evans added three more in nine minutes. Twelvetrees replied in kind and after 31 minutes, it was 12-12. Vallejos Cinalli went over for us and Evans converted but missed a long range penalty attempt. Despite the pouring rain, we were putting in a good performance and when Hawkins was binned, Evans landed the penalty for a 22-12 lead at the break. The penalties continued after and Twelvetrees knocked over his fifth and sixth but our lead was increased slightly because Guest got our second try in between (converted by Evans). With 15 minutes to go, Camacho gathered a cross-field kick from Evans and went over for the game clinching try. After Brooker was binned the Tigers were awarded a penalty try (converted by Ford) and try as they did, there was no way through to secure a losing bonus point. The 34-25 win was our first at Welford Road since 1997, a run of 14 straight defeats. Bath and Exeter also won so we were all tied at the top of Pool 4.

The Newcastle Falcons came to the Stoop on Sunday 14th November in another LV= Cup game. As it was Remembrance Sunday, a minute's silence was held and the Last Post was sounded on a bitterly cold afternoon. After just two minutes, Young was binned for hands in the ruck and before he returned, we had the lead because Sam Smith scored for Clegg to convert. Just after the Falcons had levelled with a try from Pennycook (converted by Manning), Clegg was stretchered off with a neck injury (it was a precaution and he was fine). His replacement Ben Urdapilleta landed a penalty after Pennycook had gone off for ten minutes but couldn't convert York's try three minutes later. Manning put over two penalties before the interval to make it 15-13. Urdapilleta put over a penalty and converted a penalty try but ex-Quin Charlie Amesbury went over between the posts for Manning to convert. When Swinson became the third Falcons player to visit the sin bin, Urdapilleta made no mistake with the penalty after 61 minutes. There was no further scoring and, although we had won again, it should have been by a larger margin if only because of all the yellow cards. We topped the Pool because Exeter drew and Bath lost. The Ospreys jumped into second place with a win over Leicester. Maurie "Big Mo" Fa'asavalu made his debut and would go on to make 85 appearances for us and win at least 27 caps for Samoa. He was a destructive flanker in true Samoan style and many would feel the power of his tackling over the next four seasons.

Three Aviva Premiership matches followed before rounds 3 and 4 of the Amlin Challenge Cup. Just two weeks after our LV= Cup win, we were back at Welford Road for another Friday night game. Nick Evans kicked us into an early 6-0 lead with two penalties in the first ten minutes. It was all Quins at this point, Evans was tackled just short of the line and then sent Tom Guest clear but his pass to Williams to give the winger a clear run in was forward. After this Guest ran 50 metres but Evans couldn't hold the scoring pass and another chance had gone. By half time, Twelvetrees had put Leicester in front with three penalties and in the first ten minutes of the second half landed another three to make it 18-6. He did miss one and as we tried to get back into it, more chances went begging. When Williams finally scored, Evans converted but that was the end of the game. We got a losing bonus point but really we should have won quite easily instead of going down 13-18. We dropped to ninth and once again, it was quickly becoming a case of a big gap opening up making Heineken Cup qualification (let alone a play-off place) a massive task.

Bottom club Leeds Carnegie visited on 28th November. The weather was freezing cold but we were red hot! After Thomas had put the visitors in front with a penalty after 3 minutes, we struck back with tries from Robshaw and Dickson. Evans converted both and put over a penalty. Thomas replied with his second but Evans got another and converted his own try to make it 27-6 at the interval. Leeds were struggling and it only took five minutes for us to gain the try bonus. Tom Guest got through some weak tackling and Evans converted before Blackett got a try back for Leeds. There was no let up for them though and Brown scored another. Blackett got his second (converted by Thomas) but Ross Chisholm (converted by Clegg) and Brooker scored numbers six and seven to leave the final score at 51-18. We moved up one place to eighth, well away from Leeds but still playing catch-up.

On 5th December, we played Saracens for the last time at Vicarage Road, Watford. They had recovered from their woes and were building a strong squad. Many people asked questions as to how they kept under the salary cap but the only ones who knew the answer were Sarries and they weren't giving an answer that satisfied everyone. We made a decent start when George Lowe went over after a mistake by Brits. Evans missed the conversion and that set the tone for the rest of the match. Farrell pulled back three points with a penalty and added a second after converting Strettle's try. Disaster struck when Ollie Smith went down with a nasty knee injury. He wouldn't play for us again and his career was over. Evans did get two penalties but Brits scored for Saracens in between and Farrell's conversion made it a nine point lead at half time. The game petered out in the second half and we went down without even a whimper. Farrell outscored Evans 2-1 in the penalty stakes and that was that. Sarries went into third place, we stayed in eighth.

The double header in our Amlin Challenge Cup Pool was against Connacht. We had home advantage in the first game on 12th December. Tom Guest, deputising for virus victim Nick Easter, got us off to a great start when he ran in from outside the Connacht 22. Evans converted, added a penalty and grabbed a second between two from Nikora for Connacht. Our interval lead of seven points was added to when Guest made 40 metres before supplying Brown with the scoring pass (Evans converted). Nikora landed a third penalty after 57 minutes and, despite losing Camacho for ten minutes for not rolling away in the tackle, we comfortably held on for the win. We slipped to second in the Pool on tries scored as Bayonne thrashed I Cavalieri Prato 65-7.

Just five days later, we travelled to a bitterly cold Sportsground in Galway for the return. Hundreds of tons of straw had been laid on the pitch so it was completely playable. The first half was full of errors and penalties from both sides. Evans put us in front twice only for Nikora to peg us back. In the ten minutes before half time, he landed three more but Connacht could only get one from Keatley to briefly make it 12-9. The second half began in near blizzard conditions and with us reduced to 14 men as Turner-Hall had been binned after 37 minutes for an off the ball offence. Just before he came back, Upton was sent the same way for illegal use of the elbow and before the end, Hagan went off his feet at a ruck and saw yellow as well. We soaked up the home side's pressure and were camped on their line at the end when a series of drives were inches short. No matter, we had done enough but trailed Bayonne by a point because they had again got the try bonus point against Cavalieri.

Big Game 3 took place on Monday 27th December and this time our opponents were London Irish. The entertainment included the winner of the 2010 version of ITV show X Factor, Matt Cardle and runner-up Rebecca Ferguson plus Jamie Archer from the 2009 series amongst others. The match kicked-off at 4.30 p.m. and a crowd of 74,212 turned up. The first half turned into a kicking duel between Nick Evans and old boy Chris Malone. We went ahead twice but the Irish levelled each time. Evans put over two more, Malone replied and sandwiched a fourth between two more from Evans. Just before the last one, Casey went to the bin for an offence at a ruck. Into the second half, the penalties continued; Malone scored first, Casey returned, Evans scored, Care went to the bin and Malone put over the thirteenth successful penalty of the match to make it 21-18 in our favour. While we were still down to 14 men, Turner-Hall put a kick through the defence for Lowe to reach first and score the only try of the game. Evans converted and with eleven minutes left, we led by ten points. The Irish were camped on our line for most of the time remaining but were unable to score anything despite winning a number of penalties. It was the eighth successive defeat in all competitions for the Exiles. Because only three matches were played, we leap-frogged Exeter into seventh place on 26 points level with Gloucester.

On New Year's Day 2011, we travelled to Northampton. The Saints had not been beaten at home since May 2010 and given our past record at Franklin's Gardens, a win didn't look likely. In the first ten minutes, Evans missed a couple of penalties but did get his third attempt after Myler had put the home side in front in similar fashion after 25 minutes. Right on half time, disaster struck when, from a series of scrum penalties first Andress and then Easter were sent packing for ten minutes each. The next scrum had predictable consequences when we went backwards and the referee (Dean Richards) awarded a penalty try (converted by Myler). For the first ten minutes of the second half, a series of superb driving plays ran down the clock and we held on without conceding further points before the offenders returned. After 52 minutes, Care charged down a clearance kick by Myler, recovered the ball and scored for Evans to convert. Two Evans penalties gave us a small but significant lead and Northampton's only response was a Geraghty penalty to make the final score 16-13. We were now in sixth place, level on points with London Irish.

The following Saturday, we played the return with London Wasps. We were now regularly putting out a match day squad containing 21 English qualified players out of 23 and Conor O'Shea stated that we were deliberately taking a leaf out of the books of great clubs like Leicester, Bath and Wasps who have traditionally won their trophies with a big English contingent. A number of them were products of our own academy which was now providing regularly players who would one day make the top grade. One of these opened the scoring for us after 17 minutes; Joe Marler went over in the corner but five minutes later we fell behind. Haughton scored and van Gisbergen converted but their lead was short lived because Mike Brown grabbed our second try, Evans converted but missed when Easter scored the third. We spent most of the second half on the defensive but played superbly and Wasps could only manage a penalty from Walder. Our 17-10 victory moved us ahead of Wasps into fourth spot but we still trailed Leicester by ten points. There was now a rest from the Premiership until 12th February and the gap would be filled by the last two games in the Amlin Cup and the LV= Cup respectively.

The first of these was the away fixture against I Cavalieri Prato and the least we needed was a bonus point victory. Maurie Fa'asavalu got us off to a great start with a try after 11 minutes. Rory Clegg converted and kicked a penalty between two from Wakarua-Noema. Bocca went to the bin and when he returned, we were 20-6 ahead (Care had scored, Clegg converted and added a penalty). Wakarua-Noema got his third penalty after 45 minutes but Sam Smith got a double to secure the bonus point, Clegg converted both and the game was safe entering the final quarter. Moore did get across the line for Cavalieri and Wakarua-Noema converted but Casson and Dickson finished them off. Clegg's conversion made it 48-16 and with Connacht beating Bayonne in France, we led the Pool on 19 points. Bayonne had fifteen so, even a losing bonus point in a low scoring game at home to them the following week would see us into the quarter finals.

As it was, we were starting to become consistent and the team was beginning to move into the vein of form needed to win trophies. Bayonne came to the Stoop knowing they had to win and took the lead after four minutes with a penalty by Garcia. Nick Evans quickly snuffed that out by converting his own try but Garcia put over two more penalties to regain the lead for the visitors. Evans added two penalties of his own either side of Filipo's try that ensured Bayonne led by a point at the interval (13-14). Within a minute of the restart, George Lowe went in under the posts and got his second just seven minutes later. Evans converted both and Garcia put over a penalty in between to make our lead ten points with 32 minutes left. Even when Marler saw yellow on 59 minutes, we held out and Monye and Smith scored in the last ten minutes to send us through (Evans converted the second which ended the match). In the Amlin Cup, it had been decided to enhance the competition by parachuting three teams from the

Heineken Cup into the quarter-finals alongside the five Pool winners. As the fourth seeds, we had a home tie against one of the Heineken Cup teams and after a late score, it was Wasps. At the same time, the draw was made for the semi-finals and we knew if we defeated Wasps, we would be going to either Brive or Munster.

As part of a strategy by Wasps to take their brand to a global audience, they switched the LV= Cup pool match to the Emirates Palace Hotel in Abu Dhabi. Even the specially grown grass was flown in from Panama! After Atkinson had booted Wasps into the lead inside two minutes with a penalty, we rallied strongly. As Wasps made mistakes, we scored points and Dickson and Lowe got tries for Evans to convert. Varndell went over for Wasps but an Evans penalty and conversion of a try by Ceri Jones made it 24-8 at half time. The bonus point try came through Karl Dickson's second and Evans again converted. Wade almost scored but he just clipped the touchline as he went over and there was no further scoring until Launchbury got a second try for Wasps on 72 minutes. Even that was replied to by Smith who latched on to a long kick by Williams. Clegg converted for a 38-13 win to put us top of the Pool with one game to go. Two of our players for the future made their debuts in this game, they were prop Will Collier and back row forward Joe Trayfoot. Collier came on as a substitute and would go on to make at least 88 appearances and Trayfoot would make 53.

That final game was against Cardiff Blues at the Stoop on the following Sunday (6th February). We were missing Brown, Care, Easter, Marler, Monye, Robshaw and Robson on duty with England and the Saxons so Will Skinner led the side. Despite going behind to a try from Pretorius (converted by Sweeney), we recovered to lead at the interval. Nick Evans converted his own try, kicked a penalty and added the extras to Sam Smith's effort. In the second half, Cardiff dominated for long periods but were unable to breach our defence. Evans made the game safe with penalties after 67 and 71 minutes to send us into the semi-final with our biggest home margin of victory over Cardiff since a 14-0 win back in December 1933. In the semi-final, we would play at the Stoop against Newcastle Falcons on 11th March. This was our ninth win on the trot but a lot could still go wrong in the remaining games.

The first of these was a Premiership fixture against Exeter Chiefs on 12th February at Sandy Park. In the first half, Steenson kicked four penalties to one from Evans (who also missed two others). His only success making it 3-6. Just after the break, Exeter stretched their lead with a try from Johnson before Evans got a second penalty after 53 minutes. With twelve minutes to go, Steenson slotted his fifth penalty to make the game safe and when we did manage to create a chance, Monye passed forward. A win would have kept us in the top four but defeat sent us down to seventh. Just five points separated third to seventh places so there was still everything to play for.

On 19th February tenth placed Sale Sharks visited the Stoop for another Premiership game. After messing up two early chances to get tries, we had to settle for a penalty by Clegg but the tries did come sooner rather than later. First, Joe Gray (converted by Clegg) and then Brown collected his own kick to put us 15-0 up in 17 minutes. Hodgson and Clegg then exchanged penalties after 34 and 37 minutes. Heavy rain in the morning meant that the pitch was not in the best condition and this led to a poor second half. Hodgson and Clegg again swapped penalties before almost half an hour with no scoring. Clegg did miss one and Hodgson eventually got his third with seven minutes to go but the game was safe well before then. A minute from the end, Lowe and Cohen were sent to the bin and it ended 21-9. We jumped to fifth place on the same points as Northampton (38) but they were fourth because they had won eight games to our seven.

The following Saturday, we went to Reading to take on London Irish. Malone put the Exiles in front with a penalty after 5 minutes, Clegg replied with two in five minutes before Malone did the same. With three minutes left before the half time whistle, Clegg made it 9-9. We were fortunate to be level as the Irish had missed three penalties. Into the second half, Homer got their fourth and Malone the fifth after Turner-Hall was yellow carded for offside at a ruck. Before he came back, Hodgson followed him but neither side could take advantage and a disappointing game finished 15-9 in favour of the home side. The losing bonus point left us in seventh, level on points with Northampton and London Irish but still well in the mix for a play-off spot with six games to go.

We now had a double header against Newcastle, each game was played on a Friday night. The first was at Kingston Park in the Premiership. The Falcons were in eleventh place but crucially, seven points ahead of Leeds Carnegie. After just three minutes, we went ahead when Tom Williams went over for Clegg to convert. Gopperth pulled three points back with a penalty before James Johnston and Golding were binned after there had been an altercation amongst the forwards. Ceri Jones followed them and Gopperth made it 7-6 with another penalty. On 31 minutes, Clegg got his first penalty but Gopperth put over two more before the break to snatch our lead away. It was a real see-saw tussle and Clegg put us back in front with another three pointer. We lost it when the Falcons scored two tries in four minutes through Gray and Fielden. Gopperth converted both and although Brown scored our second, Young got a third for the home side and Gopperth's conversion made the final score 33-18. A win would have put us fourth but we remained in seventh, still level with London Irish and Northampton.

The LV= Cup semi-final on Friday 11 March began so well for us when Dickson crossed the line after only 56 seconds. Clegg converted and twice exchanged penalties with Gopperth to make it 13-6 at the interval. In truth we should have been out of sight as van der Heijden had been binned for killing the ball after 22 minutes and four golden try scoring opportunities had been missed through us being penalised or knocking-on. As we attacked towards the end of the third quarter, we allowed the ball to go loose, Gopperth pounced and ran in from 60 metres to score under the posts. His conversion brought the scores level and when he added a penalty nine minutes later, the visitors were ahead. Back we came and after a period of pressure, Clegg put Brown over in the corner and converted to make it 20-16. With time up on the clock, the Falcons attacked one last time and Gopperth and Tait sent Tu'ipulotu over in the corner for a try. The conversion was missed but it didn't matter, there was no time left for another comeback. We had contrived to snatch defeat from the jaws of victory once again and Newcastle marched into the final the following week where they were beaten 34-7 by Gloucester.

The Cherry and Whites were our next league opponents at the Stoop on 26th March and were looking to consolidate their third place in the table. Gloucester failed to get off the coach and the game was all but over by half time. Clegg put over a penalty and converted Gray's try before Robinson reduced the deficit with a penalty. A two try burst in three minutes saw Robson and Monye build our lead and Clegg's conversions made it 24-3. The second half started as the first had finished with more points for us. Clegg knocked over another penalty and converted Monye's second try. When Strokosch went to the bin, Lowe scored and Clegg was successful again with the extras. Trinder started a scoring spree in the last ten minutes when he went over (Robinson converted) and Molenaar had the last word with Gloucester's second try but in between, Lowe and Monye added tries for us. Clegg converted the first but couldn't improve Monye's hat-trick try. The final score of 53-15 was our highest score and biggest winning margin against Gloucester since August 1996. A move up to sixth place followed but with four games to go, we still had to play the top two (Leicester and Saracens) at home.

When the Tigers came to town we knew we had to win and built a handy lead in the first forty minutes. Both sides had come close to opening the scoring with Evans and Flood missing penalties and Easter being denied by the TMO after putting a knee in touch as he touched down. Danny Care crossed the line after 32 minutes, Evans converted and added a penalty. When Flood missed another penalty, we led 10-0. Leicester were a different side after the break and almost immediately Alesana Tuilagi scored and Flood converted. The tide started to turn against us when Wayne Barnes sin-binned Skinner for kicking the ball out of a scrum when it looked out (to be fair, the decision really could have gone either way) and from this period of pressure on our five metre line, he then sent Lambert off for 10 minutes as well. The referee's next award was a penalty try to the Tigers which Flood converted for a 14-10 lead. The atmosphere was turning nasty now and when Ayerza head-butted Marler, the response was a punch to the face from Joe and both saw red. The provocation was too much and our prop did look to the referee to help him but when Barnes did nothing, he acted in self-defence. The whistle came too late to help when it was blown and Leicester were down to fourteen, we were temporarily reduced to twelve! Evans kicked a penalty then Williams was tackled without the ball as he tried to latch on to a kick through by Evans. The decision was a knock-on by our winger. Evans missed with a penalty chance, Flood didn't and we went down by four points (13-17). We stayed in sixth but a top four finish would now prove difficult to achieve as our eyes turned to the Amlin Challenge Cup quarter final against Wasps.

Our fourth home game on the trot took place on Friday 8th April and the team from Wycombe were in the way of a European semi-final appearance. We set off at a blistering pace and Maurie Fa'asavalu almost demolished Wasps single-handedly in the first five minutes. His drive saw Care go over in 90 seconds and barged over himself a couple of minutes later. Evans converted both before Wasps could draw breath. It was the visitors who scored next when ex-Quin Seb Jewell was awarded a try after the TMO had reviewed it, Walder converted and dropped a goal to make it 14-10. Before the interval, Evans completed a hat-trick of penalties to give us a decent lead. The third quarter saw Evans add another pair of three pointers either side of a try from Lindsay and conversion by Walder. When Haughton scored, there were seven minutes left but Nick Evans calmly dropped a goal three minutes later to send us into a semi-final showdown at Thomond Park against Munster. Before that game at the end of April, we had two away Premiership matches at Bath and Headingley to negotiate.

Although neither side might make the play-offs, both Bath and Quins were still hoping to finish in the top six to get automatic Heineken Cup qualification. The home side started better and were rewarded with a try by Claassens after 11 minutes that was converted by James. Evans then landed two penalties before James got one for Bath. Evans put over a third before the break to leave us one point behind (9-10). James added two more penalties but Evans replied in kind (the second when Vesty was binned for an offence at a ruck on the Bath line) and it was 15-16 with the final quarter to come. Before Vesty returned, James kicked his fourth penalty and try as we did, we couldn't find that match-winning score. Our last attack ended long after the clock had reached zero with a knock-on two metres from the line. Back we went to seventh place with Bath moving into sixth. Whatever we did in our final two games, we could no longer mathematically reach the play-offs. Our wait for the Premiership crown would go on for at least another season.

Leeds Carnegie were in a relegation scrap with Newcastle Falcons and both sides were on 22 points. The Falcons had a game in hand and a points difference advantage of 84. The usual scenario in these games is that the team at the bottom would lose and that is how it turned out. We played some scintillating rugby and built a fourteen point lead in the first period. Leeds old boy Danny Care chipped ahead and beat the defender to the touchdown and Joe Gray added a second. Evans converted both but it could have been even more had the home defence not played well in that first quarter. It took just three minutes for Turner-Hall to get another (Evans converted) but Lewis-Pratt replied with a penalty to stop the one-way traffic albeit briefly. At the end of the third quarter O'Shea replaced the front four and in quick succession, Care dropped a goal and Easter secured the bonus point with our fourth try. Evans converted but it was Clegg who improved Brown's try after he intercepted and ran 65 metres to score. At full time the scoreboard read 38-3 to the visitors. With one game left, we were in seventh on 51 points. Bath with a couple left were on 53 and London Irish (also with one remaining) had 54. Bath still had a slim chance of getting into the top four and we still had the possibility of automatic entry to the Heineken Cup if we could win the Amlin Cup.

Six days later on a sunny afternoon at Thomond Park, we took on the might of Munster in the Amlin Cup semi-final. They had lost only once there in 16 years of European competition – this would be no easy task. We played Munster off the park for the first 39 minutes, it was an incredible performance from the entire XV. After a great run from Camacho, the ball went right and Robson was on hand to go over for the opening score (Evans converted). It was all Quins and Monye, Brown and Lowe all came close to scoring. When it looked like Munster had weathered the storm (after Evans had failed with two penalty attempts), Care went over under the posts and with Evans injured, the scrum half converted his own try. Right on half time, Munster kicked to the corner instead of taking a shot at goal and from the lineout, the ball went right and Jones crossed unopposed in the corner. He ran round to make the conversion easier and O'Gara put it over. During the interval, Clegg replaced Evans and the home side made three changes. As one could have predicted, Munster came out of the blocks determined to blow us away in the second forty. After 46 minutes, Easter and O'Callaghan were both binned for fighting and we got the only points during this time when Clegg put over a penalty. He repeated the feat when the teams were back to full strength and we led 20-7 with the final quarter to come. As George Lowe tried to get to a kick ahead, he was impeded by Howlett. Unfortunately, the TMO didn't see it like that – no penalty try was his decision. When Howlett went over a minute later, the referee ruled the last pass was forward and the same thing happened again five minutes later. The crowd were not happy, Munster were used to getting these decisions. As the clock ticked towards the last ten minutes, the home side attacked and Easter was shown a second yellow for coming in at the side (this converted to a red and he was off). The fourteen men did us proud and when Howlett did finally go over in the corner, there were under three minutes remaining. As O'Gara lined up the conversion attempt, it was a simple equation – if he scored, Munster were still in it; if he missed, we were in the final because there was not enough time for them to score twice. He struck it well enough but it drifted to the right and we had done it! In the final on 20th May we would play Stade Français Paris. This victory showed that this squad was capable of winning tight games in the most intimidating environments; it was a good sign for the future.

Our final Premiership match was at the Stoop on 7th May against Saracens. We had lost the previous three fixtures against Sarries so a win was overdue. The first half saw the visitors take a six point lead with two Goode penalties in the first quarter only for Clegg to reply in the second to leave it all-square at the break. When the visiting pack pushed us off our own ball near our line, Farrell managed to get the ball down on the line and convert. He followed this with a penalty and all of a sudden, we were ten points down. When Burger saw yellow for persistent team offences, we had a glimmer of hope when Robshaw scored for Urdapilleta to convert. In the final three minutes, we couldn't get that elusive winning score and Saracens held on for another win by 16-13. Our final league position was seventh so, to qualify for next season's Heineken Cup, we would have to win the Amlin Cup. We saw three men make their final appearances for the Club against Saracens, they were Jon Andress, Matt Cairns and long serving Ceri Jones. Andress had made 13 appearances as a substitute but scored no points, Cairns had made 15 sub appearances and scored 5 points (1 try) and Jones came on as a sub 44 times, went to the bin on 5 occasions and scored 155 points (31 tries).

After a week off, we travelled to Cardiff City Stadium on Friday 20th May for the Amlin Challenge Cup Final against Stade Français Paris. If we thought Munster were tough opponents, this would be even harder. A crowd of 12,236 turned up to witness an enthralling encounter. The Quins team lined up as follows:- Mike Brown; Gonzalo Camacho, George Lowe, Jordan Turner-Hall, Ugo Monye; Nick Evans, Danny Care; Joe

Marler, Joe Gray, James Johnston; Ollie Kohn, George Robson; Maurie Fa'asavalu, Chris Robshaw, Nick Easter. Replacements: Matt Cairns, Ceri Jones, Mark Lambert, Pete Browne, Will Skinner, Dave Moore, Rory Clegg and Ross Chisholm. We started well and Nick Evans slotted a penalty after six minutes before Beauxis equalised seven minutes later. With the French side being penalised as we attacked, Evans put over another two but Beauxis pulled one back to make it 9-6 at half time. The second half was a different story as Stade Français took control. Within ten minutes, they were in front through a Beauxis penalty and Bastareaud's dropped goal and when Beauxis got another penalty, we trailed by six points with 22 minutes left. Will Skinner replaced Fa'asavalu for the final quarter and Evans put over his fourth penalty after missing one. With seven minutes remaining, Rodriguez (the Stade full back) dropped a goal from around 45 metres to make it 18-12. Ross Chisholm replaced George Lowe to complete the substitutions (there were only three in total in the entire tie). As the clock ticked down, Beauxis missed a penalty chance and we gave it one last go. Turner-Hall and Marler broke and the ball was passed to Care who put in a deft kick towards the right corner. As it bounced around, Gonzalo Camacho grabbed it, stepped inside and dived over for the try. Every Quins fan went mad but Evans still had to put the conversion over from wide out. He stepped up to the mark and calmly knocked it straight between the posts to give us a 19-18 lead. Two minutes remained and, as the clock ran down, a scrum was repeatedly set, we held our own as Stade shouted for a penalty but the referee (George Clancy) gave nothing and told them to "use it". The ball came out, Stade knocked-on, Care kicked it into touch and the final whistle went. Scenes of pure joy followed. We had become the first team to win three European Challenge Cups and, the other good news was that we had qualified for the Heineken Cup. After the disappointments of the Premiership and LV= Cup as well as the "Bloodgate" saga, this was a fine way to redeem ourselves. We could truly look forward to the future with renewed vigour as the squad developed together into a very experienced outfit. Only one player made his final appearance in this game and that was the hero, Gonzalo Camacho; he had made seven substitute appearances, been sent to the sin-bin once and scored 35 points (7 tries) during his all too short spell with us.

Our overall record was P39 W24 D2 L13 F1008 A613. Our points total was only the fourth time we had achieved more than one thousand points in a season and was 312 more than 2009/10. In the league our record was P22 W9 D2 L11 F482 A384 Pts 52 (BP 12 – TB 4 LB 8) Pos 7th. Out of 39 matches played, as usual, no one appeared in all of them. George Lowe was top with 35 appearances, Ollie Kohn and Jordan Turner-Hall were one behind, Will Skinner was on 33 and Brown, Jones, Lambert and Robshaw were one behind him on 32. George Lowe was top try scorer again, this time he got 11, Nick Evans and Danny Care each dropped a goal and Evans was top in penalties (80) and conversions (54). As a result, he was our top points scorer again with 371 (4 tries, 1 dropped goal, 80 penalties and 54 conversions). As a result of a good season, tries went up by 28 to 104, dropped goals doubled to 2, penalties leapt from 69 to 102 and conversions rose by 35 to 88.

2010/11

060810	SOUTHERN HEMISPHERE ALL STARS XV	TWICKENHAM STOOP	W	7G2T(59)-0
130810	CONNACHT	GALWAY	W	5G1T(40)-1G(7)
210810	ULSTER	ULSTER	W	3G1PG(24)-0
040910	LONDON WASPS(AP)	TWICKENHAM(A)	D	2G5PG(29)-2G5PG(29)
110910	NORTHAMPTON(AP)	TWICKENHAM STOOP	L	1G3PG(16)-2G2PG(20)

170910	SALE SHARKS(AP)	EDGELEY PARK	L	2G1PG(17)-1G3PG1T(21)
250910	EXETER CHIEFS(AP)	TWICKENHAM STOOP	W	4G4PG(40)-1G2PG(13)
021010	NEWCASTLE(AP)	TWICKENHAM STOOP	W	2G3PG(23)-4PG(12)
101010	BAYONNE(ACP1)	BAYONNE	L	4PG(12)-2PG2T(16)
161010	I CAVALIERI PRATO(ACP1)	TWICKENHAM STOOP	W	6G1PG2T(55)-2G1PG(17)
231010	GLOUCESTER(AP)	GLOUCESTER	L	2G4PG(26)-3G4PG(33)
311010	BATH(AP)	TWICKENHAM STOOP	D	2PG(6)-2PG(6)
051110	LEICESTER(LVCP4)	LEICESTER	W	2G5PG1T(34)-1G6PG(25)
141110	NEWCASTLE(LVCP4)	TWICKENHAM STOOP	W	2G3PG1T(28)-2G2PG(20)
191110	LEICESTER(AP)	LEICESTER	L	1G2PG(13)-6PG(18)
281110	LEEDS CARNEGIE(AP)	TWICKENHAM STOOP	W	5G2PG2T(51)-1G2PG1T(18)
051210	SARACENS(AP)	VICARAGE ROAD	L	3PG1T(14)-2G4PG(26)
121210	CONNACHT(ACP1)	TWICKENHAM STOOP	W	2G2PG(20)-3PG(9)
171210	CONNACHT(ACP1)	GALWAY	W	5PG(15)-3PG(9)
271210	LONDON IRISH(AP)	TWICKENHAM	W	1G7PG(28)-6PG(18)
010111	NORTHAMPTON(AP)	NORTHAMPTON	W	1G3PG(16)-1G2PG(13)
080111	LONDON WASPS(AP)	TWICKENHAM STOOP	W	1G2T(17)-1G1PG(10)
150111	I CAVALIERI PRATO(ACP1)	PRATO	W	6G2PG(48)-1G3PG(16)
220111	BAYONNE(ACP1)	TWICKENHAM STOOP	W	4G2PG1T(39)-4PG1T(17)
300111	LONDON WASPS(LVCP4)	ABU DHABI(A)	W	5G1PG(38)-1PG2T(13)
060211	CARDIFF BLUES(LVCP4)	TWICKENHAM STOOP	W	2G3PG(23)-1G(7)
120211	EXETER CHIEFS(AP)	EXETER	L	2PG(6)-5PG1T(20)
190211	SALE SHARKS(AP)	TWICKENHAM STOOP	W	1G3PG1T(21)-3PG(9)
260211	LONDON IRISH(AP)	READING	L	3PG(9)-5PG(15)
040311	NEWCASTLE(AP)	NEWCASTLE	L	1G2PG1T(18)-3G4PG(33)
110311	NEWCASTLE(LVCSF)	TWICKENHAM STOOP	L	2G2PG(20)-1G3PG1T(21)
260311	GLOUCESTER(AP)	TWICKENHAM STOOP	W	6G2PG1T(53)-1G1PG1T(15)
020411	LEICESTER(AP)	TWICKENHAM STOOP	L	1G2PG(13)-2G1PG(17)
080411	LONDON WASPS(ACQF)	TWICKENHAM STOOP	W	2G1DG5PG(32)-2G1DG1T(22)
160411	BATH(AP)	BATH	L	5PG(15)-1G4PG(19)

240411	LEEDS CARNEGIE(AP)	HEADINGLEY	W	5G1DG(38)-1PG(3)
300411	MUNSTER(ACSF)	THOMOND PARK, LIMERICK	W	2G2PG(20)-1G1T(12)
070511	SARACENS(AP)	TWICKENHAM STOOP	L	1G2PG(13)-1G3PG(16)
200511	STADE FRANÇAIS PARIS(ACF)	CARDIFF	W	1G4PG(19)-2DG4PG(18)

47

Were You There?

2011-2012

On 19th May 2011 it was announced that David Ellis was to be the new Chief Executive. He joined from Catalyst Housing Group and would start his work on 15th August. David Morgan (who had been the CEO on a temporary basis) would become Chairman on 1st September. Ellis had no background in rugby and time would tell if he was to be a success or not. He joined the board and Wall resigned at the same time. The year ending 30th June 2012 accounts told us that the loss this year was £2,054,693.

The seventh Rugby World Cup took place in New Zealand in September and October 2011 and this time we only had twelve players involved representing seven of the twenty countries participating. Of those, three were current players; Tomas Vallejos Cinalli (Argentina), Nick Easter (England) and Maurie Fa'asavalu (Samoa). Gonzalo Camacho and Gonzalo Tiesi (Argentina), Waisea Luveniyali (Fiji), Mike Ross (Ireland) and Junior Poluleuligaga (Samoa) had all finished their Quins careers. Future players were James Horwill (captain) (Australia), Netani Talei (Fiji) and Adam Jones and Jamie Roberts (Wales). This turned out to be a very disappointing tournament for the England team as discipline issues on and off the pitch followed them around. There were problems on a night out (Ashton, Flood, Hartley and Tindall were all featured in a news story); Ashton, Hartley and Haskell were all made to apologise to a female hotel worker after making inappropriate remarks; Armitage and Lawes missed games because of foul play and Tuilagi was fined for wearing a sponsored mouth guard; back room staff Dave Alred and Paul Stridgeon were suspended for one game after switching a ball without the referee's permission and to cap it all, Tuilagi leapt from a ferry in Auckland harbour – he was spoken to by the police and fined by England officials. Back to the actual games, England won all their Pool games against Argentina (13-9), Georgia (41-10), Romania (67-3) and Scotland (16-12) to finish top and ended up with a quarter final against France. This time it was a game too far and the French won 19-12; they would go on to contest the final with New Zealand and lose by the narrowest possible margin (7-8).

Chris Robshaw continued as captain. He was proving to be very popular and a great leader. A decision by Conor O'Shea had implications for the calculation of appearances. He decided that from the start of 2011/12 season, playing in friendly matches would no longer count as an appearance for the Club.

This time we had four friendly fixtures in August and the first of these was away to Castres Olympique on 11th. In 30 degree heat, Skinner was put over by Evans who converted but Castres equalised. Brown grabbed a second, Chisholm chipped the full back for a third and Evans added both conversions for a 21-7 lead. That was the end of our scoring and a second converted score reduced our lead to just seven points at the break. With a whole host of changes being made, we fell away in the second half and four tries (all converted) by the home side produced a full time score of 21-42.

Our second and third friendlies were at the Stoop against Esher (16th) and Nottingham (19th) respectively. Two tries in the first 12 minutes looked to have put us on the road for a resounding victory but we failed to push on. Ollie Lindsay-Hague and Charlie Walker scored them and Ben Urdapilleta added the extras. Before the interval, the visitors managed two converted scores of their own but we opened up another gap in the first 15 minutes of the second half. First Tom Casson and then Urdapilleta got over to make it 24-14. Esher scored their third converted try on 60 minutes but they got no closer and we won by three points.

The Nottingham fixture three days after Esher proved to be an easier game for us. It was all over by half time as Ross Chisholm (2), Mike Brown (2) and Tom Guest went over for tries and Rory Clegg slotted five conversions. The visitors got a penalty to briefly make it 7-3 but Sam Smith extended the lead two minutes after the break. Clegg converted this but missed the last one when Joe Trayfoot scored after Munro had scored for Nottingham (Hallett added the conversion to his earlier penalty and it finished 47-10.

A trip to Ulster the following Friday rounded off our pre-season and although not at our best, a lot would have been learned from the four games. Gilroy was lucky to score after appearing to knock-on and when Humphreys converted and kicked a penalty, it was 10-0. After good work by Turner-Hall and Chisholm, Dickson went over but the conversion by Evans hit the right hand post and bounced out. Early in the second half Marshall crossed for Humphreys to convert and Faloon got Ulster's third near the end to make it 22-5.

On 3rd September, the season started and as it was a World Cup year, a host of internationals were missing from the Premiership. Our opening fixture was at Twickenham against London Irish as part of the London Double Header. The Irish squad contained no fewer than five old or future Quins. We opened the scoring when Evans put over a penalty only for Homer to do the same. Mike Brown went close before Johnston crossed for our first try of the season. Evans converted but we lost Marler to the bin and Homer kicked the penalty. Our lead was restored when Evans slotted his second penalty before the break. We lost Tom Guest when he collided with Hala'ufia, it turned out he had broken both bones in his lower arm quite badly. He would not play in the 1st XV again until 31st December. The first score of the second half went to the Exiles when Ojo scored for Homer to convert. Evans got two more penalties either side of Ojo's second try before converting Monye's try. The last quarter saw three penalties, one from Evans between two from Homer. The second secured the Irish a losing bonus point and we were off to a winning start to the tune of 29 points to 24. After the first round, we were second to Bath. Joe Marler was cited for striking an opponent against London Irish and was subsequently banned for three weeks although this was reduced to two on appeal.

Our first home fixture was against Northampton Saints on the following Friday. Nick Evans was in excellent form with the boot and kicked four penalties in the first half. A try by Tonks (converted by Myler) split them neatly to make it 12-7. Myler put over a penalty but it was nicely sandwiched between two converted tries by Gray and Monye (Evans with the extras). There were still 27 minutes left but the only score was a Lamb penalty for the Saints. Even though Johnston went to the bin on 73 minutes and the visitors had a lot of possession, we closed the game out to go to the top of the table (albeit it for 24 hours). When the second round was completed, we slipped to third behind Exeter and Wasps who both got bonus point wins.

On 17th September, Gloucester came to the Stoop three points and one place behind us. For various reasons (World Cup duty, injuries and suspension) we had 18 players unavailable so a lot of the younger members of the squad such as Luke Wallace, Charlie Matthews and Charlie Walker were getting some serious game time. On a wet afternoon, Burns put Gloucester ahead with a penalty and our response was a try from Smith which Evans converted before adding a penalty. From a rolling maul, Wallace went over, Burns replied with a penalty and Evans put over his second to give us a twelve point lead at the half way stage. Cox was binned for persistent offences, the resulting penalty bounced off both posts and out but the pressure was maintained and eventually, Monye went over in the corner for Evans to convert. Five minutes later, Wallace was over again, Evans converted and was then replaced by Clegg who put over a penalty four minutes later. Unlike the previous week, we didn't allow Gloucester back into the game at all and Brooker rounded it off with six minutes to go with our fifth try which Clegg converted to make the final score 42-6. After this win, we went top with a three point lead over Exeter with Bath, Saracens, Sale and Wasps a further point behind. Three young players made their debuts in this game, props Darryl Marfo (substitute) and Kyle Sinckler and winger Charlie Walker (substitute). They would go on to make 34 and at least 81 and 53 appearances respectively.

A trip to Sixways to take on eleventh placed Worcester Warriors came on 24th September and our old friend Ceri Jones was waiting to greet us. The Worcester fly half Goode always seemed to get points against us whoever he played for and this game was no exception. He opened the scoring with a penalty after four minutes and added two more after Evans had equalised with one of his own. In the first 12 minutes of the second half, Goode stretched the lead with another penalty and a dropped goal from short range to make it 15-3. This was a real test for us now and we would see what the team was made of. The answer came when Smith weaved his way through to touch down under the posts. Evans converted and we were within a score. As the pressure mounted on the home side's line, the referee (Chris White) eventually decided there had been too many infringements and Abbott was sent to the bin after 73 minutes. He then awarded a penalty try, Evans converted and we held on for a great win. It was four from four and we stayed three points ahead of Saracens and Exeter with Sale one point behind them.

The last named came to the Stoop the following weekend for a fixture that was usually a high scoring affair. It began very promisingly for us when Brown scored the first try and Lowe the second inside the opening ten minutes. Evans converted both and added a penalty just after Macleod had kicked one for Sale. After 23 minutes, Miller got their first try and Macleod converted before an explosion of three tries in six minutes took us well clear. Kohn, Brown and Lambert scored them and Evans converted all three but the first half scoring was still not complete. Peel got over and Macleod converted to make it 38-17. Four minutes into the second period, Peel passed straight to Evans who ran through to score and convert. He was then replaced by Clegg who landed a penalty on 55 minutes. Within a few minutes, Miller scored Sale's third try and Macleod converted but we still led 48-24. Addison the Sale centre was stretchered off after a ten minute break in play and we must have thought the game had ended there. In a great finish for the Sharks, Cobilas (converted by Miller), Brady and Tuculet scored tries to secure both try and losing bonus points. The five points we secured in the 48-41 victory moved us four points clear of Saracens with Exeter and Sale three points further back on 15. Newcastle Falcons propped up the table with five points from five matches.

Leicester were in a lowly tenth place when we visited Welford Road on 8th October. After only two minutes, Stankovich was driven over from a lineout to put the Tigers in front but our reply was swift and within six minutes, we led 14-5. First, Brown put Smith in for a 30 metre run to the line and then our full back did the same for Stegmann. Evans added both conversions but the home side struck back to take the lead again. Hamilton went over in the corner after 20 minutes, Staunton converted and added a penalty on 33 minutes. The half time lead was ours as Evans slotted a penalty to make it 17-15. Another one made it a five point lead but Staunton replied in kind. Both kickers missed one apiece before Kohn finished off a series of drives for Evans to convert. We saw out the remaining five minutes and maintained our four point lead over Saracens (22 points). Sale and London Irish completed the top four but they were seven and nine points behind us.

The LV= Cup returned and we were in Pool 3 alongside Gloucester, Newcastle and Scarlets. The usual format saw us playing the teams in Pool 2 (Cardiff Blues, Leicester, London Irish and Sale). The first of these was against the Irish at the Stoop on 15th October. Only six players survived from the starting line-up against the Tigers as the LV= Cup was seen as a tournament for developing players. Urdapilleta, playing in the centre, went through after 6 minutes to score the opening try and Clegg converted. Homer replied with two penalties for Irish before Clegg got one for us to make it 10-6 at the interval. Clegg put over two more in the third quarter but Homer got two himself in between so when Sisi scored a try, Homer's conversion made it 19-16 to the visitors. There were only seven minutes left and Lindsay-Hague had just replaced Tom Williams at full back. With four minutes to go, Clegg levelled the scores with his fourth penalty so it was all to play for. As time ran out, both sides played for the win and two minutes into time added on, Matthews intercepted and passed to Casson who found Stegmann. As he was tackled and about to go into touch, he off-loaded to find Lindsay-Hague flying up in support and he ran in for the winning try. Clegg's conversion brought the final whistle and a scoreline of 26-19. Although we had won, we were bottom of the Pool because the three other teams had achieved bonus point wins. Second row Sam Twomey made his debut in this game and would go on to make at least 47 appearances.

At Edgeley Park, Stockport in a Friday evening fixture, we attempted to win our eighth game in a row. We had lost six on the trot at this ground so the form guide was not good. After Macleod had missed an early penalty, Stegmann opened the scoring and Clegg converted. We had to wait another 19 minutes for the next when Williams picked up a loose ball and ran in from 50 metres out to score under the posts. Clegg again converted but a productive ten minutes for the home side saw them go in front. Macleod put over a penalty, converted Addison's try but couldn't do so with Dickinson's. It was 15-14 to Sale at the break and another high scoring game was unfolding. Stegmann scored again three minutes into the second half and Clegg converted to regain the lead only for Macleod to put over another penalty to rein us in. Clegg landed his first penalty but Leota went over and Macleod converted to nudge Sale ahead by one point. With twelve minutes to go, Clegg got his second penalty and added a third a few minutes later to put us ahead by five points. Stegmann put the icing on the cake with his hat-trick try (converted by Clegg) which also gave us a bonus point. The final score of 37-25 moved us into second place in the Pool just behind Scarlets who got another bonus point win. Young centre Matt Hopper played his first game for the 1st XV when he came on as a substitute and would go on to play at least 100 times.

We now had two weeks of Aviva Premiership games before the start of the Heineken Cup campaign. Exeter visited on 29th October – this would not be an easy game as the Chiefs were fast becoming a side to be reckoned with since their promotion in 2010/11. The first half was not a high scoring one. Nick Evans put over two penalties in the first 26 minutes then Robson was sin-binned for an off the ball incident. We managed to get through the ten minutes without conceding any points and Evans extended the lead with his third penalty just after Robson returned. After Mieres opened Exeter's account on 47 minutes with a penalty, they then scored ten points in four minutes to take the lead. Mieres got his second penalty and converted Rennie's try but Evans quickly reduced the deficit to a single point with 22 minutes left. We worked our way up the pitch from the restart and Mike Brown was eventually put over for Evans to convert. After a scare or two, we did ultimately shut Exeter out to record another win by 19 points to 13. We now had 30 points, Saracens were still second on 26 with Sale (19) and Bath, London Wasps and London Irish all on 18. Newcastle were still bottom on five points.

Bath away has not been one of our favourite fixtures for a long time and we would have to be on top of our game if we were to extend our winning start to the season. After Vesty had missed two early penalties, Evans succeeded with one to put us ahead. The lead was short lived as Attwood managed to break the defence and Vesty didn't miss his kick this time. A Robshaw try and a conversion and penalty from Evans saw the first quarter end with us leading 13-7. The score did not alter until the 47th minute when Evans added a penalty. Vesty then kicked two more either side of a fourth from Evans to make it 19-13 with ten minutes left. It was left to Brown to settle the issue. He was initially stopped but managed to get free, pick up the ball from the ruck and round Abendanon to score our second try. Evans converted and despite Bath trying their hardest to get a losing bonus point, it stayed 26-13. We had won again, Saracens remained four points behind on 30, London Irish were ten points adrift on 20 and Gloucester and Sale were one point behind them. Newcastle had moved on to seven points but still remained bottom.

Our Heineken Cup Pool contained Connacht, Gloucester and Toulouse so it wouldn't be easy for us to qualify. We needed to win all our home games and at least one away. We began at home to Connacht (making their debut in the top European competition) on 11th November. In the first ten minutes of this Friday night fixture, Evans kicked penalties either side of one by Nikora but the visitors grabbed a try from O'Halloran when Robshaw was tripped, the officials missed the offence and Nikora converted for a 10-6 lead. From this point, the rest of the scoring in the first half belonged to us. Evans kicked a penalty, converted Dickson's try and added a fourth three-pointer just before the break. Quins old boy Gavin Duffy scored on his return and O'Connor converted to make it a two point game. In the final five minutes, Evans settled the nerves and the game with his fifth and sixth penalties. The 25-17 final score saw Connacht leave with nothing despite a great effort. We led the Pool on points difference after Toulouse had beaten Gloucester by a narrower margin (21-17).

The second pool game saw us travel to Kingsholm where our losing streak had reached twelve. Our winning run was now on eleven so something had to give. After six minutes, Mike Brown managed to dummy past three defenders to open the scoring. Evans converted and replied to a Burns penalty but our reply to his second was better. Matt Hopper burrowed over for a try (confirmed by the TMO), the conversion by Evans hit the post but we led by nine points at half time. In the third quarter, Evans added penalties either side of one from Burns (scored while Fa'asavalu was in the bin for a dangerous tackle) to extend the lead before Easter provided the finishing touch. He broke clear on the Gloucester 22 and with a defender hanging on to him as he crossed the line, managed to get the ball down. The home crowd were convinced the ball had been dislodged but the TMO begged to differ. Evans converted, there was no further scoring and it finished 28-9 to us. Toulouse had beaten Connacht so we were second on points difference. The double header with them in December would prove crucial if one side could win both games.

Before that we had two more weeks of Aviva Premiership fixtures. The first was a visit from the bottom side, Newcastle Falcons on Sunday 27th November. There was no score until Nick Evans slotted a penalty after 18 minutes and followed this by converting Stegmann's try ten minutes later. Manning scored for the Falcons and Care did the same for us to maintain the ten point cushion at the interval after both conversions were missed. Luke Wallace added a try (converted by Evans) when the Falcons were reduced to 13 men (Swinson and Pilgrim were the offenders) and Brown secured the bonus point before the second sin bin had expired. Between the tries Gopperth landed a penalty for the Falcons but we finally got our act together and Stegmann (converted by Clegg) and Johnston added tries to finish them off. This had been a bruising encounter and the final score of 39-8 in no way tells how hard won the victory was. Jordan Turner-Hall was injured when he ran into Maurie Fa'asavalu and, as Conor O'Shea stated afterwards, when that happens, there is only one winner! Our ninth victory was officially the best start to a Premiership season and took us to 39 points. We were now nine clear of Saracens (who lost at Northampton),

London Irish were on 24 and Northampton 22. The Falcons were nine points adrift at the bottom with just one win and a draw from their nine matches.

We had lost on our previous five visits to Adams Park (our only win had come on our first visit in 2003). Kick-off times could now be anytime between Friday and Sunday night due to the demands of TV and this one was scheduled for 4 p.m. on Sunday 4th December. We went ahead when Hopper was put over after a breakout and Evans converted but Wasps enjoyed 75% territory and 61% possession in the first half so it was a huge effort by us not to concede a try. As it was, Robinson put over two penalties to leave it close at the break. The third quarter changed the game as we scored fifteen points without reply. First, Evans kicked a penalty then Robshaw and Hopper gave Brown the chance of chipping the defence. As usual, he did it superbly and scored. After this, Care put in a brilliant cross-kick and Wallace gathered and barged his way over for Evans to convert. Suddenly it was 22-6 and another losing run could be coming to an end. Hopper went to the bin a minute after the try and Wasps scored a try through Southwell but the conversion was missed. Hopper returned but straight away Varndell went past him to score; again the conversion was missed by Robinson to leave the score at 22-16 with ten minutes left. There were no further scores and we had ten out of ten. Our points total was 43, Saracens had 34 and Exeter and London Irish were on 25 with Sale on 24. Newcastle remained six points adrift at the bottom.

The back to back games with Toulouse followed and we had won 14 in a row. If we could win both, we would also be in a commanding position in the Pool. However, it would not be easy against the four times Heineken Cup winners and so it proved. Ex-Quin Gary Botha played at hooker for the visitors and they took the lead when McAlister opened the scoring with a penalty. Evans replied but a Matanavou try and second penalty from McAlister saw the French side lead 11-3 at the break. We started the second half well and from a quickly taken penalty, Care made ground before Marler put Brown over for a try. Evans made the conversion to reduce the arrears to one point. The experience and power from Toulouse gradually began to tell and McAlister put over another penalty and converted Matanavou's second try on 65 minutes. There was no further scoring and our winning run had come to an end. Everything now depended on how we would react to this defeat. The Pool looked like this after three rounds – Toulouse 12 points, Quins 8, Gloucester 5 and Connacht 1.

Nine days later we travelled to the Stade Ernest Wallon to take on Toulouse again. This was a must win game for us if we were to have any chance of winning the Pool. Both sides made changes to their starting line-up, some of ours were forced by injury whereas Toulouse used 21 of the 23 from the previous week but most of the substitutes started this time around. McAlister opened the scoring with a penalty to which Evans quickly replied. The Toulouse kicker's second effort bounced back off an upright and a few minutes later, Evans put in a kick and Mike Brown secured the ball and the touchdown. Although Evans missed the conversion, our intent was now obvious to all watching. McAlister missed two more penalties before another Evans kick caused havoc in the Toulouse defence and Hopper, Robshaw and Care put Joe Gray over for try number two. This time Evans made no mistake and we led 15-3 with 23 minutes on the clock. Inevitably, the home side tore into us and our defence held firm until Maestri went through a gap and Doussain converted to cut our lead to five points at the break. In the first ten minutes of the second half, Doussain kicked two penalties and we were behind. His third extended the lead but we weren't giving up and a good chase of the restart by Tom Williams (who had only just replaced Stegmann) gave us possession. From this the ball went across the pitch and Easter's brilliant off-load sent Brown over and Evans converted to restore our lead. After Evans had put over a second penalty, Easter was sin-binned and from the penalty that followed, Doussain scored from the drive after the lineout but he missed the conversion and with eleven minutes remaining, the score was 25-24 to the visitors. In time remaining, Evans booted over two penalties to secure the victory. With only a minute to go, Will Skinner (who had been substituted) prevented a quick lineout by catching the ball as it went to touch and was promptly red carded by referee Alain Rolland. A famous win but it only brought us back into contention in the Pool and nothing more. Indeed, as a result of their losing bonus point, Toulouse still topped the Pool by one point with us on 12, Gloucester with 9 and Connacht on 2. Any of the top three could still qualify as Pool winners, it was going to be tight!

Nine days later on Tuesday 27th December, we were back into Aviva Premiership action with Big Game 4. This time we met Saracens at Twickenham. It was a clash of the top two sides and a World record crowd for a regular season club game of 82,000 were in attendance. The pre-match entertainment once again featured finalists from the TV show X Factor (Misha B and Amelia Lily) as well as Killer Queen and Camilla Kerslake. There were the usual fireworks which meant the first five minutes of the game were shrouded in smoke! We chose this game to give our worst performance of the season so far and gave away penalties like they were going out of fashion. Inside 18 minutes, Farrell had converted three opportunities and Evans one but when Marler attempted a pass to Easter inside our 22, unfortunately for him, Strettle intercepted and strode over. Farrell converted and added another penalty to make it 19-3 after 25 minutes. It was just the start we didn't want. Evans got his second penalty just before the break and we managed to pull ourselves together during the interval and came out fighting. As a result, Marler scored on 47 minutes but Evans couldn't convert. After this, we created opportunities as we maintained the pressure but none were taken and it ended 19-11. We had suffered our first Premiership loss of the season and Saracens closed the gap at the top to just five points. We had 43, they were on 38, London Irish were third with 29 and Sale and Leicester both had 28. At the bottom, Newcastle had just 11 points and were six adrift of Worcester.

Just four days later, we travelled to Sandy Park to take on the Exeter Chiefs in our final game of 2011. We started well enough and after we were awarded a penalty, Care took a quick one and just made the line to give us the lead. Clegg missed the conversion and a penalty six minutes later whereas Mieres kicked two for Exeter to put them ahead. Between his successes, Clegg missed another but right on half time, he got one to give us the lead back. We had butchered one golden opportunity when Brown's final pass went astray. Clegg missed two more penalty attempts on 51 and 55 minutes as the game drifted towards a nail biting conclusion. Steenson put the Chiefs ahead with a penalty with six minutes left but it had to be confirmed by the TMO as the original decision of the touch judges was that it had dropped under the bar. Amazingly, Clegg finally put one over three minutes later but, had Steenson dropped a goal a minute after that, it would have been so different. As it was, it finished 11-9 to us and we had achieved a very important win. It kept us at the top with 47 points, Saracens were still second on 40 and Northampton and Leicester came next with 32. Newcastle were now ten points adrift of Wasps and Worcester who both had 21 points. With ten rounds left, we were in prime position to get a home semi-final for only the second time.

Back in December after the home game with Toulouse, Danny Care was fined £80 for being drunk and disorderly and followed this by being banned from driving for 16 months after being found to be twice the legal limit early in the New Year. He was fined £3,100 by the court, a further £10,000 by the Club and placed on an inner-city community programme. As a result, he lost his place in the Six Nations squad and when he was arrested again for urinating against a wall in Leeds city centre after the game against Newcastle in March, there was a worry it could become an issue. Luckily, Quins got behind him, he became a changed man and settled down. Another nearly in trouble was Ollie Lindsay-Hague, he had punched someone in an argument at Mayfair's Taman Gang Club back in June 2010 (the victim needed a metal plate fitted in his cheekbone). His defence was that he had punched the man to protect a friend from racist abuse; the jury at Southwark Crown Court believed him and on 16 January 2012, he was acquitted.

There was no let-up in the difficult fixtures and another Friday night game, this time at Franklin's Gardens, would be a real test. Rory Clegg once again deputised for Nick Evans (who had a hand injury) and the time was approaching where he needed to move up to the next level in the hope that one day he would succeed the New Zealander. After 13 minutes, Lamb put the Saints ahead with a penalty and from the restart, Clegg sent it dead to immediately give Northampton the chance to attack. From a sustained period of pressure, Easter was yellow carded and Lamb dropped a goal. We just couldn't get into the game and Foden extended the lead after 25 minutes with the opening try. Easter returned and in the final ten minutes of the half, Lamb put over two more penalties either side of Clegg's effort to open our account. In truth, we simply weren't in this one and when Clegg missed two penalties in the first ten minutes of the second half, any chance we had was gone. The lead was extended further when Wilson got over and Lamb converted and there were still 24 minutes left. Even when Sorenson was sent to the bin we couldn't make any progress, there was no further scoring and the final score was 24-3 to Saints. Our lead at the top was reduced to three points with Saracens moving on to 44 points, Northampton and Leicester came next on 36 and London Irish had 33. At the bottom, Newcastle were nine points behind Wasps on 12 points. After suffering our second defeat in three games, we needed to get back on track quickly or the pack would catch us in no time.

There was now a four week break from Aviva Premiership action to enable the Heineken and LV= Cup group stages to be completed. First, we had a home European game against Gloucester to contend with and both sides had a chance to win the Pool. Evans returned to the starting line-up and promptly missed a penalty attempt. Burns put one over for the first points of the night (a 6 p.m. start for TV purposes) to which Evans replied. Five minutes later, Evans, Brown and Monye were all involved in a move that ended with Hopper going over for the first try and Evans converted. By half time, Burns had kicked a penalty and Simpson-Daniel went over for a try but Burns hit the post with his conversion attempt. A narrow one point deficit remained at the end of the third quarter because Evans and Burns landed penalties to make it 13-14. After Hopper went through, Care chipped over May at full back and he was forced to carry the ball over. From the ensuing scrums, Wood was shown yellow and from the next scrum, Care was over but the score was disallowed because he was deemed to be in an offside position. With the clock running down, we attacked again and this time, Care's kick through was reached first by Brown who scored in the left corner. Evans converted and we managed to see out the remaining time despite Gloucester attacking desperately. The position in the Pool was as follows after Toulouse gained a try bonus at home to Connacht. The French had 18 points, we were on 16, Gloucester had 10 and Connacht just 2. It was now all down to the final pool games the following week; we travelled to Connacht and Toulouse went to Gloucester. If the Cherry and Whites could do us a favour, it was still on for us to qualify as Pool winners.

Both matches kicked-off on the evening of Friday 20th January and whilst a feast of running rugby ensued at Kingsholm, the weather in Galway was absolutely atrocious and similar if not worse than that suffered by us in Ulster three years before. Connacht had been defeated in all five Heineken Cup matches so far and lost fourteen games on the trot. They were playing for pride and we knew we would be in a tough game. As the rain and wind lashed the ground, we played against the elements in the first half and it was Connacht who went in front when O'Connor kicked a penalty on 3 minutes. Four minutes later, Evans put Smith over for a try but missed the conversion. We were in front but the lead lasted just four minutes as O'Connor put over two quick penalties to make it 9-5 to the home side. There was no further scoring in the first half and surely we were well placed to make up the deficit playing with what must have been a 15-20 point wind in the second half. At Kingsholm, Toulouse led Gloucester 17-14 at the break so it couldn't have been tighter in the Pool. Into the third quarter, we were dominant and Evans ended it with a penalty but had Smith and Monye not got in each other's way when a try seemed to be the logical outcome after an Evans kick, we would have been in front. When we won a penalty on the Connacht 22, Evans lined up the kick to put us in front but somehow managed to miss it (to be fair, the wind was extremely strong). That proved to be our final chance as we got more and more desperate and Connacht defended and spoiled excellently. When the final whistle went, we had lost 9-8, the ground erupted and to top it all, news from Kingsholm came through; Gloucester had beaten Toulouse 34-24. We had blown it and were out. Toulouse won the Pool with 18 points, we were second on 17, Gloucester had 15 and Connacht finished bottom with 6. Once again we had failed in the Heineken Cup but crept in to the Amlin Challenge Cup by getting one of the three best runners-up spots – we would go to Toulon in April.

On 28th January Leicester Tigers visited and a poor start from us enabled them to take the lead with a try from Forsyth and conversion by Ford after 4 minutes. Clegg put us on the board with a penalty eight minutes later and that is how the first half ended. A more purposeful Quins side came out after the break and Clegg kicked two penalties in the third quarter to a try in between from Lewington to leave us three points behind. Try as we did in the last twenty minutes, we couldn't break through and Pienaar secured the Tigers win on 68 minutes with a third try. Ford converted and a minute from the end was sin-binned but it was too late for us to capitalise on. This defeat knocked us out of a second competition in as many weeks. The LV= Cup Pool read as follows:- Scarlets 14 points, Newcastle and Gloucester 10 and Quins 9. The best we could do was to end on the same points as Scarlets (assuming they got nothing out of their final game) but they were already on 12 tries to our six.

Our final pool game in the LV= Cup was in Cardiff against the Blues on Sunday 5th February. They were also bottom of their Pool, had lost all three games and had no points. We opened the scoring when Chris York got a try after six minutes and Clegg converted. Blair landed a penalty for the home side but Stegmann added a second try for Clegg to convert at the end of the first quarter. The second belonged to the Blues with James scoring tries either side of Hamilton's effort. Blair added all three conversions and we faced a ten point deficit at half time. There was no let-up in the scoring and James completed his hat-trick. Blair's conversion made it 31-14 but we came to life and two tries in the space of three minutes from Sam Smith and Ross Chisholm (both converted by Clegg) put us right back in the game. There was no scoring for thirteen minutes but the ninth try of the game went to Cardiff when Cook scored and James went over for his fourth. Blair converted both and with ten minutes left, it was 45-28. Still we would not lie down and on 78 minutes, Stegmann got his second, Urdapilleta converted and Chisholm went over for his second and our sixth try. The conversion was missed and it finished 45-40. An exhilarating contest had produced no fewer than twelve tries and 85 points. Although the number of points was a record for the fixture, twelve tries had been achieved before on 15th October 1988 when Cardiff had outscored us 8-4 and ran out winners 38-20. We gained two bonus points from this game and finished on eleven points, four behind Pool winners Scarlets; Gloucester and Newcastle ended on ten points.

A run of six Premiership games would take us to the end of March. The first was a visit by London Irish on 11th February and we started badly when Homer crossed for a try and converted after only two minutes. We fought back with an Evans penalty and his conversion of Tom Casson's try. Two Homer penalties ensured that the Irish led by three at the break. From the restart, Robson charged down a clearance kick by Bowden and Tom Williams won the race for the touchdown to put us back in front. Evans converted and Care dropped a goal in trademark fashion before the fifty minute mark. Two minutes later, it was all-square when Joseph scored for Homer to convert. On 55 minutes, Evans put over his second penalty and six minutes later, converted Ross Chisholm's try to give us a ten point cushion. Despite the Irish making four changes in one go on 71 minutes, they could only produce an Adrian Jarvis penalty with five minutes left that made the final score 30-23. We moved on to 51 points and maintained our three point lead over Saracens at the top with Northampton (37), Leicester (36) and Exeter (35) completing the top five. Newcastle were nine points adrift of Wasps at the bottom.

The following Saturday, Worcester came to the Stoop. They were in tenth place but nothing could be taken for granted in this league. After Gray had put Worcester in front with a penalty, Benjamin went over for a try (confirmed by the TMO) to make it an early eight point lead. On 12 minutes, Mike Brown had an effort chalked off by the TMO so it was left to Nick Evans to open our scoring with a penalty after 22 minutes. After a lengthy break because of an injury to Worcester winger Garvey, we drove a maul 25 metres up to the try line, Warriors collapsed it and the referee awarded a penalty try which was converted by Evans. For collapsing the maul, Shervington saw yellow for all but a minute of time remaining in the first half. When hostilities resumed, Evans twice exchanged penalties with Gray and, although he missed two others in the remaining 13 minutes, we held on for the win. After Saracens lost by a point to Leicester, our lead became six points (55 to 49). With seven rounds to go, Northampton, Leicester, Exeter and Gloucester made up the rest of the top six. At the wrong end, Newcastle were six points adrift of Wasps with Worcester four points ahead of them.

At Kingsholm a week later, we started slowly and quickly found ourselves ten points down in as many minutes; Burns landed a penalty and converted a try from Sharples. Two penalties from Evans put us on the board but May scored a try and Burns added two penalties before the break. Between those, Chisholm grabbed a try for us and Evans converted but we trailed by eight points at the break (13-21). In the third quarter, Evans put over another penalty but Burns did the same and Qera got their third try and we faced an uphill task to get anything out of the game. As Gloucester pushed for a bonus point try, they allowed Ross Chisholm to make a superb run from inside his own 22 to score a fantastic try. Evans converted from wide out and we had a bonus point. The final score of 23-29 was a disappointment but, our lead at the top was maintained. We had 56 points, Saracens 50, Northampton 46 and Leicester 45. It seemed that Gloucester, Exeter and Sale would be in the mix for fifth and sixth spot. The gap at the bottom was still six points and it looked as though either Newcastle or Wasps would be relegated.

A trip to Newcastle the following Friday night would not be easy given that they were literally fighting for survival. The Falcons turned up ready for a fight and ended up having two men binned and were lucky not to see red amid accusations from Conor O'Shea of punches and boots in the face and short-arm tackles. The first half lasted 58 minutes due mainly to Chris Brooker dislocating his knee – it would end his Quins career. After Evans had put us in front with a penalty after three minutes, Gopperth equalised eight minutes later. A dour first half saw no more scoring with both kickers missing opportunities and Pilgrim was binned for pulling back Turner-Hall. The half ended with a scuffle and the bad tempers continued into the second period. Evans and Gopperth again exchanged penalties, Gopperth was just wide with another and put Newcastle in front with his third success on 71 minutes. Two minutes earlier, Vickers had been binned for punching Marler. We were camped in the Falcons 22 as the clock ticked down and with the last kick of the game, Evans calmly converted a penalty chance to tie the scores at 9-9. The draw gave us two points to add to our total to make 58. Saracens moved on to 54 with Leicester making a late charge on 50 and Northampton (47), Exeter (45) and Gloucester (41) making up the top six. At the bottom, Wasps had beaten London Irish so the Falcons, despite picking up two points against us, were now eight points adrift.

We now had two weeks off as the LV= Cup semi-finals and final were played. Our next visitors were Bath on 24th March. Saracens temporarily displaced us from top spot with a 45-9 win at Sale on the Friday night before our game. After Heathcote and Evans exchanged penalties, Joe Marler was binned for a high tackle and during his time off the field, Heathcote put Bath in front with another penalty. We were struggling to find our normal rhythm and Evans missed two penalty attempts late in the half to leave us trailing. The third quarter passed without incident and Evans brought us level on 60 minutes and put us in front four minutes later with penalties. Immediately after Bath had made four changes, Cuthbert went to the bin after tackling Brown in the air and this proved to be decisive. Seven minutes into the sin bin period, we attacked and Brown was just short but a short pass from Dickson put Maurie Fa'asavalu over for the try. Evans couldn't convert but we led 14-6 with seven minutes remaining. Four minutes later, our try scorer was binned for a dangerous challenge on Heathcote and from the resulting penalty, Cuthbert hit the post. He was then wide with the last kick of the game and if either had gone over, Bath would have gone back down the M4 with at least a point. Instead they went home with nothing. We went back to the top on 62 points and led Saracens by three with Leicester (55), Northampton (52), Exeter (49) and Gloucester (42) filling the rest of the Heineken Cup slots. At the bottom, Newcastle still trailed Wasps by eight points with just four games remaining.

The following Saturday, it was a clash of the top two at Wembley Stadium. In front of a World record attendance for a club match (83,761), we turned up to perform. In the third minute, great play from Easter and Marler saw Turner-Hall go over for the opening score which Evans converted. Three penalties from Farrell put the home side in front and Robson prevented a certain try with a great tackle on Short before our second try arrived courtesy of George Lowe; Evans again converted. With the final kick of the first half, Farrell put over his fourth penalty to make it 14-12. During the interval, Nick Evans was replaced by Rory Clegg who stretched our lead with a penalty on 45 minutes. As Saracens began to up their game, we struck again when Care was put over by Brown and Guest for Clegg to convert. Our first victory over Sarries since 2009 looked on the cards but it all started to unravel as Marler went to the bin followed by Care eight minutes later and we were down to 13 men. Straight away, Wigglesworth went over from a scrum, Farrell converted and our lead was five points. Tackle after tackle prevented tries by Saracens and we held on even though Clegg missed a penalty and Easter became our third visitor to the bin. We finished the match with 13 players but a famous victory had been achieved; this team would no longer be a pushover in the big games! As a result of this latest win, we moved six points clear of Saracens who were now joined on 60 points by Leicester followed by Northampton, Exeter and Gloucester. At the foot of the table, Newcastle and Wasps both won so the gap remained at eight points with three rounds left.

A trip to Toulon followed on Friday 6th April in the quarter final of the Amlin Challenge Cup. We were trying to become the first side to retain the second tier European trophy but a disastrous opening 33 minutes effectively put paid to this. Added to this, eight changes were made to the starting XV from the previous week – the emphasis was clearly on winning the Aviva Premiership. Unfortunately, giving a kicker like Jonny Wilkinson several penalty chances was never going to end well and he got two in the first ten minutes. Clegg replied with one before Wilkinson added three more and converted a try from Tillous-Borde for a 22-3 lead at the break. Johnston was yellow carded for punching at a scrum just after Lambert looked to have scored. The TMO ruled he had knocked-on and the chance had gone. By this time, Wilkinson had been replaced and Giteau landed a penalty and converted Lapeyre's try after 58 minutes. The usual round of substitutions disrupted the flow of scoring until Steffon Armitage crossed on 72 minutes. At 37-3, the tie was lost but Danny Care did jink his way over for an unconverted try to make the final score a bit less emphatic.

So, we were out of Europe which left us with three regular season Premiership games to play. One more win would guarantee us a play-off spot and the first opportunity to do this came at the Stoop on 14th April against Wasps. Clegg continued at fly half and Robshaw returned after missing the Toulon game. Four minutes into the first half Clegg opened the scoring with a penalty and added a second after Robinson had levelled. The tries started to come after 23 minutes when Brown put Monye over and then Monye put Robson in five minutes later. Clegg missed both conversions which meant that when Wade scored for Robinson to convert, our half time lead was only 16-10. The third quarter belonged to us entirely and tries from Robshaw and Turner-Hall took us clear. Clegg converted both and added a penalty when Vunipola was binned. The final score was a try for the visitors by Filipo converted by Robinson. Aston Croall appeared for the last time making his 26th appearance as a substitute; he had been sent to the bin twice and scored 15 points (3 tries). We also said goodbye to Ben Urdapilleta, he had made 14 appearances as a sub and scored 20 points (1 try, 3 penalties, and 3 conversions). At this point, Wasps were on the verge of administration and in desperate need of a buyer. They had lost a number of players to retirement and injury during the season. They needed to stay in the Premiership and this defeat did not help their cause. We still led the way on 71 points (after our bonus point win) but Leicester were now second on 65 points with Saracens (64), Exeter (58), Northampton (56) and Sale (45) making up the top six. At the bottom, Newcastle won at Gloucester and coupled with our defeat of Wasps left them only four points adrift. It was increasingly likely that their meeting in the last game of the season would decide who went down.

On 21st April, Leicester Tigers visited the Stoop in another top of the table clash. It took the visitors six minutes to go ahead when Waldrom went over following a rolling maul. Flood converted and added a penalty after Evans had opened our account in similar fashion. Evans reduced the gap with his second success and then Monye intercepted a pass from Flood to canter home from the half way line. Evans converted and kicked another penalty when Manu Tuilagi was binned for pulling Lowe back when a try looked on. The scoring continued when Easter went over from a five metre scrum, Evans converted and Flood landed a penalty after Croft had been stretchered off. Tuilagi returned but Evans stretched our lead to 26-13 with his fourth penalty. At this point six minutes remained until the break, Leicester went into another gear and in that time scored ten points. First Mafi went over for Flood to convert and he then added a penalty with the last kick of the half after we were marched back ten metres for dissent. Flood's fourth penalty levelled the scores but George Lowe scored a great try from a chip through by Evans to put us back in front. The Tigers would not be denied and in the last fifteen minutes Alesana Tuilagi and Waldrom got tries, Flood converted both and denied us even a losing bonus point with another penalty with two minutes left. A tremendous game had finished 33-43 and the gap at the top of the table was now just one point with us just leading the way. This was Leicester's sixth bonus point win in a row, a record. Saracens were confirmed in a play-off spot and the last one would be decided between Northampton and Exeter. Newcastle and Wasps both got losing bonus points so the relegation decider would happen; the bottom side had to win with a bonus point whilst denying Wasps anything. If they got one, a 24 point winning margin would be required by the Falcons.

Because of the European semi-finals, the last weekend of the regular season took place on 5th May and we travelled to Edgeley Park, Stockport to meet Sale Sharks. It was their final game there before moving to Salford City Stadium. For us to finish top, it was a simple equation – win. Even if Leicester got another bonus point win, we had two more wins than they did and that was the first tie-breaker in case of teams being on the same points. Although Sale had been criticised for fielding an all English qualified match day squad, they were quickly out of the blocks and almost scored in the first minute. Mike Brown was impeded in the chase for the ball, a penalty was awarded and our line was cleared. Then their flanker, Bordill was held up over the line after Evans had missed a straightforward penalty chance. Just as the second quarter was beginning, Danny Care darted through under the posts for the opening score and Evans couldn't miss the conversion. Bell pulled back three points with a penalty but one from Evans and an unconverted score by Brown in the corner gave us a 15-3 lead at half time. Two more Evans penalties in the first ten minutes took us clear and although Addison scored for Bell to convert after Easter had gone to the bin we looked comfortable. Fittingly, Nick Evans slotted the final points of the regular season with a penalty after

73 minutes to make the final score 24-10. This gave us back to back away wins over Sale for the first time since the games in 1983 and 1994! Tomas Vallejos Cinalli ended his career at the Club when he came on as a sub late in the game; he had made 31 appearances from the bench, been to the bin three times and scored 5 points (1 try). We had finished top of the table for the first time ever with 75 points. We had won 17, drawn 1 and lost just 4 games and would enjoy a home semi-final against Northampton the following Saturday. It had been a great achievement but there were no celebrations at the final whistle because the job had not been done, in fact, it was only just beginning. Leicester couldn't get a bonus point against Bath but finished second just one point behind us; Saracens ended up third a further point back and, as already mentioned, Northampton got the final place and finished on 65 points. Exeter and Sale completed the top six and Newcastle were relegated. They beat Wasps 14-10 at Adams Park but finished one point behind because of the losing bonus point.

For the second time we had qualified for the Premiership semi-final and for the second time, we were at home. The difference this time was that we were not a tired team with injury problems. It would not be easy against Northampton and so it proved. An early penalty for us and Dickson tried to go quickly but his brother (Lee, also a scrum half) prevented him from doing so. The referee (Andrew Small) marched the Saints back ten metres, up stepped Nick Evans and we led 3-0. As time ticked away, more penalties followed; two for Lamb, one for Evans and another for Lamb. Then Wilson went to the bin, Evans added his third penalty but Lamb got his fourth to make it 9-12 at the break. Both kickers had missed once, it had been a nervy forty minutes. The third quarter produced two penalties for Evans to nudge us ahead but then two for Lamb to put Northampton back in front. Evans missed another chance before a sweeping move saw Artemyev, Foden and Downey put Dickson over for the first try of the game. Lamb missed what for him was a fairly easy conversion but we trailed 15-23 with under fifteen minutes left – how he would rue that miss. Into the last ten minutes and we roused ourselves for the final push. With nine to go, Evans slotted his sixth penalty and we were within range of the Saints. With five minutes remaining, Chris Robshaw asked Evans to put a penalty into the corner. He did and from the lineout, a rolling maul was set up and started to inch towards the Northampton line. As it gathered momentum, the whole team except for Tom Williams joined it and the 14 men charged over for Joe Marler to score. Quite sensibly, the referee went to the TMO who awarded the try. Evans converted and we led with just three minutes to go. We safely negotiated the remaining time and were through to our first Premiership Final. Could we do it on our first appearance just as we had done in the cup final 26 years before? Our opponents would be Leicester Tigers who had beaten Saracens at Welford Road 24-15.

We had beaten the Tigers only three times in twelve genuine one-off knockout games and had won eight and drawn one of the last forty encounters. Our only previous meeting in a final was in the Pilkington Cup in 1993 – Leicester won 23-16. The difference this time was that we were playing well as were the Tigers. This was their eighth successive Premiership final, the record was W3 L4. The weather was glorious and the squad walked over from the Stoop to Twickenham and were greeted with an honour guard of expectant Quins fans cheering them on. Gone were the days of our fans numbering a few hundred, there were tens of thousands of them. In the build up to the game there was a question mark over the fitness of the Leicester fly half, Toby Flood. He had injured an ankle against Bath on 5th May. He was named as a replacement but, on arrival at Twickenham, he reported that his groin was tight and withdrew. It was a blow to the Tigers but Ford took his place and he was a promising youngster. Our 23 was as follows:- Mike Brown; Tom Williams, George Lowe, Jordan Turner-Hall, Ugo Monye; Nick Evans, Danny Care; Joe Marler, Joe Gray, James Johnston; Olly Kohn, George Robson; Maurie Fa'asavalu, Chris Robshaw (captain) and Nick Easter. Replacements – Rob Buchanan, Mark Lambert, Will Collier, Tomas Vallejos Cinalli,

Tom Guest, Karl Dickson, Rory Clegg and Matt Hopper. This was just about our strongest match day squad – there would be no excuses for failing this time. At 3 p.m. the referee, Wayne Barnes, blew the whistle for the start of the final and we began strongly. After two minutes, Evans put us ahead with a penalty (after Manu Tuilagi had dumped Danny Care on the ground – he was lucky not to see yellow or red) and then struck a post with his second attempt. On nine minutes, great play from forwards and backs saw Williams score in the north-east corner. Evans hit the post for a second time but we led 8-0. Ford opened the scoring for Leicester with a penalty, Evans replied, Ford missed but was successful again with his third attempt to make it 11-6 with 27 minutes gone. The bounce of the ball went the way of the Tigers from our lineout inside their half and Cole fed Mafi who ran 40 metres untouched to score. Ford converted and our lead had gone. Two minutes before half time, Waldrom deliberately killed the ball at a ruck and was binned. Evans kicked the penalty and we were back in front. Before Waldrom returned in the second half, Leicester had conceded more penalties, two of which Evans kicked between the posts for a 20-13 lead. We nearly scored when Evans was put away and he probably would have made the corner but tried to return the pass to Williams and Agulla intercepted and the chance had gone. We kept pressing and after excellent driving play, Chris Robshaw (our captain fantastic) crashed over for a try which Evans converted. When Evans put over his sixth penalty eight minutes later, we unbelievably led 30-13 with a quarter of an hour to go. The Leicester surge had to come at some point and we didn't have to wait long. Ben Youngs burst through a gap from a quickly taken penalty and sent Allen under the posts for Ford to convert and three minutes later Ford added a penalty to reduce the arrears to just seven with the last ten minutes to play. After 72 minutes, Conor O'Shea made his first substitution when Tom Guest came on for Fa'asavalu and a minute later, Cockerill made four for Leicester to try and force extra time. In the last few minutes both sides gave up possession to keep the match exciting but, when Twelvetrees was penalised for holding on near our line in time expired, the Quins fans erupted into sheer joy. All that remained was for Rory Clegg (who had replaced Evans) to put the ball into the North stand and Wayne Barnes to blow the final whistle. After 25 years of league rugby, we had finally triumphed on the domestic stage – it was a fantastic day to be a Harlequin!

This was our best season ever for obvious reasons and our overall record was P35 W25 D1 L9 F823 A674. In the league it was P22 W17 D1 L4 F526 A389 Pts 75 (BP 5 – TB 4 LB 1) Pos 1st. In the play-offs, our record was P2 W2 F55 A46. Interestingly, only Newcastle scored less total bonus points than us with four.

As was nearly always the case now, no one appeared in all games. James Johnston topped the appearances with 31, Mike Brown and Joe Marler were next with 29 and Nick Evans and George Robson had 27. Nick Evans got the most points again with 333 (1 try, 78 penalties and 47 conversions), he also scored the most penalties and conversions. Danny Care dropped the only goal and Mike Brown scored the most tries (12). Overall, tries fell from 104 to 80, dropped goals fell to one, penalties were up by eleven from 102 to 113 and conversions fell from 88 to 63 in line with the reduced number of tries. Points overall were down by nearly 200 (1008 to 823).

2011/12

110811	CASTRES OLYMPIQUE	CASTRES	L	3G(21)-6G(42)
160811	ESHER	TWICKENHAM STOOP	W	2G2T(24)-3G(21)
190811	NOTTINGHAM	TWICKENHAM STOOP	W	6G1T(47)-1G1PG(10)
260811	ULSTER	ULSTER	L	1T(5)-2G1PG1T(22)

030911	LONDON IRISH(AP)	TWICKENHAM(A)	W	2G5PG(29)-1G4PG1T(24)
090911	NORTHAMPTON(AP)	TWICKENHAM STOOP	W	2G4PG(26)-1G2PG(13)
170911	GLOUCESTER(AP)	TWICKENHAM STOOP	W	4G3PG1T(42)-2PG(6)
240911	WORCESTER(AP)	WORCESTER	W	2G1PG(17)-1DG4PG(15)
011011	SALE SHARKS(AP)	TWICKENHAM STOOP	W	6G2PG(48)-4G1PG2T(41)
081011	LEICESTER(AP)	LEICESTER	W	3G2PG(27)-1G2PG1T(18)
151011	LONDON IRISH(LVCP3)	TWICKENHAM STOOP	W	2G4PG(26)-1G4PG(19)
211011	SALE SHARKS(LVCP3)	EDGELEY PARK	W	4G3PG(37)-2G2PG1T(25)
291011	EXETER CHIEFS(AP)	TWICKENHAM STOOP	W	1G4PG(19)-1G2PG(13)
051111	BATH(AP)	BATH	W	2G4PG(26)-1G2PG(13)
111111	CONNACHT(HECP6)	TWICKENHAM STOOP	W	1G6PG(25)-2G1PG(17)
191111	GLOUCESTER(HECP6)	GLOUCESTER	W	2G3PG1T(28)-3PG(9)
271111	NEWCASTLE(AP)	TWICKENHAM STOOP	W	3G1PG3T(39)-1PG1T(8)
041211	LONDON WASPS(AP)	ADAMS PARK	W	2G1PG1T(22)-2PG2T(16)
091211	TOULOUSE(HECP6)	TWICKENHAM STOOP	L	1G1PG(10)-1G3PG1T(21)
181211	TOULOUSE(HECP6)	TOULOUSE	W	2G4PG1T(31)-1G4PG1T(24)
271211	SARACENS(AP)	TWICKENHAM	L	2PG1T(11)-1G4PG(19)
311211	EXETER CHIEFS(AP)	EXETER	W	2PG1T(11)-3PG(9)
060112	NORTHAMPTON(AP)	NORTHAMPTON	L	1PG(3)-1G1DG3PG1T(24)
140112	GLOUCESTER(HECP6)	TWICKENHAM STOOP	W	2G2PG(20)-3PG1T(14)
200112	CONNACHT(HECP6)	GALWAY	L	1PG1T(8)-3PG(9)
280112	LEICESTER(LVCP3)	TWICKENHAM STOOP	L	3PG(9)-2G1T(19)
050212	CARDIFF BLUES(LVCP3)	CARDIFF	L	5G1T(40)-6G1PG(45)
110212	LONDON IRISH(AP)	TWICKENHAM STOOP	W	3G1DG2PG(30)-2G3PG(23)
180212	WORCESTER(AP)	TWICKENHAM STOOP	W	1G3PG(16)-3PG1T(14)
250212	GLOUCESTER(AP)	GLOUCESTER	L	2G3PG(23)-1G4PG1T(29)
020312	NEWCASTLE(AP)	NEWCASTLE	D	3PG(9)-3PG(9)
240312	BATH(AP)	TWICKENHAM STOOP	W	3PG1T(14)-2PG(6)
310312	SARACENS(AP)	WEMBLEY	W	3G1PG(24)-1G4PG(19)
060412	TOULON(ACQF)	TOULON	L	1PG1T(8)-2G6PG1T(37)

140412	LONDON WASPS(AP)	TWICKENHAM STOOP	W	2G3PG2T(33)-2G1PG(17)
210412	LEICESTER(AP)	TWICKENHAM STOOP	L	3G4PG(33)-4G5PG(43)
050512	SALE SHARKS(AP)	EDGELEY PARK	W	1G4PG1T(24)-1G1PG(10)
120512	NORTHAMPTON(APSF)	TWICKENHAM STOOP	W	1G6PG(25)-6PG1T(23)
260512	LEICESTER(APF)	TWICKENHAM	W	1G6PG1T(30)-2G3PG(23)

48

More Silverware and the Chance to Dominate 2012-2013

For the 2012 England tour to South Africa, we had several current players in the party. Mike Brown (sent home injured), Danny Care, Karl Dickson (called up as a replacement), Joe Gray, George Lowe (sent home injured), Joe Marler, Ugo Monye, Chris Robshaw (captain), George Robson and Jordan Turner-Hall. Old boy David Strettle and future Quin Paul Doran-Jones made the total number of representatives thirteen. Of the five matches, three were tests, the first and second were lost (17-22 and 27-36) and the third was a 14-14 draw. The other games were both won. Brown played in the first test but got injured; he was joined in the team by Marler, Robshaw and Doran-Jones (who came on as a sub). Marler, Robshaw and Strettle appeared in the second and Care and Marler were in the third.

Trevor Saving joined the Board as a Director and the annual accounts up to 30th June 2013 again produced a loss. On this occasion, it was £1,980,514; this was the eighteenth year on the trot that the Club had been in the red. This was the reality of the professional game and a large reason for this were wages. The staff number had risen to 108 full time and 59 part time and the bill now totalled £7,576,338. DHL now came on board as an official sponsor and our law firm sponsors had become Norton Rose Fulbright. Speaking to Mark Evans in 2014, he told me that he felt the Club had over achieved in 2008/09, under achieved in 2009/10 and met its potential in the following two seasons. He also said Quins should be there or thereabouts each year given the stability now enjoyed.

Chris Robshaw once again led the team and was the first Quins captain to lead a league title defending side. This time we only had three friendly fixtures and two of those were on the same day. We travelled to Castres on 9th August with a weakened side against the full strength French outfit. After Kockott had kicked an early penalty, Evans pulled us level with one of his own but two tries in the second quarter from Andreu and Wihongi (Kockott converted both) made it 3-17 at the break. After the usual host of changes, we came back with a try from Lindsay-Hague which Ben Botica converted. We were making too many errors and these allowed Andreu to score his second try. Bai converted and when Martial got a fourth, Teulet added the extras. With Lacrampe in the bin, we attacked at the end and Pete Browne got over in the corner. Botica's conversion hit the post and the match ended 15-31.

Nine days later, we met London Scottish and Connacht at the Stoop. The first game was against our old tenants, London Scottish and on a hot day, tries were aplenty. First, Stegmann went over followed by Darryl Marfo and Clegg added both conversions. The visitors came back and Lipp went over for Godman to convert. The remainder of the half saw two more tries for us through Henry Taylor and a second for Marfo, both converted by Clegg. At the end of the third quarter, the visitors scored a try through Pennycook and added another through Stevenson (both converted by Love) with sixteen minutes left to make it 28-21. Finally we woke up and Jordan Burns and Charlie Matthews wrapped the game up with further tries and Ben Botica added both conversions to leave the final score at 42-21.

After this, Connacht were played and another bunch of tries were scored. The XV who played in this one were a stronger outfit than against London Scottish and after 5 minutes, Evans wasted no time in scoring after Care has passed from a fast advancing scrum. The scorer added the points to this and when Nikora was binned, it wasn't long before Easter got our second try and Evans converted. Wallace then saw yellow and Connacht got their first points with a penalty by Jarvis. Nick Evans became the third player in the bin and Jarvis added another penalty to Connacht's tally. From the restart, George Lowe ran in from near half way beating four or five attempted tackles on the way. The conversion was missed but Chisholm scored for Care to convert and it was 26-6 at half time. Sam Smith went over at the start of the second half, Care couldn't convert and when Henshaw charged down Easter's attempted clearance to score, it was 31-11. In the remaining half an hour, we added tries through Care and Chisholm and Evans added the conversions (having re-joined the game amongst a mass of substitutions) and it finished 45-11. It has to be said that Connacht fielded a weakened side and would certainly be a different proposition when we met in the Heineken Cup in October.

The season began as usual with the London Double Header at Twickenham and our opponents were London Wasps. It turned out to be an incredible match played in perfect conditions. Wasps were not the same side that had almost been relegated back in May and literally shot out of the blocks. In the first ten minutes, Wade had gone through for a try, Robinson converted and added two penalties. After eleven minutes Varndell scored a second (Wade passed him the ball after he himself had crossed the line) for Robinson to again convert. We were twenty points down and stunned. After a quickly taken penalty by Care, Williams was sent clear for our opening try and Evans converted. Wasps responded with another Robinson penalty and Wade's second try. Two penalties from Evans after 29 and 33 minutes made it 13-28 at the break. The first eighteen minutes of the second half were a disaster for us and we conceded tries from Wentzel and Payne. Robinson added the extras to Payne's and, unbelievably, we trailed by 27 points. At this point, Dickson, Chisholm and Guest came on for Care, Hopper and Fa'asavalu. The impact was immediate and Guest scored after charging down Robinson's clearance kick and Evans converted. It was all-out attack now and Brown was put over in the corner by Evans two minutes later and the same combination produced our fourth try (this time Brown caught a superb cross-field kick by Evans). Evans had hit the post with the first conversion attempt but succeeded with the second and it was 32-40 with sixteen minutes to go. Three minutes later Evans found his own way through the defence and again converted to set things up nicely for the last ten minutes. When we were awarded a long range penalty attempt after 77 minutes, Evans stepped up to slot it through the posts and we led for the first time. It was enough and we held out for a fantastic victory by 42-40. The five points left us in fourth place after round one.

Our first visitors of the season were newly promoted London Welsh. We had first played them in 1887 but this was our first meeting in the top division. This game was our first Friday fixture of the season and these would become as regular as Sunday fixtures over the next few years. Fly half Ben Botica would come on as a substitute in this game and would go on to make 96 appearances. As always, the newcomers are expected to have a hard time of it especially when they come up against the better sides. This fixture would not be an exception to the rule but we didn't play as well as we could. George Robson got our first try after three minutes and Monye added another four minutes later. Evans converted both and although Ross opened with a penalty for the Welsh, Monye got his second and Evans converted to put us eighteen points clear at the break. Early in the second half, Ion was sent to the bin for preventing a quick tap penalty and we managed to add to our total during the period he was off. Robson got his second try for Evans to convert but there were more substitutions than points in the third quarter (we made three and London Welsh made six). After 62 minutes, George Lowe got our fifth try, Evans converted and, after Arscott took Monye out in the air, he received the second yellow of the night. Two minutes later, Botica dived over for our sixth try but he couldn't convert and the final score was 40-3. This win took us to the top of the table ahead of Leicester on points difference. At the bottom, Wasps, Worcester, Sale, London Irish and London Welsh had all lost their opening two games.

On 15th September, Sale Sharks visited the Stoop and we were looking for our third bonus point win in a row. It all began well when Monye scored in under two minutes. Evans converted but Cipriani landed a penalty and Vernon scored a try to put Sale ahead after 22 minutes. This lead lasted eleven minutes until Evans cut through and put Turner-Hall over. Evans converted and it was 14-8 at the interval. For the first half an hour of the second half, it was a case of Evans v Cipriani as the two fly-halves exchanged penalties. Evans got two, Cipriani one, Evans put over his third and Cipriani got his third as well to make it 23-14. At this point, we took the game away from the visitors with an excellent last ten minutes. Robson went over after 73 minutes followed by Brown at the end and Evans added both conversions. The final score of 37-14 flattered us slightly but it was a good win that took us two points clear at the top. Northampton were two points behind while, at the foot of the table, London Irish were still pointless and Sale had a single point.

A trip up to Leicester was our next appointment and at least we now travelled there looking to win rather than hoping. It was imperative that we made a good start and after Flood had put Leicester in front with a penalty, Evans equalised before Flood got a second. We started to play our game, Evans made a break and Robson sent Williams clear for a run to the line. Even though he pulled a hamstring a couple of metres from the line, he managed to touch down and the conversion from Evans gave us a 10-6 lead. Care dropped a goal and we had a narrow advantage going in at half time because both Flood and Evans missed penalty attempts. On 47 minutes, Evans got another penalty and when Mafi obstructed Brown as he looked set to score, the TMO only awarded a penalty. Leicester's response was a Flood penalty after 63 minutes but Evans put over his third and fourth to secure our fourth league win of the season. We stayed top with 19 points, Northampton were second on 18 and Saracens and Leicester had 12. Sale were at the bottom with one point and London Irish were three clear.

The following Sunday saw a visit from Saracens who were quickly becoming our nemesis. Just as we were getting to grips with Leicester, Northampton and Sale, it seemed we just couldn't get any sort of winning run against them. Evans put us in front after two minutes with a penalty but hit the post with his second attempt before Farrell equalised for the visitors. Evans put us in front but Farrell equalised, Kohn went to the bin and Farrell edged Sarries in front. The visitors could not take advantage of the sin bin and Care beat the defence to score near the posts. Evans got the conversion and we led 13-9 at the break. Kohn returned and Farrell promptly reduced the gap to one point with his fourth penalty. Evans missed again but Farrell didn't and we trailed after 54 minutes. Our fly half was off target again on 62 minutes but put us in front after Kruis went to the bin for ten minutes. When Evans had the opportunity to make it a four point lead, he unbelievably missed for the fourth time. When Farrell had a chance with six minutes left, he made no mistake after a bad clearance kick by Evans had put Brown in trouble. Indeed, another of his kicks hit a chap (carrying pints of beer) right on the head – it was a scene of devastation!! This was certainly a game we should have won and, but for some inexplicable misses from Evans, we would have done. It seemed that Saracens had found a way of stopping our fast off-loading game – simply go down injured every few minutes. It was boring but it worked. Our lead at the top had gone and we now trailed Northampton by two points with Saracens and Leicester four behind us on 16. Sale remained bottom on one point with Irish on 4 and Wasps with 9.

The last of the opening burst of six Premiership rounds found us on an away trip to Devon to take on Exeter Chiefs at Sandy Park on 6th October. After Steenson and Evans had exchanged penalties, Sturgess scored a try which Steenson converted and kicked his second penalty for a 13-3 lead at the end of the first quarter. Evans charged down a kick to score after putting over a penalty and even though Steenson got another penalty, Monye's try and a conversion from Evans ensured a narrow lead for us at half time (18-16). We had played badly and had enjoyed very little possession during the first forty minutes. The second half started with a try from White (converted by Steenson) and Evans was replaced by Clegg. On 57 minutes, Clegg intercepted a pass and Karl Dickson scored under the posts for Clegg to convert. We were still ahead but Exeter would not be denied and sloppy defending saw Shoemark score two tries in three minutes. Steenson converted the second as he did with Naqelevuki's effort near the end. Clegg had temporarily brought us within bonus point range with a penalty after 76 minutes but we didn't really deserve anything from this one. Mumm was binned in added time at the end but it was too late for us to make anything of it. As Conor O'Shea said afterwards - we were rubbish, we were really poor. We just didn't turn up and he promised a reaction against Biarritz the following week in the Heineken Cup. Northampton lost heavily at London Irish so the gap at the top remained the same but Leicester and Saracens moved up to twenty points with us although we remained second on points difference. Sale were now eight points adrift at the bottom having lost all six games.

The focus now shifted to the Heineken Cup and we were in Pool 3 which contained Connacht, Zebre (from Italy) as well as our first opponents, Biarritz Olympique. A 6 p.m. kick-off for TV scheduling was becoming a common sight and the players had adapted to these frequent changes to the original fixtures. It was essential to win your home games in the Pool stages and we got off to a great start with a try from Care (converted by Evans) after seven minutes. Peyrelongue got the visitors on the board with a penalty on 14 minutes before disaster struck for both sides almost at the same time. First, we lost Evans with an injury to his left ankle (he was replaced by Ben Botica) and Haylett-Petty took Tom Williams out in the air to earn a yellow card. Botica promptly landed his first penalty from forty metres before Biarritz struck back to take the lead. Héguy scored a try and Peyrelongue converted and added a penalty. Nine minutes before the break, Botica drew us level with another penalty. It was a tight game but no one could have predicted what happened in the second half. On 44 minutes, Buchanan went over for a try, Botica converted and kicked a penalty to put us ten points ahead. Our pack was dominant and in the final quarter, it showed. Another penalty from Botica stretched the lead before tries from Turner-Hall and Stegmann sealed the win in style and turned it into a five-pointer. Botica added both conversions to make the final score 40-13. Hooker Dave Ward came on as a substitute to make the first of at least 90 appearances. Unsurprisingly, we led the way after one round with Connacht in second having beaten the weakest side (Zebre) 19-10 in Italy.

Our next fixture was again in the Heineken Cup and a trip to our regular opponents Connacht in Galway. These matches were never easy and if the weather intervened again, it could be a difficult Saturday night. Botica started in place of the injured Nick Evans and promptly landed a penalty for the first points. The Connacht reply was swift and from a quickly taken penalty, McSherry was put over after a short attack. Parks converted and slotted a penalty either side of two from Botica. After 15 minutes, we trailed 9-10 but we gave away three kickable penalties in just over ten minutes and Parks got all of them to leave us with a ten point deficit. Fortunately, the weather held out and Danny Care poached two tries, Botica converted the second and got a penalty to give us a 24-19 lead at the break. Parks added a fifth penalty on 44 minutes but two more from Botica enabled us to win again and deny our hosts anything from the game. There was no scoring in the last seventeen minutes despite Connacht making a host of changes and we left Ireland with a 30-22 victory. Our lead at the top of the Pool stretched to four points; Biarritz had beaten Zebre and scored six tries in the process to get the bonus point. We were well placed to reach the quarter finals with two matches coming up against Zebre where we would be targeting two bonus point victories.

On Sunday 28th October, we travelled to Reading to meet London Irish in round seven of the Aviva Premiership. Our record on this ground against the Irish was even with two draws and four wins apiece from the ten games played since November 2000. Botica had a good start and put over two penalties in the first eight minutes but, when his clearance kick was charged down, Armitage was on hand to grab the ball and touch down. Humphreys converted and our lead had gone. We regained it quickly when Care intercepted and ran 40 metres to score under the posts. Botica converted but two penalties by Humphreys brought the scores level. Robshaw took a boot in the face and was replaced by Fa'asavalu before Botica and Humphreys exchanged penalties and Brown was yellow-carded rather harshly for a deliberate knock-on. Into the second half, Botica and Humphreys again exchanged penalties before Hopper and Botica combined to put Williams over in the corner for Botica to convert via the post. Humphreys put over three penalties in fifteen minutes, Botica missed a long range effort and we trailed 26-28 with ten minutes remaining. As the clock ticked down, we were around our 22 and in desperate need of some territory gaining phases. We drove and drove, off-loaded and gradually worked our way into the Irish 22. Monye almost scored in the corner but his pass was intercepted and the pressure was relieved. From a lineout, Monye was again almost over but Armitage tackled him and put him into touch. Luckily for us, he had passed the ball inside and as Casson tried to pick it up near the line, he knocked-on and fell on the ball in-goal. The question was referred to the TMO and it was revealed that he hadn't knocked-on but the ball had shot forward off his leg and by falling on the ball with his upper torso, had actually scored a try. It proved to be the match winner and although Botica missed the conversion, time had expired and the final whistle went to the sound of booing from the disbelieving home fans. Part of the Law relating to grounding the ball reads as follows:- Law 22.1(b) A player grounds the ball when it is on the ground in the in-goal and the player presses down on it with a hand or hands, arm or arms, or the front of the player's body from waist to neck inclusive. This confirmed that Casson's try was legal despite the Irish crying foul. We moved back to the top of the table with this win on points difference from Saracens with Gloucester (23 points) one behind and Northampton one point behind them. Sale had picked up another losing bonus point but were now eight points behind London Irish and London Welsh at the bottom.

A visit from Gloucester for another Saturday evening kick-off brought a brief spell of league action to an end and we were looking to remain top. Nick Evans came back from injury and was on the score sheet after seven minutes with a penalty. Burns equalised for Gloucester and then Brown got over for the opening try after good work from Fa'asavalu, Dickson, Evans and Williams. Evans was spot on with the conversion but Burns kept kicking penalties and three put Gloucester in front. From a quickly taken penalty by Dickson, Williams sold a massive one-handed dummy to take out three defenders and sent Hopper in for the score. Evans missed the extras but succeeded when Smith intercepted and ran in from 45 yards out. Half time came and we led 22-12 but the visitors were not yet out of it and Burns twice exchanged penalties with Evans. Two men from the visiting side saw yellow; Monahan (for taking Brown out in the air) on 47 minutes and Morgan (from a scrum infringement) after 75 minutes. With five minutes left, we led 28-18 and looked good for another win but Gloucester made a fight of it when they scored after a sweeping move from their 22. Twelvetrees rounded it off with a try under the posts and Burns quickly converted. Unluckily for them, there just wasn't enough time left to get any more scores and it finished 28-25. We stayed top by a points difference of one from Saracens. Both sides had 28 points with Leicester (25), Gloucester (24) and Northampton (23) making up the top five. At the bottom, Sale had six points with London Irish on 10 and London Welsh on 14.

The LV= Cup returned at this point and we were in Pool 1 with Exeter, Gloucester and the Dragons. Of course, as was the case with this competition, none of these sides would be played. Instead, we met the teams in Pool 4 – Bath, London Welsh, Northampton and the Ospreys. Our first encounter was at Franklin's Gardens against Northampton Saints. Conor O'Shea now deliberately used this competition to blood the younger players in the squad. It was a great way to give them the experience they would need for sterner tests to come. Lamb put over a penalty after two minutes to open the scoring but a loose pass from him ended with Sam Smith cutting in to score. Botica converted, Lamb got his second penalty and, after the Saints coughed up the ball in front of their posts, Harry Sloan was under them in a flash. Botica added the extras as he did with Smith's second try when the wing intercepted a Lamb pass on half way and romped home. Lamb completed his hat-trick on half time but we led 21-9. Northampton came out fighting after the break and a minute after Lamb's fourth penalty, Burrell went over for an unconverted score. With half an hour to go, our lead was down to just four points. A Botica penalty extended it but May scored, Lamb converted and put over another penalty to put the Saints in front. When he dropped a goal with three minutes left, it seemed they had done enough. This breed of Quins were a resilient bunch and they never gave up. Ethan Waller was binned for scrum offences and from the tap penalty, Botica went over between the posts. With the final kick of the game he converted and gave us a fantastic away win by just one point (31-30). His try was also the bonus point clincher but Exeter won by more at London Welsh (42-15) so they led the way. Back row forward Jack Clifford was a substitute in this one, it was the first of at least 54 appearances (he would also progress quickly and by the summer of 2016 had won 8 England caps) and centre Harry Sloan played from the start, he would go on to make at least 34 appearances.

Bath came to the Stoop the following Friday night for our second LV= Cup fixture. We had never beaten them in any form of cup rugby – our record was six losses out of six. Ben Botica was quickly to the fore with his place kicking and he put us in front with a penalty after just 67 seconds. He quickly added two more and replied with another to Donald's for Bath. Perinese saw yellow after repeated scrum infringements and Donald and Botica exchanged penalties again to leave us 15-6 ahead. At half time, Botica was replaced by Louis Grimoldby (who was making his debut and would go on to make 8 appearances) after taking a knock late in the half. Donald reduced the arrears after 45 minutes and after they made six substitutions, Heathcote added a fourth to make it a three point game. That was as close as they got because after Sharman was binned for a ruck offence, Grimoldby calmly landed two penalties in five minutes to see us home 21-12. Exeter also won so the situation at the top remained the same.

It was back to Premiership action the following Friday with a trip to the Rec to play our previous opponents, Bath. Our hosts were seventh in the table and eight points behind us. Early pressure brought a chance for Evans and he duly landed the penalty. Donald missed one but levelled with his next chance before Evans put us back in front. In the last five minutes of the half, Donald knocked over two more and Bath led 9-6. His fourth made it 12-6, Evans missed one and Dickson was caught on the line when it looked as though he might score the opening try of the night. From more pressure, our only reward was another Evans penalty. At the start of the third quarter, Evans brought us level, Donald edged Bath ahead, Evans made it level again and Donald nudged the home side in front once more (this came after Banahan was denied a try by the TMO). Easter went close from a charged down kick but Donald kicked his seventh penalty to make it 21-15. There was still time for Evans to get his sixth and a frantic last attack was thwarted by Bath and we had lost our third league game of the season. After 160 minutes of rugby between the two sides, no fewer than 24 penalty goals and not a single try. Because Saracens lost, we led by a point at the top with Gloucester on 28 points (the same as Sarries) and Northampton (27) and Leicester (26) not far behind. The gap at the bottom was five points, Sale had 6 and London Irish were on 11 although London Welsh (15) and Worcester (19) were not in the clear just yet.

With our England men still on Autumn International duty, we welcomed Worcester Warriors to the Stoop for another Friday encounter. After early pressure, the Warriors moved the ball from a five metre scrum and Lemi was in for a try in the corner. Goode missed the conversion but slotted a penalty to make it 8-0 after six minutes. On 20 minutes, Evans put us on the scoreboard with his first penalty but Goode hit back a minute later and the same players exchanged penalties after 25 and 30 minutes respectively. Lemi had been binned for killing the ball near his own line just before Evans landed his second penalty. When Evans set up Hopper for a straight run to the line, he converted and added a penalty to give us a half time lead (16-14). The penalty came as a result of Taulava being binned for conceding too many penalties in a desperate defensive situation. We could score nothing more during his time off the pitch but Evans did eventually put over his fourth penalty. With 13 minutes left, Claassens went over to level the scores but Goode again failed to convert. Nick Evans had the last word when he dropped a goal on 72 minutes to win the game. Another close encounter but at least we were now winning more of these than we were losing. After 10 rounds, we still led the way on 33 points with Saracens on 32, Northampton (31), Leicester (30), Gloucester (29) and Exeter (28) making up the top six. Sale still held up the table on six points with London Irish on 12, London Welsh (19) and Worcester (20).

The next two Saturdays were taken up with Heineken Cup action and a double header against the weakest side in the Pool, Zebre. We had to travel first and Stadio XXV Aprile in Parma was our destination. It was bitterly cold and there was snow around the ground but we made light of the conditions once we opened the scoring. We did have to wait 25 minutes before Evans put over a penalty and Smith quickly added our first try. Evans converted, Bergamasco went to the bin for a ruck offence and Smith scored his second for Evans to convert. Sarto scored a breakaway for the home side which Orquera converted but normal service was resumed after half time. Easter scored number three, our scrum won a penalty try for the bonus point, Hopper got another and the scrum worked its magic again. Evans converted all four tries scored in the third quarter and we were home and dry. Redolfino was binned just before the second penalty try and Buchanan scored try number seven to take us to half a century of points. Chillon got a try back from an interception (Orquera converting) but we had the last word when Botica made his way over and converted to make it 57-14. Three wins from three put us on 14 points at the top of the Pool and, as Connacht had beaten Biarritz at home, we were six points clear of them. With another try bonus likely the following Saturday, we were set fair to reach the quarter finals.

Zebre visited the Twickenham Stoop on 15th December but early Christmas presents were in short supply for our Italian friends. We started with a customary penalty from Nick Evans, Casson got the first try and Evans converted – it was 10-0 after eight minutes. The next score came from Zebre when Trevisan scored a try on 27 minutes but Evans got another penalty four minutes later. It was now a mental battle to see if we could put a far inferior side to the sword. After Halangahu saw yellow, a penalty try arrived and Evans converted for a 20-5 lead at the interval. In the third quarter we scored three tries (Botica, Easter and Smith), Evans converted the lot and Garcia went to the bin after the first of these. Care added our sixth and Dickson (who had replaced Brown) got the seventh. Evans converted Dickson's and Zebre lost their third man to the bin (Ferrarini) after Care's score. It was a stroll in the park really with the result never in doubt. The final score of 53-5 put us on 19 points with Biarritz second ten points behind, Connacht third with 8 and Zebre pointless at the bottom. Basically, with two games to go (these would be played in January), we needed only a point to win the Pool.

It was back to three weeks of Aviva Premiership action around Christmas and the New Year and we had three tough games against Northampton, London Irish and London Welsh. The first was on 22nd December at Franklin's Gardens against the Saints. The conditions would test our ability to play in the wet, it was not the time to play our off-loading game. In the first half Evans kicked penalties either side of one from Myler to leave us three points up after 40 minutes. When Johnston went to the bin, Myler equalised but three penalties from Evans in a ten minute spell at the start of the final quarter opened up a nine point gap. Lamb brought the Saints within range again with five minutes to go but an excellent attack ended with a penalty to us in front of the home posts. Evans stepped up and duly took away Northampton's losing bonus point. It was clinical but you needed to be to win the Premiership. We would be top at Christmas with 37 points, Saracens one behind on 36, Leicester (35), Gloucester (33) and Northampton had fallen away with 31. Sale were still at the bottom with seven points, the Irish had 12 and the Welsh were on 20.

Big Game 5 took place at Twickenham Stadium on 29th December and this time London Irish were our opponents. It was the final game of the year and a win would give us a good chance of heading the table going into 2013. A crowd of 82,000 turned up on a wet and windy day at HQ. As was the case when we met at the Madjeski, Evans and Humphreys had a kicking duel and twice Evans put us in front only for Humphreys to equalise. So, the first half ended 6-6 with all to play for in the final forty minutes. After the kickers had again exchanged penalties (Evans put us ahead and Humphreys brought the Irish level), the first try of the game came when Care dived under the defence and Evans converted. Humphreys got another penalty and Evans replied before the Irish kicker got his fifth of the day. With five minutes left, Phibbs went to the bin as the visiting scrum went to pieces and when the feat was repeated two minutes later, referee Greg Garner went under the posts to award the penalty try. Our victory was confirmed with a conversion from Evans, the final score was 26-15. We did lead the way because Saracens could only win by a single point at home to Northampton. The top of the tale read Quins 41 points, Saracens 40, Leicester 39, Gloucester 34, Wasps 33 and Northampton 32. At the bottom, Sale had beaten Worcester and moved to eleven points, London Irish were on 12 and London Welsh had 20. It looked as though one of those three would go down but there was still a long way to go. For so long we had always been one of the teams looking up the table but now we had the best view of all from the top!

The first match of 2013 was a trip to the Kassam Stadium, Oxford to play London Welsh. We were hoping to make it three out of three over the festive period but the Welsh were a tough team so it wouldn't be easy. This was our first visit to the stadium and we made a good start with a lot of possession and pressure. Nick Evans missed a penalty but after 15 minutes, Care broke through and scored under the posts. Evans converted and did so again when Lowe put Guest through and followed up to receive the scoring pass. When Kulemin went to the bin for a high tackle on Lindsay-Hague, the only score during his time off the field was a penalty by Ross. Robshaw got our third try for Evans to convert and Ross finished the half with his second penalty. At 21-6, we looked well set for a nice win to start the year. The third quarter saw Ross bang over two more penalties as the Welsh came back. Evans got his first penalty, Scott scored for the home side and the conversion by Ross made it a five point game. With fourteen minutes left, Lindsay-Hague sent Evans over for the bonus point try and his conversion made it 31-19. The Welsh were not finished and after Evans had missed another penalty, Botica's pass was intercepted and Jackson scored for Ross to convert. In the final eight minutes, with both sides desperate for the win, tempers frayed and Robson and Tideswell were sent to cool off for ten minutes. As we tried to score again, the home side decided they were happy with a losing bonus point and put the ball into touch. The referee (Lyr Apgeraint-Roberts) received a blast from Conor O'Shea who was not happy with his performance. However, we were still top on 46 points, Saracens were second on 44, Leicester third with 43 and Wasps next on 37. At the foot of the table, it read Sale 11, Irish 16, Welsh 21 with all to play for.

The next two weeks would determine whether we reached the Heineken Cup quarter finals and who our opponents would be in April. Connacht visited on 12th January for the eighth time but had yet to win on our home ground. The first quarter was tight and Evans kicked penalties either side of one from Jarvis. On 34 minutes with the pressure mounting on the Connacht scrum, one collapse too many sent the referee under the posts. Evans converted and completed a hat-trick of penalties to give us a 16-3 lead at the break. Immediately after the restart, Brown sent Williams over, Evans converted and when O'Connor and Vainikolo were sent to the bin for off the ball incidents, Connacht were finished. Williams scored his second try and when Marler and Reynecke went off to cool down, the visitors were briefly down to twelve men. When O'Connor came back, he scored a try but this wasn't much of a consolation because Monye, Lowe and Botica (confirmed after almost five minutes of deliberation by the TMO) added more for us. It looked like Robshaw had got the final touchdown but it was awarded to Ben in the end. Botica converted the last two to make it a resounding victory for us by 47-8. As far as Pool 3 was concerned, we had romped home and with only one game left, were confirmed in first place with 24 points; Biarritz had 14 points, Connacht 8 and Zebre brought up the rear still with no points.

The final pool fixture would decide our seeding in the quarter finals. It was the return with Biarritz and was played on the following Friday night. The conditions turned out to be horrendous and the pitch was saturated after hours of incessant rain. Biarritz had not lost a European game at Parc des Sports Aguilera since 2008 and they took the lead with a penalty from Yachvili after eleven minutes. Five minutes later, Evans brought us level and Guest went over from a lineout on 29 minutes. Evans converted and even though Marler and Lauret had a disagreement and went off for ten minutes to cool down, we led 10-3 at the interval. Two penalties from Yachvili in the first fifteen minutes of the second half made it 10-9 but Evans kicked us to victory with two of his own. We topped the Pool with six wins out of six and 28 points; Biarritz were a distant second on 15, Connacht third with 12 and Zebre at the bottom with a single point. We were the number one seeds with a guaranteed home quarter final and the way it worked was that the six Pool winners were 1-6 and the two best runners-up were 7 and 8. The top four were at home and they played the rest in reverse order (1 v 8, 2 v 7, 3 v 6, 4 v 5). When all was worked out the quarter finals were Quins v Munster, Clermont Auvergne v

Montpellier, Toulon v Leicester and Saracens v Ulster. Munster were not the force they had been before but we could not take them lightly. To do so would be suicide.

That would come in April, now we had two more weeks of LV= Cup games. The first was against London Welsh at the Stoop on 26th January. After the snow had cleared the pitch was a bit sticky but it didn't stop both teams running the ball at every opportunity. Unfortunately, lots of errors crept in and a scrappy match resulted. The visitors opened the scoring with a penalty after 13 minutes; our reply was immediate and Lambert scored after Smith was stopped just short. Botica converted and added a penalty before Davies got his second to make it 10-6. Botica stretched the lead in the second half with two more penalties and with seven minutes left, Dave Ward snapped up a loose Welsh lineout near their line and went over to make the game safe. Botica converted to make it 23-6 and we had our third win out of three games played. We led the way with 13 points, Exeter were second with 9, Gloucester next (6) and Newport-Gwent Dragons on 4. All this meant that if we got two points out of next week's game against the Ospreys in Wales, we would be through to the semi-finals. Hooker Harry Allen came on as a sub and would go on to make 5 appearances before being sacked by the Club for drugs offences.

Another rain soaked encounter at the Brewery Field, Bridgend on Sunday 3rd February saw us once again prove we could play in all conditions. After Morgan had put the home side ahead with a penalty, Botica slotted two penalties and Smith was unlucky not to score when it was 3-3. He charged down a kick, chipped the ball on but the shortened in-goal area saved the Ospreys and all he got for his efforts was a soaking! On the half hour, Hopper got over and Botica converted before a period of pressure from the home side enabled Morgan to close the gap at half time to four points with two penalties. The only score of the third quarter was another Morgan penalty and when Botica had a chance after 71 minutes, he missed. With four minutes remaining, Morgan missed with a long range effort but Botica didn't with the last kick of the game to make the final score 16-12. A great win in very difficult circumstances sent us through as Pool winners. We had 17 points from our four games, Exeter finished on 13, Dragons had 8 and Gloucester 6. We also ended up as the top seeds with Sale (15 points) second, Saracens (14) third and Bath (13) fourth. Similar to the Heineken Cup, one played four and two played three. We would play Bath at the Stoop on 9th March for a place in the final. Seb Stegmann appeared for the last time in this one having scored 70 points (14 tries) and made nine appearances as a sub.

In between that game it was back to the slog of the Premiership for four weeks. Our first one was at home to London Wasps on 9th February. It was déjà vu in the first thirteen minutes as Wasps raced into a 14-0 lead. First, Evans had a pass intercepted by Varndell and then a bad kick gave a counter-attacking chance to the visitors and Varndell, Daly and Bell put Wade in for the second try. Robinson converted both and we were stunned again. Robinson had missed a penalty at the start and Evans also missed after Varndell's try but he made up for it by getting our first points after 17 minutes. When Bell was in the bin for a high tackle on Easter, we attacked and Hopper's chip through evaded both Wade and Southwell and bounced just right for him to gather and run round behind the posts. Evans converted and added his second penalty after Daly had missed from the half-way line. After a dreadful start, we were back to 13-14 at half time. Robinson added a penalty at the end of the third quarter, Evans missed again but was on target with nine minutes left. With less than two minutes remaining, we had a penalty in front of the posts but a fair distance out. Daly had just missed another long range effort but if Evans could hit the target, our winning run in all competitions would hit eleven matches. Unfortunately, his kick fell short and Wasps held out for their first win over us since December 2009 (Big Game 2). Leicester went top on points difference (we both had 47 points), Saracens were on 44 and Wasps had 41. At the wrong end, Sale now had 15 points, Irish 20, Welsh 21 and Worcester 26.

Another home game, this time against Leicester with a 5.15 p.m. kick-off on 16th February. It was first against second and the match did not disappoint any of the 14,800 in the ground. When Evans failed a fitness test on his ankle an hour before kick-off, Ben Botica took his place among four changes from the previous week. After six minutes, we were on the attack and when Easter threw out a long pass to the wing, Flood intercepted and ran 75 yards for a try which he converted. Undeterred, we came back and Botica got us on the board with a penalty. Flood restored the gap with his first penalty, Botica got two, Flood another and Botica's fourth made it 12-13 after 34 minutes. The half would belong to Tigers though and Flood's kick through was grounded by Thompstone and confirmed by the TMO. The conversion was missed and we were six points down at the interval. A piece of magic from Danny Care put us in front nine minutes into the second half. From a quickly taken penalty around the half way, he jinked his way inside and outside of Tait and was over the line despite the attentions of Allen. Botica converted for the lead and added another penalty with twenty minutes left. With each side only making three changes, the flow of the game was not interrupted as was usually the case. With just over ten minutes left, a good move by the backs ended with Botica putting Monye over for the match clinching try but

Hopper had blocked Smith and Wayne Barnes ruled it out after consultation with the TMO. Almost immediately, Flood made the gap one point with his third penalty but Botica got his sixth with two minutes left to give us our third win over Leicester in a row. This had last been achieved between 1989 and 1992 when a run of four victories was put together. We still led the way with seven rounds to go. We passed the fifty point mark and led Saracens by two points (they had 49), Leicester were on 48 and Wasps (45) made up the top four. At the bottom, it was hotting up; Sale were on 19, London Irish had 20, London Welsh (22) and Worcester (26). All four sides now had four wins and any of them could go down.

The following Friday night saw us travel to Salford City Stadium to take on Sale Sharks. After Shepherd had opened the scoring in the second minute with a try (converted by Cipriani), we controlled the rest of the half. Botica slotted two penalties and then converted a try from Williams (scored when Tuitupou had been binned after a series of penalties against the Sharks). Botica continued his fine form with the boot into the second half and another penalty took us nine points clear. Amongst a series of substitutions, Fa'asavalu was binned for punching Jones and it was our turn to be down to fourteen men. Before he returned, Easter grabbed our second try and Botica converted. When Matthews dived over, Botica again converted and with eleven minutes left, it was 30-7. A late charge from the Sharks saw Vernon and Tuitupou go over for tries. Both were converted by Cipriani but it wasn't enough to alter the result or gain them a bonus point. It finished 30-21 and was our sixth win in a row over them. Our lead had been cut to one point by Saracens and they moved on to 54 points, Leicester had 49 and Gloucester and Wasps both had 45. After gaining nothing from the game against us, Sale lost ground at the bottom and were now three points behind London Welsh (22); London Irish had 24 and Worcester 27.

Exeter Chiefs were down in eighth place but had beaten us earlier in the season. We could not take them lightly, especially given that we were missing our England contingent of Brown, Care, Marler and Robshaw. Although Evans did return to the fly half position, we were deprived of his influence after 18 minutes when he dropped to full back because of an injury to Lindsay-Hague. Up to this point, Monye had scored a try (Evans converted) and Steenson had put over two penalties for the visitors. Steenson and Evans then exchanged penalties to leave us with a 10-9 lead at the break. Two more Steenson efforts either side of a brace from Botica still left us with a one point lead with 27 minutes to go. As the game went on, we gradually ran out of steam and when Welch scored a try to put Exeter in front (after Arscott had spilled a try-scoring pass just before) we were in trouble. We couldn't get the ball out of our half and when a bad 22 metre drop out fell to Arscott, he ran through for the match winning score. Steenson converted and even though seven minutes remained, we had no answer. In a way, it resembled our loss to them back in October and O'Shea was frustrated by the amount of ball we coughed up and our lack of ability to stretch the lead. As a result, we were knocked off the top of the table. Saracens now led the way on 59 points, we had 55, Leicester were on 54 and Northampton (49) made up the potential semi-finalists. The battle at the foot of the table had become a three horse race between Sale, London Welsh and London Irish. They gained no points between them in round 17 whereas Worcester had a bonus point win against Wasps.

The LV= Cup semi-final against Bath at the Stoop came on Saturday 9th March. Our second string took on a Bath side virtually at full strength – this would not be an easy tie. From the start, we played the style of rugby that was once again becoming synonymous with the Club. After eight minutes, the Bath defence was breached for the first time. Dickson passed to Botica, he put Williams through who fed Fa'asavalu and the final pass went to Guest for a try under the posts. Botica converted and did the same when Williams intercepted a pass from Eastmond to run 80 metres and score. From a lineout, we were driven back and Louw scored for Heathcote to convert. When Dickson went over after Guest had been stopped, Botica's conversion made it 21-7 but Heathcote kicked a penalty to narrow the deficit at half time. Right at the start of the second half Heathcote got another penalty but out fourth try came on 52 minutes. Another great piece of play saw Botica pass to Wallace who made a superb off-load to send Williams in and Botica converted to make it 28-13. A series of offside decisions ended with Smith going to the bin on 56 minutes and within a minute, Abendanon scored and Heathcote converted. When he landed his third penalty after 62 minutes, it was 28-23 and all to play for. Before Smith came back, Botica kicked the penalty after Catt had been binned for stopping a quickly taken penalty. Our fly half missed a long range effort but it didn't matter and we won 31-23. Next week would be our first domestic cup final since the defeat to Newcastle in 2001. Our opponents would be Sale Sharks who defeated Saracens 21-15 in the other semi-final.

So, on Sunday 17th March, the teams travelled to Sixways, home of Worcester Warriors to fight it out for the first trophy of the season. Both sides had lots of different starters since the league game three weeks before; we had seven and Sale had eight. Our line-up was as follows:- Ross Chisholm; Tom Williams, George Lowe, Tom Casson, Sam Smith; Ben Botica, Karl Dickson; Mark Lambert, Rob Buchanan, Will Collier; Sam Twomey, Charlie Matthews; Maurie Fa'asavalu, Luke Wallace (captain) and Tom Guest. Replacements – Dave Ward, Darryl Marfo, James Johnston, Pete Browne, Joe Trayfoot, Jordan Burns, Rory Clegg and Charlie Walker. We started well and Botica opened our account after four minutes with a penalty and when Dickson put Williams over for the opening try, we had raced into an eight point lead. Cipriani replied with two penalties but in between, Guest had picked up from a five metre scrum and driven over. Botica converted this and added a penalty to make it 18-6 at the break. Cipriani's third penalty stirred us into action and from a clean lineout take by Matthews, Dickson fed Botica who put Casson over from 25 metres out. Botica again converted and there were 35 minutes left. When Wallace also scored, Botica converted and suddenly we were 23 points clear. There were still over 25 minutes left but victory was assured even though Leota scored a consolation for Sale a couple of minutes later. At this point, O'Shea made four substitutions and with five minutes left, Burns came on to ensure every one of the 23 played. Rory Clegg made his last appearance having scored 302 points (1 try, 1 dropped goal, 58 penalties and 70 conversions) and made 36 appearances as a sub. The final score of 32-14 was our first domestic cup win since the defeat of Northampton back in May 1991. Afterwards, Conor was really pleased that the youngsters had come through to win and the experience would help them in the future. But, there was still all to play for on two fronts and we had a maximum of ten matches left. If we went all the way it would mean seven Premiership and three Heineken Cup games. Our squad would be tested to the full in the coming two months.

On Sunday 24th March, we met Saracens on their new artificial all-weather pitch at Allianz Park, Barnet. The England players returned to the fold and the first 22 minutes saw a penalty kicking duel between Evans and Farrell. The second named drew first blood then Evans put two over before Farrell equalised. Marler saw yellow trying to prevent a score and before he returned, we leaked eleven points. Two Farrell penalties and a try from Brits took them clear although Evans did land a third penalty after 29 minutes. His fourth came four minutes into the third quarter but we were making too many mistakes in attack and defence to ever hope of turning it round. When Fraser scored from a cross-kick by Farrell, the game was effectively over. Farrell converted and kicked a penalty after 67 minutes but Ashton's yellow card for a high tackle on Fa'asavalu came too late for us to do anything. All of a sudden, we had lost two Premiership games in a row and gained no points in the process. We were down to third place, eight points behind Saracens who had 63 and three behind Leicester (58). Northampton were one behind us and Gloucester were on 50 (we played them next so it had become a must win game for us).

And so to Kingsholm for a Friday fixture on a bitterly cold evening. Every Premiership game between the sides since Gloucester won at the Stoop in September 2006 had gone the way of the home side – would this one be any different? The deadlock was broken after seven minutes when Rob Buchanan scored in the corner, Burns pulled back three points with a penalty before Evans put in a superb chip and Smith gathered to score. Having missed the first conversion, Evans made no mistake with the second and we had a handy 12-3 lead at the interval. It could have been more had referee JP Doyle not wrongly adjudged that a pass from Care had been knocked on by Chisholm (Casson picked up and touched down but the decision went against us). Gloucester struck back quickly and May scored for Burns to convert. Evans put over a penalty after 54 minutes but Gray was binned with thirteen minutes left and the home side pounced two minutes later. From a five metre scrum, Qera scored and Burns converted to put them ahead. Try as we did in the final ten minutes, we couldn't get any more points and lost again, this time by a narrow two point margin (15-17). At least we got one point from this defeat and we stayed third with three rounds left. Saracens now had 67 points, Leicester 63, Quins 56 and Northampton and Gloucester both had 54. London Welsh now occupied the bottom spot because they had been deducted five points for fielding an ineligible player in ten matches. They had 18 points, Sale were on 23 and the Irish had now reached 28.

On Sunday 7th April, we entertained Munster in the Heineken Cup quarter final. Somehow, the Club administration got it all wrong with the ticket arrangements and with some Quins fans unbelievably getting tickets for or selling tickets to Munster fans, the visitors managed to get a numerical superiority of support in the ground. The decision to play at the Stoop to give us more of a home ground advantage had completely backfired. After the event, the Club publicly criticised those who had sold their allocated tickets but the damage had been done by then. When the teams came out, it seemed the Stoop was a sea of red Munster flags. After a good start, Evans put us in front with a penalty after three minutes. O'Gara had a chance to level but his kick hit a post, Evans missed a chance but doubled our lead after 18 minutes. O'Gara missed again and the Munster supporters were quiet; we had to take this opportunity to build a decent lead. We couldn't do it and O'Gara found the target either side of a third from Evans to leave us 9-6 in front at half time. The third quarter was a disaster for us as we simply didn't come out from the changing room! Munster tore into us, we gave away penalty after penalty and with O'Gara scoring regularly, our 9-6 advantage became a 9-18 deficit. Evans did pull three points back with his fourth penalty after 65 minutes but the Munster defence stood firm and we failed to score again. Yet again we had failed to reach the Heineken Cup semi-final and our European adventure was over for another season. The visitors had found some form from somewhere but had we taken advantage in the first half, it could have been a different result. As a result of this loss, none of our men in the frame for the British and Irish Lions tour to Australia made the squad.

With three games left in the Premiership regular season, we needed to win all of them to give ourselves the best possible chance of a home semi-final. On 13th April, Bath visited the Stoop knowing that defeat would almost certainly put them out of contention. We started as if we were still at La Manga Club near Cartagena, Spain (where the squad went in the early part of the week). The weather at the Stoop was wind and rain instead of sun. Donald and Devoto landed penalties in the first 21 minutes and we lost Robson and Hopper to injury. Botica replaced Hopper, was handed the place kicking duties and within ten minutes of coming on had brought us level with two penalties. Right on half time, Donald put Bath ahead again with another penalty. After 45 minutes, Evans put up a high kick and Bath conceded a lineout near their line. From this we drove, Care dummied his way over the line for Botica to convert and we led 13-9. Another Botica penalty extended our lead and on 63 minutes, we closed it out. Another high kick from Evans swirled in the wind and caused utter confusion in the Bath defence. As the ball bounced in-goal, Monye got a hand on it to grab our second try. Botica was again successful with the conversion, the last sixteen minutes remained scoreless and we had won for the first time since the LV= Cup Final. At the top, Saracens had now moved on to 72 points, Leicester had 68, Quins were next on 60 with Northampton behind us on 59. Gloucester retained an outside chance of getting into the top four but realistically, no-one else had a chance although Exeter could mathematically still make it. At the bottom, London Welsh had been relegated after a 31-14 defeat at home to Northampton.

It was back to the scene of our LV= Cup triumph on 20th April when we visited Worcester. Against the run of play, Pennell scored the opening try after a breakout. Goode converted but we got our act together and a quick fire ten points in four minutes by Evans (penalty, try and conversion) put us in front. It was a see-saw game and after Goode kicked two penalties, Williams and Care scored unconverted tries for us. Before half time there was still time for another Goode penalty. At 20-16, we needed to press on in the third quarter but the home side would not be beaten easily. Within four minutes, Grove scored a try, Goode converted and added a penalty but Care got over after Fa'asavalu had been put through by Robshaw and Evans restored our lead with a penalty. We lost Robshaw with a twisted ankle (his season was over) and then Evans somehow kept hold of a clearance kick which hit him in the throat and ran on to score. His conversion put us 35-26 ahead after 66 minutes. The final try of the game went to Mike Brown. Fa'asavalu had left three Worcester players on the floor as he rampaged through to make room for the full back to score (one of those injuries to Taulava required a fifteen minute stoppage and he was stretchered off with a serious leg injury). Evans converted and there was no way back for the Warriors even though Guest was yellow carded at the end. Saracens and Leicester both lost but picked up bonus points, we moved up to 65 points but remained one point ahead of Northampton. The top four teams were now confirmed only the order needed to be finalised. We could still get a home semi-final but Leicester would need to lose to London Irish and gain no points while we defeated Northampton.

A week off because of the European semi-finals (Toulon would go on to win the Heineken Cup) meant that our last regular season game at the Stoop against Northampton was played on 4th May. In this situation it was a difficult call, either you decided who you would rather meet in the semi-final or you played the game and either went to Allianz Park or Welford Road (assuming Leicester didn't slip up against the Irish). Both sides had a chance of the home game if they did but it was unlikely. The first score came via the boot of Evans with a penalty after eleven minutes and he converted a try by Williams on 21 minutes. Northampton then had a try disallowed by the TMO for a block but they got on the board when Elliott ran on to a kick through by Foden. In the first ten minutes of the second half, Buchanan (converted by Evans) and Casson added tries to take us 22-5 ahead. Northampton were developing into a tough unit to play against and they came back with two tries of their own from Hartley and Day (both converted by Myler) to make it 22-19 with nineteen minutes to go. Both teams now proceeded to bring on all remaining substitutes (we had five and Northampton seven) and the game ended in a victory for us. As it turned out, Saracens and Leicester won so the top of the table was as follows:- Saracens 77 points, Leicester 74, Quins 69 and Northampton 65. The semi-finals would be Saracens v Northampton and Leicester v Quins.

The week after the final round of matches came the semi-final at Welford Road, Leicester. The wind was howling and the rain lashed down just before kick-off as we played into the storm in the first half. After Flood had given the home side the lead after four minutes with a penalty, we took control and three from Evans after five, twelve and thirty one minutes gave us a 9-3 lead. Care should have scored in the corner (Croft prevented him with an excellent piece of defensive work) and if a golden opportunity had not been missed when Monye was free, the scores could have been a lot different. The Tigers were rattled and as half time approached, it was looking good for us. We had at least two opportunities to kick the ball out and go in ahead but our style of attack at all costs proved a disaster on this occasion. The ball was turned over and Goneva ran down the touchline and behind the posts after evading a desperate dive by Williams. Flood converted and it was 13-9 to Leicester at the break. During the interval, the wind dropped, the sun came out and the Tigers were rejuvenated. When Care received a yellow card for a deliberate knock-on, they took their chance. Flood kicked a penalty and converted a try from Morris. The momentum was now completely with the home side and a minute later, Croft stormed over from half way and we were a broken side. Flood missed the conversion and that of Tait's try eight minutes later. The pass to Tait was at least ten feet forward but the new approach being taken to forward passes led some to believe it was not forward including the referee! At this point, Leicester made five substitutions but we kept playing and Chisholm scorched in for a try which Evans converted. There were four minutes left and we might have scored another but it wouldn't have been nearly enough and the game finished 33-16 to the home side. James Johnston made his final appearance; he had scored 15 points (3 tries) and made 27 appearances as a sub and four trips to the bin. It was a great shame to lose an extremely promising player to Saracens and he would be sorely missed. Our season was over and Leicester went on to beat Northampton 37-17 in the final. If we had taken our chances, it would have been so different but lessons had to be learned from this in time for next season.

Although we had failed in our quest for the treble, we had won the LV= Cup and any season where you win silverware is a successful one. Overall, our playing record was P36 W27 D0 L9 F985 A672. In the league it was P22 W15 D0 L7 F560 A453 Pts 69 (BP 9 – TB 5 LB 4) Pos 3rd (our post-season was P1 L1 F16 A33). No one appeared in all 36 games, the most was Tom Guest with 32 and he was followed by Rob Buchanan (31), James Johnston and George Robson (30) and Nick Easter and Matt Hopper on 29. Top points scorer was Nick Evans for the fifth consecutive season with 331 (5 tries, 1 dropped goal, 67 penalties and 51 conversions), he also scored the most penalties and conversions and shared the dropped goals with Danny Care (one each – the same as in 2010/11). Care got the most tries with a dozen. Overall, tries rose from 80 to 96, penalties were exactly the same on 113, conversions went up from 63 to 80 and there were only two dropped goals (up one). As a result, overall points went up from 823 to 985.

2012/13

090812	CASTRES OLYMPIQUE	CASTRES	L	1G1PG1T(15)-4G1PG(31)
180812	LONDON SCOTTISH	TWICKENHAM STOOP	W	6G(42)-3G(21)
180812	CONNACHT	TWICKENHAM STOOP	W	5G2T(45)-2PG1T(11)
010912	LONDON WASPS(AP)	TWICKENHAM(A)	W	4G3PG1T(42)-3G3PG2T(40)
070912	LONDON WELSH(AP)	TWICKENHAM STOOP	W	5G1T(40)-1PG(3)
150912	SALE SHARKS(AP)	TWICKENHAM STOOP	W	4G3PG(37)-3PG1T(14)
220912	LEICESTER(AP)	LEICESTER	W	1G1DG4PG(22)-3PG(9)
300912	SARACENS(AP)	TWICKENHAM STOOP	L	1G3PG(16)-6PG(18)
061012	EXETER CHIEFS(AP)	EXETER	L	2G3PG1T(28)-4G3PG1T(42)
131012	BIARRITZ OLYMPIQUE(HECP3)	TWICKENHAM STOOP	W	4G4PG(40)-1G2PG(13)
201012	CONNACHT(HECP3)	GALWAY	W	1G6PG1T(30)-1G5PG(22)
281012	LONDON IRISH(AP)	READING	W	2G4PG1T(31)-1G7PG(28)
031112	GLOUCESTER(AP)	TWICKENHAM STOOP	W	2G3PG1T(28)-1G6PG(25)

101112	NORTHAMPTON(LVCP1)	NORTHAMPTON	W	4G1PG(31)-1G1DG5PG1T(30)
161112	BATH(LVCP1)	TWICKENHAM STOOP	W	7PG(21)-4PG(12)
231112	BATH(AP)	BATH	L	6PG(18)-7PG(21)
301112	WORCESTER(AP)	TWICKENHAM STOOP	W	1G1DG4PG(22)-3PG2T(19)
081212	ZEBRE(HECP3)	PARMA	W	7G1PG1T(57)-2G(14)
151212	ZEBRE(HECP3)	TWICKENHAM STOOP	W	6G2PG1T(53)-1T(5)
221212	NORTHAMPTON(AP)	NORTHAMPTON	W	6PG(18)-3PG(9)
291212	LONDON IRISH(AP)	TWICKENHAM	W	2G4PG(26)-5PG(15)
060113	LONDON WELSH(AP)	OXFORD	W	4G1PG(31)-2G4PG(26)
120113	CONNACHT(HECP3)	TWICKENHAM STOOP	W	4G3PG2T(47)-1PG1T(8)
180113	BIARRITZ OLYMPIQUE(HECP3)	BIARRITZ	W	1G3PG(16)-3PG(9)
260113	LONDON WELSH(LVCP1)	TWICKENHAM STOOP	W	2G3PG(23)-2PG(6)
030213	OSPREYS(LVCP1)	BRIDGEND	W	1G3PG(16)-4PG(12)
090213	LONDON WASPS(AP)	TWICKENHAM STOOP	L	1G3PG(16)-2G1PG(17)
160213	LEICESTER(AP)	TWICKENHAM STOOP	W	1G6PG(25)-1G3PG1T(21)
220213	SALE SHARKS(AP)	SALFORD	W	3G3PG(30)-3G(21)
020313	EXETER CHIEFS(AP)	TWICKENHAM STOOP	L	1G3PG(16)-1G5PG1T(27)
090313	BATH(LVCSF)	TWICKENHAM STOOP	W	4G1PG(31)-2G3PG(23)
170313	SALE SHARKS(LVCF)	WORCESTER	W	3G2PG1T(32)-3PG1T(14)
240313	SARACENS(AP)	BARNET	L	4PG(12)-1G5PG1T(27)
290313	GLOUCESTER(AP)	GLOUCESTER	L	1G1PG1T(15)-2G1PG(17)
070413	MUNSTER(HECQF)	TWICKENHAM STOOP	L	4PG(12)-6PG(18)
130413	BATH(AP)	TWICKENHAM STOOP	W	2G3PG(23)-3PG(9)
200413	WORCESTER(AP)	WORCESTER	W	3G2PG3T(42)-2G4PG(26)
040513	NORTHAMPTON(AP)	TWICKENHAM STOOP	W	2G1PG1T(22)-2G1T(19)
110513	LEICESTER(APSF)	LEICESTER	L	1G3PG(16)-2G3PG2T(33)

49

The Magic Starts to Wear Off 2013-2015

A three match tour by England to Argentina happened in June 2013 and it proved to be a 100% success with victory over a South American XV (41-21) and the two test matches against the hosts (32-3 and 51-26). Mike Brown, Rob Buchanan and Joe Marler were our current payers in the party and they were joined by past and future Quins Doran-Jones, Strettle and Marland Yarde. Brown, Doran-Jones (who came on as a sub) and Marler played in both tests, Strettle appeared in the first and Yarde started in the second.

The British and Irish Lions travelled to Australia again for their 2013 tour after a brief stop off in Hong Kong to play the Barbarians on 1st June to celebrate the 125th anniversary of the Lions. The match was won 59-8 which left just nine matches to play in Australia between 5th June and 6th July. The same two future Quins as last time were our only representation in this squad (Adam Jones and Jamie Roberts). Jones played in all three tests but Roberts only appeared in the last one and scored a try. The test series was tight to begin with - the first going to the Lions (23-21) and the second to Australia (16-15) before a commanding performance by the Lions took the series with a 41-16 victory in the deciding match. The non-test matches produced five wins and one defeat for the tourists.

The Annual Report for year ending 30th June 2014 revealed that the Stoop was valued again, this time it was £31.94 million. Vander Meersch resigned as a Director and we made another loss, the highest since 2000/01 - £2,514,725. The amount of the interest free loan from Mosaic Limited had now reached £21,817,906.

Chris Robshaw continued his successful stint as Club captain for the fourth season and he managed to juggle this and the England captaincy very well. As with the previous season, only three friendly fixtures were arranged. The first was at the Stade de Genève against Racing Metro 92 on 9th August. Racing were only a week away from the start of their season and fielded a strong side. After Dumoulin scored an early try for Sexton to convert, we applied pressure for the next twenty minutes and eventually, Monye scored and Evans converted. Lydiate got a second try for Racing, Sexton converted but we were soon level when Lowe scored for Evans to convert. All level at half time but we went behind again when Cronje scored an unconverted try. This enabled Evans to put us ahead for the first time when he converted Monye's second try. Again, the French side grabbed the lead when Mujati went over and, as regular substitutions were being made, Racing scored two more tries from Andreu and Chavancy. All three were converted to make it 40-21 with a few minutes left. We did get the final score when Lowe got his second and Botica converted. This was part of a tournament called the Legion Rugby Challenge where four teams play one game each and the overall winners are decided by public vote! The other game featured Montpellier and Leicester (the French won that one as well by a score of 52-15). Montpellier won the event and would return as defending champions for the 2014 competition held in Grenoble, France.

We followed this a week later with a friendly against London Scottish at the Stoop (again on a Friday night). On paper, a weaker side started, probably selected because of the opposition. As it was, the visitors went in front with a penalty from Millar and it took us nearly twenty minutes to get our first score. From a rolling maul, Marfo scored and Botica converted as he did when Tom Williams crossed a few minutes later. When Wallace went over after a break by Care, Botica's conversion gave us a 21-3 half time lead. The Scots were first to score after the break when Calder was driven over and Newton converted. Our reply was swift and Guest and Williams added further tries, Botica could only convert the first. Ex-Quin Miles Mantella crossed for a second try to the visitors but when Calder was sent to the bin, Clifford scored and Grimoldby converted to make it 40-15.

On Saturday 24th August, Glasgow Warriors came down to the Stoop two weeks before we opened our season against London Wasps. This was a much tighter affair than the two previous games not helped by the inclement weather. Thirteen of the starting team would begin against Wasps. After four minutes, Easter was over for the opening score and Evans converted but he couldn't do the same when Monye stretched the lead to 12-0. After 25 minutes, Wight put the Warriors on the board with a penalty and he then converted a try by McGuigan to make it 12-10 at the break. During the second half, the usual stream of substitutes entered the fray and our scoring dried up. Wight landed two penalties to put Glasgow ahead and it wasn't until later in the half that we regained the lead. From a driving maul, the ball went along the line and Hopper broke through to score our third try. Botica converted and it remained 19-16 until the end despite the best efforts of both teams.

On 7th September the 2013/14 season began with the London Double Header at Twickenham and for the second year running, we played London Wasps. There weren't as many points in this one but the drama remained. We began as we had a year ago and Varndell and Jones sent Launchbury over for the opening try in under a minute. Goode converted, Evans got a penalty and Goode replied to make it 3-10 but Lowe's superb tackle on Varndell as he sprinted down the wing saved the day. In the first ten minutes of the second half, Evans kicked two penalties to narrow the lead to a single point as we began to dominate. Dickson came on for Care and dummied his way over near the line to put us ahead for the first time and Evans converted. There were ten minutes left but there was still time for Wasps to come back. Brown made a try-saving tackle on Jacobs but the ball was moved out to the wing and Palmer scored wide out. Time had expired and it all came down to the conversion from Goode. He struck the ball sweetly and it looked to be going over but the left post intervened and we had won 16-15. If we had lost, there could have been no complaints. Paul Doran-Jones, a prop forward had joined from Northampton and came on as a sub for his first appearance; he would go on to play 19 times over the next two seasons (he had won 6 England caps) but never fulfilled his potential with us. George Merrick was a second row product of the academy and started for the first time in this one; he would go on to make at least 35 appearances. The third new boy was seasoned winger Paul Sackey. He had won 22 caps for England and would make 10 appearances during his one season with us. We were in sixth place after the first week with Exeter bottom; Northampton, Saracens and Leicester led the way after bonus point wins.

The following Friday night saw Northampton visit the Stoop but the conditions were appalling. There was a torrential downpour throughout the whole match and the ground was waterlogged. The game went ahead as planned and after Evans had missed a penalty, Myler put the Saints ahead with one. Evans and Myler missed further attempts before Evans brought the scores level in similar fashion. At the interval, it was 3-3 and our kicking didn't improve afterwards. Evans missed again, then put us in front but Myler equalised with 28 minutes left. After both sides had made four substitutions in ten minutes, the Saints went in front. Evans and Botica (from right in front of the posts) had missed further penalties before a Northampton attack saw Elliott send Wilson sliding in at the corner (whether he actually grounded the ball was debatable). Myler converted and our cause was not helped when Easter was binned for a professional foul although Myler followed him with four minutes left for a deliberate knock-on to ensure that both sides finished with fourteen. The visitors saw out the remaining time and our home record had gone in the first game. In truth we should have been 0 and 2 but we had got another point to stay in sixth. Saracens were the only side with two bonus point wins to start and led by a point from Northampton. Gloucester and Worcester propped up the table but there was a long way to go.

A second Friday night fixture was next and a trip to Sixways to take on Worcester on 20th September. The Warriors had lost their opening two games and despite taking the lead with a penalty from Mieres, we were soon in the ascendancy. Evans kicked two penalties to put us ahead, Abbott was shown yellow for deliberately killing the ball and Mieres pulled Worcester level with his second penalty. Guest, Marler and Robshaw combined to send Care over and Evans converted. Shervington was the next home player in the bin for pulling down a lineout and Marler scored for Evans to convert. At 20-6, we were well on the way to another away win. No sooner had the second half started and we were over again. Buchanan scored and Evans improved the try again. Matavesi also went off for ten minutes for a no arm tackle on Robshaw and a minute later, Mike Brown was over for the bonus point try. The conversion from Evans took us out to 34-6 and there were still thirty minutes to play. This conversion was historic as it took Nick to 1,510 points, one ahead of Bob Hiller's Club record mark set in 1976. As the Warriors tried to gain some pride, Lambert was binned and they were awarded a penalty try that Mieres converted. The final score of the game was a Botica penalty and this confirmed our resounding win by 37-13. As a result, we moved up to fourth place, level with Northampton and behind Leicester (11) and Saracens on 15. Worcester were rooted to the bottom on one point with Wasps (3) and Newcastle with 4 the teams directly above them.

Our next fixture was a visit by Saracens to the Stoop on 28th September. They still had a 100% record and already this had the tag of a must-win game. After Evans had put us ahead with a penalty, Goode was binned for a professional foul on Ugo Monye as he looked to score. It was not the only occasion when the visitors cynically killed the game but they avoided more cards. Evans doubled our lead with another penalty before Farrell got one back for Saracens. Evans restored the six point gap with his third penalty before Fa'asavalu was binned for pulling Burger's hair. During his time off the field, Farrell and Evans exchanged penalties to make it 12-6 at the break. We faced the wind and surrendered our lead after 50 minutes when Ashton scored and Farrell converted. Marler was binned and when he returned, Farrell had added two more penalties to make it 12-19. Another soon after settled the game and we had once again been nullified by the visitors. We had to find a way of playing against them and winning. We dropped to fifth place and now trailed Saracens by nine points with Northampton, Leicester and Bath making up the top four. We were simply not playing well enough although we were well above the bottom where Worcester remained on a single point. Newcastle and London Irish had five points and it was looking ominous for the team from Sixways.

The final game in the opening batch of five Aviva Premiership matches was against London Irish at the Madejski Stadium, Reading. The first half was littered with mistakes and as a result, we were unable to take advantage of all the territory and possession we enjoyed. Geraghty and Evans twice exchanged penalties to make it 6-6 at half time. Evans had missed an earlier penalty chance and Geraghty opted for a quick tap penalty when it would have been better to take the points 20 metres out and in front of the posts. The third quarter saw us lose our captain to injury and Irish gain the lead. When Cowan grabbed a try, Geraghty converted but he missed when Lewington got a second three minutes later. Evans and Botica had failed with penalties before the first try and these misses were now costing us matches. Care did get over with ten minutes left and the conversion from Evans put us within range. Despite attacking as time ran out, we couldn't get that second try and our third league defeat of the season had come after only five games! We were now seventh and already twelve points behind Saracens who were still undefeated. Worcester had two points at the bottom and were seven adrift of Wasps, Gloucester, Newcastle and London Irish.

On Saturday 12th October, it was the start of our Heineken Cup campaign and we were in Pool 4 alongside Clermont Auvergne, Racing Metro 92 and the Scarlets. First up was a meeting with the Welsh side at the Stoop. They made a great start with a try from Rhodri Williams and a conversion and two penalties from Priestland. This made it 0-13 after fourteen minutes, not the start we wanted. We did wake up in the second quarter, Evans landed a penalty and converted a try from Brown but Scott Williams added a second for the Scarlets and Priestland's conversion made it 10-20 at the break. After Lee saw yellow for making contact with Care's face with his boot, Evans dropped a goal and Priestland added two more penalties. Our tackling was not good and it led Conor O'Shea to say after the game that it wasn't a game of touch but it looked like it with some of the tries they scored. One of these came after Evans had brought us back into contention with two penalties. Jordan Williams evaded four defenders and was so close to the touchline it would only have taken the smallest of pushes to put him out; his try was the clincher because Priestland put over his seventh successful kick of the day. At 19-33 with sixteen minutes left, we attempted a comeback and Brown got his second try. Evans converted and with Rob Evans in the bin for the final three minutes, it looked on. One last chance was worked but Sackey put a foot in touch as he was scoring and our miserable start to the season continued. This was our longest losing streak since December 2009 – January 2010 when six were lost. Scarlets topped the Pool, Racing Metro won at home to Clermont and we were third on tries scored.

The next test was a stern one at the Stade Marcel Michelin against Clermont Auvergne. The French side were unbeaten at home for 64 matches and after James had kicked them into a third minute lead with a penalty, the first try arrived. Byrne scored it when he dived over unopposed in the corner. Botica got a penalty but Fofana got a try and we then lost Rob Buchanan to injury (torn pectoral muscle). At this stage, we had something like fifteen players out injured and several of them were going to be out of action for the long term. Evans got our second penalty but a third try from Lacrampe (James converted this one) ensured we had an uphill struggle. Byrne went to the bin for ten minutes but we couldn't take advantage. When he returned, we scored after good work by Robshaw, Collier, Care and Brown; Williams being the try scorer. Evans converted and we only trailed by seven at the interval (13-20). James put over a penalty after 44 minutes and despite the home side only needing one more try for the bonus point, there was no further scoring until the 81st minute. With the clock running out, Joe Trayfoot made a break from our half and charged into Clermont territory. When he was stopped, Care, Brown and Hopper carried on and from a ruck, Evans dropped a goal with the last kick to earn a losing bonus point. Scarlets and Racing Metro drew which kept us in it even though no side had ever qualified for the quarter finals after losing their opening two pool games. Scarlets led the way with six points, Racing were next also on six with Clermont (5) and Quins (2).

Back to Premiership action the following Saturday with a visit from Sale Sharks. They were currently in fifth place and had two points more than we did. Botica had the kicking duties and put us in front with a penalty after 16 minutes. Cipriani equalised but Botica eased us ahead with another penalty. Then, to add to our injury woes, Tom Guest was stretchered off causing a six minute break in play. Botica completed his hat-trick before the break to leave us 9-3 up. Danny Care was introduced after 46 minutes and played a part in a try by Wallace a minute later (an excellent cross-kick by Evans made the score). The conversion was missed but another penalty from Botica nudged us towards the win. In the eight minutes around that kick, Sale made seven substitutions but they made no impression and when Clifford (on for Guest) charged down a kick and re-gathered, he ran in for the match-clinching try. Botica converted and the last twelve minutes remained scoreless. We leap-frogged the Sharks into sixth spot and now had fifteen points. Saracens had lost 20-41 at Northampton so the gap at the top was now one point (Saracens 23, Northampton 22, Bath 18 and Exeter and Leicester on 17). Worcester were now eight points behind Gloucester and London Irish (both 10 points) and desperately needed a change in fortunes.

Leicester were fifth and we made the trip North on 2nd November for another Premiership game. We were looking to do another leap-frog as we had done with Sale the previous week. At this time of the season, the international teams had their autumn window and both sides suffered because of this but an exciting game ensued. Despite falling behind to two penalties from Williams in the first quarter, the home side didn't reach our 22 until twenty eight minutes in. When Salvi was binned for a cynical foul at the breakdown, we took full advantage either side of half time. Evans kicked a penalty and then Easter drove over for a try under the posts (Evans converted). We were now playing with the wind and, after 43 minutes, Hopper got the ball and cut inside on an angled run to the posts to score our second try. Evans converted again and we were 17-6 up. Williams pulled three points back with his third penalty but in the last quarter, two more from Evans made the game safe. Right at the end, Leicester were awarded a penalty try that Williams converted but it was too little far too late and we left with a 23-16 victory. Tim Molenaar had joined from Gloucester and would bolster the centre; he played a good game on debut and would make 19 appearances in an all too short career with us lasting just one season. We moved up to fifth with 19 points and were now nine behind Saracens at the summit. Northampton, Bath and Exeter made up the top four with Worcester still at the bottom (now nine points adrift of London Irish).

LV= Cup action was the priority for the next two weeks and we were in Pool 3 alongside Worcester, Bath and Ospreys. Of course, we played none of them, instead we met the teams in Pool 2 – Cardiff, Exeter, Leicester and Sale. The first was at Sandy Park against Exeter and we could not have got off to a better start in defence of our trophy. Sackey was on hand to finish off a move in the corner after four minutes to put us ahead. Sweeney landed two penalties to take our lead away and Charlie Walker was close to scoring our second try (he was only stopped by a great hit by Arscott). Near to half time, the Chiefs thought they had scored but Sweeney's try was ruled out by the referee because of a forward pass. The game went away from us in the third quarter with two more Sweeney penalties and a close range try from Naqelevuki that Sweeney converted. The final quarter belonged to us in attacking terms but the home defence was excellent and there was no further scoring. It was not a good way to begin our campaign but it was no different to the Aviva and Heineken competitions either. Ross Chisholm's brother James made his debut as a substitute; he was a number 8, another product of the academy and would go on to make at least 15 appearances. In our Pool, Worcester and Bath opened with four point wins, we were third and Ospreys last (both had no points).

On Friday 15th November, Sale Sharks came back three weeks after defeat in the Premiership for our second LV= Cup game in a repeat of last season's final. After eight minutes, Botica scored the opening try and converted and Wallace was unlucky not to add to the total six minutes later when Sale's full back made a try saving tackle. A few minutes later, Seymour scored for the visitors and Macleod converted. He then added a penalty and converted Miller's try (scored when Wallace was in the bin for collapsing a maul). At the end of the half, Botica got a penalty to make it 10-17. He did the same after 43 minutes but Gaskell went over for Sale and Macleod's conversion made it 13-24. The comeback continued when Walker got over, Botica converted and kicked a penalty when Fihaki was sent to the bin. Before he came back, Cipriani got over to clinch the bonus point and again Macleod converted.

With eight minutes left, Botica put over his fourth penalty but we couldn't score again. The full time score of 26-31 was another loss but we did get a bonus point. The Pool now stood as follows - Bath 9 points, Worcester 5, Quins 1 Ospreys 0. It was likely that we would not qualify for the semi-finals as Bath only needed three points from two games to surpass any points total we could get.

Premiership action returned for a couple of weeks and a home match against Gloucester was the first of these. This was played on 23rd November and came exactly 50 years after our first game at the Stoop back in 1963. Over the years we had played over 600 games; the full record was P616 W410 D22 L184. We were looking for our third league win in a row and started with a penalty from Evans after 75 seconds. This was cancelled out by a try from Twelvetrees but Evans was on target with another penalty to regain the lead. After Cowan was sin-binned for impeding Care when he tried to chase his own kick ahead, Easter and Care touched down. Evans converted both and it was 20-5 at the break. The first notable action in the second period was a yellow card for Savage (he took Robson out in the air) and almost immediately, Wallace was over for our third try. Evans again converted and when Thomas became the third Gloucester player to spend ten minutes off the field, more points would surely follow. They did but all went to the visitors. For some reason, we took our foot off the pedal and allowed them back into it. May scored, Burns converted and there was still nearly half an hour left to play. Robson saw yellow for being offside at a ruck and Williams had a try disallowed for a forward pass. Gloucester's third try came from Twelvetrees with six minutes to go, Burns converted and only a timely intervention by Evans prevented May scoring at the end. It finished 27-19 so the Cherry and Whites left empty handed. This had been a fitting way to celebrate 50 years at the Stoop. We now moved into fourth on 23 points, Saracens were on 32, Northampton had 30 and Bath 26. At the bottom, the nine point gap remained after eight rounds.

Dean Richards was now in charge of Newcastle Falcons after his three year ban in the wake of "Bloodgate" had ended. They were our next opponents on Sunday 1st December at Kingston Park. It was inevitable that Tom Williams would score and indeed he did after ten minutes. The TMO checked for a forward pass and ruled there hadn't been one. Evans converted and sandwiched two penalties between two from Godman for the Falcons to give us a 13-6 lead at half time. The match was won in the third quarter and Smith scored right at the start of it after a sweeping move. Godman kicked his third penalty but Evans got another and converted Care's try. When Smith picked up a loose ball, he sprinted 70 yards to the line for the bonus point try. Evans converted to make it 35-9 and that is how it finished. Near the end, Vickers was yellow carded but it mattered not and we stayed in fourth place. Saracens marched on but we did gain a point on them; Northampton and Bath were still second and third and Worcester were now ten points behind London Irish.

The Heineken Cup returned for the double header rounds 3 and 4 and we would meet Racing Metro 92 in Nantes first. The equation was simple, anything but a win and we would almost certainly be out. From the start, we ran the ball but it took 18 minutes to open the scoring. Evans nipped through a gap and stepped past Hernandez to score under the posts. He converted and added a penalty to give us a handy lead. Hopper was nearly in at the corner but Easter made no mistake and scored near the posts; Evans put over the conversion to give us a 17-0 lead after 30 minutes. Dambielle kicked a penalty right on half time and was substituted during the break, Sexton coming on to try and turn the tide. He had no effect and our scoring continued with a penalty from Evans. Almost immediately, Care put in a high kick, Hernandez fumbled the ball and Walker was on it in a flash. He set off, went past Machenaud and out-paced the remaining defender for our third try. Evans converted and quite incredibly it was 27-3. Racing made four changes and eventually scored their first try through Le Roux. With eight minutes to go, Dickson grabbed the bonus point try when he followed the pack as they drove over from a lineout ten yards out. The conversion was missed but this was a tremendous result against one of the big spending French sides who, it must be said, were never in the game. Nick Kennedy had joined us at the start of the season but, due to injury was unable to make his debut in the second row until he made a substitute appearance against Racing; he had won 7 England caps and would make 17 appearances for us during his only season with the Club. Clermont won again so led the way with 10 points, we were now second on 7 with the Scarlets a point behind and Racing bringing up the rear also on 6. If we won our three remaining pool games, there was every chance we would qualify.

The return with Racing Metro 92 was played the following Sunday at the Stoop. With the spending power of the French and their large squad, they were able to make fourteen changes to their starting line up from the previous week and only the full back Hernandez remained. They fielded four of the successful 2013 British and Irish Lions team but would a XV unused to playing together be a match for us? In terrible conditions (the rain swept across the ground) we steadily built a lead. Evans landed penalty goals on 7, 11 and 24 minutes (the last just before Khinchagashvili came back from the bin) to make it 9-0. Right on half time, Walker scooted in after Hopper and Molenaar had made the space. Evans was replaced by Botica at half time and with him went a lot of our spark. Botica did land a penalty on 51 minutes and Sexton replied eight minutes later but the all-stars could get no closer. For the second week running, Racing had simply not turned up but we could only play what was in front of us. Another win for Clermont put them on 15 points, we were up to 11 and Scarlets and Racing were stuck on 6. Our next fixture in the Heineken Cup was on 11th January against Clermont and the winner would hold the advantage going into the last round of pool games the following week.

The Aviva Premiership returned for the three weeks leading up to and around Christmas and the New Year. First we had an away trip to Bath and a win would most likely see us leap-frog them into third place. As had happened in the past, we struggled to carry our current form into a game at the Rec. Ford was on target three times in the opening 24 minutes with penalties and our only reply was one from Evans. A minute before the break, Walker was binned for a tip-tackle and Ford missed a penalty either side of this incident to keep us in the game. Just before Walker returned, Joseph went through and ran round Brown who was the last line of defence to score the opening try. Ford missed the conversion and there was no further scoring although Guest got over near the end but the referee (Martin Fox) decided not to refer the decision to the TMO. There was enough time left for Ford to miss another penalty but it mattered not and we had lost our fourth league game. We remained in fourth spot on 28 points but were well behind Saracens (41) and Northampton (38) with Bath still in sight on 34. Worcester had picked up another losing bonus point to move on to 3 points with London Irish nine ahead on 12 and Newcastle one ahead of them.

On 28th December, our last game of the year took place at Twickenham. It was time for Big Game 6 and this one was against the Exeter Chiefs. Although the crowd of 74,827 was down on the previous year, an entertainment package was put together with the stars of the TV show X Factor making appearances once again. On the field, we profited from an early turnover when Evans scored a try with ease. He converted and Steenson replied with a penalty but Evans then missed two chances to extend our lead. From the move which sent Walker over for a try after 31 minutes, Nowell was binned for a tip-tackle on Hopper. Evans couldn't convert but made no mistake when Care broke from a turnover and put Brown in under the posts for our third try. With Exeter back to full strength early in the second half, Steenson got his second penalty two minutes later. There was to be no comeback from the Chiefs and a lone penalty by Evans on 62 minutes wrapped the game up. We tried until the end to get that elusive fourth try for the bonus point but it wasn't to be. At the top, Saracens and Northampton won with a bonus point and Bath lost so we moved within two points of them. We were now fourteen and eleven points behind the top two respectively. Worcester suffered their eleventh loss in a row and now trailed by ten points although the Irish and Newcastle were slowly creeping away from them.

The first game of the New Year was the return with Northampton at Franklin's Gardens. On a cold night in the East Midlands, Myler put over a penalty for the first points after three minutes. By the end of the first quarter, we were in front through two penalties from Evans. When Guest went to the bin for illegally checking a lineout drive, the home side could only score a penalty from Myler just as he was about to return. It was all square at the break and a rain shower during that time didn't help the condition of the pitch. Within four minutes, Northampton had the lead again when, from a poor clearance kick, North brushed off Walker's attempted tackle and stormed over for the try. Myler converted and into the final quarter Botica and he exchanged penalties to leave us holding on to a losing bonus point. Even this was taken away when Hartley went over from an untidy lineout and Myler converted via the crossbar. We still gave it a go but could make no inroads into Northampton's lead even when Pisi was sent to the bin for a swinging arm with three minutes left. Afterwards, Conor O'Shea was frustrated by the amount of time being taken to look at various incidents using the TMO. The problem was that the TMO was here to stay and as they could look at anything on the pitch, things were likely to get worse before they got better and some games were running for 100 minutes. As a result of this 9-23 defeat, Leicester moved on to the same points as us although we stayed in fourth. Bath were now on 36, Northampton had 47 and Saracens had reached the half century. Worcester were now eleven points behind Newcastle and fourteen adrift of London Irish. Even at this stage with ten games left it didn't look good for them.

The disappointing form at Northampton would have to be left behind before our next game. It was the all-important fifth Heineken Cup pool match against Clermont Auvergne at the Stoop. The fixture was played on Saturday 11th January and would go a long way to deciding our fate in this year's competition. In the opening ten minutes, James put the visitors in front with a penalty but they blew two golden opportunities to score tries and we weathered the storm which lasted for the first 25 minutes. Then, Danny Care produced probably the best piece of skill seen on a rugby pitch for a long time. He took a tapped penalty in our half and passed to Monye who took the ball into contact. Chris Robshaw carried it on, kicked ahead, the ball bounced high and was heading into touch. Care had chased it, reached it first and with two defenders closing in, he produced a reverse pass in mid-air as he went into touch. As Matt Hopper came storming up in support, the pass found him and he ran on to score an absolutely fantastic try. With the conversion by Evans, Clermont were stunned and the momentum shifted in our favour immediately. By half time, Evans had added two penalties to give us a 13-3 lead. Five minutes into the second half, Parra put in a kick, Brown appeared to lose it in the low sun and as it hit the ground it took the most awkward turn and completely wrong-footed him. Nalaga pounced, kicked ahead and scored but the conversion was missed. Care suffered a twisted ankle and was replaced by Dickson after 49 minutes, it was a cruel blow. On 69 minutes, Evans had a penalty chance from 35 metres out in front of the posts. Inexplicably, he missed the kick that would have put us eight points ahead. We were made to pay because Sivivatu was put over after a good attacking move and James added a second penalty to put Clermont 16-13 ahead with four minutes left. With time almost up we won another penalty and Evans put it in the corner knowing only a win would do, a draw was not enough. Dave Ward threw his worst lineout throw of the season but almost made up for it by taking the ball against the head from the resulting scrum. Unfortunately, Clermont managed to kill the ball legally and the final whistle went. This match had been in our hands to win and we should have done so. As it was, we were out but could still qualify for the Amlin Cup quarter finals as one of three best runners-up. The Pool situation was as follows - Clermont 19 points, Quins 12, Scarlets 10 and Racing Metro 7.

Our final pool game was at Parc y Scarlets, Llanelli against the Scarlets on 19th January. The match was played in torrential rain and the home side took the lead with a try scored on the counter-attack by Davies after four minutes. Priestland converted but indiscipline cost the Scarlets when Shingler charged into a maul recklessly according to the referee and he was off for ten minutes. In that time, Brown ran in unopposed for Evans to even things up with the conversion. We took the lead when Lindsay-Hague scored (Evans again converted) but in the twelve minutes remaining in the first half, the Scarlets re-took the lead. Priestland landed a penalty and Shingler scored their second try when he touched down at the back of an unguarded ruck. Four minutes after the break, Dickson was put in after a good forward drive but the lead was short-lived. The Scarlets were ahead again after Scott Williams finished off another counter-attack but Priestland crucially missed the conversion. We trailed by a point and it could have been more had Jordan Williams and Priestland not missed penalty attempts. With one last push, we slowly crept towards the Scarlets line and when they were caught offside 30 metres out, Botica stepped up to slot the penalty and see us home 22-20. It was not an easy kick given the conditions but it ensured that we qualified for the Amlin Cup quarter finals in April and our reward was an away tie against Stade Français Paris. The Pool finished with Clermont on 24 points, Quins with 16, Scarlets on 11 and Racing Metro with 7. In the end, our terrible start had cost us as well as our inability to close out the game the previous week.

The LV= Cup returned for the last two rounds of pool games. We took on Leicester Tigers at the Stoop knowing that anything short of a bonus point win was likely to mean the end of our defence of the title. After Lamb had put Leicester in front with a penalty after four minutes, our reply was a try from Sackey seven minutes later. Botica missed this conversion and the one for Fa'asavalu's try after 17 minutes. Lamb and Botica exchanged penalties before half time and we led 13-6. As the Tigers tried to get back into it, Lamb sent a pass out, Tom Guest intercepted and ran the ball 50 metres to score. The conversion was successful from Botica and we had a fourteen point cushion. After 59 minutes the rain started and the wind began to pick up. Ten minutes later, a mini hurricane swept through Twickenham and advertising hoardings blew across the pitch along with assorted debris. There was a fear that scaffolding could come down so the referee (Gwyn Morris) after consulting the stadium manager called the game off after 70 minutes and 30 seconds on health and safety grounds. As stewards cleared everyone from the south-west corner, the players left the field. Within a few minutes, the storm had passed but the hail and lightning had done enough. It was decided later that the game would not be replayed and the result was confirmed to give us our first win in the competition. Bath had won with a bonus point so our elimination was confirmed. The Pool now looked like this – Bath 14 points, Quins 5, Worcester 5, Ospreys 1.

Our last pool game away against Cardiff Blues was effectively a dead rubber; we were already out and Cardiff had to get a bonus point win and hope that Sale and Exeter got nothing from their games. Rain greeted us again but we tried to play with the ball in hand and with pace to our game as was now the norm. There were no scores until 29 minutes had elapsed and it was the Blues who got the opening try. Paulo went over and this was followed by one from Evans; Humberstone converted both before Lindsay-Hague got a try back. The tie was put to bed in the opening ten minutes of the third quarter when Fish and Tom Williams got over for the Blues. Humberstone was successful with both conversions and even when Hobbs went to the bin, we still couldn't score. In the final minute, Breeze got a fifth try and Humberstone again converted to make it 5-35. We had enjoyed 70% possession and territory but had somehow contrived to lose by thirty points; this would become a worrying trend in the seasons to come. Two Academy players made their debuts as substitutes in this one; lock Kieran Treadwell and winger Henry Cheeseman. They would go on to make 6 and at least 5 appearances respectively. Results went against Cardiff and they failed to progress as well. Our Pool finished with Bath as runaway winners on 19 points, Ospreys with 6, Quins

5 and Worcester 5. In the semi-finals, Northampton beat Saracens and Exeter saw off Bath; Exeter then defeated Northampton 15-8 on their home ground to win the cup.

Six rounds of the Aviva Premiership followed and the first fixture was the return with London Wasps at the Stoop on 9th February. After their bad season last time, Wasps had improved vastly and were one point and two places behind us. Most of our England men would be missing for the next four or five games so it was crucial to pick up as many wins and points as we could in that time before the final push for play-off spots began. As they had on their previous visit, Wasps took the lead. Carlisle landed a penalty after three minutes but Evans replied in kind two minutes later. Carlisle had missed a penalty but the Wasps pack attacked our line and were rewarded with a penalty try from a scrum. Carlisle didn't miss the conversion to make it 3-10 at half time. Barely two minutes into the second half, Evans was replaced by Botica because of a leg injury. His first involvement was to miss a penalty but made no mistake with one after 50 minutes. Just before this, Maurie Fa'asavalu had put in a huge hit on Masi and this had the desired effect of rejuvenating the entire team. The visitors controlled much of the remaining time but with three minutes left, we struck a hammer blow. From a series of attacks near the Wasps line, the ball was worked out wide to Sam Smith who managed to get the ball down despite being tackled. After a lengthy review, the TMO confirmed it and although Botica missed the conversion, we held out for the one point victory. Northampton had taken over top spot on 51 points, Saracens had 50 with Bath (40), Quins and Leicester (36) and Sale (34) making up the top six. Even with nine rounds left, it looked extremely likely that the top two would be at home in the semi-finals. Poor old Worcester were still winless but had gained another losing bonus point. Newcastle were ten clear of them and London Irish on 21 points looked clear of any relegation threat.

It was Newcastle who visited the Stoop next and this meant the return of Dean Richards to the scene of "Bloodgate". It was his first visit since he left the Club after the scandal in 2009. Playing with a strong wind in the first half, we started well and after Botica had missed a penalty, Lindsay-Hague dummied the last line of defence to grab the first try on eleven minutes. After a series of infringements, Welch was binned and Botica kicked to the corner from the penalty. As the pressure came on, Smith touched down for try number two which Botica converted. Ex-Quin Rory Clegg also returned (along with Gonzalo Tiesi) and he put over a penalty two minutes later but missed a second to leave it at 12-3. When the second half started, we gave away penalty after penalty and Clegg was able to slot a couple to narrow the gap. For the second time in the match, Clegg struck an upright with a penalty attempt but the Falcons did go in front when Tait got over for a try. Lawson was binned after 74 minutes (Botica kicked the resulting penalty) and this gave us just enough leeway to create the pressure for Botica to land another penalty right on time to secure the win (18-14). Of the top six, only Sale lost (but still picked up a losing bonus point) so it was a case of as you were. Worcester lost again and Newcastle's bonus point against us took them eleven clear.

The following week, we met Gloucester at Kingsholm. The Cherry and Whites were having a miserable season and currently stood in tenth place with just four wins and 23 points from fourteen games. After 90 seconds Botica put us in front with a penalty then Lambert was yellow carded for persistent infringing. Botica doubled the lead but before Lambert came back, Kalamafoni got over for Cook to convert and we trailed by a point. A quickly taken penalty by Dickson enabled him to get past the defence and set up Lindsay-Hague for a run in under the posts. Botica converted and we had an interval lead of 13-7. The third quarter was a disaster for us as we conceded fifteen unanswered points (Cook kicked a penalty, Kvesic and Murphy got tries and Cook converted the second) and lost Grimoldby to the bin right at the end of it for a deliberate knock-on. Cook landed the penalty resulting from this to make it 13-25 and we were in trouble. When replacement Thomas became the first Gloucester player to be binned, we drove a lineout over and Ward got the try. Botica converted to set up a frantic final five minutes but Gloucester hung on for their first league win of 2014. O'Shea wasn't happy with some of the decisions but was happy with the reaction and pride of the team. The top six now read as follows – Northampton (59), Saracens (58), Bath (49), Leicester (44), Quins (41) and Sale (39). Worcester were now twelve points behind Newcastle and the games were beginning to run out.

As if it couldn't get any worse for the Warriors, their next game was a trip to the Stoop on 1st March. They had lost twelve straight games against us going back to December 2007 and there would be no better opportunity to break that run than now. We were missing several players and were not firing on all cylinders. They started well and Pennell kicked them into the lead after five minutes with a penalty. His second attempt (after Monye had been sent to the bin) rebounded off a post and when Lamb took over the kicking duties he missed as well. He made no mistake with a penalty on 23 minutes and when Lemi darted over from a ruck, his conversion made it 13-0 to the visitors. It was a shock to the system to see us behind by a reasonable margin but Botica began the recovery with a penalty right on half time. His second after 42 minutes sparked a period of pressure on Worcester which ended with Senatore being yellow carded for collapsing a maul. The defensive line was broken when Smith got over but Botica couldn't convert from the touchline. Eight minutes later, Botica nudged us ahead with his third penalty and when Worcester were back to full strength, we struck again. Smith put Harry Sloan in for a try but the TMO had to check for a forward pass. He decided there wasn't one and the try stood. Botica converted this before Senatore's day got worse as he was taken off with a suspected dislocated shoulder. The Warriors never gave up and Pennell converted his own try with six minutes left but they were one point short and we held on for the win (21-20). These victories against the lower placed sides were crucial if we were to make the top four at the end of the season. Northampton (64) and Saracens (62) continued their duel at the top with Bath and Leicester (both on 49) filling the other semi-final spots. We were fifth on 45 points and Sale were two behind us. Worcester did gain a point on the Falcons at the bottom but now with only six games left, they desperately needed a win from somewhere.

The semi-finals and final of the LV= Cup were played over the following two weekends so our next game was at Wembley against Saracens on 22nd March. Once again they set a World record for the highest attendance at a club game with a crowd of 83,889. Conor O'Shea opted to rest Brown, Care and Robshaw after their exploits with England in the 6 Nations and time would tell if this was a mistake or not as we needed all the points we could get. However, O'Shea knew his team and he stated that mentally and physically they needed the break. After five minutes, Strettle ducked into a challenge from Fa'asavalu and was stretchered off after eight minutes of treatment, a sad end to the day for the ex-Quin. Four minutes later as we attacked, Easter threw a careless pass, Ashton intercepted and 75 metres later he was touching down for the first score of the game. Farrell converted and Evans replied with a penalty before a Farrell penalty made it 3-10. Kruis charged past Kennedy to score a second try for Saracens (Farrell converted) but Dickson went over for us and Evans converted to keep us in touch. Another Farrell penalty looked to have been the final score of the first half before another ridiculous pass cost us dearly. Right on half time, Evans threw a long pass in front of our posts intended for Monye; Farrell read it, came charging in and snatched the ball to score under the posts and his conversion took the score to 27-10. Borthwick went off for ten minutes after tipping Kennedy at a lineout and we kicked the penalty to the corner. From the lineout we drove to the line and Smith was put over at the corner. Evans added the two points and we were back in it but we needed another score right away. Indeed, we had a chance from another penalty five minutes later but lost the ball. Burger got the bonus point try for Saracens on 57 minutes and with a number of substitutions being made, the game became disjointed. One final mistake by us enabled Bosch to grab another try and Hodgson's conversion made the final score 39-17. We had been well and truly beaten and it was our seventh league loss of the season. As far as we were concerned, the top two places were out of reach and the best we could hope for was third or fourth. Saracens now led the way on 67 points, Northampton came next on 64 and Bath and Leicester both had 54. Sale had gone above us with 47 and we were on 45. Worcester lost their seventeenth league game and were twelve points behind Newcastle.

London Irish came to the Stoop on 29th March and we were out for revenge after the disappointing loss back in October. We now had to win every one of our five remaining Premiership games to have any chance of a top four finish. Our England boys returned but the side couldn't get into a rhythm and it was left to Nick Evans to get us going. After eleven minutes, he chipped over the defence, gathered his own kick and scored. He converted and added a penalty after O'Connor had got one for Irish. The visiting kicker was on target twice more before the interval but when he got the chance in the second half to put Irish in front, he was just to the right of the posts with his penalty attempt. When Yarde tackled Turner-Hall without the ball, he went off for ten minutes and Evans kicked the penalty. Despite our best efforts for the next twenty minutes, we just couldn't put the game out of reach. Then, with ten minutes left, Care floated a pass to Smith from a scrum and the winger went over. The conversion was missed as it was when Brown got our third try with five minutes left. We did go for the bonus point score but it wasn't to be and we had to settle for a 23-9 win. We stayed in sixth place on 49 points and the table from fifth upwards read as follows – Sale 51, Bath 55, Leicester 58, Northampton 65 and Saracens 72. Sale had beaten Bath, Leicester won at Northampton and Worcester got their first win away to Newcastle. With four rounds left, the gap at the bottom was nine points.

It was over to the Stade Jean Bouin in Paris on Friday 4th April for the Amlin Cup quarter final against Stade Français Paris. Whereas we fielded a full strength side, the French rested several players but were still a strong outfit. The first half produced five penalties and after Steyn had missed with his first effort, Evans and he took it in turns until we had a 9-6 lead. After 28 minutes, there was an allegation of eye gouging against Marler from the Stade captain (Sempere). Despite the TMO checking, no evidence was found and he was not cited. After Steyn missed with his fourth attempt, Brown went past three defenders to score the opening try and Evans converted for a 16-6 lead after 46 minutes. Ten minutes later Evans put over his fourth penalty, Mallet missed another for Stade and when Evans dropped a goal from just inside the French ten metre line, the tie was out of Stade's reach. The icing on the cake came when Tim Molenaar crashed over with two defenders hanging on to him. Botica converted from the touchline and we were through to play Northampton in the semi-final by twenty nine points to six. Due to the various uses of the TMO, this game had a running time of 110 minutes! Paul Sackey made his final appearance when he came off the bench; he had scored 10 points (2 tries).

Another Friday fixture saw us visit Salford to take on Sale Sharks. The home side opened the scoring when Brady dived over in the corner and it took us ten minutes to get into our stride. Once we did, Sale couldn't match us and Evans grabbed a try, converted it and added a penalty before Care gave us a ten point lead at half time with another try. Smith scored another after 45 minutes and there was no further scoring for twenty six minutes. In the meantime there were eleven substitutions but we still controlled the game and Fa'asavalu made the result safe after 72 minutes. Evans converted and was immediately replaced by Botica after another excellent performance. When Matthews was binned, Sale applied some late pressure and were awarded a penalty try with two minutes left. Cipriani converted but we had triumphed with a bonus point to move above the Sharks into fifth place. Saracens were now ten points clear at the top because Northampton were suffering a late season dip in form. Leicester were only three behind them on 63, Bath had 59 and we were now on 54. Sale seemed to be safe in sixth but we needed Bath to lose at least once before the last game decider at the Stoop. Worcester picked up two points at the bottom to close the gap on Newcastle bit it was still seven.

Third placed Leicester Tigers came to the Stoop on 18th April for another must win game. After just 73 seconds Flood put Leicester ahead with a penalty and Goneva went over under the posts for Flood to convert (the final pass was adjudged by the TMO to be legal). It was 0-10 after only four minutes but we were now a solid team and early setbacks no longer knocked us out of our stride. Evans kicked two penalties either side of Flood's second and Luke Wallace was held up by Tuilagi as we came back into it. From the scrum, referee Tim Wigglesworth awarded us a penalty try and the conversion by Evans levelled matters at half time. Mike Brown was denied a try by the TMO after he ruled that the Leicester defender (Scully) had just got his hand on the ball first but Evans nudged us ahead for the first time with a penalty on 57 minutes. A minute later we were behind again as Gibson crossed after a quickly taken penalty. Flood converted and would have had a chance to extend the lead to seven points but for Matera's reckless tackle on Evans. Robson retaliated and both were yellow carded. With each side down to fourteen men, Care and Botica provided the position and pass for Brown to cross in the corner. Botica missed the conversion but when Salvi was in the bin he put over a penalty to seal the win (24-20). The only side in the top six to lose were the Tigers and Bath moved above them on games won. The lowest we could end up was sixth but it wasn't out of the question we might win the title. At the foot, Worcester were eight points adrift and one more defeat would send them down.

For our fourth Friday fixture in a row, we travelled to Franklin's Gardens to take on Northampton in the Amlin Cup semi-final. On a wet night, the first action was a yellow card for Elliott. He took Brown out in the air and our full back landed on some concrete at the edge of the pitch. He managed to get to half time but was replaced by Lindsay-Hague. We couldn't take advantage of the sin bin and the first quarter was scoreless. Myler kicked a penalty after 22 minutes and Collins just got to a cross-kick four minutes later. Myler and Botica exchanged penalties as the first half ended 11-3 to the Saints. Four minutes into the second half, the ball came loose from a ruck and shot in the air. Fotuali'i was first to it but appeared to knock-on before gathering and sprinting clear to score. The TMO took a long time to decide that he hadn't touched it and the try was confirmed (it looked the wrong decision but the touch was minimal). Myler's conversion took the Saints out to 18-3 with 35 minutes to go. Botica had missed a chance to narrow the gap just before the try with a 50 metre penalty but we began to dominate the play. On 63 minutes, Easter got over from close range and Botica converted but that was all we could manage and we were out. In the final on 23rd May, Northampton beat Bath 30-16 at Cardiff Arms Park.

At Sandy Park, Exeter on 4th May, it was our penultimate regular season game against the Chiefs. On our three previous Premiership visits here we had won one and lost two; it was time to make that a 50/50 record. After we attacked for the first five minutes, Exeter broke out and Steenson kicked a penalty and he was also on target with the conversion of a try by Lewis after fifteen minutes. Our reply was swift and saw Monye go over but two penalties from Steenson gave the Chiefs a 16-5 interval lead. It got worse when Jess was through and Steenson converted. We trailed by eighteen points with 35 minutes to go and needed something special to resurrect our play-off hopes. Nick Evans scored a minute after, converted and added two penalties while Welch was in the bin for a trip on Care. Steenson also got a penalty during this time and when Welch returned, eighteen minutes remained and the Chiefs led 26-18. When Care went through to grab our third try, Evans slotted the conversion and it was game on. On 72 minutes, Steenson banged over his fifth penalty but we would not be denied. When Ward took a quick throw to the front of the lineout, swapping passes with Guest, the back row replacement was on hand for the return and got over the line for the bonus point try. It put us one point ahead with six minutes left and we ran the clock down for a fantastic win. After Round 21, Saracens were confirmed in first place (they now had 85 points), Northampton were second with 73, Leicester had 69, Bath were on 66, Quins had 63 and Sale came next on 56. At the bottom, Worcester had been relegated because they were ten points behind Newcastle with one game left.

It all came down to the last game at the Stoop against Bath. The winner would guarantee themselves a play-off place and although there were a number of outcomes, the most likely for us was a win while allowing Bath nothing more than a losing bonus point. In that event both sides would finish on 67 points and because of us having won one more, we would qualify. There was no scoring until the fifteenth minute when Care threw a long pass out to Brown who had found space and he was over for the opening try. Evans converted but our lead only lasted six minutes as Ford ran through the defence to touch down and convert. When Easter went over from Care's pass we were back in front but the referee (Wayne Barnes) ruled a forward pass and disallowed the score. We did lead at half time because Evans put over a penalty on 35 minutes. Four minutes after the break, Ford brought the visitors level with a penalty but they lost Banahan to the bin for killing the ball. During his time off, Evans slotted two penalties to put us 16-10 up. The rest of the scoring came in a four minute spell (65-68) and Ford started it with a penalty. Evans got another when Attwood obstructed Smith from the restart and then Turner-Hall blocked Rokoduguni enabling Ford to kick his third. With the last kick of the game, Ford tried a long range drop at goal but it never got near the posts. It finished 19-16 and we were into the play-offs in fourth place. Despite our injury setbacks during the season, we had made it and would now look forward to a semi-final on 17th May at the Allianz Stadium, Barnet against Saracens. We said goodbye to Maurie "Big Mo" Fa'asavalu in this one, he had scored 25 points (5 tries), made 19 appearances as a sub and visited the bin on four occasions – he would be sorely missed. The final table had a top six of Saracens (87 points), Northampton (78), Leicester (74), Quins (67), Bath (67) and Sale (57). At the bottom, Worcester ended on 16 points and Newcastle had 22.

The following Saturday we met Saracens for the right to play Northampton in the final on 24th May at Twickenham (they had beaten Leicester the previous evening). On a hot day, we started well and Evans put over a penalty on 5 minutes but Farrell responded with two of his own. Between them, Brits tipped Sinckler up in the tackle but the TMO and the referee (Wayne Barnes) decided he had jumped just before the tackle so there was no lift. There were yellow cards for Bosch (lifting Evans in the tackle) and Stevens (deliberate knock-on) but Evans missed the penalty from the first one. Just before the first sin bin, Sinckler had absolutely smashed the Saracens danger man (Burger) into the middle of next week. He knocked the stuffing out of him and effectively put him out of the game. We did take the lead when Evans put Monye in for our first try. Evans converted but we let Brown in to score for the home side and the lead was back with them. As well as missing the conversion, Sarries had also missed two penalties and we took advantage when Robshaw kicked a loose ball on from the half way line and Mike Brown was the first one there to score. After checking with the TMO for offside and grounding of the ball, Barnes gave the try and Evans converted. As he ran up, Ashton came running off the line shouting in an attempt to put him off. Unsporting behaviour like that has no place in the game and it caused a bit of a ruck as the players left the pitch at half time but we deserved our 17-11 lead. With Saracens back to full strength, we continued to play outstandingly well and their play became more and more scrappy. We had rattled the best side in the Premiership and they were at a loss what to do. Farrell and Bosch missed further penalty attempts and as we attacked again, Care attempted a dropped goal from broken play but hit the post. On another day, we would have been awarded a penalty for offside but here is where the momentum shifted once and for all. Strettle gathered the ball, went up field with our defence out of position and from this we conceded a lineout. Barritt eventually went over for Farrell to convert and when he landed a penalty to stretch the lead, we started to unravel. Bosch thought he had scored but was offside and when Mike Brown went for an interception and missed, Kelly Brown put Ashton over for the clincher with eighteen minutes still left to play. Farrell converted and around this time we lost Brown, Molenaar, Monye and Williams to injury as the wheels came off completely. Buchanan came on for the full back and Karl

Dickson for our left wing. To our credit, we stuck to the task and only conceded one more Farrell penalty to make the final score 17-31. The effort of playing effectively seven cup finals in a row had taken its toll. On this occasion, we had shaken Saracens to their core but hadn't been able to land the knockout punch to finish them off. Maybe Care's dropped goal attempt would have been enough had it gone over. We did provide an insight into how to beat them and both Toulon in the Heineken Cup Final and Northampton in the Aviva Premiership Final took note and were successful. We said goodbye to four notable players against Saracens – Tom Guest, Nick Kennedy, Tim Molenaar and Sam Smith. Guest had scored 145 points (29 tries), captained the side once, made 98 appearances off the bench (as he had this time) and been binned 5 times during his ten seasons in the 1st XV; Kennedy came on as a sub 7 times but had been injured too much to make an impact; Molenaar scored just 5 points (one try) and was unlucky to be leaving after less than a season and Smith (appearing as a substitute for the 16th time) had scored 155 points (31 tries) and been to the bin just once.

After a very disappointing start, we gave ourselves a shot at winning a European as well as a domestic trophy but in the event won nothing. Our overall record was P35 W20 D0 L15 F675 A614. In the league it was P22 W15 D0 L7 F437 A365 Pts 67 (BP 7 – TB 4 LB 3) Pos 4th (our post-season was P1 L1 F17 A31). In the 35 games played, Nick Easter, Tom Guest and Dave Ward topped the appearances with 31, Ben Botica and Luke Wallace played in 29 and Mark Lambert, George Robson and Sam Smith came next on 28. Nick Evans again topped the points scoring with 273 (5 tries, 3 dropped goals, 55 penalties and 37 conversions) and as a result also got the most dropped goals, penalties and conversions. Mike Brown scored the most tries with 10. Overall, tries were well down from 96 to 67, penalties dropped by 34 to 79, conversions went down in line with the drop in tries from 80 to just 47 and dropped goals rose by one to 3. Amazingly, for a season which could have been so successful, our points total (675) was the lowest since the relegation season of 2004/05 when 596 were scored.

2013/14

090813	RACING METRO 92	GENEVA	L	4G(28)-5G1T(40)
160813	LONDON SCOTTISH	TWICKENHAM STOOP	W	5G1T(40)-1G1PG1T(15)
240813	GLASGOW WARRIORS	TWICKENHAM STOOP	W	2G1T(19)-1G3PG(16)
070913	LONDON WASPS(AP)	TWICKENHAM	W	1G3PG(16)-1G1PG1T(15)
130913	NORTHAMPTON(AP)	TWICKENHAM STOOP	L	2PG(6)-1G2PG(13)
200913	WORCESTER(AP)	WORCESTER	W	4G3PG(37)-1G2PG(13)
280913	SARACENS(AP)	TWICKENHAM STOOP	L	4PG(12)-1G5PG(22)
051013	LONDON IRISH(AP)	READING	L	1G2PG(13)-1G2PG1T(18)
121013	SCARLETS(HECP4)	TWICKENHAM STOOP	L	2G1DG3PG(26)-3G4PG(33)
201013	ASM CLERMONT AUVERGNE(HECP4)	CLERMONT	L	1G1DG2PG(16)-1G2PG2T(23)
261013	SALE SHARKS(AP)	TWICKENHAM STOOP	W	1G4PG1T(24)-1PG(3)
021113	LEICESTER(AP)	LEICESTER	W	2G3PG(23)-1G3PG(16)
091113	EXETER CHIEFS(LVCP3)	EXETER	L	1T(5)-1G4PG(19)
151113	SALE SHARKS(LVCP3)	TWICKENHAM STOOP	L	2G4PG(26)-4G1PG(31)
231113	GLOUCESTER(AP)	TWICKENHAM STOOP	W	3G2PG(27)-2G1T(19)

011213	NEWCASTLE(AP)	NEWCASTLE	W	3G3PG1T(35)-3PG(9)
071213	RACING METRO 92(HECP4)	PARIS	W	3G2PG1T(32)-1PG1T(8)
151213	RACING METRO 92(HECP4)	TWICKENHAM STOOP	W	4PG1T(17)-1PG(3)
211213	BATH(AP)	BATH	L	1PG(3)-3PG1T(14)
281213	EXETER CHIEFS(AP)	TWICKENHAM	W	2G1PG1T(22)-2PG(6)
030114	NORTHAMPTON(AP)	NORTHAMPTON	L	3PG(9)-2G3PG(23)
110114	ASM CLERMONT AUVERGNE(HECP4)	TWICKENHAM STOOP	L	1G2PG(13)-2PG2T(16)
190114	SCARLETS(HECP4)	LLANELLI	W	2G1PG1T(22)-1G1PG2T(20)
250114	LEICESTER(LVCP3)	TWICKENHAM STOOP	A (W)	1G1PG2T(20)-2PG(6)
310114	CARDIFF BLUES(LVCP3)	CARDIFF	L	1T(5)-5G(35)
090214	LONDON WASPS(AP)	TWICKENHAM STOOP	W	2PG1T(11)-1G1PG(10)
150214	NEWCASTLE(AP)	TWICKENHAM STOOP	W	1G2PG1T(18)-3PG1T(14)
220214	GLOUCESTER(AP)	GLOUCESTER	L	2G2PG(20)-2G2PG1T(25)
010314	WORCESTER(AP)	TWICKENHAM STOOP	W	1G3PG1T(21)-2G2PG(20)
220314	SARACENS(AP)	WEMBLEY	L	2G1PG(17)-4G2PG1T(39)
290314	LONDON IRISH(AP)	TWICKENHAM STOOP	W	1G2PG2T(23)-3PG(9)
040414	STADE FRANÇAIS PARIS(ACQF)	STADE JEAN BOUIN	W	2G1DG4PG(29)-2PG(6)
110414	SALE SHARKS(AP)	SALFORD	W	2G1PG2T(27)-1G1T(12)
190414	LEICESTER(AP)	TWICKENHAM STOOP	W	1G4PG1T(24)-2G2PG(20)
250414	NORTHAMPTON(ACSF)	NORTHAMPTON	L	1G1PG(10)-1G2PG1T(18)
040514	EXETER CHIEFS(AP)	EXETER	W	2G2PG2T(30)-2G5PG(29)
100514	BATH(AP)	TWICKENHAM STOOP	W	1G4PG(19)-1G3PG(16)
170514	SARACENS(APSF)	BARNET	L	2G1PG(17)-2G4PG1T(31)

For the 2014 four match England tour to New Zealand, we had Mike Brown, Danny Care, Joe Gray, Joe Marler, Chris Robshaw, Kyle Sinckler, Dave Ward and future Quin Marland Yarde in the party. Brown, Marler, Robshaw and Yarde all played in three tests, Gray came on as a sub in the first test and Care started in the second. The first two were crucial and with a bit more killer instinct, the tourists would have held a 2-0 lead. As it was, New Zealand won both by 20-15 and 28-27 and once the series had gone, the third as well by a bigger margin of 36-13. The other match against the Crusaders was won 38-7.

Joe Marler was named captain for the 2014/15 season after Chris Robshaw was relieved of the captaincy to enable him to concentrate on leading England to World Cup glory in late 2015. Whether this was a good decision given Marler's disciplinary record would become clear in time. DHL had succeeded Etihad as our main sponsors with a five year deal that would take them to 2019. There had been a revamp on the European rugby scene and after protracted negotiations, it was out with the old and in with the new. The European Rugby Champions Cup replaced the Heineken Cup with European Professional Club Rugby taking over from European Rugby Cup Ltd. Twenty teams would contest the trophy in five groups of four. At the end of the season, six teams from England and France and seven from the RaboDirect Pro 12 would qualify plus the winners of a play-off between one side each from England (Aviva Premiership) and France (Top 14) plus two from the RaboDirect Pro 12. The second tier competition would be called the European Rugby Challenge Cup and teams from the three leagues mentioned above would take eighteen of the twenty places, with the other two being filled by lower tier nations such as Italy, Romania and Russia.

As with the previous two seasons, three friendly fixtures were arranged. Two of these were away against Grenoble and Glasgow Warriors with a home game against Section Paloise (Pau) sandwiched between. At the Stade Des Alpes on 9th August, a 9 p.m. kick-off started our pre-season. After Buchanan opened the scoring with a try (converted by Evans), Grenoble came back with tries of their own from Edwards, Ratini and Grice all converted by Wisniewski (who also kicked a penalty after the first try). Right on half time, Evans got a penalty for us to make it 24-10. After a raft of substitutions at the break, Vanderglas got over for the hosts and Wisniewski completed the scoring with his fifth successful kick of the evening.

Against Pau the following Saturday, a side containing more younger members of the squad took to the field and it wasn't until 26 minutes had passed that the first score came. Hiriart got a try for the visitors but we were soon level after a Ben Botica try. Into the second half, Clifford put Sam Twomey over after good play by Botica but the lead was lost when Furmat scored for Marques to convert. After losing Decamps to the sin bin for a cynical tackle, Barrere went over for Pau's third try. With just over five minutes to go, Ross Chisholm kicked ahead, Walker recovered and went over in the corner. Botica converted to bring us level and it remained 17-17.

For the third and final friendly at Scotstoun against Glasgow, Conor O'Shea put out the XV who would start against London Irish two weeks later. We fell behind to a penalty by Weir but Marler got our first try for Evans to convert after 17 minutes. Off the ball incidents led to yellow cards for Nakarawa and Care and Weir added a second penalty before the break. Shortly after half time, Sinckler scored and Evans converted to open up an eight point lead but within fifteen minutes, we trailed 14-23. Matawalu (2) and van der Merwe scored tries and Weir converted the first to put us in trouble with sixteen minutes remaining. On 73 minutes, our never say die attitude was rewarded when Lindsay-Hague got a try and Marland Yarde won the match with another three minutes later to make the final score 24-23.

As the season began, a lot of questions would be answered over the coming months and those answers would tell everyone where the team ranked amongst the English and European competition. We needed to regain the consistency we had started to lose during the previous season. Our first game was against London Irish in the London Double Header at Twickenham on 6th September. We were in the second game after Saracens had beaten Wasps in a nail-biting finish (34-28). We started well and went ahead after Evans landed a penalty on 7 minutes (he had already missed one). He made no mistake with the conversion of Monye's try three minutes later before Geraghty got the Irish on the board on 24 minutes. When Sheridan was sin binned, Evans and Geraghty exchanged penalties but when Lindsay-Hague grabbed our second try, the conversion by Evans gave us a very handy 20-6 lead at half time. Had Geraghty not hit the bar with the final kick of the half (a penalty attempt from inside his own half) it would have been closer. Ninety seconds into the second half, our new captain was binned for a dangerous tackle and this set the tone for the rest of the game. Geraghty put over his third penalty followed by his fourth after Sinckler also saw yellow for a dangerous tackle. We had briefly been down to thirteen men but we still led when the sin bin periods ended. A fifth penalty from Geraghty reduced the lead to five points but they never looked capable of crossing our line. It looked as though Lindsay-Hague had scored a second try five minutes from the end but the TMO ruled it out after a knock-on by Care. From the scrum, the Irish were penalised but Evans missed for the third time and it ended 20-15. Marland Yarde (an up and coming winger) made his official debut in this one, he had joined from London Irish and was in the process of winning at least 9 England caps and would go on to make at least 49 appearances for us. Against a more competent side we would have opened with a defeat and Marler's yellow card was not a good start for the captain. As it was, we were sixth but only one point behind the four sides who achieved bonus point wins (Exeter, Northampton, Leicester and Saracens).

Six days later, we met Saracens at the Stoop in our first Friday night fixture of the season. The visitors only had six of the starting XV from the final against Northampton back in May and we made one change from the previous week (Lindsay-Hague in for Monye). This game would give us a good idea where we stood in the trophy winning stakes. Hodgson kicked Saracens into the lead on eleven minutes with a penalty and doubled the advantage ten minutes later. He then charged down a clearance kick from Evans, collected the ball and went over for the opening try. He converted and added another penalty for a 16-0 lead at half time. Our two efforts to kick to the corner instead of going for the posts (after one missed attempt) were getting nowhere and our handling skills were also not up to the mark. Evans went off at the interval, Botica replaced him and when Hodgson was binned, he could only hit the post with a penalty. The only score while Hodgson was off came from a penalty by Goode. Hargreaves went the same way as Hodgson but still the only scores were from Sarries. Their fly half was back on and added two more penalties (the second when Buchanan was in the bin). Once again, we had plenty of possession but just couldn't score and the visitors finished us off with two more tries from Ashton (he outpaced Yarde who was caught napping) and Fraser. Farrell converted both to make it 39-0. Fijian winger Asaeli Tikoirotuma made his debut, he was in the process of wining 17 caps but failed to settle and would only be with us for this season and make just 13 appearances. This was the first time since the Premiership semi-final defeat to London Irish in 2009 that we had failed to score and our heaviest defeat to Saracens since the debacle at Vicarage Road in April 2000. Conor O'Shea was not impressed and he described it as the lowest, most wretched night we have had here and it being a bitter pill to swallow in front of your home crowd. The players went out to apologise but this would set the tone for the season and excuse after excuse was trotted out; week in, week out. We dropped to eighth and Saracens led the way on nine points along with Bath and Leicester. Newly promoted London Welsh propped up the table with just one point.

A minute's silence was held before the Wasps game on 20th September for Roger Looker who had passed away on 18th August. He had been Honorary Secretary, Chairman, Chairman of Trustees and a Director during his non-playing involvement with the Club. When the action started, after a scoreless opening 13 minutes, Thompson grabbed the first try and Goode converted then Botica got two penalties to pull us to within one point. Goode then replied in kind before a third from Botica made it 9-13 at the break. We were in front for the first time on 46 minutes when Robshaw touched down after Wade had fumbled a Danny Care chip in the in-goal area. Botica converted and did the same when the TMO awarded a penalty try after he had been tripped by Myall (who was binned) as he chased his own chip. When Care dropped a goal after 57 minutes, we led 26-13 but Wasps came back. Varndell got over for a try a minute later but the conversion was missed. This meant that when Matthews was binned with five minutes left, we had some breathing space. A minute later, Young scored but again the conversion was missed and we held on to win 26-23. We moved back up to sixth but were already trailing Bath at the top by six points. Saracens remained the only other club with a 100% record and were a point behind on 13. London Welsh lost again and still had one point, the same as Newcastle above them.

The following week, we travelled to Sandy Park to play Exeter Chiefs who were currently in fourth place. At the time we played on Sunday, we knew that Saracens had won again and Northampton had defeated Bath (both on Saturday) so this was a must win fixture. We actually took the lead with a penalty from Botica after just a minute. Slade and Steenson replied in kind and the second named converted Waldrom's try (after he charged down Botica's kick) at the start of the second quarter. Botica got his second penalty but Slade and Steenson were on target again to make it 19-6 at the break. Tikoirotuma put Brown in but the pass was judged forward by the TMO and when our winger did score on 46 minutes for Botica to convert, we were back in it. Nowell was sin binned after a collision with Brown under a high ball but as against Saracens, we couldn't get anything out of the reduction in numbers. Instead, the Chiefs went further ahead with a try from Yeandle which Steenson converted to add to his earlier penalty in response to our try. With five minutes to go, Slade got Exeter's third try and Steenson converted to make it 36-13. This was our heaviest defeat by Exeter and now we were in ninth place, ten points behind Saracens. We had serious problems and it seemed obvious to everyone except the players and coaches that this team was going nowhere fast. Where had all the flair, attacking prowess, handling skills and excellent defence of 2011/12 gone? There was still a long way to go but could we recover? Our strength in depth would be challenged once we lost our England players for the autumn internationals and the injuries began to mount (as they seemed to for all teams with each passing year).

Next up were the bottom side London Welsh and anything but a massive win would be a disappointment. Nick Evans returned from injury and this would boost us because Botica was proving to be not such an able deputy as was once thought. The visitors were struggling as soon as Brown got our first try and when Care went over and Evans added a penalty and both conversions, it was game over after only 22 minutes. The Welsh had not settled down as a unit following a lot of changes made after promotion was achieved. Into the second half, Yarde got his first competitive try for the Club and Hopper sealed the bonus point with our fourth. Evans converted both as well as the penalty try awarded for a high tackle on Dickson (former Quin Stegmann was binned as a result). Three minutes later, Dickson did score and Evans again converted. After Collier and Henn were sent to the bin on 73 minutes, Yarde completed the rout and Evans converted to make the final score 52-0 with his eighth successful kick – he had missed none. We moved back up to sixth and were seven points behind Northampton. Bath were second and Saracens third after losing at the Rec. The Welsh were already looking at a swift return to the Championship after only five games. They had failed to score in two and conceded no less than 46 points per game. Our run of victories over them now stood at thirteen and you had to go back to 1984 for their last win in the series.

Another Friday night fixture followed with a trip to Leicester. The Tigers were not having a good time of it either and currently sat in tenth place. After Scully had scored the opening try, Williams converted and sandwiched a penalty between two from Evans. In windy conditions, he added two more to give the home side a ten point advantage after 40 minutes (16-6). The second half continued in the same vein with another Evans penalty followed by two from Williams. With fourteen minutes left, we trailed 9-22. Yet again, possession was not a problem for us but we had real trouble converting it into points. Dickson got over for Evans to convert with ten minutes left but there was no further scoring and we only had a losing bonus point to show for our efforts. By the end of Round six, we dropped to seventh with 14 points. Northampton led the way on 25 with Saracens on 22 and Exeter and Bath both on 20. London Welsh were still on one point but now eight behind Newcastle. An eleven point gap was already looking like a giant chasm given that we would lose our best players soon. With this victory, Leicester avoided suffering a fourth straight league defeat (it would have been the first time since 2003).

As mentioned earlier, the new European Rugby Champions Cup had replaced the Heineken Cup. We faced French side Castres at the Stoop on Friday 17th October in the opening fixture of the competition (the other sides in our Pool were Leinster and Wasps). It wasn't an impossible task for us to qualify from this Pool but home wins, as always, were essential. Castres had won only two Heineken Cup games away from France in the last ten years so their away form could only be described as awful. After 6 minutes, Kockott put over a penalty for the first points before Evans replied with one of his own to make it even at the interval. It had been a forward and defence dominated encounter and the third quarter produced much of the same. Evans put us in front, Kockott equalised and Evans added two more penalties to give us a bit of daylight. With 15 minutes left, Evans put in a great chip, re-gathered, kicked again and Danny Care reached it to score the only try. Evans converted and Kockott replied with his third penalty but victory was assured with two more penalties from Evans to make it 25-9. Wasps had gone down 20-25 at Leinster so we led the way on points difference from the Irish province.

It was nine days until the European away game with Wasps which was to be one of their final games at Adams Park before the move to Coventry. Our captain pulled out with a thigh problem so Chris Robshaw took up the mantle again. Evans put us in front with a penalty, Goode brought Wasps level before Evans nudged us ahead again. After half an hour, Simpson ripped the ball from Wallace and evaded Matthews and Robshaw on his run to the line for Goode to convert. We were only behind for six minutes because Matthews finished off a great move after Ward had made the initial break. The second row had earlier been denied a try by the TMO when he was held up over the line. Nick Evans converted and we led 13-10 at half time. We were slowly taking control but it remained tight with Evans getting another penalty before two from Goode brought the scores level on 58 minutes. When we were awarded a penalty try won by the pack, Evans converted and we led by seven after 64 minutes. The rest of the game was negotiated without further incident and we had our second win and an important away one at that. Leinster also won at Castres so the top of the Pool remained unchanged. The double header in December with Leinster could be decisive if one team won both matches.

The LV= Anglo-Welsh Cup came next during the autumn international period and our first game was at Allianz Park against Saracens. With only two players remaining from the starting XV against Wasps, it was vital to get off to a good start but we didn't. Spencer kicked a penalty to put the home side in front and there was no further scoring until Grimoldby was too slow with his clearance kick and Taylor pounced to charge down, gather and score. When Lindsay-Hague had charged down Mordt's kick earlier, the ball had bounced favourably for Saracens and they managed to clear the danger. Spencer converted and very poor and weak tackling two minutes later led to a try from Ellery. Louis Grimoldby did pull a penalty back to make it 3-15 but something needed to be done and he was replaced by Tim Swiel who came on for his debut. He was on a short term loan from the Sharks in South Africa as injury cover for Ben Botica. Our game improved and Mark Lambert got over the line for Swiel to convert. Unfortunately, a minute later, Wilson scored for Saracens and Spencer converted to restore the gap. Three minutes after this, Swiel put Charlie Walker in at the corner and converted. Lindsay-Hague was binned for tackling Wilson in the air and although Spencer missed the resulting penalty, he put one over shortly after. Swiel replied with his first but it was too little, too late and we had to settle for just one point. The other teams in our Pool were Exeter, London Welsh and Ospreys; we all played against Bath, Gloucester, Newport Gwent Dragons and Saracens. We were in second place as Exeter won by a point at home to Gloucester (28-27), Ospreys got a try bonus point against Dragons while London Welsh were thrashed by Bath.

The following Friday, we met the Dragons at the Stoop and our form continued to be poor at best. Lindsay-Hague gave us the lead after five minutes with a try but yet another charged down kick led to a try from Evans for the Dragons. After 19 minutes, Thomas got a second try for the visitors that Dorian Jones converted but Swiel kept us in it with a penalty. Jones had taken over the kicking duties from his brother Rhys and proceeded to slot another three penalties to make it 21-8 at the interval. No doubt after strong words in the changing room, we shot out of the blocks and within ten minutes, the lead had almost gone. Swiel kicked a penalty and converted James Chisholm's try (after Dee had been binned for persistent infringement). As substitutions came thick and fast, Swiel drew us level and put us ahead with two more penalties before Chisholm grabbed his second try on 69 minutes. Swiel converted and the comeback was complete although the try bonus eluded us. The Ospreys and London Welsh lost again but Exeter won so we remained in second place. We had to win our last two games when the competition returned at the end of January and hope that Exeter slipped up.

The Premiership returned the following week with the second of a run of four Friday night fixtures. This one was an away trip to Gloucester and another bad start saw us fall twelve points behind in 26 minutes with four penalties from Twelvetrees. It could have been worse had Cook not been held up over the line. We came back though and produced some good play that culminated with Easter (our captain for the night) scoring a try. Evans converted and added a penalty as the pendulum swung towards us. Into the second half, Twelvetrees missed two penalty attempts (to add to the two he missed in the first half) before Wallace was driven over to put us ahead for the first time. Evans converted but Aled Thomas was on target with Gloucester's fifth penalty to keep it tight. From a scrum near the home 22, Dickson broke right and put in a superb kick out wide for Walker to run on to and go over for the match clinching try. Evans couldn't convert but we had our first league win at Kingsholm since 1999, a run of fourteen consecutive defeats. As a result of this, we moved into sixth place on 18 points. Northampton led the way on 26 with Exeter, Bath and Saracens all on 24. There was no change at the bottom as London Welsh still trailed Newcastle by eight points.

Sale Sharks were the next visitors to the Stoop on 21st November and we needed to continue our recent winning streak. After two minutes, Cipriani put the visitors in front with the first of several penalties. Evans came back with two and Cipriani made it all square at the break. In the space of five minutes near the end of the third quarter, Evans added two more either side of another from Cipriani to give us a narrow 12-9 lead. On 68 minutes, Braid drove over for the only try of the game and Cipriani's conversion put Sale four points up. Despite throwing everything at them for the last ten minutes, nothing was achieved and another losing bonus point was gained. We dropped to eighth as Sale overtook us and by the time all matches had been completed, we trailed Northampton by eleven points. Exeter and Bath were two points behind and Saracens a further three down. London Welsh were still rooted to the bottom and London Irish were now eleventh although the gap had grown to eleven points. We just couldn't afford to lose these games because the teams at the top were winning. Before long, the gap would be too much if we kept on losing. O'Shea still talked of frustrations but the excuses were wearing thin; it was clear that this team was not good enough or playing well enough to lift any silverware let alone seriously challenge for some!

Our last Friday night game for a while was at the Rec against third placed Bath on 28th November. The prematch talk was all about Sam Burgess, the Rugby League convert who was on the bench for Bath but we had a job to do and it didn't help that our scrum was pushed around all night – it was embarrassing to say the least. Banahan and Eastmond scored unconverted tries before Evans and Devoto exchanged penalties to make it a ten point deficit at the change of ends. A minute after the restart, Evans got a second penalty but disaster struck when Bath had a series of scrums near our line. The referee (Wayne Barnes) had already spoken to our captain (Nick Easter) and his patience ran out as Sinckler, Robson and Collier all saw yellow in the space of eight minutes for various offences. As we had already lost Lambert, there were no more props to come on so uncontested scrums resulted. Just as it looked like we had survived with twelve men, Batty went over followed by Houston. Devoto converted the second and a miserable evening ended with a 25-6 defeat. After nine rounds, Northampton were top on 35 points, Bath second on 33, Exeter next with 32 and Saracens fourth on 25. We were in ninth some sixteen points behind the leaders and six off a play-off spot. There was no change at the foot of the table. In truth, our hopes of finishing top had already gone and any more defeats would seriously damage our top four hopes as well even though there were still thirteen matches to play. On current form, we couldn't hope to compete with any of the top four, we needed to find out quickly where our consistency had gone and get it back.

It was a return to European action at the Stoop against Leinster on Sunday 7th December. This was our first meeting since the infamous "Bloodgate" match back in 2009 and seven of our starting line-up appeared again (Brown, Care, Easter, Evans, Robshaw and Robson for us and Ross who now played for Leinster). The visitors had D'Arcy, Fitzgerald, Heaslip and Kearney. The first half was tight and penalty goals were the order of the day. Madigan put Leinster in front after three minutes and Evans replied soon after but was forced off with a groin injury and Swiel replaced him. He promptly put us ahead twice but each time Madigan brought the visitors level. They were ahead again after 47 minutes when Madigan hit the target but we took the initiative when Yarde was stopped just short and Easter reached behind to touch down while on his back. Swiel converted and our scrum was in charge unlike the previous week. With Leinster on the attack, Tikoirotuma intercepted a pass from Kearney to D'Arcy and set off on a 75 metre run to the line. Swiel couldn't convert and Madigan put over two more penalties to make it 21-18 with ten minutes to go. Danny Care settled it with a trademark dropped goal but the visitors left with a losing bonus point. With three wins out of three, we led the way but had no bonus points so our lead was three points over Leinster who had nine; Wasps had seven and Castres just one. As Wasps started to get their act together, it looked like any two from three could qualify.

The following Saturday at the Aviva Stadium in Dublin, the return fixture with Leinster took place. There was no score until Madigan kicked a penalty on 26 minutes, then Boss was over from a five metre scrum and Madigan added another penalty three minutes before half time. They had enjoyed large chunks of possession and territory but the 11-0 lead didn't reflect this. Back we came and the third quarter belonged to us. Swiel got our first points with a penalty (he had missed two in the first half) after Mike Brown had been denied a try by the TMO for a knock-on by Marler. It looked to be a dubious decision but it stood and we had to get on with it. Brown did get his try after several phases of possession for Swiel to convert and bring us to within a point. His second penalty and third successful kick put us 13-11 in front but Madigan was on hand to put over another penalty to edge the hosts ahead. There was a dust up near the end and Matthews was sin binned for raising his hands to the face of Ryan but at least one of the home side should have gone as well. With him went our chances but we did gain a losing bonus point. We still led the way but Leinster were on the same points as us (13) and after Wasps produced a seven try thumping of Castres at home, they now had 12. The French side still only had a point and were destined to finish bottom. As O'Shea said, our destiny was in our own hands and two wins from our final couple of games at home to Wasps and Castres away in January would almost certainly see us through as one of the best runners-up at least.

It was back to Premiership action for the following four weeks around Christmas and the New Year, the first match was at the Stoop against Newcastle on 20th December. Swiel continued in the number ten jersey and it was clear to see that he was turning into a good understudy for Evans, it was a shame we couldn't keep him permanently. He kicked us into the lead with a penalty after eight minutes but it was clear this was going to be a struggle. Easter, Marler and Robshaw were all missing and it was no surprise when the Falcons took the lead at the end of the half. Alesana Tuilagi got the try and the TMO agreed he had got the ball down. Socino converted and we had it all to do. The discipline of the visitors let them down and Swiel kicked four penalties in thirteen minutes either side of the hour mark to give us an eight point lead. There was no further scoring, we had our fifth league win of the season and we moved up to eighth. Northampton, Bath, Exeter and Saracens occupied the top four places with London Welsh still at the bottom on one point after losing 78-7 to Saracens.

Big Game 7 followed on the Saturday after Christmas Day and this year, the Saints from Northampton were our opponents. A crowd of 82,000 turned up to see us take on the Premiership's top team. We started well and George Lowe scored our first league try in four games after blanks against Sale, Bath and Newcastle. Swiel missed the conversion but added a penalty to give us an eight point lead after nine minutes. Back came the Saints and Myler got a penalty, Manoa a try and Myler converted and kicked a second penalty to put them in front. Ma'afu had been binned for a high tackle on Lowe but that penalty was the only score and once again we had failed to take advantage. Two minutes into the second half, North scored for Myler to convert and we had conceded twenty unanswered points. Swiel and Myler exchanged penalties before Swiel almost scored a try but the ball was recycled and Clifford got the five pointer for Swiel to add the extras. After a series of kicks to the corner, the visitors' pressure paid off when Fotuali'i went over for Myler to convert. Eighteen minutes remained and we were trailing 18-30. We huffed and puffed but Twomey's try on 76 minutes and Swiel's subsequent conversion brought the mere consolation of another losing bonus point. Afterwards, O'Shea talked about turning a corner in defeat – there was no end it seemed to the spin coming out of the Club every time we lost! The fact was, like it or not, we were simply not good enough. At the half way point, we were eighth on 24 points. Northampton were on top with 43, Bath were second with 42 and then a reasonable gap to Saracens (34) and Exeter (31). London Welsh trailed Newcastle by fourteen points at the bottom. Even a top four finish was starting to look beyond us because it was unlikely we could string together the number of wins required to get us there.

We travelled to Oxford for our first match of 2015 to take on London Welsh. A Sunday fixture this time and we produced one of our worst performances of the season so far. The first quarter could have seen three tries for the home side but they managed to butcher each opportunity. We were no better and even a kick to the corner from Swiel went the wrong side of the flag! After 21 minutes, our defence was broken and Rowley scored under the posts after good work from Fonua and Scott. Robinson converted and we struck back when Dickson went over from close range but the simple conversion from Swiel hit the right post. The Welsh lost their hooker (Vella) who was stretchered off and taken to hospital with an ankle injury. Robinson added a penalty to stretch the lead but we were in front by half time as Hopper put Yarde over in the corner. Swiel made no mistake with the conversion and it was 12-10. The general handling and accuracy of both sides left a lot to be desired but Sinckler grabbed our third try on 51 minutes. The conversion was again missed and Robinson reduced the deficit with his second penalty; there were 20 minutes left. With less than ten to go, Care threw out a great pass to enable Williams to dart in for the bonus point score which Swiel converted. O'Shea was happy with the bonus point but although we put out a weakened side, the Welsh were conceding on average over forty points a game and to beat them by eleven wasn't really good enough. To be fair, we should have lost and that really summed up how bad London Welsh were. We stayed in eighth spot on 29 points; the top five was now Northampton (48), Bath (42), Saracens (39) and Wasps and Leicester both on 35. You couldn't see London Welsh beating anyone so they might as well have resigned themselves to relegation because they were now fifteen points behind London Irish and Newcastle. Having said that, all the while it was mathematically possible to survive, they had to hope.

Leicester came to the Stoop on 10th January and although we didn't fear them as much as we once did (we were experiencing our best run against them for over 25 years), they were still a good team. Ben Botica started at fly half for the first time since the Exeter game back on 28th September (he had returned from injury when he came off the bench against London Welsh the previous week). Marler and Robshaw also returned to strengthen the pack but it was Leicester who scored first with two penalties from Williams in the opening ten minutes. Botica got one back, Williams replied and that was the first quarter over. The visitors had dominated the early part but Care got over for the first try (after an exquisite offload by Easter) and Botica's conversion gave us the lead. Just before half time, Jack Clifford scored the second and although Botica missed the conversion, we led 15-9. When Williams kicked straight to Yarde, he ran straight through the defence from 40 metres out to increase the lead. Botica converted and added a penalty on 50 minutes to make it 25-9. Williams put over a fourth penalty and Leicester dominated the last fifteen minutes but couldn't score. We did though with the last move of the game when Brown created the opening for Swiel to go over for the bonus point try. He added the extras to his try and the final score of 32-12 was our biggest winning margin over the Tigers since 5th March 1976. The five points took us into seventh on 34 points but Northampton were still fourteen in front although we were only two behind fourth placed Wasps. Bath and Saracens occupied second and third and with Newcastle beating the Welsh, there was now a twenty point gap between them and the Irish and the Falcons. The winning run stood at two and would need to be extended by a lot more if we were to challenge in the three competitions.

Next up were Wasps on the following Saturday at the Stoop in the return European fixture. Goode put them in front after three minutes but much worse was to come as we gifted points to the visitors like they were going out of fashion. First, Danny Care took a quick penalty and threw a pass out towards no one in particular. Unfortunately for us, Wade picked the ball up and returned it 75 metres under our posts for the opening try. Goode converted as he did with their second try when Simpson darted through a gap on the edge of a ruck. At the end of 20 minutes play, we trailed 0-17. Hughes was binned for persistent infringement and we had so much possession and territory it was unbelievable that we failed to score anything. We needed a good solid start to the second half but it was Goode with a penalty who stretched the lead. Botica got us on the board with a penalty but Daly replied from 55 metres out to make it 3-23. Despite us dominating for the rest of the game, there was no further scoring and our European adventure was left teetering on the edge of a cliff. Eighty minutes earlier, we controlled our destiny, now we didn't. A miracle was needed because Leinster thrashed Castres so the Pool looked like this with one round left – Leinster 18 points, Wasps 16, Quins 13 and Castres 1. If Wasps or Leinster got nothing out of their game, we could make it by getting a five point win at Castres the following Saturday. Yet again we had flattered to deceive and failed at home when it mattered.

The team travelled to Castres knowing that anything less than five points would mean an exit from the cup and even if we did achieve our aim, we still might not qualify. In freezing conditions and with snow falling, we set about the massive task ahead of us with a try after 11 minutes from Joe Marler that Evans converted. We had lost Will Collier in the eighth minute after rupturing his anterior cruciate ligament – his season was over. Dupont scored for Castres, Dumora converted and it was all square after 20 minutes. Walker got our second and Evans converted but Cabannes scored, Dumora converted and it was level again. In time added on, Combezou was sin binned for taking George Lowe without the ball and Care scored after some phases from a tapped penalty. Evans ended the half with his third conversion. Clifford scored the bonus point try after 48 minutes, Evans again successful and now we just had to win. Lambert got another (converted by Evans) as did Yarde and both of these were scored when Grosso was in the bin. It was a pity this free flowing game had deserted us the previous week! Beattie went over for the home side but Lowe added another for us and Evans converted again as our winning margin reached 28. O'Shea had been watching the latter stages of the match in Coventry on a laptop and it was a close one. Wasps came back from 6-20 down to level the match at 20-20. In added time, Goode skewed a dropped goal attempt wide of the posts from right in front. The match ended all square, the worst possible result for us because the Pool ended as follows:- Leinster 20, Wasps 18, Quins 18, Castres 1. Because the aggregate score between us and Wasps had to be taken into account in case both sides finished level, we finished third (the total was 26-39 in favour of Wasps). We had paid the ultimate price because of a terrible home performance the previous week. Even if Goode's dropped goal had gone over, we would still not have qualified. Our total disappointment in the top tier European competition continued for another year as both Leinster and Wasps went through.

It was back to the LV= Cup for the following two weekends and Bath visited the Stoop in the first of them on Saturday 31st January. We began badly and Homer kicked a penalty and converted Banahan's try to give them a 10-0 lead after only four minutes. We managed to pull ourselves together and Williams got a try after 23 minutes, Evans converted and kicked a penalty to level matters. Walker scored before half time, Evans hit the left post with the conversion and Homer made it a two point game with a second penalty. In the third quarter, Evans put over two penalties to give us a 21-13 lead and it was looking good. Four minutes later, he missed another and it proved crucial as Bath attacked and from a scrum in front of our posts, a penalty try was awarded and Lambert was yellow carded. Homer converted and it could not have been closer. With time running out, all we had to do was keep possession and run the clock down. We did neither and gave the ball back to Bath when Ross Chisholm put in a ridiculous kick. They broke up field, into our 22 and when the ball went loose and forward off Sloan as he made a tackle, Merrick picked it up. The referee (Ben Whitehouse) saw it as this and had no option but to award a penalty to the visitors for offside. Jennings kicked the easy three points from right in front and less than 90 seconds remained when we restarted. Bath kept the ball and we had lost another game after dominating large parts of it. Our start didn't help at all but it was Bath's first win at the Stoop since December 2006 after a run of one draw and eight defeats. The Pool situation became clear the next day when all fixtures had been played. Exeter won with a bonus point against the Dragons and the Ospreys and London Welsh got losing bonus points. Exeter were top with 13 points, we were second on 6, Ospreys next on 2 and London Welsh with 1. This meant one thing – we were out of another competition.

The final pool game at Gloucester the following Saturday was a meaningless fixture as far as we were concerned. Gloucester had to win and see what happened between Saracens and Exeter the following day. The first half was littered with mistakes but again we leaked points and found ourselves 13-0 down after 31 minutes. Aled Thomas put over a penalty, Dan Thomas scored a try and Aled converted and kicked his second penalty. Just before the interval, Monye got over and Botica converted. In the second half, there were more substitutions than points. We scored none but Gloucester got two tries through Rowan and Reynolds. There was no scoring in the final seventeen minutes and the home side won 25-7. Saracens beat Exeter on Sunday, progressed to the semi-finals at Gloucester's expense and went on to defeat the Chiefs again in the final (23-20). Our Pool finished with Exeter top on 13, Ospreys with 6, Quins 6 and London Welsh 2. The Ospreys finished second by virtue of outscoring us 9-8 in tries. Fijian back row forward Netani Talei made his debut, he was in the process of winning 33 caps and would make at least 8 appearances for the first team. Jordan Turner-Hall made his final appearance; he had scored 90 points (18 tries) during his 1st XV career, made 18 appearances as a substitute and been sin binned on four occasions. He was forced to retire on 22 July 2015 because of a hip injury and it was a sad end to his ten year career. For us it was now a case of how high we could finish in the Premiership and there were nine games left. We would probably need to win all of them with a few bonus points added to get into the play-offs. To be honest, neither looked likely given our current topsy-turvy form.

A trip to Coventry's Ricoh Arena for the fourth meeting of the season with Wasps came on Sunday 15th February. We had won our last two league games and it was essential that this run continued. We got off to another bad start and Goode punished silly mistakes with three penalties in the first 18 minutes. Evans replied with one of his own but by half time, we were out of it. Varndell and Daly got tries, Goode converted both and although Evans got his second penalty, we were looking ragged. As our defence pulled a driving lineout down, a penalty try was awarded after 46 minutes and our captain for the day (George Robson) was sin binned. Goode converted and a rout looked on the cards. Luckily for us, Wasps couldn't add to their score until three minutes from time just after Clifford became our second player in the bin. As our scrum was marched backwards, another penalty try came and this time, Lozowski converted to make the final score 37-6. This was our biggest losing margin against Wasps since December 1999 when they beat us 52-16 at the Stoop. Afterwards, Conor O'Shea trotted out the same old type of excuses like brittle confidence and youngsters being taught lessons; at least he said that next week's game against Exeter was a must win for us!! Northampton were still top on 52 points, Bath had 47, Saracens were on 43 and Wasps had 41. We were eighth with 34 points and given the way we were playing, top spot was no longer a realistic option and even the play-off spots were starting to look remote. No one would give up until it was mathematically impossible but sometimes you have to be realistic. London Welsh remained twenty points adrift at the bottom; it was obvious they were going down as they had to win at least five games to get level with the Falcons and that meant Newcastle losing five and picking up no points at all.

On Saturday 21st February, the Chiefs came to the Stoop looking to stake their claim for a play-off spot. We started well for a change and Evans put us ahead with a penalty after Whitten had been sin binned for a deliberate knock-on when a try looked certain. Before he came back, Dollman went the same way for a no-arms tackle on Yarde as he went for the corner. Evans went through for a try but missed the conversion and we were good value for our lead although it should have been more. From the restart, we conceded a penalty and Slade put Exeter on the board. Then, Care had his kick charged down and White won the race to touch down. Slade converted and fourteen man Exeter were in front. The number of kicks that had been charged down this season resulting in tries was infuriating. The Chiefs had two tries ruled out for forward passes before the break and had to settle for two more Slade penalties. Evans squeezed one between to make it 11-16. Our handling was terrible and mistake after mistake led to Slade converting his own try before Evans got another penalty. Two more from Slade effectively made the game safe with twenty minutes left. Hopper scored our second try and Evans converted but, as usual, we conceded another penalty and Slade knocked it over. When Waldrom became the third Chiefs player to be binned (this time for killing the ball) it made no difference and we had lost again (21-32). How was it possible to lose a game when the opposition had three men sin binned? Tom Casson appeared for the final time after five seasons in the first team squad; he had scored 30 points (6 tries) and captained the side on one occasion as well as appearing as a sub 17 times. We now dropped back to ninth and were 22 points behind the Saints with Bath, Saracens and Exeter filling the other top four slots. London Welsh only had one point, the gap was now the same as ours – 22 points. This defeat effectively killed off our top four hopes as well so all we could play for was a top seven finish to try and get into the Champions Cup next season.

Unfortunately for us, our next game was a Friday night trip to Franklin's Gardens to take on the leaders, Northampton. It was a game with plenty of errors and no score until Evans put over a penalty after 26 minutes. The lead didn't last long and Manoa went over for a try which was converted by Myler but we did get the final score of the half with another Evans penalty to make it 6-7. Just after Wilson had got Northampton's second try, Sinckler was binned for a dangerous tackle on Manoa. We held out until just before he came back on when Wood was driven over. We tried to get back into the game but Walker's try was ruled out for a sloppy forward pass. By the time Yarde ran in under the posts, time had expired. Botica converted to make the scoreline a bit closer but all we had was another losing bonus point. Italian international scrum half Tito Tebaldi came on as a substitute to make his debut, he was in the process of winning 20 caps but would only make 10 appearances for us. Our handling and general accuracy had been a problem all season and it made you wonder why this wasn't practiced more and more until it was perfect. Be that as it may, we did have a seven point lead over London Irish who were tenth but Northampton now moved on to 60 points after this win. Saracens, Exeter, Wasps, Bath and Leicester looked favourites to fill the other play-off spots with Sale having an outside chance. London Welsh at the bottom were reaching the point of no return as the Falcons kept picking up points.

London Irish came to the Stoop on 7th March with neither side having much to play for except our outside chance of top tier European rugby next season. After three league defeats on the trot we just had to win this one and started with two penalties from Evans in the first ten minutes. Geraghty and Evans twice exchanged penalties before Care scored a try and Evans converted for a 19-6 lead after half an hour. After we kicked to the corner, Ward overthrew the lineout, Geraghty booted the ball downfield and as Chisholm let it bounce, Short snatched it just as our full back was about to claim it and ran in unopposed. Geraghty converted and we had given away a needless seven points again! The whole side seemed obsessed with kicking to the corner but we were not disciplined enough to score many tries from the tactic. After another failed attempt, we recovered the ball, Clifford broke the line and Hopper was over for another try. Evans converted again and we continued to dominate without scoring any further points. Eventually, we let the Irish in again when Fowlie rounded off a counter attack. Geraghty added the extras and with just seconds left, Talei tried an inside flick that was intercepted by Geraghty but this time, Fowlie was put into touch and the final whistle went. When would the players learn how to close out a game again? They had been lucky on this occasion. We moved back to eighth on 39 points but were well off the top four but only four points behind Sale who were in seventh. For the record, the top five were now Northampton (62 points), Exeter (53), Saracens (52) and Bath and Leicester on 51. At the bottom, poor old London Welsh were almost down as Newcastle just needed two points or another defeat for Welsh to stay up.

Because of the LV= Cup semi-finals and final, there was now a break of two weeks for most teams. Our next game was at Wembley Stadium against Saracens. Once again, the World record attendance at a club match was beaten when 84,068 spectators turned up to watch. Easter, Marler and Robshaw all returned to the starting line-up but Mike Brown had suffered concussion on England duty against Italy and would not play again this season. From the charge down of a kick by de Kock, Clifford opened the scoring after just 25 seconds to stun the crowd. The extras were missed and normal service was soon resumed. Wyles got a try, Hodgson converted and Monye was binned for holding on. Hodgson and Evans exchanged penalties and then Ashton chipped into space down our left flank and was over before anyone could get near him. Monye returned but Goode put over two penalties to make it 21-8 at the interval. We desperately needed a strong start to the second half and Evans was on target with his second penalty after 46 minutes. By the time he got his third, the game was over because Ashton had scored again for Goode to convert. There were still 24 minutes remaining but we couldn't get anywhere and despite Ashton going to the bin for a tip-tackle on Hopper, the Saracens points kept coming. Wyles and Billy Vunipola scored tries and Goode improved both to make the final score 42-14. This was our thirteenth loss to Saracens out of the last fourteen games; not a good record at all and until we could compete and defeat them on a regular basis, the future would be bleak. London Welsh were finally relegated after losing 14-29 at home to Bath. We remained in eighth, Northampton had a ten point lead over Saracens in second but Bath, Leicester and Exeter were right behind them in the battle for the play-offs. Sale were now eight points ahead of us so it was looking like second tier European rugby for us in 2015/16 with only four games to go.

Another week off for the European quarter finals before the return with Gloucester at the Stoop on 11th April. Charlie Walker drew first blood with a try on nine minutes before Laidlaw and Evans twice exchanged penalties and Laidlaw converted a try by Meakes to edge the visitors ahead at the break. We lost Marler to the bin either side of half time and went further behind when Sharples got a try. Two penalties from Evans brought us to within a point and when Clifford also saw yellow for a late tackle on Sharples, Laidlaw put over another penalty to make it 17-21 going into the final quarter. As we applied pressure to the Gloucester line, Moriarty and Sharples were both sent to the bin and Yarde was driven over for our second try. When Lindsay-Hague got the third, Evans converted and we were suddenly 29-21 ahead and looking for the bonus point score with five minutes to go. The only further score was a try for the visitors from Robson to gain them a losing bonus point. Asaeli Tikoirotuma played his last game for the Club having scored 10 points (2 tries) during his brief spell with us. With this victory, we held our position and closed the gap between us and Sale to five points. There were six teams in contention for the top four and even with three bonus point victories, we now couldn't be one of them. Northampton, Saracens, Bath and Exeter held the positions but Leicester and Wasps were not far behind.

The European semi-finals gave us another week off before our meeting at the AJ Bell Stadium with Sale Sharks. Before kick–off it was announced that Joe Marler needed a shoulder operation and would not play in the last three games (Chris Robshaw would deputise in his absence for two of them and Care would lead the side at Newcastle). We played some good rugby in the first half and built up a nice lead but we couldn't sustain it for more than 55 minutes. Walker got the opening try after four minutes and Cipriani got Sale on the board with a penalty after 19 minutes. As we took control, Robshaw scored another, Evans converted and Yarde added a third before Cipriani got another penalty. Just before half time, Care secured the try bonus to make it 25-6. When Ward was binned after a series of collapsed driving mauls, Sale's comeback started with a try from Arscott which Cipriani converted. In the last ten minutes, the Sharks had the momentum and Arscott and Cueto scored tries but Ford (Cipriani's replacement) missed both conversions and that cost them the game. Although we stayed in eighth, the gap with Sale was now down to just one point. The battle for the top four continued and the top six all remained in contention with Northampton still on top.

Bath visited the Stoop on 8th May desperately needing to win whereas we played only for pride. The battle for seventh spot no longer applied because the European finals had taken place the previous weekend and Gloucester won the Challenge Cup at the Stoop against Edinburgh by 19-13. They entered the play-offs as a result and we would be in the Challenge Cup next season. First they played Connacht at home and won 40-32, then they faced Bordeaux Bègles at Sixways but went down to a last second dropped goal (22-23) despite leading 19-3 at one stage. Toulon won the big prize by defeating Clermont Auvergne 24-18 in the final at Twickenham. After we lost Nick Easter with concussion after five minutes, Ugo Monye scored to put us ahead. Clifford then received a yellow card and Bath took the lead with a penalty and the conversion of Louw's try by Ford. Evans put over a penalty and we went in front when a penalty try was awarded; Evans converted for the final score of the half. Just before half time, George Robson left the field injured on his last appearance. He had scored 65 points (13 tries), captained the side ten times, been a sub on 29 occasions, had eight trips to the bin and was sent off once during his ten year career. Bath were level two minutes into the second half when Agulla scored and Ford's conversion put them ahead. For ten minutes up to the hour mark it was a see-saw game. First, Evans slotted two penalties to put us ahead before Houston scored a try and Ford again converted to make it 21-24. Then Monye got his second try of the night (his 100th overall) to put us ahead for the fourth time. Evans missed his second conversion and it proved costly because Ford stepped up with six minutes left to kick the match winning penalty. We also said goodbye to Ugo Monye in this game; he had scored 500 points (100 tries), appeared 28 times as a sub and visited the bin on four occasions. He had been in the 1st XV for 13 seasons but went at the right time as his speed started to desert him. With one game left, this was the position - Northampton had 76 points and would finish top, Bath (64) were guaranteed to be second and two from Leicester (64), Exeter and Saracens (both on 63) would fill the away slots in the play-offs. Sale were now five points ahead of us on 54 and the only issue at the bottom was how big the gap would be.

On Sunday 16th May, the 2014/15 season finally came to a close for us with a visit to Kingston Park, Newcastle. Only Care, Evans, Matthews and Yarde survived from the starting line-up against London Irish back in September. The Falcons took the lead when Mayhew scored after two minutes, Evans got us on the board with a penalty but Catterick knocked over two for the home side. In the second quarter, Nick Evans landed two penalties either side of converting his own try to put us 16-11 ahead at the interval. Both sides had wasted great scoring chances but it was a full-blooded, exciting game. On 51 minutes, Lawson went over and Catterick converted but we were quickly back in front with an unconverted try from Yarde. Back came the Falcons and Blair scored followed by Powell; Catterick converted both and with seconds left, we turned the ball over at a ruck and Saull was put away for their fifth try. The final score of 37-21 summed up our season – too many bad performances from a squad not strong enough, clinical enough or accurate enough. Joe Trayfoot played his last game against the Falcons when he came on as a substitute; he had made 29 appearances as a sub but scored no points. Tom Williams retired after this game, he had scored 339 points (67 tries and 2 conversions) and made 41 appearances as a sub (including one as a temporary sub). He had been with us for twelve seasons and, thanks to the photographs taken at the time, would be forever remembered for his antics in the "Bloodgate" game against Leinster. Eventually, it was admitted that the Club had not recruited well enough and built on the solid foundations of the 2012 Premiership winning side. Something, it seems, that everyone else but the Club had known for some time! Our final position was eighth and we were 27 points behind Northampton who were top and 19 adrift of a play-off spot. The other qualifiers were Bath, Leicester and Saracens (the Chiefs failed by a points difference of 20 to oust Saracens from fourth spot). At the bottom, London Welsh ended with a single point and were 33 behind Newcastle. In the semi-finals, Northampton lost 24-29 to Saracens and Bath thrashed Leicester 47-10. In the final on 30th May, Saracens defeated Bath 28-16 to win the title for the second time.

This season had promised so much and delivered nothing again. This was not acceptable for a Club which gave the impression of one that was going to compete with the top sides. After all the spin, the players needed to deliver all the time but they failed miserably to do so. In reality, we never recovered from the heavy defeat at home to Saracens. Overall, our record was P32 W15 D0 L17 F658 A707. In the league it was P22 W10 D0 L12 F444 A514 Pts 49 (BP 9 – TB 4 LB 5) Pos 8th. No one managed more than thirty games, Charlie Matthews was top on 29, George Robson next with 26, Danny Care and Marland Yarde played in 25 and Jack Clifford and Nick Easter appeared in 24.

Nick Evans topped the points yet again with 221 (2 tries, 51 penalties and 29 conversions), he was also the leader in penalties and conversions. Marland Yarde topped the try scorers with 9 and Danny Care got the most dropped goals with 2. Overall, tries fell by one to 66, penalties dropped by three to 76, conversions stayed the same on 47 and dropped goals went down by one to 2. As a result of all this, the total points also fell by seventeen to 658.

2014/15

090814	FC GRENOBLE	GRENOBLE	L	1G1PG(10)-4G1PG(31)
160814	SECTION PALOISE	TWICKENHAM STOOP	D	1G2T(17)-1G2T(17)
230814	GLASGOW WARRIORS	GLASGOW	W	2G2T(24)-1G2PG2T(23)
060914	LONDON IRISH(AP)	TWICKENHAM(A)	W	2G2PG(20)-5PG(15)
120914	SARACENS(AP)	TWICKENHAM STOOP	L	0-3G6PG(39)
200914	WASPS(AP)	TWICKENHAM STOOP	W	2G1DG3PG(26)-1G2PG1T(23)

280914	EXETER CHIEFS(AP)	EXETER	L	1G2PG(13)-3G5PG(36)
041014	LONDON WELSH(AP)	TWICKENHAM STOOP	W	7G1PG(52)-0
101014	LEICESTER(AP)	LEICESTER	L	1G3PG(16)-1G5PG(22)
171014	CASTRES OLYMPIQUE(ERCCP2)	TWICKENHAM STOOP	W	1G6PG(25)-3PG(9)
261014	WASPS(ERCCP2)	ADAMS PARK	W	2G3PG(23)-1G3PG(16)
021114	SARACENS(LVCP4)	BARNET	L	2G2PG(20)-2G2PG1T(25)
071114	NEWPORT GWENT DRAGONS(LVCP4)	TWICKENHAM STOOP	W	2G4PG1T(31)-1G3PG1T(21)
141114	GLOUCESTER(AP)	GLOUCESTER	W	2G1PG1T(22)-5PG(15)
211114	SALE SHARKS(AP)	TWICKENHAM STOOP	L	4PG(12)-1G3PG(16)
281114	BATH(AP)	BATH	L	2PG(6)-1G1PG3T(25)
071214	LEINSTER(ERCCP2)	TWICKENHAM STOOP	W	1G1DG3PG1T(24)|-6PG(18)
131214	LEINSTER(ERCCP2)	DUBLIN	L	1G2PG(13)-3PG1T(14)
201214	NEWCASTLE(AP)	TWICKENHAM STOOP	W	5PG(15)-1G(7)
271214	NORTHAMPTON(AP)	TWICKENHAM	L	2G2PG1T(25)-3G3PG(30)
040115	LONDON WELSH(AP)	OXFORD	W	2G2T(24)-1G2PG(13)
100115	LEICESTER(AP)	TWICKENHAM STOOP	W	3G2PG1T(32)-4PG(12)
170115	WASPS(ERCCP2)	TWICKENHAM STOOP	L	1PG(3)-2G3PG(23)
240115	CASTRES OLYMPIQUE(ERCCP2)	CASTRES	W	6G1T(47)-2G1T(19)
310115	BATH(LVCP4)	TWICKENHAM STOOP	L	1G3PG1T(21)-2G3PG(23)
070215	GLOUCESTER(LVCP4)	GLOUCESTER	L	1G(7)-2G2PG1T(25)
150215	WASPS(AP)	COVENTRY	L	2PG(6)-4G3PG(37)
210215	EXETER CHIEFS(AP)	TWICKENHAM STOOP	L	1G3PG1T(21)-2G6PG(32)
270215	NORTHAMPTON(AP)	NORTHAMPTON	L	1G2PG(13)-1G2T(17)
070315	LONDON IRISH(AP)	TWICKENHAM STOOP	W	2G4PG(26)-2G2PG(20)
280315	SARACENS(AP)	WEMBLEY	L	3PG1T(14)-4G3PG1T(42)
110415	GLOUCESTER(AP)	TWICKENHAM STOOP	W	1G4PG2T(29)-1G3PG2T(26)
250415	SALE SHARKS(AP)	SALFORD	W	1G1PG3T(25)-1G2PG2T(23)
080515	BATH(AP)	TWICKENHAM STOOP	L	1G3PG2T(26)-3G2PG(27)
160515	NEWCASTLE(AP)	NEWCASTLE	L	1G3PG1T(21)-3G2PG2T(37)

50

Sevens From 2010-2016

The 2010 Middlesex tournament was the penultimate event. We won our first game against a side called Wales Amser Justin Time by 34-19 but went out to ULR Samurai International in a close contest (12-19). They went on to win in the final against London Irish by an even smaller margin (15-12). The Plate winners were Newcastle who beat our first round victims 14-10. Our squad was Nick Easter, Chris Robshaw (captain), Joe Trayfoot, Jack Clifford, Ollie Lindsay-Hague, Charlie Walker, Sam Smith, Ross Chisholm, Danny Care, Miles Mantella, Ugo Monye and Benjamin Urdapilleta. A new competition appeared in July 2010 and was known as the J.P. Morgan Asset Management Premiership Rugby 7s Series. It featured the twelve teams from the Premiership and they would be divided into three groups of four, each group would play at a separate venue on a different night. Each team would play three matches and the top two would progress through to the finals where they would be split into two groups of three. Each side would play two games this time and the group winners would play in the final. The points scoring was the same as in the Premiership and obviously red and yellow cards were also in use (a sin bin in Sevens lasts for two minutes but the effects can be devastating). The first tournament was played at the Stoop, Franklin's Gardens and Welford Road with the finals at the Rec. We beat Wasps (15-5) and lost to Saracens (5-21) and London Irish (10-12) but just scraped through on six points. Saracens won the group with thirteen and we joined Exeter, Newcastle, Northampton and Sale in the finals. We lost to Newcastle (19-26) and beat Exeter (17-5) but the nature of these small Groups was that one slip could cost you. The Falcons progressed to the final where they lost to Saracens 17-5.

On Saturday 9th July 2011, the final Middlesex Sevens tournament took place and in all truth, it was a bit of a farce in the end. The Premiership clubs were prevented from playing in it by PRL because they now had their own Sevens tournament (as mentioned above, the Premiership Sevens had started in 2010) and it ended up with sides from all over appearing. Samurai International returned to defend the crown and won it quite easily by beating Esher in the final 55-12 in front of 10,000 spectators. It's funny how the crowd started and ended up roughly the same some 86 years later. From its humble beginnings, it raised over £10 million for charity, a fantastic sum – the event would be fondly remembered by all the Quins fans who were lucky enough to see those five wins on the trot back in 1986-1990. In the London Floodlit tournament we beat Blackheath in the final by 31-7, it was our first victory there since 2007. The Premiership Sevens returned in the same format, the group stages would be played at the Rec, Franklin's Gardens and Edgeley Park and the finals would be at the Stoop. We qualified well at Bath by winning all our games against Bath (24-5), Exeter (43-0) and London Irish (26-12). Bath were second on the night and Newcastle, Sale, Saracens and Wasps made up the finalists. We won against Wasps (19-0) in our first game but slipped up again against Newcastle (12-17). They went on to win this time against Saracens in a repeat of last year's final by 31-21.

With the Middlesex Sevens now gone, the only ones of note were those held at Rosslyn Park and the Premiership Sevens. We won the London Floodlit again with victories over Loughborough Students (43-5), Marauders (36-0), Saracens (27-10) and Bath in the final (29-0). In the Premiership event, again played in July and August, we tried to qualify at the Stoop with the other grounds being Edgeley Park and Kingsholm with the finals at the Rec. We started with a win against London Irish (21-14), then got thrashed by Saracens (0-33) and recovered well to hand out a beating to Wasps (35-0). Unfortunately, the way other results went, it wasn't enough and we finished a point behind London Irish who got at least one point from all three games. At Bath, the home side were joined by Gloucester, London Irish, London Welsh, Sale and Saracens. In the final, London Irish won a tight game against Gloucester (31-28).

It was normal service at Rosslyn Park in 2013 with wins over Ealing Trailfinders (57-0), Barnes (45-0), Loughborough Students (59-12) and Serious Stuff Pups in the final (26-14). The Premiership Sevens qualifying was at Allianz Park, Franklin's Gardens and Kingsholm. We tried our luck at Barnet and won all our games again. This time we beat Wasps (26-19), London Irish (42-19) and Saracens (24-21). In the finals at Bath, we were joined by Gloucester, Leicester, Newcastle, Saracens and Worcester. Once again we slipped up and lost narrowly to Leicester (17-19) and although we beat Worcester (29-14), the damage had been done. Leicester made it to the final where they lost to Gloucester (17-24). As a result of winning the trophy, they qualified for the World Club Sevens at Twickenham later in the month. This tournament took place on 17th and 18th August and brought together twelve teams from Argentina, Australia, England (3), New Zealand, Russia (2), South Africa (2) and USA (2). The teams were divided into three Pools and each side played three games with the top two progressing to the quarter finals along with the two best runners-up. Our squad was Karl Dickson, Dave Ward (captain), Patrice Agunda, Harry Sloan, Jeremy Manning, Joe Trayfoot, Henry Cheeseman, Jack Clifford, Jordan Burns, Louis Grimoldby, Miles Mantella and Charlie Walker and in the first game against ACT Brumbies, we went behind after only thirty seconds. Mantella broke through and Grimoldby's conversion put us in front but we conceded again to trail at the interval. Ward got our second converted try but the Brumbies got one either side to run out winners 24-14. Kuban Krasnador were our second opponents but we were playing better and Grimoldby and Burns got converted tries to give us a great start. The Russians got a try back right on half time and one more when play resumed but Burns and Mantella took us clear despite Krasnodar getting a late score (24-19). Auckland had already bagged two victories but we had to win to have any chance of progressing. Mantella opened the scoring after a minute and Burns ran almost from our line to score another before Auckland got on the scoreboard. Ward almost scored in the second half but Mantella did and another try conceded made it 19-14. In the last few minutes, Walker and Burns ran in more tries to make it 31-14. As a result, we qualified as one of the best runners-up and would play Gloucester in the quarter final. We conceded an early score but Burns grabbed a try and Walker converted to level the scores. Into the second half, Walker converted his own score and Trayfoot got another to put us in the semi-final. There we met Auckland again but it was a different story this time as they went into a 14-0 lead before Burns got a try back which was converted to keep us in it at half time. They scored another at the start of the second half but Mantella went in for us to keep it a seven point game. A yellow card for Ward finished our challenge and two unconverted tries swept Auckland into the final (14-31). We did have one more match to play and that was against Buenos Aires in the 3/4th place play-off; it was a game too far and Cheeseman scored our only try in a 31-7 defeat. In the Shield (9th-12th place), Krasnodar beat Blue Bulls 19-12; New York won the Plate (5th-8th place) against Gloucester (33-14) and Brumbies won the title by scoring right at the end in a 17-14 win over Auckland.

The same happened in the London Floodlit tournament at Roehampton in 2014 by beating Loughborough Students (38-0), Richmond (29-14), Rosslyn Park (21-14) and Saracens in the final by 45-26. The Premiership Sevens lost its sponsor for a year but carried on regardless and this time, the four Welsh regions had joined the party. This led to a shake-up with the finals becoming a straight knockout (Group winners playing the runners-up) and the introduction of a Plate competition. The qualifying rounds were held at Cardiff Arms Park, Kingsholm, Franklin's Gardens and the Darlington Arena (Kingston Park was having a new all-weather pitch laid so was unavailable). We were at Northampton and started by beating the hosts (40-7), then Saracens (36-0) and finally Wasps (26-19) to race through to the finals at the Stoop. Cardiff, Leicester, Gloucester, Northampton, Newcastle and Newport Gwent Dragons also qualified. In the quarter final, we dealt with London Irish (26-10) and faced Newport Gwent Dragons in the next round. Ian Clark put us ahead after four minutes, Morgan equalised and the conversion put them in front. Just before half time, Marchant got over but somehow managed not to touch down in the eyes of the one man who counts, the referee. Burns put us ahead at the start of the second half, Morgan put the Welsh back in front before Dampies scored our third try with time almost up. Unfortunately, with time expired, Lewis scored for the Dragons and we were out (15-19). In the final, Gloucester won a tight one by 12-5 and so became the first club to successfully defend the title. In the Plate final, Leicester beat London Irish 17-0. Because the winners had already qualified for the World Club Sevens at Twickenham and there could only be one Welsh side (that was Cardiff), we were the next option. Our squad for the qualifying rounds was Lindsay-Hague, Walker, Grimoldby, Stuart, Aspland-Robinson, Jack Maslen (Worthing), Marchant, Cheeseman, Treadwell, James Chisholm, Alosio Yamoyamo (Fijian who had played for Marauders and the Army) and Izzy Foa'i (Abu Dhabi Quins). For the finals, Walker, Grimoldby, Stuart and Treadwell had to go to a training camp with the first team squad and were replaced by three non-Quins and Jordan Burns. The others were Ian Clark (Coventry), Simon Pitfield (Bletchley) and Gavin Dampies (Basingstoke). The World Club Sevens returned to Twickenham on 16th and 17th August and again brought together twelve teams, this time from Argentina, Australia, England (2), New Zealand, Russia (2), South Africa (2), USA (2) and Wales. Our squad was Izzy Foa'i, Jack Maslen, Ian Clark, Sam Aspland-Robinson, Simon Pitfield, Senitiki Nayalo (Army), Al Yamoyamo, Charlie Piper, Jordan Burns, Maika Burenivalu, Gavin Dampies and Sam Stuart (captain). In the Pool we played against Western Province (19-38), RC Enisei (12-33) and New York (7-24). To be honest, it was a disaster. The side simply didn't have the guile or the pace to get anywhere in the competition. We moved straight into the Shield and won our first game against the Waratahs (26-19) but lost to Seattle in the final by 14-28. In the Plate, Cardiff beat Blue Bulls 28-12 and in the final, Buenos Aires won 26-22 to deny Auckland again. It would be interesting to see what would happen if we could put out a full strength team free of the restraints of the fifteen-a-side season. Perhaps we would see a return to those halcyon days of the second half of the 1980s.

Setting a new record in the London Floodlit Sevens with a fifth win in a row was the aim in 2015 and the squad of Henry Cheeseman, Archie White, Sam Aspland-Robinson, Calum Waters, Kieran Treadwell, Gabriel Ibitoye, Charlie Piper, Tito Tebaldi, Asaeli Tikoirotuma, Louis Grimoldby, Jordan Burns and Joe Marchant started with Pool wins over Rambling Jesters (21-14) and Richmond (38-12). In the semi-final, Wasps were defeated narrowly by 19-17 and in the final, Worcester Warriors were beaten 33-17 after we led 12-10 at half time. They had eclipsed the record set by London Scottish between 1988 and 1991. Singha Beer were the new sponsors for the Premiership Sevens and would be in place for the next three years. This time the qualifying tournaments were held at the

Arms Park, Kingsholm, Ricoh Arena (Coventry) and Kingston Park with the final again at the Stoop. Our squad was Henry Cheeseman, Archie White, Sam Aspland-Robinson, Calum Waters, Kieran Treadwell, Gabriel Ibitoye, Robbie Nairn, Dino Lamb-Cona, Joe Marchant (captain), Luke White, Alosio Yamoyamo and Senitiki Nayalo. This was a poor team and it didn't look good as they were taken apart by Wasps (40-14) and lost to Saracens (17-24). They did recover to win against Northampton and because of the ineptitude of Northampton and Saracens, we qualified in second place courtesy of a losing bonus point. Senitiki Nayalo, Siva Naulago, Dino Lamb-Cona, Kieran Treadwell, Ed Forshaw, Gabriel Ibitoye, Joe Marchant (captain), Luke White, Calum Waters, Sam Aspland-Robinson, Robbie Nairn and Nathan Thomas (Cheeseman, Archie White and Yamoyamo had been replaced) represented the Club but didn't last long as they lost in the first game to Gloucester (26-31). In the Plate, the same happened against Sale (24-45) and perhaps one day someone will realise you are never going to win any Sevens tournament with a team that has barely met! The Newport Gwent Dragons edged out Wasps at the end to win the title (17-14) and Exeter beat Sale in the Plate final by 26-19.

For the London Floodlit Sevens in 2016, our inexperienced squad was Archie White, Kieran Ricknell, Sam Aspland-Robinson, Calum Waters, Kieran Treadwell, Gabriel Ibitoye, Niall Saunders, Harry Sloan, Beau Robinson, James Chisholm (captain) and Jonas Mikalcius. They were in Pool B with Esher and the Army and progressed to the semi-final with victories in both games by 36-7 and 19-17 respectively. Unfortunately, the Ramblin Jesters had a bit too much for us and won 28-19; they went on to beat Rosslyn Park 26-14 in the final.

The Singha Premiership Rugby 7s tournament was played again in July and August 2016. There were four Groups of four teams each. Group A was to be played on Friday 22nd July in Cardiff and contained Cardiff Blues, Newport Gwent Dragons, Ospreys and Scarlets; Group B was at Sandy Park on Saturday 23rd July and Bath, Bristol, Exeter and Wasps would compete; Group C was at Franklin's Gardens on Friday 29th July and the four teams were Gloucester, Harlequins, Northampton and Saracens; Group D was at Kingston Park on Saturday 30th July and the final teams were Leicester, Newcastle, Sale and Worcester. The top two from each Group qualified for the final night at the Ricoh Arena on Saturday 6th August (let's hope we are celebrating victory!).

51

Miscellany Throughout the Years

As previously mentioned the Harlequin Supporters' Club was formed in the early 1990s to enable fans to follow Quins, especially to away matches. The club was run entirely by supporters for supporters with Julian Easterbrook amongst the organisers. Coach trips were arranged and included a pub stop-over for lunch before continuing to the game. An annual dinner and dance was held with players and coaching staff attending and the Player of the Year award was handed out. In the summer, an annual cricket match was organised with players and Supporters' Club members forming a team to play against The Chase Farmers at one of Sir Evelyn de Rothschild's family homes (Ascott House, near Tring in Buckinghamshire). Members were kept up to date with news about the Club by way of a regular newsletter which later expanded into a magazine called The Harlequin (this also formed the basis of the online publication of the same name which was set up to attract more members worldwide). By the time professionalism came along, the concept of what supporters wanted from a supporters club needed to be redefined. The Supporters' Club became one of the founder members of the National Association of Supporters Clubs whose aim was to ensure that supporters would be charged a fair price for tickets and be treated as valued customers rather than a limitless revenue stream – something that TV money and Sponsorship would have to take on board. The problem was that a larger supporters' club could not be run by people in their spare time. Somebody would need to be contactable virtually 24/7 and with kick-off times already redefined for TV, problems were already looming. Many supporters had to travel just to get to the Stoop let alone attend away matches and coach travel from the Stoop was not necessarily the best option for everyone. European competition had seen the Supporters' Club organise some form of travel but with people coming from all points of the compass, booking of travel and match tickets needed to be made centrally rather than from someone's living room. The Supporters' Club needed time and money to evolve but before any meaningful discussions could be held with the main club, constitutional changes needed to be agreed with its membership and the club lapsed.

Quinssa, the Quins Supporters' Association, was set up on 31st March 2003 and when the Harlequin Supporters' Club folded, it established itself as the only organisation representing the Club's fans. The first General Meeting was held at the Stoop on 15th May 2003 and the first Committee was Melvin Baldock, Simon Coleman (Treasurer), Duncan Franklin, Alan Kurtz (Secretary), Barbara Richardson, Emma Stewart and Will Warner (Chair) - there were 155 members at this point. Quinssa holds events throughout the year that are open to members and non-members alike, some are rugby related such as the "Meet the..." evenings – the speakers have included Quins coaches, management, players (past, present and academy), back room staff, referees, pundits and judges and some are more social which range from meals with opposition fans to summer boat trips to the annual dinner dance. Ever since Quinssa started they have supported all aspects of the Club (the 1st XV, Ladies, Amateurs and the Academy). Support for the Academy has ranged from providing small bursaries to promising players in the early days and supporting players' trips to overseas academies to providing support for promising Elite Player Development Group players (over £25,000 has been raised to date). They have also supported a number of charities, the main one being the Shooting Star Chase Children's Hospice Care where they hold a Christmas Appeal for presents and gifts. The Club has always been very supportive in sending players along to their Christmas parties to deliver the presents. Helping fans get to away matches is something they have been involved in and run coaches to as many away games as possible. Quinssa's membership is now over 2,000 and they will have an important role in the Club's 150th anniversary celebrations, so things are looking good for the future. The current committee is Simon Bolton, Scott Cooke (Chair), Duncan Franklin, Lyn Gadd (Secretary), Louise Hopkins (Membership Secretary), Adrian Jobling, Warren Kennedy (Treasurer), Chris Munton, Emma Stewart, Robert Steers (Steve Scott was co-opted for the 2015/16 season). Other Committee members over the years have been: Sue Clayton-Smith, Chris Clements (co-opted), Stephen Engel, Jon Forster, Cliff Funnell, Sarah Gladstone, John Hartley, Emma-Jane Kurtz, David Perry and Rob White. Andrew Lawton also helped to run the coaches for a number of years. If you are interested in finding out more about Quinssa you can visit their website http://www.quinssa.org.uk, Facebook page https://www.facebook.com/QuinssaRugby, follow them on twitter at https://twitter.com/QuinssaRugby or join in the discussion at https://www.comeallwithin.co.uk.

With the introduction of professionalism some 20 years ago came a whole host of innovations rarely or never seen before at rugby clubs; indeed, far too many to mention here but there were debentures, credit cards, the Mighty Quins for junior supporters, charity collections, hospital visits and dancers (the Stoop Troupe were the originals followed by Harley's Angels, the Columbinas and the LV= Love Girls). We even had mascots and Harley Bear appeared first and was joined by Charley Bear some years later. When the Broncos were with us, they had Buck and Dusty. Some of the innovations were good, some bad and some downright terrible but it was an evolving situation and times had changed forever.

The Harlequin Ladies were formed back in 1995 after a conversation between Kirsty Heslop and Vanessa Matthews who had played together at Oxford. They decided to start a women's section and it came into being during the 1995/96 season after discussions with Dick Best, Robert Catcher and Geoff Morey and assistance from Mrs Pat Currie. They played in the 5th Division, got promoted and in 1996/97, they played in the 4th Division and introduced a 2nd XV who played in the next one down as the rules dictated. They reached Division 1 within five seasons and when the Rugby Football Union for Women restructured its league structure in 2007/08, they were placed in the Championship 2 South East League. In August 2007, they were the first ladies side to become full members of the Rugby Football Union, gaining Section 1 status and receiving full voting rights within the Union. After many ups and downs, they now play in Women's National Challenge London & SE North 2. With the announcement by the Club on 6th June 2016 of a partnership with Aylesford Bulls Ladies Rugby Club and an eventual name change on the cards, only time will tell what the future holds for the original Harlequin Ladies.

The Harlequin Amateurs were formed in the late part of the 1990s and worked their way up to Herts/Middlesex 1 in the RFU league structure. After making relatively little progress, the club began to struggle in 2006 and merged with Lockside in 2007. The Amateurs moved from their base in Roehampton to Teddington where Lockside played and the new club was officially formed on 1st August 2007. In 2012/13, they were unable to fulfil their fixture commitments in Herts/Middlesex 1, resigned their place and joined Middlesex Merit League Division 6 for 2013/14. They are now back in Herts/Middlesex 2 Phase 1.

Our list of affiliated clubs has grown over the years and now stands at eight. They are the Harlequin Club, Pretoria (known as Pretoria Harlequins) who were founded in 1902 and affiliated in 1906; Harlequin Club, Melbourne (known as Melbourne Harlequins), founded in 1928 and affiliated in 1948; Harlequin F.C., Hobart, Tasmania (known as Hobart Harlequins), founded in 1934 although it is not clear when exactly they became affiliated; Harlequin F.C., Hamilton, New Zealand (known as New Zealand Harlequins), founded in 1938 and affiliated the following year; Harlequin F.C, Kenya (known as Kenya Harlequin F.C.), formed and affiliated in 1952; Dallas Harlequins, formed in 1971 and affiliated in 1983; Future Hope Harlequins, Kolkata, India; charity founded in 1988 and affiliated in 2004 and Abu Dhabi Harlequins, founded in 1969, affiliated in 2008.

Since 2012/13, there has been an Academy Under 18 League and although we have taken part each year, we've not done too well. In the first season, we won three out of five, the next year it was four out of seven and in 2014/15, we won only one of the three games played. In 2015/16 we had success in two of six and finished fifth in the Southern Conference.

The A League was introduced for second teams in 2003/04 and we had more success in this. The first year we won against Northampton in a two-legged final 72-28 on aggregate. We got to the final again in 2005/06 but lost to Leicester 51-58 on aggregate. After a couple of years, we reached the semi-final in 2008/09 but lost to Northampton 7-16; went down to the Tigers (27-29) in the final in 2009/10 and the following season, they beat us again, this time in the semi-final. In 2011/12, Exeter beat us in the final to prevent a double (9-29) and in our fifth final the following season, we lost again to Saracens (12-37). Northampton stopped us in the semi-final in 2013/14 and we got nowhere in the next two years with records of W2 L4 and W4 L2.

In August 1997, a four page newsletter called Quins Quarterly appeared for the first time. It carried news articles on personalities around the Club and among those new to the Stoop were Ross Young, Stadium Manager and John Richardson who was to be Head Groundsman. In January 2001 the official magazine of NEC Harlequins was introduced – this was Quins Essential. It was a glossy 50-page effort and contained all the latest news from around the Club and rugby in general as well as articles on players and matches. By 2004, this had become The Jester and retained the same layout as Quins Essential but had been expanded to 84 pages. Unfortunately, like its predecessors, this publication eventually came to an end.

Our match day programme has had a long history and has changed completely over the last one hundred years or so. The earliest example I have seen is from a game against United Services, Portsmouth on 22nd October 1910. It is a single sheet of paper with the match details and teams in the centre and adverts around the edge. The teams are set out as they would line up instead of being listed side by side as is the normal method now. One from 1926 shows a single sheet with the match details and teams printed on one side. By 1930, it is an eight page programme printed on blue paper (slightly larger than our programme today), the match details are printed on the front cover, international and club fixtures are shown, the teams are printed in the centre and the rest of the space is filled with adverts. Immediately after World War 2, it becomes a single sheet of paper again (around A5 size) with everything printed on one side. By 1947, the size has grown slightly and adverts cover the back side of the single sheet but three years later, we start to see the development of the modern programme. It is eight pages again with the club badge and match details on the front cover, the teams and a small section on the visitors take up the centre pages with adverts filling the rest. For the match against Sir Wavell Wakefield's International XV in September 1952, we see a red, black and white cover with a small notes section inside plus photographs of some key players and a centre layout like the international programmes of the day. In 1953, we see a black and white cover with the Quins badge and Harlequin Football Club printed just above the match details while inside, the fixtures for the season, teams and notes plus four pages of adverts. This stayed pretty much the same until the start of the 1969/70 season although for a few seasons player profiles were introduced. Some notable exceptions were in the 1959/60 season. The Adrian Stoop Memorial Match in September 1959 when green and black was used on the cover, the programme ran to twenty pages (13 were adverts), there was an appreciation of Adrian by Wakelam and the Stoop Memorial was explained – it was to take the form of improvements and alterations to the Teddington ground; on completion, it will be renamed the Stoop Memorial Ground (history obviously intervened). An advert for season tickets quoted them at £2 2s 0d. Later on, the Twickenham Jubilee Match was played against Richmond on Boxing Day 1959 and orange and black were used on a yellowish cover. The price was one shilling (5 pence in today's money!) and another twenty page effort contained a piece on the opening of the ground, a drawing from a 1909 newspaper and a photograph of the winning Quins team; The teams from that day and fifty years on were listed and lots of adverts as usual.

In 1969/70, colour was introduced permanently when magenta was used on the cover, the Club badge appeared at the top (the year of foundation and the current year are either side) with Harlequin Football Club and the match details filling up the rest of the space. Of the remaining eleven pages, seven and a half are adverts, two pages contain fixtures for 1st XV, Wanderers and A XVs and the rest is for the teams and a few notes plus the next home match. This format continued for ten years before being cut right back to just four pages. The cover remained the same, the centre held the teams, notes and next home match and the back page had the 1st XV fixtures and an advert promoting the ground and bars at the Stoop for hire. All this for just 10p! A slightly jazzed up effort was produced for the visit of Racing Club de France in April 1983. The cover was a form of red white and blue with a message from the Presidents of Quins and the French Chamber of Commerce. For the Wavell Wakefield Memorial Match in September 1984, sixteen pages were filled with various articles about the great man, Twickenham Stadium, our captain David Cooke and the Quins sevens with related photographs. On the front page, there is a multi-coloured Club badge for the first time. That same season, a variation of the Club colours are presented diagonally on the front page with the coloured badge, Club name and a photo of the old stand at the Stoop. Twelve of the sixteen pages are a standard set up; the Club officials are given on one page with photograph of the 1st XV squad and the rest are filled with advert. A four page pink insert for each different game gives a player spotlight, teams, notes, next home match and 1st XV fixtures. In 1988/89, the cover changes to a large team badge and the price increases from 30p to 50p. The same format continues with the player spotlight being replaced by a page on today's visitors and the number of pages increases to 28. The following season, the cover changes to a group of sepia shots from the Club's history with a smaller badge, Harlequin Football Club is in blue and the size increases by four pages to hold even more adverts. For the 1991/92 season, we are back to 28 pages with a page of action shots, player profiles return, fixture lists are added for the Wanderers and some space is given to the lower teams. The Supporters' Club has a small area and a membership application form plus a page left blank for autographs. On the cover, 125th Anniversary Season 1991/92 is printed in yellow. For the midweek friendly fixtures, a simple sheet of A4 folded in half is produced with match details and a large badge on the cover, notes and the teams in the middle and an advert on the back page.

The following season, another change to the cover with a large badge on white with a light blue surround, 26 pages of adverts, a page of contacts plus the usual sections in the centre as well as a playing round up of the other teams at the Club and league tables. In 1994/95 the size increases to forty pages, the cover remains the same although purple and maroon are used as outline colours and the match detail has been added and we now see the information distributed throughout the programme rather than all together; there are still 28 pages of adverts. By 1995/96 and on the cusp of professionalism, we were now producing a 48 page programme with thirty four containing adverts. The cover had a picture of a player and was divided into four quarters, each a different colour and the price had increased to £2. The usual information was provided inside as well as some photographs from a recent game and an article looking at games from yesteryear. For the first season as a professional outfit, the programme was now called a Match Magazine and ran to 64 pages, the largest ever. Now we had a welcome page for the Chairman, Director of Rugby, the sponsors and the Director of Coaching. There was even an interview with a player, short biogs of the entire squad, referee signals explained and a plan of the ground.

From this point on, the cover has gone through a number of presentation changes but has stayed constant with a picture of a player on the front. The price increased upwards to £3 and the number of pages fluctuated between forty eight and one hundred. As more information became available on the opposition, profiles of their team became included and a huge number of photographs appeared throughout. From 1997/98, the term "Match day programme" is used for the first time. The name on the front of the programme also changed and the following were used; NEC Harlequins, The Quins, The Quin, Quins and Harlequins (in use since 2012/13). The programme now contains a welcome from the Chief Executive and the Director of Rugby; Club news about general happenings around the Stoop, work in the community, the Harlequin Foundation, a page about the past, the Mighty Quins, interviews with players, general rugby stories, nutrition tips, various quizzes between forwards and backs, Quins Academy, squad biogs, fixtures and the matchday teams and officials. It has been a long journey and an incredible transformation from those first programmes over a hundred years ago.

From the time of the name change from Hampstead to Harlequin in 1870, our shirt remained pretty much the same until 1988 when we put the name of our sponsors (Jaguar) on the left breast. When the badge was added in 1989, there was no further change apart from different sponsors until 2007 when we had to introduce an away shirt because of Premiership rules. In the late 1990s, our shirts were made by Cotton Traders, they were succeeded by Kooga, then O'Neills and finally our current company are Adidas who started in 2014/15. The home shirt has had subtle changes since 2007 and largely retains the quarters but by 2015/16, the green and black had virtually disappeared and the 2016/17 season sees a retro type shirt said to be based on a 1902 design for the 150th anniversary. There is always a different shirt for the Big Game and this is designed around the charity receiving a donation from the Club that year. The away shirt in 2007/08 retained the quarters but white replaced chocolate and French grey and this stayed the same until 2010/11 and 2011/12 when the front of the shirt was half diamonds and half white. The following two seasons saw diamonds on the sleeves, magenta and blue in the shoulder area and the front was white. In 2014/15, the design changed to larger diamonds and oblongs with various colours and a total change came in 2015/16 with a white shirt and a bar code look using the Quins colours. For the 150th anniversary season, white, blue and magenta are used in a digitised style along with the new badge carrying the Club motto, badge with the years 1866-2016 and 150 years Harlequin FC written at the bottom.

52

On the Brink of Our 150th Anniversary but No Success

On 30th September 2014, the group finalised the restructuring of debts which resulted in the formation of a new company, Harlequin RFC Holdings Limited. This became the parent of Harlequin Football Club Limited and Harlequin Estates (Twickenham) Limited. The restructuring of the debts to Mosaic Limited and the bank ensured they are placed within the most appropriate group company, leaving the trading company, Harlequin Football Club Limited, debt free from both. This effectively meant that the outstanding loan balance with Mosaic of £21,192,907 was transferred to other group companies as part of the inter-group sale of Harlequin Estates (Twickenham) Limited. The loan was provided interest free and the balance now outstanding was nil. The Club took advantage of an exemption whereby they did not disclose transactions with the ultimate parent company or any wholly owned subsidiary undertaking of the group. An all-time high of 8,818 membership applications was reached although an operating loss of £591,107 was achieved. On the same date, Blue Sky Leisure Limited disposed of its holding in Harlequin Estates (Twickenham) Limited to another group company and this created a profit on disposal of £15,688,000. The highest paid Director was on £220,000 and the number of employees now stood at 112 full-time and 52 part-time. The wage bill was now a massive £9,960,714. The Directors now comprised Mullins, Ellis, Morgan, Pope, Fitzpatrick, Brewer and Saving.

The company name changed from BlueSky Leisure Limited to Harlequin Football Club Limited on 29th July 2015. It was ultimately controlled by a Malaysian company called Union Mutual Pension Fund (L) Limited. Backing had been guaranteed until 31st December 2016 and time would tell if the Club managed to maintain a profitable status having been given a massive injection of cash to help it on its way.

On 12th June 2015, it was announced that Jason Leonard was to become the R.F.U. President for 2015/16. He became the latest in a long line of Quins to hold the post. Those before him were G Rowland Hill, Vincent Cartwright, Adrian Stoop, John Greenwood, Bernard Hartley, Sir Wavell Wakefield, Geoff Butler, Micky Steele-Bodger, Ken Chapman, David Brooks, Albert Agar, Alan Grimsdell, Donald Sanders, Ian Beer and Malcolm Phillips.

Two weeks later, it was reported that Jordan Turner-Hall had been charged with assault after being allegedly involved in an altercation with two men in Pryzm nightclub in Brighton. When the case was heard in June 2016, Jordan was acquitted of the charges but the man charged with him was found guilty.

On 5th May 2015, the Club announced that a trip to Bermuda would be undertaken between 1st and 6th June. There would be a programme of school visits, coaching workshops and fund raising activities for the Beyond Rugby Bermuda charity. They work with children on the island who are at risk of dropping out of education. The highlight was a match against the Bermuda Barbarians on Saturday 6th June at the Bermuda National Sports Centre. In a typically Barbarians type free-flowing game, we ran out winners by 68-43.

Our next friendly was a World Cup warm-up match against the USA at PPL Park, Philadelphia. An announcement made by the Club was a four year strategic partnership with USA Rugby to help the sport grow at grassroots level, develop the professional game at sevens and fifteens in both the men's and women's game and to drive the Harlequin brand across America; this was the start of that process. On 30th August the game took place and the home side were quickly in front with two penalties from MacGinty. By the end of the first quarter, Palamo stretched the lead with a try. On 27 minutes, Dickson opened our account with a try under the posts which Evans converted and six minutes before the break, Wallace went over from a rolling maul. Evans again converted and we led at half time. The first score of the second half didn't come until 59 minutes when Niua landed a penalty for the USA to tie the scores. Nine minutes later, Wallace was over again from another maul and this time Botica converted. He followed this up with a penalty from 50 metres on 79 minutes and despite the Americans scoring their second try through Test, we had done more than enough to win (24-19). Four new signings made their debuts in this game; Owen Evans came on as a replacement and would go on to make at least 10 appearances; Adam Jones (who had won 95 caps for Wales and 5 for the British and Irish Lions between 2003 and 2014) also came on as a replacement and had a wealth of experience in the front row. He would make at least 15 appearances; Mat Luamanu, a back row from New Zealand who would go on to make at least 17 appearances and Winston Stanley who had won 2 caps for Samoa in 2014 and would go on to make at least 9 appearances for the 1st XV.

The Rugby World Cup took place in England in September and October, it was the eighth tournament. This time we had six current players representing just two countries; Mike Brown, Danny Care, Nick Easter (called up to replace Billy Vunipola), Joe Marler and captain Chris Robshaw all played for England and Netani Talei was in the Fiji squad. Asaeli Tikoirotuma (Fiji), Mike Ross (Ireland) and Maurie Fa'asavalu (Samoa) had all played for us and Tim Visser (Scotland) and Jamie Roberts (Wales) would join us after their involvement had finished. Roberts was going to Cambridge University first so wouldn't actually make his debut until December. The tournament itself turned into a disaster for England as they became the first host nation not to qualify for the knockout stages. They started well enough with a 35-11 win over Fiji but then crucially lost to Wales (25-28) after leading and Australia (13-33). The final game against Uruguay was an easy win (60-3) but some key players got only their first runs out despite some of the squad quite clearly not playing well. By this time they had been eliminated and the fallout included Stuart Lancaster losing his job. New Zealand went on to become the first country to retain the trophy with a 34-17 win over Australia in the final. South Africa saw off Argentina in the Bronze Final (24-13).

Quins and London Irish had decided to play two pre-season friendly games called The Cunningham Duncombe Series in memory of Jarrod Cunningham and Nick Duncombe. The winners of the Plate would be decided on the aggregate score from both matches. The first was played on Friday 25th September and was at the Stoop (the second was also played on our home ground but was counted as the Irish home game). We started with eight of the side who would open our Premiership season against Wasps on 16th October. James Horwill, the former Australian captain, appeared for the first time although his official debut wouldn't come until the season started for real. He actually scored the first try which Botica converted before Wallace went to the bin and Narraway reduced the lead to two points. Stevens went the same way as Wallace and Botica converted his own try to give us a 14-5 lead. Lewington then scored for Irish, they lost Sheriff to the bin and Botica's penalty made it 17-10 at half time. The next score would be crucial and Walker got it to extend the lead. Ten minutes later, Lewington scored again and Brophy-Clews converted but that was as close as they got and it was all to play for in the second leg.

That took place the following Friday and we made seven changes to the starting lineup. The aggregate score was level when Ojo scored after ten minutes but Wallace soon replied and the conversion by Evans put us ahead on the night. Noakes edged the Irish in front with a penalty before Evans got two of his own and converted a try by Luamanu after 37 minutes to make it 20-8 at the break. It was one way traffic in the third quarter as Wallace and Swiel grabbed tries (Evans converted the second) and it was suddenly 32-8. On 60 minutes, Halavatu went over, Lewington did the same seven minutes later and with Lewis-Pratt converting both, the gap was down to just ten points. Owen Evans scored our fifth try leaving the Irish needing three converted scores in ten minutes to take the Series. They could only manage one when Halavatu scored for Lewis-Pratt to convert and even though Sinckler received a yellow card, there wasn't enough time left. The first Cunningham Duncombe Series winners were Quins by an aggregate score of 59-46.

Because of the World Cup, the Anglo-Welsh Cup was removed from the fixture list for a season and the Premiership didn't start until 16th October when we began at home to Wasps. It had become quite obvious to everyone including Joe Marler that he wasn't made out to be a captain and he was replaced by Danny Care with Nick Evans as his deputy. Of course, Care would not make his debut as club captain until after his involvement with England in the World Cup was at an end. James Horwill was in the process of winning 62 caps for Australia and would be a great asset in the second row. He would go on to make at least 22 appearances for us. The first points came from the boot of Gopperth with a penalty for Wasps but Evans put us in front with two of his own before Cooper-Woolley scored the first try to put the visitors ahead 6-8 after 15 minutes. We replied when a nice chip from Dickson put Evans over and his conversion ensured a half time lead as Gopperth could only reduce the deficit with a second penalty. On 46 minutes Evans put Lowe in, converted again and when Gopperth put over his third penalty with the last quarter to come, our lead was six points. Evans then kicked two more penalties as we eased our way to victory but Wasps were not quite finished. Daly scored, Jackson converted and we had to see out the final three minutes to take the spoils (26-21). Saracens had started with a bonus point win, we were fourth and amongst the pack of five other teams achieving wins in Week One.

Leicester were one place above us and Welford Road is where we went on Sunday 25th October. In a tight first half, Bell and Evans exchanged penalties but the home side led 12-6. On 34 minutes, Clifford scored from a rolling maul and Evans sent us into the break with a one point lead. Early in the second half Evans and Bell were again successful with penalties and when our man put over another from halfway after 55 minutes, we led 19-15. Just inside the final ten minutes, Pearce was driven over for Williams to convert and we trailed again. As the clock ticked down, Harrison was binned on 76 minutes and we drove Leicester back 30 yards before the maul was collapsed. The referee said no penalty try, O'Shea felt differently but the decision had been made and the Tigers held out for the win. Saracens and Leicester were the only two clubs left with 100% records after only two games as we dropped to sixth. London Irish and Newcastle were at the bottom with no points.

Another friendly had been arranged the next evening against Newport Gwent Dragons to give more senior squad members some valuable game time. The Dragons went ahead when Geraint Jones landed a penalty after 3 minutes and Botica replied two minutes later. After 15 minutes, one of the touch judges spotted a punch and Tebaldi was sent off (this was later rescinded at a hearing) but because both sides wanted to get as much out of the game as possible, it was agreed that he would be replaced. The same happened when Geraint Jones was binned after 24 minutes. Gustafson scored a try to put the Dragons in front but before half time, Archie White got over twice and Botica converted to give us a 17-8 lead. The driving maul was proving very successful for us and it worked again when Matthews scored our third try, again improved by Botica before Brew scored for Dorian Jones to convert.

When Swiel was put over by Waters, the conversion from in front of the posts by Botica took us to 31-15 and a late score by Nightingale was a small consolation for the visitors.

A trip to Bath followed and Tim Visser made his debut after finishing World Cup duties with Scotland (he was in the process of winning at least 26 caps). They had been cruelly knocked out 35-34 after the referee (Craig Joubert) had made a wrong penalty decision in Australia's favour near the end. Nick Evans opened our account with a penalty after seven minutes before Ford equalised and Evans got his second. A try from Eastmond was converted by Ford before Evans put over two more penalties but our time in front was short lived because Ford put over his second penalty for a 13-12 lead at half time. In the first ten minutes after the break, we surged ahead with more penalties from Evans who also converted Care's try scored between the two. Bath kept infringing, Evans kept punishing them and either side of Ford's third, he landed his seventh and eighth to make it 31-16. The last one broke the all-time Club record for penalties in a match by one player originally set by David Pears against Rosslyn Park back in December 1991 (Paul Burke twice and Evans had equalled it). Eastmond saw yellow for a no arms tackle on Yarde and Ward was sent over for our second try. The conversion by Nick Evans equalled John Schuster's record of 28 points in a league match also set against Bath in November 1998. In the last seven minutes including injury time, the home side scored tries through Auterac and Rokoduguni. Ford converted the second one but we had a great win under our belts (38-28). As a result, we moved back up to fourth with Saracens still leading the way on 13 points, Leicester and Exeter were just behind them. London Irish and Newcastle still had no points.

Sale Sharks were two places behind us but on the same points when they visited on Friday 6th November. After a largely forgettable opening quarter of an hour, Visser dropped an up-and-under from Cipriani, Braid grabbed the loose ball and dived over to open the scoring. Cipriani converted and our response was an Evans penalty although he missed a second effort right on half time. The first score in the second half was a second Evans penalty before Visser made amends for his earlier error when he scored from an excellent cross-field kick by Evans. He converted and added another penalty after 54 minutes to put us more than a score ahead. When James got a second try for the visitors, Cipriani's conversion made it a two point game with all to play for in the last 15 minutes. Cipriani then missed with a penalty and a last-second dropped goal either of which would have nudged the Sharks ahead. As it was, we had our third win and moved into third spot. Saracens were now the only unbeaten side and had 17 points, Exeter were on 15 and we were two points further back. The same two sides were still pointless at the bottom and already it wasn't looking good for either of them.

Because of our eighth place Premiership finish last season, we played in the European Rugby Challenge Cup this year. We were in Pool 3 along with Cardiff Blues, Montpellier and Rugby Calvisano from Italy. Our first game saw Montpellier visit the Stoop on Thursday 12th November. In wet conditions Montpellier built a lead in the first quarter with three penalties from Paillaugue. The second quarter belonged to us and after Evans and Paillaugue had exchanged penalties, tries from Wallace and Easter (the second converted by Evans) put us ahead. Nariashvili had been yellow carded before our second try but he was back on when Clifford scored on 45 minutes. Evans converted and Paillaugue landed his fifth penalty before Care secured the bonus point with another score. At the end of the third quarter, Paillaugue got another penalty but we responded in the best way possible with our fifth try. Robshaw dislodged the ball with a great tackle on Timani, Yarde chipped ahead, re-gathered and passed to Care. He continued the move, passed to Brown and his offload when tackled found Lindsay-Hague who went over. Evans converted and there was still time left for Robshaw to score try number six. Botica's conversion made the final score 41-18 - a tremendous start to our campaign. We didn't top the Pool because Cardiff had thrashed Calvisano 50-9.

The following Thursday we visited Cardiff and the previous day, the sad news broke that former Blues player and All Black legend Jonah Lomu had passed away. Players and fans paid tribute with a minute's applause before kick-off. A number of changes were made to our starting XV and we took a while to get going. Patchell put over two penalties in the first 12 minutes and Botica's reply after 33 concluded the first half scoring. We took the game by the scruff of its neck with a burst of seventeen points in a seven minute spell just after the break. First, Botica levelled matters with a penalty, then Visser intercepted a pass and ran in from half way and finally, Lindsay-Hague evaded several tacklers to score another. Botica converted both and we were suddenly 20-6 ahead. Charlie Walker scored our third try after 64 minutes before the Blues came back into it. Five minutes after Walker's score, they were awarded a penalty try from a rolling maul which Evans converted and despite having Matthew Rees sent off for stamping on Easter's face, another try came from Hobbs (converted by Evans) which brought them close. As Cardiff pressed for the winning score, we got the ball back and Care went in for the bonus point score. Swiel converted and the final score of 32-20 took us to the top of the Pool. Montpellier had done the same to Calvisano as Cardiff (winning 64-0) and they were second on tries scored and points difference.

Back to Premiership action and a Saturday visit to Exeter. With the World Cup induced late start and no Anglo-Welsh Cup, the league matches ran right through without a break except for the European fixtures. At least we would have our international players until 22nd January because there were no Autumn Internationals either. The wind was blowing, rain poured down at Sandy Park and we played into the face of it first. Steenson put the Chiefs ahead before we were awarded a penalty try which Evans converted. After Steenson's second penalty, Care put in a grubber kick and Evans latched on to it and scored. Steenson kicked another penalty before Walker was put over in the corner by Brown. Back came Exeter and Steenson kicked a penalty and converted Short's try right on half time. Because of the missed conversions by Evans, we trailed 17-19. On 42 minutes, Evans put us ahead with his first penalty but Steenson converted his own try to regain the lead with 24 minutes left. On 61 minutes, Taione was sin binned for a dangerous tackle on Lambert and a minute later, Brown put in a kick to the corner and as the ball bounced back off the flag, Visser collected it between his legs and touched down for the bonus point try. Unfortunately, Swiel couldn't convert this or a penalty with three minutes left after Johnson had become the second Exeter player to visit the bin. Our second loss of the season dropped us to fourth and we now trailed Saracens by seven points. Newcastle had drawn with Sale to move off the bottom after Irish lost for the fifth time.

The bottom club were our next visitors to the Stoop on 5th December and nothing short of a bonus point win would do. Evans opened the scoring with a penalty and after Lewington had denied Ross Chisholm a try in the corner with a great tackle, we had to wait until 32 minutes for Visser to get the first one. Evans converted for a 10-0 interval lead and when he added the extras to further scores from Care and Visser, the match as a contest was over by the end of the third quarter. A minute after the TMO had denied him (Lewington again with the try saving tackle), Visser completed his hat-trick and Evans converted. Just after Cruse went to the bin, Clifford scored our fifth try and Botica converted but the Irish grabbed a consolation score when Aulika went over for Brophy-Clews to convert and make the final score 38-7. We stayed in fourth on 20 points, one behind Leicester with Exeter (24) and Saracens (27) occupying the top two slots. A small gap of four points had opened between us and Northampton but there was a very long way to go. The Irish were anchored to the foot of the table and were in need of a miracle.

The double header with Rugby Calvisano came over the next two weekends and we travelled to the Centro Sportivo San Michele Stadium on 12th December looking to consolidate our position at the top of the Pool. Luke Wallace opened our account with a first minute try which was quickly followed by another from Lambert. Botica converted this and after Cavalieri went to the bin, Clifford scored our third which Botica converted. Buscema put over a penalty for Calvisano but further scores from Wallace and Ross Chisholm secured the bonus point before half time. It took fifteen minutes for our next try to arrive and Matt Hopper got it (Botica converted) but Mbanda scored one for the home side and Minozzi converted to make it 36-10. Two more scores in the final quarter by Sinckler and Walker enabled us to reach the fifty point mark with Botica's conversions. We were still top of the Pool at the half way mark with maximum points, Cardiff came next on 10, Montpellier below them with 6 and Calvisano bottom with no points.

In the return with the Italians at the Stoop, Jamie Roberts made his long awaited debut after ending his playing commitments with Cambridge University in the Varsity Match. He was in the process of winning at least 83 caps for Wales and 3 for the British and Irish Lions and would go on to make at least 12 appearances for us. Once again, a big win and a bonus point was expected and Yarde got us off to a good start with a try after 15 minutes. Botica converted and when Belardo went to the bin, Calvisano scored through Susio (converted by Vlaicu) to make it 7-7 after 31 minutes. We did lead at the break because Sinckler scored for Botica to convert right on half time. The second half was one way traffic and tries followed at regular intervals through Clifford, Chisholm, Roberts, Walker, Botica, Swiel and Dickson. Botica converted all bar Chisholm's and Swiel's to make it 59-7. With time almost up, Zanetti went to the bin but we couldn't add to our total. We had almost done enough to qualify and had a nine point advantage over Cardiff in second (11 points) with Montpellier on 10 and Calvisano still to get their first point. One win from our final games in January would see us qualify as Pool winners.

Big Game 8 took place on 27th December at Twickenham Stadium and our opponents this time were Gloucester. Rudimental (a drum and bass band) appeared as the headline act but a technical fault unfortunately wiped out their half time show. The attendance of 70,718 was the lowest in the series apart from the enforced 50,000 at Big Game 1 back in 2008. They witnessed a cracker that revealed the weaknesses in our game. It was fine playing an all-out attacking style of game but you needed to defend and not give away silly tries. The visitors got the opening score when Thrush scored and Laidlaw converted but a penalty from Evans and a try by Yarde put us ahead by a point. Laidlaw kicked a penalty and Hook benefited from a dubious Kvesic turnover (the ball looked to have gone forward) and ran in from 55 metres out for Laidlaw to convert. Back we came and Care scored for Evans to convert and it was 15-17 at the break. After 47 minutes, Trinder extended the Gloucester lead and Laidlaw again converted before a mad five minutes saw Easter and Ross Chisholm score, Evans convert both and Trinder grab his second to make it 29-29 (after intercepting Care's pass, Trinder pulled a hamstring and limped the last 20 metres to the line). After Laidlaw landed a penalty, Cook latched onto a bad kick from Brown, ran back 52 metres and beat seven defenders to score Gloucester's fifth try; Laidlaw's conversion left us trailing by ten points with 12 minutes to go. Evans kicked a penalty on 70 minutes and Hibberd went to the bin with five minutes left as the pressure mounted. A minute later, Chisholm was over for our fifth try and the conversion by Evans tied it up at 39-39. As we attacked with ten seconds left, Evans attempted a dropped goal from 25 metres out but it just missed to the right, he fell to the ground and both sides had three points. Saracens won for the seventh game in a row and had 31 points, we were in fourth with 23. At the bottom, London Irish had won and moved above Newcastle.

For our first game of 2016, we travelled to tenth placed Worcester Warriors. It all started so well when Walker scored after three minutes and Evans converted but Lowe went to the bin for coming in at the side of a ruck and Heathcote put the Warriors on the board with a penalty. When Lowe came back, Wallace was over after a drive from a lineout, Evans converted and added a penalty to make it 17-3 at half time. When Walker scored again after an excellent kick by Care, the conversion by Evans took us three scores clear and our eighth successive try bonus point in all competitions was in sight with 35 minutes left. At this point, our killer instinct and discipline went missing and Mama scored for Worcester. Roberts went to the bin and a penalty try followed which Mills converted and then Dowson scored (the TMO gave the try despite obstruction on Walker) and although the conversion was missed, our lead was only four points with ten minutes to go. We managed to hold on for our fifteenth successive league victory over the Warriors. Conor O'Shea moaned about some of the decisions by the referee (Wayne Barnes) but at the end of the day, this was a game we should have won by a country mile. This would be repeated many more times right up to the end of the season. As a result of this win, we moved into third place some nine points behind Saracens who would visit us next. This truly was a must win game! Newcastle moved back above Irish after getting their first Premiership win of the season.

On 9th January, the leaders came to the Stoop undefeated in 15 matches. After James Horwill went to the bin for a swinging arm that felled George Kruis and put him out of the game, Saracens scored first when we took the sensible decision to allow them to drive us back over our line rather than risk a second yellow card. The try was scored by de Kock and Farrell converted but Care went through the middle of a lineout and put Buchanan in for our first try to make it 5-7. Five minutes later, Billy Vunipola scored another and Farrell converted before we took the game to them and after an Evans penalty, we went in front with our second try. After good work from Robshaw and Yarde, Evans sent Clifford over and converted. Despite the Saracens pack having dominated, we were in with more than a chance of winning the game. The third quarter saw two penalties from Farrell to regain the lead before Botica got one for us after 61 minutes. When Farrell slotted another three minutes later, it looked as though Saracens were slowly drifting away from us again. Suddenly, Gill made a spear tackle on Lowe and was sent to the bin but the TMO intervened, the referee (Craig Maxwell-Keys) took another look, the card colour changed to red and he was off for good. Within ten minutes, Botica had knocked over two penalties as the rain lashed down and we were back in front. All attempts by Saracens to extend their run were resisted and Horwill crashed over in the final minute to secure victory (29-23). After nine rounds, Saracens were still top on 37 points, Exeter were second with 34, then Quins (31) and Leicester (29). There was a decent gap of seven points to Northampton in fifth and at the bottom, London Irish were a point ahead of Newcastle after getting their second win.

The next two weeks would decide our future in the Challenge Cup and our fifth pool game was at the Stoop against Cardiff Blues. The first half was all Quins and tries came thick and fast through Buchanan, Clifford, Yarde and Chisholm. Evans put over all the conversions, our lead at half time was 28-0 and the bonus point confirmed our top spot in the Pool and qualification for the quarter finals. As was to become a feature in the coming games, we appeared to drop off the pace having done the hard work and allowed the Blues back into it. Allen pulled a try back, Patchell converted and Fish also went over before Evans slotted a much needed penalty. A two try burst from Williams and Fish (both converted by Patchell) made the score 31-26 with nine minutes left but we held on and Botica denied Cardiff a losing bonus point with a penalty right at the end. We now had 25 points, Montpellier went above Cardiff with 15, the Blues had 12 and Calvisano still had no points.

On 20th January, the news was announced by the Club that our Director of Rugby would be leaving at the end of the season and the search was on for a replacement. After being turned down by Wayne Smith and rumoured approaches to Todd Blackadder and Gregor Townsend, the job was given to John Kingston, our Head Coach. This was announced on 27th April and Graham Rowntree (former Leicester, England and British and Irish Lions prop and England Assistant Coach) was appointed as forwards coach; Nick Easter was to become defence coach and although he would retain his playing contract, he would be first and foremost a coach; Mark Mapleftoft succeeded Kingston as Head Coach and Tony Diprose became Academy and Global Development Director. On 25th March, Italy announced that Conor O'Shea would be their new Coach. He had been linked with the role before but had always denied being approached by them. It was an odd decision the Club making it known half way through the season and it quite clearly affected the players and coupled with losing our internationals for the Six Nations Championship, it proved a disastrous mix.

The first match to be played after this was our final pool game away in Montpellier. Whereas we had qualified, the home side had to win and get a bonus point to make certain. Botica got the first points with a penalty after four minutes but Mogg scored a try and Catrakilis put over a penalty to put Montpellier ahead. Two Botica penalties nudged us in front but Liebenberg scored and Catrakilis converted for the half time lead. The second half saw another poor performance and Montpellier ran away with it. Catrakilis kicked another penalty and when Luamanu was in the bin, he added another after converting White's try. The game had gone by this point but the French kept going and in the last three minutes scored another two tries. Reilhac and Geli went over (both converted by Trinh-Duc) to make the final score 42-9. The line-up for the quarter finals in April would be Quins v London Irish, Grenoble v Connacht, Sale v Montpellier and Gloucester v Newport Gwent Dragons.

A trip to Newcastle followed the beating in France and we carried on in the same vein of form. The home side built a 10-0 lead in the first quarter but great play from Ward enabled Walker to score in the corner. Evans converted and when the second half started, we looked a different team. Ward and Walker scored tries, Evans converted the second and we led by nine points after 47 minutes. Enter our arch nemesis (Andy Goode) after 58 minutes. In just over ten minutes, our lead had gone thanks to three Goode penalties and when Vickers got over two minutes from the end, Goode converted to see the Falcons home. This was a match we should never have lost and as the wheels started to fall off, we dropped to fourth place. All the good done by the excellent win over Saracens was erased after this loss and although we were still eight points clear of Wasps in fifth, we needed to get back to winning ways immediately. The Falcons leap-frogged Irish at the bottom as a result of their win.

Back to the Stoop the following week and a visit from Northampton. In a tight first half, Myler put the Saints ahead with a penalty before George Merrick got the first try which Evans converted. Day and Burrell scored for the Saints, Myler converted both but Ross Chisholm's try converted by Evans between the two left us trailing by three points at the break (14-17). Tebaldi went to the bin after a deliberate knock-on right on half time but Northampton couldn't capitalise on it and Evans landed two penalties to edge us ahead. On 66 minutes, Wood went the same way as Tebaldi for collapsing a maul close to the line. During his time off the field, Hanrahan brought the Saints level with a penalty and Botica replied in kind to leave us in front. As Northampton attacked near the end in time expired, we turned the ball over, Swiel passed back to Botica who was just inside the dead ball line and all he had to do was step into touch. He decided to kick for touch and somehow managed to keep the ball in play. Foden gathered, passed the ball infield and eventually finished the move off with a dummy to score the winning try. Hanrahan converted and we had lost at home for the first time this season. Quite what Botica was thinking was anyone's guess but O'Shea said afterwards that it was "nothing short of unbelievable and unforgivable….you just had to walk over the dead ball line". He was not a happy man! We remained in fourth but the gap was now five points between us and Wasps with Saracens twelve clear of us at the top. Newcastle were bottom again on games won as they and London Irish were both on 12 points.

A trip to Gloucester came next and in the first half it was the James Hook show; he scored a try, converted and kicked two penalties either side of two from Evans. Chisholm went to the bin for tackling Burns without the ball but only a penalty apiece resulted. After 29 minutes, Morgan got another try, Hook converted and landed another penalty to make it 23-6 at the interval. Nick Evans was helped off and it turned out he had broken his right leg in a freak accident as he ran along with no one around him. He underwent surgery in the following week and was initially ruled out until May but in the event, he was back just over two months later. The second half was nothing like the try fest seen at Twickenham in December and the only score was a try for Gloucester by McColl after 77 minutes to make the final score 28-6. We dropped to fifth with 33 points because even though Wasps had the same total, they had won one more game. As a result, Northampton, Sale and Gloucester were all within striking distance of us now. The top three had all lost so Saracens at the top were still twelve ahead. The Irish were bottom on 12 points with Worcester (14) and Newcastle (16) also in trouble.

Against Leicester on 19th February, we desperately needed to end our run of four successive defeats. Bryant and Botica exchanged penalties three times in the first half to leave it all square. In the third quarter, Botica kicked two more and Thacker scored a try which Burns converted to put the Tigers ahead. Botica hit his sixth penalty and with five minutes left, Tuilagi spilled the ball when Hopper and Merrick tackled him, Botica picked up and kicked through for Yarde to gather and run in for the match winning try. Botica's conversion took his tally for the night to twenty points. Burns put over a penalty with two minutes to go and the Tigers went through 20 phases in our 22 after time had expired but a knock-on signalled the end of the game. We moved back into fourth at Leicester's expense, Saracens still led the way and London Irish were five points adrift of Worcester at the foot of the table.

Coventry's Ricoh Arena was our next port of call and Wasps were in form having won their last five Premiership matches with a bonus point. Our form was exactly the opposite and we held them for the first 22 minutes. Before half time, Cooper-Woolley, Wade and Hughes got tries and Gopperth converted all three. Our response was one from Wallace after Wasps' second. When Walker opened the scoring after the interval with a try on 56 minutes, we had faint hope. We couldn't score again and the home side added three more tries through Young, Siale Piutau and Macken. Gopperth converted the first two and Lozowski the last to make it 10-42. We lost Tim Swiel with a season ending ankle injury and finished the match with fourteen men. We had been blown away but as usual, O'Shea couldn't doubt the work ethic going in from our players. Something was seriously wrong and once again we had failed to adequately replace our missing internationals; it wasn't as if the Six Nations came as a surprise! Two injury replacements made their debuts in this game when they came on as substitutes; scrum half Samson Egerton and back row Beau Robinson, he had won a single Australian cap back in 2011 and would make the same number of appearances for us. We now dropped to sixth and it wasn't looking good for a top six finish let alone a play-off place. Saracens (52 points) and Exeter (49) had opened up a seven point lead over Wasps with Leicester and Northampton making up the top five. London Irish were still adrift at the foot of the table with eight games to go.

On 5th March, we travelled up to the AJ Bell Stadium to play Sale Sharks and they hadn't lost at home for eleven months. Ford got Sale off to a good start with a penalty, Botica equalised but Ford then kicked two more. Botica landed his second penalty and converted Visser's try in a five minute spell before the break but we couldn't hold on to the lead. Ioane was driven over, Ford converted and Botica's third penalty made it all square after 52 minutes. At the start of the third quarter, we lost the plot and Cipriani kicked penalties either side of Addison's try which he converted. With twelve minutes to play, we were 16-29 behind and another loss was on the way. Egerton crossed the line for Botica to convert but it was too late to give us anything more than a losing bonus point. Tito Tebaldi made his last appearance in this one, he had made 3 appearances off the bench and had been sin binned once. It was a shame we didn't see more of him. After our fifth loss in the last six league games, we dropped to eighth place. We were just not playing well enough to win the required matches to finish in the top six. The only hope was that when our internationals returned in three weeks, they would work their magic again. Saracens were 15 points clear of us now and we were level on points with Gloucester and Sale. Thankfully, Bath were having a worse season than us and trailed by ten points so it was unlikely we could finish any lower. The Irish were now eight points behind Newcastle and time was running out for the men from Reading.

Bath visited the Stoop on 11th March and we needed a win, losing again was not an option. After Botica had opened the scoring with a penalty, Sloan ran in for a try and Homer replied with two penalties either side of Botica's second to make it 11-6. When Cook was binned for a deliberate knock-on, we took full advantage in an amazing way. Botica landed a penalty and converted Walker's try to make it 21-6 at the interval. By the time Cook returned, Walker and Horwill had got us to the bonus point with tries and Botica converted both to make it 35-6. The sin bin had cost the visitors no fewer than 24 points. As was becoming the norm, we promptly dozed off and Twomey went to the bin for pulling down a jumper in the lineout only three minutes after coming on. While he was off, Mafi and Williams scored tries and Homer converted as Bath staged a fightback. With seven minutes left, Rokoduguni scored another, Homer converted and then added a penalty after Horwill was binned. It was close but we held on for the win. Had we lost, it would have been absolutely devastating. With any hopes of a top two finish now gone, we moved up to sixth and even with six matches left, it looked as though this was the best we could do. The Irish still held bottom place and the eight point gap to the Falcons remained.

Tenth placed Worcester visited the Stoop on 19th March for a game that really was a must win for us to maintain our hope of a top six finish. Botica kicked two penalties either side of two for the visitors by Heathcote before the first try came from Olivier after some terrible defending. Nine minutes later came the controversial moment. Dickson passed to Cheeseman who went along the touchline before he was forced into touch by Hougaard. The touch judge put his flag up and nearly everyone stopped except van Velze who picked up the loose ball and ran 40 metres to score. The TMO checked it and confirmed the try much to the annoyance of the Quins players and supporters. Heathcote converted and Botica put over his third penalty to make it 9-18 at half time. We played poorly in the second half and although Botica kicked two more penalties, one from Heathcote between them secured a first win over us since 2007. Although we remained in sixth place, this loss dealt a hammer blow to our title hopes and even our Champions Cup qualification looked as though it would depend on us winning the Challenge Cup. Exeter had displaced Saracens at the top with Wasps, Leicester and Northampton making up the others above us. London Irish now had 17 points but still trailed the Falcons by five and Worcester looked reasonable safe on thirty.

A trip to Franklin's Gardens was next and our England contingent returned fresh from winning the Six Nations Championship and achieving the Grand Slam in the process. We now needed them to inject that form into what had become a side incapable of putting more than one win in a row together. With Evans still some weeks off returning to the squad, Botica continued to play at fly half and kicked us into an early lead. After Waller scored a try, Botica got his second penalty but sloppy defending let Lawes in for another and Myler converted. Visser scored a good try from nothing and Botica's conversion gave us a one point lead at the interval (13-12). Right at the start of the second half, Clifford sprinted in from half way, Botica converted and we seemed to be on our way at last. Northampton came back and Myler landed a penalty and converted Foden's try to take our lead away. Botica then hit the bar with a penalty attempt and failed horribly with another before Mallinder scored the bonus point try for the Saints and Myler converted to make it 20-29 with only four minutes left. We applied pressure and were awarded a penalty in front of the posts which Botica put over. There were 70 seconds left and we needed a converted try to win it. We tried but failed and our ninth loss in the league was confirmed. We stayed in sixth, we were now five points adrift of Leicester in fifth and Sale and Gloucester were too close for comfort behind us. Saracens had gone back to the top and the gap at the bottom was now only four points.

Newcastle came to the Stoop on 2nd April and nothing else but a bonus point victory would be good enough for us now. In fact, we really needed the next four games to be the same. After Delany had put the Falcons ahead with a penalty, his second came after Visser had scored our first try which Botica converted. Clifford got our second after 12 minutes but we had to wait another twenty four minutes for the next from Gray. Botica converted both and we led 21-6 at the break. When Marchant secured the try bonus point, Botica again converted and we were well clear. At this point, Collier finally went off with a cut head after being temporarily replaced by Sinckler three times. As had happened against Bath, the Falcons came storming back and added tries through Watson and Latu. Delany converted the second, Merrick went to the bin and Latu scored again for Delany to add the extras. It was now 28-25 and there were still eight minutes of the sin bin remaining. The ship was steadied by two Botica penalties and once we were back to full strength, Visser scored his second try. We had done enough and when Delany got binned for a dangerous tackle, Yarde scored our sixth try and Botica converted to make the final score 46-25. Despite the large winning margin, this had been a close run thing and the truth was we weren't playing well enough to challenge for the title. Beating Newcastle was all well and good but how would we measure up in two weeks against the leaders, Saracens? We now trailed them by seventeen points and, mathematically, would need to win every game with a bonus point to stand any chance of a top four place. Realistically, we would be lucky to get a top six spot. There was no change at the bottom with London Irish posting a loss as well as the Falcons.

On 5th April, it was announced after a hearing that World Rugby had found Joe Marler guilty of calling Wales prop Samson Lee "Gypsy Boy" during the game at Twickenham on 12th March. He was banned for two weeks (he would miss the games against London Irish and Saracens) and fined £20,000. This was to be paid to an equality charity in the UK. The Six Nations had not found a case to answer but the ruling body had decided otherwise.

A break from the Premiership saw the visit of London Irish in the Challenge Cup quarter final on 9th April for an 8.05 p.m. kick-off. After a period of pressure, Wallace was over for the first try of the evening before Geraghty landed penalties either side of Care's try which Botica converted. Visser had a try disallowed by the TMO because of obstruction by Brown before Care's interception of McKibbin's pass and 45 metre run to the line. Our kicker then landed two penalties; these were either side of a ten point burst from Irish. Mulchrone scored a try, Geraghty converted and added his third penalty. After all that, we led 18-16 at half time. The Irish were proving to be no pushover and were playing nothing like their lowly league position. Five minutes into the second half, McKibbin scored and Geraghty converted before Paice went to the bin for a tip-tackle. Our defence went to sleep when Maitland picked up a loose ball and from nowhere produced a scintillating run through a massive hole from his own half to score another try. When Geraghty converted, we were 18-30 down with 28 minutes to go and our Challenge Cup prospects looked bad. Within a minute, Care went over, Robshaw was just short and on 62 minutes, Wallace was also through from close range. Both conversions were missed by Botica and we still trailed but now by only two points. After 72 minutes, a Botica penalty from in front of the posts edged us ahead and the job was done when Care completed his hat-trick from the back of a driving maul. Botica converted and with three minutes left, we led by eight points and that's the way it stayed (38-30). There was a new format for choosing which team got a home semi-final. This recognised performances by clubs during the Pool stages as well as the achievement of winning a quarter final match away from home. This meant that if Connacht won at Grenoble, we would be away in Ireland and if Grenoble won, we would be at home. After throwing away a big lead, Connacht went down 32-33 to a late dropped goal so we would welcome the French side to the Stoop on Friday 22nd April. The other semi would be between Montpellier who beat Sale and Newport Gwent Dragons after they defeated Gloucester.

The Saracens away match was played at Wembley Stadium for the fifth time and on this occasion, a crowd of 80,650 turned up. Instead of playing the way we had back in January, we reverted to the same old game of kicking the ball to Saracens. When would we learn that this was absolutely not the way to beat them? This was the Saracens way, they were good at it and not many teams beat them at their own game. We did take the lead with a Botica penalty after 5 minutes but when Ashton was put over by Goode, the forward pass went undetected. Botica put us back in front but a silly error after we had won a Saracens lineout on our five metre line cost us another try. The ball was set up but when Billy Vunipola took Clifford and Lambert out of the ruck, Care was exposed to Kruis coming through and he simply ripped the ball from our captain's grasp and fell over in goal to score. Hodgson converted but a third Botica penalty kept us in touch. A mistake from Care led to the third try for Saracens when he put in a kick that wasn't high enough or long enough. There was no decent chase, Sarries just made two passes, Brits went 35 metres and passed overhead to Ashton who ran in behind the posts. Another undetected forward scoring pass didn't exactly help but Hodgson's conversion made it 9-19 at half time. Botica got the first points of the second half with a fourth penalty and Chisholm was unlucky not to score after Care intercepted and kicked ahead. If Chisholm had tapped the ball left instead of right, it would have been a try, as it was, Goode touched down for a 22 drop out. Botica then wasted an opportunity when he put in a cross-field kick instead of keeping the ball in hand. At the start of the final quarter, Yarde burst through and kicked to the corner when the better option was probably the pass inside to Roberts who had two men outside him. Ward was then penalised and Farrell slotted the penalty with six minutes left. We simply couldn't keep wasting opportunities when they presented themselves. With 30 seconds left, we were awarded a penalty right in front of the posts and 41 metres out. Botica missed to the left, punched the ground and we had nothing to show for our efforts. We dropped to seventh and now had no hope of reaching the top four. It was now out of our hands as to whether we would get into the top six. Saracens, Wasps, Exeter and Leicester held the play-off slots and Newcastle beat London Irish to make the gap at the wrong end seven points.

On 18th April, the Club announced the Harlequin F.C. corporate mini-bond in a bid to raise £7.5 million. This would be invested in furthering the Club's long-term ambitions of building new audiences at home and abroad, expanding the horizons of the professional game, growing the business and remaining in the top tier of professional rugby to further develop the Harlequins name. The aim was to underpin sporting successes with commercial success to lay the foundation for the next 150 years. The Chief Executive even went so far as to say "The proceeds will enable us to invest in the Club, take us to new levels and to continue to stay ahead of the game as it grows. Our goal is to be the best rugby club in Europe and the best sports club in the World" – when you think about the size of some sports clubs, this was some statement to make! The Harlequin FC Bond was subject to a minimum investment of £2,000 per applicant and thereafter in multiples of £1,000 and offered investors interest at a rate of 5.5% (gross) per annum, paid in cash semi-annually, over an initial five year fixed-term. Harlequin F.C. Bonds were not transferable, could not be traded and were unsecured. The period was extended until 31st May to try and raise a total of £15 million but it is unclear exactly how much the final total was. When Wasps issued their 6.50% 2022 debut retail bond, £35 million was raised. Many other schemes, policies and news items were being announced all the time. Unfortunately, lots of them were never seen or heard of again or were full of mistakes. It didn't paint the Club in a good light.

On Friday 22nd April, Grenoble came to the Stoop for the Challenge Cup semi-final on a wet and miserable evening. Nick Evans was named amongst the substitutes but it remained to be seen if he was ready. Botica got us off to a good start with a penalty on 6 minutes and after Grenoble lost two men injured, Roberts crashed over from short range for Botica to convert. Wisniewski kicked two penalties although Botica got one in between to ensure we led 13-6 at the break. After 50 minutes, Nick Evans made a welcome return when he replaced Botica. We had badly missed him and he quickly showed why he was still our first choice fly half. He chipped behind the Grenoble defence and touched down for the try. He then converted, added a penalty and converted Lowe's score after 69 minutes. The French just couldn't get into the game and full time came with us ahead 30-6. During the first half, Joe Marler appeared to kick Héguy (Grenoble's hooker) in the face, he was cited and banned for another two weeks so he would be out until the final. During the course of the hearing, it became clear that Joe had been subjected to "the foulest of verbal abuse and references of a personal nature" according to Richard Smith who represented him. He became frustrated when Héguy tackled him off the ball. Marler's response was when he "flicked out" to give him a forceful message that he wouldn't be intimidated. As usual, Marler suffered and he later decided to get help in managing his temper. He had to realise he was a marked man and get used to it. We moved nicely into our first European final since 2011 and our fourth overall. We would face our Pool opponents Montpellier, they would see off Newport Gwent Dragons in the other semi-final the following day (22-12).

In the outstanding match between Bath and Sale played on 23rd April, the home side won 32-26 which gave the Sharks two points and put them three above us on 53. When we travelled to Reading on Sunday 1st May to take on London Irish for the fifth time this season, we knew that Gloucester had beaten Sale on Friday night (12-11) so a bonus point win would put our destiny back in our hands. The Irish also needed a bonus point win to keep the relegation battle going into the last round of matches. They needed at least two points and had to hope that Newcastle didn't beat Saracens. If Irish failed or Newcastle won, they would be down and out. We started well and Charlie Walker was put in by Lowe and Botica converted. Brophy-Clews landed a penalty and our response was quick if not decisive. First, Chisholm put in a grubber kick and Walker grabbed the ball from Maitland on his own goal line and touched down (Botica converted) and two minutes later, Yarde put Chisholm in for another great try. With 22 minutes gone we led 19-3 – cue taking the foot off the gas!! Clifford got binned for illegally stopping a rolling maul and Narraway and Tikoirotuma got tries to bring the Irish back into it. Brophy-Clews converted the second and Botica's penalty just before the break gave us a seven point lead. Towards the end of the third quarter, Paice scored and the conversion by Brophy-Clews drew them level. When he kicked a penalty with fourteen minutes left, the Irish were in front. Here we go again! Evans had come on some time before and his penalty brought us level. Then Kyle Sinckler burst through a tackle and raced to the line for the bonus point try. Evans converted and despite Irish trying hard to tie the game up again, there was no further scoring. The Falcons had lost 14-23 to Saracens but it didn't matter, the Exiles were relegated for the first time since 1994. Their supporters liked to sing "I'd rather be a Paddy than a Quin", perhaps this day wasn't the best time to ask them how they felt now! Saracens, Exeter, Wasps and Leicester had qualified for the play-off semi-finals, the last week would decide what the line-up would be. Northampton held fifth, we were sixth and if we won with a bonus point in our final game, we would be guaranteed a top six finish. Any other result might see us miss out but the lowest we could now finish was seventh.

On Saturday 7th May at the Stoop, Exeter Chiefs provided the opposition for Conor O'Shea's final home game in charge. If the visitors won, they would be guaranteed a home semi-final. Evans started this game and put us on the board with a penalty after 3 minutes. The Chiefs were in great form and Short, Nowell and Ewers scored tries. Steenson could only convert the last one and when Yarde and Brown put Care over in first half injury time, Evans converted to make it 10-17. No one saw it coming but the second half was an absolute disaster for us. Exeter produced some fantastic rugby and we were simply not good enough to live with them. We looked like a team at the end of a bad season instead of one looking forward to a European final in six days!! Nowell, Short and Nowell again got tries (Steenson converted the second and third) before we added to our tally. Sinckler scored another try with a great run and Botica converted to make it 17-36 after 56 minutes. Worse was to come as Dolman, Chudley and Slade went over and Steenson converted the first two to take the Chiefs past the fifty point mark. Winston Stanley scored our third try which Botica converted but the last word went to the Chiefs when the TMO awarded Salvi's try. Steenson banged over his sixth conversion to leave the final score at 24-62. This was our heaviest defeat and the most points conceded this season but we hadn't let in that many points at home ever. The previous worst was against Wasps on 17th September 1994 (26-57). As for conceding points overall, the two previous disasters were away to London Irish on 25th April 1998 (14-62) and Bath away on 29th April 2000 (19-77). To top it all off, Sale won at Newcastle to jump over us into sixth place. Saracens finished top with 80 points, Exeter claimed the other home berth with 74, Wasps came third on 72 and Leicester had 65. Northampton (60) and Sale (58) completed the top six. We ended the season in seventh on 55, Gloucester were next (49), Bath had 48, Worcester 35, Newcastle 27 and London Irish just 20.

To finish in such a terrible way at home was a sad end to Conor O'Shea's tenure and failed to do him justice. We had won more under him than any previous Coach or Director of Rugby. Credit must go of course to Dean Richards for helping to nurture the younger players who matured under Conor but the victories came on his watch and the plaudits must quite rightly go to him.

In the semi-finals on 21st May, Saracens beat Leicester 44-17 and Exeter got past Wasps 34-23; in the final a week later, Saracens retained the trophy with a 28-20 victory over the Chiefs.

Our final game of the season was the European Rugby Challenge Cup Final in the Grand Stade de Lyon against Montpellier on Friday 13th May. Under Jake White and with a lot of money backing them, they had built up a formidable side including a number of South Africans. The crowd numbered 28,556 and was crammed in as the top tier was not in use for this game. The whole build up to the final was overshadowed by the news that broke early on Monday 9th May. Seb Adeniran-Olule, our young up and coming England U20 prop forward had been killed in an accident when his car had collided with a stationary lorry on the northbound M23 motorway near Hooley in Surrey at 5.35 a.m. He was pronounced dead at the scene and was just 20 years old with his whole future ahead of him. Sadly, we would never see his full potential. A minute's silence was held before kick-off, his initials were embroidered onto the players' shirts and they also wore black armbands. Our team was as follows:- Mike Brown; Marland Yarde, George Lowe, Jamie Roberts, Tim Visser; Nick Evans, Danny Care (captain); Joe Marler, Joe Gray, Adam Jones; James Horwill, Sam Twomey; Chris Robshaw, Luke Wallace and Nick Easter. Replacements – Dave Ward, Mark Lambert, Kyle Sinckler, Mat Luamanu, Jack Clifford, Karl Dickson, Ben Botica and Ross Chisholm. We started well and Evans put over a penalty after four minutes but Catrakilis equalised with one of his own after eight minutes. After 21 minutes Montpellier won a lineout and after Care turned it over, he immediately gave it back to Nagusa. From there, the French side broke into our half, Yarde came out of position and a simple two on one put replacement Mogg over in the corner. Catrakilis converted but it would have been nice to see the TMO have a look at a possible knock-on and a foot in touch by Nagusa. Catrakilis added another penalty before Evans was on the mark with two more after hitting the post earlier to make it 9-13 at half time. Early in the second half as we won a lineout near Montpellier's 22, Care's pass to Visser went behind him and as Nagusa was put away for the score, the referee (John Lacy) brought the play back for a penalty to us for a deliberate knock-on by hooker Bismarck Du Plessis. Surprisingly, no yellow card was produced because Visser would have been clean through and it is doubtful anyone would have stopped him. Worse was to follow when Evans somehow managed to miss to the right from 25 metres out just to the right of the posts. Five minutes later, Montpellier were camped on our line right under the posts when their replacement scrum half (Paillaugue) kicked to the corner and Mogg easily outjumped Roberts to score. The TMO was asked to check for offside and the grounding, he saw no problem, Catrakilis converted and it was 9-20. The momentum swing after the missed penalty was a killer blow. Montpellier's fly half continued his successful kicking with another penalty and then, after 60 minutes, we attacked and Yarde was brought down by three defenders just short of the line. As the ball was moved left, Brown kicked to the corner after a call from Visser; all he had to do was catch it and fall over the line but he dropped it and the chance had gone. Another Catrakilis penalty made it a seventeen point deficit with just 13 minutes remaining. We had chances but were making too many mistakes and time ticked away. We gave it a go and from a Brown grubber kick, Yarde managed to get to the ball ahead of replacement centre Ebersohn as he was caught in two minds – take the ball or tackle. In the event, he tackled but Yarde's momentum got him over the line. Botica converted and the deficit was ten points with seven minutes left. As we attacked, we got a penalty almost in front of the posts, Botica put it over and we had just over two minutes to get a goal to take the final into extra time. After Botica kicked out of the 22, we won the ball back but Sinckler was penalised for not releasing. A short fracas blew up and after a lot of pushing and shoving, less than a minute remained. From Montpellier's lineout, we put them in touch and Care eventually got the ball and took a quick throw with four seconds left. We recycled the ball and had around 60 metres to go; Care passed to Botica who had three men outside him and proceeded to inexplicably kick the ball downfield into the Montpellier 22 (Roberts, Yarde and O'Shea couldn't believe what he had done to name but three). Mogg launched the ball into the stand and that was it. Botica punched the turf a few times and did a good impersonation of an upset man – he really needed to brush up on his game time management by the time he joined Montpellier for the following season.

It was so frustrating to come so close but Montpellier got the plaudits and lifted their first trophy. This game had summed up our season, a total lack of killer instinct. The number of matches we lost because of this was not good and would need to be addressed by the incoming Director of Rugby and his coaching team. Ben Botica made his final appearance in this game. He had scored 558 points (7 tries, 119 penalties and 83 conversions) and come on as a sub 54 times during his four seasons with us. It was such a shame that his last kick in our colours had not been to win the cup. Nick Easter also made his last appearance because he announced his retirement on 29th July 2016. He had scored 275 points (55 tries), captained the side 45 times, made 13 appearances as a substitute, was sent off twice for two yellow cards and visited the bin on 12 occasions. It would take a great player to fill his boots.

The season had looked so great until 17th January but then we fell apart and never looked like regaining the form we had shown before that. For all the excuses about the Six Nations, something must have been seriously wrong in the squad because a team doesn't start losing after being deprived of five or six players. Even when they returned on a high after the success with England they only achieved a record of W4 L4 and three of the wins were against the bottom two in the Premiership. Overall, our record was P32 W18 D1 L13 F883 A787. In the league it was P22 W10 D1 L11 F532 A583 Pts 55 (BP 13 – TB 6 LB 7) Pos 7th; almost the same record as last season. Top appearance makers were Kyle Sinckler and Dave Ward with 29, Lambert came next on 27 and Botica, Matthews and Wallace managed 26. After seven seasons as the top points scorer, Nick Evans was succeeded by Ben Botica. He scored 213 (1 try, 44 penalties and 38 conversions) and as a result, he also got the most penalties and conversions. Charlie Walker scored the most tries with 13 (the 10 he scored in the league were the first time double figures had been reached since Simon Keogh scored 18 in 2005/06; for the Premiership, we have to go back to the 10 scored by Ugo Monye in 2003/04). Overall, tries went up by over thirty to 98, penalties increased by five to 81, conversions rose by nearly thirty to 75 and for the first time since 1952/53, we scored no dropped goals. As a result of all this, total points were up by over 200 to 883.

2015/16

060615	BERMUDA BARBARIANS	BERMUDA	W	(68)-(43)
300815	UNITED STATES OF AMERICA	PHILADELPHIA	W	3G1PG(24)-3PG2T(19)
250915	LONDON IRISH(CUN/DUNC SERIES)	TWICKENHAM STOOP	W	2G1PG1T(22)-1G2T(17)
021015	LONDON IRISH(CUN/DUNC SERIES)	TWICKENHAM STOOP(A) (AGG 59-46)	W	3G2PG2T(37)-3G1PG1T(29)
161015	WASPS(AP)	TWICKENHAM STOOP	W	2G4PG(26)-1G3PG1T(21)
251015	LEICESTER(AP)	LEICESTER	L	1G4PG(19)-1G5PG(22)
261015	NEWPORT GWENT DRAGONS	TWICKENHAM STOOP	W	4G1PG(31)-1G1PG2T(20)
311015	BATH(AP)	BATH	W	2G8PG(38)-2G3PG1T(28)
061115	SALE SHARKS(AP)	TWICKENHAM STOOP	W	1G3PG(16)-2G(14)
121115	MONTPELLIER(ERCHCP3)	TWICKENHAM STOOP	W	4G1PG2T(41)-6PG(18)
191115	CARDIFF BLUES(ERCHCP3)	CARDIFF	W	3G2PG1T(32)-2G2PG(20)
281115	EXETER CHIEFS(AP)	EXETER	L	1G1PG3T(25)-2G4PG(26)
051215	LONDON IRISH(AP)	TWICKENHAM STOOP	W	5G1PG(38)-1G(7)
121215	RUGBY CALVISANO(ERCHCP3)	CALVISANO	W	5G3T(50)-1G1PG(10)
191215	RUGBY CALVISANO(ERCHCP3)	TWICKENHAM STOOP	W	7G2T(59)-1G(7)
271215	GLOUCESTER (AP)	TWICKENHAM	D	4G2PG1T(39)-4G2PG1T(39)
030116	WORCESTER(AP)	WORCESTER	W	3G1PG(24)-1G1PG2T(20)
090116	SARACENS(AP)	TWICKENHAM STOOP	W	1G4PG2T(29)-2G3PG(23)
170116	CARDIFF BLUES(ERCHCP3)	TWICKENHAM STOOP	W	4G2PG(34)-3G1T(26)
220116	MONTPELLIER(ERCHCP3)	MONTPELLIER	L	3PG(9)-4G3PG1T(42)
310116	NEWCASTLE(AP)	NEWCASTLE	L	2G1T(19)-2G4PG(26)
060216	NORTHAMPTON(AP)	TWICKENHAM STOOP	L	2G3PG(23)-3G2PG(27)
130216	GLOUCESTER(AP)	GLOUCESTER	L	2PG(6)-2G3PG1T(28)
190216	LEICESTER(AP)	TWICKENHAM STOOP	W	1G6PG(25)-1G4PG(19)
280216	WASPS(AP)	COVENTRY	L	2T(10)-6G(42)
050316	SALE SHARKS(AP)	SALFORD	L	2G3PG(23)-2G5PG(29)
110316	BATH(AP)	TWICKENHAM STOOP	W	3G3PG1T(35)-2G3PG1T(28)
190316	WORCESTER(AP)	TWICKENHAM STOOP	L	5PG(15)-1G3PG1T(21)

270316	NORTHAMPTON(AP)	NORTHAMPTON	L	2G3PG(23)-3G1PG1T(29)
020416	NEWCASTLE(AP)	TWICKENHAM STOOP	W	5G2PG1T(46)-2G2PG1T(25)
090416	LONDON IRISH(ERCHCQF)	TWICKENHAM STOOP	W	2G3PG3T(38)-3G3PG(30)
160416	SARACENS(AP)	WEMBLEY	L	4PG(12)-2G1PG1T(22)
220416	GRENOBLE(ERCHCSF)	TWICKENHAM STOOP	W	3G3PG(30)-2PG(6)
010516	LONDON IRISH(AP)	READING	W	3G2PG1T(32)-2G2PG1T(25)
070516	EXETER CHIEFS(AP)	TWICKENHAM STOOP	L	3G1PG(24)-6G4T(62)
130516	MONTPELLIER(ERCHCF)	LYON	L	1G4PG(19)-2G4PG(26)

53

Looking Forward to the 150th Year 2016

In June 2016, England went to Australia still searching for a first series win down under. New boss Eddie Jones had instilled a new level of discipline, belief and killer instinct in the squad and they travelled in determined mood. Brown, Care, Jack Clifford, Robshaw, Sinckler and Yarde all made the party and only Sinckler didn't get at least one test appearance. Brown, Robshaw and Care (who came on as a sub each time) appeared in all three, Yarde played in the first and Clifford was a sub in the last two. In one of the best test series ever seen, England achieved their aim and came home with a 3-0 series triumph by winning 39-28, 23-7 and 44-40.

The World Rugby Under 20 Championship had been taking place each year since 2008; England had won the title twice and been runners-up no fewer than four times. This year, the competition was in England and Sam Aspland-Robinson, Joe Marchant, Charlie Piper (called in as a replacement) and Stan South were in the squad. After beating Italy (48-10), Scotland (44-0) and Australia (17-13) in the Group, they went past South Africa in the semi-final by 39-17. In the final, they faced Ireland and reclaimed the title by a margin of twenty four points (45-21).

Events for The 150th Anniversary Season

On 17th May, the Club announced details of the plans for 2016/17. A lot of the events just had 150th attached to them and took place every year anyway.

QUINSSA Dinner, 29th July 2016

The annual supporters' club dinner will take place at The Stoop on Friday 29th July 2016.

Members Pre-season Event and Pre-season Friendly, Saturday 20th August

A one day event will take place on Saturday 20th August. Glasgow Warriors, the current Pro 12 champions, will provide the opposition for the friendly match which will be preceded by a Veterans Match featuring a Harlequin President's XV v A Jason Leonard XV.

HOPA Lunch, Friday 4th November 2016

Harlequins Old Players Association (HOPA) will hold its annual lunch at the RAC Club on Friday 4th November 2016.

Special 150th Challenge Match, Wednesday 16th November 2016
Harlequins will host the Maori All Blacks touring team in a special challenge match at The Stoop on Wednesday 16th November.

Big Game 9, Tuesday 27th December 2016
The annual highlight of the festive season will take place at Twickenham Stadium on 27th December.

150th Anniversary Golf Day, Wednesday 26th April 2017
A special golf day will be held at Royal Wimbledon Golf Club.

150th Anniversary Celebration Dinner, Tuesday 16th May 2017
A highlight of the programme, this formal dinner will be held at the Dorchester Hotel.

150th Anniversary Local Community Event, May or June 2017
A special local community 150th Anniversary event to be held at The Stoop is under discussion.

Logo
An official 150th logo has been designed in association with Adidas.

150th Anniversary Shirt
An exclusive "retro" home shirt has been designed in conjunction with Adidas.

150th Anniversary Book
A fully illustrated, coffee table style, club history book has been commissioned. The book will be published in September 2016.

150th Anniversary Documentary
A 45 minute documentary tracing the history of the Club is in hand. Presented by Ugo Monye, the documentary is a joint production with BT Sport.

150th Related Retail Merchandise
A select range of merchandise will be available in addition to the replica versions of the shirt and related Adidas merchandise.

Affiliate Clubs
The Club's eight overseas affiliate clubs will be involved in the celebrations.

Harlequins Amateurs – Mini Rugby Tournament
The Amateur Club plans to host a special 150th Anniversary Mini-Rugby Festival on 30th April 2017.

Community and Schools Events
There will be a programme of community and schools events, details to follow.

Women's and Girls' Rugby
There will be a programme of activity to encourage women's and girls' rugby. This will be undertaken by the Harlequins Foundation in association with Harlequin Ladies.

I list below the provisional fixture list for the 2016/17 season. Where there is some doubt over the actual date, I have chosen Saturday as the day for convenience but obviously, these will move around as required. We are in Pool 3 in the Anglo-Welsh Cup alongside Bristol, Cardiff and Wasps and these teams will play against Pool 2 which contains Exeter, Ospreys, Sale and Worcester. In the European Challenge Cup, we were drawn in Pool 5 with Edinburgh, Stade Français and Timisoara Saracens but the exact fixtures have not been decided as the book goes to print.

2016/17

130816	LONDON IRISH(CUN/DUNC SERIES)	TWICKENHAM STOOP
200816	GLASGOW WARRIORS	TWICKENHAM STOOP
030916	BRISTOL(AP/LDH)	TWICKENHAM
090916	SALE SHARKS(AP)	SALFORD
170916	EXETER CHIEFS(AP)	EXETER
240916	SARACENS(AP)	TWICKENHAM STOOP
021016	WASPS(AP)	COVENTRY
081016	NORTHAMPTON(AP)	TWICKENHAM STOOP
151016	EUROPEAN CHALLENGE CUP POOL ROUND 1	TBC
221016	EUROPEAN CHALLENGE CUP POOL ROUND 2	TBC
291016	WORCESTER(AP)	TWICKENHAM STOOP
051116	EXETER CHIEFS(AWCP3)	TWICKENHAM STOOP
121116	OSPREYS(AWCP3)	SWANSEA
161116	MĀORI ALL BLACKS	TWICKENHAM STOOP
201116	LEICESTER(AP)	LEICESTER
261116	BATH(AP)	TWICKENHAM STOOP
041216	NEWCASTLE(AP)	NEWCASTLE
101216	EUROPEAN CHALLENGE CUP POOL ROUND 3	TBC
171216	EUROPEAN CHALLENGE CUP POOL ROUND 4	TBC
271216	GLOUCESTER(AP/BG9)	TWICKENHAM
311217	WORCESTER(AP)	WORCESTER
070117	SALE SHARKS(AP)	TWICKENHAM STOOP
140117	EUROPEAN CHALLENGE CUP POOL ROUND 5	TBC
210117	EUROPEAN CHALLENGE CUP POOL ROUND 6	TBC
280117	WORCESTER(AWCP3)	WORCESTER
040217	SALE SHARKS(AWCP3)	TWICKENHAM STOOP

100217	BRISTOL(AP)	BRISTOL
180217	BATH(AP)	BATH
250217	LEICESTER(AP)	TWICKENHAM STOOP
040317	GLOUCESTER(AP)	GLOUCESTER
110317	ANGLO-WELSH CUP SF	TBC
180317	ANGLO-WELSH CUP F	TBC
250317	NEWCASTLE	TWICKENHAM STOOP
010417	EUROPEAN CHALLENGE CUP QF	TBC
080417	SARACENS(AP)	WEMBLEY
150417	EXETER CHIEFS(AP)	TWICKENHAM STOOP
220417	EUROPEAN CHALLENGE CUP SF	TBC
290417	WASPS(AP)	TWICKENHAM STOOP
060517	NORTHAMPTON(AP)	NORTHAMPTON
120517	EUROPEAN CHALLENGE CUP F	TBC
200517	AVIVA PREMIERSHIP SF	TBC
270517	AVIVA PREMIERSHIP F	TBC

The Senior squad for 2016/17 is as follows:- Mike Brown, Rob Buchanan, Danny Care, Ross Chisholm, James Chisholm, Jack Clifford, Will Collier, Karl Dickson, Nick Evans, Owen Evans, Joe Gray, Matt Hopper, James Horwill, Ruaridh Jackson, Adam Jones, Mark Lambert, George Lowe, Mat Luamanu, Joe Marler, Charlie Matthews, George Merrick, Aaron Morris, Charlie Mulchrone, George Naoupu, Mark Reddish, Jamie Roberts, Chris Robshaw, Matt Shields, Kyle Sinckler, Harry Sloan, Winston Stanley, Tim Swiel, Netani Talei, Sam Twomey, Tim Visser, Charlie Walker, Luke Wallace, Dave Ward and Marland Yarde. The Academy squad is Sam Aspland-Robinson, Henry Cheeseman, Gabriel Ibitoye, Josh Ibuanokpe, Dino Lamb-Cona, James Lang, Joe Marchant, Jonas Mikalcius, Robbie Nairn, Charlie Piper, Niall Saunders, Stan South, Calum Waters and Archie White. More will no doubt be added in due course but this is the official Club position at 28th July 2016.

As we move towards our 150th anniversary season, I finish with a few statistics of note - our playing record at the Stoop is P663 W448 D23 L192 (five of these were as the away side and all have been won). At our other home across the Chertsey Road (or the A316 if you prefer), we have a record of P777 W458 D42 L277 (eight have been as the away side in league matches and we have a record of W4 D1 L3; finals have been included in the main total).

Top appearance maker – Grahame Murray 307

Top points scorer – Nick Evans 2171

Top try scorer – Douglas Lambert 253

Most capped international – Jason Leonard 119 (114 England 5 British and Irish Lions)

And now it is over to the Harlequin players, officials and supporters to steer the Club through the next 150 years - let's hope success comes soon!

Nunquam Dormio

Printed in Germany
by Amazon Distribution
GmbH, Leipzig